The United Nations and El Salvador, 1990-1995

The United Nations
Blue Books Series, Volume IV

The United Nations and
El Salvador

1990-1995

**With an introduction by
Boutros Boutros-Ghali,
Secretary-General of the United Nations**

Department of Public Information
United Nations, New York

Published by the United Nations
Department of Public Information
New York, NY 10017

Editor's note:

Each of the United Nations documents and other materials reproduced in this book ("Texts of documents", pages 89-599) has been assigned a number (e.g. Document 1, Document 2, etc.). This number is used throughout the Introduction and other parts of this book to guide readers to the document texts. For other documents mentioned in the book but not reproduced, the United Nations document symbol (e.g. S/1994/645, A/47/285-S/24183) is provided. With this symbol, such documents can be consulted at the Dag Hammarskjöld Library at United Nations Headquarters in New York, at other libraries in the United Nations system or at libraries around the world which have been designated as depository libraries for United Nations documents. The information contained in this volume is correct as at 28 February 1995.

The United Nations and El Salvador, 1990-1995
The United Nations Blue Books Series
Volume IV
ISBN 92-1-100552-3

United Nations Publication
Sales No. E. 95.I.12 (Soft)

Printed by the United Nations Reproduction Section
New York, NY

Contents

CANADA

UNITED STATES OF AMERICA

ATLANTIC OCEAN

Gulf of Mexico

BAHAMAS

MEXICO

CUBA

DOMINICAN
REPUBLIC

HAITI

Puerto Rico

JAMAICA

BELIZE

ANTIGUA AND
BARBUDA

ST. KITTS
AND NEVIS

GUATEMALA

Guadeloupe

Caribbean Sea

DOMINICA

ST. LUCIA

HONDURAS

BARBADOS

ST. VINCENT AND
THE GRENADINES

EL SALVADOR

NICARAGUA

GRENADA

TRINIDAD AND
TOBAGO

COSTA RICA

PANAMA

VENEZUELA

PACIFIC OCEAN

GUYANA

SURINAME

COLOMBIA

BRAZIL

Galapagos Islands

ECUADOR

PERU

MAP NO. 3826   UNITED NATIONS
MAY 1994

Section One
Introduction

I   Overview

1   As a result of one of the most comprehensive efforts ever undertaken by the United Nations, El Salvador in 1995 could confidently be called a nation transformed. Where once human rights were violated with impunity, a new framework to ensure the rights of citizens was being put into place, bolstered by new democratic institutions. Where for years social injustice, civil strife and politically motivated violence oppressed millions of people, Salvadorians were instead devoting their labours to reconciliation, reconstruction and long-term human development. Some serious problems remained, among them incomplete reforms, fear that the former antagonists would remain polarized, and grinding poverty. None the less, El Salvador had in place what appeared to be a solid foundation for a peaceful future.

2   The United Nations played a key, catalytic role in bringing about this metamorphosis. United Nations mediators brokered the peace agreements between the Government of El Salvador and the opposition Frente Farabundo Martí para la Liberación Nacional (FMLN), putting an end to a decade-long civil conflict that claimed some 75,000 lives. United Nations peace-keepers monitored the cease-fire, the separation of forces and the formal end of hostilities. United Nations experts in human rights, civilian policing and economic development steered the country into far-reaching democratic, social and institutional reforms. United Nations observers certified that elections held in March and April 1994 were carried out under acceptable conditions, with Salvadorians freely exercising their right to take part in democratic polling.

3   The peace-keeping operation established by the United Nations Security Council to monitor and verify implementation of the Salvadorian peace accords — the United Nations Observer Mission in El Salvador (ONUSAL) — was unprecedented in several respects. ONUSAL was the first in the "second generation" of peace-keeping operations to emphasize post-conflict peace-building — efforts to strengthen and solidify peace in order to avoid a relapse into conflict. Further, at a time when United Nations peace-keepers had rarely been involved in internal conflicts, ONUSAL was granted extensive oversight to monitor and report on the human rights situation within a sovereign State Member of the United Nations. In yet another step without parallel in United Nations history, these human rights monitors were sent to El Salvador before a cease-fire had been agreed upon by the belligerent parties in the hope that their presence would defuse tensions and provide a visible deterrent to violence and rights abuses. This was indeed how events unfolded.

ONUSAL was also one of the first examples of multi-disciplinary peace-keeping, as compared to earlier, more traditional United Nations operations charged with truce observation and supervision.

4   Like most other peace-keeping operations, ONUSAL faced difficulties and challenges nearly every step of the way. Implementation of the accords fell behind schedule in several critical areas, including the demobilization of troops, the purification of the armed forces and the transfers of land intended to facilitate the reintegration into civilian society of both sides' former combatants. Confidence in the peace process was jolted by the discovery of illegal arms caches being maintained by the FMLN and by a spate of summary executions carried out by armed illegal groups, killings which called to mind the "death-squad" assassinations of the civil war years. But the peace process had powerful support in all sectors of society, and the Salvadorian people, by their scrupulous respect for the cease-fire and strong participation in the electoral process, made manifest their overwhelming desire to embrace a peaceful, democratic future. ONUSAL was thus able to report, not long into its tenure, that the peace process was irreversible, and indeed it has proven so in large measure.

5   At a time when the international community is looking increasingly to the United Nations to undertake a variety of major endeavours, the experience of ONUSAL — combining elements of peacemaking, peace-keeping and post-conflict peace-building and placing an extraordinary focus on human rights issues — has important implications for the conduct of other peace-keeping operations and for the future of the Organization itself. The high degree of success achieved by ONUSAL in fulfilling its major objectives serves to highlight the close interrelationship between the goals of peace, freedom, democracy and development. It also points towards the need for an integrated approach to human security. Under such an approach, military, political, economic, social and environmental problems should be addressed jointly and coherently rather than separately, as has traditionally been the case.

6   The account which follows, and the collection of documents reproduced on pages 89-599, are intended to support the efforts of the international community to scrutinize ONUSAL and draw lessons from its performance. Part II provides background information on the conflict in El Salvador and the early involvement of the United Nations in bringing it to a negotiated end. Part III discusses the unique conditions under which ONUSAL was inaugurated and traces the final series of talks that produced the peace accords. Parts IV, V and VI examine the progress and delays experienced as the cease-fire took hold and ONUSAL's work began to be felt throughout the country. Part VII chronicles the electoral campaign, the first round of general elections and the presidential run-off election. Part VIII discusses ONUSAL's

post-electoral efforts to monitor implementation of the peace agreements. And Part IX offers some concluding remarks on the operation, on the evolving nature of United Nations peace-keeping and on post-conflict peace-building. The documents reproduced in this book — including all the relevant resolutions and reports, the full texts of the Peace Agreement and of the report of the Commission on the Truth, and selected correspondence between myself and some of the parties in El Salvador — are listed separately on pages 77-85 and are referenced at the appropriate points in this introduction.

II   The birth of the peace process

7   The conflict in El Salvador was the product of long-standing social and economic inequities and of the many decades in which the country's repressive armed forces and public security bodies dominated Salvadorian life. When civil war erupted in 1980, the situation was aggravated by other conflicts in the region and by the ideological confrontation of the Super Powers. The end of the cold war in the late 1980s slowed the flow of weapons, training, funding and political support, but the real opportunity to forge a settlement was grasped only after the Government of El Salvador and the FMLN wearied of the fighting amid the realization that no military solution was in sight. Eventually, both sides turned to the United Nations for help in breaking the stalemate through dialogue. The following section recounts this background to the conflict, the early humanitarian involvement of United Nations agencies, the initial stages of United Nations-mediated peace talks and the creation of an international verification mission to monitor the situation of human rights in El Salvador even as the war and the negotiations continued.

Civil war and diplomacy

8   The United Nations became involved in the situation in El Salvador in December 1980, when the General Assembly adopted resolution 35/192, in which it deplored the "murders, disappearances and other violations of human rights reported in El Salvador" and urged the Government of El Salvador to "take the necessary steps to ensure full respect for human rights and fundamental freedoms in that country".

9   The General Assembly acted in response to widening turmoil in El Salvador, where a military coup in October 1979 had led to a surge in repression and public insecurity and to a climate in which, increasingly, paramilitary forces and other armed groups were engaging in terrorism and violence with impunity. One incident in particular shocked Salvadorians and the international community alike: the 24 March 1980 assassination of Archbishop Oscar Arnulfo Romero, a leading human rights advocate, as he was saying mass in San Salvador. Extreme rightists were blamed for the killing. Mourners at Romero's funeral were shot or trampled to death following explosions and gunfire and the panic that ensued.

10   The General Assembly resolution referred specifically to what it termed the "vile" killing of the Archbishop and called on the Govern-

ment to guarantee the safety of another persecuted Salvadorian church figure, Monsignor Arturo Rivera y Damas, Apostolic Administrator of the Archdiocese of San Salvador. By early 1981, the disorder in El Salvador had degenerated into full-scale civil war between the Government and the FMLN, a coalition of resistance groups formed in December 1980 after several years of active opposition by its individual constituents. This pooling of resources, as well as the FMLN's forging of links with dissident students, trade unionists, members of the clergy and others, marked a significant escalation of anti-Government activity.

11 There is wide agreement that the root causes of the conflict were twofold: the power of the armed forces and the depth of social injustice, particularly in terms of land ownership. For many decades, the army, internal security forces and police had dominated the country's Government and national affairs, often through torture and other violations of internationally agreed-upon human rights and fundamental freedoms. At the same time, in the smallest and most densely populated country in Central America, a tiny percentage of the population owned a large majority of the land and industry. The FMLN also sought changes in El Salvador's judicial and electoral systems and a variety of other social, economic and democratic reforms.

12 Reflecting the East-West confrontation that prevailed at the time, there was considerable foreign involvement in the conflict. The United States of America was opposed to the FMLN's ideology and, despite concern over the Government's record on human rights, backed the Government of El Salvador with military training, weapons and financial aid. The FMLN, for its part, received arms, sanctuary and political support from its ideological allies, Cuba, Nicaragua and the Union of Soviet Socialist Republics (USSR).

13 Tension in the region was also high because of simmering conflicts in two of El Salvador's neighbours. In Nicaragua, the leftist Frente Sandinista de Liberación Nacional came to power in 1979 following its successful rebellion against an authoritarian Government which had ruled for decades; the Sandinistas themselves subsequently faced armed opposition from forces known as "contras", some of whose bases were located in Honduras and who received assistance from the Government of the United States. In Guatemala, a more-than-thirty-year-old insurgency by the leftist Unidad Revolucionaria Nacional Guatemalteca (URNG) was continuing to press the Government for reforms and an end to repression, especially that aimed at the country's indigenous Indian population.

14 In the armed struggle that went on to consume El Salvador for more than a decade, an estimated 75,000 people were killed and well over 1 million became refugees or internally displaced persons. Arbitrary detention, death-squad killings, "disappearances", bombardments of

urban areas and other acts of brutality directed primarily against civilians were attributed to the Government or to irregular groups that supported or sympathized with it. The FMLN was also responsible for murder and violence, assassinating mayors and judges and committing acts of sabotage against electric power stations, telephone and electricity lines, public transport, commercial establishments and other important community targets. The fighting worsened long-standing problems in the nation's economic and social structure; another blow was delivered in the late 1980s and early 1990s with a downturn in external development aid and the dramatic fall in the price of coffee, El Salvador's primary commodity export.

15   The strife led the United Nations to become closely involved in efforts to negotiate a political solution. In 1981, the Commission on Human Rights appointed a Special Representative to report on the situation of human rights in El Salvador. In 1983, the Security Council adopted resolution 530 (1983) supporting the peacemaking efforts of the "Contadora Group" — Colombia, Mexico, Panama and Venezuela — which had initiated a series of consultations with five Central American Governments — Costa Rica, El Salvador, Guatemala, Honduras and Nicaragua. In 1985, a Support Group was created by the Governments of Argentina, Brazil, Peru and Uruguay in order to strengthen the Contadora effort.

16   Also in 1983, the General Assembly took up a new agenda item: "The situation in Central America: threats to international peace and security and peace initiatives". In the first in an annual series of resolutions on the question, the Assembly expressed its deep concern at the prolongation of the conflict in the region, including the continued losses of life in El Salvador, and called for the achievement of peace on a sound basis, which would make possible a genuine democratic process, respect for human rights and economic and social development. Following these initial moves, my predecessor, Secretary-General Javier Pérez de Cuéllar, maintained frequent contacts with the Central American Governments and with the Contadora and Support Group countries.

17   Nevertheless, the conflict in El Salvador persisted. Gradually, a stalemate took hold, with each side inflicting significant harm on the other without winning a decisive military victory and without gaining substantial popular support for its position. One of the only respites from the fighting during the mid-1980s occurred when the United Nations Children's Fund (UNICEF) attained the cooperation of both sides to observe "days of tranquillity", periods in which fighting would cease for a day or two at a time in order to carry out immunizations of children, particularly those under five years old, as part of a global campaign against the six deadliest childhood diseases: diphtheria, whooping cough, tetanus, measles, tuberculosis and polio. The initiative, carried out with

the help of mediation by Archbishop Arturo Rivera y Damas and in collaboration with the International Committee of the Red Cross (ICRC), the Pan American Health Organization (PAHO), the Salvadorian Government's Ministry of Health and other partners, was both a political and logistical success. It went on to inspire similar undertakings in the Sudan (Operation Lifeline Sudan), the Middle East and other emergency situations and gave rise to the related concepts of "peace corridors", "corridors of tranquillity" and "zones of tranquillity". Most importantly, it underscored the humanitarian needs and rights of women and children during times of conflict.

18   A new initiative to help break the Salvadorian impasse was taken in 1986 by my predecessor and the Secretary-General of the Organization of American States (OAS), João Clemente Baena Soares. Together, on 18 November 1986, they extended a joint offer of services to the five Central American countries as well as to the eight Contadora and Support Group nations. Two months later, in a concerted attempt to formulate a joint approach to the region's many problems, the two Secretaries-General, accompanied by the eight countries' Ministers for Foreign Affairs, visited each of the Central American nations. Earlier, the Contadora Group had circulated a draft regional agreement. Within seven months, a negotiating breakthrough occurred.

The Esquipulas II Agreement

19   On 7 August 1987, in what some have called the official birth of the peace process, the Presidents of the five Central American nations signed the "Procedure for the Establishment of a Firm and Lasting Peace in Central America", also known as the Guatemala Procedure or as Esquipulas II, after the town in Guatemala where the talks had been initiated. (Esquipulas I was a May 1986 declaration affirming the five Presidents' commitment to peace, cooperation and national sovereignty.) Under Esquipulas II, the Central American Presidents undertook to launch a process of democratization in their countries, promote a national dialogue, decree a general amnesty, bring about a genuine cease-fire and promote the holding of free, pluralistic and fair elections. They also requested all Governments concerned to terminate support for irregular forces or insurrectional movements and reiterated their commitment to prevent the use of their own territory for the destabilization of other countries in the region. To help achieve these objectives, the Presidents set up an International Verification and Follow-up Commission (CIVS), composed of the Foreign Ministers of the Contadora and Support Groups and of the Central American countries, as well as the Secretaries-General of the United Nations and the OAS.

20   The move for international verification led eventually to the establishment by the Security Council on 7 November 1989, in resolution 644 (1989), of an on-site mechanism, the United Nations Observer Group in Central America (ONUCA), the first United Nations peace-keeping operation in the western hemisphere. ONUCA's primary mandate was to patrol the borders of the five countries in order to monitor their compliance with the security commitments made in the Esquipulas II Agreement.

21   The peace process gained additional momentum with the signing, on 14 February 1989, of the Costa del Sol (El Salvador) Declaration, in which the five Presidents took three important steps towards implementation of Esquipulas II.

A. First, they agreed to establish, with the participation of the United Nations, a mechanism for verification of the Esquipulas II security commitments.

B. Second, the Government of Nicaragua decided to call general and free elections, amend its electoral laws and invite international observers, in particular the Secretaries-General of the United Nations and OAS, to verify that the electoral process was free and fair at every stage.

C. Third, the Presidents agreed to draw up a joint plan for the voluntary demobilization, repatriation or relocation of members of the Nicaraguan resistance and their families.

22   These gains led the United Nations to begin two additional undertakings essential for any durable peace: the resettlement of up-rooted populations and post-conflict peace-building through economic development. In May 1988, the General Assembly adopted a Special Plan of Economic Cooperation (PEC) for Central America, including Belize, envisaging a broad role for the United Nations Development Programme (UNDP). And in May 1989, the International Conference on Central American Refugees (CIREFCA), held in Guatemala City, adopted a comprehensive plan of action to be implemented by the Office of the United Nations High Commissioner for Refugees (UNHCR), UNDP and other organs of the United Nations system. On 27 July 1989, in resolution 637 (1989), the Security Council expressed its firm support for Esquipulas II and other agreements reached by the five Central American Presidents and lent its full support to the Secretary-General's use of his good offices.[1]

1/Document 1
See page 89;
Document 2
See page 91

Peace effort makes further headway

23   The emerging regional *détente* was given another boost when the Government of El Salvador and the FMLN agreed, on 15 September

1989, to begin a dialogue aimed at ending the armed conflict in El Salvador by political means. This was a highly encouraging development. In the more than two years since Esquipulas II, intermittent fighting between the two parties had been punctuated by fragile truces and attempts, ultimately unavailing, to hold substantive peace talks. Progress was also being made in Nicaragua during this period, most notably with the 7 August 1989 Tela (Honduras) Declaration, in which the Central American Presidents signed a joint plan for the voluntary demobilization, repatriation or relocation in Nicaragua of the Nicaraguan resistance and their families.[2] The Tela Declaration had also strongly urged the FMLN to carry out a constructive dialogue with the Government and the Government to arrange the integration of FMLN combatants into institutional and democratic life.

2/Document 3
See page 92

24   These promising developments led my predecessor to report in October 1989 that the situation had improved to the point where "we may envisage political solutions to the main conflicts in the region on the basis of the peace plan embodied in the Esquipulas II agreements".[3] By this time, too, with the end of the cold war and the *rapprochement* between the United States and the USSR, the external ideological and geopolitical factors that had helped to sustain the conflict were replaced by a common interest in shaping a solution and removing barriers to their own improved relations. The collapse of communism in Eastern Europe and the USSR had also led the FMLN to signal an ideological evolution, defusing some of the internal and external opposition to it as an interlocutor.

3/Document 4
See page 97

25   In the 15 September agreement between the Government of El Salvador and the FMLN, the parties invited the Secretary-General to send a representative as a "witness" to talks scheduled in San José, Costa Rica, on 16 and 17 October 1989. However, major stumbling-blocks remained. The FMLN was seeking agreement on wide-ranging reforms, particularly of the army, before it would agree to demobilize; the Government said it would discuss political issues and changes in the armed forces only after the resistance laid down its arms.

26   Negotiations were broken off by the FMLN following an explosion, on 31 October 1989, in a union hall which killed, among others, a prominent leader of the National Trade Union Federation of Salvadorian Workers (FENASTRAS). On 11 November, the FMLN launched what press reports described as the largest offensive of the civil war. The onslaught marked the first time that fighting engulfed parts of the capital, and was condemned by the international community; the Security Council voiced its grave concern on 8 December.[4] And on 16 November, six Jesuit priests at the José Simeón Cañas University of Central America, their housekeeper and her daughter were assassinated; the killings were widely attributed to elements of the military and sparked further international outrage as well as pressure on the two

4/Document 5
See page 100

belligerent parties to end their hostilities. The violence of late 1989 claimed hundreds of lives, but since it demonstrated the impossibility of military victory by either side it is also credited with having prompted both sides, at last, to seek resolution of their differences through serious negotiations within the Esquipulas process. In December 1989 and January 1990, the FMLN and the Government of President Alfredo Cristiani separately requested the Secretary-General of the United Nations to assist them in an uninterrupted negotiating effort to settle the conflict and eliminate its root causes.[5] This idea had the backing of the five Central American Presidents in the San Isidro de Coronado (Costa Rica) Declaration, adopted on 12 December 1989.[6]

5/Document 7
See page 102;
Document 8
See page 105

6/Document 6
See page 100

27   From this point on, the United Nations acted as a catalyst for peace. My predecessor's personal representative, Alvaro de Soto (Peru), shuttled between the parties during February and March 1990 in order to achieve agreement on an important first step: the format, mechanism and pace of the peace process. Such a framework was established in the Geneva Agreement, negotiated under the auspices of the United Nations and signed by the parties on 4 April 1990 in the presence of the Secretary-General.[7] The Agreement stipulated that the peace process would have four objectives: to end the armed conflict by political means; to promote the democratization of the country; to guarantee unrestricted respect for human rights; and to reunify Salvadorian society.

7/Document 11
See page 110;
Document 27
See page 164

28   At their next face-to-face meeting, the Government and the FMLN, with the assistance of my predecessor and his personal representative, drew up a General Agenda and Timetable for the Comprehensive Negotiating Process. The Caracas Agreement, signed on 21 May 1990, established a two-phase process that was expected to yield profound changes in Salvadorian society.[8]

8/Document 11
See page 110;
Document 28
See page 165

29   First, political agreements were to be reached on a broad range of issues — the armed forces, human rights, the judicial and electoral systems, constitutional reform, economic and social issues and verification by the United Nations — which in due course would make it possible to reach a cease-fire and then an end to the armed confrontation. All agreements, including the cease-fire and formal cessation of the conflict, would be verified by United Nations personnel.

30   Secondly, the parties would address the same issues in order to establish the necessary guarantees and conditions for reintegrating the members of the FMLN, within a framework of full legality, into the civil, institutional and political life of the country. Once those guarantees were obtained, other outstanding political agreements would be discussed.

31   A series of complex negotiations ensued, involving direct dialogue between negotiating commissions with the active participation and mediation of the Secretary-General of the United Nations and his personal representative.

32   Meanwhile, the situation in Nicaragua reached a climax with significant implications for the conflict in El Salvador. Elections on 25 February 1990, certified as "impartial and fair throughout" by the United Nations Observer Mission for the Verification of the Elections in Nicaragua, saw the defeat of one of the FMLN's main supporters, the Sandinista Government. Following the peaceful transfer of power, ONUCA — with a peak strength of 1,098 in May 1990 — assisted in monitoring a cease-fire and the separation of forces between opposing parties in Nicaragua and in demobilizing the Nicaraguan resistance. Assessing the impact of these events, press reports noted that the FMLN had lost an ally and, perhaps more important, that both sides — as well as the Salvadorian people — had been shown a successful alternative to armed conflict.

33   The demobilization by ONUCA of some 22,000 members of the Nicaraguan resistance, including the physical destruction of arms and military equipment voluntarily handed over by combatants, was a task without precedent in United Nations history. The civilian aspects of the demobilization — repatriation, relocation or resettlement — of the members of the resistance and their families were the responsibility of the International Support and Verification Commission (CIAV), a cooperative effort of the United Nations and OAS. With these and other tasks carried out successfully, ONUCA's mandate was terminated in January 1992.

The San José Agreement on Human Rights

34   The first substantive agreement of the negotiating process between the Government of El Salvador and the FMLN was reached when the two sides signed, on 26 July 1990, an accord in which they pledged unrestricted respect for international human rights laws and standards — and in which they called for an unprecedented United Nations role in monitoring compliance with such a commitment. Under the San José (Costa Rica) Agreement on Human Rights, a United Nations verification mission would be established with the following powers:

A. To receive communications from any individual, group of individuals or body in El Salvador containing reports of human rights violations;

B. To interview freely and privately any individual, group of individuals or members of bodies or institutions;

C. To visit any place or establishment freely and without prior notice;

D. To carry out an educational and informational campaign on human rights and on the functions of the Mission itself;

9/Document 9
See page107

E. To take whatever legally permissible action it deemed appropriate to promote and defend human rights and fundamental freedoms.[9]

35   Never before had the United Nations carried out such extensive, systematic human rights oversight. Moreover, although the San José Agreement stated that the Mission would take up its duties after a cessation of the armed conflict, both parties subsequently asked the Secretary-General to establish the Mission as soon as possible, even before a cease-fire — yet another move without precedent and, given the wartime conditions, rife with potential complications.

10/Document 12
See page 119

36   On 17 December 1990, the Presidents of Costa Rica, Guatemala, Honduras and Nicaragua acknowledged the valuable steps being taken by the United Nations towards a peaceful solution of the conflict.[10] Four days later, my predecessor notified the Security Council of his intention to propose the establishment of an observer mission in order to monitor all agreements concluded between the Government of El Salvador and the FMLN, beginning with the verification of the San José Agreement.[11] It was expected that, eventually, the mission would also be responsible for verification of a cease-fire and monitoring the electoral process. The Government had requested the United Nations to observe the legislative and municipal elections scheduled for March 1991, but given the absence of an agreement between the parties on this matter in the context of the negotiating process begun on the basis of the Geneva Agreement of April 1990, my predecessor informed both the Security Council and President Cristiani that he was not in a position to recommend such a mission.[12]

11/Document 10
See page 110;
Document 13
See page 129

12/Document 14
See page 132

37   The Secretary-General then sent a preliminary mission to El Salvador to evaluate the merits of trying to verify the San José Agreement without a cease-fire. The mission met with governmental representatives and a wide range of political groups — including representatives of the FMLN, in visits to zones of conflict made with the full knowledge of the Government — and concluded that "there is a strong and widespread desire in all sectors of opinion in El Salvador that the United Nations commence, as soon as possible, the verification of the Agreement without awaiting a cease-fire".[13] It was acknowledged that United Nations personnel might face risks, harassment or intimidation, particularly from some of the more strident parties in El Salvador who were resistant to the very idea of a negotiated solution. But such factors, the mission believed, were not enough of a threat to prevent the establishment of the mission before a cease-fire. In April 1991, my predecessor accepted the mission's recommendations, stating that United Nations human rights verification would promote a significant improvement in the human rights situation in El Salvador and act as a positive impetus to the negotiations.

13/Document 16
See page 134

Constitutional reforms and a surge towards peace

38   Negotiators next sought to broaden the achievements of the San José Agreement. But as talks progressed in early 1991, it became clear that in order to incorporate any peace agreements into the country's legal order, El Salvador's Constitution would have to be amended. This could be done by amending the article of the Constitution which established the actual mechanism for amending the Constitution, or by amending those articles relating to the specific issues under negotiation.

39   The possibility of changing the amendment mechanism triggered the first crisis in the negotiating process, as an important sector of the country's population feared that if the requirements for constitutional amendments were to be eased, this could affect, for instance, economic interests such as land ownership or the long-standing status of the armed forces. When the parties opted for amending specific articles of the Constitution, an unavoidable deadline imposed itself: constitutional reforms had to be approved in two consecutive legislatures, meaning that any amendments would have to be approved by the outgoing Legislative Assembly, whose term ended on 30 April 1991, in order to be ratified by the new Assembly. If the outgoing Assembly did not approve the amendments, the next chance to enact such reforms would not become available until 1994. Since the reforms were crucial to the peace process, such a delay was considered untenable.

40   A marathon negotiating effort was thus engaged, the most intense round of talks yet. Held in Mexico City, they culminated in an enormous step towards a settlement.[14] On 27 April 1991, the parties agreed, first, on a package of reforms relating to:

14/Document 29
See page 167

    A. The armed forces, including a clear definition of their subordination to civilian authority;

    B. Public security, including the creation of the National Civil Police, a body that would be independent of the armed forces, and the creation of a National Public Security Academy to train candidates for the new force;

    C. The judicial system, including a new procedure for the election of Supreme Court judges, creation of the post of National Counsel for the Defence of Human Rights and an annual allocation of no less than 6 per cent from the State budget;

    D. The electoral system, including the establishment of a Supreme Electoral Tribunal to replace the Central Board of Elections.

41   The Mexico Agreements also provided for the formation of a Commission on the Truth, to be composed of three individuals appointed by the Secretary-General of the United Nations to investigate "serious acts of violence that have occurred since 1980 and whose impact on

society urgently requires that the public should know the truth". Given this broad mandate and the sensitive nature of the task, publication of the Commission's report was expected to be a watershed in the process of healing and reunification.

42   Immediately after the signing of the Mexico Agreements, the outgoing Legislative Assembly approved nearly all of the constitutional amendments, with some alterations. Final enactment required a two-thirds majority in the following legislature. The new Assembly took early action on most of the amendments, but reforms related to the armed forces were left pending while the Assembly awaited the results of the formal negotiations on that issue. The question of the armed forces was to become the "Gordian knot" which triggered the second crisis in the negotiating process. Though there was disappointment in some quarters that the Mexico City talks had failed to arrive at arrangements for a cease-fire, press reports noted that the ability of the parties to bridge their differences over institutional issues prior to an end to armed hostilities would make the cease-fire that much stronger when, eventually, it was put into effect.

III An unprecedented mission

43   The negotiating successes achieved at San José and Mexico City paved the way for the creation of the United Nations Observer Mission in El Salvador (ONUSAL). As the first ONUSAL human rights monitors arrived in El Salvador to undertake their pioneering role — international verification within a sovereign United Nations Member State, prior to a cease-fire agreement — fighting persisted in many parts of the country. The following section focuses on the Mission's early efforts and on the months of intense, nearly uninterrupted rounds of negotiations during which the final peace plan took shape.

ONUSAL begins work

44   On 4 April 1991, one year, to the day, after the Geneva Agreement was signed and just before the signing of the Mexico Agreements, my predecessor told the Security Council that the United Nations–mediated peace process in El Salvador had evolved considerably. "[A] broad debate," he stated in his briefing, "involving all political parties and many social organizations and other institutions in El Salvador on the spectrum of issues in the negotiation is taking place. . . Issues are being aired openly which heretofore were not touched upon in public. Salvadorian society stands as if poised to undergo a profound transformation which will permit peace, once it comes about, to take hold irrevocably and irreversibly."[15]

15/Document 16
See page 134

45   My predecessor warned, however, that negotiators faced daunting difficulties. Among them was the situation of human rights, which, according to the Special Representative of the Commission on Human Rights, showed continued cause for concern during 1991 despite a decrease in the number of violations compared with 1990. In his report to the General Assembly (A/46/529), the Special Representative pointed out that, although both parties to the conflict had made some humanitarian gestures, they had also committed serious human rights violations. Members of the State apparatus continued to torture political prisoners and execute people for political reasons. The FMLN had executed persons alleged to have collaborated with the armed forces and engaged in the forcible recruitment of minors. Noting that such acts had occurred even during the peace talks, the Special Representative stated that there was a "serious and alarming gap between proclaimed intentions and results".

El Salvador

The long civil war in El Salvador devastated the country's physical infrastructure. ONUSAL was one of the first United Nations peace-keeping operations to place strong emphasis on post-conflict peace-building.

16/Document 19
See page 141

17/Document 24
See page 147

46   It was against this ambivalent background that, on 20 May 1991, in resolution 693 (1991), the United Nations Observer Mission in El Salvador (ONUSAL) was established by the Security Council with an initial mandate to verify compliance by the Government of El Salvador and the FMLN with the San José Agreement on Human Rights.[16] On 26 July 1991, with some Salvadorians claiming that the Mission infringed upon the country's sovereignty, ONUSAL was launched formally throughout the length and breadth of the country.[17]

47   Headed by Chief of Mission and Special Representative Iqbal Riza (Pakistan), the staff, by 15 September 1991, was composed of 101 international civil servants from 27 countries, including human rights observers and advisers, legal advisers, educators, political affairs officers, military advisers, police advisers and administrative support and communications personnel. During a preparatory phase, ONUSAL set up its central offices, four regional offices (San Salvador, San Miguel, Santa Ana and San Vicente) and two sub-offices (Chalatenango and Usulután) and familiarized itself with the overall human rights situation, with

problems related to the armed conflict and with the country's legal, administrative and judicial systems and institutions. On 1 October, the Mission began to investigate alleged violations of human rights and international humanitarian law.

48   In carrying out its functions, ONUSAL aimed not only to record facts objectively but also to exercise its good offices so that Salvadorian individuals, institutions and non-governmental organizations (NGOs) could remedy violations. The Mission significantly expanded its contacts with Salvadorian institutions and individuals. At the national level, it held regular meetings with a Government inter-agency group consisting of representatives of the Supreme Court of Justice, the Armed Forces General Staff, the Office of the Attorney-General and the Ministry of Foreign Affairs. At the regional and local level, ONUSAL personnel made frequent visits to mayors' offices, departmental governments, military and police units, law courts and other public entities. ONUSAL personnel also met with FMLN leaders and, in Mexico City or Managua, with the FMLN's Political and Diplomatic Commission. In addition, ONUSAL, with the support of ONUCA, continued to escort FMLN leaders in the country to and from the negotiations in Mexico and New York.

49   By the end of October 1991, the Mission had received more than 1,000 complaints of alleged human rights violations. The Special Representative of the Commission on Human Rights reported (A/46/529) that he was gratified by the positive attitude of both the Government and the FMLN with regard to the establishment and functioning of ONUSAL. The Legislative Assembly had also expressed satisfaction at ONUSAL's establishment and pledged its full support.

50   But the atmosphere was tense. Some extremist groups questioned the Mission's impartiality. Another problem was quite opposite in nature: the high, in some cases inordinate, expectations awaiting the Mission. ONUSAL's mandate was not clear to vast numbers of Salvadorians across the political spectrum, who expected the Mission to prevent, or at least punish, human rights violations. But ONUSAL had not come to El Salvador to replace the country's institutions, however deficient they might have been in investigating, prosecuting and punishing those who violated human rights. Rather, ONUSAL was to help correct such failings and draw attention to any other conduct that was incompatible with the San José Agreement. These and other early misunderstandings were attributed by ONUSAL and the Special Representative of the Commission on Human Rights to the fact that the Mission had begun its verification tasks prior to the end of the armed conflict. To explain the precise nature of its mandate to the Salvadorian people, ONUSAL published information in the country's major daily newspapers as part of its educational and information campaign.

The Gordian knot untied

51 After the Mexico Agreements of April 1991, the Government and the FMLN held numerous meetings without making any significant progress. The second crisis had occurred.

52 Concerned about the safety of its members and supporters following the end of the armed conflict, the FMLN was demanding cease-fire arrangements which would allow it to preserve its military capability. Such arrangements proved unacceptable to the Government. To break the log-jam, my predecessor began to explore whether the negotiations might be compressed into a single phase in order to establish, before a cease-fire, the necessary conditions and guarantees for the reintegration of FMLN members. Under the Geneva and Caracas agreements, this subject would have been taken up only during the second, post-cease-fire stage of the negotiations.

18/Document 20
See page 142;
Document 21
See page 144

53 Signalling again their joint interest in resolving the conflict, the Secretary of State of the United States and the Minister for Foreign Affairs of the USSR asked the Secretary-General to take personal leadership of the negotiating process.[18] My predecessor subsequently invited President Cristiani and FMLN Commanders to meet with him at United Nations Headquarters in New York on 16 and 17 September 1991.[19] The meetings in fact lasted much longer than anticipated, ending on 25 September when the parties announced major gains on many fronts.[20]

19/Document 22
See page 145;
Document 23
See page 146

20/Document 25
See page 159

54 The most important step taken in New York was their agreement on a "compressed agenda" for negotiations covering all outstanding matters, mainly those relating to the armed forces and land. This approach was devised in order to overcome the deadlock which had arisen as a result of the parties' inability to agree on mutually acceptable cease-fire terms in the framework of the original, two-stage negotiating format.

55 The Government and the FMLN also signed the New York Agreement, in which they decided, among other things:

A. To create a National Commission for the Consolidation of Peace (COPAZ) — a mechanism for civilian society, in parallel with ONUSAL itself, to monitor and participate in the process of change resulting from the agreements reached between the two parties; COPAZ was to be composed of two representatives of the Government, including a member of the armed forces, two representatives of the FMLN and one representative of each of the parties or coalitions represented in the Legislative Assembly; the Archbishop of San Salvador and a delegate of ONUSAL were to have access as observers to the Commission's work and deliberations;

B. To "purify" the armed forces on the basis of a review of all personnel serving in them by an Ad Hoc Commission, and to reduce the size of the armed forces;

C. To redefine the doctrine of the armed forces so that their function would be limited to defending the sovereignty of the State and the integrity of its territory;

D. To begin organizing the new National Civil Police immediately, without awaiting other political agreements or the cessation of the armed confrontation;

E. To use lands in excess of the constitutional limit of 245 hectares to meet the needs of peasants and small farmers who were without land;

F. To respect the current landholding situation in the conflict zones until a definitive landholding arrangement was arrived at.

56 On 30 September, in resolution 714 (1991), the Security Council commended the parties and urged them to continue their efforts.[21] On 16 November, the FMLN announced a unilateral suspension of offensive operations; the Government responded by deciding to suspend the use of aircraft and heavy artillery. The armed confrontation dwindled considerably, although in some areas fighting lingered on for several weeks. However, a considerable body of opinion in El Salvador — including members of the armed forces and others who normally supported the Government — rejected the New York Agreement and criticized President Cristiani for having given the pact his approval. The opposition was accompanied by a campaign of intimidation against the international press, ONUSAL and other international organizations working in El Salvador. In the absence of a final settlement, the situation remained fragile.[22]

21/Document 26
See page 163

22/Document 30
See page 175

The final breakthrough

23/Document 31
See page 180;
Document 38
See page 231

57 The two sides persisted in their efforts to reach a final settlement before the end of the year, a target established informally by all of the parties involved: the Government, the FMLN, the "Friends of the Secretary-General" (Colombia, Mexico, Spain and Venezuela, who had offered important diplomatic support), the United States and the USSR.[23] Further impetus towards this date was felt because it marked the end of Secretary-General Pérez de Cuéllar's tenure in office. In December 1991, following a round of talks at San Miguel de Allende, Mexico, he invited the parties to United Nations Headquarters in New York, once again at the highest level, to undertake a final push towards peace.[24] At midnight on 31 December 1991, the parties signed the Act of New York.[25]

24/Document 32
See page 186

25/Document 34
See page 187;
Document 37
See page 230

58   Combined with the agreements previously signed at San José, Mexico City and New York, the Act of New York completed the negotiations on all substantive issues of the peace process and represented a formidable display of political will. To rounds of applause, representatives of the Government and the FMLN embraced and declared that they had reached agreement on all outstanding issues, that the final Peace Agreement would be signed at Mexico City on 16 January 1992, that a cease-fire would take effect on 1 February 1992 and that the armed conflict would end formally on 31 October 1992. "This signing", said President Cristiani, "constitutes the beginning of a new era of rebuilding towards democracy and freedom." Salvador Sánchez Cerén, the leader of one of the constituent groups of the FMLN, stated, "The war in El Salvador is over. . . Our 10 years of struggle are expressed in these accords." On 3 January 1992, the Security Council warmly welcomed the agreement, which it said was "of vital importance for the normalization of the situation in El Salvador and in the region as a whole".[26]

26/Document 33
See page 187

59   Economic and social issues, specifically the mechanics of the land-transfer programme, had been the final sticking points. But a number of other details were in need of additional talks. Accordingly, the Act of New York stipulated that a meeting would be initiated on 5 January 1992 in order to negotiate the timetable for implementing the agreements and the procedure for ending the military structure of the FMLN and reintegrating its members into civilian life. Under the Act of New York, if differences on these points were not bridged by 10 January, the parties would accept formulas to be devised by the Secretary-General.

60   On 13 January 1992, without recourse to this provision, the parties resolved all outstanding issues and signed the New York Act II (with the signing of the New York Act II, the Act of New York became the New York Act I). The formal signing of the Peace Agreement took place in Mexico City on 16 January.[27] There, at a solemn ceremony in Chapultepec Castle in the presence of nine Heads of State and a number of foreign ministers, the Government of El Salvador and the FMLN began the delicate transition away from bitter confrontation.

27/Document 36
See page 113;
Document 37
See page 230

61   Having entered office on 1 January 1992, I attended the Chapultepec ceremony and paid tribute to all those whose painstaking work had engendered the conditions for a Peace Agreement and helped the people of El Salvador turn the corner from conflict towards the path of peace, reconciliation and reconstruction. "The long night of El Salvador is drawing to an end," I stated. "It is no exaggeration to say that, taken together, and given their breadth and scope, these [peace] agreements constitute a prescription for a revolution achieved by negotiation."

IV Towards an end to the armed conflict

62   Unlike other peace accords, the Peace Agreement in El Salvador sought not only to end a military conflict but to eliminate its root causes. As such, the accords provided an exhaustive blueprint for change. But as ONUSAL and the Salvadorian people began to tackle the ambitious agenda, unexpected delays disturbed the implementation timetable — which was itself an intricately designed mechanism in which each side's commitments had been carefully balanced and synchronized. It took repeated urging by myself and my representatives to keep the delays from seriously damaging the peace process. The following section describes how the Mission and the Salvadorian parties sought, amid rising tensions, to overcome the various obstacles and bring a final, formal close to the military confrontation.

A complex schedule of implementation

63   The timetable for implementation of the Peace Agreement between the Government of El Salvador and the FMLN was carefully devised so as to synchronize, on the one hand, the reintegration of the FMLN's ex-combatants into civilian life and, on the other, the reform measures that the Government had committed itself to undertake in order to facilitate that process.

64   According to the timetable, the armed conflict was to end formally on 31 October 1992. The process through which this goal would be attained consisted of four elements: the cease-fire, the separation of forces, the dismantling of the military structure of the FMLN and reintegration of its members into civilian life, and United Nations verification of these activities.

65   The cease-fire was to begin on 1 February 1992. The separation of forces was to commence five days later. Within the next 24 days, the armed forces of El Salvador were to fall back progressively to positions they would normally occupy during peacetime, while the estimated 6,000 to 8,000 FMLN combatants were to concentrate progressively in 15 designated locations within the conflict areas. Both sides were to supply ONUSAL with detailed information on their troop strength and inventories of weapons. The FMLN was to deposit all of its arms, mines, ammunition, explosives and military equipment in the

designated locations and then, between 15 and 31 October, destroy them under the sole supervision of ONUSAL. Reintegration of FMLN combatants was to be carried out in five stages between 1 May and 31 October; at each stage, 20 per cent of the FMLN members were to return officially to civilian life. The legislative decree providing for the legalization of the FMLN as a political party was to be promoted as of 1 May.

66   The reduction of the Salvadorian army from its estimated 60,000 troops to approximately half that size was to be achieved by January 1994. Two public security bodies — the Treasury Police and the National Guard — were to be abolished within 30 days of the cease-fire, and five rapid deployment infantry battalions that had been used as counter-insurgency forces were to be demobilized beginning in August 1992. An impartial Ad Hoc Commission on the Purification of the Armed Forces, composed of three Salvadorians of unimpeachable democratic credentials, was to evaluate, by 15 August, the professional competence of more than 2,000 officers, paying particular attention to respect for human rights. The Commission would then make recommendations for the military's "purification" through the transfer or discharge of individuals whose record had been found lacking. The Government, in turn, would have 60 days to comply.

67   Formation of the new National Civil Police was to follow an equally rigorous schedule. Even before the cease-fire, a preliminary bill organizing the National Public Security Academy was to be submitted to the Legislative Assembly pursuant to the September 1991 New York Agreement. Courses were to begin on 1 May 1992 and deployment of the first graduates on 1 November. On economic and social questions, the Peace Agreement stipulated, among other things, that the Government of El Salvador was to submit the National Reconstruction Plan to the FMLN within 30 days of the Agreement's signing and that transfers of land to ex-combatants on both sides would begin immediately, on 1 February.

68   The implementation process would prove to be difficult. As I noted at the time, "The agreements are complex and demand a commitment to compromise and fundamental adjustments in political and social attitudes. Nor are they self-executing. The United Nations is committed to assist the two parties but success will be assured only by their political will and their acceptance of national reconciliation as the overriding national goal."[28]

28/Document 41
See page 238

First enlargement of ONUSAL's mandate

69   These and the many other tasks entrusted to the United Nations in the Peace Agreement required a substantial enlargement of ONUSAL's mandate, which at the signing of the Peace Agreement consisted solely of its responsibilities *vis-à-vis* verification of the San José Agreement on Human Rights. On 10 January 1992, I informed the Security Council that ONUSAL would have to be supplemented by both a Military Division, to verify all aspects of the cease-fire and separation of forces, and a Police Division, to monitor the maintenance of public order during the transition period when the National Civil Police was being formed, trained and commissioned into service.[29]

29/Document 34
See page 187

70   The Security Council agreed with my assessment and decided on 14 January 1992, in resolution 729 (1992), to broaden ONUSAL's mandate and increase its strength to include 380 military observers and 631 police monitors.[30] The Council also extended ONUSAL's mandate to 31 October 1992 — the projected date for the end of the armed conflict — at which point the Mission's status would be reviewed. Given the great demand for United Nations peace-keeping services — the month of February 1992 would see the Security Council decide to undertake large and ambitious operations in Cambodia and the former Yugoslavia — it was hoped that the successful implementation of the military aspects of the Peace Agreement would allow a reduction in ONUSAL's military division at that point.

30/Document 35
See page 192

Advances and delays

71   The early months of ONUSAL's expanded role in El Salvador saw progress in many areas.[31] Three hundred and sixty-eight United Nations military observers were deployed on 31 January 1992, and the cease-fire began the following day. Deployment of the Police Division began on 7 February with 147 observers taking up their positions; by late May, 304 police observers were in place. The National Commission for the Consolidation of Peace (COPAZ) was established and two of its subcommissions designated: one to deal with the land problem, the other with the National Civil Police. On 19 May, the Ad Hoc Commission on the Purification of the Armed Forces was formed. ONUSAL's Human Rights Division reported a decline in the number of complaints it was receiving. And to the great credit of the Government and the FMLN, as of late May the cease-fire had not once been broken.[32]

31/Document 39
See page 236;
Document 41
See page 238

72   In a development carrying great practical and symbolic weight, members of the FMLN's General Command and other FMLN

32/Document 43
See page 247

leaders began to re-enter El Salvador legally, following the adoption by the Legislative Assembly on 23 January 1992 of a national reconciliation law granting a broad amnesty for political crimes and offences under ordinary law. The returning FMLN leaders, their safety guaranteed by the Government, enjoyed freedom of movement as well as ample access to the mass media. They were accompanied during the first few days by members of the National Police and, under the terms of the Peace Agreement, were allowed to make arrangements for personal body-guards.

73   At the same time, however, a variety of problems were arousing serious concern and having a negative effect on the atmosphere for implementation of the Agreements as a whole.

74   Both sides had failed to concentrate all their forces in the designated locations within the prescribed deadline. The two public security bodies that were to have been abolished — the Treasury Police and the National Guard — were instead "converted" by the Government into the Military Police and the Frontier Guards, respectively. The FMLN, for its part, delayed the reintegration of the first 20 per cent of its ex-combatants, saying, among other things, that the Government had failed to implement measures that would facilitate the reintegration process, notably those relating to land and to political activity by the FMLN. ONUSAL continued to have doubts about whether the FMLN had accurately declared its true weapons holdings.

75   The FMLN also delayed the concentration of its forces in the designated areas, citing the Government's failure to adhere to other provisions of the Agreement and a lack of infrastructure — water supply, food, shelter, the road network, health and education — at the locations. To improve the sites, which were intended to serve as a crucial bridge between war and peace, ONUSAL coordinated a collaborative effort involving UNDP, the World Food Programme (WFP), the World Health Organization (WHO), the United Nations Educational, Scientific and Cultural Organization (UNESCO), PAHO and NGOs such as Médecins sans Frontières and Caritas Internationalis of El Salvador. UNICEF, for its part, focused on the urgent needs of some 186,000 people, many of them the wives and children of the ex-combatants, clustered around the sites. UNICEF also supported the provision of water and the meeting of basic health needs.

76   Efforts to establish the National Public Security Academy were also encountering delays over personnel, legislation and the selection of the school's physical premises. This was a matter of some urgency since, under the Peace Agreement, all members of the National Civil Police had to be graduates of the Academy. In addition, common crime in El Salvador was on the upswing, a pattern attributed at least in part to the legacy of a period in which violence and the use of arms had been

for many a way of life. To assist in the establishment and operation of the Academy during its first two years, a technical mission of experts from Spain and the United States headed by the UNDP Resident Representative in El Salvador was working with the Government and the FMLN.

77   Perhaps the most critical strains at this stage concerned land. During the talks that led to the Peace Agreement, negotiators had reached only broad understandings on land issues, leaving details to be worked out during the implementation process. Thus, in mid-1992, the parties were forced to grapple anew, in an increasingly charged environment, with one of the main causes of the armed conflict.

78   The complex agrarian problem in El Salvador — a country with a predominantly agricultural economy, where land is in short supply and unevenly distributed, and where the population is large and expanding rapidly — was further complicated by the civil conflict. Fighting, fires, land mines and other wartime hazards had forced many people in the conflict zones to abandon their land; some of these plots were subsequently settled by people who had been displaced from their homes elsewhere. A multitude of such shifts had occurred during the war.

79   The Peace Agreement stated that the land-tenure situation in the conflict zones would be respected "until a satisfactory legal solution for the definitive land-tenure system" was reached. It also said that landholders would not be evicted and that they would be given financial support to purchase land and to increase agricultural production. Indeed, such activities were to provide ex-combatants from both sides, and particularly those from the FMLN, with one of their main avenues for reintegration. However, tensions rose in February and early March 1992 as a result of property seizures by various peasant groups, evictions by Government public security bodies and lawsuits by landowners. Attempts by ONUSAL to freeze the situation were unsuccessful.

80   Having received appeals for assistance from both the Government of El Salvador and the FMLN, I dispatched Mr. Marrack I. Goulding (United Kingdom), then Under-Secretary-General for Peace-keeping Operations, to El Salvador. On 13 March 1992, following extensive meetings with President Cristiani and with the FMLN General Command, agreement was reached that land seizures and evictions would be suspended in order to facilitate the processing of cases under the conflict-resolution mechanisms envisaged in the peace agreements. I subsequently reported that additional consultation mechanisms, devised as part of the March talks, were working while efforts continued to reach a pragmatic solution to the problem.[33]

33/Document 41
See page 238

Deep distrust — the legacy of conflict

34/Document 40
See page 237

35/Document 42
See page 246

81   Assessing the course of the peace process in May 1992, I noted that implementation was being impeded by the two sides' contradictory interpretations of provisions of the Peace Agreement, which had led them to exchange public accusations instead of working together constructively and pragmatically. I reminded the parties of ONUSAL's standing offer of good offices and impressed upon them my view that one breach of the agreements could not be used to justify another. I also reiterated the fact of ONUSAL's complete impartiality; at times, this position was perceived by one side as partiality towards the other. It was in this context that I reported a recurrence of threats against the security of the Mission and its personnel. I also informed the Security Council that it would be necessary to maintain temporarily the strength of ONUSAL's Military Division, which was to have been reduced after 1 June.[34] In a 3 June statement, the Security Council took note of my apprehensions and stated that it, too, was deeply concerned about the delays and the climate of mutual suspicion. "If that situation were to continue", said the Council, "it would jeopardize the very foundation of the agreements".[35]

Adjustments to the timetable

36/Document 44
See page 251

82   Conversations I had on 15 May 1992 with both President Cristiani and FMLN Coordinator-General Schafik Handal assured me of the sincere intention of the two sides to bring the implementation process back on course and recoup the time lost. On 17 June, following successful talks conducted with the help of ONUSAL, the Government and the FMLN took a major step in this direction by reprogramming those parts of the timetable that had been affected by the delays. The new arrangements spelled out revised deadlines for all the crucial commitments that had given rise to dispute: the concentration of forces, reintegration of FMLN combatants into civilian life, creation of the National Public Security Academy, abolition of the National Guard and Treasury Police, legalization of the FMLN as a political party and land tenure.[36]

83   But delays continued to occur, prompting me once again to send Under-Secretary-General Goulding to El Salvador for consultations. On 19 August, the parties agreed to a second series of changes in the timetable. Yet again, however, implementation fell behind schedule. Moreover, in both the reprogrammings, the fulfilment by the Government of certain key commitments — involving land transfers and the creation of the new National Civil Police — had to be postponed beyond

31 October. In response, the FMLN asserted that the dismantling of its military structure would also have to be reprogrammed.

84   An evaluation by the United Nations on 17 September concluded that the land issue had again emerged as a main impediment. In an attempt to overcome this obstacle, I sent Under-Secretary-General Goulding to El Salvador on 28 September for more talks. Although progress was made, the FMLN stated on 30 September that it would suspend the third phase of its demobilization of forces until new dates had been set for the start of the transfer of land and other aspects of the Agreement. More and more, the FMLN was insisting on such a linkage, saying that the lack of land deprived its members of channels for reintegration into civilian life. The Government, for its part, asserted that it was constrained in this regard by a lack of available parcels and by a shortage of funds with which to buy land from willing sellers. In any case, ONUSAL and I held to the position that each party was obliged to comply with its commitments — and to do so without making them conditional on reciprocal compliance by the other party.

85   On 13 October 1992, I presented to President Cristiani and the FMLN General Command an "equitable compromise" between the two sides' positions on the land issue.[37] Aware that the proposal would satisfy neither the Government nor the FMLN, I none the less urged the parties, in the spirit of cooperation and reconciliation, to refrain from coming forward with amendments. The proposal provided that the total number of beneficiaries of the land transfers should not exceed 47,500 — 15,000 ex-combatants from the armed forces of El Salvador, 7,500 FMLN ex-combatants and approximately 25,000 landholders in the former zones of conflict. The proposal also called for the Government to guarantee that current landholders would not be evicted from the properties they held, as specified in the Chapultepec Agreement. As I noted at the time, this was a key point which could threaten the successful implementation of the peace accords if it were ignored. COPAZ was to determine the actual amount of land available for transfer and the number of landholders on it, and other operational aspects of the proposal were to be worked out by a supervisory committee.

37/Document 46
See page 257;
Document 47
See page 257;
Document 50
See page 260;
Document 55
See page 264;
Document 56
See page 265;
Document 76
See page 443

86   The parties accepted the plan within a few days, but not without recording certain understandings about some of its provisions.[38] The FMLN stated that the size of the lots would leave the land-transfer programme's beneficiaries at current levels of subsistence and poverty. The Government, for its part, sought a number of clarifications regarding the interpretation of the proposal. On 31 October, the process of transfer started officially with the signing, in the presence of ONUSAL, by the two sides of an agreement to transfer two State properties to FMLN ex-combatants and landholders on those properties.

38/Document 48
See page 258;
Document 49
See page 259;
Document 51
See page 261;
Document 52
See page 262

87   With the agreement on the land problem, attention shifted

back to the implementation calendar. It had become evident that the cumulative delays made it unlikely that the complete demobilization of the FMLN's military structure could be achieved by 31 October 1992, as provided for in the Peace Agreement. On 23 October, I proposed to the parties a third revision of the timetable with a new target date of 15 December 1992 for the end of the armed conflict.[39]

39/Document 53
See page 263;
Document 55
See page 264

88   The FMLN accepted my proposal contingent upon its acceptance by the Government. The Government, however, reserved its position on some aspects of the proposal, conditioning demobilization, reduction and restructuring of the armed forces on submission by the FMLN of a weapons inventory and initiation of the destruction of those weapons. Press reports noted that elements of the military and of President Cristiani's political party were displaying increasing resistance to the idea of rescheduling the demobilization of the FMLN and allowing the FMLN to be converted into a political party.

89   President Cristiani also raised questions at this juncture about the schedule envisaged for implementing the recommendations of the Ad Hoc Commission on Purification of the Armed Forces. The Commission had submitted its confidential report to President Cristiani and myself on 22 September. As the Commission's recommendations became known publicly on an informal basis — several senior officers and more than 100 overall were on the list of those to be dismissed or transferred — the military grew restive over what it perceived as unexpectedly extensive changes. The armed forces were said to be particularly disturbed that the FMLN faced no similar accounting. The FMLN, for its part, was now linking its own demobilization to progress in the purification process.

90   As tensions rose — one of the three members of the Ad Hoc Commission reported receiving an anonymous death threat — and as the original 31 October 1992 deadline for ending the armed conflict passed, I sent to San Salvador both Under-Secretary-General Goulding and Assistant Secretary-General de Soto. On 6 November, following eight days of consultations, agreement was reached on the next stages of the peace process. President Cristiani agreed to inform me by 29 November of the administrative decisions he had taken concerning purification of the armed forces and to complete the process by 1 January 1993. The FMLN was to provide ONUSAL with a final inventory of weapons, conclude the concentration of those weapons on 30 November and begin their destruction on 1 December.

91   The agreement surmounted a major obstacle but marked the first time that compliance with certain key points in the calendar by one side was made contingent upon compliance with specific undertakings by the other. At the time, I described the peace process as entering "an especially delicate phase" during which it would be "imperative that both

parties act with caution and restraint in order to consolidate stability in the country". In the midst of these difficulties, the Security Council, by its resolution 784 (1992), had renewed ONUSAL's mandate for an interim period of one month, from 30 October until 30 November.[40]

92   On 30 November, in resolution 791 (1992), the Council urged both parties "to respect scrupulously and to implement in good faith the solemn commitments" they had assumed under the agreements, and extended the mandate for a period of six months, to 31 May 1993.[41]

40/Document 54
See page 264;
Document 56
See page 265

41/Document 57
See page 275

End of the armed conflict

93   Despite the late and often imperfect compliance with the peace agreements, and the polarization generated by the long years of conflict, the parties were, on the whole, advancing steadily towards the new 15 December 1992 target date for the formal cessation of the armed conflict. The peace process, I observed, was continuing to "give every sign of being irreversible".[42]

94   The impeccable observance of the cease-fire — as of late November 1992, there had yet to be a single violation — was one such indication. Further evidence of the trust and confidence growing out of the peace accords was the collaboration of the former antagonists in assisting ONUSAL in a UNICEF-led Mine Awareness Project to warn the populations in mine-ridden zones of the dangers they faced. UNICEF had decided to act upon learning that 75 per cent of those being killed or injured in mine-related accidents were children. By the end of 1992, the project had detected and demarcated well over 25,000 land-mines — believed to represent nearly all of those still in existence. In addition, a public mass media awareness campaign had been launched using television spot advertising, radio jingles and three mobile teams of educators. The Government was seeking international assistance for the next phase of the campaign — deactivating the mines.

42/Document 56
See page 265;
Document 58
See page 276

95   By this time, 60 per cent of FMLN ex-combatants had been demobilized, their weapons handed over to ONUSAL. Reduction of the armed forces was being carried out in accordance with the plan submitted to me by the Government. ONUSAL was thus able to reduce its Military Division to a strength of 226 observers and 8 medical officers, with a reduction to 103 observers expected in January 1993. The Police Division, with a strength of 303 observers, provided constant supervision and guidance to the Auxiliary Transitory Police, which was responsible for maintaining public order and security in the former zones of conflict until its replacement by the National Civil Police; observers gave daily academic instruction and logistic support to the temporary force, which

ONUSAL Deployment as of April 1992

At peak strength, ONUSAL fielded 368 observers (February 1992) and 332 police monitors (June 1993).
UN Member States contributing troops, military observers and/or police to ONUSAL included Argentina,
Austria, Brazil, Canada, Chile, Colombia, Ecuador, France, Guatemala, Guyana, India, Ireland, Italy, Mexico, Norway,
Spain, Sweden, Venezuela and Uruguay.

consisted of students from the National Public Security Academy. ONUSAL police monitors were also cooperating with the Military Division in verifying the dissolution of the Government's civil defence units, assisting in locating illegal arms caches and supporting the Human Rights Division. On 1 September 1992, with the Archbishop of San Salvador as a witness, the leadership of the FMLN swore to respect the Constitution and laws of El Salvador. Also that day, the National Public Security Academy received its first recruits, some 622 students; an additional 687 had joined by mid-November.

96   The Human Rights Division reported in August that in spite of concerns about summary executions, violent death and anonymous death threats, the overall human rights situation in El Salvador had improved during the past year, including a substantial improvement with regard to international humanitarian law.[43] The Independent Expert of the Commission on Human Rights concurred in November (A/47/596), adding, however, that unless certain characteristics were eliminated as

43/Document 45
See page 252

soon as possible, patterns of serious violations of human rights might recur. In a subsequent report (E/CN.4/1993/11), the Independent Expert added that "the number of attempts on human life originating from the practice of extrajudicial, summary or arbitrary execution" did not appear to have been high in 1992, although there did appear to have been a "significant increase in the number of homicides attributed to unknown persons or common criminals." Although the practice of torture or other ill-treatment of detainees had not been completely eliminated, the cases recorded could not be identified as forming part of a systematic policy. "At the end of the year", the Independent Expert concluded, "and with the intervention of ONUSAL, possible signs of progress began to be noted".

97   The Independent Expert had assumed his responsibilities earlier in the year, pursuant to a resolution of the Commission on Human Rights (E/CN.4/RES/1992/62), in which the Commission extended its thanks to the Special Representative and requested me to appoint an independent expert to discharge a new mandate, namely, to provide assistance in human rights matters to the Government of El Salvador; to consider the human rights situation in the country and the effects of the peace agreements on the enjoyment of human rights; and to investigate the manner in which both parties apply the recommendations contained in the final report of the Special Representative and those made by ONUSAL and the commissions established during the negotiating process.

98   The Commission on the Truth, meanwhile, formally installed on 13 July 1992 in accordance with the April 1991 Mexico Agreements, had nearly completed its investigations and interviews in El Salvador and was soon expected to present its report and recommendations. My predecessor had appointed three distinguished individuals to the Commission: Belisario Betancur, former President of Colombia; Reinaldo Figueredo Planchart, former Foreign Minister of Venezuela; and Professor Thomas Buergenthal, former President of the Inter-American Court of Human Rights and President of the Inter-American Institute for Human Rights. In October 1992, an international team of forensic anthropologists working under their direction unearthed bones and other evidence that a massacre of civilians had occurred in El Mozote and nearby hamlets in December 1981. The incident, in which hundreds of people, including children and pregnant mothers, were believed to have been killed, was one of the most brutal of the entire civil war. That Salvadorians were ready to acknowledge and discuss such painful and divisive events was taken as a positive development in the process of national reckoning and reconciliation.

99   On 1 December 1992, I received from President Cristiani a letter dated 29 November informing me that he had taken the administrative decisions to implement the recommendations of the Ad Hoc

Commission on Purification of the Armed Forces. Six days later, I informed the Government that the FMLN's inventory of weapons had been found "satisfactory" and that the destruction of the weapons had begun. The FMLN also resumed the demobilization of its combatants, completing the process on 14 December. That same day, the former rebel organization was legalized as a political party.

100 With these steps, the two parties in El Salvador were in general compliance with my proposal of 23 October 1992 and thus poised at long last to formally end the armed conflict and cross the line from an era of war into one of peace. The momentous event was marked by a ceremony in San Salvador on 15 December attended by President Cristiani, the FMLN's General Command, the Presidents of Belize, Guatemala and Nicaragua, the Vice-President of the United States and myself. "The first goal of the [peace] process has been achieved", I then remarked. "Salvadorians have every reason to be proud. At a turbulent time in history, they are providing a shining example to the world."[44]

44/Document 59
See page 281;
Document 60
See page 282;
Document 61
See page 285

V   Towards a new El Salvador

101   With peace restored, the Government and the FMLN turned their energies to the other main goals to which they had agreed: democratization, reunification and unrestricted respect for human rights. The peace process had created the necessary conditions — legal, institutional, political and social — for the practical attainment of these aspirations. But success would not follow automatically just because the armed conflict was over; rather, it would require a gradual process in which the full range of interests and wishes within Salvadorian society was aired and accommodated. "The country is now embarking on this process", reported ONUSAL's Human Rights Division in April 1993. "The basic trends are promising, but Salvadorians still have a long way to go before their chosen model of a democratic, reconciled society in which human rights are respected becomes a reality."[45] Developments during the first half of 1993 — from the watershed publication of the report of the Commission on the Truth to the discovery of secret FMLN weapons stockpiles, a dangerous setback — underscore this mixed assessment and are the focus of this section.

45/Document 70
See page 416;
Document 83
See page 466

An ambivalent human rights situation

102   By the early months of 1993, enforced disappearances and torture were virtually non-existent in El Salvador, according to ONUSAL. Freedom of expression and assembly and the exercise of political rights were widely enjoyed, not subject to any restriction and guaranteed by the State. The new National Counsel for the Defence of Human Rights was becoming increasingly active and was beginning to win the confidence of the population. The Government, workers and employers agreed on a social contract calling for significant changes in labour relations. "[T]hese positive trends", said ONUSAL in its April report, , "must first grow and then be consolidated as part of the effective functioning of democracy if they are to be lasting and not just passing phenomena."

103   A number of questions persisted. Politically motivated violence was continuing, albeit at a much lower frequency. An increase in crime and ordinary violence had led to growing public insecurity. Notwithstanding a degree of progress in the area of judicial reform, the administration of justice continued to be woefully inadequate and incapable of ensuring fulfilment by the State of its duty to guarantee human rights or respect for the right of citizens to due process of law. Doubts about the subordination of the armed forces to civilian authority grew when I reported to the Security Council on 7 January 1993 that the Government was not yet in full compliance with the recommendations of the Ad Hoc Commission on Purification of the Armed Forces.[46] I also reported that the FMLN had not completed the destruction of its arms and equipment by 29 January, contrary to prior assurances it had given.[47] On 9 February, the Security Council said it shared my concerns and strongly urged the parties to persist in their determination to bring peace to El Salvador.[48]

46/Document 62
See page 286

47/Document 64
See page 288

48/Document 65
See page 288

104   ONUSAL's Human Rights Division pointed out, however, that the problems being reported during this period were occurring in a qualitatively different framework from the situation which had existed in El Salvador in the past. Rights violations were no longer a reflection of the will of the State but, rather, "carry-overs" from the period prior to the Peace Agreement. As ONUSAL emphasized: "The political, institutional and social changes taking place in El Salvador are . . . characterized by the affirmation of the rule of law, democratic life and the protection and promotion of human rights . . . The essential factor here is that the momentum of the peace process gradually overcomes problems, even those arising from the fact that certain agreements are not yet being observed."

ONUSAL *mandate enlarged a second time*

105   On 8 January 1993, the Government of El Salvador formally asked the United Nations to observe the March 1994 general elections in which a President, a Legislative Assembly, mayors and representatives to a Central American Parliament would be chosen. I emphasized that, given the importance of the elections, they would be "the logical culmination of the entire peace process". I informed the Security Council of my intention to recommend that the Council accept the Government's request.[49]

49/Document 63
See page 287

106   A United Nations technical mission visited El Salvador from 18 to 28 April 1993 to define the terms of reference, concept of operations and financial implications of expanding ONUSAL's mandate. It met during this time with the Supreme Electoral Tribunal (the new electoral authority), COPAZ and the political parties. Several areas of concern were identified, such as the serious inadequacies of the existing electoral roll and difficulties with the timely issuance of electoral documents. One significant problem was that many records had been burned or destroyed during the war. Wartime displacements of people and other migrations had further undermined efforts at record keeping.

107   Taking into account prior United Nations electoral experience, I recommended that an Electoral Division be established as part of ONUSAL to observe the electoral process, including voter registration and the campaign, in order to ensure its impartiality and full respect for the right to vote.[50] Working in close coordination with the Human Rights and Police Divisions, the main tasks of the Electoral Division would be to monitor electoral irregularities, receive complaints and convey them, as appropriate, to electoral authorities; to observe political meetings and demonstrations; and to follow up and assess electoral advertising and electoral-related reporting in the media.

50/Document 74;
See page 427;
Document 75
See page 442

108   On election day, the number of observers would increase in order to permit monitoring at every polling site. ONUSAL would observe the counting of votes and make projections for its own use and, possibly, for sharing with the Supreme Electoral Tribunal. The electoral observation would continue after election day to cover all aspects related to the counting of votes and possible challenges to results. The observation would conclude with the official proclamation of final results by the Supreme Electoral Tribunal. On 27 May 1993, in resolution 832 (1993), the Security Council approved my plan.[51]

51/Document 78
See page 454

Commission on the Truth report made public

109   The release of the eagerly awaited report of the Commission on the Truth[52] on 15 March 1993 sparked an outcry in El Salvador on the part of the High Command of the armed forces, the President of the Supreme Court, highly placed Government officials and other targets of the report's calls for justice and punishment. Indeed, tension mounted in El Salvador as these figures, as well as some political leaders and segments of the media, vehemently and publicly rejected the Commission's findings and recommendations. It was said that the Commission had exceeded its mandate and presumed to assume judicial functions. There was strident criticism of the United Nations and renewed publication of anonymous threats against ONUSAL. Fear was voiced that the report could prompt violence, such as acts of revenge, thereby destabilizing the country at a critical stage of the peace process. The situation was complicated further because the purification of the armed forces had not yet been completed.

52/Document 67
See page 290

110   At United Nations Headquarters in New York, a ceremony was held at which the report — entitled "From madness to hope: the 12-year war in El Salvador" — was presented to me formally. Addressing an audience that included the three members of the Commission, representatives of the Government and the FMLN and representatives of the four Friends of the Secretary-General (Colombia, Mexico, Spain and Venezuela), I reiterated my belief in the importance of the Commission's work and in the power of what it represented.

111   "The philosophy underlying the decision to establish the Commission and its mandate", I stated [see UN Press Release SG/SM/4942-CA/76], "is that in order to put behind them the trauma of the war, the Salvadorians have to go through the catharsis of facing the truth. Bringing to light the truth is thus an integral component, indeed part and parcel of the process of reconciliation and reunification of Salvadorian society. There can be no reconciliation without the public knowledge of the truth . . .

"It is fair to say that the armed conflict left no Salvadorian untouched. In the same way and in the spirit of the peace accords all Salvadorians must know, by learning of this report, that the war is truly at an end . . .

"All efforts must be deployed to make sure that the Commission's report attains the farthest reaches of the nation. All Salvadorians must know of it. It should become a part of their culture and their history, so that they can better face the future . . .

"Now that the truth has been brought to light, the people of El Salvador can contemplate forgiveness."

112   During the course of its work, the Commission received more than 22,000 complaints of "serious acts of violence" that had occurred between January 1980 and July 1991. More than 60 per cent referred to extrajudicial executions, more than 25 per cent to forced disappearances and more than 20 per cent to torture. The Commission chose to focus on about 30 cases that had been selected to illustrate the different patterns of violence. These were classified as violence by agents of the State; massacres of peasants by the armed forces; assassinations by death squads; violence by the FMLN; and assassinations of judges.

113   Ninety-five per cent of this violence, the Commission found, had been carried out by the military, the security forces and the death squads, predominantly against civilians. The report identified by name senior officers who had been involved in the planning and cover-up of murders, and determined that the army had been responsible for the massacre of civilians in and around El Mozote in 1981. The FMLN was responsible for the other 5 per cent of the violence, said the report, including an assassination campaign targeting some 30 town and village mayors.

114   The report also asserted that the judicial system of El Salvador was "incapable of fairly assessing and carrying out punishment". The Commission itself, however, had been given no authority to prosecute or punish crimes. Limited to making recommendations for action, it grouped these under four headings:

A.   Recommendations arising directly from the results of the

Commission's own investigations. These related to persons found to have been involved in the cases investigated and to certain aspects of the country's judicial system. Some of these individuals were to be dismissed from their posts; others were to be disqualified from holding any public post or office for at least 10 years and disqualified permanently from any activity related to public security or national defence. In addition, the Commission recommended that the members of the Supreme Court of Justice should resign;

B. Eradication of structural causes directly connected with the incidents investigated. These included full implementation of the peace accords, reforms in the Armed Forces and in the arrangements for public security and the investigation of illegal groups;

C. Institutional reforms to prevent the repetition of such events. These related to judicial reform, the protection of human rights (including implementation of 19 recommendations already made by ONUSAL's Human Rights Division) and deployment of the National Civil Police;

D. Measures for national reconciliation. The Commission recommended the creation of a special fund for the compensation of victims and construction of a national monument bearing the names of victims, recognition of the good name of the victims and institution of a national holiday.[53]

53/Document 74
See page 427;
Document 77
See page 447

115   The report required action on the part of the Government, the FMLN and the Legislative Assembly. The Security Council, in a presidential statement, called on the parties to comply with the Commission's recommendations.[54] Mr. Schafik Handal said that, notwithstanding a number of reservations about the report, the FMLN accepted the recommendations in their entirety. However, President Cristiani expressed some reservations, stating that he was willing to comply strictly with those of the Commission's recommendations which fell within his competence, were consistent with the Constitution, were in harmony with the peace accords and contributed to national reconciliation.[55] Moreover, at his urging, the country's Legislative Assembly passed, less than a week after the report was published, a general amnesty law for people implicated in wartime violations and abuses. The move was criticized by the FMLN and other members of the Salvadorian opposition. In a statement, I expressed my concern at the haste with which this step had been taken and my view that it would have been preferable if the amnesty had been enacted after creating a broad degree of national consensus in its favour.

54/Document 66
See page 289

55/Document 68
See page 415

116   In the light of the overall reaction to the report, I decided that the United Nations would make a detailed analysis of the Commission's recommendations, examining whether any of them were outside the Commission's mandate or incompatible with the Constitution. I conveyed that analysis to the Government, the FMLN and COPAZ on

20 May 1993, emphasizing my view that implementation should be completed as far as possible before the elections. According to the analysis, only one of the Commission's recommendations could not be implemented.[56]

56/Document 71
See page 424;
Document 72
See page 425;
Document 73
See page 426;
Document 77
See page 447;
Document 86
See page 472

57/Document 74
See page 427

More progress

117   On 21 May 1993, I reported to the Security Council that the peace process was on course.[57] In addition to the formal end of the armed conflict, the conversion of the FMLN into a political party and improvements in the human rights situation, gains were being made towards many other principal objectives of the Peace Agreement. One major achievement was the full restoration of public administration in the former zones of conflict. Mayors and judges who had been forced to leave their jurisdictions during the conflict returned, many of them under arrangements negotiated by ONUSAL, and immediately organized public town meetings to identify projects for the reconstruction of their communities.

118   Meanwhile, the Government accelerated its reduction of the armed forces, finishing the task on 31 March 1993, well ahead of schedule. The Government, which had not complied with the commitment it had made in November 1992, also agreed, at the behest of the Secretary-General, to complete the purification of the armed forces by 30 June. And by 1 April, the arms listed in the FMLN inventory presented to ONUSAL, within and outside El Salvador, had been destroyed, except for a small quantity whose destruction the FMLN scheduled to coincide with full compliance by the Government with the Ad Hoc Commission's recommendations.

119   With ONUSAL's shift away from military concerns, its Military Division was able to reduce its strength again, to 74 observers as of May 1993. A reduction to 38 was to follow; these remaining observers would monitor the recovery of military weapons held by private individuals, help Salvadorian teams mark and clear minefields and conduct patrols in the former zones of conflict.

120   The National Civil Police began its deployment after the first classes graduated from the National Public Security Academy in February 1993; by the end of the year it was expected that the National Civil Police would number approximately 3,000 — half the projected total. Under the peace accords, 60 per cent of the new police personnel were to have had no direct participation in the armed conflict; former members of the FMLN or the National Police were to account for no more than 20 per cent each.

121 Certain aspects of the peace process, however, continued to be bedevilled by delays, financial difficulties and conflicting interpretations of the Peace Agreement.

122 The Government had yet to begin phasing out the National Police, which it was obligated to do under the Peace Agreement, and was strengthening the force with personnel from the National Guard and Treasury Police. The Government said these moves were necessary in order to fight common crime, but ONUSAL said they contravened the spirit of the accords.

123 The land-transfer programme was under way, but at a slow pace. The issue of greatest concern in this area involved the relocation of landholders occupying plots whose owners did not wish to sell. The 13 October 1992 agreement had stipulated that such landholders would be relocated last, after the situation of the landholders had been legalized and after combatants of both sides had been given priority in receiving land as they demobilized. But both sides had chosen to reverse this sequence — the Government because landowners were seeking to reclaim their land, and the FMLN because many of its constituents wanted land closer to their families or felt pressured to leave the lands they had occupied. The relocation of landholders at this stage could have compromised the success of the programme. Immediately, it generated price speculation and fears that owners would be less likely to sell their land if they perceived that they could simply get rid of people occupying their land. Additional land-related problems concerned insufficient credit for land purchase, housing and crop raising; the slow and complicated procedure for the legal transfer of land; variable land quality; and the likelihood that there would be a significantly higher number of landholders than the ceiling of 25,000 stipulated in the Peace Agreement. The various delays prevented many beneficiaries from beginning cultivation during the planting season that began in May 1993.

124 "The path to national reconciliation has not been without difficulties . . .", I stated in my May report, "yet the predominating characteristic of the Salvadorian peace process has been its irreversibility." On 27 May 1993, in resolution 832 (1993), the Security Council approved my recommendation that ONUSAL's mandate be extended until 30 November 1993.[58] Just prior to the Council's action, Mr. Augusto Ramirez-Ocampo (Colombia) had succeeded Mr. Iqbal Riza as my Special Representative and Chief of Mission.

58/Document 78
See page 454

FMLN *arms caches*

125 On 23 May 1993, an accidental explosion at an automobile repair shop in Managua, Nicaragua, led to the discovery of a startling array of clandestine FMLN weapons deposits. The previously undisclosed arms at the Managua site included surface-to-air missiles, large quantities of ammunition and weapons and a variety of explosives. More than 300 passports of various nationalities were also found. On the basis of the evidence uncovered, the Nicaraguan authorities linked the arms and other items to a constituent group of the FMLN, the Fuerzas Populares de Liberacion (FPL).[59]

59/Document 79
See page 455;
Document 81
See page 456

126   The FPL leadership at first denied any connection to the incident, then quickly acknowledged responsibility, steadfastly denied any intention of reverting to the use of arms as an instrument of political pressure and offered its full cooperation in clarifying the facts. Other constituent groups of the FMLN were also found be in possession of various caches of arms, ammunition and other *matériel,* which they said would soon be transferred to ONUSAL for destruction. Investigations by an ONUSAL technical team eventually uncovered 114 arms deposits in El Salvador, Honduras and Nicaragua. The incident and subsequent revelations were described by the Security Council as "the most serious violation of the peace accords to date".[60]

60/Document 80
See page 456

127   Amid profound fears that the issue of the clandestine arms caches could undermine or derail the peace process, I expressed my concern in a 12 June letter to Mr. Schafik Handal of the FMLN: "I am distressed to learn that, contrary to your assurances which I had accepted in good faith, the inventory presented to ONUSAL by the FMLN was grossly inaccurate and failed to include large quantities of warlike *matériel.* Such a deliberate attempt to mislead me places my credibility in doubt and raises in my mind very serious questions of confidence and trust . . ."[61] In response, Mr. Handal reaffirmed the FMLN's commitment to the peace process and the Secretary-General of the FPL, Mr. Salvador Sánchez Cerén, said that its action had been prompted by profound mistrust of the armed forces.[62] The FMLN subsequently agreed to disclose all its holdings of arms and munitions and destroy them by 4 August 1993.

61/Document 82
See page 458

62/Document 82
See page 458

128   Reporting to the Security Council on 29 June, I stressed that "the seriousness of the situation . . . cannot be overemphasized".[63] President Cristiani had expressed his deep concern, saying that the FMLN's conduct might be a reason to disband the FMLN as a political party. But the cancellation or suspension of the FMLN's status as a political party could itself have dealt a severe blow to the peace process. "The transformation of [the] FMLN into a political party and the full reintegration of its members . . . are at the very core of the peace accords . . . It is likewise imperative to avoid a disruption of the electoral process, in which it is essential that FMLN have every opportunity to participate." I emphasized, however, that the FMLN would have to "demonstrate anew its commitment" to the peace process, and I commended the

63/Document 82
See page 458

restraint and statesmanship shown by President Cristiani during this difficult period.

129 Following a complex and time-consuming operation by ONUSAL military and police observers, the destruction of the FMLN's weapons and equipment mandated by the peace agreements was completed on 18 August 1993.[64] ONUSAL determined that the arms discovered following the explosion in Managua represented approximately 30 per cent of the total FMLN arsenal. In order to determine whether the arms turned over to ONUSAL, both before and after the Managua incident, represented a realistic assessment of the FMLN's total inventory — the Mission had to rely on data voluntarily provided by the parties as its main source of information — ONUSAL conducted a comparative analysis based on other official and unofficial sources, including well-known international and national military research institutions and the demobilization certificates issued by ONUSAL to ex-FMLN combatants. In late August, I announced that the FMLN had been effectively dismantled and its former combatants demobilized and reintegrated into civilian life.

64/Document 85
See page 471;
Document 88
See page 473

130 The apprehensions raised by the discovery of large quantities of undeclared weapons still in the FMLN's possession seemed now to have been surmounted. In the end the incident appeared to have had at least two important dividends: it demonstrated the strength of the peace process, and it brought into sharp focus the public's condemnation of armed groups and the futility of arms as a viable means to achieve political aims.

VI A critical phase

131   I turn now to the latter half of 1993, a period in which challenges to the peace process became noticeably more acute. El Salvador's financial and economic problems were making it increasingly difficult to reconcile the spending required to implement various elements of the peace accords with the limits the Government had agreed to as part of a stabilization programme sponsored by the World Bank and International Monetary Fund (IMF). More troublesome still, a renewal of death-squad-style assassinations indicated that some groups and individuals were continuing to choose to resort to violence in order to achieve political objectives. It was within this context, discussed on the following pages, that ONUSAL began to monitor the registration of voters and to carry out its other electoral responsibilities.

The need for economic support

132   Since 1989, El Salvador had been carrying out a stabilization and structural reform programme sponsored by the World Bank and IMF to promote growth, rebuild its war-ravaged economy and improve the standard of living of the country's most downtrodden groups. UNDP, the Inter-American Development Bank and bilateral donors, particularly the United States, were also supporting this effort.

133   At the same time, the end of the war and the implementation of the Peace Agreement obligated the Government to undertake an array of new programmes entailing significant financial ramifications, among them: land transfers and other programmes for the reintegration of ex-combatants; the creation of new democratic institutions such as the National Public Security Academy, the National Counsel for the Defence of Human Rights, the National Council of the Judiciary and the Supreme Electoral Tribunal; and rehabilitation of the infrastructure (e.g. energy, water supply, sanitation, transport, housing, telecommunications, education, health and agriculture).

134   Although both processes were vital for long-term peace and well-being, questions arose as to whether the Salvadorian economy could accommodate them at the same time. The additional expenditures required to implement the peace accords, it was pointed out, had the potential to disrupt El Salvador's stabilization programme and the steady progress the country was making towards long-term economic health. Strict adherence to the fiscal targets of the stabilization programme, on the other hand, was viewed as placing restrictions on financing for programmes aimed at building long-term peace under the provisions of the Chapultepec Agreement. The two processes should have been complementary, interdependent and mutually reinforcing. The fact that they were not always so underscored the need for greater harmonization within the United Nations system.

135   On 1 April 1993, at the Consultative Group Meeting of donors convened in Paris by the World Bank, the Government of El Salvador asked the international community to fill a $600 million gap in the financing required for programmes directly related to the peace accords for the period 1993-1996. Of the $1.2 billion needed overall, the Government had already committed over $300 million and the international community just under $300 million. The Government also sought additional financing for poverty alleviation and other priority programmes. Late in the year, donor response had not yet lived up to expectations. Pledges were slightly more than the Government had requested, but contributors showed a clear preference for infrastructural and environmental projects, meaning that very little external financing would be available for the promotion of democratic institutions, the reintegration of ex-combatants (housing, purchase of land, agricultural credit, credit for small enterprises, etc.) and other peace-related programmes.

136   I made repeated appeals for international assistance and support. "The successful conclusion of this peace process", I said in May 1993, "can be achieved only if the necessary financing is forthcoming . . . two of the programmes — those relating to land and the new police force — do not at present have an adequate basis of financial support. Yet they are central to the peace accords and their failure or curtailment could threaten all that has been achieved. This state of affairs requires an urgent response. . ."[65] And in September 1993 I stated (A/48/310), "The international community must provide the financial resources necessary to consolidate and conclude this extraordinary experiment and this example of peace, reconciliation, reconstruction and development."

65/Document 74
See page 427

137   At the same time, I stressed that implementation of the peace accords could not depend entirely on external financing, and I pointed out that it was the Government's responsibility to define fiscal policies and spending priorities which would enable it to fulfil its commitment to full implementation of the accords. A study by the Economic Commission for Latin American and the Caribbean (ECLAC) conducted at my request found some room for flexibility in this regard. For example, as I noted then, the Government could adopt a less restrictive ceiling on public expenditures and on the use of international monetary reserves. In November 1993 I reported that the Government had begun to allocate

66/Document 94
See page 496

some of its own funds to finance some of the peace-related projects. Again, I emphasized that additional resources were required "rather urgently".[66]

ONUSAL *keeps pressure on Salvadorian parties*

67/Document 69
See page 416;
Document 84
See page 471;
Document 87
See page 472

138 On 7 July 1993, I reported to the Security Council that the Government of El Salvador had, more than eight months after the original deadline, taken the steps necessary to bring itself into compliance with the recommendations of the Ad Hoc Commission on the Purification of the Armed Forces.[67] In September, the ONUSAL Human Rights Division reported that there had been both definite improvements and serious violations.[68] In October, I informed the Council that some action had been taken on many of the recommendations made by the Commission on the Truth, but that more was required on several points of great importance.[69] No implementation had been reported, for example, with regard to recommendations concerning the dismissal of officials mentioned in connection with the serious acts of violence investigated by the Commission. At a high-level meeting on 8 September 1993, in which ONUSAL participated, the Government and the FMLN agreed on the need to step up the implementation process with a view to "sweeping the table clean" before the beginning of the electoral campaign, scheduled for 20 November.

68/Document 89
See page 476

69/Document 90
See page 480

139 Instead, the situation took a serious turn for the worse. On 25 October 1993, an FMLN leader and congressional candidate was murdered, death-squad style. Five days later, another leading member of the FMLN was assassinated. By mid-February 1994, at least 15 persons had been murdered, some in ways suggesting a re-emergence of the armed illegal groups that had terrorized El Salvador throughout the 1980s. Among the dead were three former commanders and four ex-combatants of the FMLN, four FMLN activists, four activists of the Alianza Republicana Nacionalista (ARENA), the brother of an FMLN candidate for mayor and an activist of the Movimiento de Solidaridad Nacional (MSN). During the same period, ONUSAL's Human Rights Division received reports of 31 additional murders described as summary executions whose perpetrators were not identified.

140 The political impact of the killings was immediate, as apprehensions swept through El Salvador and the international community at large about chronic instability that could be nearly as debilitating as a return to civil war. However, the Human Rights Division reported that the violence was not like that of the 1980s, when one group defended the established system and the other fought to change it.[70] Rather, it was directed against the democratic political system worked out by the

70/Document 98
See page 512

Government and the FMLN. This, said ONUSAL, reflected the "intransigence of fringe elements attacking the Salvadorian nation as a whole, all national political forces and the democracy proposed in the peace agreements".

141   On 3 November 1993, I expressed my shock at the killings, called for a vigorous inquiry and urged the parties to accelerate implementation of the peace accords.[71] I also stated that the killings confirmed the need for immediate implementation of the recommendations of the Commission on the Truth regarding the investigation of illegal groups. The Security Council supported my ideas two days later in a statement calling for an end to the violence.[72] I then dispatched Under-Secretary-General Goulding to El Salvador for consultations, which were held from 8 to 15 November. These led to the formation, in December, of a Joint Group for the Investigation of Politically Motivated Illegal Armed Groups, a course of action supported by the Security Council.[73] The Joint Group was composed of two independent representatives of the Government of El Salvador nominated by the President of the Republic, Dr. José Leandro Echeverría and Dr. Jerónimo Castillo; the National Counsel for the Defence of Human Rights, Dr. Carlos Mauricio Molina Fonseca; and the Director of ONUSAL's Human Rights Division, Dr. Diego García-Sayan.

71/Document 92
See page 494

72/Document 93
See page 495

73/Document 96
See page 510;
Document 97
See page 512

Electoral division begins work

142   Four elections were to be held on 20 March 1994: for President, with a second round if no candidate obtained an absolute majority in the first round; for the 84 seats in the Legislative Assembly on the basis of proportional representation; for 262 mayoral districts on the basis of a simple majority (the party obtaining the most votes would win the office of mayor and all the posts in the municipal corporation); and for the Central American Parliament, treated as a single national district, to which 20 representatives were to be elected on the basis of proportional representation.[74]

143   ONUSAL's Electoral Division concentrated first on observing the registration of voters, with ONUSAL teams making an average of six observation visits to each of the country's 262 towns. Upon closure of the electoral rolls on 19 January 1994, it was determined that there would be some 2.3 million potential voters, or roughly 85 per cent of the estimated voting-age population. I reported in February that, notwithstanding some initial delays and continuing deficiencies, the voter registration exercise was more inclusive and free of flaws than might have been predicted a few months earlier.[75]

74/Document 91
See page 491

75/Document 100
See page 521

144   One reason for this outcome was a joint effort, led by the Office of the United Nations High Commissioner for Refugees (UNHCR) in close collaboration with ONUSAL, UNDP and the Supreme Electoral Tribunal (the highest electoral authority and the general overseer of the electoral process), to restore the nation's central database, to reconstruct municipal registries destroyed during the war and to issue birth certificates, personal identity cards and identification cards for minors. These activities, initiated by UNHCR in 1987 for the benefit of refugees repatriating to El Salvador, were expanded in 1992 to target all undocumented Salvadorians. By February 1994, the project had allowed for the restoration of 3,479 municipal registry books in all 14 departments, the replacement of 1,131,250 birth certificates and the issuance of 164,166 new birth certificates, 234,332 personal identity documents and 34,484 identity cards for minors. As a result, Salvadorians who previously had been denied the full exercise of their civil rights owing to a lack of legal documents no longer faced any such obstacles.

145   With the official start of the electoral campaign on 20 November 1993, ONUSAL personnel began attending public political events, monitoring compliance with the Electoral Code and planning for the deployment of the 900 international observers who were to observe events on election day. Mission personnel also held regular meetings with the Supreme Electoral Tribunal, the Board of Vigilance (made up of representatives of all political parties) and party campaign managers. In an important step taken in response to an initiative by my Special Representative, all seven presidential candidates committed themselves to full implementation of the Peace Agreement and rejected politically motivated violence or intimidation.

146   But as the campaign was getting under way, I noticed a distinct polarization of political positions in El Salvador. In a November 1993 report to the Security Council I stated, "It is a matter of considerable concern to me that the electoral campaign should have begun when some very important elements in the accords remain only partially implemented and when there are disturbing signs of the reappearance of some ugly features of El Salvador's past."[76]

76/Document 94
See page 496

147   The spate of murders had had a nefarious impact on the political climate and undermined confidence in the peace process. Delays in the transfer of land and the provision of other benefits to ex-combatants on both sides remained a constant source of tension and instability. And there continued to be an apparent lack of commitment at some levels in the Government to the creation of a new police force, reflected in persistent delays in phasing out the National Police and the failure to provide the National Civil Police with adequate logistical and technical support such as vehicles, portable radios and funding.

148   "Until a short while ago", I added in my November report,

"impressive progress had been made in implementing the Accords despite a number of obstacles, which could usually be overcome through supplementary negotiations and agreements. But recent developments . . . have caused serious worry as to whether previous achievements are now threatened . . . I exhort [President Cristiani and the leadership of FMLN] to overcome these new challenges and make sure that the peace process continues on its course."

VII The elections

149   The electoral process offered further evidence of the eagerness on the part of the Salvadorian people to settle their differences according to the rules of democracy. The voter registration period had seen an increase in the electoral roll of nearly 30 per cent. This high degree of citizen mobilization carried over to the electoral campaign, during which hundreds of public rallies, demonstrations and other such events were held without incident. For the first time in more than a decade, the full spectrum of opinion was being heard in El Salvador in an increasingly open political environment. The final results of the elections gave ARENA the presidency and control of most mayoralties and municipal councils, but just as significantly, the FMLN emerged as the second most important political voice in the country, a considerable achievement for what was, not long before, an armed fighting force. The following section revisits the campaign and the balloting and discusses the need to keep ONUSAL in El Salvador for a brief period following the elections.

The electoral campaign

150   Battered at the outset by the murders of at least 15 persons of some political importance, the electoral campaign unfolded more smoothly in 1994 as the frequency of killings and other violence diminished and the Joint Group for the Investigation of Politically Motivated Illegal Armed Groups began to discharge its mandate. Political rallies and meetings attended by ONUSAL observation teams took place in an orderly, well-organized manner. Freedom of movement, demonstration and expression were respected. And despite some incidents of political violence and intimidation which resulted in serious injuries, and cases in which activists destroyed or pasted over a political party's mural propaganda, the overall mood of the campaign was calm.

151   ONUSAL's observation activities also included monitoring political advertising through the mass media. In this regard, the Electoral Division received a number of complaints alleging that public resources were being used to promote indirectly the party of the Government in power. ONUSAL also noted that, in violation of the electoral propaganda rules, there had been publicity by a private institute and by anonymous advertisers the content of which was strongly hostile to the FMLN and to the presidential candidate of the coalition of which it was a part.

152   Some 300 complaints of irregularities in electoral publicity and other aspects of the electoral process were presented to ONUSAL during the campaign, most of them (23 per cent) dealing with arbitrary or illegitimate action by public authorities. The remainder consisted of acts of intimidation (21 per cent), destruction of propaganda materials (18 per cent), aggression (9 per cent), murder (7 per cent) and miscellaneous (22 per cent). All complaints were transmitted by ONUSAL to the Supreme Electoral Tribunal.

153   Another source of concern lay in various flaws in the electoral roll and registration, and the consequent potential for election-day difficulties. In El Salvador, the only persons able to vote are those whose names are on the electoral roll and who, when they come to vote, are able to produce an identity document issued by the Supreme Electoral Tribunal, the data on which must tally with those on the electoral roll. One major defect was that even with the largely successful efforts of the UNHCR-led database programme, more than 74,000 persons who had requested registration were not included on the electoral roll because their applications could not be validated by a birth certificate. This number represented 2.8 per cent of the entire pool of voters, but in many former zones of conflict — areas where the FMLN reportedly had the most support — the percentage of non-validated applications amounted to 10.4 per cent. Adding to the FMLN's concern was a decision by the Supreme Electoral Tribunal to relocate four polling stations from their respective municipalities — former areas of conflict where, again, the FMLN was expected to do well on election day — to the departmental capital of Chalatenango. The Tribunal claimed that a lack of security and a relative scarcity of people in the four towns had prompted the move, but ONUSAL contested the point and reiterated that the action violated the electoral code.

154   There was also the possibility that multiple voting would be engaged in by persons in possession of several voter cards under the same or different identities; it was impossible to determine the number of people in such circumstances. The dilemma had arisen because, for technical reasons, the names of deceased citizens had not been removed from the electoral roll and because double registration was made possible under a legal framework designed to deal with displaced populations and destroyed registries. To guard against multiple voting, voters were to have their fingers stamped with indelible ink.

155   ONUSAL also reported that, for unexplained reasons, some citizens had been unable to obtain voter cards and that other citizens' names did not appear on the voting lists of the municipality where they had chosen to vote. I noted these remaining difficulties, as well as the persistent climate of mistrust among the electoral contenders, but in my final pre-election report to the Security Council concluded that "the

conditions for the holding of free and fair elections are generally adequate . . . There is good reason to expect that these elections will be a crucial stepping-stone in the consolidation of peace and national reconciliation among the Salvadorian people."[77]

77/Document 102
See page 527

Election day

156   ONUSAL monitored the proceedings on election day by deploying nearly 900 United Nations observers of 56 nationalities. (Some 3,000 additional international observers were also deployed.) They were stationed at all 355 polling centres with teams of between 2 and 30 observers — blanket coverage that made it possible for ONUSAL to resolve countless practical problems. The observers collected information on more than 7,000 forms (one for each of the 6,984 polling stations and the 355 polling centres), which were subsequently compiled by the Electoral Division and which constituted the basic documentary source for evaluating the conduct of the elections on election day.

157   According to the ONUSAL observers, monitors from the main political parties were present at all polling stations, and no interference with their work was noted. The indelible ink was applied properly. There were no serious incidents affecting law and order, and the trend towards less violence in previous months culminated in complete calm on election day. Voting took place in the four municipalities in Chalatenango following an election-eve ruling by the Supreme Electoral Tribunal that balloting would be held simultaneously in the towns and in the departmental capital. At the eleventh hour, ONUSAL organized and coordinated the moving of voting material and offices to the four areas, and the polls opened, albeit three hours late.

158   At the same time, serious irregularities occurred. Voting tables opened late. Many polling centres were overcrowded, and the pace of the voting was slow. Many voters had to travel long distances in order to vote, and lack of public transport appears to have led many to give up without voting. At least 25,000 voters — nearly 2 per cent of the electorate — possessing valid voting cards were unable to vote because their names were not on the list. In a very small number of cases, some citizens could not vote because others had already used their names to vote.

159   An estimated 1,300,000 voters participated in the election, an increase of nearly 400,000 compared with the elections of 1991 and 1989 but still only 55 per cent of the total — lower than had been expected. In my report to the Security Council on the conduct of the elections, I attributed much of the difficulties to the Supreme Electoral

Tribunal, which, despite ample and timely support from ONUSAL, the donor community and NGOs, had failed to produce a more adequate electoral roll and to give sufficient training to polling teams and party monitors.[78]

78/Document 104
See page 531

160   ONUSAL reported that the irregularities had had no impact on the presidential election but could have influenced some results in the elections for the Assembly and the municipal councils, given the smaller size of the electoral districts. Indeed, I stated, the "high visibility and frequency of the problems observed on election day . . . may have helped to leave a particularly negative impression of the overall process, especially with observers, who were concentrated in the final stage". Still, I stressed that the irregularities ought not be mistaken for significant manipulation of the election by means of fraudulent interference with its essential components, such as ballot boxes, ballot papers and tally sheets. A look at the entire process, from the registration through the events on election day, revealed, among other things, massive expansion in the voter rolls (some 700,000 new voters had been added to the list) and peaceful exercise of the right to participate in a democratic election. In the light of these considerations, my Special Representative stated on 21 March 1994 that the elections had taken place "under appropriate conditions in terms of freedom, competitiveness and security. Despite the serious flaws regarding organization and transparency . . . the elections can be considered acceptable".

161   The final results, based on a count by the Supreme Electoral Tribunal carried out in the presence of United Nations observers, showed the ruling ARENA party receiving 49.03 per cent of the votes in the election for President, while the Convergencia Democratica (CD)–FMLN–Movimiento Nacional Revolucionario (MNR) coalition received 24.9 per cent. The Partido Demócrata Cristiano (PDC) received 17.87 per cent, and the remaining votes were shared among four other parties. With no candidate obtaining more than 50 per cent of the votes, a run-off election between the two leading recipients of votes was scheduled for 24 April.

162   In the election for the 84-seat Legislative Assembly, ARENA won 39 seats, short of a majority, while the FMLN won 21 seats, making it the second largest voice in the Assembly. The PDC won 18 seats, the Partido de Conciliación Nacional (PCN) won 4 seats and 1 seat apiece went to the CD and the Partido Movimiento de Unidad (PMU). In the election for representatives to the Central American Parliament, the seats were divided as follows: ARENA, 9; FMLN, 4; PDC, 4; and 1 each to CD, PCN and PMU.

163   ARENA's strongest electoral showing came in the municipal races, in which the party won 206 out of 262 mayoral contests. The PDC came in second, winning 29 mayoralties, the FMLN was next with 16,

the PCN won 10 and the Movimiento Auténtico Cristiano (MAC) gained 1 post. The municipal results were challenged by the FMLN in 37 districts but the Supreme Electoral Tribunal subsequently decided that these appeals were not valid, leaving the election results intact. ONUSAL expressed its concern at the manner in which these cases were closed.

Towards the run-off

164   The period between the two rounds of presidential elections allowed time to try to improve on the various shortcomings that had been evident on election day. In a letter dated 24 March 1994, ONUSAL recommended that the Supreme Electoral Tribunal, among other things:

    A.   Clear up any discrepancies in the electoral rolls;

    B.   Seek reform of the Electoral Code by the Legislative Assembly so that voter cards could be issued between the first and second rounds;

    C.   Increase the number of polling centres;

    D.   Strengthen the training of electoral personnel;

    E.   Shelter the polling centres from the rain (the second round would be taking place during the onset of the rainy season);

    F.   Ensure that there was sufficient public transport;

    G.   End violations of the ground rules relating to electoral publicity;

    H.   Conduct a massive public information campaign emphasizing the deadlines for rectifying problems with the electoral rolls, urging voters to participate and informing the electorate about the location of polling centres, with an indication that public transport would be available.

165   On 7 April 1994, the Security Council congratulated the people of El Salvador on the peaceful and historic elections and called upon all concerned to take the above-mentioned and other measures in order to "guarantee a genuine and indisputable expression of the will of the people in the second round".[79] The ONUSAL Electoral Division followed up by assigning observers to work in various areas. Just prior to the run-off, however, ONUSAL expressed its regret at several continuing problems, among them the limited and uneven success of the Supreme Electoral Tribunal's training programme, the continuing inadequacy of transportation and difficulties which adversely affected the transparency of the electoral roll and the exercise of the right to vote.[80] In a positive sign, on 18 April the two presidential candidates issued a joint statement pledging, among other things, to work for the complete overhaul of the country's electoral system. Also during this period, effective 1 April, Mr. Enrique ter Horst (Venezuela) secceeded Mr. Ramirez-Ocampo as my Special Representative and ONUSAL Chief of Mission.

79/Document 106
See page 542

80/Document 107
See page 542

Election results

President, 20 March 1994

Alianza Republicana Nacionalista (ARENA): . . . . 49.03 per cent
Coalition Convergencia Democrática (CD) –
Frente Farabundo Martí para la Liberación
Nacional (FMLN)– Movimiento Nacional
Revolucionario (MNR): . . . . 24.9 per cent
Partido Demócrata Cristiano (PDC): . . . . 17.87 per cent
Partido de Conciliación Nacional (PCN): . . . . . . 5.39 per cent
Partido Movimiento de Unidad (PMU): . . . . 2.41 per cent
Movimiento de Solidaridad Nacional (MSN): . . . . 1.06 per cent
Movimiento Auténtico Cristiano (MAC): . . . . . . 0.83 per cent

President, 24 April 1994

ARENA: . . . . 68.35 per cent
Coalition CD/FMLN/MNR: . . . . 31.65 per cent

Legislative Assembly (84 seats)

ARENA: 39
FMLN: 21
PDC: 18
PCN: 4
CD: 1
PMU: 1

Mayoralties (262)

ARENA: 206
PDC: 29
FMLN: 16
PCN: 10
MAC: 1

Deputies to Central American Parliament (20)

ARENA: 9
PDC: 4
FMLN: 4
CD: 1
PCN: 1
PMU: 1

The run-off

166   The ARENA candidate, Mr. Armando Calderón Sol, won the 24 April run-off election for President against Mr. Rubén Zamora of CD/FMLN/MNR, securing 68.35 per cent of the votes against 31.65 per cent. ONUSAL again monitored the proceedings, deploying 900 observers at all polling centres in the country. They found distinct improvements in organization in several areas, including the arrangement of the voting centres, the use of guides to direct voters to voting places, the display of the Electoral Register, free public transport and the release, early on 24 April, of information on the results of the elections. Various irregularities were noted as well, but in general terms the elections again took place without vote manipulation or serious disturbances of public order.[81]

81/Document 108
See page 544

167   Still, a delicate atmosphere prevailed following Mr. Calderón Sol's victory, and in his first comments to the nation as President-elect he said, "I want to assure all our political adversaries that we will govern for all Salvadorians". He also stated that his first priority would be the full implementation of the peace accords.

VIII Beyond the elections

168   By the time of the 1994 elections, substantial advances had been made in implementation of the Peace Agreement — advances it would have been difficult to imagine when the United Nations first became involved in the effort to make peace in El Salvador. Originally, however, it had been hoped that the vast majority of the provisions of the Peace Agreement would have been carried out well before March 1994, so that the electorate could vote in an atmosphere in which the full dimensions of the new El Salvador created by the accords were already apparent to it. Instead, several important objectives had been only partly realized. Thus the United Nations continued, after the two rounds of elections, to have verification responsibilities in El Salvador.

Post-election situation

169   One such task involved the National Civil Police. The deployment of this new force was proceeding, as before, at a slower pace than envisaged in the Peace Accords. More significantly, the Government, citing an increase in the level of crime, had proposed changes in public security arrangements that would delay until at least March 1995 the full deployment of the National Civil Police (this was originally scheduled for September 1994) and the parallel phasing out of the National Police (which, according to the peace accords, was to be concluded by 31 October 1994). ONUSAL had also received little cooperation from the Government and the National Civil Police in the Mission's efforts to verify the civilian character of the new force.

170   The land-transfer programme was also continuing to suffer from delays. By the end of April 1994, 11,585 persons had received title to land — just 24 per cent of the maximum number of potential beneficiaries and slightly below the end-of-1993 target accepted by both the Government and the FMLN. An Acceleration Plan introduced by the Government in August 1993 had produced its own set of problems, prompting objections from the FMLN over new verification rules, the possibility of evictions and the imposition of deadlines for credit certificates to be used in purchasing land.

171   Problems were also afflicting programmes designed to facilitate the reintegration of ex-combatants of the FMLN and the armed forces of El Salvador. ONUSAL was encountering considerable difficulty in trying to overcome administrative obstacles and a lack of full cooperation, apparently reflecting a lack of political will in the middle-level bureaucracy.

172   Financial constraints on peace-related projects were also an ongoing consideration. During the March 1994 meeting of the Consultative Group of Donors convened by the World Bank in Paris, the Government reported a shortfall of some $376 million targeted for the National Public Security Academy, the National Civil Police, the National Counsel for the Defence of Human Rights, the judicial and electoral systems, housing needs, credits for farmers and small-business-people and the Land Bank. Donors continued to show some reluctance to provide financing for some of these vital needs, but they continued to be generous in support of infrastructural and environmental projects.

82/Document 105
See page 535

173   The human rights situation remained ambivalent, with the ONUSAL Human Rights Division documenting both progress and the persistence of violence and other serious violations.[82] The Independent Expert for the Commission on Human Rights, for his part, had also noted (E/CN.4/1994/11) several continuing problems, recommending, among other things, that the Office of the National Counsel for the Defence of Human Rights be strengthened, that the judicial system be the subject of a careful review and that the Government join the rest of the Central American nations in recognizing the jurisdiction of the Inter-American Court of Human Rights. He also stated that "the recommendations of the Commission on the Truth have to date not had any practical impact and their partial implementation cannot in general terms be taken as a declaration of intent". Several constitutional reforms were approved by the outgoing Legislative Assembly on 29 April 1994, but these fell short of the Commission's recommendations and proposals put forth by COPAZ.

174   One human rights problem — the existence of illegal armed groups, and of so-called death squads in particular — was especially troubling. In July 1994, the Joint Group for the Investigation of Politically Motivated Illegal Armed Groups released the results of its inquiry, concluding that such groups appeared to be pursuing the destabilization of the peace process, the creation of conditions which favoured the militarization of the country, the prolongation of the existence of the National Police and the neutralization of the new National Civil Police.[83]

83/Document 113
See page 568

Moreover, the Joint Group reported, these groups were seeking to engender fear among sectors of the population in order to discourage these sectors' support for, or incorporation into, political parties or social organizations that the leaders of these criminal groups perceived to be a threat to their economic or political interests or ideological perspectives.

175   The Joint Group pointed out that political violence was apparently being exercised through and camouflaged by common violence and

organized crime, and that organized criminal structures might not exist without the protection provided by some active members of state security forces. The justice system, said the Group's report, by commission or omission, continued to provide the margin for impunity that these structures required. The Joint Group recommended the purging of magistrates and judges found to have been involved in illegal infractions or professional misconduct; the approval of a temporary system for the reduction of criminal penalties for those who might provide important information about criminals acting with political motivation; the creation, within the Criminal Investigation Division of the National Civil Police, of a special unit dedicated to the investigation of illegal armed groups; and a number of other reforms.

176   The persistence of such conditions led me, as early as November 1993, to stress the desirability of keeping ONUSAL in existence at reduced strength for a few months after the elections to continue verifying compliance with the peace accords.[84] In February and March 1994, I voiced concern to President Cristiani and to the Security Council about lingering problems in a number of areas, and in May I highlighted four areas in need of especially urgent attention: agreement on measures to enhance the civilian character of the National Civil Police and to increase its strength; accelerated demobilization of the National Police and its completion by the end of 1994; a solution to the pressing problem of human settlements; and arrangements to ensure that those with title to land under the land-transfer programme also had access to agricultural credit and technical assistance in time for the planting season.[85]

177   The Security Council agreed with my periodic assessments, extending ONUSAL's mandate beyond the elections — first, in resolution 888 (1993), until 31 May 1994 and then, in resolution 920 (1994), until 30 November 1994.[86] In April 1994, I received assurances from President Cristiani that the Government of El Salvador intended to comply fully with all the pending provisions and that it viewed the peace process as irreversible. On 19 May, the Government and the FMLN reached agreement on a new "Timetable for the implementation of the most important outstanding agreements".[87] And in a 24 May meeting with me, President-elect Calderón Sol reiterated his commitment to the peace accords and his desire to see them implemented without delay for the benefit of all Salvadorians. On 1 June, Mr. Calderón Sol was inaugurated as the new President of El Salvador.[88]

Implementation under the new Government

178   In the early months of its existence, the Government of President Calderón Sol confirmed its commitment to comply fully with

84/Document 94
See page 496

85/Document 99
See page 519;
Document 101
See page 526;
Document 103
See page 530;
Document 109
See page 547

86/Document 95
See page 509;
Document 111
See page 567

87/Document 110
See page 561

88/Document 112
See page 568

those elements of the peace accords that remained to be implemented. The FMLN did likewise. The two parties issued a joint declaration on 4 October 1994 in which they stated their intent, among other things, to cooperate closely and to determine, with the participation of ONUSAL, the specific measures necessary for the fulfilment of their commitments under the accords.[89]

89/Document 117
See page 585

179   I reported to the Security Council during this period that real progress continued to be made.[90] The FMLN constituted a credible opposition in the National Assembly and maintained a presence at the regional and municipal levels. The National Civil Police approached full deployment, and the parallel demobilization of the National Police was accelerated following heightened action by the Government to combat organized crime and the involvement in criminal activities of individuals or groups within the public security apparatus. A new Supreme Electoral Tribunal was elected, providing an opportunity for much-needed reform in this area, and a new Supreme Court of Justice was established, presaging broad changes within the judicial system.

90/Document 115
See page 577;
Document 118
See page 586

180   During this last phase of the Mission, ONUSAL increasingly emphasized technical support for building and strengthening institutions to enable them to meet the post-ONUSAL demands of the peace accords. In this connection, the Human Rights Division reported that a transfer of verification tasks appeared to be under way: ONUSAL was receiving fewer complaints about human rights violations while the number of complaints received by the Office of the National Counsel for the Defence of Human Rights was on the rise. ONUSAL considered this to be natural and desirable. The Division noted, however, that human rights in El Salvador would remain "precarious" until State institutions gained the ability to prevent and punish violations. "The impunity of the perpetrators", said ONUSAL, was still "the main cause of human rights violations in El Salvador".[91]

91/Document 114
See page 574;
Document 119
See page 591

181   In other areas, key issues remained to be resolved before all commitments under the peace accords could be met. Despite the Government's accelerated land-transfer programme, only 32 per cent of the 40,648 potential beneficiaries had received land by the end of October 1994. I made a personal appeal to President Calderón Sol to facilitate the rapid completion of this programme. I also expressed concern about the programme for agricultural credit, which is vital for reactivating production in the zones of conflict. There were also delays in other reintegration efforts, particularly in housing and assistance for war-disabled persons. The most serious problem concerned human settlements. Rural settlements established by refugees and displaced persons, and urban settlements — houses vacated by their owners during the conflict and subsequently occupied by others — would create serious socio-political consequences if broken up.

182 To assist efforts to overcome these problems, both the Government and the FMLN saw a need for ongoing United Nations verification. I thus considered it essential to retain ONUSAL for an additional mandate period. I recommended the extension of ONUSAL until 30 April 1995, at a level not to exceed 100 international staff. On 16 September 1994, the Council welcomed the progress being achieved, and on 31 October, in resolution 961 (1994), the Council approved the extension of ONUSAL's mandate.[92] "It is essential", said the permanent representative of Spain before the vote (S/PV.3465), "that the United Nations fulfil its commitment to the people of El Salvador to verify full compliance with the Peace Accords."

92/Document 116
See page 584;
Document 120
See page 593

183 It became apparent during the early months of the final mandate extension that this verification work should continue even after the expiration of ONUSAL's mandate. The situation during this period was somewhat disquieting, owing to the failure to implement some parts of the peace agreements. The forcible takeover of the Legislative Assembly and the Ministry of Finance by members of the Association of Demobilized Members of the Armed Forces, which was fortunately defused with the assistance of ONUSAL, was but one symptom of this lingering discontent.

184 These considerations reaffirmed my conviction that it was essential to put in place, following the disbandment of ONUSAL *per se,* a mechanism to enable the United Nations to discharge its verification and other responsibilities without interruption — as had been requested by the Government of El Salvador and the FMLN. I therefore proposed, in a February 1995 letter to the President of the Security Council, that a small team of United Nations officials be established for an initial period of six months to perform this work.[93] The team would have the capability to provide good offices, to verify implementation of the outstanding points of the peace agreements and to provide a continuing flow of accurate and reliable information in order to keep the Security Council informed as necessary. To maintain an integrated approach in the post-conflict peace-building phase, the team would coordinate closely with the Resident Representative of the United Nations Development Programme while maintaining the separate identity required for its inherently political tasks and responsibilities. On 17 February, the Council welcomed the proposal, and preparations began for the team's deployment.[94]

93/Document 122
See page 598

94/Document 123
See page 599

IX   Conclusion

185   The peace process in El Salvador stands as a remarkable achievement for the long-suffering Salvadorian people. Exhausted from a terrible civil war, Salvadorians chose the path of national reconciliation and overcame serious obstacles to build a solid foundation for a stable and peaceful future. The war was brought to a decisive end. The FMLN was demobilized. The Government armed forces were reduced in size and reconstituted under a new doctrine stressing defence against external threats. The old military-controlled national police was disbanded and replaced by a newly trained civilian force. Reform of the judicial and the electoral systems was begun. New human rights institutions were created, and new protections written into the country's laws and constitution. Democratic elections in which the FMLN participated as a political party were successfully completed in April 1994. Substantial resources were committed by the international community to support the country's reconstruction and long-term development needs.

186   The successful transition from war to peace in El Salvador was also a signal success for the United Nations and the international community in support of it, and thus offers useful lessons. The Organization played an innovative, multi-dimensional role emphasizing peacemaking, peace-keeping and, especially, post-conflict peace-building. As the permanent representative of the United States said in the Security Council on 31 October 1994 (S/PV.3645), "The peace process in El Salvador has shown the United Nations at its best: a dynamic negotiator, innovative organizer and effective peace-keeper."

187   From the outset of the peace process, the United Nations helped the Government and the FMLN negotiate and implement not just an end to their armed confrontation but a programme of far-reaching political, economic and social measures aimed at eradicating the underlying causes of the original conflict. Another crucially important factor in forging a common destiny for the two parties was the decision to begin ONUSAL's human rights verification before a cease-fire was in place. The presence of impartial United Nations monitors amid wartime conditions helped deter abuses, encouraged the parties to arrive at additional agreements and boosted confidence in the peace process among the Salvadorian people.

188   The centrality of human rights in the peace process was demonstrated further by the work of the Commission on the Truth. Its report was a seminal contribution to the efforts of Salvadorians to seek justice for and come to terms with the abuses and excesses of the war years. But the report's conclusions and recommendations were not easily accepted by some of those individuals or institutions called to task for their actions. Still, such was the Commission's stature — and so thorough and definitive was its accomplishment — that compliance quickly became one of the leading barometers for the health of the peace process. Moreover, the success of the El Salvador Commission on the Truth led other nations seeking to make a break with conflict or civil strife to consider embarking on similarly vital exercises in national reckoning.

189   As ONUSAL prepared for the termination of its mandate on 30 April 1995, and as the United Nations prepared to deploy a team of officials to continue the mission's verification responsibilities and good offices role after the end of ONUSAL's mandate, a number of tasks critical to a durable peace remained in need of verification. These included implementation of institutional reforms in the judiciary, the recommendations of the Commission on the Truth and the reintegration programmes, especially the slow-moving land programme. At the same time, the country's reconstruction and development needs were substantial. Given the commitment of the United Nations to the people of El Salvador, the United Nations and I stand ready to assist as the Salvadorian people continue their efforts to consolidate peace in their country. A key to success will be to sustain, in this comprehensive effort, the dedication and sense of urgency that were mustered in addressing the challenges of the civil war.

BOUTROS BOUTROS-GHALI

Section Two
Chronology and Documents

I Chronology of events

15 December 1980
With the outbreak of civil war in El Salvador, the
United Nations General Assembly adopts a resolution
deploring the "murders, disappearances and other violations of human rights reported in El Salvador" and
urges the Government to "take the necessary steps to
ensure full respect for human rights and fundamental
freedoms in that country".

11 March 1981
The United Nations Commission on Human Rights
decides to appoint a Special Representative to report
on the situation of human rights in El Salvador.

18 November 1986
The Secretary-General of the United Nations and the
Secretary-General of the Organization of American
States jointly offer to help in the search for peace in
Central America.

7 August 1987
Five Central American Presidents (of Costa Rica, El
Salvador, Guatemala, Honduras and Nicaragua) sign
the Esquipulas II Agreement, in which each State commits itself to peace in the region and pledges to prevent
the use of its territory for the destabilization of the
others.

29-31 May 1989
The International Conference on Central American
Refugees is held in Guatemala City. A plan of action,
to be implemented by the Office of the United Nations
High Commissioner for Refugees, the United Nations
Development Programme and other agencies of the
United Nations system, is adopted to address the prob-
lems of people forced by the conflict to leave their
homes.

26 June 1989
The Secretary-General of the United Nations reports
on favourable developments relating to the situation in
Central America.
See Document 1, page 89

27 July 1989
The United Nations Security Council expresses its support for Esquipulas II and other agreements reached by
the five Central American Presidents and supports the
Secretary-General in his mission of good offices in the
region.
See Document 2, page 91

7 August 1989
The five Central American Presidents sign the Tela
(Honduras) Agreement which, among other things,
urges the Frente Farabundo Martí para la Liberación
Nacional (FMLN) to enter into dialogue with the Gov-
ernment of El Salvador.
See Document 3, page 92

15 September 1989
The Government of El Salvador and the FMLN agree
to initiate a dialogue aimed at ending their armed
confrontation through political means.
See Document 4, page 97

9 October 1989
The Secretary-General reports on the new climate of
détente created in Central America since the signing of
the Tela Agreement.
See Document 4, page 97

8 December 1989
Following renewed violence in El Salvador, the Security
Council expresses concern over the situation in Central
America.
See Document 5, page 100

12 December 1989
The five Central American Presidents, meeting in San
Isidro de Coronado, Costa Rica, sign a declaration
reaffirming their support for the role of the United
Nations in the region.
See Document 6, page 100

21 December 1989
The Secretary-General reports on the deterioration of
the situation in El Salvador.
See Document 7, page 102

December 1989-January 1990
The FMLN and the Government of El Salvador sepa-
rately request the help of the United Nations Secretary-
General in bringing about a resumption of the dialogue
between the two sides.
See Document 8, page 105

13 March 1990
In a gesture aimed at the resumption of peace negotiations, the FMLN declares a total suspension of acts of
sabotage and attacks on Government officials and
civilians who are not members of military or paramilitary groups belonging to the armed forces.

4 April 1990

In Geneva, the Secretary-General announces that the Government and the FMLN have agreed on a framework for negotiations under the auspices of the United Nations and that they have identified the four objectives of the peace process: to end the armed conflict through political means, to promote democratization, to guarantee unrestricted respect for human rights and to reunify Salvadorian society.
See Document 11, page 110; and Document 27, page 164

21 May 1990

In Caracas, the Government and the FMLN agree on a general agenda and timetable for the negotiations.
See Document 11, page 110; and Document 28, page 165

26 July 1990

The Government and the FMLN sign their first substantive agreement: the San José Agreement on Human Rights, which calls for the creation of a United Nations verification mission to monitor the situation of human rights in El Salvador as soon as a cease-fire is reached.
See Document 9, page 107

29 August 1990

The Secretary-General requests the approval of the Security Council to make the necessary arrangements, including the possible establishment of a small preparatory office in El Salvador, for the creation of the United Nations mission. The Council concurs on **6 September.**
See Document 10, page 110

8 November 1990

The Secretary-General states that he intends to establish a preparatory office in order to enable the mission to undertake its monitoring task as soon as developments permit.
See Document 11, page 110

November 1990

The Government and the FMLN ask the Secretary-General to establish the mission as soon as possible, without awaiting a cease-fire.
See Document 12, page 119; and Document 13, page 129

17 December 1990

The five Central American Presidents agree on the vital need to put an immediate end to the conflict by means of dialogue.
See Document 12, page 119

21 December 1990

The Secretary-General informs the Security Council that he intends to request authorization to establish a United Nations Observer Mission in El Salvador

(ONUSAL) to monitor agreements concluded between the Government and the FMLN.
See Document 13, page 129

1 January 1991

The United Nations opens a small preparatory office in San Salvador.

8 January 1991

In a letter to President Alfredo Cristiani of El Salvador, the Secretary-General explains why he is not in a position to recommend, as the Government of El Salvador had asked, that the United Nations observe the March 1991 legislative and municipal elections in El Salvador.
See Document 14, page 132

16 April 1991

The Secretary-General accepts the recommendations of a preliminary mission to El Salvador that the United Nations begin verification of the San José Agreement without awaiting a cease-fire and recommends that the Security Council authorize the initial establishment of ONUSAL.
See Document 16, page 134

27 April 1991

In Mexico City, the Government and the FMLN agree on constitutional reforms concerning the armed forces and the judicial and electoral systems; they also agree to establish a Commission on the Truth to investigate serious acts of violence that occurred during the civil war.
See Document 29, page 167

30 April 1991

The outgoing Legislative Assembly approves nearly all of the constitutional amendments to be ratified by the incoming Legislative Assembly, avoiding a major delay in the peace process.

10 May 1991

The Secretary-General writes to President Cristiani concerning the peace process and constitutional reforms.
See Document 15, page 133; Document 17, page 139; and Document 18, page 140

20 May 1991

The Security Council establishes the United Nations Observer Mission in El Salvador (ONUSAL) for an initial period of 12 months to monitor all agreements concluded between the Government and the FMLN; ONUSAL's initial mandate is limited to verification, by a Human Rights Division, of the July 1990 San José Agreement on Human Rights.
See Document 19, page 141

26 July 1991
ONUSAL is officially inaugurated.
See Document 24, page 147

1 August 1991
The Secretary of State of the United States of America and the Minister for Foreign Affairs of the Union of Soviet Socialist Republics (USSR) call on the Secretary-General to take personal leadership of the negotiating process in El Salvador and to press both sides to reach rapid agreement on remaining political issues and on a cease-fire.
See Document 20, page 142

17 August 1991
The Secretary-General responds to the Secretary of State of the United States and the Minister for Foreign Affairs of the USSR that he fully intends to continue his active engagement in the Salvadorian peace process.
See Document 21, page 144

27 August 1991
The Secretary-General invites President Cristiani and the High Command of the FMLN to come to United Nations Headquarters in New York on **16 and 17 September** for consultations.
See Document 22, page 145

28 August 1991
President Cristiani accepts the invitation of the Secretary-General to come to United Nations Headquarters in New York on **16 and 17 September** for consultations.
See Document 23, page 146

16 September 1991
The Secretary-General reports on the launch of ONUSAL. The ONUSAL Human Rights Division issues its first report, in which it defines the legal and political framework for its verification work.
See Document 24, page 147

16-25 September 1991
At United Nations Headquarters, the Government and the FMLN make progress towards a final peace settlement, agreeing on a "compressed" agenda for negotiations and on a series of measures including purification of the armed forces; reduction of the size of the armed forces; organization of a new National Civilian Police force; institution of a land-transfer programme; and establishment of a National Commission for the Consolidation of Peace (COPAZ) to oversee implementation of all political agreements reached by the parties.
See Document 25, page 159

30 September 1991
The Security Council welcomes the New York Agreement and the Compressed Negotiations of 25 September and urges the parties to proceed at an intensive and sustained pace to reach a cease-fire and peaceful settlement of the armed conflict.
See Document 26, page 163

15 November 1991
The ONUSAL Human Rights Division reports that despite the persistence of the armed conflict, it has observed an effort by the parties to respect the commitments signed at San José.
See Document 30, page 175

2 December 1991
The Secretary-General reports that steady progress has been made in the negotiations on El Salvador.
See Document 31, page 180

10 December 1991
The Secretary-General appoints the members of the Commission on the Truth: Belisario Betancur, former President of Colombia; Reinaldo Figueredo Planchart, former Foreign Minister of Venezuela; and Professor Thomas Buergenthal, former President of the Inter-American Court for Human Rights and President of the Inter-American Institute for Human Rights.

26 December 1991
With a view to bringing the negotiations between the Government and the FMLN to a successful conclusion, the Secretary-General invites President Cristiani to United Nations Headquarters.
See Document 32, page 186

31 December 1991
The Government and the FMLN sign the Act of New York, which, combined with agreements previously signed at San José, Mexico City and New York, completes the negotiations on all substantive issues of the peace process. A number of details remain unresolved.
See Document 34, page 187; and Document 37, page 230

3 January 1992
The Security Council welcomes the signing of the Act of New York.
See Document 33, page 187

10 January 1992
The new Secretary-General of the United Nations, Boutros Boutros-Ghali, conveys to the Security Council his recommendations for how ONUSAL should fulfil the various requirements arising from the Act of New York.
See Document 34, page 187

13 January 1992

The Government and the FMLN reach agreement on all outstanding issues and sign the New York Act II.
See Document 37, page 230

14 January 1992

The Security Council broadens ONUSAL's mandate, extends the mandate through **31 October** and increases the Mission's strength, adding Military and Police divisions.
See Document 35, page 192

16 January 1992

The Peace Agreement is signed formally at Chapultepec Castle in Mexico City in a ceremony attended by the Secretary-General. An informal cease-fire comes into force.
See Document 36, page 193

31 January 1992

The deployment of ONUSAL military personnel begins.
See Document 39, page 236; and Document 41, page 238

1 February 1992

The official cease-fire takes hold.
See Document 39, page 236; and Document 41, page 238

7 February 1992

The deployment of ONUSAL police observers starts.
See Document 39, page 236; and Document 41, page 238

19 February 1992

The ONUSAL Human Rights Division reports that violations of fundamental human rights are still extremely prevalent.
See Document 38, page 231

25 February 1992

The Secretary-General reports to the Security Council on developments concerning the early phases of implementing ONUSAL's widened mandate.
See Document 39, page 236

15 May 1992

The Secretary-General informs the Security Council that it will be necessary to maintain temporarily the strength of ONUSAL's Military Division, which was to have been reduced after **1 June**.
See Document 40, page 237

26 May 1992

The Secretary-General reports to the Security Council on the activities of ONUSAL since the cease-fire (**1 February**), and expresses his concern about serious delays in implementing various provisions of the Peace Agreement, including those relating to the demobiliza-

tion process, the creation of the new police force and the land-transfer programme.
See Document 41, page 238

3 June 1992

The Security Council states that it shares the Secretary-General's concern about delays in adhering to the Peace Agreement's timetable for implementation.
See Document 42, page 246

5 June 1992

The ONUSAL Human Rights Division issues its fourth report, which focuses on two topics: the right to life and to integrity and security of person, and due process of law.
See Document 43, page 247

17 June 1992

The Government and the FMLN agree to adjust the timetable for implementation of the Peace Agreement.
See Document 44, page 251

13 July 1992

The Commission on the Truth is formally installed; the Commission arrives in El Salvador on **14 July.**

12 August 1992

The ONUSAL Human Rights Division reports that, in spite of serious concerns relating to summary executions, violent death and threats, the overall human rights situation in El Salvador has improved during the past year.
See Document 45, page 252

19 August 1992

Following further setbacks in carrying out provisions of the Peace Agreement, the Government and the FMLN again adjust the implementation timetable.

22 September 1992

The Ad Hoc Commission on Purification of the Armed Forces of El Salvador established under the September 1991 New York Agreement finishes its review of individual officers' professional competence and human rights records and submits its report to the Secretary-General and to President Cristiani.

30 September 1992

The FMLN informs the United Nations that, in order to maintain the link in the original timetable between the key undertakings of the two parties, it would suspend destruction of its weapons and demobilization of its forces until new dates were set for the start of the transfer of land and other aspects of the Agreement that had fallen behind schedule.
See Document 50, page 260

13 October 1992
The Secretary-General proposes a compromise solution to the land issue.
See Document 46, pag 257; Document 47, page 257; Document 50, page 260; and Document 76, page 443

15-16 October 1992
The Government and the FMLN accept the land proposal; in replies to the Secretary-General, the FMLN records certain understandings on the proposal and the Government seeks certain clarifications.
See Document 48, page 258; Document 49, page 259; Document 51, page 261; and Document 52, page 262

23 October 1992
The Secretary-General proposes a new target date of **15 December** for the complete dismantling of the FMLN's military structure and for the formal cessation of the armed conflict; the original date had been **31 October.**

28 October 1992
The Secretary-General recommends that the mandate of ONUSAL be extended until **30 November.**
See Document 53, page 263

30 October 1992
The Security Council extends ONUSAL's mandate through **30 November.**
See Document 54, page 264

30 October 1992
With the Government delaying the purification of the armed forces, the Secretary-General sends his representatives to El Salvador for consultations.

6 November 1992
A representative of the Secretary-General announces agreement on purification of the armed forces, demobilization of the FMLN and destruction of its weaponry.
See Document 55, page 264

23 November 1992
The Secretary-General reports to the Security Council that, obstacles notwithstanding, implementation of the peace process has advanced steadily.
See Document 56, page 265

30 November 1992
The Security Council urges both parties to implement their commitments and extends ONUSAL's mandate to **31 May 1993.**
See Document 57, page 275

30 November 1992
The Secretary-General reports to the General Assembly on developments concerning El Salvador, Guatemala and the United Nations Observer Group in Central America.
See Document 58, page 276

1 December 1992
The Secretary-General confirms that he has received a letter from President Cristiani informing him of the administrative decisions that the latter had adopted to begin purification of the armed forces. The FMLN resumes demobilization of its combatants.
See Document 60, page 282

7 December 1992
The Secretary-General reports that the destruction of the FMLN's weapons has begun.
See Document 60, page 282

15 December 1992
Following the final demobilization of the FMLN's combatants and the FMLN's legalization as a political party, the armed conflict between the Government and the FMLN is brought to a formal end at a ceremony in San Salvador attended by Secretary-General Boutros Boutros-Ghali, President Cristiani, the FMLN's General Command and other dignitaries. ONUSAL's Military Division is subsequently reduced in number.
See Document 59, page 281; Document 60, page 282; and Document 61, page 285

7 January 1993
The Secretary-General reports to the Security Council that the Government of El Salvador is not yet in full compliance with the recommendations of the Ad Hoc Commission on Purification of the Armed Forces.
See Document 62, page 286

26 January 1993
The Secretary-General informs the Security Council that he intends to recommend that the United Nations agree to a request by the Government of El Salvador that the United Nations verify the elections to be held in **March 1994.**
See Document 63, page 287

29 January 1993
The Secretary-General reports to the Security Council that the FMLN did not complete the destruction of its remaining arms and equipment by the agreed deadline of **29 January.**
See Document 64, page 288

9 February 1993
The Security Council expresses its concern about continued delays in the Government's purification of the armed forces, the FMLN's destruction of arms and other matters.
See Document 65, page 288

15 March 1993
The report of the Commission on the Truth is made public; it contains the results of the investigation into human rights violations committed during the civil war and the Commission's recommendations for punishment and for preventing a repetition of such acts.
See Document 67, page 290

18 March 1993
The Security Council welcomes the report of the Commission on the Truth and calls on the parties to comply with its recommendations and with all other obligations of the peace accords that remain to be implemented.
See Document 66, page 289

20 March 1993
El Salvador's Legislative Assembly passes a broad amnesty law; the Secretary-General expresses his concern at the haste with which this step was taken.

30 March 1993
President Cristiani expresses certain reservations about the report of the Commission on the Truth.
See Document 68, page 415

2 April 1993
The Secretary-General reports to the Security Council on developments relating to the purification of the armed forces.
See Document 69, page 416

5 April 1993
The ONUSAL Human Rights Division reports that, although some disturbing practices persist, there has been a definite trend towards an overall improvement in the human rights situation in El Salvador.
See Document 70, page 416

20 May 1993
The Secretary-General transmits to the Government, the FMLN and the National Commission for the Consolidation of Peace (COPAZ) an analysis of the recommendations of the Commission on the Truth undertaken to identify the actions required by the various parties concerned. The Secretary-General emphasizes that implementation should be completed as far as possible before the elections.
See Document 71, page 424; Document 72, page 425; Document 73, page 426; and Document 77, page 447

21 May 1993
The Secretary-General reports to the Security Council on all aspects of ONUSAL's operations, including the proposed expansion of the Mission's mandate to include an Electoral Division, proposals concerning the land-transfer programme and an analysis of the recommendations of the Commission on the Truth.
See Document 74, page 427; Document 75, page 442; Document 76, page 443; and Document 77, page 447

23 May 1993
An explosion at an automobile repair shop in Managua, Nicaragua, leads to the discovery of an FMLN weapons cache; investigations by ONUSAL conducted with the cooperation of the FMLN reveal the existence of 114 previously unknown weapons deposits in El Salvador, Nicaragua and Honduras.
See Document 77, page 447

27 May 1993
The Security Council enlarges ONUSAL's mandate, adding an Electoral Division to observe the 1994 general elections.
See Document 78, page 454

11 June 1993
The Security Council describes the secret stockpiling of arms by the FMLN as "the most serious violation to date" of the peace accords.
See Document 80, page 456

12 June 1993
In a letter to the FMLN, the Secretary-General writes that the discovery of hidden arms raises "very serious questions of confidence and trust".
See Document 82, page 458

28 June 1993
In a letter to the Secretary-General, Nicaragua's Minister for Foreign Affairs describes the various actions the Government of Nicaragua has taken following the discovery of secret arms caches belonging to the FMLN.
See Document 81, page 456

29 June 1993
The Secretary-General updates the Security Council on developments relating to the discovery of illegal arms deposits belonging to the FMLN.
See Document 82, page 458

2 July 1993
The ONUSAL Human Rights Division reports that the trend towards a definite improvement continues, but that some serious and systemic violations continue to occur.
See Document 83, page 466

7 July 1993
The Secretary-General informs the Security Council that the Government has removed from active service all army officers identified for dismissal so as to fully comply with the recommendations of the Ad Hoc Commission on Purification of the Armed Forces.
See Document 84, page 471; and Document 87, page 472

12 July 1993
The Security Council expresses its continuing concern regarding the discovery of illegal arms deposits belonging to the FMLN.
See Document 85, page 471

13 July 1993
President Cristiani writes to the Secretary-General concerning the Government's compliance with the recommendations of the Commission on the Truth.
See Document 86, page 472

18 August 1993
The destruction of the FMLN's weapons and equipment under ONUSAL verification is completed.
See Document 88, page 473

15 September 1993
The ONUSAL Human Rights Division reports that the situation continues to evolve in an ambivalent manner, with signs of improvement amidst continuing violence.
See Document 89, page 476

14 October 1993
The Secretary-General urges the Government, the FMLN and others involved to step up the implementation of the recommendations of the Commission on the Truth before the electoral campaign begins on 20 November.
See Document 90, page 480

20 October 1993
The Secretary-General reports to the Security Council on the activities of the ONUSAL Electoral Division and on problems relating to the voter registration process.
See Document 91, page 491

25 October 1993
A leader of the FMLN is murdered, death-squad style, in San Salvador.

30 October 1993
Another leading member of the FMLN is murdered.

3 November 1993
The Secretary-General expresses his shock and sadness at the killings and recommends a vigorous investigation.
See Document 92, page 494

5 November 1993
The Security Council expresses its concern at the apparent pattern of politically motivated murders in El Salvador and supports the efforts of the Secretary-General to initiate an immediate investigation, as recommended in the report of the Commission on the Truth.
See Document 93, page 495

20 November 1993
The electoral campaign begins.

23 November 1993
The Secretary-General reports that although implementation of the peace accords has on the whole progressed well, recent developments have caused serious worry as to whether previous achievements are now threatened.
See Document 94, page 496

30 November 1993
The Security Council extends ONUSAL's mandate until **31 May 1994.**
See Document 95, page 509

7 December 1993
The Secretary-General informs the Security Council that a Joint Group for the investigation of politically motivated illegal armed groups has been formed.
See Document 96, page 510; and Document 97, page 512

18 January 1994
The ONUSAL Human Rights Division reports that the situation took a serious turn for the worse between August and October 1993.
See Document 98, page 512

19 January 1994
Voter registration ends.
See Document 100, page 521

15 February 1994
The Secretary-General informs President Cristiani about lingering concerns relating to the maintenance of internal order, the land-transfer programme and the reintegration of estranged groups, including former combatants.
See Document 99, page 519

16 February 1994
The Secretary-General reports to the Security Council on the electoral campaign and on difficulties with the electoral roll.
See Document 100, page 521

3 March 1994
The Secretary-General informs President Cristiani that he remains concerned about the maintenance of internal order and the reintegration of estranged groups.
See Document 101, page 526

16 March 1994
The Secretary-General reports to the Security Council that despite the remaining difficulties and the mistrust among the political contenders, the conditions for the holding of free and fair elections are generally adequate.
See Document 102, page 527

20 March 1994
Elections are held. With no candidate in the presidential contest obtaining more than 50 per cent of the vote, a run-off is required between the two parties winning the most votes — Alianza Republicana Nacionalista (ARENA), 49.26 per cent, and the Coalition Convergencia Democrática/FMLN/Movimiento Nacional Revolucionario, 25.29 per cent. Observers document some irregularities and shortcomings, but ONUSAL states that the elections, in general, took place under appropriate conditions in terms of freedom, competitiveness and security.
See Document 104, page 531

28 March 1994
The Secretary-General reports to the Security Council about ongoing concerns relating to public security, the reintegration of former combatants and the constitutional reforms recommended by the Commission on the Truth.
See Document 103, page 530

5 April 1994
The ONUSAL Human Rights Division reports a certain improvement in the situation, owing to the constructive steps — including formation of the joint investigative group — taken by the Government, the FMLN, Salvadorian society and the international community in response to the violence in previous months.
See Document 105, page 535

7 April 1994
The Security Council congratulates El Salvador on the peaceful and historic elections, calls on those concerned to carry out the measures recommended by the Secretary-General to correct the shortcomings and calls once again for full implementation of the peace accords.
See Document 106, page 542

21 April 1994
The Secretary-General, reporting on the situation just prior to the presidential run-off election, notes both progress and difficulties in efforts to rectify the flaws that occurred in the first round of elections.
See Document 107, page 542

24 April 1994
The ARENA candidate wins the presidential run-off election.
See Document 108, page 544

11 May 1994
The Secretary-General recommends that the Mission's mandate be extended until 30 November in order to verify implementation by the parties of the outstanding provisions of the peace accords.
See Document 109, page 547

19 May 1994
The Government and the FMLN reach agreement on a "Timetable for the implementation of the most important outstanding agreements".
See Document 110, page 561

26 May 1994
The Security Council welcomes the elections, expresses concern that important elements of the peace accords remain only partially implemented and extends ONUSAL's mandate until 30 November.
See Document 111, page 567

1 June 1994
Mr. Armando Calderón Sol is inaugurated as President of El Salvador.
See Document 112, page 568

28 July 1994
The Joint Group for the Investigation of Politically Motivated Illegal Armed Groups issues its report, concluding, among other things, that such groups appear to be pursuing the destabilization of the peace process.
See Document 113, page 568

28 July 1994
The ONUSAL Human Rights Division reports continuing improvement but notes that the existence of organized crime networks, coupled with the inadequate functioning of the justice system, are the greatest obstacles to the effective exercise of human rights in El Salvador.
See Document 114, page 574

26 August 1994
The Secretary-General reports that, despite some delays, progress has been made by the Government and the FMLN in carrying out the **19 May** "Timetable for the implementation of the most important outstanding agreements".
See Document 115, page 577

16 September 1994
The Security Council welcomes the steps taken by the President of El Salvador, since his inauguration, to ensure compliance with the outstanding provisions of the peace accords.
See Document 116, page 584

4 October 1994
The Government and the FMLN sign a joint declaration reflecting their determination to see the peace accords implemented fully and urgently for the benefit of all Salvadorians.
See Document 117, page 585

31 October 1994
The Secretary-General recommends that ONUSAL's mandate be extended, at much reduced strength, until **30 April 1995** to ensure that the incomplete undertakings — particularly those concerning public security — are fully implemented.
See Document 118, page 586

31 October 1994
The ONUSAL Human Rights Division reports that, in preparation for its withdrawal, it has gradually shifted its focus to reforming and strengthening El Salvador's permanent human rights institutions.
See Document 119, page 591

23 November 1994
The Security Council urges the Government and the FMLN to redouble their efforts to comply with the **19 May** timetable and extends the mandate of ONUSAL until **30 April 1995**.
See Document 120, page 593

19 December 1994
The General Assembly calls upon the Government of El Salvador and all the political forces involved in the peace process to fulfil their vital outstanding commitments and commends the efforts of the Central American peoples and Governments to consolidate peace.
See Document 121, page 594

6 February 1995
In a letter to the President of the Security Council, the Secretary-General proposes the establishment of a small team of United Nations officials to continue the verification responsibilities and the good offices functions carried out by ONUSAL after the end of the mission's mandate.
See Document 122, page 598

17 February 1995
The Security Council welcomes the Secretary-General's proposal.
See Document 123, page 599

30 April 1995
The mandate of ONUSAL is scheduled to be terminated.

II List of reproduced documents

*The documents reproduced on pages 89-599 include resolutions of the
Security Council, statements by the President of the Security Council,
statements and other communications from Member States, reports and
letters of the Secretary-General to the General Assembly and the
Security Council, correspondence of the Secretary-General, reports of
the ONUSAL Human Rights Division and other communications.*

1989

Document 1
Report of the Secretary-General concerning the situation
in Central America.
A/44/344-S/20699, 26 June 1989
See page 89

Document 2
Security Council resolution concerning the situation in
Central America and the Esquipulas II Agreement.
S/RES/637, 27 July 1989
See page 91

Document 3
Letter dated 9 August 1989 from Costa Rica, El Salvador,
Guatemala, Honduras and Nicaragua transmitting the
text of the Tela Declaration signed by the five Central
American Presidents.
A/44/451-S/20778, 9 August 1989
See page 92

Document 4
Report of the Secretary-General concerning the situation
in Central America.
A/44/344/Add.1-S/20699/Add.1, 9 October 1989
See page 97

Document 5
Statement by the President of the Security Council ex-
pressing concern over the situation in Central America.
S/21011, 8 December 1989
See page 100

Document 6
Letter dated 12 December 1989 from El Salvador trans-
mitting the Declaration of San Isidro de Coronado signed
by the five Central American Presidents.
A/44/872-S/21019, 12 December 1989
See page 100

Document 7
Report of the Secretary-General concerning the situation
in Central America.
A/44/886-S/21029, 21 December 1989
See page 102

1990

Document 8
Letter dated 29 January 1990 from President Alfredo
Cristiani of El Salvador to the Secretary-General concern-
ing the peace process and United Nations involvement.
Not issued as a United Nations document.
See page 105

Document 9
Note verbale dated 14 August 1990 from El Salvador
transmitting text of the Agreement on Human Rights
signed at San José, Costa Rica, on 26 July 1990 between
the Government of El Salvador and the Frente Farabundo
Martí para la Liberación Nacional (FMLN).
A/44/971-S/21541, 16 August 1990
See page 107

Document 10
Letter dated 29 August 1990 from the Secretary-General
to the President of the Security Council concerning the
possible establishment of a small preparatory office in El
Salvador and other arrangements for a United Nations
verification mission.
S/21717, 6 September 1990
See page 110

Document 11
Report of the Secretary-General on the situation in Cen-
tral America; contains the text of the Geneva Agreement
(4 April 1990) and the Caracas Agreement (21 May 1990)
signed by the Government of El Salvador and the
FMLN.
A/45/706-S/21931, 8 November 1990
See page 110

1991

A/46/502-S/23082, 26 September 1991, and addendum,
A/46/502/Add.1-S/23082/Add.1, 7 October 1991
See page 159

Document 26
Security Council resolution concerning agreements between the Government of El Salvador and the FMLN.
S/RES/714, 30 September 1991
See page 163

Document 27
Letter dated 8 October 1991 from El Salvador transmitting the text of the Geneva Agreement signed on 4 April 1990 by the Government of El Salvador and the FMLN.
A/46/551-S/23128, 9 October 1991
See page 164

Document 28
Letter dated 8 October 1991 from El Salvador transmitting the text of the Caracas Agreement signed on 21 May 1990 by the Government of El Salvador and the FMLN.
A/46/552-S/23129, 9 October 1991
See page 165

Document 29
Letter dated 8 October 1991 from El Salvador transmitting the text of the Mexico Agreement and annexes signed on 27 April 1991 by the Government of El Salvador and the FMLN.
A/46/553-S/23130, 9 October 1991
See page 167

Document 30
Report of the Secretary-General on ONUSAL and report of the ONUSAL Human Rights Division (extract).
A/46/658-S/23222, 15 November 1991
See page 175

Document 31
Report of the Secretary-General on the situation in Central America.
A/46/713-S/23256, 2 December 1991
See page 180

Document 32
Letter dated 26 December 1991 from the Secretary-General to President Cristiani inviting the latter to United Nations Headquarters for negotiations.
Not issued as a United Nations document.
See page 186

1992

Document 33
Statement by the President of the Security Council on the agreement signed on 31 December 1991 by the Government of El Salvador and the FMLN.
S/23360, 3 January 1992
See page 187

Document 34
Report of the Secretary-General on the monitoring of agreements by ONUSAL.
S/23402, 10 January 1992, and addendum, S/23402/Add.1, 13 January 1992
See page 187

Document 35
Security Council resolution concerning enlargement of the ONUSAL mandate.
S/RES/729, 14 January 1992
See page 192

Document 36
Letter dated 27 January 1992 from El Salvador transmitting the entire text of the Peace Agreement between the Government of El Salvador and the FMLN, signed at Chapultepec Castle in Mexico City on 16 January 1992.
A/46/864-S/23501, 30 January 1992
See page 193

Document 37
Letter dated 27 January 1992 from El Salvador transmitting the texts of the New York Act and New York Act II signed by the Government of El Salvador and the FMLN on 31 December 1991 and 13 January 1992, respectively.
A/46/863-S/23504, 30 January 1992
See page 230

Document 38
Report of the ONUSAL Human Rights Division for November and December 1991 (extract).
A/46/876-S/23580, 19 February 1992
See page 231

Document 39
Report of the Secretary-General on ONUSAL.
S/23642, 25 February 1992
See page 236

Document 40
Letter dated 15 May 1992 from the Secretary-General to the President of the Security Council concerning ONUSAL military observers.
S/23987, 20 May 1992
See page 237

Document 86

Letter dated 13 July 1993 from President Cristiani to the Secretary-General concerning the recommendations of the Commission on the Truth.
Not issued as a United Nations document.
See page 472

Document 87

Letter dated 13 July 1993 from the President of the Security Council to the Secretary-General welcoming confirmation of El Salvador's compliance with the Ad Hoc Commission's recommendations regarding the armed forces.
S/26077, 13 July 1993
See page 472

Document 88

Report of the Secretary-General on developments concerning the identification and destruction of clandestine arms deposits belonging to the FMLN.
S/26371, 30 August 1993
See page 473

Document 89

Report of the ONUSAL Human Rights Division for the period from 1 May to 31 July 1993 (extract).
A/47/1012-S/26416, 15 September 1993
See page 476

Document 90

Report of the Secretary-General on the implementation of the recommendations of the Commission on the Truth.
S/26581, 14 October 1993
See page 480

Document 91

Report of the Secretary-General on the activities of the ONUSAL Electoral Division.
S/26606, 20 October 1993
See page 491

Document 92

Letter dated 3 November 1993 from the Secretary-General to the President of the Security Council concerning the persistence of human rights violations in El Salvador.
S/26689, 3 November 1993
See page 494

Document 93

Statement by the President of the Security Council concerning the violent deaths of two FMLN leaders and other members of the FMLN.
S/26695, 5 November 1993
See page 495

Document 94

Report of the Secretary-General on ONUSAL's activities from 22 May to 20 November 1993.
S/26790, 23 November 1993
See page 496

Document 95

Security Council resolution concerning the peace process in El Salvador and the extension of ONUSAL's mandate.
S/RES/888, 30 November 1993
See page 509

Document 96

Letter dated 7 December 1993 from the Secretary-General to the President of the Security Council concerning implementation of the recommendations of the Commission on the Truth regarding the investigation of illegal groups.
S/26865, 11 December 1993
See page 510

Document 97

Letter dated 10 December 1993 from the President of the Security Council to the Secretary-General concerning the establishment of a Joint Group for the investigation of politically motivated illegal armed groups.
S/26866, 11 December 1993
See page 512

1994

Document 98

Report of the ONUSAL Human Rights Division covering the period from 1 August to 31 October 1993 (extract).
A/49/59-S/1994/47, 18 January 1994
See page 512

Document 99

Letter dated 15 February 1994 from the Secretary-General to President Cristiani about concerns relating to implementation of the peace accords.
Not issued as a United Nations document.
See page 519

Document 100

Report of the Secretary-General on the activities of the ONUSAL Electoral Division.
S/1994/179, 16 February 1994
See page 521

Document 101
Letter dated 3 March 1994 from the Secretary-General to President Cristiani about concerns relating to implementation of the peace accords.
Not issued as a United Nations document.
See page 526

Document 102
Report of the Secretary-General on the activities of the ONUSAL Electoral Division.
S/1994/304, 16 March 1994
See page 527

Document 103
Letter dated 28 March 1994 from the Secretary-General to the President of the Security Council concerning implementation of the peace accords.
S/1994/361, 30 March 1994
See page 530

Document 104
Report of the Secretary-General concerning elections held on 20 March 1994.
S/1994/375, 31 March 1994
See page 531

Document 105
Report of the ONUSAL Human Rights Division covering the period from 1 November 1993 to 28 February 1994 (extract).
A/49/116-S/1994/385, 5 April 1994
See page 535

Document 106
Statement by the President of the Security Council concerning elections held on 20 March 1994.
S/PRST/1994/15, 7 April 1994
See page 542

Document 107
Letter dated 21 April 1994 from the Secretary-General to the President of the Security Council concerning the pre-electoral situation as of 20 April 1994.
S/1994/486, 21 April 1994
See page 542

Document 108
Report of the Secretary-General concerning the second round of elections, held on 24 April 1994.
S/1994/536, 4 May 1994
See page 544

Document 109
Report of the Secretary-General on ONUSAL's activities from 21 November 1993 to 30 April 1994.
S/1994/561, 11 May 1994, and addendum, S/1994/561/Add.1, 25 May 1994
See page 547

Document 110
Letter dated 24 May 1994 from the Secretary-General to the President of the Security Council concerning agreement on a new "Timetable for the implementation of the most important outstanding agreements".
S/1994/612, 24 May 1994
See page 561

Document 111
Security Council resolution concerning the peace process in El Salvador and the extension of ONUSAL's mandate.
S/RES/920, 26 May 1994
See page 567

Document 112
Letter dated 31 May 1994 from the Secretary-General to President Cristiani conveying his regrets that he will be unable to attend the ceremony inaugurating President Cristiani's successor.
Not issued as a United Nations document.
See page 568

Document 113
Report issued on 28 July 1994 by the Joint Group for the Investigation of Politically Motivated Illegal Armed Groups (extract: conclusions and recommendations).
S/1994/989, 22 October 1994
See page 568

Document 114
Report of the ONUSAL Human Rights Division covering the period from 1 March to 30 June 1994 (extract).
A/49/281-S/1994/886, 28 July 1994
See page 574

Document 115
Report of the Secretary-General on ONUSAL's activities.
S/1994/1000, 26 August 1994
See page 577

Document 116
Statement by the President of the Security Council concerning compliance with outstanding provisions of the peace accords.
S/PRST/1994/54, 16 September 1994
See page 584

Document 117
Letter dated 6 October 1994 from the Secretary-General to the President of the Security Council transmitting the text of a joint declaration on compliance with the peace accords signed on 4 October 1994 by the Government of El Salvador and the FMLN.
S/1994/1144, 10 October 1994
See page 585

Document 118
Report of the Secretary-General on ONUSAL's activities.
S/1994/1212, 31 October 1994, and addendum, S/1994/1212/Add.1, 14 November 1994
See page 586

Document 119
Report of the ONUSAL Human Rights Division covering the period from 1 July to 30 September 1994 (extract).
A/49/585-S/1994/1220, 31 October 1994
See page 591

Document 120
Security Council resolution concerning the peace process in El Salvador and the extension of ONUSAL's mandate.
S/RES/961, 23 November 1994
See page 593

Document 121
Resolution of the General Assembly concerning the situation in Central America: procedures for the establishment of a firm and lasting peace and progress in fashioning a region of peace, freedom, democracy and development.
A/RES/49/137, 19 December 1994
See page 594

Document 122
Letter dated 6 February 1995 from the Secretary-General to the President of the Security Council concerning post-ONUSAL arrangements.
S/1995/143, 17 February 1995
See page 598

Document 123
Letter dated 17 February 1995 from the President of the Security Council to the Secretary-General concerning post-ONUSAL arrangements.
S/1995/144, 17 February 1995
See page 599

The following is a breakdown, by category, of the documents reproduced in this book.

Resolution of the General Assembly
Document 121

Resolutions of the Security Council
Documents 2, 19, 26, 35, 54, 57, 78, 95, 111, 120

Statements by the President of the Security Council on behalf of the Council
Documents 5, 33, 42, 65-66, 80, 93, 106, 116

Letters from the President of the Security Council to the Secretary-General
Documents 85, 87, 123

Statements and other communications from Member States
Documents 3, 6, 9, 12, 20, 25, 27-29, 36-37, 59, 61, 81

Reports and letters of the Secretary-General to the General Assembly and the Security Council
Documents 1, 4, 7, 10-11, 13, 16, 21, 24, 30-31, 34, 39-41, 44, 50, 53, 55-56, 58, 60, 62-64, 67, 69, 74-77, 79, 82, 84, 88, 90-92, 94, 96-97, 100, 102-104, 107-110, 115, 117-118, 122

Correspondence of the Secretary-General
Documents 8, 14-15, 17-18, 22-23, 32, 46-49, 51-52, 68, 71-73, 86, 99, 101, 112

Reports of the ONUSAL Human Rights Division
Documents 30, 38, 43, 45, 70, 83, 89, 98, 105, 114, 119

Other
Document 113

III Other documents of interest

Readers seeking additional information about the United Nations Observer Mission in El Salvador (ONUSAL) and the situation in El Salvador might wish to consult the following documents, which are available in the Dag Hammarskjöld Library at United Nations Headquarters in New York City, at other libraries in the United Nations system or at libraries around the world which have been designated as depository libraries for United Nations documents.

Resolutions and decisions of the General Assembly concerning the situation in Central America
A/RES/38/10, 11 November 1983
A/RES/39/4, 26 October 1984
A/DEC/40/470, 18 December 1985
   [decision retaining item on agenda]
A/RES/41/37, 18 November 1986
A/RES/42/1, 7 October 1987
A/RES/43/24, 15 November 1988
A/RES/44/10, 23 October 1989
A/RES/45/15, 20 November 1990
A/RES/46/109 A, 17 December 1991
A/RES/46/109 B, 17 December 1991
A/RES/47/118, 18 December 1992
A/RES/48/161, 20 December 1993

Resolutions of the General Assembly concerning the situation of human rights in El Salvador
A/RES/35/192, 15 December 1980
A/RES/36/155, 16 December 1981
A/RES/37/185, 17 December 1982
A/RES/38/101, 16 December 1983
A/RES/39/119, 14 December 1984
A/RES/40/139, 13 December 1985
A/RES/41/157, 4 December 1986
A/RES/42/137, 7 December 1987
A/RES/43/145, 8 December 1988
A/RES/44/165, 15 December 1989
A/RES/45/172, 18 December 1990
A/RES/46/133, 17 December 1991
A/RES/47/140, 18 December 1992
A/RES/48/149, 20 December 1993

Resolutions and decisions of the General Assembly concerning Central American refugees and the International Conference on Central American Refugees
A/RES/42/110, 7 December 1987
A/RES/43/118, 8 December 1988
A/RES/44/139, 15 December 1989
A/RES/45/141, 14 December 1990
A/RES/46/107, 16 December 1991
A/RES/47/103, 16 December 1992
A/RES/48/117, 20 December 1993
A/DEC/49/450, 23 December 1994

Resolutions of the General Assembly concerning economic and other assistance to El Salvador and the Special Plan of Economic Cooperation for Central America
A/RES/41/2, 14 October 1986
A/RES/41/194, 8 December 1986
A/RES/42/203, 11 December 1987
A/RES/42/204, 11 December 1987
A/RES/42/231, 12 May 1988
A/RES/43/210, 20 December 1988
A/RES/44/182, 19 December 1989
A/RES/45/231, 21 December 1990
A/RES/46/170, 19 December 1991
A/RES/47/158, 18 December 1992
A/RES/48/199, 21 December 1993
A/RES/48/203, 21 December 1993
A/RES/49/21H, 20 December 1994
A/RES/49/21J, 20 December 1994

Reports of the Secretary-General

The situation in Central America
A/48/586, 11 November 1993
A/49/489, 7 October 1994

International Conference on Central American Refugees
A/47/364, 18 August 1992
A/48/391, 23 September 1993
A/49/534, 19 October 1994

Assistance for the reconstruction and development of El Salvador
A/48/310, 3 September 1993
A/49/562, 21 October 1994

Special plan of economic cooperation for Central America
A/48/405, 11 October 1993
A/49/397, 12 October 1994

Reports on the situation of human rights in El Salvador prepared by the Special Representative of the Commission on Human Rights
A/36/608, 28 October 1981
E/CN.4/1502, 18 January 1982
A/37/611, 22 November 1982
E/CN.4/1983/20, 20 January 1983
A/38/503, 22 November 1983
E/CN.4/1984/25, 19 January 1984
A/39/636, 9 November 1984
E/CN.4/1985/18, 1 February 1985
A/40/818, 5 November 1985
E/CN.4/1986/22, 3 February 1986
A/41/710, 21 October 1986
E/CN.4/1987/21, 2 February 1987
A/42/641, 12 October 1987
E/CN.4/1988/23, 29 January 1988
A/43/736, 21 October 1988
E/CN.4/1989/23, 2 February 1989
A/44/671, 26 October 1989
E/CN.4/1990/26, 22 January 1990
A/45/630, 22 October 1990
E/CN.4/1991/34, 28 January 1991
A/46/529, 11 October 1991
E/CN.4/1992/32, 16 January 1992

Reports on the situation of human rights in El Salvador prepared by the Independent Expert of the Commission on Human Rights
A/47/596, 13 November 1992
E/CN.4/1993/11, 9 February 1993
E/CN.4/1994/11, 3 February 1994

Report to the Commission on Human Rights submitted by the United Nations Observer Mission in El Salvador (ONUSAL)
E/CN.4/1993/96, 22 February 1993

Financing ONUSAL: resolutions of the General Assembly, reports of the Secretary-General, reports of the Advisory Committee on Administrative and Budgetary Questions (ACABQ) and reports of the Fifth Committee (C.5) of the General Assembly
S/22494/Add.1, 20 May 1991
A/45/242/Add.1, 30 May 1991
A/45/1021, 12 June 1991 (ACABQ)
A/45/1026, 19 June 1991 (C.5)
A/RES/45/267, 21 June 1991
A/46/900, 22 April 1992
A/46/904, 5 May 1992 (ACABQ)
ST/ADM/SER.B/379, 12 May 1992
A/46/924, 21 May 1992 (C.5)
A/RES/46/240, 22 May 1992
ST/ADM/SER.B/381, 22 June 1992
A/47/751, 4 December 1992
A/47/797, 17 December 1992 (C.5)
A/DEC/47/452, 22 December 1992
A/47/900, 2 March 1993 (ACABQ)
A/47/797/Add.1, 12 March 1993 (C.5)
A/RES/47/223, 16 March 1993
A/47/751/Add.1, 8 July 1993
A/47/983, 27 July 1993 (ACABQ)
A/47/797/Add.2, 9 September 1993 (C.5)
A/RES/47/234, 14 September 1993
A/C.5/48/40, 9 December 1993 (C.5)
A/48/774, 17 December 1993 (ACABQ)
A/48/817, 23 December 1993 (C.5)
A/DEC/48/468 A, 23 December 1993
A/48/842, 12 January 1994 (and Corr.1, 3 March 1994)
A/48/817/Add.1, 4 March 1994 (C.5)
A/48/898, 8 March 1994 (ACABQ)
A/DEC/48/468 B, 9 March 1994
ST/ADM/SER.B/400, 16 March 1994
A/48/817/Add.2, 29 March 1994 (C.5)
A/RES/48/243, 5 April 1994
ST/ADM/SER.B/433, 25 April 1994
A/48/842/Add.1, 21 July 1994 (and Add.1/Corr.1, 21 September 1994)
A/49//458, 30 September 1994 (ACABQ)
A/49/503, 12 October 1994 (C.5)
A/49/518, 14 October 1994
A/DEC/49/405, 14 October 1994

IV Texts of documents

The texts of the 123 documents listed on the preceding pages are reproduced below. The appearance of ellipses (. . .) in the text indicates that portions of the document have been omitted. A subject index to the documents begins on page 600.

Document 1

Report of the Secretary-General concerning the situation in Central America

A/44/344-S/20699, 26 June 1989

1. This report is being submitted pursuant to resolutions 530 (1983) of 19 May 1983 and 562 (1985) of 10 May 1985 of the Security Council and resolution 43/24 of 15 November 1988 of the General Assembly.

2. In this last resolution, the General Assembly, *inter alia*, commended the desire for peace expressed by the Central American Presidents in signing on 7 August 1987 at Guatemala City the agreement on "Procedures for the establishment of a firm and lasting peace in Central America" and in issuing on 16 January 1988 at San José their Joint Declaration; expressed its strongest support for the agreement; exhorted the Governments to continue their efforts to achieve a firm and lasting peace in Central America and fervently hoped that the Central American Presidents would evaluate and give a new impetus to the process of fulfilling the undertakings assumed in the agreement concluded at the Esquipulas II summit meeting; urged the five Central American countries to adopt immediately formulae that would enable them to overcome the obstacles impeding the advancement of the regional peace process and appealed to the countries which are outside the region but which have links with it and interests in it to facilitate the implementation of the agreement concluded at the Esquipulas II summit meeting and to abstain from any action which might impede such implementation.

3. The General Assembly also exhorted the five Central American countries, with the utmost urgency, to promote and supplement the agreed verification machinery, with the cooperation of regional or extra-regional States and bodies of recognized impartiality and technical capacity, which had shown a desire to collaborate in the Central American peace process and requested me to afford the fullest possible support to the Central American Governments in their efforts to achieve peace, especially by taking the measures necessary for the development and effective functioning of the essential verification machinery.

4. Lastly, the Assembly urged the international community and international organizations to increase their technical, economic and financial cooperation with the Central American countries for the implementation of the activities supporting the goals and objectives of the Special Plan of Economic Cooperation for Central America, as stipulated in General Assembly resolution 42/231, and as a way of assisting the efforts being made by the countries of the region to achieve peace and development.

5. In the initial months following the adoption of General Assembly resolution 43/24, the situation in the region was seen to evolve favourably. An increasing number of contacts took place at various levels between Central American Governments, public recriminations ceased almost entirely and, at the same time, foreign interference seemed to be on the decline. The renewed interest shown by the Central American Governments in the establishment of impartial machinery for on-site verification of the undertakings in respect of security contained in the Esquipulas II Agreements, namely, cessation of aid to irregular forces and insurrectionist movements operating in the region and non-use of the territory of a State for attacking others was a clear manifestation of the new climate. That interest was expressed in the request from the Executive Commission set up under the Esquipulas II Agreements, consisting of the Ministers for Foreign Affairs of the five Central American States, at its sixth meeting, held on 30 November 1988 at Mexico City, that I should take steps, as a matter of urgency, for the development and effective functioning of impartial machinery for on-site verification, control and monitoring of the implementation of the undertakings in respect of security, which request I answered in detail on 5 January 1989.

6. Acting on the suggestion of the Minister for Foreign Affairs of Costa Rica, with a view to clarifying certain ideas and considerations contained in my reply of 5 January and to moving ahead with the definition of the verification machinery for the security commitments, I proposed to the five Central American Ministers for Foreign Affairs that they meet with me and my principal advisers in New York on 8 February 1989, that is, prior to the summit meeting of their Presidents in order to assist them in preparing for that meeting. At the close of the New York meeting, the Ministers for Foreign Affairs handed me a note in which they clarified the request contained in the letter of 30 November and requested, in accordance with General Assembly resolution 43/24, that I proceed to appoint a technical group of the Secretariat for the purpose of defining, with Central American representatives, the terms of reference for the establishment of the verification machinery, and on that basis, draft the relevant proposal.

7. In the Joint Declaration issued on 14 February in El Salvador (A/44/140-S/20491), the Central American Presidents adopted several specific commitments with a view to implementing the Esquipulas II Agreements and in turn entrusted three important tasks to the United Nations. Those tasks were additional to those relating to the Special Plan of Economic Cooperation referred to in paragraph 4 above and to the International Conference on Central American Refugees, which are the subject of separate reports to the General Assembly. Specifically, the Presidents entrusted the Executive Commission with the task of immediately organizing technical meetings to establish the most appropriate and effective mechanism for verification of the security commitments "in accordance with the talks held in New York with the Secretary-General of the United Nations". The Presidents, in turn, welcomed the willingness expressed by the President of Nicaragua "to undertake a process of democratization and national reconciliation in his country", by amending the electoral laws and the laws relating to the communications media to enable "political parties to organize and to be politically active in the broadest sense", to move up the elections to no later than 25 February 1990 unless the Government and opposition political parties should decide, by mutual consent, that they should be held at another date, and to invite international observers, in particular the representatives of the Secretary-General of the United Nations and the Secretary-General of the Organization of American States (OAS) to be present in all electoral districts in order to verify that the electoral process is genuine during every stage. Finally, the Presidents undertook to draw up, within a period not exceeding 90 days, "a joint plan for the voluntary demobilization, repatriation or relocation in Nicaragua or third countries

of members of the Nicaraguan resistance and their families", to which end they would request technical advice from specialized agencies of the United Nations.

8. In reply to the request made by the Ministers for Foreign Affairs in their note of 8 February, as confirmed in the Joint Declaration of their Presidents, I immediately proceeded to establish a Secretariat technical group, which prepared a working paper on a possible international mechanism to verify security commitments. This paper was considered and discussed at a technical meeting held on 14 and 15 March in New York with representatives of the Central American Governments. The paper prepared at that meeting provided for the creation of a United Nations Observer Group in Central America (ONUCA), which would operate on the basis of mobile units deployed in the territories of the five Central American countries, carry out its assignment by means of regular patrols, and unannounced visits and inspections in the event of reports of violations, and be equipped with land, air and sea transport. Although the definitive composition of ONUCA and its operational procedures would depend on the agreement of the Security Council, the paper recorded the wish of the five Central American Governments that the Group should consist of personnel from Canada, the Federal Republic of Germany and Spain, with Latin American participation.

9. The paper was submitted to the Governments of the five Central American States and, after some revisions, served as a basis for the letter dated 31 March 1989 addressed to me by the Executive Commission following its eighth meeting, held at San José (A/44/287-S/20642). The letter requested me to take the necessary steps to establish the Observer Group. That request would, in principle, have permitted me to dispatch a reconnaissance mission to the region, on the basis of whose report I would have submitted a formal proposal to the Security Council. Nevertheless, as I indicated in my letter of 14 April 1989 to the five Ministers for Foreign Affairs (A/44/288-S/20643, annex), I did not believe that I was in a position to take those steps in view of the reservation formulated by one of the signatories. Since that date, numerous but fruitless efforts have been made to overcome this obstacle. The verification of compliance with the security commitments entered into by the Presidents under Esquipulas II remains, therefore, in suspense.

10. With respect to the electoral process in Nicaragua, I received a formal request from the Government of Nicaragua to proceed, in accordance with the Joint Declaration of Costa del Sol and within the framework of the Esquipulas II Agreements, to set up a group of observers to verify implementation of the measures which had been announced, as well as the genuineness of the electoral process during every stage. I am in contact with the

Government of Nicaragua concerning the performance of this task, which, as I have mentioned on various occasions, belongs in the context of the Central American peace plan. I have twice reported to the President of the General Assembly on this subject (A/44/210 and A/44/304). Meanwhile, I have sent several missions to Nicaragua to observe the debate in the National Assembly on the reforms, which were in due course promulgated, of the electoral laws and the laws regulating the mass media, as well as to carry out a study of the new legislation. I have also been in contact with the Secretary-General of the Organization of American States with a view to performing the observation in Nicaragua jointly.

11. The joint plan for the voluntary demobilization, repatriation or relocation of members of the Nicaraguan resistance and their families, for the adoption of which the Presidents had set a deadline of 90 days from 14 February 1989, has not been approved by the Central American Presidents or by the Executive Commission.

* * *

12. In the course of my contacts with authorities and representatives of the many Member States of this Organization, I have noted the international community's serious concern regarding the continuing picture of conflict which characterizes the situation in Central America. The agreements reached in El Salvador in February 1989 raised legitimate hopes to the extent that, building on the foundations laid in Esquipulas II, they envisaged practical means of circumventing some of the principal obstacles to implementation of the agreements as planned. I have felt encouraged, particularly in the course of recent months, to redouble my efforts to help the countries of the region attain their chosen goals. Without prejudice to the need to identify fundamentally regional solutions for the crisis facing the Central American countries, and for the purpose of con-

tributing to such solutions, my colleagues and I have established contact with Governments outside the region, as well as with other forces or de facto entities operating there. These contacts are particularly important in the context of the possibility of creating the verification machinery mentioned earlier.

13. At the time of writing this report, it is my understanding that agreement has not yet been reached on the dates for the next summit meeting of the Central American Presidents. I am bound to express my concern over the difficulties that this delay entails, of itself, for the synchronized implementation of the indivisible whole which, in accordance with the Guatemala Procedure, is constituted by the measures agreed upon therein. I am, of course, aware that this is not simply due to a scheduling problem. Obviously, since the last summit, the political climate has deteriorated and, in some cases, there has been a resurgence of violence. I do not intend in this report to describe in detail the various factors which have given rise to this situation; I have referred to them on various occasions in the past, particularly in my address to the inaugural session of the International Conference on Central American Refugees on 29 May 1989 at Guatemala City (A/44/311, annex). I do consider it my duty to emphasize my view, which I believe is widely shared in the international community, that the means to address the problems affecting the Central American countries and their peoples exist in the instruments which have been signed by their leaders. More precisely, I should like to express my conviction that it is essential, if the peace process is to be set on the right track once again, to put into practice without delay the specific decisions referred to in paragraph 7 of this report, all of which envisage a role for the United Nations. For my part, I remain willing to do all in my power to ensure that the Organization may be of assistance to that end.

Document 2

Security Council resolution concerning the situation in Central America and the Esquipulas II Agreement

S/RES/637, 27 July 1989

The Security Council,

Recalling its resolutions 530 (1983) of 19 May 1983 and 562 (1985) of 10 May 1985 and General Assembly resolutions 38/10 of 11 November 1983, 39/4 of 26 October 1984, 41/37 of 18 November 1986, 42/1 of 7 October 1987 and 43/24 of 15 November 1988, as well as the initiative that the Secretary-General of the United Nations under-

took on 18 November 1986 together with the Secretary-General of the Organization of American States,

Convinced that the peoples of Central America wish to achieve a peaceful settlement of their conflicts without outside interference, including support for irregular forces, with respect for the principles of self-determination and non-intervention while ensuring full respect for human rights,

Taking note of the report of the Secretary-General of 26 June 1989 submitted in pursuance of Security Council resolutions 530 (1983) and 562 (1985) 1/,

Recognizing the important contribution of the Contadora Group and its Support Group in favour of peace in Central America,

Welcoming the agreement on "Procedures for the establishment of a firm and lasting peace in Central America" signed at Guatemala City on 7 August 1987 by the Presidents of the Republics of Costa Rica, El Salvador, Guatemala, Honduras and Nicaragua 2/ as the manifestation of the will of the peoples of Central America to achieve peace, democratization, reconciliation, development and justice, in accordance with their decision to meet the historical challenge of forging a peaceful destiny for the region,

Welcoming also the subsequent Joint Declarations issued by the Central American Presidents on 16 January 1988 at Alajuela, Costa Rica 3/ and on 14 February 1989 at Costa del Sol, El Salvador, 4/

Aware of the importance which the Central American Presidents attach to the role of international verification as an essential component for the implementation of the above-mentioned instruments, including, in particular, their commitments relating to regional security, especially non-use of territory to support destabilization of neighbouring countries and democratization, especially free and fair elections, as well as to the voluntary demobilization, repatriation or relocation of irregular forces, as agreed in the Costa del Sol accord of 14 February 1989,

Aware also that the commitments enshrined in the Guatemala agreement 2/ form a harmonious and indivisible whole,

Noting with appreciation the efforts undertaken to date by the Secretary-General in support of the Central American peace process, including his assistance in the establishment of appropriate mechanisms to verify compliance with the provisions of the Guatemala Agreement and of the Joint Declaration adopted by the Central American Presidents at their meeting held in El Salvador on 14 February 1989, 4/ and particularly the Secretary-General's agreement with Nicaragua to deploy a United Nations elections observer mission to verify the electoral process,

1. *Commends* the desire for peace expressed by the Central American Presidents in signing on 7 August 1987 at Guatemala City the agreement on "Procedures for the establishment of a firm and lasting peace in Central America" 2/ and in the Joint Declarations subsequently signed in pursuance of it;

2. *Expresses its firmest support* for the Guatemala agreement and the Joint Declarations;

3. *Calls upon* the Presidents to continue their efforts to achieve a firm and lasting peace in Central America through the faithful implementation of the commitments entered into in the Guatemala agreement and in the expressions of good will contained in the Joint Declaration of 14 February 1989;

4. *Appeals* to all States, in particular to those which have links with the region and interests in it, to back the political will of the Central American countries to comply with the provisions of the Guatemala agreement and of the Joint Declaration, particularly that regional and extra-regional Governments which either openly or covertly supply aid to irregular forces or insurrectional movements in the area immediately halt such aid, with the exception of the humanitarian aid that contributes to the goals of the Costa del Sol accord;

5. *Lends* its full support to the Secretary-General to continue his mission of good offices in consultation with the Security Council, in support of the Central American Governments in their effort to achieve the goals set forth in the Guatemala agreement;

6. *Requests* the Secretary-General to report to the Security Council regularly on the implementation of the present resolution.

1/ S/20699.
2/ S/19085.
3/ S/19447
4/ S/20491.

Document 3

Letter dated 9 August 1989 from Costa Rica, El Salvador, Guatemala, Honduras and Nicaragua transmitting the text of the Tela Declaration signed by the five Central American Presidents

A/44/451-S/20778, 9 August 1989

We have the honour to transmit to you herewith the documents adopted at the meeting of the Presidents of Costa Rica, El Salvador, Guatemala, Honduras and Nicaragua held at Tela, Honduras, on 5, 6 and 7 August 1989.

These documents are:

(a) The Tela Declaration;

(b) The Joint Plan for the voluntary demobilization, repatriation or relocation in Nicaragua or third countries of the members of the Nicaraguan resistance and their families, as well as assistance for the demobilization of all those involved in armed actions in the countries of the region when such persons voluntarily request it (annex I); and

(c) The Agreement between Honduras and Nicaragua (annex II).

We should be grateful if you would have this note and its annexes circulated as an official document of the General Assembly, under item 34 of the provisional agenda, and of the Security Council.

(*Signed*) Carlos José GUTIÉRREZ
Ambassador, Permanent Representative of Costa Rica
to the United Nations

(*Signed*) Roberto MEZA
Ambassador, Permanent Representative of El Salvador
to the United Nations

(*Signed*) Francisco VILLAGRÁN DE LEÓN
Ambassador, Permanent Representative of Guatemala
to the United Nations

(*Signed*) Roberto MARTÍNEZ ORDÓÑEZ
Ambassador, Permanent Representative of Honduras
to the United Nations

(*Signed*) Alejandro SERRANO CALDERA
Ambassador, Permanent Representative of Nicaragua
to the United Nations

Tela Declaration

The Central American Presidents, meeting at the port city of Tela, Honduras, on 5, 6 and 7 August 1989, bearing in mind and recognizing the important work done by the Executive Commission at its ninth meeting and by the Technical Working Group, whose efforts have made this meeting possible,

Considering:

That the measures agreed in the Esquipulas II agreement for the establishment of a firm and lasting peace must be implemented and the commitments made subsequently by the Presidents in their declarations and agreements at Alajuela and Costa del Sol fulfilled,

Agree:

1. To confirm their determination to promote all efforts aimed at implementing points 5 and 6 of the Esquipulas agreement in order to prevent the use of their own territory to destabilize the Governments of Central American countries. Accordingly, they have endorsed the Joint Plan for the voluntary demobilization, repatriation or relocation in Nicaragua or third countries of the Nicaraguan resistance and their families and for assistance in the demobilization of all those involved in armed actions in the countries of the region when such persons voluntarily request it.

2. To promote, by direct means, concerted solutions to any disputes that may arise directly between the various countries of Central America. Accordingly, they have endorsed the agreement between Honduras and Nicaragua regarding the application filed with the International Court of Justice, which enjoys the moral support of the Presidents of Guatemala, El Salvador and Costa Rica.

3. To endorse the appeal to armed groups in the region, particularly to FMLN, that still persist in its use of force, to halt such activities. Accordingly, they have endorsed chapter III on assistance in the voluntary demobilization of FMLN, whereby FMLN is strongly urged to put an immediate and effective end to hostilities so that a dialogue may be carried out that will lead to a rejection of armed struggle and the integration of FMLN members into institutional and democratic life.

4. The Presidents acknowledge the efforts made by the Government of Guatemala to strengthen its process of national reconciliation through a wide-ranging, ongoing dialogue in which the National Reconciliation Commission is a leading participant. They also express their hope that this dialogue will be used to strengthen the democratic, pluralistic and participatory process, in keeping with point 1 of the Esquipulas Procedure and internal legislation. They reiterate the appeal to armed groups to abandon their activities, which violate the spirit of this agreement, and to enter political life through the national reconciliation process.

5. To request the United Nations to take the necessary steps for the establishment of the security machinery by virtue of which Honduras and Nicaragua have reached an agreement in which, *inter alia*, Honduras agrees to withdraw its reservation to implementation of the Plan. They also reiterate the request by Honduras concerning the dispatch of an international peace-keeping force to Honduran territory.

6. To confirm the decision taken by the Executive Commission at its ninth meeting to convene the Central American Commission on Environment and Development for the first time at Guatemala City on 30 and 31 August 1989, so that it can begin work on the draft convention setting out its nature and functions.

7. To reiterate the importance of the Central American Parliament as a forum in which the peoples of the region can discuss and make recommendations on political, economic, social and cultural problems in Central America. Accordingly, it is imperative that the treaty establishing the

Parliament enter into force as soon as possible.

8. To condemn vigorously drug trafficking and use. The Central American Presidents agree to promulgate laws and take drastic measures to prevent the countries of Central America from becoming bases for drug trafficking. To this end, regional and international cooperation shall be sought and agreements concluded with nations affected by such illegal traffic, and activities for the effective control of drug trafficking shall be carried out.

9. The Central American Presidents agree to entrust the Executive Commission with the task of considering and adopting the document on political monitoring, which shall be ratified by the Presidents no later than at their next meeting.

As two years have passed since the signing of the Esquipulas II peace plan, the Presidents of Costa Rica, El Salvador, Guatemala, Honduras and Nicaragua reiterate their firm commitment to implement fully all commitments and agreements set out in the Guatemala Procedure and the Alajuela and Costa del Sol Declarations, particularly those which refer to the strengthening of democratic processes. Accordingly, strict compliance with these agreements is of fundamental importance.

The Central American Presidents agree to meet before the end of the year in Nicaragua.

The Central American Presidents express their gratitude to the people and Government of Honduras, and especially to its President, Mr. José Azcona Hoyo, for their hospitality.

Tela, Honduras, 7 August 1989

(*Signed*) Oscar ARIAS SÁNCHEZ
President of the Republic of Costa Rica

(*Signed*) Alfredo CRISTIANI BURKARD
President of the Republic of El Salvador

(*Signed*) Vinicio CEREZO ARÉVALO
President of the Republic of Guatemala

(*Signed*) José AZCONA HOYO
President of the Republic of Honduras

(*Signed*) Daniel ORTEGA SAAVEDRA
President of the Republic of Nicaragua

Annex I

Joint Plan for the voluntary demobilization, repatriation or relocation of the members of the Nicaraguan resistance and their families, as well as assistance in the demobilization of all those involved in armed actions in the countries of the region when they voluntarily seek it

The Presidents of Costa Rica, El Salvador, Guatemala, Honduras and Nicaragua,

Honouring their historic commitment to achieve a firm and lasting peace in Central America,

Remembering the Guatemala Procedure, adopted on 7 August 1987, and the Alajuela and Costa del Sol Declarations,

In accordance with resolution 637 (1989) adopted unanimously by the United Nations Security Council on 27 June 1989,

With the purpose of advancing toward achievement of the objectives of the Central American peace process and as a firm example of their decisive commitment to the full strength of the principles of international law, have agreed to this Joint Plan for the voluntary demobilization, repatriation or relocation of the members of the Nicaraguan resistance and their families, as well as assistance in the demobilization of all those involved in armed actions in the countries of the region when such persons voluntarily request it,

Chapter I

Voluntary demobilization, repatriation or relocation in Nicaragua or third countries of the members of the Nicaraguan resistance and their families.

Introduction

The purpose of this chapter is to develop what was agreed on by the Presidents in this matter, taking into consideration also:

(1) The report of the Secretary-General of the Organization of American States;

(2) The national Political Agreement between the Government of Nicaragua and the 21 political parties existing in the country, in which, after arrival at important political agreements on the democratic process, an appeal is made to the Central American Presidents for approval of the Plan for voluntary demobilization, relocation or repatriation.

This chapter defines the machinery and methodology for the voluntary demobilization, repatriation or relocation of the members of the Nicaraguan resistance, as well as the material and security conditions to be encountered by the persons covered by this Plan, which will be implemented with the cooperation of international organizations. This Plan will also apply to the voluntary repatriation or relocation of the families of the members of the Nicaraguan resistance and of Nicaraguan refugees, without prejudice to the agreements signed on this subject.

The Government of Nicaragua has made clear, in conformity with the Esquipulas Procedure and the Costa del Sol Declaration, its disposition to strengthen its process of national reconciliation and democratization, in order to encourage the voluntary repatriation of the

Nicaraguan resistance and has accordingly determined to sign this Plan, which will try to achieve the repatriation of the majority, relocation in third countries being the exception.

The five Central American Governments reaffirm their commitment to halt the use of their own territory by persons, organizations or groups to destabilize other States and to cease all types of aid to armed groups, with the exception of humanitarian aid that serves the purposes that the Presidents have defined for this Plan.

Machinery

1. For the purposes of the execution and implementation of this Plan, an International Support and Verification Commission will be created, hereinafter called "CIAV", which the Secretary-General of the United Nations and the Secretary-General of the Organization of American States, who may act through their representatives, will be asked to form.

2. The International Support and Verification Commission (CIAV) should be established within 30 days of the signing of this agreement. The five Central American Presidents urge the Nicaraguan resistance to accept the execution of this Plan within 90 days of the date of the Constitution of CIAV. During these 90 days, the Nicaraguan Government and CIAV will maintain direct contacts with the Nicaraguan resistance in order to promote its return to the nation and its integration in the political process. At the end of this period, CIAV will submit a report on the implementation of this Plan, which will be submitted to the Central American Presidents.

3. CIAV will be responsible for all activities that make possible the voluntary demobilization, repatriation or relocation, including the reception and installation of repatriated persons at their destinations. In addition, it will ensure that necessary conditions exist or are maintained to permit the full incorporation of repatriated persons into civilian life and will carry out the follow-up and control that those processes require.

4. CIAV will carry out its activities with the collaboration of the Central American Governments and will seek the support of specialized organs or organizations with experience in the region and others that may be considered necessary and are officially invited by the Governments.

One of the objectives of that support will be to facilitate the execution of the Plan, and to that end it will collaborate in monitoring the full exercise of the fundamental rights and freedoms of those repatriated, as well as in efforts to ensure economic security.

5. Once established, CIAV will immediately proceed to

(a) Carry out necessary consultations with the authorities of the Government of Nicaragua, the other Central American Governments and the Nicaraguan resistance and officials of humanitarian organizations, as required for the purpose of expediting the execution of this Plan;

(b) Visit the camps of the Nicaraguan resistance and the refugees for the purpose of:

(i) Making known the achievements and benefits of this Plan;

(ii) Ascertaining existing human and material resources;

(iii) Organizing the distribution of humanitarian aid;

(c) Taking responsibility, as much as possible, for the distribution of food, medical attention, clothing and other basic necessities in the resistance camps through the support organs and organizations;

(d) Carry out negotiations for the reception by third countries of those who do not desire to be repatriated and give them the necessary assistance.

6. CIAV will issue a certificate to each Nicaraguan who takes advantage of this Plan and will put into effect a voluntary repatriation programme for those who desire to return to Nicaragua.

Exit and entry routes will be through the frontier posts set up by the Governments by mutual agreement. At these posts, the Government of Nicaragua, in the presence of representatives of CIAV will issue the necessary documentation to guarantee the full exercise of civil rights.

At the same time, the relocation in third countries of those who do not choose repatriation during the period of the execution of this Plan will be initiated. For that purpose, the Government of Nicaragua, with the cooperation of CIAV, will facilitate the issue of passports to those who apply for them.

The five Presidents exhort the international community to offer financial support to the present demobilization Plan.

Procedures

7. Upon its establishment, CIAV will determine the procedures by which it will, in compliance with the Plan for voluntary demobilization, repatriation or relocation in Nicaragua or third countries proceed to receive arms equipment and military supplies from the members of the Nicaraguan resistance, which will remain in its custody until the five Presidents decide their destination.

8. CIAV will verify the dismantling of the camps left behind by the resistance and Nicaraguan refugees.

9. Those repatriated will, if circumstances permit, be taken directly by CIAV to their places of final settlement, which will be chosen by mutual agreement between

the Government of Nicaragua and CIAV. To that end, temporary residence areas may be established in Nicaragua, under the control and supervision of CIAV, while the final location is being determined.

Land, economic assistance and technical assistance will be provided to repatriated persons who wish to devote themselves to agricultural production, in accordance with the possibilities of the Nicaraguan Government, according to the experience of specialized international organizations and in accordance with the amount of funds obtained for such purposes.

10. In collaboration with the Government of Nicaragua, CIAV will establish reception centres capable of providing basic services, first aid, family counselling, economic assistance, transport to settlement areas and other social services.

11. In order to guarantee the necessary security for repatriated persons, CIAV will establish, from the beginning of the programme, follow-up offices so that people can, where necessary, expose any non-compliance with the guarantees originally offered for their repatriation. These offices will function as long as CIAV, in consultation with the Central American Governments deems them necessary.

Personnel from these offices will periodically visit the repatriates to verify compliance with this Plan and report thereon. The report shall be sent by CIAV to the five Central American Presidents.

12. Situations not envisaged in this chapter will be resolved by CIAV, in consultation with the Central American Governments and the institutions or persons involved.

Chapter II

Assistance in the demobilization of all persons involved in armed actions in the countries of the region when they voluntarily request it.

The objective of this chapter is assistance in the demobilization of all persons involved in armed actions in the countries of the region when they voluntarily request it. The demobilization of these persons should be carried out in conformity with the procedures of Esquipulas II and the laws and internal procedures of the country concerned.

CIAV may be officially invited by the Central American Governments to guarantee this assistance.

Chapter III

Assistance in the voluntary demobilization of the members of FMLN.

In conformity with what was established in the Guatemala Procedure and the Alajuela and Costa del Sol Declarations and with the purpose of assisting in the cessation of the armed actions now being suffered by the Republic of El Salvador, the Governments of Costa Rica, Guatemala, Honduras and Nicaragua reiterate their firm belief in the necessity of an immediate and effective end to hostilities in this fraternal country. They therefore strongly urge the Frente Farabundo Martí para la Liberación Nacional (FMLN) to carry out a constructive dialogue for the purpose of achieving a just and lasting peace. Similarly, the aforementioned Governments urge the Government of El Salvador to arrange, with full guarantees and in the spirit of point II of the Guatemala Procedure, the integration of the members of FMLN into peaceful life.

The Government of El Salvador expresses its unequivocal respect for its commitments to national reconciliation and to continuing strengthening the existing process of pluralistic, participatory and representative democratization by means of which social justice and full respect for all human rights and fundamental freedoms of Salvadorians is promoted.

Once FMLN agrees to abandon the struggle and to incorporate itself into the democratic and institutional life by means of dialogue, the mobilization of the members of FMLN will proceed with the use of the procedure laid down in chapter I of this Plan, where applicable, with the modifications required by the situation and for the purpose of facilitating their demobilization.

The above notwithstanding, members of FMLN who at any moment voluntarily decide to abandon their arms in order to incorporate themselves into the civilian political life in El Salvador will also enjoy the benefits of this Plan. To that end, the Government of El Salvador, by means of CIAV and adequate national and international procedures, exhorts such persons to accept and receive the benefits established here, using all the appropriate available means.

Agreed and signed in the city of Puerta de Tela, Honduras, on 7 August 1989.

(*Signed*) Oscar ARIAS SÁNCHEZ
President of the Republic of Costa Rica

(*Signed*) Alfredo CRISTIANI
President of the Republic of El Salvador

(*Signed*) Vinicio CEREZO ARÉVALO
President of the Republic of Guatemala

(*Signed*) José AZCONA HOYO
President of the Republic of Honduras

(*Signed*) Daniel ORTEGA SAAVEDRA
President of the Republic of Nicaragua

Annex II

Agreement

The President of the Republic of Honduras, José Azcona Hoyo, and the President of the Republic of Nicaragua, Daniel Ortega Saavedra,

Acting in their capacity as the Executive Heads of their respective States and enjoying the moral and political support of President Marco Vinicio Cerezo Arévalo of Guatemala, Alfredo Cristiani of El Salvador and Oscar Arias Sánchez of Costa Rica,

Motivated by the noble task of maintaining peace, cordiality and cooperation among the Republics of Nicaragua and Honduras, countries united by close historical ties of friendship and brotherhood,

Recalling the commitment undertaken in the Esquipulas agreements of 7 August 1987 not to allow their territory to be used for the purpose of attacking other States,

Bearing in mind also the Costa del Sol Declaration of 14 February 1989, in which the Central American Presidents undertook "to draw up, within a period not exceeding 90 days, a joint plan for the voluntary demobilization, repatriation or relocation in Nicaragua or third countries of members of the Nicaraguan resistance and their families", and

Motivated by the desire always to be able to avail themselves of peaceful means for the settlement of disputes, including recourse to the International Court of Justice, in resolving any situations or disputes that may threaten peace and security between the two States,

Have agreed

To reach an extrajudicial agreement regarding the legal action instituted by Nicaragua against Honduras before the International Court of Justice on 28 July 1986. This agreement is based on the following:

(a) As an agreement was reached on 7 August 1989 on the Joint Plan for the voluntary demobilization, repatriation or relocation of the Nicaraguan resistance and their families, implementation of the Plan should commence as soon as the International Support and Verification Commission (CIAV) is established, no later than 6 September 1989, and should be completed 90 days after the commencement, with the Secretary-General of the United Nations and the Secretary-General of the Organization of American States certifying that the Plan has been fully implemented.

(b) Bearing in mind that the presence of the *contras* and their camps does not contribute to the development of the democratic process already under way in Nicaragua, the President of Honduras undertakes to make official, in the appropriate manner, his Government's request to the United Nations Security Council for the establishment and dispatch to Honduran territory of an international peace-keeping force to prevent the use of that territory by irregular forces.

(c) When all of the above has been completed and the corresponding report on the implementation of the Plan has been issued by CIAV, in accordance with the Joint Plan for demobilization, Nicaragua shall withdraw the application it has filed against Honduras with the International Court of Justice.

The President of Nicaragua, confident that the Government of Honduras will cooperate fully to ensure that the Joint Plan for demobilization is implemented in good faith within the period of time specified in the Plan, agrees that the Government of Nicaragua shall request the International Court of Justice to extend the deadline set for the submission of the memorandum on the merits of the application until the date on which, according to the Joint Plan, the official report on the implementation of the Plan is to be submitted.

When Nicaragua receives the official report from CIAV on the implementation of the Joint Plan under the agreed terms, Nicaragua shall withdraw the application filed against Honduras with the International Court of Justice.

Done at Tela, Republic of Honduras, on 7 August 1989.

(*Signed*) Daniel ORTEGA SAAVEDRA
President of the Republic of Nicaragua

(*Signed*) José AZCONA HOYO
President of the Republic of Honduras

Document 4

Report of the Secretary-General concerning the situation in Central America

A/44/344/Add.1-S/20699/Add.1, 9 October 1989

Addendum

1. The events that have taken place in Central America during the past three months, particularly following the summit meeting of the five Central American Presidents held at Tela, Honduras, from 5 to 7 August 1989 (see A/44/451-S/20778), have prompted me to submit another report, in addition to the one I submitted to the General Assembly and the Security Council over three months ago, on 26 June 1989 (A/44/344-S/20699).

2. One month prior to the Tela meeting, and in response to the invitation addressed to me on 3 March 1989 by the Minister for Foreign Affairs of Nicaragua, I informed

the Government of Nicaragua that I was prepared to establish a United Nations Observer Mission for the Verification of the Electoral Process in Nicaragua (ONUVEN). The Mission's first report is being issued separately.

3. On 27 July 1989, the Security Council adopted resolution 637 (1989), its first since the start of the Central American peace process. In it the Security Council *inter alia* took note of the importance which the Central American Presidents attach to the role of international verification as an essential component of the peace plan, including, in particular, their commitments relating to regional security, especially non-use of territory to support destabilization of neighbouring countries and democratization, especially free and fair elections, as well as to the voluntary demobilization, repatriation or relocation of irregular forces, and of the efforts undertaken to date by the Secretary-General in support of the peace process, including his assistance in the establishment of appropriate mechanisms to verify compliance with the provisions of the Guatemala Agreement and of the Joint Declaration adopted by the Central American Presidents at their meeting at Costa del Sol, El Salvador, on 14 February 1989, and particularly the Secretary-General's agreement with Nicaragua to deploy a United Nations elections observer mission in that country.

4. The Council also commended the desire for peace expressed by the Central American Presidents in the Guatemala Agreement and the subsequent Joint Declarations and expressed its firmest support for them. It called upon the Presidents to continue their efforts to achieve a firm and lasting peace in Central America through the faithful implementation of the commitments entered into in the Guatemala Agreement and in the expressions of good will contained in the Joint Declaration of Costa del Sol. It appealed to all States, in particular to those with links to and interests in the region, to back the political will of the Central American countries to comply with the provisions of the Guatemala Agreement and of the Joint Declaration, and particularly to regional and extra-regional Governments which either openly or covertly supply aid to irregular forces or insurrectional movements in the area, to halt such aid immediately, with the exception of the humanitarian aid that contributes to the goals of the Tesoro Beach Agreement. I was given its full support to continue my mission of good offices in consultation with the Security Council, in support of the Central American Governments in their efforts to achieve the goals set forth in the Guatemala Agreement.

5. At the summit meeting held at Tela, Honduras, the Central American Presidents signed a number of documents (A/44/451-S/20778) which, in my view, were an important step forward in the process of pacification

in the region because they provided for the immediate implementation of the decisions adopted, in principle, at the Presidents' previous meeting at Costa del Sol, El Salvador, in February. With respect specifically to the United Nations, the Presidents adopted a Joint Plan for the voluntary demobilization, repatriation or relocation in Nicaragua or third countries of the members of the Nicaraguan resistance and their families, as well as assistance in the demobilization of all those involved in armed actions in the countries of the region when they voluntarily seek it (*ibid.*, annex I), and invited the Secretary-General of the Organization of American States and me to establish the International Support and Verification Commission (CIAV) for the execution and implementation of that Plan.

6. The Presidents also requested that the United Nations should take the necessary steps for the establishment of the United Nations Observer Group in Central America (ONUCA), as the security verification machinery, by virtue of the Agreement between the Presidents of Honduras and Nicaragua regarding the action instituted by Nicaragua against Honduras before the International Court of Justice on 28 July 1986 (*ibid.*, annex II). This Agreement includes the withdrawal by Honduras of the reservation it had made in the letter which the Executive Commission sent me on 31 March 1989 (A/44/287-S/20642). As I had pointed out in my previous report, that reservation had prevented me from adopting the measures necessary to put the machinery in question into operation. The withdrawal of the reservation by the Government of Honduras was subsequently confirmed by the Minister for Foreign Affairs of Honduras in a letter which he addressed to me on 10 August 1989 (A/44/459-S/20786).

7. In response to this request I sent a reconnaissance mission to the region with the aim of drawing up a definitive plan on the basis of the working document prepared in March by a technical group of the Secretariat with the participation of the representatives of the Central American Governments. As a result, I was able to submit a formal proposal to the Security Council. The mission, headed by Brigadier Péricles Ferreira Gomes, Head of the United Nations Angola Verification Mission (UNAVEM), carried out a reconnaissance of the five countries of the region from 3 to 23 September 1989. Taking into account its recommendations, I am submitting a report to the Security Council so that it may be able to reply effectively to the request made by the five Central American Governments.

8. As regards the request, reiterated by the representatives of the five Central American countries in a letter dated 14 August 1989 (A/44/464-S/20791), to set up the International Support and Verification Mission

(CIAV), which would begin operations within 30 days of the signature of the Joint Plan agreed to in Tela, the Secretary-General of the Organization of American States and I agreed on 25 August 1989 to establish it with effect from 6 September 1989. On that same date we informed the five Presidents and their respective Foreign Ministers of our decision and conveyed to them certain comments and specific data regarding the execution of the Joint Plan, its timetable and the conditions necessary for its smooth operation. Subsequently, the Secretary-General of the Organization of American States and I agreed on the terms of reference necessary to carry out the tasks entrusted to CIAV.

9. These tasks are extensive, complex and delicate. They include such complex matters as good offices, disarmament and the custody of weapons, and operations of a humanitarian nature and assistance for development. At the same time the time-limits established in the Joint Plan are extremely short. In any case, I am fully prepared, for my part, to tackle these tasks in the best possible way and with the greatest possible speed, aware of the confidence which the Central American Presidents have placed in the United Nations. I have informed the Security Council of the steps we have taken and in particular I have expressed my opinion that the collection of weapons and other military equipment and their custody require the establishment of a military body. The Security Council has informed me of its approval of the steps taken and has welcomed with satisfaction my intention to adopt in due course the measures necessary to establish such a military unit. On the other hand, I have requested the cooperation of the United Nations High Commissioner for Refugees (UNHCR) for the activities of CIAV related to the voluntary repatriation or, as the case may be, the voluntary relocation of the members of the Nicaraguan resistance and their families and activities for the follow-up and protection of the returnees. Similarly, the special plan of cooperation for Central America, approved by the General Assembly in resolution 42/204, dated 11 December 1987, provides a basis on which CIAV may provide assistance for carrying out economic and social development projects in the areas settled by the returnees.

10. Since the establishment of CIAV, in the exercise of the responsibilities conferred upon us by the Tela Agreement, we have held frequent consultations with the governmental authorities of Nicaragua and Honduras and the other Central American Governments and also with the United States and with representatives of the Nicaraguan resistance. These contacts, established so far in New York, Washington, Managua and Tegucigalpa, and also in the camps of the Nicaraguan resistance, are designed to establish the bases for the execution of the Joint Plan with the consent of the persons concerned. I

am convinced that with patience and tenacity and with the good faith, cooperation and flexibility of all the interested parties, CIAV will be able to carry out its task.

11. The new climate of *détente* created in Central America since the Tela meeting has been strengthened by the agreement reached on 15 September in Mexico City between the Government of El Salvador and the Frente Farabundo Martí para la Liberación Nacional (FMLN) and designed to initiate a dialogue aimed at ending the armed conflict in El Salvador by political means. In view of the invitation extended by both parties to the United Nations to participate as observers in the next meeting to be held in San José, Costa Rica, on 16 and 17 October 1989, and in pursuance of the request by the Security Council in resolution 637 (1989) that I should continue my good offices, I have decided to accept the invitation. The meeting will be attended by Mr. Alvaro de Soto, Assistant Secretary-General, whom I appointed my personal representative for the peace process in Central America on 1 September 1989.

12. Three and a half months have passed since I submitted my last report. In this short space of time the situation in Central America has considerably improved to the point where we may envisage political solutions to the main conflicts in the region on the basis of the peace plan embodied in the Esquipulas II agreements. The electoral process in Nicaragua and the execution of the Joint Plan for the voluntary demobilization, repatriation or relocation of the members of the Nicaraguan resistance and their families provide us with an opportunity to achieve the national reconciliation provided for in Esquipulas II on the basis of democratization and a cease-fire in the country. If, as I hope, the Security Council soon establishes the United Nations Observer Group in Central America (ONUCA), we shall finally be able to verify impartially the fulfilment of the obligations undertaken in Esquipulas II on the cessation of aid to the irregular forces and the insurrectional movements and the non-use of the territory to attack other States. The establishment of ONUCA similarly constitutes a means of creating confidence in the region and should help to promote an environment more favourable to dialogue, particularly that which has been initiated between the Government of El Salvador and FMLN. To this may be added the appreciable reduction of foreign intervention in the region. In this context Security Council resolution 637 (1989) represents highly important political support for the peace process in the region. For my part, I hope that my good offices mission, with the support of the Security Council, may help to establish a just and lasting peace in Central America. To this end, I warmly welcome the support I have received from all my interlocutors both within and outside the region.

Document 5

Statement by the President of the Security Council expressing concern over the situation in Central America

S/21011, 8 December 1989

The members of the Security Council, after hearing statements by the representatives of El Salvador and Nicaragua at the 2896th meeting of the Security Council, on 30 November 1989, express their grave concern over the present situation in Central America, in particular over the numerous acts of violence resulting in loss of lives and sufferings of the civilian population.

The members of the Council reiterate their firm support for the Esquipulas process of peaceful settlement in Central America and appeal to all States to contribute to the urgent implementation of the agreements reached by the five Central American Presidents. In this regard the members of the Council welcome the announcement by the five Central American Presidents to meet on 10 and 11 December at San José, Costa Rica, in order to discuss within the framework of the Esquipulas peace process, solutions to the problems confronting them.

The members of the Council consider that it is primarily the responsibility of the five Central American Presidents to find solutions to the regional problems, in accordance with the Esquipulas Agreements. Therefore, they reiterate their appeal to all States, including those with links to the region and interests in it, to refrain from all actions that could impede the achievement of a real and lasting settlement in Central America through negotiations.

The members of the Security Council urge all parties concerned to cooperate in the search for peace and a political solution.

They also express their firm support for the efforts being made by the Secretary-General of the United Nations and the Secretary-General of the Organization of American States in the peace process. In particular, they reiterate their full support for the Secretary-General of the United Nations in the exercise of the missions entrusted to him by the General Assembly and the Security Council, as well as for the early deployment of the United Nations Observer Group in Central America.

Document 6

Letter dated 12 December 1989 from El Salvador transmitting the Declaration of San Isidro de Coronado signed by the five Central American Presidents

A/44/872-S/21019, 12 December 1989

I have the honour to transmit to you herewith the Declaration of San Isidro de Coronado, signed today at San Isidro de Coronado, Costa Rica, by the five Central American Presidents (see annex).

I should be grateful if you would have this note and its annex circulated as an official document of the General Assembly, under agenda item 34, and of the Security Council.

(*Signed*) Ricardo CASTAÑEDA
Ambassador
Permanent Representative

Annex

Declaration of San Isidro de Coronado

The Presidents of Costa Rica, El Salvador, Guatemala, Honduras and Nicaragua, meeting at a special session at San Isidro de Coronado, Costa Rica, on 10, 11 and 12 December 1989, for the purpose of reviewing the delicate situation in Central America, which seriously affects the peace process, ratified the agreement contained in the preamble to the Procedure for the establishment of a firm and lasting peace in Central America (Esquipulas II), and particularly those points in which they agreed to take up fully the historic challenge of forging a peaceful destiny for Central America, to eliminate war and to make dialogue prevail over violence and reason over hatred. To this end, they have agreed as follows:

1. They reaffirm their most vigorous condemnation of the armed action and terrorism being waged by irregular forces in the region and reiterate their deep conviction that the people must be made to realize that they must reject the use of force and terror to achieve political ends and objectives.

2. The Presidents of Costa Rica, Guatemala, Honduras and Nicaragua expressed their determined support for the President of El Salvador, Mr. Alfredo Cristiani, and his Government, as a genuine demonstration of their unwavering policy of supporting Governments that have been established through democratic, pluralistic and participatory processes.

3. The Presidents of Guatemala, Honduras, Nicaragua and Costa Rica support the Government of El Salvador in its often-stated intent to find a solution to the conflict in El Salvador by peaceful and democratic means; to that end, they reiterated their vigorous appeal to FMLN immediately and effectively to cease hostilities in that fraternal country and to resume the dialogue that has been initiated. They also demand that FMLN publicly renounce any type of violent action that may directly or indirectly affect the civilian population. The five Presidents agreed to request respectfully the Secretary-General of the United Nations to do everything within his power to take the necessary steps to ensure the resumption of the dialogue between the Government of El Salvador and FMLN, thereby facilitating its successful continuation.

4. In accordance with the Alajuela, Costa del Sol and Tela declarations, the provisions of chapters I and III of the Joint Plan for demobilization constitute an integral and indivisible whole. Accordingly, they request the International Support and Verification Commission (CIAV) to proceed at once with the demobilization of the Frente Farabundo Martí para la Liberación Nacional, in keeping with the procedures set out in the aforementioned Plan.

5. The Presidents support the Nicaraguan Government of President Daniel Ortega in its wish to have the funds appropriated for the Nicaraguan resistance turned over to CIAV as of the signing of this agreement, with a view to implementing the voluntary demobilization, repatriation or relocation in Nicaragua or third countries of the members of the Nicaraguan resistance and their families.

The Presidents appeal to the Nicaraguan resistance to cease any action which may jeopardize the electoral process and the civilian population, so that that process may evolve in an atmosphere of normalcy, in accordance with the Esquipulas II Agreement.

6. Initiation of the demobilization of the Nicaraguan resistance and FMLN is a key factor in overcoming the crisis besetting the peace process; accordingly, the United Nations Observer Group in Central America (ONUCA) must step up its activities to prevent the supply of weapons to FMLN and the Nicaraguan resistance.

7. The Government of Nicaragua reiterates the offer it made to the Nicaraguan resistance in Washington, D.C., United States of America, to take the necessary steps to ensure that those members of the resistance who are repatriated before 5 February 1990 may register to vote in the general elections to be held on 25 February 1990.

The Government of Nicaragua shall proceed at once to make the necessary contacts with ONUCA and CIAV so that the demobilization of the Nicaraguan resistance forces in Honduras may begin as of the signing of this agreement, in accordance with the provisions of the Tela Agreement.

8. The Presidents reiterated the importance of international cooperation as a parallel and indispensable element in the political efforts to bring peace to the region, and urged the international community to increase its support. They expressed the commitment of the region to pursue joint efforts in this area, in the conviction that economic and social development is a constant in efforts to secure peace. They expressed their gratitude for the progress made in this connection under the Special Plan of Economic Cooperation for Central America, approved by the United Nations Development Programme (UNDP), and to the European Economic Community for its support in providing cooperation under the Luxembourg agreements.

9. The Central American Presidents, in accordance with the Esquipulas II Agreements, reaffirmed their commitment fully to respect human rights, including the civil, political, economic, social and cultural rights laid down in their respective Constitutions and in the international agreements they have signed and ratified.

10. The Presidents agreed to request the Secretary-General of the United Nations to make the necessary connections to involve States with interests in the region more directly in the peace effort, within the framework of the Esquipulas II Agreements and subsequent declarations. They also request that the mandate of the United Nations Observer Group in Central America (ONUCA) should be expanded to include verification of any cessation of hostilities and demobilization of irregular forces that may be agreed upon in the region.

11. In view of recent events, the Presidents confirmed that the complete deployment of the ONUCA machinery is of the utmost urgency for compliance with the commitments set forth in sections 5 and 6 of the Esquipulas II Agreements. By the same token, they also

decided to request that the Secretary-General of the United Nations should take appropriate action to expedite the work of ONUCA, and that ONUCA should keep the Central American Presidents informed of developments.

12. The Presidents of Guatemala, Honduras and Costa Rica, on the basis of their commitment to seek negotiated solutions as a means of overcoming the conflicts resulting from the Central American crisis, fraternally urge the Presidents of El Salvador and Nicaragua to put an end, through negotiation and dialogue, to the estrangement between their Governments, and to continue their diplomatic and consular relations.

13. In connection with the application entered before the International Court of Justice by the Government of Nicaragua against the Government of Honduras, entitled *Border and Transborder Armed Actions*, the Governments of those countries agree to set up a commission with bilateral representation to seek an out-of-court settlement to the dispute within six months of today's date. In order to facilitate the work of the commission, they also agree to instruct their respective agents in the case immediately to communicate this agreement, jointly or separately, to the Court (the agreement being recognized, upon presentation, as fully and immediately valid between the Litigants), and to request the Court to postpone until 11 June 1990 the setting of the deadline for submission of the Honduran counter-memorial.

They also agree, in case by the date indicated no out-of-court settlement has been reached, that the agents for either country should request the Court to allow the Government of Honduras a period of six months for the submission of the said counter-memorial.

The Central American Presidents thank the people and Government of Costa Rica for their hospitality, and all those, men and women, whose efforts have contributed to the outcome of this meeting. In the light of what has been agreed, and in the certainty that it will be carried out, they agree to meet during the first quarter of 1990 at the regular session scheduled to be held in the city of Managua, Nicaragua.

San Isidro de Coronado, 12 December 1989

(*Signed*) Oscar ARIAS SÁNCHEZ
President of the Republic of Costa Rica

(*Signed*) Alfredo CRISTIANI BURKARD
President of the Republic of El Salvador

(*Signed*) Vinicio CEREZO ARÉVALO
President of the Republic of Guatemala

(*Signed*) José AZCONA HOYO
President of the Republic of Honduras

(*Signed*) Daniel ORTEGA SAAVEDRA
President of the Republic of Nicaragua

Document 7

Report of the Secretary-General concerning the situation in Central America

A/44/886-S/21029, 21 December 1989

1. This report has been prepared pursuant to Security Council resolution 637 (1989) of 27 July 1989 and General Assembly resolution 44/10 of 24 October 1989.

2. In the preamble to resolution 44/10, the General Assembly, *inter alia*, took note with special satisfaction of the agreements reached by the Central American Presidents at Tela, Honduras, on 7 August 1989 (A/44/451-S/20778), comprising the Tela Declaration, the Joint Plan for the demobilization, repatriation or voluntary relocation in Nicaragua or third countries of the members of the Nicaraguan resistance and their families, as well as assistance for the demobilization of all those involved in armed actions in the countries of the region, when such persons voluntarily request it, and the agreement signed by Honduras and Nicaragua. It also took note of the

action taken by the Secretaries-General of the United Nations and the Organization of American States in support of the agreements of the Central American Presidents, in particular those relating to the establishment and functioning of the International Verification and Follow-Up Commission (CIAV) entrusted with the implementation of the Joint Plan, and recognized the importance of the action taken by me for the establishment of the United Nations Observer Group in Central America (ONUCA) in order to set in motion on-site verification machinery in fulfilment of the security commitments emanating from the Esquipulas II Agreements (A/42/521-S/91085, annex) and subsequent declarations. Lastly, it took note of the importance attached to the function of international verification of the electoral processes in the region and my positive response to the invitation from the Government of Nicaragua to establish, within the context of the Central American peace process, a group of observers to verify each and every stage of the electoral process in Nicaragua, and welcomed with interest the agreement signed on 15 September 1989 at Mexico City by the Government of El Salvador and the Frente Farabundo Martí para la Liberación Nacional (FMLN) to continue the process of dialogue in an effort to reach an understanding through political agreements that would put an end to the armed conflict by political means in the shortest possible time, as well as to encourage the democratization of the country and to reunify Salvadorian society, and my decision to accept the invitation extended by the parties for the United Nations to participate as a witness in the meeting held at San José from 16 to 18 October 1989.

3. In the operative part of the resolution, the General Assembly commended the desire for peace expressed by the Central American Presidents in the agreement on the "Procedure for the establishment of a firm and lasting peace in Central America", signed on 7 August 1987 at Guatemala City at the Esquipulas II summit meeting (A/42/521-S/19085, annex), and in subsequent declarations and agreements, and expressed its strongest support for those agreements; exhorted the Governments to continue their efforts to achieve a firm and lasting peace in Central America and expressed its fervent hopes for the effective implementation of the agreements signed at Tela, Honduras, on 7 August 1989; appealed to the countries which are outside the region but have links with it and interests in it to facilitate the implementation of the agreements concluded by the Central American Presidents and to refrain from any action which might impede such implementation; pledged me its full support in the performance of the functions entrusted to me, at the Tela summit meeting, as a member of CIAV, together with the Secretary-General of the Organization of American States, and requested me to continue to afford the fullest possible support to the Governments of the region in their efforts to achieve peace, especially by taking the measures necessary for the development and effective functioning of the verification machinery in respect of security, through ONUCA; supported my agreement with the Government of Nicaragua concerning the establishment of the United Nations Observer Mission to verify the electoral process in Nicaragua (ONUVEN) (see A/44/375) and requested me to report to it periodically on the Mission's progress; and urged the international community and international organizations to increase their technical, economic and financial cooperation with the Central American countries for the implementation of the goals and objectives of the Special Plan of Economic Cooperation for Central America (A/42/949, annex).

4. In my last report, dated 9 October 1989 (A/44/344/Add.1-S/20699/Add.1), I described the steps which I and the Secretary-General of the Organization of American States had taken to establish CIAV, as well as its timetable, the conditions necessary for its smooth operation and the activities so far carried out.

5. In the past two months CIAV, fulfilling the complex responsibilities entrusted to it under the Joint Plan adopted at Tela, continued to hold frequent consultations with the authorities of the Governments of Nicaragua, Honduras, other Central American countries and the United States of America, as well as with representatives of the Nicaraguan resistance. In addition to such contacts, in New York, Washington, Managua and Tegucigalpa, mention should be made of a visit to camps of the Nicaraguan resistance at Yamales, Honduras, in mid-October. CIAV was also in contact with the the the Nicaraguan Atlantic Coast Indigenous Movement.

6. In the course of such talks, CIAV put forward a number of ideas, concerning, *inter alia*: the need to create a climate of trust in Nicaragua so as encourage a voluntary approach on the part of the Nicaraguan resistance with regard to repatriation; the usefulness of establishing direct contact between the Government of Nicaragua and the Nicaraguan resistance; the advisability of visits by CIAV representatives to resistance camps in order to publicize the scope and benefits of the Joint Plan and learn about the existing human and material resources, and in that connection, the need to take a census of the members of the resistance and their relatives; the sending of a survey mission to the area by the Secretary-General of the United Nations for the purpose of assessing the personnel and equipment requirements for the collection and custody of arms and other military *matériel* of the resistance. Towards the end of October, in view of persisting differences between the Government of Nicaragua and the Nicaraguan resistance relating to the implementation of the Joint Plan, CIAV proposed that the two parties should hold direct and confidential talks in its presence, according to the provisions of the Joint Plan adopted at Tela.

7. At the same time, there was a breach of the cease-fire in Nicaragua. After denouncing attacks by forces of the Nicaraguan resistance in the interior of the country and a massive infiltration by resistance troops across the border, the Government of Nicaragua announced, with effect from 1 November, its decision not to extend the unilateral declaration of the cease-fire which it had been renewing on a monthly basis since March 1988. In the days preceding the suspension of the cease-fire, I expressed, among other things, my concern, and pointed out that the deterioration of the situation could not fail to have an adverse effect on the Central American peace process as a whole. After various initiatives, a series

of meetings between delegations of the Government of Nicaragua and the Nicaraguan resistance were held under the auspices of CIAV; they were attended by a representative of the Government of Honduras, in the capacity of an observer, and by Cardinal Miguel Obando y Bravo, in the capacity of a witness. The meetings were held on 9 and 10 November at United Nations Headquarters in New York, and from 13 to 21 November at the headquarters of the Organization of American States in Washington, D.C.

8. In the report submitted on 5 December to the five Central American Presidents pursuant to the Joint Plan, the Secretary-General of the Organization of American States and I were obliged to place on record, much to our regret, that for reasons beyond our control, it had not been possible for us to set in motion the Joint Plan formulated at Tela. It should be pointed out, however, that preliminary steps have been taken to lay the foundation for subsequent implementation of the Plan, and that it would therefore be useful to persevere. In that connection, attention should be drawn to the measures taken to date in conjunction with the United Nations High Commissioner for Refugees, the United Nations Development Programme and specialized agencies of the United Nations system and the Organization of American States, with a view to preparing a detailed scheme for implementation of the Joint Plan and to permitting us, at the proper time, to appeal to the international community for financial support.

9. As announced in my previous report, on 11 October 1989 I submitted a report to the Security Council (S/20895) recommending the establishment of ONUCA to verify in an impartial manner the fulfilment of the security commitments set forth in sections 5 and 6 of the Guatemala Procedures (A/42/521-S/19085, annex), namely, termination of aid to irregular forces and insurrectionist movements operating in the region, and non-use of territory for attacks on other States. As will be recalled, the establishment of such a mechanism had been requested by the five Central American Presidents under the agreement between the Presidents of Honduras and Nicaragua signed at Tela, Honduras (A/44/451-S/20778, annex II). My proposal to the Council took into account the results and recommendations of the survey mission which I sent to the five countries of the region from 3 to 23 September 1989, and gave specific details regarding the functions that ONUCA was to fulfil, as well as its *modus operandi*, the personnel required and the phases of its deployment.

10. The Security Council approved the establishment of ONUCA in its resolution 644 (1989) of 7 November 1989 for an initial renewable period of six months and requested me to take the necessary steps to

that effect. Following consultations with the parties and with the consent of the Security Council, I proceeded to request military observers from Canada, Colombia, Ireland, Spain and Venezuela; logistics units from Canada and Venezuela and civilian elements from the Federal Republic of Germany (S/20979 and S/20980). Following the same procedure, I appointed Major-General Agustín Quesada Gómez of Spain as Chief Military Observer of ONUCA (S/20981 and S/20982). ONUCA began the deployment of phase I on 2 December 1989 with the departure for Tegucigalpa of an advance contingent composed of approximately 30 officials, as well as civilian support personnel, led by the Chief Military Observer. The team is currently making visits to the five countries of the region with a view to establishing liaison offices in the respective capitals and making the necessary preparations for the subsequent establishment of other verification centres.

11. The General Assembly approved the financing of ONUCA in its resolution 44/44 of 7 December 1989.

12. Since the submission of my last report, ONUVEN has submitted two reports dated 17 October 1989 (A/44/642 and Corr.1) and 7 December 1989 (A/44/834), respectively. The first covers the period from the establishment of the mission up to the beginning of October and describes, *inter alia*, the functions of the mission, the establishment of the electoral authority, the organization of the political parties and the initiation of the politico-electoral activity. The second covers the period between the months of October and November and includes, *inter alia*, the voter registration process and the preparation of the electoral rolls, the functioning of the electoral authority and the progress of the electoral campaign and the use of the mass media, as well as the complaints and allegations received by the mission. Twenty-two international observers have joined the staff of ONUVEN already *in situ*, which has made it possible to establish offices in practically all parts of the country to cover the period of the electoral campaign which began on 4 December.

13. My Personal Representative for the Verification of Elections in Nicaragua visited that country from 18 to 23 October and informed me personally of his assessment of the electoral situation in the country and the functioning of ONUVEN. From the reports that I have received to date, I consider that, in spite of the interruption of the cease-fire, the electoral process in Nicaragua is proceeding in a generally positive way. At the present time, my main reason for concern is the outbreaks of violence that have occurred in the first days of the electoral campaign. I hope that these are isolated incidents and that political passions will remain under control so as to make it possible for the campaign to develop peacefully, thus contributing to the process of

democratic construction and national reconciliation to which the country aspires. I am convinced that the holding of honest elections, whose results are respected by all, is the key to the normalization of the situation in this country.

14.   I have followed with deep concern the alarming deterioration of the situation in El Salvador. I consider it urgent that substantive conversations be reinitiated between the Government and FMLN with a view to arrival at a just and lasting peace in this tormented country, and I am prepared to make every effort to contribute to that end.

15.   At the extraordinary meeting held in San Isidro de Coronado, Costa Rica, from 10 to 12 December, the Central American Presidents signed a declaration (A/44/872- S/21019 and annex) which reinforced the role of the United Nations in the region. The Presidents requested me to ensure the acceleration of the full deployment and the functioning of ONUCA and the expansion of the mandate of ONUCA to include verification of any cessation of hostilities and demobilization of irregular forces that may be agreed upon in the regions. The Presidents also requested me to take the necessary steps for the reinitiation of the dialogue between the Government of El Salvador and FMLN and thereby contribute to its successful development. The Presidents requested me also to make the necessary connections to involve States with interests in the region more directly in the peace effort, within the framework of the Esquipulas II Agreements and subsequent declarations. I am taking the necessary steps to carry out these tasks, which are an indication of the confidence which they have placed in the United Nations. These tasks correspond to the advisability of utilizing already existing international verification mechanisms, particularly ONUCA, in order to underpin the peace process in the region and the need to find procedures or mechanisms for incorporating in it those States which, because of their special connections in the region, have the capacity to promote or frustrate that process. I hope that the decisions adopted by the Central American Presidents will definitively guide the peace process in Central America along the right lines and that the cycle of great expectations and deep disappointments that have characterized it will finally be broken.

Document 8

Letter dated 29 January 1990 from President Alfredo Cristiani of El Salvador to the Secretary-General concerning the peace process and United Nations involvement

Not issued as a United Nations document; original in Spanish

I have the honour to extend to you my cordial greetings and sincere wishes for your continued success in your difficult functions, and to express the very special thanks of my Government, on behalf of the Salvadorian people, for the generous and enthusiastic welcome you have extended to the various requests made by the Central American Presidents to the United Nations in their quest for a firm, lasting peace in the region, which has been suffering for more than a decade from totalitarian conflicts and threats, during which time huge efforts have been made to establish and consolidate genuine representative democracy and real political pluralism in all our countries, so as to make Central America a region of secure stability and progress in the foreseeable future.

  With specific reference to El Salvador, and before addressing the concrete reason for my visit, I am very pleased to express our deepest gratitude that you agreed to send a special observer to the dialogue between my Government and the representatives of the Frente Farabundo Martí para la Liberación Nacional (FMLN), which was held in San José, Costa Rica, on 16, 17 and 18 October 1989. My Government hopes that, if it is possible to hold the agreed dialogue in Mexico, the presence of an observer representing the Secretary-General of the United Nations will continue to ensure the seriousness and genuine permanence of a process in which my Government has been intensely and unequivocally involved since 1 June 1989, when I had the honour to assume the Presidency of the Republic by express mandate of the people, whose most fervent desire and most just aspiration are to find peace through a political settlement, within the legal framework of democracy.

  As you are aware, Sir, the Presidents of the five Central American countries met at San Isidro de Coronado on 10, 11 and 12 December 1989, at a special session from which they issued a declaration containing new elements, specifications and decisions to make the quest for regional peace more coherent. You will not have failed to note that the document contains a much more explicit condemnation of all forms of violence and terror and an explicit repudiation of the armed action and terrorism being waged by the irregular forces in the region, one of these being FMLN. This has been once again demonstrated by the indiscriminate, reprehensible FMLN offensive of 19 November 1989, supported by other countries and with the direct participation of foreign elements, which, by violating the commitment to seek a peaceful solution at the negotiating table, and directly attacking the civilian population in densely populated sectors of San Salvador and the surrounding area, together with other important cities of El Salvador, gave ample proof that it is a terrorist organization. In that regard, it should be recalled that the United Nations has a laudable tradition of condemning terrorism, wherever and by whom it is committed.

This aggressive attitude on the part of FMLN, grounded in its own nature, moved the Central American Presidents to agree as follows, at San Isidro de Coronado: "The Presidents of Guatemala, Honduras, Nicaragua and Costa Rica support the Government of El Salvador in its oft-stated intent to find a solution to the conflict in El Salvador by peaceful and democratic means; to that end, they reiterated their vigorous appeal to FMLN immediately and effectively to cease hostilities in that fraternal country and to resume the dialogue that has been initiated". This vigorous appeal, which reiterates more clearly the appeal made at the meeting held at Tela, Honduras, is this time accompanied by the following emphatic demand, which is the natural result of the Presidents' condemnation of the terrorist offensive of November and all similar actions: "They also demand that FMLN publicly renounce any type of violent action that may directly or indirectly affect the civilian population."

Despite all these difficulties, my Government has not at any time abandoned, nor will it abandon, its sincere efforts to achieve peace by all reasonable means. For our part, this has not been, is not, and will not be a tactical or circumstantial manoeuvre, nor is it an attitude subject to the vagaries of political self-interest. It is a consciously assumed patriotic decision, which we will not renounce, although we may deplore and denounce at every step the insincerity of FMLN and its tactical use of the dialogue for the purpose of gaining domestic or international advantage. Our position as a Government which is responsible for the fate of the country, having received a legitimate, unquestionable mandate from the people in fair, open elections, is that of complying with the historic commitment to hold a permanent dialogue, which will allow us to find a firm, lasting solution through negotiations.

The Central American Presidents, imbued with the will to find a peaceful solution, have alluded, in a number of resolutions contained in the Declaration of San Isidro de Coronado, to the supreme representation of the United Nations, trusting that, by being privileged to have the personal assistance of the Secretary-General, they will be better able to achieve the objectives sought by the presidential resolutions. Accordingly, we requested you to "do everything within [your] power to take the necessary steps to ensure the resumption of the dialogue between the Government of El Salvador and FMLN, thereby facilitating its successful continuation". The essential reason for my presence at United Nations Headquarters is to reiterate this request in a most respectful and urgent manner.

Your effective and admirable contribution, Sir, to peace-building in various areas of the world makes us certain that your actions and efforts to ensure the resumption of the agreed dialogue will be a firm support for the cause of democratic pacification in El Salvador.

Of course, we are well aware of certain events and situations at this moment, as we resume the effort at dialogue and request your decisive cooperation in that regard. Two events must be taken into account, namely, the unilateral violation, on the part of FMLN, of the Mexico City agreement, in which the two parties seated at the negotiating table had agreed not to leave the table unilaterally, because they had undertaken to hold a permanent dialogue; and the offensive launched by FMLN in November, whose last-minute preparations were made even as the dialogue was in progress with the aim of finding a political solution. This means that the situation in which the effort is being resumed today is different from that of September, when the procedure for continuing to work towards a negotiated settlement was agreed. The belief in the sincere desire on the part of FMLN to hold a dialogue, which was already very precarious because of the background of the process, has practically disappeared today; for this reason, the Central American Presidents, as a logical consequence, called on FMLN to cease hostilities immediately and requested it to renounce publicly the use of violence.

My Government feels, therefore, that one of the necessary actions that must be taken in order for dialogue to be resumed would be for FMLN to show clear, verifiable signs that it will sit down at the negotiating table with a genuine desire to find a political solution to the conflict, and not as a simple tactic to cover up or make possible the continuation of armed struggle. My Government, being flexible in its efforts for peace, makes a special request to you, Sir, to direct your first invaluable steps, in seeking the resumption of dialogue, towards obtaining such assurances of seriousness and responsibility on the part of FMLN. The high moral and political backing of the Secretary-General of the United Nations will without doubt be a key factor in the success of the process towards a serious, responsible and lasting dialogue.

The Declaration of San Isidro de Coronado contains other important requests which my Government wishes to reiterate: that addressed to the International Support and Verification Commission (CIAV)—in which the Secretary-General of the Organization of American States is also participating—requesting it to proceed at once with the demobilization of FMLN; and that addressed to the United Nations Observer Group in Central America (ONUCA), requesting it to verify any cessation of hostilities and demobilization of FMLN. My Government feels that the very undertaking of these fundamental tasks, with appropriate, timely measures, will open new prospects favourable to a political solution in El Salvador.

The Salvadorian conflict is not an isolated one, but rather part of a complex Central American and global problem. This is why your contribution to its successful development goes beyond your extremely important efforts towards the resumption of dialogue, because it will, at other international political levels, make it possible for the changes and readjustments that are occurring in the world to have a beneficial impact on the settlement of the Salvadorian conflict, as part of the Central American crisis. Your high-level presence in this effort will also greatly enhance the possibility of making contact with other factors which, at various levels of world power, have a determining influence, or at least a conditioning one. My Government therefore places special emphasis on the request contained in the Declaration of San Isidro de Coronado, which reads as follows: "The Presidents agreed to request the Secretary-General of the United Nations to make the necessary connections to involve States with interests in the region more directly in the peace effort, within the framework of the Esquipulas II Agreements and subsequent declarations". This request is a very significant step, both towards a deeper understanding of the Central American problem and in terms of the valiant effort to face it with true realism on the part of the Central American Presidents.

All the foregoing, Sir, is based on the letter and spirit of the Declaration of San Isidro de Coronado, which embodies the unanimous thinking of the five Central American Presidents, who, rising above their ideological and political differences, were able to define at this meeting with more precision and openness the means and requirements of the regional process. Moreover, the above-mentioned explanation gives you an idea of the magnitude of our governmental efforts for peace, and the quest for effective support to achieve it. In its tireless peace effort, my Government calls on your help, Sir, with the most open, sincere desire. Despite all the vicissitudes and, especially, the manoeuvres of those who claim to seek peace without renouncing armed conflict, a position which has no justification or future, our goal of achieving peace through civilized understanding remains firm, because peace is the outcry of a people who have suffered the unjust havoc of fratricidal conflict for more than a decade. We call on you to help us to end this collective suffering, trusting that you more than anyone else, as a universal and Latin American human being, will understand our reasons and purposes.

Accept, Sir, the assurances of the highest consideration of the Salvadorian people and of my Government.

(Signed) Alfredo CRISTIANI

Document 9

Note verbale dated 14 August 1990 from El Salvador transmitting text of the Agreement on Human Rights signed at San José, Costa Rica, on 26 July 1990 between the Government of El Salvador and the Frente Farabundo Martí para la Liberación Nacional (FMLN)

A/44/971-S/21541, 16 August 1990

The Chargé d'affaires a.i. of the Permanent Mission of El Salvador to the United Nations presents his compliments to the Secretary-General of the United Nations and has the honour to transmit the annexed text of the "Agreement on Human Rights" signed in San José, Costa Rica, on 26 July between the Government of El Salvador and the Frente Farabundo Martí para la Liberación Nacional (FMLN).

The Chargé d'affaires a.i. respectfully requests that this note and its annex should be circulated as an official document of the forty-fourth session of the General Assembly, under agenda item 34, and of the Security Council.

Annex

Agreement on human rights*

I. Respect for and Guarantee of Human Rights

The Government of El Salvador and the Frente Farabundo Martí para la Liberación Nacional (hereinafter referred to as "the Parties"),

Bearing in mind that the legal system of El Salvador provides for the recognition of human rights and the duty of the State to respect and guarantee such rights;

Considering also that the State has assumed obligations of this nature under the many international conventions to which it is a party;

Bearing in mind that the Frente Farabundo Martí para la Liberación Nacional has the capacity and the will and assumes the commitment to respect the inherent attributes of the human person;

Reiterating the common purpose, expressed in the Geneva Agreement, to guarantee unrestricted respect for human rights in El Salvador;

Further reiterating their willingness, also expressed in the Geneva Agreement, to submit in this matter to verification by the United Nations;

On the understanding that for the purposes of the present political agreement, "human rights" shall mean those rights recognized by the Salvadorian legal system, including treaties to which El Salvador is a party, and by the declarations and principles on human rights and humanitarian law adopted by the United Nations and the Organization of American States;

Have concluded the following agreement in pursuance of the initial objective of the Geneva Agreement:

1. All necessary steps and measures shall be taken immediately to avoid any act or practice which constitutes an attempt upon the life, integrity, security or freedom of the individual. Similarly, all necessary steps and measures shall be taken to eliminate any practice involving enforced disappearances and abductions. Priority shall be given to the investigation of any cases of this kind which may arise and to the identification and punishment of the persons found guilty.

2. The full guarantee of the freedom and the integrity of the person requires that certain immediate measures be taken in order to ensure the following:

(a) No one may be arrested for the lawful exercise of his political rights;

(b) An arrest may be made only if ordered by the competent authority in writing and in accordance with the law, and the arrest must be carried out by officers who are properly identified as such;

(c) Anyone arrested must be informed while the arrest is being made of the reasons for the arrest and must be apprised without delay of the charge or charges against him;

(d) No one shall be placed under arrest as a means of intimidation. In particular, arrests shall not be made at night, except in the case of individuals caught *in flagrante delicto*;

(e) No one in custody shall be held incommunicado. Any person who has been arrested shall have the right to be assisted without delay by legal counsel of his own choosing and the right to communicate freely and privately with such counsel;

(f) No one shall be subjected to torture or other cruel, inhuman or degrading treatment or punishment.

3. In the course of the present negotiations, appropriate legal procedures and timetables shall be determined for the release of individuals who have been imprisoned for political reasons.

4. The fullest possible support shall be given to ensuring the effectiveness of the remedies of *amparo* and *habeas corpus*. To this end, the broadest possible publicity shall be given to this Agreement among the public at large and, in particular, among authorities or officers in charge of detention centres. Anyone who hampers the operation of these remedies or provides false information to the judicial authorities shall be punished.

5. The right of all persons to associate freely with others for ideological, religious, political, economic, labour, social, cultural, sporting or other purposes shall be fully guaranteed. Trade union freedom shall be fully respected.

6. Freedom of expression and of the press, the right of reply and the activities of the press shall be fully guaranteed.

7. Displaced persons and returnees shall be provided with the identity documents required by law and shall be guaranteed freedom of movement. They shall also be guaranteed the freedom to carry on their economic activities and to exercise their political and social rights within the framework of the country's institutions.

8. All persons shall be guaranteed freedom of movement in the areas involved in conflict, and the necessary steps shall be taken to provide the inhabitants of such areas with the identity documents required by law.

9. The Parties recognize the necessity of guaranteeing the effective enjoyment of labour rights. This subject will be considered under the agenda item on economic and social problems.

II. International Verification

10. In accordance with the provisions of the Geneva Agreement and the agenda for the negotiations which was adopted in Caracas, the Parties hereby agree to the terms of reference for the United Nations human

---

* It is the understanding of the Parties that this Agreement does not exhaust the consideration of the item on human rights and that it is, accordingly, a partial agreement. With the exception of points that are immediately applicable, the Agreement is subject to the package of political agreements to be negotiated for the achievement of the initial objective envisaged in the Geneva Agreement.

rights verification mission (hereinafter referred to as "the Mission"), as set out below.

11. The Mission shall devote special attention to the observance of the rights to life, to the integrity and security of the person, to due process of law, to personal liberty, to freedom of expression and to freedom of association.

In this context, a special effort shall be made to clarify any situation which appears to reveal the systematic practice of human rights violations and, in such cases, to recommend appropriate measures for the elimination of the practice to the Party concerned. The foregoing shall be without prejudice to any powers granted to the Mission to consider individual cases.

12. A Director designated by the Secretary-General of the United Nations shall be in charge of the Mission. The Director shall work in close cooperation with existing human rights organizations and bodies in El Salvador. He shall also be assisted by expert advisers. In addition, the Mission shall include as many verification personnel as may be necessary.

13. The purpose of the Mission shall be to investigate the human rights situation in El Salvador as regards acts committed or situations existing as from the date of its establishment and to take any steps it deems appropriate to promote and defend such rights. Accordingly, it shall perform its functions with a view to promoting respect for human rights and their guarantee in El Salvador and helping to do away with those situations in which such respect and guarantees are not duly observed.

14. The Mission's mandate shall include the following powers:

(a) To verify the observance of human rights in El Salvador;

(b) To receive communications from any individual, group of individuals or body in El Salvador, containing reports of human rights violations;

(c) To visit any place or establishment freely and without prior notice;

(d) To hold its meetings freely anywhere in the national territory;

(e) To interview freely and privately any individual, group of individuals or members of bodies or institutions;

(f) To collect by any means it deems appropriate such information as it considers relevant;

(g) To make recommendations to the Parties on the basis of any conclusions it has reached with respect to cases or situations it may have been called upon to consider;

(h) To offer its support to the judicial authorities of El Salvador in order to help improve the judicial procedures for the protection of human rights and increase respect for the rules of due process of law;

(i) To consult the Attorney-General of the Republic;

(j) To plan and carry out an educational and informational campaign on human rights and on the functions of the Mission itself;

(k) To use the media to the extent useful for the fulfilment of its mandate;

(l) To report regularly to the Secretary-General of the United Nations and through him to the General Assembly.

15. The Parties undertake to give their full support to the Mission. To that end, they pledge:

(a) To grant the Mission whatever facilities it may require for the performance of its functions;

(b) To ensure the security of the members of the Mission and of such persons as may have provided it with information, testimony or evidence of any kind;

(c) To provide, as expeditiously as possible, whatever information may be required by the Mission;

(d) To give their earliest consideration to any recommendations made to them by the Mission;

(e) Not to hinder the fulfilment of the Mission's mandate.

16. Each of the Parties shall appoint a delegate to serve as liaison with the Mission.

17. Should the Mission receive communications referring to acts or situations which occurred prior to its establishment, it may transmit them, if it deems it appropriate, to the competent authorities.

18. The fact that a case or situation has been considered by the Mission shall not preclude the application thereto of international procedures for the promotion and protection of human rights.

19. Subject to any arrangements which must be made prior to its establishment, the Mission shall take up its duties as of the cessation of the armed conflict. The Mission shall be established initially for one year and may be renewed.

San José, 26 July 1990

For the Government of El Salvador:	*For the Frente Farabundo Martí para la Liberación Nacional:*
(Signed)	*(Signed)*
Oscar Alfredo SANTAMARÍA	Commander Schafik HÁNDAL
Colonel Juan A. MARTÍNEZ VARELA	Commander Eduardo SANCHO
Colonel Mauricio Ernesto VARGAS	Ana Guadalupe MARTÍNEZ
Abelardo TORRES	Salvador SAMAYOA
David ESCOBAR GALINDO	Dagoberto GUTIÉRREZ
Rafael Hernán CONTRERAS	Marta VALLADARES
	Roberto CAÑAS

(Signed) Alvaro DE SOTO
Representative of the Secretary-General
of the United Nations

Document 10

Letter dated 29 August 1990 from the Secretary-General to the President of the Security Council concerning the possible establishment of a small preparatory office in El Salvador and other arrangements for a United Nations verification mission

S/21717, 6 September 1990

I wish to refer to the negotiations which are under way between the Government of El Salvador and the Frente Farabundo Martí para la Liberación Nacional (FMLN) under my auspices. As I informed the Council in my statement in informal consultations of 3 August 1990, it is envisaged that the United Nations will in due course be formally requested to carry out a certain number of tasks relating to the monitoring of a cessation of armed confrontation, the verification of respect of human rights and the monitoring of the forthcoming electoral process.

As a result of the most recent round of direct talks just concluded in Costa Rica, it emerges that the parties share the wish that preparations for carrying out the responsibilities envisaged should be initiated at the earliest possible date. My Representative, Mr. Alvaro de Soto, who was in El Salvador shortly before the latest round, has ascertained in his consultations with a broad spectrum of representatives of Salvadorian society, as well as all political parties, that the wish of the Government and of the FMLN is widely shared.

While in the absence of a formal and verifiable cessation of combat there is no certainty that conditions exist for carrying out these tasks in a systematic fashion throughout El Salvador, I believe that the time has come to take steps which would put the United Nations in a position to assess the local situation and initiate preparations so as to undertake the monitoring tasks as soon as circumstances permit. I am therefore at this time seeking the concurrence of the Security Council to my making the necessary arrangements, as soon as practicable, including the possible establishment of a small preparatory office in El Salvador, for the United Nations verification mission which is to be set up at the appropriate time. Verification *per se* would await further consultation with the members of the Council.

I would appreciate hearing from you on this matter at an early stage.

(*Signed*) Javier PÉREZ DE CUÉLLAR

Document 11

Report of the Secretary-General on the situation in Central America; contains the text of the Geneva Agreement (4 April 1990) and the Caracas Agreement (21 May 1990) signed by the Government of El Salvador and the FMLN

A/45/706-S/21931, 8 November 1990

1. The present report is submitted pursuant to Security Council resolution 637 (1989) of 27 July 1989 and General Assembly resolution 44/10 of 24 October 1989.

2. In my last report, dated 21 December 1989 (A/44/886-S/21029), I described the activities of the International Support and Verification Commission (CIAV) carried out by myself and the Secretary-General of the Organization of American States (OAS), the establishment of the United Nations Observer Group in Central America (ONUCA) and the progress made by the United Nations Observer Mission to verify the electoral process in Nicaragua (ONUVEN). I also noted that in the extraordinary meeting held at San Isidro de Coronado, Costa Rica, on 12 December 1989, the Central American Presidents, in addition to requesting the full deployment of ONUCA and the expansion of its mandate to include verification of any cessation of hostilities and demobilization of irregular forces that might be agreed upon in the region, also requested me to take the necessary steps for the reinitiation of the dialogue between the Government of El Salvador and the Farabundo Martí National Liberation Front (FMLN) and to involve States with interests in the region more directly in the peace effort.

3. In the past 10 months, the pace of events in Central America and the United Nations involvement in the region have accelerated considerably.

4. At the time of the submission of my last report to the General Assembly, ONUVEN had issued two reports on the electoral process in Nicaragua (A/44/642 and A/44/834). The third report, issued on 31 January 1990 (A/44/917), covered the period from the beginning of the electoral campaign in early December to the end of January 1990. By the beginning of December, the core group of observers had been enlarged by 20 additional personnel and ONUVEN regional offices had been opened in eight of the nine regions of Nicaragua. The report described, *inter alia*, the administration of the electoral process, the conduct of the electoral campaign, including external and internal financing, electoral strategies of the different parties, military actions in conflict areas and the role in the campaign of the mass media, including television, radio stations and the written press.

5. The fourth report of ONUVEN (A/44/921) was timed to appear on the day following the closing of the electoral campaign on 21 February. It covered the events that occurred in the last three weeks of the campaign and, more importantly, gave an overall assessment of the electoral process since its inception and up to the close of the campaign. In the opinion of ONUVEN, the people of Nicaragua were in a position to decide between alternatives which had been given a reasonable chance to be aired and would be free to determine their future government through the verdict of the ballot boxes on 25 February.

6. The final task of ONUVEN, to verify the fairness of the polling and counting of votes, was carried out by over 240 observers representing over 50 different nationalities. To those drawn from the United Nations Secretariat as well as from organizations and agencies of the United Nations system based in the region were added poll-watchers from over 20 Member States. These included Austria, Belgium, Canada, Cape Verde, Colombia, Czechoslovakia, Denmark, Finland, the Federal Republic of Germany, the German Democratic Republic, Hungary, India, Italy, Japan, Morocco, the Netherlands, New Zealand, Poland, Spain and Sweden.

7. In the early morning of 26 February 1990, my Personal Representative informed me of the preliminary assessment of ONUVEN that the voting had been conducted under normal conditions without intimidation or violence and could be considered free and fair. The last ONUVEN report (A/44/927) of 30 March 1990 confirmed the preliminary assessment by stating that the electoral process had been impartial and fair throughout.

8. On 26 February, the accurate projection of the voting results made the previous night by ONUVEN had been confirmed by the results officially announced by the Supreme Electoral Council. President Daniel Ortega Saavedra publicly accepted the results and declared the readiness of the Sandinista Front of National Liberation to transfer power on 25 April 1990 to the new Government to be formed by the National Opposition Union through a peaceful and orderly transition process. Both the President and the President-elect, Mrs. Violeta Barrios de Chamorro, requested me, through my Personal Representative, to maintain a United Nations presence in Nicaragua to ensure a peaceful and orderly transition process leading to the transfer of power on 25 April 1990. I replied positively and assigned for this purpose a small team to remain in the country. The team was to assist both in the remaining electoral issues as well as in the political aspects of the transition.

9. In the post-electoral atmosphere, charged with uncertainty, the demobilization of the Nicaraguan resistance, an essential element in the Central American peace process, became a high priority. To that end, at the beginning of March, I reached agreement with the Secretary-General of OAS on the *modus operandi* of CIAV in relation to the two organizations' responsibilities in the demobilization and voluntary repatriation of members of the Nicaraguan resistance and their families. Under that agreement, subsequently complemented by another one arrived at in June, the United Nations component of CIAV (CIAV/UN) was assigned responsibility for the assistance to and repatriation of demobilized members of the Nicaraguan resistance, their families and others related to the Nicaraguan resistance in Honduras and Costa Rica. The OAS component of CIAV (CIAV/OAS) was to provide assistance to those members of the Nicaraguan resistance who demobilized inside Nicaragua, as well as to the members of the Nicaraguan resistance and their families repatriated by CIAV/UN once they had reached Nicaraguan soil. In addition, CIAV/UN was to be responsible for the voluntary repatriation of Nicaraguan refugees, as well as for all follow-up activities and their assistance in Nicaragua. The United Nations High Commissioner for Refugees (UNHCR) acted as the operational arm of CIAV/UN, conducting all support and repatriation activities.

10. In a report to the Security Council, dated 15 March (S/21194), I sought from the Council its urgent approval, on a contingency basis, of an enlargement of the mandate of ONUCA and the addition of armed personnel to its strength in order to enable it to play a part in the voluntary demobilization of the Nicaraguan resistance. I recalled that, in a letter to the President of the Security Council (S/20856) on 28 August 1989, I had pointed out that the task of collecting the weapons, *matériel* and military equipment of the Nicaraguan resistance would need to be entrusted to military units

equipped with defensive weapons. The Council had welcomed my intention to seek its approval at the appropriate time (S/20857). My request of 15 March was based on consultations held earlier that month at Managua between the Under-Secretary-General for Special Political Affairs and the Chief Military Observer of ONUCA and the Nicaraguan authorities. An understanding had then been reached in principle according to which ONUCA would be responsible for implementing the military aspects of the Tela Accord (A/44/451-S/20778) and would receive the weapons, *matériel* and military equipment from members of the Nicaraguan resistance. Having done so, the individuals concerned would become the responsibility of CIAV, which would arrange for their repatriation or resettlement. ONUCA would also establish and ensure the security of temporary assembly points in Honduras and Nicaragua and in certain locations in Costa Rica. It would further be responsible for the custody of the weapons and other *matériel* handed over to it until their final disposal was decided upon by the five Central American Presidents.

11. The Security Council, in resolution 650 (1990) of 27 March 1990, authorized an enlargement of the mandate of ONUCA and the addition of armed personnel to its strength, as requested in my report.

12. On 27 March 1990, the two transition teams designated by the President and the President-elect of Nicaragua signed a Protocol of Procedure for the transfer of power which, *inter alia*, considered the demobilization of the resistance forces before 23 April 1990 as essential in creating the climate for a peaceful transfer (A/44/927, appendix VIII).

13. On 3 April 1990, the Central American Presidents signed a Declaration at their summit meeting at Montelimar, Nicaragua (A/44/936-S/21235), in which, *inter alia*, they agreed to emphasize the urgent need for the immediate demobilization of the Nicaraguan resistance, pursuant to the Joint Plan signed at Tela on 7 August 1989 and to support the Protocol of Procedure for the Transfer of Presidential Authority of the Republic of Nicaragua. They also agreed to request ONUCA and CIAV to take the necessary steps to assist in the demobilization and disarmament of the members of the resistance inside or outside Nicaragua, a process to be initiated immediately and concluded no later than 25 April 1990. They also decided that the weapons to be received by ONUCA were to be destroyed *in situ*, as I had suggested.

14. The demobilization of the first group of the Nicaraguan resistance took place in Honduras on 16 April 1990, where a company of an armed Venezuelan infantry battalion temporarily added to ONUCA for that purpose began the process of receiving and destroying the weapons. However, by that date, most of the resistance forces had moved to Nicaragua where, on 18 April 1990, following intense negotiations, definitive cease-fire agreements were concluded in Managua between the Government of Nicaragua and the Northern, Central and Atlantic fronts of the Nicaraguan resistance. The talks, which were attended by the ONUCA Chief Military Observer and my Alternate Personal Representative, concluded with an agreement that the demobilization of the resistance forces in Nicaragua should start on 25 April 1990 and be completed no later than 10 June 1990 (A/44/941-S/21272).

15. On 19 April 1990, I informed the Security Council (S/21259) that the agreements arrived at by the Nicaraguan parties required a further broadening of the ONUCA mandate to include the tasks of monitoring a cease-fire and separation of forces; that the security zones envisaged in the agreements, where the resistance was to concentrate, were considerably larger than the temporary assembly points envisaged in my March report; and that CIAV would provide humanitarian assistance to members of the resistance as soon as they arrived in the zones, i.e., before demobilization was complete. By resolution 653 (1990) of 20 April, the Security Council approved my proposals concerning ONUCA's additional task of monitoring the cease-fire and separation of forces resulting from the withdrawal of the Nicaraguan Government's forces from the established security zones and surrounding areas.

16. On 27 April, I submitted a report to the Security Council recommending the extension of the ONUCA mandate for a further period of six months on the understanding that ONUCA's task of monitoring the cease-fire and separation of forces in Nicaragua and the demobilization of the Nicaraguan resistance would lapse with the completion of the demobilization process no later than 10 June 1990. The Council approved my recommendation on 4 May 1990 by resolution 654 (1990). On the same day in Managua, the Nicaraguan resistance had stated its willingness to proceed to its voluntary demobilization to be completed by 10 June. On 22 May 1990, however, the slow pace of demobilization of the Nicaraguan resistance prompted me to convey my concern to the Council, stressing that, unless there was a rapid increase in the rate of demobilization, the deadline for its completion would not be met. This would create for the Security Council, responsible for ONUCA, and the OAS, responsible for CIAV in Nicaragua, a difficult choice, since continuation of the current arrangement would have implied assistance to a group which stood in defiance of its commitments to the Nicaraguan Government, whereas a withdrawal could have precipitated a crisis in the country which, at worse, could have led to a resumption of civil conflict. The following day, the President of

the Council made a statement (S/21331) calling upon the resistance to meet fully and urgently the commitments it had made in agreeing to demobilize. The Council supported the Government of Nicaragua in its efforts to facilitate timely demobilization and called upon all others with influence in this matter to take action to ensure that demobilization would proceed in accordance with the agreements and, in particular, that the 10 June deadline would be respected. This position was conveyed to the five Central American Presidents as well as to the Secretary-General of OAS.

17. In my report of 4 June 1990 (S/21341), I informed the Council about a set of complaints investigated by ONUCA referring to the situation surrounding the security zones and the demilitarized zones in Nicaragua. In general, it remained my assessment that there had not been serious violations of the cease-fire. Some breaches of the agreement on the separation of forces in certain areas were attributable to the lack of trust between the two sides following eight years of hostilities. As far as demobilization was concerned, I noted that, although there had recently been a welcome increase in its rate, the leaders of the Nicaraguan resistance had still not achieved the minimum target to which they had committed themselves. In a further report to the Security Council on 8 June (S/21349), I recommended that ONUCA's mandate of monitoring the cease-fire and separation of forces in Nicaragua and demobilizing members of the Nicaraguan resistance be extended, on the understanding that these tasks would lapse with the completion of the demobilization process not later than 29 June 1990 (resolution 656 (1990)).

18. By the end of June 1990, I was in a position to inform the Security Council that demobilization of the Nicaraguan resistance had been essentially completed on 28 June (S/21379). In a letter addressed to the Chief Military Observer, the Nicaraguan Government had stated its full satisfaction with the process of demobilization that ONUCA had carried out in fulfilment of its mandate. The demobilization of over 22,400 members of the Nicaraguan resistance and the destruction of their weapons, including small arms, grenade launchers and missiles, appeared to close a chapter of a conflict with 30,000 casualties which had taken its toll on every Nicaraguan family. All the problems, however, were not solved by the demobilization itself. While a major international effort gave the people of Nicaragua the opportunity to vote freely and brought an end to the civil war, the country unfortunately still faces a daunting task of reconciliation and reconstruction. It deserves all possible assistance from the international community.

19. A wider task awaited the United Nations in the assistance and repatriation of members of families of former combatants, as well as thousands of Nicaraguan refugees and "indocumentados" living in Honduras and Costa Rica. On 18 April 1990, I addressed a letter to all Member States in which, after delineating the respective responsibilities of the United Nations and OAS within CIAV, I launched an appeal to Member Governments to support the task to be undertaken by CIAV/UN. 1/ A pledging conference to that effect took place on 25 April 1990.

20. On 1 May 1990, CIAV/UN initiated its activities in Honduras. So far CIAV/UN, with the operational support of UNHCR and the United Nations Development Programme (UNDP) has provided assistance to over 60,000 people. Assistance to former members of the Nicaraguan resistance and their families was taken over from the United States Agency for International Development (USAID) in coordination with Honduran authorities and the Honduran Red Cross. In the absence of data, CIAV/UN conducted a census, in which 36,684 former combatants and their families, former beneficiaries of USAID, were registered in Honduras. Their voluntary repatriation to Nicaragua began on 5 July 1990 and is scheduled to conclude by the end of 1990. By mid-October, 15,124 persons had been repatriated and at the beginning of November there were about 2,500 CIAV/UN beneficiaries pending for repatriation. The majority of remaining ones are believed to have gone back by their own means. In addition, CIAV/UN conducted a census of 23,463 Nicaraguan refugees, 20,385 of whom have so far been repatriated. Their assistance and follow-up activities will continue to be provided in Nicaragua by UNHCR on behalf of CIAV/UN.

21. According to the latest tentative figures available, the number of CIAV beneficiaries inside Nicaragua for 1991 would be approximately 90,000 people. I wish to express my sincere appreciation to the donor countries for their assistance to CIAV and to pay tribute to all those dedicated workers of the United Nations and other international agencies who have carried out their task so efficiently in often difficult circumstances.

22. During the period under review, I have actively pursued my efforts, with the full support of the Security Council in its resolutions 637 (1989) and 654 (1990), to find a negotiated settlement to the conflict in El Salvador. In the San Isidro de Coronado Declaration of December 1989, the five Central American Presidents requested me to do everything within my power to ensure the resumption of the dialogue between the Salvadorian Government and FMLN. These efforts intensified following a visit to Headquarters by President Cristiani in January 1990, and after receiving assurances from both the Salvadorian Government and FMLN that they were seriously intent on seeking an end to the armed conflict in that country through negotiations. A series of consultations were un-

1/ SG/CONF.5/1.

dertaken by my Personal Representative, Mr. Alvaro de Soto, with both parties in order to agree on the format, mechanism and pace of a process aimed at bringing about as speedily as possible, under my auspices, a definitive end to the armed conflict in that country.

23. At a joint meeting held in my presence at Geneva on 4 April 1990, the Government of El Salvador and FMLN signed an agreement in which they agreed to a process of negotiations under my auspices to end the armed conflict by political means as speedily as possible, promote democratization of the country, guarantee unrestricted respect of human rights and reunify Salvadorian society (see annex I). The initial objective was to achieve political agreements for arranging a halt to the armed confrontation and any acts that infringe the rights of the civilian population which would have to be verified by the United Nations subject to the approval of the Security Council. Once that had been achieved, the process was to lead to the establishment of necessary guarantees and conditions for reintegrating the members of FMLN, within a framework of full legality, into the civil, institutional and political life of the country. The parties agreed to a method of negotiation by means of two complementary activities: direct dialogue between the negotiating commissions of the two parties with the active participation of the Secretary-General or his representative, and an intermediary role by the Secretary-General or his representative between the parties to ensure that both the Government and FMLN were committed at the highest level.

24. Following a second round of direct talks held at Caracas with the participation of my Personal Representative, the Government and FMLN agreed to an agenda and a schedule for negotiations, in which mid-September was set as a target date for achieving the initial objective described above (see annex II). As had been agreed at Geneva, the initial objective for the process will be to achieve political agreements for a halt to the armed confrontation and any acts that infringe the rights of the civilian population, which will have to be verified by the United Nations, subject to the approval of the Security Council. The issues on which political agreements, as described in the Caracas agenda, were to be reached relate to the following: armed forces, human rights, judicial system, electoral system, constitutional reform, economic and social issues and verification by the United Nations.

25. Following the agreement on the agenda, two substantive rounds of negotiations were held in Mexico and Costa Rica in June and July, respectively. On 26 July 1990, the parties concluded an agreement on human rights (A/44/971-S/21541) which contains detailed commitments to guarantee unrestricted respect for human rights in El Salvador, and which provides for the establishment of a United Nations verification mission under a Director appointed by the Secretary-General and with such verification personnel as may be necessary. The mission is to be given powers to take whatever legally permissible action it may deem appropriate for promoting and protecting human rights as part of the intention to promote respect for and guarantee of such rights in El Salvador and to contribute towards improving those situations in which such respect and guarantee are not duly observed. The agreement on human rights is the first substantive achievement of the negotiating process. The implementation of the verification mission, which is to last for one year, but which may be renewed, was conditioned in the agreement on a halt to the armed confrontation. The parties have since agreed that it need not await the fulfilment of that condition.

26. As I informed the Security Council on 3 August 1990, it is envisaged that, in the context of the achievement of the "initial objective" established in the Geneva agreement, the United Nations will be requested to carry out a certain number of tasks relating to the verification of a cease-fire, the monitoring of the electoral process and the human rights verification mentioned above. It is my view that these tasks are being cast as essential components of a peaceful solution to the Salvadorian conflict and that, in order to ensure proper coordination on the ground and the rational use of resources, an integrated operation should be established under the authority of the Security Council. In the mean time, having obtained the previous authorization of the Security Council (S/21717 and S/21718), I intend to establish shortly a small preparatory office for the United Nations verification mission, in order to enable the latter to undertake the monitoring task as soon as developments permit.

27. The human rights agreement arrived at in San José was followed by two direct meetings held also at San José in August and September 1990 between the representatives of the Government and the FMLN with the participation of my Representative. My Personal Representative has also undertaken frequent trips to meet with President Cristiani and senior commanders of the FMLN. He has also been in frequent contact with leaders and representatives of a wide array of political parties, social organizations and church leaders in El Salvador. I myself met with President Cristiani during his recent visit to the United Nations. I also met with a high-level delegation of the FMLN. The question of El Salvador has come up frequently in my meetings with leaders of Member States who are in a position to assist in my efforts, as envisaged in the Geneva Agreement.

28. While significant progress has been recorded to date, it is fair to say that considerable problems have been encountered in negotiations, particularly on the most

difficult, sensitive and complex issue on the agenda, the armed forces, on which, despite continuous efforts, it has not yet been possible to reach an agreement. In an effort to reinvigorate the negotiating process, at a direct meeting held in Mexico City from 29 to 31 October 1990, the two parties, with the participation of my Representative, reached consensus on the need to make adjustments in the mechanics followed so far. To this end, they decided to place greater emphasis on the active role of the Secretary-General's Representative and his role as intermediary and on the confidential character of future direct meetings. Procedural improvements will not by themselves solve the remaining problems. However, I remain persuaded that, given the necessary will, coupled with perseverance and flexibility on the substance of the issues on both sides, and with the support from outside Powers in a position to support these efforts, the goal of peace in El Salvador can be achieved in the not-too-distant future.

29. On 30 March 1990, a delegation of the National Reconciliation Commission of Guatemala, acting with the full support of the Government of the Republic, and a delegation of the Unidad Revolucionaria Nacional Guatemalteca (URNG), with the full support of its General Command, signed in Oslo a "Basic Agreement for the Search for Peace by Political Means", with a view to initiating a serious process which, by seeking ways to bring about a peaceful solution of the nation's problems, would culminate in the attainment of peace and the enhancement of functional and participatory democracy in Guatemala (see annex III). To that end, the National Reconciliation Commission and URNG agreed to carry out a series of activities and, by mutual agreement, appointed as Conciliator Monsignor Rodolfo Quezada Toruño in his capacity as Chairman of the National Reconciliation Commission, a body established by the Government of Guatemala in accordance with the Esquipulas II Agreements. The two parties agreed to request that I should observe the activities to be carried out and I, with the express support of the President of the Republic, accepted that request on 21 May 1990, bearing in mind that the Agreement fell within the framework of the Esquipulas II Agreements, as endorsed by Security Council resolution 637 (1989).

30. Pursuant to the Oslo Agreement, five meetings have been held, under the auspices of the National Reconciliation Commission and in the presence of the Conciliator and my appointed Observer, between representatives of URNG and representatives of political parties, private enterprises, religious and popular groups and a mixed sector representing academics, professionals and small- and medium-sized businesses. These meetings were held at El Escorial, Spain, from 27 May to 1 June (A/44/959); at Ottawa, from 31 August to 1 September;

at Quito, from 24 to 26 September; and at Metepec (Puebla), Mexico, from 23 to 25 October and from 27 to 28 October, respectively. The next phase envisaged under the Oslo Agreement would be the holding of talks between representatives of the Government of the Republic, the Guatemalan Army and the General Command of URNG with a view to achieving a political solution of the internal armed confrontation. I cherish the hope that the process initiated by the signature of the Oslo Agreement will continue and pave the way for a process of reconciliation and peace in Guatemala.

31. The Central American Presidents, and the President of Panama as an observer, attended a summit meeting at Antigua, Guatemala, in June 1990. In the Antigua Declaration of 17 June 1990 (A/44/958), they agreed, *inter alia*, to pursue negotiations on security, verification and control and limitation of weapons, in accordance with the Esquipulas II Agreement, and to seek technical advice from the Secretariats of the United Nations and OAS. In order to provide such advice, officials from the United Nations Secretariat participated as observers in the meetings of the Security Commission, established under Esquipulas II, held at San José, on 31 July and at San Salvador on 12 and 13 September 1990, respectively.

32. At the San José meeting, the members of the Security Commission agreed that its objectives were to ensure the defensive nature of armed forces of the countries of the region, establish a reasonable balance among them, define a new model for security relations and secure commitments with respect to the foreign military presence in the region (A/44/970). At its second meeting (A/45/642), the Security Commission established a technical sub-commission for the purpose of drawing up a draft format or model for conducting inventories of the military installations, personnel and weapons of the military and security forces of the Central American countries. The sub-commission, at a meeting held at Guatemala City in mid-October, prepared, with the assistance of Secretariat representatives, such a model, which will be considered by the Security Commission at its next meeting to be held in Honduras in November.

Annex I

Press communiqué issued following the Geneva meeting presided over by the Secretary-General between representatives of the Government of El Salvador and of the Frente Farabundo Martí para la Liberación Nacional

At the request of the Central American Presidents and within the framework of the mandate of good offices conferred on me by the Security Council under resolution 637 of 27 July 1989, I have held consultations with the

Government of El Salvador and the Frente Farabundo Martí para la Liberación Nacional (FMLN) in order to agree on the format, mechanism and pace of a process aimed at bringing about as speedily as possible, under my auspices, a definitive end to the armed conflict in that country. I have agreed to carry out this effort at the request of the Government and FMLN and because I have received assurances from both parties that there is a serious intention and good faith to seek to bring about such an end through negotiations. As a result of my consultations, the Government and FMLN have agreed on the points set forth below, which are designed to ensure that the process proceeds in an efficient and serious manner and promotes mutual trust through appropriate guarantees.

I believe that the scrupulous maintenance of these guarantees, over and above their intrinsic importance, will demonstrate the desire and ability of the parties to carry out the commitments that they undertake during the negotiations. On this understanding, the Government and FMLN have pledged not to renounce the negotiation process.

1. The purpose of the process shall be to end the armed conflict through political means as speedily as possible, promote the democratization of the country, guarantee unrestricted respect for human rights and re-unify Salvadorian society.

The initial objective shall be to achieve political agreements for arranging a halt to the armed confrontation and any acts that infringe the rights of the civilian population, which will have to be verified by the United Nations, subject to the approval of the Security Council. Once that has been achieved, the process shall lead to the establishment of the necessary guarantees and conditions for reintegrating the members of FMLN, within a framework of full legality, into the civil, institutional and political life of the country.

2. The process shall be carried out under the auspices of the Secretary-General and in a continuing and ongoing manner.

3. In order to ensure the success of the negotiation process, the Government and FMLN agree to a method which will be elaborated by means of two types of complementary activities: direct dialogue between the negotiation commissions with the active participation of the Secretary-General or his Representative, and an intermediary role by the Secretary-General or his Representative between the parties to ensure that both the Government and FMLN are committed at the highest level. The Secretary-General shall see to it that these activities are conducted in a manner that truly contributes to the success of the process. The Government and FMLN

shall ensure that their negotiation commissions are fully authorized to discuss and conclude agreements.

4. The Government and FMLN agree that the process shall be conducted in the strictest confidence. The only public information on the development of this process shall be that which is provided by the Secretary-General or his authorized Representative.

5. The Secretary-General, at his discretion, may maintain confidential contacts with Governments of States Members of the United Nations or groups of such Governments which may contribute to the success of the process through their advice and support.

6. The Government of El Salvador and FMLN agree that the political parties and other existing representative social organizations in El Salvador have an important role to play in achieving peace. In the same way, they recognize the need for both the Government and FMLN to maintain adequate and standing information and consultation mechanisms with these parties and social organizations in the country and that the latter must undertake to ensure the necessary confidentiality for the success of the dialogue process. When it is deemed appropriate and on the basis of mutual agreement, the commissions may call upon the representatives of these parties and organizations in order to receive their contributions.

7. The Government and FMLN likewise recognize that it is useful for the Secretary-General to maintain contacts with Salvadorian persons and groups whose contribution may be of use in his efforts.

Representing the Government of El Salvador:	*Representing the Frente Farabundo Martí para la Liberación Nacional:*
(*Signed*)	(*Signed*)
Dr. Oscar SANTAMARÍA	Comandante Schafik HÁNDAL
Ambassador Guillermo PAZ LARIN	Licenciado Salvador SAMAYOA
Ambassador Ana Cristina SOL	Comandante Ana Guadalupe MARTÍNEZ
Ambassador Carlos Ernesto MENDOZA	Comandante Roberto CAÑAS

In the capacity assigned to me by the United Nations Security Council in resolution 637 (1989)

(*Signed*) Javier PÉREZ DE CUÉLLAR
Secretary-General of the United Nations

Annex II

General agenda and schedule for the comprehensive negotiation process, issued at Caracas on 21 May 1990

A. *General agenda*

I. The initial objective shall be to achieve political agreements for a halt to the armed confrontation and any acts that infringe the rights of the civilian population, which will have to be verified by the United Nations, subject to the approval of the Security Council.

(a) First: POLITICAL AGREEMENTS
1. Armed forces
2. Human rights
3. Judicial system
4. Electoral system
5. Constitutional reform
6. Economic and social issues
7. Verification by the United Nations

(b) Second: AGREEMENT ON A HALT TO THE ARMED CONFRONTATION AND ANY ACTS THAT IN-FRINGE THE RIGHTS OF THE CIVILIAN POPULA-TION

II. Establishment of the necessary guarantees and conditions for reintegrating the members of FMLN, within a framework of full legality, into the civilian, institutional and political life of the country.
1. Armed forces
2. Human rights
3. Judicial system
4. Electoral system
5. Constitutional reform
6. Economic and social issues
7. Reintegration of FMLN members
8. Verification by the United Nations

III. Final agreements for the consolidation of the objectives of the Geneva Agreement, and verification by the United Nations, as appropriate.

Note: The sequence of the items listed for the respective phases is not a strict order of consideration, and may be changed by common agreement.

The agreements should be precisely tailored to the nature of the phase involved. Political items have been referred to their respective phases; but since some of them are quite complex, certain aspects might be addressed in other phases. It all depends on the dynamics of the negotiations.

B. *Schedule*

In the light of the general agenda for the comprehensive negotiation process in the preceding section, the Government of El Salvador and FMLN agree that the initial objective set forth in paragraph 1 of the Geneva Agreement of 4 April 1990 should be achieved by the middle of September 1990, provided that the parties reach synchronized agreements which have schedules for implementation and are subject to verification as appropriate, so as to ensure that all the components of the initial objective are duly coordinated.

The additional advantage of that deadline is that it would help to ensure that an electoral process is conducted at the legislative and municipal levels in an atmosphere of tranquillity, broad participation and freedom from intimidation.

It is difficult to set a strict time-limit for the conclusion of the comprehensive process. That would depend on factors that cannot yet be considered, such as the range and scope of the political agreements referred to in section I, which are to be negotiated, and the relationship between the negotiations and the electoral process. On the other hand, there is also a possibility that the initial objective might be achieved before the deadline. For these reasons, formulations regarding the conclusion of the process should not be in terms of dates, but in terms of a certain number of months from the achievement of the initial objective: tentatively, two to six months.

On the basis of the above understandings, the Government and FMLN shall concentrate, as the primary substantive priority, on the negotiation of the political agreements envisaged under the initial objective.

Caracas, 21 May 1990

Representing the Government of El Salvador:	*Representing the Frente Farabundo Martí para la Liberación Nacional:*
(*Signed*) Colonel Juan A. MARTÍNEZ VARELA	(*Signed*) Comandante Schafik HÁNDAL
Dr. Oscar Alfredo SANTAMARIÁ	Comandante Eduardo SANCHO
Colonel Mauricio Ernesto VARGAS	Ana Guadalupe MARTÍNEZ
Dr. Abelardo TORRES	Salvador SAMAYOA
Dr. David ESCOBAR GALINDO	Dagoberto GUTIÉRREZ
Dr. Rafael HERNAN CONTRERAS	Marta VALLADARES
	Roberto CAÑAS

(*Signed*) Alvaro DE SOTO
Representative of the Secretary-General
of the United Nations

Annex III

Oslo agreement

The delegation of the Reconciliation Commission of Guatemala, acting with the full support of the Government of the Republic and in the conciliatory role attributed to it under the Esquipulas II Agreement, and the delegation of the Unidad Revolucionaria Nacional Guatemalteca (URNG), acting with the full support of its General Command, express their profound satisfaction upon the signature of the

Basic agreement for the search for peace by political means

following the serious, wide-ranging and frank discussions held from 26 to 30 March 1990 in the welcoming city of Oslo, with the kind hospitality of the Government of Norway and under the auspices of the Lutheran World Federation.

In conclusion, the two delegations attending the Oslo meeting wish to record their deep gratitude to the exemplary people and Government of Norway for having made it possible to hold this extremely important meeting in their territory. We are most particularly grateful for the presence of Mr. Kjell Magne Bondevik, Minister for Foreign Affairs of Norway.

Thanks are also due to the Lutheran World Federation, which sponsored and made this meeting possible by virtue of its persistent efforts. We mention especially its Secretary-General, Dr. Gunnar Stålsett, the Under-Secretary-General for International Affairs and Human Rights, Dr. Paul Wee, and Dr. Leopoldo J. Niilus, Special Adviser on International Affairs to the Lutheran World Federation.

We are grateful too for the support and solidarity of the Norwegian Church and its Council for External Relations. Our thanks also go to the Reverend Andreas Aarflot, Bishop of Oslo.

DONE in the city of Oslo, Norway, this 29th day of March, 1990.

Delegation of the National Reconciliation Commission of Guatemala, representing the Guatemalan Government:

(*Signed*) Jorge SERRANO ELÍAS
(*Signed*) Mario PERMUTH
(*Signed*) Eduardo P. VILLATORO

Delegation of the General Command of the Unidad Revolucionaria Nacional Guatemalteca:
(*Signed*) Luis BECKER GUZMÁN
(*Signed*) Francisco VILLAGRÁN
(*Signed*) Jorge E. ROSAL

Basic agreement for the search for peace by political means

In the city of Oslo, Norway, the delegation of the National Reconciliation Commission (CNR) of Guatemala, acting with the full support of the Government of the Republic of Guatemala and in the conciliatory role attributed to it under the Esquipulas II Agreement, and the delegation of the Unidad Revolucionaria Nacional Guatemalteca (URNG), with the full support of its General Command, having met from 26 to 30 March 1990 expressly for the purpose of finding ways to bring about a peaceful solution of the nation's problems by political means, and recognizing that this objective is fundamental to the achievement of reconciliation between Guatemalans and to the solution of the nation's problems, do agree to initiate a serious process which will culminate in the attainment of peace and the enhancement of functional and participatory democracy in Guatemala.

The two delegations shall, by mutual agreement, proceed to exercise their

Good offices

In accordance with the spirit of the Esquipulas II Agreement, the National Reconciliation Commission shall take steps to facilitate and sustain the peace-seeking activities to which this Agreement refers, through its good offices and the appointment as Conciliator, by agreement with URNG, of Monsignor Rodolfo Quezada Toruño in his capacity as Chairman of the National Reconciliation Commission.

It shall be the function of the Conciliator to propose initiatives to all the parties, to facilitate and sustain dialogue and negotiation and to impart momentum to that process, and to analyse whatever similarities or differences there may be between the positions of the parties. He shall be entitled to propose initiatives and solutions for discussion and agreement and shall perform all other functions required for the proper fulfilment of his commitment.

The National Reconciliation Commission and the Unidad Revolucionaria Nacional Guatemalteca agree to request the Secretary-General of the United Nations, Dr. Javier Pérez de Cuéllar, to observe the activities to be carried out and to act as guarantor of compliance with the agreements and commitments entered into upon signature of this document.

Activities to be carried out

The two delegations agree to launch activities which will generate conditions permitting the definitive attainment of peace and the enhancement of democracy.

(a) A meeting shall be held between representatives of the political parties of the Republic of Guatemala and representatives of the Unidad Revolucionaria Nacional Guatemalteca. The National Reconciliation Commission and the Unidad Revolucionaria Nacional Guatemalteca shall, by mutual agreement, decide the conditions under which this meeting will take place. The parties shall make the efforts required for the meeting to be held in the second fortnight of May 1990.

(b) The National Reconciliation Commission shall, by mutual agreement with URNG, create the mechanisms required for the convening, preferably in June 1990, of the necessary meetings between the Unidad Revolucionaria Nacional Guatemalteca and representatives of the country's popular, religious and business sectors, as well as other politically representative entities, with a view to finding ways of solving the nation's problems.

(c) Talks with a view to achieving a political solution of the internal armed confrontation shall be held, on a date to be established by mutual agreement between the Government of Guatemala and the Unidad Revolucionaria Nacional Guatemalteca, between representatives—with decision-making powers—of the Government of the Republic, the Guatemalan Army and the General Command of the Unidad Revolucionaria Nacional Guatemalteca. The National Reconciliation Commission shall take part in these meetings for purposes of confirmation and verification, in accordance with the functions attributed to it under the Esquipulas II Agreement.

SIGNED in the city of Oslo this 30th day of March 1990.

For the delegation of the National Reconciliation Commission:
(*Signed*) Jorge SERRANO ELÍAS
(*Signed*) Mario PERMUTH
(*Signed*) Eduardo P. VILLATORO
　　　　　Executive Secretary of CNR

For the delegation of the Unidad Revolucionaria Nacional Guatemalteca:
(*Signed*) Luis BECKER GUZMÁN
(*Signed*) Francisco VILLAGRÁN M.
(*Signed*) Jorge E. ROSAL

Document 12

Letter dated 17 December 1990 from Costa Rica, El Salvador, Guatemala, Honduras and Nicaragua transmitting the Declaration of Puntarenas adopted by the Presidents of the five Central American countries and the Declaration on the Situation in El Salvador signed by the Presidents of Costa Rica, Guatemala, Honduras and Nicaragua

A/45/906-S/22032, 21 December 1990

We have the honour to transmit to you herewith the Declaration of Puntarenas (see annex), which was adopted on this date by the Presidents of the five Central American countries and to which is appended the Declaration on the situation in El Salvador, signed by the Presidents of Costa Rica, Guatemala, Honduras and Nicaragua. The President of the Republic of Panama participated as an invited observer.

We should be grateful if you would have the text of this note and its annex circulated as an official document of the General Assembly, under agenda item 28, and of the Security Council.

(*Signed*) Cristián TATTENBACH
　　　　　Permanent Representative
　　　　　Permanent Mission of Costa
　　　　　Rica to the United Nations

(*Signed*) Ricardo CASTAÑEDA CORNEJO
　　　　　Permanent Representative
　　　　　Permanent Mission of El Salvador
　　　　　to the United Nations

(*Signed*) Francisco VILLAGRÁN DE LEÓN
　　　　　Permanent Representative
　　　　　Permanent Mission of Guatemala
　　　　　to the United Nations

(*Signed*) Roberto FLORES BERMÚDEZ
　　　　　Permanent Representative
　　　　　Permanent Mission of Honduras
　　　　　to the United Nations

(*Signed*) Roberto MAYORGA CORTÉS
　　　　　Permanent Representative
　　　　　Permanent Mission of Nicaragua
　　　　　to the United Nations

Annex

Declaration of Puntarenas

The Central American Presidents, meeting in Puntarenas, Costa Rica, from 15 to 17 December 1990, and acting in accordance with the wishes of the peoples of the isthmus, declare Central America to be a region of peace, freedom, democracy and development. In this spirit, they reaffirm their commitment to the establishment of a firm and lasting peace in Central America; their decision to strengthen relations of friendship, cooperation and good-neighbourliness; and their determination to improve the democratic systems in the region through Governments which have been elected by universal, equal, free and secret suffrage in each of the countries.

They declare that it is imperative to incorporate the irregular forces into the political process and to do away with violence. They express their commitment to protecting, defending and promoting human rights. They reiterate their decision to bring about reconciliation in the divided Central American societies.

They recognize that peace in Central America is one, undivided and indivisible, and that any situation of violence, wherever it occurs, has a negative impact on the entire region. Consequently, the countries of the region are bound by a legitimate concern and a mutual, inescapable duty of solidarity in their efforts to do away with all violent action and terrorism and their undertaking to overcome extreme poverty and promote sustained development, as an expression of the basic interdependence and the common origin and destiny of the countries of the isthmus. Accordingly, they commit themselves to the establishment of a new model of regional security.

They recognize that there must be no delay in developing education for peace and establishing a new regional ecological order. They declare their joint commitment to the protection of the environment, recognizing the responsibility they share with the developed countries for its preservation.

They take note of the report submitted by the Ministers responsible for regional integration and development and welcome the progress made in implementing the Central American Economic Plan of Action (PAECA). Likewise, they decide to continue to promote the establishment of a new kind of Central American integration, the aim being to make the region into a stronger economic bloc that can be integrated successfully into the global economy, through such measures as the following: liberalizing regional and extra-regional trade; pursuing a regional policy on prices and the supply of agricultural products in order to guarantee food security in Central America; supporting the development of the productive sectors through modernization and conversion programmes, specific proposals for resolving the serious debt problem facing our countries, and regional action to eliminate discriminatory barriers to our exports in other countries.

On the basis of these common principles and purposes, the Presidents agree as follows:

1. Renewing their commitment to strengthening democratic institutions in the isthmus, they decide to request the international community and the relevant specialized agencies to increase cooperation aimed at enhancing the functioning of the various branches of government and, in particular, improving the administrative and judicial machinery guaranteeing the full observance of basic human rights.

They draw particular attention to their decision to promote and strengthen the full observance of human rights, and agree on the advisability of establishing regional programmes to publicize and provide education on human rights.

2. They express their profound satisfaction at the extent of the progress achieved in the negotiations being carried out by the Security Commission with a view to concluding a Central American agreement on security, verification and the control and limitation of weapons and military forces, despite the obstacle created by the persistence of armed actions by the irregular groups still operating in the region. They also express their approval of the work being done by the Security Commission on the establishment of measures of trust between the Central American States.

They underscore the advances made in such important matters as the establishment of inventories and factor charts, the deactivation of land mines or the disarming of civilians, in accordance with internal laws, and the prevention of incidents; and they acknowledge the cooperation being provided by the international community through the United Nations and the Organization of American States in political and material support of such work.

They instruct the Security Commission to fulfil as soon as possible the mandate conferred upon it in Antigua, Guatemala, with a view to the adoption of an agreement on security, verification and the control and limitation of weapons and military forces.

They uphold the firm determination of their Governments to continue to take whatever action is necessary to strengthen the decisions of the legitimately constituted civil authorities. They underscore the importance in this respect of enabling the armed forces and the security forces to take specific action to support the civil authorities in the implementation of social welfare and environmental protection projects.

In this context, the Presidents of Costa Rica, El

Salvador, Guatemala and Honduras praise the successful efforts of the Government of Nicaragua to effect the gradual reduction of its army, in the spirit of strengthening civil institutions and freeing resources for economic and social development.

3. They agree, in the light of the reports of the Executive Commission, to establish a committee to verify the political commitments entered into as part of the Esquipulas process. This committee shall be composed of five Central American citizens of recognized independence, suitability and prestige, to be appointed by the National Reconciliation Commissions. Within the next 60 days, each Commission shall inform its respective Government regarding the person it has selected to be a member of the committee. The Presidents also agree to request the Secretary-General of the Organization of American States, in consultation with the Executive Commission, to identify the areas in which technical support and advice are to be provided to the committee.

The Presidents of Costa Rica, El Salvador, Honduras and Nicaragua recognize the work done by the National Reconciliation Commission of Guatemala to develop a broad national dialogue aimed at reaching consensus agreements and proposals that will meet the aspirations of all sectors of society. In addition, they underscore its effectiveness in sponsoring, with the support of the Government of Guatemala, talks between the various sectors of Guatemalan society and the Unidad Revolucionaria Nacional Guatamalteca (URNG), in an attempt to persuade the latter to abandon armed struggle and be incorporated into the peaceful political pre ss.

4. The Presidents of Costa Rica, Guatemala, Honduras and Nicaragua have reviewed with the President of El Salvador the developments in the armed conflict in that country and the current status of the ongoing dialogue between the Government of El Salvador and the irregular armed force of the Frente Farabundo Martí para la Liberación Nacional.

In connection with the latest outbreak of hostilities, they are issuing the Declaration on the situation in El Salvador appended hereto.

The Presidents of Costa Rica, Guatemala, Honduras and Nicaragua, together with the President of El Salvador, reiterate their resolute support for the efforts being made by the United Nations Secretary-General on behalf of peace in El Salvador, and they express their firm hope that steps can shortly be agreed and taken under international supervision to ensure a cease-fire and its verification by United Nations observers and the establishment, as agreed, of machinery to guarantee the observance of human rights and bring about full national reconciliation in El Salvador.

5. They are following closely the action taken over the past year by the United Nations Observer Group in Central America (ONUCA) and underscore the positive contribution it has made to the current situation in the region. They express their satisfaction that Security Council resolution 675 (1990) has extended the mandate of ONUCA for six months.

They have carefully studied the recommendations made by the Security Commission at its latest meeting in Tegucigalpa, Honduras, aimed at strengthening and bringing up to date the organizational and operational structure of ONUCA and making the verification activities more effective. They agree to support the recommendations that relate to communication, investigation, detection and coordination, and they instruct the Executive Commission to initiate talks as soon as possible with the United Nations Secretariat with a view to the early adoption of the aforementioned recommendations and the establishment of an arrangement whereby the United Nations will keep the Executive Commission regularly informed about ONUCA activities.

6. In order that the continuing flows of returnees, displaced persons and refugees into individual countries of the region may receive proper attention, including protection and assistance, they urge that specific international support should be organized for the implementation of the proposals and projects submitted by the Governments which convened the first international meeting of the Follow-up Committee of the International Conference on Central American Refugees (CIREFCA), held at United Nations Headquarters, New York on 27 and 28 June 1990, and that the contributions pledged should be used as soon as possible to assist these groups of people.

7. They agree on the need to maintain and strengthen direct relations between the European Community and Central America, with the participation of the Group of Three, using the existing institutional forums.

They also express the hope that the forthcoming seventh meeting at San José, which is scheduled to be held at Managua on 18 and 19 March 1991, will mark an advance in the new stage of enhanced dialogue and cooperation between the two regions.

Underscoring the importance of their forthcoming meeting with the President of Mexico, Carlos Salinas de Gortari, they decide to take whatever steps are needed to strengthen the relations of the region with the United Mexican States and express the hope that agreements reflecting this goal can be signed at the meeting.

They express their firm conviction that the new initiatives towards cooperation in the region will complement the bilateral and multilateral programmes currently in effect and will help to expand cooperation in development and trade.

8. Aware that education and development are related, they reaffirm their decision to examine and meet the conspicuous needs that still exist in the region. Accordingly, they support the steps taken towards educational and cultural coordination in Central America aimed at expanding and strengthening pre-school education programmes, adopting strategies to broaden educational coverage, improve the quality of education, enhance the retention of pupils in schools and promote education, encouraging adult education programmes and policies and furthering education for peace, democracy, development, health and the environment.

They draw particular attention to the imperative need to eliminate illiteracy in the region, and to revise the educational curricula adapting them to the requirements of development and to the cultural conditions of the different sectors of the population.

9. Convinced that the current state of the region's natural resources and environment requires drastic action in terms of preservation, renewal and development, supported by the most emphatic political decisiveness, they recognize the work done by the Central American Commission on Environment and Development and decide to instruct it to identify, within 90 days, the measures needed to:

(a) Prepare a strategy for an "external debt for nature swap", with the aim of financing sustained development and environmental protection programmes, using as a starting-point the Americas Initiative and the commercial and bilateral debt of the Central American Bank for Economic Integration (BCIE). Such a strategy should envisage both the incurring of commercial debts and the write-off of institutional debts;

(b) Establish a regional inventory and a regional census of zones and species requiring special protection, and identify the protected areas to be given priority in border areas;

(c) Draw up a regional agreement setting out the commitment of the Central American Governments to the establishment of a system of protection for the zones and species that have been identified, to be submitted for consideration at the forthcoming Summit Meeting of the Central American Presidents;

(d) Work out, in coordination with the Executive Commission, a Central American position and strategy for the next World Conference on the Environment, to be held in Brazil in 1992;

(e) Participate actively in the negotiations being held within the United Nations system with a view to concluding international conventions on biological diversity and climatic change;

(f) Take practical steps to keep the Central American countries from becoming dumps for toxic waste and for substances harmful to the environment and to health, and to prevent the transit of such wastes and substances through the area, observing the stipulations of the Basel Convention on the subject;

(g) Ensure prompt and full application of the plan of action for forestry in Central America and the respective national plans in each country; and

(h) Devise machinery to establish national environment and development funds as well as a regional fund, and begin work on formulating a Central American agenda on the environment and development, in coordination with the national bodies dealing with the matter.

The Presidents of El Salvador, Guatemala, Honduras and Nicaragua share the conviction expressed by the President of Costa Rica, Rafael Angel Calderón Fournier, to the effect that concerted international action must be taken to confront the environmental challenges from a standpoint of respect for nature and solidarity and harmony with it. They enthusiastically give their support to the proclamation concerning a new ecological order of international cooperation, issued on 14 December 1990 by the President of Costa Rica, and they appeal to the international community to support with concrete action the initiatives set forth in that proclamation, because they are convinced that they constitute a basis for ensuring that human beings will enjoy their right to a liveable world.

10. In view of the threat which drug trafficking poses to the stability of the democratic institutions and the well-being of the Central American peoples, they resolve:

(a) To appeal to the international community to step up action to combat drug trafficking by means of technical and financial cooperation and to work effectively towards the adoption of a multilateral policy covering drug production, consumption, processing and trafficking, the control of chemical precursors and related financial offences;

(b) To emphasize the importance of improving the economic and social conditions of developing countries as a means of curtailing illicit drug production or trafficking in those countries, and to stress the need for the industrialized countries to take appropriate steps to eradicate the illicit consumption of drugs and to control the production and export of the chemical substances used in their processing;

(c) To take joint and coordinated action to prevent, control and eradicate drug trafficking, and to adopt all possible measures to enhance the effectiveness of the agreement on regional cooperation for the eradication of illicit traffic in drugs;

(d) To establish a Central American standing commission for the eradication of the production, consumption, trafficking and abuse of narcotic drugs and psychotropic substances and of related crimes, particularly money laundering and the legalization of other property, and to set up regional machinery for the exchange of information on this subject;

(e) To coordinate monitoring at borders and by customs with a view to averting illicit traffic in drugs;

(f) To draw up a regional educational programme to prevent illicit drug consumption and use;

(g) To instruct the appropriate bodies in each of the countries to carry out the actions enumerated, and to request support from the international community and the specialized agencies for the same purpose.

11. Convinced that it is necessary in the strictest respect for human rights, to regulate and organize migratory flows in, to and from the region, they agree to instruct the respective national authorities to take concerted action with a view to:

(a) Harmonizing legislation and systems relating to migration in the region;

(b) Eliminating visas in diplomatic and official passports, and establishing a multiple visa for merchants, businessmen, professionals and other categories of persons;

(c) Establishing a common format for passports and migrants' documents;

(d) Designing a Central American information system for migration control.

12. They express their support to the Central American Parliament in recognizing its potential value as a political forum which will strengthen the ongoing dialogue and the search for regional consensus. They urge the European Economic Community to make good its offer of assistance for the holding of parliamentary elections to those countries which require it.

13. They recognize and emphasize that the meetings of First Ladies of Central America, initiated in 1987, make an important and meaningful contribution to the peace process and to the development of the social and cultural agenda for the region in such major areas as assistance to children affected by armed violence in Central America, responsibility towards adolescent women, and the situation of women and families in the region. They accordingly instruct their Governments, subject to the coordinating role of the First Ladies, to adopt and implement wherever possible the conclusions and recommendations formulated at those meetings. At forthcoming summits, the First Ladies will play an active part in the consideration of the social agenda.

14. The Presidents of Costa Rica, El Salvador, Guatemala and Honduras express their belief that the economic and social problems of Nicaragua must be dealt with as a matter of urgency and in the spirit of generosity which the circumstances require, since otherwise there may be a serious deterioration in the democratic processes of that nation and in the stability of the region in general. In this regard, they consider that what is required in order to surmount those problems, in addition to the support provided by the Central American countries, which serves as an example, is a vast and effective programme of assistance by the international community.

15. They therefore instruct the Central American forum for consultations and coordination in external debt matters, consisting of the Ministers of the Treasury and the Presidents of the Central Banks of the countries of the region, to devise, by 31 March 1991 at the latest, an exceptional and realistic way of dealing with Nicaragua's interregional debt.

In the light of the above, they urge the international community to implement an emergency plan of an exceptional nature which would provide additional resources designed to effect immediate solutions to the problems which Nicaragua faces in the areas of external indebtedness and financing for the economic and social reconstruction of the country. They also request the Inter-American Development Bank and the World Bank to assume joint responsibility for coordinating and executing a programme to surmount the above-mentioned problems.

16. Considering the importance to the socio-economic development of the region of securing greater openness and effective participation in international trade, they instruct the Ministers responsible for regional integration and development to draw up a Central American policy of tariff and customs alignment which would be compatible with the policies for the regional development of external openness and to modernize the instruments used as its basis.

To enable the countries to achieve uniformity in a gradual, concurrent and concerted process, they set the following time-limits:

(a) 31 March 1991, for the establishment of the parameters of the negotiation;

(b) 31 May 1991, for the general tariff review and the entry into effect of the tariffs on which there is consensus;

(c) 31 December 1992, for the conclusion of the negotiations and the entry into effect of the uniform tariff;

(d) 31 December 1991, for the adoption of the tariff nomenclature known as the "harmonized system" and of the Central American Anti-Dumping Code.

They further instruct the Executive Council of the General Treaty of Central American Economic Integration to take any necessary steps to ensure that regional commitments pertaining to tariffs and customs are honoured.

17. In view of the urgent need for the Central

American countries to develop and transform the productive sectors, and as a complement to the tariff policy to be adopted, they instruct the Ministers responsible for regional integration and development, acting in coordination with the sectors concerned, to draw up within three months a regional programme for the conversion and modernization of the productive sectors, without prejudice to the actions being carried out at the national level. This programme shall be implemented from June 1991 onwards.

To this end, they appeal to the international financial institutions, especially the Inter-American Development Bank (BID), to provide the necessary support for the implementation of the programme.

18. They approve the proposed regional science and technology policy elaborated by the competent authorities and commission them to prepare the profile of an investment plan for the scientific and technological development of the productive sectors which is designed to strengthen those sectors' competitiveness and capacity for technological innovation and is in keeping with the regional programme for the conversion and modernization of the sectors and the regional tariff programme.

19. With a view to facilitating the exchange of basic agricultural products among the countries of the region and guaranteeing food security, they instruct the Ministers of Agriculture, acting in coordination with the Ministers responsible for regional integration and development and other competent authorities, to:

(a) Give priority, in the harmonization of agricultural policies, to the question of regional pricing and marketing of basic commodities, with a view to meeting fully consumer demand within the region;

(b) Take immediate action to design a system for the exchange of information on markets;

(c) Draw up regional policies on the administration of grants, the purchase and sale of products and inputs, concessional imports, and negotiations concerning surpluses and deficits of basic agricultural commodities.

Draft agreements in this area are to be submitted to the summit convened to deal principally with agricultural development.

20. Aware that external public debt has become a serious obstacle to the economic and social development of the Central American countries, is holding back efforts to achieve peace and democracy in the region and, furthermore, is a joint responsibility of debtors and creditors, urge that:

(a) The multilateral financial institutions, acting in concert with the competent authorities of the Central American countries, establish as a matter of urgency comprehensive machinery for rescheduling loans, reducing the effective level of payments and arranging terms compatible with the economic realities of the countries of the region; and modify the existing procedures for administering, approving and disbursing loans with a view to making them more flexible and expeditious;

(b) The creditor countries forgive a significant portion of the debt, the remainder to be refinanced on concessional terms, with payment in national currency, so that it can be used to finance projects designed to reduce poverty, generate foreign exchange and protect the environment.

They further instruct the Ministers responsible for regional integration and development, acting together with the competent authorities, to establish machinery for devising solutions to the problem of indebtedness among the countries of the region.

21. They express their support for the actions taken by the Ministers responsible for regional integration and development and by the Presidents of the Central Banks for the restructuring and revitalization of the Central American Economic Integration Bank (BCIE), with a view to its becoming the financial instrument required to reactivate the economies of the countries in the region, on the basis of the documents containing the country representatives' descriptions of the current situation and the outlook for BCIE (15 and 16 October and 11 December 1990, Washington, D.C.).

In reference to the foregoing, they urge the Inter-American Development Bank to finance the countries of the region so that they will be able to capitalize BCIE and make it financially sound.

22. They express their satisfaction with the entry into force of the new regional payments system, designed to give impetus to Central American regional trade. They undertake to operate it according to sound financial standards and are particularly grateful for the support which the European Economic Community (EEC) has provided for its functioning within the framework of the Community's cooperative relations with Central America.

23. They express their appreciation to the European Economic Community for the granting of special treatment under the generalized system of preferences (GSP) to four Latin American countries in support of their struggle against drug production and trafficking. As this decision places the Central American countries at a disadvantage, they urge EEC to extend, without delay, the same benefits as were granted to those nations to the products exported by the Central American countries.

They also instruct their Ministers for Foreign Affairs to make arrangements with EEC for the extension of those benefits to the Central American countries.

24. Considering that, within the framework of cooperation between EEC and the Central American isth-

mus, the banana has been recognized as important in the trade between the two regions and as vital to the economies of the area, they reiterate the urgency, as part of the negotiations being conducted in the current round of multilateral negotiations and the strategy for a single European market in 1992, that the banana be guaranteed exemption from import levies and quotas.

25. They reiterate their satisfaction at the Americas Initiative proposed by the President of the United States of America, George Bush. The source of high hopes for the economic development of Central America, the Americas Initiative advocates a system of free trade, the promotion of investments in the region and the adoption of debt conversion arrangements designed to foster environmental protection.

In this connection, they urge the Congress of the United States of America to support the Initiative.

At the same time, they instruct the competent authorities of their countries to establish machinery for consultations and coordination for the purpose of signing with the United States of America a treaty on fair trade with the region, stimulating greater flows of investment to Central America and developing environmental impact projects. The foregoing is without prejudice to activities promoted by individual countries.

26. They welcome the proposal to establish the Association for Democracy and Development in Central America (ADD), which would serve as a forum for strengthening peace and democracy and contributing to the economic development of Central America.

They believe that Central America's leading role in the Association is of vital importance and that the management of such an Association must be broadly based, as evidenced by standards of equality and the equitable representation of all its participants.

They instruct the Executive Commission, composed of Ministers for Foreign Affairs, and the Ministers responsible for regional integration and development to work together in adopting measures and making arrangements for the establishment of ADD.

In order for this initiative to be effective and designed to fulfil the above-mentioned purposes, they urge the Inter-American Development Bank to coordinate the work of a regional consultative group, with the participation of international organizations, cooperation agencies and donor countries, whose purpose would be to support the Central American countries in establishing conditions which would facilitate the attainment of common social, political and economic goals.

27. They express their satisfaction at the intention of Colombia, Mexico and Venezuela to launch national and regional projects which would identify and develop new sources of energy, thereby helping to reduce the Central American countries' dependency on oil, which is particularly heavy in times of crisis.

28. They express their appreciation for the resolution adopted by the General Assembly of the United Nations to extend the Special Plan of Economic Cooperation (PEC) for another three years. They also urge the Governing Council of the United Nations Development Programme to approve the request submitted by the region and to grant the amount sought, which would enable PEC to continue functioning as a fundamental source of support for the development of the area, with a view to enhancing the effectiveness of funded programmes and deepening relations between the Plan and the isthmus countries. In order to give economic and technical substance to the priorities of PAECA, they reiterate their appeal that the secretariat of PAECA should be established in a country of the region.

29. They welcome the favourable treatment granted by the friendly nations of Mexico and Venezuela in the matter of the payment of oil bills by Central American countries and express their hope that the relations thus far established in the current economic context of the oil crisis be consolidated in lasting ties of cooperation, promotion of investments and increased trade.

30. They recognize the importance of the recent establishment of the Mexican Commission for Cooperation with Central America both to integration efforts and to the implementation of measures for the strengthening of trade relations between Mexico and Central America.

31. They recognize the progress achieved in the implementation of PAECA, according to the report submitted to the Ministers responsible for regional integration and development, including: an analysis of the legal framework for integration by the Commission of Jurists; the entry into force of the regional payments system; some important preliminary steps towards the signing of an interim multilateral free trade agreement between Honduras and the other countries of the region; the launching of physical infrastructure programmes; the streamlining of regional transport and customs procedures; the harmonization of regional policies in priority areas of the agricultural sector; the elaboration of a proposal on the regional policy and programme for science and technology; and progress regarding the environment and development.

32. They instruct the Ministers responsible for regional integration and development, acting in compliance with the provisions of PAECA and working together with the competent authorities, to complete the following tasks no later than 31 December 1991:

(a) Formulation of a regional tourism policy, based on the development of the natural and cultural heritage;

(b) Study of the feasibility of a flexible air space policy based on negotiation;

(c) Elaboration of a plan for the regional development of fisheries;

(d) Review and adjustment of the mechanisms for achieving the free movement of cultural property in the region;

(e) Adoption of a regional programme for the development of the productive sectors of society;

(f) Adoption of a regional housing and human settlements programme;

(g) Development of a programme for airport facilities.

They are grateful for the active participation of all sectors and organizations involved in PAECA and urge the competent authorities to pursue their efforts to implement PAECA and this Declaration.

33. In view of the importance of the institutional and legal basis of Central American integration, they instruct the Ministers concerned to submit to this forum at the next summit a proposal for a basic regulatory framework which would legitimize and guarantee the legal security required to strengthen the integration process.

34. With the aim of enhancing the presence of Central American countries in international organizations and of heightening the importance of the regional group within those organizations, they agree to establish machinery for coordinating votes and candidacies, based on a strict rotation system in putting forward nominations for offices, posts, venues and membership in bodies of the inter-American system and the United Nations system, including agencies and specialized agencies. In this connection, they instruct the Executive Commission and the Ministers responsible for regional integration and development to set up the above-mentioned machinery.

35. They reaffirm the mandate whereby the various forums already established are to regulate, promote and facilitate the implementation of the agreements, as well as to carry out their principal function which is to verify, control and follow up all commitments set forth in the Guatemala Procedure and subsequent Declarations.

They further agree to the following additional institutional arrangements, designed to systematize and strengthen the organization and coordination of summits:

(a) Presidential meetings shall take place semi-annually in the months of June and December. They will be preceded by a preparatory meeting of the Executive Commission and the Ministers responsible for regional integration and development, which shall be attended by Ministers and authorities responsible for other areas of government, as required in order to prepare summit agendas;

(b) The host country of the summit shall act as secretariat thereof through its Ministry of Foreign Affairs

during the six months following the summit, in order to facilitate the analysis and dissemination of documents and relations with third countries and international organizations. In this connection, the host country shall be the spokesman for Central America during the corresponding six-month period.

Future host countries, by rotation, shall be as follows:

January-June 1991 ... Costa Rica
July-December 1991 ... El Salvador
January-June 1992 ... Honduras
July-December 1992 ... Nicaragua
January-June 1993 ... Guatemala

(c) The secretariat of the summit shall transmit the reports, conclusions and recommendations of the summits to the appropriate forums and to the Executive Commission for the Proceedure, with a view to ensuring effective and coordinated action thereon.

36. They welcome the proposal put forward by the Rio Group at its last meeting, held at Caracas, Venezuela, that Central America should participate in the Permanent Mechanism for Consultation and Concerted Political Action and agree to send their representatives in accordance with the order of rotation established.

37. They reaffirm their gratitude for the efforts and progress made by the Government of the Republic of Panama in the domestic consultative process taking place there, with a view to determining whether it should strengthen its economic ties with the Central American isthmus.

They also welcome with deep satisfaction the clear statements by the Government of Panama that it will participate to a greater extent in the Central American political and economic forums and strengthen its ties with regional organizations.

38. Recognizing the significant support given to the cause of peace and international *détente* by the President of the Union of Soviet Socialist Republics, Mikhail Gorbachev, recipient of the 1990 Nobel Peace Prize, and in the conviction that his visit to Central America would help to highlight the importance of the cause of peace and democracy in the region and strongly promote it, they agreed to invite him to pay an offical visit to Central America.

39. The Presidents of Costa Rica, El Salvador, Honduras and Nicaragua, in view of the fact that the term of the President of Guatemala, Marco Vinicio Cerezo Arevalo is drawing to a close, express their gratitude for the fundamental role he has played in favour of regional peace and emphasize that it was his initiative which brought together the five Central American leaders in Esquipulas. They are grateful for his constant devotion and efforts throughout the process of Esquipulas II,

whose importance in the attainment of the agreed objectives is such that Central Americans today can look forward to the prospect of achieving firm and lasting peace in the region.

40. Aware of the fundamental role of farming, forestry and cattle-raising activities in the economic and social life of the Central American countries, and convinced of the need to stimulate their development in every way, they agree that a forthcoming summit will be devoted primarily to the agricultural sector.

41. They agree to meet again during the first half of 1991 in the Republic of El Salvador.

42. The Presidents of El Salvador, Guatemala, Honduras, Nicaragua and Panama express their profound appreciation to the President of Costa Rica, Rafael Angel Calderón Fournier, and to the Costa Rican Government and people for the hospitality and kindness, which significantly contributed to the success of the meeting.

Puntarenas, 17 December 1990

(*Signed*) Rafael Angel CALDERÓN FOURNIER
President of the Republic of Costa Rica

(*Signed*) Marco Vinicio CEREZO ARÉVALO
President of the Republic of Guatemala

(*Signed*) Alfredo CRISTIANI BURKARD
President of the Republic of El Salvador

(*Signed*) Rafael Leonardo CALLEJAS ROMERO
President of the Republic of Honduras

(*Signed*) Violeta BARRIOS DE CHAMORRO
President of the Republic of Nicaragua

As invited Observer:
(*Signed*) Guillermo ENDARA GALIMANY
President of the Republic of Panama

Appendix

Declaration on the situation in El Salvador

The Presidents of Costa Rica, Guatemala, Honduras and Nicaragua, together recognizing the current difficult situation in the fraternal Republic of El Salvador, recently exacerbated by the actions of FMLN, which have affected the civilian population and led to a qualitative escalation of the armed conflict in that country, as a result of the use by the aforementioned irregular force of sophisticated and highly destructive weapons,

Recalling the commitments entered into by the Central American Governments in the context of the Esquipulas process concerning an appeal for an end to hostilities and national reconciliation, whereby they are to: "make dialogue prevail over violence and reason over hatred"; "... initiate a dialogue with all the domestic political opposition groups which have laid down their arms and those which have availed themselves of the amnesty"; and "... take all necessary steps, in accordance with the constitution, to bring about a genuine cease-fire",

Acknowledging once again the efforts made since 1 June 1989 by the President of El Salvador, Alfredo Cristiani, with a view to ending the country's armed conflict by means of dialogue with FMLN, in order that the members of that irregular armed group may be fully incorporated into peaceful and democratic life,

Reiterating that peace, freedom, democracy and development must be based on respect for the constitutional juridical order, which may be amended only by established lawful means and by legitimate constituted authorities, representing as they do the sovereign will of the people freely expressed through the ballot-boxes,

Reaffirming the need for peace to be achieved by means of reconciliation and lasting stability throughout Central America, in order to permit the economic and social development sought by our peoples, at a time when such reconciliation and stability are obstructed by the existence of conflicts in some countries of the region, and particularly by the situation prevailing in El Salvador,

Bearing in mind that the process of dialogue to achieve peace between the Government of El Salvador and FMLN has been obstructed by persistent acts of violence on the part of FMLN,

Recalling the Declaration of San Isidro de Coronado, which included a decision, with a view to involving the international community as represented by the Secretary-General of the United Nations, to invite the Secretary-General to take the necessary steps to ensure the resumption of the dialogue between the Government of El Salvador and FMLN, thereby facilitating its successful continuation,

Emphasizing and acknowledging the valuable contribution of Mr. Javier Pérez de Cuéllar, Secretary-General of the United Nations, under whose auspices the Geneva Agreement of 4 April 1990 was signed, thus permitting the resumption of the El Salvador peace process, in which both parties assured him that there was "a serious intention and good faith" to seek a definitive settlement of the armed conflict through negotiations,

Drawing attention to the constructive position of the Government of El Salvador in accepting a wide-ranging and serious discussion of all items making up the agenda for that process, including the Salvadorian armed forces, whose existence is governed by the Constitution of that Republic,

Noting that the attitude of FMLN in the dialogue with the Government of El Salvador has made it more difficult to achieve a rapid solution of the armed conflict and that its new offensive constitutes a violation of the Agreement on Human Rights signed at San José, Costa Rica, on 26 July 1990, which includes a commitment to "... avoid any act or practice which constitutes an attempt upon the life, integrity, security or freedom of the individual",

Hereby agree:

1. *To support* the desire for peace, democracy and reconciliation of the fraternal Salvadorian people, as repeatedly expressed in recent years in honest and pluralistic electoral processes;

2. *To acknowledge* the political will of the constitutional Government of El Salvador and its determination to comply with the commitments to peace and democracy into which it entered under the "Procedure for the establishment of a firm and lasting peace in Central America", Esquipulas II and subsequent declarations, particularly those adopted at Tela and San Isidro de Coronado;

3. *To reaffirm* their decisive support for the constitutional President of El Salvador, Alfredo Cristiani, in his repeated and continuous efforts to achieve peace through the peaceful procedures of dialogue and negotiation;

4. *To reiterate* the need for immediate and effective compliance with the Agreement on Human Rights and, in that context, to applaud the firm stand taken by President Alfredo Cristiani;

5. *To acknowledge and emphasize* the valuable steps taken by the Secretary-General of the United Nations with a view to achieving a peaceful solution of the Salvadorian conflict, which threatens the peace and stability of the entire Central American region;

6. *To condemn* the acts of violence carried out by FMLN, which have caused anguish and death among the Salvadorian civilian population and inflicted serious damage on that country's economic infrastructure;

7. *To insist* that FMLN immediately halt its use of sophisticated weapons such as those employed in the recent offensive, and to call on the United Nations Observer Group in Central America (ONUCA) to carry out, as soon as possible, the necessary investigations to identify the origin of those weapons;

8. *To demand* that FMLN observe an immediate and effective cease-fire, display its political will to enter, at the earliest opportunity, into agreements permitting the achievement of a firm and lasting peace in the region, refrain from obstructing the elections, abandon the armed struggle and join the democratic process;

Call upon all peoples and Governments of the world:

1. *To give their firm and decisive support* to this initiative of the Central American Governments, which is a legitimate expression of the will of its peoples;

2. *To assist* in persuading FMLN of the vital need to negotiate and take advantage of the desire for dialogue displayed by the Salvadorian Government with a view to achieving peace;

3. *To help*, as a means of promoting the process of bringing about a peaceful settlement of the conflict, to end all military, economic, logistical and publicity assistance which is still available to FMLN in various parts of the world;

And undertake, for their part:

1. *To support*, through their actions, the negotiations being held under the auspices of the Secretary-General of the United Nations;

2. *To constitute themselves* as a mechanism to follow up the process of negotiations between the Government and FMLN, with a view to promoting and contributing to the objectives proposed for the achievement of a peaceful and democratic solution in El Salvador, in accordance with the commitments entered into by the various parties;

3. *To request*, both directly and through Central American diplomatic missions, support for this initiative from the Secretary-General of the United Nations and the Security Council and the Secretary-General and the Permanent Council of the Organization of American States and to call upon Governments, churches and bodies of other sorts to provide it with political and material support;

4. *To promote*, in support of this peace process, an intensive joint coordinated campaign of diplomatic activity directed toward the international community, and particularly towards those Governments which have links with and interests in the Salvadorian conflict;

5. *To instruct* the Ministers for Foreign Affairs to agree promptly on the measures and steps to be taken in order to attain the objectives herein defined.

In conclusion, the Presidents agree on the vital need to put an immediate end to this conflict, whose continuation can only bring more grief to the Central American people.

(*Signed*) Rafael Angel CALDERÓN FOURNIER
President
Republic of Costa Rica

(*Signed*) Rafael Leonardo CALLEJAS
President
Republic of Honduras

(*Signed*) Marco Vinicio CEREZO ARÉVALO
President
Republic of Guatemala

(*Signed*) Violeta BARRIOS DE CHAMORRO
President
Republic of Nicaragua

Document 13

Report of the Secretary-General on efforts towards a negotiated political solution to the conflict in El Salvador

S/22031, 21 December 1990

1. The present report is submitted in pursuance of Security Council resolution 637 (1989). Its purpose is to give the Council an up-to-date account of my efforts to promote the achievement of a negotiated political solution to the conflict in El Salvador.

2. In my previous report to the General Assembly and to the Security Council of 8 November 1990, 1/ I reported on the agreements between the Government of El Salvador and the Frente Farabundo Martí para la Liberación Nacional (FMLN) arrived at, under my auspices, at Geneva on 4 April 1990, on the framework for the negotiations, and in Caracas on 21 May 1990, on the agenda and calendar of the negotiating process. 2/ I also referred to the agreement on human rights 3/ reached at San José, Costa Rica, on 26 July 1990, between the Government of El Salvador and FMLN, which contains detailed commitments to guarantee unrestricted respect for human rights in El Salvador, and which provides for the establishment of a United Nations verification mission under a Director appointed by the Secretary-General and with such verification personnel as might be necessary.

3. Since then, several direct meetings have been held between representatives of the Government and of FMLN, with the participation of my Representative, and my Representative has made frequent trips to meet with President Cristiani and senior commanders of FMLN. He has also been in contact on numerous occasions with leaders and representatives of a wide array of political parties, social organizations and religious leaders in El Salvador. For my part, I met this fall with President Cristiani, as well as with a high-level delegation of FMLN. The question of El Salvador has been addressed frequently in my meetings with leaders of Member States who are in a position to assist in my efforts, as envisaged in the Geneva Agreement.

4. As pointed out in my report to the General Assembly, 1/ while significant progress has been accomplished to date, as exemplified by the San José Agreement on Human Rights, it is fair to say that considerable problems have been encountered in reaching agreement on armed forces, the most sensitive and complex issue on the agenda. Given the pervasive character of this question, it has not been possible to make substantive progress on other items. Conscious of the need to reinvigorate the negotiating process, the two parties, with the participation of my Representative, agreed on 31 October 1990 at a direct meeting held at Mexico City to make adjustments in the mechanics of the negotiations, laying greater emphasis on the active role of my Representative and on the confidential nature of the process. While procedural improvements by themselves will not solve the remaining problems, whose magnitude must not be underestimated, I am persuaded that, given the necessary political will, coupled with support from outside Powers in a position to assist me in my efforts, the goal of peace in El Salvador can be achieved in the not too distant future.

5. I now wish to refer to my statement, made in informal consultations on 3 August 1990, the full text of which is annexed hereto, as well as to the letter that I addressed to the President of the Security Council on 29 August 1990 4/ and to his reply of 6 September 1990, 5/ which, *inter alia*, dealt with the verification tasks envisaged for the United Nations under the Geneva and Caracas agreements.

6. It will be recalled that, having regard to the complex and interrelated character of the tasks involved, I had put to the members of the Council the concept of an integrated operation to ensure proper coordination of operations on the ground and the rational use of resources, bearing in mind recent experience in undertakings of similar scale and complexity. In his letter dated 6 September 1990, 5/ the President of the Security Council conveyed to me the Council's concurrence with this concept.

7. The Caracas accord envisaged a series of synchronized agreements, and the verification mechanism under the San José Agreement was intended to enter into effect upon the cessation of the armed conflict. However, both parties have since signified their desire to have the human rights mechanism in place as soon as possible without waiting for other agreements to be concluded. I should emphasize that such a desire is in keeping with the objectives laid down in the Esquipulas II Agreement, 6/ which have received the endorsement of the Security Council in resolution 637 (1989), with its emphasis on democratization and respect for human rights as key components of the peace process. At the same time, the importance of international verification of Central

1/ A/45/706-S/21931.
2/ Ibid., annexes I and II.
3/ A/44/971-S/21541.
4/ S/21717.
5/ S/21718.
6/ A/42/541-S/19085, annex.

American peace agreements has been underlined by the Central American Governments as well as in successive resolutions adopted by the General Assembly. At their recent meeting in Puntarenas, Costa Rica, the five Central American Presidents urged me to deploy the human rights verification mission without delay. Reference should be made in this respect to resolution 45/15, in which the General Assembly requested me to "continue to afford the fullest possible support to the Central American Governments in their efforts to consolidate peace, especially by taking the measures necessary for the maintenance, establishment and effective functioning of the appropriate verification machinery".

8. I wish therefore to inform the Council of my intention shortly to request authorization to establish a United Nations Observer Mission in El Salvador, hereinafter referred to as ONUSAL, with the task of monitoring agreements concluded between the Government of El Salvador and FMLN. Pending the conclusion of other agreements, I would recommend that, as a first step towards establishing this integrated operation, the human rights verification component of ONUSAL be established as soon as the necessary preparations have been made on the ground and, in particular, the extent to which the tasks of the Mission can be conducted in the absence of a cease-fire has been determined; the personnel required for such a complex operation, for which no precedent exists in the annals of the United Nations, has been recruited; and satisfactory arrangements have been worked out with the Government and with FMLN to ensure the safe deployment and effective functioning of ONUSAL. I shall be dispatching to El Salvador, as early as practicable in 1991, a technical mission in order to assist me in preparing an operational plan for submission to the Council. Given the difficulty of the preparatory work involved and the positive contribution that the deployment of this mission is likely to make towards the achievement of the goals of the negotiating process as well as to the improvement of the human rights situation in El Salvador, I shall, when the time comes, urge the Council to take early action on my recommendation.

9. As regards the observation of the process leading up to the legislative and municipal elections in March 1991, members of the Council will note that the Geneva accord refers to verification by the United Nations of agreements reached between the Government of El Salvador and FMLN. No agreement at present exists between the parties for observation of the March 1991 elections by the United Nations. Under the circumstances, I am not in a position to recommend at this time that it be carried out. I should mention in passing that it is my understanding that the Organization of American States has decided to undertake the observation of the elections,

although the criteria involved are different from those that apply for the United Nations.

10. I shall, at the appropriate time, seek the Council's authorization for the deployment of the other components of ONUSAL to cover verification of other political agreements that might be arrived at, as well as of a cease-fire, in keeping with the concept of a single, integrated operation in El Salvador as outlined by me at the Council's informal consultations on 3 August 1990 and reiterated in my letter of 29 August. 4/

11. Meanwhile I have taken steps to establish the preparatory office in El Salvador referred to in my 29 August letter, with which the Council has already concurred. The preparatory office is concentrating in particular on planning human rights verification activities, preparing procedures, establishing contacts with government agencies and non-governmental organizations and carrying out a public information programme.

Annex

Statement made by the Secretary-General in informal consultations on 3 August 1990

I wish to inform the members of the Security Council about progress made to date in relation to El Salvador.

You will recall that, on 4 April 1990, representatives of the Government of El Salvador and the Frente Farabundo Martí para la Liberación Nacional (FMLN) signed at Geneva, in my presence, an agreement to launch a negotiating process under my auspices in order to "end the armed conflict through political means as speedily as possible, promote the democratization of the country, guarantee unrestricted respect for human rights and reunify Salvadorian society".

Pursuant to the Agreement arrived at in Geneva, intensive efforts have been conducted, including three rounds of direct talks between representatives of the Government and of FMLN, with the active participation of my Representative, Mr. Alvaro de Soto, at Caracas from 16 to 21 May 1990, at Oaxtepec, Mexico, from 19 to 25 June 1990, and most recently at San José, Costa Rica, from 20 to 26 July 1990. Between the rounds of direct talks, in accordance with the Geneva Agreement, my Representative is in frequent communication with both sides, travelling to the region to meet with President Cristiani and members of the High Command of FMLN. Also, the Government and FMLN consult during these periods with Salvadorian political parties and social organizations. When my Representative visits San Salvador, he also meets with leaders of political parties and social organizations.

In the May round of talks at Caracas a general agenda and schedule for the negotiating process were agreed upon.

As had been agreed in Geneva, the initial objective of the process will be "to achieve political agreements for a halt to the armed confrontation and any acts that infringe the rights of the civilian population, which will have to be verified by the United Nations, subject to the approval of the Security Council".

The issues on which such political agreements need to be reached relate to the following:

(a) Armed forces;
(b) Human rights;
(c) Judicial system;
(d) Electoral system;
(e) Constitutional reform;
(f) Economic and social issues;
(g) Verification by the United Nations.

As agreed in the schedule, the Government and FMLN began to address the substantive issues on the agenda at the June meeting in Mexico, where the armed forces issue was addressed in depth, and human rights were discussed in a preliminary fashion.

At their recent meeting in San José, the Government and FMLN took up the armed forces question once again, but were not able to reach agreement.

Turning to human rights, the parties were able to agree on a text that contains detailed commitments to guarantee unrestricted respect for human rights in El Salvador, and that provides for the establishment of a United Nations verification mission under a Director appointed by the Secretary-General and with such verification personnel as may be necessary. The mission is to be given powers to take whatever legally permissible action it may deem appropriate for promoting and protecting human rights, as part of the intention to promote respect for and guarantee of such rights in El Salvador and to contribute towards improving those situations in which such respect and guarantee are not duly observed.

The text on human rights constitutes the first substantive achievement of the negotiating process. As stipulated in a footnote on the first page of the text, its implementation is subject to the package of political agreements to be negotiated for the achievement of the initial objective envisaged in the Agreement signed at Geneva, to which I referred earlier. I should therefore make it clear that I am not at present faced with a formal request to set up such a mission, nor am I at this stage making such a proposal to the Council.

At Caracas, the Government and FMLN had agreed that the initial objective should be achieved by the middle of September 1990, provided that the parties reach synchronized agreements with schedules for implementation, subject to verification as appropriate, so as to ensure that all the components of the initial objective are duly coordinated. It was also stated on that occasion that an additional advantage of that date was that it would help to ensure that the process leading to the legislative and municipal elections of March 1991 is conducted in an atmosphere of tranquillity, broad participation and freedom from intimidation.

Given the complexity and the pace of the negotiating process, it is not certain that it will be possible to meet the mid-September target date. Indeed, it is not possible to guarantee success at all. None the less, I wish to lay before the members of the Security Council the elements that are likely to be included in a proposal flowing from the targeted set of agreements and to say a few words about the way in which I would propose that the tasks be implemented. In this context, I remain most mindful of the fact that in resolution 637 (1989), the Security Council lent me its full support to continue my mission of good offices in consultation with the Security Council in support of the Central American Governments in their effort to achieve the goals set forth in the Guatemala Agreement, a/ and that in resolution 654 (1990), it specifically welcomed my efforts to promote the achievement of a negotiated political solution to the conflict in El Salvador.

Responsibilities devolving upon the United Nations as a result of the achievement of the initial objective established in the Geneva Agreement are likely to be considerable and to some extent innovative. If current trends continue, they would, in all probability, include the verification of a cease-fire, the monitoring of the electoral process and the verification of respect for human rights as described earlier. While the pending negotiations on the other points under discussion must be awaited, these tasks are being cast as essential and inseparable components of the peaceful solution to the Salvadorian conflict. They all fall clearly under the umbrella of the Guatemala Agreement of August 1987, which lays down the basis for the peace process in Central America and which received the endorsement of the Security Council.

These considerations, the need to ensure proper coordination of operations on the ground and to use resources rationally, as well as recent experience in undertakings of similar scale and complexity, lead me even at this stage to conclude that the operation would most appropriately be carried out as an integrated whole under the authority of the Security Council rather than as separate enterprises. It is against this background that I would be making proposals to the Council when the time comes and that I intend soon to send a technical mission to El Salvador to assess personnel and infrastructure needs on the ground.

Finally, I wish to inform you that the next round of direct talks will take place from 17 to 22 August at San José. My Representative will be in the region next week.

a/ A/42/521-S/19085.

Document 14

Letter dated 8 January 1991 from the Secretary-General to President Cristiani concerning United Nations observation of the March 1991 elections in El Salvador

Not issued as a United Nations document; original in Spanish

I have the honour to refer to the request that you made in your address to the General Assembly on 1 October 1990 that the United Nations should mount an operation to observe the process leading to the legislative and municipal elections to take place in March 1991.

You will have read the report that I submitted to the Security Council on 21 December 1990 on the action I have taken to promote the achievement of a negotiated political solution to the conflict in El Salvador, in which I refer, in paragraph 9, to the issue of electoral observation. The report, which is attached to this letter, is self-explanatory. However, in view of the keen interest you have shown in the conduct of such an observation, expressed recently by Minister Oscar Santamaría to my representative, Alvaro de Soto, I should like to make a few more points in order to familiarize you with United Nations principles and practice in this area. To this end, I am transmitting to you herewith a copy of my annual report on the work of the Organization, submitted to the General Assembly in September 1990, in which I discuss the type of action in question in some detail (chap. III).

The relevant United Nations principles are based on Article 2, paragraph 7, of the Charter of the United Nations, which specifies that the Organization may not intervene in matters which are essentially within the domestic jurisdiction of any State. I realize that in requesting the United Nations to observe the electoral process, which clearly falls within the domestic jurisdiction of El Salvador, your Government is indicating that it has no objection to the United Nations carrying out such an operation. However, that is not sufficient to enable the United Nations to do so without violating the article in question, since it is also necessary for one of the major organs duly empowered to do so—the General Assembly or the Security Council—to take a decision to that effect.

In view of these conclusions, it is not the practice of the United Nations to observe elections; quite the contrary. Normally, in instances where a Member State requests the United Nations to observe its elections, we decline to do so. The possibility of departing from that practice was seriously discussed for the first time precisely in the case of Nicaragua, because that country posed a problem that was placed clearly and unmistakably in the context of the Central American peace process, and the international dimension of the electoral contest was thus clearly established. There was an opportunity to observe the process from the outset and throughout the country without any significant restrictions. Furthermore, all Nicaraguan political players were in favour of the elections and of their observation by the United Nations. Lastly—and this is a very important point—the elections clearly offered a historic opportunity to facilitate the establishment of the necessary conditions for bringing the conflict in Nicaragua to an end and leading the way to a new era of peace and reconstruction.

Armed with these arguments, I proceeded to hold broad consultations with States Members of the United Nations, and it was only once I had ascertained that I had broad support for such an innovative step that we played an active role in the preparation of electoral rules and negotiated with the Electoral Council, the political parties and the Nicaraguan resistance the best conditions for satisfactorily carrying out the task in question. Even so, we were able to start observation at the stage of the registration campaign. I received broad support from the General Assembly for the action I took, and the elections and their observation by the United Nations were an unquestionably major success at that time of transition in Nicaragua.

More recently the United Nations received a request from Haiti to observe the electoral process in that country. In this case the international dimension of the contest was not as clear as in the case of Nicaragua, although it was indeed clear that the contest could play a decisive role in enabling Haiti to break out of the very grim pattern of the past. It was in the light of these very special circumstances and only after an anguishing process of hesitation and deliberation that the decision was taken by Member States that the United Nations should observe the elections.

In the past 12 months the United Nations has received three specific requests from Member States, including a Central American country, to observe their elections, and in all three cases we have declined to do so, which shows that there has been no departure from normal United Nations practice. I wish to stress that the cases of Nicaragua and Haiti were exceptions.

In the case of El Salvador, even if the obstacle to which I refer in my recent report to the Security Council did not exist—namely, the lack of an agreement in the context of the negotiation process begun on the basis of the Geneva agreement of 4 April 1990, it is not clear that the requirements referred to in my most recent annual report are met.

It was in the light of the foregoing that I decided to make the reference to the issue of electoral observation in my report to the Security Council. You will note that in the report I confined myself to invoking the technical grounds for the lack of agreement on this point in the context of the peace negotiations. I did so deliberately, in order to avoid triggering a debate within the United Nations on whether or not the requirements for electoral observation were met. I have chosen instead to set out in this private letter my reasons for believing that it would not be appropriate for you to maintain your request for observation in your country during the electoral process now under way.

Accept, Sir, the assurances of my highest consideration.

(Signed) Javier PÉREZ DE CUÉLLAR

Document 15

Letter dated 12 April 1991 from the Secretary-General to President Cristiani concerning constitutional reforms

Not issued as a United Nations document; original in Spanish

I am writing to you in order to express my deep concern about the status of the negotiations currently taking place in Mexico between your Government and the Farabundo Martí National Liberation Front (FMLN). I believe that the new accelerated scheme of negotiations provides an unprecedented opportunity to establish an essentially irreversible cease-fire in the near future, but this will require decisions whose difficulty I do not by any means underestimate. I also believe that if this opportunity is not seized, the conflict in El Salvador may flare up again and continue indefinitely, and the negotiations may be delayed in a manner unacceptable to the Salvadorian people and the international community.

At the beginning of the current round, on 4 April, my representative explained to both parties our view concerning the prospects for an agreement at this stage of the negotiations, bearing in mind that the terms of the current legislature will end on 30 April. That view consisted in four elements relating to the three subjects proposed as the agenda for the accelerated negotiations:

(a) A political agreement on the subject of armed forces;

(b) An agreement on the ending of the armed confrontation under United Nations supervision;

(c) Specific agreements on constitutional reforms which will be recommended during the current term of the legislature; and

(d) A reform of Article 248 of the Constitution which would be recommended during the current term of the legislature, with a view to making possible the approval at an early date of those reforms that may remain to be negotiated, and in any case during a single legislative term, in the second stage of the process.

Needless to say, a timetable for the implementation of the above-described agreements would also have to be negotiated.

The foregoing view is, of course, the result of the consultations we have been conducting with the parties and of careful prior preparation, and it represents our considered opinion with regard to what appears to be feasible in the present circumstances. This was made clear to the parties on 4 April, the day on which the current round began, with a view not to obtaining a formal agreement but to establishing understandings through which the details could, in so far as possible, be negotiated within a tentatively agreed framework. Although there was no agreement in the proper sense with regard to this framework, my representative gained from his consultations the clear impression that, in general terms and subject to negotiation of the specific content of each of the four areas and the relevant timetable, the framework seemed realistic and possible.

On the morning of 5 April, at the hour for which a face-to-face meeting between the parties had been scheduled with the consent of both, with a view to taking up the subject of the constitutional reform (and when the other party's delegation was already present in the meeting room), the Government's Negotiating Commission asked to see my representative privately and informed him, upon your instructions, that it was not prepared to agree with FMLN on a reform of Article 248 of the Constitution and to recommend it for adoption in the Legislative Assembly during the current term.

My representative said to the Government's Negotiating Commission that, in his view, this new attitude fundamentally altered the previously described scheme, which was based, among other considerations, on the Government's acceptance of the possibility of considering a reform of Article 248 if it proved impossible to negotiate a satisfactory package of specific reforms in time to have them dealt with during the current legislative term. Thereafter, my representative spoke with you on the subject at some length, so that I know you are aware of my concern.

My representative informed me of your reasons for giving such instructions to your Negotiating Commission, and I realize the internal campaign you are facing on this subject. This being said, we have always known that a certain sector in your country still remains to be convinced of the need for a negotiated political solution to the conflict, and it is not surprising that as the time for definitions approaches, that sector should launch a campaign which I would almost go so far as to call intimidating.

I am also aware, from the information I have been receiving from El Salvador and Mexico, of the juridical and political arguments that have been advanced for and against a reform of Article 248.

Notwithstanding all these considerations, in view of the importance of this element within the indivisible set of agreements that must be achieved in order to ensure success in the current stage of the negotiations and to make possible the establishment of a cease-fire in El Salvador in the near future, I believe that one consideration is being lost from sight amid this debate, namely, that we are working in the abstract, that is to say, without knowing what reforms are being negotiated. You are certainly the one who fixes the position of your Negotiating Commission, and you know to what extent you are prepared to make concessions, but we cannot dismiss the possibility that there will be changes, perhaps significant ones, in the light of all the questions that are being negotiated. Nobody is in a position at this point to say what the result of the negotiations will be. For that reason, I believe that it would be necessary and desirable—for everyone—to reserve any definitive position on whether or not Article 248 should be reformed until the results of the present negotiations are known.

In this connection, I have noted hopefully the fact that in your address to the nation on 9 April 1991—which I interpreted as the beginning of the great effort you will have to make in order to persuade Salvadorians to accept the historic challenge of peace, with all its consequences—you did not preclude the possibility of reforming Article 248.

I am preparing to travel to Europe today in order to fulfil some important official commitments. This does not, however, mean that I will stop following carefully and constantly the negotiations that I have been carrying on. I know that a short recess in the negotiations is about to be declared, and I regard this as very timely, since it will enable both sides to consider the present situation in depth; they will have available for that purpose the document which I have asked my representative to deliver to them and in which the decisions that should be taken during the next few days are stated with the utmost clarity.

I take this opportunity to extend to you, Sir, the renewed assurances of my highest and most distinguished consideration.

(*Signed*) Javier PÉREZ DE CUÉLLAR

Document 16

Report of the Secretary-General on the preliminary mission sent to El Salvador

S/22494, 16 April 1991 and addendum, S/22494/Add.1, 20 May 1991

1. The present report is submitted further to my report of 21 December 1990, 1/ in which I had informed the Security Council of my intention to request authorization to establish a United Nations Observer Mission in El Salvador (ONUSAL) to monitor agreements concluded between the Government of El Salvador and the Frente Farabundo Martí para la Liberación Nacional (FMLN), commencing with the verification of the Agreement on Human Rights signed by both parties at San José on 26 July 1990 (hereinafter referred to as "the Agreement"). 2/ In my statement during their consultations on 4 April 1991 (annex I), I informed the members of the Council that in this connection a preliminary mission, headed by my Alternate Personal Representative for the Central American Peace Process, and including experts in the field of human rights and technical advisers (see list in annex II), recently visited El Salvador. Its purpose was to assist me in determining the extent to which the verification tasks could be conducted before the cessation of the armed

1/ S/22031.
2/ S/21541.

conflict, and in preparing an operational plan for implementing the verification functions outlined in the Agreement. The mission was supported by the small preparatory office opened in San Salvador in January 1991.

2. The preliminary mission evaluated, in the context of its mandate, the situation in El Salvador through in-depth discussions with representatives of a wide spectrum of political opinion. These included government Ministers, the Supreme Court, the Attorney General and the Military High Command as well as leaders of political parties, religious organizations, non-governmental organizations active in the field of human rights, trade unions and employers' associations. The mission also visited, the Government being kept informed, four zones of conflict where it met representatives of the FMLN to discuss operational modalities of the projected verification functions.

3. In the light of these discussions and its evaluation of the political situation, the preliminary mission concluded that there is a strong and widespread desire in all sectors of opinion in El Salvador that the United Nations commence, as soon as possible, the verification of the Agreement without awaiting a cease-fire. This desire arises from the hope and expectation that such verification by the United Nations would bring about a diminution of the violence which affects the lives of the people of El Salvador. Virtually all sectors of political opinion pledged full support for the projected United Nations Verification Mission (hereinafter referred to as "the Mission") once it was established.

4. Notwithstanding these strong expressions of expectation and support, the preliminary mission recognized that the absence of the other political agreements envisaged in the framework of the Geneva agreement of 4 April 1990 and the Caracas agenda of 21 May 1990, 3/ raised a number of questions and concerns. One such concern is that, with the agreements on the armed forces and the judicial system not yet in place, the verification of the Agreement would necessitate the Mission's reaching specific working arrangements on an ad hoc basis with the military, security and judicial authorities and the FMLN. In view of the explicit assurances of support received from these authorities, the preliminary mission is of the view that such arrangements would be feasible.

5. The risks that a situation of armed conflict would pose to the tasks of the Mission and to the security of its personnel also were addressed by the preliminary mission. It concluded that, while a cease-fire obviously would provide optimal conditions, until this was secured, the verification tasks envisaged under the Agreement could be implemented to a significant extent, and that therefore this factor should not impede the establishment of the Mission before a cease-fire. The preliminary mission also concluded that, while the armed conflict could pose risks to security of personnel not usually encountered in United Nations observation or verification missions, these were not to a degree that should prevent the establishment of the Mission before a cease-fire. In reaching this conclusion the preliminary mission took into consideration not only the assurances received from the Government of El Salvador and the FMLN, but also the fact that the armed actions tend to be limited in time and place, rather than being prolonged and widespread.

6. In relation to security aspects, the preliminary mission noted further that certain extremist groups who tend to utilize violence to achieve their goals or to eliminate obstacles to them could resort to intimidation against the Mission's personnel, and precaution in this regard would be advisable.

7. In the light of the above and other relevant considerations, I have decided to accept the preliminary mission's recommendations that the human rights component of ONUSAL be established at the earliest feasible moment in advance of an agreement on a cease-fire. The Council already is informed that this measure would be in response to requests to this effect from both parties, which would need to be formalized in order to amend the reference to the cessation of the armed conflict in paragraph 19 of the Agreement, which at present provides that the Mission shall take up its duties as of the cessation of the armed conflict. In addition, measures would be required to ensure the security of the Mission, and its independence in functioning, especially the unrestricted freedom of movement and communication, as well as other rights and facilities necessary for its tasks. For this purpose, the United Nations and the Government of El Salvador would conclude an agreement on the status of ONUSAL and its privileges and immunities. Simultaneously, the FMLN would be required to make a declaration that it will fully cooperate in assuring the safety of the Mission and in facilitating the fulfilment of its functions.

8. In practical terms, the verification tasks of the human rights component of ONUSAL under the Agreement concluded between the Government of El Salvador and the FMLN may broadly be categorized as follows:

(a) Active monitoring of the human rights situation in El Salvador;

(b) Investigation of specific cases of alleged violations of human rights;

(c) Promotion of human rights in El Salvador;

(d) Recommendations to eliminate violations of, and to promote respect for, human rights;

(e) Reports to the Secretary-General and, through him, to the Security Council and the General Assembly.

3/ S/21931, annexes I and II.

It would be of fundamental importance that all parties accept that, from the first day of its establishment, ONUSAL has the authority to exercise all the functions assigned to it under the Agreement in investigating the human rights situation in El Salvador, such as full freedom of movement and access.

9. Nevertheless, in assuming these tasks before a cease-fire, it appears highly advisable that ONUSAL adopt a progressive approach. Accordingly, in the first phase it would concentrate on the active monitoring of the human rights situation, and of the processing by the parties of cases involving the allegations of violations of human rights. During this phase ONUSAL would not itself undertake direct investigations of specific cases, except when they are of an especially significant nature, this determination being made by its Director. In this phase, ONUSAL would establish its regional offices and sub-offices. Its personnel would undertake extensive and frequent travel to demonstrate its presence in all parts of El Salvador, particularly in places, including detention centres, with a history of frequent allegations of violations of human rights. Simultaneously, it would initiate a public information campaign to inform the public about the capabilities and limitations of the Mission under the Agreement. It also would present initial recommendations to the parties if it considered this advisable and feasible. Essentially, ONUSAL's priority during this phase would be to familiarize itself with the system and conditions in El Salvador in proceeding to the subsequent full deployment of its tasks, while retaining the right to exercise any functions it deems necessary in terms of the Agreement. It would present periodic reports to the Secretary-General.

10. After the first phase, which would last 60 to 90 days, ONUSAL's human rights component would enter into the second phase, in which it would exercise all the functions assigned to it under the Agreement. It would intensify direct investigations, promotion of respect for human rights through courses imparted to various sectors of society, and the formulation of specific and substantive recommendations to promote respect for human rights in El Salvador.

11. The structure of ONUSAL in these phases (in which it would absorb the preparatory office, which would have completed its functions) would be the following:

(a) Office of the Chief of Mission (San Salvador): A small advance component would provide overall political direction for the human rights component of ONUSAL and would deal with political matters that might arise from the performance of the verification functions. It also would prepare for the establishment of additional components of ONUSAL consequent on further political agreements that may be signed between the two parties.

(b) Office of the Director for Human Rights (San Salvador): The Director, who would be a person with an established record in the field of human rights, would have the principal responsibility for the verification of the Agreement. He would be assisted by a team of experts on human rights, a team of human rights investigators, and legal, judicial and police advisers. This office also would include a team of educators on human rights, public information activities being undertaken by the Office of the Chief of Mission.

(c) Regional offices at San Salvador, San Miguel, San Vincente and Santa Ana: Each regional office (map in annex III shows jurisdictions) would be headed by a Regional Coordinator, who would be assisted by Human Rights Officers, Legal Protection Officers, Police Monitors, Military Liaison Officers and a Political Adviser.

The San Salvador and San Miguel regions would have small sub-offices at Chalatenango and Usulután respectively, owing to the difficulty of access to certain areas in these two departments.

12. Planning for ONUSAL's personnel and logistics requirements is proceeding in the context of the preliminary mission's recommendations. Tentative projections for substantive international personnel are estimated at approximately 70 professional and above (coordinators, monitors, educators, legal and political affairs officers, etc.), 28 police personnel and 15 Military Liaison Officers. For the second phase, additional personnel are estimated at 20 professional and above and 38 police personnel, whose actual deployment would be adjusted according to the extent of activities becoming manifest in the first phase.

13. Given the nature of the tasks for which ONUSAL would be responsible, it would be essential to equip it with a reliable communications system to enhance its effectiveness and the security of its functions and personnel. Adequate transport resources also would be required to give it the mobility essential for its effective operation. The total cost of ONUSAL for an initial 12-month period, including one-time major procurements of vehicles and communications equipment, is estimated to be approximately $32 million. It is recommended that should the Council decide to set up ONUSAL, its costs should be considered as expenses of the Organization relating to the maintenance of regional peace and security and should be treated outside the procedures related to the contingency fund.

14. In conclusion, I strongly recommend that the Security Council give early authorization for the initial establishment of ONUSAL as outlined above. Should the

Council give this authorization, detailed personnel and logistical proposals and their financial implications would be submitted to the General Assembly at its resumed forty-fifth session later in April. The Secretariat can then proceed with the administrative, logistical and personnel procedures required, especially the recruitment of appropriately qualified personnel, which would be the key to the Mission's effectiveness, with the aim of ONUSAL initiating its functions on the ground by June 1991.

15. I reported to the members of the Security Council on 4 April 1991 on the progress in and the prospects for negotiations on the remaining questions agreed between the Government of El Salvador and the FMLN. While these are advancing, I would not advise linking the approval of the proposal contained in this report to the success of the negotiations as a whole. As I have stated before, I am convinced that the commencement of the verification of human rights by ONUSAL would promote a significant improvement in the human rights situation in El Salvador, and also would act as a positive impetus to the negotiations. I am of the strong view that the proposed establishment of the first component of ONUSAL should proceed by itself, without awaiting the outcome of the negotiation effort in progress. Once there is agreement on the cease-fire and the United Nations is called upon to play a broader role as envisaged, the corresponding resources to be included in ONUSAL's structure would be established with the aim of its being able to operate effectively as an integrated whole.

Annex I

Secretary-General's statement on El Salvador of 4 April 1991

One year ago today, the Government of El Salvador and the Frente Farabundo Martí para la Liberación Nacional (FMLN) agreed to initiate a process of negotiation, under my auspices, in order to end the armed conflict in El Salvador through political means as speedily as possible, promote the democratization of the country, guarantee unrestricted respected for human rights and reunify Salvadorian society.

Lives continue to be lost in combat in El Salvador, and peace is not yet at hand. But the negotiation is now entering an intensified new phase which, if successful, could lead to an early cease-fire under the supervision of the United Nations.

The road travelled in the last 12 months has been rough. This was to be expected, given the depth and complexity of the issues at stake, as illustrated in the agenda set last May and its provision that political agreements on a broad range of subjects be reached before a cease-fire could be contemplated.

Much time has been spent on the pervasive issue of the armed forces. It would not be appropriate for me to reveal what transpires in a negotiation which must of necessity remain confidential. But it is fair to say that, though no agreement has yet been struck, much progress has been made.

Last July, the parties signed a far-reaching agreement on human rights which provided for the establishment of an unprecedented, long-term, nationwide United Nations verification mission. A small preparatory office was set up in San Salvador in January. After much preparatory work and deliberation, and following a 10-day preliminary mission which I dispatched to El Salvador I am about to submit a formal proposal to the Security Council for the establishment of the verification mission as the initial component of an operation that I intend to call ONUSAL, which will undertake the responsibilities that will fall upon the United Nations as agreements emerge from the negotiation, and which are expected to include, in due course, a separation of forces and a cease-fire.

The phase of the process which is about to begin involves the simultaneous negotiation of a restricted set of issues, including the armed forces, constitutional reform and cease-fire arrangements which will for the first time permit the treatment of related issues in context and in perspective. Time is limited for these negotiations: constitutional reforms must be approved in two consecutive legislatures, and if they are not agreed upon and submitted to the current legislature before the end of its term on 30 April 1991, the possibility of adopting reforms which may well be crucial to the success of the negotiation may not become available again before 1994.

The situation in El Salvador has evolved considerably since the negotiations began. As provided for in the Geneva agreement, a broad debate involving all political parties and many social organizations and other institutions in El Salvador on the spectrum of issues in the negotiation is taking place. The armed forces as an institution are fully engaged in the process of negotiation itself. Issues are being aired openly which heretofore were not touched upon in public. Salvadorian society stands as if poised to undergo a profound transformation which will permit peace, once it comes about, to take hold irrevocably and irreversibly. At the same time, while the hope which is now offered is great, we must be wary of rising expectations. While the prospects for progress and indeed agreement have clearly improved, and recent contacts by my representative and myself with the parties reveal a desire to push ahead the sincerity of which I dare not doubt, the difficulties facing the negotiators and the short time available are daunting.

Throughout this process, I and my representative have worked closely with a certain number of Governments in a position to assist my efforts. I wish to record my appreciation to them. I would also add that we remain in touch with other Governments from outside Central America which are, I believe, called upon to play an essential role to ensure that the effort under way is successful. I fully intend to continue engaging these Governments in the process.

I will in due course be reporting to the Security Council about progress in the negotiations. Meanwhile, I intend to bring to the Council my proposal for the establishment of the human rights component of ONUSAL, which should go ahead as if it were a self-contained unit in view of its importance for the improvement of the situation in El Salvador and for the contribution that it can bring to helping the negotiation along.

Annex II

Members of the preliminary mission to El Salvador
from 13 to 23 March 1991

CHIEF OF MISSION:
Mr. Iqbal RIZA
Alternate Personal Representative of the Secretary-General

EXPERTS:
Dr. Pedro NIKKEN (Venezuela)
Vice-President of the Inter-American Institute of Human Rights and former President of the Inter-American Court of Human Rights

Dr. Philippe TEXIER (France)
Judge in the Court of Evry in France and Special Representative for Haiti of the Human Rights Commission

H.E. Mr. Carl Johan GROTH (Sweden)
Ambassador of Sweden in Denmark and formerly Representative of Sweden to the Human Rights Commission

Mr. Diego GARCÍA-SAYAN (Peru)
Professor of Human Rights in the Catholic University of Peru and Executive Director of the Andean Commission of Jurists

ADVISERS:
Lt. Col. Francisco Javier ZORZO FERRER
(Spanish Army)

Cmdt. Enrique VEGA FERNAÑDEZ (Spanish Army)
Supdt. Peter FITZGERALD (Irish Police)

SECRETARIAT:
Mr. NGUYEN H. Dong
Political Affairs Officer

Mr. Mario ZAMORANO
Director of UNIC in Mexico

Mr. Miguel DE LA LAMA
Centre for Human Rights in Geneva

Mrs. Silvia GAYMER
Secretary

PREPARATORY OFFICE OF ONUSAL IN SAN SALVADOR:
Dr. Ricardo VIGIL, Chief

Political Affairs Officers:
- Mr. Francesco MANCA
- Mr. Gino COSTA
- Miss Denise COOK

Annex III

Map of El Salvador [See Introduction, page 18.]

Addendum (S/22494/Add.1)

1. In my report to the Council, 1/ I indicated in paragraph 13 that the total cost of the United Nations Observer Mission in El Salvador (ONUSAL) for an initial 12-month period was estimated at approximately $32 million. I further indicated that, should the Council decide to set up ONUSAL, its costs should be considered as an expense of the Organization relating to the maintenance of regional peace and security and should be treated outside the procedures related to the contingency funds.

2. Following informal consultations with certain members of the Council regarding the method of financing, I consider it appropriate to provide the following clarification.

3. It would be my recommendation to the General Assembly that the cost of ONUSAL be considered an expense of the Organization to be borne by Member States in accordance with article 17, paragraph 2, of the Charter of the United Nations and that the assessments to be levied on Member States be credited to a special account that would be established for this purpose.

1/ S/22494 and Corr.1.

Document 17

Letter dated 19 April 1991 from President Cristiani to the Secretary-General concerning constitutional reforms

Not issued as a United Nations document; original in Spanish

Acknowledging receipt of your letter of 12 April 1991, I wish to say that I share your concern about the way in which the peace process is unfolding. Like you, we were very optimistic about the possibility of holding intensive meetings, without a time-limit and with a wide-ranging agenda. Furthermore, we regarded it as an encouraging sign that FMLN indicated that the only agreements that would need to be reached prior to the cessation of the armed confrontation were agreements on the subjects of the armed forces, constitutional reform and the cease-fire.

However, we were very surprised when your representative included reform of article 248 of our Constitution as a fourth fundamental aspect of a possible agreement. It is very disturbing that you say that this is the result of the consultations carried out with the parties, because the Government of El Salvador at no time told its representative to agree to reform that article.

Months earlier your representative, explaining that it was his idea and not an idea of FMLN, requested me to consider the possibility of introducing a transitional provision in article 248 so as to leave open the possibility for the subject of constitutional reform to be agreed upon after the completion of the term of the current Legislative Assembly. At that time I told him that this would give a negative signal regarding the early achievement of a cease-fire and that it would be better to reach specific agreements on constitutional reforms, since there would be a time-limit for putting them into effect.

About one month ago, after the elections for deputies and mayors, your representative again insisted that we should consider the possibility of analysing the proposed mechanism, and we told him that we would do so and would later inform him of our position in that regard.

At that same time, a massive campaign was unleashed by left-wing groups in our country to press for reform of article 248 of the Constitution. FMLN also began to exert pressure for the same purpose. This campaign gave rise to public debate, sometimes very heated, and at other times very serious and at the legal level.

For our part, we proceeded to analyse your representative's request, not only with the members of our delegation, but also with renowned lawyers and members of the various political parties. This process of consultation and analysis led us to take a position on the matter which was put forward by our delegation at the current meeting at Mexico City, and explained very clearly to your representative on 5 April. In addition, I had a direct telephone conversation with your representative and explained to him our reasons for arriving at that position; I told him that we preferred to be honest with him from the outset of the meeting so that no hopes would be generated on that subject and we would be able to take advantage of the time available to develop a set of specific reforms and there would be sufficient time for the current Legislative Assembly to have an opportunity to analyse them and initiate the reform process with the reforms it could accept.

As you may note, our position on this matter has not changed and cannot therefore be regarded as a new attitude. What took place was an extensive and thorough legal and political analysis which culminated in a very clear position on our part on this point.

You state in your letter that your representative explained to you the reasons which gave rise to our position, but I wish to stress some of the most important reasons:

1. In view of the legal debate on the constitutionality of the reform, there is a risk that a declaration on its unconstitutionality would totally preclude the possibility of constitutional reform until after the 1994 elections. There is a better chance of achieving the objective if specific reforms are submitted to this Legislative Assembly.

2. In view of the insecurity and instability experienced by our country since 1980, it is not advisable to add destabilizing elements which may give rise to grave and unpredictable situations in all areas of national life. This is now being aggravated by the appearance of a document found on a high-level member of FMLN who recently died in combat; the document shows a very destabilizing attitude which FMLN may be planning to take in its claims at the negotiating table.

3. The majority political parties of our country, Alianza Republicana Nacionalista (ARENA), Partido Demócrata Cristiano and Partido de Conciliación Nacional, publicly came out against reforming article 248, but expressed their willingness to analyse and promote specific reforms. The cooperation of these three political forces is essential for approving possible reforms, both in this legislature and in the next one.

As you will appreciate, our position is not capricious, but is based on realities, which lead us to conclude that, in order to advance in the peace process, there is an urgent need to reach agreements on the necessary reforms and not to waste valuable time in discussions on article 248.

We firmly believe that this is possible if FMLN takes a flexible and realistic position with regard to seeking agreements on the constitutional reforms which are necessary for the implementation of the political agreements deriving from the agenda agreed upon at Caracas, Venezuela. If this is achieved, some pending matters for the second phase of the process can be resolved basically through secondary legislation, which would have immediate application, and that would mean that very little or nothing would remain to be resolved by the Legislative Assembly elected in 1994.

We consider, therefore, that if pressure needs to be exerted to make possible an agreement that would put an end to the armed confrontation, that pressure should be exerted on FMLN. Our Government has shown great flexibility during the process and we believe that our proposals on possible constitutional reforms are broad and respond essentially to the demands they have been making, and to the aspirations of the political forces of our country.

I wish to state that we are maintaining a constructive position in the current work so that the negotiations will lead to final results; we appeal to you very respectfully to ensure that your representative at the negotiating table makes a more consistent effort to seek common ground between the opposing positions. Of course, any attitude of the intermediary which could be interpreted as an inclination in favour of one of the parties, particularly if it was transferred to the group of friends of the Secretary-General, would be an obstacle to progress towards the peace agreements we desire.

I wish to emphasize, again, our desire to find a solution to the conflict afflicting our country, and to stress that we will continue to work hard to achieve it. Thus, you will find in us a flexible and realistic attitude, although always within the bounds of legality and of what is reasonable.

Once again, on behalf of the people and Government of El Salvador, I wish to express our eternal gratitude for the cooperation and efforts you are making for peace in our country.

(*Signed*) Alfredo CRISTIANI
President of the Republic

cc: President of the Republic of Colombia
President of the Spanish Government
President of the United States of America
President of the United Mexican States
President of the Republic of Venezuela

Document 18

Letter dated 10 May 1991 from the Secretary-General to President Cristiani concerning constitutional reforms

Not issued as a United Nations document; original in Spanish

I have preferred to await the conclusion—which was fortunately successful—of the intensive round of negotiations between your Government and the Frente Farabundo Martí para la Liberación Nacional (FMLN) recently held in Mexico before replying to your letter of 19 April 1991, which was in turn a reply to my letter of 12 April in which I expressed my concern about the status of the negotiations. I think that it would be useful for me to make a few comments on the contents of your letter.

Firstly, you expressed surprise at the fact that my representative had included reform of article 248 of the Constitution as one of the four elements of a possible agreement in that round of negotiations, since your Government had never expressed its agreement to amend the said article.

In my view, there is no contradiction between the proposal which my representative made and the position of your Government. He never claimed that your Government had agreed to reform article 248 and merely expressed his opinion, which in no way committed the parties, that in order to achieve agreement on the three issues under negotiation—constitutional reform, armed forces and cease-fire—such an amendment would have to be one of the ingredients. This opinion was based on his knowledge of the position of FMLN, which was insisting on the reform as a quid pro quo for the cease-fire. Mentioning the possibility of that reform was reasonable in so far as up to 4 April the possibility that your Government would accept it had not been ruled out and, as you confirmed, was still under consideration. In any case, my representative was not taking a position on an issue which, in the final analysis, was for Salvadorians alone to decide, but rather expressing an opinion about the needs of the negotiating process.

In retrospect, the opinion of my representative was confirmed when your Government ruled out an amendment of article 248 and FMLN said that, under those conditions, it was not prepared to accept a cease-fire as part of the agreement.

During that round of negotiations, my representative, in order to avoid wasting time with the problem of article 248, urged FMLN to spare no effort in working for specific constitutional reforms which could be submitted to the Assembly in the outgoing legislature, an effort which culminated in the results that are known to all and whose passage through the Legislative Assembly you yourself facilitated, as I am fully aware, with skill and courage in the face of considerable resistance.

It is not for me to comment on the reasons you state which led to the position adopted by your Government on the reform of article 248. I wish to refer, rather, to your appeal for my representative to make a more consistent effort in seeking common ground between the opposing positions, and to your observation that any attitude of the mediation process which might be interpreted as an inclination in favour of one of the parties would be an obstacle to progress towards the achievement of the peace agreements which we desire.

I do not need to assure you, Sir, that my representative and I have spared no effort to seek common ground between the parties. It would be inappropriate to list all our efforts to put an end to the conflict in El Salvador, which is clearly the most destabilizing situation which your country faces. Nevertheless, I wish to reiterate that if my representative or I at any time suggested any course of action to either of the parties, this should never be interpreted as a value judgement on the position of one or other of the parties. During the course of this negotiation *sui generis*, we have frequently been compelled, at the insistence of the parties, to compensate for the diffi-culty which they experience in holding direct negotiations and to provide working documents which have been the only basis on which they have been able to reach agreement—in Geneva, Caracas, San José and now in Mexico. We have done so, and in so doing have run the risks that this entailed—including the risk that some might hint that we were partial, which is certainly not the case.

I believe that the incident about which we are writing is a manifestation of the very special nature of the conflict in your country and of the negotiations which are under way to put an end to that conflict. I do not underestimate the difficulties of your task in negotiating with an insurgent group; on the contrary, I fully appreciate those difficulties and admire your courage in facing them with patriotism and perseverance. At the same time, it is necessary to bear in mind that my representative is in the unenviable position of having to interpret to you the thinking and positions of said group, with the danger that, at times, the messenger might be identified with the message.

My representative and I, Sir, will continue to make every effort to assist the parties in their search for a solution to the Salvadorian conflict, in conformity with the mandate entrusted to us in the Geneva and subsequent Agreements. This task has the highest priority. I trust that with this letter any misapprehensions which may have inspired your letter of 19 April may be fully dissipated. I am very pleased that my representative and yourself have been in close and constant contact by telephone since the Mexico Agreements were concluded. The stage ahead of us is extremely complex and difficult and will require a great human and political effort, which I have no doubt that Salvadorians will be ready to make.

Accept, Sir, the assurance of my highest and most distinguished consideration.

(Signed) Javier PÉREZ DE CUÉLLAR

Document 19

Security Council resolution concerning establishment of the United Nations Observer Mission in El Salvador (ONUSAL)

S/RES/693 (1991), 20 May 1991

The Security Council,

Recalling its resolution 637 (1989) of 27 July 1989, in which it lent its full support to the Secretary-General for the continuation of his mission of good offices in Central America,

Recalling also the Geneva Agreement of 4 April 1990 1/ and the Caracas Agenda of 21 May 1990 2/ concluded between the Government of El Salvador and the Frente Farabundo Martí para la Liberación Nacional,

Deeply concerned at the persistence of and the increase in the climate of violence in El Salvador, which

1/ S/21931, annex I.
2/ Ibid., annex II.

seriously affects the civilian population, and thus stressing the importance of the full implementation of the Agreement on Human Rights signed by the two parties at San José on 26 July 1990, 3/

Welcoming the Mexico Agreements between the two parties of 27 April 1991, 4/

Having considered the reports of the Secretary-General, of 21 December 1990, 5/ and 16 April and 20 May 1991, 6/

Commending the Secretary-General and his Personal Representative for Central America for their efforts at good offices, and expressing its full support for their continuing efforts to facilitate a peaceful settlement to the conflict in El Salvador,

Underlining the great importance that it attaches to the exercise of moderation and restraint by both sides to ensure the security of all United Nations-employed personnel as well as to the adoption by them of all other appropriate and necessary measures to facilitate the negotiations leading to the achievement of the objectives set forth in the Geneva and other above-mentioned agreements as soon as possible, including their full cooperation with the Secretary-General and his Personal Representative to this end,

Recognizing the right of the parties to determine their own negotiating process,

Calling upon both parties to pursue the current negotiations urgently and with flexibility, in a concentrated format on the items agreed upon in the Caracas Agenda, in order to reach, as a matter of priority, a political agreement on the armed forces and the accords necessary for the cessation of the armed confrontation, and to achieve as soon as possible thereafter a process which will lead to the establishment of the necessary guarantees and conditions for reintegrating the members of the Frente Farabundo Martí para la Liberación Nacional within a framework of full legality into the civil, institutional and political life of the country,

Expressing its conviction that a peaceful settlement in El Salvador will contribute to a successful outcome in the Central American peace process,

1. *Approves* the report of the Secretary-General of 16 April and 20 May 1991; 6/

2. *Decides* to establish, under its authority, and based on the Secretary-General's report referred to in paragraph 1, a United Nations Observer Mission in El Salvador to monitor all agreements concluded between the two parties, whose initial mandate in its first phase as an integrated peace-keeping operation, will be to verify the compliance by the parties with the Agreement on Human Rights signed at San José on 26 July 1990, 3/ and also decides that the subsequent tasks or phases of the Observer Mission will be subject to approval by the Council;

3. *Also decides* that the United Nations Observer Mission in El Salvador will be established for an initial period of twelve months;

4. *Requests* the Secretary-General to take the necessary measures to establish the first phase of the Mission as described in paragraphs 2 and 3 above;

5. *Calls upon* both parties, as agreed by them, to pursue a continuous process of negotiations in order to reach at the earliest possible date the objectives set forth in the Mexico Agreements of 27 April 1991, 4/ and all other objectives contained in the Geneva Agreement of 4 April 1990, 1/ and to this end to cooperate fully with the Secretary-General and his Personal Representative in their efforts;

6. *Requests* the Secretary-General to keep the Security Council fully informed on the implementation of the present resolution.

3/ S/21541.
4/ S/23130.
5/ S/22031.
6/ S/22494 and Corr.1 and Add.1.

Document 20

Joint letter dated 1 August 1991 from the Secretary of State of the United States of America and the Minister for Foreign Affairs of the Union of Soviet Socialist Republics (USSR) concerning the peace process in Central America, and a joint statement on USSR-United States cooperation in Central America

S/22947, 15 August 1991

We have the honour to transmit herewith the texts of a joint letter from the Secretary of State of the United States of America, James A. Baker, III, and the Minister for Foreign Affairs of the Union of Soviet Socialist Republics,

Aleksandr A. Bessmertnykh, to you regarding the peace process in Central America, and a joint statement on USSR-United States cooperation in Central America (see annexes).

We should be grateful if you would have the present letter and its annex and enclosure circulated as a document of the Security Council.

(*Signed*) Thomas R. PICKERING
Permanent Representative of the United States
of America to the United Nations

(*Signed*) Valentin V. LOZINSKIY
Acting Permanent Representative of the Union of
Soviet Socialist Republics to the United Nations

Annex

*Letter dated 1 August 1991 from the Minister for
Foreign Affairs of the Union of Soviet Socialist
Republics and the Secretary of State
of the United States of America
addressed to the Secretary-General*

The Presidents of the Union of Soviet Socialist Republics and the United States of America have just concluded a summit meeting in Moscow at which our two Governments agreed to significant reductions in strategic arms and to cooperate closely in the search for peace throughout the world. We discussed the progress being made to complete the Central American peace process by bringing peace to El Salvador and Guatemala. We took note of the great strides made in El Salvador last April under your leadership to reach fundamental agreement on constitutional amendments on all the major issues before the parties: armed forces reform, separation of the security forces from the army, judicial and electoral reform and human rights. We also recognized the progress made in defining terms and modalities of a cease-fire and are pleased that the ONUSAL human rights monitoring group began to function last month.

At the same time, we are deeply concerned that the peace process has not continued to move forward since May. We consider it imperative to reach an early cease-fire agreement in order to avoid putting the major gains made in the peace process at risk. After 15 months of negotiations, it is critical to bring this tragic conflict to an end and permit the normalization and economic growth of all of Central America.

Accordingly, we join in calling on you, Mr. Secretary-General, to take personal leadership of the negotiating process and press both sides to reach rapid agreement on remaining political issues, agreement on a cease-fire, creating appropriate conditions for the full integration of all groups into political life and for national reconcili-

ation. The United States and the Soviet Union are prepared to extend full cooperation to this intensified effort in the context of the Security Council and bilaterally. We offer to join together with you and with the Friends of the Secretary-General to cooperate with a new negotiating round on an intensive basis so that we might offer our full support to help bring the parties to a resolution and help overcome any difficulties. Your own role in this process is critical, of course. The sense of urgency and high priority which your personal and direct leadership of a new negotiating round will send are essential for its success. We look forward to your early response.

James A. BAKER, III
Secretary of State

Aleksandr A. BESSMERTNYKH
Minister for Foreign Affairs

Enclosure

*Joint statement of 1 August 1991 on USSR-United
States cooperation in Central America*

Minister for Foreign Affairs Aleksandr Bessmertnykh and United States Secretary of State James Baker noted positive trends in Central America towards a settlement of contentious regional problems at the negotiating table and relaxation of tension through national reconciliation. Within this context, the Soviet Foreign Minister and the United States Secretary of State welcomed the resolution of the conflict in Nicaragua, the important accords reached in April between the Government of El Salvador and the Farabundo Martí National Liberation Front, and the launching of a dialogue between the Government of Guatemala and the Guatemalan National Revolutionary Unity Group.

They pointed out that the Soviet-United States cooperation in Central America and the adjacent areas promotes stronger stability in Latin America. The two sides agreed that additional joint steps should be made in the interest of assisting the entire spectrum of the Esquipulas accords, including democratization, cease-fire, and a settlement of the current conflicts, national reconciliation, economic development and regional disarmament.

The Soviet Foreign Minister and the United States Secretary of State urged the United Nations and other international organizations, as well as countries outside the region, including Cuba, to intensify their efforts to resolve the remaining political problems, ensure a cease-fire and finally settle the conflict in El Salvador peacefully. They expressed resolute support for the United Nations Secretary-General's efforts to help negotiate an end to the conflict in El Salvador and urged him to participate personally in the talks to promote a final settlement. They also firmly declared in support of an active involvement of the Secretary-General's Friends—Venezuela, Colombia, Mexico and Spain—in the peace process. As members of the United Nations Security Council, the two sides expressed readiness to play an active constructive role in supporting the talks and implementing accords on a final settlement.

The Soviet Union and the United States are convinced that an end to the conflict in El Salvador will promote the economic development of Central America and will help eliminate the remaining seats of tension in the Caribbean, thereby contributing to further peaceful integration of Latin America.

Document 21

Letters dated 17 August 1991 from the Secretary-General to the President of the Security Council transmitting the texts of letters from the Secretary-General to the Minister for Foreign Affairs of the USSR and the Secretary of State of the United States concerning the negotiations to solve the conflict in El Salvador

S/22963, 20 August 1991

The attached letters dated 17 August 1991 were addressed by the Secretary-General to the Minister for Foreign Affairs of the Union of Soviet Socialist Republics and the Secretary of State of the United States of America, respectively.

Annex I

Letter dated 17 August 1991 from the Secretary-General addressed to the Minister for Foreign Affairs of the Union of Soviet Socialist Republics

I am writing in reply to your joint letter with the United States Secretary of State of 1 August 1991, transmitted to me on 14 August, which in particular refers to the negotiations under my auspices to solve the conflict in El Salvador. I very much appreciate your expressions of support for my efforts on El Salvador, and I take note of your urging me to take personal leadership of the negotiating process.

As I indicated to you on 7 August, in reference to the 1 August U.S.-Soviet communiqué on the same subject, I fully intend to continue my active engagement in the Salvadorean peace negotiations. I need hardly say that Mr. Alvaro de Soto, as my personal representative, acts entirely on my behalf and with my full support, and I am therefore constantly and fully engaged in the process. I stand prepared to become involved directly and personally again, as I have done in several instances, most recently in Guadalajara. My personal participation in direct negotiating rounds is an option which has always existed and which remains open for consideration at the appropriate time and assuming that the level of representation of the two sides justifies such participation.

On 7 August I advised you of a number of concrete

ideas regarding the current critical juncture in the negotiations and the way in which you could be of assistance in helping me to cut the Gordian knot now facing the process. The problems bedevilling the negotiation are not, in my view, of a methodological nature. As has been demonstrated on several occasions during this process, including in Mexico last April, great strides are possible without my being physically present at direct meetings. Direct meetings are indeed only a relatively small part of the negotiating process. There are, however, fundamental issues which must be grappled with in order to go beyond the success so far achieved, and specifically to obtain a cease-fire. These are the subject of Mr. de Soto's shuttling between President Cristiani and the FMLN commanders during the past and coming weeks.

I noted with particular pleasure the offer contained in your joint communiqué to play an active and constructive role in supporting the talks and implementing accords on a final settlement. I therefore very much look forward to receiving your reaction to the ideas which I have presented.

(Signed) Javier PÉREZ DE CUÉLLAR

Annex II

Letter dated 17 August 1991 from the Secretary-General addressed to the Secretary of State of the United States of America

I am writing in reply to your joint letter with the Soviet Foreign Minister of 1 August 1991, transmitted to me on 14 August, which in particular refers to the negotiations under my auspices to solve the conflict in El Salvador. I very much appreciate your expressions of support for my efforts on El Salvador, and I take note of your urging me to take personal leadership of the negotiating process.

As I indicated to you on 7 August, in reference to the 1 August U.S.-Soviet communiqué on the same subject, I fully intend to continue my active engagement in the Salvadorean peace negotiations. I need hardly say that Mr. Alvaro de Soto, as my personal representative, acts entirely on my behalf and with my full support, and I am therefore constantly and fully engaged in the process. I stand prepared to become involved directly and personally again, as I have done in several instances, most recently in Guadalajara.

My personal participation in direct negotiating rounds is an option which has always existed and which remains open for consideration at the appropriate time and assuming that the level of representation of the two sides justifies such participation. I trust that for this purpose there would be no difficulty in ensuring the presence at United Nations Headquarters of members of the FMLN General Command, even on short notice.

On 7 August I advised you of a number of concrete ideas regarding the current critical juncture in the nego-tiations and the way in which you could be of assistance in helping me to cut the Gordian knot now facing the process. The problems bedevilling the negotiation are not, in my view, of a methodological nature. As has been demonstrated on several occasions during this process, including in Mexico last April, great strides are possible without my being physically present at direct meetings. Direct meetings are indeed only a relatively small part of the negotiating process. There are, however, fundamental issues which must be grappled with in order to go beyond the success so far achieved, and specifically to obtain a cease-fire. These are the subject of Mr. de Soto's shuttling between President Cristiani and the FMLN commanders during the past and coming weeks.

I noted with particular pleasure the offer contained in your joint communiqué to play an active and constructive role in supporting the talks and implementing accords on a final settlement. I therefore very much look forward to receiving your reaction to the ideas which I have presented.

(*Signed*) Javier PÉREZ DE CUÉLLAR

Document 22

Letter dated 27 August 1991 from the Secretary-General to President Cristiani concerning consultations to be held at United Nations Headquarters on 16 and 17 September

Not issued as a United Nations document; original in Spanish

I am writing to you in connection with the conversation we had at Guadalajara on 18 July 1991, on the occasion of the First Ibero-American Summit, and the consultations with you and with the High Command of the Frente Farabundo Martí para la Liberación Nacional (FMLN) carried out during the past few weeks by my Representative, Mr. Alvaro de Soto, within the context of the negotiating process initiated under my auspices at Geneva on 4 April 1990.

I am glad to find that as a result of those consultations, an agreement in principle has been reached with regard to compressing the negotiations into a single phase. I know we agree that this is an essential first step, without which it would be difficult to open the way towards achieving a cessation of the armed confrontation. I am confident that in the very near future it will be possible to confirm in writing the objectives of the compressed negotiations and the principles which will govern their conduct, as well as their agenda.

This first positive step is, of course, not a sufficient basis for believing in the success of the negotiations. That will require tackling the central problem which has thus far prevented the first phase of the negotiations from coming to a successful conclusion. This problem was manifested in the substantive statements by FMLN which accompanied its June proposal and which relate to the conditions and guarantees for the reincorporation of the members of FMLN, within a framework of full legality, into the country's civil, institutional and political life.

In the light of recent experience in the process, and on the basis of my knowledge of the positions held by the parties, I have good reason to fear that if an attempt were made to renew the direct negotiations without first confronting the problems associated with the aforementioned conditions and guarantees, the negotiations would quickly bog down and inevitably result in disappointing the people's hopes and discrediting the process.

I am prepared to make a personal and direct commitment to participate in the efforts that must be made at the present juncture in the process, but I believe that in order to do that, the parties must also be committed at the highest decision-making level.

Consequently, I believe that it is of the utmost importance to consult with you personally on the subjects described above, and to that end, I take pleasure in inviting you to United Nations Headquarters in New York for 16 and 17 September of this year.

With the same purpose in mind, a similar invitation is being sent today to the High Command of FMLN.

Awaiting your reply to my invitation, I take this opportunity to extend to you, Sir, the renewed assurances of my highest and most distinguished consideration.

(*Signed*) Javier PÉREZ DE CUÉLLAR

Document 23

Letter dated 28 August 1991 from President Cristiani to the Secretary-General concerning consultations to be held at United Nations Headquarters on 16 and 17 September

Not issued as a United Nations document; original in Spanish

With reference to your kind note of 27 August 1991, inviting me to United Nations Headquarters in New York on 16 and 17 September 1991 for consultations on specific issues relating to the peace process, particularly with regard to the conditions and guarantees for the reintegration of FMLN members within the context of full legality into the country's civil, institutional and political life.

In that regard, I should like to reply that I would be very happy to come to United Nations Headquarters to explore with you various avenues for moving ahead in the process towards definitive agreements. Nevertheless, since 15 September is Independence Day in our country, I would be unable to arrive in New York until very late on 16 September. Accordingly, I should be very happy to meet with you as of 17 September, for as long as you feel necessary and appropriate, to discuss specifically the points which will make it possible to achieve the final outcome in the shortest possible time.

I should also like to make a few comments on some ideas you expressed in your letter. Firstly, as you quite rightly pointed out, an agreement of principle has been reached regarding the compression of negotiations into a single phase. However, as we have stated on various occasions to your representative, Mr. Alvaro de Soto, our position is with the proviso that whatever agenda is agreed upon should not be a means for delaying the process but, quite the contrary, should facilitate a prompt conclusion of the process since any delaying tactic by FMLN at this stage in the negotiations would rightly be rejected by the Salvadorian people, the friends of the process and by the international community in general.

Secondly, and this follows on from the foregoing, I wish to reiterate, as I did in Guadalajara, that we are aware that the reintegration of FMLN into the country's civil, institutional and political life calls for the implementation of conditions and guarantees that will facilitate this transition. Nevertheless, FMLN's claim that members of FMLN groups should be included in the armed forces of El Salvador, by any means, cannot be considered in any way a condition or guarantee and, in reality, it is a purely political claim intended to satisfy its own interests. The inclusion of FMLN personnel by any means in the armed forces is totally unacceptable for obvious institutional reasons and from whatever practical standpoint it may be considered. On the issue of guarantees, the effort must be directed at working out concrete and reasonable measures, without forgetting that the best guarantee is United Nations verification of all the agreements reached.

The foregoing is merely intended to ensure that the effort which you have decided to undertake may culminate in success and that its outcome may contribute to and facilitate the achievement of the firm and lasting peace which the Salvadorian people wish and urgently call for.

Finally, I should like to emphasize that we have always been and will continue to be committed to the process of pacification in our country and that the bulk of our efforts have been directed to this end. Accordingly, I should again like to thank you for the efforts you have been making in this regard, especially now that you have decided to do so personally. Naturally, we also appreciate the efforts made by Mr. de Soto.

Looking forward to seeing you soon, accept, Sir, the assurances of my highest consideration.

(*Signed*) Alfredo F. CRISTIANI

Document 24

Report of the Secretary-General on ONUSAL and first report of the ONUSAL Human Rights Division

A/45/1055-S/23037, 16 September 1991

1. The attached document contains the first report of the United Nations Observer Mission in El Salvador (ONUSAL), established pursuant to Security Council resolution 693 (1991) of 20 May 1991. Appended thereto is the first report of the Director for Human Rights, whose mandate it is to verify compliance with the Agreement on Human Rights signed by the Government of El Salvador and the Frente Farabundo Martí para la Liberación Nacional (FMLN) at San José on 26 July 1990 (A/44/971-S/21541, annex).

2. The report was prepared during the Mission's preparatory phase and does not therefore attempt to analyse the human rights situation in El Salvador in depth but rather to establish a basis for future reports which will take up the substantive aspects of its present mandate.

3. I gratefully acknowledge the warm welcome and sincere cooperation extended to ONUSAL by the two parties signatories to the San José Agreement, which augur well for the Mission's contribution to the promotion of respect for human rights in El Salvador and to the peace process to which the parties have committed themselves.

Annex

First report of the United Nations Observer Mission in El Salvador

I. Establishment and mandate of the mission

1. As part of the negotiating process which they are conducting under the auspices of the Secretary-General, in accordance with the Geneva Agreement (4 April 1990) and the Caracas agenda (21 May 1990), the Government of El Salvador and FMLN signed at San José on 26 July 1990 an Agreement on Human Rights (henceforth referred to as the Agreement) (A/44/971-S/21541, annex) which provides, *inter alia*, for the establishment of a United Nations verification mission to monitor nationwide, for an initial period of one year, respect for and the guarantee of human rights and fundamental freedoms. The tasks of verification include actively monitoring the human rights situation; investigating specific cases of alleged human rights violations; making recommendations; and, lastly, reporting to the Secretary-General and, through him, to the United Nations Security Council and

General Assembly. The powers conferred on the Mission are very broad and include the possibility of visiting any place or establishment freely and without prior notice; receiving communications from any Salvadorian individual, group or entity and interviewing freely any individual or group; conducting direct investigations; and using the media to the extent useful for the fulfilment of its mandate. The Agreement thus assigns to the Mission a role unprecedented in the history of the United Nations.

2. Article 19 of the Agreement provided for the Mission to take up its duties as of the cessation of the armed conflict. Shortly after signing the Agreement, the two parties independently requested that the Mission be set up without waiting for a cease-fire. In December 1990, the Secretary-General informed the Security Council that it intended to propose the establishment of the United Nations Observer Mission in El Salvador (ONUSAL) to begin verification of the Agreement (S/22031). In March 1991, he sent a preliminary mission consisting of a select group of human rights experts and technical advisers to help him determine the extent to which verification activities could be conducted before the cessation of the armed conflict. The Mission received support from a small preparatory office set up in San Salvador in January 1991.

3. The preliminary mission reached the conclusion that there was a widespread desire in all sectors of opinion in El Salvador that the United Nations should commence verification of the Agreement as soon as possible, without awaiting a cease-fire. It also concluded that the risks posed by the armed conflict to the tasks of verification and to the security of personnel were not to a degree that should prevent the establishment of the Mission, as long as it exercised reasonable caution in performing its verification functions. Both the Government of El Salvador and FMLN, by letters dated 2 May, reiterated their request that the Mission be established before a cease-fire.

4. The Secretary-General endorsed the Mission's conclusions and transmitted them to the Security Council (S/22494), which on 20 May 1991 unanimously adopted resolution 693 (1991) establishing ONUSAL to monitor, as an integrated operation, all agreements concluded between the Government and FMLN. ONUSAL's initial mandate was to be to verify compliance with the San José Agreement, and the Council authorized the launching of the Mission without preconditions. The Secretary-General appointed Mr. Iqbal Riza as his Special Representative and

Chief of Mission of ONUSAL and Mr. Philippe Texier as Director of the Human Rights Verification Mission provided for in the San José Agreement. The latter post will correspond to that of Director of the Human Rights Division within the integrated structure of ONUSAL.

5. The Headquarters Agreement with the Government of El Salvador was formalized on 23 July 1991, through an exchange of letters between the Secretary-General and the Minister for Foreign Affairs which grants the Mission all the powers provided for in the San José Agreement, determines the Mission's legal status and defines the privileges and immunities of its members and property.

6. On 30 August, by means of an exchange of letters between the Personal Representative of the Secretary-General and the FMLN representative to the United Nations, FMLN undertook to respect the rights and powers necessary for ONUSAL to carry out its activities.

II. *Launching of the mission*

7. ONUSAL was launched on 26 July 1991. As indicated in the report of the Secretary-General (S/22494) and in view of the fact that ONUSAL has been established in advance of a cease-fire, the Mission is taking a progressive approach to its work. During the preparatory phase, which lasts until the end of September, the Mission is concerned with: establishing offices throughout El Salvador; organizing its personnel and familiarizing them with the country's Constitution, relevant laws and administrative system; establishing contacts with the two parties at various levels; and studying, proposing and agreeing on working arrangements for fulfilling its mandate. In so doing, it is preparing to enter the second phase, in October, performing all the functions assigned to it under the San José Agreement.

8. The Mission's organizational structure at this preliminary stage is relatively simple. The Office of the Chief of Mission will provide overall political direction and will deal with political matters that may arise from the performance of verification functions. It will also prepare for the establishment of additional components consequent on further political agreements that may be signed between the parties. The Office of the Director for Human Rights will be responsible for verifying the Agreement. The Director will be assisted by a team of human rights advisers and investigators and by legal and police advisers. The Office will also have a team of educators on human rights. Each of the regional offices will be headed by a regional coordinator, assisted by human rights officers, legal officers, police investigators, military liaison officers and a political adviser.

9. By 15 September, a total of 101 international civil servants from 27 countries had joined the Mission, comprising five senior management staff, 42 human rights observers

and advisers, legal advisers, educators and political affairs officers; 15 military advisers; 16 police advisers; and 23 administrative support and communications staff. When the Mission's preparatory phase ends, personnel needs will be re-evaluated and the staff assigned to the different offices and regions will be supplemented accordingly.

10. ONUSAL has already set up regional offices in San Salvador (central region), San Vicente (paracentral region), San Miguel (eastern region) and Santa Ana (western region), with suboffices in Chalatenango and Usulután.[See map in Introduction, page 32.] It also embarked immediately on an extensive programme of visits both to official institutions (ministries, the judiciary, the armed forces and local authorities) and to non-governmental organizations working in the field of human rights, as well as to marginal populations, communities of returnees and other vulnerable sectors of Salvadorian society. Towards the end of the period covered by this report, visits began to populations living in conflict zones. The purpose of the visits is to verify certain conditions in the place visited when, according to the information available, acts or situations contrary to respect for human rights may have occurred there or information useful to their investigation may be found. The presence of observers also helps to prevent acts or situations contrary to human rights from occurring, continuing or escalating. Reports of human rights violations also began to be received, and these are being transmitted to the competent authorities and given the necessary follow-up. Activities will intensify in the coming days and it is estimated that, by the time the initial phase of ONUSAL's establishment is complete, almost all the municipalities in the country will have been visited.

11. The first report of the Director of the ONUSAL Human Rights Division, covering the period 26 July-31 August 1991, is appended.

12. The report was prepared during the Mission's preparatory phase and does not therefore include an analysis of the human rights situation in El Salvador. Instead, it contains valuable information on the background to the Mission, the context in which it will have to operate and, in particular, the difficulties of verifying the San José Agreement before the cessation of the armed conflict and the resulting legal problems. It also contains a description of El Salvador's institutional structure in the area of human rights; a description of the types of violations of the San José Agreement, which will serve as a guide for classifying the reports that are received, investigated and processed; a reference to the most important cases so far referred to the Mission; and the report's conclusions.

13. It should be mentioned that the Mission is receiving support and cooperation from the Government of El Salvador and its authorities.

14. Similar support and cooperation have been received from FMLN, although technical difficulties have so far prevented the establishment of steady, smooth communication.

15. The welcome extended by Salvadorian civilian society has been equally positive. We have only to mention the unanimous agreement adopted by the Legislative Assembly on 25 July 1991 whereby the Assembly, as the representative of the sovereign will of the State, extended ONUSAL its entire support and backing.

16. The positive attitude of the Government of El Salvador and FMLN make it possible to predict realistically that the tasks entrusted to the Mission will be duly carried out. If both parties show their readiness to respect the commitments entered into in the San José Agreement and if, in addition, they contribute through their cooperation to the successful performance of the Mission's tasks, we can predict with optimism that the human rights situation in El Salvador will improve substantially. What is more, success in this area can be expected to make a positive contribution to the negotiating process aimed at restoring peace and creating the conditions necessary for democratic coexistence.

Appendix

First report of the Director of the Human Rights Division

I. Launching of verification activities

1. When the Human Rights Verification Mission was set up, the first step it took was to establish working arrangements with the two parties signatories to the San José Agreement.

2. A series of meetings was held with a governmental working group to define the mechanisms for processing reports of human rights violations. Although the Government has appointed the Executive Secretary of the Human Rights Commission as its liaison with the Mission, agreement was reached that the Mission will be able to directly contact the various principal organs of the State and their auxiliary services, as well as the Public Prosecutor's Office, the armed forces and local authorities. The Mission's other liaisons at the national level will be the Chief of Psychological Operations and Civilian Affairs of the Armed Forces Joint Staff and the Assistant Prosecutor for Human Rights. To this end, there is agreement that the Mission may establish links with the authorities directly competent to support the objectives pursued, whether in obtaining information or in requesting action by them, without prejudice to timely notification of the corresponding senior official or body designated for this purpose.

3. At meetings held with FMLN at Mexico City and Managua, the necessary mechanisms for contacts and liaison in the field were established and the corresponding arrangements were discussed. Meetings with both the parties were conducted in a very cordial atmosphere and in a spirit of full cooperation and it is hoped that the establishment of working arrangements will be completed in the next few days.

4. The San José Agreement stipulates that the Mission shall use the media to the extent useful for the fulfilment of its mandate. A massive public information campaign has been prepared to publicize the content and scope of the San José Agreement and the Mission's tasks. There has already been excellent, highly positive journalistic coverage.

5. The Mission is preparing to conduct its human rights education campaign, which it plans to carry out with programmes aimed at national governmental and non-governmental bodies and with mass organizations that are promoting human rights education projects in a variety of ways. Programmes will also involve institutions of both the parties which have responsibilities related to the protection and promotion of human rights. Programmes will be based on an analysis of existing activities, needs and deficiencies in the area of human rights promotion and education and will be aimed essentially at providing specific inputs into the training of national personnel, developing a human rights publicity campaign and advising on conceptual, methodological and didactic aspects of human rights promotion. ONUSAL is also working on the preparation of educational documents on human rights which will be disseminated widely among the population.

II. Context in which the human rights verification mission in El Salvador is performing its tasks

6. As expressly stipulated in the San José Agreement, the Mission will investigate acts committed or situations existing as of the date of its establishment. Its mandate therefore covers the present and future situation of human rights in El Salvador, not the past. However, in exceptional cases and as provided for in article 17 of the Agreement, the Mission will be able to transmit to the competent organs communications received concerning acts or situations which occurred before it was set up, if the case so warrants and there is new evidence which might help to solve it. The Mission will also be able to verify the current prosecution of past cases, in the light of the priority which the Agreement attaches to the right to due process. It will likewise be able to take the past as a reference point for determining whether current acts or situations, given their persistence over time, form part of a systematic practice of human rights violations inherited from the past. Except in the cases mentioned above, acts occurring before 26 July 1991 fall outside the Mission's mandate and could fall within the competence of the

Commission on the Truth, whose establishment the parties agreed to in April 1991 in Mexico.

7. Human rights violations in El Salvador have attracted national and international attention. Different, and in some cases conflicting, interpretations have been given as to their causes, their scale and those responsible for them. Salvadorian society is particularly divided in its interpretation of such violations. The persistence of the armed conflict has resulted in an extreme polarization which has helped politicize the issue of human rights. In this situation, verification of the Agreement will be a difficult and delicate task and will require that the Mission play the role of educator in order to establish objectively both the obligations of the parties and their conduct in relation thereto.

8. For more than a decade, the United Nations and the Organization of American States have given priority attention to developments in the human rights situation in El Salvador. In 1981, the United Nations Commission on Human Rights appointed Professor José Antonio Pastor Ridruejo its Special Representative on El Salvador. Successive reports of the Special Representative and reports by national and foreign governmental and non-governmental organizations have documented the very serious human rights violations that have occurred in El Salvador in recent years. It is no accident therefore that the parties have attached importance to this issue in the negotiations, that the first agreement in the negotiating process concerns human rights and that ONUSAL is beginning its activities by verifying them.

9. Although acts which occurred in the past do not, save in exceptional cases, fall within the competence of the Mission, a brief description of the human rights situation since the signing of the Agreement is needed to give an idea of the situation in which ONUSAL is beginning its activities. By its resolution 1991/75 of 6 March 1991, the Commission on Human Rights noted that, despite the reduction in the number of violations of human rights and the efforts made by the parties to improve the human rights situation, numerous politically motivated violations of human rights, such as enforced disappearances, abductions and, in particular, summary executions, are continuing in El Salvador and that a climate of intimidation persists against certain sectors of the population.

10. Although the figures provided by Salvadorian governmental and non-governmental organizations generally support this assessment, they differ as to the magnitude of the violations mentioned and the degree of responsibility of the alleged perpetrators. Non-governmental organizations also often differ among themselves in their assessments. For purposes of illustration, let us look at the figures given by human rights organizations in the following tables. [See opposite page.]

11. In addition to reflecting an alarming human rights situation, the above figures show that human rights organizations do not use uniform criteria for classifying violations or for establishing periods within which these occur. This presents difficulties for making a comparative analysis of human rights violations based on existing sources. As a result, the Mission will make an effort to typify violations of the Agreement precisely and to establish a criterion for measuring their occurrence in time.

12. The absence of a cease-fire complicates the Mission's verification task in a variety of ways. One complication, clearly, is a juridical one related to the verification, in the midst of an armed conflict, of an agreement conceived for a peace-time situation. The legal framework which the Mission will use for verification in a war situation is described in the next section.

13. A second complication relates to the fact that the agreement is a partial one, no other political agreements having been reached on issues which in one way or another have an impact on human rights. In addition to issues related directly to human rights, there are others related to the judiciary and the armed forces. The parties had, in fact, provided for verification of the Agreement to take place only after a cease-fire and in the context of institutional reforms designed, *inter alia*, to ensure respect for human rights. As a result, verification of the Agreement is taking place not only in a very different military context from what was envisaged but also in a different institutional context.

14. The need to protect members of the Mission in a situation of armed conflict complicates verification of the Agreement. In his report to the Security Council, the Secretary-General said that the risks posed by the armed conflict would be acceptable. However, he also noted that certain extremist groups might attempt to intimidate Mission members. This issue received considerable attention in the Security Council, where some members let their concerns be known. Shortly before the Mission was set up, flyers of the self-styled Salvadorian Anti-Communist Front came to light which openly threatened the Mission. Other groups, such as the Crusade for Peace and Work, although different from the Front, helped arouse hostility towards ONUSAL among certain sectors by questioning its constitutionality. Both the President of the Republic and the Ministers for Foreign Affairs and Defence reported in due course that they were investigating the situation and that ONUSAL could count on all the necessary guarantees for performing its functions, for which the Mission thanked them. ONUSAL was also pleased to learn that, by a unanimous agreement adopted on 25 July 1991, the Legislative Assembly had expressed profound satisfaction at ONUSAL's establishment and had pledged it its full support.

Table 1.

Persons killed or injured as a result of the violence

	First six months of 1990	Second six months of 1990	First six months of 1991
Killed out of combat	206	156	152
Killed in combat	737	1 043	944
Total	923	1 219	1 096
Injured out of combat	318	327	391
Injured in combat	900	1 508	1 149
Total	1 218	1 835	1 540

Source: El Salvador Human Rights Commission (governmental).

Table 2.

Unlawful arrests, enforced disappearances and extrajudicial executions

	First six months of 1990	Second six months of 1990	First six months of 1991
Unlawful arrests	702	249	367
Enforced disappearances	101	60	79
Extrajudicial executions	498	621	576

Source: El Salvador Human Rights Commission (non-governmental).

Table 3.

Politically motivated murders, arrests, arrests followed by disappearance, and disappearances

	April-July 1990	August-November 1990	December 1990-March 1991
Murders	74	30	40
Arrests	322	147	193
Arrests/ disappearances	23	10	8
Disappearances	41	23	35

Source: Human Rights Institute of José Simeón Cañas Central American University.

Table 4.

Human rights violations by the Frente Farabundo Martí para la Liberación Nacional, August 1990-June 1991

Murders	29
Abductions	139
Threats	63

Source: Human Rights Office of the Armed Forces Joint Staff.

Table 5.

Human rights violations

	1990	First six months of 1991
Arrests	208	80
Arrests/disappearances	60	22
Disappearances	102	33
Abductions attributed to FMLN	33	5
Murders attributed to FMLN	14	8
Murders attributed to death squads	53	24
Murders attributed to the armed forces	64	52
Deaths occurring in armed forces military operations a/	396	34
Deaths occurring in armed forces combat actions b/	456	285
Armed forces casualties	592	310

Source: Legal Protection Office of the Archdiocese of San Salvador.

a/ Includes FMLN combatants and the civilian population. The corresponding category was not determined because there was no on-site investigation, but most of the deaths were among the civilian population.

b/ Includes FMLN combatants and the civilian population. The corresponding category was not determined because there was no on-site investigation, but most of the deaths were of FMLN combatants.

15. The launching of verification activities while negotiations are going on and the armed conflict is continuing creates a number of additional problems for the Mission. On the one hand, it can be expected that groups will emerge that will question ONUSAL's objectivity and impartiality. This risk will require that the Mission act with caution. If it is understood by the parties and by the various sectors of Salvadorian society and if everyone makes an effort to guarantee the Mission's credibility and respect for it, that will help create a climate of *détente* which might permit a settlement of the conflict.

16. This latter situation itself creates difficulties. There are very high, and in some cases inordinate, expectations of the Mission. Vast numbers of Salvadorians right across the political spectrum believe that the Mission will be able to prevent, or at least punish, human rights violations. Even though the Mission will try to fulfil the expectations which the Salvadorian people have of it, it is worth remembering that while its verification possibilities are considerable, it does not have the power to prevent violations or to punish violators. As a result, far from attempting to replace the institutions responsible for ensuring the protection and promotion of and respect for human rights, the Mission will assist Salvadorians in the effort to ensure unrestricted exercise of those rights. To that end, it will attempt to persuade the parties to modify conduct that is incompatible with the Agreement, and its sole support in that task will be the moral authority of the United Nations.

III. *Human rights and humanitarian law in the context of the San José Agreement*

17. The Mission was not conceived to deal with violations of human rights—or of the attributes of the human person—resulting directly from the armed conflict. The intention of the parties to the San José Agreement, and the structure of the Agreement itself, corresponded to the objective of creating additional guarantees for the observance of human rights in the new era in El Salvador's history that was to begin once a cease-fire went into effect.

18. The fact that the parties requested that the Mission begin before a cease-fire was achieved does not alter the nature, the structure or the purpose of the San José Agreement, nor the Mission's mandate or the priorities that it must assign to its tasks. Their request cannot in itself be interpreted as demonstrating their intention of entrusting the Mission with a task which was not envisaged in its original mandate, namely, that of dealing systematically with cases directly linked to the armed conflict. It seems more logical to interpret that request as meaning that the parties wanted the Mission to begin to play, ahead of time, the role they had assigned to it for the stage that would follow the cease-fire, in which it was not, as a general rule, to deal with cases directly related to the hostilities.

19. The normative framework within which the Mission must act is defined by the sixth preambular paragraph of the Agreement, according to which human rights shall be understood to mean "those rights recognized by the Salvadorian legal system, including treaties to which El Salvador is a party, and by the declarations and principles on human rights and humanitarian law adopted by the United Nations and the Organization of American States". 1/

20. International human rights law and international humanitarian law are two separate legal systems, each with its own foundations and mechanisms, but they share the same goal, namely, protection of the human person. Even though the specific legal system for situations of armed conflict is international humanitarian law, the international system for the protection of human rights continues to apply concurrently during armed conflicts. 2/

21. Although in exceptional situations which threaten the life of the nation, States may take measures derogating from some of the rights recognized by international instruments, this does not authorize any derogation from rights that are considered "untouchable" (art. 4 of the International Covenant on Civil and Political Rights). These are the fundamental human rights of the human person which guarantee respect for his or her physical and mental integrity. This irreducible core of human rights constitutes a minimum standard corresponding to the lowest level of protection to which any person can aspire at any time and in any place or circumstance. 3/

22. Although there is some overlapping between the provisions of human rights instruments and those of humanitarian law treaties, the Mission's verification

1/ The second paragraph of the preamble to Additional Protocol II of 1977 to the Geneva Conventions of 12 August 1949 establishes a link between international human rights law and international humanitarian law relating to armed conflicts, in recalling "that international instruments relating to human rights offer a basic protection to the human person". The "Commentary" to this Protocol, published by the International Committee of the Red Cross, specifies that "international instruments relating to human rights" should be understood to mean instruments adopted by the United Nations such as the Universal Declaration of Human Rights and the Covenants derived therefrom (in particular, the International Covenant on Civil and Political Rights); instruments concerning specific aspects of the protection of human rights; and regional instruments, among which it mentions the American Convention on Human Rights. This is the first time that such a reference has appeared explicitly in a treatise on humanitarian law.

2/ Cf. General Assembly resolution 2675 (XXV) of 19 December 1970.

3/ Protocol II contains practically all the "untouchable" rights contained in the International Covenant on Civil and Political Rights. These rights are principles which have universal validity beyond any treaty obligation.

tasks differ from the functions entrusted to such humanitarian agencies as the International Committee of the Red Cross (ICRC) and relief agencies. 4/ It should be borne in mind that, since the conclusions and recommendations of ICRC must be kept confidential while those of the Mission are intended to be made public, it would not seem advisable for there to be any overlapping between their work in relation to acts occurring in the armed conflict.

23.   This does not, however, mean that the Mission has absolutely no powers to verify and even investigate cases or situations related to the armed conflict. Both the reference to international humanitarian law in the preamble to the San José Agreement, and paragraph 18 of the Agreement authorizing the application of the Mission's procedures concurrently with other international procedures for the promotion and protection of human rights, permit the conclusion that the presence of ICRC would not be incompatible with action by the Mission in certain cases of this kind in which the minimum standard of protection of the human person is at stake.

24.   It should also be recalled that, in exercise of its verification mission and of its power to take any steps it deems appropriate to promote and defend human rights (para. 13 of the Agreement), the Mission, guided by international human rights instruments, will devote special attention to observance of the rights to life, to integrity and security of the person and to personal liberty (para. 11, first part) in the continuing situation of armed conflict in El Salvador. It will also pay special attention to protection of the civilian population and the right to personal freedom of displaced persons and returnees (para. 7) and of all persons in conflict zones (para. 8).

25.   For all the above reasons, the most reasonable conclusion which can be drawn at the present time is that the Mission will have to perform its task within the context and the sphere in which it was conceived, but that it will also have to deal with situations related to the armed conflict, to which international humanitarian law is applicable, only in cases which can be considered especially significant, giving top priority to protecting the human rights of the civilian population.

IV.   *The Salvadorian institutional system*

26.   This first report will give a brief description of the Salvadorian institutional system, with special emphasis on those institutions having some link with the Mission's current work. This description will not be repeated in subsequent reports, except when specific analyses and recommendations are made for some of these institutions.

27.   In the executive branch, the governmental Human Rights Commission, established in 1982 as an authority under the President of the Republic, receives and investigates reports of possible human rights violations and provides information on them to the victims or their relatives and to the appropriate authorities, in accordance with its by-laws and procedures. It also has a human rights education and promotion policy and a social and medical action component. It executes the foreign policy of the executive branch in the field of human rights.

28.   More specifically, the Mission has noted the existence of the Criminal Investigation Commission which is under the authority of the executive branch. Despite the technical, material and professional resources of this body, there are those who feel that its dependence on the political and military authorities prevents it from cooperating effectively with the judiciary.

29.   As the Mission begins its work, the legislative branch is in the midst of a major institutional reform and human rights effort, which includes ratification of the constitutional reforms agreed upon in Mexico on 27 April 1991 between the Government and FMLN. These reforms concern the armed forces, the electoral system, significant aspects of the judicial system, and mechanisms for guaranteeing human rights. This initiative, as well as the promulgation of secondary legislation or the formulation of new political agreements which expand on the Constitution in other areas, constitutes a very important step in the creation of a new institutional framework and is an encouraging sign of the desire for peace and national reconciliation.

30.   In any State subject to the rule of law, the judicial branch is vitally important for the effective exercise of human rights, and the Mission has the power to offer it its support "in order to help improve the judicial procedures for the protection of human rights and increase respect for the rules of due process of law" (Agreement, para. 14 (h)). The Mission welcomes, as a praiseworthy initiative, the establishment of the Detainee Information Department, whose purpose is to keep track of detainees in order to guarantee their rights and give information to interested persons (Agreement No. 267 of the Supreme Court of Justice). The Supreme Court has a clear interest in expediting the work of this Department.

31.   The Mission is aware, however, that the actual operation of the Department could be improved, in that it receives no information from the army and very little from the security forces and from justices of the peace in conflict zones such as Chalatenango and Morazán, to the great detriment of its potential effectiveness. The Mission is interested in helping fulfil the objectives of the Detainee Information Department, which helps to provide reliable information on the circumstances of detentions and on

---

4/ Cf. article 3 of the four Geneva Conventions and article 18 of Protocol II respectively.

the identity of detainees. The Mission has also taken note of other initiatives by the Supreme Court of Justice to improve the administration of justice, such as the introduction of itinerant judges, judicial assessors, prison supervision agents, a Judicial Training School, an Institute of Forensic Medicine and a Department for the Promotion, Dissemination and Study of Human Rights. The Mission will follow these measures to safeguard human rights with particular attention.

32. The Public Prosecutor's Office consists of the *Fiscaléa General de la República* and the *Procuraduréa General de la República,* to which is now being added the post of a National Prosecutor (*Procurador Nacional*) for the Protection of Human Rights who will be responsible essentially for promoting and ensuring respect for human rights. The *Fiscaléa General* currently has an Assistant Prosecutor (*Fiscal Adjunto*) for Human Rights whose express mandate is to ensure respect for human rights and constitutional guarantees. The Mission will pay special attention to the work of the Public Prosecutor's Office in the field of human rights.

33. The armed forces play a leading role in the country, with the result that their decisions and conduct are decisive for the effective exercise of human rights.

34. The Mission has noted that the armed forces have established a Human Rights Office under the authority of their Joint Staff to try to correct practices by their members which represent an assault on the dignity of the human person. This initiative, taken in response to past errors and criticisms, will also warrant the closest attention in the Mission's future work, and initial contacts have therefore been made with the authorities responsible. Particular mention should be made of the almost unanimous view which all sectors of Salvadorian society have of the civil defence forces, which have acted under military orders throughout this period and are accused of abuses and of violating human rights with virtual impunity.

35. It should be mentioned that the functions of the public security forces, particularly the National Guard, the National Police and the Treasury Police, are currently twofold. On the one hand, as noted previously, they belong to the armed forces and, on the other hand, they act as auxiliary bodies of the system for the administration of justice in investigating crimes and offences which must be prosecuted officially and in performing other duties assigned to them by the law on penal procedure. It does not seem advisable to prolong this situation if, as is desired, the justice system is to become more effective in meeting the whole of society's expectations. One important point, therefore, is the constitutional reform that will separate the police from the armed forces.

36. In general, viewing the institutional order as a whole, the Mission cannot ignore the fact that many reports by the United Nations and by national and international human rights organizations have testified to the practical ineffectiveness of existing mechanisms in El Salvador for the defence, protection and promotion of human rights. This is especially important when we observe that, despite the high incidence of violations of human rights and humanitarian law, the investigation, prosecution and punishment of those responsible has been virtually non-existent, creating a perception of widespread impunity. The Mission is aware of this situation and will, in the course of its work, point out any failings it observes in all the institutions with which it comes in contact.

37. Recently, the public authorities have promoted initiatives which have a direct bearing on the issue of human rights and which take practical account of the agreements reached at the negotiating table. These initiatives point to the development of a new sensitivity to the need to improve the human rights situation. Contributing to their effectiveness and hence to their credibility in the eyes of all of Salvadorian society would appear to be a task which the Mission can carry out only with the cooperation of all the country's institutions and social sectors.

38. The Mission has observed that FMLN has a relatively stable presence in conflict zones and has a decisive influence on the life of the population. It also exerts a strong influence among certain sectors of Salvadorian society. Given this situation, the Mission was interested in finding out what kind of relations FMLN establishes in conflict zones. As is clear from the San José Agreement, the Mission is not seeking to establish any kind of symmetry between what FMLN does and what the State does within any organized community, as this is not relevant, but rather to find out what pre-established rules of conduct regulate life in conflict zones. FMLN has a Secretariat for the Promotion and Protection of Human Rights, which was set up in 1987 to file documented reports of human rights violations attributed to the Government and to investigate cases of violations attributed to FMLN in order to uphold the legitimacy of its methods of struggle. FMLN provided the Mission with a set of criteria which it applies in taking prisoners and in the treatment of prisoners. FMLN prisoners may be its own combatants who have violated the rules of international law; informers or individuals who have infiltrated its ranks; members of the armed forces captured in combat; or members of the civilian population who have committed ordinary crimes in conflict zones. In some cases, FMLN has also resorted to abduction in order to force payment of the so-called "war tax". The Mission has made it clear that abduction on any grounds is a violation of the San José Agreement. Concerning the other points,

the Mission will try to find out in greater detail what criteria are applied to the treatment of prisoners. It will continue to try to clarify these and other points concerning FMLN conduct.

V. *Categories of cases and situations*

39. As established by the San José Agreement, the purpose of the Mission is to "investigate the human rights situation in El Salvador". According to the Agreement, "human rights" shall mean the following: (a) those rights recognized by the Salvadorian legal system, including treaties to which El Salvador is a party, in other words, the rights recognized by El Salvador's Constitution and secondary legislation and those guaranteed by the universal and regional international treaties ratified by it; 5/ and (b) those rights included in the declarations and principles on human rights and humanitarian law adopted by the United Nations and the Organization of American States, in other words, the rights contained in, inter alia, the Charter of the United Nations and the Universal Declaration of Human Rights, international humanitarian law treaties, the Charter of the Organization of American States and the American Declaration on the Rights and Duties of Man. 6/

A. *Verification of observance of human rights*

40. As this first report emphasizes, the priorities for international verification by the Mission are established in the San José Agreement (para. 11), according to which the Mission shall devote special attention to the following rights or groups of rights: the rights to life and to the integrity and security of the person; the right to due process; the right to personal liberty; the right to freedom of expression; and the right to freedom of association. The content of those rights for the purposes of international verification is outlined below.

1. *Right to life and to the integrity and security of the person 7/*

41. These rights are covered by paragraph 1 of the San José Agreement. In its international verification functions, the Mission will devote special attention to the following violations of these rights:

(a) *Summary executions*

42. This category covers:

(a) Executions or deaths which may have occurred in violation of the safeguards designed to protect the right to life contained in the domestic laws and the international law in force;

(b) Death threats.

(b) *Enforced or involuntary disappearances*

43. This category covers the abduction or arrest of a person by an agent of the State, or by a person whose action is supported or tolerated by the State, when no information is provided as to the destination or whereabouts of the victim.

(c) *Abductions*

44. This category will cover cases of politically motivated abduction by individuals or private groups, according to the legal provisions which create the normative framework for verification.

(d) *Torture and cruel, inhuman or degrading treatment or punishment 8/*

45. These practices are prohibited by the San José Agreement (para. 2 (f)) and cover all cases which may involve the following violations:

(a) Torture;

(b) Cruel, inhuman or degrading treatment or punishment;

(c) Violation of the right of anyone deprived of his liberty to be treated humanely and with the respect due to human dignity.

2. *Right to due process 9/*

46. The San José Agreement refers to this right in its paragraphs 11 and 14 (h) and guarantees the remedies of *amparo* and *habeas corpus* (para. 4). Verification will cover, *inter alia*, observance of the following rights:

(a) The right of anyone to be heard within a reasonable time by a competent, independent and impartial tribunal;

(b) The right to an effective legal remedy for the protection of fundamental rights, which includes the obligation not to obstruct the remedies of *amparo* and *habeas corpus* and not to provide false information to the judicial authority;

5/ El Salvador has ratified a number of the main universal and regional international human rights treaties, including the International Covenant on Economic, Social and Cultural Rights and the International Covenant on Civil and Political Rights of the United Nations and the American Convention on Human Rights of the Organization of American States.
6/ The term "declarations and principles" also covers other United Nations legal norms such as the Standard Minimum Rules for the Treatment of Prisoners, the Declaration of Basic Principles of Justice for Victims of Crime and Abuse of Power and the Principles on the Effective Prevention and Investigation of Extralegal, Arbitrary and Summary Executions. In the area of international humanitarian law, El Salvador is a party to the four Geneva Conventions of 1949, article 3 of which applies to domestic armed conflicts, and to Additional Protocols I and II of 8 June 1977, of which the latter applies to such conflicts.
7/ Cf. Political Constitution of the Republic of El Salvador, art. 2; Universal Declaration of Human Rights, art. 3; International Covenant on Civil and Political Rights, art. 6; and American Convention on Human Rights, art. 4.
8/ Cf. Universal Declaration, art. 5; International Covenant, art. 7; American Convention, art. 5.
9/ Cf. Political Constitution, arts. 11, 12, 13, 14, 15, 16, 17 and 21; Universal Declaration, arts. 6, 7, 8, 10 and 11; International Covenant, arts. 14, 15 and 16; American Convention, arts. 8, 9, 10 and 25; Declaration of Basic Principles of Justice for Victims of Crime and Abuse of Power; and General Assembly resolution 40/34 of 29 November 1985.

(c) The right to procedural guarantees, including the right to defend oneself during trial, the right to be presumed innocent and the right not to be compelled to testify against oneself;

(d) The right to justice for victims of crimes and abuse of power.

3. *Right to personal liberty* 10/

47. This right, including freedom of movement, is guaranteed in the San José Agreement (paras. 1, 2, 4, 7 and 8). The Mission will also verify observance of, *inter alia*, the following rights:

(a) The right of anyone who is threatened with deprivation of liberty to appeal to the competent judge for a decision on the lawfulness of such a threat;

(b) The right of everyone lawfully within the territory of the country to freedom of movement and freedom to choose his residence within that territory, subject only to the restrictions provided by law and in applicable international treaties.

4. *Freedom of expression* 11/

48. The San José Agreement (para. 6) guarantees this right. Verification will cover the following rights:

(a) Freedom of thought, expression and the press;

(b) The right to a correction or response;

(c) The right to engage in the profession of journalism.

5. *Freedom of association* 12/

49. This right is guaranteed by the San José Agreement (para. 5). Verification will cover the following rights:

(a) The right of everyone to freedom of association for all lawful purposes, including, *inter alia*, those of organizations for the protection and promotion of human rights;

(b) The right to trade union freedom, which includes the right of everyone to form and join trade unions for the protection of his interests.

B. *Verification of cases involving humanitarian law* 13/

50. Within the limits indicated in section III of this report, the Mission will devote attention to especially significant cases or situations related to the following violations of international humanitarian law.

1. *Humane treatment*

51. Violations of fundamental guarantees whereby all persons who are not participating directly in hostilities or have ceased to participate in them must be treated humanely in all circumstances.

2. *Civilian population*

52. The following violations, *inter alia*, will be given special attention:

(a) Attacks on the civilian population as such and on civilians;

(b) Acts or threats of violence whose main purpose is to intimidate the civilian population;

(c) Acts involving attacks on material goods essential to the survival of the civilian population or the obstruction of relief operations;

(d) Arbitrary relocation of the civilian population.

VI. *Significant situations*

53. Although the Mission's tasks are in their preparatory phase, some comments are called for on a number of situations that have occurred in this period and are covered by the Mission's mandate.

A. *Abductions*

54. On 27 July, the Mission received a report of the abduction, on 12 July, of a well-known coffee grower in Usulután, which was attributed to an FMLN commando. According to the report, the victim met with FMLN on the day of the abduction to agree on details for the payment of a "war tax" which FMLN had been demanding from him. The victim was in poor health and required permanent medical treatment. While an FMLN leader publicly denied responsibility for the abduction, another privately admitted responsibility.

55. Although this incident occurred before the Mission was set up and before it had agreed on arrangements with FMLN for the processing of reports, the Mission contacted FMLN immediately to find out whether the report was true and expressed concern at the possible violation of the commitment made in the San José Agreement to eliminate any practice involving abductions. After a series of contacts, FMLN admitted to the Mission on 5 August that it was responsible and sent it a public communiqué issued the same day justifying abduction as a valid method for demanding payment of the war tax. In direct talks at Mexico City, the Mission urged FMLN to fulfil its commitments and rejected the practice of abduction, as well as the justifications given for it. On 24 August, the victim was released and handed over to the Auxiliary Bishop of San Salvador who, together with ICRC, had also taken action to resolve the case satisfactorily.

56. The Mission also received another report of the abduction of a well-known leader of the Nationalist Republican Alliance (ARENA). Although it made repeated efforts to communicate with the relatives of the

10/ Cf. Political Constitution, arts. 2, 4, 5, 10 and 11; Universal Declaration, arts. 3, 8 and 13; International Covenant, arts. 9 and 12; and American Convention, arts. 7 and 22.
11/ Cf. Political Constitution, art. 6; Universal Declaration, art. 19; International Covenant, art. 19; and American Convention, arts. 13 and 14.
12/ Cf. Political Constitution, arts. 7 and 47; Universal Declaration, art. 20; International Covenant, art. 22; and American Convention, art. 16.
13/ Cf. article 3 of the four Geneva Conventions of 12 August 1949; articles 4, 13, 14 and 17 of Additional Protocol II; and General Assembly resolution 2675 (XXV) of 9 December 1970.

victim and the authors of the report in order to obtain more information, it was unable to do so. FMLN emphatically denied to ONUSAL that it had had any part in the incident. The Mission is still making efforts to shed light on the case.

57. The Mission reiterates that abduction, like the enforced disappearance of persons, is a violation of the San José Agreement, and it urges that measures be taken immediately to eliminate this practice.

B. Impact of the armed conflict on the rights of the civilian population

1. Segundo Montes community

58. On 20 August, the ONUSAL regional office in San Miguel received information about military operations carried out on 17 and 18 August in the Segundo Montes community, in which members of the civilian population were injured and their property damaged. The community, a settlement of returnees, is situated near the Torola river, on both sides of the main road leading to northern Morazán. This is a conflict zone with a large FMLN presence. According to members of the community, military units entered the community at 9.30 p.m. on 17 August, firing grenades and mortars and machine-gunning the Los Hatos and San Luis settlements. According to the same source, the next day military units took up positions in the hills near the community and carried out military actions against it. As a result, nine people were seriously wounded, including a pregnant woman who later had to be given an abortion. A further 25 people were injured in the confusion caused by the explosions and 23 more were poisoned by tear-gas bombs. A number of dwellings and animals in the community were hit by bullets or fragments or affected by explosions.

59. The armed forces claimed that the raid on Segundo Montes took place on the afternoon of 17 August when armed members of FMLN opened fire on army units from dwellings in the settlement and, later, groups of civilians armed with machetes, sickles and clubs attacked the soldiers. It also claimed that the military units were conducting operations pursuant to the constitutional order to ensure the integrity of the national territory. 14/

60. On 21 August, the Mission visited the community and talked to a number of people who had been affected by the use of tear-gas bombs and injured by bullets and fragments. It noted the traces left by the impact of bullets and fragments on dwellings and the effects of mortars and grenades landing on community property. It later requested information from various reliable sources who had been present during the incident, including representatives of the Office of the United Nations High Commissioner for Refugees (UNHCR).

61. On the basis of all the information received and its on-site investigations, the Mission concludes that there is no decisive evidence that armed members of FMLN were in the community at the time of the incidents. Everything would seem to indicate that the purpose of the military actions was to intimidate the civilian population in order to facilitate a military operation in northern Morazán. In any case, the army's response was out of all proportion to the alleged attack by members of the community.

62. The Mission believes that acts against the civilian population such as that mentioned above violate the San José Agreement, and it appeals for an end to such acts in the future.

2. San José de las Flores community

63. The ONUSAL regional sub-office in Chalatenango was set up on 28 August. That same day, a verification team visited a number of communities in the conflict zone, including San José de las Flores, without giving advance warning. While it was visiting San José de las Flores, the team noticed the presence of FMLN combatants in the community. It was also able to detect the presence of military units not far from the community, who were conducting military operations that had begun a number of days previously.

64. The community told ONUSAL that it had long been the object of frequent acts of intimidation by military units, which would subject it to artillery bombardments and had imposed a permanent economic blockade. The military operation in the zone was stepped up on 3 September, with the result that a number of members of the community were wounded and a nine-month-old girl was killed by a bullet which hit her while she was in her own home.

65. On 4 September, members of the community gathered outside the Mission's offices to report the child's death. They later went to the main square in Chalatenango, across from where a military unit was stationed. Incidents occurred with members of the unit and, according to witnesses, from there they went to the bishopric for protection.

66. The armed forces told the Mission that the military operations being conducted in the zone form part of routine surveillance activities and can in no way be viewed as actions aimed directly at the civilian population.

67. From its investigations, the Mission concluded that there was a line of fire from the place where the military units were posted near San José de las Flores to

14/ The armed forces also reported an incident that occurred on 25 August, in which a soldier who was seriously wounded died while he was being transferred in a military ambulance. ONUSAL, which has received very conflicting versions of the incident, is following an investigation into it.

the place where a number of members of the community received bullet wounds. However, it was unable to determine whether FMLN combatants were in the community when the incidents occurred, although, as indicated above, a Mission team had noted the presence of FMLN combatants a few days earlier.

68. The Mission is concerned at the incidents and urges the parties to take urgent, immediate steps to prevent actions which might cause civilian casualties.

69. These two cases illustrate the difficulties of finding out the truth about incidents when the San José Agreement is being verified before the cessation of the armed conflict.

C. *Right to due process*

Prosecution of the Jesuit case

70. The murder of six Jesuit priests and their housekeeper and one of her daughters, which took place on 16 November 1989 on the campus of José Siméon Cañas Central American University in San Salvador, is considered one of the most glaring cases of human rights violations to have occurred in the country. Prosecution of this case can be seen as an opportunity to test the alleged impunity in the area of human rights to which different national and international sources have repeatedly drawn attention.

71. The case will soon come before a jury which, after the public hearing, will have to give a verdict. Immediately thereafter, the Fourth Criminal Judge who is in charge of the case will have to pass sentence. Of the nine accused, all of whom are soldiers, eight are in detention, including a colonel.

72. The investigation of this murder, and of other human rights violations that occurred prior to 26 July 1991, does not strictly fall within the competence of the Mission but rather, potentially, of the Commission on the Truth. However, in order to verify respect for due process in the current proceedings, the Mission will follow them closely.

VII. *Comments and conclusions*

73. The purpose of this first report is to define the legal and political framework for verification based on an analysis of the San José Agreement, taking into account the fact that the Mission was set up before the parties signed an agreement on cessation of the armed conflict.

74. These circumstances have been discussed with the two parties signatories to the San José Agreement and a publicity campaign has been launched to inform Salvadorian society, through non-governmental organizations, about the scope of the Agreement.

75. The progressive deployment of the Mission throughout the territory, the visits to all sectors of society, both governmental and non-governmental, and the Mis-

sion's presence in the field reflect its desire both to fulfil the mandate established by articles 10-18 of the Agreement and by Security Council resolution 693 (1991) and to explain the content of the Agreement and the importance of the ONUSAL presence in the country. To that end, the Mission took advantage of its generally very favourable reception by the Salvadorian people, the parties to the conflict, Government institutions and civilian society at large.

76. As of the date of drafting this report, six weeks after the Mission's arrival, while it was not possible to give a detailed analysis of a particularly complex situation, it was necessary, having described the circumstances in which the Mission was set up, to define a preliminary legal framework for action, establish priorities and begin to devise a methodology for working arrangements and a programme for human rights promotion and education.

77. The desire of the Government of El Salvador and FMLN that the Mission be set up as soon as possible, even in the absence of a cease-fire, made it necessary for the Mission to analyse the scope of its powers. While the priorities set forth in paragraph 11 of the Agreement, to which a number of references are made in this report, are perfectly clear, the Mission could not ignore the persistence of the armed conflict, its impact on the overall level of violence and the need for vigilance in ensuring the protection of the human rights of the civilian population. It was not, therefore, a question of interpreting the Agreement but rather of taking into account the intention of the parties in not waiting for a cease-fire agreement to be signed before requesting verification by the Mission.

78. Nor was it feasible, in this period in which the Mission is being organized, is finding out at first hand about the country's institutions and their structure and functioning and is making its first contacts with FMLN and civilian society, to embark on a detailed analysis of the reports submitted to it. However, the significance of certain incidents that occurred in the first weeks after the Mission was set up and of certain situations affecting vulnerable civilian populations made it necessary to mention a number of cases in one section of the report.

79. The persistence of the armed conflict and, since mid-August, its escalation in certain parts of the country are creating a considerable amount of tension which affects fundamental rights that are a priority for the Mission: the rights to life and to the integrity and security of the person. Although direct investigation of the observance of human rights cannot begin in the first phase of verification, particular vigilance does however seem to be called for in especially serious situations.

80. In future reports, it will be possible to follow the progress made in implementing the Agreement since

the Mission was set up. The description of the institutional framework and of the overall situation of human rights in El Salvador marks a starting point, based on the situation existing at the time of ONUSAL's arrival. We shall not attempt, therefore, to make definitive judgements but rather, on the basis of field visits and the observation and investigation of incidents, to help improve the functioning of institutions and ensure respect for the Agreement by the two parties.

81. After it has made recommendations to the Government of El Salvador and FMLN, the Mission will be able to observe the efforts they make to ensure increasingly full observance of human rights.

82. While we cannot of course apply standards which might be used in countries with a solid tradition of respect for human rights, we shall attempt in this case to apply criteria which take the country's situation into account and shall encourage the parties to make positive changes in this area.

83. The welcome given the Mission in its first activities by the Salvadorian Government, FMLN, political parties and mass organizations and the beginnnings of cooperation with human rights bodies reveal a readiness to facilitate the Mission's verification task and to make progress towards a lasting peace.

Document 25

Letters dated 26 September 1991 and 4 October 1991 from El Salvador transmitting texts of the New York Agreement and the Compressed Negotiations, signed on 25 September 1991 by the Government of El Salvador and the FMLN

A/46/502-S/23082, 26 September 1991, and addendum, A/46/502/Add.1-S/23082/Add.1, 7 October 1991

I have the honour to transmit herewith the text of the "New York Agreement" signed at United Nations Headquarters on 25 September 1991, containing the results of the negotiations held from 16 to 25 September between the Government of El Salvador and the Frente Farabundo Martí para la Liberación Nacional.

I should be very grateful if you could have this note and its annex circulated as an official document of the General Assembly, under item 31, and of the Security Council.

(*Signed*) Ricardo G. CASTAÑEDA
Ambassador
Permanent Representative

Annex

New York agreement

The Government of El Salvador and the Frente Farabundo Martí para la Liberación Nacional (hereinafter called "the Parties"),

Convinced of the need to give a final impetus to the process of negotiations currently taking place with the active participation of the Secretary-General of the United Nations, so that the set of political agreements required to bring a definitive end to the armed conflict in our country can be reached as speedily as possible,

Conscious of the fact that, in order to achieve the aforementioned objective, it is essential to establish a set of conditions and guarantees which will ensure the full implementation of those political agreements by both Parties,

Have reached the following political agreement:

I. *Comisión Nacional para la Consolidación de la Paz*

1. The Comisión Nacional para la Consolidación de la Paz (National Commission for the Consolidation of Peace) (COPAZ) shall be responsible for overseeing the implementation of all the political agreements reached by the Parties. COPAZ is a mechanism for the monitoring of and the participation of civilian society in the process of the changes resulting from the negotiations, in relation both to the armed forces, in particular, and to the other items on the agenda.

2. *Composition*
a. COPAZ shall be composed of two representatives of the Government, including a member of the armed forces, two representatives of FMLN and one representative of each of the parties or coalitions represented in the Legislative Assembly.
b. The Archbishop of San Salvador and a delegate of ONUSAL shall have access to the work and deliberations of COPAZ, as observers.

3. *Decisions*

COPAZ shall adopt its decisions by majority vote.

4. *Powers*

a. COPAZ shall not have executive powers since it is for the Parties, through their internal machinery, to carry out the peace agreements.

b. The Parties shall be obliged to consult COPAZ before adopting decisions or measures relating to relevant aspects of the peace agreements. Similarly, COPAZ may consult the Parties, at the highest level, whenever it deems it appropriate to do so. In the event of a difference of opinion as to whether a matter should be submitted to COPAZ, the question shall be decided by COPAZ.

c. At the request of three or more of its members, COPAZ shall be convened immediately and its opinion heard.

d. COPAZ shall have direct access to the President of the Republic and shall meet with him whenever CO-PAZ itself or the President deems it appropriate.

e. COPAZ shall have access to and may inspect any activity or site connected with the implementation of the peace agreements.

f. COPAZ shall have the power to issue conclusions and recommendations of any kind relating to the implementation of the peace agreements and to make them public. The Parties undertake to comply with those conclusions and recommendations.

g. COPAZ shall have the power to prepare the preliminary legislative drafts necessary for the development of the agreements which have been reached, both on the subject of the armed forces and on the other items on the agenda.

h. COPAZ shall have the power to oversee the implementation of the agreements reached by the Parties, both on the subject of the armed forces and on the other items on the agenda.

i. COPAZ shall be responsible for the preparation of the preliminary legislative drafts necessary to ensure that all those wounded in the war and, where appropriate, the families of combatants who have died, on both sides, are incorporated into the social security system of the State or receive adequate economic compensation, as provided for by law.

j. In the performance of its functions, COPAZ shall be authorized to address the relevant organs of the United Nations, through the Secretary-General.

k. COPAZ shall have full powers to organize its work in the manner which it deems most appropriate and to appoint any groups or subcommissions which it may deem useful in the discharge of its mission. For that purpose, it shall have its own budget.

5. *Form*

In addition to being the product of this political agreement, COPAZ shall be confirmed by law.

6. *Duration*

a. Between the date of this agreement and the cessation of the armed conflict, two representatives of the Government, including one member of the armed forces, two representatives of FMLN and one representative of each of the parties or coalitions represented in the Legislative Assembly shall work under a special operational régime of a transitional nature which they themselves shall define. This work shall include the preparation of the preliminary draft legislation to formalize the establishment of COPAZ.

b. The preliminary draft legislation to formalize the establishment of COPAZ shall be submitted to the Legislative Assembly within eight (8) days following the signing of the cessation of armed conflict. The formal establishment of COPAZ shall take place within eight (8) days following the promulgation of the said law.

c. COPAZ shall be dissolved once the implementation of the peace agreements has been completed. Its dissolution shall be decided upon by COPAZ itself, by means of an agreement receiving a favourable vote from at least two thirds of its members.

7. *International guarantees*

a. The establishment of COPAZ shall be explicitly endorsed by a resolution to be adopted by the Security Council concerning the peace agreements.

b. The Secretary-General shall keep the Security Council informed regarding the activities and effectiveness of COPAZ.

c. COPAZ shall be endorsed by Governments which are in a position to support effectively the guarantee required under the agreements as well as the work of COPAZ. In particular, the cooperation of those Governments shall be expressed and given in such a way as to promote the proposals set forth in the peace agreements as well as their full implementation.

II. *Purification* 1/

1. A process of purification of the armed forces is agreed upon, on the basis of a vetting of all personnel serving in them by an ad hoc Commission.

2. Participation by the armed forces will comprise two of their personnel, who shall have access only to the deliberations of the Commission.

III. *Reduction of the armed forces*

1. The criteria for reduction of the armed forces shall be agreed upon between the Parties.

1/ The mechanisms for selecting all participants in the ad hoc Commission, as well as the voting criteria and other measures relating to the purification, will be dealt with in the compressed negotiations.

2. The criteria shall determine inter alia the guidelines on the basis of which:

a. The size to which the armed forces shall be reduced in peacetime shall be determined;

b. The plan for the reduction (manner, timetable, budget, etc.) shall be drawn up.

IV. *Doctrine of the armed forces*

Agreement shall be reached on the redefinition of the doctrine of the armed forces based on the ideas that emerge from the agreements on this subject and from the constitutional reform. It is understood that the function of the armed forces is to defend the sovereignty of the State and the integrity of its territory, and that this doctrine should be based on the principle that the activities and regime of the armed forces shall be consistent with the principles deriving from the concept of the legally-constituted State governed by the rule of law, the primacy of the dignity of the human person and respect for human rights; defence of and respect for the sovereignty of the Salvadorian people; the concept of the armed forces as an institution in the service of the nation, free from all considerations of politics, ideology or social standing, and from all other forms of discrimination; and the subordination of the armed services to the constitutional authorities.

V. *Training system for the armed forces*

Full effect will be given in its entirety to the agreement reached in Mexico on 27 April 1991 whereby the professional training of personnel serving in the armed forces shall place emphasis on the pre-eminence of human dignity and democratic values, respect for human rights and the subordination of such forces to the constitutional authorities. The agreements reached in this respect shall comprise regulatory provisions guaranteeing the foregoing points as well as the admission and instruction systems.

VI. *National civil police*

The agenda for the negotiations on the National Civil Police provided for in the constitutional reform approved in the Mexico agreements shall include the following items: 2/

a. Establishment of the NCP. 3/ Doctrine. Juridical regime;

b. Disbandment of the National Guard and the Treasury Police, as Public Security Forces;

c. Personnel of the NCP:

1. Vetting of National Police personnel.

2. Enlistment of new personnel. Pluralistic and non-discriminatory selection and training system.

3. Profiles and training.

4. International advisory services and support coordinated by the United Nations. The organization of the NCP and of the National Public Security Academy and the selection of their personnel will be the subject of close international cooperation and supervision.

5. Transitional regime.

VII. *Economic and social questions*

1. Lands in excess of the constitutional limit of 245 hectares, as well as lands owned by the State which are not currently legally designated forest reserves, shall be used to meet the needs of peasants and small farmers who are without land. To this end, the Government shall also make arrangements to purchase lands offered for sale to the State.

2. The current land-holding situation in the conflict zones shall be respected until a satisfactory legal solution for the definitive land-holding regime is arrived at. The procedures and deadlines for the implementation of this agreement shall be agreed upon in the compressed negotiations.

3. The policies for granting loans to the agriculture and livestock sector shall be revised.

4. The Parties refer to the compressed negotiations, as part of the economic and social subject area, consideration of the following topics:

a. Measures required to alleviate the social cost of structural adjustment programmes;

b. Appropriate procedures for direct external cooperation designed to encourage community assistance and development projects;

c. Establishment of a Forum for economic and social accommodation, with participation by the governmental, labour and business sectors, for the purpose of continuing to resolve economic and social problems. The Forum may be open to participation by other social and political sectors as observers, under terms to be determined by it.

VIII. *Remainder of the agenda*

1. Other aspects still pending under the "Armed Forces" item relate to the guarantees of compliance with the agreements. No direct mention is made of these, because they are subject to agreement in the compressed negotiations. In any event, their fulfilment and implementation will be the responsibility of COPAZ.

2. On the same date, the Parties have agreed on an agenda for the compressed negotiations on the pending

2/ The negotiations on the National Civil Police and on the Public Security Forces are at an advanced stage. The Parties have in their possession a working paper which reflects the progress made.

3/ Given the complexity of the task and the time required to carry it out, the process of organizing the new National Civil Police needs to begin immediately, i.e. without awaiting other political agreements or the cessation of the armed confrontation. To this end, provision of the international advisory services required has already begun.

items, which shall be deemed to form part of the present agreement. Those items on this agenda which have been the subject of agreements in principle in the present agreement shall be subject to consideration and negotiation in conformity with the criteria and principles defined herein.

New York, 25 September 1991

Representing the Government of El Salvador:	*Representing the Frente Farabundo Martí para la Liberación Nacional:*
(Signed) Dr. Oscar SANTAMARÍA	*(Signed)* Cmdr. Schafik HÁNDAL
Col. Mauricio Ernesto VARGAS	Cmdr. Francisco JOVEL
Dr. David ESCOBAR GALINDO	Cmdr. Salvador SÁNCHEZ CERÉN
	Cmdr. Eduardo SANCHO
	Cmdr. Joaquín VILLALOBOS

Alvaro DE SOTO
Representative of the Secretary-General
of the United Nations

Addendum

I have the honour to transmit the document entitled "The Compressed Negotiations" signed at United Nations Headquarters on 25 September 1991 by representatives of the Government of El Salvador and of Frente Farabundo Martí para la Liberación Nacional (FMLN).

I should be very grateful if you would have this note and its annex circulated as an official document of the General Assembly, under item 31, and of the Security Council, as an addendum to document A/46/502-S/23082 of 26 September 1991.

(Signed) Ricardo G. CASTAÑEDA
Ambassador
Permanent Representative

Annex

The Compressed Negotiations

Article 1. *Aims and principles*

Compression of the negotiations aims to secure, at one go, political agreements to:

(a) Coordinate an end to the armed conflict and to every act that violates the rights of the civilian population, under United Nations verification, subject to the approval of the Security Council; and

(b) Establish the guarantees and conditions needed to reintegrate members of FMLN into the civilian, institutional and political life of the country in absolute legality.

Accordingly, all the substantive items on the Agenda would be negotiated and settled prior to the end of the armed conflict. This will mean a cease-fire of predetermined length, short and dynamic, during which there would not be any substantive negotiations but only the measures necessary to put the agreements reached into practice.

This implies that the Agenda approved at Caracas should be reshaped to take account of the above aims and of the outcome of the negotiations conducted since then.

Article 2. *Subjects for negotiation*

The matters to be negotiated are as follows:

I. Armed forces 1/

This item includes:

1. Doctrine.
2. Training system.
3. Purification.
4. Reduction. 2/
5. Waiver of impunity. 3/
6. Public Security Forces: 4/
   - Establishment of the NCP. 5/ Doctrine. Juridical regime.
   - Disbandment of the National Guard and the Treasury Police, as Public Security Forces.
   - Personnel of the NCP. Vetting of National Police personnel. Enlistment of new personnel. Pluralistic and non-discriminatory selection and training system.
   - Profiles and training.
   - International advisory services and support.
   - Transitional regime.
6. [*sic*] Intelligence services: 6/
   - Disbandment of the DNI.
   - Establishment of the OIE. Doctrine. Juridical regime.
   - Personnel of the OIE.
   - Monitoring.

1/ Most of the sub-items under this point are fairly advanced on the basis of the working document prepared by the intermediary.
2/ The question will be considered within the scope defined by the New York Agreement.
3/ See "Comisión de la Verdad" (Truth Commission) in the Mexico agreements of 27 April 1991. The working paper on the Armed Forces sets forth the connection between the subject and that Commission.
4/ This question has also reached an advanced stage, on the basis of an additional document prepared by the intermediary.
5/ In view of the complexity of the task and the time required to carry it out, the process of organizing the new National Civil Police needs to begin immediately, i.e. without awaiting other political agreements or the cessation of the armed confrontation.
6/ This question has also reached an advanced stage, on the basis of an additional document prepared by the intermediary.

7. Rapid deployment infantry battalions.
8. Subordination to the civil power.
9. Paramilitary entities:
   - Civil defence.
   - Regime of the Salvadorian Armed Forces reserves.
   - Eradication of illegal groups.
   - Regulation of private security.
   - Monitoring.
10. Suspension of conscription.
11. Preventive and promotional methods.
12. Relocation and reduction.
13. International verification.

II. Judicial system

Implementation of the political agreements for the development of the constitutional reform adopted in the Mexico agreements of 27 April 1991.

III. Electoral system

Implementation of the political agreements for the development of the constitutional reform adopted in the Mexico agreements of 27 April 1991.

IV. Ratification of the constitutional reform

This item is inferred from the Mexico agreements of 27 April 1991. It is an indispensable prerequisite for the concretization of other political agreements, such as many of those referring to the electoral and judicial systems, as well as the agreement relating to the National Civil Police, for example. Consequently, progress should be made in that direction without further delay.

V. Economic and social questions

VI. Conditions for the cessation of the armed confrontation

The work that has been done with regard to this question will have to be adapted to the arrangements for the cease-fire described above, and particularly to its dynamic character, the consequence of the compression of the negotiations.

VII. Political participation by FMLN

VIII. Verification by the United Nations

IX. Timetable for implementation

New York, 25 September 1991

Representing the Government of El Salvador:	Representing Frente Farabundo Martí para la Liberación Nacional:
(Signed) Dr. Oscar SANTAMARÍA	*(Signed)* Cmdr. Schafik HÁNDAL
Col. Mauricio Ernesto VARGAS	Cmdr. Francisco JOVEL
Dr. David ESCOBAR GALINDO	Cmdr. Salvador SÁNCHEZ CERÉN
	Cmdr. Eduardo SANCHO
	Cmdr. Joaquín VILLALOBOS

Alvaro DE SOTO
Representative of the Secretary-General
of the United Nations

Document 26

Security Council resolution concerning agreements between the Government of El Salvador and the FMLN

S/RES/714 (1991), 30 September 1991

The Security Council,

Recalling its resolution 637 (1989) of 27 July 1989, by which it lent its full support to the Secretary-General for his mission of good offices in Central America,

Also recalling its resolution 693 (1991) of 20 May 1991, by which it established the United Nations Observer Mission in El Salvador,

Welcoming the New York Agreement signed 25 September 1991 by the Government of El Salvador and the Frente Farabundo Martí para la Liberación Nacional, 1/ which provides guarantees and conditions on which to reach a peaceful settlement to the armed conflict, including, *inter alia*, the provisions concerning the National Commission for the Consolidation of Peace, permitting the reintegration of the members of the Frente Farabundo Martí, within a framework of full legality, into the civil, institutional and political life of the country,

Welcoming also the oral report of the Secretary-General, made at the consultations held on 30 September 1991,

1. *Commends* the parties for the flexibility and seriousness which they demonstrated during the course of the recent talks in New York;

2. *Congratulates* the Secretary-General and his Personal Representative for Central America for their skilful and tireless efforts which have been vital to the peace process;

3. *Expresses* appreciation for the contributions of the Governments of the Group of Friends of the Secretary-General, Colombia, Mexico, Spain, and Venezuela, which have advanced the peace process in El Salvador;

4. *Urges* both parties at the next negotiating round, which will begin on 12 October 1991 to proceed at an intensive and sustained pace to reach at the earliest possible date a cease-fire and a peaceful settlement to the armed conflict in accordance with the framework of the New York Agreement; 1/

5. *Reaffirms* its *full support* for the urgent completion of the peace process in El Salvador, and expresses its readiness to support the implementation of a settlement;

6. *Urges* both parties to exercise maximum and continuing restraint, particularly with respect to the civilian population, in order to create the best climate for a successful last stage of the negotiations;

7. *Calls upon* both parties to continue to cooperate fully with the United Nations Observer Mission in El Salvador.

1/ S/23082.

Document 27

Letter dated 8 October 1991 from El Salvador transmitting the text of the Geneva Agreement signed on 4 April 1990 by the Government of El Salvador and the FMLN

A/46/551-S/23128, 9 October 1991

I have the honour to transmit to you herewith a copy of the "Geneva Agreement" signed at Geneva, Switzerland, on 4 April 1990 by representatives of the Government of El Salvador and of the Frente Farabundo Martí para la Liberación Nacional (see annex).

I should be grateful if you would have this note and its annex distributed as an official document of the General Assembly, under agenda item 31, and of the Security Council.

(*Signed*) Ricardo G. CASTANEDA
Ambassador
Permanent Representative

Annex

Geneva Agreement

(4 April 1991)

At the request of the Central American Presidents and within the framework of the mandate of good offices conferred on me by the Security Council under resolution 637 of 27 July 1989, I have held consultations with the Government of El Salvador and the Frente Farabundo Martí para la Liberación Nacional (FMLN) in order to agree on the format, mechanism and pace of a process aimed at bringing about as speedily as possible, under my auspices, a definitive end to the armed conflict in that country. I have agreed to carry out this effort at the request of the Government and FMLN and because I have received assurances from both parties that there is a serious and good faith intention to seek to bring about such an end through negotiations. As a result of my consultations, the Government and FMLN have agreed on the points set forth below, which are designed to ensure that the process is conducted in an efficient and serious manner and promotes mutual trust through appropriate guarantees.

I believe that in addition to their intrinsic importance, the scrupulous maintenance of these guarantees will demonstrate the desire and ability of the parties to carry out any commitments they make during the negotiations. On this understanding, the Government and FMLN have pledged not to abandon the negotiating process.

1. The purpose of the process shall be to end the armed conflict by political means as speedily as possible, promote the democratization of the country, guarantee unrestricted respect for human rights and reunify Salvadorian society.

The initial objective shall be to reach political agreements which lay the basis for a cessation of the armed conflict and of any acts that infringe the rights of the civilian population, which will have to be verified by the United Nations, subject to the approval of the Security Council. Once that has been achieved, the process shall lead to the establishment of the necessary guarantees and conditions for reintegrating the members of FMLN, within a framework of full legality, into the civil, institutional and political life of the country.

2. The process shall be conducted under the auspices of the Secretary-General, on a continuous and uninterrupted basis.

3. In order to ensure the success of the negotiating process, the Government and FMLN agree to an approach which shall involve two types of complementary activities: direct dialogue between the negotiating commissions with the active participation of the Secretary-General or his Representative, and an intermediary role by the Secretary-General or his Representative between the parties to ensure that both the Government and FMLN are committed at the highest level. The Secretary-General shall seek to ensure that these activities are conducted in a manner that genuinely contributes to the success of the process. The Government and FMLN shall ensure that their negotiating commissions have full powers to discuss and conclude agreements.

4. The Government and FMLN agree that the process shall be conducted in the strictest secrecy. The only public information on its progress shall be that provided by the Secretary-General or his authorized Representative.

5. The Secretary-General, at his discretion, may maintain confidential contacts with Governments of States Members of the United Nations or groups thereof that can contribute to the success of the process through their advice and support.

6. The Government of El Salvador and FMLN agree that the political parties and other representative social organizations existing in El Salvador have an important role to play in the attainment of peace. They also recognize the need for both the Government and FMLN to maintain appropriate, ongoing information and consultation mechanisms with such parties and social organizations in the country, and that the latter must undertake to preserve the secrecy necessary to the success of the dialogue process. When it is deemed appropriate and on the basis of mutual consent, the commissions may call upon representatives of these parties and organizations in order to receive their inputs.

7. The Government and FMLN likewise recognize that it is useful for the Secretary-General to maintain contacts with Salvadorian individuals and groups whose input may benefit his efforts.

Geneva, 4 April 1990

Representing the Government of El Salvador:	*Representing the Frente Farabundo Martí para la Liberación Nacional:*
(Signed)	*(Signed)*
Mr. Oscar SANTAMARÍA	Commander Schafik HÁNDAL
Ambassador Guillermo PAZ LARIN	Mr. Salvador SAMAYOA
Ambassador Ana Cristina SOL	Commander Ana Guadalupe MARTÍNEZ
Ambassador Carlos Ernesto MENDOZA	Commander Roberto CAÑAS

In the capacity assigned to me by the United Nations Security Council in resolution 637 (1989)

(Signed) Javier PÉREZ DE CUÉLLAR
Secretary-General of the United Nations

Document 28

Letter dated 8 October 1991 from El Salvador transmitting the text of the Caracas Agreement signed on 21 May 1990 by the Government of El Salvador and the FMLN

A/46/552-S/23129, 9 October 1991

I have the honour to transmit to you herewith a copy of the "General Agenda and Timetable for the Comprehensive Negotiating Process" signed at Caracas, Venezuela, on 21 May 1990 by representatives of the Government of El Salvador and of the Frente Farabundo Martí para la Liberación Nacional (see annex).

I should be grateful if you would have this note and its annex distributed as an official document of the General Assembly, under agenda item 31, and of the Security Council.

(Signed) Ricardo G. CASTAÑEDA
Ambassador
Permanent Representative

Annex

*General agenda and timetable for the
comprehensive negotiating process*

A. *General agenda*

I. The initial objective shall be to reach political agreements which lay the basis for a cessation of the armed conflict and of any acts that infringe the rights of the civilian population, which will have to be verified by the United Nations, subject to the approval of the Security Council.

(a) First: Political agreements
(1) Armed forces
(2) Human rights
(3) Judicial system
(4) Electoral system
(5) Constitutional reform
(6) Economic and social issues
(7) Verification by the United Nations

(b) Second: Cessation of the armed conflict and of any acts that infringe the rights of the civilian population

II. Establishment of the necessary guarantees and conditions for reintegrating the members of FMLN, within a framework of full legality, into the civil, institutional and political life of the country.
(1) Armed forces
(2) Human rights
(3) Judicial system
(4) Electoral system
(5) Constitutional reform
(6) Economic and social issues
(7) Reintegration of FMLN members
(8) Verification by the United Nations

III. Final agreements for the consolidation of the objectives of the Geneva Agreement and verification, where appropriate, by the United Nations.

Note: The sequence of the items listed for each phase does not imply a strict order of consideration and may be changed by mutual consent.

Agreements must be tailored to the nature of the phase involved. Political issues have been placed in their respective phases but, given the complexity of some of them, aspects thereof may be addressed in other phases. All this depends on the dynamic of the negotiations.

B. *Timetable*

In the light of the general agenda for the comprehensive negotiating process set forth in the preceding section, the Government of El Salvador and FMLN agree that the initial objective set forth in paragraph 1 of the Geneva Agreement of 4 April 1990 should be achieved by the middle of September 1990, provided that agreements are reached which are synchronized, have implementation timetables and can be verified where appropriate, so as to ensure that all the components of the initial objective are duly coordinated.

This deadline would offer the additional advantage of helping to ensure that a legislative and municipal electoral process is conducted in an atmosphere of tranquillity, broad participation and freedom from intimidation.

It is difficult to set a fixed date for the conclusion of the comprehensive process. This will depend on factors that cannot be weighed at the present time, such as the extent and scope of the political agreements reached under paragraph I, which are a matter of negotiation, and the relationship between the negotiations and the electoral process. There is also a possibility that the initial objective may be achieved before the deadline. For these reasons, the conclusion of the process should be envisaged not in terms of dates but rather in terms of a given number of months after the achievement of the initial objective: tentatively, two to six months.

On the basis of the above understandings, the Government and FMLN shall, as their first substantive priority, concentrate on negotiating the political agreements envisaged under the initial objective.

Caracas, 21 May 1990

*Representing the
Government of
El Salvador:*

(Signed)
Colonel Juan A.
MARTÍNEZ VARELA

Mr. Oscar Alfredo
SANTAMARIÁ

Colonel Mauricio
Ernesto VARGAS

Mr. Abelardo TORRES

Mr. David ESCOBAR
GALINDO

Mr. Rafael HERNÁN
CONTRERAS

*Representing the
Frente Farabundo
Martí para la
Liberación Nacional:*

(Signed)
Commander Schafik
HÁNDAL

Commander Eduardo
SANCHO

Ana Guadelupe
MARTÍNEZ

Salvador SAMAYOA

Dagoberto
GUTIÉRREZ

Marta VALLADARES

Roberto CAÑAS

(Signed) Alvaro DE SOTO
Representative of the Secretary-General
of the United Nations

Document 29

Letter dated 8 October 1991 from El Salvador transmitting the text of the Mexico Agreement and annexes signed on 27 April 1991 by the Government of El Salvador and the FMLN

A/46/553-S/23130, 9 October 1991

I have the honour to transmit to you herewith a copy of the "Mexico Agreement" and the annexes thereto signed at Mexico City, Mexico, on 27 April 1991 by representatives of the Government of El Salvador and of the Frente Farabundo Martí para la Liberación Nacional (see annex).

I should be grateful if you would have this note and its annex distributed as an official document of the General Assembly, under agenda item 31, and of the Security Council.

(*Signed*) Ricardo G. CASTAÑEDA
Ambassador
Permanent Representative

Annex

Mexico agreements

The Government of El Salvador and the Frente Farabundo Martí para la Liberación Nacional (hereinafter referred to as "the Parties"),

Reaffirming their intention to make speedy progress towards the restoration of peace, national reconciliation and the reunification of Salvadorian society, in accordance with the common will of the Salvadorian people as expressed by both Parties in the Geneva Agreement of 4 April 1990;

Considering that the peace negotiations being conducted pursuant to the Geneva Agreement and to the Caracas Agenda of 21 May 1990 call for a number of constitutional reforms embodying the political agreements emanating therefrom;

Bearing in mind the urgent need to submit to the Legislative Assembly whose term expires on 30 April 1991 those constitutional reforms on which the Parties have reached agreement, even where such agreements are partial and do not deal with all aspects under the item as envisaged in the Caracas Agenda;

Considering that various points on which agreement has been reached can be put into practice through secondary legislation or through further political agreements elaborating on the Constitution;

Have reached the agreements summarized below, which comprise constitutional reforms and issues referred to secondary legislation, as well as other political agreements:

I. *Armed forces*

1. Agreements on constitutional reforms aimed at:

(a) A clearer definition of the subordination of the armed forces to civilian authority.

(b) The creation of a National Civil Police for the maintenance of peace, tranquillity, order and public safety in both urban and rural areas, under the control of civilian authorities. It is expressly understood that the National Civil Police and the armed forces shall be independent and shall be placed under the authority of different ministries.

(c) The creation of a State Intelligence Agency independent of the armed forces and under the direct authority of the President of the Republic.

(d) Redefinition of the system of military justice with a view to ensuring that only those cases which affect a strictly military legal interest are submitted to it.

2. Other issues considered in the negotiations were referred to secondary legislation or to the set of political agreements on the armed forces. These include:

(a) Paramilitary forces.

(b) Forcible recruitment.

(c) Aspects relating to the management of the security forces and State intelligence.

(d) Aspects relating to the personnel of the armed forces and the National Civil Police.

(e) The emphasis which must be given, in the professional training of members of the defence and public security forces, to the pre-eminence of human dignity and democratic values, to respect for human rights and to the subordination of such forces to the constitutional authorities.

The foregoing is without prejudice to the other outstanding issues under the item on the armed forces, with respect to which the Parties reaffirm that they stand ready, and hope, to reach overall agreements in the next phase of the negotiating process.

II. *Judicial system and human rights*

1. Agreements on constitutional reforms designed to improve significant aspects of the judicial system and establish mechanisms for safeguarding human rights, such as:

(a) Reorganization of the Supreme Court of Justice and a new procedure for the election of Supreme Court judges. Henceforth, a two-thirds majority of deputies elected to the Legislative Assembly shall be required to elect judges to the Supreme Court of Justice.

(b) An annual allocation from the State budget to the judiciary amounting to no less than 6 per cent of current income.

(c) Creation of the post of a National Counsel for the Defence of Human Rights, whose primary function shall be to promote and ensure respect for human rights.

(d) Election of the Attorney-General of the Republic, the Chief State Counsel and the National Counsel for the Defence of Human Rights by a two-thirds majority of deputies elected to the Legislative Assembly.

2. Other issues raised in the negotiations were referred to secondary legislation and to other political agreements. Although the set of political agreements on the judicial system envisaged by the Parties in the Caracas Agenda has still to be negotiated, the following agreements have been reached during the current round:

(a) National Council of the Judiciary

Agreement has been reached to restructure the National Council of the Judiciary so that its composition guarantees its independence from the organs of State and from political parties and its membership includes not only judges but also sectors of society not directly connected with the administration of justice.

(b) Judicial Training School

The National Council of the Judiciary shall be responsible for organizing and operating the Judicial Training School, whose purpose shall be to ensure a steady improvement in the professional training of judges and other judicial officials.

(c) Career judicial service

The secondary legislation shall contain provisions to ensure that admission to the career judicial service is based on mechanisms guaranteeing objective selection, equal opportunities for all candidates and the selection of the best-qualified candidates. Such mechanisms shall include competitive examinations and attendance at the Judicial Training School.

III. *Electoral system*

1. Agreements on constitutional reforms aimed at:

(a) The establishment of a Supreme Electoral Tribunal to replace the Central Board of Elections. The Supreme Electoral Tribunal shall be the highest administrative authority and jurisdiction with respect to electoral matters. It has been agreed that the composition of the Tribunal shall be determined by secondary legislation, making sure that no party or coalition of parties predominates it. It has also been agreed that the Supreme Electoral Tribunal shall include members without any party affiliation, elected by a qualified majority of the Legislative Assembly.

(b) It has also been agreed that legally registered political parties shall have the right to monitor the compilation, organization, publication and updating of the electoral roll.

2. Other issues raised in the negotiations were referred to secondary legislation and to other political agreements. Although the set of political agreements on the electoral system envisaged by the Parties in the Caracas Agenda has still to be negotiated, the following agreements have been reached during the current round:

(a) The electoral roll shall be compiled in such a way that the lists of citizens eligible to vote are published at least 20 days before the date of the election. A simple and expeditious procedure shall be established for making legitimate corrections requested by any interested party.

(b) Within 60 days after the establishment of the new Supreme Electoral Tribunal, a Special Commission presided over by the Tribunal and composed of representatives of all legally registered parties and, possibly, independent experts shall be established to prepare a comprehensive proposal for reform of the electoral system.

IV. *Commission on the Truth*

Agreement has been reached to establish a Commission on the Truth, which shall be composed of three individuals appointed by the Secretary-General of the United Nations after consultation with the Parties. The Commission shall elect its Chairman. The Commission shall be entrusted with the task of investigating serious acts of violence that have occurred since 1980 and whose impact on society urgently requires that the public should know the truth. The Commission shall take into account:

(a) The exceptional importance that may be attached to the acts to be investigated, their characteristics and impact, and the social unrest to which they gave rise; and

(b) The need to create confidence in the positive changes which the peace process is promoting and to assist the transition to national reconciliation.

The characteristics, functions and powers of the Commission on the Truth and other related issues are set forth in the corresponding annex.

V. *Final declaration*

The Parties state for the record that the foregoing is a summary of the main political agreements which they reached during the round of negotiations held at Mexico City between 4 April 1991 and today's date. This summary shall in no way detract from, distort or contradict the authentic text of all the agreements reached, which are annexed to this document.

The Parties likewise reaffirm their commitment to take all necessary steps to execute the agreements fully. In particular, the Government of El Salvador solemnly undertakes to promote the approval by the current legislature of the constitutional reforms agreed to by the Parties in this round of negotiations. Matters relating to the ratification of these reforms shall be considered in the framework of the ongoing negotiations, under the timetable for the implementation of future agreements.

The Parties undertake to pursue the negotiations on an intensive basis, continuing the discussion of the list of issues agreed upon in the Caracas Agenda, with a view to reaching, as a matter of priority, a political agreement on the armed forces and the necessary agreements for the cessation of the armed conflict under United Nations supervision.

These negotiations will require careful additional preparation based on the important work done in recent months and, more especially, in recent weeks. Such preparation is an integral part of the negotiating process and the latter process shall not, therefore, be considered suspended. A brief direct meeting of an organizational nature is in fact planned for early May and direct negotiations are scheduled to resume in the latter half of the month. As usual, neither the exact dates nor the venue shall be announced in advance.

VI. *Unilateral declaration by FMLN*

FMLN stated for the record that the wording of article 211, where the armed forces are described as a "permanent" institution, is incompatible with its position on the matter. It made it clear that it considers there to be certain constitutional reforms still awaiting negotiation, including demilitarization, article 105 on the limit on rural land ownership and the need to open up the mechanism for reform of the Constitution, either by amending article 248 or by other procedures such as popular referendum. FMLN maintains its position on all these points.

Mexico City, 27 April 1991

Representing
the Government
of El Salvador:

Representing the
Frente Farabundo
Martí para la
Liberación Nacional:

(*Signed*)
Mr. Oscar
SANTAMARÍA

(*Signed*)
Commander Schafik
HÁNDAL

Colonel Juan MARTÍNEZ
VARELA

Commander Joaquín
VILLALOBOS

Colonel Mauricio Ernesto
VARGAS

Salvador SAMAYOA

Mr. David
ESCOBAR GALINDO

Ana Guadalupe
MARTÍNEZ

Mr. Abelardo TORRES

Mr. Rafael HERNÁN
CONTRERAS

(*Signed*) Alvaro DE SOTO
Representative of the Secretary-General
of the United Nations

The legislative assembly of the Republic of El Salvador:

I. Whereas it is the firm intention and duty of this Assembly to contribute to the restoration of peace, to national reconciliation and to the reunification of Salvadorian society, in accordance with the common will of our people,

II. Whereas the peace negotiations being conducted pursuant to the Geneva Agreement of 4 April 1990 and the Caracas Agenda of 21 May 1990 call for a number of constitutional reforms in support of the political agreements emanating therefrom,

In exercise of the powers conferred upon it by article 248 of the current Political Constitution,

Hereby adopts the following constitutional reform:

Article 1. Article 30 is hereby repealed.

Article 2. In article 77, the words "Central Board of Elections" are hereby replaced by the words "Supreme Electoral Tribunal" and a new paragraph is hereby added, to read as follows:

"Legally registered political parties shall have the right to monitor the compilation, organization, publication and updating of the electoral roll."

Article 3. Article 131 (37) is hereby amended to read as follows:

"To recommend to the Office of the President of the Republic the dismissal of Ministers of State, or to the relevant bodies the dismissal of officials of autonomous official institutions, whenever it deems appropriate on the basis of an investigation by its special commissions or an appeal, as the case may be. The Assembly's decision shall be binding with regard to heads of public security or State intelligence when the cause is serious human rights violations."

Article 4. Article 162 is hereby amended to read as follows:

"Article 162. The President of the Republic shall be responsible for appointing, dismissing, accepting the resignation of and granting leave to Ministers and Deputy Ministers of State and heads of public security and State intelligence."

Article 5. Article 163 is hereby amended to read as follows:

"Article 163. Decrees, decisions, orders and rulings of the President of the Republic must be countersigned and transmitted by Ministers, or by Deputy Ministers where appropriate, in their respective departments. Failure to comply with these requirements shall render such instruments null and void."

Article 6. Paragraphs (11) and (12) of article 168 are hereby amended, and three new paragraphs numbered (17), (18) and (19) are hereby added, to read as follows:

"(11) To command, organize and maintain the armed forces, confer military ranks and order postings and duties or the discharge of officers, in accordance with the law.

"(12) To use the armed forces to defend the sovereignty of the State and the integrity of its territory. In exceptional cases, where the normal means for the maintenance of domestic peace and public tranquillity and safety have been exhausted, the President of the Republic may use the armed forces for that purpose. Such action by the armed forces shall be limited to the period and extent strictly necessary to restore order and shall cease once that task has been fulfilled. The President of the Republic shall keep the Legislative Assembly informed of such action and the Assembly may, at any time, order the cessation of such exceptional measures. In any event, within two weeks of the termination of such measures, the President of the Republic shall submit to the Legislative Assembly a detailed report on the action taken by the armed forces.

"(17) To command, organize and maintain the National Civil Police to preserve peace, tranquillity, order and public safety in both urban and rural areas, adhering strictly to respect for human rights and under the control of civilian authorities. The National Civil Police and the armed forces shall be independent and shall be placed under the authority of different ministries.

"(18) To command, organize and maintain the State Intelligence Agency.

"(19) To determine annually a reasonable manpower level for the armed forces and the National Civil Police."

Article 7. A new paragraph is hereby added to article 172, to read as follows:

"The judiciary shall receive an annual allocation from the State budget of no less than 6 per cent of current income."

Article 8. Article 174, second paragraph, is hereby amended to read as follows:

"The Constitutional Division shall comprise five judges appointed for that purpose by the Legislative Assembly. The President of the Constitutional Division shall be appointed by the Legislative Assembly whenever the latter elects judges to the Supreme Court of Justice. The same appointee shall serve as President of the Supreme Court of Justice and of the judiciary."

Article 9. Article 180 is hereby amended to read as follows:

"Article 180. Any person wishing to be a justice of the peace shall, as a minimum, be a Salvadorian citizen, a lawyer, a layman, over 21 years old, and known to be competent and of good character; he must have rights of citizenship and have had them for the three years preceding his appointment. Justices of the peace shall be considered members of the career judicial service.

"In cases where the National Council of the Judiciary so decides, the duties of justice of the peace may be carried out by a person who is not a lawyer or does not belong to the career judicial service. In such cases, the term of office shall be one year."

Article 10. Paragraph 9 of article 182 is hereby amended to read as follows:

"9. To appoint magistrates and judges of courts of first and second instance and justices of the peace from lists of three candidates submitted by the National Council of the Judiciary; forensic physicians and employees of offices of the Court; and dismiss them, accept their resignation and grant them leave."

Article 11. Article 186 is hereby amended to read as follows:

"*Article 186.* A career judicial service is hereby established.

"Judges of the Supreme Court of Justice shall be elected by the Legislative Assembly for a term of nine years, with one third of the judges coming up for renewal every three years. Their tenure shall be deemed to be renewed by right unless, at the end of a judge's term of office, the Legislative Assembly decides otherwise or a judge is dismissed for cause, the causes for dismissal having been previously established by law. The affirmative vote of at least two thirds of the elected deputies shall be required for a decision to be taken in each of the above cases.

"Judges of the Supreme Court of Justice shall be elected from a list of candidates drawn up by the National Council of the Judiciary in the manner prescribed by law, half of the names being proposed by the associations representing lawyers in El Salvador; the list shall comprise candidates representative of the main schools of legal thought.

"Magistrates and judges of courts of first and second instance and justices of the peace who are members of the career judicial service shall enjoy security of tenure.

"The law shall afford judges protection so that they can carry out their duties in complete freedom, impartially and free of any influence on the cases that come before them; it shall also afford them the means guaranteeing them fair remuneration and a standard of living commensurate with the level of their responsibilities.

"The law shall regulate the requirements and procedures for admission to the career judicial service, promotions, transfers, disciplinary measures against members of the service, and other matters relating to the service."

Article 12. Article 188 is hereby amended to read as follows:

"Article 188. No person serving as a magistrate or judge may practise as a lawyer or notary or serve as an employee of the other organs of State, except as a teacher or a diplomat on temporary assignment."

Article 13. Article 191 is hereby amended to read as follows:

"Article 191. The function of public prosecutor shall be performed by the Attorney-General of the Republic, the Chief State Counsel, the National Counsel for the Defence of Human Rights and such other officials as may be prescribed by law."

Article 14. Article 192 is hereby amended to read as follows:

"Article 192. The Attorney-General of the Republic, the Chief State Counsel and the National Counsel for the Defence of Human Rights shall be elected by the Legislative Assembly, by a qualified majority of two thirds of the elected deputies. Their term of office shall be three years and they may be re-elected.

"The qualifications required for the post of Attorney-General of the Republic or Chief State Counsel shall be the same as those for judges of courts of second instance.

"The requirements to fill the post of National Counsel for the Defence of Human Rights shall be prescribed by law."

Article 15. In Article 193, a new paragraph (3) is hereby added; paragraphs (2) and (3) are hereby amended, the latter becoming paragraph (4); and paragraph (9) is hereby repealed. The new paragraphs read as follows:

"2. To institute judicial proceedings, *proprio motu* or at the request of a party, in defence of the legal order.

"3. To direct the investigation of the offence, particularly of any criminal acts that are liable to criminal prosecution. To that end, under the direction of the Office of the Attorney-General of the Republic, there shall be established a Criminal Investigation Agency whose mandate shall be prescribed by law. This shall not limit the independence of the judge in investigating matters submitted to him. The Crimi-

nal Investigation Agency shall take without delay any action that a judge may request of it for the purposes stated.

"4. To institute criminal proceedings *proprio motu* or at the request of a party."

Article 16. A new article is hereby added after article 194, to read as follows:

"Article 194. The National Counsel for the Defence of Human Rights shall be responsible for promoting human rights and making sure that they are respected. He may have permanent departmental and local representatives.

"The functions of the National Counsel shall be:

1. To make sure that human rights are respected and guaranteed.

2. To investigate, either *proprio motu* or on the basis of a complaint he has received, cases of human rights violations.

3. To assist alleged victims of human rights violations.

4. To promote judicial or administrative remedies for the protection of human rights.

5. To monitor the situation of persons deprived of their liberty. He shall be notified of all arrests and shall make sure that the legal limits on administrative detention are respected.

6. To carry out inspections, where he deems necessary, in order to ensure respect for human rights.

7. To supervise the conduct of the administration towards citizens.

8. To propose to the organs of State reforms for promoting human rights.

9. To give opinions on proposed legislation that would affect the exercise of human rights.

10. To promote and propose such measures as he deems necessary to prevent human rights violations.

11. To formulate conclusions and recommendations, either publicly or in private.

12. To prepare and issue reports.

13. To develop a permanent programme of activities to promote a knowledge of, and respect for, human rights.

14. Such other functions as may be assigned to him by the Constitution or the law."

Article 17. The heading of chapter VII of title VI is hereby amended to read:

"CHAPTER VII
SUPREME ELECTORAL TRIBUNAL"

Article 18. Article 208 is hereby amended to read as follows:

"Article 208. The Supreme Electoral Tribunal shall be the highest administrative authority and jurisdiction with respect to electoral matters. Its decisions shall not be subject to appeal, other than appeals to the Tribunal itself for a review, in the cases established by the law, and appeals provided for in this Constitution against violations hereof.

"The composition of the Supreme Electoral Tribunal shall be determined by law, making sure that no party or coalition of parties predominates in it. Likewise, appropriate provision shall be made for the Supreme Electoral Tribunal to include members without any party affiliation, elected by a two-thirds majority of the deputies elected to the Legislative Assembly."

Article 19. Article 209 is hereby amended to read as follows:

"Article 209. The agencies necessary for collecting, counting and checking ballots and for other activities connected with the exercise of suffrage shall be established by law, making sure that no party or coalition of parties predominates in them. Contending political parties shall have the right to monitor the entire electoral process."

Article 20. Article 211 is hereby amended to read as follows:

"Article 211. The armed forces are a permanent institution in the service of the nation. They shall be obedient, professional, apolitical and non-deliberative."

Article 21. Article 212 is hereby amended to read as follows:

"Article 212. The mission of the armed forces shall be to defend the sovereignty of the State and the integrity of its territory. In exceptional cases, the President of the Republic may use the armed forces to maintain domestic peace, in accordance with the provisions of this Constitution.

"The main organs of government referred to in article 86 may use the armed forces to enforce the provisions which they have adopted, within their respective spheres of competence under this Constitution, to ensure compliance with the Constitution.

"The armed forces shall cooperate in public works assigned to them by the executive branch and shall assist the public in cases of national disaster."

Article 22. Article 213 is hereby amended to read as follows:

"Article 213. The armed forces shall form part of the executive branch and shall be subject to the authority of the President of the Republic in his capacity as Commander-in-Chief. The structure, legal regime, doctrine, composition and functioning of the armed forces shall be defined by law, by regulation and by special provisions adopted by the President of the Republic."

Article 23. Article 216 is hereby amended to read as follows:

"Article 216. Military jurisdiction is hereby established. For the trial of purely military offences and misdemeanours, there shall be special procedures and courts as provided by law. Military jurisdiction, as an exception to the unity of the system of justice, shall be limited to the trial of purely military offences and misdemeanours, understood to be those affecting only a strictly military legal interest.

"Members of the armed forces on active duty shall be subject to military jurisdiction in respect of purely military offences and misdemeanours."

Article 24. Article 217 is hereby amended to read as follows:

"Article 217. The manufacture, import, export, trading, possession and bearing of weapons, ammunition, explosives and similar articles shall be permitted only with the authorization and under the direct supervision of the executive branch in the defence area.

"This matter shall be regulated by a special law."

Transitional provisions

FIRST: The National Counsel for the Defence of Human Rights whose post is created by this Decree shall be elected within 90 days following ratification of the constitutional reform by the Legislative Assembly whose term begins on 1 May 1991.

SECOND: The secondary legislation on electoral matters shall be amended within 90 days following ratification of the constitutional reform by the Legislative Assembly whose term begins on 1 May 1991. The new Supreme Electoral Tribunal shall be appointed within 30 days following approval of that legislative reform.

THIRD: For the purpose of implementing the provisions of the fourth paragraph of article 172, budgetary resources shall be allocated gradually and proportionally until the full amount is covered, within a period of no more than four years from the date of entry into force of this Decree.

Political agreements elaborating on the constitutional reform

With a view to elaborating on some of the aspects which the agreed constitutional reform refers to secondary legislation, the Parties have agreed to the following:

A. *Judicial system*

(a) Supreme Court of Justice

For the purposes of the appointment of judges to the Supreme Court of Justice as envisaged in the constitutional reform, the National Council of the Judiciary shall keep a list of 60 candidates representative of the main schools of legal thought, which shall be renewed after each election of judges. Thirty of the candidates shall be nominated by the lawyers associations of the different regions of the country.

(b) National Council of the Judiciary

Agreement has been reached to restructure the National Council of the Judiciary as follows:

1. The composition of the National Council of the Judiciary shall be such as to guarantee its independence from the organs of State and from political parties, and to ensure as far as possible that its membership includes not only judges but also representatives of sectors of society not directly connected with the administration of justice. The act regulating the National Council of the Judiciary shall be amended to bring it into line with the provisions of this Agreement within 90 days following ratification of the constitutional reform by the Legislative Assembly whose term begins on 1 May 1991. A new National Council of the Judiciary shall be elected within 90 days following approval of that legislative reform.

2. The National Council of the Judiciary shall be responsible for organizing and operating the Judicial Training School, whose purpose shall be to ensure a steady improvement in the professional training of judges and other judicial officials and of members of the Office of the Attorney-General of the Republic; to investigate the country's judicial problems and promote solutions thereto; and to foster greater bonds of solidarity among members of the judiciary and a coherent overall vision of the function of the judiciary in a democratic State.

(c) Career judicial service

The secondary legislation on the career judicial service shall satisfy the following requirements:

1. The secondary legislation shall contain provisions to ensure that admission to the career judicial service is based on mechanisms guaranteeing objective selection, equal opportunities for all candidates and the selection of the best-qualified candidates. Such mechanisms shall include competitive examinations and attendance at the Judicial Training School.

2. Candidates shall be admitted to the career judicial service only if they fulfil the admission requirements established by law.

B. *Electoral system*

1. The electoral roll shall be compiled in such a way that the lists of citizens eligible to vote are published at least 20 days before the date of the election. A simple and expeditious procedure shall be established for making legitimate corrections requested by any interested party.

2. Within 60 days after the establishment of the new Supreme Electoral Tribunal, a Special Commission presided over by the Tribunal and composed of representatives of all legally registered parties and, possibly, independent experts shall be established to prepare a comprehensive proposal for reform of the electoral system, to be completed and submitted to the Legislative Assembly within 120 days of the Commission's establishment. The Special Commission shall in any case be set up at least two years before the next legislative elections, and the Assembly shall vote on the proposed reforms at least one year before the date of those elections.

C. *Armed forces*

The political agreements on the armed forces are being referred for consideration under the corresponding item of the Caracas Agenda. Nevertheless, the Parties agree that those agreements shall include the following points:

1. The professional training of members of the defence and public security forces shall emphasize the pre-eminence of human dignity and democratic values, respect for human rights and the subordination of those forces to the constitutional authorities.

2. The secondary legislation on military jurisdiction shall be amended, where necessary, to ensure that under no circumstances shall any offences whose victims are civilians or include civilians be deemed to be purely military offences or misdemeanours and, likewise, that civilians shall not be subject to military jurisdiction under any circumstances, except in the case of military offences committed in connection with an international armed conflict involving El Salvador.

Commission on the Truth

The Government of El Salvador and the Frente Farabundo Martí para la Liberación Nacional (hereinafter referred to as "the Parties"),

Reaffirming their intention to contribute to the reconciliation of Salvadorian society;

Recognizing the need to clear up without delay those exceptionally important acts of violence whose characteristics and impact, and the social unrest to which they gave rise, urgently require that the complete truth be made known and that the resolve and means to establish the truth be strengthened;

Considering that, although the need to put an end to impunity was raised in the discussion on the item on the armed forces of the Agenda for the negotiations adopted at Caracas on 21 May 1990, the means of investigation which the Parties themselves have been prepared to set up are addressing situations whose complexity warrants independent treatment;

Agreeing on the advisability of fulfilling that task through a procedure which is both reliable and expeditious and may yield results in the short term, without prejudice to the obligations incumbent on the Salvadorian courts to solve such cases and impose the appropriate penalties on the culprits;

Have arrived at the following political agreement:

1. There is hereby established a Commission on the Truth (hereinafter referred to as "the Commission"). The Commission shall be composed of three individuals appointed by the Secretary-General of the United Nations after consultation with the Parties. The Commission shall elect its Chairman.

Functions

2. The Commission shall have the task of investigating serious acts of violence that have occurred since 1980 and whose impact on society urgently demands that the public should know the truth. The Commission shall take into account:

(a) The exceptional importance that may be attached to the acts to be investigated, their characteristics and impact, and the social unrest to which they gave rise; and

(b) The need to create confidence in the positive changes which the peace process is promoting and to assist the transition to national reconciliation.

3. The mandate of the Commission shall include recommending the legal, political or administrative measures which can be inferred from the results of the investigation. Such recommendations may include measures to prevent the repetition of such acts, and initiatives to promote national reconciliation.

4. The Commission shall endeavour to adopt its decisions unanimously. However, if this is not possible, a vote by the majority of its members shall suffice.

5. The Commission shall not function in the manner of a judicial body.

6. If the Commission believes that any case brought to its attention does not meet the criteria set forth in paragraph 2 of this agreement, it may refer the case to the Attorney-General of the Republic, should it deem appropriate, for handling through the judicial channel.

Powers

7. The Commission shall have broad powers to organize its work and its functioning. Its activities shall be conducted on a confidential basis.

8. For the purposes of the investigation, the Commission shall have the power to:

(a) Gather, by the means it deems appropriate, any information it considers relevant. The Commission shall be completely free to use whatever sources of information it deems useful and reliable. It shall receive such information within the period of time and in the manner which it determines.

(b) Interview, freely and in private, any individuals, groups or members of organizations or institutions.

(c) Visit any establishment or place freely without giving prior notice.

(d) Carry out any other measures or inquiries which it considers useful to the performance of its mandate, including requesting reports, records or documents from the Parties or any other information from State authorities and departments.

Undertaking by the parties

9. The Parties undertake to extend to the Commission whatever cooperation it requests of them in order to gain access to sources of information available to them.

10. The Parties undertake to carry out the Commision's recommendations.

Report

11. The Commission shall submit a final report, with its conclusions and recommendations, within a period of six months after its establishment.

12. The Commission shall transmit its report to the Parties and to the Secretary-General of the United Nations, who shall make it public and shall take the decisions or initiatives that he deems appropriate.

13. Once the report has been handed over, the Commission's mandate shall be considered terminated and the Commission shall be dissolved.

14. The provisions of this agreement shall not prevent the normal investigation of any situation or case, whether or not the Commission has investigated it, nor the application of the relevant legal provisions to any act that is contrary to law.

Document 30

Report of the Secretary-General on ONUSAL and report of the ONUSAL Human Rights Division (extract)

A/46/658-S/23222, 15 November 1991

1. The attached document contains the second report of the United Nations Observer Mission in El Salvador (ONUSAL). The Mission has begun to exercise in full the verification powers granted it by the Agreement on Human Rights signed at San José on 26 July 1990 between the Government of El Salvador and the Frente Farabundo Martí para la Liberación Nacional (FMLN) (A/44/971-S/21541, annex).

2. The report of the Director of the ONUSAL Human Rights Division, which appears in the annex to this document, briefly describes the Mission's verification activities and the situation of human rights in El Salvador, indicating specific cases and relevant situations. The report of the Chief of the Mission describes the circumstances in which ONUSAL has had to operate as a result of its having been established prior to the cessation of the armed conflict, contrary to what was envisaged in the San José Agreement.

3. In presenting this second report, I should like to express my gratitude to the Governments of Spain, France and Italy for having made their police officers available for service in the verification Mission and the Governments of Brazil, Canada, Ecuador, Venezuela and, again, Spain for having offered the services of their military officials to provide liaison with the military chiefs of the two parties, in order to facilitate the Mission's complex and difficult tasks.

4. I should also like to express my gratitude to the Government of El Salvador and to FMLN, who have continued to extend their full support and cooperation to ONUSAL in its verification work.

Second report of the United Nations Observer Mission in El Salvador

1. The first component of the United Nations Observer Mission in El Salvador (ONUSAL), authorized by the Security Council in its resolution 693 (1991), is now firmly established in the field, with four regional offices and two regional suboffices. The Human Rights Division, which is responsible for verifying the Agreement on Human Rights signed at San José on 26 July 1990 by the Government of El Salvador and the Frente Farabundo Martí para la Liberación Nacional (FMLN) (A/44/971-S/21541, annex), completed its preparatory phase at the end of September, and on 1 October 1991 began to perform in full the functions assigned to it by the San José

Agreement. Its report, which covers the period between 1 September and 31 October 1991, is annexed to this document. Its previous report (A/45/1055-S/23037) covered the period from the establishment of the Mission on 26 July to 31 August 1991.

2. ONUSAL is currently operating in a tense atmosphere, which is exacerbated by the polarization of the political situation in El Salvador. The signing of the New York Agreement on 25 September 1991 (A/46/502-S/23082, annex) gives reason to believe that the armed conflict is drawing to an end. This belief is reinforced by what could be considered a first breakthrough towards national reconciliation, newly perceptible in the functioning of the working group constituting the National Commission for the Consolidation of Peace (COPAZ) envisaged in the New York Agreement. The latter is still in its informal phase, in which delegates from all the political parties represented in the National Assembly come together to discuss and establish guidelines for the preliminary drafting of secondary legislation enabling the political agreements adopted at the negotiating table to be incorporated into El Salvador's legal system. However, some sectors of both parties have voiced strong reservations about the direction and rate of the negotiations and apprehension at the political, legal and social insecurity that might arise as a result of the end of the conflict. This dichotomy is reflected in the fact that while the National Assembly is ratifying constitutional reforms emanating from the political agreements reached at the negotiating table the fighting has intensified, resulting in an escalation of violence in the country. However, the announcement by FMLN of a unilateral cessation of offensive operations, just as this report was being completed, and the positive response of the Government of El Salvador are encouraging signs.

3. The continuation of the armed conflict during the period covered by this report has direct repercussions for ONUSAL. It is true that the Mission has received every cooperation from both parties in performing its functions and has established, for that purpose, a coordinating mechanism and a working method with both parties at a number of levels. In this sense, it seems to enjoy complete freedom of movement and access in its efforts to verify human rights and has encountered no deliberate obstruction. However, ONUSAL has recently come under criticism from some political sectors which apparently do not

have a clear idea of its mandate and functions. The Mission has therefore taken the necessary steps to correct misinterpretations by publishing information in the country's major dailies.

4. The misconception of the Mission's mandate seems to derive from the expectation that ONUSAL will give its opinion on military actions or aspects which do not fall within its mandate. This expectation has arisen because ONUSAL began its verification work before the cessation of the armed conflict. In some cases, there is misunderstanding as to the actual nature of its mandate. Its mandate is to verify compliance with the San José Agreement and to report thereon to the Secretary-General; its mandate does not include making public statements on what it has observed.

5. One particularly sensitive issue is that military clashes or operations which seriously threaten the safety of ONUSAL personnel often occur while such personnel are performing verification functions in the field. As a result, although the advice of the Mission's military advisers and the measures taken in this regard serve to reduce the danger, they do not completely eliminate it, and this is cause for concern.

6. In this connection, ONUSAL is convinced that the chiefs of the armed forces of El Salvador and of FMLN combatants are honouring fully their pledge to guarantee the safety of Mission personnel. It is clear that the Government of El Salvador has taken effective action to deal with the anonymous threats which ONUSAL received in the past, for which ONUSAL is grateful.

Annex

Report of the Director of the Human Rights Division

I. Context in which verification is taking place

1. During the period covered by this report, ONUSAL has continued to carry out its activities in a context of armed conflict which was not envisaged in the San José Agreement. However, the New York Agreement and the possibility of a cessation of the armed conflict make it likely that ONUSAL will soon be able to carry out its verification work in optimum conditions, in other words, in a context of peace and institutional reform in which the agreements currently under negotiation will be put into practice. This will not only eliminate many of the risks to which its personnel are exposed in their work, but also reduce the legal and political drawbacks which verification of the San José Agreement in a situation of armed conflict entails. An end to the conflict will also mean that ONUSAL will not be asked to give an opinion on purely military actions, to which the verification powers deriving from its mandate do not extend.

2. Despite the progress made in the negotiations and in the institutional reform, the armed conflict continues unabated, above all in the Departments of Cabañas, Chalatenango, Cuscatlán, Morazán and Usulafter. Although military operations have been limited in the San Salvador metropolitan area, the mountainous area of Guazapa and the outskirts of Apopa, both of them close to the capital city on the trunk road heading north, have continued to see heavy fighting. This is unfortunate not only because the persistence of the conflict continues to cause casualties among the combatants, but also because it seriously affects the civilian population, creating situations in which human rights are violated. Since protecting the rights of the civilian population in this conflict situation is one of the Mission's main concerns, ONUSAL is not only maintaining an active presence in the areas most affected by the fighting but has also urged the parties to take the necessary precautions to minimize civilian casualties.

II. Activities of the human rights division

3. During the preparatory phase which ended on 30 September, ONUSAL set up its regional offices and laid the operational and conceptual bases for its future work. ONUSAL teams travelled all over the country, making contact with political, judicial and military authorities at the local, regional and national levels. Initial contacts were made with organizations representing civilian society, including human rights organizations and communities of resettled, repatriated and displaced persons, and others whose activities are relevant to the Mission's mandate. Despite the difficulties created by the conflict, ONUSAL also made its first contacts in the field with FMLN. It used the preparatory phase not only to establish its internal structure and its channels of communication with Salvadorian society, but also to familiarize itself with national institutions, problems related to the armed conflict, and the situation of human rights in the country. During this phase, the Mission also received the first complaints of alleged human rights violations, which it followed up on a preliminary basis but did not investigate, save in exceptional cases.

4. On 1 October, ONUSAL entered its second phase of operations in which, in addition to continuing the activities described above, it has begun to investigate cases and situations involving human rights violations and to follow them up systematically with the competent State organs. The Mission has also maintained an ongoing dialogue with FMLN concerning its alleged violations of the San José Agreement. The purpose of all these activities has been to establish that allegations are true and to find out what the party concerned has done to

punish the culprits and to prevent such violations in future.

5. During this phase, ONUSAL has significantly expanded its contacts with the parties, establishing flexible, stable coordination mechanisms with them. For instance, it holds regular working meetings with an inter-agency group of the Salvadorian Government; the group is coordinated by the Executive Secretary of the governmental Human Rights Commission and consists of representatives of the Supreme Court of Justice, the Armed Forces General Staff, the Office of the Attorney General and the Ministry of Foreign Affairs. It also holds regular coordination meetings at the highest level with the main State organs. In addition, it has expanded its local and regional contacts with the main political, judicial and military authorities, making frequent visits to mayor's offices, departmental governments, military and police units, law courts and other public entities. It also holds periodic coordination meetings at Mexico City or Managua with the FMLN Political and Diplomatic Commission and has ongoing functional contacts with local FMLN leaders inside the country.

6. The Mission's contacts with the parties are characterized by frankness and transparency; ONUSAL not only informs them of cases of alleged human rights violations attributed to them, but also gives its views and assessments as to how the parties are fulfilling their commitments under the San José Agreement. This direct dialogue has served to build mutual trust and has allowed ONUSAL to make recommendations in the hope that these will lead to an improvement in the human rights situation in the country.

7. The beginning of the second phase also saw the launching of the Mission's educational activities and of an information campaign designed to publicize its functions as widely as possible. In the first phase, the team of ONUSAL educators had worked in consultation with human rights organizations to design a programme for the promotion of human rights. This programme is already in operation, its initial aim being to publicize the Mission's mandate and the content of the San José Agreement. It is directed mainly at the armed forces, FMLN and social organizations and is intended to reinforce the educational activities carried out by national institutions. The Mission also launched a media campaign on 6 October to publicize its mandate as widely as possible among the population. The success of the campaign can be measured by the marked increase in the number of people and institutions who approach ONUSAL either to file complaints or to request information or support for educational activities.

8. The San José Agreement stipulates that the Mission shall work in close cooperation with human rights organizations, which it has in fact been doing ever since it was established. ONUSAL has set up coordination mechanisms with non-governmental human rights organizations ... in order to take advantage of the existence of common and complementary areas of activity. It is also cooperating with humanitarian organizations which, although not directly involved with human rights problems, have ties to certain vulnerable sectors of Salvadorian society, 1/ such as communities of persons repatriated from places of refuge abroad and/or persons displaced within the national territory.

9. It should be mentioned that, over the past decade, non-governmental human rights organizations have played a vital role in protecting and promoting the human rights of the most vulnerable sectors of society, in difficult and sometimes tragic circumstances. Quite a number of human rights activists were forced to go into exile, and some even lost their lives in the course of their work. Human rights organizations have been among the few organizations to investigate human rights violations and to protect their victims.

10. These organizations' vast experience makes them a valuable source of information for ONUSAL. Moreover, the Mission's presence serves to support and encourage non-governmental organizations. ONUSAL welcomes the opening of human rights offices inside the country. The Mission wishes to place on record its gratitude to the non-governmental organizations which supply it with information on the human rights situation, share with it their analyses of certain human rights problems and promote human rights in the country; these organizations include the non-governmental Human Rights Commission of El Salvador, the Human Rights Institute of José Simeón Cañas Central American University and the Legal Protection Office of the Archdiocese of San Salvador.

. . .

1/ The Concertación Nacional de Instituciones de Apoyo y Organismos de la Población Refugiada, Repoblada y Desplazada (National Coalition of Support Institutions and Agencies of Refugees and Resettled and Displaced Persons) consists of the following organizations: the Asociación Salvadoreña de Desarrollo Integral (Salvadorian Association for Integrated Development), the Fundación para la Autogestión y Solidaridad de los Trabajadores Salvadoreños (Foundation for the Self-Management and Solidarity of Salvadorian Workers), the Fundación para la Cooperación con Repobladores y Desplazados (Foundation for Cooperation with Resettled and Displaced Persons), the Coordinación Ecuménica de Servicios y Ayuda Humanitaria (Ecumenical Coordinator of Services and Humanitarian Aid), the Fundación Salvadoreña para la construcción y el Desarrollo (Salvadorian Foundation for Construction and Development), the Coordinadora de Repoblaciones Salvadoreñas (Coordinator of Salvadorian Resettlement), the Patronato para el Desarrollo de las Comunidades de El Salvador (Community Development Board of El Salvador), the Comité Cristiano Por Desplazados de El Salvador (Christian Committee for Displaced Persons in El Salvador), the Comité Nacional de Repobladores (National Committee of Resettled Persons) and the Comité de Repobladores de Cabañas y Cuscatlán (Committee of Resettled Persons in Cabañas and Cuscatlán).

V. Conclusions and recommendations

146. While the purpose of the first report was to establish a legal and political framework for the verification of human rights in El Salvador before the cessation of the armed conflict, the second report presents a more precise analysis of the situation, based on the study of cases related to human rights and of situations, related or otherwise to the conflict, which because of their impact on human rights deserve special consideration and could justify some preliminary recommendations.

147. Once the preparatory phase of its activities was concluded, ONUSAL began in October to investigate cases and situations arising since the beginning of the Mission and to follow them up with State institutions. With FMLN, it has also verified the measures taken to avoid certain practices that are contrary to the San José Agreement. In fact, the preamble to the Agreement bears in mind that El Salvador's legal system provides for the recognition of human rights and the duty of the State to respect and safeguard them. In paragraph 16 of this report, the Mission referred expressly to this obligation to provide safeguards. The State has also assumed the obligation to respect and safeguard human rights under many international conventions. FMLN, for its part, as indicated in the preamble to the Agreement, has declared that it has the capacity and the will and assumes the commitment to respect the inherent attributes of the human person. In particular, it must be understood that this declaration includes the rules of international humanitarian law contained in article 3 of the four Geneva Conventions of 12 August 1949 and in the Protocol additional to those Conventions, and relating to the protection of victims of non-international armed conflicts (Protocol II).

148. On the basis of the information received at the Mission's offices, either directly from individual complaints or from organizations responsible for the protection of human rights or State institutions, it can be said that the level of human rights violations is cause for concern, notwithstanding the real efforts made to improve the situation. While not all difficulties are linked to the armed conflict, the persistence of a very tense situation is not conducive to a spirit of reconciliation, the consolidation of which seems inseparable from the effective exercise of human rights.

Right to life and to integrity and security of person

149. The Mission has been able to confirm that a number of summary executions by unidentified individuals or paramilitary groups have taken place during the period covered by this report. In many of these cases, notwithstanding the seriousness of the events, no special investigation has been made by the security forces or the judiciary. The lack of effective measures for investigating the facts heightens the feeling of insecurity which prevails in El Salvador.

Recommendations

150. ONUSAL recommends that the Government of El Salvador, the Office of the Attorney General of the Republic and the judiciary organ establish the necessary mechanisms to ensure that cases of attacks on the life of persons are systematically investigated, in order to find and punish the perpetrators. In particular, it thinks it would be very useful if account were taken of the Principles on the Effective Prevention and Investigation of Extra-legal, Arbitrary and Summary Executions referred to in General Assembly resolution 44/162 of 15 December 1987.

151. Vigorous action should also be taken to put an end to the practices of intimidation and threats by clandestine groups. The immediate disposal of bodies should be avoided in cases of violent death or death in questionable circumstances and an adequate autopsy should be conducted in accordance with the conditions recommended in the Principles mentioned above.

152. Lastly, the authorities should take all possible measures to identify the authors of flyers signed by apparently clandestine organizations and adopt regulations prohibiting the radio or television broadcasting of threatening messages.

153. The Mission considers that it is not yet in a position to make an exhaustive evaluation of the phenomenon of enforced or involuntary disappearances. The complaints received often relate to illegal detentions or recruitment and further study of the problem is needed in order to determine its exact extent. Certain measures would, however, make it possible to avoid a large number of complaints of disappearance, which do not always correspond to an enforced or involuntary disappearance.

Recommendation

154. The authorities should set up simple, flexible mechanisms to enable complainants to ascertain the whereabouts of the person concerned quickly. The Mission recommends, in particular, that the armed forces should systematically report each detention they carry out to the Detainee Information Department set up by the Supreme Court of Justice.

155. On the issue of torture and cruel, inhuman or degrading treatment or punishment, the Mission will continue to verify this problem carefully, as well as the efforts made by the authorities to eliminate certain existing practices.

Recommendation

156. Scrupulous respect for the legal norms regulating administrative detention, particularly the prohibi-

tion on holding a detained person incommunicado established by article 2 (e) of the San José Agreement, should facilitate better supervision of the treatment of detainees by the judiciary. Allowing lawyers to defend detainees during the period of administrative detention, as also envisaged in the same article, would likewise help to avoid practices of torture and cruel, inhuman or degrading treatment or punishment.

Civilian population

157. Concerning the protection of the civilian population, ONUSAL has noted that both parties' troops have made efforts to avoid civilian deaths. Nevertheless, the scale of the armed clashes of recent weeks continues to affect the civilian population.

Recommendations

158. As long as the armed conflict continues, the Mission can only reiterate its recommendation to both parties to take all necessary measures and precautions, as a matter of urgency, to avoid attacks and acts or threats of violence against the civilian population. The Mission also recommends that the parties refrain from actions liable to cause civilian casualties and, in particular, avoid indiscriminate attacks and excessive use of force in military operations.

159. The Mission, stressing once again that its mandate does not give it the power to verify the armed conflict as such, considers that, in exceptional cases, it must take into account the fundamental guarantees of humane treatment for all persons not directly participating, or no longer participating, in hostilities. ONUSAL therefore urges the parties to not only respect all the norms of international humanitarian law but also take all necessary steps to observe the principles of humanity referred to in the fourth preambular paragraph of Protocol II relating to the protection of victims of non-international armed conflicts.

Personal documentation

160. Taking into account the number of complaints received, the importance of the problems raised and the possibility of finding short-term or medium-term solutions, the Mission has devoted particular attention to certain situations with a view to following them up in the future. Regarding documentation for displaced persons, returnees and people living in conflict zones, articles 7 and 8 of the San José Agreement recognize the right to personal documentation, as does the Constitution of the Republic of El Salvador.

161. The situation of undocumented persons is the direct result of the armed conflict. The large number of internally displaced persons and the massive repatriation that began in 1987 have intensified the problem, creating very difficult situations for the populations concerned, particularly as regards their safety and personal liberty.

162. Although a number of initiatives have been taken by the Government of El Salvador, UNHCR, the churches and some non-governmental organizations concerned with the problem, according to information available to ONUSAL, the draft bill discussed between the Ministry of Interior and UNHCR, on which there seemed to be a broad consensus, has not been submitted to the Legislative Assembly. A provisional law might solve this problem, which is given priority under the San José Agreement.

Recommendations

163. In view of the extent of the problem and its serious consequences for the populations concerned, the Mission recommends that the Government of El Salvador submit an urgent proposal to the Legislative Assembly for the adoption of a special provisional law establishing simple, flexible methods, based on the principles of equality before the law and non-discrimination, for providing proper documentation at no charge to displaced persons, returnees and all persons living in conflict zones.

164. In the short term, even before such a law is adopted, it would be advisable for the Government to step up its efforts to ensure that the existing legislation is applied more effectively, providing mayors with clear, uniform instructions to facilitate civil status registration. It is also suggested that the Central Board of Elections assist the documentation process by making its microfilm archives available.

Military recruitment

165. It has been emphasized that, as in many countries, the Constitution of the Republic establishes compulsory military service. The armed forces, recognizing that recruitment practices may be at variance with individual rights and freedoms, have issued two sets of instructions regulating military recruitment procedures and the granting of exemptions from compulsory military service.

166. The report analyses this effort to regulate military recruitment practices and points to shortcomings in recruitment methods: frequent failure to show the written order from the chief of the military region, to notify the families of recruits, and to post a list of the young men recruited in each commander's area. The military authorities have responded favourably to the Mission's comments, demonstrating their interest in finding solutions. The basic problem is the absence of a law standardizing the recruitment process and making it known to all Salvadorian citizens.

167. The continuing armed conflict has caused the

Mission to also examine recruitment by FMLN. It has been noted that there are a significant number of children under 15 in the ranks of the guerrillas, in violation of the provisions of Protocol II concerning the protection of children. FMLN leaders have pledged to discontinue the recruitment of children under 15 and to assign other tasks to those already recruited.

Recommendations

168. The Mission recommends that the special law regulating compulsory military service provided for in the Constitution of the Republic be enacted as soon as possible. In the meantime, it suggests that the Ministry of Defence regulations on military recruitment procedures and the granting of exemptions from compulsory military service should be given wide publicity.

169. It also recommends that the military authorities find a way of informing relatives that a member of the family has been recruited, using a speedy, flexible mechanism such as systematic notification of relatives through a centralized information department in the General Staff or another institution.

170. Lastly, ONUSAL recommends that FMLN honour its pledge to observe the rules of international humanitarian law concerning the recruitment of minors and reminds it that minors may not take part in any kind of military operations, even if these are not directly linked with the fighting.

Due process of law

171. Due process of law is also a priority for the Mission, which has begun to follow it up by observing a significant verdict recently reached by a jury and by beginning to analyse the day-to-day practice of the courts.

172. The Mission considers it premature, after only three months in El Salvador, to make an overall evaluation of the judicial system and, in particular, of penal procedures. However, it must emphasize the fact that, for the first time, a jury has convicted a high-ranking officer in a case of serious human rights violations.

173. Setting aside the symbolic value attached to the case of the Jesuit priests, despite the shortcomings evident in the public hearing, ONUSAL has been able to infer from this and other trials that certain defects in the pre-trial stage of penal proceedings make it difficult to establish the truth and to try and punish the culprits. The obvious inadequacy of the technical and material means available to the judicial system is a serious obstacle to its proper functioning. The lack of a civilian police force specialized in judicial matters and answerable to a civilian authority responsible for bringing public action is another major difficulty. The Mission's examination of this trial has demonstrated the need for serious reflection on the criminal justice system, with a view to improving it through the adoption of structural reforms.

174. The problems relating to investigation and penal procedures will be analysed in subsequent reports. In the meantime, the Mission would like to be able to contribute to a positive development, within the strict framework of its mandate.

175. Although the human rights situation in El Salvador is still cause for concern, ONUSAL has observed, throughout the first three months of its presence in the country, an effort by the parties to respect the commitments signed at San José. So far, it has not met with any real difficulties in performing its verification mission, thanks to the cooperation of the parties and of the people of El Salvador in general. However, it regrets that the persistence of the armed conflict remains a real obstacle to the implementation of effective, lasting measures which might significantly improve the human rights situation. Through its work in the field and its constant contacts with the Government and the armed forces, FMLN and human rights organizations, the Mission is trying to contribute to the enormous task of consolidating the rule of law in El Salvador.

Document 31

Report of the Secretary-General on the situation in Central America

A/46/713-S/23256, 2 December 1991

1. The present report is submitted pursuant to Security Council resolution 637 (1989) and General Assembly resolution 45/15 of 20 November 1990.

El Salvador

2. Since my last report, dated 8 November 1990 (A/45/706-S/21931), steady progress has been made in the negotiations on El Salvador. On 31 October last year the parties agreed that a more active role should be played by my Personal Representative. This was deemed necessary in view of the inability of the parties, in two successive rounds of talks held in Costa Rica in August and

September, to make progress on the substantive agenda which had been agreed upon in Caracas, Venezuela, in May 1990 (A/46/552-S/23129) and particularly on the question of the armed forces, following the adoption of the San José Agreement on Human Rights on 26 July 1990 (A/44/971-S/21541). The enhanced role requested from my Representative involved putting forward formulae that would be used as the basis for negotiations. My Representative on that same day submitted a working paper on the armed forces that has been the subject of several revisions in the course of negotiations since.

3. From December 1990 through February 1991, my Representative participated in the four rounds of direct talks held between the parties and shuttled frequently between them. Although some cumulative progress was made on the question of the armed forces, the parties were not able to reach a formal agreement on this item. In March 1990, following a proposal to that effect by the Farabundo Martí National Liberation Front (FMLN), the parties agreed to continue negotiations within a concentrated scheme, giving priority to three issues included in the first stage of negotiations: the armed forces, constitutional reforms and cease-fire arrangements.

4. On 4 April 1991, I informed the Security Council (S/22494, annex I) of the above-mentioned development, and I stressed that time was limited for these negotiations as constitutional reforms had to be approved in two consecutive legislatures and had therefore to be submitted before 30 April 1991, which was the closing date of the outgoing Legislature.

5. Following several weeks of protracted negotiations, on 27 April 1991 the Government of El Salvador and the FMLN signed the Mexico Agreements (A/46/553-S/23130) covering a series of constitutional reforms relating, *inter alia*, to the role of the armed forces and their subordination to civilian authorities, the creation of a National Civil Police separate from the armed forces, the judicial system and human rights, and the electoral system. A number of complementary agreements on these issues, including the need for secondary legislation, were also reached. The parties also agreed to the establishment of a Commission on the Truth, to be composed of three individuals appointed by the Secretary-General after hearing the opinion of the parties. The Commission shall have the task of investigating serious acts of violence that have occurred since 1980, the impact of which on society urgently demands that the public should know the truth. During the April talks in Mexico, considerable ground was covered on the subject of cease-fire arrangements in separate talks with each of the parties held by the Under-Secretary-General for Special Political Affairs, who prepared a working paper that was submitted to the parties.

6. In May and June 1991, two successive rounds of talks proceeded in Caraballeda, Venezuela, and Querétaro, Mexico, within a concentrated framework as agreed in Mexico on 27 April. The aim was to reach, as a matter of priority, a political agreement on the armed forces and the necessary accords for the cessation of the armed confrontation under United Nations verification. In addition to my Personal Representative, the Under-Secretary-General for Special Political Affairs participated in talks on cease-fire arrangements. Although progress was made, particularly on the question of the creation of a National Civil Police, it was not possible to make substantive headway regarding cease-fire arrangements.

7. The talks following the Mexico Agreements evinced a fundamental difficulty in achieving a cease-fire within the two-stage framework laid down in the Geneva and Caracas Agreements, which provided for a cease-fire coupled with continued, open-ended negotiations, the result of which could not be assured. Within this framework, FMLN insisted on the need for cease-fire arrangements which would allow it to preserve its military capability, arrangements which proved unacceptable to the Government.

8. On the occasion of the First Ibero-American Summit held in Guadalajara, Mexico, in July 1991, I met separately with President Cristiani and with the FMLN General Command. I also met with the Presidents of Colombia, Mexico and Venezuela and the President of the Spanish Government—the Friends of the Secretary-General—in order to evaluate the status of the process. At those meetings we discussed, *inter alia*, the advisability of reviewing the two-phase format of the negotiating process to see whether the negotiations could be compressed into a single phase in order to establish before a cease-fire the necessary conditions and guarantees for the reintegration of the FMLN members into the country's civilian, institutional and political life within a framework of full legality. At Guadalajara, the four above-mentioned Presidents issued a strong statement in support of the negotiating process and in particular for my own efforts.

9. In connection with and in reply to a joint letter of 1 August 1991 from the Secretary of State of the United States of America and the Minister for Foreign Affairs of the Union of Soviet Socialist Republics, I put to them a number of concrete ideas regarding the critical juncture of the negotiations existing at the time and the way in which they could be of assistance in helping me to break the deadlock in the negotiations (S/22963). I noted that there were fundamental issues that had to be grappled with in order to go beyond the success so far achieved and, specifically, to obtain a cease-fire. These were the subject of my Personal Representative's shuttling between

President Cristiani and the FMLN commanders during that period.

10. On 30 August 1991, I informed the members of the Security Council that I had issued invitations to President Cristiani and to the FMLN General Command to visit United Nations Headquarters in New York on 16 and 17 September so that I could consult with them personally to address squarely the question of the guarantees and conditions for the reintegration of the members of FMLN into society, which under the Geneva and Caracas Agreements would only have been taken up during the second, post-cease-fire stage of the negotiations, and thus to give the process new impetus. The consultations, in fact, lasted until 25 September, on which date an agreement, known as the New York Agreement, was signed in my presence by Representatives of the Government of El Salvador and by the General Command of FMLN.

11. It was my firm expectation that the New York Agreement (A/46/502-S/23082) would break the deadlock in the negotiations. The text of the Agreement consists of two parts. It provides for the creation of a National Commission for the Consolidation of Peace (COPAZ) to be composed of two representatives of the Government, two of FMLN and one member of each of the political parties or coalitions currently represented in the Legislative Assembly of El Salvador. The Archbishop of San Salvador and a representative of ONUSAL would participate as observers. The purpose of COPAZ was to oversee and supervise the implementation of all political agreements reached by the parties. COPAZ was conceived as a machinery for the control and participation of Salvadorian civilian society in the process of changes resulting from the negotiations, both in relation to the armed forces as well as to all other matters on the agenda. It was to be a compulsory consultative mechanism for all major decisions affecting the implementation of the agreements, and it would begin formal operation within eight days of the signing of a cease-fire. Its creation was to be sanctioned by law. The Agreement also contains provisions regarding the purification of the armed forces, its doctrine and training system, the establishment of the National Civil Police (NCP) and on economic and social questions. The parties also agreed to a document entitled "The Compressed Negotiations" (A/46/502/Add.1-S/23082/Add.1, annex), which is an integral part of the New York Agreement and which established that all substantive items would be negotiated and agreed before the cease-fire; that the cease-fire would be of a predetermined duration, short and dynamic; and that no substantive negotiations would take place during the cease-fire, only the implementation of agreements. It also spelled out the substantive items on the agenda that would be negotiated and settled prior to the cease-fire.

12. On 30 September 1991, I informed the Security Council that negotiations would resume on 12 October and that following the New York Agreement, conditions had been established for the opening of the final phase in the negotiations. I suggested that the moment might have come for the parties to the armed confrontation to reach a *modus vivendi* for the gradual cessation of hostilities. I also suggested that, if accepted, such a *modus vivendi* might include a simple liaison mechanism consisting in the detachment of United Nations military observers to the command of both parties. In its resolution 714 (1991), the Security Council, *inter alia*, reaffirmed its strong support for the urgent completion of the peace process, expressed its readiness to support the implementation of a settlement and urged both sides to exercise maximum and continuing restraint, particularly with respect to the civilian population, in order to create the best climate for a successful last stage of the negotiations.

13. In the New York Agreement, the Organization was requested to assist in the implementation of the accords. One such request was to coordinate advisory services and support for the establishment of the National Civil Police. In this context, I sent a group of five experts to El Salvador from 8 to 23 October 1991 in order to formulate recommendations on this matter on the basis of understandings and agreements reached in the course of the negotiations and tailored to the specific needs and idiosyncracies of El Salvador. For this purpose, they conducted interviews with Salvadorian authorities as well as with FMLN representatives and representatives of many sectors of society who would have an interest or particular knowledge in this field. A report containing their conclusions and recommendations on the establishment and functioning of the National Civil Police has been made available to the negotiating parties.

14. The decision reached in New York to create COPAZ had generated intensive activity by the political parties and thus broadened the political base of support for the peace process. The future members of COPAZ have already held several meetings, laying the groundwork to assume the substantive responsibilities which they will have to shoulder, without awaiting the formal establishment of the Commission. I commend these developments.

15. Negotiations took place from 13 to 21 October and from 3 to 16 November 1991 and are currently under way in Mexico on an intensive, virtually uninterrupted basis, with the continued active participation of my Representative. Both sides have repeatedly affirmed their desire to reach agreement as rapidly as possible on the remaining pending issues, which are of considerable complexity. The FMLN decision to cease offensive operations unilaterally on 16 November was a positive development,

as was President Cristiani's rapid, favourable reaction. Armed confrontation appears to have considerably dwindled since then. This is an encouraging development, which cannot but raise the level of confidence of the Salvadorian people in the prospects for a negotiated political solution to the conflict, but which, in the absence of specific agreements and independent monitoring, is inherently fragile. There continue to be in El Salvador groups which, though increasingly isolated, are extremely strident in their opposition to the negotiating process, and which persist in issuing threatening statements against all whom they perceive as supporting it. I am confident, however, that the parties to the negotiations, as well as the Salvadorian body politic and people as a whole, will hold steadfastly to the course they have set themselves, during this final stretch in the negotiations. The strong support of the international community will continue to be needed until a cease-fire is reached and beyond, in the delicate phase of transition to a durable peace.

16. Throughout this process, I and my Personal Representative, Mr. Alvaro de Soto, have continued to work closely with a certain number of Governments in a position to assist in my efforts. I wish to record my sincere appreciation to them, and in particular to those of Colombia, Mexico, Spain and Venezuela, which have provided strong support and encouragement.

Guatemala

17. In my last report, I noted that on 30 March 1990, a delegation of the National Reconciliation Commission of Guatemala, acting with the full support of the Government of the Republic, and a delegation of the Unidad Revolucionaria Nacional Guatemalteca (URNG) had signed at Oslo a "Basic Agreement for the Search for Peace by Political Means", with a view to initiating a process which, by seeking ways to bring about a peaceful solution of the nation's problems, would culminate in the attainment of peace and the enhancement of functional and participatory democracy in Guatemala (see A/45/706-S/21931, paras. 29 and 30). I also mentioned that, pursuant to the Oslo Agreement, five meetings had been held in 1990 between representatives of URNG and representatives of various political, business, religious and social sectors in Guatemala, in the presence of the Conciliator and Chairman of the National Reconciliation Commission and of my appointed Observer. I expressed the hope that the process initiated by the signing of the Oslo Agreement would continue and pave the way for a process of reconciliation and peace in Guatemala.

18. On 26 April 1991 at Mexico City, the Government of Guatemala, whose President, as a result of the elections held in late 1990, was now Mr. Jorge Serrano Eléas, and the Unidad Revolucionaria Nacional Guate-malteca (URNG) signed an Agreement on the procedure for the search for peace by political means (A/45/1007-S/22563, annex) in which they agreed to hold talks with the Chairman of the National Reconciliation Commission of Guatemala, Monsignor Rodolfo Quezada Toruño, acting as Conciliator and with the Representative of the Secretary-General of the United Nations, Mr. Francesc Vendrell, acting as Observer. Under this Agreement, the two parties undertook to conduct a process of negotiation that would permit, in the shortest possible time, the signing of an agreement on a firm and lasting peace which would set out political agreements, how they were to be implemented and executed by the parties and how their fulfilment was to be verified by the United Nations and such other bodies as the parties might designate by mutual agreement. The Government and URNG agreed to hold negotiations through direct meetings between the parties, with the active participation of the Conciliator and in the presence of the Observer, or through indirect meetings through the Conciliator and in the presence of the Observer. The two parties also agreed not to abandon the negotiating process unilaterally and to pursue it without interruption, in accordance with the agreed procedure, until the negotiating agenda was exhausted. In so doing, they undertook to act in good faith in an atmosphere of complete mutual respect and reiterated their express determination to reach political agreements for achieving a firm and lasting peace that would bring the internal armed conflict in Guatemala to an early, definitive end. The Government and URNG undertook to be duly represented in the negotiations by high-level delegates, in order to negotiate and conclude political agreements in accordance with the existing constitutional framework.

19. At the same meeting, held at Mexico City in April with the participation of the Conciliator and my Representative, the Government and URNG signed an Agreement on a general agenda (A/45/1009-S/22573, annex) comprising the following items: democratization, human rights, strengthening of civilian authority and the role of the army in a democratic society, identity and rights of indigenous peoples, constitutional reforms and electoral system, socio-economic aspects, agrarian situation, resettlement of populations uprooted by the armed conflict, bases for bringing URNG into the political life of the country, arrangements for the cease-fire, timetable for the implementation, fulfilment and verification of agreements, signing of the agreement on a firm and lasting peace, and demobilization.

20. After reaching the agreements on procedure and the agenda, the parties held two rounds of direct negotiations on substantive issues at Cuernavaca and Querétaro, Mexico, in June and July respectively. These

culminated in the signing at Querétaro on 25 July 1991 of a framework agreement on democratization in the search for peace by political means which is annexed to this report. The parties then held two rounds of talks at Mexico City in September and October 1991 on the item of human rights. Although valuable progress was made at these meetings towards narrowing the differences between the parties, it was agreed at the end of October that the Conciliator and the Observer would hold a series of shuttle meetings with the two parties in order to give greater impetus to the process and to reach substantive agreements on the very important issue of human rights. The Conciliator and my Representative are currently engaged in these meetings, which I hope will bear fruit in the not too distant future. I consider it my duty to point out that, despite the speed with which the two parties agreed to the procedure and the general agenda, the negotiations have not progressed at the desired rate. I hope that the conclusion of an agreement on specific, verifiable measures in the area of human rights will reinvigorate the process, which I consider vitally important for overcoming the serious problems which Guatemala has faced for so many years.

21. Since the beginning of the year, my Representative has travelled frequently to meet with President Serrano and with URNG commanders. I myself met with President Serrano twice, first at Guadalajara, Mexico, in July 1991 on the occasion of the First Ibero-American Summit and again during President Serrano's recent visit to the United Nations.

United Nations Observer Mission in El Salvador

22. By its resolution 693 (1991), the Security Council, on 20 May 1991, decided to establish under its authority a United Nations Observer Mission in El Salvador (ONUSAL), based on my recommendation (S/22494 and Corr.1 and Add.1). ONUSAL's mandate is to monitor, as an integrated peace-keeping operation subject to approval by the Council, all agreements concluded between the Government of El Salvador and FMLN. ONUSAL's initial mandate, extending up to 30 June 1992, is to verify the compliance by the parties with the San José Agreement on Human Rights (A/44/971-S/21541, annex). ONUSAL became operational on 26 July 1991 and is now firmly established, with its headquarters in San Salvador. It has established four regional offices in San Salvador, San Miguel, San Vicente and Santa Ana and two sub-offices in Chalatenango and Usulután. Its operational teams include human rights observers, legal officers, political officers, police observers and military liaison officers. It has established working contacts with both parties at the political and the opera-

tional levels and has received full cooperation from them. ONUSAL's activities and observations have been presented in two reports covering the period up to 30 October 1991 (A/45/1055-S/23037 and A/46/658-S/23222).

United Nations Observer Group for Central America

23. Since last year's report, the Security Council has approved, on three separate occasions, in resolutions 675 (1990) of 5 November 1990, 691 (1991) of 6 May 1991, and 719 (1991) of 6 November 1991, the extension of the mandate of the United Nations Observer Group in Central America (ONUCA) as defined in resolution 644 (1989). The size of ONUCA has been reduced in the meantime to a total number of 132 military observers. The current mandate of ONUCA terminates on 30 April 1992. The Security Council has requested me to report before 6 February 1992, taking account of any developments in the region which indicate that the present size of the Observer Group or its future should be reconsidered.

Security Commission

24. The meetings of the Security Commission, established under Esquipulas II, continued with the participation of officials from the United Nations Secretariat and OAS. The meetings were held at Tegucigalpa, Honduras, on 23 and 24 November 1990, at Managua, Nicaragua, on 12 and 13 April 1991, at Guatemala City, on 19 and 20 September 1991, and at San José, Costa Rica, on 24 and 25 October 1991.

25. At the Tegucigalpa meeting, the Commission dealt with such matters as the model report on weapons inventories, verification of inventories, the question of mines and the disarming of civilians. This work was continued at the Managua meeting, which also dealt with the strengthening of ONUCA. As regards the inventories of weapons, the Commission agreed to postpone consideration of this matter to the next meeting, but little progress was made in Guatemala City on this issue. The Commission did, however, endorse the verification mechanisms that had been elaborated by its Technical Subcommission, which met on several occasions during the year.

26. The Commission held a special meeting in San José to discuss the Security Treaty which had been submitted by Honduras at the Central American Presidents' summit held in El Salvador in July 1991.

Annex

Querétaro Agreement

The Government of the Republic of Guatemala, the Unidad Revolucionaria Nacional Guatemalteca (URNG) and the National Reconciliation Commission (CNR), at the close of the meeting on democratization in the search for peace by political means, express their appreciation for the generous hospitality and support shown for the Guatemalan peace process by the Government and people of Mexico during the meeting held in the city of Querétaro from 22 to 25 July, which culminated today in the signing of this historic Agreement.

Querétaro, Mexico, 25 July 1991

Framework Agreement on Democratization in the Search for Peace by Political Means

"*Querétaro Agreement*"

With the aim of achieving the objectives set forth in the Esquipulas II Agreement of 7 August 1987 and in accordance with the Oslo Agreement of 30 March 1990, the delegations of the Government of the Republic of Guatemala and the Unidad Revolucionaria Nacional Guatemalteca (URNG), having pursued negotiations under the Oslo Agreement with the Chairman of the National Reconciliation Commission, Mr. Rodolfo Quezada Toruño, acting as Conciliator, with the participation of the National Reconciliation Commission (CNR) and with the Representative of the Secretary-General of the United Nations Mr. Francesc Vendrell, acting as Observer, and hereby placing on record the agreements which they have reached on the item "democratization" of the general agenda adopted at Mexico City on 26 April 1991,

CONSIDER THAT:

1. The political forces and the various sectors which make up Guatemalan society have expressed their desire for the achievement of peace, democracy and social justice.

2. The Government of the Republic of Guatemala and the Unidad Revolucionaria Nacional Guatemalteca (URNG) have agreed to pursue a process of negotiations whose final objective is the search for peace by political means, the enhancement of functional and participatory democracy and the laying of foundations on which to build national development and progress, thereby ensuring democratic co-existence and the attainment of the common good.

3. Considering the issue of democratization makes it possible to establish a general framework within which to approach coherently the other items to be discussed in the negotiating process.

4. Guatemala requires measures which ensure the development of political, economic, social and cultural democratization.

The Government of the Republic of Guatemala recognizes its responsibility to implement measures which are in the population's interest and guarantee the country's democratization.

5. The procedures and agreements resulting from the discussion of the general agenda adopted in Mexico

are fundamental to the process of enhancing functional and participatory democracy, and the Conciliator should therefore inform the Guatemalan people objectively and fairly about their content.

6. Any political agreements reached by the Government of the Republic of Guatemala and the Unidad Revolucionaria Nacional Guatemalteca (URNG) must reflect the legitimate aspirations of all Guatemalans and lead to institutional measures and the proposal of constitutional reforms to the Congress of the Republic, within the framework and in the spirit of the Political Constitution of the Republic of Guatemala and the Oslo, El Escorial and Mexico Agreements.

Accordingly, the Government of the Republic of Guatemala and the Unidad Revolucionaria Nacional Guatemalteca (URNG),

AGREE:

I. That the strengthening of functional and participatory democracy requires:

(a) The pre-eminence of civilian society;

(b) The development of democratic institutions;

(c) The effective functioning of a State subject to the rule of law;

(d) The permanent elimination of political repression, electoral fraud and coercion, military abuses and pressures, and anti-democratic, destabilizing actions;

(e) Unconditional respect for human rights;

(f) Subordination of the role of the armed forces to civilian authority;

(g) Recognition of and respect for the identity and rights of indigenous peoples;

(h) Access by all Guatemalans to the benefits of national production and natural resources, and enjoyment thereof, which must be based on principles of social justice;

(i) Effective resettlement of populations uprooted by the internal armed conflict.

II. That democratization means guaranteeing and promoting participation, whether direct or indirect, by civilian society in general in the formulation, implementation and evaluation of government policies at the various levels of government, recognizing the right of all social groups in the nation to enjoy fair and equitable labour relations, their own forms of culture and organization, and full respect for human rights and the law.

III. That this Agreement must be disseminated widely to the people of Guatemala and, in particular, to the sectors which took part in the dialogue at the meetings held under the Oslo Agreement and the National Dialogue, and that they must be informed by the Conciliator in order to ensure that the Agreement is duly understood.

IV. This Agreement shall be placed on record and form part of the Agreement on a firm and lasting peace, and shall serve as a framework for considering the other items to be negotiated, taking into account the particular aspects and specific concerns relating to each one.

Querétaro, Mexico, 25 July 1991

FOR THE GOVERNMENT OF THE REPUBLIC
OF GUATEMALA

(Signed) Manuel CONDE ORELLANA
Secretary-General of the Presidency of the Republic

(Signed) Fernando HURTADO PREM
Minister of the Interior

(Signed) Brigadier General
Mario René ENRÍQUEZ MORALES
Commander of the Military Brigade Guard of Honour

(Signed) Staff Colonel
Marco A. GONZÁLEZ TARACENA
Director of Intelligence of the National Defence Staff

(Signed) Rubén Amílcar BURGOS SOLÍS
Special Counsellor to the Presidency of the Republic

(Signed) Manolo BENDFELDT ALEJOS
Minister of Urban and Rural Development

(Signed) Brigadier General
José D. GARCÍA SAMAYOA
Deputy Chief of the National Defence Staff

(Signed) Staff Colonel
Julio A. BALCONI TURCIOS
Commander of the Mobile Military Police

(Signed) Ernesto VITERI ECHEVERRÍA
Special Counsellor to the Presidency of the Republic

(Signed) José Luis ASENSIO AGUIRRE
Adviser to the President of the Republic

FOR THE UNIDAD REVOLUCIONARIA
NACIONAL GUATEMALTECA (URNG)

General Command

(Signed) Commander Gaspar ILOM
(Signed) Commander Pablo MONSANTO
(Signed) Commander Rolando MORÁN

Political and Diplomatic Commission

(Signed) Francisco VILLAGRÁN MUÑOZ
(Signed) Luis BEKKER GUZMÁN
(Signed) Miguel Angel SANDOVAL
(Signed) Mario CASTAÑEDA
Adviser

FOR THE NATIONAL RECONCILIATION COMMISSION

(Signed) Teresa BOLAÑOS DE ZARCO

(Signed) Alfonso CABRERA HIDALGO

(Signed) Mario PERMUTH LISTWA

(Signed) Oliverio GARCÍA RODAS

(Signed) Monsignor Rodolfo QUEZADA TORUÑO
Conciliator
Chairman of the National Reconciliation Commission

FOR THE UNITED NATIONS

(Signed) Francesc VENDRELL
Representative of the Secretary-General
of the United Nations

Document 32

Letter dated 26 December 1991 from the Secretary-General to President Cristiani inviting the latter to United Nations Headquarters for negotiations

Not issued as a United Nations document; original in Spanish

I am writing to you regarding the ongoing negotiations between your Government and the Frente Farabundo Martí para la Liberación Nacional (FMLN). As you know, I am making an intense effort in the remaining days of my term of office to try and bring these negotiations, if possible, to a successful conclusion.

I have a responsibility to the Security Council, under whose authority I am carrying out this mission of good offices, to submit a report to it before handing over to my successor. I should like to be in a position, in this report, to affirm that all efforts have been exhausted. To that end, and convinced that your presence may be decisive for the success of the negotiations, I wish to invite you to come to New York, if possible, today, or tomorrow, 27 December 1991. With your presence and direct and personal participation, the negotiations will, I am convinced, receive a decisive impetus which they cannot have without it.

Accept, Sir, the assurances of my highest consideration.

(*Signed*) Javier PÉREZ DE CUÉLLAR

Document 33

Statement by the President of the Security Council on the agreement signed on 31 December 1991 by the Government of El Salvador and the FMLN

S/23360, 3 January 1992

The members of the Security Council have noted with appreciation the briefing provided by the Secretary-General on the agreement signed late in the night of 31 December by the Government of El Salvador and the Frente Farabundo Martí para la Liberación Nacional which, when implemented, will put a definite end to the Salvadorean armed conflict. The members of the Council warmly welcomed the agreement which is of vital importance for the normalization of the situation in El Salvador and in the region as a whole. They place on record their thanks and appreciation for the enormous contribution of the Secretary-General and his Personal Envoy for Central America, their collaborators, and all the Governments, especially those of Colombia, Mexico, Spain and Venezuela, that have assisted the Secretary-General in his efforts.

The members of the Council urge the parties to show maximum flexibility in resolving the pending issues in the negotiations at United Nations Headquarters in New York starting this weekend. They also urge the parties to exercise maximum restraint and to take no action in the coming days which would be contrary to the agreement reached in New York and to the excellent spirit in which these talks took place.

They welcomed the Secretary-General's intention, stated today, to submit a written report and proposals early next week with a view to Council action both regarding verification of cease-fire arrangements and the monitoring of the maintenance of public order pending the establishment of the new National Civil Police. This will require the approval by the Council of new tasks for the United Nations Observer Mission in El Salvador. The members of the Council stand ready to deal expeditiously with any recommendations that the Secretary-General may make.

Document 34

Report of the Secretary-General on the monitoring of agreements by ONUSAL

S/23402, 10 January 1992, and addendum, S/23402/Add.1, 13 January 1992

Introduction

1. The present report is submitted in pursuance of Security Council resolution 693 (1991) of 20 May 1991 by which the Council, *inter alia*, decided to establish the United Nations Observer Mission in El Salvador (ONUSAL) to monitor all agreements concluded between the Government of El Salvador and the Frente Farabundo Martí para la Liberación Nacional (FMLN) and requested the Secretary-General to keep the Council fully informed on the implementation of that resolution.

2. As the members of the Security Council will be aware, the results of the latest round of negotiations between the two parties in New York were announced in the "Act of New York", which was signed at midnight on 31 December 1991 and whose text is attached as an annex to the present report. That document recorded that the two parties had concluded a number of further agreements which, following a final round of negotiations on two outstanding issues, would be signed in Mexico City on 16 January 1992.

3. The agreements reached include two in particular which, subject to the Council's approval, will require

an immediate and substantial increase in ONUSAL's strength if it is to assume the verification and monitoring functions desired of it by the two parties. These are the agreement on the cessation of the armed confrontation, in which it is envisaged that ONUSAL will verify all aspects of the cease-fire and the separation of forces, and the agreement on the National Civil Police, which envisages that ONUSAL will monitor the maintenance of public order during the transitional period while the new National Civil Police is set up. The purpose of the present report is to convey to the Security Council my recommendations on how ONUSAL should undertake these functions and on the consequent changes that will be required in its organization and strength.

I. *Verification requirements arising from the agreement on the cessation of the armed confrontation*

4. The Agreement provides that the process of ending the armed confrontation will begin on 1 February 1992 (D-day) and will be completed by 31 October 1992. During the period between the signature of the Agreement on 16 January 1992 and D-day the parties will observe an informal cease-fire. The cease-fire will formally enter into force on D-day. Any alleged violation of it will be investigated by ONUSAL. A separation of forces will be carried out in two stages, the first ending on D+5 day (6 February 1992) and the second on D+30 day (2 March 1992), with the armed force of El Salvador (FAES) redeploying progressively to the positions it would maintain in normal peace-time deployment and the FMLN forces concentrating progressively in agreed "designated locations" in the areas of conflict. During the period of the informal cease-fire (16 January-31 January 1992), the Chief Military Observer of ONUSAL, in consultation with the two sides, will have defined precisely the designated locations for FMLN forces and worked out phased programmes for the movements of both sides' forces to those locations. These movements will be supervised by ONUSAL. As soon as possible after signature of the Agreement, the two sides will have conveyed to the Chief Military Observer of ONUSAL detailed information about the strength and armament of their forces. ONUSAL will verify that all declared personnel and equipment are brought to the agreed locations. The Agreement specifies the purposes for which personnel may leave the agreed locations in coordination with, and sometimes accompanied by, ONUSAL. ONUSAL is also given certain responsibilities in relation to alleged violations of the cease-fire committed by clandestine forces to non-combat flights by military aircraft and to a possible decision by the President of the Republic to exercise his constitutional right to use FAES exceptionally to help to deal with a public order crisis.

II. *Requirements arising from the agreement on the National Civil Police*

5. As part of the overall agreement to establish peace in El Salvador, two of the existing security bodies will be disbanded early in the process and the third will be phased out over a longer period. These measures will be implemented simultaneously with the organization of a new National Civil Police, in accordance with the terms of the agreement, with close international cooperation and supervision, coordinated by the United Nations.

6. In order to facilitate the difficult transition phase following the cease-fire and to generate confidence among all sectors of the population, the United Nations is expected to play a role that entails more than mere verification, and which includes the monitoring of the maintenance of public order, in particular the monitoring of operations and conduct of the existing National Police until the new National Civil Police is deployed throughout the country, which is to be done progressively. The concept for such monitoring is drawn from recent United Nations experience. Its objective is to permit the Salvadorian people to feel sufficiently secure during the delicate phase of transition from armed confrontation to national reconciliation, while the new National Civil Police, which is to be created, with the agreement of the two sides, to meet the country's requirements in the new era, is formed, trained and commissioned into service.

7. The United Nations police monitors will work closely with the Salvadorian police, monitoring their activities in order to ensure that they are conducted with professionalism, objectivity and impartiality. The police contingent of ONUSAL would deploy monitors at all levels of the present National Police. In particular, ONUSAL police monitors would establish their presence at the National Police central and regional headquarters and other decision-making and operational levels. Such presence would extend to as many fixed National Police installations as considered necessary, in both urban and rural areas. ONUSAL police monitors would also be deployed in areas where a special regime will prevail under the terms of the transitional provisions of the agreement on the creation of the National Civil Police. Mobile monitoring also would be a major activity, both by accompanying police patrols and monitoring their activities by random checks. The aim of United Nations monitoring will be to deter intimidation, reprisals or other violations of the civil rights of all sectors of the population, as well as to promote the impartial and non-discriminatory enforcement of laws and regulations in a manner that will encourage and promote national reconciliation. As the strength of the National Police is progressively reduced in accordance with a timetable to

be established, the number of ONUSAL police monitors also would be reduced.

III. *Changes in the organization and strength of ONUSAL*

8. It will be recalled that in its first phase of operation ONUSAL's verification responsibilities have related to implementation by the parties of the Agreement on Human Rights 1/ which they signed at San José on 26 July 1990. This task is carried out by a Human Rights Division which has been established in ONUSAL. If the Security Council agrees that ONUSAL's strength should be increased to permit it to fulfil the new verification requirements described above, it will be necessary to establish two additional divisions, a Military Division and a Police Division. Like the Human Rights Division, these new divisions would be under the overall control of the Chief of Mission, Mr. Iqbal Riza.

9. The Military Division would be commanded by an officer in the rank of Brigadier-General, who would be appointed by the Secretary-General after consultation with the parties and with the consent of the Security Council. The military observers would be contributed by Member States, at the request of the Secretary-General, who will consult the parties and obtain the Security Council's approval. The core strength of the Military Division, which will be required until the cessation of the armed confrontation is completed by 31 October 1992, will be 244 military observers. In addition it will be necessary to deploy an additional 128 military observers to enable ONUSAL to carry out the extensive responsibilities entrusted to it during the 30-day period when the separation of forces will be implemented. The headquarters of the Military Division will be in San Salvador and it will have four regional offices, which will be colocated with the existing regional offices established by the Human Rights Division.

10. I intend to meet as much as possible of the personnel requirements of ONUSAL's Military Division by transferring to that mission officers currently serving with the United Nations Observer Group for Central America (ONUCA), with the concurrence of the contributing Governments concerned. Aircraft, vehicles and other equipment will similarly be transferred. In pursuance of paragraph 3 of Security Council resolution 719 (1991), I shall shortly convey to the Council my recommendation that, with the end of the armed conflict in El Salvador now in sight, the mandate of ONUCA should be terminated. I have already informed the Governments of the five countries in which ONUCA is deployed that this is my intention.

11. The Police Division would be commanded by an officer of rank equivalent to Brigadier-General, who also would be appointed by the Secretary-General. The police

monitors also would be contributed by Member States, at the request of the Secretary-General. The preliminary estimate for the core strength of the Police Division until 31 December 1992 is 631 observers, to be deployed in all departments of El Salvador. It is hoped that this estimate would be adequate to implement ONUSAL's police monitoring functions effectively. Again, should it transpire that additional monitors become indispensable, the Council's authority would be requested.

12. The headquarters of the Police Division would be in San Salvador. It would have four regional offices, colocated with the existing ONUSAL regional offices, with suboffices being established to correspond to National Police deployment. The Police Division would work in close coordination with the Human Rights Division, which also is concerned with the functioning of the Salvadorian public security forces in relation to the human rights of the population.

13. The intention would be to reduce the strength of the Police Division after 1 January 1993 in concordance with the phasing out of the National Police. More precise proposals would be submitted to the Council towards the end of 1992.

IV. *Observations*

14. The present report is being presented to the Security Council in advance of signature of the agreements, which will give rise to the additional responsibilities for ONUSAL described above. I am confident that the remaining issues in the negotiation (a timetable for implementation of all the agreements and modalities for the ending of the military structure of FMLN and the reintegration of its members, within a framework of full legality, into the civil, institutional and political life of the country) will rapidly be agreed and that signature of all the agreements will take place on 16 January 1992, as scheduled. In these circumstances, I hope that the Security Council will be ready to adopt, in advance of signature, the decisions that will be necessary to permit a very rapid enlargement of ONUSAL so that it will be in a position to fulfil its new responsibilities as soon as the cessation of the armed confrontation begins on 1 February 1992.

15. The agreed modalities for the ending of the military structure of the FMLN and the reintegration of its members, within a framework of full legality, into the civil, institutional and political life of the country will give rise to some further verification tasks for ONUSAL but these can be performed with the increased strength recommended in this report. If verification of other agreements which are to be signed in Mexico City should give rise to requirements beyond the capacity of the personnel levels recommended in this report, I shall revert to the Council.

1/ S/21541.

16. The recommendation for the rapid enlargement of ONUSAL refers to the urgent operational needs prompted by the agreement to cease fire on 1 February 1992. However, the Geneva Agreement of 4 April 1990, which lays down the framework for the process which is to lead to the end of the armed conflict in El Salvador, under the auspices of the Secretary-General, provides for the verification of all agreements by the United Nations. This was approved by the Security Council in its resolution 693 (1991). The agreements which are to be signed on 16 January 1992, together with those already signed by the parties, cover a very wide agenda and involve considerable demands upon the Organization. I hope soon to put before the Council any further needs that arise out of these demands and that might entail consequences in terms of resources going beyond those currently in existence.

17. The Geneva Agreement of 4 April 1990 specifically provided in paragraph 5 for the Secretary-General to maintain, at his discretion, confidential contacts with the Governments of States Members of the United Nations or groups thereof that can contribute to the success of the process through their advice and support. Throughout the negotiating stage of the process, my predecessor and his Personal Representative have, within this framework, regularly consulted with a number of Governments that have lent assistance through their own channels of communication with the parties, as well as helping financially and logistically. My predecessor has had occasion to express his appreciation for this assistance. I wish to reiterate it on the Organization's behalf. Among these States it is appropriate to single out the Governments of Colombia, Mexico, Spain and Venezuela, which have come informally to be known as the "friends of the Secretary-General".

18. The responsibilities as entrusted to me under the aforementioned agreement, and those of the United Nations pursuant to subsequent agreements, continue well beyond the negotiating phase which is now drawing to an end. The period to come, combining implementation of agreements under United Nations verification and national reconciliation as well as reconstruction, will require a large and sustained effort on the part of the Salvadorian Government and people and the strong support of the international community. Clearly the central role in promoting the implementation of agreements falls upon the Security Council, which has expressed support for peace efforts in Central America and specifically in El Salvador on a number of occasions.

19. Using the discretionary faculties entrusted to me by the parties to the Geneva Agreement, I fully intend to continue to call upon Governments of member States for assistance in the period to come. I will in particular continue to rely on Colombia, Mexico, Spain and Venezuela, whose Governments have reiterated to me their willingness to continue playing a support role which I consider to be essential both to buttress me in the exercise of my responsibilities as described above, as well as in coming reconstruction endeavours. I will also be approaching other States and groups of States, both within and outside the region, towards this same end. I intend in the coming days and weeks to continue to explore with the parties and with others ways and means to ensure a follow-up in the coming stages of the Salvadorian process whose goals, as stated in the Geneva Agreement, were not only to bring an end to the armed conflict, but also to promote respect for human rights, democracy and the reunification of the Salvadorian people.

20. In conclusion, I recommend that the Security Council now take the decision to enlarge ONUSAL's mandate and increase its strength as proposed in this report. I shall, as always, ensure that these additional tasks are carried out as economically as possible. It is my intention to summit a further report to the Council in mid-October 1992 with my recommendations concerning ONUSAL's continuing operations and strength in the period following the end of that month.

Annex

Act of New York

The Government of El Salvador and the Frente Farabundo Martí para la Liberación Nacional (FMLN) hereby declare that they have reached definitive agreements which, combined with those previously signed at San José, Mexico City and New York, complete the negotiations on all substantive items of the Caracas Agenda and the New York "Compressed Negotiations". Their implementation will put a final end to the Salvadorian armed conflict.

An agreement has also been reached on all technical and military aspects relating to the separation of the warring parties and the cessation of the armed conflict, which includes the end of the military structure of the FMLN and the reintegration of its members, within a framework of full legality, into the civil, political and institutional life of the country.

The parties have also agreed that the cessation of the armed conflict shall take effect formally on 1 February 1992 and shall conclude on 31 October 1992.

A further meeting between the parties has been scheduled for 5 January 1992 to negotiate the timetable for implementing the agreements and the procedure for ending the military structure of FMLN and reintegrating its members, within a framework of full legality, into the civil, political and institutional life of the country.

Such negotiations must be successfully concluded by 10 January 1992 at the latest. Otherwise, the parties undertake to accept, by 14 January 1992 at the latest, a formula for resolving outstanding issues to be proposed to them by the Secretary-General of the United Nations. The Final Peace Agreements will be signed at Mexico City on 16 January 1992.

The parties undertake to preserve the atmosphere necessary for maintaining and expanding the unilateral decisions which they have taken in order to avoid all military activity.

New York, 31 December 1991

Representing the Government of El Salvador:

(*Signed*)
Dr. Oscar SANTAMARÍA

Colonel Mauricio Ernesto VARGAS

Dr. David ESCOBAR GALINDO

Colonel Juan MARTÍNEZ VARELA

Dr. Abelardo TORRES

Dr. Rafael HERNÁN CONTRERAS

Representing the Frente Farabundo Martí para la Liberación Nacional:

(*Signed*)
Commander Schafik HÁNDAL

Commander Francisco JOVEL

Commander Salvador SÁNCHEZ CORÉN

Colonel Eduardo SANCHO

Commander Joaquín VILLALOBOS

(*Signed*) Alvaro DE SOTO
Representative of the Secretary-General
of the United Nations

Addendum (S/23402/Add.1)

1. In paragraph 3 of my report to the Security Council (S/23402) I indicated the need for an immediate and substantial increase in the strength of the United Nations Observer Mission in El Salvador (ONUSAL) if it were to assume the verification and monitoring functions desired of it by the two parties. In this regard, I have put forward to the Security Counci my recommendations on how ONUSAL should undertake these functions and on the consequent changes that will be required in its organization and strength.

2. As stated in paragraphs 8 through 11 of the report, in order to fulfil the new verification requirements as proposed, it would be necessary for ONUSAL to establish two additional divisions, a Military Division and a Police Division. The core strength of the Military Division, consisting of 244 observers, will be required until the cessation of the armed confrontation, that is, through 31 October 1994. Moreover, it will be necesary to deploy an additional 128 Military Observers to enable ONUSAL to carry out the extensive responsibilities entrusted to it during the 30-day period when the separation of forces will be implemented. In order to implement ONUSAL's police monitoring functions effectively, the Police Division will require 631 police observers, to be deployed in all departments of El Salvador. In addition 95 civilian staff would be required to provide administrative, transport, communication and procurement support to ONUSAL. There would also be additional requirements for premises/accommodation, transport and air operations, communication and miscellaneous equipment, supplies and services.

3. Should the Security Council decide to expand the mandate of ONUSAL on the basis of the recommendation set out in my report of 10 January 1992 (S/23402), it is estimated that the cost of ONUSAL would be approximately $58.9 million, as shown in the annex. This amount includes the requirements of the present ONUSAL mandate, covering the verification of compliance on human rights for 10 months through 31 October 1992 and the estimated requirements for the expansion for the phased separation of forces beginning in February 1992.

4. It would be my recommendation to the General Assembly, should the Security Council decide to expand ONUSAL's mandate, that the cost relating thereto should be considered an expense of the Organization to be borne by Member States in accordance with Article 17, paragraph 2, of the Charter of the United Nations and that the assessments to be levied on Member States be credited to the ONUSAL Special Account.

Cost estimates by main expenditure groups
(in thousands of United States dollars)

Serial	(1)	(2)	(3)
1. Military and police observers			
(a) Military observers, including travel to mission area	300.0	5 570.0	5 870.0
(b) Police observers, including travel to mission area	1 010.0	11 580.0	12 590.0
(c) Death and disability	0.0	750.0	750.0
2. Civilian personnel, including travel to mission area	11 750.0	3 760.0	15 510.0
3. Premises, construction and maintenance	520.0	2 990.0	3 510.0
4. Vehicle operations	440.0	6 150.0	6 590.0
5. Aircraft operations	0.0	7 250.0	7 250.0
6. Communications	230.0	3 300.0	3 530.0
7. Miscellaneous equipment	50.0	980.0	1 030.0
8. Miscellaneous supplies, services, freight and support costs	1 160.0	1 150.0	2 310.0
Totals	15 460.0	43 480.0	58 940.0

(1) Projected requirements for ONUSAL, prior to expansion, for 10 months from 1 January to 31 October 1992.

(2) Estimated requirements for the expanded ONUSAL operations, from approximately mid-January to 31 October 1992.

(3) Combined estimated requirements for the expanded ONUSAL operations, through 31 October 1992.

Document 35

Security Council resolution concerning enlargement of the ONUSAL mandate

S/RES/729 (1992), 14 January 1992

The Security Council,

Recalling its resolution 637 (1989) of 27 July 1989,

Recalling also its resolution 714 (1991) of 30 September 1991, as well as the statement made by the President of the Council on behalf of its members on 3 January 1992 1/ following the signature of the Act of New York on 31 December 1991,

Recalling further its resolution 693 (1991) of 20 May 1991 by which it established the United Nations Observer Mission in El Salvador,

Welcoming the conclusion of agreements between the Government of El Salvador and the Frente Farabundo Martí para la Liberación Nacional, which are to be signed at Mexico City on 16 January 1992 and which, when implemented, will put a definitive end to the Salvadorian armed conflict, and will open the way for national reconciliation,

Calling upon both parties to continue to exercise maximum moderation and restraint and to take no action which would be contrary to or adversely affect the agreements to be signed in Mexico City,

Expressing its conviction that a peaceful settlement in El Salvador will make a decisive contribution to the Central American peace process,

1/ S/23360.

Welcoming the intention of the Secretary-General to convey shortly to the Council his recommendation on the termination of the mandate of the United Nations Observer Group in Central America,

1. *Approves* the report of the Secretary-General of 10 and 13 January 1992; 2/

2. *Decides*, on the basis of the report of the Secretary-General and in accordance with the provisions of resolution 693 (1991), to enlarge the mandate of the United Nations Observer Mission in El Salvador to include the verification and monitoring of the implementation of all the agreements once these are signed in Mexico City between the Government of El Salvador and the Frente Farabundo Martí para la Liberación Nacional, in particular the Agreement on the Cessation of the Armed Conflict and the Agreement on the Establishment of a National Civil Police;

3. *Also decides* that the mandate of the Mission, enlarged in accordance with the present resolution, will be extended to 31 October 1992 and that it will be reviewed at that time on the basis of recommendations to be presented by the Secretary-General;

4. *Requests* the Secretary-General to take the necessary measures to increase the strength of the Mission as recommended in his report;

5. *Calls upon* both parties to respect scrupulously and to implement in good faith the commitments assumed by them under the agreements which are to be signed at Mexico City, and to cooperate fully with the Mission in its task of verifying the implementation of these agreements;

6. *Reaffirms* its support for the Secretary-General's continuing mission of good offices with regard to the Central American peace process, and in particular for his observations in paragraphs 17 to 19 of the report regarding his intention to continue, as was foreseen in the Geneva Agreement of 4 April 1990 3/ concerning the process which is to end definitively the armed conflict, to rely on the Governments of Colombia, Mexico, Spain and Venezuela, as well as other States and groups of States, to support him in the exercise of his responsibilities;

7. *Requests* the Secretary-General to keep the Security Council fully informed of developments relating to the implementation of this resolution and to report on the operations of the Mission before the expiry of the new mandate period.

2/ S/24302, annex.
3/ S/21931, annex I.

Document 36

Letter dated 27 January 1992 from El Salvador transmitting the entire text of the Peace Agreement between the Government of El Salvador and the FMLN, signed at Chapultepec Castle in Mexico City on 16 January 1992

A/46/864-S/23501, 30 January 1992

I have the honour to transmit herewith the "Peace Agreement" signed at Mexico City on 16 January 1992 between the Government of El Salvador and the Frente Farabundo Martí para la Liberación Nacional (see annex), which contains the set of political agreements designed to put a definitive end to the Salvadorian armed conflict.

I should be grateful if you would have this note and its annex circulated as an official document of the General Assembly, under agenda item 31, and of the Security Council.

(*Signed*) Ricardo G. CASTAÑEDA
Ambassador
Permanent Representative

Annex

Peace Agreement

The Government of El Salvador and the Frente Farabundo Martí para la Liberación Nacional (hereinafter referred to as "the Parties"),

Reaffirming that their purpose, as set forth in the Geneva Agreement of 4 April 1990, is "to end the armed conflict by political means as speedily as possible, promote the democratization of the country, guarantee unrestricted respect for human rights and reunify Salvadorian society",

Bearing in mind the San José, Mexico and New York Agreements of 26 July 1990, 27 April 1991 and 25 September 1991 respectively, arrived at by them in the course of the negotiating process conducted with the active participation of the Secretary-General of the United Nations and of his Representative, which Agreements form a whole with the Agreement signed today,

Having concluded negotiations on all the substantive items of the Caracas Agenda of 21 May 1990 and of the New York Compressed Negotiations of 25 September 1991,

Have arrived at the set of political agreements that follow, whose implementation, together with that of the earlier Agreements mentioned above, will put a definitive end to the Salvadorian armed conflict:

CHAPTER I
ARMED FORCES

1. *Doctrinal principles of the armed forces*

The doctrine for the armed forces, on the basis of the constitutional reform agreed to in April 1991, as defined by law, shall conform to the principles set forth below, and henceforth their institutional regime and educational system shall be based exclusively on those principles and their operations shall be bound by strict observance of them:

A. The mission of the armed forces is to defend the sovereignty of the State and the integrity of its territory, according to the terms of the regime defined for them by the Constitution and the laws. The performance of this mission is inseparable from democratic values and strict respect for all parts of the Constitution.

B. As established in the Constitution, the armed forces are a permanent institution in the service of the nation. They shall be obedient, professional, apolitical and non-deliberative. Their institutional regime and operations shall also be consistent with the principles deriving from the rule of law, the primacy of the dignity of the human person and respect for human rights; respect for and defence of the sovereignty of the Salvadorian people; the concept of the armed forces as an institution free from all considerations of politics, ideology or social position or any other discrimination; and the subordination of the armed forces to the constitutional authorities.

C. The armed forces owe respect to the political order determined by the sovereign will of the people and all political or social changes generated by that will, in accordance with democratic procedures consistent with the Constitution. Their institutional regime and operations shall be defined in terms ensuring a harmonious relationship at all times with civilian society and the normal activities of their members as part of that society.

D. As a State institution, the armed forces play an instrumental, non-decision-making role in the political field. Consequently, only the President of the Republic and the basic organs of government may use the armed forces to implement the provisions they have adopted, within their respective constitutional areas of competence, to enforce the Constitution. Similarly, those authorities have exclusive competence to verify whether the political or social changes referred to in the preceding paragraph are consistent with the Constitution.

E. The doctrine of the armed forces is based on a distinction between the concepts of security and defence. National defence, the responsibility of the armed forces, is intended to safeguard sovereignty and territorial integrity against outside military threat. Security, even when it includes this notion, is a broader concept based on unrestricted respect for the individual and social rights of the person. It includes, in addition to national defence, economic, political and social aspects which go beyond the constitutional sphere of competence of the armed forces and are the responsibility of other sectors of society and of the State.

F. The maintenance of internal peace, tranquillity, order and public security lies outside the normal functions of the armed forces as an institution responsible for national defence. The armed forces play a role in this sphere only in very exceptional circumstances, where the normal means have been exhausted, on the terms established in the constitutional reform approved in April 1991.

2. *Educational system of the armed forces*

Reiterating fully their previous agreements, whereby the professional training of members of the armed forces shall emphasize the pre-eminence of human dignity and democratic values, respect for human rights and the subordination of such forces to the constitutional authorities, the Parties have reached the following agreements:

A. The legal framework of the armed forces educational and training system shall be defined on the basis of the provisions of articles 212 and 213 of the constitutional reform agreed to in April 1991.

B. The doctrinal framework of the armed forces educational system shall be defined by the doctrinal principles set forth in this chapter. Those principles shall be the doctrinal foundation of all armed forces educational and training programmes at all levels.

C. Curricula and study programmes for the training and education of the armed forces shall include, in addition to military and technical subjects, scientific and humanistic studies in order to provide an all-round education which gives students the necessary skills to participate actively in the institutional life of the country and promotes at all times an harmonious relationship with civilian society, as well as their normal activities as members of that society.

D. In order to attain fully the goals outlined in the

preceding paragraph, members of the armed forces shall be encouraged to take professional and postgraduate courses at the country's universities.

E. The Military College shall be run on a collegiate basis in teaching matters. Its Director shall be the President of an Academic Council which shall include members of the military and civilians from the academic world. Members of the Academic Council shall be appointed by the President of the Republic.

F. COPAZ shall decide on the number of members of the Academic Council, which shall comprise an equal number of civilians and military personnel.

G. Civilian members of the Academic Council shall be appointed by the President of the Republic, on the basis of criteria of political pluralism, from lists of three candidates proposed by COPAZ.

H. The teaching staff shall be appointed by the Academic Council, which shall ensure that no political tendency predominates among that staff.

I. The Director of the Military College shall be appointed by the President of the Republic.

J. The admissions system shall be determined by the Academic Council, which shall ensure that it is not discriminatory.

K. COPAZ shall oversee, in particular, the implementation of paragraphs (G), (H) and (J), under the terms laid down in the New York Agreement of 25 September 1991.

3. *Purification*

The Parties agree to a process of purification of the armed forces, within the framework of the peace process and with a view to the supreme objective of national reconciliation, based on evaluation of all members of the armed forces by an ad hoc Commission.

A. The evaluation shall take into account the past performance of each officer, including, in particular: (1) his record of observance of the legal order, with particular emphasis on respect for human rights, both in his personal conduct and in the rigour with which he has ordered the redress and punishment of unlawful acts, excesses or human rights violations committed under his command, especially if there have been serious or systematic omissions in the latter respect; (2) his professional competence; and (3) his capacity to function in the new situation of peace, within the context of a democratic society, and to promote the democratization of the country, guarantee unrestricted respect for human rights and reunify Salvadorian society, which is the common purpose agreed upon by the Parties in the Geneva Agreement. The existence of serious deficiencies in any one of the above-mentioned areas could be sufficient grounds for the ad hoc Commission to take the decisions required under paragraph (G) of this section.

B. The evaluation shall be carried out by a rigorously impartial ad hoc Commission composed of three Salvadorians of recognized independence of judgement and unimpeachable democratic credentials. It shall also include two officers of the armed forces with impeccable professional records, who shall have access only to the deliberations of the Commission; they shall not have access to the investigation phase to be carried out by the ad hoc Commission, nor be involved in the final phase of the investigation, but they may have access to its conclusions.

The selection of the three civilian members of the ad hoc Commission is the result of a process of consultations carried out by the Secretary-General of the United Nations, the outcome of which has already been communicated to both Parties. The President of the Republic shall issue, within five days from the signing of this Agreement, his endorsement giving legal form and force to the Commission. If necessary, the same procedure shall be used to replace any member of the Commission who is permanently unable to serve. The two officers of the armed forces who are to participate in the ad hoc Commission on the conditions indicated above shall be appointed by the President of the Republic.

C. The Commission on the Truth established by the Mexico Agreements of 26 April 1991 (hereinafter referred to as "the Commission on the Truth") may appoint an observer to the ad hoc Commission.

D. The ad hoc Commission shall be provided with such civilian support staff as it considers necessary.

E. The Ministry of Defence and Public Security, 1/ as well as any public entity, shall supply the ad hoc Commission with any information it requests, including information on the service record of each officer. In any case, the ad hoc Commission may avail itself of information from any source which it considers reliable.

F. The ad hoc Commission shall adopt and, where necessary, request the adoption of any measure which, in its view, is necessary for its own safety and to ensure the safety and physical and moral integrity of persons who, in any form or manner, cooperate with it in the fulfilment of its mission.

G. The ad hoc Commission shall adopt its conclusions, after hearing the parties concerned, on the basis of the provisions of paragraph (A) of this section. Its conclusions may include a change of duty station and, where necessary, the discharge of the staff evaluated.

H. The ad hoc Commission shall endeavour to adopt its decisions unanimously, but if this is not possible a vote by the majority of its members shall suffice.

I. The evaluation shall be extended to non-commissioned officers when, in the judgement of the ad hoc Commission, there is justification for doing so.

1/ The results of the constitutional reform will be taken into account.

J. The ad hoc Commission shall conclude its evaluation within a maximum period of three months from the date of its establishment. The corresponding administrative decisions shall be taken within 30 days from the date on which the conclusions are communicated to the Government by the ad hoc Commission and shall be implemented within 60 days from that date.

K. The results of the evaluation shall not prevent the implementation of such recommendations as the Commission on the Truth may make at the appropriate time.

4. *Reduction*

The new situation of peace shall include the reduction of the armed forces to a size appropriate to their doctrine and to the functions assigned to them by the Constitution within the framework of the constitutional reform resulting from the Mexico Agreements. Accordingly, pursuant to the New York Agreement, the Government has submitted to the Secretary-General of the United Nations a plan for the reduction of the armed forces, which the Secretary-General has made known to FMLN. The implementation of the plan must have the practical consequence of making reductions in the various branches of the armed forces.

A. *Organization*

The organization of the armed forces shall be adapted to their institutional mission in peacetime, in keeping with the functions assigned to them by the Constitution. This means:

a. The type of units appropriate for performing the various tasks corresponding to that mission;

b. The appropriate structure, organization and equipment for such units by branch, service, category (rank) and speciality; and

c. Staffing requirements, by unit, mission and rank.

B. *Units*

a. Reduction of units shall be based on the reorganization of the armed forces. The number and type of units shall be in keeping with the new organization;

b. In any case, the reduction covers units established as a consequence of the conflict.

C. *Personnel*

The reorganization and the reduction of units involve cutting back personnel in the various categories, branches and services or specialities of the armed forces. The number of officers shall be reduced in accordance with the reduction plan and shall be commensurate with the normal needs of an army.

D. Matériel *and equipment*

Matériel and equipment shall be in keeping with the new organization, the doctrine and constitutional mission of the armed forces.

E. *Facilities*

Reduction involves the conversion, return or disposal of facilities no longer used by the armed forces.

F. *Administrative and service structures*

All administrative and service structures shall be adapted to the new situation of peace and to the doctrine and the new constitutional mission of the armed forces.

G. *Military spending*

5. *End to impunity*

The Parties recognize the need to clarify and put an end to any indication of impunity on the part of officers of the armed forces, particularly in cases where respect for human rights is jeopardized. To that end, the Parties refer this issue to the Commission on the Truth for consideration and resolution. All of this shall be without prejudice to the principle, which the Parties also recognize, that acts of this nature, regardless of the sector to which their perpetrators belong, must be the object of exemplary action by the law courts so that the punishment prescribed by law is meted out to those found responsible.

6. *Public security forces*

A. Under the constitutional reform resulting from the Mexico Agreements, the safeguarding of peace, tranquillity, order and public security in both urban and rural areas shall be the responsibility of the National Civil Police, which shall be under the control of civilian authorities. The National Civil Police and the armed forces shall be independent and shall be placed under the authority of different ministries.

B. According to the terms of chapter II of this Agreement, the National Civil Police shall be a new force, with a new organization, new officers, new education and training mechanisms and a new doctrine.

C. The National Guard and the Treasury Police shall be abolished as public security forces and their members shall be incorporated into the army.

7. *Intelligence services*

A. The National Intelligence Department shall be abolished and State intelligence services shall be entrusted to a new entity to be called the State Intelligence Agency, which shall be subordinated to civilian authority and come under the direct authority of the President of the Republic. During the transitional period, the Director of the State Intelligence Agency shall be a civilian appointed by the President of the Republic on the basis of his ability to attract broad acceptance. He may be dismissed by resolution of the Legislative Assembly on grounds of serious human rights violations.

B. The legal regime, staff training, organizational lines, operational guidelines and, in general, the doctrine of the State Intelligence Agency shall accord with democratic principles; the concept of State intelligence as a State function for the common good, free from all considerations of politics, ideology or social position or any other discrimination; and strict respect for human rights.

C. The activities of the State Intelligence Agency shall be restricted to those required for compiling and analysing information in the general interest, by the means and within the limits authorized by the legal order and, in particular, on the basis of strict respect for human rights.

D. The activities of the State Intelligence Agency shall be supervised by the Legislative Assembly, using the oversight mechanisms established by the Constitution.

E. Alternative employment and compensation shall be offered to staff currently attached to the National Intelligence Department who are not incorporated into the new State Intelligence Agency. International support shall be sought for that purpose.

F. The incorporation into the State Intelligence Agency of staff of the National Intelligence Department who so request shall be permitted only after rigorous evaluation of their past performance, abilities and capacity to adapt to the new doctrine. Such evaluation shall be made by the Director of the Agency, under the authority of the President of the Republic, with the support of international advisory services and United Nations verification.

G. The State Intelligence Agency shall be organized by its Director, under the authority of the President of the Republic.

8. Rapid deployment infantry battalions

The Parties recognize that the rapid deployment infantry battalions were created at a specific moment in the conflict and that their existence must therefore be reviewed as circumstances dictate. Consequently, they also recognize that the rapid deployment infantry battalions will not be needed in the new situation of peace, with the result that in these circumstances it will be possible to disband them and to redeploy or discharge personnel currently assigned to them.

9. Subordination to civilian authority

The President of the Republic, in exercise of the power of discretion conferred on him by the Constitution,

may appoint civilians to head the Ministry of Defence. In any case, appointees must be persons fully committed to observing the peace agreements.

10. Paramilitary bodies

A. The Parties recognize the principle that any paramilitary force or group must be proscribed in a State governed by the rule of law.

B. *Civil defence.* Civil defence units shall be disbanded. This process shall be gradual and shall be subject to the implementation timetable for the peace agreements.

C. *System of armed forces reserves.* A new system of armed forces reserves shall replace the present system of territorial service, according to the following terms:

a. The system shall be responsible for the organization and functioning of the following aspects: (1) up-to-date registration of citizens in reserve status and citizens fit for military service; (2) updating of the military skills of reserves; (3) when necessary, calling reserves up for active duty to perform the mission entrusted to the armed forces by the Constitution.

b. The new system shall be under the authority of the Ministry of Defence.

c. Armed forces reserves may undertake missions only if assigned to active duty in the armed forces and in conformity with the Constitution, and shall not perform any function related to public security or monitoring of the population or the territory.

d. The laws, regulations and orders in force on this subject shall be made compatible with the terms of this Agreement.

D. *Regulation of private security services.* The Parties recognize the need to regulate the activities of all those entities, groups or persons who provide security or protection to private individuals, corporations or State institutions, in order to guarantee the transparency of their activities and also their strict subordination to the law and to respect for human rights. To that end:

a. A special law shall regulate the activities of entities, groups or persons who provide security or protection to private individuals, corporations or State institutions. That law shall establish the requirements which must be met in order to offer and provide such services; a system for the public registration of the staff, weapons and offices, if any, of such groups, entities or persons; appropriate oversight mechanisms, including their supervision by the National Civil Police; and, in general, the necessary limitations and prohibitions to ensure that such security services operate exclusively within the framework of the law.

b. The law shall also establish peremptory deadlines for fulfilling the above requirements, where relevant.

Once those deadlines have expired, entities which have not fulfilled the above requirements shall be considered illegal and their members and organizers shall be subject to application of the corresponding legal penalties.

c. To that end, the Parties express their agreement with the outline of the preliminary legislative draft included as an annex to this Agreement, which they refer to COPAZ, together with the above considerations, for it to prepare the corresponding preliminary draft.

11. *Suspension of forcible recruitment*

A. Any form of forcible recruitment shall be suspended when the cessation of the armed conflict comes into effect, pending the entry into force of the law referred to in the next paragraph.

B. A new law governing military service and reserve service shall be promulgated. That law shall establish as fundamental principles of military service that it shall be universal and compulsory and shall be imposed fairly and without discrimination.

C. Pursuant to the above, the law shall establish that all Salvadorians must present themselves at the proper time at the corresponding registration centres. Recruitment shall be effected exclusively by calling up individuals through the drawing of lots, and by registering volunteers. Military service may be performed over one continuous period or over several periods of time.

D. The above law shall envisage administrative penalties for failure to fulfil the obligations provided for therein and shall determine the grounds for temporary or permanent exemption from military service, equivalences between types of military service and other general provisions.

E. The law shall also regulate the armed forces reserves in accordance with paragraph (C) of section 10 of this chapter.

12. *Preventive and promotional measures*

Within the context of the objectives of this Agreement, the Parties recognize the need to adopt a number of measures designed to promote enhanced respect for the rules which must govern the armed forces and to prevent infringements of those rules. These measures include the following:

A. Supervision of armed forces operations by the Legislative Assembly.

B. Effective functioning of the Armed Forces General Inspectorate. The Inspector General shall be a member of the armed forces with an impeccable professional record, appointed by the President of the Republic.

C. Creation of an armed forces court of honour to try acts which, although not necessarily punishable, are contrary to military honour. This shall be without prejudice to the requirement that soldiers who have broken the law must be brought before the courts.

D. Amendment of the law penalizing unlawful enrichment to expressly include within its jurisdiction senior commanders of military units and those performing administrative functions at the same levels.

E. Cancellation of licences for private individuals to bear weapons that are for the exclusive use of the armed forces, and immediate recall of such weapons.

F. Dissemination of the doctrine of the armed forces so that the whole of society is familiar with it.

G. Adaptation of the legislation on the armed forces to the constitutional reform approved in April 1991, to the New York Agreement and to this Agreement.

13. *Redeployment and discharge*

A. Troops belonging to units that are to be abolished or disbanded shall be redeployed within the armed forces where such redeployment is compatible with the armed forces troop strength required by the objectives of this Agreement, and with the conclusions and recommendations of the ad hoc Commission provided for in section 3 of this chapter.

B. All troops discharged as a result of these agreements shall be given compensation equivalent to one year's pay at their wage level and the Government shall promote projects permitting the integration of such individuals into civilian life.

CHAPTER II
NATIONAL CIVIL POLICE

1. *Establishment of the national civil police*

The National Civil Police shall be established in accordance with the constitutional reform resulting from the Mexico Agreements. The National Civil Police shall be a new force with a new organization, new officers, new education and training mechanisms and a new doctrine.

A. The National Civil Police shall be the only armed police body with national jurisdiction. Its mission shall be to protect and safeguard the free exercise of the rights and freedoms of individuals, to prevent and combat all types of crimes, and to maintain internal peace, tranquillity, order and public security in both urban and rural areas.

B. In accordance with the provisions of the New York Agreement, the organization of the National Civil Police and the general outlines of its staff profile shall be determined, on the terms set forth in this Agreement, under close international cooperation and supervision, coordinated by the United Nations. 2/

2/ The international cooperation referred to in these Agreements shall be coordinated by the United Nations and shall be subject to a formal request by the Government, compliance with the official procedures and the corresponding consultations.

2. *Doctrine*

A. The legal regime, staff training, organizational lines, operational guidelines and, in general, the institutional definition and operation of the National Civil Police shall accord with democratic principles; the concept of public security as a service provided by the State to its citizens, free from all considerations of politics, ideology or social position or any other discrimination; respect for human rights; the effort to prevent crime; and the subordination of the force to the constitutional authorities. Citizens' exercise of their political rights may not be impaired by police activities.

B. The National Civil Police shall be a professional body, independent of the armed forces and free from all partisan activity. Without prejudice to the right of its members to make, as citizens, their own political choices, they shall not be able to use their status for partisan purposes.

C. Members of the National Civil Police shall at all times observe the duties imposed on them by law, serving the community and protecting all persons from illegal acts, in keeping with the high degree of responsibility required by their profession.

D. In the performance of their tasks, members of the National Civil Police shall respect and protect human dignity and shall preserve and defend the human rights of all persons.

E. Members of the National Civil Police may use force only when strictly necessary and to the extent required for the fulfilment of their tasks.

F. Questions of a confidential nature of which members of the National Civil Police have knowledge shall be kept secret, unless compliance with duty or the needs of justice strictly demand otherwise.

G. No member of the National Civil Police may inflict, instigate or tolerate any act of torture or other cruel, inhuman or degrading treatment or punishment, nor invoke the orders of a superior or special circumstances, such as a state of war or threat of war, threats to national security, internal political instability or any other public emergency to justify torture or other cruel, inhuman or degrading treatment or punishment.

H. All orders from above shall be in keeping with the laws of the Republic. Obeying the orders of a superior is no justification for committing acts which are clearly punishable.

I. Members of the National Civil Police shall ensure full protection of the health of persons in their custody and, in particular, shall take immediate steps to provide medical care when necessary.

J. Members of the National Civil Police shall not commit any act of corruption. They shall also strongly oppose such acts and shall combat them.

K. Members of the National Civil Police who have reason to believe that a breach of these rules of conduct has occurred or is about to occur shall so inform their superiors and, if necessary, any authority or appropriate agency having powers of control or correction.

L. In the performance of their functions, members of the National Civil Police shall, as far as possible, utilize non-violent means before resorting to the use of force and firearms. They may use force and firearms only when other means prove ineffective or do not in any way guarantee the achievement of the legitimate anticipated result.

M. Members of the National Civil Police shall not use firearms against people except in self-defence or in defence of other people, or in case of imminent danger of death or serious injury, or with the intention of preventing the commission of a particularly serious crime involving a serious threat to life, or for the purpose of arresting a person who represents such a threat and resists their authority, and only where less extreme means prove insufficient to achieve such objectives. In any case, lethal weapons may be used intentionally only when strictly unavoidable for the protection of a life.

N. As part of the performance of their duty to safeguard the exercise of the rights of individuals, members of the National Civil Police shall protect the exercise of the right of assembly and demonstration. When, for legal reasons, they are compelled to break up a demonstration or a meeting, they shall use the least dangerous means and only to the minimum extent necessary. Members of the National Civil Police shall refrain from using firearms in such cases, save where the meetings are violent and other means have been exhausted, and only under the circumstances provided for in the preceding paragraph.

3. *Functional and territorial structure*

The functional and territorial structure to be adopted by the National Civil Police is defined in the following general framework. This structure shall be reflected in the organizational chart and in the law on the organization of the National Civil Police.

A. *General legal framework*

a. *National Civil Police authorities*

(1) The National Civil Police shall be under the control of civilian authorities (art. 168, para. 17, of the Constitution). These shall be: the President of the Republic, the Minister, the Vice-Minister, the Director-General of Police, the Deputy Directors-General, the Inspector General, the division chiefs of each service and the chiefs of departmental delegations.

(2) The Director-General of the National Civil Po-

lice shall be appointed by the President of the Republic. He may be dismissed by resolution of the Legislative Assembly for serious violations of human rights. The leadership of the National Civil Police shall be civilian.

(3) Without prejudice to the provisions of this chapter concerning the transitional regime, the National Civil Police shall be placed under the authority of a new Ministry of the Interior and Public Security. To that end, the existing Ministry of the Interior shall be restructured. A Vice-Ministry of Public Security shall be established and shall be responsible for relations with the National Civil Police. The public security structure shall be entirely new.

b. *Nature of the organization*

The National Civil Police shall have a centralized organization, in that it will be structured at the national level in such a way as to cover all tasks assigned to the police. Its operation, on the other hand, shall be decentralized, because there shall be departmental police delegations in accordance with the administrative divisions of the country.

Owing to the nature of the functions assigned to certain units which belong organizationally to the National Civil Police, these units may remain under the functional control of other authorities, under the terms set forth in this chapter.

B. *Organs reporting to the Director-General*

a. *Offices of Deputy Directors-General*

b. *The General Inspectorate*

Under the authority of the Director-General, the General Inspectorate of Police shall be responsible for monitoring and supervising the activities of the operational services of the force.

The Inspector General shall be appointed by the Director-General, in consultation with the Attorney-General of the Republic and the National Counsel for the Defence of Human Rights.

The General Inspectorate shall comprise a Monitoring Division, which shall have the function of monitoring all police services, and a Disciplinary Investigation Division, which shall have the function of investigating breaches of discipline by police officers.

c. *Legal advisory services*

These services shall be staffed by legal experts specialized in police matters. They shall be organized in accordance with the needs of the various functional and territorial police structures.

d. *International legal advisory services*

International legal advisory services shall be staffed by suitable personnel and high-level specialists. They shall be coordinated by the United Nations and are envisaged as a transitional arrangement.

C. *Office of the Deputy Director-General for Operations*

a. *Divisions*
(1) *Public Security Division*

The Public Security Division shall be responsible for the maintenance of tranquillity, order and public security. It shall have the following departments: prevention, traffic, public order, control of private security, juveniles 3/ and general coordination with departmental delegations.

(2) *Criminal Investigation Division*

Under the functional control of the Attorney-General of the Republic, the Criminal Investigation Division shall be responsible for investigating criminal acts and gathering evidence to identify the perpetrators of such acts. It shall also carry out investigations and other activities within its field of competence as required by the Attorney-General of the Republic, judges and courts.

The Chief of the Division shall be appointed by the Director-General of the National Police, in consultation with the Attorney-General and the President of the Supreme Court of Justice.

The spheres of operation of this Division shall be organized on the basis of punishable offences having the greatest social impact. It shall also have technical support departments.

The legal regime applicable to this Division shall be harmonized with the provisions of the Constitution concerning auxiliary organs of the system of justice.

(3) *Frontiers Division*

This Division shall be responsible for monitoring and supervising the admission, departure, activities and expulsion of aliens and the migration of nationals and for the monitoring and supervision of public and private civilian airports, without prejudice to the constitutional duty of the armed forces to defend the integrity of the territory of the State.

(4) *Finance Division*

Under the functional control of the Ministry of Finance and without prejudice to the fiscal oversight or other functions performed by it, this Division shall be responsible for preventing and combating infringements of tax law. It shall be the police support organ of the Ministry of Finance. It shall have two departments: customs and taxes.

The Finance Division shall be the only police organ with competence in the areas of customs and taxes. Consequently, following its entry into operation, all provisions and structures incompatible with this principle shall cease to exist.

The Chief of the Finance Division shall be appointed by the Director-General of the National Police with the prior approval of the Minister of Finance.

3/ This department shall provide support for the Juvenile Office of the Ministry of Justice.

(5) *Arms and Explosives Division*

This Division shall be responsible for preventing and combating infringements of the constitutional and legal regime on the manufacture, import, export, trading, possession and bearing of weapons, ammunition, explosives and similar articles.

(6) *Division for the Protection of Eminent Persons*

This Division shall be responsible for protecting and escorting senior State officials; foreign dignitaries visiting the country; and other persons on the basis of decisions of the Government or of the courts; and for guarding public buildings and the offices of diplomatic missions or international organizations.

(7) *Environment Division*

Under the functional control of the Ministry of Agriculture and Livestock, this Division shall be responsible for preventing and combating crimes and misdemeanours against the environment.

The Chief of the Environment Division shall be appointed by the Director-General of the National Civil Police with the prior approval of the Minister of Agriculture and Livestock.

b. *Territorial distribution*

One police delegation per department and one metropolitan delegation for San Salvador shall be established. The headquarters of delegations shall be located in departmental capitals. Within each delegation, there may also be sub-delegations located in the main urban centres and also police posts in rural areas.

(1) *Departmental delegations*

The chiefs of departmental delegations shall have authority over all the units in their department. They shall be appointed by the Director-General of the National Police on the proposal of the Deputy Director-General for Operations, who shall be their direct supervisor. The organizational structure of delegations shall be adapted to the needs of each department.

(2) *Sub-delegations and police posts*

Sub-delegations shall be established in urban centres and shall be organized on the basis of local needs. Police posts shall operate in rural areas.

D. *Office of the Deputy Director-General for Management*

The Office of the Deputy Director-General for Management shall be responsible for implementing and coordinating the administrative and logistical support activities of the police. Its initial structure shall consist of the following divisions:
- Infrastructure Division
- Data-Processing Division
- Administration Division
- Logistics Division
- Planning and Budget Division

4. *Personnel of the National Civil Police*

The personnel of the National Civil Police shall be organized on the basis of a hierarchized manning table with three levels: basic, executive and senior. Each level shall consist of the ranks determined by law. The staff profile and general regime shall be in keeping with the terms of this Agreement.

A. *Profile*

a. Personnel of the National Civil Police must have a vocation of service to the community, a capacity for human relations and emotional maturity, and the conduct and physical condition required to serve as a police officer. They must also be suited to serving in a police force which is designed, structured and operated as a civilian institution with the purpose of protecting and guaranteeing the free exercise of the rights and freedoms of individuals; preventing and combating all types of crimes; and maintaining internal peace, tranquillity, order and public security. They must also be able to adjust their conduct satisfactorily to the doctrine and legal regime of the National Civil Police.

Both admission to the National Public Security Academy and final admission to the police force shall require checking the profile of candidates. Specific evaluation criteria shall be established for this purpose, with rigorous standards set for each level of responsibility.

b. *Educational level*

(1) Basic level.

(a) Police officers must have completed the ninth grade of education.

(b) Police sergeants must hold a high school diploma.

(2) Executive level. The successful completion of three years of university studies or their equivalent is required.

(3) Senior level. A university degree or its equivalent is required.

c. *General requirements for admission to the Academy*

In order to enter the National Public Security Academy, applicants are required to:

(1) Be Salvadorian by birth.

(2) Have reached the age of 18 before submitting the application.

(3) Have completed the level of studies required for the category concerned.

(4) Be physically fit.

(5) Have full exercise of their civic rights.

(6) Have no criminal record, i.e. convictions resulting from a final verdict.

(7) Pass the entrance examinations, which shall be designed to ensure that candidates fit the profile required to belong to the National Civil Police, according to each

of the levels of responsibility defined in this chapter. The entrance examinations shall consist of a test of general knowledge, a physical examination, a medical examination and a psychological examination. These examinations shall be supplemented by personal interviews with the candidates.

d. The preparation of the examinations referred to in the preceding paragraph and the formation of the boards of examiners responsible for administering them shall be carried out on the basis of exclusively technical criteria.

e. Special emphasis shall be placed on the training of police personnel, so that they are given the best possible preparation and are trained to perform their duties in strict conformity with the doctrine of the police force, with special emphasis on unrestricted respect for human rights.

B. *General regime*

a. Members of the National Civil Police shall be career professionals and agents of authority.

b. The duties, rights, responsibilities and disciplinary regime of the members of the National Civil Police shall be determined by law.

c. Members of the National Civil Police shall be required to serve in any part of the national territory.

d. Members of the National Civil Police shall wear the regulation uniform whenever they are on active duty. In exceptional cases, the Minister, or in his absence, the Vice-Minister or the Director-General may give authorization for not wearing uniforms for certain tasks.

e. Members of the National Civil Police shall bear firearms when warranted by the needs of the service. They shall use only small arms, which are appropriate to police duties and cannot be considered war *matériel.* Special weapons shall be stored in the arsenal of the National Civil Police, to be used by personnel trained for this purpose when, in the opinion of the Minister concerned or, in his absence, of the Vice-Minister or the Director-General, special circumstances exist which require their use.

f. Members of the National Civil Police shall respect the Constitution and the law and shall at all times adjust their conduct to the doctrine of the force, as defined in this Agreement.

g. Members of the National Civil Police shall not normally be required to live in barracks. Such a regime shall be applied only in exceptional circumstances and for the time strictly necessary.

h. The law shall define the regime of labour rights of members of the National Civil Police, bearing in mind the nature of the function they are required to perform.

i. Members of the National Civil Police shall enjoy job security. They may not be dismissed except for specific legal reasons.

j. Members of the National Civil Police shall be entitled to a level of remuneration that ensures a decent standard of living for themselves and their families and also accords with their rank and length of service.

k. Vehicles, communications systems, uniforms, facilities and, in general, any equipment used by members of the National Civil Police shall be suited to the requirements of a police force of the type defined in this Agreement.

5. *National Public Security Academy*

A. The National Public Security Academy shall be responsible for:

a. Basic training, training of middle-ranking and senior officers and specialized training of the National Civil Police.

b. Selecting personnel for the National Civil Police.

c. Investigating, studying and publicizing matters relating to the National Civil Police and public security.

d. Making an annual evaluation of all National Civil Police personnel.

B. The National Public Security Academy shall be an autonomous body placed directly under the authority of the Minister concerned.

C. The National Public Security Academy shall be run by a Director-General and an Academic Council. The Academic Council shall perform standard-setting and comptrolling functions in its sphere of competence. The Director-General shall be President of the Academic Council and shall exercise the executive and administrative powers of the Academy.

D. The Director-General shall be appointed by the President of the Republic.

E. The Academic Council shall consist of civilians prominent in civilian, cultural, legal, technical, police or academic life, appointed by the President of the Republic on the proposal of the Minister concerned and on the basis of criteria of political pluralism.

F. The admissions system shall be determined by the Academic Council, which shall ensure that it is not discriminatory.

G. The teaching staff of the Academy shall be appointed by the Academic Council. No political tendency shall predominate among that staff. The law shall establish suitable mechanisms for ensuring this last goal.

6. *Legal regime*

The National Civil Police and the National Public Security Academy shall each be regulated by special laws. To that end, the Parties express their general agreement with the proposed preliminary legislative drafts included as annexes to this Agreement (annexes II and III), provided that the proposed drafts do not depart from the

Agreement. Consequently, in implementation of the New York Agreement, they hereby refer those proposals to COPAZ, along with this Agreement, for it to prepare the corresponding preliminary drafts.

7. *Transitional regime*

A. *Organization*

a. During the transition, the National Civil Police shall not be attached to any Ministry. The Director-General shall be under the direct authority of the President of the Republic.

b. The National Civil Police shall be run by the Director-General, under the terms laid down in this Agreement and in the New York Agreement. Until the establishment of the National Civil Police has been legally formalized, the organizational work shall be done by a Coordinator chosen for his ability to receive wide acceptance.

c. During the transition, the Director-General of the National Civil Police shall be appointed by the President of the Republic from a list of three candidates proposed by the National Commission for the Consolidation of Peace (COPAZ).

d. The Coordinator and, subsequently, the Director-General, shall establish appropriate machinery for information and communication with COPAZ or, before the latter's final formalization, with its transitional body, so that the Commission can perform its function of supervising the organization of the National Civil Police. As part of the normal exercise of its functions, COPAZ shall designate a subcommission to carry out this task, which shall serve as an advisory commission to the Coordinator or to the Director-General for the adoption of relevant decisions or measures concerning the organization of the National Civil Police, the assumption of its functions and, in general, matters relating to the transitional regime which have not been expressly resolved in this chapter.

e. In accordance with the provisions of the New York Agreement, the organization of the National Civil Police shall be determined, on the terms set forth in this Agreement, under close international cooperation and supervision, coordinated by the United Nations.

B. *Assumption of functions*

a. The National Civil Police shall take up its functions gradually, as contingents graduating from the National Public Security Academy make it possible to staff fully each of the functional and territorial structures provided for in this chapter. The Director-General shall determine the priorities and order according to which this assumption of functions shall take place.

b. The process of replacing the former security forces shall be carried out by geographical department, making sure that there are no gaps in authority. Within 21 months of the launching of this process, all departments must be covered by contingents of the National Civil Police.

c. During the first two years of the formation of the new force, the goal of 5,700 officers at the basic level and 240 at the executive and senior levels must be achieved. Over the following five years, the final figures for the National Civil Police, estimated tentatively at some 10,000 officers at the basic level and about 500 at the executive and senior levels, shall be attained.

d. While the first senior and executive officers of the National Police Force are being trained, the Director-General may order the creation of provisional commands, exclusively for the National Civil Police, which shall act during a predetermined period and shall be supported by experts and advisers, under a programme of close international cooperation and supervision, coordinated by the United Nations, on the terms laid down in this Agreement.

e. While the progressive deployment of the new force is taking place under the terms laid down in this Agreement, the existing National Police shall continue to perform its current public security functions, with the exception laid down in the next paragraph. The National Police shall be the only one of the current public security forces to retain functions of this nature during the transitional period. The international verification of agreements to be undertaken by the United Nations through ONUSAL shall include the activities of a group of specialists from countries with experience in the organization and operation of civilian police forces. The tasks of those specialists shall include, in addition to cooperating in ensuring a smooth transition and assisting police authorities, that of accompanying officers and members of the National Police in the performance of their duties.

f. During the progressive deployment of the new force to zones which were traditionally conflict zones during the armed conflict, public security in those zones shall be subject to a special regime to be determined by the Director-General of the National Civil Police. That regime shall, in any case, envisage activities by the group of specialists referred to in the preceding paragraph.

g. Personnel of the National Civil Police graduating from the National Public Security Academy shall be subject to the general rule laid down in this chapter that police shall not be required to live in barracks. During the initial period, however, exceptions may be made where this is justified by lack of personnel in the early phases of the deployment of the new force. This exceptional regime may not be extended under any circumstances beyond 31 December 1993.

h. In any case, during the preparatory phase and, in general, during the transitional period until the National Police is completely replaced by the National Civil

Police, the role of international advisory services and verification shall be strengthened.

C. National Public Security Academy

a. During the transition, the National Public Security Academy shall not be attached to any Ministry. Its Director shall be under the direct authority of the President of the Republic.

b. During the transition, the Director-General of the National Public Security Academy shall be appointed by the President of the Republic from a list of three candidates proposed by COPAZ.

c. COPAZ shall determine how many members the Academic Council of the National Public Security Academy should have during the transition. In this same period, those members shall be appointed by the President of the Republic from lists of three candidates proposed by COPAZ. In any case, the Council shall consist of civilians prominent in civilian, cultural, legal, police or academic life, in accordance with this chapter. The lists proposed by COPAZ and the final appointments made by the President of the Republic must ensure pluralism of the Academic Council.

d. The admissions system shall be determined by the Academic Council, which shall ensure that it is not discriminatory.

e. Admission shall be contingent on passing the entrance examinations provided for in section 4 of this chapter, adapted to the criteria and procedures referred to in the New York Agreement. The examinations shall be prepared on the basis of exclusively technical criteria and the formation of the boards of examiners responsible for administering them must be such as to ensure the juries' absolute impartiality. To that end, where it is necessary to obtain additional technical resources because there are not enough suitable resources in the country, the support of experts shall be sought through the United Nations under the terms laid down in this Agreement, as indicated in the next paragraph of this section. COPAZ shall pay special attention to monitoring the fulfilment of this provision.

f. In selecting the initial academic personnel, every effort shall be made to find the best human resources available in Salvadorian society so as to provide a group of teachers which is sufficiently broad and pluralistic and of sufficiently high quality to give the new police force a cultural identity in keeping with its nature and doctrine. To that end, assistance shall be sought from university lecturers, expert jurists, doctors and other professionals involved in police matters. COPAZ shall establish appropriate mechanisms to ensure that no political tendency predominates in that academic body. Such mechanisms must be included in the preliminary bill on the National Public Security Academy.

g. In those areas of study where there are not sufficient teachers in the country to meet the initial needs of the Academy, the support of experts shall be sought through the United Nations under the terms laid down in this Agreement, as indicated in the following paragraph.

h. For the purposes of the recruitment, selection, preparation and training of new personnel, the support of experts from countries which are able to provide the assistance required for the needs of this process shall be sought through the United Nations, under the terms laid down in this Agreement.

D. Personnel

a. The criteria and mechanisms for the selection and training of personnel shall accord with the concept of the National Civil Police as a new force, with a new organization, new officers, new education and training mechanisms and a new doctrine. In this context, personnel who did not participate directly in the armed conflict shall be encouraged to join the force, without prejudice to the right of former members of the National Police and former FMLN combatants not to be discriminated against in the selection of such personnel and their right to join the National Civil Police under the terms of the New York Agreement and of this Agreement.

b. A publicity campaign to promote the recruitment of new personnel for the National Civil Police shall be designed and implemented as soon as possible. Special consideration shall be given to the recruitment of women.

c. Former members of the National Police may join the National Civil Police under the terms of this Agreement, after an evaluation of their conduct, provided that they meet the admission requirements and go through the new National Public Security Academy. This evaluation shall be made by the Director-General of the National Civil Police, under the supervision of COPAZ, and shall be subject to verification by the United Nations.

d. Former FMLN combatants may join the National Civil Police provided that they fulfil the admission criteria and procedures established for them by COPAZ and go through the new National Public Security Academy. As part of the verification of the cessation of the armed conflict, ONUSAL shall check that applicants who identify themselves in this category have actually and irrevocably abandoned the armed struggle. All this shall be supervised and guaranteed by COPAZ.

e. For the recruitment of personnel referred to in the preceding paragraphs, in the case of the basic level of the National Civil Police, the level of general knowledge and/or the zones in which personnel are to be recruited and serve shall be taken into account. Those who do not have the level of formal education required for admission must pass an aptitude and skills test to evaluate their ability to follow the study programmes of the National Public Security Academy satisfactorily. Special courses shall be organized to prepare for this test, under the auspices of the National Public Security Academy and with support from the Ministry of Education and the country's universities.

f. For courses at the basic level, 330 recruits shall be selected per month, for a 6-month training course, during the first 24 months of the mass training programme. Candidates shall be selected in such a way as to ensure that most recruits did not participate directly in the armed conflict and that the proportion of former FMLN combatants is no greater than that of former members of the National Police, and vice versa. COPAZ shall take special care to ensure that these requirements are met.

g. The recruitment of officers for the executive and senior levels of the National Civil Police shall be carried out by means of rigorous selection, in accordance with the criteria and procedures laid down in this Agreement, and shall fully respect the principles of equality of opportunity among applicants and non-discrimination. Courses shall last a year, according to the level and manning table concerned. A total of 120 officers shall be trained each year.

h. Posts at the executive and senior levels shall be allocated to graduates of the National Public Security Academy by the Director-General according to the needs of the service. However, the top five students each year shall be entitled to choose from the various vacant posts corresponding to the level of responsibility of their studies.

i. Without prejudice to the provisions of the preceding paragraph, zones that were traditionally conflict zones during the armed conflict shall be the object of special treatment designed to promote national reconciliation and stability during the transition. Such treatment shall involve the formation of police units comprising personnel of different origins who have graduated from the National Public Security Academy. The chiefs of the corresponding delegations shall be appointed following consultations with the advisory commission of COPAZ.

j. All personnel joining the National Civil Police in accordance with this Agreement shall be considered to be civilians, regardless of their origin.

E. Any other matter relating to the transitional regime which has not been resolved by this Agreement or by other agreements already adopted by the Parties shall be decided by COPAZ, under the terms laid down in the New York Agreement.

CHAPTER III
JUDICIAL SYSTEM

1. National Council of the Judiciary

A. The Parties reaffirm that, as already agreed in the Mexico Agreements, the composition of the National Council of the Judiciary shall be such as to guarantee its independence from the organs of the State and from political parties and its membership shall, as far as possible, include not only judges but also sectors of society not directly connected with the administration of justice. In accordance with the New York Agreement, they refer the matter to COPAZ to prepare the corresponding preliminary legislative draft.

B. Judicial Training School

a. Pursuant to the Mexico Agreements, the preliminary draft referred to in the preceding paragraph shall include provisions regulating the Judicial Training School, which shall function under the responsibility of the National Council of the Judiciary and whose purpose shall be to ensure a steady improvement in the professional training of judges and other judicial officials and of members of the Office of the Attorney-General of the Republic; to investigate the country's judicial problems and promote solutions thereto; and to foster greater bonds of solidarity among members of the judiciary and a coherent overall vision of the function of the judiciary in a democratic State.

b. The rules for the administration and organization of the Judicial Training School shall be such as to ensure its academic independence and its openness to the various schools of legal thought.

2. Office of the National Counsel for the Defence of Human Rights

A. The National Counsel for the Defence of Human Rights shall be appointed within 90 days following the entry into force of the constitutional reform resulting from the Mexico Agreements.

B. COPAZ shall be entrusted with preparing the preliminary bill organizing the Office of the National Counsel for the Defence of Human Rights.

C. The preliminary bill shall establish appropriate means for putting into effect the firm commitment assumed by the Parties in the course of the negotiations to identify and eradicate any groups which engage in a systematic practice of human rights violations, in particular, arbitrary arrests, abductions and summary executions, as well as other attempts on the liberty, integrity and security of persons. This includes the commitment to identify and, where appropriate, abolish and dismantle any clandestine jail or place of detention. In any event, the Parties agree to give top priority to the investigation of such cases, under ONUSAL verification.

CHAPTER IV
ELECTORAL SYSTEM

The Parties reaffirm their commitment, made in the Mexico Agreements, to promote a comprehensive proposal for reform of the electoral system. To that end, they request COPAZ to appoint the Special Commission envisaged for that purpose in the Mexico Agreements. That Commission shall study the preliminary draft amendments to the Electoral Code submitted to the Legislative Assembly by the Central Board of Elections, as well as any proposals put forward by its members or by independent experts invited for that purpose. The Special Commission shall organize its work in such a way that the results can be used within the time-limits set for the reform of the electoral system.

CHAPTER V
ECONOMIC AND SOCIAL QUESTIONS

1. *Preamble*

One of the prerequisites for the democratic reunification of Salvadorian society is the sustained economic and social development of the country. At the same time, reunification of Salvadorian society and a growing degree of social cohesion are indispensable for fostering development. Hence, the set of agreements required to put a definitive end to the armed conflict in El Salvador must include certain minimum commitments to promote development for the benefit of all sectors of the population.

In accordance with the New York Agreement, the issues covered by this instrument are: the agrarian problem, loans to the agricultural sector, measures required to alleviate the social cost of structural adjustment programmes, appropriate procedures for direct external cooperation designed to encourage community development and assistance projects, establishment of a forum for economic and social consultation and the National Reconstruction Plan. Also, although the general philosophy or orientation of the Government's economic policy, which FMLN does not necessarily share, is not covered by this Agreement, both Parties agree on the need to provide certain basic guidelines so as to ensure the requisite social stability during the transitional period, consolidate peace and make progress towards the reunification of Salvadorian society.

2. *The agrarian problem*

A. *Lands in excess of the constitutional limit of 245 hectares*

The Government of El Salvador shall transfer rural farmland that has not yet been transferred under articles 105 and 267 of the Constitution of the Republic.

It likewise undertakes to ensure that implementation of the relevant constitutional requirements is not evaded by owners of rural holdings in excess of 245 hectares.

B. *State-owned lands which are not currently part of a forestry reserve*

The Government of El Salvador shall transfer to beneficiaries of the agrarian reform, as provided in article 104 of the Constitution, State-owned rural farmland which is not part of a forestry reserve.

Under the various land-transfer programmes which the Government of El Salvador is carrying out with State-owned farmland, preference shall be given to former combatants of both Parties who so request voluntarily, are of peasant origin and familiar with farming, and possess no land of any kind. The size of the lots shall be determined by the amount of land available, as mentioned above, and the number of beneficiaries who meet the conditions set out in this section.

C. *Lands offered for sale to the State*

Making use of the legal, technical and financial resources available to it, the Government of El Salvador shall seek to acquire and transfer through the Land Bank lands voluntarily offered for sale by their owners. Once the said lands are acquired, they shall be transferred to beneficiaries of the agrarian reform.

D. *Recipients of lands transferred in accordance with the preceding sections*

The lands acquired under sections A, B and C of this chapter shall be used to satisfy the need for land of landless peasants and small farmers. Specifically, title to the land shall be transferred legally to the peasants and small farmers designated by law as beneficiaries of the agrarian reform.

E. *Payments for land*

The lands referred to in the preceding sections shall be transferred at market prices and on the same credit terms as are granted to beneficiaries of the reformed sector. At the same time, a system of payments may be established on the basis of a fixed price and long-term financing at low, fixed interest rates not subject to interest capitalization. Domestic credit shall be supplemented with financing from international cooperation, for which a special fund, financed from external resources, shall be established for the purchase of land.

F. *New legislation*

Since the current agrarian legislation is haphazard, contradictory and incomplete, the Parties agree that it must be harmonized and unified into an agrarian code. To this end, the Government shall submit the relevant draft legislation to the Legislative Assembly no later than 12 months after the signing of this Agreement. If it fails to do so, COPAZ shall take on the task of preparing the corresponding preliminary draft.

3. *Lands within conflict zones*

A. *The land-tenure system in conflict zones*

In accordance with the New York Agreement, the current land-tenure situation in conflict zones shall be respected until a satisfactory legal solution for the definitive land-tenure system is arrived at. Consequently, landholders shall not be evicted pending agreement on such a solution; moreover, they shall be given financial support to increase agricultural production.

In view of the irregularity of the land-tenure system in conflict zones, the Parties agree on the following:

B. *Determination as to who are the "current landholders"*

"Landholders" shall mean those currently occupying and/or working the land in conflict zones.

C. *Inventory of cases covered by this part of the Agreement*

Within 30 days from the signing of the Agreement, FMLN shall submit an inventory of land or buildings affected by the Agreement. Upon verification that such land or buildings are in fact subject to the provisions of this Agreement, and in accordance with the procedure set forth in the next section, the Government of El Salvador shall seek to provide a satisfactory legal solution for their final disposal through the voluntary sale of such property by the rightful owners to the current holders, on the terms referred to in section 3 (F) of this chapter.

Should a rightful owner not wish to sell his property, the Government of El Salvador shall make use of the legal mechanisms at its disposal to try to resettle the peasants or small farmers on such land as may be available for the purpose and shall, as far as possible, seek to ensure that such land is situated in the same zones.

D. *Establishment of a Special Commission*

COPAZ shall appoint a special commission whose members shall be of recognized integrity and ability. The special commission, to be formed within 20 days following the signing of this Agreement, shall be entrusted with the following tasks and duties:

a. To verify the inventory of affected land or buildings within conflict zones. Once the inventory has been verified, the special commission shall submit copies to the Government of El Salvador and to COPAZ;

b. Should the need arise, to facilitate the settlement of disputes between current holders and rightful owners;

c. To take any decisions and measures it deems necessary and proper for the prompt and effective fulfilment of the agreements set forth in this chapter.

E. *Legalization of land tenure*

Except for particularly complex cases, the Government of El Salvador shall legalize the land-tenure situation in conflict zones definitively within six months from the signing of the cease-fire agreement, granting, as appropriate, individual or collective title to the land.

F. *Payment for lands*

Lands shall be purchased from their former owners at market prices. The sale to the current holders shall be subject to the same conditions as those granted to beneficiaries of the reformed sector. However, special conditions may be agreed to in the interests of the peace process.

G. *Verification by COPAZ*

COPAZ shall guarantee fulfilment of the agreements set forth in sections 2 and 3.

4. *3 July 1991 agreement on occupied lands*

The agreement on occupied lands between the Government of El Salvador and peasant organizations shall be respected.

With regard to lands occupied illegally after the date of that agreement, the Government of El Salvador gives notice that it reserves the right to enforce the relevant legal provisions so as to ensure that the rule of law prevails. FMLN holds that the agrarian problem, including land occupations, should be dealt with through consultation and the channels and mechanisms provided by the peace agreements.

5. *Loans to the agricultural sector and to micro- and small-scale enterprise*

A. *Loans to the sector as a whole*

The Government of El Salvador shall see to it that the national financial system has the resources it needs to meet the demand for credit of the agricultural sector in general and of micro- and small-scale enterprise and small-scale peasant production, including cooperatives in the reformed and the non-reformed sector, in particular.

It shall also establish rules governing loans for agricultural and industrial production so that such loans are granted in a timely manner and in amounts sufficient to sustain productive capacity and the marketing of the goods produced. To that end, it shall promote an increase in loans by the commercial banking system to small businessmen and small-scale enterprises.

B. *Active involvement of target sectors*

The Government also undertakes to permit and promote the active involvement of target sectors in both the design and the administration of special credit programmes for those sectors. To that end, the Government undertakes to increase the participation of organizations representing the sectors referred to in the preceding section in developing policies of the Agricultural Guarantee Fund, FIGAPE, FEDECREDITO and BFA, and to ensure that the financial position of these institutions remains sound and that they become conduits for channelling external resources into loans for micro- and small-scale enterprise, small-scale peasant production and cooperatives in both the reformed and the non-reformed sector.

C. *Technical assistance*

The Government of El Salvador shall design and promote new programmes of technical assistance to help increase the productivity of peasant farmers and smallholders, especially in conflict zones.

D. *International cooperation for the agricultural sector*

Given the increase in the demand for agricultural credit that will follow the signing of the Peace Agreement, the Government of El Salvador undertakes to seek additional external resources to cover the new needs of the sector. In this connection, the Government shall seek external financial resources to increase the operations of the Agricultural Guarantee Fund as a mechanism for facilitating lending to small- and medium-sized farmers and their cooperatives, without adversely affecting the financial health of lending institutions.

6. *Measures to alleviate the social cost of structural adjustment programmes*

A. *Consumer protection*

The Government of El Salvador undertakes to adopt policies and create effective mechanisms for consumer protection in accordance with the requirements set out in the last part of article 101, paragraph 2, of the Constitution. In order to comply with this constitutional requirement, the Government undertakes to submit to the Legislative Assembly, within 60 days from the signing of this Agreement, a consumer protection bill providing for the strengthening of the Ministry of Economic Affairs, which could be a first step towards the establishment of an Office of Consumer Protection Advocate (Procuraduría General de Defensa del Consumidor).

B. *Privatization*

The policy of privatization shall increase society's share of ownership by affording workers access to ownership of privatized companies. It shall also avoid monopolistic practices, while guaranteeing business freedom and consumer protection, in accordance with the provisions of article 110 of the Constitution.

C. *Social welfare programmes*

The Government of El Salvador shall seek to strengthen existing social welfare programmes designed to alleviate extreme poverty. Additional external resources shall be sought for this purpose.

7. *Procedures for direct external cooperation for community development and assistance projects*

The Government of El Salvador shall facilitate private direct external cooperation for community development and assistance projects, provided that assistance is channelled in accordance with foreign exchange and lending regulations. Official direct external cooperation may also be approved, subject to the provision of the requisite information on the purposes of such cooperation.

The Government shall grant legal and institutional facilities to private sources of direct external cooperation benefiting communities, social organizations and national non-governmental organizations: it shall not discriminate among the latter, provided that it is ascertained that they are engaged in or wish to engage in integrated development projects. Former combatants of both Parties shall have access to external cooperation funds.

8. *Forum for economic and social consultation*

A. *Purpose of the Forum*

A forum shall be established in which representatives of the Government, labour and the business community shall participate on an equal footing for the purpose of working out a set of broad agreements on the economic and social development of the country for the benefit of all its inhabitants. The consultation process shall be a sustained effort and shall be conducted in phases, bearing in mind that the aim is to reach some agreements that are to be implemented immediately to achieve stabilization, others that are designed to tackle the economic and social problems that will ensue from the end of the conflict and still others that are geared specifically to reconstruction.

Among other things, the Government shall propose to the Forum for Economic and Social Consultation that existing labour legislation be revised in order to promote and maintain a climate of harmonious labour relations, without prejudice to the unemployed and the public at large. It shall also propose that the situation of disadvantaged urban and outlying urban communities be analysed with a view to proposing solutions to problems resulting from the armed conflict of recent years. In general terms, the Forum shall be the mechanism for agreeing on measures to alleviate the social cost of the structural adjustment programme.

B. Establishment of the Forum

COPAZ shall convene the Forum for Economic and Social Consultation for the first time no later than one month after the signing of this Agreement.

C. Composition of and representation in the Forum

The composition of the Forum and the representation in it of the various sectors and the Government shall be as follows:

a. The Government of El Salvador shall be represented at a high level, its representatives being empowered to take decisions on economic and social matters;

b. The most representative labour and business organizations shall be invited to represent those sectors.

In addition, the Forum may invite other social and political sectors to participate in its work as observers, on terms to be determined by it.

D. Powers of the Forum

The Forum shall determine its own operational structure and the issues for discussion and consultations. The sectors represented in the Forum shall have equal rights and shall enjoy equal opportunities for expressing their views.

In order to guarantee the effectiveness of the agreements reached by the Forum by consensus, the Government undertakes to issue, amend or repeal decrees or provisions within its sphere of competence and to submit relevant proposals to the other organs of State.

E. Secretariat of the Forum

The Forum shall appoint a secretariat to provide it with technical support and ensure the continuity of its work.

9. National Reconstruction Plan

Within 30 days from the signing of the agreement on the cessation of the armed conflict, the Government of El Salvador shall submit to FMLN the National Reconstruction Plan which it has drawn up, so that the recommendations and suggestions of FMLN, like those of the various sectors of national life, may be taken into account, ensuring that the Plan reflects the country's collective wishes.

The main objectives of the Plan shall be the integrated development of zones affected by the conflict, satisfaction of the most immediate needs of the population hardest hit by the conflict and of former combatants of both Parties, and the reconstruction of damaged infrastructure. In particular, in the context of the corresponding national programmes, measures shall be taken to facilitate the reintegration of FMLN into the country's civil, institutional and political life, including fellowship, employment and pension programmes, housing programmes and programmes for starting up new businesses.

The Plan shall pay special attention to the need to promote job creation on a massive scale and to increase the production of basic foodstuffs, which shall be a priority for the State. To that end, the Government shall promote the integrated development of agricultural, stockbreeding, fisheries, forestry and agro-industrial activities, guarantee the provision of basic social services and launch the construction and rehabilitation of economic and social infrastructures. The National Reconstruction Plan shall also include programmes for the war-disabled and the relatives of victims among the civilian population.

Given the magnitude of the additional resources that will be required for the implementation of the Plan, both Parties appeal to the international community to lend its fullest support to the fund-raising effort. To this end, a national reconstruction fund shall be established, to be supported by the United Nations Development Programme.

The role of UNDP shall include advising the Government on all matters relating to the mobilization of external support, assisting in the preparation of projects and programmes likely to attract such support, facilitating approaches to official bilateral and multilateral agencies, mobilizing technical assistance and cooperating with the Government in harmonizing the Plan with the activities of non-governmental organizations involved in local and regional development activities.

CHAPTER VI
POLITICAL PARTICIPATION BY FMLN

The following agreements have been reached concerning political participation by FMLN, and shall be subject to the implementation timetable contained in this Agreement:

1. Adoption of legislative or other measures needed to guarantee former FMLN combatants the full exercise of their civil and political rights, with a view to their reintegration, within a framework of full legality, into the civil, political, and institutional life of the country.

2. Freedom for all political prisoners.

3. Full guarantees and security for the return of exiles, war-wounded and other persons currently outside the country for reasons related to the armed conflict.

4. Granting of licences for FMLN mass media.

5. Cessation of the armed conflict implies the commitment and the right of FMLN to full political participation, without any restrictions other than those deriving from the new institutional and legal framework estab-

lished by the agreements reached during the negotiations.

6. Legalization of FMLN as a political party, through the adoption of a legislative decree to that end.

7. Guarantee that FMLN will be able to conduct its activities normally when it becomes a political party, meaning:

(a) Freedom to canvass for new members;

(b) The right to set up an appropriate infrastructure (premises, printing works, etc.);

(c) Free exercise of the right of assembly and mobilization for FMLN leaders, activists and members;

(d) Freedom for FMLN to purchase and use advertising space in the mass media.

8. Legal solution to the participation of FMLN members in COPAZ, once the latter formalizes its existence.

9. *Special security measures*

Immediately after the signing of this Agreement, special security measures shall be taken to protect any FMLN leaders who may require such protection. The aforesaid measures, which may include their being accompanied by diplomatic personnel and also technical support from friendly Governments, shall offer all the facilities required for FMLN leaders to be able to organize their own security in accordance with the law. COPAZ shall supervise the arrangements agreed to herein and shall, if necessary, promote the adoption of the relevant legislative or other provisions to ensure that such security measures are fully effective and properly established. As part of its responsibility for the security of FMLN leaders, the Government of El Salvador shall provide the necessary facilities for implementing the agreed arrangements. ONUSAL shall verify the adoption of the above measures.

CHAPTER VII
CESSATION OF THE ARMED CONFLICT

1. The cessation of the armed conflict (hereinafter referred to as the CAC) is a brief, dynamic and irreversible process of predetermined duration which must be implemented throughout the national territory of El Salvador. During the CAC, there shall be no substantive negotiations but only the measures necessary to put into practice the agreements reached during the negotiating process.

2. The CAC shall begin on 1 February 1992 (hereinafter referred to as D-Day) and shall be completed on 31 October 1992.

3. The CAC consists of four elements, as defined herein:

(a) The cease-fire;

(b) The separation of forces;

(c) The end of the military structure of FMLN and the reintegration of its members, within a framework of full legality, into the civil, political and institutional life of the country;

(d) United Nations verification of all the above-mentioned activities.

This chapter also includes agreements on the restoration of public administration in conflict zones and the use of the mass media to promote reconciliation (see annexes E and F).

The cease-fire

4. The cease-fire shall enter into force officially on D-Day.

5. As of that date, each of the parties shall, as appropriate, refrain from carrying out any hostile act or operation by means of forces or individuals under its control, meaning that neither party shall carry out any kind of attack by land, sea or air, organize patrols or offensive manoeuvres, occupy new positions, lay mines, interfere with military communications or carry out any kind of reconnaissance operations, acts of sabotage or any other military activity which, in the opinion of ONUSAL, might violate the cease-fire, or any act that infringes the rights of the civilian population.

6. Official verification of compliance with the undertaking described in the preceding paragraph shall begin on D-Day. Any alleged violation of the cease-fire shall be investigated by ONUSAL.

7. During the period between the signing of this Agreement and D-Day, the two parties shall observe an informal cease-fire under which they undertake not to carry out any of the activities described in paragraph 5.

8. ONUSAL shall deploy its personnel and equipment during the informal cease-fire period, so as to be able to verify all aspects of the CAC as of D-Day.

Separation of forces

9. The purpose of the separation of forces is to reduce the risk of incidents, to build trust and to allow ONUSAL to verify both parties' compliance with this Agreement.

10. The separation of forces shall take place in two stages, so that the Salvadorian armed forces (FAES) fall back progressively from their present positions until deployed as they would normally be in peacetime and the FMLN forces are concentrated progressively in designated locations within conflict areas as determined in annex D.

11. During the first stage, which shall coincide with the five days following D-Day, FAES land forces shall go to the barracks, bases, existing semi-permanent facilities and other locations listed in annex A and FMLN forces, except for the combatants mentioned in paragraph 18, shall go to the places listed in annex B. The places listed in annexes A and B generally reflect the present deployment of the two parties' forces.

12. The movements described in the preceding

paragraph shall be made under the supervision of ONUSAL. Neither party shall do anything to prevent or jeopardize the movement of the other party's forces during this period. ONUSAL military observers shall closely supervise all the places listed in annexes A and B and shall in principle be present 24 hours a day in each of those places as of D-Day.

13. During the period between D-Day + 6 days and D-Day + 30 days, FAES land forces shall fall back to their peacetime positions as listed in annex C and FMLN forces, except for the combatants mentioned in paragraph 18, shall fall back to the locations indicated in annex D. The precise designation of such locations shall be determined by the ONUSAL Chief Military Observer, in consultation with the two parties, during the informal cease-fire period.

14. The movements described in the preceding paragraph, which shall also be supervised by ONUSAL, shall be carried out according to phased programmes agreed between the ONUSAL Chief Military Observer and the two parties during the informal cease-fire period, through the joint working group to which reference is made in paragraph 32. During this task, the group shall be guided as appropriate by the agreed timetable for the implementation of the agreements reached.

15. As soon as possible after the signing of this Agreement but no later than two weeks before D-Day, the FAES shall transmit to the ONUSAL Chief Military Observer detailed information on the number of their troops and weapons to be concentrated in the places listed in annex A.

16. As soon as possible after the signing of this Agreement but no later than two weeks before D-Day, FMLN shall supply the ONUSAL Chief Military Observer with detailed information on its troop strength and inventories of arms, ammunition, mines, other explosives and military equipment located anywhere within the national territory. These arms, etc. shall be concentrated in the places listed in annex B, with the exception of those of its clandestine forces, which shall be concentrated in the places listed in annex D during the second stage of the separation of forces.

17. Upon completion of the first stage of the separation of forces, that is, as of D-Day + 6, ONUSAL shall verify that all troops and military equipment declared by the parties, other than the arms, etc. referred to in the last sentence of the preceding paragraph, have been concentrated in the locations listed in annexes A and B. ONUSAL shall investigate any report or allegation of the presence of troops or military equipment in any place other than those locations, apart from the movements authorized in paragraphs 20-22.

18. The arrangements just described relate to FAES land forces and FMLN forces as defined in paragraph 11. Although it is not possible, for practical reasons, to arrange a similar separation of clandestine forces, the latter shall remain fully subject to the undertaking to refrain from carrying out any hostile act or operation. As provided in paragraph 6, any alleged violation of this undertaking shall be investigated by ONUSAL.

19. As of D-Day, the naval and air force components of the FAES shall refrain from carrying out any offensive operation. They shall carry out only such non-hostile missions as are necessary for the discharge of their duties unrelated to the armed conflict. ONUSAL shall be advised in advance of all military flight plans. Such flights shall not be carried out over places where FMLN forces have been concentrated.

20. During the CAC period, ONUSAL liaison officers shall be posted in FAES units, bases and barracks to coordinate in advance the movements of FAES forces throughout the national territory and to verify that such movements will neither violate the cease-fire nor jeopardize in any other way the process of implementing this Agreement.

21. With special reference to FAES forces deployed near places where there are FMLN forces, in other words, those listed in appendix 1 to annex A and those listed in appendix 1 to annex C, the Government agrees that such forces shall be authorized to leave their locations only with the consent of ONUSAL and for the following purposes:

(a) To carry out troop rotations and relief;

(b) To carry out liaison and coordination activities between commands at battalion level and above;

(c) To deliver logistical supplies;

(d) To take part in programmes for the deactivation, removal and destruction of mines;

(e) To go on leave or seek medical care or for other humanitarian reasons, individually, in civilian clothing and unarmed.

However, ONUSAL shall not grant permission for any movement, even in the above cases, if it believes that such movement could jeopardize the cease-fire or other aspects of this Agreement or disturb the process of *détente* and reconciliation. Forces that leave their locations for the purposes listed in paragraphs (a), (b), (c) and (d) shall be accompanied by ONUSAL, which shall verify that such movements are in keeping with this Agreement.

22. Similarly, during the CAC period ONUSAL liaison officers shall be posted in the listed locations where FMLN forces are to be concentrated in order to coordinate movements by those forces. FMLN agrees that its forces may leave the locations in question only with the consent of ONUSAL and for the following purposes:

(a) To carry out liaison and coordination activities

between its high command and the commands of the forces stationed at the various locations indicated;

(b) To supply provisions, clothing or vital necessities;

(c) To take part in programmes for the deactivation, removal and destruction of mines;

(d) To go on leave or seek medical care or for other humanitarian reasons, individually, in civilian clothing and unarmed.

However, ONUSAL shall not grant permission for any movement, even in the above cases, if it believes that such movement could jeopardize the cease-fire or other aspects of this Agreement or disturb the process of *détente* and reconciliation. Forces that leave their locations for the purposes listed in paragraphs (a), (b) and (c) shall be accompanied by ONUSAL, which shall verify that such movements are in keeping with this Agreement.

23. ONUSAL shall verify that the supplies delivered to each party do not include lethal articles. However, the FAES shall be allowed to maintain stocks of ammunition normal for peacetime. The mechanisms for such verification shall be established by the ONUSAL Chief Military Observer in consultation with the two parties.

24. During the cease-fire, COPAZ shall systematically evaluate the progress being made in implementing the Agreements. If it notes that a situation is developing which might result in a crisis, it shall draw such conclusions and make such recommendations as may be necessary to prevent a collapse of the cease-fire or a crisis of public order. It shall transmit its conclusions and recommendations to the Chief of ONUSAL.

25. Should a public order crisis occur despite the above provisions and if the normal means for the maintenance of domestic peace and public security have been exhausted, with the result that the President of the Republic deems it necessary to make use of the exceptional measures provided for in the amendment to article 168 (12) of the Constitution adopted in April 1991, the President shall, before giving the relevant order, inform the Chief of ONUSAL to enable him to make any appropriate remarks. The actions of the FAES under such circumstances shall be monitored closely by ONUSAL to ensure that they are consistent with all the peace Agreements.

End of the military structure of FMLN and reintegration of its members, within a framework of full legality, into the civil, institutional and political life of the country

26. Between D-Day + 6 and D-Day + 30, according to the phased programmes referred to in paragraph 14, FMLN shall concentrate in the 15 designated locations listed in annex D all arms, ammunition, mines, other explosives and military equipment belonging to its forces, both those concentrated during the first stage in the places

listed in annex B and those belonging to its clandestine forces, and ONUSAL shall verify that they tally with the information given in the inventories it has received in accordance with paragraph 16.

27. In each of the 15 designated locations, all the arms and equipment mentioned above, save for the personal weapons and equipment of combatants present in the place, shall be kept in locked warehouses. Each warehouse shall have two locks, one key to which shall be kept by ONUSAL and the other by the FMLN commander in the place. ONUSAL shall verify the contents of such warehouses periodically to ensure that there has been no change in them.

28. During the CAC period, FMLN members shall keep their personal weapons and equipment as long as they remain in the designated locations. When they leave those places in order to be reintegrated, within a framework of full legality, into the civil, political and institutional life of the country, their personal weapons shall also be deposited in the locked warehouses referred to in the preceding paragraph. Combatants who are still in the designated locations when the programme for the destruction of arms, etc. provided for in the next paragraph begins, shall deposit their personal weapons and equipment in the locked warehouses, for verification by ONUSAL, immediately prior to their destruction according to a programme agreed with ONUSAL.

29. Between 15 and 31 October 1992, FMLN shall destroy all arms and equipment deposited in designated locations according to the arrangement described above, in the presence and under the sole supervision of ONUSAL and with its technical advice. Such destruction shall be carried out simultaneously in all 15 places designated for FMLN. FMLN shall dispose of the remains of the destroyed weapons.

United Nations verification

30. The numbers of ONUSAL military and civilian personnel shall be increased to enable it to fulfil its tasks related to the agreed processes, as described in this Agreement.

31. The Secretary-General shall request the Security Council to approve this increase in the mandate and personnel of ONUSAL. He shall also request the General Assembly to provide the necessary funding from the budget. The composition by country of the military component of ONUSAL and the appointment of the commander of its military division shall be decided by the Security Council on the recommendation of the Secretary-General, who shall first consult with the two parties. In order to fulfil its new tasks effectively, ONUSAL will require, as in the other aspects of its mandate, complete freedom of movement throughout the territory of El Salvador.

32. To facilitate the application of this Agreement, a joint working group shall be set up immediately after the Agreement has been signed. The working group shall consist of the ONUSAL Chief Military Observer, as Chairman, and one representative from each of the parties. The members of the working group may be accompanied by the necessary advisers. The Chairman of the working group shall convene its meetings on his own initiative or at the request of either or both of the parties.

Annex A

*Places where FAES forces shall be
concentrated by D-Day + 5*

A. AHUACHACAN
1. Llano del Espino, Beneficio Agua Chica and Geotérmica Ausoles (Ausoles geothermal station) and Finca San Luis
2. Beneficio Molino, Beneficio Sta. Rita, Repetidora Apaneca (Apaneca relay station), Puente Sunzacate, Finca Alta Cresta
3. Military Detachment No. 7 (DM-7)

B. SONSONATE
4. Complejo Industrial Acajutla (Acajutla industrial complex), Puente Hacienda Km 5, Puente Río Bandera
5. Military Detachment No. 6 (DM-6)

C. SANTA ANA
6. Beneficio Tazumal, Beneficio Venecia, Beneficio La Mia and Cerro Singüil
7. Planta San Luis Uno and San Luis Dos
8. El Rodeo
9. Sitio Plan El Tablón
10. Cerro El Zacatío
11. Santa Rosa Huachipilín
12. Banderas
13. Cerro El Zacamil
14. Second Brigade

D. CHALATENANGO
15. Cantón and Caserío El Encumbrado (El Encumbrado canton and hamlet)
16. Cantón and Caserío Potrero Sula (Potrero Sula canton and hamlet)
17. Cantón and Caserío El Carrizal (El Carrizal canton and hamlet)
18. San Rafael
19. La Laguna
20. Concepción Quezaltepeque

21. Potonico
22. Fourth Infantry Brigade
23. Military Detachment No. 1 (DM-1)
24. El Refugio base

E. LA LIBERTAD
25. Presa San Lorenzo (San Lorenzo dam), Beneficio Río Claro and Beneficio Atapasco
26. San Juan de los Planes
27. Cantón and Caserío Las Granadillas (Las Granadillas canton and hamlet)
28. ESTRANFA (Transport Unit)
29. Artillery Brigade
30. Atlacatl BIRI (Rapid Deployment Infantry Brigade)
31. Cavalry Regiment
32. Huizúcar

F. SAN SALVADOR
33. Bernal - El Carmen
34. Beneficio Mecafé, Ingenio El Angel (El Angel sugar mill), Nejapa substation
35. Cantón and Caserío Calle Nueva (Calle Nueva canton and hamlet)
36. First Infantry Brigade
37. FAES Headquarters
38. CITFA
39. Military College
40. CALFA
41. Belloso BIRI
42. Parachute Battalion (Ilopango)
43. National Navy Headquarters

G. CUSCATLAN
44. San Rafael-El Terrero
45. Oratorio Concepción
46. Rosario-El Tablón
47. Military Detachment No. 5 (DM-5)
48. El Roblar military base

H. LA PAZ
49. San Pedro Nonualco
50. Guadalupe
51. Centro Acopio IRA (IRA storage centre)
52. Fábrica Acero (steelworks), COPAL and ANDA plant
53. El Nilo
54. El Rosario
55. Army Engineers Unit
56. Bracamonte BIRI

I. CABAÑAS
57. Ilobasco
58. Tejutepeque
59. Guayabito
60. Cerro Pelón
61. Military Detachment No. 2 (DM-2)

J. SAN VICENTE
62. San Felipe
63. Tecoluca
64. Fifth Infantry Brigade

K. USULUTAN
65. Los Cantaritos
66. Beneficios Marquez, Lourdes, Oromontique and Venecia
67. El Triunfo
68. Cantón and Caserío El Volcán (El Volcán canton and hamlet)
69. San Jorge
70. La Placita
71. Jucuarán
72. FENADESAL base
73. Jiquilisco
74. Sixth Infantry Brigade
75. Atonal BIRI

L. SAN MIGUEL
76. San Gerardo
77. San Luis de la Reina
78. Carolina
79. Ciudad Barrios
80. Chapeltique
81. Concepción Corozal
82. Cantón El Niño (El Niño canton)
83. Chirilagua
84. Comacarán
85. Third Infantry Brigade
86. Arce BIRI

M. MORAZAN
87. Gualococti
88. Oscicala
89. Cacaopera
90. Las Flores
91. Sensembra
92. San Carlos
93. Sesori
94. Military Detachment No. 4 (DM-4)

N. LA UNION
95. Yucoaiquín
96. Santa Rosa de Lima
97. Lislique
98. Porolós
99. Military Detachment No. 3 (DM-3)
100. CEMFA

REMARKS

- The exact location of the sites will be determined during the informal cease-fire period.

- The guarding of non-military facilities of national importance by the FAES will be carried out with the minimum number of troops necessary.

- The task of guarding these facilities will be gradually handed over to the newly formed National Civil Police, as soon as it is in a position to take over these functions.

Appendix 1 to Annex A

List of military facilities, bases, barracks and other locations which FAES forces may not leave without ONUSAL authorization

A. SANTA ANA
1. El Rodeo

B. CHALATENANGO
2. El Encumbrado canton and hamlet
3. El Carrizal canton and hamlet
4. San Rafael
5. La Laguna
6. Concepción Quezaltepeque
7. Pontonico
8. Headquarters of the Fourth Infantry Brigade
9. Headquarters of Military Detachment No. 1

C. LA LIBERTAD
10. Las Granadillas canton and hamlet
11. Huizúcar

D. SAN SALVADOR
12. Area including Beneficio de Mecafé, El Angel sugar mill and Nejapa substation
13. Calle Nueva canton and hamlet

E. CUSCATLAN
14. San Rafael-El Terrero
15. Oratorio Concepción
16. Rosario-El Tablón
17. Headquarters of Military Detachment No. 5
18. El Roblar military base

F. LA PAZ

19. San Pedro Nonualco
20. Guadalupe
21. IRA storage centre
22. Steelworks, COPAL and ANDA plant
23. El Nilo
24. Headquarters of Army Engineers Unit
25. Headquarters of Bracamonte BIRI

G. CABAÑAS

26. Ilobasco
27. Tejutepeque
28. Guayabito
29. Cerro Pelón
30. Headquarters of Military Detachment No. 2

H. SAN VICENTE

31. San Felipe
32. Tecoluca
33. Headquarters of the Fifth Infantry Brigade

I. USULUTAN

34. Los Cantaritos
35. Beneficios Marqués, Lourdes, Oromontique and Venecia
36. El Triunfo
37. El Volcán canton and hamlet
38. San Jorge
39. La Planta
40. Jucuarán
41. FENADESAL base
42. Headquarters of the Fourth Infantry Brigade
43. Headquarters of Atonal BIRI

J. SAN MIGUEL

44. San Gerardo
45. San Luis de la Reina
46. Carolina
47. Ciudad Barrios
48. Chapeltique
49. Concepción Corozal

K. MORAZAN

50. Gualococti
51. Osicala
52. Cacaopera
53. Las Flores
54. Sensembra
55. Sesori
56. Headquarters of Military Detachment No. 4

L. LA UNION

57. Santa Rosa de Lima

Annex B

Places where FMLN forces shall be concentrated by D-Day + 5

A. SANTA ANA

1. Los Méndez

B. LA LIBERTAD

1. San Sebastián

C. SAN SALVADOR

1. Jicaron
2. Los Mazariego
3. Volcán (El Cerrito) (Finca San Francisco and La Presa)

D. CUSCATLAN

1. Aguacayo, Milinco
2. Lébano
3. La Cruz (Piedra Labrada, Santa Inez)
4. Tenancingo

E. CABAÑAS

1. Cinquera
2. Jutiapa
3. El Carrasco
4. Las Huertas
5. Santa Marta

F. CHALATENANGO

1. La Reyna
2. San Antonio Los Ranchos (El Gramal)
3. Las Flores
4. San Francisco Morazán
5. Santa Rosa
6. La Palma
7. Las Vueltas
8. Nueva Trinidad
9. Dulce Nombre de María

G. SAN VICENTE

1. Santa Rosa (Tortuguero)
2. La Laguna (Apastepeque)
3. El Tablón
4. Socorrón - Ojushte (Tecoluca)
5. San Carlos - Pacun

H. LA PAZ

1. El Carmen (Zacatecoluca) - southern slope of Chinchontepec volcano

2. Zacatecoluca Costa - La Isleta

I. USULUTAN

1. Nueva Granada (Loma Grande - Carrizal)
2. Los Horcones (FMLN)
3. Cantón San Judas (Jiquilisco)
4. Cantón Amaton (Jucuapa)
5. Cantón Chilamate (Jucuapa)
6. California - San Pedro Arenales - Las Maréas
7. Santa Cruz (Berlén)
8. Moropala (Jucuarán)

J. SAN MIGUEL

1. San Francisco - Lolotique
2. Hacienda Sierra Morena (San Gerardo)
3. Hacienda Cuscatlán (Sesori)

K. MORAZAN

1. Southern area of Guatajiagua
2. Torola
3. Perquín
4. Joateca
5. Joqoaitique
6. La Estancia
7. El Tablón (Sociedad)
8. Isletas - Los Castillos (Yamabal)

L. LA UNION

1. El Copetillo (Santa Rosa de Lima)

REMARKS

- The exact location of the sites will be determined during the informal cease-fire period.

Annex C

Places where FAES forces shall be concentrated as from D-Day + 6

A. PEACETIME FACILITIES

1. Headquarters of Military Detachment No. 4
2. Headquarters of Military Detachment No. 3
3. Headquarters of the Third Infantry Brigade
4. Headquarters of Arce BIRI
5. Headquarters of the Sixth Infantry Brigade
6. Headquarters of Atonal BIRI
7. Headquarters of DMIFA
8. Headquarters of Military Detachment No. 2
9. Headquarters of Military Detachment No. 1
10. Headquarters of Military Detachment No. 5
11. Headquarters of Bracamonte BIRI
12. Headquarters of Belloso BIRI
13. Headquarters of the Fourth Infantry Brigade
14. El Roblar military base
15. FAES headquarters at San Salvador
16. CITFA headquarters at San Salvador
17. Headquarters of the First Infantry Brigade
18. Capitán General Gerardo Barrios Military College at San Salvador
19. Parachute Battalion (Ilopango)
20. Logistical Support Command (General Stores and Military Industries) at San Salvador
21. Headquarters of the Cavalry Regiment at Sitio del Niño
22. Headquarters of Atlacatl BIRI at Sitio del Niño
23. Headquarters of the Artillery Brigade at San Juan Opico
24. Headquarters of the Second Infantry Brigade
25. Headquarters of Military Detachment No. 6
26. Headquarters of Military Detachment No. 7
27. Headquarters of the Fifth Infantry Brigade
28. Armed Forces Transport Unit
29. Armed Forces Military Training Centre
30. Ilopango air base
31. Comalapa air base
32. National Navy Headquarters at San Salvador
33. La Unión naval base
34. Port of El Triunfo
35. Acajutla naval base
36. La Libertad naval base
37. La Herradura navy post
38. El Cuco navy post
39. El Tamarindo navy post

B. MILITARY AND CIVILIAN FACILITIES OF NATIONAL IMPORTANCE

40. El Pichaco relay station
41. La Torrecilla relay station in La Unión
42. Conchagua relay station
43. Cerro del Aguacate relay station in Morazán
44. Cacahuatique relay station in Morazán
45. El Pacayal relay station in Morazán
46. Las Delicias relay station in San Vicente
47. El Faro relay station in Santa Ana
48. 15 de Septiembre dam
49. 5 de Noviembre dam
50. Cerrón Grande dam
51. El Guajoyo plant in Santa Ana
52. Ausoles geothermal plant in Ahuachapán
53. La Laguna military base in Chalatenango
54. Las Pavas relay station
55. Los Naranjos relay station
56. Loma Larga relay station

57. Santa Rosa de Lima military base
58. Ciudad Barrios military base
59. Victoria military base
60. Apaneca relay station
61. El Refugio military base
62. RASA refinery

C. REMARKS

1. The guarding of non-military facilities of national importance will be determined by their strategic importance from an economic and military standpoint. The personnel assigned to this task will in all cases be the minimum necessary.

2. The task of guarding these facilities will be gradually handed over to the newly formed National Civil Police, as soon as the latter is in a position to take over these functions.

3. Both technical military personnel and guards will be assigned to relay stations, with the number of guards kept to the minimum necessary. During the informal cease-fire, the ONUSAL Chief Military Observer, in consultation with the Government, will establish a ceiling for the number of troops to be stationed at each relay station for the above reasons. A similar ceiling will be established for the El Roblar military base.

4. The Government of El Salvador will not concentrate troops or build military facilities at the navy posts listed in 37, 38 and 39.

5. The list of peacetime facilities does not take into account the possible outcome of the application of agreements on the armed forces.

6. The maintenance of a number of military bases in peacetime is justified by the need to protect El Salvador's borders, and the appropriate arrangements will be adopted for this purpose. Those peacetime facilities whose occupation during the CAC might arouse concern will not be occupied. In this connection, the ONUSAL Chief Military Observer may determine, in consultation with the parties, which peacetime facilities should not be occupied during the CAC period.

Appendix 1 to Annex C

List of military facilities which FAES forces may not leave without ONUSAL authorization

A. PEACETIME FACILITIES

1. Headquarters of Military Detachment No. 4
2. Headquarters of the Sixth Infantry Brigade
3. Headquarters of Atonal BIRI
4. Headquarters of DMIFA
5. Headquarters of Military Detachment No. 2
6. Headquarters of Military Detachment No. 1
7. Headquarters of the Fourth Infantry Brigade
8. El Roblar military base
9. Headquarters of the Fifth Infantry Brigade
10. Third Infantry Brigade
11. Arce BIRI
12. Belloso BIRI
13. Bracamonte BIRI
14. Atlacatl BIRI
15. Parachute Battalion

B. MILITARY AND CIVILIAN FACILITIES OF NATIONAL IMPORTANCE

16. Cerro del Aguacate relay station in Morazán
17. Cacahuatique relay station in Morazán
18. El Pacayal relay station in Morazán
19. Las Delicias relay station in San Vicente
20. 15 de Septiembre dam
21. 5 de Noviembre dam
22. Cerrón Grande dam
23. La Laguna military base in Chalatenango
24. Ciudad Barrios military base
25. Victoria military base
26. El Refugio military base

Annex D

Places where FMLN forces shall be concentrated as from D-Day + 6

1. Area of La Reyna, Chalatenango
2. Area of Dulce Nombre de María, Chalatenango
3. Area of San Antonio Los Ranchos, Chalatenango
4. Area of El Paisnal, San Salvador
5. Area of the Cerro de Guazapa, Cuscatlán
6. Area of El Zapote de Tejutepeque, Cabañas
7. Area of Santa Marta, Cabañas
8. Area of Santa Clara, San Vicente
9. Area of Tecoluca, San Vicente
10. Area of El Carmen canton (southern slope of Chichontepec volcano), La Paz
11. Area of San Agustín-San Francisco Javier, Usulután
12. Area of La Peña, Las Marías and Jocote Dulce, Usulután
13. Area of Perquín and Jocoaitique, Morazán
14. Area of Isletas, Los Castillos (Yamabal), Morazán
15. Area between Sesori and Nueva Granada, San Miguel/Usulután

Annex E

Restoration of public administration in conflict zones

With the entry into force of the cease-fire, public administration shall gradually be restored in conflict zones, in accordance with the following principles:

A. The full range of public services (such as water, electricity, telecommunications and roads) and other services provided by the State in such areas as agriculture, education and health shall be restored as soon as possible.

B. Mayors who, because of the armed conflict, have performed their functions on an itinerant basis shall take up residence in their respective municipalities as soon as possible, in close consultation with ONUSAL, in order to strengthen the process of *détente* and reconciliation.

C. The administration of justice shall be re-established in a manner appropriate to the purposes of this Agreement and, in particular, to the process of peace and reconciliation. Accordingly:

(a) The administration of justice shall be re-established as soon as possible, in close consultation with ONUSAL, in order to strengthen the process of *détente* and reconciliation.

(b) The Government shall take appropriate steps to ensure that the re-establishment of the administration of justice does not impair the effectiveness of the legislative or other measures adopted within the framework of this Agreement and of the peace and reconciliation process to guarantee members of FMLN the full exercise of their civil and political rights.

D. The restoration of public administration shall not be detrimental to either the existence or the functioning of the non-governmental organizations of a cultural, economic or social nature that have been established in conflict zones. As part of the process of peace and reconciliation, appropriate channels between these organizations and the respective authorities shall be maintained, with the support of ONUSAL.

Annex F

Use of the mass media to promote reconciliation

For the purpose of assisting the process of *détente* and reconciliation:

A. Once this Agreement is signed, the Government shall not jam FMLN radio stations.

B. As from D-day, both Parties undertake to:

(a) Promote, through the various mass media at their disposal, a national publicity campaign in favour of the reunification and reconciliation of Salvadorian society.

(b) Refrain from any propaganda or information policy that is inconsistent with this Agreement or with the process of *détente* and reconciliation.

C. COPAZ shall monitor the above undertakings and shall transmit to the Parties any recommendations it deems relevant. It may also make suggestions for the participation of the various sectors of civilian society and, in particular, the mass media in the national reconciliation campaign.

D. ONUSAL shall verify fulfilment of these undertakings.

CHAPTER VIII
UNITED NATIONS VERIFICATION

1. The United Nations shall verify compliance with this Agreement and with the San José, Mexico City and New York Agreements of 26 July 1990, 27 April 1991 and 25 September 1991, respectively, with the cooperation of the Parties and of the authorities whose duty it is to enforce them.

2. The international cooperation referred to in this Agreement shall be coordinated by the United Nations and shall be subject to a formal application by the Government, compliance with official formalities and the appropriate consultations.

CHAPTER IX
IMPLEMENTATION TIMETABLE

1. COPAZ

1.1 Submission to the Legislative Assembly of the preliminary bill formalizing COPAZ: A+8 at the latest.

1.2 Establishment: D-day.

2. ARMED FORCES

2.1 *Ratification of the constitutional reform*

2.1.1 Ratification by the Legislative Assembly: between A- and D-days.

2.1.2 Publication: D+15 at the latest.

2.2 *Educational system*

2.2.1 Determination of the number of members and submission by COPAZ of the lists of three candidates for the appointment of civilian members of the Academic Council of the Military College: D+90.

2.2.2 Designation of the Academic Council of the Military College: D+100 at the latest.

2.2.3 Designation of the teaching staff: between D+120 and D+180.

2.2.4 Reforms in the educational system: D+210 at the latest.

2.2.5 Determination of the admissions system by the Academic Council: D+210 at the latest.

2.3 Purification

2.3.1 Issuance of the agreement giving legal form to and formalizing the ad hoc Commission: A+5.

2.3.2 Establishment of the ad hoc Commission: D+105.

2.3.3 Result of the evaluation: D+195.

2.3.4 Corresponding administrative decisions: D+225.

2.3.5 Implementation: D+255.

2.4 Reduction

The Government of El Salvador has submitted to the Secretary-General of the United Nations the timetable for implementing the reduction plan referred to in section 4 of chapter I of this Agreement. The Secretary-General has made the timetable known to FMLN. The United Nations shall verify compliance with that timetable.

2.5 Public security forces: abolition of the Treasury Police and the National Guard as public security forces and transfer of their members to the army: D+30.

2.6 State intelligence

2.6.1 Dissolution of the National Intelligence Department: D+135 at the latest.

2.6.2 Creation of the State Intelligence Agency: D+30 at the latest.

2.6.3 Designation of the Director: D+45 at the latest.

2.6.4 Launching of the evaluation of NID staff: D+60.

2.7 Rapid deployment infantry battalions (BIRI)

The following statement is made with regard to the rapid deployment infantry battalions in the relevant part of the timetable for implementing the reduction plan mentioned in paragraph 2.4 of this chapter:

› "The demobilization of the BIRIs shall begin in the third week of the sixth month and shall last four weeks. Once the demobilization has begun, the battalions shall be considered to have lost their offensive battle capability.

"The BIRIs shall be demobilized as detailed below:

6th month: General Ramón Belloso BIRI

7th month: Atonal BIRI

8th month: Atlacatl BIRI

9th month: General Eusebio Bracamonte BIRI

10th month: General José Manuel Arce BIRI."

2.8 Paramilitary bodies

2.8.1 Civil defence

2.8.1.1 Registration and location: D+60 at the latest.

2.8.1.2 Disarming: D+120 at the latest.

2.8.1.3 Total disbanding: D+150 at the latest.

2.8.2 System of armed forces reserves

2.8.2.1 Submission to the Legislative Assembly of the preliminary bill on military service and armed forces reserves: D+60 at the latest.

2.8.2.2 Promulgation of the law on the new system of military service and armed forces reserves: D+90 at the latest.

2.8.2.3 Replacement of territorial service by a new system of armed forces reserves: D+120 at the latest.

2.8.3 Private security services: Submission of the preliminary bill to the Legislative Assembly: D+45 at the latest.

2.9 Suspension of forcible recruitment

2.9.1 Implementation of the suspension: D-day.

2.9.2 Wide publicity in all the media, especially radio: as of D-day.

2.9.3 Submission to the Legislative Assembly of the preliminary bill on military service and armed forces reserves: D+60 at the latest.

2.9.4 Promulgation of the law: D+90.

2.10 Preventive and promotional measures

2.10.1 Organization of the Armed Forces General Inspectorate: D+90 at the latest.

2.10.2 Functioning of the armed forces court of honour: as of D+255.

2.10.3 Submission to the Legislative Assembly of the preliminary draft amendments to the law on unlawful enrichment: D+90.

2.10.4 Suspension of the issuance of licences to private individuals to bear weapons that are for the exclusive use of the armed forces: A-day.

2.10.5 Cancellation of licences for private individuals to bear weapons that are for the exclusive use of the armed forces: D+30 at the latest.

2.10.6 Recall of such weapons: between D+30 and D+270.

2.10.7 Dissemination of the doctrine of the armed forces: as of D+30.

2.10.8 Adaptation of the legislation on the armed forces: between D-day and D+270.

3. NATIONAL CIVIL POLICE

3.1 Submission to the Legislative Assembly of the preliminary bill organizing the National Civil Police: D+20.

3.2 Submission to the Legislative Assembly of the preliminary bill organizing the National Public Security Academy: between A- and D-days.

3.3 Appointment of the Coordinator: before D-day.

3.4 Submission by COPAZ of the list of three candidates for the post of Director-General of the National Civil Police: D+20 at the latest.

3.5 Appointment of the Director-General of the National Civil Police: D+30 at the latest.

3.6 Submission by COPAZ of the list of three candidates for the post of Director-General of the National Public Security Academy: D+5.

3.7 Determination of the number of members and submission by COPAZ of the lists of three candidates for appointments to the Academic Council of the National Public Security Academy: D+5.

3.8 Appointments of the Director and of the members of the Academic Council of the National Public Security Academy: D+15.

3.9 Designation of the COPAZ subcommission for the National Civil Police: D-day at the latest.

3.10 Design of the publicity campaign for recruitment: D+10 at the latest.

3.11 Launching of the publicity campaign for recruitment: D+15 at the latest.

3.12 Design of the aptitude test for former members of the National Police and former FMLN combatants: D+30 at the latest.

3.13 Organization of courses for this test: D+45 at the latest.

3.14 Evaluation of former members of the National Police: from D+30 until the end of the transitional period.

3.15 Aptitude and skills test: D+80 at the latest.

3.16 Introduction of the admissions system for the National Public Security Academy: D+80 at the latest.

3.17 Formation of boards of examiners: D+60 at the latest.

3.18 Admission of the first group of candidates: D+90 at the latest.

3.19 Start of courses at the National Public Security Academy: D+90 at the latest.4/

3.20 Establishment of the entire functional structure of the National Civil Police: D+240.

3.21 Elimination of structures incompatible with the Finance Division of the National Civil Police: D+240.

3.22 Launching of the territorial deployment of the National Civil Police: D+270 at the latest.

3.23 Completion of the territorial deployment of the National Civil Police: 21 months from the start of territorial deployment.

3.24 End of the transitional regime for the National Civil Police and of the functions of the National Police: 2 years after the start of territorial deployment.

3.25 Expiry of the possible requirement to live in barracks: 31 December 1992.

4. JUDICIAL SYSTEM

4.1 National Council of the Judiciary:

    4.1.1 Submission to the Legislative Assembly of the preliminary draft amendments to the law: D+60 at the latest.

    4.1.2 Adoption of the new law: D+90.

    4.1.3 Election and establishment: at the latest, +90 after the adoption of the new law.

4.2 Judicial Training School: at the latest, +180 after the establishment of the National Council of the Judiciary.

4.3 Formation of lists of candidates for the National Council of the Judiciary: April 1994.

4.4 Judicial career: submission to the Legislative Assembly of a preliminary draft for legal reform: D+90 at the latest.

4.5 Military jurisdiction: submission to the Legislative Assembly of a preliminary draft for legal reform: D+90 at the latest.

4.6 Office of the National Counsel for the Defence of Human Rights:

    4.6.1 Submission to the Legislative Assembly of a preliminary draft organic law: D+60 at the latest.

    4.6.2 Designation of the National Counsel: D+30 at the latest.

5. ELECTORAL SYSTEM

5.1 Designation of the Supreme Electoral Tribunal: D+15 at the latest.

5.2 Designation by COPAZ of the Special Commission: D+15 at the latest.

5.3 Legal reform: D+120 at the latest.

4/ Both Parties recognize that this is an ambitious goal which they pledge their political will to achieving; however, attaining this goal depends on the optimum operation of all the national and international factors involved, which cannot be assured at this time.

5.4 Full implementation of the right of legally registered parties to monitor the preparation, organization, publication and updating of the electoral rolls: one year before the elections, at the latest.

5.5 Publication of the register of electors: at least 20 days before the elections.

6. ECONOMIC AND SOCIAL QUESTIONS

6.1 Submission by FMLN of the inventory of affected land or buildings within conflict zones: A+30.

6.2 Designation by COPAZ of a special commission: A+20 at the latest.

6.3 Legalization of land tenure in conflict zones: A+180 at the latest.

6.4 Submission to the Legislative Assembly of the preliminary consumer protection bill: A+60 at the latest.

6.5 Convening by COPAZ of the Economic and Social Forum: A+30 at the latest.

6.6 Submission of the National Reconstruction Plan by the Government of El Salvador to FMLN: A+30 at the latest.

6.7 Establishment of the Reconstruction Fund: D+60 at the latest.

6.8 Start of implementation of the agreements on loans to the agricultural sector and for micro- and small-scale enterprise: as of D+120.

6.9 Start of the transfer of lands in excess of 245 hectares, as of D-day.

6.10 Starting date for requests for State land by former combatants of both Parties: D+60.

6.11 Start of the preferential transfer of land by the State to former combatants of both Parties who have so requested and who are of peasant origin and familiar with farming, and possess no land of any kind: D+90.

6.12 Submission to the Legislative Assembly of the preliminary draft agrarian code: A+12 months at the latest.

6.13 Implementation of agreements on privatization and social welfare: as of A.

6.14 Implementation of agreements on external co-operation: as of D-Day.

6.15 Implementation of programmes to facilitate the integration of former FMLN combatants: before D+60.

7. POLITICAL PARTICIPATION BY FMLN

7.1 Adoption of legislative or other measures to guarantee former FMLN combatants the full exercise of their rights: between A and D. 5/

7.2 Arrangements for the security of FMLN leaders and FMLN participants in COPAZ and other commissions: between A and D.

7.3 Release of political prisoners: D+30.

7.4 Promotion of the legislative decree for the legalization of FMLN as a political party: as of D+90.

7.5 Granting of licences for mass media: as of D+30.

7.6 Full guarantees and security for returnees: as of D+40.

8. CESSATION OF THE ARMED CONFLICT

8.1 Informal cessation of the armed conflict: between A and D.

8.2 Establishment of the Joint Working Group: A-day.

8.3 Launching of the reconciliation campaign: A+1.

8.4 Transmittal by the Salvadorian armed forces to ONUSAL of detailed information on the number of their troops and weapons to be concentrated in the places listed in annex A: D-7 at the latest.

8.5 Provision by FMLN to ONUSAL of detailed information on its troop strength and inventories of arms, ammunition, mines, other explosives and military equipment located anywhere in the national territory, and its plans for concentrating them in the places listed in annex B: D-7 at the latest.

8.6 Precise designation of the places to which the Salvadorian armed forces and FMLN are to fall back: between A and D.

8.7 First stage of the separation of forces: between D and D+5.

8.8 Second stage of the separation of forces: between D+5 and D+30.

8.9 Concentration by FMLN in each of the 15 designated locations, under ONUSAL supervision, of all FMLN arms, ammunition, mines, explosives and military equipment, including those belonging to its clandestine forces, pursuant to paragraph 26 of chapter VII (Cessation of the Armed Conflict): between D+6 and D+30.

8.10 Monitoring by ONUSAL of all FMLN arms, ammunition, mines, explosives and military equipment, including those belonging to its clandestine forces, pursuant to paragraphs 27 and 28 of chapter VII (Cessation of the Armed Conflict): as of D+30.

5/ It is understood that these measures will take effect in time for members of FMLN to be able to join COPAZ and other commissions without restrictions of any kind. It is also understood that these legislative and other measures are broadly conceived and do not exclude any former FMLN combatants of any kind. Consequently, they include arrangements for obtaining documentation and do not discriminate against any member of FMLN.

8.11 Reintegration of former FMLN combatants, within a framework of full legality, into the civil, political and institutional life of the country:

8.11.1 D+90: No less than 20 per cent.
8.11.2 D+120: No less than 40 per cent.
8.11.3 D+180: No less than 60 per cent.
8.11.4 D+240: No less than 80 per cent.
8.11.5 31 October 1992: 100 per cent.

8.12 End of the military structure of FMLN: between 15 October 1992 and 31 October 1992.

FINAL PROVISION

The time allotted for implementing any agreements not included in this timetable, and any adjustments to the above timetable that may be required, for any reason, shall be decided by ONUSAL in consultation with the Parties.

FINAL DECLARATION

The Parties express their firm determination to observe scrupulously and to fulfil in good faith all the undertakings given in this Agreement and in the other agreements reached during the negotiating process, under the terms and through the mechanisms provided for therein, and to cooperate with ONUSAL in its task of verifying compliance with such agreements. The Government of El Salvador solemnly undertakes to work actively for the adoption of the agreed legislative reforms in time for them to be promulgated on the envisaged dates.

Mexico City, 16 January 1992

Representing the Government of El Salvador:

(*Signed*)
Mr. Oscar SANTAMARÍA
Col. Juan MARTÍNEZ VARELA
Gen. Mauricio Ernesto VARGAS
Mr. David Escobar GALINDO
Mr. Abelardo TORRES
Mr. Rafael Hernán CONTRERAS

Representing the Frente Farabundo Martí para la Liberación Nacional:

(*Signed*)
Cmdr. Schafik HÁNDAL
Cmdr. Francisco JOVEL
Cmdr. Salvador SÁNCHEZ CERÉN
Cmdr. Eduardo SANCHO
Cmdr. Joaquín VILLALOBOS
Salvador SAMAYOA
Ana Guadalupe MARTÍNEZ
María Marta VALLADARES
Roberto CAÑAS
Dagoberto GUTIÉRREZ

(*Signed*) Boutros BOUTROS-GHALI
Secretary-General of the United Nations

Annex I

Outline for the drafting of the act concerning the authorization, registration and monitoring of security groups or units for protecting the property of the State, corporations or individuals, and private security personnel

I. PREAMBULAR PARAGRAPHS:

1. Refer to the relevant articles and subparagraphs of the Constitution which may have a bearing on the purposes of the act.

2. Need to regulate, coordinate and integrate these functions, setting up a body responsible for monitoring them.

3. Develop a suitable framework for regulating the functioning of these types of groups, units and persons who provide security services, in relation to their role in a democratic society.

II. ARTICLES:

1. Purpose of the act.

2. Scope:

a. Any group, unit or person providing security services to State institutions, other public or private institutions, and individuals;

b. The following shall be regulated according to the type of security provided:

(1) The number and type of personnel;

(2) The number and type of weapons, and equipment in general;

(3) Facilities for housing security personnel, training, and also storing weapons, ammunition and equipment.

c. Determination of mechanisms for the monitoring and supervision of security groups, entities and personnel by the National Civil Police, without prejudice to the jurisdiction of other organs and officials authorized by the Constitution or by the law;

d. Determination of the powers and responsibilities of the monitoring body.

3. Establishment of the judicial and legal formalities for obtaining the necessary authorization to provide security services regulated by this act.

4. Establishment of the regime of powers granted to such groups, units or persons for the discharge of their functions.

5. Determination of the monitoring mechanisms to be used by the monitoring body and of the specific requirements to be fulfilled by such groups, units or persons:

a. Registration of firms or individuals specifically providing security services;

b. Special requirements to be fulfilled by persons responsible for the organization and operation of such firms;

c. Registration of the personnel of security firms;

d. Requirements and conditions for the recruitment of personnel by such firms, and conditions to be fulfilled by persons providing security services individually, including evidence of their respect for human rights;

e. Registration of facilities, weapons, ammunition and equipment.

6. Prohibitions:

Prohibit the existence or the functioning of any private armed groups which are not regulated and which do not fulfil the requirements established by this act.

7. Request by the monitoring body to such firms, groups or persons for information on the type of security to be developed for the provision of such services.

8. Establishment of the requisite procedures to enable any individual or legal entity to obtain authorization to hire security personnel.

9. Regulations for the establishment, functioning and monitoring of private detective agencies.

10. Determination of compliance with any special registers which may have been established by other laws with respect to certain necessary weapons, equipment or supplies to be used by such firms or groups.

11. Determination of the limits on personnel, weapons, ammunition, equipment and *matériel* in general, according to the type of security to be provided, and the proportions which must exist among them.

12. Determination of the deadlines for fulfilling the requirements set forth in this act.

13. Issuance by the monitoring body of whatever regulations and instructions may be necessary for carrying out the activities regulated by this act.

14. Establishment of various penalties for failure to comply with the provisions of this act.

15. Establishment of a transitional regime laying down peremptory deadlines for verifying that such entities and their personnel meet the requirements established by law for performing such functions, as a condition of their continuing to provide such services; surrender of weapons, ammunition and equipment not authorized under this act; and harmonization of juridical procedures in this area. ·

16. Establishment of an evaluation mechanism which will, within two years from this agreement, give an opinion on the advisability of continuing to authorize the functioning of the entities in question.

17. Repeal of any laws or provisions which conflict with this act.

Annex II

Preliminary bill organizing the National Civil Police

THE LEGISLATIVE ASSEMBLY OF THE REPUBLIC OF EL SALVADOR
Whereas

In accordance with paragraph 17 of article 168 of the Constitution, it is the responsibility of the President of the Republic: "To command, organize and maintain the National Civil Police to preserve peace, tranquillity, order and public security, in both urban and rural areas, adhering strictly to respect for human rights and under the control of civilian authorities. The National Civil Police and the armed forces shall be independent and shall be placed under the authority of different ministries",

The establishment of the National Civil Police must be accompanied by an act organizing and regulating it institutionally,
HEREBY DECREES

TITLE I
GENERAL PROVISIONS

Article 1

The National Civil Police of El Salvador shall have the mission of protecting and safeguarding the free exercise of the rights and freedoms of individuals, preventing and combating all types of crimes and maintaining internal peace, tranquillity, order and public security throughout the national territory.

There shall be no other armed police body with national jurisdiction.

Article 2

The National Civil Police shall be an armed institution which is civilian and professional in nature and is free from all partisan activity. Its structure and organization shall be hierarchical, under the supreme command of the President of the Republic, who shall exercise such command through the Minister of the Interior and Public Security and the Vice-Minister for Public Security.

Article 3

Under the authority of the Minister and of the Vice-Minister for Public Security, the day-to-day command of the police shall be exercised by the Director-General of Police. The Director-General shall direct and monitor the implementation of the public security policy formulated by the Government. He shall also be the supreme administrative authority of the National Civil Police.

The Director-General of Police shall be appointed by the President of the Republic. He may be dismissed by resolution of the Legislative Assembly for serious violations of human rights, as provided in the Constitution.

Article 4

Under the authority of the Director-General, the General Inspectorate of Police shall be responsible for monitoring and supervising the activities of the operational services of the force.

The Inspector General shall be appointed by the Director-General, in consultation with the Attorney-General of the Republic and the National Counsel for the Defence of Human Rights.

The General Inspectorate shall comprise a Monitoring Division, which shall have the function of monitoring all police services, and a Disciplinary Investigation Division, which shall have the function of investigating breaches of discipline by police officers.

Article 5

The Director-General shall be assisted by a Deputy Director-General for Operations and a Deputy Director-General for Management.

The Deputy Director-General for Operations shall be responsible for implementing and coordinating the activities of central divisions and departmental police delegations.

The Deputy Director-General for Management shall be responsible for implementing and coordinating the administrative and logistical support activities of the police.

Article 6

The National Civil Police shall have the following central divisions: Public Security; Criminal Investigation; Frontiers; Finance; Arms and Explosives; Protection of Eminent Persons; Environment; and others to be established by order of the President of the Republic. Chiefs of division shall be appointed by the Director-General of Police, on the proposal of the Deputy Director-General for Operations. In the case of the Chief of the Criminal Investigation Division, prior consultation shall also be required with the President of the Judiciary and the Attorney-General of the Republic. In the case of the Chief of the Finance Division, the prior approval of the Minister of Finance shall be required.

Article 7

The Public Security Division shall be responsible for the maintenance of tranquillity, order and public security.

Article 8

Under the functional control of the Attorney-General of the Republic, the Criminal Investigation Division shall be responsible for investigating criminal acts and gathering evidence to identify the perpetrators of such acts. It shall also carry out investigations and other activities within its field of competence as required by the Attorney-General of the Republic, judges and courts.

...

Article 9

The Frontiers Division shall be responsible for monitoring and supervising the admission, departure, activities and, where necessary, expulsion of aliens and the migration of nationals and for the monitoring and supervision of public and private national airports, without prejudice to the constitutional duty of the armed forces to defend the integrity of the territory of the State.

Article 10

Under the functional control of the Ministry of Finance, the Finance Division shall be responsible for preventing and combating infringements of tax law, without prejudice to the fiscal oversight or other functions performed by that Ministry, for which it shall serve as police support organ. It shall have two departments: customs and taxes.

The Finance Division shall be the only police organ with competence in the areas of customs and taxes. Consequently, following its entry into operation, all provisions and structures incompatible with this principle shall cease to exist.

Article 11

The Arms and Explosives Division shall be responsible for preventing and combating infringements of the constitutional and legal regime on the manufacture, import, export, trading, possession and bearing of weapons, ammunition, explosives and similar articles.

Article 12

The Division for the Protection of Eminent Persons shall be responsible for protecting and escorting senior State officials; foreign dignitaries visiting the country; and other persons on the basis of decisions of the Government or of the courts; and for guarding public buildings and the offices of diplomatic missions or international organizations.

Article 13

Under the functional control of the Ministry of Agriculture and Livestock, the Environment Division shall be responsible for preventing and combating crimes and misdemeanours against the environment.

Article 14

There shall be one police delegation per department and one metropolitan delegation for the city of San Salvador, to which all police units of the corresponding district shall report. The organizational structure of delegations shall be adapted to the needs and characteristics of each department.

Chiefs of delegations shall be appointed by the Director-General of Police on the proposal of the Deputy Director-General for Operations, who shall be their direct supervisor. The headquarters of delegations shall be located in departmental capitals.

Within each delegation, there shall be subdelegations and police posts as required for local needs.

Article 15

The Office of the Deputy Director-General for Management shall be responsible for implementing and coordinating the administrative and logistical support activities of the police. It shall consist of the following divisions: Infrastructure Division; Data-Processing Division; Administration Division; Logistics Division; Planning and Budget Division; and others to be established by order of the President of the Republic. Chiefs of division shall be appointed by the Director-General of Police, on the proposal of the Deputy Director-General for Management.

Article 16

Ordinary courts shall be competent to try crimes committed against members of the National Civil Police, as well as crimes committed by them, even in the exercise of their functions.

TITLE II
FUNCTIONS OF THE POLICE

Article 17

The functions of the National Civil Police shall be to:

1. Protect and safeguard the free exercise of the rights and freedoms of citizens throughout the national territory.

2. Maintain internal peace, tranquillity, order and public security.

3. Prevent and combat all types of crimes.

4. Make arrests in the cases provided by law.

5. Monitor and supervise the admission, departure, activities and expulsion of aliens and the migration of nationals and monitor and supervise public and private national airports, without prejudice to the constitutional duty of the armed forces to defend the integrity of the territory of the State.

6. Prevent and combat infringements of tax law, under the terms set out in article 10.

7. Grant protection to persons and property throughout the national territory, under the terms set out in article 12.

8. Prevent and combat infringements of the constitutional and legal regime on the manufacture, import, export, trading, possession and bearing of weapons, ammunition, explosives and similar articles.

9. Monitor private security entities or services.

10. Oversee passenger and goods traffic on public thoroughfares and ensure the safety of the roads.

11. Safeguard all land, sea and air communication routes from frontiers, ports and airports.

12. Enforce provisions relating to the protection of the environment.

13. Guard the perimeter of penitentiaries and escort prisoners and detainees.

14. Provide members of the judiciary with the support they need to enforce their decisions.

15. Provide the Attorney-General of the Republic with the support he needs to investigate crimes and, in particular, criminal acts which must be subject to criminal jurisdiction.

16. Provide the National Counsel for the Defence of Human Rights with the support he needs to discharge his duties.

17. Compile and classify data for the preparation of national crime statistics.

18. Assist citizens in cases of public disaster.

19. Participate in any social, civic, cultural or educational programmes which the Government may order through the Minister or Vice-Minister.

20. Any other functions which may be assigned to it by law.

For the purpose of exercising the powers mentioned in subparagraphs 14, 15 and 16 of this article, the Director-General of Police shall detach the necessary police officers at the request of the judge, the Attorney-General of the Republic or the National Counsel for the Defence of Human Rights, as the case may be. In such circumstances, the officers thus detached shall remain within the organizational structure of the National Civil Police, but shall be under the functional authority of the judge, the Attorney-General of the Republic or the National Counsel for the Defence of Human Rights, as the case may be. The request or authorization of the latter authorities shall be essential in order to release such officers from the duties thus entrusted to them.

Article 18

The exercise of police functions shall be subject to the following code of conduct:

1. Members of the National Civil Police shall at all times observe the duties imposed on them by law, serving the community and protecting all persons from illegal acts, in keeping with the high degree of responsibility required by their profession.

2. In the performance of their tasks, members of the National Civil Police shall respect and protect human dignity and shall preserve and defend the human rights of all persons.

3. Questions of a confidential nature of which members of the National Civil Police have knowledge shall be kept secret, unless compliance with duty or the needs of justice strictly demand otherwise.

4. No member of the National Civil Police may inflict, instigate or tolerate any act of torture or other cruel, inhuman or degrading treatment or punishment, nor invoke the orders of a superior or special circumstances, such as a state of war or threat of war, threats to national security, internal political instability or any other public emergency to justify torture or other cruel, inhuman or degrading treatment or punishment.

5. Members of the National Civil Police shall ensure full protection of the integrity and health of persons in their custody and, in particular, shall take immediate steps to provide medical care when necessary.

6. Members of the National Civil Police shall not commit any act of corruption. They shall also strongly oppose such acts and shall combat them.

7. Members of the National Civil Police who have reason to believe that a breach of these rules of conduct has occurred or is about to occur shall so inform their superiors and, if necessary, any authority or appropriate agency having powers of control or correction.

Article 19

Members of the National Civil Police shall wear the regulation uniform whenever they are on active duty. In exceptional cases, the Minister, or in his absence, the Vice-Minister or the Director-General may give authorization for not wearing uniforms for certain tasks.

Article 20

Members of the National Civil Police shall bear regulation firearms when warranted by the circumstances and their duties.

The use of firearms shall be governed by the following norms:

1. In the performance of their functions, members of the National Civil Police shall, as far as possible, utilize non-violent means before resorting to the use of force and firearms. They may use force and firearms only when other means prove ineffective or do not in any way guarantee the achievement of the legitimate anticipated result.

2. Members of the National Civil Police shall not use firearms against people except in self-defence or in defence of other people, or in case of imminent danger of death or serious injury, or with the intention of preventing the commission of a particularly serious crime involving a serious threat to life, or for the purpose of arresting a person who represents such a threat and resists their authority, and only where less extreme means prove insufficient to achieve such objectives. In any case, lethal weapons may be used intentionally only when strictly unavoidable for the protection of a life.

3. When the use of firearms becomes unavoidable, members of the National Civil Police shall:

(a) Exercise restraint and take action proportional to the seriousness of the crime and the legitimate objective pursued;

(b) Reduce damage and injury to a minimum and respect and protect human life;

(c) Ensure that medical assistance and services are provided as soon as possible to persons who are injured or otherwise affected;

(d) Endeavour to notify, as soon as possible, the relatives or close friends of injured or otherwise affected persons.

4. Where members of the National Civil Police cause injuries or death through the use of force or firearms, they shall report the fact immediately to their superiors.

5. As part of the performance of their duty to safeguard the exercise of the rights of individuals, members of the National Civil Police shall protect the exercise of the right of assembly and demonstration. Where, for legal reasons, they are compelled to break up a demonstration or a meeting, they shall use the least dangerous means and only to the minimum extent necessary. Members of the National Civil Police shall refrain from using firearms in such cases, save where the meetings are violent and other means have been exhausted, and only under the circumstances provided for in subparagraph 2 of this article.

6. Exceptional circumstances, such as internal political instability or any other public emergency situation, may not be invoked to justify non-compliance with these norms.

Article 21

Members of the National Civil Police shall not normally be required to live in barracks. Such a regime shall be applied only in exceptional circumstances and for the time strictly necessary.

Article 22

Vehicles, communications systems, uniforms, facilities and, in general, any equipment used by members of the National Civil Police shall be suited to the requirements of a police force of the type defined in this act.

TITLE III
POLICE REGULATIONS

Article 23

Members of the National Civil Police shall, in the performance of their duties, be deferred to as representatives of authority for all legal purposes.

Article 24

The duties of the police shall be to:

1. Respect human rights, the Constitution and the

law, whatever the circumstances in which they are required to fulfil their mission.

2. Obey and carry out orders and instructions given by their hierarchical superiors, which shall always be consistent with the Constitution and laws of the Republic. Obedience to an order from above shall not be justification for committing acts which are clearly punishable.

3. Show due consideration and courtesy in their relations with the public and with their subordinates. Police shall identify themselves before taking measures that restrict freedom, except where circumstances of *in flagrante delicto* prevent them from doing so.

4. Intervene where necessary, even when off duty, to protect persons and property and to prevent a crime.

5. Refrain from engaging in any other remunerated activity and from receiving gifts or rewards related to the performance of their duties.

6. Refrain from taking an active part, while on duty, in political meetings or demonstrations.

7. Refrain from organizing themselves into unions or other groups pursuing similar aims and from participating in strikes.

Article 25

The rights of the policeman are as follows:

1. A policeman shall enjoy job security. He may not be dismissed except for the reasons provided by law.

2. A policeman shall have the right to be informed by his superiors of the missions, organization and functioning of the service to which he belongs.

3. A policeman shall have the right to be promoted within the ranks of the police force, under the conditions provided for in this act.

4. A policeman shall have the right to remuneration consistent with his rank and length of service.

5. A policeman shall have the right to annual leave of no less than 15 working days. The leave period shall be increased after the fifth year of service, on such conditions as are determined by the rules.

6. A policeman shall have the right to a pension and to social security.

7. In the exercise of his functions, a policeman shall have the following prerogatives:

a. To request the cooperation of any authority;

b. To have access without charge to collective public transport services;

c. To be treated free of charge and on a priority basis in hospitals, clinics and health services, if he is injured in the performance of his duties;

d. To be granted facilities for pursuing studies that will enable him to improve his academic level.

Article 26

A policeman shall be responsible for acts committed in the performance of his duties.

Article 27

Members of the National Civil Police shall be subject to the following disciplinary measures, depending on the gravity of the misdemeanour committed:

1. Verbal warning.
2. Written warning.
3. Suspension without pay.
4. Arrest for a maximum period of 15 days.
5. Demotion.
6. Dismissal.

Verbal or written warnings shall be within the competence of each chief of service; the policeman shall, however, have the right of appeal to a disciplinary committee.

The other penalties shall be imposed by a disciplinary committee under the authority of the General Inspectorate. Such penalties may be imposed only by means of a procedure which gives the policeman access to the dossier and which respects the rights of defence.

The investigation of misdemeanours shall be the responsibility of the General Inspectorate, which may act *propio motu* or on a complaint from any citizen, the chief of service of the policeman concerned, the Attorney-General of the Republic or the National Counsel for the Defence of Human Rights.

Article 28

Members of the National Civil Police may be suspended, with pay, where the best interests of an administrative or judicial investigation so require.

TITLE IV
POLICE CAREER AND MANNING TABLE

Article 29

Personnel of the National Civil Police must have a vocation of service to the community, a capacity for human relations and emotional maturity, and the physical condition required to serve as a police officer. They must be suited to serving in a police force which is designed, structured and operated as a civilian institution with the purpose of protecting and guaranteeing the free exercise of the rights and freedoms of individuals; preventing and combating all types of crimes; and maintaining internal peace, tranquillity, order and public security. They must also be able to adjust their conduct satisfactorily to the doctrine and legal regime of the National Civil Police.

Article 30

The manning table of the National Civil Police shall consist of the following levels and categories:

1. Basic level, with the categories of: constable, officer [corporal] and sergeant.

2. Executive level, with the categories of: deputy inspector, inspector and chief inspector.

3. Senior level, with the categories of: [intendant, senior intendant and superintendent].

Article 31

Admission to the National Civil Police shall be contingent on passing the entrance examinations to the National Public Security Academy and completing the selective basic training course provided there.

The entrance examinations shall be designed to ensure that candidates fit the profile required to belong to the National Civil Police, according to each of the levels of responsibility defined in this act, and shall consist of: a test of general knowledge, a physical examination, a medical examination and a psychological examination. These examinations shall be supplemented by personal interviews with the candidates.

Article 32

The minimum requirements for applicants for the entrance examinations are:

1. Be Salvadorian by birth.

2. Have reached the age of 18 before submitting the application.

3. Have completed the level of studies required for the category concerned.

4. Be physically fit.

5. Have full exercise of their civic rights.

6. Have no criminal record, i.e., convictions resulting from a final verdict.

Article 33

For the categories of constable and officer [corporal], applicants are required to have completed the ninth grade of education or its equivalent. For other categories of the basic level, a high school diploma is required. The executive level requires an intermediate university diploma, or the successful completion of three years of university studies or their equivalent. The senior level requires a university degree or its equivalent.

Article 34

Members of the National Civil Police may be promoted within the categories of the basic level by means of competitive examinations among those with more than two years' service in the lower category who meet the requirements for the category for which they are applying. Those selected must also successfully complete the course organized for the purpose by the National Public Security Academy.

Article 35

At the executive and senior levels, half the posts shall be reserved for internal promotion. The remaining half may be filled by external competitive examination.

Promotion within these categories shall also be by competitive examination among those with more than three years' service in the lower category who meet the requirements for the category for which they are applying. Those selected must also successfully complete the course organized for the purpose by the National Public Security Academy.

Article 36

Administrative, technical and service staff employed by the National Civil Police shall be subject to civil service regulations and shall not belong to the police.

TITLE V
TRANSITIONAL REGIME

Article 37

The transitional period for the establishment of the National Civil Police shall be 24 months, starting from the entry of the first contingent of basic-level students to the National Public Security Academy.

Article 38

During the transition, the National Civil Police shall not be attached to any Ministry. The Director-General shall be under the direct authority of the President of the Republic.

Article 39

The National Civil Police shall be run by the Director-General, under the terms laid down by this act.

Article 40

During the period of transition until the functional and territorial structures of the National Civil Police are operating normally, the Director-General shall be appointed by the President of the Republic from a list of three candidates proposed by the National Commission for the Consolidation of Peace (COPAZ).

Article 41

During the transition, the Director-General shall establish appropriate machinery for information and communication with COPAZ so that the Commission can perform its function of supervising the organization of the National Civil Police. As part of the normal exercise of its functions, COPAZ shall designate a subcommission to carry out this task, which shall serve as an advisory commission to the Coordinator or to the Director-General.

Article 42

The National Civil Police shall take up its functions gradually, as contingents graduating from the National Public Security Academy make it possible to staff fully each of the functional and territorial structures provided for in this act. The Director-General shall determine the priorities and order according to which this assumption of functions shall take place.

Article 43

The process of replacing the former security forces shall be carried out by geographical department, making sure that there are no gaps in authority. Within 21 months of the launching of this process, all departments must be covered by contingents of the National Civil Police.

Article 44

While the first senior and executive officers of the National Civil Police are being trained, the Director-General may order the creation of provisional commands for a predetermined period.

Annex III

Preliminary bill on the National Public Security Academy

Article 1

(1) The National Public Security Academy of El Salvador shall be established as an autonomous body under the authority of the Ministry of the Interior and Public Security.

(2) In order to achieve its purposes, the Academy shall be accorded its own juridical personality, shall enjoy administrative autonomy and shall be fully qualified to act in accordance with the legislation in force.

(3) The Academy shall operate with financial autonomy and must have sufficient resources made available to it. To that end, it shall have its own budget.

Article 2

The Academy may conduct its activities throughout the national territory. The Academy's headquarters shall be situated in ...

Article 3

(1) The Academy shall have the following functions, among others:

(a) To train members of the National Civil Police;

(b) To develop selection procedures and to conduct the corresponding examinations for admission to, and promotion in, the National Civil Police;

(c) To investigate, to study and to publicize matters relating to the National Civil Police and public security.

(2) The Academy shall provide the tuition corresponding to training courses set up for the National Civil Police, in accordance with the curricula to be established.

(3) In order to attain and develop the above objectives, the Academy shall promote institutional cooperation with universities, the judiciary, the Public Prosecutor's Office and other national or foreign institutions relevant to the teaching purposes referred to above.

Article 4

The administration and management organs of the Academy shall be the Director and the Academic Council.

Article 5

The Director, who shall have the same rank as the Director-General of the National Civil Police, shall be appointed, on the same conditions as the Director-General of Police, on the proposal of the Ministry of the Interior and Public Security.

The Director shall have a three-year term of office.

Article 6

The Academic Council shall comprise eight members, all civilians prominent in civilian, cultural, legal, police and academic life, appointed by the Minister, on the proposal of the Director and on the basis of criteria of pluralism. Their term of office shall be the same as that of the Director of the Academy.

Article 7

The Director of the Academy shall be responsible for:

(a) Managing the services and staff of the Academy;

(b) Authorizing expenditure and payments;

(c) Issuing diplomas and certificates;

(d) Granting the appointments and contracts of the teaching staff of the Academy, designated by the Academic Council;

(e) Hiring the administrative staff of the Academy;

(f) Drawing up the preliminary budget proposal;

(g) Managing the implementation of training and selection plans.

Article 8

The Academic Council shall be responsible for:

(a) Designating the teaching staff, in such a manner as to ensure that no political tendency shall predominate among that staff;

(b) Determining the admissions system and ensuring that it is not discriminatory;

(c) Giving opinions and recommendations on the Academy's teaching activities;

(d) Reporting to the Director on matters which he submits to it for consideration;

(e) Preparing an annual report on the activities of the Academy.

Article 9

The Academy's assets shall comprise the following resources:

(a) Contributions by the Government;

(b) Contributions by international organizations;

(c) Subsidies and other public or private contributions;

(d) Considerations granted under agreements;

(e) Other resources which may be granted to it.

Article 10

(1) The organizational structure of the Academy shall be determined by decree;

(2) The permanent staff of the Academy shall have the status of civil servants.

Article 11

When designating the first Director and the first Academic Council of the Academy, the following principles shall apply, on an interim basis:

(1) The Director shall be appointed by the President of the Republic, from a list of three candidates proposed by the National Commission for the Consolidation of Peace (COPAZ);

(2) The members of the Academic Council shall be proposed in lists of three candidates by COPAZ on the basis of criteria of political pluralism, for appointment by the President of the Republic;

(3) During the transition, the National Public Security Academy shall not be attached to any Ministry. Its Director shall be under the direct authority of the President of the Republic.

Document 37

Letter dated 27 January 1992 from El Salvador transmitting the texts of the New York Act and New York Act II signed by the Government of El Salvador and the FMLN on 31 December 1991 and 13 January 1992, respectively

A/46/863-S/23504, 30 January 1992

I have the honour to transmit to you the New York Act (see annex I) and the New York Act II (see annex II) signed at United Nations Headquarters on 31 December 1991 and 13 January 1992 respectively by the Government of El Salvador and the Frente Farabundo Martí para la Liberación Nacional.

I should be grateful if you would have this note and its annexes circulated as an official document of the General Assembly, under agenda item 31, and of the Security Council.

(*Signed*) Ricardo G. CASTAÑEDA
Ambassador
Permanent Representative

Annex I

New York Act

The Government of El Salvador and the Frente Farabundo Martí para la Liberación Nacional (FMLN) hereby declare that they have reached definitive agreements which, combined with those previously signed at San José, Mexico City and New York, complete the negotiations on all substantive items of the Caracas Agenda and the New York "Compressed Negotiations".

Their implementation will put a final end to the Salvadorian armed conflict.

An agreement has also been reached on all technical and military aspects relating to the separation of the warring parties and the cessation of the armed conflict, which includes the end of the military structure of the FMLN and the reintegration of its members, within a framework of full legality, into the civil, political and institutional life of the country.

The parties have also agreed that the cessation of the armed conflict shall take effect formally on 1 February 1992 and shall conclude on 31 October 1992.

A further meeting between the parties has been scheduled for 5 January 1992 to negotiate the timetable for implementing the agreements and the procedure for ending the military structure of the FMLN and reintegrating its members, within a framework of full legality, into the civil, political and institutional life of the country.

Such negotiations must be successfully concluded by 10 January 1992 at the latest. Otherwise, the parties undertake to accept, by 14 January 1992 at the latest, a formula for resolving outstanding issues to be proposed to them by the Secretary-General of the United Nations. The Final Peace Agreements will be signed at Mexico City on 16 January 1992.

The parties undertake to preserve the atmosphere necessary for maintaining and expanding the unilateral decisions which they have taken in order to avoid all military activity.

New York, 31 December 1991

Representing the
Government of
El Salvador:

(*Signed*) Mr. Oscar
SANTAMARÍA

(*Signed*) Col. Mauricio
Ernesto VARGAS

(*Signed*) Mr. David
ESCOBAR GALINDO

(*Signed*) Col. Juan
MARTÍNEZ VARELA

(*Signed*) Mr. Abelardo
TORRES

(*Signed*) Mr. Rafael
HERNÁN CONTRERAS

*Representing the
Frente Farabundo
Martí para la
Liberación Nacional:*

(*Signed*) Cmdr. Schafik
HÁNDAL

(*Signed*) Cmdr. Francisco
JOVEL

(*Signed*) Cmdr. Salvador
SÁNCHEZ CERÉN

(*Signed*) Cmdr. Eduardo
SANCHO

(*Signed*) Cmdr. Joaquín
VILLALOBOS

(*Signed*) Alvaro DE SOTO
Representative of the Secretary-General
of the United Nations

Annex II

New York Act II

The Government of El Salvador and the Frente Farabundo Martí para la Liberación Nacional, meeting at United Nations Headquarters, have reached agreements which complete the negotiations on all issues outstanding when the New York Act was signed on 31 December 1991. This opens the way for the signing of the Peace Agreement in Mexico City on 16 January 1992.

New York, 13 January 1992

*Representing the
Government of
El Salvador:*

(*Signed*) Mr. Oscar
Alfredo SANTAMARÍA

(*Signed*) Mr. David
ESCOBAR GALINDO

(*Signed*) Col. Mauricio
Ernesto VARGAS

(*Signed*) Mr. Rafael
HERNÁN CONTRERAS

*Representing the
Frente Farabundo
Martí para la
Liberación Nacional:*

(*Signed*) Cmdr. Schafik
HÁNDAL

(*Signed*) Cmdr. Salvador
SÁNCHEZ CERÉN

(*Signed*) Cmdr. Eduardo
SANCHO

(*Signed*) Ana Guadalupe
MARTÍNEZ

(*Signed*) María Marta
VALLADARES

(*Signed*) Alvaro DE SOTO
Representative of the Secretary-General
of the United Nations

Document 38

Report of the ONUSAL Human Rights Division for November and December 1991 (extract)

A/46/876-S/23580, 19 February 1992

1. The attached document contains the third report of the United Nations Observer Mission in El Salvador (ONUSAL) and consists of the report of the Director of the Mission's Human Rights Division for November and December 1991.

2. It should be recalled that, from the time when ONUSAL was established until the signing of the Peace Agreement on 16 January 1992, the Human Rights Division was the only component of ONUSAL that was functioning fully. Pursuant to Security Council resolution 729 (1992), ONUSAL now also has a Military Division and a Police Division. A subsequent report will cover functions related to these aspects of the Mission's mandate.

Annex

Report of the Director of the Human Rights Division

I. *Introduction*

1. The two main events since the Division's previous report (A/46/658-S/23222 and Corr.1) have been the signing of the Peace Agreement on 16 January and the entry into force of the cessation of the armed conflict on 1 February (see A/46/864-S/23501, annex). Both events radically transform the context in which the ONUSAL Human Rights Division is operating. On the one hand, the Division will finally be able to perform its task within the framework originally conceived by the San José

Agreement. On the other, it will have to coordinate its activities with the Mission's new divisions, the Police and Military Divisions.

2. Although the cessation of the armed conflict went into effect on 1 February, both the unilateral cease-fire declaration by FMLN on 16 November 1991 and the signing of the New York Act on 31 December 1991 helped to substantially reduce the level of military activities in the country and their adverse effects on the civilian population. It is to be hoped that a whole series of acts and situations which violate human rights and are related to the armed conflict will now rapidly disappear. Indeed, there are already clear signs of a significant decline in such problems as recruitment, restrictions on freedom of movement, harm done to the civilian population in the course of the armed conflict and, in general, violations of international humanitarian law by both parties. It will be some time before certain other problems, such as the lack of personal documentation of large sectors of the population, are finally solved, but the end of the conflict removes the political impediments to their solution.

3. Hopefully, the changes agreed to at the negotiating table concerning the armed forces, public security and the military structure of FMLN, and also the expansion of the Mission's mandate and the increase in its police and military observers, will likewise help to improve the human rights situation in the country substantially. However, the transitional period now beginning is fraught with uncertainty and may see attempts at destabilization and, possibly, an increase in certain practices which, like summary executions by paramilitary groups, still seem alarmingly prevalent. There have also been further cases of death threats, many of them coming, by all indications, from organized groups, to which the competent State organs have yet to respond effectively. This will require the Human Rights Division to redouble its efforts in order to help ensure that the agreements reached translate into practices and conducts that respect human rights, that all practices and conducts that might violate human rights are eradicated and that the institutions responsible for protecting and guaranteeing citizens' rights fulfil their task.

4. During the period covered by this report, the Human Rights Division continued to carry out all the activities begun on 1 October and described in detail in paragraphs 4-7 of its previous report. The Division's contacts with the parties are now operating smoothly and its exchanges with them are frank. Contacts with the Government of El Salvador and with its political, military, judicial and municipal authorities were strengthened at both the regional and the national level during the reporting period. In the latter connection, mention should be made of the valuable coordination mechanism pro-

vided by the inter-agency group coordinated by the Executive Secretary of the governmental Human Rights Commission. Contacts with FMLN have also increased, especially at the local level, having been greatly facilitated first by the reduction and then by the total suspension of military activities. In addition to these contacts, meetings outside the country with the FMLN Political and Diplomatic Commission have continued. Such meetings will henceforth take place within the country. Links between the Division, its regional offices and suboffices and civilian society, as represented by trade union, social and political organizations and organizations for the promotion and protection of human rights, have also increased.

5. As on earlier occasions, various political and social sectors have understandably insisted on requesting the Division to perform functions not entrusted to it under the San José Agreement. Such requests have forced the Division to continue to define its role more precisely. Three types of situations have prompted further requests for action by the Division: land seizures, the levying of the so-called war tax and labour disputes. On the first of these, the Division has maintained that it has no mandate to give an opinion on agrarian disputes or to prevent land seizures or evictions. However, it has made it clear that, where land problems are concerned, it will verify that the rights to life, security and integrity of person, personal liberty and due process, to which the San José Agreement attaches priority, are not being violated. The Division has, nevertheless, acting through its regional coordinators and under the direction of the Chief of Mission, used its good offices to help find negotiated solutions to problems that may arise at the local level between the lawful owners and the occupants of land. On the levying of the so-called war tax, the Division has stated that this is either an activity related to the armed conflict or, when not carried out by FMLN, simply a criminal activity. Neither of these is covered by the Mission's mandate. However, ONUSAL has reiterated that it will verify whether, in the course of such activities, human rights to which the San José Agreement gives priority are being violated. The Mission has taken a similar position on labour disputes, stating that while it is not competent to give an opinion on their substance, it will verify that, in the settlement of such disputes, established procedures are observed and priority human rights, particularly freedom of association, are not violated.

...

V. Conclusions and recommendations

150. The prospect of a final cessation of the armed conflict as of 1 February and the informal cease-fire which went into effect on 15 January put the Human Rights Division in the situation originally envisaged by the San José Agreement for the performance of its mandate. Paragraph 19

of that Agreement in fact envisaged that the Mission would take up its duties as of the cessation of the armed conflict.

151. The determination of both parties to respect the cease-fire and their request for ONUSAL to monitor it, as well as the verification and supervision of the operations of the National Police until the new National Civil Police is deployed throughout the country, are important elements for facilitating the task of the Human Rights Division and for human rights verification, promotion and education. What is required in the overall context of progress towards lasting peace and institutional change, is to promote, through vigilant observation of the real situation, behavioural changes and legal reforms conducive to the essential spirit of reconciliation and, in the longer term, to the consolidation of the rule of law and unrestricted respect for and the safeguarding of human rights.

152. The period covered by this report saw a significant decline in the fighting, particularly after the unilateral truce declaration by FMLN on 16 November 1991 and the positive response by the President of the Republic in deciding to suspend the use of the aircraft and heavy artillery. In some areas, however, particularly Chalatenango, fighting continued for several more weeks. During the same period, a number of incidents caused the Mission considerable concern: an increase in the number of summary executions or deaths, many of them attributable to unidentified organized groups, particularly in the San Salvador area and in the Departments of La Libertad and Santa Ana; death threats, also by organized groups, against members of non-governmental organizations or churches; and the attack on the vehicle of a foreign press correspondent at the precise moment when the New York Act was being signed.

153. Military recruitment, which had declined in the final days of 1991, was particularly intense in certain regions of the country in the first two weeks of January 1992. The undertaking signed by the Government to suspend all recruitment as of 1 February and to present a bill on military service within 60 days should put an end to the difficulties caused by this problem to which the Mission has been drawing attention from the outset. Freedom of movement has also improved considerably in recent weeks, particularly in the conflict zones of Morazán and Chalatenango, and this situation should continue to improve after 1 February until it is completely normalized.

A. Human rights

1. Right to life and to integrity and security of person

(a) Summary executions or deaths in violation of juridical guarantees

154. During the period covered by this report, a considerable number of violations of the right to life occurred in the country, particularly in the regions of San Salvador and Santa Ana. The cases considered in the report show that the auxiliary organs of the system of justice, and often judges themselves, have not taken all necessary steps to comply with the recommendations made to States by the General Assembly concerning the prevention and investigation of summary executions, particularly in the Principles endorsed by the General Assembly in its resolution 44/162. In most cases, the action taken to collect evidence and to find, identify and arrest the alleged perpetrators in order to bring them to justice has been inadequate and at times even non-existent.

155. If the current sense of impunity is to be overcome and conditions are to be created for the genuine public security that is particularly necessary in the transitional period now beginning, the duty to protect or safeguard the fundamental right to life and to integrity of person must be observed. In this connection, ONUSAL feels bound to reiterate the recommendations made in its second report (para. 150).

(b) Death threats

156. The death threats dealt with in this report are equally disturbing. Many of them were directed at leaders and members of non-governmental organizations, trade unions or churches. Some organized but anonymous groups, which became active before ONUSAL arrived and have remained so since, continue to make death threats and yet the alleged authors have so far been neither identified, investigated nor brought to trial. The actions of such groups were mentioned in the Mission's second report, which recommended that vigorous action should be taken to put an end to the practices of intimidation and threats by clandestine groups.

157. In this connection, the Mission emphatically reiterates its recommendation to the authorities that they should take all necessary steps to provide effective protection to persons who receive such threats, as recommended in Principle 4 already mentioned.

(c) Torture and cruel, inhuman or degrading treatment or punishment

158. A number of cases of torture or cruel, inhuman or degrading treatment or punishment have been described in this report. ONUSAL considers it important and encouraging that the military authorities have imposed administrative penalties on the perpetrators. However, it must emphasize that such abuses are crimes, and it therefore recommends that the public authorities institute legal proceedings, wherever necessary, in accordance with domestic law and the international norms referred to in the corresponding section. It also reiterates its recommendation that the periods of administrative deten-

tion provided for in domestic law should be respected and that incommunicado detention, which is prohibited by the San José Agreement, should be prevented.

159. Lastly, the Mission recommends that in setting up the new National Civil Police provided for in the Peace Agreement, account should be taken of the provisions of the General Assembly Declaration on the Protection of All Persons from Being Subjected to Torture or Other Cruel, Inhuman or Degrading Treatment or Punishment, to ensure that future members of the police are given appropriate training emphasizing that such practices are absolutely prohibited.

2. Right to due process of law

160. The Mission has continued to monitor due process of law, to which the San José Agreement gives priority, by observing the pre-trial or adversarial proceedings of trials now in progress. In this connection, it feels bound to recommend, first of all, strict respect for domestic law on the collection of evidence: in cases of violent or suspicious deaths, the judge must make an immediate visual inspection, the body must be examined and, wherever possible, a thorough autopsy must be performed. The recommendations to States contained in the Principles on the Effective Prevention and Investigation of Extra-legal, Arbitrary and Summary Executions, endorsed by the General Assembly in its resolution 44/162, should also be borne in mind.

161. Concerning the proceedings brought in the El Mozote case, which are very important for institutional reasons, the Mission reiterates the comments made in analysing the current status of the pre-trial proceedings, especially those relating to the need to use systematic anthropological techniques to study skeletal remains and the need to request assistance from international experts in forensic anthropology so that they can be there to supervise the exhumation and laboratory analyses, along with local professionals.

162. Concerning the conduct of the public hearing, which is the main part of the trial stage of the proceedings under El Salvador's present system of criminal justice, the Mission wishes to refer to the comments made in the corresponding section. In particular, it recommends strict compliance with the procedural rules requiring that the summary be read out clearly and that the judge observe the obligation to ask members of the jury whether they wish to question the accused or the witnesses.

3. Right to personal liberty

(a) Arrest of juveniles

163. This problem was examined during the period covered by this report in the light of applicable national and international norms. The Mission has observed such

practices as illegal or arbitrary arrests, omissions or delays by the authorities in handing over minors to the juvenile courts and failure to observe the requirement that juveniles and adults be confined separately in prisons and detention centres. The authorities seem to be aware of the seriousness of these problems, which are attributable in part to limited human and material resources. However, as the report indicates, such constraints are not sufficient to justify failure to comply with binding rules.

164. The Mission wishes to recommend increased supervision of police officers and juvenile reform centres and improved staff training in order to ensure full respect for the human rights of juveniles in custody or detention.

(b) Arrests by military personnel

165. During the period covered by this report, the Mission found that the armed forces frequently make arrests in cases not involving in flagrante delicto, generally on mere suspicion of belonging to subversive groups, and usually hold detainees for varying periods of time. By law, the armed forces may make arrests only in cases of in flagrante delicto and must hand over detainees immediately to an auxiliary organ of justice. Since such arrests are illegal and violate the San José Agreement and domestic and international law, the Mission recommends that the armed forces refrain from such practices in future. It is its expectation that these practices will disappear in the period now beginning, since they were directly related to the armed conflict.

4. Freedom of movement

166. This report analyses the situation of freedom of movement from when the Mission was established on 26 July 1991 to 31 January of this year. The corresponding section emphasizes the complexity of verifying the right to movement of persons and goods in a situation of internal armed conflict. It also draws attention to the applicable legal norms and legally acceptable restrictions. Freedom of movement, particularly to and from conflict zones, was severely restricted in the early months of the period analysed. Later on, around mid-November, it was noted that both sides were beginning to make efforts to ease such restrictions, although these efforts were not uniform and there were a number of exceptions. Lastly, as of 16 January of this year, a number of checkpoints have been removed, others have been dismantled and still others, although manned by soldiers, do not actually check vehicles.

167. The Mission welcomes the fact that restrictions on the movement of civilians and civilian goods have been eased and thinks they should soon disappear altogether given the situation now prevailing in the country. Its field observations show this to be the trend at present.

5. Personal documentation

168. The Mission welcomes the initiative taken by the Central Board of Elections in providing a town hall with photocopies of the registers of births, deaths and marriages and reiterates the suggestion made in its previous report that this measure should be implemented nation-wide. At the same time, the Mission reiterates its recommendation that the special law to establish the civil status of undocumented persons affected by the conflict should be submitted to the Legislative Assembly as soon as possible and that it should include provisions making it easier to obtain personal identity cards.

6. Freedom of association

169. This report considers the legal framework, under domestic and international law, for the freedom of association guaranteed by the San José Agreement (paras. 5 and 11), and specifies the conditions in which ONUSAL will fulfil its mandate in this connection. The Mission has received various reports of irregularities in the exercise of trade union freedom. While it seems premature to draw conclusions from the information received so far, ONUSAL will continue to investigate this problem and will make a more detailed analysis of it in a subsequent report.

B. Humanitarian law

1. Humane treatment

170. The entry into effect of the cease-fire should mark the end of consideration by the Human Rights Division of situations such as those described in paragraphs 110 and 116, which should be seen as a thing of the past. The Mission feels bound to recall that, in the case of a non-international armed conflict, persons who do not take a direct part or who have ceased to take part in hostilities are protected by the Geneva Conventions of 12 August 1949 and by Additional Protocol II thereto. The wounded and sick are entitled to immediate protection and care. Failure to observe this rule of conduct is a serious violation of the norms of international humanitarian law. Furthermore, while international humanitarian law allows insurgent forces to engage in summary executions, it imposes a number of minimum mandatory requirements: existence of a court offering the essential guarantees of independence and impartiality, respect for the principle of legality, procedural guarantees and, in particular, the right of defence both before and during trial. ONUSAL hopes that, in future reports, its recommendations on respect for humane treatment will no longer be necessary.

2. Civilian population

171. The consideration given to indiscriminate attacks in this report should not be necessary in future.

However, it should be emphasized that in the cases mentioned in the corresponding section, the armed forces did not take the necessary precautions in their attacks, nor did they attempt to establish responsibility for incidents the investigation of which required that disciplinary or criminal proceedings should have been brought. FMLN, for its part, violated established norms on the precautions to be taken against the effects of attacks, as indicated in the corresponding section.

172. It has not been possible to determine responsibility for the injuries caused to a civilian as a result of the explosion of a mine. It should be recalled in this connection that mines must not be used indiscriminately, a requirement established by the norms of international humanitarian law applicable to non-international armed conflicts mentioned in discussing this case in the corresponding section.

3. War tax

173. It is very likely that the cessation of the armed conflict will be accompanied by the virtual disappearance of this problem. Although the Mission has taken the position that complaints relating to this issue are, strictly speaking, outside its mandate, it has in all cases received them and transmitted them to FMLN to find out whether they are true. When FMLN has denied the charges, the Mission has advised complainants to make application to the competent State organs, since there is clear evidence that criminal groups, using the name of FMLN, are engaging in extortion. In cases where FMLN has acknowledged responsibility, the Mission has called on it to avoid any action which might jeopardize the process of peace and national reconciliation and to refrain from violating rights to which the San José Agreement gives priority, which could occur in the course of levying the so-called war tax.

174. Lastly, the Mission believes that its main course of action in dealing with the parties is to make recommendations on the basis of the conclusions drawn from cases or situations which it has considered (San José Agreement, para. 14 (g)). The parties, in turn, have undertaken to give their earliest consideration to recommendations made by the Mission (San José Agreement, para. 15 (d)). Accordingly, on 7 January last, the Mission sent notes to both the Government of El Salvador and FMLN asking each of them to kindly let it know what consideration is being given to the recommendations made in its second report (paras. 146 ff.). The notes included a recapitulation of those recommendations.

175. A new era is beginning for El Salvador, filled with hopes and misgivings. The end of the armed conflict should ensure that the State and FMLN, as long as they remain parties to the San José Agreement, will devote themselves more fully to respect for and the protection of

human rights. A number of problems which have been of concern to the Mission ever since its establishment should be substantially resolved or disappear: restrictions on freedom of movement, military recruitment and violations of international humanitarian law.

176. However, violations of fundamental human rights are still extremely prevalent. Not only is the number of such violations cause for concern, but also the nature of some of those which have occurred frequently in recent weeks. These include summary executions and death threats by organized groups. It is also disturbing that State organs, including the judicial system and its auxiliary bodies, remain incapable of preventing, investigating and punishing violations of fundamental human

rights. Other consequences of the conflict, such as problems relating to the lack of personal documentation, also persist.

177. Because of all this, the Mission will have to remain vigilant in verifying the human rights situation in El Salvador. It will have to make a greater effort to help improve the judicial procedures for the protection of human rights and increase respect for the rules of due process of law (San José Agreement, para. 14 (h)). The Mission will also step up its activities in the area of human rights education, publicity and promotion in order to help restore the climate of harmony essential to respect for all the agreements signed.

...

Document 39

Report of the Secretary-General on ONUSAL

S/23642, 25 February 1992

1. The present report is submitted to the Security Council in response to paragraph 6 of resolution 693 (1991) of 20 May 1991, in which the Council, having established the United Nations Observer Mission in El Salvador (ONUSAL) as an integrated peace-keeping operation with the initial mandate of verifying compliance by the parties with the San José Agreement, 1/ requested the Secretary-General to keep the Council fully informed of the implementation of the resolution. It is also based on the similar request contained in paragraph 7 of resolution 729 (1992) of 14 January 1992, by which the Council decided to enlarge the mandate of ONUSAL to include the verification and monitoring of the implementation of all the agreements that were to be signed by the parties in Mexico City on 16 January 1992 and extended that mandate until 31 October 1992.

2. In implementation of resolution 729 (1992), ONUSAL proceeded to take the necessary measures in order to carry out the new tasks assigned to the Mission. Priority was given to establishing the Military Division, which was entrusted with verifying the cessation of the armed confrontation and was placed under the command of Brigadier-General Victor Suanzes Pardo (Spain), who previously had been chief of the United Nations Observer Group for Central America (ONUCA). During the informal cease-fire (16 to 31 January 1992), the Military Division received its first contingents, which came both from ONUCA and directly from a number of contributing countries. The Military Division deployed its personnel at all the verification points on 31 January and one day later, as agreed, began its verification activities. Under its supervi-

sion, the first stage of the separation of forces was completed without any major incident. To date, the Military Division has 368 of the 373 authorized observers.

3. At the beginning of February, the Police Division was established under the command of Colonel Pierre Gastelu (France), as acting chief. This Division will have the responsibility, within the framework of the agreement on the establishment of the national civil police, of facilitating the transition in the field of public security until the new police corps becomes fully operational by the middle of 1994. The deployment of the Division, which will coincide with that of the national police, has already begun. To date, the Division has 147 of the 631 authorized observers. It is expected that 120 more will arrive by the first week of March.

4. In the meantime, the Human Rights Division, which, to date, is staffed with 51 civilian professionals and 14 police observers assigned by the Police Division (which are included in the total of 147 referred to in the previous paragraph), has continued its task of verifying compliance by the parties with the Agreement on Human Rights. 2/ The report of its Director, which covers the period from 1 November to 31 December 1991, while including some references to events that occurred in January 1992, is the subject of a report that is being published separately.

5. The long and complex negotiation process begun on 4 April 1990 under the auspices of the Secretary-General, culminated in the signing on 16 January 1992

1/ S/21541, annex.
2/ S/23580, annex.

in Mexico City of the Peace Agreement between the Government of El Salvador and the Frente Farabundo Martí para la Liberación Nacional (FMLN). 3/ The success achieved in this process put an end to 12 years of cruel and bloody conflict and opened up, with the cessation of the armed confrontation on 1 February 1992, the path towards national reconciliation and the establishment of just and lasting peace. At a time like this, a change in political thinking is essential in order to consolidate the process of national reconciliation. In general, the leaders of the main political forces have demonstrated their desire to speed up this change. Owing to this, the main leaders of FMLN returned to El Salvador under conditions of security guaranteed by the Government. In the same context, the first stage of the separation of forces was completed without incident. There have also been other developments which are of fundamental importance, such as the establishment of the National Commission for the Consolidation of Peace and the designation of two of its commissions: the special commission to deal with the agrarian problem and the commission on the National Civil Police. Furthermore, the Legislative Assembly has adopted the National Reconciliation Act, which provides for a broad amnesty, with exceptions, however, concerning cases which will be brought to the attention of the Commission on the Truth.

6. I had the pleasure of participating in the signing of the Peace Agreement in Mexico City on 16 January 1992 and of travelling immediately afterwards to El Salvador. Through my visit I sought to underscore the importance for the international community of the decision by the Salvadorians to leave behind an era of violence and embark upon the path of peace. It is obvious that the signing of the Peace Agreement is due to the determination of President Alfredo Cristiani and the leadership of FMLN to achieve a negotiated solution to the conflict. I should not fail to mention that it was the personal participation of my predecessor that ensured, in the final hours of his mandate, the success of the negotiations. Similarly, I should express once again my appreciation to the Governments of Colombia, Mexico, Spain and Venezuela, as well as others, for the support provided in order to achieve peace. On behalf of the international community, I congratulate the parties and extend to the Salvadorian people my best wishes for a future of peace and stability.

7. I shall report to the Security Council, at regular intervals, on the further implementation of ONUSAL's mandate.

3/ S/23501, annex.

Document 40

Letter dated 15 May 1992 from the Secretary-General to the President of the Security Council concerning ONUSAL military observers

S/23987, 20 May 1992

I have recently been informed by the Chief of Mission of ONUSAL that, based on recent experience in verifying the relevant provisions of the Peace Agreement and in the expectation that the Military Division of ONUSAL will soon be required to monitor additional activities foreseen under the Agreement, the Chief Military Observer of ONUSAL has come to the conclusion that, for these tasks to be completed, it will be necessary to maintain temporarily the strength of the Military Division, which currently stands at 290 military observers. Under the original plan, the strength of the Division was to have been reduced after 1 June 1992.

For these reasons, I endorse the recommendation of the Chief Military Observer, conveyed to me by the Chief of Mission, to extend for a three-month period, i.e., until 1 September 1992, the services of 39 military observers who are presently due to leave the Mission on 1 June 1992.

Every attempt will be made to absorb the additional resources required for these extra personnel within the appropriations made available by the General Assembly for ONUSAL. Should this not be possible, the additional requirements will be reported to the General Assembly.

I should be grateful if you would bring this matter to the attention of the members of the Security Council.

(*Signed*) Boutros BOUTROS-GHALI

Document 41

Report of the Secretary-General on the activities of ONUSAL since the cease-fire (1 February 1992) between the Government of El Salvador and the FMLN

S/23999, 26 May 1992

Introduction

1. The present report, submitted in accordance with Security Council resolution 729 (1992), describes the activities of the United Nations Observer Mission in El Salvador (ONUSAL) since the cease-fire between the Government of El Salvador and the Frente Farabundo Martí para la Liberación Nacional (FMLN) came formally into effect on 1 February 1992.

2. Mr. Iqbal Riza continues to serve as my Special Representative and Chief of Mission of ONUSAL. The Mission has been carrying out all the various verification tasks assigned to it in the agreements signed by the Government of El Salvador and the FMLN between 4 April 1990 and 16 January 1992. It has also used its good offices to help the two parties to overcome difficulties that have arisen in implementation of the agreements, in particular through promoting, and attending, meetings between them. In addition ONUSAL has been participating as an observer in the work of the National Commission for the Consolidation of Peace (COPAZ), whose composition and functions were defined in the New York Agreement of 25 September 1991. 1/

3. The work of the Mission is described below in eight sections devoted respectively to the verification of the cessation of the armed conflict; the Armed Forces of El Salvador; public security matters; economic and social matters; political participation by FMLN; the restoration of public administration in conflict zones; the judicial system; and the electoral system. ONUSAL's work in relation to the San José Agreement on Human Rights 2/ will continue to be the subject of a separate series of reports, the most recent of which was submitted to the General Assembly and the Security Council under my note of 19 February 1992. 3/

4. ONUSAL continues to be helped in its work by the four "Friends of the Secretary-General" (Colombia, Mexico, Spain and Venezuela) and by other interested Governments.

I. Verification of the cessation of the armed conflict

A. Composition and tasks of the Military Division

5. The Military Division of ONUSAL, which is responsible for verifying the agreement on the cessation of the armed conflict, was established on 20 January 1992

and is under the command of Brigadier-General Victor Suanzes Pardo (Spain). The Division, which began with an authorized strength of 380, currently has 292 military observers from Brazil, Canada, Colombia, Ecuador, India, Ireland, Norway, Spain, Sweden and Venezuela. In addition to the above, eight medical officers provided by Argentina assist ONUSAL in its mission. The Security Council has recently agreed to my recommendation that the Military Division should be retained at its current strength until 1 September 1992. 4/, 5/

6. The Military Division monitors the troops of the Armed Forces of El Salvador and FMLN at the locations where they have been concentrated in accordance with the Peace Agreement; 6/ verifies the inventories of weapons and personnel furnished by the two parties; authorizes and accompanies the movements of both forces; and receives and investigates complaints of violations. It is deployed among 4 regional military offices and 15 verification centres, as shown in the map annexed to the present report. [See Introduction, page 32.] The military observers constantly patrol, by air and land, the entire area under their responsibility.

B. Separation and concentration of forces

7. As stipulated in the Peace Agreement, a joint working group, consisting of the Chief Military Observer of ONUSAL as Chairman, one representative of the Government and one of FMLN, was established on 22 January 1992 to define precisely the designated locations for the two parties' troops and to deal with other aspects relating to the separation and concentration of the opposing forces.

8. Difficulties arose with regard to the definition of some of the 15 locations designated for the concentration of FMLN combatants. In two cases where it proved impossible to achieve an agreed definition, both the Government and FMLN accepted the delimitations determined by the Chief Military Observer, although the Government placed on record its objection to them. As indicated below, there have been difficulties with regard

1/ S/23082.
2/ S/21541, annex.
3/ S/23580.
4/ S/23987.
5/ S/23988.
6/ S/23501, annex.

to the locations for the concentration of the troops of the Armed Forces of El Salvador. These have proved more difficult to resolve.

9. By 6 February, which marked the end of the first stage of the separation of forces, the Armed Forces of El Salvador had concentrated its troops at the 100 locations designated in the Peace Agreement. By 2 March, the end of the second stage, the majority of the troops of the Armed Forces of El Salvador had been concentrated at the 62 designated locations. However, at that time the Armed Forces of El Salvador also remained at about 16 additional locations, on the grounds that they were necessary to protect installations of national importance and, at 2 others, on the grounds of lack of space to accommodate all the concentrated personnel. This was not in conformity with the Agreement. ONUSAL accordingly pressed the Armed Forces of El Salvador to withdraw and they gradually did so. By 25 May 1992 they remained at only one disputed location, other than the two mentioned in paragraph 10 below. ONUSAL continues its efforts to resolve this problem.

10. Considerable difficulties have arisen over the two public security bodies, the Treasury Police and the National Guard, which, under the Peace Agreement, were supposed to be abolished by 1 March 1992, with their members being incorporated into the Army. These difficulties, which are described more fully in section II below, have contributed to the failure to complete the concentration of the two sides' troops in accordance with the Peace Agreement. This is because, for several weeks after their incorporation into the Army, the ex-members of these two bodies remained in their original barracks, even though these were not included in the 62 locations designated for the Armed Forces of El Salvador. This was denounced as a violation of the Peace Agreement by FMLN, which refused to complete concentration of its own forces until the problem was resolved. By 23 April the majority of the ex-Treasury Police and ex-National Guard personnel had been moved into the 62 locations of the Armed Forces of El Salvador but some 3,500 of them remained at the two ex-bodies' headquarters in San Salvador, neither of which is included in the 62 locations. This problem remains unresolved.

11. As for FMLN, its forces had, by 6 February, concentrated at the 50 locations designated for the first stage. FMLN did not, however, complete its second stage concentration by the due date of 2 March. It cited lack of infrastructure at the agreed locations and failure by the Government to comply with other provisions of the Agreement. A series of further deadlines were established but not observed, with FMLN continuing to insist that it would complete its concentration only when the Armed Forces of El Salvador completed their own. A further delay arose in late April when FMLN objected to a law adopted by the Legislative Assembly on the night of 23-24 April concerning the Treasury Police and National Guard (see para. 17 below). At the time of writing the present report, some 8 per cent of FMLN combatants have yet to complete their concentration at the agreed locations. These include combatants who, during the conflict, had belonged to "Committees for Citizen Security" and who still remain at 11 locations. Both sides have assured ONUSAL that, despite these delays, they are committed to comply with their obligations. ONUSAL continues its efforts to resolve this problem, which has had a negative impact on the atmosphere for the implementation of the agreements as a whole.

C. *Inventories of troop strengths and armaments*

12. Under the Peace Agreement both sides were obliged to submit, by 23 January, detailed information on the number of their troops and armaments to the Chief Military Observer of ONUSAL. With regard to FMLN, this was done on time and without incident. However, ONUSAL has serious doubts as to whether the number, quality and age of the weapons declared and presented accurately reflect FMLN's true holdings. FMLN has been repeatedly informed, both in El Salvador and in New York, of these doubts, but it continues to insist that the information provided is accurate.

13. Difficulties also arose over the inventories submitted by the Armed Forces of El Salvador, as some unit commanders maintained that the Agreement did not cover the personnel or weapons of permanent garrisons that were not being moved. ONUSAL clarified that the required information must include all the personnel and armaments to be concentrated, including those already present at some of the locations when the process began. However, there was considerable delay before ONUSAL received all the relevant information. The last inventory was submitted by the Armed Forces of El Salvador on 27 March 1992 and has been verified by ONUSAL.

D. *Logistical situation in the areas of FMLN concentration*

14. At the beginning of February ONUSAL was asked to help to provide logistical assistance at the 15 areas designated for the concentration of FMLN troops. A coordination mechanism was accordingly established with the United Nations Development Programme (UNDP), which appealed to the international community for funding. Simultaneously, other agencies of the United Nations system, such as the World Food Programme (WFP), the World Health Organization (WHO), working through the Pan American Health Organization (PAHO), and the United Nations Educational, Scientific and Cultural Organization (UNESCO), contributed support in

their respective fields of competence. Non-governmental organizations (NGOs) also cooperated, especially Médecins sans Frontières and Caritas Internationalis of El Salvador. The Government, for its part, facilitated these efforts, which included the supply of water, food and shelter, improvement of the road network and assistance in health and education. This collaborative effort is achieving good results with the generous support of the Governments of Canada, Denmark, Japan, Norway, Sweden and the United States of America, and of the European Economic Community.

E. *Reintegration of FMLN ex-combatants*

15. Under the Peace Agreement at least 20 per cent of FMLN ex-combatants were to have been reintegrated "within a framework of full legality, into the civil, political and institutional life of the country" on 1 May. FMLN has not complied with this provision, citing, *inter alia*, the Government's delay in implementing those aspects of the Agreement that would facilitate the reintegration of ex-combatants into civilian life, notably those relating to land, the formation of the new National Civil Police and political activity by FMLN. This renders urgent the need to give effect to the relevant aspects of the Agreements. ONUSAL and UNDP have therefore been urging the Government to ensure that these are implemented in accordance with the agreed timetable and that a special effort be made to catch up on delays that have already occurred. ONUSAL has equally urged FMLN to cooperate with the Government in this work.

II. *Armed forces of El Salvador*

16. The Legislative Assembly has adhered to the agreed timetable for approving constitutional reforms affecting the Armed Forces of El Salvador and for the suspension of forcible recruitment as of 1 February. Action has also been taken to give legal form and force to the ad hoc Commission on the purification of the Armed Forces of El Salvador. ONUSAL has been in touch with the members of the Commission to cooperate in planning that body's future activities.

17. On 1 March 1992, the Government announced that the Treasury Police and National Guard were being converted into Military Police and Frontier Guards, respectively, and this change was duly effected at ceremonies on 2 March. This action elicited negative reactions from many who saw in it more a change of form than the substantive change called for in the Agreement. ONUSAL asked the Government for information on how many members of the two former public security bodies were being transferred to the Army, how many were being assigned to new duties as Military Police or Frontier Guards, and how many were being discharged. While ONUSAL was awaiting this information, the Govern-

ment created further misgivings by securing rapid adoption in the Assembly of legislation that did not clearly abolish the Treasury Police and National Guard. ONUSAL has made it clear to the Government that the law, as adopted, does not comply with the Agreement. The Government has stated that further legislative steps will be taken to abolish the Treasury Police and the National Guard. ONUSAL has asked for clarification of what is intended. This is another matter that has had a negative effect on the atmosphere for implementation of the Agreements as a whole.

18. The preliminary draft legislation on military and armed forces reserve service was submitted to the Legislative Assembly on 7 April. However, some work remains to be done to bring the draft fully into line with the provisions of the Peace Agreement.

19. With regard to the paramilitary bodies mentioned in the Peace Agreement, the civil defence units were registered and located in accordance with the plan presented by the Joint Chiefs of Staff of the Armed Forces. The implementation of the Agreement on this issue has begun and is being verified by ONUSAL. ONUSAL has also requested the Armed Forces of El Salvador to provide details about personnel in the territorial service system, especially the so-called "*escoltas militares*" or "*patrullas cantonales*". Several related deadlines have expired and ONUSAL is awaiting information from the Government in this regard. Similarly, while permits enabling individuals to carry military weapons for private use have been suspended or cancelled, no details are available on how such weapons are to be recalled. That process was to have started on 2 March and is to be completed by 28 October.

20. As regards the reduction of the armed forces, a timetable was submitted by the Government to the Secretary-General who, as stipulated in the Agreement, duly informed FMLN. This reduction process is to be supervised by ONUSAL on the basis of information that is being obtained from the Government.

III. *Public security matters*

21. The creation of a new police force, completely civilian in its membership and command, is one of the fundamental components of the Peace Agreement. Under the Agreement this new force, the National Civil Police, is to replace the three existing public security bodies. As reported above, two of these, the National Guard and the Treasury Police, were to be abolished as public security forces and their members incorporated into the Army, although some doubts have arisen as to the adequacy of the Government's compliance with this provision. The third, the National Police, is to continue to operate during the transitional period but will be progressively replaced by the new National Civil Police. Meanwhile the Na-

tional Police is being closely monitored by the Police Division of ONUSAL.

22. The Division consists mostly of specialists from countries experienced in the organization and operation of civilian police forces. The observers are from Austria, Chile, France, Guyana, Italy, Mexico, Norway, Spain and Sweden, under the command of General Homero Vaz Bresque (Uruguay). The Division currently has 304 of the 631 observers authorized.

23. The deployment of police observers throughout the territory of El Salvador began on 7 February 1992. They are currently deployed among six regional offices and four regional sub-offices, from where they monitor National Police activities through visits and day and night patrols, which average 100 daily. In order to ensure that the National Police functions as the sole body responsible for law and order pending the full deployment of the new National Civil Police and to ensure that the transition from one to the other takes place smoothly, the Division lends its support to the police authorities and accompanies police officials and officers as they discharge their duties.

A. Establishment of the National Civil Police

24. In order to proceed with the organization of the National Civil Police, the President of the Republic, after consulting with FMLN through the United Nations, selected a Coordinator on 28 December 1991. Although this took place ahead of schedule, other measures have been subject to delays of varying durations: on 10 February 1992 (10 days late), COPAZ appointed the eight members of its Subcommission on the National Civil Police; the President of the Republic, choosing from lists submitted by COPAZ, appointed the Director-General and the members of the Academic Council of the new National Academy for Public Security on 20 March (5 days late) and 26 March (11 days late), respectively. The preparation by the Subcommission of the draft laws relating to the Academy and the National Civil Police was also delayed and, whereas the former was adopted by the Legislative Assembly on 2 April 1992, full discussion of the latter by COPAZ is still pending. Since under the Peace Agreement all the members of the National Civil Police must be graduates of the Academy, it is a matter of extreme urgency that the latter begin operating without delay. Another most serious delay has been in the appointment of the Director-General of the National Civil Police, which was supposed to take place by 2 March 1992 but is still awaited. It had originally been envisaged that the Coordinator would be quickly confirmed as Director-General, which would have enabled him to take concrete and effective steps towards the establishment of the National Civil Police and thus avoid the unfortunate delays that have occurred.

25. To assist in the establishment and operation of the Academy during its first two years, a technical mission of experts from Spain and the United States, headed by the UNDP Resident Representative in El Salvador, has been in the country since 3 March 1992. Since the mission operates in the framework of the joint activities of UNDP and the Government of El Salvador for the establishment and operation of the Academy, it has been working with a government team.

26. FMLN has pointed out that, as one of the parties to the Peace Agreement, its views on matters relating to the Academy should also be taken into consideration. ONUSAL and UNDP have now ascertained FMLN's views. They are being transmitted to the Academic Council which is the body overseeing the establishment of the Academy.

27. It is intended that, in the first two years, the Academy will train 5,700 new police officers at the basic level and 240 at the executive and senior levels and that, during the following five years, the corresponding numbers will reach some 10,000 and 500 respectively. This will require a sizeable budget, to which the Governments of Spain and the United States have already expressed their willingness to contribute. The generous financial support of other members of the international community will also be needed.

28. The Government of El Salvador has committed itself to providing premises for the Academy, together with the necessary infrastructure for its operation. The United Nations asked that the Academy should be installed either in the headquarters of the Atlacatl Rapid Deployment Infantry Battalion or in the current Military Academy, which was originally the Academy for Public Security and which was taken over by the Army in December 1991. However, after considerable delays, the Government declined to make either of these sites available and suggested a number of alternatives. Of these, the technical mission has chosen the headquarters of the Bracamonte Rapid Deployment Infantry Battalion, which is to be disbanded under the Peace Agreement. These premises were initially to be made available in late May 1992 but this has been postponed to the end of July 1992. The technical mission has accordingly suggested that the Academy operate provisionally on the premises of the Technical Centre for Police Training, which are to become available in late May, although the latest indications are that it will not be possible to begin tuition until early July. Under this procedure, the Academy would be obliged to reduce the number of recruits from 330 to 270 a month until it can use the Bracamonte premises. From then on, the Technical Centre for Police Training premises would be used exclusively for the training of executive and senior officers. FMLN has expressed strong objec-

tions to this approach. ONUSAL has urged the Government to ensure that the training of police personnel at all levels begin simultaneously. It is still awaiting a response.

29. Disagreement has also arisen over whether former members of the Treasury Police and the National Guard may be admitted to the Academy. The Government maintains that both categories could eventually be eligible provided the personnel concerned were properly discharged and had become civilians. ONUSAL views this position as contrary to the Agreement's concept of a completely new civilian police force which would replace the previous military public security bodies. The Government has given assurances that it will not present former members of the two bodies as candidates in the immediate future.

B. *Transfer of ex-Treasury Police and ex-National Guard personnel to the National Police*

30. It is generally acknowledged that common crime has recently increased in El Salvador and that, following the transfer of the members of the Treasury Police and the National Guard to the Army, the National Police does not have sufficient human and material resources to combat it. On this basis, the Government has transferred large numbers of personnel from the two former public security bodies to the National Police on the grounds that its responsibility for public security gives it no alternative. The Government argues that there is no express prohibition of this in the Agreements. ONUSAL has made it clear that in its view this argument is irreconcilable with the whole thrust of the Agreements, which is to replace the existing public security bodies with a new civilian police force. The first step in this process was precisely the disbanding and abolition of the Treasury Police and the National Guard. To reassign their ex-members to law and order functions thus runs directly counter to the Agreements. ONUSAL has asked for details of the personnel concerned so that it can closely monitor their activities in the National Police.

IV. *Economic and social matters*

A. *Land-tenure system*

31. The complex agrarian problem in El Salvador has deep-seated historical roots that the present report does not attempt to analyse. It has, however, been recognized as one of the main causes of the armed conflict, as a result of which many properties were abandoned and the inhabitants of many rural areas displaced. It is estimated that about half a million persons were displaced persons and approximately 45,000 became refugees. Many of the displaced persons have settled in communities, some of them on abandoned lands. These flows of population, along with other phenomena associated with the war, have altered the pattern of land ownership in the conflict zones.

32. The subject of land was taken up in the New York Agreement of 25 September 1991, and again in the Peace Agreement of 16 January 1992, in which reference is also made to an agreement signed between the Government and peasant organizations on 3 July 1991. The Peace Agreement stipulates that, pending agreement on various issues under this item, the current land-tenure situation will be respected in former conflict zones and landholders will not be evicted. It also assigns to COPAZ the task of verifying the implementation of the provisions relating to these issues through a special commission. The Special Commission, which has the same composition as COPAZ, took up the problem of land tenure in the conflict zones one week later than called for in the implementation timetable. One of the difficulties it faces is that the Peace Agreement does not define the conflict zones.

33. The months of February and early March saw a continuation in the countryside of the tension that had begun there after the signing of the New York Agreement. Various peasant groups seized properties in a number of departments and many were evicted by the public security bodies, in some cases with the support of the armed forces and without a court order. These actions gave rise to insecurity and concern among FMLN combatants who were awaiting concentration at the designated locations. On 15 February, COPAZ appealed to both peasants and landowners to permit the operation of the conflict-resolution mechanisms envisaged in the agreements. This appeal, however, was only partially successful as further occupations took place and landowners initiated lawsuits demanding that their properties be vacated and the institutional framework respected. These developments affected properties in and outside the conflict zones.

34. Subsequent efforts by ONUSAL, on the basis of the appeal made by COPAZ, to freeze the situation with regard to land occupations and evictions were unsuccessful. As this was affecting the atmosphere for the implementation of the agreements as a whole, and at the request of both the Government and FMLN, I sent Mr. Marrack Goulding, Under-Secretary-General for Peacekeeping Operations, to El Salvador to examine with the parties how to restore the necessary climate of trust. In the course of his visit, from 11 to 14 March 1992, Mr. Goulding and Mr. Riza had several meetings with the President of the Republic and his advisers and with the General Command of FMLN. At a final joint meeting on 13 March it was agreed that land seizures and evictions would be suspended in order to facilitate the processing of the cases submitted to the Special Commission of COPAZ. In addition, consultation mechanisms were es-

tablished between the Government and FMLN, with the good offices of ONUSAL, to devise pragmatic solutions to these cases. These mechanisms are working, and it is to be hoped that the goodwill expressed by both parties at recent high-level joint meetings convened under the good offices of ONUSAL will be translated into an early solution of this problem.

B. *Forum for Economic and Social Consultation*

35. The convening of the Forum for Economic and Social Consultation had been scheduled for 15 February. To that end, COPAZ invited the leaders of the most representative business and labour organizations to participate in a discussion, *inter alia*, on the composition and organization of the Forum.

36. During the meetings which, owing to the very full COPAZ schedule, did not begin until 26 February, the business representatives publicly expressed their concern with what they described as the climate of insecurity resulting from land seizures and labour conflicts. On 23 March, at a meeting of the World Bank Advisory Group in Washington, in which representatives of the Government, FMLN and the political parties participated, the Director of the National Private Enterprise Association indicated that he would participate in the Forum, which COPAZ then convened for 11 May. Subsequently, however, the National Private Enterprise Association informed COPAZ that it would postpone its participation. Given the Forum's responsibilities under the Agreement for securing agreements on the economic and social development of the country, the prompt and full participation of all sectors is essential.

C. *National reconstruction plan*

37. The Government submitted the national reconstruction plan to FMLN on time, for its suggestions. In addition to projects for the rebuilding of infrastructure in the municipalities affected by the conflict and for production schemes, agreement was reached on making funds available for the strengthening of the democratic institutions provided for in the Agreement and for technical assistance. In order to obtain the additional funds needed for its implementation, the plan was presented at the meeting of the World Bank Advisory Group referred to above and received a positive response from the international community. Despite reservations in certain sectors, the implementation of a small number of projects has begun with the Government's own resources, pending the receipt of the external assistance that has been pledged. The Government has said that, for the plan to become fully operational, public administration must be restored in the conflict zones.

38. Another important aspect is the formulation of programmes to promote the reintegration of ex-combat-
ants of both sides into civilian life. The delay in establishing such programmes is cited by FMLN as another factor in its decision to postpone the reintegration of the first contingent of its combat personnel.

V. *Political participation by FMLN*

39. On 23 January 1992, the Legislative Assembly of El Salvador adopted a law on national reconciliation granting amnesty for political crimes and offences under ordinary law, with the exception of cases within the purview of the Commission on the Truth or those committed by individuals already convicted in a jury trial. The measure applies to FMLN leaders who are members of COPAZ, as well as those who are members of other bodies dealing with the implementation of the Agreements. Also amnestied are non-combatant members of FMLN, war-wounded persons living outside the country and those detained for political offences. The amnesty does not extend to those members of FMLN who, under the Peace Agreement, have been temporarily concentrated with their arms, at designated locations. The law does provide, however, that any criminal or civil action against such individuals for acts covered by the amnesty shall be suspended.

40. The adoption of the law on reconciliation has enabled the members of the General Command and other FMLN leaders to re-enter El Salvador legally. Since their return, they have had freedom of movement and ample access to the mass media, and they have obtained licences for two radio stations and one television channel. On 1 February, the FMLN representatives in the recently formed COPAZ swore allegiance to the Constitution together with the other members of that body. Political detainees have been released, with the exceptions provided for in the law on national reconciliation.

41. The returning FMLN leaders, their safety guaranteed by the Government, were accompanied during the first few days by members of the National Police and were allowed, under the terms of the Agreement, to make arrangements for personal bodyguards. The support of the representatives in El Salvador of the four "Friends of the Secretary-General" in this process was of great importance, as was the assistance provided by several other Governments, notably those of Brazil, Chile, France, Nicaragua and the United Kingdom of Great Britain and Northern Ireland. Some problems have nevertheless arisen over various aspects of the security of FMLN leaders. Efforts are being made by ONUSAL with the government authorities to streamline the relevant procedures. At the same time, COPAZ is examining this question and has stated its intention to promote the legislative or other steps that may be necessary.

42. According to the Peace Agreement, the Govern-

ment was to have promoted a decree for the legalization of FMLN as a political party in the Legislative Assembly starting on 1 May 1992. The Government has informed ONUSAL that, rather than present a draft decree—which, in its view, would provoke a strong debate—it needed to prepare the ground to ensure a consensus in the Assembly. It has since contacted various political parties to that effect.

43. Prior to 1 May 1992, ONUSAL had taken up with FMLN occasional complaints by the Government that FMLN was violating the Agreement by setting up offices at various locations and by other political activities by its leaders and other personnel, especially ex-combatants concentrated in the designated locations. Since 1 May 1992, however, the Government has indicated that, while the process of legalization is proceeding, FMLN can take steps to organize itself as a party. For its part, FMLN urges quick action by the Government, arguing that until it is legalized it will be hindered in its political activities. Nevertheless, a rally by FMLN to launch itself as a political party took place without incident on 23 May 1992.

44. The Government has shown its willingness to facilitate the return of the war-wounded currently outside the country through the Office of the United Nations High Commissioner for Refugees (UNHCR). Among those expected to return are a number of individuals living in Cuba, whose repatriation has been delayed because Cuba and El Salvador do not have diplomatic relations. UNHCR is attempting to solve the problem with the cooperation of a third country acting as intermediary.

VI. *Restoration of public administration in conflict zones*

45. Following the entry into force of the cease-fire agreement, restoration of public administration in conflict zones began gradually, in most cases in consultation with ONUSAL, at a pace that varied from region to region. In some locations, judges and mayors returned without any difficulty, although some are now facing problems in carrying out their functions as a result of inadequate infrastructure or lack of support and cooperation from the community and NGOs. In other locations, judges and mayors have been unable to return because of opposition from FMLN, the community and NGOs and the absence of communication with such groups which is necessary to facilitate the restoration process. Sixty-eight of the 262 mayors elected in El Salvador in 1991 had been forced by the conflict to operate away from their municipalities; some 24 of them have now returned.

46. ONUSAL is convinced that the return of judges and mayors and their effective functioning can succeed only in a context of open dialogue between local authorities and the bodies that performed the functions of local government during the armed conflict. Not only will such dialogue guarantee peace and reconciliation in the zones most severely affected by the armed conflict, but it will permit local consultation mechanisms to revive and ensure broad community participation in municipal government, without adversely affecting the institutional framework. ONUSAL has called upon the parties to show the greatest possible flexibility and is working at the regional level to promote a consensus in the various locations affected.

VII. *Judicial system*

47. The measures provided in the Peace Agreement concerning this subject and their implementation according to the agreed timetable will be discussed in future reports of the ONUSAL Human Rights Division, in keeping with the mandate given to it by the San José Agreement to "offer its support to the judicial authorities of El Salvador in order to help improve the judicial procedures for the protection of human rights and increase respect for the rules of due process of law". 7/

48. Meanwhile COPAZ and the Legislative Assembly have approved, prior to the prescribed date, the law establishing the Office of the National Counsel for the Defence of Human Rights. The Counsel has been appointed, but his office is not yet fully functional owing to the fact that the budget has only recently been approved. In addition to the resources provided by the Government of El Salvador, it is hoped that additional financial assistance will be made available by Governments and international bodies.

VIII. *Electoral system*

49. As stipulated in the Mexico Agreements of 27 April 1991, 8/ COPAZ appointed a Special Commission on this issue, which will study the preliminary draft amendments to the Electoral Code. Subsequently, the Legislative Assembly appointed, with some delay, the Supreme Electoral Tribunal, which will have as its main task the preparation of the 1994 legislative and presidential elections.

IX. *Financial aspects*

50. The General Assembly by its resolution 46/240 of 22 May 1992 appropriated an amount of $39 million gross ($37 million net) for the operation of ONUSAL for the period from 1 January to 31 October 1992. This appropriation includes provision for the expanded mandate of ONUSAL based on Security Council resolution 729 (1992).

51. As at 26 May 1992, unpaid assessed contributions to the ONUSAL special account for the first six

7/ S/21541, annex, para. 14 (h).
8/ S/23130, annex.

months from 1 July to 31 December 1991 amounted to $1.98 million.

X. *Observations*

52. The agreements that the Government and FMLN signed, under the auspices of the United Nations, between 4 April 1990 and 16 January 1992, established the framework for implementation of the political understandings between them. The goal is to end 12 years of civil conflict, consolidate peace in El Salvador and return to a normal political process, which should culminate in 1994 in free and fair elections with broad participation. This process is not an easy one. The agreements are complex and demand a commitment to compromise and fundamental adjustments in political and social attitudes. Nor are they self-executing. The United Nations is committed to assist the two parties but success will be assured only by their political will and their acceptance of national reconciliation as the overriding national goal.

53. The Government and FMLN are to be commended for their success in maintaining the cease-fire, which has not once been broken. Nor has there been any major incident to threaten this fragile first phase of national reconciliation. There have, however, been some serious delays in implementing various provisions of the agreements and these have undermined each side's confidence in the other's good faith.

54. I am particularly concerned by the continuing failure of both sides to concentrate all their forces in the designated locations, which was supposed to have been completed by 2 March 1992, i.e. almost three months ago. On the Government's side, substantial numbers of armed personnel are still outside the designated locations at the headquarters of the former National Guard and Treasury Police. FMLN's failure to concentrate its remaining forces is equally unacceptable. It is essential that both parties comply, independently and without further delay, with their respective obligations. I have also expressed to FMLN my doubts about whether the inventories of arms that it has presented to ONUSAL accurately reflect its true holdings. Suspicions that FMLN is retaining clandestine caches of arms and ammunition have had a destabilizing effect on the whole implementation process.

55. Other sources of serious concern are the Government's failure to establish the National Public Security Academy and begin recruitment for the National Civil Police on the programmed date of 1 May 1992 and FMLN's failure, on the same date, to return the first 20 per cent of its combatants to civilian life. 1 May 1992 was also the date on which the Government was supposed to begin promoting legislation to legalize FMLN as a political party. ONUSAL has from the outset taken the position that one breach of the agreements cannot be used to justify another. It cannot, however, be ignored that the timetable for implementation, contained in chapter IX of the Peace Agreement, does not constitute a haphazard sequence of actions that can easily be altered. It is, on the contrary, an intricately designed and carefully negotiated mechanism whose purpose is to synchronize (a) the reintegration of FMLN's ex-combatants into civilian life and (b) the measures that the Government has committed itself to undertake in order to facilitate that process, especially as regards agriculture, political activity and recruitment into the National Civil Police. It is for this reason that the delays that have occurred on these latter issues arouse such serious concern.

56. In other cases implementation has been impeded by the two parties' contradictory interpretations of specific provisions in the agreements. This has sometimes led them to exchange public accusations rather than working together, with the good offices of ONUSAL, to find practical and pragmatic ways of putting the agreements into effect by honouring their spirit rather than insisting on legalistic interpretations of their letter. This has been a particular problem in relation to land tenure, which was one of the main roots of the conflict. Notwithstanding the role assigned to COPAZ by the agreements, which COPAZ has not been able to discharge in full, ONUSAL has, at the request of the parties, used its good offices to help the two sides to tackle the land issue in a constructive spirit at the highest level. I am grateful to both sides for honouring the commitments they gave in March to halt occupations of, and evictions from, lands while a pragmatic solution is sought to this problem.

57. There are other issues on which a similarly restrained and pragmatic search for solutions is needed. These include the restoration of public administration in zones of former conflict and certain questions relating to the former Treasury Police and National Guard. It was agreed in the negotiations that these two bodies would be dissolved and would exercise no further public security functions. Their personnel, after being transferred to the Armed Forces, were to be included in the reduction of those forces. As already stated in this report, the manner in which these two bodies were dissolved and the subsequent induction of some of their ex-members into the National Police have raised serious questions about whether the Government has complied with the agreements on these points.

58. The present report gives an idea of the complex, varied and delicate nature of the verification tasks entrusted to ONUSAL. In addition to its specific verification responsibilities, ONUSAL is also exercising its good offices to help the parties to implement the agreements. In these endeavours, it receives valuable support from the four "Friends of the Secretary-General", as well as others who are in a position to help.

59. ONUSAL is operating in an atmosphere of deep distrust, which may be an inevitable consequence of a long and bitter conflict. Its insistence on maintaining its impartiality is sometimes misperceived by each side as being partiality towards the other. In this context, I regret to have to report to the Security Council that there has recently been a recurrence of threats against the security of the Mission and its personnel. 9/ The Salvadorian authorities have been informed and I am confident that they will succeed in identifying the authors of these threats, which until now have been anonymous, and in preventing any hostile acts against the Mission's personnel.

60. In telephone conversations on 15 May 1992, after I had reviewed a first draft of the present report, I spoke to President Cristiani of El Salvador and to Mr. Schafik Handal of the General Command of FMLN about my concerns at both sides' failure to comply fully with the timetable established by the agreements, making special reference to the points mentioned in the preceding paragraphs. President Cristiani told me that the two sides were meeting regularly in order to establish a timetable for recovering the time lost. He gave me an assurance that everything that had been delayed would be put back on track and described various steps he had taken to that end. Mr. Handal also spoke of the meetings between the two sides to set new deadlines for implementation of various points in the agreements. He said that FMLN's admitted failures to comply with the existing timetable were due to the Government's non-compliance with many of its commitments. FMLN would have no problem in complying with the timetable, without waiting for the Government to do so, if it was given assurances that third parties would ensure that the Government also would comply. Mr. Handal assured me that FMLN was participating seriously in the meetings with the Government; it wanted to adhere to the existing agreements and not renegotiate them. I assured both my interlocutors of my steadfast support for the agreements and my readiness to do all I could to help both sides to implement them. I said that I would refer in this report to what they had said and looked forward to being able to state in the next report that the process was indeed back on course.

61. In conclusion, I should like to pay tribute to my Special Representative, Mr. Iqbal Riza, and to all the personnel of ONUSAL who, under his leadership, are tackling with perseverance and courage the difficult but noble task of helping to establish a just and lasting peace in El Salvador.

9/ S/22494, para. 6.

Document 42

Statement by the President of the Security Council urging both parties to implement the peace agreements

S/24058, 3 June 1992

The members of the Security Council have taken note of the report of the Secretary-General of 26 May 1992 and 12 June 1992 on the United Nations Observer Mission in El Salvador. 1/

The members of the Council are pleased that the cease-fire is holding and there has not been a single violation since it came into force on 1 February 1992.

However, the members of the Council are deeply concerned about the many delays by both parties in implementing agreements concluded between the Government of El Salvador and the Frente Farabundo Martí para la Liberación Nacional and the climate of mutual suspicion that still remains. If that situation were to continue, it would jeopardize the very foundation of the agreements.

The members of the Council urge both parties to demonstrate good faith in implementing the agreements fully, to abide by the agreed time-limits, to exert every effort to bring about national reconciliation in El Salvador and to implement the process of demobilization and reform.

The members of the Council reaffirm their full support for the efforts made by the Secretary-General and his Special Representative for El Salvador, with the assistance of the Governments of the Groups of Friends of the Secretary-General and other Governments concerned. They commend the staff of the Mission, who are working under very difficult conditions, and express their concern about the threats to their safety. They remind the parties of their obligation to take all necessary measures to guarantee the safety of the Mission and its members.

The members of the Council will continue to monitor closely developments in the implementation of the peace agreements in El Salvador.

1/ S/23999 and Add.1.

Document 43

Report of the ONUSAL Human Rights Division for the period from 1 January to 30 April 1992 (extract)

A/46/935-S/24066, 5 June 1992

Introduction

1. This report covers the period from 1 January to 30 April 1992 and has been prepared in accordance with the mandate entrusted to the Human Rights Verification Mission by the San José Agreement (para. 14 (l)). The Peace Agreement signed on 16 January (A/46/864-S/23501) and the actual cessation of hostilities on 1 February brought about a major change in the activities of the ONUSAL Human Rights Division. Difficulties directly linked to the armed conflict have gradually disappeared. The cease-fire has been fully observed, and in principle no civilian or military casualties have been recorded, with the exception of the incidents that are being investigated, which are reported on in the chapter on cases and situations relating to international humanitarian law. Irregular recruitment, by either the Armed Forces or the Frente Farabundo Martí para la Liberación Nacional (FMLN), has gradually ceased. Freedom of movement, which was the subject of numerous complaints up until 16 January 1992, has been completely restored.

2. As a result of the new situation the number of complaints has declined, particularly in what were the conflict zones. a/ However, the overall picture still gives rise to concern: summary executions and violent deaths—above all in the Departments of San Salvador, La Libertad and Santa Ana—have continued after the cease-fire, and no effective action has been taken to put an end to them, investigate them or punish the perpetrators. Moreover, there has been a recurrence of the threats against certain non-governmental organizations (NGOs), trade unions, churches and political leaders; even though clandestine organized groups are still active, no measures are being taken to prevent them from carrying out their activities or to clarify the situation. Violations of the right to life, as well as death threats, were a fundamental cause for concern referred to by the Mission in its second and third reports (A/46/658-S/23222 and Corr.1 and A/46/876-S/23580), in which specific recommendations were made to the authorities, concerning both the incidents in question and the State's duty of prevention and investigation. Unfortunately, those recommendations have as yet not been heeded in the manner prescribed in the San José Agreement (para. 15 (d)). Another source of concern was that Maj. José Alfredo Jiménez Moreno escaped from the

facilities of the new Military Police. This incident was reported on 7 April 1992, the day before he was sentenced to 30 years' imprisonment for abducting five prominent businessmen, and it was regarded as a sign of the continuing impunity of perpetrators and the complicity that makes such impunity possible, particularly in the military institutions. The Mission recently addressed a letter to the Ministry of Defence on this incident.

3. Forty-two individuals were released under the National Reconciliation Act of 23 January 1992, under which amnesty is granted to perpetrators of political crimes and related ordinary offences and which is designed to facilitate the progressive reintegration of FMLN members into political and civilian life. That measure means that the provision of the San José Agreement on the release of individuals who have been imprisoned for political reasons (para. 3) is being implemented. Moreover, the Legislative Assembly has enacted two laws to ensure that citizens affected by the armed conflict are provided with identity documents, a step that is required in order to solve the serious problem of personal documentation as required by the San José Agreement (paras. 7 and 8).

4. Furthermore, the organic law on the Office of the National Counsel for the Defence of Human Rights was enacted on 20 February and the National Counsel was appointed on 27 February. The Counsel, who is to perform a very important role, was granted a budget far lower than that requested and has as yet been unable to start his activities. The National Council of the Judiciary Act, which according to the Peace Agreement was to be made public not later than 1 April 1992, has not yet been presented.

5. The Mexico Agreements of 27 April 1991, reaffirmed by the Peace Agreement of 16 January 1992, provide for a major reform of the judicial system, which has been adopted by the Legislative Assembly and has now been incorporated in the Constitution of the Republic. The judiciary receives an allocation from the State budget amounting to no less than 6 per cent of current income. The minimum eligibility requirements for Justice of the Peace are being changed, and it is now necessary

a/ The number of complaints received by the Mission from January to March 1992 declined by 19.7 per cent as compared with October-December 1991. The decline was even more drastic with regard to complaints of violations of international humanitarian law—as much as 79.1 per cent. Complaints of irregular recruitments dropped by 58.7 per cent.

to be a counsel of the Republic and of established competence to qualify. A career judicial service has been set up, and there is now a new method of appointing judges to the Supreme Court of Justice. Judges of the Courts of Second Instance and of the Courts of First Instance and Justices of the Peace, who are now integrated into the career judicial service, will enjoy stability and independence in performing their duties. Magistrates or Judges cannot serve as lawyers or as officials of other State organs. Important functions have been assigned to the National Council of the Judiciary.

6. The Attorney-General of the Republic has been given new powers: to conduct the investigation of crimes, through a body whose attributes are to be prescribed by law, without prejudice to the independence of judges in investigating the facts. A change has also been made in military jurisdiction: the special military courts no longer can exercise jurisdiction in the event of a state of emergency. Military courts will now be confined to trying crimes and minor offences committed while on duty of a purely military nature perpetrated by members of the Armed Forces in active service.

7. On 17 March 1992 at the Court of First Instance at Chinameca, Department of San Miguel, the Mission witnessed the handing over of two FMLN combatants allegedly implicated in the death of the two United States advisers David Pickett and Earnest Dawson in January 1991. ONUSAL will follow this trial closely. With regard to the case concerning the El Mozote incidents, the reader is referred to the relevant comments made in the third report, particularly those concerning the need to examine skeletal remains using appropriate anthropological techniques, and the desirability of calling in international experts in the field to assist in the investigations.

8. This report will concentrate chiefly on two topics. Firstly, it will deal with the right to life and to integrity and security of person (San José Agreement, para. 11), with special reference to the investigation of deaths due to other than natural causes. It will then consider the issue of due process of law (San José Agreement, paras. 11 and 14 (h)), in order to identify crucial issues relating to the administration of criminal justice regarded as being of high priority as a result of the verification activities carried out by the Mission. The two topics are interrelated, since criminal investigations, even at the pre-trial stage, are closely linked to criminal procedure. Those questions will be given special treatment because this report is an introduction to one of the Mission's priority tasks at the next stage, namely, to "help improve the judicial procedures for the protection of human rights and increase respect for the rules of due process of law" (San José Agreement, para. 14 (h)). This report will also deal with the issue of identity documents (San José Agreement, paras. 7 and 8) and with cases and situations relating to humanitarian international law now that the armed conflict has ceased.

...

IV. *Conclusions*

44. The problems of the criminal justice system have many causes, some inherent in its structure and others resulting from the past and linked, in particular, to the internal armed conflict in El Salvador. An example of the latter is the large number of judges, known as "judges in exile", who have not been able to perform their functions in conflict zones, in nine of the 14 Departments of El Salvador. It is clear that the criminal justice system as a whole should be completely overhauled as part of a broader reform of the administration of justice, its auxiliary bodies, the Chief State Counsel's office and the function of defence lawyers. This process may be prepared through gradual reforms which, although partial, must be systematic, and which depend, for their success, on consensus and social participation. The initiatives developed in this respect in the Ministry of Justice are positive and should be encouraged as necessary steps towards far-reaching reform of the judicial system and, in particular, of the criminal justice system. In this context, all the social sectors have a specific role to play, but some are pivotal for the process of change. That is the case of the mass communications media, which to a large extent can promote or fail to promote the process of criminal justice reforms during the transitional stage.

45. The problems discussed in this report represent challenges which require not only legislative solutions, but political and institutional responses, not only from the State but from the citizenry as a whole. The flaws in the judicial system, demonstrated chiefly by its inability to investigate violent deaths, the selectivity of the criminal justice system and delays in sentencing, cannot be remedied without basic reforms which must be made sooner or later and require painstaking campaigns of discussion and explanation. Only then will it be time to cope with structural defects, such as those which now exist. One example of those defects, organic in nature, is that the examining magistrate who investigates the facts of the case is at the same time the presiding judge who directs the proceedings and passes sentence. There will be no basic solution unless the independence and impartiality of the judiciary is upheld, and there is an increase in the number of judges, as well as an improvement in their training and of the human and material resources that support their work. In this respect, the Agreement on Peace and Constitutional Reform referred to earlier has laid the basis for the necessary changes. Education concerning the law and the legal system is an important factor

in creating an awareness of the urgent need for the changes required in the existing criminal justice system. In order to strengthen this aspect of the protection and promotion of human rights, the Mission will make specific recommendations in this first report in which it has considered in more detail the problems of due process of law, in fulfilment of the mandate conferred on it by the San José Agreement (paras. 11 and 14 (h)).

V. *Recommendations*

46. In this section the Mission makes recommendations to the parties based on the conclusions drawn from the cases or situations it has reviewed (San José Agreement, para. 14 (g)). The parties have undertaken to give their earliest consideration to any recommendations made to them by the Mission (San José Agreement, para. 15 (d)).

A. *Right to life and to security and integrity of person*

Investigation of the facts

47. The Mission reiterates the recommendations contained in its second and third reports (para. 150 and paras. 154 and 155 respectively) and calls on the Government of El Salvador, the Office of the Attorney-General of the Republic and the Judiciary to take decisive and firm measures for the prevention and investigation of violations of the right to life and to security and integrity of person. The National Police should be provided with the necessary material resources to carry out its functions and ensure that it maintains professional standards in carrying out proper investigations. Judges should use the powers of investigation accorded under the law and improve coordination with the National Police. Judges of the first instance should personally conduct the investigations in cases that have given rise to serious social unrest and in particular to encroachments on the right to life. The autonomy and independence of the Chief State Counsel's Office should be strengthened. Prosecutors should play an active role in initiating proceedings and investigating crimes, and the Attorney-General of the Republic should use all the powers available to him under the judicial system, including that of appointing special commissions (Constitution, art. 193 (7)), which could be done selectively to clear up relevant cases. m/ Prosecutors should take into account the United Nations Guidelines on the Role of Prosecutors and, in particular, those concerning prosecutors in criminal cases. Furthermore, a register of victims of deaths from other than natural causes could be established.

B. *Right to due process of law*

1. *Extrajudicial confessions*

48. Until a measure such as a draft law prohibiting extrajudicial confession is approved, the duration of any interrogation of a detained or imprisoned person and of the intervals between interrogations as well as the identity of the officials who conducted the interrogations and other persons present should be recorded and legally certified. A detained or imprisoned person, or his counsel, must have access to that information in accordance with the Body of Principles for the Protection of All Persons under Any Form of Detention or Imprisonment adopted by the General Assembly in resolution 43/173 of 9 December 1988 (*Principle 23*). Furthermore, the principles invalidating statements made in an atmosphere of intimidation, or under any form of coercion, must be observed. In particular, acts of psychological coercion or classic coercion (torture and other cruel, inhuman or degrading treatment or punishment) during interrogation must be severely punished. In addition to the provisions of domestic law and of international treaties ratified by El Salvador, the recommendations contained in the Body of Principles cited above and of the Code of Conduct for Law Enforcement Officials should be taken into account.

2. *Administrative detention*

49. The police should hold accused persons in administrative detention for a maximum of 72 hours only where the gravity of the charge and the difficulties of the investigation make this strictly necessary. Under no circumstances should this period be exceeded. Courts should monitor the administrative detention of accused persons from the moment of their detention. Courts of first instance should undertake such monitoring in all cases in which the circumstances of the crime or the position of the accused or of the victims have provoked social unrest. Courts should exercise more rigorous supervision over places of administrative detention, through regular visits and inspection of the records. Also, through legislative reform such as that proposed in the bill prepared by the Ministry of Justice, efforts should be made to reduce the maximum period of administrative detention to a reasonable length.

3. *Incommunicado detention*

50. The commitment given in the San José Agreement concerning the prohibition of incommunicado detention must be scrupulously respected. There should be no derogation from this principle nor can it be modified by the application of disciplinary measures in prison or during pre-trial detention. Any person deprived of his freedom should therefore be allowed, from the very beginning of his detention, to communicate, especially with his family, relatives and counsel and with humanitarian

m/ Guidelines on the Role of Prosecutors adopted by the Eighth United Nations Congress on the Prevention of Crime and the Treatment of Offenders held at Havana, Cuba, from 27 August to 7 September 1990 (A/CONF.144/28).

organizations. In this connection, the Mission recommends that a study be undertaken of legislative reform that would explicitly incorporate this guarantee in the Code of Criminal Procedure.

4. The right to legal counsel

51. Without prejudice to the application of the new legal norms governing legal assistance and public defenders, upon the entry into force of those norms, the competent authorities should effectively advise any person, whether or not detained, against whom an investigation by the auxiliary organs of justice is being initiated of his right to appoint legal counsel. The accused should be advised of this right from the moment he is charged. Any person arrested or detained, on a criminal or other charge, shall be guaranteed access to counsel immediately and in all cases within 48 hours of his arrest or detention, in accordance with the basic principles on the role of lawyers (*Principle* 7). n/ A special effort should also be made to train public defenders.

5. Pre-trial detention

52. A person may be subject to pre-trial detention only where such detention is necessary to ensure his presence at the trial or to prevent any obstacles being placed in the way of the investigation. Courts should use the maximum term of 72 hours for their investigations (art. 244 of the Code of Criminal Procedure) only where the gravity of the offence and the difficulties of the investigation render this strictly necessary. The rules governing the length of pre-trial detention set forth in paragraph 37 of this report should be respected and a legal provision should be adopted establishing procedures for automatic release based on the above-mentioned rules, when the emergency law to resolve the problem of untried detainees ceases to have force.

6. Delay in the administration of justice

53. A special effort should be made to observe the time-limits prescribed by law for concluding the pre-trial proceedings in criminal cases and to ensure that those proceedings in no case exceed what may be considered a reasonable period. Also, the delays provided for the trial itself from its commencement to the rendering of the judgement and notification of a final sentence should be respected. In order to promote respect for the right to be tried without undue delay, the Mission recommends that the organization of the administration of justice and of the Office of the Chief State Counsel should be strengthened by implementing the judicial system reforms that have been incorporated into the Constitution of the Republic as a result of the signing of the Peace Agreement.

C. National Counsel for the Defence of Human Rights

54. The financial and capital resources provided for in the law establishing the National Counsel for the Defence of Human Rights must be made available, particularly the contributions and grants made by the Central Government, and steps must be taken to ensure the transfer of the funds necessary for the start-up operations of this new institution.

D. Identity documents

55. The central authorities and local bodies must assist mayors in applying the new laws in this field, as well as all the other procedures for the documentation of personal identity. Such assistance should include clear and consistent instructions to municipalities on the application of the new norms in conformity with the principles of equality before the law and non-discrimination. The process of documentation must be completed in the shortest possible period to facilitate the full reintegration of the persons concerned into national life.

E. Respect for international humanitarian law

56. The Mission recommends that the parties, during the entire period of cessation of armed conflict, should strictly observe the norms of article 3 which are common to the four Geneva Conventions of 12 August 1949 and to Additional Protocol II o/ to those Conventions, particularly with regard to the fundamental guarantees concerning the treatment of human beings and the protection of civilian populations.

F. Follow-up to recommendations

57. On 7 January 1992, the Mission sent notes to both the Government of El Salvador and FMLN seeking to ascertain the manner in which the recommendations contained in its second report (paras. 146 and ff.) were being followed. The notes included a reminder of the thrust of those recommendations. FMLN, on 27 April 1992, sent a letter in reply to the note of the Mission. The Government of El Salvador has not yet responded to the Mission's request.

n/ Basic Principles on the Role of Lawyers adopted by the Eighth United Nations Congress on the Prevention of Crime and the Treatment of Offenders (op. cit.).
o/ *United Nations Treaty Series*, vol. 75, Nos. 970-973 and ibid., vol. 1125, No. 17513.

Document 44

Report of the Secretary-General on the rescheduled timetable for implementation of the Peace Agreement

S/23999/Add.1, 19 June 1992

Addendum

1. In my report of 26 May 1992 (S/23999, para. 60), I informed the Security Council of my conversations earlier that month with President Cristiani and Mr. Handal of the General Command of the Frente Farabundo Martí para la Liberación Nacional (FMLN) about my concerns at both sides' failure to comply fully with the timetable established by the Peace Agreement of 16 January 1992. 1/ As I reported to the Council, both had assured me that they were making efforts to bring back on course the process of implementing the agreements signed by them.

2. It is my pleasure to report to the Security Council that, in discussions conducted in recent days with the assistance of the good offices of the United Nations Observer Mission in El Salvador (ONUSAL), both parties have now resolved the issues that had delayed the implementation process. Certain of the dates mentioned in the implementation timetable of the Peace Agreement, which had not been complied with, have been readjusted, in accordance with the provisions of the timetable itself.

3. These arrangements, which were finalized on 12 June 1992, provide for the completion of the following steps, envisaged in the Peace Agreement, on the rescheduled dates indicated:

(a) By 25 June, the forces of both sides will have been fully concentrated at the locations designated for them;

(b) By 30 June, the first contingent of former FMLN combatants will commence their reintegration into civilian life. The reintegration process of all former FMLN combatants will be completed by 31 October 1992, as provided for in the timetable;

(c) Within 15 days after 30 June, the National Academy for Public Security will commence its first course for training recruits for the new National Civil Police, including personnel from the present National Police and former FMLN combatants in agreed proportions;

(d) By 30 June, the Government will present to the Legislative Assembly a bill for the definitive abolition of the National Guard and Treasury Police and will establish a "Special Brigade for Military Security" which will consist of a unit for frontier protection duties and a unit for military police duties. The Special Brigade will have no public security responsibilities in the civilian sphere. Personnel of the former National Guard and Treasury Police will not be eligible for recruitment into the new National Civil Police and there will be no further transfers of such personnel into the present National Police;

(e) By 30 June, the Government will propose to the Legislative Assembly reforms to the Electoral Code in order to facilitate the legalization of FMLN as a political party;

(f) By 15 July, the Government will finalize programmes to facilitate the reintegration of the former FMLN combatants into civilian life, providing contingency plans to benefit those who reintegrate before that date;

(g) By 30 June, the verification of the inventory of lands presented by FMLN to the National Commission for the Consolidation of Peace (COPAZ) will commence, certain properties being given priority owing to their being subject to legal process.

4. I should like to express to the Government of El Salvador and to the leadership of FMLN my profound satisfaction at the constructive spirit in which they have resolved the impasse that was holding up progress in the implementation of the Peace Agreement. I am confident that they will continue to demonstrate the same positive and pragmatic approach in the implementation of their remaining commitments under the Agreement.

1/ S/23501, annex.

Document 45

Report of the ONUSAL Human Rights Division for the period from 1 May to 30 June 1992 (extract)

A/46/955-S/24375, 12 August 1992

I. *Introduction*

1. In signing the Geneva Agreement on 4 April 1990, the Government of El Salvador and the Frente Farabundo Martí para la Liberación Nacional (FMLN) expressed their shared aim of guaranteeing "unrestricted respect for human rights" in El Salvador, thereby demonstrating their clear intention of ending the human rights violations which for more than a decade had been a cause of major concern to the international community, particularly the United Nations and the Organization of American States.

2. The signing of the San José Agreement on Human Rights (A/44/971-S/21541, annex) on 26 July 1990 reaffirmed the desire of the parties to agree on immediate measures for the protection of fundamental rights and freedoms and to allow international verification of their observance. On 26 July 1991, the first anniversary of the San José Agreement, the United Nations human rights verification mission was established with a mandate to "investigate the human rights situation in El Salvador as regards acts committed or situations existing as from the date of its establishment and to take any steps it deems appropriate to promote and defend such rights" (sect. II, para. 13 of the Agreement).

3. Under the San José Agreement, the Mission was to take up its duties as of the cessation of the armed conflict. At the request of the parties, the Security Council decided by its resolution 693 (1991) of 20 May 1991 to establish the Mission as soon as possible. Its mandate included wide-ranging powers unprecedented in the history of the United Nations. As was recognized from the outset, the fact that ONUSAL was established before the end of the armed conflict made its verification duties even more complex.

4. The commitment by the parties immediately to take all necessary steps to avoid any act or practice which constituted an attempt upon the life, integrity, security or freedom of the individual demonstrated a clear awareness of the gravity of the situation. Both the history of recent decades and the persistence of internal armed conflict over a period of more than 10 years have resulted in a deeply ingrained climate of violence in El Salvador, which has undermined certain institutions and generated widespread social intolerance and general scepticism towards the law. The peace agreements undoubtedly express the willingness of the parties and of the people of El Salvador

to embark on a new phase in their history, although it must be recognized that it is not possible in the space of a few months to eliminate the consequences of a turbulent past, where social tensions were resolved by confrontation and conflict rather than through dialogue and cooperation.

5. Now that the Mission's initial mandate has ended, this report is intended to provide an assessment of the situation regarding those human rights whose verification was given priority in the San José Agreement, taking as a starting point the situation in El Salvador in July 1991 and highlighting the course of current trends. It will examine the extent to which essential human rights and international humanitarian law have been respected and safeguarded through the verification duties undertaken by ONUSAL, the analysis of the statistical trends, the human rights education and promotion campaigns, the recommendations put forward, the replies of the parties and the prospects for the immediate future.

6. In performing his international verification duties, the Director of the Human Rights Division paid special attention to the valuable work done by existing organizations for the protection and promotion of human rights in El Salvador, in accordance with the provisions of the San José Agreement (para. 12). In this connection, he attached particular weight to the reports and analyses provided by these organizations on the development of the human rights situation in the country following the establishment of the Mission, and to the Mission's own work in this area.

7. ONUSAL fulfilled the preventive role assigned to it, and the civilian population gradually gained confidence in the protection afforded by the Mission. The parties themselves realized that the Mission's verification of the observance of human rights and its power to visit any place or establishment without prior notice meant that they must redouble their efforts to comply with the undertakings given in the San José Agreement.

8. Following the cease-fire, breaches of international humanitarian law were kept to a minimum and substantial improvements were recorded with regard to certain rights. However, some traces of violent behaviour continue to persist. Despite the commendable efforts of broad sectors of the population to create a climate of tolerance and *détente*, there are still instances of unwarranted use of force or firearms and threats of violence and

intimidation, while the behaviour of a significant minority remains incompatible with progress towards lasting social peace. The challenge currently facing the Mission is, within the limits of its mandate, to help encourage the far-reaching changes vital if peace is to be consolidated and a culture of reconciliation and human rights established.

9. Now that the direct consequences of the armed conflict are receding, the main guarantor of human rights is the State, in compliance with the undertakings it has given at national and international level. All sectors of society, including FMLN, must help to create the conditions necessary to ensure that human rights are respected and guaranteed, since this is an essential part of a modern State governed by the rule of law and is vital to the building of a lasting peace.

...

VI. Recommendations

89. The Mission's mandate included the power to make recommendations to the parties on the basis of any conclusions it had reached with respect to cases or situations it might have been called upon to consider (San José Agreement, para. 14 (g)). Such recommendations have been contained in all the Mission's reports and, from the second report onwards, they have been the subject of a separate section (A/45/1055-S/23037, paras. 57 and 68; A/46/568-S/23222, paras. 146 et seq.; A/46/876-S/23580, paras. 150 et seq.; A/46/935-S/24066, paras. 46 et seq.).

A. Human rights

1. Right to life and to integrity and security of person

(a) Summary executions or deaths in violation of juridical guarantees

90. It was recommended that the National Police should be provided with the necessary material resources to carry out its functions and to ensure that it maintains professional standards in carrying out proper investigations. The Mission recommended that judges should use the powers of investigation accorded under the law and should improve coordination with the National Police. In cases of violent or suspicious deaths, the Mission recommended that the judge must make an immediate visual inspection, the body must be examined and a thorough autopsy must be performed. The Mission also recommended that the judges of first instance should personally conduct the investigations in cases that have given rise to serious social unrest and in particular to encroachments on the right to life.

91. In one of the cases reviewed, the investigation of the complaint concerning group summary executions in El Mozote, Department of Morazán, in December 1981, the Mission recommended that the skeletal remains should be exhumed with the necessary precautions and should be studied according to systematic anthropological techniques. For these purposes, it recommended the use of the services of international experts in forensic anthropology, who could be present, together with local professionals, to supervise the exhumation and laboratory analyses. It also recommended that all possible witnesses of the alleged incidents must be found and interviewed and that all those potentially implicated in the reported summary executions should be removed from the investigation.

92. The Mission stressed that the autonomy and independence of the Public Prosecutor's Office should be strengthened. To this end, it recommended that prosecutors should play an active role in initiating proceedings and investigating crimes and that the Attorney-General of the Republic should use all the powers available to him under the judicial system, including that of appointing special commissions (Constitution, art. 193 (7)), which could be done selectively to clear up relevant cases. At the same time, the Mission recommended that a register of victims of deaths from other than natural causes could be established . Among recent special legal instruments, the Mission drew attention to the United Nations Guidelines on the Role of Prosecutors and, in particular, those concerning prosecutors in criminal cases.

93. The Mission also repeated its recommendation that the Principles on the Effective Prevention and Investigation of Extra-legal, Arbitrary and Summary Executions, endorsed by the General Assembly in its resolution 44/162 of 15 December 1989, should be fully observed.

(b) Death threats

94. Emphasis was placed on the need to provide effective protection for the victims of death threats and to implement measures to halt such practices, such as those established by the General Assembly Principles referred to in the previous paragraph. Among such measures, the Mission recommended that measures should be taken to identify the authors of flyers signed by apparently clandestine organizations and adopt regulations prohibiting the radio or television broadcasting of threatening messages, without prejudicing the liberty of the press.

(c) Enforced disappearances

95. The Mission recommended that simple, flexible mechanisms should be set up to enable complainants to ascertain the whereabouts of the person concerned quickly. When the arrests were carried out by the armed

forces, it recommended systematic reporting to the Detainee Information Department set up by the Supreme Court of Justice.

(d) Abductions

96. The Mission reiterated that abduction, like the enforced or involuntary disappearance, is a violation of the San José Agreement, and stressed the need for immediate measures to eliminate this practice.

(e) Torture and cruel, inhuman or degrading treatment or punishment

97. ONUSAL recommended that in all verified cases of such abuses, legal proceedings should be instituted to investigate the facts and to detain, prosecute and punish the perpetrators, in accordance with domestic and international law. It also repeated its recommendation that the periods of administrative detention provided for in domestic law should be strictly adhered to and that incommunicado detention, which is prohibited by the San José Agreement, should be prevented. At the same time, the Mission recommended that, in setting up the new National Civil Police, account should be taken of the legal safeguards against torture and other cruel, inhuman or degrading treatment or punishment, to ensure that future members of the police were given appropriate training.

2. Right to due process of law

98. The Mission took note of the public hearing in the Jesuit case, a legal action of historic importance in El Salvador. An extensive analysis of this procedural act, and of its successes and failures from the point of view of the criminal justice system, was provided in the Mission's second report (paras. 128-142). Note was also taken of the public hearings in other cases which revealed the judicial practices at work in the trial stage of criminal proceedings. This monitoring work by the Mission led it to recommend that the judge should give the members of the jury guidance in understanding the list of evidence in a case and should help them weigh evidence and prepare them properly for the exercise of their functions. The Mission also recommended that the judge should comply strictly with the provisions of the law requiring that the summary should be read out in a manner that is clear and comprehensible to the members of the jury. It also recommended that the judge, in all cases, should ask the members of the jury whether they wish to question the accused or any of the witnesses who have already appeared on the stand.

99. In addition to the recommendations on strict respect for domestic law and the United Nations principles on the collection of evidence, already referred to in connection with summary executions, the Mission's fourth report contains a series of recommendations designed to improve legal measures for the safeguarding of human rights and to enhance respect for the due process of law. The recommendations cover extrajudicial confessions, administrative detention, incommunicado detention, the right to legal counsel, pre-trial detention and delays in the administration of justice. The recommendations cover both specific measures which could be taken on an immediate basis, and proposed legislative reforms, training courses or efforts to strengthen the organization of the administration of justice and of the Public Prosecutor's Office, to be implemented at a later stage. A more detailed consideration is contained in the relevant section of the report in question (A/46/935-S/24066, paras. 48-53).

3. Right to personal liberty

100. Where the arrest of juveniles is concerned, it was recommended that the authorities should hand minors over to the juvenile courts without delay and that adults and juveniles should be confined separately in detention centres. At the same time, the Mission recommended increased supervision of police officials and juvenile reform centres and improved staff training.

101. During the conflict the armed forces were recommended to refrain from the practice of making arrests without legal justification and to confine restrictions on freedom of movement to what was necessary to ensure the safety of the civilian population. In regard to military recruitment, it was recommended that wide publicity be given to the Ministry of Defence regulations on recruitment procedures and exemptions from military service should be widely publicized and that the relatives of recruits should be informed through a speedy and flexible mechanism. The Government was also advised to enact without delay the special law on compulsory military service provided for by the Constitution. FMLN was recommended to observe the rules of international humanitarian law concerning the prohibition of the recruitment of minors under the age of 15 and their participation in hostilities.

4. Personal documentation

102. The adoption of legislation to regularize the situation of undocumented persons is a positive response to the Mission's repeated recommendations to that effect. Without prejudice to this, emphasis is placed on the recommendation to facilitate civil status registration in practice and the intervention of the Central Board of Elections—now the Supreme Electoral Tribunal—in order to facilitate access to microfilmed archives.

B. International humanitarian law

103. With regard to the norms of humane treatment, it was pointed out that persons who do not take

part directly or who have ceased to take part in hostilities are protected by article 3 which is common to the four Geneva Conventions of 1949 and by Additional Protocol II thereto. It was emphasized that the wounded and the sick are entitled to immediate protection and care. It was pointed out that, while international humanitarian law allows insurgent forces to hold trials, it imposes a number of minimum mandatory requirements: existence of an independent and impartial court, respect for the principle of legality, procedural guarantees and, in particular, the right of defence.

104. With regard to the protection of the civilian population, attention was drawn to the responsibilities of the armed forces in cases where they had not taken the necessary precautions in their attacks, and to those of FMLN where it had not respected the norms on precautions against the effects of attacks. Similarly, the Mission reminded the parties that they must not use mines indiscriminately.

105. The Mission recommended the parties, throughout the entire period of the cessation of the armed conflict, to comply strictly with international humanitarian law, particularly regarding the fundamental guarantees of humane treatment and the protection of the civilian population.

C. War tax

106. Although the Mission considered that the question of the so-called "war tax" falls outside its mandate, it called on FMLN, in those cases in which it had acknowledged responsibility, to avoid any action which might jeopardize the process of peace and national reconciliation and to refrain from violating rights to which the San José Agreement gave priority, which could occur in the course of levying the so-called war tax.

D. Follow-up to recommendations

107. The main means of instigating action by the parties available to the Mission is the making of recommendations. For their part, the parties have undertaken to give their earliest consideration to any recommendations made to them by the Mission (San José Agreement, para. 15 (d)). Thus, in addition to sending a series of notes last January to the Government of El Salvador and to FMLN requesting them to provide information on the action taken by them in response to the recommendations made, the Mission has made a point of following up the matter more actively. This was done through regular working meetings with the parties, correspondence in writing on individual subjects and the participation of the Mission in seminars and workshops on topics that were considered to be of importance.

108. Nevertheless, and as shown by the evaluation made in this report, serious problems remain concerning the observance of the fundamental human rights to life, integrity and security of person, due process of law and the right to personal liberty; complaints—in one case, an accusation of the utmost gravity—are still being received on infringements of international humanitarian law. In other words, the Mission's recommendations appear so far to have been complied with in a piecemeal rather than a systematic manner and to have led to the resolution of individual cases rather than to general and qualitative transformations. This is indicative of the magnitude of the task that still remains to be carried out, a subject to which reference will be made in the conclusions.

VII. Conclusions

109. The cessation of the armed conflict has led to major changes in regard to recruitment and freedom of movement, and since its commencement almost no civilian victims or military casualties have been recorded. It must be pointed out that perceptible changes in these respects had begun even before the agreements were signed.

110. One matter of concern, however, is the lack of any institutional response with regard to the protection of the right to life and to integrity and security of person. No significant progress has been made in the systematic investigation of attempts on human life or on the eradication of the practices of intimidation and threat by organized clandestine groups.

111. It is evident that not many improvements in the present situation will be possible in the immediate future; this is due in part to the shortage of economic or human resources, to the need for legislative reforms or the enhancement of personnel training in various State sectors. But certain measures could be adopted quickly to modify behaviour which violates human rights. For example, judicial action could be initiated against the presumed perpetrators of torture or of cruel, inhuman or degrading treatment or punishment. Similarly, it would be possible to provide clear national policy guidelines to ensure strict compliance with the legal rules on detention with reference to legal aid for detainees and to the prohibition of incommunicado detention. Similarly, the norms which refuse to recognize the validity of statements made under duress could be observed, and pre-trial detention imposed only when it is necessary in order to ensure the presence of the accused and to avoid difficulties in the investigation. The conditions under which minors are detained should also be monitored.

112. Although the presence and recommendations of the Mission, through personal contact with the parties

and through periodic reports, have undoubtedly produced positive changes, it is necessary that behaviour which respects human rights should be dependent not solely on the ad hoc intervention of the Mission, but rather on the will of the State expressed in clear guidelines resulting in consistent behaviour.

113. It must be recognized, however, that, in spite of the serious concerns that have been expressed on the subject of summary executions, violent death and threats, the overall human rights situation in El Salvador has improved during the past year. It cannot be claimed that there is at present any systematic practice involving torture, enforced disappearances or abductions. But this positive trend by no means indicates the firm and definitive consolidation of a State ruled by law. In particular, fundamental guarantees to ensure the right to due process of law require far-reaching reform both of the structures of the judicial system, the Public Prosecutor's Office and the auxiliary bodies, and of criminal law and procedure, the law relating to minor offences and of prison legislation. The right of *habeas corpus* has still not become an effective means of protecting individual liberty and the integrity and security of the person. Illegal and arbitrary detention continues to be practised, cruel, inhuman or degrading treatment or punishments are still applied and people are detained under inhuman conditions. There are still no satisfactory guarantees of freedom of association and trade union freedom. The effective application of the right of displaced persons and returnees and of the inhabitants of former conflict areas to be provided with adequate personal documentation, recognized by recent legislation, is being seriously delayed.

114. In order to promote the consolidation of the advances achieved, it is necessary to strengthen the machinery of reconciliation in a society which is still highly polarized, and progressively to create a climate of confidence in institutions. The recently created National Counsel for the Defence of Human Rights forms part of the monitoring arrangements needed by El Salvador. This institution has not yet become fully operational and it will be some time before it begins to play its role. The Mission has begun to support it and is to continue to do so until such time as the Counsel becomes a highly regarded participant in dialogue with the State and with society and takes direct action to rectify situations in which human rights are violated. The cooperation of ONUSAL is expected to enable this new institution progressively to take over the present task of the Mission, and eventually to replace it when its mandate comes to an end.

115. A fully independent judiciary and a strong and active Public Prosecutor's Office with a professional and effective criminal investigation body operating under its guidance are the other indispensable elements for the full enjoyment of human rights. In compliance with paragraph 14 (h) of the San José Agreement which confers on the Mission a mandate "To offer its support to the judicial authorities of El Salvador in order to help improve the judicial procedures for the protection of human rights and increase respect for the rules of due process of law", the Mission has supported the judicial authorities through seminars and advice which should serve as a basis for extending the contribution of ONUSAL to other participants in the legal process, prosecutors, attorneys and lawyers in particular.

116. The structural reform of the administration of justice, of the Public Prosecutor's Office and of the auxiliary bodies, which resulted from the Peace Agreement and from measures provided for in the Constitution and in secondary legislation, implies a series of changes to which reference has already been made in the fourth report. The Mission has begun to verify compliance with the agreements on this matter and now has to extend its support to the complex task of the transformation of the judicial system. The dissemination of the special instruments adopted by the United Nations congresses on the prevention of crime and the treatment of offenders, between 1955 and 1990, may have a significant contribution to make to the change that has now begun, subject to the realities of the situation in El Salvador. Similarly, the Mission is in a position to make a worthwhile contribution to the process of penal reform and the reform of criminal procedures currently in hand through the dissemination of provisions of the United Nations regarding human rights in the administration of justice which are the expression of a broad international consensus on the subject. It is of fundamental importance that this task be followed through in the near future so as to achieve the twofold objective, set forth in the San José Agreement, of improving the judicial protection of human rights and the rules of due process of law.

Document 46

Letter dated 13 October 1992 from the Secretary-General to President Cristiani concerning a United Nations proposal for a solution to the problem relating to the land-transfer programme

Not issued as a United Nations document

I have the honour to enclose the United Nations' proposal [See Document 76, page 443] for a solution to the problem which has arisen concerning the provisions relating to the transfer of land in the Peace Agreement of 16 January 1992.

The preparation of this proposal, in close consultation with my Special Representative, Mr. Riza, has taken longer than was expected. This is for three main reasons. First, the issue is complex and of great sensitivity for both sides. Secondly, I thought it necessary to consult widely in order to satisfy myself that the United Nations' proposal constitutes a fair and reasonable solution to the problem. Thirdly, delays have resulted from the pressure of other work on the department concerned, especially the setting up of new United Nations operations in Mozambique and Somalia and critical developments in existing operations in Angola, Cambodia and the former Yugoslavia.

I am conscious that the enclosed proposal will fully satisfy neither the Government nor the FMLN. Extensive discussions with both sides have confirmed that wide differences exist between them, especially concerning the size of plots to be transferred and the number of potential beneficiaries. The views of both sides, as well as those of outside experts, in particular from the IMF, the World Bank and FAO, have all been given careful consideration in preparing the propsosal. I hope that both sides will be ready to accept it as an equitable compromise.

The proposal is designed to ensure both the early and rapid transfer of substantial quantities of land to the ex-combatants of the FMLN (who are given priority over those of the FAES in the first phase) and formalization of the tenancy, or if necessary the relocation, of substantial numbers of *tenedores* in the zones of former conflict. This is a central element in the peace settlement and I am convinced that priority must be given to its early implementation.

I accordingly urge you, Mr. President, to accept and put into immediate effect the terms and conditions set out in the proposal. I am forwarding it today to the General Command of the FMLN and urging them to commit themselves to working with the Government, in a spirit of cooperation and reconciliation, to facilitate its earliest possible implementation. I am asking them, as I ask you, to refrain from coming forward with amendments.

Please be assured, Mr. President, of my continued commitment to do everything possible to assist the full implementation of the Peace Agreements and the reestablishment of lasting peace in your country.

Please accept, Mr. President, the assurances of my highest consideration.

(Signed) Boutros BOUTROS-GHALI

Document 47

Letter dated 13 October 1992 from the Secretary-General to the General Command of the FMLN concerning a United Nations proposal for a solution to the problem relating to the land-transfer programme

Not issued as a United Nations document

I have the honour to enclose the United Nations' proposal [See Document 76, page 443] for a solution to the problem which has arisen concerning the provisions relating to the transfer of land in the Peace Agreement of 16 January 1992.

The preparation of this proposal, in close consultation with my Special Representative, Mr. Riza, has taken longer than was expected. This is for three main reasons. First, the issue is complex and of great sensitivity for both sides. Secondly, I thought it necessary to consult widely in order to satisfy myself that the United Nations' proposal constitutes a fair and reasonable solution to the problem. Thirdly, delays have resulted from the pressure of other work on the department concerned, especially the setting up of new United Nations operations in Mozambique and Somalia and critical developments in existing operations in Angola, Cambodia and the former Yugoslavia.

I am conscious that the enclosed proposal will fully satisfy neither the FMLN nor the Government. Extensive discussions with both sides have confirmed that wide differences exist between them, especially concerning the size of plots to be transferred and the number of potential beneficiaries. The views of both sides, as well as those of outside experts, in particular from the IMF, the World Bank and FAO, have all been given careful consideration in preparing the proposal. I hope that both sides will be ready to accept it as an equitable compromise.

The proposal is designed to ensure both the early and rapid transfer of substantial quantities of land to the ex-combatants of the FMLN (who are given priority over those of the FAES in the first phase) and formalization of the tenancy, or if necessary the relocation, of substantial numbers of *tenedores* in the zones of former conflict. This is a central element in the peace settlement and I am convinced that priority must be given to its early implementation.

I accordingly urge you, Gentlemen, to accept the terms and conditions set out in the proposal and to work with the Government, in a spirit of cooperation and reconciliation, to facilitate its earliest possible implementation. I am forwarding the proposal today to President Cristiani and urging him to accept it and put it into immediate effect. I am asking him, as I ask you, to refrain from coming forward with amendments.

Please be assured, Gentlemen, of my continued commitment to do everything possible to assist the full implementation of the Peace Agreements and the reestablishment of lasting peace in your country.

Please accept, Gentlemen, the assurances of my highest consideration.

(Signed) Boutros BOUTROS-GHALI

Document 48

Letter dated 15 October 1992 from Mr. Schafik Handal, in the name of the FMLN, to the Secretary-General concerning the United Nations proposal for a solution to the problem relating to the land-transfer programme

Not issued as a United Nations document; original in Spanish

After having studied the proposal that you sent to us on 13 October, we respectfully submit to you the following considerations:

1) As you yourself expected, we find the proposal unsatisfactory, especially with regard to point #5, which if applied rigidly, would leave no option to individual beneficiaries but to remain at their current levels of subsistence and in conditions of poverty. The table in point #5 expresses equivalencies at the subsistence level and does not address criteria of minimum profitability.

We note that the proposal has been prepared in close consultation with your special representative. Mr. Riza is perfectly aware of the fact that the majority of technical studies establish that greater surface areas are necessary in order to make plots productive and profitable. He also knows that the Government itself had offered larger plots depending on soil categories. We are surprised that he did not transmit this data to you. For its part, the European Economic Community, also established larger plots for its project in the Department of Usulután. In addition, the sizes established by the Lands Bank law are also greater.

We hoped that the proposal would seek a happy medium but it has turned out to be lower than all the above-mentioned parameters.

2) Without relinquishing these considerations, the Comandancia General of the FMLN has decided to accept the proposal that you have sent us and to work intensely and constructively to make it work.

Our decision is based on two considerations:

a) our respect for your authority and our recognition of your efforts to find a solution;

b) our desire to strengthen the viability of the peace process.

3) We think it appropriate to state that we understand that your proposal:

a) establishes that landholders are entitled to plots of the same size as those for combatants, unless the size of the plots they currently hold is smaller (#6);

b) excludes the idea of a fixed financial ceiling and obliges the Government to ensure the established plot sizes (#7 and #8);

c) proposes a table which will not necessarily be interpreted as a fixed ceiling for all soil categories, as adjustments will be required to ensure the averages put forward in the proposal (#11), especially with regards to categories II, III and IV;

d) obliges the Government to approve solid, clear legislative measures to prevent evictions until the situation is resolved;

e) calls for guarantees for the compliance with this proposal that have yet to be developed and specified.

We hope, Mr. Secretary-General, that this decision by the FMLN will contribute to facilitating a proposal by you to ensure that all pending agreements be complied with as soon as possible, ruling out unviable expectations of forcing a unilateral demobilization by the FMLN and the adherence to purportedly fatal dates which would endanger the peace process.

Accept, Mr. Secretary-General, our most sincere assurances of esteem and consideration.

(*Signed*) Schafik Jorge HÁNDAL

in the name of the
Comandancia General del FMLN

Document 49

Letter dated 16 October 1992 from President Cristiani to the Secretary-General concerning the United Nations proposal for a solution to the problem relating to the land-transfer programme

Not issued as a United Nations document; original in Spanish

I have the honour to inform you that on 14 October 1992 we received your letter CYU 262 P2/14, which transmits the proposal for a solution of the problem relating to land-transfer measures for ex-combatants and landholders referred to in the Peace Agreement of 16 January 1992.

We understand that the issue's complexity, as well as the many other matters requiring your attention, made it impossible to produce the aforesaid document as promptly as we had foreseen. We are, however, grateful for your personal interest and your determined cooperation with our country to advance the peace process in which all we Salvadorians are engaged.

We wish to inform you that we accept the proposal submitted for our consideration in its entirety. This acceptance is a further demonstration of our firm political will and commitment to consolidate the peace process, as expressed to you during my recent visit to United Nations Headquarters. Furthermore, we are aware that it is only by fulfilling our commitments on time that we can create the confidence and credibility required for the Salvadorian population to maintain its trust and hope in the construction of a firm and lasting peace which will allow it finally to forget the fateful days of conflict.

Having carefully read your proposal, we feel the need to repeat the ideas and comments concerning the proper interpretation of some of its points which I have today communicated to Mr. Marrack Goulding by telephone. We believe that the following points should be made sufficiently clear and precise to ensure they are applied correctly:

(a) Items 3 and 4: the returnees mentioned under item 3 are included among the 25,000 landholders.

(b) If a landholder is occupying a property smaller than those provided for in the proposal, wishes to remain on that property and has the agreement of the owner to do so, the property shall be transferred to him even though its size is below the limit established in the general rule.

(c) The Secretary-General will provide special support to the Government of El Salvador and request additional resources from the international community to ensure full implementation of the programme.

(d) Item 17: the landholders whose tenure is to be established formally in phases I, II and III are included among the total number of 25,000 landholders referred to under item 4.

The allocation of land to ex-combatants and landholders shall always be limited to the terms of items 4 and 5 of the proposal.

(e) The Government of El Salvador shall appoint the manager of the programme.

(f) Item 22: the mandate of CEA-COPAZ for verification of matters under the Peace Agreement relating to land shall be discharged within the limits and for the purposes established in the Secretary-General's proposal.

In order to formalize and complete the process according to schedule, it is essential that FMLN should as soon as possible submit the list of ex-combatants, duly certified by ONUSAL. FMLN will also have to provide the list of landholders and the properties they are occupying. This list will be added to the list of landholders whose situation is to be formally established in phases I, II and III of the programme, bringing the total number up to the maximum of 25,000 landholders.

Meanwhile, we assume that the commitment on the part of FMLN to respect the right of property and to halt any illegal occupation of land will be carried out in a serious and responsible manner, thus helping to maintain the climate of stability and reconciliation which is indispensable for consolidation of the peace process.

We wish to emphasize, Sir, that we are prepared to apply the terms and conditions included in your proposal immediately. It would be our hope that the FMLN leadership show a similar attitude and determination to work together for the shared objectives of our country's peace, in a spirit of cooperation and reconciliation, which are key factors in our current environment. However, it is also most important to note that, in taking this step, we are in fact doing what you called for in your latest report on verification of the process of implementation and compliance with agreements, dated 17 September 1992, through Mr. Marrack Goulding. In that report, you con-

cluded that if the Government, as a result of its efforts, were to establish terms for land transfer deemed by yourself to be reasonable, you would then consider that the conditions were met for the total demobilization of FMLN to be completed by 31 October 1992.

Sir, we believe it essential to insist that FMLN completes its final demobilization by 31 October 1992. We hope that the international community, through the Organization which you so worthily represent, will support our efforts to that end, designed as they are to promote the interests of all Salvadorians who believe in the peace process.

(Signed) Alfredo CRISTIANI

Document 50

Letter dated 19 October 1992 from the Secretary-General to the President of the Security Council concerning implementation of the Peace Agreement

S/24688, 19 October 1992

I have the honour to refer to the situation in El Salvador on which I last briefed the Security Council, at informal consultations, on 10 September 1992.

Since that date, important progress has been achieved in implementing the Peace Agreements but there have also been further delays in the agreed schedule.

The most important progress has been on the problem of land to which I referred in my statement on 10 September and on which the Secretariat has worked intensively. After receiving technical advice from FAO, IMF and the World Bank, I sent Under-Secretary-General Marrack Goulding to San Salvador on 28 September to help my Special Representative search with both parties for solutions which might bring them closer together. As a result of the visit a number of issues were clarified and progress was made.

The work begun in San Salvador was continued in New York, in close consultation with experts inside and outside the United Nations system. As a result, on 13 October, I presented to President Cristiani and to the General Command of FMLN a proposal which, in my judgement, was an equitable compromise between their positions. It set out terms and conditions for the transfer of land to former combatants of both sides and for the formalization of the land-tenure system, or if necessary the relocation on new land, of persons who during the hostilities had moved onto land in the conflict zones.

I am happy to be able to report to the Security Council that I received letters from both parties dated 15 and 16 October confirming that they accepted my proposal and were committed to working with each other to implement it as soon as possible. Intensive efforts by the Government and full cooperation from FMLN will be required if we are to achieve a prompt and speedy transfer of large areas of land, especially to the former combatants of FMLN as provided for in the Agreement.

It is now necessary to resolve as soon as possible the problem posed by the further delays that have occurred in the schedule of implementation of the Peace Agreements. In this connection, it will be recalled that according to the original schedule, which forms an integral part of the Agreements, the transfer of land was to be completed by the end of July 1992. Another important element of the Agreements was the establishment of the new National Civil Police, whose first units were to be deployed no later than 28 October 1992. Both these essential commitments by the Government were thus to have been completed before completion of the demobilization of FMLN which is scheduled for 31 October. The purpose of the changes made to the schedule on 17 June and 19 August was therefore to adjust the phasing of the demobilization of FMLN combatants to take account of the delays in the implementation of the land transfer programme and the police project, always with the intention of retaining 31 October as the date by which demobilization of FMLN was to be completed.

As of now 40 per cent of FMLN combatants have returned to civilian life. One third of the 60 per cent who still have their weapons were due to leave the assembly areas on 30 September and a further one third on 15 October; the final one third were to be demobilized on 31 October. On 30 September members of the FMLN General Command informed Mr. Goulding that they had decided to suspend the demobilization of their forces until new dates had been set for the start of the transfer of land and for the implementation of other aspects of the Agreements which had fallen behind schedule. Mr. Goulding urged them to reconsider this decision but without success.

This development is cause for great concern. So, too, are continuing suspicions that significant quantities of arms held by FMLN were not included in the inventories presented to ONUSAL at the beginning of the cease-fire. In face of these difficulties, I have concentrated on resolving the problem of land, believing that it constituted the most serious obstacle to timely implementation of the Peace Agreements and that its solution would open the way to rapid progress.

Now that this problem is on the way to being resolved, a concerted effort is necessary to get the process back on track. For essentially practical reasons, related to the complicated process of demobilization in 15 different locations, I do not believe that it will be possible to complete the dismantling of the military structures of FMLN by 31 October 1992, as provided for in the Peace Agreements.

Accordingly, within the next few days I shall present to the parties a proposal for overcoming this difficulty and, if necessary, undertaking a third revision of the agreed timetable. In that case I would emphasize that this revision must be the final one, and that both parties must fully commit themselves to abiding by the new schedule. I shall remind the parties that I am required, before the end of October, to submit recommendations to the Security Council on the future strength and mandate of ONUSAL after its current mandate comes to an end on 31 October 1992. I shall further draw their attention to the fact that United Nations peace-keeping services are currently in great demand and to the consequent need to avoid any undue extension of the planned schedule for ONUSAL. At the same time, I shall assure them that I shall recommend that ONUSAL remain in place, albeit at reduced strength, until it has discharged all the responsibilities assigned to it under the Peace Agreements.

I should be grateful if you would bring the matters in this letter to the attention of the members of the Security Council. Meanwhile, I am having it circulated as a document of the Council.

(*Signed*) Boutros BOUTROS-GHALI

Document 51

Letter dated 20 October 1992 from the Secretary-General to President Cristiani concerning the United Nations proposal for a solution to the problem relating to the land-transfer programme

Not issued as a United Nations document

I received your kind letter of 16 October 1992, delivered to me personally by Dr. Oscar Alfredo Santamaría, Minister of the Presidency, which contains your affirmative reply to the proposal on the question of lands which I sent you through my Special Representative on 14 October last.

This is indeed a positive step which, taken together with the FMLN's acceptance of the same proposal which was conveyed to me on 15 October, clears the way to go forward with the implementation of the Peace Agreements between the Government and the FMLN.

You have sought a number of clarifications regarding the interpretation of my proposal on land. I wish to reply to these as follows:

a) Repatriated people (former refugees) are indeed included in the category of *tenedores*. The maximum number of *tenedores* will be 25,000, but this figure might be adjusted downward once COPAZ completes its work of verifying the lands in the FMLN inventory and the number of *tenedores* on them.

b) The *tenedor* is welcome to stay in a smaller size of plot if he wishes, but only if the original owner is willing to sell. If he is not, the tenedor will have to be relocated.

c) The Secretary-General has interceded, and will continue to intercede, with the multilateral institutions and bilateral donors to seek resources, both financial and technical, to facilitate the implementation of the land-transfer programme.

d) As stated in a) above, the number of *tenedores* cannot exceed 25,000 people.

e) The Government will indeed appoint the manager/coordinator of the programme since it is the Government that will implement the transfer of land and carry out the logistics. I want to emphasize, however, the importance of appointing someone to this post who is a supporter of the programme and can carry it out in a pragmatic and professional way, in close collaboration with all concerned.

f) Without prejudice to the responsibilities of CO-PAZ as spelled out in the Mexico Agreement, the CEA-COPAZ mechanism will have to carry out its tasks within the framework described in my proposal and accepted by the Government and the FMLN. As stated in paragraph 22 of the proposal, the work of the Committee should complement the verification work of COPAZ.

I agree with you, Mr. President, on the need for the FMLN to cooperate fully in the implementation of the Agreements in order to ensure that the proposal can be carried out. It is essential that both sides faithfully adhere to their commitment to work in concert to this end and to refrain from any action which might jeopardize the implementation of the Agreements.

You have alluded in your letter to the evaluation by my Special Representative and Under-Secretary-General Marrack Goulding on 17 September, and specifically to the statement that with a solution to the problem of land, all obstacles will have been removed and the conditions will exist for the total demobilization of the FMLN to be completed on 31 October 1992. I wish to point out in this regard that it was clearly stated in that evaluation that if those conditions were to be in place it would be necessary for the Government to have concluded the formulation of conditions for the transfer of lands, considered reasonable by the Secretary-General, before the end of September. Since we are now approaching the end of October, it no longer appears possible to meet that goal. Accordingly, I am today informing the President of the Security Council that for essentially practical reasons related to the logistics of the demobilization in fifteen different locations, I do not feel that it is possible to achieve by 31 October 1992 the dismantling of the military structure of the FMLN as provided in the Peace Agreements. I am also informing the President of my intention to present shortly to the parties a proposal aimed at overcoming this difficulty and, if necessary, at revising, for the last time, the calendar of implementation of the Agreements.

Please accept, Mr. President, the assurances of my highest consideration.

(Signed) Boutros BOUTROS-GHALI

Document 52

Letter dated 23 October 1992 from the Secretary-General to the FMLN concerning the United Nations proposal for a solution to the problem relating to the land-transfer programme

Not issued as a United Nations document

I received your letter of 15 October 1992, delivered to me through my Special Representative, which contains your affirmative reply to the proposal on the question of lands which I sent you on 13 October last.

This is indeed a positive step which, taken together with the Government's acceptance of the same proposal clears the way for further progress in the implementation of the Peace Agreements between the FMLN and the Government.

The FMLN and the Government need to cooperate fully in the implementation of the Agreements in order to ensure that the proposal can be carried out. It is essential that both sides faithfully adhere to their commitment to work in concert to this end and to refrain from any action which might jeopardize the implementation of the Agreements. I am encouraged by your commitment to work intensively and constructively in this regard.

I want to assure you that Mr. Riza has transmitted to us all the pertinent information to which you refer in your letter. Indeed, he transmitted much more. I am satisfied, therefore, that the proposal that was prepared in close consultation with him takes into account all those factors and that, all variables considered, it represents the best possible solution.

In your letter you record certain understandings on the proposal. I wish to make the following points in this regard:

a) *Tenedores* can receive the same amount of land as ex-combatants if they presently occupy an extension of land equal to or larger than what is indicated in the table. If, however, they occupy smaller plots (but above the minimum), they would remain in them if owners are willing to sell. Otherwise, they will have to be relocated to another plot under comparable conditions.

b) Paragraph 7 of the accepted United Nations proposal makes it clear that the Government should guarantee the extension of land to which ex-combatants and *tenedores* are entitled (paras. 5-6). There is no ceiling on financing. The Government has committed itself to providing enough financing so that beneficiaries can buy the amount of land to which they are entitled.

c) The table establishes the maximum amount of land to which ex-combatants are entitled according to the different types of soil. The same plot might have more than one type of soil and this will have to be taken into account. However, the average specified in para. 11 is used solely for the purpose of estimating the total amount of land and financial resources required. This average will not affect the allocation of land which will be done exclusively according to the table.

d) Paragraph 24 of the United Nations proposal states that the Government will guarantee that *tenedores* in the zones of the former conflict will not be evicted and that the *status quo* will be maintained until the situation is resolved. ONUSAL is studying the question whether this guarantee needs to be enshrined in new legislation.

e) The United Nations proposal contains new mechanisms which are to be put in place to ensure the implementation of the agreements. These are complements to the guarantees offered by COPAZ as set forth in the New York Agreement of 25 September 1991.

Please accept, Gentlemen, the assurances of my highest consideration and my best regards.

(*Signed*) Boutros BOUTROS-GHALI

Document 53

Letter dated 28 October 1992 from the Secretary-General to the President of the Security Council recommending that the mandate of ONUSAL be extended until 30 November 1992

S/24731, 29 October 1992

I have the honour to refer to the United Nations Observer Mission in El Salvador (ONUSAL).

The members of the Security Council will recall that by its resolution 729 (1992), adopted on 14 January 1992, the Council decided to enlarge the mandate of ONUSAL to include the verification and monitoring of the implementation of all the agreements signed between the Government of El Salvador and the Frente Farabundo Martí para la Liberación Nacional (FMLN), and that it also decided that the mandate of the Mission would be extended to 31 October 1992 and would be reviewed at that time on the basis of recommendations to be presented by the Secretary-General.

It is also worth recalling that the date of 31 October was chosen for the review of the mandate of ONUSAL because, under the terms of the Agreement signed at Mexico City on 16 January 1992 (S/23501, annex), that was the date on which the process of cessation of the armed conflict in El Salvador would be completed. This did not mean that the application of the peace agreements would be completed, but that it would be possible to reduce the military division of ONUSAL and to review the human and material resources needed by the Mission to verify the application of the remaining provisions of the agreements.

As I indicated in my letter of 19 October 1992 (S/24688), because of the difficulties that have emerged, it will not be possible to complete the dismantling of the military structures of FMLN by 31 October 1992. I have therefore presented proposals for overcoming these difficulties to both parties. At the present time, consultations are continuing, and I have recently asked Mr. Marrack Goulding and Mr. Alvaro de Soto to travel to El Salvador for that purpose. I continue to hope that the process of cessation of the armed conflict can be completed towards mid-December, but I do not at present have the information I would need to formulate long-term recommendations to the Security Council regarding the mandate and strength of ONUSAL and their financial implications.

In the circumstances, I can see no other solution than to recommend to the Security Council that it extend the current mandate of ONUSAL for an interim period of one month, that is, until 30 November 1992. I am convinced that, with the cooperation of the two parties to the peace agreements, I shall by then be able to make a specific recommendation on the mandate and strength that ONUSAL will need in order to verify implementation of the final phases of the peace process in El Salvador.

I should be grateful if you would bring this letter to the attention of the members of the Security Council.

(*Signed*) Boutros BOUTROS-GHALI

Document 54

Security Council resolution concerning the extension of ONUSAL's mandate

S/RES/784 (1992), 30 October 1992

The Security Council,

Recalling its resolution 637 (1989) of 27 July 1989,

Recalling also its resolutions 693 (1991) of 20 May 1991, 714 (1991) of 30 September 1991 and 729 (1992) of 14 January 1992,

Taking note of the letter from the Secretary-General of 19 October 1992 addressed to the President of the Security Council, 1/ in which he announced a delay in the schedule laid down in resolution 729 (1992),

Taking note also of the letter from the Secretary-General of 28 October 1992 addressed to the President of the Security Council, 2/ in which he proposed an interim extension of the current mandate of the United Nations Observer Mission in El Salvador,

1. *Approves* the proposal of the Secretary-General to extend the current mandate of the United Nations Observer Mission in El Salvador for a period ending on 30 November 1992;

2. *Requests* the Secretary-General to submit to the Security Council, between now and that date, recommendations on the period of extension of the mandate, on the mandate itself and on the strength that the Mission will need, taking into account progress already made, in order to verify the implementation of the final phases of the peace process in El Salvador, together with their financial implications;

3. *Urges* both parties to respect scrupulously and to implement in good faith the commitments assumed by them under the agreements signed on 16 January 1992 at Mexico City 3/ and to respond positively to the Secretary-General's latest proposals to them aimed at overcoming the current difficulties;

4. *Decides* to remain seized of the matter.

1/ S/24688.
2/ S/24731.
3/ S/23501, annex.

Document 55

Letter dated 11 November 1992 from the Secretary-General to the President of the Security Council concerning implementation of the Peace Agreement

S/24805, 13 November 1992

I refer to my letter to the President of the Security Council dated 28 October (S/24731) in which I reported that due to certain difficulties which had developed, it would not be possible to conclude the dismantling of the military structure of the FMLN on the date originally envisaged, and that I had asked Messrs. Marrack Goulding and Alvaro de Soto to travel to San Salvador to assist in overcoming those difficulties. In the meantime, I recommended, and the Council agreed in resolution 784 (1992), to extend the mandate of ONUSAL until 30 November 1992. In approving my proposal, the Council urged both parties "to respect scrupulously and to implement in good faith the commitments assumed by them under the agreements signed on 16 January 1992 at Mexico City and to respond positively to the Secretary-General's latest proposals to them aimed at overcoming the current difficulties".

On 23 October I had proposed to the Government of El Salvador and the FMLN a set of adjustments to the timetable in the Peace Agreements according to which the phase of the cessation of the armed conflict would be completed on 15 December. The FMLN accepted my proposal contingent upon agreement by the Government. President Cristiani, however, reserved his position on a number of aspects of my proposal, conditioning demobilization, reduction and restructuring of the Armed Forces on submission by the FMLN of a weapons inventory satisfactory to the Secretary-General and initiation of the destruction of those weapons. President Cristiani raised some questions concerning the schedule envisaged for implementation of the recommendations of the Ad Hoc Commission on Purification of the Armed Forces.

Mr. Goulding and Mr. de Soto arrived in San Salvador on 30 October and immediately began consultations with President Cristiani and, separately, with the General Command of the FMLN. On 2 November I had to ask Mr. Goulding to return to New York and go to Angola because of the situation which had arisen there.

Mr. de Soto stayed on in San Salvador and returned on 7 November, having successfully concluded arrangements with the parties which would formally bring the armed conflict to an end on 15 December 1992. This is the date which I had proposed in my 23 October letter to the two sides.

President Cristiani has agreed to complete the implementation of the recommendations of the Ad Hoc Commission on Purification of the Armed Forces within a specified time-frame. A certain adjustment was necessary for the practical reason that decisions regarding military personnel are issued and made public on the last day of each month and become effective on the first day of the following month. President Cristiani has agreed to inform me by 29 November of the administrative decisions he has taken on this matter. Assuming these decisions match the recommendations of the Ad Hoc Commission (all of which have remained confidential), the FMLN is to provide ONUSAL with a final inventory of weapons, conclude the concentration of those weapons on 30 November and begin their destruction on 1 December. These are also the dates which I had proposed. Contin-

gent upon my confirmation that these actions have been duly completed, the Government would promptly resume the dissolution of military units as previously agreed.

It is important to note that it has been expressly stipulated, for the first time, that compliance with certain key points in the calendar by one side is contingent upon compliance with specific undertakings by the other side. Careful monitoring by ONUSAL will therefore be necessary to ensure that compliance takes place on schedule. I shall keep the Security Council duly informed of progress in this regard.

It is evident that the peace process is entering an especially delicate phase during which it will be imperative that both parties act with caution and restraint in order to consolidate stability in the country. It will be equally important that such caution and restraint be ensured for an extended period after 15 December, especially in the former zones of conflict, so that national reconciliation may become a reality.

As requested in resolution 784 (1992), I will present to the Council in the second half of November a report on the progress of the peace process and my recommendations regarding the extension of the mandate of ONUSAL.

(Signed) Boutros BOUTROS-GHALI

Document 56

Report of the Secretary-General on the activities of ONUSAL

S/24833, 23 November 1992, and addendum, S/24833/Add.1, 30 November 1992

I. Introduction

1. The present report is presented in compliance with resolution 729 (1992) of 14 January 1992 and resolution 784 (1992) of 29 October 1992, by which the Security Council agreed to extend the mandate of the United Nations Observer Mission in El Salvador (ONUSAL) for a period ending on 30 November 1992. It describes the activities of ONUSAL during the period since my last reports in May and June 1992 (S/23999 and Add.1). In the meantime, in letters dated 19 and 28 October and 11 November 1992 (S/24688; S/24731 and S/24805), I informed the members of the Security Council of certain obstacles that had arisen in the implementation of the peace process in El Salvador and of how these had been overcome.

2. ONUSAL, headed by my Special Representative, Mr. Iqbal Riza, has continued to carry out all the verification functions assigned to it under the several agreements ("the Peace Accords") signed by the Government

of El Salvador and the Frente Farabundo Martí para la Liberación Nacional (FMLN) between 4 April 1990 and 16 January 1992. ONUSAL has also intensified its participation as an observer in the work of the National Commission for the Consolidation of Peace (COPAZ), composed of the two signatories of the accords and the political parties represented in the National Legislative Assembly. COPAZ drafts legislative measures related to the accords and supervises their execution. In response to difficulties that have arisen in execution of the peace accords, and with the cooperation of the parties, ONUSAL has expanded its function beyond the verification role envisaged in its original mandate and now uses its good offices in a variety of ways to facilitate implementation of the accords.

3. Under the timetable for the implementation of the accords, the process of ending the armed conflict was to have been completed by 31 October 1992. By that date, the Government was to have completed several major

commitments of a political and institutional nature and FMLN was to have demobilized all its combatants, destroyed their armament and reintegrated them into civilian life under programmes provided by the Government.

4. The tightness of the timetable, an integral component of the accords, together with the complexity of the various commitments undertaken by the two sides, led to major delays in completing certain crucial commitments. Within a few months the accumulation of these delays became an obstacle to the implementation of the peace process. Consequently, in consultation with the two parties, ONUSAL on 17 June 1992 reprogrammed those parts of the timetable that had been affected by the delays. In the face of further delays, a second reprogramming was agreed on 19 August 1992 following a visit to El Salvador by Mr. Marrack Goulding, Under-Secretary-General for Peace-keeping Operations.

5. In both these reprogrammings the fulfilment of certain key commitments that the Government was to complete by 31 October 1992 had to be postponed beyond that date. These included the provision of agricultural land in the former zones of conflict to persons who had occupied properties there during the conflict; this was originally to have been completed by the end of July 1992. Another concerned the establishment of the National Public Security Academy to train the new National Civil Police; this had been due on 1 May 1992. In response to delays in the implementation by the Government of its undertakings, FMLN had asserted that the dismantling of its military structure would also have to be reprogrammed in order to maintain the link in the original timetable between the key undertakings of the two parties.

6. While the United Nations has maintained the position that, in principle, each party is obliged to comply with its commitments without making this conditional on reciprocal compliance by the other party, it must be kept in mind that the original timetable was conceived as a carefully synchronized whole, comprising parallel actions by both sides. The delays described above disturbed the balance established in the timetable and, even after the two reprogrammings, it became evident that that balance had not been re-established.

7. An evaluation by the United Nations on 17 September 1992 of the two sides' compliance with the second reprogramming concluded that the land issue had emerged as a main obstacle to the effective implementation of the accords. To overcome this obstacle, I sought the advice of specialized bodies in the United Nations system and on 13 October 1992 I presented to the parties a proposal that I considered to be a reasonable solution to the land issue taking all relevant factors into account. My proposal was accepted by FMLN and the Government on 15 and 16 October 1992 respectively.

8. Notwithstanding this, it soon became evident that the cumulative delays, and the reactions of the parties to them, were leading the peace process into an impasse, each party holding the other responsible and insisting on contradictory interpretations of key clauses of the accords. In this situation, I presented on 23 October 1992 a proposal under which the schedule for compliance would undergo further adjustments. In this proposal, the final phase of the dismantling of the military structure of FMLN was to commence by 31 October 1992 and be completed by 15 December 1992.

9. As I informed the Members of the Security Council on 11 November 1992 (S/24805), FMLN accepted my proposal contingent upon acceptance of it by the Government. The Government, however, reserved its position on some aspects of the proposal and raised questions related both to the inventory of weapons submitted by FMLN and to the schedule for the implementation of the recommendations of the Ad Hoc Commission on the Purification of the Armed Forces. President Cristiani also announced that, pending clarification of these questions, the Government was suspending implementation of the agreed programme for the restructuring, reduction and demobilization of the Armed Forces. In these circumstances I decided to send Mr. Goulding and Mr. de Soto, my Senior Political Adviser, to San Salvador to assist in overcoming the difficulties which had arisen. They arrived there on 30 October 1992.

10. Following extensive consultations separately with the Government and FMLN, Mr. de Soto (I had requested Mr. Goulding to leave San Salvador for Angola on 2 November) reported to me on 6 November that he had successfully concluded with the parties arrangements which, if implemented, would formally bring the armed conflict to an end on 15 December 1992. Agreement on these arrangements was recorded in letters that Mr. de Soto exchanged on my behalf with President Cristiani and the High Command of FMLN respectively. In these letters, it was expressly stipulated that compliance with specific undertakings by one side would be contingent upon compliance with specific undertakings by the other side. In light of the outcome of these consultations and in accordance with the final provision of the calendar of implementation contained in the Chapultepec Agreement, I made the necessary adjustments to the timetable for implementation of the accords, and ONUSAL is now verifying, with close attention, the implementation by the parties of the arrangements which each of them agreed with Mr. de Soto.

11. It is in this context that the present report, describing ONUSAL's activities in support of the peace process, is presented to the Council, together with my

recommendations on ONUSAL's future mandate and strength.

II. Verification of the cessation of the armed conflict

A. *Composition and tasks of the Military Division*

12. The Military Division, which remains under the command of Brigadier-General Victor Suanzes Pardo (Spain), had a strength of 375 military observers in February 1992. It now consists of 226 military observers from Brazil, Canada, Colombia, Ecuador, India, Ireland, Spain, Sweden and Venezuela and 8 medical officers from Argentina. This reduction has been made possible by the progress achieved in implementation of the agreement relating to the cessation of the armed conflict.

13. While continuing to ensure the observance of the cease-fire, the Division has assumed further tasks related to the verification of the reduction of the Armed Forces of El Salvador (FAES) and the reintegration of FMLN ex-combatants into civilian life. After 15 December 1992, the Division's main functions will be to continue to verify the reduction of FAES and the introduction of the new armed forces reserve system, to coordinate the clearance of minefields and to help consolidate peaceful conditions, particularly in the former zones of conflict. During January 1993, the Division will, if my recommendations are approved by the Security Council, be reorganized and further reduced to 103 military observers. Thereafter, its size will be reviewed periodically.

B. *Separation and concentration of forces*

14. Under the first reprogramming of 17 June 1992, certain adjustments were made in the concentration points allocated to FAES. With some delay, FAES completed its concentration on 26 June 1992, including withdrawals from specified installations, such as the headquarters of the former Treasury Police.

15. Under the same reprogramming, FMLN presented a schedule for the final concentration of its combatants. This was completed on 26 June 1992, except in several locations where there remained small groups of armed and uniformed personnel in support of so-called "public security committees" (see para. 44 below). In response to ONUSAL's continued insistence, these personnel eventually completed their concentration, after considerable delay, by 30 August 1992.

C. *Reintegration of FMLN ex-combatants and hand over of weapons*

16. In accordance with the first reprogramming, the initial contingent of 20 per cent of FMLN ex-combatants was demobilized on 30 June 1992, two months after the date stipulated in the original timetable. However, ONUSAL considered the number of weapons handed over to be insufficient. FMLN attributed the low number to the fact that this first contingent included mainly support personnel who were normally unarmed. At ONUSAL's insistence, it agreed to hand over additional weapons to approximate to 20 per cent of its inventory. This was completed on 18 August 1992 after several delays, but the majority of weapons received were in poor condition and this raised further doubts about the authenticity of this first demobilization.

17. The reintegration of the second contingent of 20 per cent of FMLN ex-combatants, which had been reprogrammed for 31 July 1992, was suspended a few days before that date by FMLN, which protested that the Government was not complying with the first reprogramming. This second contingent was finally demobilized on 24 September 1992, following the second reprogramming of 19 August 1992. A further 20 per cent of FMLN's arms inventory was handed over. On this occasion most weapons were in reasonable condition.

18. In my proposal of 23 October 1992 the dates for the demobilization of the remaining three contingents of 20 per cent of FMLN ex-combatants were set for 31 October, 20 November and 15 December 1992. The third contingent was duly demobilized on 30 and 31 October 1992. The arms handed over to ONUSAL were mostly in good condition. Demobilization of the fourth contingent duly began on 20 November 1992.

19. The demobilization of FMLN personnel disabled in the war began on 31 August 1992 and continues to this date.

D. *Inventory of FMLN troop strengths and armaments*

20. I have referred in earlier reports to my concern about whether the inventory presented to ONUSAL by FMLN in February 1992 represented a full accounting of FMLN's holding of arms. As part of the second reprogramming, FMLN, after some delays, presented an updated inventory, which is currently being verified by ONUSAL. Following the consultations described in paragraphs 9 and 10 above, FMLN is to submit a final inventory of its weapons on 30 November 1992, concentrate them in the designated zones by that date and begin their destruction on 1 December 1992.

E. *Marking of minefields and removal of mines*

21. A working group composed of the United Nations Children's Fund (UNICEF), ONUSAL, FAES and FMLN established to study the problem of minefields has collected all available information on their types and location and is currently signposting mined areas. A plan for the removal of the mines is to be coordinated by the Military Division at the request of the Government and

FMLN. A delegation of the Inter-American Defense Board of the Organization of American States (OAS) visited El Salvador on 15 August 1992 to study how it might participate in this plan. Meanwhile, ONUSAL is supporting a UNICEF public education campaign to make the population aware of the dangers posed by minefields and the work being done to clear the mines.

III. Armed forces of El Salvador

A. *Civil defence*

22. The disarming and disbandment of the civil defence units was carried out in April and May 1992 in accordance with the FAES reduction plan. The Military Division has verified that the process was completed by 30 June 1992. Routine patrolling has confirmed that the command structures of these units have been dissolved, but monitoring is being maintained to establish that their disbandment is effective.

B. *Reduction of the armed forces*

23. The Military Division is verifying that the reduction of the armed forces called for by the peace accords is being carried out in accordance with the reduction plan submitted by the Government to the Secretary-General. The strength reductions carried out up to late October conformed with that plan. As described in paragraph 9 above, President Cristiani announced on 28 October a temporary suspension of implementation of the plan, but this will be restored in early December as a result of the consultations described in paragraph 10 above. The Division's verification, through visits to units and review of relevant documents, has determined that the majority of demobilized personnel were released directly into civilian life, while a number were transferred to non-military service. In cases where units are disbanded but their personnel are transferred to other military service, the Division continues to verify that such transfers do not conflict with the accords.

24. On 6 July 1992, the Joint Chiefs of Staff of FAES submitted a revised force reduction plan to ONUSAL. To date, two immediate reaction infantry battalions (Bracamonte and Belloso) have been dismantled. Information was requested on the location of their demobilized personnel after it was ascertained that former personnel of the Belloso Battalion had been recruited by the National Police. This development and its possible extension to other immediate reaction infantry battalions is being investigated to determine whether it can be reconciled with the relevant provisions of the accords. The dismantling of a third immediate reaction infantry battalion (Atlacatl) began on 22 September 1992 but was suspended by the Government in late October. It will now be completed by 8 December 1992, subject to the arrangements discussed in paragraph 10 above.

C. *Substitution of the Territorial Service by an armed forces reserve system*

25. The Military Service and Reserve Law called for by the accords was promulgated on 30 July 1992 but was ambiguous on the legal and operational dissolution of the Territorial Service. As part of the second reprogramming of 19 August 1992, the Government issued an "interpretation decree" on 7 September 1992 confirming that the Territorial Service had effectively been dissolved. The Ministry of Defence immediately commenced implementation of the dissolution process with ceremonies in the various regional military headquarters. The Military Division monitored this operation and received lists indicating where the former local commanders had been relocated and confirming the closing of their offices. Verification is being maintained to establish that the dissolution is effective.

26. Implementation of the new armed forces reserve system has not yet begun because the regulations to implement the new Military Service and Reserve Law have not yet been issued. The date on which ONUSAL is to be informed of the regulations is now 30 November 1992.

D. Other issues

27. The Academic Council of the Military College was appointed on 31 July 1992, rather than on 11 May 1992 as originally scheduled. The Council has drawn up new admission criteria, as required under the accords.

28. Although the new State Intelligence Agency was constituted on 28 April 1992, six weeks behind schedule, and the appointment of its director was three months late, the former National Intelligence Department was disbanded by a general order of the Ministry of Defence on 9 June 1992, a few days ahead of schedule. The Military Division has verified that the Department has officially been disbanded, that its facilities have been handed over to other units of FAES, that its military personnel have been transferred to other units and that some civilian personnel have also been relocated in the FAES civilian administration. However, FMLN has expressed concern that FAES continues to undertake intelligence activities related to the internal situation in El Salvador. ONUSAL has not been able to establish clearly what functions the transferred personnel are performing in their new posts and, despite repeated requests, the location of the records of the former Department has not been divulged. Apparently no civilian personnel were transferred to the new agency. Efforts continue to obtain information from FAES on these various points.

29. Although military weapons held by private individuals were to be recovered by FAES starting on 1 September 1992, there is no indication that this process has begun. ONUSAL has requested, but not yet received, the recovery plan, so that it can verify its implementation.

IV. Public security matters

A. *Police Division*

30. The Police Division has fully assumed its assigned role of monitoring and assisting the National Police during the period of transition until the deployment of the new police established by the accords, the National Civil Police. Specific tasks were not defined in the accords, but the Division was able to develop its functions and procedures quickly.

31. The strength of the Division, which continues to be commanded by General Homero Vaz Bresque (Uruguay), is currently 303 police observers. They are contributed by Austria, Chile, France, Guyana, Italy, Mexico, Norway, Spain and Sweden. The establishment of some 60 new National Police posts throughout the country since the cease-fire has considerably increased demands on the Division. The early deployment of some 50 additional police observers will be required to supervise the Auxiliary Transitory Police (*Policéa Auxiliar Transitoria*) (see paras. 44-46 below). In the longer term the Division, which at present carries out an average of 100 patrols every 24 hours, will be reduced with the progressive deployment of the National Civil Police.

32. The Police Division has cooperated with the Military Division in verifying the dissolution of civil defence units and coordinated monitoring will continue. Police observers have assisted in locating illegal arms caches. The Division also supports the Human Rights Division, to which 18 police observers are seconded, and conducts special inquiries when required.

33. The Division ensures that special security measures are provided for FMLN leaders, as required by the Agreements.

B. *National Public Security Academy*

34. The National Public Security Academy, which will train the new National Civil Police, started its activities on 1 September 1992, four months behind schedule, partly owing to problems regarding premises and funds. The latter difficulty remains and adequate financing is assured only until the end of 1992. The Academy has requested additional funds for 1993 but a decision on this matter will not be taken before the end of December 1992. Although the Governments of Norway, Spain and the United States of America are presently supporting the Academy financially, major additional financial support from the international community will be necessary to ensure that it can train the required personnel over the next two years, so that the National Civil Police can be fully and effectively deployed.

35. The Academy is provisionally housed in the premises of the former Bracamonte Battalion and the former Public Security Academy. The Government is negotiating the possible purchase of permanent premises for the Academy.

36. Under the accords the Academy is to receive some 330 basic-level recruits each month for training in order to complete the replacement of the National Police by the National Civil Police by mid-1994. Two groups totalling 622 students joined the Academy on 1 September 1992, 357 more on 15 October 1992 and another 330 on 16 November 1992. Of the 120 candidates for the senior and executive levels who also joined the Academy on 15 October 1992, 60 are now being trained in Puerto Rico and 15 others are training in Spain. The remainder are being trained at the Academy. Although the accords establish that applicants from the National Police should be evaluated by the Director-General of the National Civil Police before the admission examinations, this requirement was not fulfilled and evaluations are well behind schedule.

37. The accords stipulate that candidates for the Academy shall be selected in such a way as to ensure that most recruits did not participate directly in the armed conflict and that the proportion of former FMLN combatants is no greater than that of former members of the National Police and vice versa. It has been agreed that candidates from FMLN and the National Police will each constitute 20 per cent of the intake. As I have reported to the Council (see S/23999, para. 29), the Government had undertaken not to present former members of the Treasury Police and the National Guard as candidates in the immediate future. However, several candidates from the National Police who recently applied for the senior and executive levels were found to have belonged to the National Guard, the Treasury Police or FAES before being transferred to the National Police after signature of the agreement of 16 January 1992. The Academic Council has decided to accept these candidates despite ONUSAL's objections that this contravenes the accords and subsequent undertakings by the Government. This problem is still awaiting resolution in ONUSAL's discussions with the Government.

38. The Academic Council has also accepted the prior training and service of candidates in the National Police as being equivalent to the university studies required for enrolment in the courses for senior and executive levels. ONUSAL is still awaiting a reply to its request for information as to the technical grounds on which such a decision was taken.

39. ONUSAL is monitoring closely the Government's compliance with its commitment not to use National Police, ex-public security forces or FAES personnel as advisors or instructors in the Academy and in the National Civil Police.

40. The Academy has been receiving the support of an international technical team of experts from Spain and the United States. Having fulfilled its main task of assisting in setting up the Academy, the team is now providing the Director and the Academic Council with advice on the finances of the Academy, the recruitment and selection processes, the curricula, the disciplinary regime, etc. Instructors from Chile, Norway and Spain are fully involved in training activities. ONUSAL has also provided the Academy with instructors on a provisional basis. Further, ONUSAL is monitoring the admission examinations and has recommended improvements in these.

41. Effective monitoring of the functioning of the Academy is being obstructed by failure to accept ONUSAL's proposal that it attend the meetings of the Academic Council as an observer. ONUSAL is attempting to resolve this matter with the Government in order to ensure proper verification of this important aspect of the accords.

C. National Civil Police

42. The deployment of the National Civil Police is due to start by the end of January 1993 with the graduation of the first group of police personnel from the Academy. According to the accords, the organization of the National Civil Police is to be defined with close international cooperation and supervision, coordinated by the United Nations. ONUSAL already has offered technical assistance to the Director-General of the National Civil Police, who is in the process of preparing the organizational structure of this new body.

D. Transfer of armed forces personnel to the National Police

43. Following ONUSAL's intervention (see S/23999, para. 30), the Government halted the transfer of ex-Treasury Police and ex-National Guard personnel to the National Police. However, the Police Division recently ascertained that self-contained units from one of the demobilized immediate reaction infantry battalions, including officers, had been integrated into the National Police. Upon inquiry, the Government confirmed this, asserting that this was not expressly prohibited by the agreements. ONUSAL has taken the position that such transfers clearly contravene the spirit of the agreements and increase distrust at a time when it is essential to build confidence. The Government continues to insist that it is entitled to effect such transfers of trained personnel in order to cope with the increase in crime, especially in the rural areas where the former National Guard and Treasury Police used to function. In this situation and in order to minimize the negative effects of such transfers, ONUSAL has insisted that they be on an individual basis, and not in units or sub-units, as this would amount to a redeployment of army personnel. Further, ONUSAL should be informed in advance of such transfers and should receive relevant lists of personnel.

E. Special regime

44. Delays in the concentration of forces and in the designation of the Director-General of the National Civil Police held up the definition of the special regime for the maintenance of public security in the zones of former conflict as required by the accords. Meanwhile, armed FMLN ex-combatants and civilian supporters had established "public security committees" to assume public order functions. Under the second reprogramming of 19 August 1992, FMLN concentrated these ex-combatants in the designated areas. In late September the Director-General, in close consultation with ONUSAL, defined the special regime and established the Auxiliary Transitory Police (see para. 31 above).

45. The deployment of the Auxiliary Transitory Police commenced in early October. It is responsible for maintaining public order and security in former conflict zones until its replacement by the new National Civil Police. Its members are drawn from recruits to the Academy who, after a 15-day preparatory course, serve in the Auxiliary Transitory Police for short periods. They then return to the Academy to complete their formal training.

46. Under the command of the Director-General of the National Civil Police, the Auxiliary Transitory Police is being deployed in about 30 posts in former conflict zones. Twelve posts had been established by mid-November 1992. Each of the Auxiliary Transitory Police's contingents is under the constant supervision and guidance of officers from the Police Division of ONUSAL, who also provide daily academic instruction. Further, ONUSAL provides the Auxiliary Transitory Police with logistical support. The special regime will be phased out gradually, following the deployment of the National Civil Police in the former zones of conflict. Meanwhile, the National Police is to enter these zones only in special situations under orders from the Director-General of the National Civil Police and with ONUSAL escort.

47. The problems referred to in this section, and particularly those mentioned in subsections B, C and D above, give rise to concern in so far as they reflect a certain reluctance, in some quarters, to accept fully the spirit and the thrust of the peace accords as regards public security matters. The essence of these is to move from public order agencies controlled by the armed forces to a new National

Civil Police exclusively controlled by civilian authorities, as a new body, with a new organization, new cadres, new training and educational mechanisms and a new doctrine.

V. Human rights

48. In the most recent report of the Director of the Human Rights Division (A/46/955-S/24375), issued at the beginning of August 1992, it was stated that, following the cease-fire on 1 February, substantial improvements had been recorded with regard to rights linked to humanitarian law, as well as to other rights related to life and to personal integrity and liberty. Nevertheless, concerns were also expressed regarding the persistence of apparent violations such as summary executions, death threats, systematic maltreatment of detainees and, especially, shortcomings in the due process of law and in the obligation of the State to provide safeguards to its citizens.

49. The persistence of anonymous death threats which, in the majority of cases, are directed at potential witnesses, or relatives of victims, and of unsolved violent deaths, continues to be a cause for concern. With regard to those cases that have been reported to the various government authorities, there is no indication to date that adequate measures have been taken either to investigate the threats or to protect the threatened persons.

50. During the past several months, ONUSAL has been deeply concerned by frequent incidents of violent death and threats to personal security, many of which might have political motivations. It was agreed in the second reprogramming of 19 August 1992 that the Division would give special attention to such cases. The Police Division can be of particular help in obtaining pertinent information. However, it is difficult to reach clear conclusions in such cases as the Government's investigation system is deficient and ONUSAL cannot be a substitute for it. The Mission continues to impress upon the authorities the urgent need to investigate such cases thoroughly and to take appropriate action.

51. Mr. Philippe Texier, who established and directed the Division of Human Rights under difficult conditions before the cease-fire came into effect, completed his assignment on 30 June 1992. I wish to place on record my recognition of his valuable services. The recently appointed Director of the Division, Mr. Diego García-Sayan, will give priority to the strengthening of the Division's verification activities under the San José Agreement (see S/21541, annex), and the various international human rights instruments to which El Salvador is a party. The Director will continue to present periodic reports in compliance with the San José Agreement.

52. In this context, the Division will place special emphasis on the evolution of the situation of fundamental human rights, including trade union and labour rights. In addition, it will concentrate its efforts on an extensive set of actions in support of the judicial system. This will be complemented by education programmes to promote respect for human rights.

VI. Economic and social matters

A. *Land-tenure system*

53. The complexity of the land issue, which, as reported above, has delayed implementation of the accords, arises from two causes. One is inherent in the economic, political and social sensitivity of land questions in countries with predominantly agricultural economies where, as in El Salvador, land is in short supply and unevenly distributed, and where the population is large and increasing rapidly. The second is that the accords reflect only in general terms broad understandings that were reached during the negotiations, leaving details to be worked out during the implementation process.

54. The accords required that arrangements for the transfer of land to ex-combatants of both sides and for the legalization of the situation relating to land occupied during the conflict be completed by 31 July 1992. This implied completion of all stages of the process, including verification by COPAZ of the inventory of affected lands presented by FMLN, definition of conditions of transfer (determination of the number of potential beneficiaries, their entitlements, terms of payment, etc.) and the actual transfer of titles. Prolonged delays were encountered from the outset. The inventory presented by FMLN in February 1992 was incomplete and underwent several revisions before the final version was submitted in June 1992. Extended discussions in COPAZ delayed verification of the inventory.

55. Conditions for land transfer presented by the Government at the end of August 1992 led to complex discussions. ONUSAL, concerned at the consequence of further delays in initiating the transfer of land, which was supposed to have begun by 1 May 1992, became progressively more involved in the land issue. Taking into account the recommendations of experts from the International Monetary Fund (IMF), the World Bank and the Food and Agriculture Organization of the United Nations (FAO) who, at my request, visited El Salvador and worked with ONUSAL on this issue, I presented a proposal to the two sides on 13 October 1992 which was quickly accepted by both of them.

56. The proposal provided that the total number of beneficiaries should not exceed 47,500, consisting of 15,000 ex-combatants from FAES, 7,500 FMLN ex-combatants and approximately 25,000 landholders in the former zones of conflict. Given the complexity of the

transfer process and the limited land and financing immediately available, my proposal established a three-phase programme for the provision of land to ex-combatants and to current landholders. If the latter occupy lands whose owners are unwilling to sell, they are to be relocated on alternative lands. Meanwhile, as required by the accords, the Government is to guarantee that current landholders will not be evicted from the properties they hold. This is a key point which, if it is ignored, could threaten the successful implementation of the peace accords. The Government has informed ONUSAL that it intends to provide the necessary guarantees. The actual amount of land available for transfer and the number of landholders on it will be known only after COPAZ has completed its verification of FMLN inventory and other Government's holdings of State land have also been verified.

57. Various operational aspects of the programme of land transfer need to be worked out by the supervisory committee established under my proposal. The programme manager and the Government's representative to the committee were appointed only recently, after considerable delay. Meanwhile, on 31 October 1992, the process of transfer started officially with the signing by the Government and FMLN, in the presence of ONUSAL, of an agreement to transfer two State properties to FMLN ex-combatants and current landholders on those properties. Several additional steps must yet be completed to define individual entitlements before the legal transfer and issue of titles can take place.

58. Since a large proportion of the land to be transferred is private land that must be purchased from its owners at market prices and with cash, the availability of adequate financing is of critical importance to the success of the programme. I shall be appealing to international and regional organizations and to bilateral donors to supplement the limited financing now available for the purchase of land, which will suffice to carry out land transfers to only 40 per cent of the beneficiaries.

59. New occupations of lands in the former zones of conflict, some of them by FMLN ex-combatants, have created new tensions. The ex-combatants assert that they are returning to lands on which they had been working before concentrating in the designated zones. One incident in October led to the Government's deploying a police contingent consisting of recently demobilized troops, a move which threatened the cease-fire. A clash was averted through the intervention of ONUSAL and the Archbishop of San Salvador. This incident illustrates the sensitive nature of the land issue in the former zones of conflict and the urgency of implementing the provisions of the accords, in accordance with my proposal of 13 October 1992.

60. FMLN has publicly called for a halt to further occupations of land in order to facilitate the land transfer programme. However, reports of occupations are still being received and are being investigated by ONUSAL.

B. *Forum for Economic and Social Consultation*

61. Following the second reprogramming of 19 August 1992, the National Private Enterprise Association finally decided to participate in the Forum, which was formally installed on 9 September. So far, the three participating sectors—Government, private employers and unions—have agreed upon internal regulations.

C. *National reconstruction plan*

62. The Government has maintained that public administration must be restored in the former zones of conflict so that the reconstruction plan can become fully operational. This requirement is now being met under procedures established by ONUSAL (see sect. VIII below).

63. With regard to the reintegration of ex-combatants into civilian life, the emergency assistance programmes for the first contingent of demobilized FMLN personnel were initiated with minor delays. The partial implementation of programmes for the second contingent began in early October 1992 and in early November 1992 for the third contingent. Problems in the programme for agricultural training were overcome by the Government and FMLN working together with ONUSAL and the United Nations Development Programme (UNDP). The programme for the medical care of disabled ex-combatants has started, but long-term rehabilitation programmes are still to be defined by the Government. Legislation in this respect has been pending in COPAZ but will be given priority once it is received in the Legislative Assembly.

64. Reintegration programmes for the medium term were prepared by the due date by the Government. However, the lack of financing continues to be a problem. Implementation procedures are still to be finalized and ONUSAL is pressing for their completion.

VII. Political participation by FMLN

65. The Government completed a vital undertaking when, on 30 July 1992, FMLN was given the status of a "political party in formation". For this purpose, the Legislative Assembly approved a number of temporary reforms to the Electoral Code. The main obstacle raised had been article 7 of the Constitution which bans the existence of armed political groups. Objections on this ground were ultimately overcome since the disarming of FMLN ex-combatants was in progress under ONUSAL supervision.

66. Meanwhile, FMLN moved to establish itself as a political party, collecting the required number of signatures and presenting them to the Supreme Electoral Tribunal. After a large public meeting, FMLN proceeded to formalize the required documents at a ceremony on 1 September 1992 attended by political personalities and members of the diplomatic corps. With the Archbishop of San Salvador as a witness, FMLN leadership swore to respect the Constitution and the laws of El Salvador. The Government has not hindered FMLN's political activities, including proselytization, which were carried out with only minor problems and with open access to the media.

67. The unconstitutionality of armed political groups re-emerged as an issue when it became evident that the dismantling of the military structure of FMLN might not be completed by 31 October 1992. The governing party, ARENA, submitted to the Tribunal a formal, though non-binding, request that final registration of FMLN not be granted until it had fully demobilized. After deferring action for some time, the Tribunal issued a resolution on 12 November 1992. The resolution, approved by the majority of the Tribunal, stated that, while FMLN had complied with the established requirements, final registration could not be granted before evidence of total disarming and demobilization, duly documented by ONUSAL, was presented to the Tribunal, which would then grant final registration within 24 hours. On 19 November 1992 the Legislative Assembly extended for 30 days the temporary reforms to the Electoral Code, which were due to expire on 27 November 1992.

68. The Government has granted provisional licences, pending completion of some technical requirements, for two FMLN radio stations which were already broadcasting. The FMLN's request to be assigned a television licence has not been granted.

69. The Government has promised to take measures to accelerate the documentation of ex-combatants and to continue providing the facilities required for the protection of FMLN leaders.

VIII. Restoration of public administration in the former zones of conflict

70. Soon after the cease-fire on 1 February 1992, 24 of the 68 mayors then in exile returned to their municipalities. However, despite ONUSAL's efforts at the local and regional level, it was not possible to effect the return of the rest. This was due to the existence of particularly tense situations in their jurisdictions where the concentration of forces was still incomplete, and also to resistance by community organizations that had performed certain administrative functions in these areas during the conflict.

71. In July 1992, at the request of the national mayors' association (COMURES) and the association of community organizations (Concertación), ONUSAL initiated contacts between the mayors in exile and the local organizations which were resisting their return. In the second reprogramming of 19 August 1992, the Government and FMLN requested ONUSAL to prepare a programme for the restoration of public administration in the former zones of conflict. After consultation with both sides, this was finalized on 16 September 1992. Under the programme, a third of the mayors who were still in exile in July 1992 have now returned, and the rest will return by the year's end. The return of the judges in exile will now be coordinated by ONUSAL with the Supreme Court of Justice. ONUSAL will continue to exercise its good offices to ensure that the restoration of public administration in the former zones of conflict progresses smoothly without resurgence of tensions, especially after 15 December 1992.

IX. Judicial system

72. The majority of reforms to the judicial system required by the accords have been incorporated into the Constitution. However, there have been delays on secondary legislation. For example, bills pertaining to military jurisdiction, the National Council of the Judiciary and the judicial career were to have been enacted by 1 May 1992. The first was adopted only recently and the other two are pending in the Political Commission of the Legislative Assembly and are still to be revised by COPAZ.

X. Electoral system

73. After several months of discussion, in which important progress was made in narrowing differences among the parties, COPAZ is expected to submit shortly to the Legislative Assembly draft amendments to the Electoral Code. It is expected that the Assembly will approve the reformed Code by the proposed date of 10 December 1992.

74. The Government and FMLN were informed on 23 October 1992 that the United Nations had been approached by several opposition political parties, as well as by certain Member States, urging that the United Nations verify the 1994 elections, which will be the first to take place after the end of the conflict. COPAZ also has recommended unanimously to the President that an official request be made for such verification. The Government has informed the Secretary-General that it has requested the Supreme Electoral Tribunal, as the competent authority, to consider this proposal.

75. In August 1992, a United Nations mission under a UNDP technical assistance project visited El Salvador at the request of the Supreme Electoral Tribunal.

It presented recommendations on the feasibility of introducing a personal identity document which would also be valid for the 1994 elections; it also provided other technical advice to the Tribunal.

XI. Financial aspects

76. Should the Security Council decide to extend ONUSAL beyond its current mandate period, I shall request the General Assembly at its present session to make appropriate financial provisions for the maintenance of the Observer Mission during the period of extension.

77. As at 12 November 1992, unpaid assessed contributions to the ONUSAL Special Account for the period from inception through 11 November 1992 amounted to $11,625,882.

XII. Observations

78. The difficulties encountered throughout the negotiations to end the conflict in El Salvador and address its underlying causes were an early indication of the complexities awaiting the unprecedented United Nations endeavour that was to follow. It is no surprise that the implementation of these intricate agreements has encountered obstacles. But what is significant, and a cause of great satisfaction, is that, despite these problems and despite the distrust and polarization that a fratricidal conflict creates, the implementation of the peace process has advanced steadily and the obstacles have been overcome. The impeccable observance of the cease-fire and the ability of FMLN to engage in political activities in advance of its full legalization as a party are an impressive demonstration of the will of both the Government and FMLN to consolidate peace in their country. The peace process in El Salvador continues to give every sign of being irreversible.

79. None the less both parties to the peace accords have been responsible for late and/or imperfect compliance with many of their commitments, including the most sensitive and important ones. There have been a number of occasions when action or inaction on the part of one or other of the parties has put the whole process at serious risk. On such occasions considerable effort has been required from the United Nations, with unstinting help from the "Friends of the Secretary-General" (Colombia, Mexico, Spain, Venezuela), the United States of America and other interested Governments, to get the process back on track. The most serious threat to the process emerged when it became clear, simultaneously, that the formal ending of the armed conflict could not be achieved by the programmed date of 31 October 1992 and that there were difficulties over the schedule for the purification of the Armed Forces in accordance with the Chapultepec Agreement. It was in this situation that I proposed to the parties certain adjustments to the implementation process, with the results described in paragraphs 9 and 10 above. I am grateful to both parties for the flexibility which they showed in assisting me to overcome what I hope will be the last major obstacle to full and faithful implementation of the peace accords in their entirety.

80. The achievement of that goal will however continue to require flexibility and restraint on the part of the Government and FMLN, especially in the zones of former conflict, where the population has suffered directly from, and often been displaced by, military operations and where tensions remain. It is incumbent upon the Government and FMLN to ensure that the restoration of normal conditions in these zones is achieved in a spirit of *détente* and reconciliation. The same is true of the intricate process for the transfer of lands to ex-combatants and the regularization of the situation of those who occupied lands during the conflict. That programme, which will extend well into 1993 and perhaps beyond, will require from all concerned patience and willingness to work constructively together.

81. Successful completion of the peace process will also require continuing support from the international community both through the continued existence of ONUSAL and through the provision of voluntary contributions to support activities that the Government cannot finance itself but which it would not be appropriate to include in ONUSAL's budget. The most important of these are the third phase of the lands transfer programme, for which an estimated $85 million will be required, and the National Public Security Academy, for which, as reported in paragraph 34 above, funds are not presently available beyond the end of the current year. I shall be appealing to Governments to contribute generously in support of both these programmes.

82. As regards ONUSAL, its mandate under paragraph 2 of resolution 693 (1991) is "to monitor all agreements concluded between the two parties". These are the agreements signed by the Government and FMLN on 26 July 1990, 27 April 1991, 25 September 1991 and 16 January 1992. Since certain major undertakings, such as the reduction of the Armed Forces and the deployment of the National Civil Police, extend into 1994, it is my intention to submit to the Security Council at appropriate intervals my recommendations on the future activities and strength of ONUSAL, taking into account progress made in implementing the peace process. My reports will of course recommend such reductions in the strength of ONUSAL as the evolution of its mandate permits.

83. The Military Division has already been reduced to a strength of 226 and it will be reduced further to 103 officers in January 1993. The Police Division may also be

reduced from March 1993 in step with the progressive deployment of the new National Civil Police, and it will be phased out once this deployment is completed in early 1994. In the event that ONUSAL is required to verify the elections, the personnel required for this task would be phased in as required by the electoral process and their assignment would end immediately after the elections in March 1994. It can thus be anticipated that ONUSAL will complete its mission by mid-1994. For the present, I recommend that the Security Council extend the mission's mandate for a further period of six months, to 31 May 1993.

84. A decision in this sense by the Security Council will be another token of the international community's commitment to support the peace process in El Salvador. This commitment is of course based on the belief that Salvadorians themselves will show a matching commitment. It is only through determined efforts by all sectors of Salvadorian society to overcome the rancours caused by the conflict that the country will return to the path of lasting peace. Not only must the parties dedicate themselves to such efforts, but the Salvadorian media also must play a positive role in exercising the power that they possess to educate public opinion and influence positively the hearts and minds of the people. A special concern at present is the anonymous threats that have frequently appeared of late in the newspapers and which, along with more direct anonymous threats, are aimed at FMLN leaders, political personalities and members of ONUSAL. The Government has been asked repeatedly to investigate these threats and to take effective action before any serious incidents occur.

85. In conclusion, I should like to take this opportunity to express my support for, and pay tribute to, my Special Representative, Mr. Iqbal Riza, and to the military, police and civilian personnel of ONUSAL who under his leadership are tackling with courage, impartiality and determination the challenging task of helping the people of El Salvador to achieve just and lasting peace in their country.

Addendum (S/24833/Add.1)

1. In my report to the Security Council of 23 November 1992 (S/24833), I recommended that the Council extend the mandate of the United Nations Observer Mission in El Salvador (ONUSAL) for a further period of six months, to 31 May 1993. A preliminary cost estimate of such an extension, should the Security Council decide to approve it, is provided for information purposes in the annex to the present addendum.

2. It would be my recommendation to the General Assembly that the cost relating to the extension of ONUSAL's mandate should be considered an expense of the Organization to be borne by Member States in accordance with Article 17, paragraph 2, of the Charter of the United Nations and that the assessments to be levied on Member States be credited to the ONUSAL special account.

Annex

Cost estimates by main expenditure groups

(Thousands of United States dollars)

Serial		
1.	Military observers	2 106
2.	Civilian police	4 914
3.	Civilian personnel	9 624
4.	Rental and maintenance of premises	450
5.	Vehicle operations	624
6.	Aircraft operations	1 494
7.	Communications	78
8.	Miscellaneous equipment	78
9.	Miscellaneous supplies, services, freight and support costs	1 218
	Total	20 586

Document 57

Security Council resolution concerning the extension of ONUSAL's mandate

S/RES/791, 30 November 1992

The Security Council,

Recalling its resolution 637 (1989) of 27 July 1989,

Recalling also its resolutions 693 (1991) of 20 May 1991, 714 (1991) of 30 September 1991, 729 (1992) of 14 January 1992 and 784 (1992) of 30 October 1992,

Having studied the report of the Secretary-General on the United Nations Observer Mission in El Salvador of 23 and 30 November 1992, 1/

Noting with appreciation the continuing efforts of the Secretary-General to support implementation of the several agreements signed between 4 April 1990 and 16 January 1992 by the Government of El Salvador and the

Frente Farabundo Martí para la Liberación Nacional to re-establish peace and promote reconciliation in El Salvador,

Noting the intention of the Secretary-General to continue, in this as in other peace-keeping operations, to monitor expenditures carefully during this period of increasing demands on peace-keeping resources,

1. *Approves* the report of the Secretary-General on the United Nations Observer Mission in El Salvador of 23 and 30 November 1992; 1/

2. *Decides* to extend the mandate of the Mission as defined in resolutions 693 (1991) and 729 (1992), for a further period of six months ending on 31 May 1993;

3. *Welcomes* the intention of the Secretary-General to adapt the future activities and strength of the Mission, taking into account progress made in implementing the peace process;

4. *Urges* both parties to respect scrupulously and to implement in good faith the solemn commitments they have assumed under the agreements signed on 16 January 1992 at Mexico City 2/ and to exercise the utmost moderation and restraint, both at present and following the conclusion of the cease-fire phase, in order to respect the new deadlines agreed upon by them for the successful completion of the peace process and for the restoration

of normal conditions, especially in the zones of former conflict;

5. *Shares*, in this context, the preoccupations expressed by the Secretary-General in paragraph 84 of his report;

6. *Reaffirms* its support for the Secretary-General's use of his good offices in the El Salvador peace process and calls upon both parties to cooperate fully with the Special Representative of the Secretary-General for El Salvador and the Mission in their tasks of assisting and verifying the parties' implementation of their commitments;

7. *Requests* all States, as well as the international institutions in the fields of development and finance, to continue to support the peace process, in particular through voluntary contributions;

8. *Requests* the Secretary-General to keep the Security Council fully informed of further developments in the El Salvador peace process and to report, as necessary, on all aspects of the operations of the Mission, at the latest before the expiry of the new mandate period;

9. *Decides* to remain seized of the matter.

1/ S/24833 and Add.1.
2/ S/23501, annex.

Document 58

Report of the Secretary-General on the situation in Central America

A/47/739-S/24871, 30 November 1992

Report of the Secretary-General

1. The present report is submitted pursuant to Security Council resolution 637 (1989) of 27 July 1989 and General Assembly resolution 46/109 of 17 December 1991.

A. *El Salvador*

2. Since my last report, dated 2 December 1991 (A/46/713-S/23256), the long and complex negotiation process, begun on 4 April 1990 under the auspices of my predecessor, culminated in the signing in Mexico City on 16 January 1992 of the Peace Agreement between the Government of El Salvador and the Frente Farabundo Martí para la Liberación Nacional (FMLN) (A/46/864-S/23501, annex).

3. The signing of the Peace Agreement was preceded by the signing of the New York Act, on 31 December 1991, reached as a result of direct negotiations between the parties held in New York, through the good offices of the Secretary-General. In the New York Act (S/23402, annex), the

parties declared, *inter alia*, that they had reached definitive agreements which, combined with those previously signed at San José, Mexico City and New York, completed the negotiations on all substantive items of the Caracas Agenda and the New York "Compressed Negotiations". The Act provided that the cessation of the armed conflict should take effect formally on 1 February 1992 and should conclude on 31 October 1992. The parties also agreed to finalize before 16 January 1992 the timetable for the implementation of the agreements and the modalities for the dissolution of the military structure of the FMLN and the reintegration of its members into the civil and institutional life of the country.

4. On 13 January 1992, following an intensive final round of negotiations at United Nations Headquarters under the leadership of my Personal Representative for the Central American Peace Process, Mr. Alvaro de Soto, the parties signed the New York Act II (A/46/863-S/23504, annex II). In it the parties stated that they had reached agreements which completed the negotiations on

all issues outstanding when the New York Act was signed on 31 December 1991, thus opening the way for the signing of the Peace Agreement in Mexico City on 16 January 1992.

5. The Peace Agreement between the Government of El Salvador and the FMLN constitutes a comprehensive package of interrelated undertakings by both parties which aims not only at the cessation of the 12-year civil war in El Salvador, but also at tackling some of the root causes of the conflict by promoting democratization and reconciliation among Salvadorians. In that respect, it may serve as an inspiration for the settlement of other conflicts. It provides, *inter alia,* for significant reforms in the doctrine, structure and strength of the armed forces and security bodies (chap. I); the creation of an entirely new National Civil Police under exclusive civilian control, together with a new National Public Security Academy (chap. II); judicial reforms, including the creation of an Office of the National Counsel for the Defence of Human Rights (chap. III); reforms of the electoral system (chap. IV); modalities for land transfer, particularly in conflict zones, as well as measures of economic and social development (chap. V); and measures for the political participation of FMLN (chap. VI). The Peace Agreement also outlines modalities for the cessation of the armed conflict (chap. VII), provides for the United Nations to verify the implementation of its provisions as well as prior agreements between the parties (chap. VIII), and sets forth a detailed timetable of all actions to be undertaken by the parties (chap. IX).

6. It should be stressed that the signing of the Peace Agreement was due primarily to the determination of President Cristiani and the leadership of the FMLN to achieve a negotiated solution to the conflict. I also wish to recall that the personal participation of my predecessor helped to ensure, in the final hours of his mandate, the success of the negotiations. Similarly, I should express once again my appreciation to the Governments of Colombia, Mexico, Spain and Venezuela, as well as others, for the support provided in order to achieve peace. After participating in the signing of the Peace Agreement in Mexico on 16 January 1992, I had the opportunity to travel to El Salvador, where I sought to underscore the importance for the international community of the decision by the Salvadorians to leave behind an era of violence and embark upon the path of peace.

7. The peace agreements provided for the establishment of a Commission of the Truth, mandated to investigate serious acts of violence that have occurred since 1980 and whose impact on society urgently demands that the public should know the truth. Pursuant to the agreements, my predecessor appointed the three members of the Commission: Mr. Belisario Betancur,

former President of Colombia; Mr. Reinaldo Figueredo, former Foreign Minister of Venezuela; and Professor Thomas Buergenthal, former President of the Inter-American Court for Human Rights and Honorary President of the Inter-American Institute for Human Rights. On 13 July 1992, the Commission was formally installed in my presence at United Nations Headquarters in New York. The members of the Commission then travelled to El Salvador to commence their activities. The Commission has established a secretariat in San Salvador. It is expected that a report will be prepared and will be made public by mid-January 1993.

United Nations Observer Mission in El Salvador

8. It will be recalled that the Security Council, in resolution 693 (1991) of 20 May 1991, had established, under its authority, a United Nations Observer Mission in El Salvador (ONUSAL) to monitor all agreements concluded between the Government of El Salvador and FMLN. In the initial phase, its mandate was to verify the compliance by the parties with the Agreement on Human Rights (A/44/971-S/21541, annex), signed at San José on 26 July 1990. ONUSAL became operational on 26 July 1991 and, in addition to its headquarters in San Salvador, it opened four regional offices in San Salvador, San Miguel, San Vicente and Santa Ana, and two suboffices in Chalatenango and Usulután.

9. Soon after the signing of the New York Act, I recommended to the Security Council in my report of 10 January 1992 (S/23402 and Add.l), the enlargement of the mandate of the Mission and an immediate and substantial increase in its strength in order to assume the new verification and monitoring functions entrusted to it by the parties. I indicated, in particular, the need to establish a Military Division to verify all aspects of the cease-fire and the separation of forces, and a Police Division to monitor the maintenance of public order during a transitional period while the new National Civil Police was set up. The new Divisions, together with the existing Human Rights Division, would come under the authority of my Special Representative and Chief of Mission, Mr. Iqbal Riza. The Security Council, in its resolution 729 (1992) of 14 January 1992, approved the above-mentioned report, and decided to enlarge and extend the mandate of ONUSAL until 31 October 1992 to include the verification and monitoring of the implementation of all the agreements that were to be signed in Mexico City between the Government of El Salvador and FMLN.

10. Prior to 1 February 1992, the agreed date for the cease-fire, ONUSAL proceeded to take the necessary measures in order to carry out the new tasks assigned to the Mission. Priority was given to establishing the Military Division, which was entrusted with verifying the cessation of the armed confrontation and was placed

under the command of Brigadier-General Victor Suanzes Pardo (Spain), who previously had been chief of the United Nations Observer Group for Central America (ONUCA). During the informal cease-fire (16-31 January 1992), the Military Division received its first contingents, which came both from ONUCA and directly from a number of contributing countries. The Military Division deployed its personnel at all the verification points on 31 January 1992 and one day later, as agreed, began its verification activities.

11. Since that date, the Mission has been carrying out the various verification tasks assigned to it in the agreements signed by the two parties between 4 April 1990 and 16 January 1991. In addition, I should point out that the Mission has been increasingly called upon to use its good offices to help the two parties overcome difficulties that have arisen in the implementation of the agreements. It has done so by promoting a continuing dialogue between them, but also by elaborating, at their request, proposals conducive to overcoming existing differences. On several occasions, the Under-Secretary-General for Peace-Keeping Operations, Mr. Marrack Goulding, visited San Salvador to assist in the process of implementation. I have also been in contact with President Cristiani and the leadership of FMLN during critical periods of the process.

12. Regarding the implementation of the San José Agreement on Human Rights, as mentioned in paragraph 8 above, the Human Rights Division of ONUSAL started operating on 26 July 1992, before the signing of the Peace Agreement and the proclamation of the cease-fire. It has been functioning with a staff of 51 civilian professionals and 14 police observers. It was decided that the work of ONUSAL in relation to the San José Agreement would be the subject of a separate series of reports. The Director of the Human Rights Division has submitted five reports covering the period from 26 July 1991 to 30 June 1992 (A/45/1055-S/23037 of 16 September 1991; A/46/658-S/23222 and Corr.1, of 15 November 1992; A/46/876-S/23580 of 19 February 1992; A/46/935-S/24066 of 5 June 1992; and A/46/955-S/24375 of 12 August 1992). The last report of the Human Rights Division offers an assessment of the situation regarding those human rights whose verification was given priority in the San José Agreement, taking as a starting point the situation in El Salvador in July 1991 and highlighting the course of current events. In that report, the Director of the Human Rights Division stated that, following the cease-fire on 1 February 1992, substantial improvements were recorded with regard to rights linked to humanitarian law, as well as to other rights related to the right to life, personal liberty and personal integrity. Nevertheless, concerns were expressed regarding the persistence of alleged violations such as summary executions, death threats, systematic maltreatment of detainees and, particularly, the shortcomings of due process of law and of the obligation of the State in providing safeguards to its citizens.

13. Regarding the various processes relating to the cessation of the armed conflict, the first stage of the separation of forces following the 1 February 1992 cease-fire was completed without major incident by 6 February 1992. However, the second phase of the separation scheduled for 2 March 1992, and the concentration of the troops of both parties, suffered considerable delays. Major difficulties arose over the two public security bodies, the Treasury Police and the National Guard, which, under the Peace Agreement, were supposed to be abolished by 1 March 1992, and their members incorporated into the Army. Actions by the Government at that time raised questions on its compliance with the agreements on these points. The FMLN did not complete its second stage of concentration of troops. In addition to the above-mentioned issue, it cited the lack of infrastructure at the locations where its troops were to concentrate, as well as failure by the Government to comply with other provisions of the Agreement. For its part, the Government pointed to the inadequacy of the inventory of arms presented by the FMLN. As I indicated in my report to the Security Council of 26 May 1992 (S/23999), suspicions that the FMLN was retaining clandestine caches of arms and ammunitions have had a destabilizing effect on the implementation process. Following discussions conducted in early June with the assistance of ONUSAL, the parties were able to resolve the impasse, in particular by rescheduling several of the deadlines included in the initial timetable. I reported to the Security Council on those developments on 19 June 1992 (S/23999/Add.1). The complete concentration of troops was finally achieved by 30 August 1992.

14. Since the beginning of the implementation process, considerable difficulty has been experienced in ensuring that political agreements were implemented together with agreements related to the demobilization of FMLN forces. As mentioned in my report to the Security Council of 26 May 1992, while one breach of the agreement cannot be used to justify another, it cannot be ignored that the implementation timetable set forth in chapter IX of the Peace Agreement was designed to synchronize the reintegration of FMLN ex-combatants and the measures to be undertaken by the Government in order to facilitate that process. Under the agreements, reintegration of FMLN ex-combatants into civilian life was to take place in five stages between 1 May and 31 October 1992. The FMLN, however, argued on several occasions that it could not comply with its calendar of demobilization unless the Government met the deadlines

for the implementation of political agreements, especially those related to land, political participation by FMLN and recruitment into the National Civil Police. As mentioned in paragraph 13 above, in view of serious delays in the implementation of various provisions of the agreements, ONUSAL was called upon to assist the parties in adopting changes in the original timetable with a view to ensuring synchronization between the reintegration of FMLN combatants and the implementation of government programmes. A second revision of the timetable was agreed on 19 August 1992. As a result of those rescheduling exercises, the first two contingents of FMLN combatants—comprising 40 per cent of FMLN strength—were demobilized on 30 June 1992 and 24 September 1992.

15. As I indicated in my letter to the President of the Security Council of 19 October 1992 (S/24688), despite those delays, the intention was to retain 31 October 1992 as the date by which demobilization of the FMLN was to be completed. On 30 September 1992, however, Under-Secretary-General Goulding was informed that further FMLN demobilization would be suspended until new dates had been set for the start of the transfer of land and other aspects of the Agreements that had fallen behind schedule. On 13 October 1992, after intensive work by ONUSAL on the land issue, with the cooperation of experts inside and outside the United Nations system, I presented a proposal to the parties, which they accepted. While the problem of land was resolved, it appeared, however, that the complete dismantling of the military structure of FMLN by 31 October 1992 would be difficult to achieve, making it necessary to proceed with a final revision of the implementation timetable. On 23 October 1992, I presented a proposal in that respect to the parties, which included an extension to 15 December 1992 of the current phase of the implementation of the Peace Agreement, and I recommended to the Security Council an extension of the mandate of ONUSAL. The Security Council, in its resolution 784 (1992) of 30 October 1992, approved an extension of the current mandate of ONUSAL for a period ending 30 November 1992. On 31 October 1992, FMLN demobilized a third contingent. To date, 60 per cent of FMLN ex-combatants have been reintegrated into civilian life.

16. The peace agreements also provided for the establishment of an ad hoc Commission mandated to evaluate the members of the Salvadorian armed forces with a view to a process of purification of the army. As a result of consultations carried out by my predecessor, three civilian personalities, Mr. Reynaldo Galindo Pohl, Mr. Abraham Rodriguez and Mr. Eduardo Molina Olivares, were appointed members of the ad hoc Commission, which was established on 19 May 1992. On 22 September,

the Commission submitted its report in New York to President Cristiani of El Salvador and to me. Under the agreements, the conclusions must be followed by corresponding administrative decisions within 30 days, and implemented within 60 days of their submission. However, difficulties emerged, *inter alia*, regarding that timetable. On 30 October 1992, Under-Secretary-General Marrack Goulding and Assistant Secretary-General Alvaro de Soto travelled to El Salvador to discuss with the parties those and other difficulties related to the peace process. During those consultations, the Government of El Salvador and FMLN were able to reach agreement on the coming stages of the peace process, which are to culminate with the formal end of the armed conflict on 15 December 1992.

17. In addition to verifying the implementation of the agreement related to the cessation of the armed conflict, ONUSAL has been carrying out other verification tasks entrusted to it by the agreements signed by the two parties. The Military Division, which now consists of 234 military observers, has been verifying, *inter alia*, the reduction of Government Armed Forces, and the introduction of the new Armed Forces Reserve System. It will continue to coordinate the clearance of minefields and to monitor the situation affecting ex-combatants on both sides. The Police Division, with a total strength of 303 police observers, has been assisting the existing National Police during the transition period until the deployment of the new National Civil Police.

18. As I mentioned in paragraph 15 above, the United Nations has been actively involved in assisting the parties to overcome their differences on the land issue. The Mission has also followed closely all issues related to the creation of the new National Civil Police, the political participation of FMLN, the restoration of public administration in former zones of conflict, and reforms of the judicial and electoral systems. In addition, ONUSAL participates as an observer in the National Commission for the Consolidation of Peace (COPAZ), mandated to oversee the implementation of all political agreements reached by the parties.

19. I should point out that ONUSAL has been operating in an atmosphere of deep distrust. The insistence of the Mission on maintaining its impartiality has sometimes been misunderstood by each side as partiality towards the other. On 26 May 1992, I had to report to the Security Council (S/23999) that there had been a recurrence of threats against the security of the Mission and its personnel. Since then, further similar incidents have taken place, and I expect that all of them will be duly investigated and measures taken to prevent any future hostile acts against personnel of the Mission.

20. The implementation of the agreements signed

by the Government of El Salvador and FMLN is proving a difficult exercise for all parties concerned. Obstacles, including differences in the interpretation of the agreements and the sheer magnitude of the undertakings, have exceeded the ability of both sides to meet the deadlines of a complex timetable. This, in turn, has continued to fuel existing suspicions, which are a natural legacy of a protracted and bloody civil conflict. It is all the more important for the parties, whose determination to achieve peace made the 16 January Agreement possible, to keep in mind the overriding goal of consolidating this fragile initial phase of the peace-building process in El Salvador. The United Nations will continue to help them meet the challenges of that process.

21. In conclusion, I should like to pay tribute to my Special Representative, Mr. Iqbal Riza, and to all the personnel of ONUSAL who, under his leadership, have worked with dedication and courage, in often very difficult circumstances, to accomplish their demanding mission.

B. *Guatemala*

22. In my last report, I noted that, on 26 April 1991 in Mexico City, the Government of Guatemala and the Unidad Revoluciónaria Nacional Guatemalteca (URNG) had signed an Agreement on the procedure for the search for peace by political means (A/45/1007-S/22563, annex), in which they agreed to hold talks, with the Chairman of the National Reconciliation Commission of Guatemala acting as Conciliator, and in the presence of the Representative of the Secretary-General, acting as Observer. At the same time, the parties signed an agreement on a general agenda for their negotiations (A/45/1009-S/22573, annex). On 25 July 1991 in Queretaro, Mexico, after reaching a "Framework Agreement on Democratization in the Search for Peace by Political Means" (A/46/713-S/23256, annex), the parties proceeded to discuss the issue of human rights.

23. By the beginning of this year, the parties were able to agree on several provisions to be included in a future agreement on human rights, including the principle of international verification by the United Nations. Serious differences emerged, however, regarding the issues of human rights in the framework of the internal armed conflict, the "Voluntary Civil Defence Committees", the establishment of a commission mandated to inquire into violations of human rights since the beginning of the conflict, and the time of entry into force of the agreement on human rights. A long series of indirect meetings, held through the Conciliator and in the presence of the Observer, was instrumental in maintaining the dialogue between the parties from February to August 1992. The publication in May by the URNG of its proposals on other items of the agenda agreed in April 1991, and the

response of the Government the following month, helped to keep attention focused on the peace process despite the impasse on the issue of human rights. Finally, in August 1992, progress was achieved on the issue of "Voluntary Civil Defence Committees". The parties, at a face-to-face meeting in Mexico, were able to agree on a provision whereby, *inter alia*, the Ombudsman (Procurador) for Human Rights of Guatemala would be empowered, upon complaint, to inquire whether members of the patrols were indeed volunteers, and whether they had committed human rights abuses. In addition, the agreed text contained a pledge by the Government not to encourage the creation of new patrols, unless warranted, and laid down procedures should new patrols be established. The parties decided to make that agreed provision public.

24. The parties also agreed to try to overcome outstanding differences through a new round of indirect meetings convened by the Conciliator and in the presence of the Observer. During the past two months, little progress has been made. Therefore, I must reiterate my concern, expressed last year, that the negotiations have not proceeded at a desirable pace. While the parties, in spite of sharp differences, have fulfilled their pledge given in 1991 in Mexico not to abandon the process of negotiation, both should now strive to reinvigorate the process and redouble their efforts towards the goal of a firm and lasting peace.

C. *United Nations Observer Group in Central America*

25. As I mentioned in my report to the Security Council on ONUCA (S/23421 of 14 January 1992), my predecessor had indicated in October 1991 that an early and successful conclusion to the peace process in El Salvador would make it necessary to reconsider the future of ONUCA. In view of the major additional tasks of verification that fell to ONUSAL as a result of the peace agreements between the Government of El Salvador and the FMLN, I believed that the time had come for the Security Council to decide to terminate the operational mandate of ONUCA, so as to enable me to proceed with the transfer of certain personnel and equipment from ONUCA to ONUSAL and complete this deployment in El Salvador by 1 February 1992. In resolution 730 (1992) of 16 January 1992, the Security Council decided to terminate the mandate of ONUCA with effect from 17 January 1992.

26. At this juncture, I should like to pay tribute once again to the Chief Military Observer of ONUCA, Brigadier-General Victor Suanzes Pardo (Spain), to his predecessors in command and to all military and civilian personnel who served in ONUCA, for their success in establishing this first large-scale peace-keeping operation of the United Nations in the Americas and for the contribution they have made to the restoration of peace and stability in Central America.

Document 59

Letter dated 17 December 1992 from Colombia, Mexico, Spain, Venezuela and the United States transmitting a joint statement issued on 15 December 1992 on the occasion of the ceremony to celebrate the end of the first phase of the implementation of the Peace Agreement in El Salvador

A/47/842-S/25007, 23 December 1992

We have the honour to transmit the text of a joint statement issued by the Governments of Colombia, Mexico, Spain, Venezuela and the United States of America on 15 December 1992 on the occasion of the ceremony of national reconciliation held in San Salvador to celebrate the end of the first phase of the implementation of the Peace Agreements in El Salvador, with the culmination of the cessation of the armed conflict (see annex).

We should be grateful if you would have the text of this letter and its annex circulated as a document of the General Assembly, under agenda item 36, and of the Security Council.

(Signed) Luis Fernando JARAMILLO
Permanent Representative of Colombia
to the United Nations

(Signed) Juan A. YAÑEZ-BARNUEVO
Permanent Representative of Spain
to the United Nations

(Signed) Antonio VILLEGAS
Chargé d'affaires a.i. of Mexico to the United Nations

(Signed) Diego ARRIA
Permanent Representative of Venezuela
to the United Nations

(Signed) Edward J. PERKINS
Permanent Representative of the United States of America to the United Nations

Annex

Joint statement issued on the occasion of the ceremony on 15 December 1992 in San Salvador

The Governments of Colombia, Mexico, Spain and Venezuela have served in the capacity of friends of the Salvadorian peace process since October 1990 at the request of the Secretary-General of the United Nations. The Government of the United States of America has also provided its full support for the negotiation and implementation of the Peace Agreements in El Salvador. The Presidents of Colombia, Mexico and Venezuela and the Prime Minister of Spain, and the Secretary of State of the United States of America participated on 16 January 1992 in the ceremony for the signing of the Peace Agreement between the Government of El Salvador and the Frente Farabundo Martí para la Liberación Nacional (FMLN), held in Mexico City, to demonstrate their full support for the Agreements.

The Governments of Colombia, Mexico, Spain, Venezuela and the United States of America congratulate the Salvadorian parties and the Secretary-General of the United Nations on the great progress made in the implementation of the Peace Agreements. Throughout the past year, the five Governments have worked with the Secretary-General, his Special Representative and the United Nations Observer Mission in El Salvador (ONUSAL) to this end.

On this important occasion, the Governments of Colombia, Mexico, Spain, Venezuela and the United States of America reiterate their firm commitment to assist the Secretary-General and Salvadorian institutions and political and social forces in their efforts to ensure that the Salvadorian Peace Agreements are fully implemented and to promote the reconciliation and reconstruction of the country. The five Governments will continue their efforts to gain the support of the international community for the important process of national reconciliation and reconstruction in El Salvador, within the framework of the attainment of democracy, peace, stability and the development of all Central America.

San Salvador, 15 December 1992

Document 60

Report of the Secretary-General concerning the formal end of the armed conflict in El Salvador

S/25006, 23 December 1992

1. The purpose of the present report is to inform the Security Council that, on 15 December 1992, the armed conflict between the Government of El Salvador and the Frente Farabundo Martí para la Liberación Nacional (FMLN) was brought formally to an end in accordance with the adjustment in the timetable for implementing the Peace Accords which the two sides had agreed on the basis of my proposal of 23 October 1992.

2. This event, which had been preceded the previous evening by the legalization of the FMLN as a political party, does not mark the end of implementation of the El Salvador Peace Accords. But it was a defining moment in the history of El Salvador, whose long suffering people can now look forward to a future in which political, economic and social arguments will be settled through the processes of democracy and not by war. The event was marked by a ceremony presided over by President Cristiani, to whom a special tribute is due for his wisdom and courage in promoting peace in his country. I had the honour of being the first speaker at the ceremony and was followed by Mr. Schafik Handal of the FMLN, Vice-President Quayle of the United States of America, Mr. Narcis Serra, Vice-President of the Government of Spain on behalf of the four "Friends of the Secretary-General", President Serrano of Guatemala on behalf of the Central American States, and President Cristiani himself. The text of my statement is at Annex I.

3. During the preceding weeks, the parties had, in general, complied with their commitments in accordance with the adjustments to the timetable in my proposal of 23 October 1992. Both COPAZ and the Legislative Assembly had made a determined effort to complete pending legislation. Informal reports on progress in recent weeks had been presented to the members of the Security Council. The following points are worth special mention:

(a) Demobilization and demilitarization

The demobilization of the fourth FMLN contingent, due on 20 November, was completed after considerable delay. However, the fifth and final contingent was demobilized on time. The relevant statistics are at Annex II.

(b) FMLN arms

The inventory was presented and the FMLN's arms concentrated in the designated zones on time by 30 November. After analysis by ONUSAL, the inventory was accepted as satisfactory. It included details both of sophisticated weapons and of armament located outside El Salvador. The destruction of the arms by FMLN began with only a slight delay. However, for technical reasons, destruction could not be completed by 15 December, by when only about 50 per cent of the inventory had been destroyed. The process continues under ONUSAL's supervision and should finish by the end of December. The destruction of weapons located outside El Salvador should be completed in early January 1993.

(c) Recall of weapons distributed to civilian groups and individuals

This recall was to have been effected by 8 December 1992. However, notwithstanding constant urgings by ONUSAL, the Government failed to take any effective steps to ensure the return of the weapons. As of 8 December 1992, less than 100 (out of an estimated total of several thousands) had been recovered. ONUSAL has been assured by the Government that its efforts will be intensified. It will continue to press the Government for effective action.

(d) Ad Hoc Commission and Truth Commission

The administrative decisions on the implementation of the recommendations of the Ad Hoc Commission were presented punctually by the Government. The actual implementation is to follow shortly. The Commission on the Truth has completed its investigations and will present its report and recommendations in February 1993.

4. It is important that both parties, and the international community, should persevere in their efforts to ensure punctual implementation of the remaining provisions of the Peace Accords. Much remains to be done. All provisions of the Accords are to be regarded as solemn commitments but certain of them merit special emphasis. One is the programme for effective land transfers outlined in my proposal of 13 October 1992, which was accepted by the parties and therefore constitutes an agreement between them, including guarantees for the non-eviction

of current landholders until a legal solution is achieved. Another is the effective implementation of programmes for the reintegration into civilian life of ex-combatants from both sides, with special attention to the war-disabled. A third is improvement in the effective international supervision of the National Public Security Academy and its establishment in permanent premises. A fourth is the establishment of the National Civilian Police, and its progressive and timely deployment, with the corresponding phasing out of the present National Police. A fifth is the completion of the planned reduction of the Armed Forces. A sixth is the concertation in the Forum for Economic and Social Consultation of long-term plans for the economic and social development of El Salvador. The role of COPAZ in ensuring the effective implementation of these and other pending commitments is central and must be supported and strengthened by both parties.

5. It is to be noted in this context that FMLN, which negotiated and signed the Peace Accords as an armed movement and is now a fully legal political party, retains its status as one of the two signatories to these Accords until they have been fully implemented. I have no doubt that the Government of El Salvador will maintain, in this respect, the positive and constructive attitude it has previously demonstrated.

6. As the remaining provisions of the Accords are implemented, under the constant supervision of ONUSAL, both parties will have a continuing responsibility to foster political stability and the climate of *détente* and reconciliation referred to in the Accords. Special care will be required in the former zones of conflict where ill-judged action by either party could cause tensions to resurface. The Presidential, legislative and municipal elections which are to be held in March 1994 will be the logical culmination of the entire peace process. Only then will peace, which has been achieved at such high cost, be firmly consolidated in El Salvador. Until then the watchword must be restraint, tolerance and national reconciliation.

7. The transition from war to peace does not come spontaneously or easily. Twelve years of strife inevitably leave deep scars, bitter memories and rancour. Peace is won only by effort and resolve. There must therefore be a change in attitudes, a change in mentalities. Reconciliation must be the new challenge; social justice and the struggle against poverty, the new goals. As I declared in the ceremony on 15 December, as long as the people of El Salvador remain steadfast in the commitments which they undertook at Chapultepec, the international community will be behind them and support them in building peace in the wake of war. But the primary responsibility belongs to the Salvadorians themselves.

Annex I

Statement of Secretary-General at the ceremony marking the end of the armed conflict in El Salvador, San Salvador, 15 December 1992

President Cristiani,
Presidents and Vice-Presidents from other nations,
Members of the Comandancia of the FMLN,
Excellencies,
Ladies and gentlemen,

The armed conflict in El Salvador has come to an end.

Thirty-two months ago, the Government of El Salvador and the Frente Farabundo Martí para la Liberación Nacional began a negotiating process under the auspices of my predecessor, Javier Pérez de Cuéllar. The purpose of the process was "to end the armed conflict by political means as speedily as possible, promote the democratization of the country, guarantee unrestricted respect for human rights and reunify Salvadorian society".

Today, following almost a year without armed combat, El Salvador crosses the line from armed peace into a new era. It is a momentous occasion indeed. The first goal of the process has been achieved. Salvadorians have every reason to be proud. At a turbulent time in history, they are providing a shining example to the world.

Many steps have been taken toward achieving the second goal, that of promoting the democratization of the country. Many more are yet to come. This process is to build on the solid foundations laid down in the negotiation, in the reforms of the Constitution ratified earlier this year. But democracy is an elusive goal. It must permeate the minds of all. Salvadorians must become accustomed to tolerance. This means accepting that others may have different ideas. This means that others may have different attitudes. This means that others may have different policies. This means respecting the right of others to freely express those ideas; to hold those attitudes; to promote those policies. The broad spectrum of society represented in this ceremony testifies to the giant strides already taken in the direction of pluralism.

Monitoring of respect for human rights is an important element of the work of the United Nations in El Salvador. It sends a signal to the people, even in the farthest reaches of the country: the changes occurring are meant to provide them with an environment in which their rights are respected. ONUSAL has been monitoring respect for human rights for almost a year and a half. This will continue to be done throughout the country, on a long-term basis. Thus the third goal of the process is being gradually consolidated.

The last goal, the reunification of Salvadorian society, is still not within reach. The scars of the past are still present. It is essential that those in a position of responsibility should play a leading role in the healing of wounds. As President Cristiani put it in his remarkable speech at Chapultepec Castle:

> "... what is beginning to occur in El Salvador is not the re-establishment of a pre-existing peace. It is the inauguration of an authentic peace based on social consensus; on the basic harmony between social, political and ideological sectors, and above all on the concept of the country as a whole without exclusion."

The two warring parties negotiated the peace. But many sectors of society played a role in the great national debate which took place during the negotiation. They must also play a part in bringing Salvadorians back together. COPAZ has a central role to play in this mission, as does the Forum for Economic and Social Consultation.

The reunification of society is a long-term goal. It will not come about by miracle. The parties to the peace agreement must give the example by complying scrupulously with their solemn undertakings. They must also play a determined, active role in assisting the process of *détente* and reconciliation. They are specifically committed to do so under the Peace Agreement. This is fundamentally important.

I am well aware of the difficulties which have been encountered in implementing the Peace Agreement. I know of the tensions that have arisen as a result of the challenges inherent in meeting a very tight timetable. The timetable was an ambitious mechanism, as intricate as clockwork. It could not be otherwise. Its purpose was to synchronize two distinct but interlocking processes: the reintegration of the members of the FMLN, within a framework of full legality, into the civil, institutional and political life of the country, on the one hand; and the establishment of the necessary guarantees and conditions to bring about that reintegration, on the other.

It is not entirely surprising that problems should have arisen in implementing this timetable. It is a reason for rejoicing that these problems have largely been overcome. For example, a serious crisis was faced in dealing with the problem of the land. This led to the suspension of the demobilization of the FMLN. The entire process was in danger. The provisions of the land issue had not been spelled out with sufficient clarity in the Chapultepec Agreement.

Fortunately, with assistance from various quarters and the cooperation of the parties, it proved possible to resolve the land question in October. This permitted the demobilization of the FMLN to resume.

Further difficulties and much public debate arose in reference to the recommendations of the Ad hoc Commission on the Purification of the Armed Forces. These have fortunately been overcome. I wish to pay tribute to the members of that Commission. They have discharged an onerous and sensitive task in the service of their country. The beneficiary will be the Salvadorian people, who will have at their service a professional institution, under civilian authority, adapted to the needs of tomorrow.

It is quite possible that the watershed in the process of reuniting Salvadorian society will come only when the report of the Commission on the Truth becomes available. The scriptures tell us that the truth shall set you free. Salvadorians will only put the past behind them once the truth about the past is brought to light. We await with expectation the results of the courageous labour which these three eminent and wise men have undertaken.

For the United Nations, involvement in El Salvador has been a pioneering experience. It is the first in a new generation of United Nations operations whose purpose is post-conflict peace-building. In addition to the verification of respect for human rights, the United Nations is variously involved in a complex and integrated set of tasks. These tasks are carried out under the aegis of ONUSAL headed by Mr. Iqbal Riza, my Special Representative. We assist the National Police and monitor its activities. We participate in the creation of a new National Civil Police. We monitor the transition to a new, leaner Armed Forces, better suited to its role as defined in the reformed Constitution. We play an active role in overseeing the implementation of the agreement on land. We stand ready to assist so that the land programme can be implemented. In short, we are trying to help in ensuring that the causes of the conflict do not recur.

The Security Council and I myself place the greatest emphasis on the consolidation of stable conditions following the definitive end of the armed conflict today. But the primary responsibility lies with the people of El Salvador. The Security Council cannot substitute for you, the Salvadorian people. Neither the Secretary-General, nor the "Friends of the Secretary-General", nor indeed any other country can replace the people of El Salvador. I can assure you, however, that as long as the people of El Salvador remain steadfast in the commitments which they undertook at Chapultepec, the international community is behind you. The international community will support you.

FMLN Demobilization as at 17 December 1992

Military Regional Office	Military Verification Team	Disarmed Combatants
San Salvador	La Reina	415
	San Antonio los Ranchos	1 084
	El Ocotal	277
	El Paisnal	244
	Guazapa	1 760
	Sub-Total	3 780
San Vicente	Murillo	202
	Tecoluca	266
	Santa Clara	253
	Santa Marta	558
	El Zapote	436
	Sub-Total	1 715
San Miguel	Perquín	1 403
	Isleta	202
	San Francisco Javier	526
	Las Marias	553
	Nueva Granada	697
	Sub-Total	3 381
	TOTAL	8 876*
	Weapons	*Percentage of Inventory*
	Collected	93.4%
	Destroyed	46.8%

*Note: In addition, there are 3,486 war handicapped and injured members of the FMLN. These have also been demobilized.

Document 61

Letter dated 30 December 1992 from the Russian Federation and the United States transmitting a joint statement on El Salvador issued 28 December 1992

A/47/853-S/25056, 6 January 1993

We have the honour to send you herewith the text of the joint statement on El Salvador of 28 December 1992 by the Department of State of the United States of America and the Ministry of Foreign Affairs of the Russian Federation (see annex).

We would appreciate the distribution of the texts of the present letter and of the joint statement as an official document of the General Assembly, under agenda item 36, and of the Security Council.

(*Signed*) Edward J. PERKINS
Ambassador
Permanent Representative of the United States
of America to the United Nations

(*Signed*) Yuli M. VORONTSOV
Ambassador
Permanent Representative of the Russian Federation
to the United Nations

*Joint statement on El Salvador issued on
28 December 1992 by the Ministry of Foreign
Affairs of the Russian Federation and the
Department of State of the United States of America*

The Russian Federation and the United States of America, whose constructive interaction on Central American issues the last several years has helped defuse tensions in this area, note with great satisfaction that the peace process in El Salvador started at Esquípulas and pursued further within the framework of the Chapultepec Accords has entered a promising new phase.

Russia and the United States applaud the political resolve displayed by the Government of El Salvador and the leadership of the Frente Farabundo Martí para la Liberación Nacional (FMLN), which overcame mutual distrust to implement the main provisions of the Chapultepec Accords. Russia and the United States are grateful for the role played by the United Nations, above all its Secretary-General, and for the support given the peace process by Mexico, Spain, Colombia and Venezuela. The high level of representation at the reconciliation ceremony on 15 December 1992 bears testimony to the intention of the international community to continue its support of the peace process.

As El Salvador moves forward to implement fully the Peace Accords and to realize the full potential of progress to date, Russia and the United States express confidence that the Government of El Salvador and the FMLN will continue their dialogue and cooperation with the United Nations, show restraint, and demonstrate renewed determination to achieve their country's socio-economic reconstruction. They reiterate their readiness to continue to assist in this effort and express hope that other interested States and international and regional organizations will offer their support.

Document 62

Letter dated 7 January 1993 from the Secretary-General to the President of the Security Council concerning implementation of the provisions of the peace agreements relating to the purification of the armed forces

S/25078, 9 January 1993

The purpose of this letter is to report to you and through you to the members of the Security Council on the latest developments relating to implementation of the provisions of the Peace Accords for El Salvador concerning the purification of the armed forces (S/23501, annex, chap. I, sect. 3).

It will be recalled that in my letter to the President of the Security Council of 13 November 1992 (S/24805) I reported on arrangements which had been successfully concluded with the Government and the FMLN to bring the armed conflict in El Salvador formally to an end on 15 December 1992. Those arrangements included agreement by President Cristiani to complete implementation of the recommendations of the Ad Hoc Commission on Purification of the Armed Forces within a specified time-frame. In particular, President Cristiani had agreed to inform me by 29 November 1992 of the administrative decisions he had taken on this matter. As I subsequently reported to the Security Council in paragraph 3 (d) of my report of 23 December 1992 (S/25006), the administrative decisions were punctually communicated to me by President Cristiani. In his letter, President Cristiani in-formed me that he had adopted administrative decisions concerning all the officers included in the Ad Hoc Commission's report. These decisions would be made known on 31 December 1992 at the latest and would become effective as of 1 January 1993.

On 5 January 1993, in my absence in Africa, the Under-Secretary-General for Peace-keeping Operations and my Senior Political Adviser received, by hand of Dr. Oscar Santamaria, Minister of the Presidency, and General Mauricio Vargas, Deputy Chief of Staff of the Armed Forces of El Salvador, a letter dated 1 January 1993 in which President Cristiani conveyed to me details of the measures adopted to implement the recommendations of the Ad Hoc Commission.

The recommendations of the Ad Hoc Commission concerned 103 officers. One of these was no longer a serving member of the Armed Forces. Of the remaining 102 officers, it was recommended that 26 should be transferred to other functions and 76 should be discharged. President Cristiani informed me in his letter that the following measures had been adopted in relation to 94 of these 102 officers:

(1) Twenty-five officers had been transferred to other functions;

(2) Four officers had been discharged for disciplinary reasons (one of them being the 26th officer recommended for a transfer to other functions);

(3) Nineteen officers had been discharged for administrative reasons;

(4) Thirty-eight officers had been placed on leave with pay, pending completion of the procedures for their retirement which would take place within a period not exceeding six months;

(5) Seven officers had been appointed as Military Attachés to Salvadorian embassies abroad;

(6) One officer had, for personal reasons, been permitted to remain in active service until he retired on 1 March 1993.

President Cristiani's letter went on to say that administrative decisions relating to the other eight officers would be deferred during "the period of transition", which is understood to mean during the remainder of President Cristiani's mandate as President of the Republic.

Enclosed with President Cristiani's letter were copies of the administrative orders relating to categories (1), (2), (3), (4) and (5) above. I have verified that the names correspond with those in the report of the Ad Hoc Commission.

Having carefully studied President Cristiani's letter and its enclosures, I have come to the following conclusions:

(a) The measures adopted in relation to categories (1), (2) and (3) above comply fully with the recommendations of the Ad Hoc Commission;

(b) The measures adopted in relation to categories (4) and (6) also comply broadly with the recommendations of the Ad Hoc Commission. The officers concerned will not perform any official functions with effect from 1 January 1993, but their discharge will not become effective until the legal formalities for their retirement are complete, which could in some cases take as long as six months. I nevertheless consider that these measures can be accepted as satisfactory in the circumstances;

(c) The appointment of the seven officers in category (5) to Military Attaché posts does not comply with the Ad Hoc Commission's recommendations which require these officers to be discharged;

(d) The deferral of decisions relating to the remaining eight officers is similarly not in compliance with the Commission's recommendations.

I have from the outset been conscious of the particular difficulty and sensitivity of this aspect of the Peace Accords. As indicated above, I am ready to accept as satisfactory the measures adopted and implemented by the Government of El Salvador with respect to 87 of the 102 officers covered by the Ad Hoc Commission's recommendations, even though a number of them do not conform in all respects with those recommendations. However, the measures adopted in respect of the other 15 officers do not comply with those recommendations and are thus not in conformity with the Peace Accords. The mandate entrusted to me by the Security Council requires me to seek full compliance by each side with all the commitments it has entered into in signing the Peace Accords. I have therefore asked President Cristiani to take early action to regularize the position of the 15 officers in respect of whom the Ad Hoc Commission's recommendations have not yet been fully implemented.

I shall continue to report to the Security Council as appropriate on the implementation of this and other aspects of the Peace Accords.

(*Signed*) Boutros BOUTROS-GHALI

Document 63

Letter dated 26 January 1993 from the Secretary-General to the President of the Security Council concerning United Nations verification of elections to be held in El Salvador in March 1994

S/25241, 4 February 1993

I have the honour to refer to the United Nations Observer Mission in El Salvador (ONUSAL).

The members of the Security Council will recall that, in my report to the Council of 23 November 1992 (S/24833, para. 74), I stated that the Government of El Salvador had informed me that it had requested the Supreme Electoral Tribunal, as the competent authority, to consider a proposal that the United Nations verify the next presidential, legislative and municipal elections due to be held in El Salvador in March 1994.

I now wish to inform the Security Council that I have received from the Salvadorian authorities a letter dated 8 January 1993, informing me that, based on the reply received from the Supreme Electoral Tribunal, the Government had decided to request the United Nations to verify the forthcoming general elections.

Given the importance of these elections, which will be the first to take place after the end of the conflict and should in the normal course of events constitute the logical culmination of the entire peace process, it would be my intention to recommend the acceptance of the request of the Government of El Salvador. As I indicated in my report of 23 November 1992 (S/24833, para. 83), the personnel needed for this task would be phased in as required by the electoral process and their assignment would end immediately after the elections in March 1994. I shall present to the Security Council, in the report requested of me in paragraph 8 of resolution 791 (1992), my recommendations regarding the administrative and financial implications of the request.

I should be grateful if you would bring this letter to the attention of the members of the Security Council.

(*Signed*) Boutros BOUTROS-GHALI

Document 64

Letter dated 29 January 1993 from the Secretary-General to the President of the Security Council concerning developments relating to the destruction of FMLN arms and equipment

S/25200, 29 January 1993

I wish to report to you and through you to the members of the Security Council on developments relating to the destruction of the arms and equipment which, in accordance with the provisions of the Peace Accords for El Salvador, were deposited by the Frente Farabundo Martí para la Liberación Nacional (FMLN) in previously designated locations and placed under the supervision of ONUSAL.

It will be recalled that in my report to the Security Council of 23 December 1992 (S/25006) I indicated that the armed conflict between the Government of El Salvador and the FMLN had been brought formally to an end on 15 December in accordance with the adjustment in the timetable which the two sides had agreed on the basis of my proposal of 23 October 1992. The destruction by the FMLN of its arms inventory was to have been completed on 15 December, except for certain categories of weapons which would take longer to destroy for technical reasons. Towards the end of December the FMLN suspended the process of destruction of its remaining arms and equipment. After repeated requests for compliance by the United Nations Observer Mission in El Salvador (ONUSAL), my Special Representative informed the FMLN leadership that, should the FMLN fail to take action to resume the process, alternative ways to ensure compliance would have to be put into effect.

On 21 January 1993, my Special Representative informed me that, at a meeting the previous day, the FMLN had undertaken to resume the destruction of its arms and equipment on 22 January and to complete it by 29 January. Although the process did resume on the date indicated, I regret to have to report to the Security Council that the FMLN, despite prior assurances, did not complete the destruction of its weapons by the agreed deadline and that it is therefore not yet in compliance with its undertakings under the Peace Accords.

(*Signed*) Boutros BOUTROS-GHALI

Document 65

Statement by the President of the Security Council emphasizing the solemn nature of the undertakings made by each of the parties when they signed the peace agreements for El Salvador

S/25257, 9 February 1993

The Security Council welcomes with satisfaction the important progress made thus far towards the full implementation of the peace accords for El Salvador and the cooperation shown by the parties to this end. The Council takes note of the report of the Secretary-General of 23 December 1992 1/ in which he indicates that the armed conflict between the Government of El Salvador and the Frente Farabundo Martí para la Liberación Nacional (FMLN) was formally brought to an end on 15 December 1992. The Council emphasizes this event, which puts an end to more than 10 years of armed conflict.

However, the Council expresses concern at the observations made by the Secretary-General in his letter dated 7 January 1993 to the President of the Security Council, 2/ by which he reported on the situation with regard to the implementation of the recommendations of the Ad Hoc Commission concerning the purification of the armed forces of El Salvador and, basically, at the fact that those recommendations have yet to be fully complied with despite prior assurances by the Government of El Salvador. The Council also expresses concern at the indication in the letter dated 29 January 1993 from the Secretary-General to the President of the Security Council 3/ that FMLN, despite prior assurances, did not complete the destruction of its weapons by the agreed deadline and that it is therefore not yet in full compliance with its undertakings under the peace accords.

In this connection, the Council emphasizes the solemn nature of the undertakings made by each of the parties when they signed the peace accords and reaffirms the obligation of the parties to comply fully and in a timely fashion with those undertakings.

The Council welcomes with satisfaction the decision of the Government of El Salvador to request the United Nations to verify the forthcoming general elections and the intention of the Secretary-General, communicated in his letter dated 26 January 1993 to the President of the Security Council, 4/ to recommend to the Security Council that it accede to this request.

The Security Council strongly urges the parties to persist in their determination to complete the process of bringing peace and national reconciliation to El Salvador and to continue cooperating with the Secretary-General in the efforts that he is making to ensure that the peace accords are implemented fully. To that end, the Council will follow closely the progress and results of those efforts.

1/ S/25006.
2/ S/25078.
3/ S/25200.
4/ S/25241.

Document 66

Statement by the President of the Security Council calling upon the parties to comply with the recommendations contained in the report of the Commission on the Truth

S/25427, 18 March 1993

The Security Council welcomes the recent efforts to apply fully the peace accords in El Salvador and acknowledges the sense of responsibility and cooperation demonstrated by the Government of El Salvador and the Frente Farabundo Martí para la Liberación Nacional to reach this objective.

In this context, the Security Council welcomes the submission of the report of the Commission on the Truth and of its recommendations intended to prevent the repetition of the acts of violence committed during the twelve years of armed confrontation, as well as to create confidence in the positive changes caused by the peace process and stimulate national reconciliation.

The Council underlines the need for the parties, in accordance with the peace accords, to comply with the recommendations contained in the report of the Commission on the Truth, as well as all other obligations which remain to be implemented. In addition, it calls upon Salvadorian society to continue acting with the responsibility which it has demonstrated throughout this process, in order to contribute to the consolidation of internal peace and the maintenance of a genuine and lasting atmosphere of national harmony.

The Council invites the Secretary-General to keep it informed regarding the implementation of the parties' pending commitments and reiterates that it will continue to follow closely the evolution of the peace process in El Salvador and that it stands ready to assist the parties as appropriate to achieve the successful completion of that process.

Document 67

Letter dated 29 March 1993 from the Secretary-General to the President of the Security Council transmitting the report presented on 15 March 1993 by the Commission on the Truth

S/25500, 1 April 1993

I have the honour to transmit herewith the report presented on 15 March 1993 by the Commission on the Truth established under the peace agreements between the Government of El Salvador and the Frente Farabundo Martí para la Liberación Nacional (FMLN) (see annex).

As you are aware, the report contains a set of recommendations that are binding on the Parties. As part of the mandate entrusted to the United Nations to verify implementation of all agreements reached between the Government of El Salvador and FMLN, I have today addressed to the President of El Salvador and the General Coordinator of FMLN requests that each of them inform ONUSAL of the measures he intends to take to implement the recommendations of the Commission, together with the timetable for the execution of such measures.

Also today, the Acting Chief of the United Nations Observer Mission in El Salvador, General Victor Suanzes, has been instructed to address a letter to the Comisión Nacional para la Consolidación de la Paz (COPAZ), which, under the peace agreements, is mandated to supervise the implementation of political agreements reached between the Parties. In that letter, General Suanzes will inform COPAZ of the request for information which I have addressed to the Government of El Salvador and FMLN and will ask the Commission to inform ONUSAL of the steps it intends to take to discharge the responsibilities entrusted to it under the peace agreements.

I should be grateful if you would bring this information to the attention of the members of the Security Council.

(Signed) Boutros BOUTROS-GHALI

Annex

FROM MADNESS TO HOPE

The 12-year war in El Salvador

REPORT OF THE COMMISSION ON THE TRUTH FOR EL SALVADOR

THE COMMISSION ON THE TRUTH FOR EL SALVADOR

Belisario Betancur, *Chairman*
Reinaldo Figueredo Planchart
Thomas Buergenthal

CONTENTS

*The annexes are available for consultation in the language of submission (Spanish) in the Dag Hammarsjköld Library.

"... all these things happened among us ..."

—*Mayan poem*

I. Introduction

Between 1980 and 1991, the Republic of El Salvador in Central America was engulfed in a war which plunged Salvadorian society into violence, left it with thousands and thousands of people dead and exposed it to appalling crimes, until the day—16 January 1992—when the parties, reconciled, signed the Peace Agreement in the Castle of Chapultepec, Mexico, and brought back the light and the chance to re-emerge from madness to hope.

A. *Institutions and names*

Violence was a fire which swept over the fields of El Salvador; it burst into villages, cut off roads and destroyed highways and bridges, energy sources and transmission lines; it reached the cities and entered families, sacred areas and educational centres; it struck at justice and filled the public administration with victims; and it singled out as an enemy anyone who was not on the list of friends. Violence turned everything to death and destruction, for such is the senselessness of that breach of the calm plenitude which accompanies the rule of law, the essential nature of violence being suddenly or gradually to alter the certainty which the law nurtures in human beings when this change does not take place through the normal mechanisms of the rule of law. The victims were Salvadorians and foreigners of all backgrounds and all social and economic classes, for in its blind cruelty violence leaves everyone equally defenceless.

When there came pause for thought, Salvadorians put their hands to their hearts and felt them pound with joy. No one was winning the war, everyone was losing it. Governments of friendly countries and organizations the world over that had looked on in anguish at the tragic events in that Central American country which, although small, was made great by the creativity of its people—all contributed their ideas to the process of reflection. A visionary, Javier Pérez de Cuéllar, then Secretary-General of the United Nations, heeded the unanimous outcry and answered it. The Presidents of Colombia, Mexico, Spain and Venezuela supported him. The Chapultepec Agreement expressed the support of the new Secretary-General, Mr. Boutros Boutros-Ghali, for the search for reconciliation.

B. *The creative consequences*

On the long road of the peace negotiations, the need to reach agreement on a Commission on the Truth arose from the Parties' recognition that the communism which had encouraged one side had collapsed, and perhaps also from the disillusionment of the Power which had encouraged the other. It emerged as a link in the chain of reflection and agreement and was motivated, ultimately, by the impact of events on Salvadorian society, which now faced the urgent task of confronting the issue of the widespread, institutionalized impunity which had struck at its very heart: under the protection of State bodies but outside the law, repeated human rights violations had been committed by members of the armed forces; these same rights had also been violated by members of the guerrilla forces.

In response to this situation, the negotiators agreed that such repugnant acts should be referred to a Commission on the Truth, which was the name they agreed to give it from the outset. Unlike the Ad Hoc Commission, so named because there was no agreement on what to call the body created to purify the armed forces, the Commission on the Truth was so named because its very purpose and function were to seek, find and publicize the truth about the acts of violence committed by both sides during the war.

The truth, the whole truth and nothing but the truth, as the oath goes. The overall truth and the specific truth, the radiant but quiet truth. The whole and its parts, in other words, the bright light shone onto a surface to illuminate it and the parts of this same surface lit up case by case, regardless of the identity of the perpetrators, always in the search for lessons that would contribute to reconciliation and to abolishing such patterns of behaviour in the new society.

Learning the truth and strengthening and tempering the determination to find it out; putting an end to impunity and cover-up; settling political and social differences by means of agreement instead of violent action: these are the creative consequences of an analytical search for the truth.

C. *The mandate*

Furthermore, by virtue of the scope which the negotiators gave to the agreements, it was understood that the Commission on the Truth would have to examine systematic atrocities both individually and collectively, since the flagrant human rights violations which had shocked Salvadorian society and the international community had been carried out not only by members of the armed forces but also by members of the insurgent forces.

The peace agreements were unambiguous when, in article 2, they defined the mandate and scope of the Commission as follows: "The Commission shall have the task of investigating serious acts of violence that have occurred since 1980 and whose impact on society urgently demands that the public should know the truth". Article 5 of the Chapultepec Peace Agreement gives the Commission the task of clarifying and putting an end to any indication of impunity on the part of officers of the armed forces and gives this explanation: "acts of this nature, regardless of the sector to which their perpetrators belong, must be the object of exemplary action by the law courts so that the punishment prescribed by law is meted out to those found responsible".

It is clear that the peace negotiators wanted this new peace to be founded, raised and built on the transparency of a knowledge which speaks its name. It is also clear that this truth must be made public as a matter of urgency if it is to be not the servant of impunity but an instrument of the justice that is essential for the synchronized implementation of the agreements which the Commission is meant to facilitate.

D. *"Open-door" policy*

From the outset of their work, which began on 13 July 1992 when they were entrusted with their task by the Secretary-General of the United Nations, the Commissioners could perceive the skill of those who had negotiated the agreements in the breadth of the mandate and authority given to the Commission. They realized that the Secretary-General, upon learning from competent Salvadorian judges of the numerous acts of violence and atrocities of 12 years of war, had not been wrong in seeking to preserve the Commission's credibility by looking beyond considerations of sovereignty and entrusting this task to three scholars from other countries, in contrast to what had been done in Argentina and Chile after the military dictatorships there had ended. The Commissioners also saw a glimmer of hope dawn in the hearts of the Salvadorian people when it became clear that the truth would soon be revealed, not through bias or pressure but in its entirety and with complete impartiality, a fact which helped to restore the faith of people at all levels that justice would be effective and fitting. Accordingly, in their first meeting with the media upon arriving in El Salvador, the Commissioners stated that they would not let themselves be pressured or impressed: they were after the objective truth and the hard facts.

The Commissioners and the group of professionals who collaborated with them in the investigations succeeded in overcoming obstacles and limitations that made it difficult to establish what had really happened, starting with the brief period of time—six months—afforded them under the Chapultepec Agreement. Given the magnitude of their task, this time-frame, which seemed to stretch into Kafkaesque infinity when they embarked upon their task, ultimately seemed meagre and barely sufficient to allow them to complete their work satisfactorily.

Throughout its mandate and while drafting its report, the Commission consistently sought to distance itself from events that had not been verified before it reached any conclusions. The whole of Salvadorian society, institutions and individuals familiar with acts of violence were invited to make them known to the Commission, under the guarantee of confidentiality and discretion provided for in the agreements. Paid announcements were placed in the press and on the radio and television to this end, and written and oral invitations were extended to the Parties to testify without restriction. Offices of the Commission were opened in various departmental capitals, including Chalatenango, Santa Ana and San Miguel. Written statements were taken, witnesses were heard, information from the sites of various incidents (e.g. El Calabozo, El Mozote, Sumpul river and Guancorita) was obtained. The Commission itself went to various departments with members of the professional team, occasionally travelling overland but more often in helicopters provided promptly and efficiently by ONUSAL. As the investigation moved forward, it continued to yield new pieces of evidence: anyone who might have been involved was summoned to testify without restriction as to time or place, usually in the Commission's offices or in secret locations, often outside El Salvador in order to afford witnesses greater protection.

The Commission maintained an "open-door" policy for hearing testimony and a "closed-door" policy for preserving confidentiality. Its findings illustrate the horrors of a war in which madness prevailed, and confirm beyond the shadow of a doubt that the incidents denounced, recorded and substantiated in this report actually took place. Whenever the Commission decided that its investigation of a specific case had yielded sufficient evidence, the matter was recorded in detail, with mention of the guilty parties. When it was determined that no

further progress could be made for the time being, the corresponding documentation that was not subject to secrecy was delivered to the courts or else kept confidential until new information enabled it to be reactivated.

One fact must be squarely denounced: owing to the destruction or concealment of documents, or the failure to divulge the locations where numerous persons were imprisoned or bodies were buried, the burden of proof occasionally reverted to the Commission, the judiciary and citizens, who found themselves forced to reconstruct events. It will be up to those who administer the new system of justice to pursue these investigations and take whatever final decisions they consider appropriate at this moment in history.

Inevitably, the list of victims is incomplete: it was compiled on the basis of the complaints and testimony received and confirmed by the Commission.

E. A convulsion of violence

The warped psychology engendered by the conflict led to a convulsion of violence. The civilian population in disputed or guerrilla-controlled areas was automatically assumed to be the enemy, as at El Mozote and the Sumpul river. The opposing side behaved likewise, as when mayors were executed, the killings justified as acts of war because the victims had obstructed the delivery of supplies to combatants, or when defenceless pleasure-seekers became military targets, as in the case of the United States marines in the Zona Rosa of San Salvador. Meanwhile, the doctrine of national salvation and the principle of "he who is not for me is against me" were cited to ignore the neutrality, passivity and defencelessness of journalists and church workers, who served the community in various ways.

Such behaviour also led to the clandestine refinement of the death squads: the bullet which struck Monsignor Romero in the chest while he was celebrating mass on 24 March 1980 in a San Salvador church is a brutal symbol of the nightmare the country experienced during the war. And the murder of the six Jesuit priests 10 years later was the final outburst of the delirium that had infected the armed forces and the innermost recesses of certain government circles. The bullet in the portrait of Monsignor Romero, mute witness to this latest crime, repeats the nightmare image of those days.

F. Phenomenology of violence

It is a universally accepted premise that the individual is the subject of any criminal situation, since humans alone possess will and can therefore take decisions based on will: it is individuals that commit crimes, not the institutions they have created. As a result, it is to individuals and not their institutions that the corresponding penalties established by law must be applied.

However, there could be some situations in which the repetition of acts in time and space would seem to contradict the above premise. A situation of repeated criminal acts may arise in which different individuals act within the same institution in unmistakably similar ways, independently of the political ideology of Governments and decision makers. This gives reason to believe that institutions may indeed commit crimes, if the same behaviour becomes a constant of the institution and, especially, if clear-cut accusations are met with a cover-up by the institution to which the accused belong and the institution is slow to act when investigations reveal who is responsible. In such circumstances, it is easy to succumb to the argument that repeated crimes mean that the institution is to blame.

The Commission on the Truth did not fall into that temptation: at the beginning of its mandate, it received hints from the highest level to the effect that institutions do not commit crimes and therefore that responsibilities must be established by naming names. At the end of its mandate, it again received hints from the highest level, this time to the opposite effect, namely, that it should not name names, perhaps in order to protect certain individuals in recognition of their genuine and commendable eagerness to help create situations which facilitated the peace agreements and national reconciliation.

However, the Commission believes that responsibility for anything that happened during the period of the conflict could not and should not be laid at the door of the institution, but rather of those who ordered the procedures for operating in the way that members of the institution did and also of those who, having been in a position to prevent such procedures, were compromised by the degree of tolerance and permissiveness with which they acted from their positions of authority or leadership or by the fact that they covered up incidents which came to their knowledge or themselves gave the order which led to the action in question. This approach protects institutions and punishes criminals.

G. *The recovery of faith*

As this Commission submits its report, El Salvador is embarked on a positive and irreversible process of consolidation of internal peace and modification of conduct for the maintenance of a genuine, lasting climate of national coexistence. The process of reconciliation is restoring the nation's faith in itself and in its leaders and institutions. This does not mean that all the obstacles and difficulties in implementing the commitments made in the negotiations have been overcome: the particular sensitivity of some of these commitments, such as the commitment to purify the armed forces, is creating resistance to the administrative action which must be taken by President Alfredo Cristiani, who on many counts deserves widespread recognition as the driving force behind the peace agreements.

One fundamental element of the agreements, and one which is critical for El Salvador's democratic future, is the unreserved, unconditional subordination of the military authorities to civilian authority, not only on paper but in reality: in a democratic system based on respect for the constitutional order and governed by the rule of law, there is room neither for conditions, personal compromises or the possibility of subverting order for personal reasons, nor for acts of intimidation against the President of the Republic who, by virtue of his office, is the Commander-in-Chief of the armed forces.

H. *The risk of delays*

The purification which is to follow the reports of the Ad Hoc Commission and the Commission on the Truth may seem inadvisable in cases where a person guilty of a serious crime in the past rectified his behaviour and contributed to the negotiated peace. This, however, is the small price that those who engage in punishable acts must pay, regardless of their position: they must accept it for the good of the country and the democratic future of the new Salvadorian society. Moreover, it is not up to the Commission to act on complaints, requests for pardon or pleas of attenuating circumstances from persons dismissed from the armed forces, because it has no binding judicial powers. It is not by resignation but by its creative attitude towards its new commitments and the new order of democratic coexistence that Salvadorian society as a whole will ultimately strike a balance in dealing with those who must take the blame for what they did during the conflict but deserve praise for what they did in the peace process.

El Salvador needs new souls. By its response to the murder of the Jesuits, 10 years after the assassination of Monsignor Romero by that nightmarish creation the "death squads", the military leadership showed just how far its position had hardened in daring to eliminate those it viewed as opponents, either because they were opponents or because they voiced concern, including church workers and journalists. In the uproar that followed, the most perverse sentiments came to the fore and the most absurd obfuscation was used in an attempt to cover up the truth as to who had given the orders.

What is more, it would tarnish the image of the

armed forces if they were to retain sufficient power to block the process of purification or impose conditions on it: if the guilty were not singled out and punished, the institution itself would be incriminated; no other interpretation is possible. Those who would have the armed forces choose this course must weigh the price of such an attitude in the eyes of history.

I. *Foundation for the Truth*

The mass of reports, testimony, newspaper and magazine articles and books published in Spanish and other languages that was accumulated prompted the establishment within the Commission on the Truth itself of a centre for documentation on the different forms of violence in El Salvador. The public information relating to the war (books, pamphlets, research carried out by Salvadorian and international bodies); testimony from 2,000 primary sources referring to more than 7,000 victims; information from secondary sources relating to more than 20,000 victims; information from official bodies in the United States and other countries; information provided by government bodies and FMLN; an abundant photographic and videotape record of the conflict and even of the Commission's own activities; all of this material constitutes an invaluable resource—a part of El Salvador's heritage because (despite the painful reality it records) a part of the country's contemporary history—for historians and analysts of this most distressing period and for those who wish to study this painful reality in order to reinforce the effort to spread the message "never again".

What is to be done with this wealth of material in order to make it available to those around the world who are seeking peace, to bring these personal experiences to the attention of those who defend human rights? What is to be done when one is bound by the requirement of confidentiality for documents and testimony? What use is to be made of this example of the creativity of the United Nations at a time in contemporary history which is fraught with conflict and turmoil and for which the parallels and the answers found in the Salvadorian conflict may be of some relevance?

To guarantee the confidentiality of testimony and of the many documents supplied by institutions and even by Governments and, at the same time, to provide for the possibility of consultation by academic researchers while preserving such confidentiality, the Commission obtained the agreement of the Parties and the consent and support of the International Rule of Law Center of George Washington University in Washington, D.C., which, since 1992, has been administering and maintaining the collection of documents relating to the transition to peace in

countries under the rule of oppression and countries emerging from armed conflicts. In addition, the Commission has already sought the cooperation of Governments, academic institutions and international foundations, always on the clear understanding that it holds itself personally responsible for guaranteeing confidentiality before finally handing the archives over to their lawful owners.

The Foundation for the Truth would be a not-for-profit academic body governed by statutes conforming to United States law. It would be managed by an international Board of Directors, with Salvadorian participation; a representative of the Secretary-General of the United Nations and the members of the Commission would also be members of the Board. The Foundation would be operated under the direction of Professor Thomas Buergenthal and would maintain close contacts with leaders and researchers in El Salvador, with the group of European, United States and Latin American professionals who worked with the Commission, and with scientists from around the world. For those documents which were not subject to secrecy, duplicate copies and computer terminals for accessing the collection would be available in Salvadorian institutions requesting them.

The Foundation would be inaugurated in June 1993, in Washington, with a multidisciplinary encounter to discuss the report of the Commission on the Truth.

J. *Expressions of gratitude*

The Commission places on record its admiration for and gratitude to the Salvadorian people, without exception, for the courage they have shown throughout the terrible ordeal of the conflict and for the outstanding spirit which they have generously demonstrated in the peace process. It also expresses its gratitude to President Cristiani and the members of his Government, and to the Commanders and members of the Frente Farabundo Martí para la Liberación Nacional (FMLN), for cooperating with it in the performance of its tasks.

The Commission further expresses its gratitude to the Secretaries-General of the United Nations, Mr. Javier Pérez de Cuéllar and Mr. Boutros Boutros-Ghali, and to Assistant Secretary-General Mr. Alvaro de Soto and his staff for their efficient cooperation. It also thanks ONUSAL, in particular, its Director, Mr. Iqbal Riza, for their diligence and expeditiousness in providing logistical and security support, and legal expert Mr. Pedro Nikken, whose knowledge of Central America is extensive.

We owe a debt of gratitude to the President of Colombia, Mr. César Gaviria Trujillo; the President of

Mexico, Mr. Carlos Salinas de Gortari; the Prime Minister of Spain, Mr. Felipe González; and the President of Venezuela, Mr. Carlos Andrés Pérez known as "the four friends of the Secretary-General", and their ambassadors to the United Nations and El Salvador, for their constant and full support.

We also express our gratitude to Salvadorian political parties and their leaders; Salvadorian and international non-governmental organizations; the Catholic Church and its hierarchy and all religious faiths; the Directors and staff of the information media; and important public figures in El Salvador and outstanding international figures who have followed the conflict closely: without the cooperation of all these people it would have been impossible to penetrate the maze in which the truth often lay hidden.

This report would not have been possible without the collaboration of the interdisciplinary group of professionals from around the world who, under the direction of Ms. Patricia Valdez, for eight months devoted themselves with professionalism, objectivity and dedication to the task of seeking, unravelling and, on more than a few occasions, unearthing the truth.

K. *The dominant idea*

The members of the Commission are convinced from what they observed during six months of close association with Salvadorian society, that there is no place among the sorely tried Salvadorian people for bitterness or vengeance. There is likewise no intention to cause humiliation; nor does anyone today seek to harm the dignity of any human being by any action. Peace is always made by those who have fought the war, and all the former combatants have established forums for reconciliation in the new society. All are called upon to make a contribution, each according to the pain he has suffered and the love he has for his country. It falls to President Cristiani—the peace President—and his Government and the former insurgents, especially the former Commanders of FMLN, once again to play the leading role by setting a new course for El Salvador.

Salvadorian society—a society of sacrifice and hope—is watching them from the vantage point of history. The future of the nation summons them, a nation which is moving forward under the influence of one dominant idea: to lift itself out of the ruins in order to hold high like a banner the vision of its future. The nations of the international community are watching them in gladness. A new people is rising from the ashes of a war in which all were unjust. Those who perished are watching them from the great beyond. Those who hope are watching them from the heights of hope.

II. The mandate

A. *The mandate*

The Commission on the Truth owes its existence and authority to the El Salvador peace agreements, a set of agreements negotiated over a period of more than three years (1989-1992) between the Government of El Salvador and FMLN. The negotiating process, which took place under United Nations auspices with the special cooperation of Colombia, Mexico, Spain and Venezuela (the so-called "friends of the Secretary-General"), culminated in the Peace Agreement signed at Chapultepec, Mexico, on 16 January 1992. 1/ [Editor's note: Footnotes can be found at the end of the document, starting on page 392.]

The decision to set up the Commission on the Truth was taken by the Parties in the Mexico Agreements, signed at Mexico City on 27 April 1991. 2/ These Agreements define the functions and powers of the Commission, while its authority is expanded by article 5 of the Chapultepec Peace Agreement, entitled "End to Impunity". 3/ Together, these provisions constitute the Commission's "mandate".

The mandate defines the Commission's functions as follows:

"The Commission shall have the task of investigating serious acts of violence that have occurred since 1980 and whose impact on society urgently demands that the public should know the truth."

It then states that the Commission shall take the following into account:

"(a) The exceptional importance that may be attached to the acts to be investigated, their characteristics and impact, and the social unrest to which they gave rise; and

"(b) The need to create confidence in the positive changes which the peace process is promoting and to assist the transition to national reconciliation."

The specific functions assigned to the Commission as regards impunity are defined, in part, in the Chapultepec Agreement, which provides as follows:

"The Parties recognize the need to clarify and put an end to any indication of impunity on the part of officers of the armed forces, particularly in cases where respect for human rights is jeopardized. To that end, the Parties refer this issue to the Commission on the Truth for consideration and resolution."

In addition to granting the Commission powers with respect to impunity and the investigation of serious acts of violence, the peace agreements entrust the Commission with making "legal, political or administrative" recommendations. Such recommendations may relate to specific cases or may be more general. In the latter case, they "may include measures to prevent the repetition of such acts, and initiatives to promote national reconciliation".

The Commission was thus given two specific powers: the power to make investigations and the power to make recommendations. The latter power is particularly important since, under the mandate, "the Parties undertake to carry out the Commission's recommendations". The Parties thus agree to be bound by the Commission's recommendations.

As regards the Commission's other task, the mandate entrusted it with investigating "serious acts of violence ... whose impact on society urgently demands that the public should know the truth". In other words, in deciding which acts to focus on, the Commission would have to take into account the particular importance of each act, its repercussions and the social unrest to which it gave rise. However, the mandate did not list or identify any specific cases for investigation; nor did it distinguish between large-scale acts of violence and acts involving only a handful of people. Instead, the mandate emphasized *serious acts of violence* and their impact or repercussions. On the basis of these criteria, the Commission investigated two types of cases:

(a) Individual cases or acts which, by their nature, outraged Salvadorian society and/or international opinion;

(b) A series of individual cases with similar characteristics revealing a systematic pattern of violence or ill-treatment which, taken together, equally outraged Salvadorian society, especially since their aim was to intimidate certain sectors of that society.

The Commission attaches equal importance to uncovering the truth in both kinds of cases. Moreover, these two types of cases are not mutually exclusive. Many of the so-called individual acts of violence which had the greatest impact on public opinion also had characteristics revealing systematic patterns of violence.

In investigating these acts, the Commission took into account three additional factors which have a bearing on the fulfilment of its mandate. The first was that it must investigate serious or flagrant acts committed by both sides in the Salvadorian conflict and not just by one of the Parties. Secondly, in referring the issue of the impunity "of officers of the armed forces, particularly in cases where respect for human rights is jeopardized" to the Commission, the Chapultepec Agreement urged the Commission to pay particular attention to this area and to acts of violence committed by officers of the armed forces which were never investigated or punished. Thirdly, the Commission was given six months in which to perform its task.

If we consider that the Salvadorian conflict lasted 12 years and resulted in a huge number of deaths and other serious acts of violence, it was clearly impossible for the Commission to deal with every act that could have been included within its sphere of competence. In deciding to investigate one case rather than another, it had to weigh such considerations as the representative nature of the case, the availability of sufficient evidence, the investigatory resources available to the Commission, the time needed to conduct an exhaustive investigation and the issue of impunity as defined in the mandate.

B. Applicable law

The Commission's mandate entrusts it with investigating *serious acts of violence*, but does not specify the principles of law that must be applied in order to define such acts and to determine responsibility for them. Nevertheless, the concept of serious acts of violence used in the peace agreements obviously does not exist in a normative vacuum and must therefore be analysed on the basis of certain relevant principles of law.

In defining the legal norms applicable to this task, it should be pointed out that, during the Salvadorian conflict, both Parties were under an obligation to observe a number of rules of international law, including those stipulated in international human rights law or in international humanitarian law, or in both. Furthermore, throughout the period in question, the State of El Salvador was under an obligation to adjust its domestic law to its obligations under international law.

These rules of international law must be considered as providing the basis for the criteria applicable to the functions which the peace agreements entrust to the Commission. 4/ Throughout the Salvadorian conflict, these two sets of rules were only rarely mutually exclusive.

It is true that, in theory, international human rights law is applicable only to Governments, while in some armed conflicts international humanitarian law is binding on both sides: in other words, binding on both insurgents and Government forces. However, it must be recognized that when insurgents assume government powers in territories under their control, they too can be required to observe certain human rights obligations that are binding on the State under international law. This would make them responsible for breaches of those obligations.

The official position of FMLN was that certain parts of the national territory were under its control, and it did in fact exercise that control. 5/

1. International human rights law

The international human rights law applicable to the present situation comprises a number of international instruments adopted within the framework of the United Nations and the Organization of American States (OAS). These instruments, which are binding on the State of El Salvador, include, in addition to the Charters of the United Nations and OAS, the following human rights treaties: the International Covenant on Civil and Political Rights and the American Convention on Human Rights. El Salvador ratified the Covenant on 30 November 1979 and the American Convention on 23 June 1978. Both instruments entered into force for El Salvador before 1980 and were thus in force throughout the conflict to which the Commission's mandate refers.

Clearly, not every violation of a right guaranteed in those instruments can be characterized as a "serious act of violence". Those instruments themselves recognize that some violations are more serious than others. This position is reflected in a provision which appears in both instruments and which distinguishes between rights from which no derogation is possible, even in time of war or other state of national emergency, and those from which derogations can be made in such circumstances. It is appropriate, therefore, that the Commission should classify the seriousness of each "act of violence" on the basis of the rights which the two instruments list as not being subject to derogation, in particular, rights related directly to the right to life and to physical integrity.

Accordingly, the following rights listed in article 4 of the Covenant as not being subject to derogation would come within the Commission's sphere of competence: the right to life ("No one shall be arbitrarily deprived of his life"); the right not to be subjected to torture or to cruel, inhuman or degrading treatment or punishment; and the right not to be held in slavery or any form of servitude. Article 27 of the American Convention on Human Rights provides that these same rights cannot be suspended even "in time of war, public danger, or other emergency that threatens the independence or security of a State Party".

Under international law, it is illegal for a State, or for persons acting on its behalf, to violate any of the above rights for whatever reason. Violation of these rights may even constitute an international crime in situations where acts are of a consistent type or reflect a systematic practice whose purpose is the large-scale violation of these fundamental rights of the human person.

2. International humanitarian law

The principles of international humanitarian law applicable to the Salvadorian conflict are contained in article 3 common to the four Geneva Conventions of 1949 and in Additional Protocol II thereto. El Salvador ratified these instruments before 1980.

Although the armed conflict in El Salvador was not an international conflict as defined by the Conventions, it did meet the requirements for the application of article 3 common to the four Conventions. That article defines some fundamental humanitarian rules applicable to non-international armed conflicts. The same is true of Protocol II Additional to the Geneva Conventions, relating to the protection of victims of non-international armed conflicts. The provisions of common article 3 and of Additional Protocol II are legally binding on both the Government and the insurgent forces.

Without going into those provisions in detail, it is clear that violations—by either of the two parties to the conflict—of common article 3 6/ and of the fundamental guarantees contained in Additional Protocol II, 7/ especially if committed systematically, could be characterized as serious acts of violence for the purposes of the interpretation and application of the Commission's mandate. Such violations would include arbitrary deprivation of life; torture; cruel, inhuman or degrading treatment; taking of hostages; and denial of certain indispensable guarantees of due process before serious criminal penalties are imposed and carried out.

3. Conclusions

With few exceptions, serious acts of violence prohibited by the rules of humanitarian law applicable to the Salvadorian conflict are also violations of the non-repealable provisions of the International Covenant on Civil and Political Rights and the American Convention on Human Rights, the two human rights treaties ratified by the State of El Salvador. The two instruments also prohibit derogation from any rights guaranteed in any humanitarian law treaty to which the State is a party.

As a result, neither the Salvadorian State nor persons acting on its behalf or in its place can claim that the existence of an armed conflict justified the commission of serious acts of violence in contravention of one or other of the human rights treaties mentioned above or of the applicable instruments of humanitarian law binding on the State.

C. Methodology

In determining the methodology that would govern the conduct of the investigations essential to the preparation of this report, the Commission took a number of factors into account.

The text of its mandate was a binding condition and a starting-point for the Commission, in that it stated the Parties' intentions in this connection. The preamble to the mandate indicates that the Commission was established because the Parties recognized "the need to clear up without delay those exceptionally important acts of violence whose characteristics and impact ... urgently require that the complete truth be made known ...".

In establishing the procedure that the Commission was to follow in performing its functions, paragraph 7 of the mandate provided that the Commission would conduct its activities "on a confidential basis". Paragraph 5 established that "The Commission shall not function in the manner of a judicial body". Paragraph 8 (a) stipulated that "The Commission shall be completely free to use whatever sources of information it deems useful and reliable", while paragraph 8 (b) gave the Commission the power to "Interview, freely and in private, any individuals, groups or members of organizations or institutions". Lastly, in the fourth preambular paragraph of the mandate, the Parties agreed that the task entrusted to the Commission should be fulfilled "through a procedure which is both reliable and expeditious and may yield results in the short term, without prejudice to the obligations incumbent on the Salvadorian courts to solve such cases and impose the appropriate penalties on the culprits".

In analysing these provisions of the mandate, the Commission thought it important that the Parties had emphasized that "the Commission shall not function in the manner of a judicial body". In other words, not only did the Parties not establish a court or tribunal, but they made it very clear that the Commission should not function as if it were a judicial body. They wanted to make sure that the Commission was able to act on a confidential basis and receive information from any sources, public or private, that it deemed useful and reliable. It was given these powers so that it could conduct an investigation procedure that was both expeditious and, in its view, reliable in order to "clear up without delay those exceptionally important acts of violence whose characteristics and impact ... urgently require that the complete truth be made known ...".

So it is clear that the Parties opted for an investigation procedure that, within the short period of time allotted, would be best fitted to establishing the truth about acts of violence falling within the Commission's sphere of competence, without requiring the Commission to observe the procedures and rules that normally govern the activities of any judicial or quasi-judicial body. Any judicial function that had to be performed would be reserved expressly for the courts of El Salvador. For the Parties, the paramount concern was to find out the truth without delay.

Another important overall consideration which influenced the Commission's methodology was the reality of the situation in El Salvador today. Not only was this reflected in the Commission's mandate, but it also had a profound impact on the Commission's investigation process and *modus operandi*. It forced the Commission to gather its most valuable information in exchange for assurances of confidentiality.

It was not just that the Parties authorized the Commission, in the peace agreements, to act on a confidential basis and to receive information in private; the reality of the situation in El Salvador forced it to do so for two reasons: first, to protect the lives of witnesses and, secondly, to obtain information from witnesses who, be-cause of the climate of terror in which they continue to live, would not have provided such information if the Commission had not guaranteed them absolute confidentiality.

The situation in El Salvador is such that the population at large continues to believe that many military and police officers in active service or in retirement, Government officials, judges, members of FMLN and people who at one time or another were connected with the death squads are in a position to cause serious physical and material injury to any person or institution that shows a readiness to testify about acts of violence committed between 1980 and 1991. The Commission believes that this suspicion is not unreasonable, given El Salvador's recent history and the power still wielded or, in many cases, wielded until recently by people whose direct involvement in serious acts of violence or in covering up such acts is well known but who have not been required to account for their actions or omissions.

Even though the fears expressed by some potential witnesses may have been exaggerated, the fact is that in their minds the danger is real. As a result, they were not prepared to testify unless they were guaranteed absolute secrecy. It should be pointed out that many witnesses refused to give information to other investigatory bodies in the past precisely because they were afraid that their identity would be divulged.

The Commission can itself testify to the extreme fear of reprisals frequently expressed, both verbally and through their behaviour, by many of the witnesses it interviewed. It is also important to emphasize that the Commission was not in a position to offer any significant protection to witnesses apart from this guarantee of confidentiality. Unlike the national courts, for instance, the Commission did not have the authority to order precautionary measures; neither, of course, did it have police powers. Besides, it is the perception of the public at large that the Salvadorian judicial system is unable to offer the necessary guarantees.

The Commission also received reports from some Governments and international bodies, on condition that the source was not revealed. This information was subjected to the same test of reliability as the other information received and was used principally to confirm or verify personal testimony and to guide the Commission in its search for other areas of investigation.

From the outset, the Commission was aware that accusations made and evidence received in secret run a far greater risk of being considered less trustworthy than those which are subjected to the normal judicial tests for determining the truth and to other related requirements of due process of law, including the right of the accused to confront and examine witnesses brought against him.

Accordingly, the Commission felt that it had a special obligation to take all possible steps to ensure the reliability of the evidence used to arrive at a finding. In cases where it had to identify specific individuals as having committed, ordered or tolerated specific acts of violence, it applied a stricter test of reliability.

The Commission decided that, in each of the cases described in this report, it would specify the degree of certainty on which its ultimate finding was based. The different degrees of certainty were as follows:

1. Overwhelming evidence—conclusive or highly convincing evidence to support the Commission's finding;

2. Substantial evidence—very solid evidence to support the Commission's finding;

3. Sufficient evidence—more evidence to support the Commission's finding than to contradict it.

The Commission decided not to arrive at any specific finding on cases or situations, or any aspect thereof, in which there was less than "sufficient" evidence to support such a finding.

In order to guarantee the reliability of the evidence it gathered, the Commission insisted on verifying, substantiating and reviewing all statements as to facts, checking them against a large number of sources whose veracity had already been established. It was decided that no single source or witness would be considered sufficiently reliable to establish the truth on any issue of fact needed for the Commission to arrive at a finding. It was also decided that secondary sources, for instance, reports from national or international governmental or private bodies and assertions by people without first-hand knowledge of the facts they reported, did not on their own constitute a sufficient basis for arriving at findings. However, these secondary sources were used, along with circumstantial evidence, to verify findings based on primary sources.

It could be argued that, since the Commission's investigation methodology does not meet the normal requirements of due process, the report should not name the people whom the Commission considers to be implicated in specific acts of violence. The Commission believes that it had no alternative but to do so.

In the peace agreements, the Parties made it quite clear that it was necessary that the "complete truth be made known", and that was why the Commission was established. Now, the whole truth cannot be told without naming names. After all, the Commission was not asked to write an academic report on El Salvador, it was asked to investigate and describe exceptionally important acts of violence and to recommend measures to prevent the repetition of such acts. This task cannot be performed in the abstract, suppressing information (for instance, the names of persons responsible for such acts) where there

is reliable testimony available, especially when the persons identified occupy senior positions and perform official functions directly related to violations or the cover-up of violations. Not to name names would be to reinforce the very impunity to which the Parties instructed the Commission to put an end.

In weighing aspects related to the need to protect the lives of witnesses against the interests of people who might be adversely affected in some way by the publication of their names in the report, the Commission also took into consideration the fact that the report is not a judicial or quasijudicial determination as to the rights or obligations of certain individuals under the law. As a result, the Commission is not, in theory, subject to the requirements of due process which normally apply, in proceedings which produce these consequences.

Furthermore, the Commission's application of strict criteria to determine the degree of reliability of the evidence in situations where people have been identified by name, and the fact that it named names only when it was absolutely convinced by the evidence, were additional factors which influenced the Commission when it came to take a decision on this analysis. As a result, the Commission is satisfied that the criteria of impartiality and reliability which it applied throughout the process were fully compatible with the functions entrusted to it and with the interests it had to balance.

The considerations which prompted the Commission to receive confidential information without revealing the source also forced it to omit references from both the body and the footnotes of the reports on individual cases, with the exception of references to certain public, official sources. As a result, reference is made to official trial proceedings and other similar sources, but not to testimony or other information gathered by the Commission. The Commission took this approach in order to reduce the likelihood that those responsible for the acts of violence described herein, or their defenders, would be able to identify the confidential sources of information used by the Commission. In some of the reports on individual cases, the Commission also omitted details that might reveal the identity of certain witnesses.

III. Chronology of the violence

Introduction

The Commission on the Truth had the task of investigating and analysing serious acts of violence that had occurred in El Salvador between January 1980 and July 1991.

In taking into account "the exceptional importance that may be attached to the acts to be investigated, their characteristics and impact, and the social unrest to which

Frequency of reports in the Salvadorian press concerning acts of violence

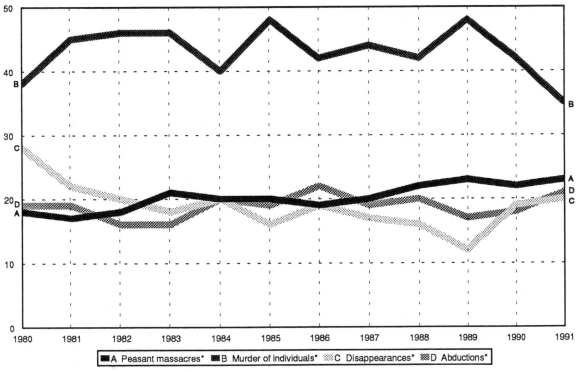

A Peasant massacres* B Murder of individuals* C Disappearances* D Abductions*

they gave rise", 8/ the Commission, for methodological reasons, divided the years 1980-1991 into four periods, namely: 1980-1983, 1983-1987, 1987-1989 and 1989-1991. Each of these periods corresponds to political changes in the country, developments in the war and the systematic nature or frequency of certain practices that violated human rights and international humanitarian law.

I. 1980-1983: The institutionalization of violence

The main characteristics of this period were that violence became systematic and terror and distrust reigned among the civilian population. The fragmentation of any opposition or dissident movement by means of arbitrary arrests, murders and selective and indiscriminate disappearances of leaders became common practice. Repression in the cities targeted political organizations, trade unions and organized sectors of Salvadorian society, as exemplified by the persecution of organizations such as the Asociación Nacional de Educadores Sal-

vadoreños (ANDES), 9/ murders of political leaders 10/ and attacks on human rights bodies. 11/

The Frente Farabundo Martí para la Liberación Nacional (FMLN) was formed in late 1980 and in January 1981, the first large-scale military offensive left hundreds of people dead. Starting in 1980, there was a succession of indiscriminate attacks on the non-combatant civilian population and also collective summary executions, particularly against the rural population. 12/ There were appalling massacres, such as those at the Sumpul river (14-15 May 1980), the Lempa river (20-29 October 1981) and El Mozote (December 1981). Organized terrorism, in the form of the so-called "death squads", became the most aberrant manifestation of the escalation of violence. Civilian and military groups engaged in a systematic murder campaign with total impunity, while State institutions turned a blind eye. 13/ The murder of Monsignor Romero exemplified the limitless, devastating power of these groups. This period saw the greatest number of deaths and human rights violations.

1980

The Government of General Carlos Humberto Romero (July 1977-October 1979) was overthrown on 15 October 1979. The Revolutionary Government Junta (JRG) composed of Colonel Jaime Abdul Gutiérrez and Colonel Adolfo Majano announced its main goals: an end to violence and corruption, guarantees for the exercise of human rights, adoption of measures to ensure the fair distribution of national wealth and a positive approach to external relations. 14/

On 18 October 1979, elections were announced for February 1982. Measures were enacted restricting landholdings to a maximum of 100 hectares (Decree No. 43 of 6 December 1979). The organization ORDEN 15/ was dissolved on 6 November 1979 and the Salvadorian national security agency (ANSESAL) was dismantled. 16/

The political struggle between civilians and conservative military sectors intensified, against a backdrop of social upheaval and mobilization. Left-wing organizations such as the Bloque Popular Revolucionario (BPR), the Ligas Populares 28 de Febrero (LP-28) and the Frente de Acción Popular Unificada (FAPU), among others, held public demonstrations, occupied ministries and organized strikes demanding the release of political prisoners. Economic measures and land tenure reforms were adopted. The organizations BPR, FAPU, LP-28 and the Unión Democratíca Nacionalista (UDN) came together to form the Coordinadora Revolucionaria de Masas (CRM). 17/ On 22 January, the National Guard attacked a massive CRM demonstration, described by Monsignor Romero as peaceful, killing somewhere between 22 and 50 people and wounding hundreds more.

Anti-Government violence erupted in the form of occupations of radio stations, bombings of newspapers (*La Prensa Gráfica* and *El Diario de Hoy*), abductions, executions and attacks on military targets, particularly by the Fuerzas Populares de Liberación (FPL) and the Ejército Revolucionario del Pueblo (ERP).

On 3 January 1980, the three civilian members of the Junta resigned, along with 10 of the 11 cabinet ministers. 18/ The Junta was again in crisis. The Agrarian Reform Act 19/ and the nationalization of banks were announced. On 9 March, José Napoleón Duarte became a member of the Junta when the Christian Democratic Party expelled Dada Hizeri, Rubén Zamora and other leaders from its ranks. The process of political polarization triggered an unprecedented increase in death squad activities.

On 6 February, United States Ambassador Frank Devine informed the State Department that mutilated bodies were appearing on roadsides as they had done in the worst days of the Romero regime and that the extreme right was arming itself and preparing for a

confrontation in which it clearly expected to ally itself with the military. 20/

On 22 February, PDC leader and Chief State Counsel Mario Zamora was murdered at his home, only days after the Frente Amplio Nacional (FAN), headed by former National Guard Major Roberto D'Aubuisson, had accused him publicly of being a member of subversive groups (see the case in chap. IV).

On 24 March, Monsignor Oscar Arnulfo Romero was shot dead by a sniper as he celebrated mass in the Chapel of the Hospital de la Divina Providencia 21/ (see the case in chap. IV). This crime further polarized Salvadorian society and became a milestone, symbolizing the point at which human rights violations reached their peak and presaging the all-out war between the Government and the guerrillas that was to come. During the funeral, a bomb went off outside San Salvador Cathedral. The panic-stricken crowd, estimated at 50,000 people, was machine-gunned, leaving an estimated 27 to 40 people dead and more than 200 wounded. 22/

On 7 May 1980, Major Roberto D'Aubuisson 23/ was arrested on a farm, along with a group of civilians and soldiers. In the raid, a significant quantity of weapons and documents were found implicating the group in the organization and financing of death squads allegedly involved in Archbishop Romero's murder. The arrests triggered a wave of terrorist threats and institutional pressures which culminated in D'Aubuisson's release. This strengthened the most conservative sector in the Government 24/ and was a clear example of the passivity and inertia of the judiciary during this period. 25/

Government measures 26/ and illegal repressive measures were taken to dismantle the country's legal structure and neutralize the opposition. 27/

Between 12 and 15 August, a general strike called by FDR, a coalition of centre-left parties, was violently suppressed, leaving 129 people dead. 28/ On 27 November, Alvarez Córdoba and six FDR leaders were abducted. Their bodies were found later, bearing signs of torture (see the case in chap. IV). A few days later, the Brigada Anticomunista General Maximiliano Hernández Martínez issued a communiqué claiming responsibility for the killings.

Between October and November 1980, the five armed opposition groups—Fuerzas Populares de Liberación (FPL), Ejército Revolucionario del Pueblo (ERP), Fuerzas Armadas de Liberación (FAL), Fuerzas Armadas de Resistencia Nacional (FARN) and Partido Revolucionario de los Trabajadores de Centroamérica (PRTC)—formed the Frente Farabundo Martí para la Liberación Nacional (FMLN).

In late 1980, as a change of Administration was taking place in the United States, the violence in El Salvador reached United States citizens. On 2 December, four churchwomen were arrested, raped and murdered by members of the National Guard (see the case in chap. IV). At the end of the year, Colonel Majano was removed from the Junta and Napoleón Duarte became President. 29/

The Commission on the Truth received direct complaints concerning 2,597 victims of serious acts of violence occurring in 1980. 30/

1981

Individual extrajudicial executions continued and mass executions in rural areas increased. On 3 January, the President of the Salvadorian Institute for Agrarian Reform and two United States advisers were murdered in the Sheraton Hotel 31/ (see the case in chap. IV). This incident was part of a campaign of murders of cooperative leaders and beneficiaries of the agrarian reform.

On 10 January, FMLN launched the "final offensive" announced in late 1980. 32/ Attacks were launched on military targets throughout the country, leaving hundreds of people dead. Government sources reported that "at least 500 extremists" had died in the final offensive. Because of FMLN actions, the state of siege decreed by the Junta was maintained until October 1981.

The violence in El Salvador began to attract international attention and to have international repercussions. External political forces began to claim that the Salvadorian conflict was part of the East-West confrontation. Other forces worked for a negotiated settlement of the conflict. 33/ Many sectors began to envisage the possibility of a negotiated settlement, provided that the necessary resources were available. On 14 January, the United States Administration restored military aid, which had been suspended after the murder of the United States churchwomen. 34/ The United States Government also significantly increased its military and economic assistance. The increasing flow of resources was intended to train, modernize and expand the structure of a number of elements of the armed forces. The Rapid Deployment Infantry Battalions (BIRI), specialized in anti-guerrilla warfare, also began to be created (Atlacatl: March 1981, Atonal: January 1982, Belloso: May 1982, etc.).

Counter-insurgency military operations affected the non-combatant civilian population, causing a high death toll and the emergence of a new phenomenon—displaced persons.

On 17 March, as they tried to cross the Lempa river to Honduras, a group of thousands of peasants was attacked from the air and from land. Between 20 and 30 people were reported killed and a further 189 reported missing as a result of the attack. Something similar happened in October on the banks of the same river, on which occasion 147 peasants were killed, including 44 minors. In November, in Cabañas Department, a counter-insurgency operation surrounded and kept under attack for 13 days a group of 1,000 people who were trying to escape to Honduras. This time, between 50 and 100 people were reported killed. 35/ In late December, the Atlacatl Battalion carried out one of the worst massacres of the war, in various hamlets in and around El Mozote (see the case in chap. IV).

According to the Fundación Salvadoreña para el Desarrollo (FUSADES), by 1981 there were 164,000 displaced persons. The number of displaced persons leaving the country in search of refuge also increased, according to the report of the Office of the United Nations High Commissioner for Refugees (UNHCR). 36/ Furthermore, Christian Legal Aid reported 12,501 deaths in 1981. 37/

The Commission on the Truth received direct testimony concerning 1,633 victims of serious acts of violence occurring in 1981.

1982

The 60-member Constituent Assembly 38/ adopted a new Constitution and elected an interim Government. Although PDC won the most votes (40.3 per cent), ARENA (29.3 per cent), in alliance with the Partido de Conciliación Nacional (PCN) (19 per cent) and other minority parties, won control of the Assembly. Roberto D'Aubuisson was elected President of the Constituent Assembly and two PCN members were elected Vice-Presidents. The Assembly ratified the 1962 Political Constitution. 39/ It also elected Alvaro Magaña Provisional President of the Republic and Raúl Molina Martínez (PDC), Gabriel Mauricio Gutiérrez Castro (ARENA) and Pablo Mauricio Alvergue (PCN), Vice-Presidents.

Decree No. 6 of the National Assembly suspended phase III 40/ of the implementation of the agrarian reform, and was itself later amended. The Apaneca Pact was signed on 3 August 1982, establishing a Government of National Unity, whose objectives were peace, democratization, human rights, economic recovery, security and a strengthened international position. An attempt was made to form a transitional Government which would establish a democratic system. Lack of agreement among the forces that made up the Government and the pressures of the armed conflict prevented any substantive changes from being made during Magaña's Presidency.

FMLN attacked the Ilopango Air Force Base, destroying six of the Air Force's 14 UH-1H helicopters, five Ouragan aircraft and three C-47s. 41/ The guerrillas stepped up their activities against economic targets. Between February and April, a total of 439 acts of sabotage were reported 42/ and the number of acts of sabotage involving explosives or arson rose to 782 between January and September. 43/ The United States Embassy estimated the damage to the economic infrastructure at US$ 98 million. 44/ FMLN also carried out large-scale operations in the capital city and temporarily occupied urban centres in the country's interior. According to some reports, the number of rebels ranged between 4,000 and 5,000; other sources put the number at between 6,000 and 9,000. 45/

Combined land-air military operations by the armed forces sought to regain control of populated areas controlled by the rebels. In one of these operations (31 January), 150 civilians were reported killed by military forces in Nueva Trinidad and Chalatenango. On 10 March, some 5,000 peasants were fired at from helicopters and shelled as they fled the combat zone in San Esteban Catarina. In August, a military campaign of "pacification" in San Vicente reported 300 to 400 peasants killed. 46/ In late November, 5,000 soldiers took part in a 10-day counter-offensive in northern San Salvador. The Ministry of Defence reported at the end of the operation that four districts had been recovered, with 20 soldiers and 232 guerrilla fighters killed. 47/

On 31 August, the Comisión Nacional de Asistencia a la Población Desplazada (CONADES) reported that there were 226,744 internally displaced persons. By June of that year, the number of Salvadorian refugees in Latin American countries totalled between 175,000 and 295,000. 48/

The United States Embassy reported a total of 5,639 people killed, of whom 2,330 were civilians, 762 were members of the armed forces and 2,547 were members of the guerrilla forces. Christian Legal Aid reported that during the first eight months of 1982, there was a total of 3,059 political murders, "nearly all of them the result of action by Government agents against civilians not involved in military combat". 49/ The same source reported that the total number of civilian deaths in 1982 was 5,962. 50/

The death squads 51/ continued to operate with impunity in 1982. On 10 March, the Alianza Anticomunista de El Salvador published a list of 34 people who had been condemned to death for "discrediting the armed forces". Most of them were journalists. The Inter-American Commission on Human Rights, referring to the discovery of clandestine graves of death squad victims, reported that on 24 May the bodies of more than 150 people had been dumped at Puerta del Diablo, Panchimalco. 52/ On 27 May, the bodies of six members of the Christian Democratic Party were found at El Playón, another clandestine mass grave used by the death squads. 53/ President Duarte publicly denounced the extreme right wing, holding it responsible for the murder of

hundreds of PDC members and mayors. Four Dutch journalists were killed on 17 March 1982 (see the case in chap. IV).

The Commission on the Truth received direct testimony concerning 1,145 victims of serious acts of violence occurring in 1982.

II. 1983-1987: Violations within the context of the armed conflict

Violations of life, physical integrity and security continued to occur in urban centres. The number of violations fell but was accompanied by greater selectivity. In 1982, 5,962 people died at the hands of government forces; by 1985 the number had fallen to 1,655. 54/

There began to be a marked decrease in the activities of the death squads. During a visit to El Salvador, in December 1983, Vice-President Bush publicly condemned the death squads. He demanded the removal of certain armed forces and security officers who were associated with human rights violations. The visit demonstrated that United States diplomatic pressure could bring about a reduction in the number of violations.

FMLN strengthened its structure and demonstrated strength in the military sphere. It carried out large-scale operations and exercised territorial control, albeit temporarily, in various parts of the country. In 1985, it began to use mines indiscriminately, causing many deaths among the civilian population. An intensive campaign for the destruction of economic targets unfolded, resulting in major property damage. Hostage-taking and murder, particularly of town mayors and government officials in areas of, or close to, the conflict became commonplace. The guerrillas sought thus to demonstrate, both within and outside the country, the existence of a "duality of power" in El Salvador.

During this phase, the military development of the war caused the armed forces to view the civilian population in the areas of conflict as "legitimate targets for attack". Indiscriminate aerial bombings, massive artillery attacks and infantry advances were carried out, all of which resulted in massacres and the destruction of communities in an effort to deprive the guerrillas of all means of survival. Because of the systematic use of this tactic by the armed forces, in violation of human rights, this phase was characterized by vast numbers of displaced persons and refugees. By 1984, there were reported to be 500,000 displaced persons within the country 55/ and 245,500 Salvadorian refugees abroad, bringing the total number of displaced persons to approximately one and a half million. Following much international criticism, the armed forces cut back on the use of air attacks against the civilian population.

1983

On 4 May, the Constituent Assembly passed an Amnesty Law for civilians involved in political offences. 56/ In November, it was agreed that the presidential elections, originally scheduled for December 1983, would be held on 25 March 1984. On 15 December, following 20 months of debate, the new Constitution was approved. 57/

Talks began between the Government and FDR-FMLN, although no positive results were achieved. Delegations from both sides met on 29 and 30 August in San José, Costa Rica, and on 29 September in Bogotá, under the auspices of the Presidents of the Contadora Group. 58/ On 7 October, President Magaña announced that the next round of talks had been cancelled, citing the refusal by FMLN to participate in elections. That same day, Víctor Manuel Quintanilla, the senior FDR representative residing in El Salvador, was found dead, together with three other persons. The Brigada Anticomunista Maximiliano Hernández Martínez claimed responsibility. 59/

FMLN continued its campaign of economic sabotage and its escalation of large-scale military actions. Between 15 and 18 January, the guerrillas launched an offensive and temporarily occupied towns in Morazán. On 29 January, in a similar action, FMLN occupied Berlín, a city of 35,000 inhabitants, for a period of three days, destroying the Police and the National Guard headquarters. For its part, the Government responded with a large-scale counter-offensive. Some days later, Monsignor Rivera y Damas accused the armed forces of being responsible for the high number of civilians killed—estimated at between 50 and 170—and the property damage caused. On 22 February, uniformed soldiers kidnapped and summarily executed a group of peasants from a cooperative at Las Hojas, Sonsonate; the number of dead was estimated at 70 (see this case in chap. IV). On 16 March, Marianela García Villas, President of the Human Rights Commission of El Salvador (non-governmental) was executed by security forces. 60/

Between January and June, there were 37 large-scale military operations by government forces. On 25-26 September, FMLN attacked army positions in Tenancingo, and A-37 aircraft responded with aerial bombings; some 100 civilians were killed in this operation. 61/ In November, troops from Atlacatl Battalion invaded an area close to Lake Suchitlán under rebel control, and 118 people were reported killed as a result of the action. 62/ Towards the end of the year, FMLN embarked on its biggest military action against El Paraíso military base in Chalatenango; it is estimated that more than 100 soldiers were killed in the attack. On 25 May, the Clara Elizabeth Ramírez urban unit of FPL executed Marine Colonel Albert Schaufelberger, the second-ranking officer among the 55 United States military advisers in El Salvador. 63/

On 6 April, Mélida Amaya Montes (Commander Ana María), the second in command of FPL, was murdered in Managua. A few days later, on learning that a close collaborator of his had committed the crime, Salvador Cayetano Carpio, founder and leader of the majority faction of FMLN, committed suicide.

In 1983, the death squads continued operating; a high proportion of those murdered were leaders of the political opposition, trade union leaders, educators and church officials. According to a State Department briefing, death squad activities picked up again in May, and they became very active in October and November, primarily as a result of the continuing, though limited, dialogue between the Peace Commission and the left. 64/

On 1 November, the Brigada Anticomunista Maximiliano Hernández Martínez issued a death threat to Bishops Rivera y Damas and Rosas Chávez, warning them "to desist immediately from their disruptive sermons". In his farewell message, Ambassador Hinton referred to this event saying that he had never been able to understand the private sector's silence with regard to the activities of the death squads. 65/

On 4 November, the new Ambassador, Thomas Pickering, referred to the pressure being put on the Government of El Salvador to take action against the leaders of the death squads, mentioning, *inter alia*, Héctor Regalado, Chief of Security of the Constituent Assembly; Major José Ricardo Pozo, Chief of Intelligence of the Treasury Police; Lieutenant Colonel Arístides Alfonso Márquez, Chief of Intelligence of the National Police and Colonels Denis Morán, Elmer Araujo González and Miguel Alfredo Vasconcelos. 66/

The most important event in this respect was the visit by the Vice-President of the United States, George Bush, to San Salvador on 9 December. Bush took the opportunity to state publicly that the death squads must disappear because they constituted a threat to the political stability of the Government. Later on he handed the Government a list of civilian and military personnel suspected of belonging to those clandestine organizations. 67/ From that time on there was a significant decrease in the activities of the squads and several government bodies announced that they planned to conduct investigations into the matter. 68/

On 25 December, Monsignor Gregorio Rosas Chávez reported that 6,096 Salvadorians had died in 1983 as a result of political violence. The number of people killed by the army and the death squads was 4,700; the number of army and security forces personnel killed was 1,300. 69/

In the interior of the country, the number of displaced persons climbed to 400,000; this, added to the approximately 500,000 Salvadorians which UNHCR estimated to be in the United States and the 200,000 in Mexico and Central America, represented 20 per cent of the country's total population. 70/

In his annual report, the Special Representative of the United Nations Commission on Human Rights, José Antonio Pastor Ridruejo, said:

"... the number of civilians murdered for political reasons in El Salvador continues to be very high. This is, unfortunately, the feature of the human rights situation ... which causes the greatest concern." 71/

The Commission on the Truth received direct testimony concerning 513 victims of serious acts of violence occurring in 1983.

1984

PDC placed first in the March 1984 elections, with 43.41 per cent of the vote, followed by ARENA, with 29.76 per cent, and PCN, with 20 per cent. Since no party had obtained an absolute majority, a second round of balloting was held on 6 May between the two parties that placed highest. José Napoleón Duarte won 53.6 per cent and the ARENA candidate, Roberto D'Aubuisson, won 46.4 per cent. Duarte took office on 1 June and became the first civilian to be elected President in 50 years.

The trial of the members of the National Guard accused of murdering the American churchwomen in December 1980 was held during the interval between the elections and the time Duarte took office. The Government and institutions of the United States brought strong pressure to bear on the proceedings, for the United States Congress was considering emergency assistance to El Salvador. On 23 May, after finding them guilty, Judge Bernardo Rauda Murcia sentenced the five members of the National Guard to 30 years in prison. 72/

In October, President Duarte invited FMLN to talks. The meeting took place in La Palma, Chalatenango, on 15 October and was followed by a further meeting on 30 November in Ayagualo, La Libertad. Neither meeting was a success because of the positions taken regarding the conditions of a possible incorporation of FMLN into political life. 73/

As the war proceeded there was a decrease in the number of political murders but, at the same time, acts of war increased, as manifested by countless confrontations, acts of economic sabotage 74/ and massive counter-insurgency operations by the military in conflict zones. 75/

On 23 October, the Ejército Revolucionario del Pueblo (ERP) tricked Colonel Domingo Monterosa,

Commander of the Third Infantry Brigade, into locating and seizing what was thought to be the Radio Venceremos transmission centre. An explosive device which had been planted in the transmitter exploded while the unit was being transported by helicopter. The Colonel and those accompanying him were killed.

Despite indiscriminate and disproportionate attacks on the civilian population, the number of air attacks on the population dropped. At the same time, there was a marked decrease in the activities of death squads during the first months of the year. 76/ In April, however, Legal Protection reported that murders by death squads were on the increase again, following a two-month lull. 77/

In a document issued in September, Legal Aid reported that, during the first eight months of 1984, the number of civilian deaths attributed to the army, security forces and death squads came to 1,965. In his annual report, the Special Representative of the United Nations Commission on Human Rights stated that "... the persistence of civilian deaths in or as a result of combat weakens the favourable impression created by a decline in the number of political murders in non-combat situations." 78/

The Commission on the Truth received direct testimony concerning 290 victims of serious acts of violence occurring in 1984.

1985

Elections for the Legislative Assembly and the municipalities were held on 31 March and the Christian Democrats won. The loss of relative political control by ARENA led to a process of internal realignments which culminated, on 29 September, in the election of Alfredo Cristiani as President of the National Executive Committee of that party.

In the course of the year, the dialogue process remained at a standstill, because of the non-acceptance of the proposal that talks should continue without publicity so that the peacemaking effort might progress.

There was a marked stepping up of violence in military confrontations and operations in the areas where guerrillas were active. At the same time, FMLN had been carrying out a series of abductions and summary executions. 79/ The action having the greatest consequences was the attack carried out on 19 June, on a restaurant in the Zona Rosa in San Salvador, by the Partido Revolucionario de Trabajadores Centroamericanos (PRTC). Four United States Marines from the United States Embassy were killed in the attack, together with nine civilians (see this case in chap. IV).

During 1985, FMLN carried out a series of abductions of mayors and municipal officials and, by September, 20 mayors had been abducted. The army captured Nidia Díaz,

Commander of PRTC, in combat and Commander Miguel Castellanos deserted (see the case in chap. IV).

FMLN abducted President Duarte's daughter. 80/ Following several weeks of negotiation with the mediation of the church and foreign Governments, FMLN exchanged Inés Guadalupe Duarte and 22 mayors for Nidia Díaz and a group of 21 leaders; 101 war-wounded FMLN combatants left the country.

FMLN began to make widespread tactical use of mines in areas under its influence. As a result of this practice, a great many civilians were killed or maimed. Legal Protection put the number of persons killed by mines in 1985 at 31 and the Human Rights Commission of El Salvador (governmental) reported 46 people killed and 100 injured as a result of contact mines. 81/

No large-scale collective executions were carried out during the numerous military counter-insurgency operations. However, there were intensive aerial bombings and mass displacement of the peasant population in rural areas. 82/ Christian Legal Aid put the number of civilian non-combatant deaths attributable to government forces at 1,655. 83/ Legal Protection put the number of dead at 371. 84/

Death squad activity continued in 1985. Legal Protection cited 136 murders by death squads, as against 39 during the latter half of 1984. At the same time the Ejército Secreto Anticomunista (ESA) issued death threats to 11 members of the University of El Salvador and 9 of those threatened went into exile. Major D'Aubuisson, commenting on the squads, pointed out that they "had been operating in El Salvador since 1969, when the terrorist groups of the Communist Party were formed". 85/

Different sources cited different figures for the number of persons injured and killed as a result of the fighting. The actual number was probably around 2,000. 86/

The Commission on the Truth received testimony concerning 141 victims of acts of serious violence occurring in 1985.

1986

The process of political dialogue on resolving the conflict remained deadlocked because of the radicalization of the parties. The war had a negative impact on production, and the process of recovery was slow. President Duarte adopted a programme of stabilization and reactivation of the economy; at the same time protests increased and the crisis deepened.

The Unión Nacional de los Trabajadores Salvadoreños (UNTS) and the Unión Nacional Obrero-Campesina (UNOC) began to act, organizing protests and popular demonstrations. They put forward economic demands and called for a dialogue between the Government and FMLN-FDR. UNTS and the Federación de Estudiantes Universitarios (FEUS), as well as other organizations, held three major protest demonstrations. In January, so-called "Operation Phoenix" began with the objective of regaining the Guazapa area from FMLN control. This operation continued throughout the year.

Vast numbers of people were displaced from their places of origin when they fled the counter-insurgency operations. Those affected established the Coordinadora Nacional de la Repoblación (CNR), which sought to regain the right of the civilian population to live in the areas from which they had come. These resettlement movements had the backing of the Church.

President Napoleón Duarte proposed a new peace plan which FMLN rejected because the Salvadorian guerrilla movement refused to be compared to the Nicaraguan rebels. 87/ Throughout the year, President Duarte pressed for the convening of talks and the international community did likewise, in an effort to bring peace to the region. In June, after a second attempt to sign the Central American peace agreement failed, 13 Latin American nations made one final attempt to save the Contadora peace process. 88/ In September, President Duarte again proposed talks with FMLN-FDR in Sesori, San Miguel, but the guerrillas did not attend.

The violence continued. The counter-insurgency operations and repressive measures of the State security forces produced casualties as did abductions, summary executions, attacks on mayors' offices and the laying of mines by FMLN. The activity of the death squads continued and the Ejército Salvadoreño de Salvación was born. In October, an earthquake in San Salvador caused hundreds of casualties and considerable property damage. A state of emergency was declared.

The Commission on the Truth received testimony concerning a total of 155 victims of serious acts of violence occurring in 1986.

III. 1987-1989: The military conflict as an obstacle to peace

The Esquipulas II Agreement 89/ signed by President Duarte provided a political opportunity for leaders of FDR to come back at the end of 1987. They participated as a coalition in the 1989 presidential elections.

Although progress was made in what the international community termed "the humanization of the conflict", 90/ there was a resurgence of violence, with a definite increase in attacks on the labour movement, human rights groups and social organizations. FMLN carried out a campaign of abductions, summary executions and murders against civilians affiliated with or sympathetic to the Government and the armed forces. The dialogue among the parties came to a standstill and it became clear that human rights violations were being fostered by institutional shortcomings, complicity or negligence and that they were the main obstacles to the peace process.

1987

Protests against tax measures and electoral reforms became more widespread, as did workers' demonstrations and violence against leaders of the cooperative movement. 91/ In August 1987, the five Central American Presidents meeting in Guatemala signed the Esquipulas II Agreement, which called for the establishment of national reconciliation commissions in each country, an International Verification Commission and amnesty legislation. The Papal Nuncio, for his part, offered to host meetings between the Government and FMLN-FDR, with Archbishop Rivera y Damas acting as moderator. The parties publicly endorsed the Esquipulas II Agreement and announced the establishment of commissions to deal with the cease-fire and other areas covered by the Agreement.

The Legislative Assembly adopted Legislative Decree No. 805, entitled "Amnesty Act aimed at achieving National Reconciliation". 92/ The Special Representative for El Salvador of the United Nations Commission on Human Rights 93/ and such human rights organizations as Americas Watch criticized the scope of the amnesty. 94/ In fact, Christian Legal Aid went so far as to bring an action challenging the constitutionality of the article which extended the benefit of amnesty to all kinds of offences. 95/

Moreover, the coordinator of the Salvadorian Human Rights Commission (non-governmental), Herbert Anaya Sanabria, was murdered. The incident caused great outrage in the country. 96/ The United Nations Special Representative, José Antonio Pastor Ridruejo, reported more humanitarian patterns of conduct in the armed forces compared with the previous year. He also noted that he had not received any reports of mass murders attributed to the armed forces or of the use of torture. 97/ The Special Representative concluded by assigning responsibility to the guerrillas for most of the civilian deaths or injuries caused by the explosion of contact mines. He also referred to the forcible recruitment of minors by the guerrilla forces. 98/ Overall, however, there was a decline in the number of victims compared with 1986.

General Adolfo Blandón, Chief of the Armed Forces Joint Staff, presented his annual balance sheet, which stated that 75 per cent of the armed forces, estimated at over 50,000 men, had taken part in a total of 132 military operations. Government forces had suffered 3,285 casualties: 470 dead and 2,815 wounded, 90 per cent of whom had returned to active duty. Rebel casualties totalled 2,586: 1,004 dead, 670 wounded, 847 taken prisoner and 65 deserters. 99/

The Commission on the Truth received testimony concerning a total of 136 victims of serious acts of violence occurring in 1987.

1988

The elections for the National Assembly and municipal councils resulted in a majority for ARENA. FMLN attempted to boycott the elections with transport stoppages, kidnappings and murders, and by car-bombings. The Supreme Court, in application of the Amnesty Act, exonerated the officers and alleged perpetrators of the Las Hojas massacre, as well as those implicated in the murder of the American agrarian reform advisers and the Director of ISTA. 100/

The army reverted to the practice of mass executions, the most serious having occurred in the district of San Sebastián, San Vicente, where 10 peasants were killed (see reference to the case in chap. IV). Furthermore, the number of those killed by the death squads was three times higher than in 1987, averaging eight victims a month. 101/

FMLN began to target as military objectives municipal officials and suspected army informers. Thus, the guerrillas killed eight mayors (see reference to the case in chap. IV) and threatened to execute a similar number of informers. 102/ More than 150 people are estimated to have been killed by mines in 1988.

The Commission on the Truth received testimony concerning 138 victims of serious acts of violence occurring in 1988.

IV. 1989-1991: From the "final offensive" to the signing of the peace agreements

At 8 p.m. on Saturday, 11 November 1989, FMLN launched the biggest offensive of the war just a few days after the bombing of FENASTRAS headquarters. The impact of the offensive on the capital and other cities led the Government to decree a state of emergency. Beginning on 13 November, a 6 p.m. to 6 a.m. curfew went into effect. 103/ The fighting that raged up to 12 December cost the lives of over 2,000 from both sides and caused material damage amounting to approximately 6 billion colones. 104/

The 1989 offensive was one of the most violent episodes of the war. The guerrilla forces took cover in densely populated areas during the skirmishes and urban areas were the targets of indiscriminate aerial bombardment. The critical situation in the country bred such violations as the arrest, torture, murder and disappearance of hundreds of non-combatant civilians. It was against this backdrop that the Jesuit priests and two women were murdered.

The parties realized that a decisive military victory

was not within their grasp and resumed in greater earnest the negotiating process which led to the signing of the peace agreements.

Security Council resolution 637 (27 July 1989) endorsed the use of the good offices of the United Nations Secretary-General. The United Nations became a direct participant, mediating between the parties, until the ultimate signing of the agreements. The United Nations Secretary-General and his representatives intervened at crucial moments to keep one or the other of the parties from leaving the negotiating table.

The Geneva Agreement (April 1990), witnessed by the Secretary-General, marked the beginning of an irreversible embracing process drawing up an agenda and timetable (Caracas Agenda, 21 May 1990); human rights (San José Agreement, 26 July 1990); reforms in the army and the judicial and electoral systems and the establishment of the Commission on the Truth (Mexico Agreements, 27 April 1991), and finally the Chapultepec Agreement, the starting-point for the cessation of hostilities, disarmament and the implementation of the agreed institutional reforms.

1989

Two contradictory trends characterized Salvadorian society in 1989. On the one hand, acts of violence became more common, as did complaints of human rights violations, while on the other, talks between representatives of the Government of El Salvador and members of the FMLN leadership went forward with a view to achieving a negotiated and political settlement of the conflict. 105/

In the presidential elections, Alfredo Cristiani, 106/ the ARENA candidate, was elected while FMLN called for a boycott of the elections and a transport stoppage during election week. A number of incidents occurred in university centres. 107/ Systematic intimidation and threats against pastoral workers of various churches and social workers of different church institutions continued. 108/

FMLN continued its policy of *"ajusticiamientos"* (summary executions) and threats against mayors, forcing them to leave office; one third of the territory of El Salvador was affected. 109/ In addition, the number of politically motivated murders increased, most of them attributed to the rebels. The cases which caused the most outrage were the murder of former guerrilla commander Miguel Castellanos (17 February) (see chap. IV); the execution of Mr. Francisco Peccorini Letona; the murder of the Attorney General of the Republic, Roberto García Alvarado; the murder of José Antonio Rodríguez Porth, who only days before had assumed the post of the President's Chief of Staff, together with his chauffeur and another person with him. Mr. Rodríguez Porth, who was 74 years of age, was wounded by several

gunshots in front of his house and died a few days later in the hospital. In addition there was the murder of conservative ideologue Edgard Chacón; the execution of Gabriel Eugenio Payes Interiano 110/ and the death of prominent politician Francisco José Guerrero, former President of the Supreme Court, on 24 November in an operation which the Government claimed was carried out by the urban commandos of FMLN (see chap. IV).

Progress was made in the dialogue between FMLN and the Salvadorian Government. 111/ The talks continued in Mexico City from 13 to 15 September, in San José, Costa Rica, beginning on 16 October and in Caracas a month later. Observers from the Catholic Church of El Salvador, the United Nations and the Organization of American States were present.

Following the bombing of the offices of the Federación Nacional Sindical de Trabajadores Salvadoeñes (FENASTRAS) 112/ (see chap. IV), FMLN suspended talks with the Government.

On 16 November 1989 army units murdered the Jesuit priests of the Central American University (UCA): Ignacio Ellacuría, Rector of the University, Segundo Montes, Ignacio Martín-Baró, Armando López, Juan Ramón Moreno and Joaquín López, together with housekeeper Elba Ramos and her 15-year-old daughter, Celina Ramos (see chap. IV).

Colonel René Emilio Ponce, Chief of the Armed Forces Joint Staff, reported that the body count was 446 soldiers dead and 1,228 wounded, and 1,902 guerrillas killed and 1,109 wounded. 113/

The Commission on the Truth received direct testimony concerning 292 victims of serious acts of violence occurring in 1989.

1990

In 1990, negotiations proceeded and made real progress, while at the same time the war continued. Héctor Oquelí Colindres (see chap. IV.), leader of the Movimiento Nacional Revolucionario (MNR) 114/ was abducted and killed in Guatemala. Former President José Napoleón Duarte died and FMLN marked the occasion by proclaiming a unilateral cease-fire on the 24th and 25th.

According to the Annual Report of the Inter-American Commission on Human Rights 1990-1991, 119 people, 53 of whom were executed by death squads and 42 by the army, died as a result of political murders attributable to military or paramilitary groups. FMLN executed 21 persons, 14 of those executions being considered political murders. 115/

There were fewer civilian deaths than in 1989. The numbers dropped sharply after the signing of the San José Agreement on Human Rights on 26 July 1990. The army's military operations accounted for 852 victims, but it is not known how many were FMLN combatants and how many were civilians. 116/

In his report on the human rights situation for 1990, the Special Representative of the United Nations shared the concern of the Commission on Human Rights about the alarming frequency with which members of civil defence units had been involved in serious acts of murder, robbery, assault, rape and abuse of authority, keeping the population in a permanent state of fear and insecurity. 117/

The delegations of the Government and the Frente Farabundo Martí para la Liberación Nacional met in Geneva and agreed to resume talks. On 20 May 1990, the parties signed an agreement in Caracas which contained the agenda for the negotiations aimed at ending the conflict and established a definite timetable. 118/ The parties continued to meet on 19 June in Oaxtepec, Mexico, to discuss demilitarization and military impunity. The round of talks concluded without producing any agreement. As part of the process, what was regarded as the first substantive agreement, dealing with respect for human rights, was signed on 26 July, which has come to be known as the San José Agreement. Both parties undertook to respect the most fundamental rights of the human person and to institute a procedure for international verification by a United Nations mission.

In August, there was another round of talks to discuss the armed forces that ended once again without agreement. The deadlock in the talks led the United Nations Secretary-General to announce on 31 October that henceforth the negotiations would be held in secret.

Towards the middle of November, FMLN stepped up its military operations in various areas as a means of exerting military pressure to get the stalled negotiating process moving again. The international community responded with appeals to FMLN to desist from those operations. 119/

The Commission on the Truth received direct testimony concerning 107 victims of serious acts of violence occurring in 1990.

1991

The negotiating process between the Government of El Salvador and FMLN went forward during 1991. At the same time, the parties were faulted for serious acts of violence. On 2 January, in San Miguel, FMLN forces shot down a helicopter manned by three American advisers and executed the two survivors (see chap. IV). On 21 January, persons in uniform in El Zapote executed 15 members of a family. 120/ On 28 February, Mr. Guillermo Manuel Ungo died after a long illness. The same day, FMLN announced that it would not, as it

had in the past, boycott the March elections. On 10 March, 53 per cent of registered voters took part in the general legislative and municipal elections held in El Salvador. 121/

The process of dialogue advanced with two rounds of negotiations: one in Mexico from 3 to 6 January and the other in San José from 19 to 21 February, yielding no concrete results. Meanwhile, the level of violence of the war intensified throughout the country. 122/

On 4 April, Mexico City played host to the representatives of the Government and FMLN for the eighth round of negotiations, which went on until 27 April. Significant agreements were reached involving constitutional reforms affecting such aspects as the armed forces and the judicial and electoral systems, which were adopted by the Legislative Assembly on 29 April. It was in these Agreements that the parties decided to establish the Commission on the Truth. 123/

On 26 July, with the prior and full support of the United Nations Security Council resolution 693 (1991) and of the Legislative Assembly of El Salvador, the United Nations Observer Mission in El Salvador (ONUSAL) was launched and its Human Rights Division immediately became operational. The United Nations Secretary-General invited the parties to meet with him in New York. On 25 September they concluded the agreement known as the New York Act, which established the National Commission for the Consolidation of Peace (COPAZ). A process of purification and reduction of the armed forces was set in motion, the parties undertook to redefine the doctrine for the armed forces and confirmed the applicability of the Mexico Agreements of 27 April 1991. Furthermore, several economic and social agreements were concluded and an agenda was drawn up for negotiations on all outstanding issues.

The signing of the El Salvador Peace Agreement at Chapultepec, Mexico, on 16 January 1992, marked the culmination of the negotiating process and the beginning of the implementation phase of the agreements. It was also specifically agreed at Chapultepec to link the work of the Commission on the Truth with the clarification and ending of impunity. 124/

For the first six months of 1991, the Commission on the Truth received testimony concerning 28 victims of serious acts of violence.

The signing of the Peace Agreement in Chapultepec put an end to 12 years of armed conflict in El Salvador and the events mentioned in this brief chronology are only part of the tragic events of El Salvador's recent history. The Chapultepec Peace Agreement should also be the beginning of a new period that augurs a promising future for this Central American nation through national reconciliation.

IV. Cases and patterns of violence 125/

A. *General overview of cases and patterns of violence*

The Commission on the Truth registered more than 22,000 complaints of serious acts of violence that occurred in El Salvador between January 1980 and July 1991. 126/ Over 7,000 were received directly at the Commission's offices in various locations. The remainder were received through governmental and non-governmental institutions. 127/

Over 60 per cent of all complaints concerned extrajudicial executions, over 25 per cent concerned enforced disappearances, and over 20 per cent included complaints of torture.

Those giving testimony attributed almost 85 per cent of cases to agents of the State, paramilitary groups allied to them, and the death squads.

Armed forces personnel were accused in almost 60 per cent of complaints, members of the security forces in approximately 25 per cent, members of military escorts and civil defence units in approximately 20 per cent, and members of the death squads in more than 10 per cent of cases. The complaints registered accused FMLN in approximately 5 per cent of cases.

Despite their large number, these complaints do not cover every act of violence. The Commission was able to receive only a significant sample in its three months of gathering testimony.

This also does not mean that each act occurred as described in the testimony. The Commission investigated certain specific cases in particular circumstances, as well as overall patterns of violence. Some 30 of the cases dealt with in the report are illustrative of patterns of violence, in other words, involve systematic practices attested to by thousands of complainants.

Both the specific cases and the patterns of violence show that, during the 1980s, the country experienced an unusually high level of political violence. All Salvadorians without exception, albeit to differing degrees, suffered from this violence.

The introduction to the report and the section on methodology contain an explanation of this phenomenon.

Patterns of violence by agents of the State and their collaborators

All the complaints indicate that this violence originated in a political mind-set that viewed political opponents as subversives and enemies. Anyone who expressed views that differed from the Government line ran the risk of being eliminated as if they were armed enemies on the field of battle. This situation is epitomized by the extrajudicial executions, enforced disappearances and murders of political opponents described in this chapter.

Any organization in a position to promote opposing ideas that questioned official policy was automatically labelled as working for the guerrillas. To belong to such an organization meant being branded a subversive.

Counter-insurgency policy found its most extreme expression in a general practice of "cutting the guerrillas' lifeline". The inhabitants of areas where the guerrillas were active were automatically suspected of belonging to the guerrilla movement or collaborating with it and thus ran the risk of being eliminated. El Mozote is a deplorable example of this practice, which persisted for some years.

In the early years of the decade, the violence in rural areas was indiscriminate in the extreme.

Roughly 50 per cent of all the complaints analysed concern incidents which took place during the first two years, 1980 and 1981; more than 20 per cent took place in the following two years, 1982 and 1983. In other words, over 75 per cent of the serious acts of violence reported to the Commission on the Truth took place during the first four years of the decade.

The violence was less indiscriminate in urban areas, and also in rural areas after 1983 (95 per cent of complaints concerned incidents in rural areas and 5 per cent concerned incidents in more urban areas).

Patterns of FMLN violence

The Commission registered more than 800 complaints of serious acts of violence attributed to FMLN. This violence occurred mainly in conflict zones, over which FMLN at times maintained firm military control.

Nearly half the complaints against FMLN concern deaths, mostly extrajudicial executions. The rest concern enforced disappearances and forcible recruitment.

The patterns show that this violence began with the armed conflict. It was considered legitimate to physically eliminate people who were labelled military targets, traitors or "orejas" (informers), and even political opponents. The murders of mayors, right-wing intellectuals, public officials and judges are examples of this mentality.

Members of a given guerrilla organization would investigate the activities of the person who might be designated a military target, a spy or a traitor; they would then make an evaluation and take a collective decision to execute that person; special groups or commandoes would plan the action and the execution would then be carried out. After the extrajudicial execution, the corresponding organization would publicly claim responsibility for propaganda purposes. FMLN called such executions "ajusticiamientos".

These executions were carried out without due process. The case of Romero García, alias Miguel Castellanos, in 1989 is typical of extrajudicial executions ordered by FMLN because the victims were considered traitors. He was not given a trial. After a time, FMLN claimed responsibility for having ordered the killing. It never revealed which organization had carried out the execution.

The killings of mayors and the murder of United States military personnel in the Zona Rosa were carried out in response to orders or general directives issued by the FMLN Command to its organizations.

In the Zona Rosa case in 1985, the execution of Mr. Peccorini in 1989, and the execution of Mr. García Alvarado that same year, different member organizations of FMLN interpreted general policy directives restrictively and applied them sporadically, thereby triggering an upsurge in the violence.

In the case of executions of mayors, on the other hand, instructions from the FMLN General Command were interpreted broadly and applied extensively. During the period 1985-1989, the Ejército Revolucionario del Pueblo repeatedly carried out extrajudicial executions of non-combatant civilians. There is no concept under international humanitarian law whereby such people could have been considered military targets.

The Commission was not able to verify the existence of general directives from the FMLN leadership to its constituent organizations authorizing enforced disappearances. It did receive complaints of some 300 cases of disappearance, which occurred mainly in areas where FMLN exercised greater military control. It was not possible to establish the existence of any pattern from an analysis of these complaints. Nevertheless, links were observed between disappearances, forcible recruitment by FMLN and cases of extrajudicial execution by FMLN members of individuals labelled spies or traitors.

The extrajudicial execution of the United States military personnel who survived the attack on their helicopter in San Miguel in 1991 cannot be viewed as the norm. FMLN admitted that some of its members had been responsible, and stated publicly that it had been a mistake. However, there is no record that those who carried out the execution were actually punished.

Lastly, although the number of complaints of the alleged use of land-mines by guerrilla forces was small, the Commission considered accusations made by various organizations against FMLN to that effect. Members of FMLN admitted to the Commission that they had laid mines with little or no supervision, so much so that civilians and their own members who were not sufficiently familiar with the location of minefields had been affected. The Commission did not find any other evidence on this subject.

B. *Violence against opponents by agents of the State*

1. *Illustrative case: the murders of the Jesuit priests*

Summary of the case

In the early hours on 16 November 1989, six Jesuit priests, a cook and her 16-year-old daughter were shot and killed at the Pastoral Centre of José Simeón Cañas Central American University (UCA) in San Salvador. The victims were Fathers Ignacio Ellacuría, Rector of the University; Ignacio Martín-Baró, Vice-Rector; Segundo Montes, Director of the Human Rights Institute; Amando López, Joaquín López y López and Juan Ramón Moreno, all teachers at UCA; and Julia Elba Ramos and her daughter, Celina Mariceth Ramos.

Criminal proceedings were subsequently brought against members of the armed forces for the murders; they included Colonel Guillermo Alfredo Benavides Moreno, Director of the Military College, accused of having given the order to murder the priests; Lieutenant Yusshy René Mendoza Vallecillos, an officer of the Military College, and Lieutenants José Ricardo Espinoza Guerra and Gonzalo Guevara Cerritos, officers of the Atlacatl Battalion, all of them accused of commanding the operation; and five soldiers of the Atlacatl Battalion, accused of committing the murders.

In 1991, a jury found Colonel Benavides guilty of all the murders and Lieutenant Mendoza Vallecillos guilty of the murder of the young girl, Celina Mariceth Ramos. The judge imposed the maximum sentence, 30 years in prison, which they are currently serving. The judge also found Colonel Benavides and Lieutenant Mendoza guilty of instigation and conspiracy to commit acts of terrorism. Lieutenants Espinoza and Guevara Cerritos were sentenced to three years for instigation and conspiracy to commit acts of terrorism. Lieutenant Colonel Hernández was convicted by the judge of being an accessory, as was Mendoza Vallecillos. All, except for Colonel Benavides and Lieutenant Mendoza, were released on bail and remained in the armed forces.

The Commission on the Truth makes the following findings and recommendations:

1. On the night of 15 November 1989, then Colonel René Emilio Ponce, in the presence of and in collusion with General Juan Rafael Bustillo, then Colonel Juan Orlando Zepeda, Colonel Inocente Orlando Montano and Colonel Francisco Elena Fuentes, gave Colonel Guillermo Alfredo Benavides the order to kill Father Ignacio Ellacuría and to leave no witnesses. For that purpose, Colonel Benavides was given the use of a unit from the Atlacatl Battalion, which had been sent to search the priests' residence two days previously.

2. Subsequently, all these officers and others, including General Gilberto Rubio Rubio, knowing what had happened, took steps to conceal the truth.

3. That same night, Colonel Guillermo Alfredo Benavides informed the officers at the Military College of the order for the murder. When he asked whether anyone had any objection, they all remained silent.

4. The operation was organized by then Major Carlos Camilo Hernández Barahona and carried out by a group of soldiers from the Atlacatl Battalion under the command of Lieutenant José Ricardo Espinoza Guerra and Second Lieutenant Gonzalo Guevara Cerritos, accompanied by Lieutenant Yusshy René Mendoza Vallecillos.

5. Colonel Oscar Alberto León Linares, Commander of the Atlacatl Battalion, knew of the murder and concealed incriminating evidence.

6. Colonel Manuel Antonio Rivas Mejía, Head of the Commission for the Investigation of Criminal Acts (CIHD), learnt the facts and concealed the truth; he also recommended to Colonel Benavides measures for the destruction of incriminating evidence.

7. Colonel Nelson Iván López y López, who was assigned to assist in the CIHD investigation, learnt what had happened and concealed the truth.

8. Rodolfo Antonio Parker Soto, a lawyer and member of the Special Honour Commission, altered statements in order to conceal the responsibility of senior officers for the murder.

9. The Commission believes that it is unfair that Colonel Guillermo Alfredo Benavides Moreno and Lieutenant Yusshy René Mendoza Vallecillos should still be in prison when the people responsible for planning the murders and the person who gave the order remain at liberty. In the Commission's view, the request by the Society of Jesus that Colonel Guillermo Alfredo Benavides Moreno and Lieutenant Yusshy René Mendoza Vallecillos be pardoned should be granted by the relevant authorities.

Description of the facts 128/

In the early hours of 16 November 1989, a group of soldiers from the Atlacatl Battalion entered the campus of José Simeón Cañas Central American University (UCA) in San Salvador. They made their way to the Pastoral Centre, which was the residence of Jesuit priests Ignacio Ellacuría, Rector of the University; Ignacio Martín-Baró, Vice-Rector; Segundo Montes, Director of the Human Rights Institute; and Amando López, Joaquín López y López and Juan Ramón Moreno, all teachers at UCA.

The soldiers tried to force their way into the Pastoral Centre. When the priests realized what was happening, they let the soldiers in voluntarily. The soldiers searched the building and ordered the priests to go out into the back garden and lie face down on the ground.

The lieutenant in command, José Ricardo Espi-noza Guerra, gave the order to kill the priests. Fathers Ellacuría, Martín-Baró and Montes were shot and killed by Private Oscar Mariano Amaya Grimaldi, Fathers López and Moreno by Deputy Sergeant Antonio Ramiro Avalos Vargas. Shortly afterwards, the soldiers, including Corporal Angel Pérez Vásquez, found Father Joaquín López y López inside the residence and killed him. Deputy Sergeant Tomás Zarpate Castillo shot Julia Elva Ramos, who was working in the residence, and her 16-year-old daughter, Celina Mariceth Ramos. Private José Alberto Sierra Ascencio shot them again, finishing them off.

The soldiers took a small suitcase belonging to the priests, with photographs, documents and $5,000.

They fired a machine gun at the façade of the residence and launched rockets and grenades. Before leaving, they wrote on a piece of cardboard: "FMLN executed those who informed on it. Victory or death, FMLN."

Preceding events

A few hours earlier, on 15 November between 10 p.m. and 11 p.m., Colonel Guillermo Alfredo Benavides Moreno, Director of the Military College, met with the officers under his command. The officers present included Major Carlos Camilo Hernández Barahona, Captain José Fuentes Rodas, Lieutenants Mario Arévalo Meléndez, Nelson Alberto Barra Zamora, Francisco Mónico Gallardo Mata, José Vicente Hernández Ayala, Ramón Eduardo López Larios, René Roberto López Morales, Yusshy René Mendoza Vallecillos, Edgar Santiago Martínez Marroquín and Second Lieutenant Juan de Jesús Guzmán Morales.

Colonel Benavides told them that he had just come from a meeting at the General Staff at which special measures had been adopted to combat the FMLN offensive, which had begun on 11 November. Those present at the meeting had been informed that the situation was critical and it had been decided that artillery and armoured vehicles should be used.

Those present at the meeting had also been informed that all known subversive elements must be eliminated. Colonel Benavides said that he had received orders to eliminate Father Ignacio Ellacuría and to leave no witnesses.

Colonel Benavides asked any officers who objected to the order to raise their hands. No one did.

Major Hernández Barahona organized the operation. Troops from the Atlacatl Battalion were used, under the command of Lieutenant José Ricardo Espinoza Guerra. In order to overcome any reluctance on his part, it was arranged that Lieutenant Yusshy René Mendoza Vallecillos, who had graduated from officer training school in the same class ("tanda") as him, would also participate.

After the meeting, Major Hernández Barahona met

with Lieutenant Mendoza Vallecillos, Lieutenant Espinoza Guerra and Second Lieutenant Gonzalo Guevara Cerritos of the Atlacatl Battalion. In order to pin responsibility for the deaths on FMLN, they decided not to use regulation firearms and to leave no witnesses. After the murders, they would simulate an attack and leave a sign mentioning FMLN.

It was decided to use an AK-47 rifle belonging to Major Hernández Barahona, because the weapon had been captured from FMLN and was identifiable. The rifle was entrusted to Private Mariano Amaya Grimaldi, who knew how to use it.

In order to reach UCA, it was necessary to pass through the defence cordons of the military complex. Lieutenant Martínez Marroquín arranged for the Atlacatl soldiers to pass.

Lieutenants Espinoza Guerra and Mendoza Vallecillos and Second Lieutenant Guevara Cerritos left the Military College in two pick-up trucks with the soldiers from the Atlacatl Battalion. They went to some empty buildings which are close to the UCA campus, where other soldiers of the Atlacatl Battalion were waiting. There, Lieutenant Espinoza indicated who would keep watch and who would enter the Jesuits' residence.

Background

Members of the armed forces used to call UCA a "refuge of subversives". Colonel Juan Orlando Zepeda, Vice-Minister for Defence, publicly accused UCA of being the centre of operations where FMLN terrorist strategy was planned. Colonel Inocente Montano, Vice-Minister for Public Security, stated publicly that the Jesuits were fully identified with subversive movements.

Father Ellacuría had played an important role in the search for a negotiated, peaceful solution to the armed conflict. Sectors of the armed forces identified the Jesuit priests with FMLN because of the priests' special concern for those sectors of Salvadorian society who were poorest and most affected by the war.

On two earlier occasions that same year, 1989, bombs had gone off at the University printing house.

The offensive

The offensive launched by FMLN on 11 November reached proportions that the armed forces had not expected and which alarmed them. The guerrillas gained control of various areas in and around San Salvador. They attacked the official and private residences of the President of the Republic and the residence of the President of the Legislative Assembly. They also attacked the barracks of the First, Third and Sixth Infantry Brigades and those of the National Police. On 12 November, the Government declared a state of emergency and imposed a 6 p.m. to 6 a.m. curfew.

At a meeting of the General Staff on 13 November, security commands were created to deal with the offensive. Each command was headed by an officer under the operational control of Colonel René Emilio Ponce, Chief of the Armed Forces Joint Staff. Colonel Benavides Moreno was designated to head the military complex security command, a zone which included the Military College, the Ministry of Defence, the Joint Staff, the National Intelligence Department (DNI), the Arce and Palermo districts (most of whose residents were members of the armed forces), the residence of the United States Ambassador and the UCA campus.

A national radio channel was also established, the pilot station being Radio Cuscatlán of the armed forces. Telephone calls to the station were broadcast in a "phone-in" in which callers levelled accusations at Father Ellacuría and went so far as to call for his death.

On 11 November, guerrillas blew up one of the main gates of the University and crossed the University campus. The next day, a military detachment was stationed to watch who went in and out of the University. From 13 November onwards no one was permitted onto the campus.

On 13 November, Colonel Ponce ordered Colonel Joaquín Arnoldo Cerna Flores, head of unit III of the General Staff, to arrange for a search of UCA premises. According to Colonel Ponce, he ordered the search because he had been informed that there were over 200 guerrillas inside the University.

Colonel Cerna Flores entrusted the search to Lieutenant José Ricardo Espinoza Guerra, who took some 100 men from the Atlacatl Battalion. Lieutenant Héctor Ulises Cuenca Ocampo of the National Intelligence Department (DNI) joined the troops at the entrance to UCA to assist with the search. Lieutenant Espinoza Guerra personally directed the search of the Jesuits' residence. They found no signs of any guerrilla presence, war *matériel* or propaganda.

On completing the search, Lieutenant Espinoza Guerra reported to Major Hernández Barahona. He then went to the General Staff where he reported to Colonel Cerna Flores.

At 6.30 p.m. on 15 November there was a meeting of the General Staff with military heads and commanders to adopt new measures to deal with the offensive. Colonel Ponce authorized the elimination of ringleaders, trade unionists and known leaders of FMLN and a decision was taken to step up bombing by the Air Force and to use artillery and armoured vehicles to dislodge FMLN from the areas it controlled.

The Minister of Defence, General Rafael Humberto Larios López, asked whether anyone objected. No hand was raised. It was agreed that President Cristiani would be consulted about the measures.

After the meeting, the officers stayed in the room talking in groups. One of these groups consisted of Colonel Réne Emilio Ponce, General Juan Rafael Bustillo, Colonel Francisco Elena Fuentes, Colonel Juan Orlando Zepeda and Colonel Inocente Orlando Montano. Colonel Ponce called over Colonel Guillermo Alfredo Benavides and, in front of the four other officers, ordered him to eliminate Father Ellacuría and to leave no witnesses. He also ordered him to use the unit from the Atlacatl Battalion which had carried out the search two days earlier.

From 12 to 1.30 a.m. the next day, 16 November, President Cristiani met with the High Command. According to his statement, the President approved a new arrangement for using armoured units of the cavalry regiment and artillery pieces; at no time during this meeting was anything said about UCA.

The cover-up

During the early hours of the morning of 16 November, Major Carlos Camilo Hernández Barahona and Lieutenant José Vicente Hernández Ayala went in person to Colonel Ponce's office to report on everything that had happened at UCA. They reported that they had a small suitcase with photographs, documents and money which the soldiers had stolen from the Jesuits a few hours earlier. Colonel Ponce ordered it destroyed because it was evidence of the armed forces' responsibility. They destroyed the suitcase at the Military College.

On returning to his unit, Lieutenant Espinoza Guerra informed the Commander of the Atlacatl Battalion, Lieutenant Colonel Oscar Alberto León Linares, of what had happened.

President Cristiani entrusted the investigation of the crime to the Commission for the Investigation of Criminal Acts (CIHD).

Colonel Benavides told Lieutenant Colonel Manuel Antonio Rivas Mejía, Head of CIHD, what had happened and asked him for help. Mejía recommended that the barrels of the weapons which had been used be destroyed and replaced with others in order to prevent them from being identified during ballistic tests. This was later done with the assistance of Lieutenant Colonel Oscar Alberto León Linares.

Lieutenant Colonel Rivas Mejía also advised Colonel Benavides to make sure that no record remained of those entering and leaving the Military College that would make it possible to identify the culprits. Subsequently, Colonel Benavides and Major Hernández Barahona ordered that all Military College arrival and departure logs for that year and the previous year be burned.

Shortly after the investigation began, Colonel René Emilio Ponce arranged for Colonel Nelson Iván López y López, head of unit I of the General Staff, who had also been in charge of the General Staff Tactical Operations Centre during the entire night of 15 to 16 November, to join CIHD in order to assist in the investigation of the case.

In November, CIHD heard two witnesses, Deputy Sergeant Germán Orellana Vázquez and police officer Victor Manuel Orellana Hernández, who testified that they had seen soldiers of the Atlacatl Battalion near UCA that night; they later changed their statements.

Another witness also retracted her initial statement. Lucía Barrera de Cerna, an employee at the University, said that she had seen, from a building adjacent to the Jesuits' residence, soldiers in camouflage and berets. In the United States, where she went for protection, she was questioned by the Federal Bureau of Investigation (FBI) and retracted her earlier statement. Lieutenant Colonel Rivas Mejía, Head of CIHD, was present when she was questioned. Subsequently, she confirmed her original statement.

CIHD did not take a statement from Colonel Benavides, even though the incident had occurred within his command zone. According to the court dossier, the first statement Benavides made was on 11 January 1990 to the Special Honour Commission.

On 2 January 1990, a month and a half after the murders, Major Eric Warren Buckland, an officer of the United States Army and an adviser to the armed forces of El Salvador, reported to his superior, Lieutenant Colonel William Hunter, a conversation he had some days previously with Colonel Carlos Armando Avilés Buitrago. During that conversation, Avilés Buitrago had told him that he had learnt, through Colonel López y López, that Benavides had arranged the murders and that a unit from the Atlacatl Battalion had carried them out. He also said that Benavides had asked Lieutenant Colonel Rivas Mejía for help.

Lieutenant Colonel William Hunter informed the Chief of the United States Military Mission, Colonel Milton Menjívar, who arranged a meeting in Colonel Ponce's office where Buckland and Avilés were brought face to face. Avilés denied having given Buckland such information.

A few days after Buckland's statements were reported, the Minister of Defence established a Special Honour Commission, consisting of five officers and two civilians, to investigate the murders.

On learning what CIHD had found out, the Honour Commission questioned some 30 members of the Atlacatl Battalion, including Lieutenant Espinoza Guerra and Second Lieutenant Guevara Cerritos, and a number of officers of the Military College, including Colonel Benavides and Lieutenant Mendoza Vallecillos.

Lieutenants Espinoza and Mendoza and Second Lieutenant Guevara, as well as the soldiers who had participated in the murders, confessed their crime in extrajudicial statements to the Honour Commission.

A civilian member of the Commission, Rodolfo Antonio Parker Soto, legal adviser to the General Staff, altered their statements in order to delete any reference to the existence of orders from above. He also deleted the references to some officers, including the one to Major Carlos Camilo Hernández Barahona.

On 12 January, the Commission submitted its report to President Cristiani. The report identified nine people as being responsible for the murders, four officers and five soldiers; they were arrested and later brought to trial. Subsequently, newly promoted Lieutenant Colonel Carlos Camilo Hernández Barahona was included in the trial.

The pre-trial proceedings took nearly two years. During this time, Colonel (now General) René Emilio Ponce, Colonel (now General) Juan Orlando Zepeda, Colonel Inocente Orlando Montano and Colonel (now General) Gilberto Rubio Rubio pressured lower-ranking officers not to mention orders from above in their testimony to the court.

Finally, the trial by jury took place on 26, 27 and 28 September 1991 in the building of the Supreme Court of Justice. The identity of the five members of the jury was kept secret. The accused and the charges were as follows:

Colonel Guillermo Alfredo Benavides Moreno, Lieutenant José Ricardo Espinoza Guerra and Second Lieutenant Gonzalo Guevara Cerritos: accused of murder, acts of terrorism, acts preparatory to terrorism and instigation and conspiracy to commit acts of terrorism.

Lieutenant Yusshy René Mendoza Vallecillos: accused of murder, acts of terrorism, acts preparatory to terrorism, instigation and conspiracy to commit acts of terrorism and of being an accessory.

Deputy Sergeant Antonio Ramiro Avalos Vargas, Deputy Sergeant Tomás Zarpate Castillo, Corporal Angel Pérez Vásquez and Private Oscar Mariano Amaya Grimaldi: accused of murder, acts of terrorism and acts preparatory to terrorism.

Private Jorge Alberto Sierra Ascencio: tried in absentia for murder. Lieutenant Colonel Carlos Camilo Hernández Barahona: accused of being an accessory.

The jury had to decide only with respect to the charges of murder and acts of terrorism. The other charges were left to the judge to decide.

Only Colonel Guillermo Alfredo Benavides Moreno and Lieutenant Yusshy René Mendoza Vallecillos were found guilty of murder. The judge gave them the maximum sentence, 30 years in prison, which they are currently serving. The judge also found Colonel Benavides and Lieutenant Mendoza guilty of instigation and conspiracy to commit acts of terrorism. Lieutenants Espinoza and Guevara Cerritos were sentenced to three years for instigation and conspiracy to commit acts of terrorism. Lieutenant Colonel Hernández was also sentenced by the judge to three years for being an accessory and Mendoza Vallecillos was also convicted on that charge. Espinoza, Guevara and Hernández were released and continued in active service in the armed forces.

Findings

The Commission on the Truth makes the following findings and recommendations:

1. There is substantial evidence that on the night of 15 November 1989, then Colonel René Emilio Ponce, in the presence of and in collusion with General Juan Rafael Bustillo, then Colonel Juan Orlando Zepeda, Colonel Inocente Orlando Montano and Colonel Francisco Elena Fuentes, gave Colonel Guillermo Alfredo Benavides the order to kill Father Ignacio Ellacuría and to leave no witnesses. For that purpose, Colonel Benavides was given the use of a unit from the Atlacatl Battalion, which two days previously had been sent to search the priest's residence.

2. There is evidence that, subsequently, all these officers and others, knowing what had happened, took steps to conceal the truth. There is sufficient evidence that General Gilberto Rubio Rubio, knowing what had happened, took steps to conceal the truth.

3. There is full evidence that:

(a) That same night of 15 November, Colonel Guillermo Alfredo Benavides informed the officers at the Military College of the order he had been given for the murder. When he asked whether anyone had any objection, they all remained silent.

(b) The operation was organized by then Major Carlos Camilo Hernández Barahona and carried out by a group of soldiers from the Atlacatl Battalion under the command of Lieutenant José Ricardo Espinoza Guerra and Second Lieutenant Gonzalo Guevara Cerritos, accompanied by Lieutenant Yusshy René Mendoza Vallecillos.

4. There is substantial evidence that:

(a) Colonel Oscar Alberto León Linares, Commander of the Atlacatl Battalion, knew of the murder and concealed incriminating evidence.

(b) Colonel Manual Antonio Rivas Mejía of the Commission for the Investigation of Criminal Acts (CIHD) learnt the facts and concealed the truth and also recommended to Colonel Benavides measures for the destruction of incriminating evidence.

(c) Colonel Nelson Iván López y López, who was assigned to assist in the CIHD investigation, learnt what had happened and concealed the truth.

5. There is full evidence that Rodolfo Antonio Parker Soto, a member of the Special Honour Commission, altered statements in order to conceal the responsibility of senior officers for the murder.

6. The Commission believes that it is unfair that Colonel Guillermo Alfredo Benavides Moreno and Lieutenant Yusshy René Mendoza Vallecillos should still be in prison when the people responsible for planning the murders and the person who gave the order for the murder remain at liberty. In the Commission's view, the request by the Society of Jesus that Colonel Guillermo Alfredo Benavides Moreno and Lieutenant Yusshy René Mendoza Vallecillos be pardoned should be granted by the relevant authorities.

2. Extrajudicial executions

(a) San Francisco Guajoyo

Summary of the case

In the early hours of 29 May 1980, 58 members of the security forces and the Second Infantry Brigade arrived at San Francisco Guajoyo cooperative in Belén Güijat canton, Metapán district, Department of Santa Ana, dragged members of the cooperative from their homes in the adjoining houses and took them to the central area of the farm.

That same morning, the bodies of 12 victims were found, covered with a blanket on which were written the words "killed as traitors". Shortly afterwards, the justice of the peace carried out the requisite procedures.

The Commission finds the following:

1. On 29 May 1980, two employees of the Salvadorian Institute for Agrarian Reform (ISTA) and 10 members of the San Francisco Guajoyo cooperative were executed with large-calibre firearms in the central area of the cooperative, after having been dragged from their homes.

2. The deaths did not occur during an armed confrontation.

3. Members of the Second Infantry Brigade and of the security forces having jurisdiction in the Department of Santa Ana were responsible for the incident.

4. The Salvadorian State bears full responsibility for the execution of the cooperative members, which was a violation of international humanitarian law and international human rights law, and for having taken no action to identify and punish those responsible.

Description of the facts 129/

General background

The San Francisco Guajoyo cooperative was founded in 1977 and there were some 260 families who were members. The organization did a great deal of educational and advocacy work.

The army and security forces launched a smear campaign against members of the cooperative, accusing them of being guerrillas. In 1979, the threats increased. There were constant army patrols and persecution was stepped up. Most members of the cooperative used to sleep in the hills for fear of being dragged from their homes in the night.

The operations were carried out by troops from the Second Brigade and by security forces, often accompanied by civil defence members. The accusation was always the alleged ties between cooperative members and the guerrillas, but cooperative members believed that the real motive was to block their demands.

The military operation

In the early hours of 29 May 1980, between 50 and 80 members of the Second Infantry Brigade, the National Police, the Treasury Police and the National Guard, including some National Guard members who were responsible for guarding the Guajoyo CEL, approached the San Francisco Guajoyo cooperative building.

The military contingent entered the cooperative from two equidistant points, moving in on the stable and dwellings located near its centre. They dragged cooperative members from their homes and took them to the central area of the farm. People were arrested according to a list, "although towards the end, they were taking anyone to the courtyard of the house".

Soldiers simultaneously burst into the cooperative offices, seizing three members of the cooperative who were looking after the premises. The group that entered the offices was headed by Adán Figueroa, 130/ known as "calache", of the Treasury Police, originally from Tahuilapa canton. They took the three to the central area of the farm. One of the survivors observed that "the others had already been made to lie face down, ready to be killed". Everyone was asked who they were and where they were hiding the weapons. A few minutes later the shooting began.

On realizing the operation was under way, particularly on hearing the noise of houses being searched, other members of the cooperative ran from their homes. One witness stated that a member who was on guard in the cooperative's tobacco storeroom came to his house to warn him that a military truck had arrived. He was able to hide in time, but he heard the shots and "the cries and suffering" of those who had been arrested.

The executions

Twelve people were executed. According to the records of the Metapán Second Magistrate's Court, the bodies were found in the central area of the farm. Seven bodies were found in the farmhouse courtyard, lying at intervals of about half a metre apart. The remaining five bodies were lying at a short distance from the first group. According to the forensic examination, all the wounds were caused by large-calibre weapons.

They executed people who apparently were not on the list. This was true of José Angel Mira, a mentally handicapped person who was arrested. When his father asked them to let his son go, the officer told him to lie down next to his son so that they could die together. This is what in fact happened.

Members of the cooperative who had fled to the hills found the bodies when they returned after the attack. Near the bodies they found a blanket on which were written the words "killed as traitors". According to witnesses, combined forces often did this to create confusion as to who was responsible.

Public version of the incident

The next day, a press source reported that a guerrilla camp had been discovered in an area close to Metapán "hours after alleged left-wing guerrillas killed 12 peasants, members of a cooperative which was working a farm taken over as part of the agrarian reform, in the area where the camp was discovered". It went on to say that "the Armed Forces Press Committee told ACAN-EFE" that some 30 guerrillas had joined the battle with the members of the National Guard who discovered the camp. According to the source, there had been no military casualties; however, it did not specify the number of guerrilla casualties either.

Another source, under the headline "12 killed at farm in subversive attack", reported an armed confrontation in which 12 people had been killed; "mostly peasants, and two ISTA employees wounded, at the San Francisco farm in Metapán district". It also reported that troops had been deployed: "men in olive-green uniforms entered the farm at Guajoyo in La Joya canton, Metapán district".

Action taken by the judiciary

On the morning of the executions, the competent justice of the peace went to the cooperative with his secretary and two forensic doctors to carry out the requisite legal procedures. The main findings in the record are as follows:

(a) Twelve people were shot and killed in the early hours of that day;

(b) Witnesses stated that a group of individuals in olive-green uniforms accompanied by civilians, who had dragged the victims from their homes, were responsible for the execution;

(c) According to the forensic examination, a number of the victims had been shot in the back and several of the bodies had been shot at close range. 131/ Further-

more it was not possible to determine where the bullets had entered and exited the bodies. 132/ Several of the victims were barefoot and only half dressed.

Having completed the preliminary inquiries, the justice of the peace transmitted the information to the ordinary court to institute the corresponding judicial investigation. That court took no further action and filed the information.

Findings

The Commission finds the following:

1. There is full evidence that, on 29 May 1980, two employees of the Salvadorian Institute for Agrarian Reform (ISTA) and 10 members of the San Francisco Guajoyo cooperative were executed with large-calibre firearms in the central area of the cooperative, after having been dragged from their homes.

2. There is sufficient evidence to attribute responsibility for the incident to members of the Second Infantry Brigade and of the security forces having jurisdiction in the Department of Santa Ana.

3. The Salvadorian State bears full responsibility for the execution of the cooperative members, which was a violation of international humanitarian law and international human rights law, and for having taken no action to identify and punish those responsible.

(b) *The leaders of the Frente Democrático Revolucionario*

Summary of the case

On 27 November 1980, Enrique Alvarez Córdoba, 133/ Juan Chacón, 134/ Enrique Escobar Barrera, 135/ Manuel de Jesús Franco Ramírez, 136/ Humberto Mendoza 137/ and Doroteo Hernández, 138/ political leaders of the Frente Democrático Revolucionario (FDR), 139/ representing an important sector of Salvadorian society, were abducted, tortured and, after a short period in captivity, executed in San Salvador.

The abduction was carried out during the morning at the Colegio San José by a large number of heavily armed men.

The climate of violence and insecurity prevailing in the country at the time was such that, had it not been for who the victims were, the place and time of the abduction, the type of operation and the public outrage it caused, it would have been just one more in the long list of abuses that were occurring at the time.

The Commission on the Truth concludes that it was an operation carried out by one or more public security forces and that the Treasury Police were responsible for the external security operation which aided and abetted the perpetrators. By commission and, in failing to properly investigate the incident, by omission, the State failed to comply with its obligations under international human rights law to protect and guarantee the enjoyment by individuals of their most elementary rights.

Description of the incident

The six victims were abducted from the Colegio San José, a Jesuit School Society in the very heart of the capital city, San Salvador, between 9.30 a.m. and 11 a.m. on 27 November 1980. In the immediate vicinity of the school, there are other educational centres, a number of hospitals and, to the north, the former United States Embassy, which at the time was under heavy guard.

The ground floor of the central building housed the rector's office, the administration and the Christian Legal Aid office, which had been in existence since 1975 when the school had started working with the neediest social sectors.

The workload of Christian Legal Aid had increased appreciably because, in addition to the normal stream of people coming to seek assistance, other entities which had been doing the same kind of work had closed their doors because of the prevailing climate of terror. 140/

Despite the large numbers of people going in and out of the school, the building had no security system. There were just a few unarmed porters at the central entrance to the educational complex. That morning there was only one porter at the main entrance.

The facts

The operation was carried out between 9.30 a.m. and 11 a.m. Initially, an unspecified number of men seized the porter, took him some 500 metres from the entrance and radioed to other people that they could go in.

They opened the gate and let in a number of vehicles carrying people who were heavily armed with machine-guns and "G3" rifles. 141/ The group went swiftly over to the central entrance of the main building and placed people against the wall ordering them to lie on the ground and close their eyes. Members of the group also stationed themselves at the entrances to the school and dealt in similar fashion with anyone who approached. Reports at the time put the total number of men who participated in the operation at between 13 and 200. 142/ According to the information received, the speed with which the bodies were dumped in the street in full view of passers-by was clearly intended to ensure that they were readily identified, so as to lessen the political pressure on the case.

The first four bodies and that of Alvarez Córdoba were found on the outskirts of the resort city of Apulo, in Ilopango district, approximately one hour by car from San Salvador. The Ilopango justice of the peace made the legal examination and opened a dossier which was later sent to the Fourth Criminal Court in San Salvador.

The Commission did not find that any judicial, police or administrative remedy had been sought to preserve the physical integrity of the abducted men. In its view, this was because people were very afraid and distrustful of using judicial bodies.

The Court dossier which the Commission studied shows clearly that the organ entrusted with investigating the case did not conduct a proper investigation; it finally closed the case on 8 October 1982. In fact, only bureaucratic measures were taken; no autopsy was performed, nor was anything else done to clarify the facts and find out who was responsible. 143/

Analysis

Once the news broke, a war of communiqués ensued over who had committed the deed, whether part of the security forces or else the death squads acting without the direct participation of government forces. The possibility of it being the work of left-wing groups was also considered. 144/ The government Junta, for its part, urged that the physical and psychological integrity of the abducted leaders be respected. 145/

At the political level, the abduction of the opposition leaders closed the door to negotiations and fuelled demands for armed confrontation against the third Revolutionary Government Junta. It is worth recalling that the very day the incident occurred, the former Foreign Minister, Fidel Chávez Mena, was in Washington, D.C. at the General Assembly of the Organization of American States (OAS), talking with church and opposition circles in an effort to secure a negotiated outcome to the crisis. 146/

The Revolutionary Government Junta (JRG) offered to carry out an exhaustive investigation into the incident and emphatically denied that security forces under its command had participated. The investigations that were carried out were purely a formality. For example, although a considerable number of people had been present when the incident took place, only four of them were interviewed. The Commission requested, but was not given, the report of the National Police. 147/

The incident outraged public opinion, prompting the armed forces and the Office of the President to interview some of the eyewitnesses. All political sectors in the country disclaimed responsibility for the incident, accusing other sectors.

FDR turned the funeral into a political rally, introducing the organization's new leadership and asserting that paramilitary groups, with the complicity at least of the security forces, were responsible for the murders. 148/

From all the evidence which the Commission has gathered, it is clear that the purpose of the operation was to arrest the FDR leaders. It does not seem possible that the operation and its outcome could have occurred by chance or that it could have had any other purpose. The manner in which those participating in the operation entered the building and the surrounding area leaves no doubt that it was, indeed, an operation designed specifically to capture the leaders.

According to the various theories that have been put forward, the operation was carried out by paramilitary groups, by security forces or by a combination of the two; it may also have been an independent operation by members of those State organs.

For example, the Brigada Anticomunista General Maximiliano Hernández Martínez claimed responsibility for the murders. This group has been identified as one of several which the extreme right-wing used to claim responsibility for such actions. One witness told the Commission that, at the time the incident occurred, some soldiers in active service were members of the Brigade.

In the Commission's view, the characteristics of the operation show that, while there may not have been unified planning by some security forces, the coverage provided for the execution of the crime was centralized and, without it, the operation would have been highly risky or very difficult to carry out. In any event, it is unlikely that the operation could have been carried out so openly without at least the complicity of the security forces which, moreover, were keeping a close watch on the political leaders and on the school itself because of the activities that were going on there.

Indeed, the time, the place, the number of personnel, the radio equipment, vehicles, weapons and uniforms used, the slang and the chain of command, the fact that the participants withdrew without any problem and the absence of a proper investigation by the security forces indicate the extent to which those forces were involved.

According to diplomatic reports, it was widely believed that the crime had been committed by security forces including, possibly, the Treasury Police. The testimony given by several people points in this direction. The Commission has substantial evidence that the Treasury Police carried out the security operation on the school's perimeter. The Commission summonsed several officers who held positions of responsibility at the time in that institution. The few who did appear roundly denied having had anything to do with the incident.

Other information received by the Commission concerning the activities of the security and intelligence forces indicates that the National Guard carried out the operation, acting independently of the General Staff.

As indicated earlier, the Commission cannot, in any case, accept the idea that the operation was carried out without the cooperation of senior commanders of one or more security forces, which at the time were headed by military officers.

Based on the available information, it is difficult to determine whether the operation was planned at the highest level of the armed forces or whether, instead, it was instigated by middle-ranking commanders of the security forces, resulting in *de facto* situations that were difficult to reverse.

Lastly, the Commission tried in vain to establish who gave the order to kill the FDR leaders and whether that was part of the original plan or was decided upon subsequently. Given the conditions of violence prevailing at the time, an operation of this kind clearly involved a very high risk that the persons captured would be eliminated.

The Commission received reliable information that the final execution order was discussed at the highest level of right-wing sectors. It is alleged that there were telephone calls between those who carried out the murders and those who planned them. According to the testimony received, the latter allegedly decided to act as swiftly as possible in order to reduce the political pressure created by the capture of the victims.

Findings

The Commission finds that:

1. The abduction, torture and subsequent murder of the political and trade union leaders was an act that outraged national and international public opinion and closed the door to any possibility of a negotiated solution to the political crisis at the end of 1980. It was a very serious act which warranted the most thorough investigation by the Commission on the Truth.

2. It is not possible to determine precisely which public security force carried out these criminal operations. Nevertheless, the Commission considers that there is sufficient evidence to indicate that State bodies were jointly responsible for this incident, which violated international human rights law.

3. The Commission has substantial evidence that the Treasury Police carried out the external security operation which aided and abetted those who committed the murders.

4. There has been an obvious lack of interest in ordering an exhaustive investigation by an independent State organ to clarify the facts, find out who was responsible and bring those responsible to justice.

(c) *The American churchwomen*

Summary of the case

On 2 December 1980, members of the National Guard of El Salvador arrested four churchwomen after they left the international airport. Churchwomen Ita Ford, Maura Clarke, Dorothy Kazel and Jean Donovan were taken to an isolated spot and subsequently executed by being shot at close range.

In 1984, Deputy Sergeant Luis Antonio Colindres Alemán and National Guard members Daniel Canales

Ramírez, Carlos Joaquín Contreras Palacios, Francisco Orlando Contreras Recinos and José Roberto Moreno Canjura were sentenced to 30 years in prison for murder.

The Commission on the Truth finds that:

1. The arrest and execution of the churchwomen was planned prior to their arrival at the airport. Deputy Sergeant Luis Antonio Colindres Alemán carried out orders of a superior to execute them.

2. Then Colonel Carlos Eugenio Vides Casanova, Director-General of the National Guard, Lieutenant Colonel Oscar Edgardo Casanova Vejar, Commander of the Zacatecoluca military detachment, Colonel Roberto Monterrosa, Major Lizandro Zepeda Velasco and Sergeant Dagoberto Martínez, among other military personnel, knew that members of the National Guard had committed the murders pursuant to orders of a superior. The subsequent cover-up of the facts adversely affected the judicial investigation process.

3. The Minister of Defence at the time, General José Guillermo García, made no serious effort to conduct a thorough investigation of responsibility for the murders.

4. Local commissioner José Dolores Meléndez also knew of the executions carried out by members of the security forces and covered them up.

5. The State of El Salvador failed in its responsibility to investigate the facts thoroughly, to find the culprits and to punish them in accordance with the law and the requirements of international human rights law.

Description of the facts 149/

The murders

Shortly after 7 p.m. on 2 December 1980, members of the National Guard of El Salvador arrested four churchwomen as they were leaving Comalapa International Airport. Churchwomen Ita Ford, Maura Clarke, Dorothy Kazel and Jean Donovan were taken to an isolated spot where they were shot dead at close range.

Two of the four murdered churchwomen, Ita Ford and Maura Clarke, worked in Chalatenango and were returning from Nicaragua. The other two had come from La Libertad to pick them up at the airport.

The arrests were planned in advance. Approximately two hours before the churchwomen's arrival, National Guard Deputy Sergeant Luis Antonio Colindres Alemán informed five of his subordinates that they were to arrest some people who were coming from Nicaragua.

Colindres then went to the San Luis Talpa command post to warn the commander that, if he heard some disturbing noises, he should ignore them, because they would be the result of an action which Colindres and his men would be carrying out.

Once the members of the security forces had brought the churchwomen to an isolated spot, Colindres returned to his post near the airport. On returning to the place where they had taken the churchwomen, he told his men that he had been given orders to kill the churchwomen.

The investigation

1. The burial

The next morning, 3 December, the bodies were found on the road. When the justice of the peace arrived, he immediately agreed that they should be buried, as local commissioner José Dolores Meléndez had indicated. Accordingly, local residents buried the churchwomen's bodies in the vicinity.

The United States Ambassador, Robert White, found out on 4 December where the churchwomen's bodies were. As a result of his intervention and once authorization had been obtained from the justice of the peace, the corpses were exhumed and taken to San Salvador. There, a group of forensic doctors refused to perform autopsies on the grounds that they had no surgical masks.

2. The Rogers-Bowdler mission

Between 6 and 9 December 1980, a special mission arrived in San Salvador, headed by Mr. William D. Rogers, a former official in the Administration of President Gerald Ford, and Mr. William G. Bowdler, a State Department official.

They found no direct evidence of the crime, nor any evidence implicating the Salvadorian authorities. They concluded that the operation had involved a cover-up of the murders. 150/ They also urged the Federal Bureau of Investigation (FBI) to play an active role in the investigation. 151/

3. The Monterrosa commission and the Zepeda investigation

The Government Junta put Colonel Roberto Monterrosa in charge of an official commission of investigation. Colonel Carlos Eugenio Vides Casanova, Director-General of the National Guard, put Major Lizandro Zepeda 152/ in charge of another investigation. Neither official took the case seriously or sought to resolve it. Subsequently, Judge Harold R. Tyler, Jr., appointed by the United States Secretary of State, carried out a third investigation. It found that the purpose of the two previous investigations had been to establish a written precedent clearing the Salvadorian security forces of blame for the killings. 153/

(a) The Monterrosa commission

Colonel Monterrosa admitted that his commission had ruled out the possibility that security forces had been involved in the crime; to have acknowledged it would have created serious difficulties for the armed forces.

In fact, Monterrosa kept back the evidence implicating Colindres. In February 1981, he sent the United States Embassy the fingerprints of three out of four National

Guard members from whom the commission had taken statements. However, none of them appeared to have been involved in the murders. Colonel Monterrosa failed to provide the fingerprints of the fourth man, Colindres, from whom testimony had also apparently been taken. Judge Tyler therefore concluded that Colonel Monterrosa had not forwarded Colindres' fingerprints because he knew from Major Zepeda that Colindres was responsible for the executions. 154/

(b) The Zepeda investigation

Major Zepeda reported that there was no evidence that members of the National Guard had executed the churchwomen. 155/ According to testimony, Major Zepeda personally took charge of covering up for the murderers by ordering them to replace their rifles so as not to be detected, and to remain loyal to the National Guard by suppressing the facts.

There is also sufficient evidence that Major Zepeda informed his superior, Vides Casanova, of his activities. 156/

4. Resolution of the case

In April 1981, 157/ the United States Embassy provided the Salvadorian authorities with evidence incriminating Colindres and his men. Despite the existence of evidence against Colindres, such as the presence of his fingerprints on the churchwomen's minibus, neither he nor his subordinates were charged with any crime. 158/

In December 1981, Colonel Vides Casanova appointed Major José Adolfo Medrano to carry out a new investigation. In February 1982, one of the persons involved confessed his guilt and implicated the others, including Colindres. All of them were charged with the deaths of the churchwomen.

On 10 February, President Duarte, in a televised message, reported that the case had been resolved. He also gave to understand that Colindres and his men had acted independently and not on orders of a superior. In conclusion, he said that the Government was convinced that the accused were guilty. 159/

The judicial process

1. The judicial investigation

The judicial investigation did not represent any substantial progress over what the Medrano working group had done. Nevertheless, under questioning by the FBI, Sergeant Dagoberto Martínez, then Colindres' immediate superior, admitted to having been told by Colindres himself about the churchwomen's murders and about his direct role in them. On that occasion, Martínez had warned Colindres not to say anything unless his superiors asked him about it. Martínez also said that he had not been aware that orders had been given by a superior. 160/

2. The trial

On 23 and 24 May 1984, members of the National Guard were found guilty of the executions of the churchwomen and were sentenced to 30 years in prison. 161/

It was the first time in Salvadorian history that a member of the armed forces had been convicted of murder by a judge. 162/ Despite ambiguous statements by some of its official representatives, 163/ the United States Government had made its economic and military aid contingent on a resolution of the case. 164/

The involvement of senior officers

Although the Tyler Report concluded in 1983, "... based on existing evidence", 165/ that senior officers had not been involved, the Commission believes that there is sufficient evidence to show that Colindres acted on orders of a superior.

There is also substantial evidence that Lieutenant Colonel Oscar Edgardo Casanova Vejar, Commander of the Zacatecoluca detachment, was in charge of the National Guard at the national airport at the time when the murders of the churchwomen occurred.

General Vides Casanova and Colonel Casanova Vejar have denied any personal involvement in the arrest and execution or in the subsequent cover-up of the crime. Nevertheless, there is sufficient evidence to show that both General Vides Casanova and Colonel Casanova Vejar knew that members of the National Guard had murdered the churchwomen, and that their efforts to impede the gathering of evidence adversely affected the judicial investigation.

Cooperation with the Commission on the Truth

On several occasions from October 1992 onwards, the judge of the First Criminal Court of Zacatecoluca, Mr. Pleitus Lemus, refused to cooperate with the Commission on the Truth and to provide the evidence and the full court dossiers of the case. He transmitted only a condensed version which does not include testimony and other critical evidence on the possible involvement of senior officers 166/ in the case.

It was only after much insisting that, on 8 January 1993, the Commission finally obtained all the dossiers of the case from the Supreme Court, barely a week before its mandate expired.

Findings

The Commission on the Truth finds that:

1. There is sufficient evidence that:

(a) The arrest of the churchwomen at the airport was planned prior to their arrival.

(b) In arresting and executing the four churchwomen, Deputy Sergeant Luis Antonio Colindres Alemán was acting on orders of a superior.

2. There is substantial evidence that:

(a) Then Colonel Carlos Eugenio Vides Casanova,

Director-General of the National Guard, Lieutenant Colonel Oscar Edgardo Casanova Vejar, Commander of the Zacatecoluca military detachment, Colonel Roberto Monterrosa, Major Lizandro Zepeda Velasco and Sergeant Dagoberto Martínez, among other officers, knew that members of the National Guard had committed the murders and, through their actions, facilitated the cover-up of the facts which obstructed the corresponding judicial investigation.

(b) The Minister of Defence at the time, General José Guillermo García, made no serious effort to conduct a thorough investigation of responsibility for the murders of the churchwomen.

(c) Local commissioner José Dolores Meléndez also knew of the murders and covered up for the members of the security forces who committed them.

3. The State of El Salvador failed in its obligation under international human rights law to investigate the case, to bring to trial those responsible for ordering and carrying out the executions and, lastly, to compensate the victims' relatives.

(d) El Junquillo

Summary of the case

On 3 March 1981, a military operation took place in the north of the Department of Morazán. Units under Captain Carlos Napoleón Medina Garay arrived at El Junquillo and stayed there for 8 to 12 days. On leaving, Captain Medina Garay ordered the execution of the civilian population in El Junquillo canton.

On 12 March 1981, soldiers and members of the Cacaopera civil defence unit attacked the population, consisting solely of women, young children and old people. They killed the inhabitants and raped a number of women and little girls under the age of 12. They set fire to houses, cornfields and barns.

The Commission finds that:

1. On 12 March 1981, units of the Military Detachment at Sonsonate and members of the civil defence unit at Cacaopera indiscriminately attacked and summarily executed men, women and children of El Junquillo canton in the district of Cacaopera, Department of Morazán.

2. Captain Carlos Napoleón Medina Garay ordered the execution of the inhabitants of El Junquillo canton.

3. Colonel Alejandro Cisneros, the military commander in charge of the operation carried out in March 1981 in northern Morazán, involving units from Military Detachment No. 6 at Sonsonate under the command of Captain Medina Garay, failed in his duty to investigate whether troops under his command had executed members of the civilian population of El Junquillo canton.

4. The Government and the judiciary of El Salvador failed to conduct investigations into the incident. The State thus failed in its duty under international human rights law to investigate, bring to trial and punish those responsible and to compensate the victims or their families.

5. The Minister of Defence and Public Security, General René Emilio Ponce, is responsible for failing to provide this Commission with information on the military operation carried out in the area of El Junquillo canton, thereby failing to honour the obligation to cooperate with the Commission on the Truth entered into by the Government when it signed the peace agreements, and thus for preventing the identification of other soldiers who took part in the massacre.

Description of the facts 167/

The massacre

On 3 March 1981, a military operation was launched in northern Morazán, with Colonel Alejandro Cisneros in charge. In the course of the operation, soldiers from the Military Detachment at Sonsonate, under the command of Captain Carlos Napoleón Medina Garay, went to El Junquillo.

The unit set up camp in the El Junquillo area, where it remained for 8 to 12 days. According to the testimony received, as the unit was preparing to withdraw to a different location, Captain Medina Garay ordered another officer to do the job they had agreed on before leaving the hamlet.

On the night of 11 March 1981, soldiers occupied the hills near El Junquillo canton. The next day, they shelled the canton for 15 minutes. After the shelling, soldiers entered the canton in large numbers and closed in on the houses.

According to the testimony, soldiers and civil defence members proceeded to kill the following persons: Francisca Díaz, her daughters Juana and Santana Díaz, and nine children all under the age of 10; Guillerma Díaz, her 13-year-old daughter María Santos Díaz, and five children under the age of 12; Doroteo Chicas Díaz, his wife and his one-day-old son, and seven children under the age of 10; Eulalio Chicas, his wife and his three sons; Rosa Ottilia Díaz, her daughter-in-law María Argentina Chicas Chicas, and the children who were present; Santos Majín Chicas, his wife and his daughters Lencha aged 12 and Gertrudis aged 9; Tránsito Chicas, aged 58, and Filomena Chicas, aged 68; Luciano Argueta, his wife Ufemia Sánchez, and two sons, under the age of seven; Leopoldo Chicas, an 80-year-old man, and Esteban and Vicente Argueta, both aged over 70; and Petronila and two of her sons, under the age of 11. Some of the victims were shot in the back of the head; some of the children's bodies had knife wounds in the chest and bullet holes in the back of the head. In some cases, the bodies had been burned. According to testimony, some of the women and little girls had been raped.

The soldiers and civil defence members set fire to the houses in the hamlet and to cornfields and barns. They stole some of the corn which the farmers had stored and killed a number of animals.

The survivors fled. The next day, a peasant returned to see what had happened. In the house of Doroteo Chicas, he saw the dead bodies of the Chicas children. The soldiers noticed he was there and shot at him several times. He fled to the hills to hide. One survivor of the massacre returned to the canton to try to bury the victims. As the soldiers were still occupying the canton, he went back into hiding.

The survivors stayed in hiding in the hills for several days. One of them found the remains of a number of people. The survivors dug several mass graves where they buried the remains.

One survivor went to a guerrilla camp at La Guacamaya, where he recounted the episode to a priest, who took care of him.

Total absence of official investigations

When it heard about the survivors' reports, FMLN condemned the massacre on Radio Venceremos and in various statements and press releases.

Despite these public complaints, the Government, the armed forces and the judiciary of El Salvador made no attempt to investigate the incident.

Findings

The Commission finds that:

1. There is substantial evidence that on 12 March 1981, units of the Military Detachment at Sonsonate and members of the civil defence unit at Cacaopera indiscriminately attacked and summarily executed men, women and children of El Junquillo canton in the district of Cacaopera, Department of Morazán.

2. There is sufficient evidence to show that Captain Carlos Napoleón Medina Garay ordered the execution of the inhabitants of El Junquillo canton.

3. There is sufficient evidence to show that Colonel Alejandro Cisneros, the military commander in charge of the operation carried out in March 1981 in northern Morazán, involving units from Military Detachment No. 6 at Sonsonate under the command of Captain Medina Garay, failed in his duty to investigate whether troops under his command had executed members of the civilian population of El Junquillo canton.

4. There is full evidence that the Government, the armed forces and the judiciary of El Salvador failed to conduct investigations into the incident. The State thus failed in its duty under international human rights law to

investigate, bring to trial and punish those responsible and to compensate the victims or their families.

5. The Minister of Defence and Public Security, General René Emilio Ponce, is responsible for failing to provide this Commission with information on the military operation carried out in the area of El Junquillo canton, thereby failing to honour the obligation to cooperate with the Commission on the Truth entered into by the Government when it signed the peace agreements, and thus far preventing the identification of other soldiers who took part in the massacre.

(e) The Dutch journalists

Summary of the case

On the afternoon of 17 March 1982, four Dutch journalists accompanied by five or six members of FMLN, some of them armed, were ambushed by a patrol of the Atonal Battalion of the Salvadorian armed forces while on their way to territory under FMLN control. The incident occurred not far from the San Salvador-Chalatenango road, near the turn-off to Santa Rita. The four journalists were killed in the ambush and only one member of FMLN survived. Having analysed the evidence available, the Commission on the Truth has reached the conclusion that the ambush was set up deliberately to surprise and kill the journalists and their escort; that the decision to ambush them was taken by Colonel Mario A. Reyes Mena, Commander of the Fourth Infantry Brigade, with the knowledge of other officers; that no major skirmish preceded or coincided with the shootout in which the journalists were killed; and, lastly, that the officer named above and other soldiers concealed the truth and obstructed the judicial investigation.

Description of the facts

The days before the ambush

A large number of foreign journalists were in El Salvador to cover the 1982 elections to the Constituent Assembly. The political situation in the country had aroused the interest of world public opinion. 168/

At that time, violence in the country was widespread. A number of journalists had received threats, presumably from death squads, and there had been accusations that their reporting favoured the guerrillas.

In March 1982, Koos Jacobus Andries Koster, a Dutch journalist, was in El Salvador making a report on the political and military situation in the country for the Dutch television company IKON. 169/ Producer and editor Jan Cornelius Kuiper Joop, sound technician Hans Lodewijk ter Laag and cameraman Johannes Jan Willemsen, all of them Dutch nationals, had come from Holland especially to make the report.

The team was headed by Koster, who was familiar

with the political situation in the country, spoke Spanish and had the necessary contacts, since he had been working in Latin America for years. 170/

In 1980, Koster had produced a report on the civil defence units and the death squads which had had a great impact abroad. The Government had considered the report to be favourable to FMLN.

This latest report was to cover the situation in San Salvador and in a number of areas under FMLN control. According to diplomatic sources, it was "public knowledge" that the Dutch journalists were producing a report favourable to the guerrillas, similar to that of 1980.

On 7 March, as part of their work, the journalists visited Mariona prison in San Salvador to interview and film prisoners accused of belonging to the guerrilla forces. During a cultural event at the prison, one of the leaders thanked the journalists for their support for political prisoners in El Salvador. The videos filmed by the journalists included shots of prisoners' scars, which the prisoners said were the result of torture. 171/

In order to make preliminary contact with FMLN, Koster met with an FMLN member. Koster gave the man a piece of paper with his name, nationality and where he could be reached. After the meeting, the guerrilla member was followed by several men. While attempting to escape over a fence, he apparently dropped his papers, where he had put the piece of paper for safe keeping.

According to a statement made by Francisco Antonio Morán, Director-General of the Treasury Police, around that time Morán received a report from the Commander of the Military Detachment at Usulafter him. As a result, Colonel Morán gave orders that Koster be brought to Treasury Police headquarters for questioning. 174/

At around 6 a.m. on 11 March 1982, members of the Treasury Police in civilian clothing brought Koster and the three other journalists to Colonel Morán's office. 175/ Colonel Morán asked Koster about the piece of paper. Koster denied knowing any terrorists in the country and explained that the information about him might have been provided by another journalist. 176/ Before releasing the journalists, 177/ Colonel Morán warned Koster to be careful because subversive elements knew that he was in the country. 178/

The next day, 12 March, photographs of Koster and the three other journalists appeared in the newspaper, together with a press release from the Armed Forces Press Committee (COPREFA) containing a transcript of the interrogation. The article was headlined "Foreign journalist a contact for subversives" and the caption to Koster's photograph said that he had been summoned to make a statement to the Treasury Police because some of his personal papers had been found on terrorist Jorge Luis Méndez, along with a piece of paper identifying him as a "contact". 179/

That same day, Dutch journalist Jan Pierre Lucien Schmeitz, who also worked for the company IKON, arrived in the country to cover the elections. Journalists of other nationalities told him that Koster had been arrested and taken to Treasury Police headquarters, accompanied by the three other Dutch journalists.

On the night of 12 March, the four journalists met with Schmeitz. Remembering what El Salvador had been like in 1977, Schmeitz advised them to be very careful of the possible consequences of the interrogation by Colonel Morán. In spite of everything, they decided to go on with their work. 180/ Koster's FMLN contacts also urged him to leave the country for a while, but he consistently refused to postpone the journey he wanted to make for his report.

On Monday, 15 March, 181/ Schmeitz lent them his minibus but did not offer to drive it. On Tuesday, 16 March, Armin Friedrich Wertz, an independent journalist of German nationality, agreed to act as driver for a fee of $100. That same day, Koster held a further meeting with members of FMLN, at which it was agreed that they would leave the next day, 17 March. Also present at the meeting, in addition to Koster's previous contacts, was "Commander Oscar", a member of the FDR/FMLN command in Chalatenango, who was to travel with them and could act as interpreter because he knew English.

On the night of 16 March, the journalists discovered that their rooms had been searched.

The journey to Chalatenango

On the morning of Wednesday, 17 March, they picked up Schmeitz's minibus, which had the words "PRENSA-TV" painted in large letters on the sides, as was customary in El Salvador. In the afternoon, the four journalists met up with Wertz and went to a restaurant car park, where they met "Commander Oscar" of FPL (Fuerzas Populares de Liberación) Forces. A boy named "Rubén", aged between 12 and 15, also arrived; he was the guide and the only one who knew where the meeting was to take place.

At around 3 p.m., they set out from San Salvador for Chalatenango, passing through the town of Aguilares. 182/

A few kilometres before the El Paraíso barracks, Wertz noticed in the rear-view mirror that a dark brown Cherokee Chief jeep with tinted windows appeared to be following them. He slowed down, but the vehicle did not overtake; he then speeded up, but the vehicle stayed in sight. They continued on the Chalatenango road to about kilometre 65, where they took the turn-off to Santa Rita. About 1 kilometre before the turn-off, the Cherokee Chief disappeared from sight. 183/

They had driven nearly 1 kilometre on the side road when they saw a group of people. Immediately "Rubén" got out of the minibus and signalled to them. 184/ It was the contacts, who were waiting for them.

According to Wertz, the four members of the escort party were waiting on a piece of ground below the level of the dirt road and behind a barbed wire fence. One of them was carrying an automatic rifle, probably an FAL, the second a pistol, and the third a rifle of some kind. The fourth man was unarmed. According to a statement given by "Martín", 185/ the man in charge of the escort who was armed with an M-1 rifle, he went to meet the journalists with two other men, "Carlos", who had an M-16, and "Tello", who was carrying a 9-mm pistol.

When they approached the vehicle, Wertz apparently agreed with "Martín" that he would return to pick up the group at 8 a.m. on Sunday, 21 March. 186/ The journalists unloaded their equipment and, at around 5.10 p.m., took a path leading into a hollow opposite a hill.

Wertz says he then returned to San Salvador with the radio on high volume and neither saw soldiers nor heard shots during the journey. 187/

The ambush

According to "Martín" he was given the order to go and meet the group on 14 March 1982. He knew "Commander Oscar" and "Rubén". He also knew that the others were foreign journalists. He took seven men and left base camp at 4 p.m. the next day, 15 March. 188/

At around 5 a.m. on 17 March, the escort party reached a refuge 2 kilometres from the meeting place. Two men went out to reconnoitre the area over a radius of 1 kilometre, but found nothing unusual.

In their statements, "Martín" said that he had never had any problems on that route in the past, 189/ but Colonel Mario A. Reyes Mena said that the army had information that the route was being used to supply nearby guerrilla camps. During the trial, "Commander Miguel Castellanos", a former member of FMLN, said that the route was known to the army. 190/

When the escort arrived at the agreed place, the journalists put on their rucksacks, took the rest of their equipment and set off overland.

According to "Martín", the group was walking in a single file, at a distance of 4 metres apart. "Commander Oscar" led the way, followed by "Rubén", Martín was among the journalists, and "Carlos" brought up the rear with his M-16. 191/ They had gone about 250 metres when they came under heavy fire from M-16 rifles and M-60 machine-guns, coming from two hills about 100 metres away. Martín saw two of the journalists fall to the ground. They were hit by the first shots and never moved again. 192/ He headed towards the road, dodging the soldiers' fire, climbed over the barbed wire fence and escaped. 193/

Most of "Martín"'s account was confirmed by the statement made by Sergeant Mario Canizales Espinoza, who was in command of the military patrol that staged the ambush. 194/ The sergeant also said that he noticed that some members of the group were carrying equipment and were taller than the average Salvadorian; at the time, however, it did not occur to him that they might be foreigners and he assumed that they were armed. He added that, towards the end of the shoot-out, he noticed that two of the tall men were attempting to escape towards the river-bed. He came down the hill in pursuit of them and shot and killed them with his M-16 from a distance of about 25 metres. In his statements, he said he did not know for certain whether the men had been armed. 195/

The statements by the sergeant and the soldiers differ in some respects from those made by "Martín", as well as among themselves. They claim that the first shots were fired from a hill by FMLN guerrillas and that the shoot-out with the group of journalists and their escorts was part of a larger skirmish involving a second group of FMLN combatants. As indicated below, these statements do not appear to be true.

Origin of the patrol

According to the statements by Sergeant Mario Canizales Espinoza, the patrol he was commanding consisted of 25 soldiers and had been sent to inspect the area because information had been received that it was being used as a supply route for the guerrillas. According to the sergeant, his men had set the ambush because, just before the encounter, they had seen a small group of armed guerrillas heading towards the Santa Rita road and had decided to surprise them on their return. He denies having any prior knowledge that a particular group would be using that route or that it would include foreign journalists. 196/

This version of events is essentially the same as the one which subsequently appeared in the press release issued by the Armed Forces Press Committee (COPREFA).

However, according to statements made to the Commission on the Truth by officers stationed at the El Paraíso barracks at the time, a meeting was held in which officers of the General Staff of the Fourth Brigade, including its Commander, Colonel Mario A. Reyes Mena, and officers of the Atonal Rapid Deployment Infantry Battalion (BIRI) took part. According to those interviewed, the ambush was planned at that meeting, on the basis of precise intelligence data indicating that the journalists would try to enter the zone controlled by FMLN via that route the next day. 197/ The mission was entrusted to a patrol from the Atonal Battalion, which left the El Paraíso barracks at 5 a.m. on 17 March in order to avoid detection and remained in the hills all day awaiting the group's arrival.

Subsequent events

Sergeant Canizales says that, when the ambush was over, he informed barracks by radio of the outcome. 198/ Colonel Reyes Mena 199/ then dispatched a vehicle patrol which, when it arrived at the scene, found the eight bodies. 200/ The lieutenant in command sent some of his men for the Santa Rita justice of the peace, who arrived half an hour later.

According to one officer of the detachment, the lieutenant's decision to notify the justice of the peace and take the bodies to the El Paraíso barracks surprised and greatly annoyed Colonel Reyes Mena. In the end, however, Colonel Reyes Mena decided to inform the General Staff.

The next morning, 18 March, the judicial inquiry continued at the El Paraíso barracks. 201/ Because of his physical features, "Commander Oscar" was taken for a foreigner and his body was sent with those of the Dutch journalists to San Salvador.

According to Schmeitz, at around 9 a.m. he received a telephone call from Howard Lane, press attaché at the United States Embassy in El Salvador, confirming that his four colleagues were dead. 202/ He later went to CO-PREFA, where an official handed out a statement explaining briefly that the journalists had been killed in cross-fire during a clash between guerrillas and the army. 203/

When Schmeitz was back in his hotel room, he received a threatening phone call telling him to "stop his inquiries and leave the country, because there was a fifth coffin ready for him". He received three more such calls in the course of that night. On 20 March, Schmeitz left El Salvador.

In the days that followed, the Dutch Ambassador met with a member of the Revolutionary Government Junta to transmit his country's request to the Salvadorian authorities that it be allowed to conduct a full investigation into the incident. One key element would be to interview the sergeant and soldiers who staged the ambush, but the Salvadorian Government would not give authorization for this. In its second report, the Dutch Commission of inquiry noted that "at the request of the Government of the Netherlands, the United States Government endorsed this request to the Salvadorian authorities". 204/

"Martín", the guerrilla who survived the ambush, was taken to Holland, where he testified on 4 and 5 May 1982. Subsequently, on 19 May, the Dutch commission interviewed the sergeant at length in private. 205/

The judicial proceedings on the case came to a halt in 1988, when the judge, Dora del Carmen Gómez de Claros, sought and obtained asylum abroad. In a letter, she said that she had received anonymous threats.

The Commission requested a copy of the dossier from Margarita de los Angeles Fuente Sanabria, the current judge of the Court of First Instance at El Dulce Nombre de María, Chalatenango. Although initially prepared to hand over the dossier, she later said that she had received instructions that the Commission should apply to the President of the Supreme Court of Justice for a copy. The Commission repeatedly telephoned and wrote to Mr. Mauricio Gutiérrez Castro, President of the Supreme Court of El Salvador, requesting a copy, but received no answer. It was the Chief State Counsel of the Republic who transmitted a copy of his dossier to the Commission.

Findings

1. The Commission on the Truth considers that there is full evidence that Dutch journalists Koos Jacobus Andries Koster, Jan Cornelius Kuiper Joop, Hans Lodewijk ter Laag and Johannes Jan Willemsen were killed on 17 March 1982 in an ambush which was planned in advance by the Commander of the Fourth Infantry Brigade, Colonel Mario A. Reyes Mena, with the knowledge of other officers at the El Paraíso barracks, on the basis of intelligence data alerting them to the journalists' presence, and was carried out by a patrol of soldiers from the Atonal BIRI, under the command of Sergeant Mario Canizales Espinoza.

2. These same officers, the sergeant and others subsequently covered up the truth and obstructed the investigations carried out by the judiciary and other competent authorities.

3. These murders violated international human rights law and international humanitarian law, which stipulates that civilians shall not be the object of attack.

4. The State failed in its obligation to investigate, bring to trial and punish the guilty parties, as required under international law.

5. The President of the Supreme Court, Mr. Mauricio Gutiérrez Castro, failed to cooperate with the Commission on the Truth.

(f) Las Hojas

Summary of the case

On 22 February 1983, members of the Jaguar Battalion, under the command of Captain Carlos Alfonso Figueroa Morales, participated in an operation in Las Hojas canton, San Antonio del Monte Municipality, Department of Sonsonate. Soldiers arrested 16 peasants, took them to the Cuyuapa river and shot and killed them at point-blank range.

The accused have consistently maintained that this was a clash with terrorists. An investigation by the Ministry of Defence concluded that no members of the armed forces were responsible for the incident.

The judicial proceedings were dismissed by the Supreme Court of Justice under the 1987 Amnesty Act. In 1992, the Inter-American Commission on Human Rights accused the Government of El Salvador of failing in its duty to investigate and punish those responsible for violations of the American Convention on Human Rights.

On the basis of various degrees of evidence, the Commission finds the following:

1. Colonel Elmer González Araujo, then Commander of Military Detachment No. 6 at Sonsonate, Major Oscar León Linares and Captain Carlos Alfonso Figueroa Morales (deceased) planned the operation in Las Hojas canton for the purpose of arresting and eliminating alleged subversives.

2. The orders of execution were transmitted to the actual perpetrators by then Second Lieutenants Carlos Sasso Landaverry and Francisco del Cid Díaz.

3. Colonel Gonzáles Araujo, Major León Linares and Captain Carlos Alfonso Figueroa Morales learnt immediately of the massacre, but covered it up.

4. Colonel Napoleón Alvarado, who conducted the Ministry of Defence investigation, also covered up the massacre and obstructed the judicial investigation.

5. The Commission on the Truth recommends that the Government of El Salvador comply fully with the resolution of the Inter-American Commission on Human Rights in this case.

Description of the facts 206/

The massacre

In the early morning of 22 February 1983, Captain Carlos Alfonso Figueroa Morales, commanding the Jaguar Battalion based in Military Detachment No. 6 at Sonsonate, mobilized three units from there belonging to the first company. One unit was under the command of Second Lieutenant Carlos Sasso Landaverry, one under the command of Second Lieutenant Cadet Francisco del Cid Díaz and the third under the command of Sergeant José Reyes Pérez Ponce. 207/

At about 6 a.m., a unit entered the Las Hojas coop-erative of the Asociación Nacional de Indígenas (ANIS). With the help of members of the local civil defence unit, who had scarves tied around their faces to conceal their identities, they arrested seven members of the cooperative. The soldiers had a list of alleged subversives and several members of the civil defence unit pointed out the people whose names were on the list. They were dragged from their houses, beaten and bound, then taken from the cooperative along the road towards the Cuyuapa river.

The members of the cooperative arrested were Gerardo Cruz Sandoval (34 years), 208/ José Guido García (21 years), 209/ Benito Pérez Zetino (35 years), 210/ Pedro Pérez Zetino (24 years), 211/ Marcelino Sánchez Viscarra (80 years), 212/ Juan Bautista Mártir Pérez (75 years) 213/ and Héctor Manuel Márquez (60 years). 214/

Another unit of about 40 soldiers entered the San Antonio farm in Agua Santa canton, near the Las Hojas cooperative, arrested a number of people and took them also towards the Cuyuapa river. 215/ The people arrested there included Antonio Mejía Alvarado, 216/ Romelio Mejía Alvarado, 217/ Lorenzo Mejía Carabante, 218/ Ricardo García Elena (19 years), 219/ Francisco Alemán Mejía (36 years), 220/ Leonardo López Morales (22 years), 221/ Alfredo Ayala 222/ and Martín Mejía Castillo. 223/

When the leader of ANIS, Adrián Esquino, was informed of the arrest of the members of the cooperative, he went immediately, at 7 a.m., to speak to Colonel Elmer González Araujo, 224/ Commander of Military Detachment No. 6 at Sonsonate. Colonel González Araujo told him he knew nothing about the arrest of the members of the ANIS cooperative, but that he knew that a number of subversives with the surname Mejía had been captured.

Later that morning, a group of ANIS members found 16 bodies on the banks of the Cuyuapa river; there were marks that showed that their hands had been tied, their faces were disfigured by bullets and they had all been shot at point-blank range in the forehead or behind the ear.

That same day, 22 February, Roberto Rogelio Magaña, the justice of the peace and experts examined the bodies. Alfredo Ayala's body still had "... his arms and forearms behind his back with the thumbs tied together with a piece of string ...". 225/ The other victims also showed signs of having had their thumbs tied together and had been riddled with bullets at point-blank range.

The official version

The operation was discussed and decided upon the previous day by Colonel González Araujo, Major Oscar León Linares, the commanding officer of the Battalion, and Captain Figueroa Morales, the Chief of S-2. According to their version, they were informed of the presence of subversives and the purpose of the operation was to search the area.

Later, Captain Figueroa Morales said that during the operation he heard shots coming from up ahead. 226/ When he arrived at the Cuyuapa river, the two Second Lieutenants informed him that there had been a clash with guerrillas. They found a number of bodies there, but none of them were bound. 227/

Although in several depositions soldiers alleged that there had been a clash with guerrillas, none of them admitted to having witnessed such a clash and all of them said that they had only heard it.

After the clash, Captain Figueroa Morales made a report to Colonel González Araujo. 228/ Major León Linares also received reports on arriving at the Detachment at about 8 a.m.

The investigations

Three investigations followed. President Magaña ordered the newly established governmental Human Rights Commission to investigate the case. Thus, before the case went to the Attorney-General's Office, family members were interviewed and a first account of the incident was drawn up.

The Minister of Defence, General José Guillermo García Merino, entrusted Colonel Napoleón Alvarado with investigating the case. Statements were taken from several witnesses as part of the investigation, but not from the two Second Lieutenants, Cid Díaz and Sasso Landaverry, who were in Morazán. 229/ According to the testimony of Captain Figueroa Morales, it was they who had headed the unit which took part in the alleged clash.

In April 1983, Colonal Alvarado determined that no proof had been found of the guilt of any member of the armed forces and that the deaths had occurred in a clash. He also expressed the view that the investigation by the Human Rights Commission had been biased. He added that the case had been politicized by enemies of the armed forces and that "... the armed forces cannot take any responsibility for what may happen to Mr. Adrián Esquino Lisco, since he ... it would appear, is protecting guerrilla elements within the association he heads". 230/

The judicial investigation followed a different course. In March 1984, on the basis of a recommendation by the Office of the Attorney General, 231/ the preventive detention of seven civil defence members and other members of the military escort was ordered, but the order did not extend to soldiers. 232/ However, in December 1984, the judge of Sonsonate First Criminal Court ordered a stay of proceedings and in July 1985, the criminal court approved the case's dismissal. It also determined that the law on complicity could not be applied to civil defence members without any proof as to the main perpetrators. It had been established only that the escorts had assisted the army in the arrest. However, the court did not indicate who the immediate perpetrators were. 233/

As to the dismissal of the case against Captain Figueroa Morales and Major Léon Linares, the court affirmed that there was not enough evidence to bring charges against them. 234/

In July 1986, through the intervention of the United States Embassy and with new evidence that soldiers had been involved, criminal proceedings were reopened against a number of defendants, including Colonel González Araujo, Major León Linares and Captain Figueroa Morales. 235/

In March 1987, however, the judge of the Court of First Instance again dismissed the case; 236/ in August, the appeal court revoked his decision and ordered the case brought to trial. 237/

Colonel González Araujo then filed a remedy of *habeas corpus* with the Supreme Court, when it was not yet certain that the National Assembly would approve the Amnesty Act (27 October 1987). 238/ In July 1988, the Supreme Court held that the Amnesty Act should apply to the Las Hojas case, and dismissed the case against all the defendants. 239/

Resolution of the Inter-American Commission on Human Rights on the application of the 1987 Amnesty Act in the Las Hojas case

The Inter-American Commission on Human Rights received a petition in 1989 240/ denouncing the application of the 1987 Amnesty Act as a violation of the obligation of the Government of El Salvador to investigate and punish the violations of the rights of the Las Hojas victims and to make reparation for the injury caused. 241/ On 24 September 1992, the Commission issued a resolution in which it determined that the amnesty decree adopted after the order to arrest officers of the armed forces had legally foreclosed the possibility of an effective investigation, the prosecution of the culprits and appropriate compensation for the victims. 242/

The Commission stated that the Government of El Salvador had failed in its obligation to guarantee the free and full exercise of human rights and fundamental guarantees for all persons under its jurisdiction. 243/ It further recommended that the Government of El Salvador should: (1) conduct an exhaustive, rapid, complete and impartial investigation of the facts in order to identify all the victims and the culprits and bring the latter to justice; (2) take the necessary steps to prevent the occurrence of similar incidents in future; (3) make reparation for the consequences of the situation and pay fair compensation to the victims' families. 244/

The Commission gave the Government of El Salvador three months in which to implement its recommendations, i.e., up to 24 December 1992. So far, no action has been taken to comply with the Commission's recommendations.

Findings

The Commission finds the following:

1. There is substantial evidence that Colonel Elmer González Araujo, then Commander of Military Detachment No. 6 at Sonsonate, Major Oscar León Linares and Captain Figueroa Morales (deceased) planned the operation in Las Hojas canton for the purpose of arresting and eliminating alleged subversives.

2. There is full evidence that Captain Figueroa Morales, as captain of the Jaguar Battalion, was in command of the operation. Also, that during the operation, 16 peasants were arrested, bound and summarily executed, and that there was no clash with guerrillas.

3. There is substantial evidence that the orders of execution were transmitted to the actual perpetrators by then Second Lieutenants Carlos Sasso Landaverry and Francisco del Cid Díaz.

4. There is substantial evidence that Colonel González Araujo, Major León Linares and Captain Figueroa Morales, learnt immediately of the massacre but covered it up.

5. There is sufficient evidence that Colonel Napoleón Alvarado, who conducted the Ministry of Defence investigation, also covered up the massacre and later obstructed the judicial investigation.

6. The Commission on the Truth recommends that the Government of El Salvador comply fully with the resolution of the Inter-American Commission on Human Rights in this case.

(g) San Sebastián

Summary of the case

On 21 September 1988, members of the Jiboa Battalion detained 10 people in San Francisco canton in the district of San Sebastián. That same morning, Major Mauricio Jesús Beltrán Granados, chief of the Intelligence Department of the Fifth Brigade, under orders from Colonel José Emilio Chávez Cáceres, Chief of the Fifth Brigade, arrived at San Francisco canton. After interrogating several of the detainees, he ordered all 10 of them executed and the staging of a fictitious ambush.

In March 1989, an Honour Commission of the armed forces conducted an investigation in which members of the Jiboa Battalion said that Major Beltrán Granados had ordered them to execute the detainees and cover up the incident. Beltrán Granados, another officer and other non-commissioned officers and soldiers were brought before the judge, who ordered their detention. They were then released, except for Beltrán who is awaiting judgement.

The Commission on the Truth finds the following:

1. Colonel José Emilio Chávez Cáceres gave the order to execute the detainees.

2. Major Mauricio de Jesús Beltrán Granados ordered members of the Jiboa Battalion to execute the 10 detained peasants.

3. Colonel José Emilio Chávez Cáceres covered up the execution of the 10 detainees and Major Mauricio de Jesús Beltrán Granados took steps to cover up the execution.

4. Second Lieutenant Arnoldo Antonio Vásquez Alvarenga transmitted Major Beltrán's order to designate some soldiers to finish off the victims and also provided the necessary materials to activate the mines which seriously wounded them.

5. Sergeant Jorge Alberto Tobar Guzmán activated the mechanism that detonated the mines, knowing that they would explode in the place where the detained peasants were.

6. Deputy Sergeant Rafael Rosales Villalobos and soldiers Fermín Cruz Castro, José Carlos Hernández Matute, José Alfredo Méndez Beltrán and Francisco Ponce Ramírez shot and killed the detainees.

7. Colonel Luis Mariano Turcios and Lieutenant Colonel José Antonio Rodríguez Molina knew about the order to execute the detainees and did nothing to prevent their execution.

8. The Honour Commission of the armed forces, the Commission for the Investigation of Criminal Acts and the judge of the Criminal Court of First Instance of the city of San Sebastián failed to take steps to determine the responsibility of Colonel José Emilio Chávez Cáceres, Colonel Luis Mariano Turcios and Lieutenant Colonel José Antonio Rodríguez Molina.

Description of the facts 245/

The executions

On 20 September 1988, the second company of the Jiboa Battalion of the Fifth Brigade arrived in the municipality of San Sebastián in the Department of San Vicente. Lieutenant Manuel de Jesús Gálvez Gálvez, commander of the unit, was informed that four men were involved in subversive activities. He ordered Second Lieutenant Arnoldo Antonio Vásquez Alvarenga to go to San Francisco canton and detain them.

Second Lieutenant Vásquez Alvarenga detained one of these men that same night. The detainee took the soldiers to a place where they found subversive propaganda, explosive devices, rucksacks, wire and two M-16 rifles. 246/

Second Lieutenant Vásquez Alvarenga informed Lieutenant Gálvez Gálvez of the find. 247/ Captain Oscar Armando Peña Durán heard the information on the radio and transmitted it to the Fifth Brigade. Early next morning, over the Cerro Las Delicias radio relay station, Captain Peña Durán was ordered to "eliminate" the detainee. Captain Peña Durán said that his officers (Gálvez and Vásquez) could not obey that order. He then informed Gálvez Gálvez of the order, and the latter also refused to carry it out. Gálvez told him that if the order was repeated, the Brigade should be requested to give the order in writing.

During the night, Second Lieutenant Vásquez Alvarenga continued to interrogate the detainee and the latter agreed to point out the house of the other three suspects. 248/ All of them were subsequently detained.

The four detainees were taken to the village school. Second Lieutenant Vásquez received a message over the radio from Lieutenant Gálvez informing him that he would come to San Francisco canton and telling him to assemble the residents of the canton in the school. 249/

At 7.30 a.m. on 21 December, Lieutenant Gálvez arrived and interrogated one of the detainees again. 250/ He again contacted Captain Peña and told him that he would not kill the detainees without a written order from the Commander of the Brigade. 251/ The Commander of the Fifth Brigade, and of the Fifth Military Zone, was Colonel José Emilio Chávez Cáceres. Peña requested permission to go to the Brigade and explain the situation in San Francisco. Major Beltrán Granados refused permission. 252/ He added that he would go to San Francisco canton with two interrogators. Peña Durán then contacted Gálvez Gálvez to inform him that Major Beltrán was coming, and told him to make a report to him. 253/

On the morning of 21 September, under orders from Colonel Chávez Cáceres, Major Beltrán went to San Francisco canton. He arrived the same morning, with two other interrogators and his assistant.

Captain Peña Durán, for his part, arrived at the Brigade 254/ at midday. He reported to Major Rodríguez, informing him of what had happened and of the order to eliminate the detainee. According to Captain Peña, Major Rodríguez said that the detainee should be taken to Brigade headquarters, in accordance with the procedure for normal operations. The two of them informed Lieutenant Colonel Turcios of the situation and of the order to eliminate the detainee. Peña then gave the same report to Colonel Chávez Cáceres. According to Chávez Cáceres, he told Peña that the detainee should be transferred to the Brigade. 255/

When Major Beltrán Granados arrived in the canton, Gálvez Gálvez made a report to him. 256/ Beltrán had three detainees brought out for interrogation. On his return from the interrogation, Major Beltrán, who as intelligence officer was not in command of the unit, informed Lieutenant Gálvez Gálvez that they had to execute the detainees. Gálvez Gálvez replied that he would not obey that order and that he would hand over command of the unit that was carrying out the operation to Major Beltrán. 257/

Beltrán Granados told Gálvez to order the detention of other persons, which he did. The total number of detainees increased to 10. 258/ Then, according to testimony, Major Beltrán Granados gave the order to execute them by simulating a guerrilla ambush. 259/

Major Beltrán Granados ordered Sergeant Tobar Guzmán to look for a place down in the street in which to lay the confiscated mines to prepare an ambush. 260/ Tobar laid the mines and connected the wire to them. 261/

Second Lieutenant Vásquez ordered the soldiers to take the rest of the confiscated material to the site of the ambush. Second Lieutenant Vásquez told soldiers "Churute" (Fermín Cruz Castro), Matute (José Carlos Hernández Matute) and "Ciguanabo" (José Alfredo Méndez Beltrán) that they would finish off any detainee who was left alive. 262/

The detainees' hands were tied behind their backs (except for the women) and they were blindfolded. At about 3 p.m., they were taken to the place where they were to be executed, on the road. Vásquez gave a battery to Tobar, who installed it and activated the mines. 263/

Some soldiers shot off their weapons to simulate an ambush, as ordered by Major Beltrán. 264/ The gunfire lasted five minutes. Since the detainees did not die as a result of the mines, Major Beltrán ordered some soldiers to finish them off. One of them, Manuel de Jesús Herrera Rivera, refused to obey the order. Soldiers "Churute" (Fermín Cruz Castro), "Balazo" (Francisco Ponce Ramírez) and Matute (José Carlos Hernández Matute) finished off the detainees. 265/

Major Beltrán Granados ordered Deputy Sergeant Rosales Villalobos to shoot the detainees, and he did so. He also ordered a soldier to take the blindfolds off the bodies and ordered soldier Hernández Alfaro to smear blood on the uniform of soldier Méndez Beltrán ("Ciguanabo") and put a dressing on him to make it look as if he had been wounded in combat.

Major Beltrán then ordered Lieutenant Gálvez Gálvez to inform the Brigade that terrorists had ambushed them and that eight detainees and two terrorists had been killed, and to request a helicopter to transport a wounded soldier. 266/

A helicopter arrived with a lawyer from Department 5 of the Brigade and a United States adviser. Beltrán got into the helicopter with the allegedly wounded soldier and they went to Brigade headquarters.

The cover-up and the official investigations

The next day, the San Sebastián justice of the peace identified the murdered peasants and COPREFA reported that 10 subversives had died in a clash between troops of the Jiboa Battalion and guerrillas. On 23 September,

COPREFA published the version that Colonel Chávez Cáceres says he received from Major Beltrán Granados.

Officials from non-governmental human rights bodies (Legal Protection and the non-governmental Human Rights Commission) and journalists went to San Francisco canton on 22 September. A number of witnesses reported that the peasants had been murdered by the soldiers. In public statements, President Duarte refuted the accusations.

General Blandón, Chief of Staff, communicated with Colonel Chávez Cáceres on 23 September and told him that the version of the incident he had been given was untrue.

On 24 September, Major Beltrán Granados learnt that a soldier called Escoto had been wounded by guerrillas. He suggested to Escoto that he pretend to have been wounded at San Francisco on 21 September, so as to help them find a way out of the problem. Two days later, he presented him to the other members of the second section of the second company of the Jiboa Battalion and told them that they should say that Escoto had been at San Francisco on 21 September and that he had been wounded there. Escoto was then presented as having been at San Francisco that day. 267/

On the night of 26 September, Major Beltrán Granados assembled the officers, non-commissioned officers and soldiers who had been at San Francisco. He indicated the places where each of them had been when they left San Francisco canton and said that was the version they should give. Later, there were other meetings to remind the soldiers what they had to say.

On one occasion, Second Lieutenant Vásquez Alvarenga took the soldiers to San Francisco canton and placed each soldier in the position that had been indicated to him, so that each soldier would recognize his position and not forget what he had to say.

On 27 and 28 September, members of the Commission for the Investigation of Criminal Acts interviewed Major Beltrán, Lieutenant Gálvez, Second Lieutenant Vásquez and the non-commissioned officers and soldiers. They all adhered to the cover-up version.

Some days later, lawyers Paredes and Parker of the Ministry of Defence and of the General Staff, respectively, interrogated the personnel of the Fifth Brigade who had been in San Francisco canton. All of them kept to the version of an ambush. An investigator administered lie detector tests. The results showed that some people were giving "dubious" replies. The lawyers then drew up a report which Chávez Cáceres sent to the General Staff and the Ministry of Defence.

Nine days after the incident, a member of the Jiboa Battalion told Colonel Chávez Cáceres that Major Beltrán had ordered the execution of the detainees and that they had been murdered. On 5 October, the corpses were exhumed and the forensic analysis revealed that the peasants had died after being shot at close range and not during combat. 268/

On 29 October 1988, the Commander of the Fifth Brigade announced at a press conference that the detainees had died in an ambush and that the guerrillas had returned during the night and mutilated the bodies to make it look as if they had been executed at close range.

Between 8 and 10 December 1988, investigators from the Commission for the Investigation of Criminal Acts again interrogated the officers, non-commissioned officers and soldiers. All of them kept to the cover-up version.

On 3 February 1989, United States Vice-President Dan Quayle visited El Salvador and called for the punishment of those responsible for the San Sebastián massacre. He handed over a list of three officers who were implicated: Colonel Chávez Cáceres, Major Beltrán Granados and Second Lieutenant Vásquez Alvarenga.

Some days later, Colonel Chávez Cáceres left the Brigade and Lieutenant Colonel Turcios was put in command. The other officers were then relieved of their duties. Lieutenant Gálvez Gálvez was held at Treasury Police headquarters, along with Second Lieutenant Vásquez Alvarenga.

In the course of February and March 1989, the military personnel who had been in San Francisco canton were questioned again. With the exception of Major Beltrán Granados, all of them abandoned the version of an ambush and said that Major Beltrán had ordered the execution and also the cover-up version of the incident.

The Commission for the Investigation of Criminal Acts identified Major Beltrán Granados as having ordered the executions and Second Lieutenant Vásquez Alvarenga, Sergeant Tobar Guzmán, Deputy Sergeant Rosales Villalobos, Corporal Ayala Arias and soldiers Cruz Castro, Hernández Matute, Mendéz Beltrán and Ponce Ramírez as having been responsible for carrying them out. 269/

Colonel Chávez Cáceres was not summonsed to make a statement or accused of or held responsible for any act or omission.

The judicial proceedings

The results of the investigations were sent to the judge of the Court of First Instance of San Sebastián on 11 March 1989. 270/ The judicial detention of nine people was ordered. 271/ In February 1990, the judge released all of them except Major Beltrán 272/ and Deputy Sergeant Rosales Villalobos. 273/

In May 1990, the court of San Vicente confirmed the judgement ordering the detainees' release and revoked the decision to bring Deputy Sergeant Rafael Rosales Villalobos to trial. 274/

As of the date of drafting of this report, Major Beltrán was still in prison awaiting the public hearing.

Findings

The Commission finds the following:

1. There is sufficient evidence that Colonel José Emilio Chávez Cáceres gave the order to execute the detainees.

2. There is full evidence that Major Mauricio de Jesús Beltrán Granados ordered members of the Jiboa Battalion to execute the 10 detained peasants.

3. There is substantial evidence that Colonel José Emilio Chávez Cáceres covered up the execution of the 10 detainees, and full evidence that Major Mauricio de Jesús Beltrán Granados took steps to cover up the execution.

4. There is substantial evidence that Second Lieutenant Arnoldo Antonio Vásquez Alvarenga transmitted the order from Major Beltrán Granados to designate some soldiers to finish off the victims and sufficient evidence that he provided the necessary materials to activate the mines which seriously wounded the victims.

5. There is substantial evidence that Sergeant Jorge Alberto Tobar Guzmán activated the mechanism that detonated the mines, knowing that they would explode in the place where the detained peasants were.

6. There is substantial evidence that Deputy Sergeant Rafael Rosales Villalobos and soldiers Fermín Cruz Castro, José Carlos Hernández Matute, José Alfredo Méndez Beltrán and Francisco Ponce Ramírez shot and killed the detainees.

7. There is sufficient evidence that Colonel Luis Mariano Turcios and Lieutenant Colonel José Antonio Rodríguez Molina knew about the order to execute the detainees and did nothing to prevent their execution.

8. There is substantial evidence that the Honour Commission of the armed forces, the Commission for the Investigation of Criminal Acts and the judge of the Criminal Court of First Instance of the city of San Sebastián failed to take steps to determine the responsibility of Colonel José Emilio Chávez Cáceres, Colonel Luis Mariano Turcios and Lieutenant Colonel José Antonio Rodríguez Molina.

(h) Attack on an FMLN hospital and execution of a nurse

Summary of the case

On 15 April 1989, air force units attacked an FMLN mobile hospital. 275/ Five of the 15 people in the hospital were killed: three Salvadorians—Juan Antonio (a patient), Clelia Concepción Díaz (a literacy instructor)

and María Cristina Hernández (a nurse and radio operator)—and two foreigners: José Ignacio Isla Casares (an Argentine doctor) and Madeleine Marie Francine Lagadec (a French nurse).

A Salvadorian air force unit attacked the hospital. Members of that unit deliberately attacked the medical staff in violation of international humanitarian law and captured the French nurse Madeleine Lagadac alive and executed her. Since no autopsies were performed on the other persons killed, it was not possible to ascertain with the same degree of accuracy whether they too were executed.

Description of the facts

The attack

According to witnesses, at about 7 a.m. or 8 a.m. on 15 April 1989, two low-flying A-37 aircraft bombed the area surrounding an FMLN mobile hospital located near the Catarina farm in El Tortugal canton, San Ildefonso district, Department of San Vicente. Three UH 1M helicopter gunships, a Hughes-500 helicopter and a "Push-Pull" light aeroplane took part in the attack. A few minutes later, six helicopters carrying paratroopers armed with M-16 rifles arrived on the scene. At 8.15 a.m., the helicopters dropped the troops near the hospital. The bombardment lasted 15 minutes.

Fifteen people were in the hospital when the attack started. Most of them started to escape; one of the patients returned the attackers' fire before fleeing. María Cristina Hernández, a nurse and radio operator, and Juan Antonio, one of the hospital's patients, were seriously injured in the attack.

Madeleine Lagadec, a French nurse who had been working with FMLN for three years, refused to run away and stayed behind to attend to María Cristina. José Ignacio Isla Casares, the Argentine doctor in charge of the hospital, and Clelia Concepción Díaz Salazar, the literacy instructor, also stayed behind.

Those who escaped witnessed what happened next. The soldiers closed in and the radio operator for the group of paratroopers informed his commanding officer that "mercenaries" had been captured and requested instructions. The soldiers then questioned the three captives and screams were heard, the loudest being those of Madeleine Lagadec. Next, some shots rang out. The soldiers left that afternoon. 276/

There is substantial evidence that the operation was carried out by a group belonging to the "Special Operations" unit of the Salvadorian air force (paratroopers backed by artillery and aircraft fire). They were part of "Operación Rayo", designed to destroy the logistical and command structure of the Partido Revolucionario de Trabajadores Centroamericanos (PRTC) in the area.

The investigation

On 17 April, a COPREFA communiqué was published announcing that nine people had died in an army attack on a PRTC command post. It also reported that weapons and medical equipment had been seized. 277/

That same day, FMLN members found the bodies at the scene. According to two of them, only Madeleine Lagadec's torso was clothed, her trousers had been pulled down to the knees, she did not have any underwear on under them 278/ and her left hand had been severed at the wrist. There were bullet holes in the skulls of the five bodies. 279/

The autopsy

An autopsy was performed only on the French nurse, in France on 2 May 1989. 280/

The autopsy found at least five gunshot wounds on Madeleine Lagadec. Two wounds—to the head and in the left shoulder blade region—were potentially lethal. The wounds were significant for the small calibre of the bullets used (between 5 and 6 mm) and their considerable destructive power, for which the only possible explanation is great velocity. No precise explanation was found for the amputation of the left hand. The French doctors said that the diversity of the trajectory of the projectiles made the theory of an execution highly unlikely. 281/

However, Dr. Robert Kirschner, 282/ who analysed the autopsy reports written in France and the sketches and documentation in the possession of this Commission, concluded that Madeleine Lagadec had been executed. 283/

In the analysis he made for the Commission, Dr. Kirschner, one of the world's foremost analysts of summary executions, explained that "The wounds and their trajectories provide significant evidence of the manner in which Madeleine Lagadec was killed. There were six gunshot wounds of the body, including three to the chest, one in the medial aspect of each thigh, and one to the head. All of these wounds passed from front to rear, upward, and in a medial to lateral direction . . . The pathologists who performed the autopsy were of the opinion that the diversity of the trajectory of the projectiles made it unlikely that this was an execution. I disagree with this conclusion. While the gunshot wounds to the chest might have occurred while the victim was standing, the wounds to the thighs almost certainly were inflicted while she was lying on the ground, and those of the chest are more consistent with having been inflicted while she was supine. Of special importance, the gunshot wound of the right temporal region of the head, which passed on a horizontal plane and exited from the left temporoparietal region of the scalp, was a characteristic *coup de grace* wound, and a trademark of the extrajudicial execution." 284/

Dr. Kirschner's conclusion that Madeleine Lagadec was executed is also supported in a separate analysis made by experts in electronic microscopy in France. 285/ They first ascertained that the victim had been shot when already half-naked: "(...) there are no traces of bullets on the brassière, briefs and trousers, while there are gunshot wounds to the right breast, the pelvis and the lower limbs (...) It can be deduced that the victim was not wearing those three items of clothing when the shots were fired." 286/

As for the distance from which the shots were fired, the above Centre puts forward two theories that contradict the assertion that Madeleine Lagadec's wounds were inflicted from a distance. 287/

Findings

The Commission finds the following:

1. There is sufficient evidence that a unit of the Salvadorian air force attacked the field hospital, and substantial evidence that it deliberately attacked medical personnel in violation of international humanitarian law.

2. There is substantial evidence that members of the unit captured the French nurse Madelaine Lagadec alive and executed her.

3. The State of El Salvador failed in its responsibility to investigate the case, bring the culprits to trial and punish them. The Commission was unable to determine whether the other people were also executed, since no autopsies were performed on their bodies.

(i) *García Arandigoyen*

Summary of the case

On 10 September 1990, Dr. Begoña García Arandigoyen was summarily executed in the Department of Santa Ana. The Spanish doctor, who was 24 years old, died in an alleged clash between a patrol of the 4th Company BIC PIPIL of the Second Infantry Brigade of the armed forces of El Salvador and a column of the Ejército Revolucioniario del Pueblo (ERP) of FMLN.

The Commission finds the following:

1. Begoña García Arandigoyen was executed extrajudicially by troops of the 4th Company BIC PIPIL of the Second Infantry Brigade, under immediate command of Lieutenant Roberto Salvador Hernández García and the overall command of Army Lieutenant Colonel José Antonio Almendáriz, commanding officer of the Second Brigade.

2. The above officers covered up the crime with the collaboration of the National Police Third Command, Santa Ana unit, and the experts and judicial authorities who took part in the examination of the corpse of Begoña García.

The death

Dr. Begoña García Arandigoyen, a Spanish doctor, entered El Salvador in September 1989 to work as a doctor for FMLN. She was executed, following her arrest, on 10 September 1990 in the Department of Santa Ana by troops of the 4th Company BIC PIPIL of the Second Infantry Brigade.

According to the official version, a patrol which was conducting a search of the area to the south of the Santa Ana volcano, near the Montañita estate, clashed with FMLN troops at approximately 1 p.m. on 10 September on the La Graciela estate.

According to a statement by Army Lieutenant Colonel José Antonio Almendáriz Rivas, commanding officer and Chief of Staff of the Second Brigade, he was advised by radio when fire contact was made with the enemy and was later informed of the death of 10 guerrillas, including two women, one of whom was a foreigner. 289/

According to the official version, FMLN troops managed to retrieve the bodies of eight of the dead, and the troops of 4th Company BIC PIPIL found only the bodies of two women. One of them looked like a foreigner.

At nightfall, other soldiers transferred the bodies of the two women from the place where the events had allegedly occurred to the main building of the Malacara estate, in Potrero Grande Arriba canton, Santa Ana district.

On the morning of 11 September, Army Lieutenant Colonel José Antonio Almendáriz Rivas, COPREFA staff and members of the National Police Third Command, Santa Ana unit, under the command of Lieutenant Gilberto García Cisneros, arrived at the Malacara estate by helicopter. COPREFA staff photographed the bodies and, according to the official version, members of the Third Command performed paraffin tests to see whether the women had fired weapons. There was no judicial examination of the bodies. 290/ At the request of the military personnel, local residents proceeded to bury the bodies.

The official examination of the corpse

On 14 September, the corpses were exhumed and the body of Dr. Begoña García was examined by the forensic doctor on duty, Dr. Neftalí Figueroa Juárez, in the presence of the judge of the First Criminal Court of the Santa Ana judicial district, Oscar Armando Avilés Magaña. Those present included a representative of the Embassy of Spain and Lieutenant Colonel Almendáriz Rivas.

The examination report states that "[they] examined the corpse of BEGOÑA GARCIA ARANDIGOYEN, which has a destructive wound on the outer right-hand surface of the right forearm, with a total and displaced fracture, a destructive wound on the lateral surface of the right buttock and wounds on the outer surface of the right elbow and the left thigh. The corpse is rapidly decomposing, death having occurred at least four days ago, there is no evidence of tattooing, burns or powder marks around any of the above-mentioned wounds, from which it can be inferred that the wounds were inflicted from a distance. The corpse was exhumed and the direct cause of death was hypovolemic shock resulting from multiple wounds." 291/

The autopsy in Spain

After the corpse of Begoña García had been transferred to Spain, the Pathology Department of Navarra Government Hospital performed a clinical autopsy. That autopsy, and the report by Dr. Carlos Martín Beristaín on the medical and forensic findings, 292/ established the following:

1. The corpse had multiple wounds, especially to the head, neck and upper and lower extremities.

2. There was a large wound on the left forearm, corresponding to a total fracture, which implied the use of a blunt instrument or the impact of a bullet.

3. There were two round bullet entry holes, from 2.4 to 3 cm in diameter, above both elbow joints, although no exit holes could be detected, the wounds being very selective and occurring only on the extremities and symmetrically on the arms, without other wounds on the thorax which could have been caused by a line of fire.

4. The wounds on the arms and the left thigh could have been made by a sharp bayonet-type instrument, since they were too large in diameter to have been caused by a firearm without being accompanied by greater destruction, other exit holes or the presence of bullets in the flesh.

5. An entry hole 1.8 cm in diameter in the lower central occipital region, the trajectory being upwards and forwards.

6. A round hole 2.5 cm in diameter at the base of the neck, just above the sternal manubrium.

7. Death must have occurred instantaneously as a result of the firearm wounds to the cranium, because of the destruction of vital nerve centres and not because of the bleeding which the wounds may have caused.

Dr. Beristaín's report notes that a biochemical analysis detected the existence of a large quantity of powder around the edges of the neck wound (above the sternal manubrium), confirming that the wound had been caused by a shot fired from a distance of a few centimetres. The bullet wounds in the occipital region and the sternal manubrium had similar characteristics and had been made from a distance of a few centimetres.

The report further notes that when the corpse was officially examined in El Salvador, neither of the two head wounds which were made from a distance of a few centimetres (in the nape of the neck and in the region above the sternum) was recorded.

Report by the expert of the Commission on the Truth

At the request of the Commission on the Truth, Dr. Robert H. Kirschner, a forensic pathologist, studied the examination made by Dr. José Neftalí Figueroa on 14 September 1990 and the clinical autopsy report from Navarra Hospital. In the opinion of Dr. Kirschner, the Navarra autopsy directly contradicts the El Salvador examination and supports the contention that Begoña García was captured and executed. Dr. Kirschner notes that the Navarra autopsy report describes wounds which are inconsistent with those occurring in combat and typical of those caused by execution, including the wound at the base of the cranium, fired from a gun almost in contact with the nape of the neck, and another in the upper chest, caused by a shot fired from a distance of a few centimetres.

Findings

The Commission finds the following:

1. There is full evidence that Begoña García Arandigoyen was executed extrajudicially, in flagrant violation of international humanitarian law and international human rights law, by units of the Second Infantry Brigade under the immediate command of Lieutenant Roberto Salvador Hernández García and the overall command of Army Lieutenant Colonel José Antonio Almendáriz Rivas, commanding officer of the Second Brigade.

2. There is full evidence that the above officers covered up the crime.

3. There is full evidence of the responsibility of the judicial authorities, as shown by the actions of the judge of the First Criminal Court of the Santa Ana judicial district, Oscar Armando Avilés Magaña, and of the forensic doctor on duty, Dr. Neftalí Figueroa Juárez, who took part in the examination of the corpse of Begoña García and who omitted from the record the two gunshot wounds made at a distance of a few centimetres, thus failing in their duty to carry out a full and impartial investigation of the causes of her death.

(j) COMADRES and FENASTRAS

Summary of the case

In the early morning of 31 October 1989, persons unknown placed a bomb at the entrance to the offices of the Comité de Madres y Familiares de Presos Políticos, Desaparecidos y Asesinados de El Salvador Monseñor Oscar Arnulfo Romero (COMADRES) in San Salvador. Four people, including a child, were injured.

At midday, a bomb was placed in the offices of the Federación Nacional Sindical de Trabajadores Salvadoreños (FENASTRAS) in San Salvador. Nine people were killed and over 40 injured. As a result of the attack, FMLN decided to suspend peace negotiations with the Government.

The Commission on the Truth finds the following:

1. The bomb attacks on the offices of COMADRES and FENASTRAS on 31 October 1989 were part of a systematic pattern of attacks on the lives, physical integrity and freedom of members of those organizations.

2. The Government of El Salvador failed in its duty to guarantee the human rights to which the members of these organizations are entitled as individuals and as members of their organizations.

3. The attack on FENASTRAS was carried out using a bomb which persons unknown placed outside its offices.

4. The competent authorities of El Salvador did not carry out a full and impartial investigation of the attacks on the offices of COMADRES and FENASTRAS.

5. There is no countervailing evidence that FMLN or FENASTRAS members carried out the attack.

Description of the facts 293/

COMADRES is a non-governmental organization established to provide support for mothers and relatives of victims of politically motivated disappearances or murders. It was founded in December 1977 at the suggestion of Monsignor Oscar Arnulfo Romero.

FENASTRAS is an independent confederation formed in 1974 to strengthen trade unions and promote the interests of Salvadorian workers. It has 25,000 individual members and 16 member trade unions. It is the largest industrial trade union confederation in El Salvador. Its main office is located two blocks away from the National Police in San Salvador.

The attacks

In the early morning of 31 October 1989, two men in uniform allegedly placed a bomb at the entrance to the COMADRES offices in San Salvador. A large lorry was also reportedly heard leaving the scene moments later. Four people, including a child of four months, were injured. The National Police blamed the crime on the guerrillas. 294/

At approximately 12.30 p.m. the same day, a worker who was a member of FENASTRAS noticed someone propping a sack against the outside wall of the FENASTRAS cafeteria. He smelt gunpowder and ran inside to warn his companions. Another witness, a scrap dealer, noticed two young men entering FENASTRAS grounds through the door in the access wall. One of them was carrying a suitcase in a jute sack. Through the door in the wall, we saw one of them "crouch down as if he was setting light to something". As he came out, he shouted that they had planted a bomb and the two of them ran off northwards.

Outside, someone yelled "bomb!" and people began running. At that moment, the bomb exploded. The building was enveloped in smoke and powder and the offices were destroyed. More than 40 people were injured and the following were killed: Ricardo Humberto Cestoni, trade unionist; Carmen Catalina Hernández Ramos, FENASTRAS cook; José Daniel López Meléndez, trade unionist; Julia Tatiana Mendoza Aguirre, trade unionist and daughter of a leader of the Frente Democrático Revolucionario (FDR) assassinated in 1980; Vicente Salvador Melgar, trade unionist; María Magdalena Rosales, student and daughter of a trade union leader; Rosa Hilda Saravia de Elias, FENASTRAS cook and trade union member; Luis Edgardo Vásquez Márquez, trade unionist; and Febe Elizabeth Velásquez, International Secretary of FENASTRAS and a member of the Executive Committee of the Unidad Nacional de Trabajadores Salvadoreños (UNTS).

FENASTRAS members and the main trade unions blamed the armed forces. UNTS accused the Ministry of Defence of "summarily executing" the workers in retaliation for an FMLN attack on the Armed Forces Joint Staff the previous day.

Background

These attacks on the offices of COMADRES and FENASTRAS occurred in a specific political and chronological context. It was common knowledge that the two organizations were critical of government policy, especially with regard to human rights violations, and that FENASTRAS was critical of governmental measures which, from its point of view, were detrimental to workers' interests. The armed forces considered FENASTRAS a "front" for FMLN. 295/

The security forces had several members of COMADRES and FENASTRAS, as well as their offices, under constant surveillance. The offices of the two organizations were raided repeatedly and their members were regularly threatened, harassed and detained by the authorities. 296/ On 22 February and 5 September, explosive devices were thrown at FENASTRAS headquarters. Hundreds of incidents of violence, persecution and threats against the two organizations have been reported.

In this political and chronological context, it should be noted that during October 1989, there had been a number of attacks against the army and against opponents of the Government. 297/ The day before the attacks on COMADRES and FENASTRAS, FMLN members had attacked the Armed Forces Joint Staff using explosive devices. 298/

The investigation of the attacks

Immediately after the attack on FENASTRAS, the Commission for the Investigation of Criminal Acts (CIHD), the judiciary and the National Police launched their respective investigations. The Second Justice of the Peace, Nelson Ulises Umaña Bojórquez, attempted to make a judicial inspection 299/ on 31 October. He was forced to abandon his efforts owing to "the congestion and commotion caused by the crowd which [was] present at the scene". 300/ CIHD experts arrived half an hour after the attack to make a visual inspection. Neither they nor staff from the Police Explosives Unit were able to gain access to the inside of the building. 301/

There are many doubts as to the seriousness and impartiality with which the investigations proceeded. That same day, CIHD representatives expressed the view that "the cause of the explosion was the mishandling of explosive materials inside the building itself". 302/ Members of the Police Explosives Unit concluded that the attack "... formed part of the conspiracy to discredit the Government of El Salvador by making the national and international community believe that the attack was a government response to the artillery attack launched by FMLN on 30 October 1989 against the Armed Forces Joint Staff ... which leads us to conclude that FMLN carried out the attack against itself in order to confuse public opinion, making it believe that it was an act of revenge for the earlier attack".

The CIHD dossier suggests that its investigation was based on the conclusions of the investigation carried out by the Technical Assistance Department of the "Sargento Carlos Sosa Santos" Explosives and Demolition Unit of the National Police, which ruled out the possibility that the explosive device had been planted at FENASTRAS offices "by an unknown person unconnected with that organization, since a meeting was being held inside the building and it is possible that access to it was being monitored by FENASTRAS staff". 303/ One of the first steps taken by CIHD was to request the security forces "urgently" to provide any political or ordinary information on the people killed and injured in the explosion. 304/

In November 1989, at the request of President Cristiani, the United States Department of State sent FBI experts to inspect the site of the explosion at the FENASTRAS offices. 305/ In its report, the FBI concluded that the disturbance of the scene of the crime, the passage of time and the conditions in which the crime had occurred reduced the possibility of identifying the type of explosive used. 306/ It was able to determine only that a high-power explosive, weighing approximately 15 pounds, had been used, and that the explosion had occurred in the area between the access wall and the outside wall of the building itself. 307/

It has been heard that the Government allegedly pressured some detainees to blame FMLN for the attack or to issue false statements to the press.

Findings

The Commission finds the following:

1. There is sufficient evidence that the bomb attacks on the offices of COMADRES and FENASTRAS on 31 October 1989 were part of a systematic pattern of attacks on the lives, physical integrity and freedom of members of those organizations.

2. There is full evidence that the Government of El Salvador failed in its duty to guarantee the human rights to which the members of these organizations are entitled as individuals and as members of their organizations.

3. There is full evidence that the attack on the FENASTRAS offices was carried out using a bomb which persons unknown placed outside the building.

4. There is substantial evidence that the competent authorities of El Salvador did not carry out a full and impartial investigation of the attacks on the offices of COMADRES and FENESTRAS.

5. There is no countervailing evidence that FMLN or FENASTRAS members might have carried out the attack.

(k) Oquelí and Flores

Summary of the case

On 12 January 1990, Héctor Oquelí Colindres and Gilda Flores Arévalo were abducted in Guatemala City, Republic of Guatemala. Their bodies were found the same day in the village of San José El Coco in the Jalpatagua district of Guatemala, 5 kilometres from the border with El Salvador.

The facts of the killings are not in dispute. However, views differ as to who bears criminal and political responsibility.

Within the constraints imposed on it, the Commission made an exhaustive effort to determine who was responsible for the murders. It received some of the results of the investigations made by the Office of the President of the Republic of Guatemala, made inquiries with the authorities of that country, evaluated information supplied by the Government of El Salvador, studied the report prepared by Professors Tom Farer and Robert Goldman, and received some relevant testimony.

Having analysed the information available, it can say with certainty that members of the Guatemalan security forces, acting in conjunction with Salvadorians, took part in the crime.

It also notes that the incident was not properly investigated and that some essential procedures were omitted.

The Governments of Guatemala and El Salvador must make a thorough investigation of this double murder.

Description of the facts

Background

Héctor Oquelí, a leader of the Movimiento Nacional Revolucionario (MNR) of El Salvador, 308/ enjoyed tremendous national and international prestige and had been active for many years in the Socialist International. 309/ He was widely regarded as the likely successor to MNR leader Guillermo Ungo. 310/

Gilda Flores Arévalo, a citizen and resident of Guatemala, was actively involved in the Partido Socialista Democrático (PSD).

The murder occurred shortly after the biggest military offensive of the Salvadorian conflict, launched by FMLN in November 1989.

The fact that Héctor Oquelí was an opposition politician in El Salvador and the outrage which this crime prompted make this case a serious act of violence falling within the Commission's mandate, regardless of the place where the incident occurred.

Some considerations

After the Government of President Vinicio Cerezo came to power in Guatemala, some opponents of the Salvadorian regime, including Oquelí, began to engage in low profile political activities on Guatemalan territory. 311/

As a member of MNR, Oquelí had returned to El Salvador and was publicly active in politics. In November 1989, during an FMLN offensive, he took refuge in the Venezuelan Embassy. He then moved to Mexico, where he continued his political activities within the Socialist International.

The facts

On 11 January 1990, Oquelí was travelling from Mexico to Nicaragua to take part in a Socialist International meeting in Managua. He planned to make a one-day stopover in Guatemala and leave the next day for Managua.

The reason for this stopover was to hold a political meeting with Mr. René Flores, a member of the same political group as Oquelí. René Flores travelled from San Salvador specifically to meet with Oquelí. Oquelí also planned to visit Gilda Flores in Guatemala.

On 11 January, Oquelí arrived in Guatemala City. In the international arrivals area, he met up with René Flores, who was arriving on a flight from San Salvador.

Oquelí went through immigration control without a problem. Two immigration officials then came up to him and asked him to show his passport again, on some administrative pretext, and detained him for over half an hour. Because of this, Oquelí was unable to leave the baggage area or go through customs because he did not have his passport. Gilda Flores and René Flores were waiting for him outside and could not understand why he had been delayed.

Oquelí's passport was new and absolutely in order and there was no reason why it could not be checked simply by looking at it. However, when the immigration officials returned it to him, they wrote in by hand over the date on the entry stamp the instruction "read this".

Once outside, Oquelí met up with René Flores and Gilda Flores. They talked about the passport episode that had occurred in the baggage area and drove to the home of Gilda Flores.

As they were leaving the airport, they noticed that some people who looked like plain clothes policemen were watching them, but nothing happened as they drove into the city.

When they reached Gilda Flores' home, there were some people they did not know outside but since there was a foreign embassy there they did not see anything significant in this.

Once inside the house, Oquelí made a number of telephone calls. He and René Flores talked about the overall political situation in El Salvador and René Flores gave him some documents.

Gilda Flores and Oquelí then took René Flores to the airport. René Flores told the Commission on the Truth that he had been surprised that they went with him to the airport, as there was no need for this and it was not in line with the security measures that Oquelí always scrupulously observed.

Gilda Flores invited Héctor Oquelí to have dinner at her home. The maid left when dinner was over. Next morning, Flores and Oquelí set out early for the airport for Oquelí to take a plane to Managua. Gilda Flores was driving.

At approximately 5.45 a.m., on the Avenida Sexta in Zona Nueve, they were intercepted by a private vehicle from which a group of people got out. 312/ Oquelí, who was in the front passenger seat, tried to escape but was overpowered. He and Gilda were forced into the vehicle which had intercepted them.

Luis Ayala, the General Secretary of the Socialist International, and people at the International's meeting in Managua, began to wonder why Oquelí had not arrived.

That same day, Guatemalan police went to the scene of the abduction and found papers in the vehicle abandoned on the street establishing that the vehicle belonged to Gilda Flores. That morning, a complaint had been lodged with the police that two individuals had violently stolen a vehicle from a Guatemalan citizen in Guatemala City. In doing so, the assailants had identified themselves as members of the police. 313/ The vehicle turned out to be the same one in which the bodies of Oquelí and Flores were found later. There were bullet wounds in the bodies and they appeared to have been injected with an unidentified substance. 314/

At 5 p.m. the same day, 12 January, the two bodies were found in a vehicle abandoned on the main road to the border with El Salvador. Héctor Oquelí's papers were in his clothing.

Subsequent events

The Guatemalan authorities concluded on the spot that the body was indeed that of Héctor Oquelí Colindres. The body of Gilda Flores was identified by members of her family.

President Cerezo ordered an investigation of the case. The result of these investigations was the so-called "Third Report". The report made no findings and assigned no responsibilities, but simply set forth a number of theories, on which the Guatemalan Government had based its investigation, as to the possible motives for the crime. The investigation went nowhere, even though the report itself maintained that intelligence services obtained information that persons with ties to the activities of Salvadorian terrorist groups in recent years might be operating in Guatemala. Among the names obtained were those of Francisco Ricardo de Sola and Orlando de Sola. Although there is no definite evidence linking them to the crime, the investigation found that they were in Guatemala on the exact days on which the abduction and murder took place. 315/ The report added that "information was found pointing to Infantry Colonel Mario Denis Morán Echeverría of the Salvadorian army, El Salvador's Military Attaché in Guatemala, as someone whose background gave grounds to suspect that he might be providing a cover for clandestine terrorist groups coming from El Salvador. 316/

Reacting to the report, the Salvadorian Government claimed that Salvadorian citizens had been implicated without grounds. President Cristiani ordered the Attorney-General of the Republic to launch an investigation. However, this investigation did not yield any results either.

At the request of the Socialist International, Professors Tom Farer and Robert Goldman, human rights experts, evaluated the action taken by the Guatemalan Government. The Farer-Goldman report found that the deficiencies of the Government's reports were so obvious that one could conclude that the investigation had been meant to fail. 317/

The Oquelí-Flores case is still awaiting a judicial resolution in both El Salvador and Guatemala.

Analysis

The Commission interviewed a considerable number of people who had been close to Oquelí, both members of his family and political contacts, and made all kinds of inquiries in order to obtain more precise information on the official investigations made in Guatemala and El Salvador. It had access to information about many of the possible motives for the double murder. Unfortunately, the most important information needed to conduct an in-depth investigation and answer some of the questions which were suggested to the Commission as a basis for its work could not be substantiated when the Commission requested that it be given access to all the information gathered by the Salvadorian Government on the Oquelí-Flores case. The reluctance in both Guatemala and El Salvador to give the Commission access to the information it requested during its investigation imposed serious constraints on it.

In this case, the facts are documented and the characteristics of the abduction and murder of Héctor Oquelí and Gilda Flores are not in question. However, neither those who planned the double homicide nor those who carried it out have been identified.

It was never made clear why the Guatemalan authorities had detained Oquelí at the airport and confiscated his passport for over half an hour. Nor was the liquid injected into the victims before their death identified. The records of persons entering and leaving the country were not checked—not even the records of the frontier post that was five kilometres away from the place where the bodies were found. No statement was taken from anyone whose testimony was decisive for shedding light on the facts and no one took the fingerprints left on the vehicles. Lastly, there was no investigation of the fact that the individuals who stole the car used for the crime identified themselves as police.

The dossier does not contain any new information other than letters and reports from police units and purely procedural judicial documents.

The Commission requested all existing information on this case from the highest level of the Government of the Republic of Guatemala. 318/ Despite the latter's pledge to cooperate in the Commission's work, no relevant information was received. 319/

The Office of the Attorney-General of the Republic of El Salvador provided the Commission with a copy of the dossier of the investigation made at the request of President Cristiani. In fact, the dossier is nothing more than a compilation of press clippings on the case. 320/

Moreover, the Office of the Attorney-General did not interview the Salvadorians named in the "Third Report", some of whom were public officials in El Salvador.

Among the theories as to possible motives for the crime is the fact that Héctor Oquelí was an international political figure. This is the theory underlying the Guatemalan Government's "Third Report", which speculates that the killers could have been from the most radical sectors of FMLN, the Guatemalan army, the Salvadorian authorities or the Salvadorian extreme right wing.

MNR provided the Commission with the original of a military identity card, belonging to a major René Grande Martínez, which had been handed over to it by President Vinicio Cerezo and which the Guatemalan authorities had apparently found at the scene of the murder.

The Ministry of Defence did little to respond to the request by the Commission on the Truth that it locate Major Grande Martínez. The Commission summoned him repeatedly but he never came to testify.

The Commission determined that the most important features of this murder were: (a) that the murderers knew beforehand that Oquelí would be in Guatemala; (b) that Oquelí was detained at the airport by authorities; (c) that his movements were constantly watched; (d) that persons claiming to be police stole the vehicle in which the bodies were later found; (e) that Oquelí was abducted in Guatemala City in broad daylight in the middle of the street; (f) and that the murderers were able to drive without incident from the capital city to the border with the two victims in a stolen car. All of this makes it absolutely clear that the Guatemalan authorities must have collaborated with or tolerated these crimes.

Findings

1. The Governments of Guatemala and El Salvador have not done enough to thoroughly investigate the reasons for the murder of Héctor Oquelí Colindres and Gilda Flores or to find out who was responsible. The Commission on the Truth urges the two Governments separately to order the necessary action to clear up the crime and jointly, with the cooperation of such international bodies as are able to help them clarify this tragic event, to provide the international community with information establishing what happened, without prejudice to the corresponding judicial action.

2. The Commission believes that there is a direct link between the following facts: the fact that Héctor Oquelí Colindres and Gilda Flores Arévalo were members of their countries' political opposition; the fact that Oquelí was inexplicably detained by Guatemalan authorities at the airport; the fact that the home of Gilda Flores was being watched; the subsequent abduction and murder of Oquelí and Flores; and alleged police involve-

ment in the theft of the car in which the bodies were found.

3. The Commission has found sufficient evidence that members of the Salvadorian security forces, acting in conjunction with or tolerated by Guatemalan security forces, were responsible for the murders.

4. There is sufficient evidence that the Salvadorian authorities did not investigate this crime properly. There is also sufficient evidence that the investigations made by the Guatemalan authorities were deficient and that the omission of basic evidence, even if not intended as a cover-up, had that effect.

3. Enforced disappearances

(a) Ventura and Mejía

Summary of the case

Francisco Arnulfo Ventura and José Humberto Mejía, law students at the University of El Salvador, were arrested by members of the National Guard in the parking lot of the United States Embassy on 22 January 1980 after a student demonstration. According to witnesses, members of the National Guard handed the students over to some men in civilian clothing who drove off with them in a private car. Despite the judicial investigations and remedies carried out since that date, the students' whereabouts are still unknown.

The Commission made the following findings:

1. Members of the National Guard arrested Francisco Arnulfo Ventura and José Humberto Mejía, detained them in the parking lot of the United States Embassy and then handed them over to some men in civilian clothing who drove off with them in a private vehicle.

2. While in the custody of those men, the students disappeared and there is no evidence that they are still alive.

3. By denying that the students had been arrested and failing to act quickly to investigate the incident and identify precisely who was responsible, then Colonel Eugenio Vides Casanova, Commander of the National Guard, was guilty, at the least of complicity through negligence and of obstructing the resulting judicial investigation.

4. The State failed in its duty to investigate, bring to trial and punish the guilty parties, compensate the victims' relatives and inform them of the whereabouts of the disappeared persons. The State must comply fully and promptly with these obligations.

Description of the facts 321/

On the morning of 22 January 1980, a student demonstration which had marched from the University of El Salvador to the centre of San Salvador was violently dispersed by security forces in front of the cathedral; a number of people were killed or injured. 322/

Two of the demonstrators, Francisco Arnulfo Ventura Reyes (age 24) and José Humberto Mejía (age 25), both law students, went through the main entrance of the United States Embassy after the demonstration, at about 2.30 in the afternoon.

According to a number of witnesses, members of the National Guard arrested them at the Embassy gate and took them into the parking lot, where they stayed for a few minutes in the custody of the National Guard. Shortly afterwards, a private car 323/ entered the Embassy parking lot and the National Guard handed the students over to some men in civilian clothing who put them in the car boot and drove off. That was the last that was seen of the students.

The investigation

The same afternoon, a relative of Francisco Ventura went looking for him. Near the cathedral, a number of people told him that they had heard that Francisco Ventura and José Humberto Mejía had been arrested in front of the United States Embassy by guards. The next day, he received confirmation of this information when he went to the Asociación General de Estudiantes Universitarios Salvadoreños (AGEUS).

At the request of AGEUS, Mr. Santiago Orellana Amador and Mr. Florentín Menéndez were appointed to file writs of *habeas corpus* for the two students. According to their judicial statements, they spoke to Mr. Vytantos A. Dambrava, Director of the International Communications Agency of the United States Embassy, and to the Embassy's chief of security. Both Embassy officials said that they had known about the students' arrest and that the United States Marines had not been involved. They also said that the members of the National Guard who had been guarding the Embassy had brought the students into the courtyard to search them, and had kept them there. They added that, shortly afterwards, the two young men had been taken out of the Embassy. Mr. Dambrava said that they had been taken away by members of the National Guard, 324/ while the chief of security said that men in olive drab trousers and ordinary shirts had driven off with them in a private vehicle.

Mr. Orellana and Mr. Meléndez later interviewed Colonel Eugenio Vides Casanova, then Commander of the National Guard, who denied the statements by the Embassy officials. The lawyers then requested the Supreme Court to rule on the conflicting information given by the Embassy and the National Guard Command. 325/

At the same time, the Chief State Counsel, Mario Zamora, filed a complaint with the Second Criminal Court. Testimony was heard from relatives of the disappeared students. The judge also requested information from the United States Embassy and the National Guard, but did not receive a reply.

On 22 February 1980, the Supreme Court authorized the judge of the Second Criminal Court to initiate an investigation into the whereabouts of the disappeared students. That same night, Mario Zamora was murdered. 326/ After that, no further investigations were carried out.

However, the lawyers pursued their investigation, visiting National Guard barracks, 327/ while the students' relatives searched everywhere, even among the bodies that were turning up on the outskirts of San Salvador. Neither the young men nor their bodies were found.

Three months later, the death squad known as the "Ejército Secreto Anti-Comunista" published a list of names which included people who had already been murdered or disappeared, such as Monsignor Romero, Father Rutilio Grande and Chief State Counsel Mario Zamora. The names of Francisco Arnulfo Ventura and José Humberto Mejía were on the list. At the end of the list was an exhortation which read, "... help us get rid of all these traitors and criminal communists. The country will thank you for it." 328/

Findings

The Commission finds the following:

1. There is full evidence that members of the National Guard arrested Francisco Arnulfo Ventura and José Humberto Mejía, detained them in the parking lot of the United States Embassy and handed them over to men in civilian clothing who drove off with them in a private car.

2. While in the custody of these men who drove into the Embassy parking lot and to whom they were handed over by the guards who arrested them, Ventura and Mejía disappeared. There is no evidence that they are still alive.

3. There is substantial evidence that by failing to act quickly to investigate the incident and identify precisely who was responsible, then Colonel Eugenio Vides Casanova was guilty, at least of complicity through negligence and of obstructing the resulting judicial investigation.

The State failed in its duty to investigate, bring to trial and punish the guilty parties, compensate victims' relatives and inform them of the whereabouts of the disappeared persons. The State must comply with its obligations.

(b) *Rivas Hernández*

Summary of the case

Miguel Angel Rivas Hernández, aged 17, disappeared on Saturday, 29 November 1986, near the Ilopango air force base in San Salvador. Witnesses attributed his arrest to members of the air force, to whom his family went to demand his return; at the base however, they were told that he was not being detained. Despite this official denial, the family received confirmation that the young man was at the base. Accordingly, they reported his disappearance to human rights organizations.

In January 1987 the young man was allegedly transferred to the National Guard central barracks in San Salvador. In March 1988, the victim's father maintains that he saw him from a distance at the National Guard barracks.

The Commission finds that:

1. Miguel Angel Rivas Hernández was arrested on 29 November 1986 by members of the Salvadorian air force.

2. He was transferred from the air force base to the National Guard central barracks, where he disappeared, there being no evidence that he is still alive.

3. The Salvadorian air force and the National Guard covered up his arrest and detention.

4. The Commission for the Investigation of Criminal Acts (CIHD) did not cooperate properly with the Commission. It transmitted incomplete information concerning its investigation of the case.

Miguel Angel Rivas Hernández was arrested by members of the air force and subsequently transferred to the National Guard central barracks; not only did he disappear while in the custody of the National Guard, but there is no evidence that he is still alive. Air force and National Guard personnel covered up his detention. The State cannot evade its duty to investigate the case thoroughly.

Description of the facts

Miguel Angel Rivas Hernández, son of Guillermo Rivas Compas, a bus driver, and Rosa Elba Rivas, a housewife, lived in the Ilopango district adjacent to the Salvadorian air force base in San Salvador. He was not known in the community to be involved in political activities.

When he was 17, Miguel Angel got a job as attendant at the Texaco service station located on the Pan American Highway, just beyond the limits of air force base property. He walked to and from work every day.

It was common to see motorized patrols circulating at various times, as well as members of the Salvadorian air force on foot. Residents of the area usually knew airmen who worked at the base.

Arrest and disappearance

On Saturday, 29 November 1986, Miguel Angel's boss at the Texaco service station gave him permission to leave at approximately 7.30 p.m. As usual, he headed straight for home.

Miguel Angel's parents were expecting him at around 8 p.m. The young man did not arrive home. Worried, they inquired at the filling station, where they were assured that he had left shortly before 7.30 p.m.

His mother managed to find out that individuals in civilian clothing, driving a red pick-up truck with no doors on the cab, had detained a boy wearing white trousers and a black shirt. The description fitted Miguel Angel. His captors, from the description given, appeared to be members of the "7.30 p.m. air force patrol".

Very early the next day, Miguel Angel's parents went to the air force base to inquire about him, but were told that he was not being detained. They then went to various police and military departments, but these also denied that they were holding him.

A neighbour told Miguel Angel's mother that a young man had witnessed the arrest and had recognized an airman from the base as one of the captors. The airman was nicknamed "El Mango".

An air force member, nicknamed "El Chino", also confirmed to a friend of Miguel Angel that he was being held at the Ilopango air force base. This friend told Miguel Angel's mother. At the base, however, they still officially denied his detention.

Complaints and searches

In view of these continuing denials, the family decided, in December 1986, to report Miguel Angel's disappearance to several human rights bodies: the Human Rights Commission of El Salvador (governmental), the Archdiocesan Legal Protection Office, the International Committee of the Red Cross (ICRC), Amnesty International and Americas Watch. Americas Watch brought the case to the attention of the Inter-American Commission on Human Rights (IACHR). 329/

In January 1987, the family was informed of Miguel Angel's transfer to the National Guard barracks in San Salvador. 330/ However, when they went there, his detention was again denied.

The transfer of Miguel Angel Rivas Hernández from the air force to the National Guard was apparently recorded in the Guard's books in January 1987. 331/

In February 1987, the case was presented to the United States Embassy in El Salvador. Some members of the United States Congress wrote letters to their own Embassy in El Salvador 332/ and to the then President of El Salvador, José Napoleón Duarte, 333/ expressing concern at Miguel Angel's disappearance. In March, an Amnesty International mission visited the National Guard barracks, but did not find the young man there.

The investigation

CIHD took charge of the investigation of the case in April 1987. 334/ *Detective Sergeant Roberto Palacios Iraheta was assigned to the investigation. 335/*

Sergeant Palacios found out from an informant that a National Guard lieutenant had called a meeting of five Guard members and had ordered them to hide the books containing the records of the interrogations to which Rivas Hernández 336/ had been subjected and the place where he was being held: National Guard cell (*bartolina*) No. 4, S-II.

On receiving this information, Lieutenant Colonel Nelson Iván López y López, Chief of the CIHD Executive Unit, decided to intervene directly in the case and went to the National Guard barracks, but did not find the young man. 337/

In a report dated 26 May, Lieutenant Colonel López noted that "... the investigations concerning Mr. Rivas Hernández are running into complications which require decisions at another level and which will shortly be reported ... (to the Head of CIHD)". 338/

On 2 June 1987, in another report, Lieutenant Colonel López "... described, in general terms, the difficulties encountered in the case of the disappearance of Mr. Rivas Hernández". 339/

Meanwhile, the family received regular information from its own source concerning Miguel Angel's state of health and place of detention. (The family's source was the same as that of CIHD.)

The family also transmitted regularly to this source various sums of money, which were carefully recorded by the victim's mother, during the period from June 1987 to February 1989. The informant reported seeing the detained youth in person and also gave an account of various transfers, both to official National Guard locations and to private houses; on several occasions, ICRC visited the official locations, without finding the young man.

On 23 March 1988, IACHR adopted resolution No. 21/88 in which it assumed that the facts of the complaint on the disappearance were true, advised the Government of El Salvador that the case involved extremely grave violations of human rights and recommended that it investigate and punish those responsible.

A few days later, nearly 16 months after the disappearance, the young man's father, Guillermo Rivas Campos, claims he caught sight of Miguel Angel for a few moments at the National Guard Command in San Pablo Tacachico.

The United States Embassy, through one of its officials, constantly supported the family in the search for the young man. Colonel Rivas Rivas of CIHD interviewed a colonel and a lieutenant of the National Guard, without success.

Following the FMLN offensive in 1989, the father

of Miguel Angel Rivas Hernández was detained on charges of being linked to the guerrilla movement. His release was obtained with the help of the United States Embassy.

Findings

The Commission finds the following:

1. There is substantial evidence that Miguel Angel Rivas Hernández was arrested by members of the Salvadorian air force.

2. There is substantial evidence that he was transferred to the National Guard.

3. There is substantial evidence that, while in the custody of the National Guard, the young man disappeared; there is no evidence that he is still alive.

4. There is substantial evidence that the air force subsequently covered up his arrest and detention and that the National Guard covered up his detention.

5. The State failed in its responsibility under international human rights law to investigate the case and to bring to trial and punish those responsible.

(c) *Chan Chan and Massi*

Summary of the case

The Commission on the Truth received abundant complaints of disappearances and studied most of them in depth. The present case is symptomatic of the disregard shown for family values, family feelings, maternal grief and trade union solidarity, which is why the Commission chose to focus on it.

On 18 August 1989, trade unionists Sara Cristina Chan Chan Medina and Juan Francisco Massi Chávez were walking home along the Boulevard del Ejército, near San Salvador. She was 20 years old and a photographer for the trade union confederation FENASTRAS; he was 25, a student and worked for the LIDO factory. As they passed the Reprocentro factory, 2.5 kilometres from the capital city, six air force members arrested them in front of the main gate: passengers in the buses driving by on the road recognized the young people and saw them standing against the wall with their hands in the air while being interrogated by the soldiers. This occurred at approximately 6 p.m. They have not been seen since.

Description of the facts 340/

Background

Juan Francisco was born on 25 February 1973 in Quezaltepeque, La Libertad, to Carmen Chávez de Massi and Simeón Massi. He lived with his family in the Las Margaritas district in Soyapango, was a worker, was public relations secretary of the trade union at the LIDO company, worked with FENASTRAS members on various trade union projects, had never been arrested and had no criminal record.

Sara Cristina Chan Chan was the eldest daughter of Jorge Eduardo Chan Chan Jiménez and María Juana Antonia Medina. The family used to live in the city of Santa Ana, where her father was an office worker and a well-known leader of the trade union ANDA. She had never been arrested either and had no criminal record. She had however, suffered the consequences of her family's trade union activities.

On 16 June 1980, when Sara Cristina was barely 10 years old, men in civilian clothing came to her home and murdered her father in the presence of Sara Cristina, her three younger brothers and sisters and her mother. The men arrived at 2 a.m. and identified themselves as members of the National Guard. When Sara Cristina's father refused to open the door, the men broke one of the windows and shot him. They also fired at the propane gas cylinder in the kitchen, and one of the men was about to light a match when he saw Sara Cristina and her brothers and sisters hiding under a bed. They left without setting fire to the house because there were "quite a few children" in it.

Because of the murder of Jorge Eduardo Chan Chan Jiménez, the family went to live in San Salvador. It was only after "quite some time" that Sara Cristina's mother decided to return to Santa Ana. In July 1989, according to witnesses, a group of uniformed soldiers from the Second Brigade, together with some civilians, came to her house. They blindfolded her and put her into a vehicle to take her to the Santa Ana barracks; on the way, she was tortured. After her release that same month, the family returned to the capital to live. There, Sara Cristina had obtained a job as a photographer for FENASTRAS, one of the country's largest and most active trade unions. Because FENASTRAS took positions critical of the armed forces, it was labelled a "front for FMLN". In 1989, threats against FENASTRAS were common and its members were accused in the media of having organizational links to FMLN. A month before the disappearance of Sara Cristina and Juan Francisco, a paid advertisement in the newspaper *El Diario de Hoy* blamed leaders of FMLN, priests Ignacio Ellacuría and Segundo Montes and leaders of FENASTRAS for the country's destruction by terrorism. The same advertisement asked President Cristiani to institute the death penalty and summary trials for these people.

Such characterizations, and the persecution of members of the trade union movement in general, added to the years of confrontation between FENASTRAS and the armed forces, created a situation in which the armed forces viewed anyone belonging to FENASTRAS as suspect. As a result, FENASTRAS members and persons linked to the trade union movement were generally considered by the Salvadorian authorities to be a threat to the security of the State.

The arrests

On Saturday, 18 August, Sara Cristina spent the entire morning at FENASTRAS. She then took a bus to go and visit Juan Francisco, who worked at the LIDO factory on the Boulevard del Ejército. She met him and they set off on foot towards San Salvador. The young people lived in the Santa Lucía district, near Juan Francisco's work.

As they passed the Reprocentro commercial factory, 2.5 kilometres from the capital, six air force members stopped them in front of the main factory gate. The soldiers were armed with M-16 rifles and wore red berets with the air force metal badge. Three of them were in olive-green uniform, the others in camouflage.

Air force motor patrols and soldiers on foot were a common sight. The air force maintained checkpoints and patrols on the Boulevard del Ejército, near its base, 24 hours a day. It also had soldiers stationed inside several commercial firms located on the Boulevard, close to the base.

Between 6 and 6.30 p.m., several people travelling past the place recognized Sara Cristina and Juan Francisco. The first to go by was a colleague from work who recognized the two detainees, got out of the vehicle in which he was travelling and returned to San Salvador to report the arrests to FENASTRAS. Minutes later, two colleagues went by in a minibus; when they realized that the two had been arrested, they too got out and returned to the city. Febe Elizabeth Vásquez, General Secretary of FENASTRAS, also drove by; she witnessed the arrest and returned to the office to inform her colleagues.

According to the log of incoming and outgoing vehicles kept by the Paratroop Battalion, a driver left at 6.50 p.m. to drop off patrols on the Boulevard. Others also left to patrol the Boulevard at this time. 341/

According to testimony, one of the soldiers asked Sara Cristina and Juan Francisco for their identity papers, while others stood guard. Other witnesses said that the soldiers had surrounded them and had placed them against a wall with their hands in the air, directly in front of the Reprocentro factory.

Some people were waiting for a bus nearby and must have witnessed the arrest. Out of fear, they did not approach, but they commented that the soldiers "had some detainees over there". That is what people usually said in those days.

The Paratroop Battalion was in charge of patrolling the Boulevard del Ejército and, that day, its third squadron was the unit assigned to guard the Boulevard. The officer in charge was Captain Oscar Arnulfo Díaz Amaya. In August 1989, some six or eight air force members were on duty 24 hours a day at the Reprocentro factory. These soldiers had orders to stay inside the factory premises. The air force did not provide the Commission on the Truth with the names of the officers of the unit which was guarding that company. The arrests were reported immediately to FENASTRAS which telephoned the media to report the incident. A FENASTRAS member left within 15 minutes to investigate; when he arrived on the scene, the young people were still being held. Later, two other people drove to the place, but the young people were no longer there. A total of five people witnessed the arrests.

The soldiers allegedly took Sara Cristina and Juan Francisco to the air force barracks, although no one saw a military vehicle at the scene. Lieutenant Colonel René Alcides Rodríguez Hurtado, Commander of the Paratroop Battalion at the time, told the Commission that, when Battalion troops made arrests, the normal procedure was to communicate with the duty officer through the air force base radio station; a vehicle would then be sent to bring the detainees to the base, where they would be interrogated. Following interrogation, the detainee was either released or handed over to the Treasury Police, the National Police or the National Guard. Lieutenant Colonel Rodríguez Hurtado, who was chief duty officer at the time, did not record the arrest of Sara Cristina and Juan Francisco. 342/ When FENASTRAS telephoned the air force to find out whether they had been transferred to the barracks, the duty commander denied that any arrest had been reported.

Efforts made by relatives

The next day, Sara Cristina's mother was informed of her daughter's arrest. Juan Francisco's family, however, learnt of the arrests the same day, through a relative.

According to testimony, on Monday, 20 August, a representative of the Human Rights Commission of El Salvador who was at the Ilopango air force base investigating the arrests of Sara Cristina and Juan Francisco said that he had been informed that the young people had been arrested by members of the air force, but that they had already been handed over to the Treasury Police central barracks. A sister of Juan Francisco and a FENASTRAS lawyer also went to the air force base but were not allowed in. The Paratroop Battalion log of incoming and outgoing vehicles for the period from 18 to 20 August 1989, however, has no entry concerning the detainees. 343/

From that moment on, the authorities systematically denied even the fact that the arrests had occurred, and hence all knowledge of the victims' whereabouts and fate. That same day, Monday, 20 August, Sara Cristina's mother had gone to the Ilopango air force base to ask about her daughter. The soldier on duty took out a list and then went to call another officer. A few minutes later, an officer by the name of Flores arrived. He told the mother to "do me a big favour, tell those FENASTRAS people to stop putting that propaganda on television. We don't have them".

From that moment on, Sara Cristina's mother found herself embarked on a futile quest. She went to various military and police departments around the city in search of information; from the National Police to the air force; from the air force to the Treasury Police; from the Treasury Police to the air force. All her efforts were in vain.

Juan Francisco's sister also went to the Treasury Police, where she was told that the air force had not transferred anyone. Returning to the air force base, she was told that she had been misinformed and the air force had not arrested anyone by the name of Juan Francisco Massi or Sara Cristina Chan Chan.

Sara Cristina's mother went to the air force a third time, at 8 a.m., on Tuesday, 21 August, where they insisted that she look for her daughter at the National Guard barracks. From there, she went round in circles again: from the National Guard to the Treasury Police; from the Treasury Police to the National Police; from the National Police to the Treasury Police; from the Treasury Police to the National Guard. Again, all her efforts were in vain.

On Wednesday, 22 August, she returned to the air force base, accompanied by a FENASTRAS lawyer. At the entrance to the base, she met Juan Francisco's father, who was taking similar steps to find his son.

The same air force officer dealt with them. This time, he told Sara Cristina's mother that if she came back one more time, "the same thing would happen to her", in other words, they might make her disappear. The officer denied the arrests, but took the opportunity to tell them that Juan Francisco was an FMLN commander and that young people who joined the guerrillas often died.

Since the mother insisted that various people had witnessed the arrests by members of the air force a few days earlier, another officer was finally called in; he took the mother to the *bartolinas*. She inspected six cells, but saw neither Sara Cristina nor Juan Francisco. The officer shouted, "Don't come back unless you want this to happen to you!" Out of fear, she never returned.

On Thursday, 23 August, Sara Cristina's younger sister went to the air force base, accompanied by a lawyer. The officer who dealt with them said to her: "You must be her sister, you look a lot like her. But we don't have her. Stop coming here to ask about her, because we don't have her here!" Sara Cristina's sister returned to the air force base with a sister of Juan Francisco on Friday, 24 August. Despite her pleas, the soldiers again denied the arrests.

The families of Sara Cristina and Juan Francisco left

no stone unturned: they put paid advertisements in the newspaper demanding the release of both young people; 344/ they made countless visits to hospitals, cemeteries and police and military departments; they filed complaints with the (governmental) Human Rights Commission, the (non-governmental) Human Rights Commission, the Archdiocesan Legal Protection Office, the International Committee of the Red Cross (ICRC) and other human rights bodies; and they filed writs of *habeas corpus* with the Supreme Court. 345/

Letters were also sent to the Legislative Assembly and the Ministry of Justice. Two members of the Assembly informed Sara Cristina's mother that the young people's names were recorded in the air force's internal prisoner logs and that they were being held in the cellar of the air force barracks. The arrest and transfer to Ilopango air force base were thus confirmed.

The Director of the Archdiocesan Legal Protection Office sent letters to the Director-General of the Treasury Police at the time, Colonel Héctor Heriberto Hernández; the Commander of the air force, Colonel Juan Rafael Bustillo; the Chief of the Armed Forces Joint Staff at the time, Colonel René Emilio Ponce; the Minister of Defence and Public Security at the time, General Rafael Humberto Larios López; the Vice-Minister for Public Security, Colonel Inocente Orlando Montano; and the Vice-Minister for Defence, Colonel Juan Orlando Zepeda.

The only reply received was from the Treasury Police. In a letter dated 23 August 1989, Colonel Héctor Heriberto Hernández replied that he had "painstakingly" searched "the archives" and that Juan Francisco and Sara Cristina were not being held and had not been held by that body. 346/

The governmental Human Rights Commission searched for Sara Cristina and Juan Francisco at the air force base, the Artillery Brigade, the Cavalry Regiment, the National Police central barracks, the National Guard, the Treasury Police, the First Infantry Brigade, the Fourth Infantry Brigade and Military Detachment No. 1. 347/ These efforts proved fruitless and the investigation was apparently limited to asking the officer in charge of each unit to fill out a form stating that he was not holding the young people. The Human Rights Commission finally stated that it had been unable to find out any information on the case.

The Commission on the Truth asked the air force, the National Police, the Treasury Police and the National Guard for information on all the people arrested by them during the period from 16 to 20 August. It also asked for the list of people transferred from the air force to the other security forces during that week. The air force transmitted the list of people arrested by its units during the period from

16 to 20 August 1989; however, the list was not the original, but a typewritten copy, and listed only six people as having been arrested on 17 August. There was no record of the arrest of Sara Cristina or Juan Francisco. 348/

The National Police transmitted a list of people arrested by its units during the period from 17 to 19 August 1989. This list, a typewritten copy of the names of several people arrested on those days, also contained no record of the arrest of Sara Cristina or Juan Francisco. 349/ The National Guard transmitted copies of the pages of the book in which it kept a record of people arrested on 17, 18, 19 and 20 August. There was no record of Sara Cristina or Juan Francisco. It stated that, on those days, "no one was transferred to it from the Salvadorian air force". 350/

The Massi family received several telegrams telling them to go to the National Police to get Juan Francisco. Juan Francisco's father established a relationship with an individual who allegedly belonged to the National Police and who told him that his son was at the police barracks in the Monserrat district and that he could communicate with him. According to that source, his son had injuries from the blows he had received and needed clothes and money. Although Juan Francisco's father took him food, clothing and money, he was never allowed to see him. He was told that Juan Francisco was in bad shape and that he had to wait until the young man was better. The father stayed in contact with the policeman until 1991, but Juan Francisco never appeared. Finally, the family gave up the search.

A month after the disappearance of Sara Cristina and Juan Francisco, on 18 September 1989, Sara Cristina's mother took part in a demonstration organized by FENASTRAS to demand the release of the two young people. Along with 63 other people, she was arrested by members of the National Police and transferred to the central barracks. She was threatened, beaten and tortured. The next month, her younger daughter was injured when a bomb exploded at FENASTRAS headquarters. After this last incident, the mother stopped looking for her daughter.

The official investigations

The military authorities, the Government and the judiciary all refused to investigate the incident. Because of the publicity surrounding the case, however, the air force asked then Lieutenant Edgardo Ernesto Echeverría, Chief of the C-II Tactical Support Division, to carry out an internal investigation. Lieutenant Echeverría questioned the soldiers in his division and, upon receiving negative replies, reported that no one in his unit had seen the two young people.

In testimony before the Commission, Lieutenant Echeverría described the investigation as "a bureaucratic investigation", confined to asking questions orally. He said that such cases had been common during the two years in which he worked in the intelligence division. The air force commander or chief had requested internal investigations on various occasions, and Lieutenant Echeverría could not recall a single case in which the air force had admitted responsibility.

Findings

The Commission finds the following:

1. There is full evidence that members of the air force arrested Sara Cristina Chan Chan and Juan Francisco Massi.

2. There is sufficient evidence that the detainees were transferred to the air force base.

3. There is sufficient evidence that they disappeared while in the custody of the air force, and there is no evidence that they are still alive.

4. There is full evidence of a cover-up by air force personnel, who denied the arrests of Sara Cristina Chan Chan and Juan Francisco Massi.

5. The judiciary and the police investigation units which have so far refused to act must launch a special investigation into the air force to clear up the circumstances of the arrest and subsequent disappearance of the two young people. The Commission on the Truth considers it unacceptable that people seeking evidence in this case, which is typical of many such cases of disappearance, have been denied access to individuals or archives. It is incumbent on the judiciary, headed by the Supreme Court of Justice, to open this exhaustive investigation into the air force. As the expression of Salvadorian society, the State has an obligation to history to investigate the incident in a transparent manner, to punish the culprits and to compensate the families of the young victims Sara Cristina Chan Chan and Juan Francisco Massi.

C. Massacres of peasants by the armed forces

In 1980, 1981 and 1982, several massacres of peasants were carried out by troops of the armed forces of El Salvador. An account of three of them follows.

1. Illustrative case: El Mozote

Summary of the case

On 10 December 1981, in the village of El Mozote in the Department of Morazán, units of the Atlacatl Battalion detained, without resistance, all the men, women and children who were in the place. The following day, 11 December, after spending the night locked in their homes, they were deliberately and systematically executed in groups. First, the men were tortured and executed, then the women were executed and, lastly, the children, in the place where they had been locked up. The number of victims identified was over 200. The figure is higher if other unidentified victims are taken into account.

These events occurred in the course of an anti-guerrilla action known as "Operación Rescate" in which, in addition to the Atlacatl Battalion, units from the Third Infantry Brigade and the San Francisco Gotera Commando Training Centre took part.

In the course of "Operación Rescate", massacres of civilians also occurred in the following places: 11 December, more than 20 people in La Joya canton; 12 December, some 30 people in the village of La Ranchería; the same day, by units of the Atlacatl Battalion, the inhabitants of the village of Los Toriles; and 13 December, the inhabitants of the village of Jocote Amarillo and Cerro Pando canton. More than 500 identified victims perished at El Mozote and in the other villages. Many other victims have not been identified.

We have accounts of these massacres provided by eyewitnesses and by other witnesses who later saw the bodies, which were left unburied. In the case of El Mozote, the accounts were fully corroborated by the results of the 1992 exhumation of the remains.

Despite the public complaints of a massacre and the ease with which they could have been verified, the Salvadorian authorities did not order an investigation and consistently denied that the massacre had taken place.

The Minister of Defence and the Chief of the Armed Forces Joint Staff have denied to the Commission on the Truth that they have any information that would make it possible to identify the units and officers who participated in "Operación Rescate". They say that there are no records for the period.

The President of the Supreme Court has interfered in a biased and political way in the judicial proceedings on the massacre instituted in 1990.

Description of the facts

Village of El Mozote

On the afternoon of 10 December 1981, units of the Atlacatl Rapid Deployment Infantry Battalion (BIRI) arrived in the village of El Mozote, Department of Morazán, after a clash with guerrillas in the vicinity.

The village consisted of about 20 houses situated on open ground around a square. Facing onto the square was a church and behind it a small building known as "the convent", used by the priest to change into his vestments when he came to the village to celebrate mass. Not far from the village was a school, the Grupo Escolar.

When the soldiers arrived in the village they found, in addition to the residents, other peasants who were refugees from the surrounding areas. They ordered every-

one out of the houses and into the square; they made them lie face down, searched them and asked them about the guerrillas. They then ordered them to lock themselves in their houses until the next day, warning that anyone coming out would be shot. The soldiers remained in the village during the night.

Early next morning, 11 December, the soldiers reassembled the entire population in the square. They separated the men from the women and children and locked everyone up in different groups in the church, the convent and various houses.

During the morning, they proceeded to interrogate, torture and execute the men in various locations. Around noon, they began taking out the women in groups, separating them from their children and machine-gunning them. Finally, they killed the children. A group of children who had been locked in the convent were machine-gunned through the windows. After exterminating the entire population, the soldiers set fire to the buildings.

The soldiers remained in El Mozote that might. The next day, they went through the village of Los Toriles, situated 2 kilometres away. Some of the inhabitants managed to escape. The others, men, women and children, were taken from their homes, lined up and machine-gunned.

The victims at El Mozote were left unburied. During the weeks that followed the bodies were seen by many people who passed by there. In Los Toriles, the survivors subsequently buried the bodies.

Background

The Atlacatl Battalion arrived at El Mozote in the course of a military action known as "Operación Rescate", which had begun two days earlier on 6 December and also involved units from the Third Brigade and the San Francisco Gotera Commando Training Centre.

The Atlacatl Battalion was a "Rapid Deployment Infantry Battalion" or "BIRI", that is, a unit specially trained for "counter-insurgency" warfare. It was the first unit of its kind in the armed forces and had completed its training, under the supervision of United States military advisers, at the beginning of that year, 1981.

Nine months before "Operación Rescate" took place, a company of the Atlacatl Battalion, under the command of Captain Juan Ernesto Méndez, had taken part in an anti-guerrilla operation in the same northern zone of Morazán. On that occasion, it had come under heavy attack from guerrillas and had had to withdraw with heavy casualties without achieving its military objective. This setback for the brand new "Rapid Deployment Infantry Battalion" made it the butt of criticism and jokes by officers of other units, who nicknamed it the "Rapid Retreat Infantry Battalion".

The goal of "Operación Rescate" was to eliminate the guerrilla presence in a small sector in northern Morazán, where the guerrillas had a camp and a training centre at a place called La Guacamaya.

Colonel Jaime Flórez Grijalva, Commander of the Third Brigade, was responsible for overseeing the operation. Lieutenant Colonel Domingo Monterrosa Barrios, Commander of the Atlacatl BIRI, was in command of the units taking part.

On 9 December, clashes took place between Government troops and the guerrillas. That same day, a company of the Atlacatl BIRI entered the town of Arambala. They rounded up the population in the town square and separated the men from the women and children. They locked the women and children in the church and ordered the men to lie face down in the square. A number of men were accused of being guerrilla collaborators. They were tied up, blindfolded and tortured. Residents later found the bodies of three of them, stabbed to death.

In Cumaro canton as well, residents were rounded up in the main square by Atlacatl units on the morning of 10 December. There, however, no one was killed.

There is sufficient evidence that units of the Atlacatl BIRI participated in all these actions. In the course of "Operación Rescate", however, other mass executions were carried out by units which it has not been possible to identify with certainty.

In all instances, troops acted in the same way: they killed anyone they came across, men, women and children, and then set fire to the houses. This is what happened in La Joya canton on 11 December, in the village of La Ranchería on 12 December, and in the village of Jocote Amarillo and Cerro Pando canton on 13 December.

Subsequent events

The El Mozote massacre became public knowledge on 27 January 1982, when *The New York Times* and *The Washington Post* published articles by Raymond Bonner and Alma Guillermoprieto, respectively, reporting the massacre. In January, they had visited the scene of the massacre and had seen the bodies and the ruined houses.

In the course of the year, a number of human rights organizations denounced the massacre. The Salvadorian authorities categorically denied that a massacre had taken place. No judicial investigation was launched and there was no word of any investigation by the Government or the armed forces.

On 26 October 1990, on a criminal complaint brought by Pedro Chicas Romero, criminal proceedings were instituted in the San Francisco Gotera Court of the First Instance. During the trial, which is still going on, statements were taken from witnesses for the prosecution; eventually, the remains were ordered exhumed, and this provided irrefutable evidence of the El Mozote massacre. The judge asked the Government repeatedly for a list of the officers who took part in the military operation. He received the reply that the Government did not have such information.

The results of the exhumation

The exhumation of the remains in the ruins of the little building known as the convent, adjacent to the El Mozote church, took place between 13 and 17 November 1992.

The material found in the convent was analysed by expert anthropologists and then studied in minute detail in the laboratories of the Santa Tecla Institute of Forensic Medicine and of the Commission for the Investigation of Criminal Acts by Dr. Clyde Snow (forensic anthropologist), Dr. Robert H. Kirschner (forensic pathologist), Dr. Douglas Scott (archaeologist and ballistics analyst), and Dr. John Fitzpatrick (radiologist), in collaboration with the Argentine Team of Forensic Anthropologists made up of Patricia Bernardi, Mercedes Doretti and Luis Fondebrider.

The study made by the experts led to the following conclusions:

1. "All the skeletons recovered from the site and the associated evidence were deposited during the same temporal event ...". 351/ The physical evidence recovered in the site excludes the possibility that the site could have been used as a clandestine cemetery in which the dead were placed at different times.

2. "The events under investigation are unlikely to have occurred later than 1981". 352/ Coins and bullet cartridges bearing their date of manufacture were found in the convent. In no case was this date later than 1981.

3. In the convent, bone remains of at least 143 people were found. 353/ However, the laboratory analysis indicates that "there may, in fact, have been a greater number of deaths. This uncertainty regarding the number of skeletons is a reflection of the extensive perimortem skeletal injuries, postmortem skeletal damage and associated commingling. Many young infants may have been entirely cremated; other children may not have been counted because of extensive fragmentation of body parts". 354/

4. The bone remains and other evidence found in the convent show numerous signs of damage caused by crushing and by fire.

5. Most of the victims were minors.

The experts determined, initially, after the exhumation, that "approximately 85 per cent of the 117 victims were children under 12 years of age", 355/ and indicated that a more precise estimate of the victims' ages would be made in the laboratory. 356/

In the laboratory, the skeletal remains of 143 bodies were identified, including 131 children under the age of 12, 5 adolescents and 7 adults. The experts noted, in addition, that "the average age of the children was approximately 6 years". 357/

6. One of the victims was a pregnant woman. 358/

7. Although it could not be determined with certainty that all the victims were alive when they were brought into the convent, "it can be concluded that at least some of the victims were struck by bullets, with an effect that may well have been lethal, inside the building". 359/

This conclusion is based on various factors:

(1) A "large quantity of bullet fragments [were] found inside the building ...". 360/ "Virtually all the ballistic evidence was found at level 3, in direct contact with or imbedded in the bone remains, clothing, household goods and floor of the building". 361/ Moreover, "the spatial distribution of most of the bullet fragments coincides with the area of greatest concentration of skeletons and with concentrations of bone remains". 362/ Also, the second and third areas of concentration of bullet fragments coincide with the second and third areas of concentration of skeletons, respectively.

(2) "Of 117 skeletons identified in the field, 67 were associated with bullet fragments. In 43 out of this subtotal of 67, the fragments were found in the areas of the skull and/or the thorax, i.e., parts of the body where they could have been the cause of death." 363/

(3) "In at least nine cases, the victims were shot inside the building while lying in a horizontal position on the floor. The shots were fired downwards. In at least six of the nine cases mentioned, these shots could have caused the victims' deaths." 364/

(4) "Direct skeletal examination showed intact gunshot wounds of entrance in only a few skulls because of the extensive fracturing that is characteristically associated with such high-velocity injuries. Skull reconstruction identified many more entrance wounds, but relatively few exit wounds. This is consistent with the ballistic evidence that the ammunition involved in the shootings was of a type likely to fragment upon impact, becoming essentially frangible bullets. Radiologic examination of skull bones demonstrated small metallic densities consistent with bullet fragments in 45.2 per cent (51/115).

In long bones, vertebrae, pelvis and ribs there were defects characteristic of high velocity gunshot wounds." 365/

(5) The weapons used to fire at the victims were M-16 rifles.

As the ballistics analyst described, "two hundred forty-five cartridge cases recovered from the El Mozote site were studied. Of these, 184 had discernible headstamps, identifying the ammunition as having been manufactured for the United States Government at Lake City, Missouri. Thirty-four cartridges were sufficiently well preserved to analyse for individual as well as class characteristics. All of the projectiles except one appear to have been fired from United States-manufactured M-16 rifles". 366/

(6) At least 24 people participated in the shooting. 367/ They fired "from within the house, from the doorway, and probably through a window to the right of the door". 368/

An important point that emerges from the results of the observations is that "no bullet fragments were found in the outside west facade of the stone wall". 369/

The evidence presented above is full proof that the victims were summarily executed, as the witnesses have testified.

The experts who carried out the exhumation reached the following conclusion: "All these facts tend to indicate the perpetration of a massive crime, there being no evidence to support the theory of a confrontation between two groups". 370/

For their part, the experts who conducted the laboratory analysis said that "the physical evidence from the exhumation of the convent house at El Mozote confirms the allegations of a mass murder". 371/ They went on to say, on the same point: "There is no evidence to support the contention that these victims, almost all young children, were involved in combat or were caught in the crossfire of combat forces. Rather the evidence strongly supports the conclusion that they were the intentional victims of a mass extra-judicial execution". 372/

Action by the Commission

Before the Commission on the Truth began its work, the Director of the Human Rights Division of the United Nations Observer Mission in El Salvador (ONUSAL) brought a motion before the judge hearing the case to have qualified foreign experts appointed.

The Commission on the Truth, from the moment it was set up, took a special interest in having the exhumation conducted under conditions that guaranteed the necessary scientific rigour and impartiality.

The Commission also reviewed the available publications, documentation and court records. It took testimony directly from eyewitnesses and was present at the exhumation site.

The Commission wrote three times to the Minister of Defence and once to the Chief of the Armed Forces Joint Staff requesting information about the units and officers who took part in "Operación Rescate", and about any orders, reports or other documents relating to that operation that might be in the archives. The only response it received was that there were no records for that period.

Special mention must be made of the interference in the case by the President of the Supreme Court of El Salvador, Mr. Mauricio Gutiérrez Castro. When on 17 July 1991 representatives of the Legal Protection Office asked the trial judge to appoint qualified foreign experts to conduct the exhumations, he told them that this would require the approval of Mr. Gutiérrez Castro. It was not until nine months later, on 29 April 1992, after ONUSAL stepped in, that he proceeded to appoint them.

On 16 July 1992, when the members of the Commission on the Truth went to see him, Mr. Gutiérrez Castro said that the exhumation ordered by the trial judge would prove that "only dead guerrillas are buried" at El Mozote.

A few days later, the court hearing the case ruled that its appointment of foreign experts was not valid without a complicated procedure of consultation with foreign Governments through the Supreme Court of Justice, with the result that the exhumation was on the point of going ahead without the presence of such experts.

On 21 October, Mr. Mauricio Gutiérrez Castro came to the exhumation site and, in giving his opinion on how future excavations in the zone should be carried out, said that care should be taken not to "favour one of the parties" (presumably the Government and FMLN) "because of the political implications of this process, which override legal considerations".

Findings

There is full proof that on 11 December 1981, in the village of El Mozote, units of the Atlacatl Battalion deliberately and systematically killed a group of more than 200 men, women and children, constituting the entire civilian population that they had found there the previous day and had since been holding prisoner.

The officers in command of the Atlacatl Battalion at the time of the operation whom the Commission has managed to identify are the following: Battalion Commander: Lieutenant Colonel Domingo Monterrosa Barrios (deceased); Commanding Officer: Major Natividad de Jesús Cáceres Cabrera (now Colonel); Chief of Operations: Major José Armando Azmitia Melara (deceased); Company Commanders: Juan Ernesto Méndez Rodríguez (now Colonel); Roberto Alfonso Mendoza Portillo (deceased); José Antonio Rodríguez Molina (now Lieutenant Colonel), Captain Walter Oswaldo Salazar (now Lieutenant Colonel) and José Alfredo Jiménez (currently a fugitive from justice).

There is sufficient evidence that in the days preceding and following the El Mozote massacre, troops participating in "Operación Rescate" massacred the non-combatant civilian population in La Joya canton, in the villages of La Ranchería, Jocote Amarillo y Los Toriles, and in Cerro Pando canton.

Participating in this operation, in addition to the Atlacatl Battalion, were units of the Third Infantry Brigade, commanded by Colonel Jaime Flórez Grijalba (now retired) who was also responsible for supervising the operation, and units from the San Francisco Gotera Commando Training Centre commanded by Colonel Alejandro Cisneros (now retired).

Although it received news of the massacre, which would have been easy to corroborate because of the profusion of unburied bodies, the Armed Forces High Command did not conduct or did not give any word of an investigation and repeatedly denied that the massacre had occurred. There is full evidence that General José Guillermo García, then Minister of Defence, initiated no investigations that might have enabled the facts to be established. There is sufficient evidence that General Rafael Flórez Lima, Chief of the Armed Forces Joint Staff at the time, was aware that the massacre had occurred and also failed to undertake any investigation.

The High Command also took no steps whatsoever to prevent the repetition of such acts, with the result that the same units were used in other operations and followed the same procedures.

The El Mozote massacre was a serious violation of international humanitarian law and international human rights law.

The President of the Supreme Court of Justice of El Salvador, Mr. Mauricio Gutiérrez Castro, has interfered unduly and prejudicially, for biased political reasons, in the ongoing judicial proceedings on the case.

The Commission recommends that the competent authorities implement the recommendations made in the experts' reports . . .

2. *Sumpul river*

Summary of the case

On 14 May 1990, units of Military Detachment No. 1, the National Guard and the paramilitary Organización Nacional Democrática (ORDEN) deliberately killed at least 300 non-combatants, including women and children, who were trying to flee to Honduras across the Sumpul river beside the hamlet of Las Aradas, Department of Chalatenango. The massacre was made possible by the cooperation of the Honduran armed forces, who prevented the Salvadorian villagers from landing on the other side.

The Salvadorian military operation had begun the previous day as an anti-guerrilla operation. Troops advanced from various points, gradually converging on the hamlet of Las Aradas on the banks of the Sumpul river. In the course of the operation, there had been a number of encounters with the guerrillas.

There is sufficient evidence that, as they advanced, Government forces committed acts of violence against the population, and this caused numerous people to flee, many of whom congregated in the hamlet, consisting of some dozen houses.

Troops attacked the hamlet with artillery and fire from two helicopters. The villagers and other people displaced by the operation attempted to cross the Sumpul river to take refuge in Honduras. Honduran troops deployed on the opposite bank of the river barred their way. They were then killed by Salvadorian troops who fired on them in cold blood.

Description of the facts

Background

In 1970, when the so-called "Soccer War" between Honduras and El Salvador ended, a demilitarized zone was established comprising a strip of land three kilometres wide on each side of the border. The zone was monitored by an observer mission of the Organization of American States. The armed forces of both countries were prohibited from entering the zone.

When the conflict in El Salvador began, many Salvadorian peasants took refuge in Honduras, where they set up camps. When anti-guerrilla actions increased in early 1980, a large number of Salvadorian peasants crossed the border, leaving a number of villages, including Las Aradas, almost deserted. The Honduran Government became increasingly concerned as Salvadorian refugees entered and remained in Honduras. It should be recalled that one of the reasons for the war between the two countries had been the settlement of Salvadorian peasants in border areas in Honduran territory.

The Salvadorian Government, for its part, believed that the demilitarized zone and Honduran territory were serving as a base of operations and a refuge for guerrillas whose activities had intensified in the adjacent area, in the north of the Department of Chalatenango.

A large part of the peasant population in the zone also belonged to the Federación de Trabajadores del Campo, which had joined the struggle for agrarian reform and was viewed by the Salvadorian Government as a guerrilla support organization.

In the last two weeks of March 1980, Honduran authorities put pressure on the refugees to return to their country. A group of refugees returned to Las Aradas.

Anti-guerrilla operations by the Government of El Salvador continued in the zone. After the villagers' return to Las Aradas and before the May massacre, National Guard and ORDEN troops, who were able to enter the zone freely, twice advanced as far as Las Aradas. On both occasions, residents fled across the river to Honduran territory.

On 5 May, nine days before the massacre, Honduran and Salvadorian military leaders met on the border,

according to the Honduran press, to work out a way of preventing Salvadorian guerrillas from entering Honduras. A few days later, Honduran soldiers again put pressure on Salvadorian refugees and a group of them returned to Las Aradas.

When the operation which would lead to the massacre began a week later, many fleeing peasants converged on Las Aradas, confident that from there they would be able to cross the hanging bridge over the Sumpul river, which was running high because of the rainy season, and take refuge in Honduran territory. They also hoped that Salvadorian soldiers would not enter the demilitarized zone.

Subsequent events

The armies of the two countries left the zone that same day. The National Guard continued to patrol the area to prevent residents from returning. The bodies were not buried.

In Honduras, the massacre received extensive media coverage. The first news report was transmitted on 21 May by a morning news programme on Radio Noticias del Continente, which operates out of Costa Rica. A few days later, the newspaper *Tiempo* published an interview with Father Roberto Yalaga, a priest in the diocese of Santa Rosa de Copán, who confirmed that at least 325 Salvadorians had been killed by the army and that a Honduran military detachment had cordoned off the bank of the Sumpul river.

Two foreign journalists, Gabriel Sanhuesa and Ursula Ferdinand, managed to get to Las Aradas from the Honduran side and obtain visual evidence of the massacre. They also managed to interview a number of survivors who had taken refuge in Honduran border villages. They published a leaflet on the incident.

A formal complaint about the massacre was filed by the priests and nuns of the Honduran diocese of Santa Rosa de Copán on 19 June 1980, signed by the diocese's 38 pastoral workers. The complaint was based on the visual evidence and the testimony gathered by the diocese as part of its investigations.

The complaint accused the Government and the armed forces of the Republic of Honduras of complicity in the massacre and in the subsequent cover-up and the Organization of American States (OAS) of complicity in covering up the tragic event. This accusation was endorsed by the entire Honduran Conference of Bishops, headed by the Archbishop of Tegucigalpa, Monsignor Héctor E. Santos, in a statement published by the press on 1 July 1980. From El Salvador, the Archdiocese of San Salvador endorsed and associated itself with the complaint by the diocese of Santa Rosa de Copán, in a communiqué published on 29 June 1980.

The Minister of Defence of El Salvador, General José Guillermo García, denied that the massacre had occurred. A year later, in an interview, he admitted that a number of people had died in a clash on 14 May 1980 at the Sumpul river, but said that the number of deaths had been greatly exaggerated. 373/

In October 1980, President José Napoleón Duarte, in an interview with the Canadian publication *United Church Observer*, acknowledged that a military operation had taken place in the Sumpul river area and said that some 300 people, all of them "communist guerrillas", had died. 374/

The charges made by the diocese of Santa Rosa de Copán were also denied in an official statement issued by the Government and armed forces of Honduras describing the accusations as libellous and irresponsible. 375/ The Honduran President, Policarpo Paz, denied the truth of the complaint in a speech broadcast on national radio and television. The Minister of Government, Colonel Cristóbal Díaz García, told the press that Honduras would not set up any commission of investigation. Replying to a question, he said that no one doubted that there had been a massacre on the other side of the river, but that Honduras had not been involved.

Colonel Alfonso Rodríguez Rincón, Chief of the OAS observers, dismissed the accusation by the Honduran Church as the product of an overactive imagination. He said that as Chief of the observers, he could confirm that they had known nothing about the incident. He added that there were numerous operations on the Salvadorian side and it was conceivable that many guerrillas had been killed; he wondered whether the incident was perhaps being confused with another one.

However, the Commission found out that OAS observers did report a major clash between Salvadorian troops and FMLN guerrillas as having occurred between 14 and 16 May 1980 on the border in that region. According to their report, over 200 people had been killed and some civilians had been caught in the crossfire, but there was no evidence that innocent civilians had been massacred.

On 26 October 1992, surviving witnesses of the Sumpul river massacre filed a judicial complaint with the Chalatenango Court of First Instance, which was declared admissible under the title "on verifying the murder of 600 people". 376/

Action taken by the Commission

The Commission received some 100 direct testimonies on the incident and examined an equivalent number of testimonies presented to other organizations. It examined the documentation available, including photographs, and interviewed the original complainants. A Commission official travelled to Honduras to gather direct testimony. Members of the Commission personally inspected the scene of the massacre.

The Commission repeatedly requested the cooperation of the Salvadorian military authorities in conducting the investigation, but the only reply it received was that there were no records for that period. The Commander of Military Detachment No. 1 at the time, Colonel Ricardo Augusto Peña Arbaiza, was summonsed to testify but did not appear.

Findings

There is substantial evidence that on 13 and 14 May 1980, troops from Military Detachment No. 1 and members of the National Guard and of the paramilitary Organización Nacional Demócratica (ORDEN), backed by the air force, massacred no less than 300 unarmed civilians on the banks of the Sumpul river.

The Commission believes that the Salvadorian military authorities were guilty of a cover-up of the incident. There is sufficient evidence that Colonel Ricardo Augusto Peña Arbaiza, Commander of Military Detachment No. 1 in May 1980, made no serious investigation of the incident.

The Sumpul river massacre was a serious violation of international humanitarian law and international human rights law.

3. El Calabozo

Summary of the case

On 22 August 1982, in the place known as El Calabozo situated beside the Amatitán river in the north of the Department of San Vicente, troops of the Atlacatl Rapid Deployment Infantry Battalion (BIRI) killed over 200 men, women and children whom they were holding prisoner.

The victims had converged on El Calabozo from various directions, fleeing a vast anti-guerrilla military operation which had begun three days earlier in the area of Los Cerros de San Pedro and which involved, in addition to the Atlacatl BIRI, other infantry, artillery and aerial support units.

There was a major guerrilla presence, supported by the local population, in the area of the operation. Government forces had penetrated the area on earlier occasions, but the guerrillas had avoided combat. This time the operation, which bore the name "Teniente Coronel Mario Azenón Palma", involved some 6,000 troops and was designed to clear the area of guerrillas. As the troops advanced, the civilian population fled, fearing the shelling and the soldiers' violence. One of the places where a large number of fugitives congregated was El Calabozo.

According to witnesses, the fugitives were surprised

by the Atlacatl Battalion unit. Some of them managed to escape; the rest were rounded up and machine-gunned.

The military operation continued for several more days. The Government informed the public that it had been a success: many guerrillas had been killed, camps had been destroyed and weapons and other supplies had been seized.

On 8 September, two weeks after the incident, the massacre was reported in *The Washington Post*. The Minister of Defence, General José Guillermo García, said that an investigation had been made and that no massacre had occurred. He repeated this assertion in an interview with the Commission.

In July 1992, the San Sebastián Mixed Court of First Instance launched a judicial investigation of the incident on the basis of a private complaint.

The Commission received eye witness testimony and examined available documentation. Commission members inspected the scene of the massacre. When the Commission requested information on the military operation, the units which had taken part in it and the outcome of the alleged investigation, the Minister of Defence replied that there were no records for that period.

Findings

There is sufficient evidence that on 22 August 1982, troops of the Atlacatl Battalion deliberately killed over 200 civilians—men, women and children—who had been taken prisoner without offering any resistance. The incident occurred at the place known as El Calabozo, near the canton of Amatitán Abajo, Department of San Vicente.

Although the massacre was reported publicly, the Salvadorian authorities denied it. Despite their claim to have made an investigation, there is absolutely no evidence that such an investigation took place.

The El Calabozo massacre was a serious violation of international humanitarian law and international human rights law.

4. Pattern of conduct

In addition to the massacres described here, the Commission received direct testimony concerning numerous other mass executions that occurred during the years 1980, 1981 and 1982, in which members of the armed forces, in the course of anti-guerrilla operations, executed peasants—men, women and children who had offered no resistance—simply because they considered them to be guerrilla collaborators.

Because the number of such individual and group executions is so high and the reports are so thoroughly substantiated, the Commission rules out any possibility that these might have been isolated incidents where soldiers or their immediate superiors went to extremes.

Everything points to the fact that these deaths formed part of a pattern of conduct, a deliberate strategy of eliminating or terrifying the peasant population in areas where the guerrillas were active, the purpose being to deprive the guerrilla forces of this source of supplies and information and of the possibility of hiding or concealing themselves among that population.

It is impossible to blame this pattern of conduct on local commanders and to claim that senior commanders did not know anything about it. As we have described, massacres of the peasant population were reported repeatedly. There is no evidence that any effort was made to investigate them. The authorities dismissed these reports as enemy propaganda. Were it not for the children's skeletons at El Mozote, some people would still be disputing that such massacres took place.

Those small skeletons are proof not only of the existence of the cold-blooded massacre at El Mozote but also of the collusion of senior commanders of the armed forces, for they show that the evidence of the unburied bodies was there for a long time for anyone who wanted to investigate the facts. In this case, we cannot accept the excuse that senior commanders knew nothing of what had happened.

No action was taken to avoid incidents such as this. On the contrary, the deliberate, systematic and indiscriminate violence against the peasant population in areas of military operations went on for years.

D. Death squad assassinations

1. Illustrative case: Archbishop Romero

Summary of the case

On 24 March 1980, the Archbishop of San Salvador, Monsignor Oscar Arnulfo Romero y Galdámez, was assassinated while celebrating mass in the Chapel of the Hospital de la Divina Providencia.

The Commission finds the following:

1. Former Major Roberto D'Aubuisson gave the order to assassinate the Archbishop and gave precise instructions to members of his security service, acting as a "death squad", to organize and supervise the assassination.

2. Captains Alvaro Saravia and Eduardo Avila, together with Fernando Sagrera and Mario Molina, were actively involved in planning and carrying out the assassination.

3. Amado Antonio Garay, the driver of former Captain Saravia, was assigned to drive the gunman to the Chapel. Mr. Garay was a direct witness when, from a red, four-door Volkswagen, the gunman fired a single high velocity .22 calibre bullet to kill the Archbishop.

4. Walter Antonio "Musa" Alvarez, together with former Captain Saravia, was involved in paying the "fees" of the actual assassin.

5. The failed assassination attempt against Judge Atilio Ramírez Amaya was a deliberate attempt to deter investigation of the case.

6. The Supreme Court played an active role in preventing the extradition of former Captain Saravia from the United States and his subsequent imprisonment in El Salvador. In so doing, it ensured, *inter alia*, impunity for those who planned the assassination.

Description of the facts 377/

The assassination

On Monday, 24 March 1980, the Archbishop of San Salvador, Monsignor Oscar Arnulfo Romero y Galdámez, was celebrating mass 378/ in the Chapel of the Hospital de la Divina Providencia 379/ when he was killed by a professional assassin who fired a single .22 or .223 calibre bullet from a red, four-door Volkswagen vehicle. The bullet hit its mark, causing the Archbishop's death from severe bleeding.

Background

Monsignor Romero had become a well-known critic of violence and injustice and, as such, was perceived in right-wing civilian and military circles as a dangerous enemy. His sermons deeply irritated these circles because they included human rights violations produced by the Archdiocesan Legal Aid Office.

As a result, members of the Government and the armed forces viewed his actions as favouring subversives.

Newspapers criticized him in unequivocally hostile terms, such as "... a demagogic and violent Archbishop ... (who) preached terrorism from his cathedral ...", 380/ or "... the armed forces should begin to oil their weapons (...)". 381/

In his sermon on 17 February 1980, he expressed opposition to United States military aid to El Salvador, pointing out that "(...) neither the (Government) Junta nor the Christian Democrats govern this country. Political power is in the hands of the armed forces which are unscrupulous in their use of this power. They only know how to repress the people and defend the interests of the Salvadorian oligarchy (...)". 382/

That same month, he received death threats 383/ and therefore decided that his colleagues should not accompany him when he went out, so as not to expose themselves to unnecessary risks. 384/ On Monday, 10 March, the day after he had celebrated a mass for Mario Zamora, assassinated on 23 February, 385/ an attaché case was found near the High Altar behind the pulpit, 386/ which the Explosives and Demolition Unit of the National Police found to contain a bomb that had failed to go off. 387/

In his sermon on Sunday, 23 March, the Archbishop appealed to Salvadorian soldiers themselves: "... I beseech you, I beg you, I order you, in the name of God, to stop the repression!". 388/

The official investigation

The investigation to determine who was responsible for the Archbishop's assassination was not only inefficient but also highly controversial and plagued by political motivations. Some of the main elements which the Commission took into account in its own investigation are described below.

Initial inquiries and incidents

The National Police went to the Chapel of the Hospital de la Divina Providencia to gather evidence. They did not do this properly, however, since they failed to collect material evidence of the crime at the scene.

Atilio Ramírez Amaya, the Judge of the Fourth Criminal Court, gave instructions for the Salvadorian Polyclinic to perform an autopsy on the prelate: a small entry wound barely 5 millimetres in diameter in the right thorax indicated the point of entry of the bullet. It had fragmented without exiting the Archbishop's body, causing fatal internal bleeding. Three fragments of the bullet were extracted for further study. 389/ Judge Ramírez Amaya maintained that the bullet used must have been a .22 or similar. 390/ Going by the weight of the fragments, the National Police confirmed that the bullet was a .22 calibre but did not reach any more precise conclusions. 391/ Following an attempt to assassinate him at his home on 27 March, Judge Ramírez Amaya tendered his resignation and left the country. 392/

The "Saravia Diary" and other documents found at the San Luis estate

On 7 May 1980, in a raid on the San Luis estate in Santa Tecla, 12 active and retired military personnel and 12 civilians, 393/ including former Major Roberto D'Aubuisson, who had gathered there were arrested and formally accused of plotting to overthrow the Government by means of a coup d'état. 394/

The documents seized during the raid included a "List of accusations made by a South American informant against Monsignor Oscar Arnulfo Romero, Archbishop of San Salvador. Informant is prepared to provide filmed and written evidence within a period not exceeding 15 days", 395/ a diary belonging to former Captain Alvaro Rafael Saravia and two lists of names of commanders and officers (of the Salvadorian armed forces). 396/

The "Saravia Diary" contained various important pieces of information concerning the assassination of Monsignor Romero. It referred to purchases and deliveries of large quantities of arms and ammunition, some of which, based on the ballistic study made by Judge Ramírez Amaya, were of the type used in the assassination. 397/ In addition, several names which appeared over and over again in the diary were of people concerning whose involvement in planning, carrying out or covering up the assassination the Commission has already received sufficient evidence. 398/ Other details include the name "Amado"— Amado Garay, the driver assigned to drive the assassin— and receipts for petrol purchased for a red vehicle used by former Captain Saravia.

A third document, entitled "General Framework for the Organization of the Anti-Marxist Struggle in El Salvador", reflected the approach and objectives of the San Luis group. Their goal was to seize power in El Salvador and their political plan provided for "direct action", so-called "activities of combat networks", including "attacks on selected individuals". 399/

None of the documents seized at the San Luis estate was made available to the Judge of the Fourth Criminal Court, and it was only years later that the court gained access to a copy of the diary. The Judge's efforts to locate the original diary proved unsuccessful.

The accusations by former Major D'Aubuisson

In March 1984, former Major Roberto D'Aubuisson appeared on television during the presidential election campaign and showed a recording of an alleged FMLN commander, "Pedro Lobo", confessing to having been an accomplice in the assassination of Monsignor Romero. Almost immediately, "Pedro Lobo" was identified as a common criminal who had been in prison from 1979 to 1981. 400/

He said that he had been offered US$ 50,000 to claim responsibility for the assassination. 401/ Former Major D'Aubuisson nevertheless continued to insist that the guerrillas had assassinated Monsignor Romero, 402/ and officially the armed forces continue to hold to this position. 403/

The work of the Commission for the Investigation of Criminal Acts

The Commission for the Investigation of Criminal Acts (CIHD) began its investigation into Monsignor Romero's assassination in January 1986. 404/

In November 1987, Amado Antonio Garay, one of the San Luis detainees and former Captain Alvaro Saravia's driver revealed that on 24 March 1980, Saravia had ordered him to drive a red Volkswagen to the Hospital de la Divina Providencia in the Miramonte district. He had parked opposite the Chapel. His passenger, a bearded stranger, had ordered him to crouch down and pretend to be repairing something. He had heard a shot, turned around and seen the individual "holding a

gun with both hands pointing towards the right side of the rear right window of the vehicle (...)". He had immediately smelt gunpowder and at that moment the bearded man had calmly told him: "drive slowly, take it easy" and they had driven off. 405/

Garay alleged that he had driven the individual to former Captain Saravia, to whom the stranger had said "mission accomplished". Three days later, Garay had driven Saravia to a house where former Major D'Aubuisson was and Saravia had said in front of D'Aubuisson: "We've already done what we planned about killing Monsignor Arnulfo Romero". 406/

The Attorney-General's Office presented Garay to make a statement to Judge Ricardo Alberto Zamora Pérez on 20 November 1987. Based on the description of the gunman provided by Garay 407/ and the investigation of places mentioned by the witness, 408/ on 24 November the judge ordered the arrest of former Captain Saravia 409/ and officially requested the Central Board of Elections to certify the status of former Major D'Aubuisson as a member of the Legislative Assembly, the first step towards requesting that his parliamentary immunity be withdrawn and that he appear in court. 410/

Saravia filed a writ of *habeas corpus*, on which the Supreme Court took a year to rule. In December 1988, the Supreme Court ruled that "(...) the aforementioned testimony (of Garay) is invalid (...) the witness made his statement seven years, seven months and 24 days after the event about which he is testifying, (which) makes his testimony lose all credibility (...)". It also took the view that the Attorney-General did not have the power to request extradition. 411/

The accusation of the alleged gunman

CIHD made other investigations. Garay picked out a 1969 photograph 412/ of Mr. Héctor Antonio Regalado with a beard drawn in as being closest to his description of the gunman. After Saravia, Regalado had been responsible for D'Aubuisson's personal security. 413/ When he appeared before the Commission, Regalado denied having fired the shot. CIHD found no convincing evidence that he had participated in the assassination.

The investigation by the Commission on the Truth

The Commission on the Truth had access to sufficient evidence to find that:

Former Major Roberto D'Aubuisson, former Captain Alvaro Saravia and Fernando Sagrera 414/ were present on 24 March 1980 at the home of Alejandro Cáceres in San Salvador. Captain Eduardo Avila arrived and told them that Archbishop Romero would be celebrating a mass that day. Captain Avila said that this would be a good opportunity to assassinate the Archbishop. D'Aubuisson ordered that this be done and put Saravia in charge of the operation. When it was pointed out that a sniper would be needed, Captain Avila said he would contact one through Mario Molina. Amado Garay was assigned to drive the assassin to the Chapel.

The parking lot of the Camino Real Hotel was the assembly point before proceeding to the Chapel. There, the bearded gunman, carrying the murder weapon, got into a red, four-door Volkswagen driven by Garay. At least two vehicles drove from the Camino Real Hotel to the scene of the crime. Outside the main entrance to the Chapel, the assassin fired a single bullet from the vehicle, killing Archbishop Romero. D'Aubuisson ordered that 1,000 colones be handed over to Walter Antonio "Musa" Alvarez, who received the payment in question, as did the bearded assassin. Alvarez was abducted in September 1981 and was found dead not long afterwards.

Findings

The Commission finds the following:

1. There is full evidence that:

(a) Former Major Roberto D'Aubuisson gave the order to assassinate the Archbishop and gave precise instructions to members of his security service, acting as a "death squad", to organize and supervise the assassination.

(b) Captains Alvaro Saravia and Eduardo Avila, together with Fernando Sagrera and Mario Molina, were actively involved in planning and carrying out the assassination.

(c) Amado Antonio Garay, the driver of former Captain Saravia, was assigned to drive the gunman to the Chapel. Mr. Garay was a direct witness when, from a red, four-door Volkswagen, the gunman fired a single high velocity .22 bullet to kill the Archbishop.

2. There is sufficient evidence that Walter Antonio "Musa" Alvarez, together with former Captain Saravia, was involved in paying the "fees" of the actual assassin.

3. There is sufficient evidence that the failed assassination attempt against Judge Atilio Ramírez Amaya was a deliberate attempt to deter investigation of the case.

4. There is full evidence that the Supreme Court played an active role in preventing the extradition of former Captain Saravia from the United States and his subsequent imprisonment in El Salvador. In so doing, it ensured, *inter alia*, impunity for those who planned the assassination.

2. The death squad pattern

The Commission on the Truth received a great many complaints of serious acts of violence allegedly perpetrated by death squads. The direct testimony received concerns a total of 817 victims of abductions, disappear-ances and executions that occurred between 1980 and 1991. 415/

There is no question that what have been classified as murders committed by the death squads in rural areas account for a significant proportion of all killings in El Salvador between 1980 and 1991. The Commission on the Truth has obtained extensive information from the testimony of many witnesses, including several members of the armed forces and civilian members of the death squads, who admitted and gave details of their involvement at the highest levels in the organization, operation and financing of the death squads.

The undeniable impact of the extensive evidence received about the death squads leads us to share the fervent conviction of the Salvadorian people that it is crucial not only to comprehend the scope of this phenomenon in El Salvador but also to inform the international community about what it was that, by commission or omission, caused the death squads to insinuate themselves so perniciously into the formal State structure. Decisive action is needed to root out this infamous phenomenon that has so grievously compromised human rights.

Between 1980 and 1991, human rights violations were committed in a systematic and organized manner by groups acting as death squads. The members of such groups usually wore civilian clothing, were heavily armed, operated clandestinely and hid their affiliation and identity. They abducted members of the civilian population and of rebel groups. They tortured their hostages, were responsible for their disappearance and usually executed them. 416/

The death squads, in which members of State structures were actively involved or to which they turned a blind eye, gained such control that they ceased to be an isolated or marginal phenomenon and became an instrument of terror used systematically for the physical elimination of political opponents. Many of the civilian and military authorities in power during the 1980s participated in, encouraged and tolerated the activities of these groups. Although there is no evidence of latent structures for these clandestine organizations, they could be reactivated when those in high Government circles issue warnings that might trigger the resumption of a dirty war in El Salvador. Since the death squad phenomenon was the problem *par excellence* of that dirty war which ultimately destroyed all vestiges of the rule of law during the armed conflict, the Salvadorian Government must not only be ready and willing to prevent the resurgence of this phenomenon but also seek international cooperation in eradicating it completely. 417/

Origins and history

El Salvador has a long history of violence committed by groups that are neither part of the Government nor ordinary criminals. For decades, it has been a fragmented society with a weak system of justice and a tradition of impunity for officials and members of the most powerful families who commit abuses. At the same time, it is a country with little land, a large population and tremendous social tensions. All this has helped create a climate in which violence has been a part of everyday life.

Violence has formed part of the exercise of official authority, directly guided by State officials. This has been reflected, throughout the country's history, in a pattern of conduct within the Government and power élites of using violence as a means to control civilian society. The roots of this situation run deep. In the past 150 years, a number of uprisings by peasants and indigenous groups have been violently suppressed by the State and by civilian groups armed by landowners.

A kind of complicity developed between businessmen and landowners, who entered into a close relationship with the army and intelligence and security forces. The aim was to ferret out alleged subversives among the civilian population in order to defend the country against the threat of an alleged foreign conspiracy. When controlling internal subversion became a priority for defending the State, repression increased.

There were several stages in the process of formation of the death squads in this century. The National Guard was created and organized in 1910 and the following years. From its inception, members cooperated actively with large landowners, at times going so far as to crack down brutally on the peasant leagues and other rural groups that threatened their interests.

Local National Guard commanders "offered their services" or hired out guardsmen to protect landowners' material interests. The practice of using the services of "paramilitary personnel", chosen and armed by the army or the large landowners, began soon afterwards. They became a kind of "intelligence network" against "subversives" or a "local instrument of terror".

In other words, from virtually the beginning of the century, a Salvadorian State security force, through a misperception of its true function, was directed against the bulk of the civilian population. In 1932, National Guard members, the army and paramilitary groups, with the collaboration of local landowners, carried out a massacre known as "La Matanza", in which they murdered at least 10,000 peasants in the western part of the country in order to put down a rural insurrection.

Between 1967 and 1979, General José Alberto Medrano, who headed the National Guard, organized the paramilitary group known as ORDEN. 418/ The function of this organization was to identify and eliminate alleged communists among the rural population. He also organized the national intelligence agency, ANSESAL.

These institutions helped consolidate an era of military hegemony in El Salvador, sowing terror selectively among alleged subversives identified by the intelligence services. In this way, the army's domination over civilian society was consolidated through repression in order to keep society under control. During those years of military dictatorship, the Government kept itself in power basically by using "selective violence".

The reformist coup by young military officers in 1979 ushered in a new period of intense violence. Various circles in the armed forces and the private sector vied for control of the repressive apparatus. Hundreds and even thousands of people perceived as supporters or active members of a growing guerrilla movement—the Frente Farabundo Martí para la Liberación Nacional (FMLN)—were murdered. Members of the army, the Treasury Police, the National Guard and the National Police formed "squads" to do away with enemies. Private and semi-official groups also set up their own squads or linked up with existing structures within the armed forces.

The Commission on the Truth received testimony describing this phenomenon of local violence, such as that which occurred in the village of Cojutepeque and in the towns of San Rafael de los Cedros, El Rosario and Monte San Juan in the south-eastern part of the Department of Cuscatlán. In this area, civil defence forces, soldiers from the local military detachment, members of the National Guard and civilian members of ORDEN took part in death squads that killed hundreds of people. In the Second Court of Cojutepeque, the judge showed the court register for 1980, which listed 141 cases of homicide. He said that 2,000 people had been murdered in the Department of Cuscatlán that year and that probably less than 20 per cent of those murders had been registered in court.

It should be said that, while it is possible to differentiate the armed forces death squads from the civilian death squads, the borderline between the two was often blurred. For instance, even the death squads that were not organized as part of any State structure were often supported or tolerated by State institutions. Frequently, death squads operated in coordination with the armed forces and acted as a support structure for their activities. The clandestine nature of these activities made it possible to conceal the State's responsibility for them and created an atmosphere of complete impunity for the murderers who worked in the squads. This mentality and actual exercise of impunity is a danger for Salvadorian society.

Two cases illustrate the composition and operation of the death squads during this stage: the group around Major D'Aubuisson and the death squads that operated out of the S-II or C-II intelligence sections of military institutions. The Commission on the Truth considers it appropriate to describe these two groups because their activities caused anxiety, fear and great harm to civilian society in El Salvador. These, of course, were not the only death squads active in the country.

The group headed by former Major D'Aubuisson

The 1979 coup d'état altered the political landscape in El Salvador. 419/ One of the competing factions directly affected by the coup was a core of military officers who sought to pre-empt the groups that had staged the coup and also any reform movement. 420/ They considered the Government Junta to be "infiltrated by Marxist officers, which could be fatal for the independence and freedom of the Salvadorian fatherland if the anti-communists in the population failed to act". 421/ The leader of this faction was former Major Roberto D'Aubuisson, who up until 1979 had been third in command of ANSE-SAL and who, on being retired, kept part of the agency's archives.

Former Major D'Aubuisson drew considerable support from wealthy civilians who feared that their interests would be affected by the reform programme announced by the Government Junta. They were convinced that the country faced a serious threat of Marxist insurrection which they had to overcome. The Commission on the Truth obtained testimony from many sources that some of the richest landowners and businessmen inside and outside the country offered their estates, homes, vehicles and bodyguards to help the death squads. They also provided the funds used to organize and maintain the squads, especially those directed by former Major D'Aubuisson.

As the social conflict in El Salvador intensified, subversive operations increased. D'Aubuisson was well placed to provide a link between a very aggressive sector of Salvadorian society and the intelligence network and operations of the S-II sections of the security forces. He was virtually catapulted to undisputed national political leadership of the only faction capable "of preventing a left-wing takeover". 422/ He then opted for applying what he saw as the only method used by the subversives: the illegal use of force. "An eye for an eye, a tooth for a tooth", as the saying goes.

D'Aubuisson arranged meetings between powerful civilians and economic interests and groups in the armed forces, thereby combining two elements in a strategic relationship: the input of resources (money, vehicles, weapons, homes, etc.) by civilians and the definition of a political line for the operations of the S-II intelligence sections. This gave political meaning and purpose to the attacks on and intimidation of civilian opponents and individuals suspected of collaborating with or belonging to the guerrilla movement.

For D'Aubuisson, having access to intelligence reports was of the utmost importance, because it served the cause and the functioning of his political plans. He lost no opportunity to infiltrate the security forces and the armed forces and elicit information from them. In line with D'Aubuisson's political project, all such information was used for "direct action", which explicitly included assassination attempts on individuals, abductions, "recovery of funds" and sabotage. 423/

After the assassination of Monsignor Romero, which, in very closed circles, D'Aubuisson took credit for having planned (see the case of the assassination of Archbishop Romero), his prestige and influence grew among the groups that wielded economic power, gaining him further support and resources. The San Luis estate incident and his temporary stay in Guatemala did not interrupt his political plans, since it was in Guatemala that he was able to establish contacts with internationally linked anti-communist networks and organizations and individual anti-communists such as Mario Sandoval Alarcón, Luis Mondizabal and Ricardo Lao.

From Guatemala, D'Aubuisson continued to plan and direct numerous attacks by groups identified as "death squads" and, on his return to El Salvador, had access to sources which kept him permanently supplied with abundant, up-to-date intelligence information from most armed units or territorial districts, whose leaders shared his political views. They also offered him actual logistical support for his activities, seconding and rotating troops for his personal protection and supplying weapons.

Although members of the Armed Forces Joint Staff knew about this steady leak of information, not only was nothing ever done to control it but intelligence leaks were even organized intentionally: in fact, there were serving members of the armed forces who participated actively in D'Aubuisson's group.

There is substantial evidence that D'Aubuisson operated during this period through concealed channels in which civilians and both serving and discharged members of the armed forces mixed politics, murder and the defence of their own economic interests in their zeal to combat both the peaceful and the armed opposition.

One of those closest to D'Aubuisson was his Chief of Security, Héctor Antonio Regalado. The Commission on the Truth obtained sufficient evidence to conclude that Regalado not only formed his own death squad in the town of Santiago de María but also used to coordinate and train D'Aubuisson's networks in the capital. Regalado ran D'Aubuisson's death squad from his office in the National Assembly, where he was Chief of Security when D'Aubuisson was President of the Assembly. 424/

Death squads operating in the
S-II Intelligence Sections

In many armed forces units, the intelligence section (S-II) operated on the death squad model. Operations were carried out by members of the armed forces, usually wearing civilian clothing, without insignias, and driving unmarked vehicles.

The Salvadorian armed forces also maintained within the Joint Staff under Department 5—Civilian Affairs, a secret, clandestine intelligence unit for the surveillance of civilian political targets, which received information from the S-II sections of each military unit or security force. The purpose of this unit was to obtain information for the planning of direct actions that included the "elimination" of individuals. In some cases, such plans were transmitted as actual orders to operational units in the various security forces or the armed forces themselves.

The following is only one example of the many death squads of this kind.

The death squads of the National Guard Intelligence Section

Testimony and information received by the Commission on the Truth from former members of the S-II section of the National Guard show that the murder of Rodolfo Viera, President of the Salvadorian Institute for Agrarian Reform (ISTA), and two United States advisers in January 1981 was not an isolated event. Members of this section, with the complicity of economically influential civilians, operated as a death squad dedicated to eliminating political opponents and people considered to be supporters of the armed left wing.

A group of extreme right-wing civilians that included Hans Christ, Ricardo Sol Meza, Constantino Rampone and Ernest Panamá acted as "advisers" to the S-II section of the National Guard and influenced its work. They often visited headquarters to meet with the Chief of Section II, Major Mario Denis Morán, and his second-in-command, Lieutenant Isidro López Sibrián. On various occasions, they provided money and weapons. There is also evidence and testimony that Argentine nationals frequented S-II headquarters and were commissioned by the above-mentioned group of civilians to carry out assignments that included murders.

Information from a wide variety of sources also indicates that Major Morán, Lieutenant López Sibrián and Captain Eduardo Avila—all three of whom held leadership positions in the S-II were connected with it— were members of death squads with links to the civilians mentioned.

The Intelligence Section had subsections such as operations and intelligence. Within the intelligence subsection, there was a smaller group in charge of "dirty work", which specialized in interrogations, torture and executions. This group enjoyed the full confidence of its superiors and acted as a special corps in the service of Morán and López Sibrián, who were numbers one and two respectively in the S-II. This group comprised, *inter alia*, Rodolfo Orellana Osorio, Enoc Abel Campos ("Heidi"), René Mauricio Cruz González, Oscar Reinaldo Bonilla Monge and Mario Ernesto Aparicio. The group did not observe the hierarchical chain of command but took orders only from Morán and López Sibrián, and its members came and went at will.

Findings

Because of the clandestine nature of their operations, it is not easy to establish all the links existing between private businessmen and the death squads. However, the Commission on the Truth has absolutely no doubt that a close relationship existed, or that the possibility that businessmen or members of moneyed families might feel the need and might be able to act with impunity in financing murderous paramilitary groups, as they did in the past, poses a threat to the future of Salvadorian society.

At the same time, it must be pointed out that the United States Government tolerated, and apparently paid little official heed to the activities of Salvadorian exiles living in Miami, especially between 1979 and 1983. According to testimony received by the Commission, this group of exiles directly financed and indirectly helped run certain death squads. It would be useful if other investigators with more resources and more time were to shed light on this tragic story so as to ensure that persons linked to terrorist acts in other countries are never tolerated again in the United States.

1. The State of El Salvador, through the activities of members of the armed forces and/or civilian officials, is responsible for having taken part in, encouraged and tolerated the operations of the death squads which illegally attacked members of the civilian population.

2. Salvadorian institutions must make serious efforts to investigate the structural connection that has been found to exist between the death squads and State bodies. The fact that there are hundreds of former civil defence members in rural areas who are still armed is particular cause for concern. These people could easily mobilize to commit new acts of violence in future if they are not clearly identified and disarmed.

3. It is especially important to call attention to the repeated abuses committed by the intelligence services of the security forces and the armed forces. It is crucial for the future of El Salvador that the State pay attention to the use of intelligence services and to the exploitation of this arm of the Government to identify targets for murder or disappearance. Any investigation must result both in an institutional clean-up of the intelligence services and in the identification of those responsible for this aberrant practice.

4. The lack of effective action by the judicial system

was a factor that reinforced the impunity that shielded and continues to shield members and promoters of the death squads in El Salvador.

5. The links of some private businessmen and moneyed families to the funding and use of death squads must be clarified.

6. The Government must recognize that, given their organizational structure and the fact that they possess weapons, there is a serious danger that the death squads may become involved, as has happened in some cases, in illegal activities such as drug trafficking, arms trafficking and abductions for ransom.

7. The issue of the death squads in El Salvador is so important that it requires special investigation. More resolute action by national institutions, with the cooperation and assistance of foreign authorities who have any information on the subject, is especially needed. In order to verify a number of specific violations and ascertain who was responsible, it will be necessary to investigate the serious acts of violence committed by death squads on a case-by-case basis.

3. Zamora

Summary of the case

Lawyer Mario Zamora Rivas, a leader of the Christian Democratic Party and Chief State Counsel of the Republic, was murdered at his home on 23 February 1980.

Considered one of his party's most important leaders, Zamora was also a major public figure outside the party; given the political violence in the country, this exposed him to reprisals.

Members of a security force were responsible for Zamora's murder, which forms part of a pattern of conduct adopted by such forces in their illegal activities. Although the Commission has no doubt about the details of the murder, the identity of the murderers cannot be established from the testimony, investigations, evidence and proceedings on the case.

The Government did not make a proper investigation which would have resulted in the identification and punishment of the guilty parties.

Description of the facts 425/

Background

The Christian Democratic Party (PDC) joined other centrist and centre-left parties in the first Government Junta which overthrew General Romero in October 1979.

The Christian Democrats did not withdraw from the Government, as other groups did, and in December 1979 they joined the second Revolutionary Government Junta.

This attitude drew the opposition of Zamora and other leaders within the party, who believed that the armed forces did not offer sufficient guarantees for their political project.

As a condition for remaining in the second Junta, the Christian Democratic Party (PDC) proposed a meeting with the Armed Forces Joint Staff at the highest level. It presented a document on the violations being committed against its members and stated the bases for the party's relationship with the armed forces. One of the proponents of this strategy was Mr. Zamora. The armed forces maintained that they could not respond to the document because it contained serious accusations, and they asked for time to consider it. 426/

Other evidence submitted to the Commission suggests that Zamora had begun talks aimed at opening a dialogue with Cayetano Carpio, 427/ leader of the Fuerzas Populares de Liberación (FPL), a party to the left of PDC.

The PDC Convention, which was scheduled to take place the day after Zamora's assassination, was to have heard an explanation of the choices facing the Christian Democratic Party at that moment in time.

Zamora was the only party leader strong and persuasive enough to be able to alter the course of the policy of alliances pursued by the party, then headed by Mr. Duarte, 428/ and the importance of this in Salvadorian public life was well understood.

A few days before the assassination, Major Roberto D'Aubuisson publicly accused Zamora and other PDC leaders of being communists and members of the guerrilla group FPL. 429/ Because of this, Zamora, in his capacity as a public official, filed a complaint of defamation against D'Aubuisson with the Criminal Court, basing his right to do so on the duty of any public official to challenge an unfounded accusation before the courts. According to testimony, this was the first complaint lodged in El Salvador in an attempt to contain the far right through the use of criminal proceedings.

Two days before Zamora's assassination, two staff members of the Office of the Chief State Counsel were riddled with bullets while driving an official car. Some testimony claims that the shooting was a mistake and that Zamora was the intended target.

The facts

Mr. Zamora was at a party in his home with approximately seven other people. The party ended at midnight. Without warning, a group of six individuals entered the victim's house from the roof. Their faces were covered by ski masks and they carried small arms with silencers and some rifles. They immediately forced everyone there to lie down on the floor.

They demanded the keys to the front gate which

Aronette, Zamora's wife, 430/ said she did not have. The group's leader spoke with a foreign accent and asked specifically for Mario Zamora. Zamora identified himself; they made him get up and took him to another room, while turning up the volume of the music. After killing Zamora, they left the house in an orderly manner.

Zamora's brother, Rubén 431/ lived in the house next door and had gone home to bed moments before the armed men entered. He was woken by shouting and thought that people at the party had drunk too much. He decided to go over to his brother's house but at his wife's request he telephoned instead; the line was dead. 432/

When the assailants left, the rest of the people in the house began to look for Mario Zamora and to telephone party leaders, police authorities and Government officials, including then Colonel Eugenio Vides Casanova, Director-General of the National Guard. At that point, the telephone was working normally. At first, they thought that Zamora had been abducted, but when they searched the house, they found his body riddled with bullets, in the bathroom.

It was approximately three to four hours after the murder was reported that the first security forces patrol arrived to conduct the preliminary investigation.

Although judicial proceedings were instituted on this case, no one was ever accused of the crime and the case was finally closed in 1981.

Analysis

The operation was carried out with extreme precision and skill in order to eliminate the victim without letting the identity of the killers be known.

The Commission has received sufficient evidence that the operation was carried out by the intelligence section of a State security force without consulting the Intelligence Department of the High Command, the institution which usually decided on this type of operation. The evidence also shows that the same security force had devised a plan for eliminating the victim and that the Intelligence Department of the High Command knew all about it. The security force repeatedly requested approval for the plan and when it did not receive the go-ahead, decided to proceed without authorization.

The High Command's reaction to the incident was to request military intelligence to verify internally who had carried out the operation. According to the information received, the purpose of the investigation was to establish whether the murder had been committed by one of the security forces, a death squad or a gang of kidnappers.

The decision by the security force to go ahead without authorization would explain the alleged involvement of foreign personnel in the operation, as a strategy to conceal identities and obstruct a subsequent investigation by the High Command itself or by any other security force. Furthermore, there is sufficient evidence that some security forces used people from other countries, for instance, Argentina and Nicaragua, to do the "dirty work" of eliminating political opponents.

Although the killers did not know Zamora personally, they were aware of his position and prestige; it was clear that the plan was devised in such a way as to minimize the risks of the operation, so as to prevent any subsequent public reaction.

Findings

Based on the investigation it made and the testimony it received, the Commission believes it has sufficient evidence to conclude that Mr. Zamora was assassinated by members of a State security force in an operation decided on by that force and carried out as part of its illegal activities.

Likewise, the Commission has sufficient evidence to affirm that the Intelligence Department of the High Command established precisely which security force had committed the crime and that the military hierarchy at that time kept this information secret in order to conceal the identity of the perpetrators and made no report to the proper authorities, with the result that the necessary investigation was never made.

4. Tehuicho

Summary of the case

On 23 July 1980, 13 inhabitants of El Bartolillo hamlet in Tehuicho canton were executed by heavily armed civilians who identified themselves as guerrillas. Other people died in the surrounding area.

The justice of the peace arrived at the scene the next morning accompanied by troops of the Artillery Brigade. He left without carrying out the required procedures. For three days, soldiers prevented the burial of the bodies.

The Commission finds the following:

(a) On 23 July 1980, in Tehuicho canton, 13 civilians were executed by a death squad consisting of members of the "Lieutenant Colonel Oscar Osorio" Artillery Brigade and members of the civil defence unit for the San Juan Opico district.

(b) Troops from the Artillery Brigade went to the scene the next day and for three days prevented the burial of the victims.

(c) The justice of the peace did not carry out the procedures required by law. Nor did he institute criminal proceedings to investigate what had happened.

(d) Miguel Lemus, a former member of the local civil defence unit participated as a member of the death squad.

(e) Carlos Azcúnaga Sánchez, now a lieutenant colonel, planned the crime; his motive was personal revenge.

Description of the facts 433/

The collective execution

Shortly after midday on 23 July 1980, a group of approximately 100 civilians arrived at El Bartolillo hamlet in Tehuicho canton. Their faces were painted and they were dressed as peasants. They were very well-armed and dispersed throughout the canton. Witnesses identified Miguel Lemus, who was a civil defence member at the time.

They identified themselves as guerrillas and called a meeting on the football field, supposedly to distribute weapons. As the operation proceeded, they started to force people to assemble.

The villagers congregated on the sports field, where they were blindfolded. The strangers then identified themselves as a "death squad" and accused the villagers of having links with the guerrillas.

They proceeded to make a selection. Apparently they had a list. "*Orejas*" 434/ identified people on the list and singled out 14 of them, 12 men and 2 women. The men were taken to a ravine, the two women were taken elsewhere. Shots were heard. Some houses were looted and burned.

The bodies of the women and the men were found in the course of the night. There was physical evidence that they had been tortured.

On returning to their homes, the survivors found the words "death squad" painted on a wall.

Background

One year before the incident, a private dispute had arisen over the ownership of a property between Pedro Franco Molina, a villager from Tehuicho canton who supported the guerrillas, and Antonio Azcúnaga, a villager from Los Amates canton who was the father of then Captain Carlos Azcúnaga Sánchez. The dispute intensified when it was rumoured that Franco had offered a reward for Antonio Azcúnaga's death.

In October 1979, according to testimony, a group of guerrillas murdered Antonio Azcúnaga.

There was information that the group was from Santa Ana, but villagers from Tehuicho canton, including Pedro Franco, were also blamed. Carlos Azcúnaga made various threatening comments.

Subsequent events

Uniformed soldiers from the "Lieutenant Colonel Oscar Osorio" Artillery Brigade, accompanying justice of the peace Rodolfo Sánchez 435/ and the forensic doctor, went to the scene of the incident the following day. The soldiers prevented the villagers from burying the bodies.

Neither the justice of the peace nor the forensic doctor carried out the required procedures before leaving the canton. No judicial investigation was undertaken.

Troops remained in the area for three days and prevented the burial of the bodies. The villagers buried the bodies in a mass grave as soon as the soldiers left.

Subsequently, then-Captain Carlos Azcúnaga Sánchez, according to witnesses, made comments incriminating himself. When he appeared before the Commission, however, he denied that he had participated in the incident.

Findings

The Commission finds the following:

1. There is substantial evidence of the following:

(a) On 23 July 1980, in Tehuicho canton, 13 civilians were executed by a death squad consisting of members of the "Lieutenant Colonel Oscar Osorio" Artillery Brigade and members of the civil defence unit for San Juan Opico district.

(b) Troops from the Artillery Brigade went to the scene the next day and stayed there for three days and prevented the burial of the victims.

(c) The justice of the peace did not carry out the required procedures, or institute criminal proceedings to investigate what had happened.

2. There is sufficient evidence of the following:

(a) Miguel Lemus, a former member of the local civil defence unit, participated as a member of the death squad.

(b) Carlos Azcúnaga Sánchez, now a lieutenant colonel, planned the massacre; his motive was personal revenge.

5. Viera, Hammer and Pearlman

Summary of the case

On the night of 3 January 1981, in the Sheraton Hotel in San Salvador, two National Guard agents killed José Rodolfo Viera Lizama, President of the Salvadorian Institute for Agrarian Reform (ISTA), and Michael P. Hammer and Mark David Pearlman, United States advisers from the American Institute for Free Labor Development (AIFLD).

The actual murderers, Santiago Gómez González and José Dimas Valle Acevedo, who were National Guard agents, were convicted and later released under the 1987 Amnesty Act. The other individuals involved in planning and ordering the murders, Lieutenant Rodolfo Isidro López Sibrián, second-in-command of the Intelligence Section of the National Guard, Captain Eduardo Ernesto Alfonso Avila and businessman Hans Christ, were never convicted.

The Intelligence Section of the National Guard had

planned to eliminate Viera months before his murder. National Guard agents carried out the murders in the manner characteristic of the death squads.

Lieutenant Colonel Mario Denis Morán Echeverría, then Chief of the Intelligence Section of the National Guard, covered up information about the murders, and Judge Héctor Enrique Jiménez Zaldívar allowed one of the suspects to disguise himself so as to conceal his identity.

Description of the facts 436/

The agrarian reform and the death threats

When the General Secretary of the Union Comunal Salvadoreña (UCS), Rodolfo Viera, was murdered, he was also President of ISTA, a Government agency set up to carry out the agrarian reform programme. Michael P. Hammer and Mark David Pearlman, both of them officials of AIFLD, were in El Salvador to provide support and technical assistance for the agrarian reform process.

As President of ISTA and General Secretary of UCS, Viera was viewed as a dangerous adversary by those who were opposed to the agrarian reform. He received death threats on a number of occasions. In May 1980, the Ejército Secreto Anticomunista referred to Viera as a "Communist traitor" who should be eliminated by the "patriots" who were fighting for a Government that would respect "private property". There were two attempts to murder him in 1980. 437/ There is sufficient evidence that they were planned by Section II of the National Guard.

The murders of Viera, Hammer and Pearlman 438/

It is not clear whether those who planned the murders set the specific place and time in advance. However, there is full evidence that they did take advantage of the unexpected opportunity in the Sheraton Hotel to murder people who were a previously selected target.

On the night of 3 January 1981, López Sibrián ordered Valle Acevedo, a National Guard agent, to accompany him to the home of businessman Hans Christ. 439/ López Sibrián 440/ was carrying a 9-mm pistol and an Ingram sub-machine-gun 441/ obtained from the National Guard depot. 442/ At approximately 10 p.m., Christ, López Sibrián and Avila arrived at the hotel and went to eat in the hotel restaurant.

Viera, Hammer and Pearlman arrived sometime after 10 p.m. They went into the restaurant where Christ, Avila and López Sibrián were sitting. Since the restaurant was full, they asked for somewhere more private. An employee recommended the Americas room, which is spacious. Christ recognized Viera and commented to Avila: "Look! There's that son of a bitch!" 443/ Avila

said that someone in the group commented that he had grown a beard and that it would be good if he were dead. 444/ Avila also mentioned that when López Sibrián saw Viera he said that that was a good opportunity to kill him. 445/ At least one of the three left the table and watched where Viera's group was going. 446/

Moments later López Sibrián, Avila and Christ left the hotel, went to the parking lot and got into a car. There, they told Valle Acevedo to kill the President of ISTA and the other two, 447/ but he refused to do the job alone. 448/ López Sibrián got out of the car, went back to the parking lot and went over to National Guard agent Gómez González, who was watching Morán's vehicle. López Sibrián told him to go with him. 449/ When Gómez González replied that he could do nothing without Major Morán's authorization, 450/ López Sibrián went into the hotel, returned immediately and told Gómez that Morán had authorized him to accompany him. 451/

López Sibrián and Gómez González then walked towards Sibrián's vehicle, in which Valle Acevedo, Christ and Avila were sitting. 452/ López Sibrián ordered Valle Acevedo and Gómez González to accompany Christ to the hotel and kill the three men there. 453/ He also gave Gómez González the 9-millimetre Ingram sub-machine-gun, while Avila gave Valle Acevedo another .45-millimetre sub-machine-gun and a khaki sweater to conceal the weapon. 454/ Christ told them that he would identify the men. 455/

The two National Guard agents entered the hotel behind Christ, who showed them where Viera, Hammer and Pearlman were sitting. 456/ They waited only a few moments, then Valle Acevedo and Gómez González opened fire on Viera and his two companions. 457/ There is sufficient evidence, based on the wounds received and the place where the bodies were, that, in addition to Viera, both Hammer and Pearlman were a target of the gunmen.

The two gunmen left the hotel immediately and escaped in López Sibrián's vehicle to a house near the auxiliary funeral service, followed by Avila in his vehicle. 458/ There, they returned the weapons to their respective owners 459/ and López Sibrián then ordered them to return to National Guard headquarters. 460/ After the murders of Viera, Hammer and Pearlman, it became known in the National Guard that members of Section II, including Valle Acevedo and Gómez González, had committed the murders. 461/

On 14 February 1986, five years after the murder, the two agents were convicted and sentenced to 30 years in prison. On 19 December 1987, they were released under the Amnesty Act. The case against Avila was dismissed for the same reason. 462/

The investigation

The seven years of investigation of the murders of Viera, Hammer and Pearlman are well documented elsewhere and there is no need to review them here. However, two aspects of this incident warranted careful consideration by the Commission.

The role of Major Morán

There is substantial evidence that Major Morán, then Chief of Intelligence of the National Guard, learnt, after the murders, that his second-in-command, López Sibrián, had ordered two guards in the unit he commanded to carry them out. Morán also neglected to inform the appropriate authorities of those facts. 463/

It is also clear that Morán's role in the murders was never properly investigated. One of the convicted guards said that Major Medrano, who headed the military investigation of the case, told him to blame López Sibrián, 464/ apparently so as not to implicate his superior, Morán. 465/ Furthermore, there is no indication that when the Commission for the Investigation of Criminal Acts reopened the case in 1985, it investigated Morán's role in the murders, even though it had received evidence that Morán participated in a meeting of the Intelligence Section of the National Guard on 3 January, when the murder may have been planned. The Commission for the Investigation of Criminal Acts was also given evidence that on 5 January, Morán received payment for completing a "job".

The identification of López Sibrián

Although the testimony gathered by the Medrano commission shed new light on López Sibrián's role in the murders, there is full evidence that Judge Jiménez Zaldívar cooperated actively with López Sibrián by allowing him to disguise himself 466/ so that it was impossible for a key witness to recognize him. The next day, Judge Jiménez Zaldívar ordered López Sibrián released for lack of evidence. 467/

Findings

The Commission finds the following:

1. There is full evidence that on 3 January 1981, José Dimas Valle Acevedo and Santiago Gómez González killed José Rodolfo Viera, Michael Hammer and Mark David Pearlman in the Sheraton Hotel.

2. There is full evidence that Lieutenant López Sibrián was involved in planning the operation to murder Viera, Hammer and Pearlman and in ordering two members of the National Guard to carry it out. He also gave a weapon to Gómez González and helped the killers escape from the scene of the crime.

3. There is full evidence that Captain Eduardo Avila was involved in planning the murder operation and collaborated with López Sibrián in carrying it out.

4. There is sufficient evidence that Hans Christ 468/ was involved in planning the murder operation and assisted in carrying it out.

5. As to the role of Lieutenant Colonel Mario Denis Morán, there is substantial evidence that he covered up the murders by neglecting to report the facts.

6. There is full evidence that Judge Héctor Enrique Jiménez Zaldívar cooperated with the main suspect, López Sibrián, hindering his identification which would have led to the institution of criminal proceedings.

E. Violence against Opponents by the Frente Farabundo Martí para la Liberacion Nacional

This section deals with the use of violence by FMLN against real or alleged opponents in violation of the rules of international humanitarian law and international human rights law. It covers the use of violence against non-combatants and also the execution of alleged criminals without due process.

The section begins with a representative case, the execution of mayors in conflict zones. Then, after an explanation of the pattern observed in this type of violence, an account follows of some of the cases attributed to FMLN which had a major impact on Salvadorian society. In some cases, it has not been possible to prove who planned the attacks, in others it is impossible to determine, or to determine with certainty, who carried them out.

Lastly, this section includes a case which, in the Commission's view, is an isolated incident which does not conform to any pattern of unlawful use of violence. The section concludes with the Commission's findings.

1. Illustrative case: summary execution of mayors 469/

Summary of the case

Between 1985 and 1988, a large number of mayors of towns situated in conflict zones were executed, without any kind of a trial, by the Ejército Revolucionario del Pueblo (ERP), one of the organizations in FMLN. These executions were carried out pursuant to a policy which FMLN has openly acknowledged.

The present report describes 11 executions, but there were more than that.

The Commission finds the following:

1. The FMLN General Command approved and adopted a policy of murdering mayors whom it considered to be working against it.

2. The ERP leadership carried out the policy and ordered its local commanders to murder mayors whom it considered to be working against FMLN.

3. The following persons, among others, were part

of the ERP leadership at various times when mayors within territory under ERP control were murdered, and they were parties to the decisions to carry out—and are therefore responsible for—those summary executions: Joaquín Villalobos ("Atilio"), Jorge Meléndez ("Jonas"), Ana Sonia Medina ("Mariana"), Mercedes del Carmen Letona ("Luisa"), Ana Guadalupe Martínez ("María") and Marisol Galindo.

4. Joaquín Villalobos, as General-Secretary of ERP, held the highest position in that organization and bears special responsibility for the murders of mayors by ERP.

5. Local ERP commanders, either under orders from the leadership or with its approval and backing, murdered the mayors listed in this summary.

6. The murders of mayors José Alberto López, Francisco Israel Díaz Vásquez, Pedro Ventura, María Ovidia Graciela Mónico Vargas, José Domingo Avilés Vargas, Dolores Molina, Napoleón Villafuerte, Edgar Mauricio Valenzuela and Terencio Rodríguez were part of an established pattern, based on a deliberate FMLN policy, and were carried out by local ERP commanders on orders from and with the express approval of members of the ERP leadership.

7. The mayor of Guatajiagua, José Alberto López, was murdered in October 1988, while in the power of commander "Amadeo".

8. The execution of mayors by FMLN was a violation of the rules of international humanitarian law and international human rights law.

Description of the facts

Execution of José Alberto López, mayor of Guatajiagua

Mr. José Alberto López was elected mayor of the town of Guatajiagua, Department of Morazán, in March 1988. According to an FMLN source after his election, López received a letter from FMLN warning him to resign and stating that it was FMLN policy to execute any mayor in the area. López replied that he would not resign.

The mayor was summoned three times by FMLN to go to the guerrilla camp in San Bartolo canton, but López never went. Out of fear, he did not stay in Guatajiagua, but usually worked in San Francisco Gotera. In any case, the mayor's office in Guatajiagua had been destroyed by the guerrillas.

On Saturday, 25 October 1988, López was at home with his wife, Leticia Canales, and their four minor children. The house was in the El Calvario district of the town of Guatajiagua. An FMLN combatant whom López knew came to the house that morning and told the mayor that his commander wanted to speak to him. Fearing what would happen if he refused a fourth time, López agreed

to go. Leticia, his wife, decided to go with him and the three left for San Bartolo canton on foot.

When they reached the Gualavo river, a man in uniform carrying a rifle was waiting for them. The combatant who had brought them told the man in uniform that he had the mayor with him and handed him over. The man in uniform told the mayor's wife that she could not cross the river or go to the guerrilla camp. He told her to go home, saying that her husband would be sent back that afternoon.

On arriving at the camp, the mayor was taken to the commander, who went by the name of "Amadeo". There is sufficient proof that, after speaking to the mayor, "Amadeo" ordered his execution.

That same night, Radio Venceremos announced that FMLN had summarily executed the mayor of Guatajiagua, José Alberto López.

Execution of Francisco Israel Díaz Vásquez, mayor of Lolotique

On 2 May 1985, Francisco Israel Díaz Vásquez took office as mayor, after being elected by popular vote. There is full evidence that on 2 June that year, he was abducted by FMLN and kept hostage until 24 October, when he was released along with other mayors who had also been abducted by FMLN. He was released following negotiations in Panama between FMLN and the Government.

On 2 June 1986, Díaz resumed office as mayor. In December of that year, he received death threats from the guerrillas and resigned. However, the guerrillas believed that he was still working for the Government.

On 5 December 1988, an unknown man went to Francisco Israel Díaz's home and handed his wife a note ordering him to go the next day to the place known as "la Entrada de Tempisque", near Santa Bárbara.

Díaz left on the morning of 6 December with a neighbour. They passed the place known as "la Entrada de Tempisque" and continued on to Santa Bárbara canton, arriving around noon. Three uniformed combatants with rifles suddenly appeared and arrested Mr. Díaz. Five minutes later one of them returned and told Mr. Díaz's companion to go home because they were going to hold the mayor for several days.

The next afternoon, 7 December, two unknown men went to Lolotique church and reported that Díaz was dead and handed over his wallet containing his identity papers.

That same night, several relatives and friends of Díaz went looking for his body. When they found it, they saw that "he had been shot once, behind the ear, and that the bullet, in exiting, had shot out one eye and his teeth. On one calf there was a piece of paper saying "summarily executed by FMLN" and, on the other, a piece of paper saying "as a traitor".

In October 1992, FMLN informed the Commission officially that ERP, pursuant to a policy approved by FMLN, had executed mayor Díaz.

Executions of other mayors

In its communication dated 18 October 1992, replying to a request for information from the Commission on the Truth, FMLN said that ERP, pursuant to a policy approved by FMLN, had also executed the following mayors:

Pedro Ventura, mayor of San Isidro, Department of Morazán, on 15 April 1988.

María Ovidia Graciela Mónico Vargas, mayor of San Jorge, Department of San Miguel, on 18 January 1985.

José Domingo Avilés Vargas, mayor of Santa Elena, Department of Usulután, on 8 January 1985.

Dolores Molina, mayor of Lolotiquillo, Department of Morazán, 19 August 1988.

Napoleón Villafuerte, mayor of Sesorí, Department of San Miguel, 25 November 1988.

Edgar Mauricio Valenzuela, mayor of San Jorge, Department of San Miguel, 4 March 1985.

The communication contained the text of two FMLN communiqués, dated 22 August and 26 November 1988, announcing the execution of Napoleón Villafuerte and Dolores [Molina] respectively.

Furthermore, there is sufficient evidence that on 11 May 1988, Mr. Terencio Rodríguez, mayor of Perquín, Department of Morazán, was executed without trial.

Applicable law

In considering the facts in the light of international humanitarian law and international human rights law, the Commission examined the arguments put forward by FMLN to justify its policy of executing mayors.

FMLN justified these executions on the grounds that "mayors and mayors' offices had come to engage in what were clearly counter-insurgency activities. The mayors, in close coordination with the commanders of the garrisons of the various towns, had embarked on the task of creating paramilitary forces (civil defence units) and direct repressive activity against the civilian population and had developed spy networks to detect FMLN members and supporters, or simply people opposed to the regime among the population and to obtain information about members of popular organizations and their plans; this information was then passed on to the army." It also stated that the mayors' activities affected supply lines.

FMLN went on to say that "when mass arrests of villagers, murders, repression by civil defence forces and operations by the armed forces of El Salvador based on information supplied by the mayors' spy networks began to occur, the mayors joined the ranks of those whom FMLN, since 1980, had considered military targets whose summary execution was hence legitimate: spies, paramilitary personnel, those who collaborated with the death squads and anyone whose actions triggered repression or murder of the civilian population".

The Commission does not accept these arguments. If by calling the mayors "military targets", FMLN is trying to say that they were combatants, it must be pointed out that there is nothing to support the claim that the executed mayors were combatants according to the provisions of humanitarian law.

However, whether the executed mayors might or might not at some point have been considered "military targets" is irrelevant, since there is no evidence that any of them lost their lives as a result of any combat operation by FMLN. The execution of an individual, whether a combatant or a non-combatant, who is in the power of a guerrilla force and who does not put up any resistance is not a combat operation.

There is nothing in international humanitarian law or international human rights law to prohibit belligerents from punishing, in areas under their control, individuals who commit acts that, according to the applicable laws, are criminal in nature. In the aforesaid document, FMLN says that it considered the summary execution of "spies, paramilitary personnel, those who collaborated with the death squads and anyone whose actions triggered repression or murder of the civilian population" a legitimate action. 470/

The Commission recalls that, when punishing persons accused of crimes, it is necessary to observe the basic elements of due process. International humanitarian law does not in any way exempt the parties to a conflict from that obligation, and international human rights law does not exempt the party which has effective control of a territory from that obligation with respect to persons within its jurisdiction. On the contrary, those two sources of law expressly prohibit the passing of sentences and the carrying out of executions without previous judgement pronounced by a regularly constituted independent and impartial tribunal attaching all the judicial guarantees generally recognized as indispensable.

In none of the cases mentioned above is there any evidence that a proper trial was held prior to the execution. Nor is there any evidence that any of the individuals died in a combat operation or that they resisted their executioners.

Findings

The Commission finds the following:

1. There is full evidence that the FMLN General Command approved and adopted a policy of murdering mayors whom it considered to be working against it.

2. There is full evidence that members of the ERP leadership, among others, carried out the policy and ordered their local commanders to murder mayors whom they considered to be working against FMLN.

3. There is full evidence that the following persons, among others, were part of the ERP leadership at various times when mayors within territory under ERP control were murdered, and that they were parties to the decisions to carry out—and are therefore responsible for—those summary executions: Joaquín Villalobos ("Atilio"), Jorge Meléndez ("Jonas"), Ana Sonia Medina ("Mariana"), Mercedes del Carmen Letona ("Luisa"), Ana Guadalupe Martínez ("María") and Marisol Galindo.

4. There is full evidence that Joaquín Villalobos, as General-Secretary of ERP, held the highest position in that organization and bears special responsibility for the murders of mayors by ERP.

5. There is full evidence that local ERP commanders, either under orders from the leadership or with its approval and backing, murdered the mayors listed in this summary.

6. There is full evidence that the murders of mayors José Alberto López, Francisco Israel Díaz Vásquez, Pedro Ventura, María Ovidia Graciela Mónico Vargas, José Domingo Avilés Vargas, Dolores Molina, Edgar Mauricio Valenzuela, Napoleón Villafuerte, and Terencio Rodríguez were part of an established pattern, based on a deliberate FMLN policy, and were carried out by local ERP commanders on orders from and with the express approval of members of the ERP leadership.

7. There is full evidence that the mayor of Guatajigua, José Alberto López, was murdered in October 1988, while in the power of commander "Amadeo".

8. The execution of mayors by FMLN was a violation of the rules of international humanitarian law and international human rights law.

2. Extrajudicial executions

(a) Zona Rosa

Summary of the case

At around 9 p.m. on 19 June 1985, in an area of San Salvador known as the "Zona Rosa" where there are many restaurants, a group of armed men opened fire on a group of United States marines. The assailants were members of the Partido Revolucionario de Trabajadores Centroamericanos (PRTC), one of the organizations in FMLN. The marines, who were serving as security guards at the United States Embassy in San Salvador, were in civilian clothing and were unarmed. Four marines, nine civilians and one of the assailants died in the shoot-out. The "Mardoqueo Cruz" urban commando of PRTC claimed responsibility for the killings; FMLN defended

the attack in a communiqué. In a subsequent trial, three people were tried and convicted. Two other trials were instituted for the same attack. One of them did not reach the sentencing stage, since the accused was amnestied; in the other, sentence has yet to be passed on the accused.

The Commission finds the following:

1. The attack on the United States marines was part of the FMLN policy of considering United States military personnel a legitimate target.

2. A PRTC commando carried out the attack.

3. Ismael Dimas Aguila and José Roberto Salazar Mendoza were involved in planning and carrying out the attack.

4. Pedro Antonio Andrade was also involved in planning the attack.

5. The attack on the marines in the Zona Rosa was a violation of the rules of international humanitarian law.

Description of the facts 471/

Background

In 1985, the General Command of the Frente Farabundo Martí para la Liberación Nacional took the decision to consider United States military personnel in El Salvador legitimate military targets. It gave its members broad and sweeping orders to implement the decision. 472/

Planning the attack

In early June 1985, some members of the Partido Revolucionario de Trabajadores Centroamericanos (PRTC), one of the five political-military organizations in FMLN, planned an attack which they called "Yankee aggressor in El Salvador, another Viet Nam awaits you". The aim was to execute United States military personnel assigned to El Salvador and responded to the general directive to that effect issued earlier by the General Command. The attack was to be carried out by members of the "Mardoqueo Cruz" urban commando.

The commando operated from an auto repair shop in which Ismael Dimas Aguilar and his brother José Abraham were partners and from the "La Estrella" upholstery shop in which William Celio Rivas Bolaños and Juan Miguel García Meléndez were partners. The main planning meetings were therefore held in those places. 473/

The attack

At around 8.30 p.m. on 19 June 1985, six United States marines who were responsible for security at the United States Embassy sat down at an outside table at Chili's restaurant in the area known as the "Zona Rosa" in the San Benito district. They were regular customers known to the owners of restaurants and cafes in the area and to those who worked there. They used to go there in groups whenever they were off duty. 474/ After a while, two of them left the group and went to sit down at a table in the Flashback restaurant a few yards away from their companions at Chili's. 475/

At around 9 p.m., a white pick-up truck with dark stripes parked outside the La Hola restaurant; a group of some seven individuals got out and walked over to Chili's and, without warning, fired a volley of shots at United States marines 476/ Thomas Handwork, Patrick R. Kwiatkoski, Bobbie J. Dickson and Gregory H. Weber. The marines were in civilian clothing. There is no evidence that they were carrying weapons.

While the attackers were firing at the United States marines, someone returned their fire from inside Chili's and the Mediterranée restaurant. 477/

A member of the commando was wounded in the cross-fire. 478/ The following people were also shot and died at the scene: Humberto Sáenz Cevallos, lawyer, Secretary of the Faculty of Law at José Matías Delgado University; Humberto Antonio Rosales Pineda, Executive Director of Inter Data Corporation; Arturo Alonso Silva Hoff, student; José Elmer Vidal Peñalva, university student; Oswaldo González Zambroni, Guatemalan businessman; Richard Ernest Mac Ardie Venturino, Chilean executive of the WANG corporation; George Viney, United States citizen, Regional Director of WANG; and Roberto Alvidrez, United States citizen and WANG executive. Some of these people had been sitting in Chile's, others in the Mediterranée. 479/ There is no evidence that any of the civilians who died were armed. 480/ Other people at the scene were wounded.

A few minutes after the commando withdrew, staff from the United States Embassy arrived on the scene and drove the four marines to a first aid post.

At 9.30 p.m., members of the National Police arrived on the scene but, according to their report, were unable to make a satisfactory inspection because only eight of the bodies were there and the scene of the incident had already been disturbed. 481/

That same night, the other members of the commando took José Roberto Salazar Mendoza, who had been seriously wounded in the attack, to a Salvadorian Red Cross post. He died from his wound. 482/

Subsequent statements

Three days later, on 22 June 1985, the Partido Revolucionario de Trabajadores Centroamericanos (PRTC) claimed responsibility for the operation in a communiqué signed by "Fernando Gallardo" of the political and military headquarters of the "Mardoqueo Cruz" urban guerrilla commando of PRTC.

On 25 June 1985, the FMLN General Command issued a communiqué supporting the operation and asserting that the four marines were a legitimate military target. 483/ The Commission has full evidence, however, that the United States marines were not combatants. Their function was to guard the United States Embassy and there is no indication whatsoever that they took part in combat actions in El Salvador. Furthermore, international humanitarian law defines the category of "combatant" restrictively. The allegation that they were performing "intelligence functions" has not been substantiated. In any event, carrying out intelligence functions does not, in itself, automatically place an individual in the category of combatant.

In a subsequent broadcast on Radio Venceremos, Ismael Dimas Aguilar acknowledged that, as one of the military chiefs of the "Mardoqueo Cruz" urban commando responsible for the operation, he had participated in its planning and in the execution of the marines. 484/

On 28 August 1985, then President of the Republic José Napoleón Duarte held a press conference to report on the results of the investigation into what he called the "Zona Rosa Massacre". He said that three of the people responsible for the operation had been arrested. José Abraham Dimas Aguilar and Juan Miguel García Meléndez, who had planned the operation, and William Celio Rivas Bolaños, who had helped carry it out.

The judicial proceedings

On 27 August 1985, the National Guard placed the three accused at the disposal of the military court and handed over the results of the investigation, including the confession of the three defendants. 485/ Rivas and García later said that their confessions had been obtained under torture. The documents of the investigation were incomplete, since they did not include autopsy or ballistic reports, a reconstruction of events, or other reports customary in the investigation of a case of this kind. 486/

Sentence was passed only five years later, on 30 April 1991, in the court of first instance. Although it appears from the dossier that the extrajudicial confessions were generally confirmed, there is no record that the defendants ever appeared in court, that any statement was taken from them or that any effort whatsoever was made to clarify the facts.

Two years after the trial began, the defendants' lawyer requested the dismissal of proceedings against them under the 1987 Amnesty Act. 487/ On 12 November 1987, the court granted the request and dismissed all charges against the three defendants. 488/

The United States Consul-General in San Salvador representing the family of one of the dead United States marines went to court to file an appeal against the amnesty. 489/ On 4 December 1987, the military court confirmed the dismissal on grounds that the offences had been political. 490/

On 22 February 1988, President Napoleón Duarte, to whom, as Commander-in-Chief of the Armed Forces, the decision of the military court was referred, overturned it on the grounds 491/ that the Zona Rosa killings were ordinary crimes of international significance and, as such, not subject to amnesty. The Supreme Court of Justice, before which the matter was brought by means of a remedy of *habeas corpus*, confirmed the decision.

On 30 April 1991, sentence was passed in the court of the first instance and the three defendants were found guilty; the sentence was confirmed, almost in its entirety, on 5 March by the relevant court.

On 25 September 1992, the military judge decided to wait until he had seen the report of the Commission on the Truth before ruling on the request from the defendants' lawyer that the National Reconciliation Act be applied to the defendants, saying that the report was indispensable in order to determine whether the amnesty provided for in that Act was applicable. 492/

While this trial was going on, two other defendants went on trial for the same incident.

One trial, that of Juan Antonio Morales, began in 1988. Morales confessed to the Treasury Police that he had been part of the commando that had carried out the Zona Rosa operation and he confirmed his statement to the judge of the Fifth Criminal Court. Although his version of events is substantially the same as the one given by Rivas, García and Dimas, he did not name them as having been among the participants. There was no joinder of the two trials, and he has still not been sentenced. After a number of procedural vicissitudes, those implicated were denied the benefit of amnesty. Morales is still being held. 493/

The other trial, for complicity, was instituted in 1989 before the Third Criminal Court against Pedro Antonio Andrade, *nom de querre* "Mario González". 494/ This trial too was not joined to the earlier one. Unlike the other defendants, Andrade benefited from the 1987 amnesty.

The Commission has received sufficient evidence that Andrade was one of the people who planned the attack. Andrade was head of the "Mardoqueo Cruz" urban commando at the time the incident occurred and he confessed in court to having had prior knowledge of an attack planned against "los cheles" (foreigners) and having made arrangements for a safe house and for medical care in case anyone was wounded in the operation. However, the Commission has received credible information that Andrade had a wider role in the selection of specific targets and in other aspects of the attack.

Findings

The Commission finds the following:

1. There is full evidence that the attack on the United States marines was part of the FMLN policy of considering United States military personnel a legitimate target of war.

2. There is full evidence that the "Mardoqueo Cruz" urban commando of PRTC carried out the attack and that PRTC, as the organization to which this commando belongs, bears responsibility for the incident.

3. There is substantial evidence that Ismael Dimas Aguilar planned the attack and that he himself fired on the marines.

4. There is sufficient evidence that Pedro Antonio Andrade was involved in planning the attack.

5. The attack on the marines in the Zona Rosa was a violation by FMLN of the rules of international humanitarian law.

(b) *Anaya Sanabria*

Summary of the case

Herbert Ernesto Anaya Sanabria, leader of the Human Rights Commission (non-governmental), was shot and killed on the morning of 26 October 1987 in the parking lot outside his home in San Salvador.

Two months later, National Police arrested a young man, Jorge Alberto Miranda Arévalo, a member of ERP, who initially stated that he had taken part in the murder as the look-out. He later retracted his confession. In 1991, a jury found him guilty and he was sentenced to the maximum penalty of 30 years in prison.

The Commission finds that:

1. For this case, it did not have sufficient time to resolve the following dilemma: the fact that there was evidence that a State security force or a death squad might have been responsible, and also evidence that the Ejército Revolucionario del Pueblo (ERP) might have been responsible for the murder of Herbert Ernesto Anaya Sanabria.

2. Miranda's trial and his treatment by the police violated his basic rights.

3. The State failed in its duty under international law to protect human rights, properly investigate the murder of Herbert Anaya and bring to trial and punish the culprits.

Description of the facts 495/

The murder

On 26 October 1987, Herbert Anaya was shot to death in the parking lot of his home in the Zacamil district. According to witnesses, three men took a direct part in the murder: one fired the shots, another acted as look-out for the first and the third 496/ drove the vehicle. 497/ The murderers escaped in an old, yellow pick-up truck.

Ballistic tests showed that the six cartridges had been

fired from the same weapon, 498/ and also that the six bullets found had been fired from the same weapon. 499/ The Commission for the Investigation of Criminal Acts (CIHD) maintained that the bullets were not typical of the ammunition available to the armed forces of El Salvador. 500/

Background

At the time he was murdered, Herbert Anaya was general coordinator of the Human Rights Commission (non-governmental) (CDHES-NG) 501/ and used to speak out regularly against human rights violations. He was also a member of the Ejército Revolucionario del Pueblo. 502/ Before his death, he apparently advocated a peaceful solution to the armed conflict in his country. 503/

On 26 May 1986, he was arrested by members of the Treasury Police who were dressed in civilian clothing and heavily armed. 504/ He was interrogated and imprisoned 505/ until 2 February 1987, when he was released in an exchange of prisoners.

Reaction to the murder

The murder triggered a strong reaction both within El Salvador and abroad. There were demonstrations in the capital and national and international human rights groups and civilian associations expressed their concern. 506/

President Duarte asked CIHD to investigate the case and also offered a reward of 50,000 colones (US$ 10,000). 507/ The investigation did not produce any significant results, and the possibility that Anaya might have been murdered by Government forces or right-wing sectors was not seriously investigated.

Arrest and detention of Jorge Alberto Miranda Arévalo

On 23 December 1987, National Police arrested Jorge Alberto Miranda Arévalo, a member of a union of the ERP urban commandos. 508/ Miranda and a companion had attacked a truck carrying soft drinks. His companion "Carlos", who, according to Miranda's first statement, shot at Anaya, managed to escape.

Miranda was interrogated 509/ and, according to the National Police, made an extrajudicial statement confessing to having participated as look-out in Anaya's murder. According to the court dossier, that same day he led members of the National Police to arms caches.

During the first weeks of his detention, Miranda said that he had been subjected to psychological pressure. 510/ He said he had been injected with an unknown substance, 511/ and also that he had been subjected to sleep deprivation.

The Government concluded that Miranda was guilty. When the Government paid Miranda 12,000 colones on 4 January 1988, saying that the payment was being made under a programme announced in December 1987, the Minister of Justice denied that Miranda was being rewarded for taking the blame for the murder. 512/

During the first weeks of his imprisonment, Miranda received special treatment: he was interviewed on camera and visited alone by foreign reporters 513/ and also by senior officials. Miranda says he was also visited by members of the National Police and by some Venezuelans who offered him comforts if he stuck to his original statement. 514/

For its part, CIHD concluded its investigation shortly after Miranda's arrest. According to the dossier, CIHD did not pursue leads or update important information, spoke to few witnesses and did not compare the results of ballistic tests of the ammunition used in the murder with ammunition handed over by Miranda.

Judicial proceedings against Miranda

When he had been held nine days longer than the maximum time allowed by the Salvadorian Constitution without being brought before a judge, 515/ Miranda was brought before the judge of the First Criminal Court of San Salvador 516/ [on 4 January 1988], the day he received his payment from the Government. That same day, Miranda confirmed his extrajudicial statement before the judge. Nevertheless, one month later, he retracted his statement about the assassination, although he reaffirmed that he was a member of ERP. 517/

After two years during which little headway was made, the judge ordered a partial stay of proceedings in Miranda's favour in April 1990, "... because of the absence of the necessary evidence of his participation". 518/ Subsequently, the First Criminal Chamber of the First Central Section revoked the stay 519/ and brought the case to trial.

In October 1991, a jury of five persons found Jorge Miranda guilty of murder and acts of terrorism. 520/

In March 1992, the judge applied the National Reconciliation Act to Miranda in respect of the offence of acts of terrorism and subversive association, but not in respect of the murder, and gave Miranda the maximum sentence of 30 years in prison. 521/

The evidence 522/

ERP

No ERP member interviewed by the Commission has claimed responsibility for Anaya's murder, nor has any witness identified Miranda as a participant. One eyewitness who claimed to have seen the murderers from close up was unable to identify Miranda when shown a series of photographs of young men, including Miranda. 523/

Nonetheless, there is evidence that ERP and Miranda may have participated in the murder, and there are even credible motives. There were disagreements between Anaya and ERP. There is evidence that Anaya already wanted to see an end to the violence, whereas ERP had embarked on an initiative which would require violence in San Salvador.

Moreover, in his first two statements, Miranda put the blame on himself and on ERP. He had, and continues to have, a grasp of the facts. 524/

To the Commission, Miranda continued to deny his involvement. He even claimed that he had made up everything he had said about the murder and its planning. Nevertheless, he gave details of the murder and the way in which it was apparently planned that tally with other facts and that, according to our investigations, he had not given before. He provided information on: the time of a meeting held the night before the murder, where the pick-up truck came from, who obtained it and how he got to Anaya's parking lot in order to be able to act as look-out before the murder.

The Government

Salvadorian and international human rights organizations have expressed concern that the armed forces or a death squad may have killed Anaya in order to put an end to his criticisms of human rights violations. 525/

There is evidence that this could be true. According to his colleagues, Anaya received a number of direct and indirect threats from the Government throughout 1987. 526/ According to a leader of CDHES-NG, two weeks before his murder a woman who worked for the Commission was arrested by the National Police, who informed her that they knew that Anaya was the leader of the organization and that "they were going to disrupt the entire work" of the organization. 527/

Throughout the 1980s, there were constant acts of violence against CDHES-NG and Anaya was the fourth leader of the Commission to be murdered or to disappear. Not one of these cases has been satisfactorily resolved. 528/

Moreover, according to Anaya's widow, at 6.10 a.m on the day of the murder, neighbours saw a group of National Police some 200 metres from the family's house. 529/ She argues that since the police were so close by, the murderers could not have been from FMLN.

Findings

The Commission finds that:

1. For this case, it did not have sufficient time to resolve the following dilemma: the fact that there was evidence showing that a State security force or a death squad might have been responsible, and also evidence that the Ejército Revolucionario del Pueblo (ERP) might have

been responsible for the murder of Herbert Ernesto Anaya Sanabria.

2. Miranda's trial and his treatment by the police violated his basic rights.

3. The State failed in its duty under international law to protect human rights, properly investigate the murder of Herbert Anaya and bring to trial and punish the culprits.

(c) Romero Garcia, "Miguel Castellanos"

Summary of the case

Miguel Castellanos, whose real name was Napoleón Romero García, was murdered at 6.30 p.m. on 16 February 1989, shortly after leaving his office in the Centro para Estudios de la Realidad Nacional (CEREN) in the Flor Blanca district of San Salvador. FMLN urban commandos machine-gunned the vehicle in which Castellanos was travelling with his bodyguard, Rafael Quijada López, on the 43 Avenida Sur and Sexta Décima calle PONENTE. Castellanos was taken to the military hospital, where he died soon after. Quijada López received three bullet wounds, two in the legs and one in the stomach, but he survived the attack.

The attackers were not identified.

In a Radio Venceremos broadcast and in statements to the press, FMLN took responsibility for the attack.

Background

Castellanos, aged 39, had been a member of the Political Commission of the Fuerzas Populares de Liberación (FPL), one of the member organizations of FMLN, until mid-April 1985, when he was arrested by members of the National Guard. During the first days of his detention, he agreed to change his position and to collaborate with the authorities.

Before his arrest, Castellanos had been a member of the Political Commission of FPL and, in that capacity, the political and military official in charge of the special metropolitan area, as well as a member of the FMLN Joint Command in San Salvador. According to a report submitted to the Commission on the Truth by FMLN, Castellanos handled a great deal of secret information and, after his arrest in 1985, advised the National Guard and other intelligence bodies of the armed forces on matters relating to the campaign against FPL in particular and FMLN in general.

After changing his position, Miguel Castellanos started working at CEREN. He was also editor of the magazine Análisis.

Action by the Commission

The facts of the case are not in dispute. Nevertheless, the Commission examined the available evidence and sought information from FMLN, which it obtained.

The position of FMLN is that the death of Miguel Castellanos was a legitimate execution, since he was a traitor who was contributing in a direct and effective manner to repression against FMLN.

Findings

Notwithstanding the arguments put forward by FMLN, international humanitarian law does not permit the execution of civilians without a proper trial.

(d) Peccorini Lettona

Francisco Peccorini Lettona, aged 73, a doctor of philosophy and university lecturer, was a contributor to *El Diario de Hoy*, a morning newspaper in El Salvador, in which he had written a number of articles opposing the activities of FMLN.

Mr. Peccorini took an active and public part in a group dedicated to what it termed "winning back" the University of El Salvador, which, in its view, had been infiltrated by guerrillas.

On 15 March 1989 in San Salvador, while driving his car, Mr. Peccorini was the target of an attack in which he was shot. He was taken to the military hospital, where he died.

At the Cocoyoc meeting, held in Mexico from 21 to 24 July 1989 between prominent persons from the United States of America and representatives of FMLN, FMLN acknowledged responsibility for Mr. Peccorini's death.

(e) García Alvarado

On 19 April 1989, Mr. José Roberto García Alvarado, Attorney-General of the Republic, was killed when a bomb planted in the car he was driving exploded. The incident occurred in the San Miguelito area of San Salvador and the two passengers in the car were injured.

At the Cocoyoc meeting in Mexico in July 1989, FMLN took responsibility for Mr. García Alvarado's death, which it attributed to the Fuerzas Armadas de Liberación (FAL), one of its member organizations.

(f) Guerrero

Summary of the case

On 28 November 1989, Mr. Francisco José Guerrero, former President of the Supreme Court of El Salvador, was assassinated in his car at the intersection of Boulevard de los Héroes and Alameda Juan Pablo II in San Salvador. One of the attackers was killed, another escaped and the third, César Ernesto Erazo Cruz, was wounded.

In the hospital, Erazo Cruz said he had killed Guer-rero on orders from FMLN. He later changed his story and finally denied participating at all. When he came to trial, the jury acquitted him.

At the time of his death, Mr. Guerrero was investigating the assassination of the Jesuit priests and apparently had found evidence. One of the possible motives for his murder may have been precisely to conceal that evidence.

Mr. Guerrero died as a result of deliberate action aimed at killing him. Although César Ernesto Erazo Cruz was acquitted at the trial, there is every evidence that he participated in the assassination. The Commission tried unsuccessfully to obtain significant information both within and outside El Salvador to confirm or disprove its investigating hypotheses. Although there is sufficient evidence that Erazo Cruz was at the time an active FMLN member, a fact which suggests that a more thorough investigation of FMLN responsibility for the assassination is called for, the available evidence did not allow the Commission, on completion of its work, to reach full agreement on this case.

Description of the facts 530/

Mr. Francisco José Guerrero, a prominent conservative politician, was active in public life for more than three decades. 531/ He was President of the Supreme Court, worked as an adviser to President Cristiani to promote the dialogue with FMLN and was also a member of the Ministry of Foreign Affairs advisory council. 532/

Mr. Guerrero was investigating the assassination of the Jesuit priests, which took place 12 days before he was killed. He had contacted the Jesuits immediately after the crime occurred and offered to cooperate in solving it.

The death of Mr. Guerrero

On the morning of 28 November 1989, Mr. Guerrero left his house in the Escalón district with his daughter-in-law to drive her to the San Salvador judicial centre, where she worked. Mr. Guerrero was driving, his daughter-in-law was sitting in the front passenger seat, and his bodyguard, Víctor Manuel Rivera Monterrosa, was sitting in the back seat. Mr. Guerrero was usually accompanied by two bodyguards, but that morning one of them did not show up.

They reached the intersection of Boulevard de los Héroes and Alameda Juan Pablo II without incident, and there they stopped at a traffic light near the "Biggest" restaurant. A man—later identified as Angel Aníbal Alvarez Martínez—ran up along the pavement and stationed himself behind Mr. Guerrero's car. Another unidentified man stationed himself to the left of the car and a third, later identified as César Ernesto Erazo Cruz, stood on the right side. Without addressing a word to the occupants of the car, they opened fire with their weapons. 533/ Mr. Guerrero's bodyguard noticed the men before they aimed their first shots at him, but only had time to react and counter-attack. 534/

According to witnesses, the attackers had followed Mr. Guerrero to the intersection in a yellow Volkswagen, from which they emerged and surrounded him. Other witnesses asserted that the attackers arrived on foot. 535/

The vehicle was hit from three sides by nine bullets. 536/ Apparently, the attackers fired first at Mr. Rivera Monterrosa, who was wounded, lost control for a few seconds, then managed to fire back at his attackers with a 357 calibre revolver and an M-16 rifle. At that moment, he was hit again and emptied the entire magazine at the attackers. 537/

Mr. Guerrero was hit by five bullets. 538/ All the bullets extracted from his body were 45 calibre, 539/ three of them having been fired from a revolver which, according to the person who handed it over to the police two days later, was found on the body of Alvarez Martínez. 540/ The other two bullets had been fired from another weapon that was never recovered.

Erazo Cruz and Alvarez Martínez were standing on the pavement in front of the "Biggest" restaurant when on-the-spot witnesses saw at least one man get out of a Cherokee-type vehicle two or three cars behind that of Mr. Guerrero, and fire a rifle, apparently an M-16, at Erazo Cruz and Alvarez Martínez. 541/ Alvarez Martínez was killed instantly. 542/ Erazo Cruz was wounded. 543/ The calibre of the bullet extracted from the body of Alvarez Martínez was 5.56 mm, 544/ which is the calibre used in the M-16.

The third attacker fled the scene and has never been identified. The Cherokee picked up the man with the M-16 and likewise left the scene for an unknown destination. 545/

Mr. Guerrero and his bodyguard were taken to the Medical Surgical Hospital, where Mr. Guerrero died the same day. His daughter-in-law survived the attack unharmed.

Subsequent events

The paraffin tests performed on Alvarez Martínez and Erazo Cruz the following day by officers of the National Police were positive. 546/

Erazo Cruz stated at the National Police medical clinic that he was a member of the FPL urban commandos and had participated in the assassination on the orders of the FMLN command, transmitted through another member of the organization. According to this statement, all he knew was that an important politician was to be assassinated. On further questioning, he changed his story and said that a certain "Manuel" had simply told him they were going to commandeer a vehicle. 547/

In his second statement, made to the judge of the Sixth Criminal Court, Erazo Cruz confirmed his first statement, with some changes. According to this version, "Manuel" had told him they were going to commandeer a vehicle with tinted glass windows. They had gone up and down the boulevard several times without finding the vehicle. When they came to the corner where the "Biggest" restaurant is situated, his two companions suddenly started running towards a vehicle. "Manuel" took up position behind the vehicle and shot into the back of it, while "Efraín" stood in front and shot into the front of it.

According to Erazo Cruz, when this happened he ran to the pavement in front of the "Biggest" restaurant. From there he saw a man with a rifle get out of a car behind the vehicle at which "Manuel" and "Efraín" were firing and shoot at "Manuel". At that moment he himself felt an impact and fell to the ground. He did not know where "Efraín" went or whether he had been wounded. 548/

On the basis of these statements, the trial judge ordered that Erazo Cruz be detained pending trial. 549/ After recovering from his wounds, he was held in the Mariona prison. This prison was attacked by FAL members; Erazo Cruz escaped with other prisoners and reached an FMLN camp. 550/

In September 1991, troops of the Atlacatl Battalion wounded and captured Erazo Cruz. The soldiers took him to hospital and he was subsequently committed to prison.

The public hearing was held on 21 July 1992 in the Sixth Criminal Court. Erazo Cruz was accused of aggravated homicide, 551/ causing grievous bodily harm, 552/ being a member of a subversive association, 553/ and escape involving the use of violence. 554/ During the trial, Erazo Cruz denied participating in the crime, despite his judicial confession. He claimed that he was passing by the scene of the crime when he found himself caught in the gunfire; he was wounded and was, he alleged, forced to confess that he was responsible.

The jury acquitted Erazo Cruz of the charges of homicide and causing grievous bodily harm. 555/ He was freed in mid-August 1992.

Responsibility of the guerrillas and participation of Erazo Cruz

FMLN admitted a certain degree of responsibility for the assassination of Mr. Guerrero. Shortly after the crime, FMLN spokesmen said he had been killed when the members of the urban commandos tried to steal his car. This version coincides with parts of the original statements by Erazo Cruz, including his judicial confession.

Furthermore, the 45 calibre and 9 mm revolvers used in the assassination were typical of the weapons used by the urban commandos. Moreover, although Erazo Cruz was acquitted and denied any participation when he appeared before the Commission, there is substantial evidence that he took part in the crime. An eyewitness who had not spoken before identified him as one of the attackers. The paraffin test was positive, showing he had fired a gun. There are also contradictions in parts of his testimony to CIHD. *556/*

The FMLN members interviewed by the Commission said that they did not know Erazo Cruz before the assassination and did not have any information on Alvarez Martínez and the other participants, nor did they know anything about the crime. Nevertheless, the Commission received reliable evidence indicating that Erazo Cruz belonged to the guerrilla forces at the time when Mr. Guerrero was assassinated.

On the other hand, the Commission received information to the effect that Mr. Guerrero was assassinated because he had obtained incriminating evidence on those allegedly responsible in the Jesuit case. This version was made public in January 1992, when Marta Aracely Guerrero de Paredes, Mr. Guerrero's daughter, said that on the day he died her father had been carrying documents revealing the identity of those who had killed the six Jesuit priests. *557/*

Mr. Guerrero had used his political influence to obtain information. A few days before he died, at least one friend warned him that his life was in danger and that he should stop investigating the Jesuit case.

The attack on Mr. Guerrero certainly did not occur as a result of an attempt to steal his car. The attackers never addressed a word to the occupants of the car, which was, moreover, hit by so many bullets that it could not be used again.

The role which the Cherokee-type vehicle played in the incident casts further doubts on the identity of those responsible for planning the assassination. Generally speaking, Cherokee vehicles were used in official circles and, similarly, M-16 rifles were used by members of the armed forces and bodyguards. The whereabouts of the Cherokee and its occupants is unknown.

Findings

Taking into account its consideration of the available documents and the direct testimony received, including the new evidence, the Commission finds that there is full evidence that Mr. Guerrero's death resulted not from an attempt to steal his car but from an intention to kill the driver of the car, i.e. Mr. Guerrero.

Mr. Guerrero died as a result of deliberate action aimed at killing him. Although César Ernesto Erazo Cruz was acquitted at the trial, there is every evidence that he participated in the assassination. The Commission tried unsuccessfully to obtain significant information both within and outside El Salvador to confirm or disprove its investigating hypotheses. Although there is sufficient evidence that Erazo Cruz was at the time an active FMLN member, a fact which suggests that a more thorough investigation of FMLN responsibility for the assassination is called for, the available evidence did not allow the Commission, on completion of its work, to reach full agreement on this case.

(g) United States soldiers who survived the shooting down of a helicopter

Summary of the case

On 2 January 1991, a United States helicopter gunship was shot down by an FMLN patrol in San Francisco canton, Lolotique district, Department of San Miguel, while flying at low altitude towards its base at Soto Cano, Honduras.

The pilot, Daniel F. Scott, was killed in the crash and Lt. Colonel David H. Pickett and Corporal Earnest G. Dawson were wounded; all were United States nationals. Members of the patrol approached the helicopter and fired at the survivors from a certain distance. The patrol left the dead United States soldier and the two wounded soldiers at the scene and departed, carrying off weapons and equipment from the helicopter. Shortly afterwards, a member of the patrol was sent back to the scene and killed the two wounded men.

Description of the facts

At about 1.40 p.m. on 2 January 1991, a United States armed forces UH-1H helicopter took off from the Ilopango airport, San Salvador, with a crew consisting of the following United States military personnel: Lt. Colonel David H. Pickett, Corporal Earnest G. Dawson and the pilot, Daniel F. Scott. Pickett was Commander of the Fourth Battalion of the 22nd Airborne Regiment, based in Soto Cano, Honduras, where they expected to arrive shortly after 5 p.m.

At about 2 p.m., the helicopter was flying over San Francisco canton at an altitude of between 30 and 50 metres. It was flying low in order to be less vulnerable to possible guerrilla missile attacks, and also because, if it was shot down, there would be more likelihood of the occupants surviving.

That day, seven armed combatants of the Ejército Revolucionario del Pueblo (ERP) an FMLN member organization, were on patrol in San Francisco canton, Lolotique district, Department of San Miguel. Severiano Fuentes Fuentes, "Aparicio", a political leader of that organization in the area, was in command of the patrol, which in addition consisted of Antonio Bonilla Rivas, "Ulises", Daniel Alvarado Guevara, "Macaco", Digna Chicas, "Doris", and María Lita Fernández, "Carmen".

They were accompanied by Santos Guevara Portillo, "Domínguez", and Fernán Fernández Arévalo, "Porfirio".

On sighting the helicopter, the patrol fired their M-16 and AK-47 rifles at it. The helicopter crashed some 500 metres away.

As the autopsy subsequently showed, the pilot, Scott, was killed when the helicopter crashed. The ERP patrol approached firing and wounded the two survivors.

One member of the patrol went to San Francisco canton, some 500 metres away, and came back with about 10 of the inhabitants. They placed the two wounded men and Scott's body some metres away from the helicopter and took back to San Francisco the articles which the combatants pointed out to them. The latter then set fire to the helicopter.

There is sufficient proof that Severiano Fuentes Fuentes, "Aparicio", ordered Daniel Alvarado Guevara, "Macaco", to kill the two wounded men and that "Macaco" refused to obey. When the patrol had moved about 100 metres away, Fernán Fernández Arévalo, "Porfirio", on the orders of Fuentes, came back and killed the wounded men.

Subsequent events

Some inhabitants of San Francisco told the authorities what had happened. The same night, the bodies were found and transferred by helicopter to Third Brigade headquarters, where they were examined by a justice of the peace. They were subsequently transferred to Ilopango airport, in San Salvador, where they were handed over to the United States authorities.

The following day, 3 January, a group of United States military personnel, accompanied by Salvadorian officers, inspected the remains of the helicopter and interviewed a number of local inhabitants.

The news of the shooting down of the helicopter and the execution of the wounded soldiers was disseminated the same day.

FMLN, via Radio Venceremos, began by denying that any wounded men had been executed. On 7 January, it acknowledged that this might have happened and announced that an investigation would be undertaken. On 9 January, it admitted that the wounded men had been executed and on 18 January it announced that "Domínguez" and "Porfirio" would be tried for the offence. A correction was subsequently issued to the effect that "Aparicio" and not "Domínguez" was involved.

On 17 March 1992, Fuentes ("Aparicio") and Fernández ("Porfirio") voluntarily appeared before the Cinameca Court of First Instance and were sent to the Mariona Prison, where they remain.

Action by the Commission

The Commission on the Truth examined the materials in the judicial dossier, the results of the investigations carried out by United States experts and the documentation relating to the investigation made by FMLN, which was supplied by the latter. It interviewed five of the seven combatants who participated in the incident, together with a number of inhabitants of San Francisco canton and other people who could provide relevant information.

Findings

The Commission considers that there is sufficient proof that United States soldiers Lt. Colonel David H. Pickett and Corporal Earnest G. Dawson, who survived the shooting down of the helicopter by an ERP unit, but were wounded and defenceless, were executed, in violation of international humanitarian law, by Fernán Fernández Arévalo, acting on the orders of Severiano Fuentes Fuentes. The Commission has found no evidence that other members of the unit participated in the execution.

The Commission has likewise found no evidence that the executions were ordered by higher levels of command, or that they were carried out in accordance with an ERP or FMLN policy of killing prisoners. FMLN acknowledged the criminal nature of the incident and detained and tried the accused.

3. Abductions

Duarte and Villeda

On 10 September 1985, Inés Guadalupe Duarte Durán, daughter of President José Napoleón Duarte, and her friend, Ana Cecilia Villeda, arrived by car at the gates of a private university in San Salvador. They were followed in a van by two bodyguards assigned to protect them. As the two vehicles came to a stop, other vehicles positioned themselves so as to block traffic, while a number of armed individuals killed the bodyguards and forced the two women into a truck. 558/ The two women were taken to a guerrilla camp.

Four days after the incident, the self-styled Pedro Pablo Castillo commando of FMLN publicly announced that it was responsible.

On 24 October, after several weeks of negotiations in which the Salvadorian church and diplomats from the region acted as mediators in secret talks, Inés Duarte and her friend were released in exchange for 22 political prisoners. 559/ The operation also included the release of 25 mayors and local officials abducted by FMLN in exchange for 101 war-wounded guerrillas, whom the Government allowed to leave the country. The entire process of exchanging prisoners, which took place in various parts of the country, was carried out through the International Committee of the Red Cross.

In a communiqué from the FMLN General Command broadcast by Radio Venceremos on the day Inés Duarte was released, the General Command assumed full responsibility for the operation and described the actions of the commando, including the killing of the bodyguards, as "impeccable".

The abduction of Inés Duarte and Ana Cecilia Villeda constitutes a taking of hostages and is therefore a violation of international humanitarian law. 560/

F. Murders of judges

In the 1980s, it was dangerous to be a judge in El Salvador. As can be seen from the reports in this chapter concerning the murders of Monsignor Romero and the Dutch journalists, some judges, after being threatened or attacked, were forced to resign and even to flee the country.

What is more, according to a report given to the Commission on the Truth by the Supreme Court of Justice, 28 judges were murdered in El Salvador in the 1980s. 561/

One of them, Mr. Francisco José Guerrero, was assassinated after completing his term of office as President of the Supreme Court. Three others murdered were judges of courts of first instance and the remaining 24 were justices of the peace; of the latter, 20 were murdered during the period 1980-1982.

The Commission received complaints and testimony from independent sources regarding some of the cases referred to it by the Supreme Court and was able to investigate two of them. As to the other murders, there was evidence that some had been perpetrated by FMLN and others by the death squads and in two cases the judges appear to have died in combat.

The case investigated in depth was the assassination of Mr. Francisco José Guerrero, the report of which is contained in this chapter. The results of the investigation of the murder of a justice of the peace are given below.

Justice of the peace of Carolina

José Apolinar Martínez, justice of the peace of the town of Carolina in the Department of San Miguel, was shot to death at his home on 14 June 1988. His three-year-old daughter was also wounded in the attack and subsequently underwent weeks of medical treatment.

There is strong evidence that FMLN was responsible. About one year previously, the judge had received threatening letters from the Ejército Revolucionario del Pueblo, one of the armed groups in FMLN. The murder took place in an area at least partially controlled by FMLN. The killers subsequently fled towards an area under greater FMLN control. They were wearing military uniforms and carrying rifles. A piece of paper indicating that FMLN assumed responsibility for the murder was found at the scene of the crime.

On the other hand, a long time elapsed between the threats and the murder. Furthermore, there was no pattern of executing justices of the peace at that time. Although many justices of the peace were murdered in the period 1980-1982, only two such murders, including this one, occurred between 1986 and 1988.

Nevertheless, taking into account all the circumstances and all the evidence, the Commission finds that there is sufficient evidence to attribute this murder to FMLN members. The murder of justice of the peace José Apolinar Martínez violated international humanitarian law.

V. Recommendations

Introduction

As part of its mandate, the Commission is called upon to make recommendations. Indeed, under the terms of its mandate,

"The mandate of the Commission shall include recommending the legal, political or administrative measures which can be inferred from the results of the investigation. Such recommendations may include measures to prevent the repetition of such acts, and initiatives to promote national reconciliation".

The Commission decided to first comment generally on the results of its investigations, the principles on which these investigations and its recommendations are based and the persons and institutions to whom they are addressed, before making specific recommendations.

1. General conclusions

The causes and conditions which generated the large number of serious acts of violence in El Salvador derive from very complex circumstances. The country's history and its deeply rooted relations of injustice cannot be attributed simply to one sector of the population or one group of persons. This or that Government institution, certain historical traditions, even the ideological struggle between East and West which went on until only recently, and of which El Salvador was a victim and an episode, are mere components. All these factors help to explain the complex situation in El Salvador during the 12-year period which concerns us. The Commission was not called upon to deal with all these factors, nor could it do so. Instead, it focused on certain considerations which prompted it to formulate its basic recommendations in such a way that this situation might be fully understood.

The lack of human rights guarantees in El Salvador and the fact that a society has operated outside the principles of a State subject to the rule of law imposes a serious responsibility on the Salvadorian State itself, rather than on one or other of its Governments. The political, legislative and institutional mechanisms required to ensure the existence of a society subject to the rule of law existed in theory, at least in part, but the reality was not what it should have been, perhaps as a consequence of excessive pragmatism. With the passage of time, the military establishment and, more specifically, some elements within the armed forces, having embarked upon a course from which they found it difficult to extricate themselves, ended up totally controlling the civilian authorities, frequently in collusion with some influential civilians.

None of the three branches of Government—judicial, legislative or executive—was capable of restraining the military's overwhelming control of society. The judiciary was weakened as it fell victim to intimidation and the foundations were laid for its corruption; since it had never enjoyed genuine institutional independence from the legislative and executive branches, its ineffectiveness steadily increased until it became, through its inaction or its appalling submissiveness, a factor which contributed to the tragedy suffered by the country. The various, frequently opportunistic, alliances which political leaders (legislators as well as members of the executive branch) forged with the military establishment and with members of the judiciary had the effect of further weakening civilian control over the military, police and security forces, all of which formed part of the military establishment.

The wide network of illegal armed groups, known as "death squads", which operated both within and outside the institutional framework with complete impunity, spread terror throughout Salvadorian society. They originated basically as a civilian operation, designed, financed and controlled by civilians. The core of serving officers, whose role was originally limited to that of mere executants and executioners, gradually seized control of the death squads for personal gain or to promote certain ideological or political objectives. Thus, within the military establishment and in contradiction with its real purpose and mandate, impunity *vis-à-vis* the civilian authorities became the rule. The institution as a whole was a hostage to specific groups of officers, which were sometimes formed even as their members graduated from officer training school, abused their power and their relations with certain civilian circles and intimidated fellow officers who were reluctant to join in or to collaborate with their corrupt and illegal practices.

The internal armed conflict between opposing forces grew in intensity and magnitude. The inevitable outcome was acts of violence, some of which were brought before the Commission with anxiety and anticipation. The more bloody the conflict became, and the more widespread, the greater the power of the military hierarchy and of those who commanded armed insurgent groups. The outcome of that vicious circle was a situation in which certain elements of society found themselves immune from any governmental or political restraints and thus forged for themselves the most abject impunity. It was they who wielded the real power of the State, expressed in the most primitive terms, while the executive, legislative and judicial branches were unable to play any real role as branches of government. The sad fact is that they were transformed, in practice, into mere façades with marginal governmental authority.

How else can the *modus operandi* of the death squads be understood? The disappearance of large numbers of people, the assassination attempts on important Government officials, church leaders and judges, and the fact that the perpetrators of these atrocities were only rarely brought to trial. What is ironic is that the web of corruption, timidity and weakness within the judiciary and its investigative bodies greatly impeded the effective functioning of the judicial system even where crimes attributed to FMLN were involved.

In order to avoid any risk of reverting to the *status quo ante*, it is essential that El Salvador establish and strengthen the proper balance of power among the executive, legislative and judicial branches and that it institute full and indisputable civilian control over all military, paramilitary, intelligence and security forces. The recommendations which follow are intended to outline the basic prerequisites for this transition and to ensure that it leads to a democratic society in which the rule of law prevails and human rights are fully respected and guaranteed.

2. *Principles*

The report which the Commission is submitting is part of a process initiated, according to the Geneva Agreement of 4 April 1990, for the purpose of ending the armed conflict by political means as speedily as possible, promoting the democratization of the country, guaranteeing unrestricted respect for human rights and reunifying Salvadorian society. The first of these objectives has already been achieved. The remaining goals, however, require a continuous and, in some respects, permanent effort. These goals are complementary: democracy loses ground when human rights are not fully respected; human rights cannot be protected from arbitrariness without the rule of law which is the expression of the democratic system of government; and unless rights and freedoms are respected and guaranteed for all, it will be difficult to speak of a reunified society.

The Commission's recommendations, while they bear fully on the results of its investigations, provide the means for pursuing these objectives, which were defined in the context of the country's recent history by the Salvadorians who negotiated the peace agreements, and by the decisive majority which supported them, as the objectives which must be achieved in the society which they are now beginning to build. Accordingly, these recommendations are based on the following principles:

One: Democracy, which leaves the fundamental decisions as to the destiny of society in the hands of the people, and which gives priority to dialogue and negotiation as basic political tools.

Two: Participation, which integrates minorities with the majority and gives pride of place to democracy as a model respectful of the individual and collective dimensions of human coexistence; also, a participation which promotes solidarity and respect among individuals.

Three: The rule of law, in which the primacy of and respect for the law is the basis of a culture which guarantees equality and proscribes all arbitrariness.

Four: Respect for human rights, which are the *raison d'être* of the above principles and the basis of a society organized to serve people, all of whom are vested with equal freedom and dignity.

The consolidation of the supremacy of civilian authority in Salvadorian society and the necessary subordination of the armed forces to it stem directly from the democratic concept of the rule of law, the primordial value of the dignity of the human person and, hence, full respect for his rights.

The peace agreements envisage a new concept of national defence and public security which represents significant progress towards establishing the supremacy of civilian authority. It is essential that all, absolutely all, the agreements on these issues be complied with fully.

The Commission also underscores the special care which must be taken in implementing the provisions of the peace agreements, and the recommendations in this report, for strengthening a comprehensive system for the protection of human rights and an independent, strong and effective judiciary. The glaring deficiencies experienced by the country in this regard were a prime cause of the occurrence and systematic repetition of extremely grave human rights violations, and such violations will be deemed to have been completely eradicated only when this objective is achieved.

3. Persons and institutions to whom the recommendations are addressed

The Commission's mandate does not specify or limit the persons or institutions to whom its recommendations are to be addressed. What it does establish is a procedure as regards the undertaking given by the Parties, namely, the Government and FMLN, concerning these recommendations. In signing the Mexico Agreements, the Parties created the mechanism which is now completing its work. They undertook to carry out the Commission's recommendations (agreement on the Commission on the Truth, para. 10) and must therefore implement, without delay, those recommendations which are addressed directly to them. Where the recommendations are addressed to others or, particularly in the case of the Government, where they require action or initiatives by State organs other than the executive branch, the Government's undertaking means that it must take the necessary action and initiatives to ensure that the recommendations are put into practice by the appropriate State machinery.

It should also be noted that, with the armed conflict at an end, it is natural that the bulk of the recommendations, being institutional in nature, should be addressed to the official sector. The most crucial recommendation which would have had to be made to FMLN would have been to abandon the use of arms as a means of political struggle and, in any case, to renounce acts and practices such as those described in this report. This objective has been achieved through the peace agreements and their implementation, although this does not prevent the Commission from making a strong appeal to FMLN to ensure that its action as a political force is always accompanied by militant renunciation of all forms of violent struggle and constant adherence to the legal and civilized means proper to democracy, renouncing for ever the methods which resulted in the serious acts of violence described herein that were committed under its authority.

The Commission will now make its recommendations. Clearly, not all of them have the same importance or the same meaning. Some of them, which are inferred directly from the results of the investigation and must be acted on urgently, are aimed at the immediate removal of factors relating directly to the acts investigated or to the fact that the latter were not cleared up when they should have been. Another group of recommendations seeks to remedy certain structural defects linked directly to the acts examined by the Commission. A third group concerns institutional reforms designed to prevent the repetition of such acts. Lastly, the Commission will present its considerations and recommendations concerning national reconciliation.

I. Recommendations inferred directly from the results of the investigation

In this section, the Commission will make recommendations which are the direct and inevitable consequence of its findings concerning acts which it has been called upon to investigate and clarify, in the light of realities connected directly with them which still pervade the country. By their nature, these recommendations are the ones which must be carried out most urgently.

The Commission makes the following recommendations which must be carried out without delay:

A. *Dismissal from the armed forces*

The findings on the cases investigated by the Commission on the Truth and published in this report give the names of officers of the Salvadorian armed forces who are personally implicated in the perpetration or cover-up of serious acts of violence, or who did not fulfil their professional obligation to initiate or cooperate in the investigation and punishment of such acts. For those officers who are still serving in the armed forces, the Commission recommends that they be dismissed from their posts and discharged from the armed forces. For those now in retirement or discharged, the Commission recommends application of the measure described in paragraph C below.

B. *Dismissal from the civil service*

The findings on the cases investigated by the Commission on the Truth also give the names of civilian officials in the civil service and the judiciary. These officials, acting in their professional capacity, covered up serious acts of violence or failed to discharge their responsibilities in the investigation of such acts. For these persons, the Commission recommends that they be dismissed from the civil service or judicial posts they currently occupy. For those who no longer occupy such posts, the Commission recommends application of the measure described in paragraph C below.

C. *Disqualification from holding public office*

Under no circumstances would it be advisable to allow persons who committed acts of violence such as those which the Commission has investigated to participate in the running of the State. The Commission therefore believes that the persons referred to in the preceding paragraphs, as well as any others equally implicated in the perpetration of the acts of violence described in this report, including the civilians and members of the FMLN Command named in the findings on individual cases, should be disqualified from holding any public post or office for a period of not less than 10 years, and should be disqualified permanently from any activity related to public security or national defence. While the Commission does not have the power to apply such a provision directly, it does have the power to recommend to the National Commission for the Consolidation of Peace (COPAZ) that it prepare a preliminary legislative draft on this issue, offering proper guarantees in accordance with Salvadorian law, and that it submit such draft to the Legislative Assembly for early approval. It also has the power to recommend to the bodies authorized to make appointments to public office that they refrain from appointing the persons referred to above.

D. *Judicial reform*

All aspects of the agreed judicial reform must be put into practice. Even if this reform must be complemented by additional measures, some of which will be the subject of other recommendations by the Commission, the agreements reached on this issue during the peace process must be complied with immediately and in full. Two specific aspects should be noted:

(a) *Reform of the Supreme Court of Justice*

The constitutional reform approved as part of the peace process provided a new procedure for the election of judges to the Supreme Court of Justice, the body which heads the judicial branch. Those innovations cannot be put into effect until the current judges' terms expire, with the result that the Court continues to consist of persons elected in accordance with the rules that applied before the constitutional reform and the peace agreements. Given the tremendous responsibility which the judiciary bears for the impunity with which serious acts of violence such as those described in this report occurred, there is no justification for further postponing the appointment of a new Supreme Court of Justice, whose current members should make way for the immediate implementation of the constitutional reform by resigning from their posts.

(b) *National Council of the Judiciary*

The peace agreements provided for the establishment of a National Council of the Judiciary independent from the organs of State and from political parties (Mexico Agreements: "Political agreements elaborating on the constitutional reform", A (b) (1); Chapultepec Peace Agreement, chap. III (1) (A)). However, the National Council of the Judiciary Act, adopted in December 1992 by the Legislative Assembly, contains provisions which, in practice, leave the dismissal of some members of that Council to the discretion of the Supreme Court of Justice. The Commission recommends that this system be changed and that it be possible to dismiss members of the Council only for precise legal causes, to be weighed by the Legislative Assembly which, being the body constitutionally authorized to appoint such members, should, logically, also be the one to decide on their dismissal.

E. *Judges*

The Career Judicial Service Act, the amendment of which, the Commission understands, is under discussion for the date on which this report will be submitted, should establish that only those judges who, according to a rigorous evaluation made by the National Council of the Judiciary, have demonstrated judicial aptitude, efficiency and concern for human rights and offer every guarantee of independence, judicial discretion, honesty and impartiality in their actions may remain in the career judicial service.

F. *Penalties*

One of the direct consequences of the clarification of the serious acts which the Commission has investigated should, under normal circumstances, be the punishment which those responsible for such acts deserve. However, in view of current conditions in the country and the situation of the administration of justice, the Commission is facing insurmountable difficulties which it will describe below.

It is not within the Commission's powers to directly impose penalties on those responsible: it does not have judicial functions and cannot therefore decide to impose a particular penalty on a person. That is a function which, by its nature, properly belongs to the courts, a question which raises serious problems for the Commission. Accordingly, the problem and possible solutions to it cannot be discussed in isolation from the current situation in the country.

One painfully clear aspect of that situation is the glaring inability of the judicial system either to investigate crimes or to enforce the law, especially when it comes to crimes committed with the direct or indirect support of State institutions. It was because these shortcomings were so apparent that the Government and FMLN agreed to create an instrument such as the Commission on the Truth to perform tasks which should normally be undertaken by the bodies responsible for the administration of justice. Had the judiciary functioned satisfactorily, not only would the acts which the Commission has had to investigate have been cleared up at the proper time, but the corresponding penalties would have been imposed. The inability of the courts to apply the law to acts of violence committed under the direct or indirect cover of the public authorities is part and parcel of the situation in which those acts took place and is inseparable from them. This is a conclusion which emerges clearly from most of the cases of this kind examined in this report.

We must ask ourselves, therefore, whether the judiciary is capable, all things being equal, of fulfilling the requirements of justice. If we take a detached view of the situation, this question cannot be answered in the affirmative. The structure of the judiciary is still substantially the same as it was when the acts described in this report took place. The reforms of the judicial system agreed on during the peace process have been implemented to only a limited extent, so that they have yet to have a significant impact which translates into a transformation of the administration of justice. What is more, the judiciary is still run by people whose omissions were part of the situation which must now be overcome, and there is

nothing to indicate that their customary practices will change in the near future.

These considerations confront the Commission with a serious dilemma. The question is not whether the guilty should be punished, but whether justice can be done. Public morality demands that those responsible for the crimes described here be punished. However, El Salvador has no system for the administration of justice which meets the minimum requirements of objectivity and impartiality so that justice can be rendered reliably. This is a part of the country's current reality and overcoming it urgently should be a primary objective for Salvadorian society.

The Commission does not believe that a reliable solution can be found to the problems it has examined by tackling them in the context which is primarily responsible for them. The situation described in this report would not have occurred if the judicial system had functioned properly. Clearly, that system has still not changed enough to foster a feeling of justice which could promote national reconciliation. On the contrary, a judicial debate in the current context, far from satisfying a legitimate desire for justice, could revive old frustrations, thereby impeding the achievement of that cardinal objective, reconciliation. That being the current situation, it is clear that, for now, the only judicial system which the Commission could trust to administer justice in a full and timely manner would be one which had been restructured in the light of the peace agreements.

II. *Eradication of structural causes linked directly to the acts examined*

The peace process led to a set of political agreements which are clearly supported by society as a whole and which introduce major structural reforms and address many defects which contributed to the situation described in this report. As a general principle, the Commission recommends most emphatically that all the agreements be implemented in full: that was the undertaking made by those who negotiated and concluded the agreements and it is also what the Salvadorian people expects, believes in and hopes for.

Without prejudice to these general comments, the Commission wishes to make some additional recommendations:

A. *Reforms in the armed forces*

1. The transition to the new model of the armed forces outlined in the peace agreements and in the constitutional reform should be made rapidly and transparently, under the close supervision of the civilian authorities. It is recommended that a special committee of the Legislative Assembly be appointed for that purpose, comprising the various political forces represented

in the Assembly. Special attention should be paid to the subordination of the military establishment to the civilian authorities, democratic control over promotions to senior ranks and positions of command, rigorous budgetary management, greater decentralization of the military structure, application of the new doctrine and new educational system of the armed forces and steady professionalization of officers.

2. The comprehensive review of the military legislation in force should be completed without delay, in order to bring it fully into line with the new Political Constitution, the new doctrine of the armed forces and the requirements of respect for human rights.

3. Among the reforms referred to in the preceding paragraph, a simple and practical mechanism must be established to resolve the situation of subordinates who receive illegal orders, so that they are protected if they refuse to obey. The provision of article 173 of army regulations which requires a subordinate to obey, at all times and irrespective of risk, the orders he receives from a superior, should be repealed, and the pledge so to obey should be eliminated from the formula used when swearing the solemn oath of allegiance to the flag as part of military ceremonial. It must be made clear, in any case, that so-called "due obedience" does not exonerate a person who carries out an order which is clearly illegal.

4. The above-mentioned reforms should also provide that all actions whereby members of the armed forces take advantage of their status to commit abuses of power or violations of human rights are to be regarded as serious offences against the military institution, and should stipulate the administrative and legal penalties to which the perpetrators are liable, including discharge, without prejudice to the imposition of the corresponding criminal penalties, where appropriate. A strict system of discharges should not allow persons who have been discharged for the type of conduct described, or for other reasons which adversely affect the service or the institution, to be readmitted to the institution.

5. Military curricula, from the Military College to General Staff courses, should include thorough training in human rights. The assistance of a highly qualified civilian teaching staff will be required for this.

6. In selecting advanced training courses for officers of the armed forces to follow abroad, care will have to be taken to ensure that such courses are based on a doctrine of democracy and respect for human rights.

7. The armed forces Court of Honour created by the peace agreements should give priority to the eradication of any vestige of a relationship between serving and retired members of the armed forces and now-disbanded paramilitary bodies or any illegal armed group.

B. *Reforms in the area of public security*

One of the prominent features of the peace agreements was the decision to disband the former public security forces (CUSEP), which were organically linked to the armed forces, and to entrust civilian security to the National Civil Police, a new and absolutely civilian entity. The Commission recommends most emphatically that the guidelines for the new body be scrupulously observed. The demilitarization of the police is a big step forward in El Salvador and it must be ensured that there are no links between the National Civil Police and the former security forces or any other branch of the armed forces.

C. *Investigation of illegal groups*

One of the most horrendous sources of the violence which swept the country in recent years was the activity of private armed groups which operated with complete impunity. All necessary measures must be taken to ensure that they are disbanded. Given the country's history, prevention is essential in this area. There is always a risk that such groups may become active again. The Commission recommends that a thorough investigation of this issue be undertaken immediately and that, since the newly established National Civil Police is still in its early stages, assistance be sought, through channels which the confidentiality of the issue requires, from the police of friendly countries which are in a position to offer it.

III. *Institutional reforms to prevent the repetition of such acts*

This too is an issue which is intrinsically linked to the implementation of the reforms agreed to in all the peace agreements, which are designed to provide the country with a modern, democratic institutional framework adapted to the requirements of the rule of law.

The Commission believes, however, that there are some points which should be emphasized, either because of their importance or because they were not clearly resolved in the peace agreements.

A. *Administration of justice*

One of the most pressing requirements if democracy in El Salvador is to be consolidated into the genuine rule of law is the transformation of its judicial system. The judicial reform programmes currently being worked out should be intensified and put into practice as soon as possible. The effort which the Ministry of Justice is making to link judicial reform to the democratization process is highly commendable and should be carried to its conclusion.

There are also some issues which are important enough to warrant a separate comment by the Commission:

1. One of the most glaring deficiencies which must be overcome in the Salvadorian judicial system is the tremendous concentration of functions in the Supreme Court of Justice, and in its President in particular, as the body which heads the judiciary. This concentration of functions seriously undermines the independence of lower court judges and lawyers, to the detriment of the system as a whole. The formal origin of this problem is constitutional, with the result that solving it requires analysing whether the relevant provisions should be amended, through the procedure provided for in the Constitution itself, so that the Court, without losing its status as the country's highest court, is not also the administrative head of the judiciary.

2. Judges should not be appointed and removed by the Supreme Court of Justice, but by an independent National Council of the Judiciary.

3. Each judge should be responsible for administering the resources of the court under his jurisdiction and should be accountable for them to the National Council of the Judiciary.

4. The functions of granting authorization to practise as a lawyer or notary and suspending or penalizing members of those professions should be attributed to a special independent body and not to the Supreme Court of Justice.

5. The budget allocation for the administration of justice provided for in the Constitution should be used to create new courts and improve judges' salaries.

6. The Commission recommends the adoption of the following measures to reinforce the application of the right to due process:

(a) Invalidate extrajudicial confessions.

(b) Ensure that accused persons, in all circumstances, exercise their right to be presumed innocent.

(c) Ensure strict compliance with the maximum time-limits for police and judicial detention, establishing immediate penalties for violators.

(d) Reinforce exercise of the right to defence starting from the very first actions in a proceeding.

7. The utmost priority should be given to the proper functioning of the Judicial Training School, conceived as a study centre not only for professional training but also to establish bonds of solidarity among judges and a coherent overall vision of the function of the judiciary in the State—to quote the peace agreements. There is also a short-term need to train new, sound human resources to staff new courts or to replace members of the judiciary who, according to the evaluation which the Commission has recommended, should not remain in the judiciary. This is an area susceptible to constructive, tangible international cooperation. The Commission calls on those in a position to offer such assistance to do so without delay, as part of an accelerated programme of implementation, and even ventures to appeal first and foremost to the European Economic Community, because of the similarities between the Salvadorian legal system and that of several of its member countries.

B. Protection of human rights

Many agreements were reached on this issue during the peace negotiations, including constitutional and legal reforms and the deployment of a United Nations human rights verification mission, something unprecedented in the history of the Organization. The Commission's first recommendation is that these agreements should be complied with strictly and that ONUSAL recommendations on human rights should be implemented.

In addition to all the proposals advanced in this area as part of the peace process, the Commission would like to make the following recommendations, fully realizing that some of them can be implemented only through a constitutional reform:

1. The Office of the National Counsel for the Defence of Human Rights must be strengthened:

(a) It would be desirable if the Counsel, with the support of ONUSAL and the participation of all governmental and non-governmental sectors concerned, made an assessment of the Office's current situation and its most immediate priorities and needs, in order to secure the means, including international cooperation, to achieve those objectives.

(b) The Office's presence should be extended throughout the country through offices in the various departments.

(c) The Office should make more frequent use of its powers to inspect any site or installation in the country, especially where places of detention are concerned.

2. Measures must be taken to make the remedies of *amparo* and *habeas corpus* truly effective. To that end, the Commission recommends the following:

(a) Competence to hear these remedies should be broadened in order to make them more accessible to the population. All judges of first instance should be competent, within their sphere of jurisdiction, to hear remedies of *amparo* or *habeas corpus*, and this competence could be extended to justices of the peace. The Supreme Court of Justice should only be the final instance in such proceedings.

(b) Express provision should be made that the remedies of *amparo* and *habeas corpus*, like the rules of due process, cannot be suspended under any circumstances, including during a state of emergency.

3. The constitutional force of human rights provisions should be reaffirmed, including those not set forth expressly in the Constitution but in other instruments such as human rights conventions binding on El Salvador.

4. The system of administrative detention also warrants a number of changes. This is a matter of prime importance, since violations of integrity of person and even disappearances can occur during such detention:

(a) The restrictions as to which officials can order administrative detention, which officials can carry it out and for what reasons should be spelled out.

(b) The duration of administrative detention should be kept to the absolute minimum.

(c) The administrative authorities should be stripped of their power to impose penalties involving deprivation of liberty. Such penalties should be imposed only by the law courts, in the context of due process.

5. It is recommended that the current system of information on detainees should be expanded. Through the Office of the National Counsel for the Defence of Human Rights, a centralized, up-to-date list should be kept of all persons detained for any reason, indicating their location and legal status. The competent authorities must inform the Office of any detention that is carried out and the personnel involved in the arrest.

6. Any future reform of criminal legislation should give due consideration to crimes committed with the direct or indirect support of the State apparatus, either by establishing new categories of crimes, modifying existing ones or introducing special aggravating circumstances.

7. Legislation should be passed granting a simple, swift and accessible remedy to anyone who has been a victim of a human rights violation enabling them to obtain material compensation for the harm suffered.

8. Certain decisions should also be taken at the international level to reinforce the country's adherence to global and regional systems for the protection of human rights. To that end, the Commission recommends that El Salvador:

(a) Ratify the following international instruments: Optional Protocol to the International Covenant on Civil and Political Rights, Optional Protocol to the American Convention on Human Rights (Protocol of San Salvador), Conventions Nos. 87 and 98 of the International Labour Organisation, Convention on the Non-Applicability of Statutory Limitations to War Crimes and Crimes against Humanity, United Nations Convention against Torture and Other Cruel, Inhuman or Degrading Treatment or Punishment and the Inter-American Convention to Prevent and Punish Torture.

(b) Recognize the compulsory jurisdiction of the Inter-American Court of Human Rights established by the American Convention on Human Rights, as all the other Central American Republics have done.

C. National Civil Police

The Commission emphasizes the importance of the establishment and functioning of the National Civil Police, in accordance with the model defined in the peace agreements, for defending the population and preventing human rights violations. In addition to making a general recommendation to this effect, it wishes to emphasize criminal investigation, an issue closely linked to the impunity which accompanied the serious acts of violence described in this report. First, it recommends that every effort be made to put into practice as soon as possible the criminal investigation mechanism decided on in the peace agreements, which entails joint action by the National Civil Police and the Office of the Attorney-General of the Republic. This is also an area where international technical and financial cooperation can make a substantial contribution. Second, it recommends that the Commission for the Investigation of Criminal Acts be dissolved: it was through its omissions that serious human rights violations during the period under investigation were covered up.

IV. Steps towards national reconciliation

The Geneva Agreement of 4 April 1990, which provided the framework for the negotiations and thus for the peace agreements, defined as objectives of the process, in addition to guaranteeing unrestricted respect for human rights and promoting the democratization of the country, the restoration of peace, national reconciliation and the reunification of Salvadorian society. These last two goals are complex and do not depend only on the cessation of hostilities but also on a process involving several stages that cannot be bypassed. We are again faced with inseparable goals. There will be no reunification of Salvadorian society without national reconciliation, and the latter will be impossible without the fraternal unity of the Salvadorian people.

The country must move on from a situation of confrontation to one of calm assimilation of all that has happened, in order to banish such occurrences from a future characterized by a new relationship of solidarity, coexistence and tolerance. In order to achieve this, a process of collective reflection on the reality of the past few years is crucial, as is a universal determination to eradicate this experience forever.

One bitter but unavoidable step is to look at and acknowledge what happened and must never happen again. The Commission took on the difficult task of clarifying significant aspects of this reality, which it hopes it has fulfilled through this report. The truth is not enough, however, to achieve the goals of national reconciliation and the reunification of Salvadorian society. Pardon is essential: not a formal pardon which is limited to not imposing penalties, but one founded on a universal determination to rectify the mistakes of the past and on the certainty that this process will not be complete unless it emphasizes the future rather than a past which, no matter how abhorrent the acts which occurred, cannot now be altered.

However, in order to achieve the goal of a pardon, we must pause and weigh certain consequences which can be inferred from knowledge of the truth about the serious acts described in this report. One such consequence, perhaps the most difficult to address in the country's current situation, is that of fulfilling the twofold requirements of justice: punishing the guilty and adequately compensating the victims and their families.

The Commission has already referred in its introduction to this chapter of the report to the insurmountable difficulties it has encountered in this regard. Such difficulties, which it is beyond its power to resolve directly, can be attributed to the glaring deficiencies of the judicial system.

In this connection, the Commission would simply add that, since it is not possible to guarantee a proper trial for all those responsible for the crimes described here, it is unfair to keep some of them in prison while others who planned the crimes or also took part in them remain at liberty. It is not within the Commission's power to address this situation, which can only be resolved through a pardon after justice has been served.

However, the Commission fervently hopes that knowledge of the truth, and the immediate implementation of the above recommendations which can be inferred directly from the investigation, will be an adequate starting-point for national reconciliation and for the desired reunification of Salvadorian society.

But justice does not stop at punishment; it also demands reparation. The victims and, in most cases, their families, are entitled to moral and material compensation. FMLN must provide such compensation where it is found to have been responsible, while this obligation devolves on the State in cases where the actions or omissions of the public authorities or their agencies were among the causes of the acts of violence described, or in cases where the persons responsible enjoyed impunity. However, since the country's financial constraints and national reconstruction needs cannot be ignored complementary mechanisms along the lines recommended below should be envisaged.

A. *Material compensation*

1. It is recommended that a special fund be established, as an autonomous body with the necessary legal and administrative powers, to award appropriate material compensation to the victims of violence in the shortest time possible. The fund should take into account the information on the victims reported to the Commission on the Truth contained in the annexes to this report.

2. The fund should receive an appropriate contribution from the State but, in view of prevailing economic conditions, should receive a substantial contribution from the international community. Therefore, without prejudice to the obligations of the State and of FMLN, the Commission urgently appeals to the international community, especially the wealthier countries and those that showed most interest in the conflict and its settlement, to establish a fund for that purpose. It also suggests that the United Nations Secretariat promote and coordinate this initiative. It further recommends that not less than 1 per cent of all international assistance that reaches El Salvador be set aside for this purpose.

3. The fund could be managed by a board of directors consisting of three members: one appointed by the Government of El Salvador, one appointed by the Secretary-General of the United Nations and a third chosen by mutual agreement between the two appointed members.

4. The fund must be free to establish its own rules of procedure and to act in accordance with the Commission's recommendations, Salvadorian law, international law and general legal principles.

B. *Moral compensation*

The Commission recommends:

1. The construction of a national monument in El Salvador bearing the names of all the victims of the conflict.

2. Recognition of the good name of the victims and of the serious crimes of which they were victims.

3. The institution of a national holiday in memory of the victims of the conflict and to serve as a symbol of national reconciliation.

C. *Forum for Truth and Reconciliation*

The Commission feels it would be useful if this report and its conclusions and recommendations and progress towards national reconciliation were analysed not only by the Salvadorian people as a whole but also by a special forum comprising the most representative sectors of society which, in addition to the above-mentioned objectives, should strive to monitor strict compliance with the recommendations.

It is not for the Commission to indicate how such a forum should be established. However, a National Commission for the Consolidation of Peace (COPAZ) was established under the peace agreements as "a mechanism for the monitoring of and the participation of civilian society in the process of change resulting from the negotiations". It therefore seems appropriate that the task referred to by the Commission should be entrusted primarily to COPAZ. However, given the scope and the importance of the subject-matter dealt with in this report, the Commission would like to suggest to COPAZ that, to this end, it consider expanding its membership so that sectors of civilian society that are not directly represented in COPAZ can participate in this analysis.

Moreover, COPAZ is the body entrusted by the agreements with preparing preliminary legislative drafts related to the peace process. In this sphere, it has a crucial role to play in the implementation of the recommendations in the present report that call for legal reforms.

D. *International follow-up*

The Commission has carried out its mandate as part of an extraordinary process which is a milestone in the history of United Nations operations for the maintenance of international peace and security. The tragedy in El Salvador absorbed the attention of the international community. As a result, the current peace process continues to arouse expectations throughout the world. The United Nations is also responsible for verifying all the agreements, which includes ensuring that the recommendations of the Commission on the Truth, which the Parties undertook to carry out, are implemented.

The Commission requests the Independent Expert for El Salvador of the United Nations Commission on Human Rights, in the report he is to submit to the Commission on Human Rights pursuant to his mandate and to the extent allowed by that mandate, to make corresponding evaluation of the implementation of the recommendations of the Commission on the Truth.

VI. Epilogue: the seekers after peace

Yes indeed, as the Mayan poem goes, all these things happened among us. Each one of us projected his own version of the truth as the universal truth. Each group or party saw its banner as the only banner in the Manicheism that held sway. And every individual or party loyalty was held to be the only real allegiance. In those days, all Salvadorians were so unfair in one way or another to their fellow countrymen that the heroism of some became the immediate misfortune of others. Moreover, the nation was a pawn in the East-West conflict; Salvadorians were buffeted by a turbulent sea of waning ideologies and global contradictions. Although the victims hailed from many countries, they were mainly Salvadorians. One way or another, blame for this can be attributed to a complex web of events in El Salvador's history and to unique circumstances in world history, so that it would be unfair to assign it to a particular individual, organization or party.

When there came pause for thought, each Salvadorian once again responded to the only true allegiance—allegiance to the nation. The Salvadorian nation looked deep into its soul and saw, as the preamble to the Constitution says, its destiny written in the stars. Many brilliant war-time figures have also shone in peacetime: the old contradictions and intransigence contrast sharply

with the current rapprochements and agreements. Former combatants of all parties have embraced one another in a sign of reconciliation. There are neither victors nor vanquished, since everyone gains from the agreements. As in classical painting, the loftier sentiments that make law the agreed bulwark against unbridled freedom and mindless anarchy triumph over the pain of battle.

The report of the Commission on the Truth records the acts of violence that occurred repeatedly during the 12 years of war in order to prevent such events from ever happening again.

Pursuant to its mandate under the peace agreements, the Commission is presenting this background to the country's painful recent history as a lesson for reconciliation: this is the motivation behind the recommendations of this report, submitted on 15 March 1993 to the President of El Salvador, Mr. Alfredo Cristiani; to former Commanders of the Frente Farabundo Martí para la Liberación Nacional (FMLN), Schafik Handal, Salvador Samayoa and Ana Gualupe Martínez; and to the Secretary-General of the United Nations, Mr. Boutros Boutros-Ghali.

The collective spirit underlying the agreements also runs through this report, which is the contribution of the Commission on the Truth to restoring the institutional fabric of El Salvador. However, it is for Salvadorians themselves to take the fundamental decisions that will lead to a full-fledged peace. Salvadorian society must decide about accountability for past actions and new statutes of limitations. It has the power to grant pardons. It is also this society, steeped in the painful lessons of war, that will have to settle the dispute about new appointments to high office.

The members of the Commission on the Truth hope—as the only compensation for the pact made with their own consciences—that this report will help the seekers after peace, the protagonists of the new history of El Salvador, to find answers.

VII. Instruments establishing the Commission's mandate

The following are the passages pertaining to the Commission on the Truth contained in the peace agreements between the Government of El Salvador and the Frente Farabundo Martí para la Liberación Nacional (FMLN):

Mexico Agreements, 27 April 1991

[...]

IV. *Commission on the Truth*

Agreement has been reached to establish a Commission on the Truth, which shall be composed of three individuals appointed by the Secretary-General of the United Nations after consultation with the Parties. The

Commission shall elect its Chairman. The Commission shall be entrusted with the task of investigating serious acts of violence that have occurred since 1980 and whose impact on society urgently requires that the public should know the truth. The Commission shall take into account:

(a) The exceptional importance that may be attached to the acts to be investigated, their characteristics and impact, and the social unrest to which they gave rise; and

(b) The need to create confidence in the positive changes which the peace process is promoting and to assist the transition to national reconciliation.

The characteristics, functions and powers of the Commission on the Truth and other related issues are set forth in the corresponding annex.

[...]

Annex to the Mexico Agreements, 27 April 1991

Commission on the Truth

The Government of El Salvador and the Frente Farabundo Martí para la Liberación Nacional (hereinafter referred to as "the Parties"),

Reaffirming their intention to contribute to the reconciliation of Salvadorian society;

Recognizing the need to clear up without delay those exceptionally important acts of violence whose characteristics and impact, and the social unrest to which they gave rise, urgently require that the complete truth be made known and that the resolve and means to establish the truth be strengthened;

Considering that, although the need to put an end to impunity was raised in the discussion on the item on the armed forces of the Agenda for the negotiations adopted at Caracas on 21 May 1990, the means of investigation which the Parties themselves have been prepared to set up are addressing situations whose complexity warrants independent treatment;

Agreeing on the advisability of fulfilling that task through a procedure which is both reliable and expeditious and may yield results in the short term, without prejudice to the obligations incumbent on the Salvadorian courts to solve such cases and impose the appropriate penalties on the culprits;

Have arrived at the following political agreement:

1. There is hereby established a Commission on the Truth (hereinafter referred to as "the Commission"). The Commission shall be composed of three individuals appointed by the Secretary-General of the United Nations after consultation with the Parties. The Commission shall elect its Chairman.

Functions

2. The Commission shall have the task of investigating serious acts of violence that have occurred since 1980 and whose impact on society urgently demands that the public should know the truth. The Commission shall take into account:

(a) The exceptional importance that may be attached to the acts to be investigated, their characteristics and impact, and the social unrest to which they gave rise; and

(b) The need to create confidence in the positive changes which the peace process is promoting and to assist the transition to national reconciliation.

3. The mandate of the Commission shall include recommending the legal, political or administrative measures which can be inferred from the results of the investigation. Such recommendations may include measures to prevent the repetition of such acts, and initiatives to promote national reconciliation.

4. The Commission shall endeavour to adopt its decisions unanimously. However, if this is not possible, a vote by the majority of its members shall suffice.

5. The Commission shall not function in the manner of a judicial body.

6. If the Commission believes that any case brought to its attention does not meet the criteria set forth in paragraph 2 of this agreement, it may refer the case to the Attorney-General of the Republic, should it deem appropriate, for handling through the judicial channel.

Powers

7. The Commission shall have broad powers to organize its work and its functioning. Its activities shall be conducted on a confidential basis.

8. For the purposes of the investigation, the Commission shall have the power to:

(a) Gather, by the means it deems appropriate, any information it considers relevant. The Commission shall be completely free to use whatever sources of information it deems useful and reliable. It shall receive such information within the period of time and in the manner which it determines.

(b) Interview, freely and in private, any individuals, groups or members of organizations or institutions.

(c) Visit any establishment or place freely without giving prior notice.

(d) Carry out any other measures or inquiries which it considers useful to the performance of its mandate, including requesting reports, records or documents from the Parties or any other information from State authorities and departments.

Undertaking by the parties

9. The Parties undertake to extend to the Commission whatever cooperation it requests of them in order to gain access to sources of information available to them.

10. The Parties undertake to carry out the Commission's recommendations.

Report

11. The Commission shall submit a final report, with its conclusions and recommendations, within a period of six months after its establishment.

12. The Commission shall transmit its report to the Parties and to the Secretary-General of the United Nations, who shall make it public and shall take the decisions or initiatives that he deems appropriate.

13. Once the report has been handed over, the Commission's mandate shall be considered terminated and the Commission shall be dissolved.

14. The provisions of this agreement shall not prevent the normal investigation of any situation or case, whether or not the Commission has investigated it, nor the application of the relevant legal provisions to any act that is contrary to law.

[...]

El Salvador Peace Agreement signed at Chapultepec on 16 January 1992

[...]

3. C. The Commission on the Truth established by the Mexico Agreements of 26 April 1991 (hereinafter referred to as "the Commission on the Truth"), may appoint an observer to the ad hoc Commission.

[...]

5. End to impunity

The Parties recognize the need to clarify and put an end to any indication of impunity on the part of officers of the armed forces, particularly in cases where respect for human rights is jeopardized. To that end, the Parties refer this issue to the Commission on the Truth for consideration and resolution. All of this shall be without prejudice to the principle, which the Parties also recognize, that acts of this nature, regardless of the sector to which their perpetrators belong, must be the object of exemplary action by the law courts so that the punishment prescribed by law is meted out to those found responsible.

[...]

VIII. **Persons working on the Commission on the Truth**

I. The Commissioners
Belisario Betancur, Chairman; Reinaldo Figueredo Planchart; Thomas Buergenthal

II. *Advisers to the Commissioners*
Douglass Cassel; Guillermo Fernández de Soto; Luis Herrera Marcano; Robert E. Norris

III. *Executive Director*
Patricia Tappatá de Valdez

IV. *Consultants and researchers*
Carlos Chipoco; Mabel Colalongo; Jayni Edelstein;

Stener Ekern; Guillermo Fernández-Maldonado; Alfredo Forti; Lauren Gilbert; Juan Gabriel Gómez; Javier Hernández; Sergio Hevia; Elena Jenny-Williams; Felipe Michelini; Theodore Piccone; Clifford C. Rohde; Carlos Somigliana; Ana María Tello; Lucía Vásquez

V. *Personal assistants to the Commissioners*
Lourdes Zambrano; Alba Reyes; Abigail Mellin

VI. *Experts*
Clyde Snow, forensic anthropologist; Robert H. Kirschner, forensic pathologist; John Fitzpatrick, trauma radiologist; Douglas D. Scott, archaeologist and ballistics analyst;

Argentine Team of Forensic Anthropologists: Patricia Bernardi, forensic anthropologist; Mercedes C. Doretti, forensic anthropologist; Luis B. Fondebrider, forensic anthropologist; Claudia Bernardi, Ph. D.

Alberto Binder, lawyer; Alejandro Garro, lawyer; Robert Goldman, lawyer; José Ugaz, lawyer; María del Carmen Bermúdez, journalist; Gabriel Rodríguez, journalist

VII. *Codification team*
Coordinator: José Ignacio Cano

Team: Daniel Angrisano; Gabriel Catena; Cristina Lemus; Judith Kallick; Nila Pérez; Margreet Smit; Miguel Angel Ventura; Ken Ward

VIII. *Administrative personnel*
Lilian Delgado; Guillermo Lizarzaburu; Sharon Singer

IX. *Permanent security personnel*
Joseph Leal (Chief); Manuel Arcos; Alfredo Figueroa; Leo Powell; Kenneth Rosario; Wilfredo Vega

X. *Interns*
William Cartwright; Denise Gilman; Chris Guarnota; Priscilla Hayner; Mary Beth Hastings; Jean Leong; Maggie Miqueo

XI. *Offices*
San Salvador, El Salvador; United Nations, New York

I. *The Commissioners*

Belisario Betancur. Colombian, B.A. in Law and Economics, Bolivarian Pontifical University of Medellín (1955). Married to Rosa Helena Alvarez, three children, five grandchildren. University professor, member of the Spanish Language Academy and the Colombian Academy of Jurisprudence. Former Senator, Ambassador, Minister of Labour. Former President of Colombia (1982-1986). Honorary doctorates from Georgetown University, Washington, D.C. (1984) and University of

Colorado, Boulder, Colorado (1988). Member of the Pontifical Commission for Justice and Peace in Rome. Vice-President for Latin America of the Club of Rome and President of the Santillana Foundation for Iberoamerica in Santa Fé de Bogotá.

Reinaldo Figueredo Planchart. Member of the Venezuelan National Congress. Chairman of the Congressional Special Committee on Privatization and the Subcommittee on Analysis and Planning of the Standing Committee for Defence. Former Minister for Foreign Affairs of the Republic of Venezuela (1989-1991); Secretary-General of the Presidency (1989); Special Commissioner for the President of the Republic (1984-1985); Director of the Manufactures Division of the United Nations Conference on Trade and Development (UNCTAD), Geneva (1980-1984); President of the Foreign Trade Institute (1974-1979). Has participated in many international meetings and conferences sponsored by the United Nations, the Organization of Petroleum Exporting Countries (OPEC), financial organizations, the Andean Group, the Non-Aligned Movement, the Group of 15. Head of delegation on various international missions. Columnist on petroleum topics for the periodical *El Nacional* of Caracas since 1970. Has published a variety of articles in specialized journals. Economist by profession, graduated *cum laude* from the Free University of Brussels, Belgium.

Thomas Buergenthal. Lobingier Professor of International and Comparative Law, George Washington University Law School, and Director of the George Washington University National Law Center. Served as Judge (1979-1991), Vice-President (1983-1985) and President (1985-1987) of the Inter-American Court of Human Rights. Currently Vice-President of the Administrative Tribunal of the Inter-American Development Bank. Formerly Dean of the Law School, American University, Washington, D.C. (1980-1985) and I. T. Cohen Professor of Human Rights at Emory University Law School. Former Director of the Human Rights Programme of the Carter Center, Atlanta, Georgia (1985-1989). Founded the Inter-American Institute of Human Rights, San José, Costa Rica, in 1980; President (1980-1992); currently Honorary President. Former President of the Human Rights Committee, Section of International Law and Practice, American Bar Association (early 1980 and 1991-1992). Former Vice-President of the American Society of International Law. Author of more than a dozen books and many articles on international law. Graduate of Bethany College, West Virginia; J.D., New York University Law School; LL.M. and S.J.D. in International Legal Studies, Harvard Law School. Honorary doctorates from Bethany College and the University of Heidelberg, Germany.

II. *Advisers to the Commissioners*

Douglass W. Cassel, Jr. DePaul University: Executive Director of the International Human Rights Law Institute, Professor of International Human Rights Law, and Director, Jeanne and Joseph Sullivan Programme on Human Rights in the Americas. Formerly, Counsel, Judge Advocate General's Corps, United States Navy (1973-1976); Staff Counsel (1976-1982) and General Counsel (1982-1992), Business and Professional People for the Public Interest, a not-for-profit legal centre in Chicago involved in litigation and research on civil rights, civil liberties and other legal issues. Travels regularly to Central America for matters involving human rights. Official observer (1991) on behalf of the American Bar Association at the trial in El Salvador of the military personnel accused of murdering the Jesuit priests and two women at the Central American University in 1989. Has published articles on international human rights law in specialized reviews and other periodicals. B.A. in Economics, Yale University; J.D. (1972), Harvard Law School, where he served as editor of the *Harvard Civil Rights-Civil Liberties Law Review.*

Guillermo Fernández de Soto. Colombian, age 40, married, three children. B.A. in Law and Economics, Xaverian University of Bogotá and Georgetown University, Washington, D.C. Deputy Minister for Foreign Affairs of Colombia. Formerly, Legal Adviser to the Inter-American Commission on Human Rights of the Organization of American States (1979-1985). Consultant to the United Nations Development Programme (1987). Head, United Nations technical mission for the drafting of the Special Plan of Economic Cooperation for Central America (1988). Executive Director of the "Foro Interamericano" Centre for International Studies (1988-1990). Currently Dean of the Faculty of International Studies of the Jorge Tadeo Lozano University in Bogotá; Secretary-General of Nueva Fuerza Democrática in Colombia. Author of various books on international politics.

Luis Herrera Marcano. Venezuelan. LL.D., Central University of Venezuela. Ambassador. Former International Policy Director and Legal Counsel, Ministry of Foreign Affairs of Venezuela. Professor of International Law, Central University of Venezuela. Former Director of the School of Law and Dean of the Faculty of Juridical and Political Sciences. Member and former President, Inter-American Legal Committee.

Robert E. Norris. United States national. Lecturer, Stephen F. Austin State University, and Managing Attorney, East Texas Legal Services. Ph.D. in Ibero-American Studies, University of New Mexico, and J.D., University of Texas Law School, Austin. Senior Human Rights Specialist, Inter-American Commission on Human

Rights; contributed to the United Nations Centre for Human Rights study *The Rights of Indigenous Peoples*. Co-author of the textbook *Protecting Human Rights in the Americas: Selected Problems*, and of a series of volumes entitled *Human Rights: the Inter-American System*. Lecturer at the International Institute of Human Rights in Strasbourg (1979-1990) and at the Inter-American Institute of Human Rights (1990-1992).

III. *Executive director*

Patricia Tappatá de Valdez. Born in Bahía Blanca, Argentina. Researcher and consultant on human rights issues in Latin America. B.A. in Social Work, Faculty of Law and Social Sciences, National University of Córdoba. Studies towards an M.A. in Political Science, Latin American Faculty of Social Sciences (FLACSO), Buenos Aires. Director, Human Rights Department of the Episcopal Commission for Social Action of Peru (1977-1987). Adviser to the Peace Commission of the Office of the President of Peru (1985-1986). Founder and member of the Executive Committee of the National Human Rights Federation in Peru (1985-1987). Fellowship from the International Human Rights Programme (1988). Since 1991, coordinator of the "Justice in Argentina" programme of the Citizens' Foundation in Buenos Aires.

IV. *Consultants and researchers*

Carlos Chipoco. Born in Lima, Peru. LL.B. *summa cum laude* from the Pontifical Catholic University of Peru. LL.M., Harvard Law School and M.A. in International Law, Fletcher School of Law and Diplomacy (1990). Professor, Faculty of Law, Pontifical Catholic University of Peru and National University of San Marcos. Visiting Professor, School of Law, University of Puerto Rico. Adviser to the Inter-American Commission on Human Rights before the Inter-American Court of Human Rights. Former Director of the Legal Defence Institute of Peru (1983-1988) and fellow of Americas Watch (1988-1989). Author of *En Defensa de la Vida. Ensayos sobre Derechos Humanos y Derecho Internacional Humanitario* (CEP, Lima).

Mabel Colalongo. Argentine national. Procurator and lawyer, graduated from the Faculty of Law of the National University of Buenos Aires, 1984. Associate Professor, Faculty of Law, University of Buenos Aires and National University of Lomas de Zamora. Appointed to the Procurator's Office of the Federal Criminal and Correctional Court of Buenos Aires (1985-1987; 1991-1992). UNDP consultant to the commission set up to reform the national criminal prosecution system in Argentina. Chief, Judicial Department of the Sub-Secretariat for Human Rights (1984-1986).

Jayni Edelstein. United States national. B.A. with distinction, University of Wisconsin (1988), and J.D., New York Law School (1992). Worked for three years for the Lawyers Committee for Human Rights, New York. Internships with the International Commission of Jurors (Geneva) and the Centro de Investigación y Educación Popular (Colombia), and clerkships in the United States Court of International Trade, New York, and the United States District Court, Eastern District, New York.

Stener Ekern. Norwegian. B.A. in Social Anthropology, University of Bergen, Norway (1986). Project Coordinator, FAFO International. Project Officer, programme for assistance to indigenous peoples of the Central American area, Norwegian Agency for International Development (NORAD), NGO Division. Formerly, Project Officer for the Central American area, CARITAS Norway.

Guillermo Arturo Fernández-Maldonado Castro. Born in Lima, Peru. LL.B., Pontifical Catholic University of Peru, and LL.D. *cum laude*, University of Alcalá de Henares, Spain. M.A. in Public Administration, National Institute of Public Administration, Spain; Visiting Professor, 1987. External Studies Diploma in Human Rights and Humanitarian Law, Academy of International Law, The Hague. Graduate in international relations from the International Studies Society of Madrid. Since 1987, Professor in the Faculty of Law and on the M.A. programmes in constitutional law and international law, Pontifical Catholic University of Peru. Legal adviser to the Senate of Peru (1982-1992). Since 1988, chief adviser to the Senate Special Committee on the Causes of Violence and Peaceful Alternatives in Peru; chief adviser to the Chairman of the United Nations Commission on Human Rights (1991).

Alfredo Waldo Forti. Argentine national. B.A. *cum laude* in International Relations, American University, Washington, D.C. Senior Fellow of the Center for International Policy, Washington, D.C. Former Director of the Committee on United States-Latin American Relations, The International Center, Washington, D.C. (1986-1992). Consultant to agencies of the Argentine Government (1989-1991) and consultant on electoral issues for the United States Agency for International Development (USAID), Georgetown University. Former coordinator of the Latin American Human Rights Secretariat, Caracas, Venezuela (1978-1980).

Lauren Gilbert. United States national. B.A. *magna cum laude* in Government, Harvard University (1983). J.D. *cum laude*, University of Michigan (1988). Associate, Arnold & Porter law firm, Washington, D.C. (1988-1991). Pro Bono Service Award from the International Human Rights Law Group for monitoring the elections in Chile (1990). Adviser to the Venezuelan Government on its accession to the General Agreement on Tariffs and Trade (GATT) and on the drafting of an anti-dumping law. Received a Fulbright award to study the Americas Initiative in Costa Rica and taught a course in foreign trade at the School of International Relations of the National University in Heredia (1991). Worked with the Deputy Director of the Inter-American Institute of Human Rights on the peace process in El Salvador (1992).

Juan Gabriel Gómez Albarello. Born in Ibagué, Colombia, in 1968. LL.B. from the External Studies University of Colombia (1989). Adviser to Francisco Rojas Birry, the indigenous delegate to the National Constituent Assembly, and researcher for the Committee to Overcome Violence. Won second prize in a Latin American essay contest on legal criticism and alternative uses of the law, organized by the Inter-American Legal Services Association (ILSA) in 1989, and first prize in the essay contest on the new Colombian Constitution organized by the Department of Public Law of the External Studies University of Colombia in 1992.

Javier Hernández Valencia. Born in Lima, Peru. LL.B. from the Pontifical Catholic University of Peru. Adviser to the Senate of Peru (1985-1990) and member of the Senate Legislative Research Centre (1992). Team member of the congressional commission of inquiry into the 1986 prison massacres in Lima (1987). Adviser to the Ministry of Education (1990), and to the National Planning Institute on Project SITOD concerning government decision-making (1991). Researcher for the IDS Institute for Popular Politics in Lima since 1988: has developed institutional reform projects to promote peace in Peru. Has published various articles on the subject in Peru.

Sergio Hevia Larenas. Born in Santiago, Chile. B.A. Juridical and Social Sciences, Faculty of Law, University of Chile. Specialized studies in criminology and forensic medicine. Legal adviser and staff member of the Vicaría de la Solidaridad of the Archdiocese of Santiago.

Elena Jenny-Williams. Swiss national born in Panama. M.A., Harvard University (1967), LL.B., University of Geneva (1984). Legal consultant on private law, international law, criminal law and tax law. Has participated in missions in Europe and Latin America.

Felipe Raúl Michelini Delle Piane. Born in Montevideo, Uruguay. Doctorate in Law and Social Sciences, Faculty of Law and Social Sciences, University of the Republic, Montevideo (1987). LL.M., Columbia University School of Law, New York (1992). Former legal adviser to victims in Uruguay and before the Inter-American Commission on Human Rights. Professor of Human Rights, Faculty of Law, University of the Republic, Montevideo (1991). Professor of Legal Architecture, Faculty of Architecture, University of the Republic, Montevideo (1988). Member of the Centre for Labour and Social Research and Advisory Services (CEALS), Uruguay.

Theodore J. Piccone. United States national. B.A. *magna cum laude* in History, University of Pennsylvania, 1984. J.D., Columbia University School of Law (1990); former Editor-in-Chief, *Columbia Human Rights Law Review.* International Fellow, Harlan Fiske Stone Scholar. Former Director, Youth Policy Institute. Congressional assistance in United States Congress and rapporteur in the Council on Foreign Relations. Law clerk for Federal Judge Stanley S. Brotman (United States District Court of New Jersey and District Court of the Virgin Islands). Summer associate, Patton, Boggs & Blow, Cahill, Gordon & Reindel and Dewey, Ballantine (Washington, D.C.). Currently, Litigation Associate, Schnader, Harrison, Segal & Lewis, Philadelphia, Pennsylvania.

Clifford C. Rohde. United States national. Graduated with special distinction from Cornell University, Ithaca, New York, majoring in Latin American History. Completed one year of study at the National Law Center, George Washington University, Washington, D.C. Since 1988, researcher for Americas Watch on Mexico, Guatemala and Colombia.

Carlos Somigliana. Argentine national. Forensic anthropologist, member of the Argentine Team of Forensic Anthropologists since 1987, and as such served as an expert in Guatemala. Co-author of various articles on forensic anthropology. Worked in the Procurator's Office of the Federal Criminal Court of the Argentine Republic (1985-1987). Studied law and anthropology at the University of Buenos Aires.

Ana María Tello. Born in Montevideo, Uruguay. Researcher and lecturer in History and Social Sciences. Human rights documents librarian. Worked with the Centre for Latin American Studies (CEL) of the University of the Republic, Montevideo (1986). Graduate of the Artigas Teachers Institute, Montevideo, 1986. Guidance counsellor and lecturer, Institutes for Advanced Technical Training, Labour University of Uruguay, Montevideo (1981).

Lucía Carmen Vásquez Rodríguez. Born in Lima, Peru. B.A. in Social Work from the Pontifical Catholic University of Peru. Has worked with the Episcopal Commission for Social Action in Peru since 1983: Director of the Human Rights Department (1987-1989) and the Solidarity and Development Department (1990-1991). Member of the Executive Committee of the Office of the National Human Rights Federation (1987-1989). Adviser to the Archdiocese of Lima on its programmes of pastoral work in prisons.

V. *Personal assistants to the Commissioners*

Lourdes Margarita Cobo de Zambrano. Born in Caracas, Venezuela. M.A. in Political Science, Central

University of Venezuela (1979). M.A. in Political Science, Simón Bolívar University (1981). Has worked in Ministry of Foreign Affairs of Venezuela. Member of the Board and researcher, Venezuelan Institute of International Relations (IVRI). Former consultant, Tinker Foundation, Commission for State Reform in Venezuela (COPRE). Edited and contributed to *Análisis*, a specialized review of the Pedro Gual Diplomatic Academy. Author of "La Política de Fronteras hacia Colombia: Toma de Decisiones, Disgregación y Consenso; El Estudio de las Relaciones Internacionales en Venezuela; Prioridades de la Política Exterior de Venezuela para el Año 2000".

Alba Reyes. Colombian, age 35, economist, married, two children. Assistance in the Office of the President of Colombia (1982-1986). Personal assistant to former President Betancur (1986-1993).

Abigail Mellin. United States national. B.A. *magna cum laude*, Southwestern University; J.D. candidate, George Washington University National Law Center (May 1993). Studied at the Institute for Comparative Politics and Economic Systems, Goldsmith's College, University of London. Former legislative assistance to Senator Tejeda, State Assembly, Texas, and programme coordinator for The Fund for American Studies, Washington, D.C. Has also worked with the House Ways and Means Committee and the Congressional Sunbelt Caucus.

Notes

1/ Published by the United Nations under the title *El Salvador Agreements: The Path to Peace* (DPI/1208, May 1992).

2/ El Salvador Agreements, supra, p. 30.

3/ El Salvador Peace Agreement (signed at Chapultepec), *supra*, p. 55.

4/ It is important to mention that, in the San José Agreement on Human Rights, it was the understanding of the Parties to the peace agreements that "human rights" shall mean "those rights recognized by the Salvadorian legal system, including treaties to which El Salvador is a party, and by the declarations and principles on human rights and humanitarian law adopted by the United Nations and the Organization of American States".

5/ See, for example, FMLN, *La situación de los derechos humanos a la Luz de los Convenios de Ginebra*, p. 5 (1983).

6/ Article 3 (common to the four Conventions): conflicts not of an international character

In the case of armed conflict not of an international character occurring in the territory of one of the High Contracting Parties, each Party to the conflict shall be bound to apply, as a minimum, the following provisions:

(1) Persons taking no active part in the hostilities, including members of armed forces who have laid down their arms and those placed *hors de combat* by sickness, wounds, detention, or any other cause, shall in all circumstances be treated humanely, without any adverse distinction founded on race, colour, religion or faith, sex, birth or wealth, or any other similar criteria. To this end, the following acts are and shall remain prohibited at any time and in any place whatsoever with respect to the above-mentioned persons:

(*a*) violence to life and person, in particular murder of all kinds, mutilation, cruel treatment and torture;

(*b*) taking of hostages;

(*c*) outrages upon personal dignity, in particular humiliating and degrading treatment;

(*d*) the passing of sentences and the carrying out of executions without previous judgement pronounced by a regularly constituted court, affording all the judicial guarantees which are recognized as indispensable by civilized peoples.

(2) The wounded and sick shall be collected and cared for ...

7/ See, for example, article 4 of Protocol II.

8/ United Nations, Mexico Agreements, 27 April 1991, Commission on the Truth, "Functions" section, para. 2 (a). Document A/46/553-S/23130, p. 16.

9/ The Asociación Nacional de Educadores Salvadoreños (ANDES) reported that in the period January-June 1981, 136 schoolteachers were executed. United Nations, Report of the Special Representative of the Commission on Human Rights, 1981.

10/ The Inter-American Commission on Human Rights, quoting the United States Embassy, reported that the average number of political murders in El Salvador was approximately 300 a month in 1982. According to the Catholic Legal Aid Office, the figure was 500 a month. OAS-IACHR, *Annual Report*, 1981-1982, p. 121.

The Archbishop Oscar Romero Christian Legal Aid Office reported the following numbers of civilian victims:

1980: 11,903
1981: 16,266
1982: 5,962

Source: Central American Human Rights Institute (IDHUCA), *Los Derechos Humanos en El Salvador durante 1985*, vol. II, José Simeón Cañas Central American University, San Salvador, 12 April 1986, p. 39.

11/ In September 1980, the house containing the office of the Human Rights Commission of El Salvador was blown up. Damage was considerable and the bodies of three young people, showing signs of having been brutally tortured, were found at the front door of the office. OAS-IACHR, *Annual Report*, p. 124.

Attacks against the non-governmental Human Rights Commission were systematic during this period:

On 3 October 1980, Maria Magdalena Henríquez, press secretary of the Commission, was abducted by uniformed police. Her body was found later. On 25 October, Ramón Valladares, the Commission's administrator, was murdered. On 4 December 1981, security forces abducted the Commission's director,

Carlos Eduardo Vides, who then disappeared. In August 1982, the Treasury Police abducted América Perdomo, Director of Public Relations, who also disappeared. On 16 March 1983, Marianela García Villas, the Commission's President, was killed when a military patrol ambushed a group of displaced persons. *Americas Watch, El Salvador's Decade of Terror. Human Rights since the Assassination of Archbishop Romero*, Yale University Press, 1991, pp. 44-45, 144-148.

12/ According to Christian Legal Aid, 16,266 people, 7,916 of them peasants, were killed between January and December 1981.
Source: Archbishop Oscar Romero Christian Legal Aid Office. *See* Central American Human Rights Institute (IDHUCA), *Los Derechos Humanos en El Salvador durante 1985*, San Salvador, April 1986, p. 41.

13/ On 11 November 1981, the non-governmental Human Rights Commission of El Salvador reported that in recent months the bodies of over 400 people had been dumped at the place known as El Playón.

14/ The General Secretary of MNR, Guillermo Manuel Ungo, the Rector of the Central American University, Román Mayorga Quiroz, and businessman Mario Antonio Andino became part of the Junta. Colonels José Guillermo García and Nicolás Carranza were appointed Minister and Deputy Minister of Defence respectively. Other members of the cabinet included Salvador Samayoa (Education), Enrique Alvarez Córdoba (Agriculture), Colonel René Francisco Guerra y Guerra (Under-Secretary of the Interior), Héctor Dada Hirezi and Héctor Oquelí Colindres (Foreign Affairs).

15/ The Organización Democrática Nacionalista (ORDEN) was a civil defence body set up by General Medrano in the 1960s to keep an eye on the peasant population. It became one of the precursors of the death squads.

16/ The Agencia Nacional de Servicios Especiales de El Salvador (ANSESAL) was the State intelligence agency set up by General Medrano. Its last director was Colonel Santibañez. National Security Archives, *El Salvador: The Making of US Policy, 1977-1984*, Chadwick-Healey, Inc., Alexandria, VA, p. 73.

17/ The Bloque Popular Revolucionario was the largest coalition of organizations in the late 1970s and early 1980s. It was established in 1975 and the sectors represented in it included peasants (the Federación Cristiana de Campesinos Salvadoreños (FECCAS) and the Unión de Trabajadores del Campo (UTC)); teachers (the Asociación Nacional de Educadores de El Salvador (ANDES)); shanty-town residents (the Unión de Pobladores de Tugurios (UPT)); and students (the Movimiento Estudiantil Revolucionario de Secundaria (MERS)).
The Ligas Populares 28 de Febrero (LP-28) was a smaller, urban-based organization controlled by students. It took its name from the date—28 February 1977—when dozens of demonstrators were killed in

protests denouncing electoral fraud in the elections in which General Carlos Humberto Romero became President.
The Frente Popular de Acción Unificada (FAPU), founded in 1974, was an organization composed of trade unions, student organizations, peasants and schoolteachers.
The Unión Democratíca Nacionalista (UDN), founded in 1969, was the legal mouthpiece of the banned Salvadorian Communist Party.

18/ By agreement between the Revolutionary Government Junta and the Christian Democratic Party (PDC), the members who resigned were replaced on 10 January by PDC members Héctor Dada Hizeri and José Antonio Morales Elrich and independent José Ramón Avalos Navarrete.

19/ The Agrarian Reform Act decreed the expropriation of landholdings in excess of 1,250 acres. This affected some 372 landowners and a total of 625,000 acres of land. Approximately 85 per cent of the rural population were to benefit. To forestall a reaction by the landowners concerned, the Junta issued Decree No. 155 imposing a state of siege for 30 days.
National Security Archives, *El Salvador: The Making of US Policy, 1977-1984*, Janet Di Vicenzo, project editor, Chadwick-Healey, Inc., Alexandria, VA, 1984, p. 33.

20/ United States Embassy in El Salvador, cable 00837, 6 February 1980.

21/ In his last Sunday sermon, on 23 March, Monsignor Romero had said: "In the name of God, in the name of this suffering people whose cries rise up to Heaven more urgently with each day that passes, I beseech you, I beg you, I order you to stop the repression."

22/ United States Embassy in San Salvador, cable 02296, 31 March 1980. *The Washington Post*, 31 March 1980. Op. cit., National Security Archives, *El Salvador: The Making of US Policy, 1977-1984*, p. 34.

23/ National Guard Major and Director of ANSESAL until the 15 October coup, when he was forced to resign.

24/ On 12 May, Majano lost his influence when Colonel Jaime Abdul Gutiérrez, of the conservative wing, was appointed President of the Revolutionary Government Junta by the armed forces and, as such, became their Commander-in-Chief.
That same day, a communiqué from a group calling itself "death squad" was read out over the telephone to the press, demanding the release of Major D'Aubuisson and the others arrested at Santa Tecla and threatening to blow up any newspapers that did not publish the message. *La Prensa Gráfica*, 12 May 1980, p. 25.

25/ D'Aubuisson and the other detainees were never brought before the courts, despite the seriousness of the accusations about the death squads and the murder of Monsignor Romero.

26/ On 22 May, the Junta issued Decrees Nos. 264 and 265 amending the Code of Criminal Procedure. The first of these expanded the definition of terrorist activities and prohibited the occupation of public buildings, workplaces and religious establishments. The second decree prohibited bail for persons accused of or sentenced for political offences.

On 24 June, Decree No. 296 prohibited officials and employees of State bodies from taking part in strikes, and ordered immediate dismissal for anyone who promoted or organized work stoppages.

On 22 August, Decree No. 366 gave the executive branch the power to withdraw legal recognition from any State union for taking part in strikes or causing the interruption of essential public services.

On 3 December, the Junta issued Decree No. 507 giving military courts jurisdiction over political offences against the State.

27/ On 26 June 1980, after a national strike, the army and the National Guard attacked the National University, killing between 22 and 40 students and destroying facilities. The Rector of the University, Félix Antonio Ulloa, was assassinated on 29 October.

28/ Op. cit., National Security Archives, *The Making of US Policy, 1977-1984*, p. 35.

29/ After a brief period in detention, Majano went into exile in March 1981.

30/ The direct complaints received by the Commission on the Truth and referred to in this chronology concerned both parties to the conflict. Most complaints concerned violations committed by members of the armed forces or paramilitary organizations. Only those complaints which, in the Commission's view, were sufficiently substantiated were processed (see annex 5).

31/ The victims were José Rodolfo Viera, President of ISTA, and two AIFLD agricultural advisers, Mark David Pearlman and Michael Hammer.

32/ On 27 December, during one of the first large-scale attacks launched by FMLN on military garrisons, Commander Fermán Cienfuegos of FARN announced that a final offensive would be launched before Reagan's inauguration on 20 January 1981. Op. cit., National Security Archives, *El Salvador: The Making of US Policy*, p. 38.

33/ On 28 August 1981, a communiqué issued by the Governments of Mexico and France referred to FDR-FMLN as a representative political force for seeking a political solution to the conflict.

34/ On 14 January, in one of his last foreign policy measures, President Carter announced the sending of $5 million in military aid to El Salvador. Among the reasons cited was evidence of Nicaraguan aid to the Salvadorian rebels. Op. cit., National Security Archives, *El Salvador: The Making of US Policy*, p. 34. Not long after the Government of Ronald Reagan took office, the State Department sent a cable to the Embassy in San Salvador instructing it to inform the Duarte Government that the United States was planning to launch a diplomatic offensive the following week in Europe and Latin America to demonstrate Cuban and Nicaraguan involvement with the insur-

gents in El Salvador. Department of State (draft), 2/4/1981.

35/ Op. cit., Americas Watch, pp. 48-49 and 146.

36/ *The Miami Herald*, 23 August 1981. Op. cit, National Security Archives, p. 42.

37/ Christian Legal Aid, San Salvador, 1984 report.

38/ The breakdown of the Assembly by party was as follows:
Christian Democratic Party: 24 members
Alianza Republicana Nacionalista: 19 members
Partido de Conciliación Nacional: 14 members
Acción Democrática: 2 members
Partido Popular Salvadoreño: 1 member

39/ Decree No. 3 of the Constituent Assembly. The Decree also repealed Decree No. 114, containing the basic legal provisions governing the agrarian reform.

40/ Phase III of the agrarian reform was launched by Decree No. 207 of the Revolutionary Government Junta and enabled peasants who were leasing small plots of land to buy them and gain title to them with financial assistance from the Government. Op. cit, National Security Archives, p. 79.

41/ *The New York Times*, 7 February 1982.
Newly elected President Reagan, citing the attack on the Ilopango Base, also signed an Executive Order on 1 February authorizing $55 million in emergency military aid for El Salvador (see *The Washington Post*, 2 February 1982).

42/ According to statistics, acts of sabotage focused on means of transport (46 per cent), the electricity distribution and supply system (23.7 per cent) and roads and railways (5.7 per cent). During the first quarter of 1982, the following bridges were destroyed or damaged: 4 in Santa Ana, 1 in San Salvador, 3 in Usulután, 2 in San Miguel and 1 in Morazán. Centro Universitario de Documentación e Información, *Proceso*, Año 3, No. 98, February-April 1982.

43/ Op cit., United Nations, Report of the Special Representative of the Commission on Human Rights, 1982, p. 33. Armed Forces of El Salvador, National Police, Datos estadísticos sobre atentados dinamiteros, incendiarios y sabotajes diversos realizados por las diversas agrupaciones terroristas con el fin de destruir la economía nacional, San Salvador, 22 September 1982.

44/ United States Embassy in San Salvador (cable 02165), 3 March 1983.

45/ United States Embassy in San Salvador (cable 00437), 3 December 1982. The information also indicates that the armed forces troop strength was 31,757.

46/ Op cit., Americas Watch, 1991, pp. 146-147.

47/ *The Washington Post*, 28 December 1982.

48/ Office of the United Nations High Commissioner for Refugees, *UNHCR Information*, Central America, June 1982, No. 5.

49/ Op. cit., United Nations, Report of the Special Representative of the Commission on Human Rights, p. 20.

50/ Central American Human Rights Institute (IDHUCA), *Los Derechos Humanos en El Salvador durante 1985*, vol. II, José Simeón Cañas Central American University, San Salvador, 12 April 1986, p. 41.

51/ "Death squads" is a generic term referring to the *modus operandi* of such groups. They were used as instruments of terror and introduced the systematic practice of massive human rights violations.

52/ Op. cit., OAS-IACHR, *Annual Report*, 1981-1982, pp. 115-116.

53/ United Nations, Report of the Special Representative of the Commission on Human Rights, 22 November 1982, p. 24.

54/ Archbishop Oscar Romero Christian Legal Aid *Víctimas de la Población Civil desde 1977 hasta 1985*, February 1986 (mimeo).

55/ Op. cit., Americas Watch, 1991, p. 108.

56/ Decree 210 of the Constituent Assembly referred to the Amnesty and Citizen Rehabilitation Act presented by the President of the Republic; 533 political prisoners were freed by 24 June. The Act also granted amnesty to any rebel who abandoned the armed struggle before 4 July.

57/ The Constitution contained 247 articles and provided for greater control over presidential power. It also reduced the impact of the land reform on landowners. According to a report issued in December by United States labour advisers, only 57,000 of the 117,000 who were eligible to benefit from the reform had exercised their right to purchase up to 17.5 acres of land which they were leasing; more than 10 per cent of those who did exercise that right were either displaced or murdered. *The New York Times*, 28 December 1983.

58/ The Government was represented by the Salvadorian Peace Commission set up by the Apaneca Pact. Possible participation of the rebels in presidential elections was one of the main issues discussed. The talks failed because FDR-FMLN rejected the conditions of the Peace Commission.

59/ The other bodies were identified as those of Santiago Hernández Jiménez, Secretary-General of FUSS, who disappeared on 25 September, José Antonio García Vázquez and Dr. Dora Muñoz Castillo. *La Prensa Gráfica*, "El conflicto en El Salvador", second edition, 1983.

60/ Op. cit., Americas Watch, 1991, p. 148.

61/ Op. cit., Americas Watch, 1991, p. 148. *The Miami Herald*, 1 October 1983.

62/ According to newspaper reports, a group of 20 women and children were surrounded in a dwelling and executed. Another 30 people drowned in Lake Suchitlán while being shot at by soldiers. Op. cit., Americas Watch, 1991, p. 148. *The Christian Science Monitor*, 21 November 1983.

63/ Congress had set the ceiling on the number of advisers at 55. Starting in June 1983, a contingent of 130 Green Berets stationed in Honduras began training a first group of 2,400 Salvadorian soldiers in anti-guerrilla tactics.

64/ Department of State press briefing, 29 November 1983.

65/ United States Embassy, San Salvador (06349), 18 July 1983.

66/ *The New York Times*, 5 and 19 November 1983, quoted in op. cit., National Security Archives, pp. 64-65.

67/ United States Embassy, San Salvador (11503), 12 December 1983, *The New York Times*, 15 December 1983.

68/ On 14 December, the High Command ordered all security forces to look into the existence of the death squads. On 19 December, Captain Eduardo Ernesto Alfonso Avila was arrested on orders of the High Command on suspicion of having participated in the murder of the United States advisers in the Sheraton case. On 21 December, Colonel Nicolás Carranza, Director of the Treasury Police, announced that his forces had captured one member of a squad, though no name was given. *La Prensa Gráfica*, "El Conflicto en El Salvador", second edition, 1983, pp. 61-62.

69/ *The Los Angeles Times*, 27 December 1983.

70/ Op. cit., the National Security Archives, p. 63.

71/ Report of the Special Representative, 22 November 1983 (A/38/503).

72/ The following day the House of Representatives approved $67.75 million in emergency aid to El Salvador. Op. cit., the National Security Archives, p. 72.

73/ President Duarte offered to grant amnesty to FMLN and to recognize it so that it could participate as a political party in the elections, if it agreed to lay down its arms. FMLN responded with a counterproposal that would have involved its participating in a provisional Government that would call elections and would reorganize the armed forces. Op. cit., Americas Watch, 1991, p. 12.

74/ On 1 January, the rebels blew up Cuscatlán bridge, the longest in the country, connecting the eastern and western regions. On several occasions, the northern and eastern areas of the country were left without electricity as a result of continuing acts of sabotage. On 21 June, FMLN attacked and occupied the Cerrón Grande hydroelectric power station, leaving 120 people dead. On 30 July, following a number of attacks involving dynamite, train service in the country was suspended. Towards the end of the year, it was reported that FMLN attacks on the economic infrastructure had cost the country 238 million colones. Op. cit., *La Prensa Gráfica*, "El Conflicto en El Salvador", 1984.

75/ Between 17 and 22 July, 68 civilians were executed by army troops during a military operation in Los Llanitos, Cabañas. Between 28 and 30 August a further military operation by the Atlacatl Battalion in Las Vueltas, Chalatenango, resulted in the massacre of some 50 civilians on the banks of the Guaslinga river. Op. cit., Americas Watch, 1991, p. 148.

76/ According to a cable from the United States Embassy, no murder had been attributed to any known death squad since the end of 1983. United States Embassy, San Salvador (02547), 8 March 1984.

77/ Op. cit., the National Security Archives, p. 70.

78/ Report on the situation of human rights in El Salvador (A/39/636), 9 November 1984.

79/ On 7 March, Lt. Col. Ricardo Arístides Cienfuegos, Head of COPREFA, was executed. On 23 March, General José Alberto Medrano, former Director of the National Guard and founder of ORDEN and ANSESAL, was murdered. On 17 May, Mr. José Rodolfo Araujo Baños, military judge of the Court of First Instance, was killed in an attack. Op. cit., *La Prensa Gráfica*, "El Conflicto en El Salvador", p. 81.

80/ Inés Guadalupe Duarte Durán was abducted, together with her friend, Ana Cecilia Villeda. On the 16th, an organization calling itself Frente Pablo Castillo claimed responsibility for the abduction. Op. cit., *La Prensa Gráfica*, "El Conflicto en El Salvador", p. 81.

81/ Op. cit., Central American Human Rights Institute (IDHUCA), *Los derechos humanos en El Salvador durante el año 1985*, fascicle II, pp. 79-81.

82/ In a letter dated October 1985 to Monsignor Rivera y Damas, the population of Suchitoto reported that the following damage had occurred between May and October 1985: 39 bombings, 4 landings, 32 machine-gunnings, 28 raids, 252 captures, 26 dead, 9 wounded, 28 houses destroyed, 41 *manzanas* (approximately 25 hectares) of farmland and considerable quantities of corn destroyed. Op. cit., IDHUCA, *Los derechos humanos en El Salvador durante el año 1985*, fascicle II, p. 43.

83/ Op. cit, IDHUCA, *Los derechos humanos en El Salvador durante el año 1985*, fascicle II, p. 39.

84/ This list refers only to cases for which testimony from survivors has been received. Op. cit., IDHUCA, *Los derechos humanos en El Salvador ...*, p. 67.

85/ Op. cit., *La Prensa Gráfica* "El Conflicto en El Salvador", p. 76.

86/ The figures given by the various sources are as follows: Legal Protection: 3,306; Legal Aid: 1,714; Human Rights Commission of El Salvador (non-governmental): 1,995; Human Rights Commission of El Salvador (governmental): 1,810; and United States Embassy: 1,855. Op. cit., IDHUCA, *Los derechos humanos en El Salvador ...*, p. 36.

87/ Op. cit., *La Prensa Gráfica*, "El Conflicto en El Salvador", p. 86.

88/ Op. cit., *La Prensa Gráfica*, p. 85.

89/ The document entitled "Procedure for the establishment of a firm and lasting peace in Central America", known as the "Esquipulas II Agreement", was signed by the Central American Presidents on 7 August 1987 in Guatemala City. Among the main points of the Agreement are the objective of concluding a cease-fire within 90 days, the establishment of national reconciliation commissions, a general amnesty, formation of an International Verification Commission and the termination of logistical assistance and arms supplies to all armed groups in the region.

90/ "The humanization of the conflict" refers to the objectives of halting such practices as abductions, bombings, indiscriminate attacks on civilians, summary executions and the indiscriminate planting of mines, etc.

91/ In a paper issued on 22 July 1987, Amnesty International expressed concern about what appeared to be a campaign of repression against the cooperative movement. Over 80 cooperative workers and leaders had disappeared, been summarily executed, arbitrarily detained or beaten.
United Nations, Report of the Special Representative to the Commission on Human Rights, 1988, p 3.

92/ The Act conferred unconditional amnesty on anyone who had been involved in political offences or politically motivated ordinary offences committed prior to 22 October 1987 in which fewer than 20 persons had participated. This option was also applicable to the rebels if they came forward, renounced the use of violence and manifested their desire to be amnestied within 15 days following the promulgation of the Act. The Act would not apply to persons who: (a) participated in the murder of Monsignor Romero; (b) engaged in kidnappings for profit; (c) were involved in drug trafficking; or (d) participated in the murder of Herbert Anaya.
Op. cit., United Nations, Report of the Special Representative to the Commission on Human Rights, 1988, p. 19. OAS-ICHR: *Report on the situation of human rights in El Salvador*, 1978, p. 299. Amnesty International: *Annual Report*, 1988, p. 137.

93/ The United Nations Special Representative said that the broad scope of the Act that had been promulgated might make it even more difficult to overcome the climate of impunity that existed in El Salvador.

94/ "... the Esquipulas II Agreement is not being served by an act that pardons the murderers of non-combatants and whose authors are connected with FMLN, the armed forces or the death squads".

95/ Op. cit., United Nations, Report of the Special Representative to the Commission on Human Rights, 1988, p. 19.

96/ Op. cit., United Nations, Report of the Special Representative, 1988, p. 5.

97/ Op. cit., United Nations, Report of the Special Representative to the Commission on Human Rights, 1988, p. 12.

98/ Op. cit., United Nations, Report of the Special Representative to the Commission on Human Rights, 1987, p. 18.

99/ Op. cit., OAS-ICHR, *Annual Report of the Inter-American Commission on Human Rights*, 1987-1988, p. 294. This report estimates the loss of life caused by the civil war at 60,000 persons.

100/ On grounds of an error in procedure, the Supreme Court revoked the request for the extradition of Captain Alvaro Saravia, who was implicated in the murder of Monsignor Romero.
With regard to the implementation of the Amnesty Act, military judge Jorgé Alberto Serrano Panameño, just before handing down his decision on the case of abductions for purposes of extortion, stated that he opposed granting amnesty to the officers implicated in those cases. The following day, 11 May, he was shot dead by persons unknown in the doorway of his home.

101/ Op. cit., *Proceso*, "Annual Summary", San Salvador, December 1988, p. 27.

102/ *Source*: IDHUCA. See in *Proceso*, "Annual Summary", December 1988, p. 30.

103/ Americas Watch pointed out that "... both the Government and FMLN appear to have violated the rules of war during the first week of the offensive. Op. cit., United Nations, Report of the Special Representative ..." 1990, p. 4.

104/ Op. cit., *La Prensa Gráfica*, 1989, p. 111.

105/ Op. cit., OAS-ICHR, *Annual Report*, 1989-1990, p. 140.

106/ Alfredo Cristiani received 53.83 per cent of the 939,078 valid votes counted, higher than the 36.03 per cent received by the Christian Democratic candidate, Fidel Chávez Mena.

107/ On 28 August, army units opened fire on 15 university students, killing one and wounding six others. On 16 December, Imelda González, a lecturer at the National University in Santa Ana, was killed.

108/ Op. cit., OAS-ICHR, *Report on the human rights situation in El Salvador*, 1989-1990, p. 145.

109/ Op. cit., United Nations, Report of the Special Representative of the Commission on Human Rights, 1989, p. 14.

110/ Edgard Antonio Chacón was President of the Institute of International Relations and a columnist known to have extreme anti-communist opinions. On 30 June, while driving with his wife, he was attacked and died of gunshot wounds.

Both COPREFA and the widow of the deceased blamed FMLN urban commandos for the killing, but the charge was denied by FMLN.

Gabriel Eugenio Payes Interiano was a computer engineer affiliated with ARENA. He was shot in the street on 19 July and died on 21 August after a stay in hospital.

111/ The fourth Summit, Esquipulas IV, was held at Tela, Honduras, from 5 to 7 August 1989 with the five Central American Presidents in attendance. In chapter III of the annex, the Governments of the Central American countries urged FMLN to hold a constructive dialogue with a view to achieving a just and lasting peace. At the same time, the Central American Governments urged the Government of El Salvador to arrange, with full guarantees, the integration of the members of FMLN in peaceful life.

Op. cit., United Nations, Report of the Special Representative to the Commission on Human Rights, 1990, p. 4.

112/ On 31 October 1989, the bombing of FENASTRAS headquarters left 10 trade unionists dead and about 30 injured. Among the dead was the leader of Febe Velázquez. That same day, a bomb injured four people at the headquarters of the Comité de Madres de Presos Políticos, Desaparecidos y Asesinados de El Salvador (COMADRES).

Op. cit., Americas Watch, *El Salvador's Decade of Terror*, p. 156.

113/ Op. cit., *La Prensa Gráfica*, San Salvador, p. 109.

114/ The Special Representative, in theory, conceded that the perpetrators might have ties to members of the armed forces and security forces or be tolerated and protected by them.

United Nations, Report of the Special Representative of the Commission on Human Rights, 1990, p. 10.

115/ Noteworthy among those acts was the murder of the Chief of the Legal Department of the Armed Forces Joint Staff, Major Carlos Figueroa Morales, for which the FMLN "Modesto Ramírez" commando unit claimed responsibility.

Op. cit., United Nations, Report of the Special Representative of the Commission on Human Rights, 1990, p. 13.

116/ OAS-ICHR, *Report on the situation of human rights in El Salvador*, 1990-1991, p. 472.

117/ Op. cit., United Nations, Report of the Special Representative of the Commission on Human Rights, 1990, p. 11.

118/ According to the timetable, the process would comprise two phases. The first phase would be aimed at reaching a set of political agreements leading to a cease-fire and would cover the topics of the armed forces, human rights, the judicial and electoral systems, constitutional reforms, economic and social issues and United Nations verifications reached of the agreements. The second phase would be devoted to establishing the necessary conditions and guarantees for reintegration of the members of FMLN into the institutional, civil and political life of the country.

Op. cit. United Nations, Report of the Special Representative of the Commission on Human Rights, 1991, p. 4.

119/ On 19 November, the United Nations Secretary-General, Javier Pérez de Cuéllar, called on FMLN not to jeopardize the negotiating process. Mexico, Canada and the Central American Governments also appealed to FMLN to suspend its new offensive. Finally, on 17 December, the Presidents of the region, at a summit meeting held at Puntarenas, Costa Rica, demanded that FMLN declare a cease-fire.

120/ In his Sunday sermon on 3 February, Monsignor Rivera y Damas accused members of the First Infantry Brigade of this mass murder. Op. cit., *La Prensa Gráfica*, p. 115. Op. cit., Americas Watch, *El Salvador's Decade of Terror*, p. 160.

121/ The new Legislative Assembly, enlarged from 60 to 84 representatives in 1991, comprised 39 deputies from ARENA, 26 from the Christian Democratic Party, 9 from the Partido de Reconciliación Nacional, 8 from Convergencia Democratica and 1 each from the Unión Democrática Nacionalista and the Movimiento Auténtico Cristiano.

122/ On 9 February, the offices and typewriters of *Diario Latino* were destroyed by arson. Five days of truce at the beginning of March were followed by an escalation of clashes, attacks on military installations and army personnel, etc. resulting in more than 100 people killed in action.

123/ Among its most important provisions are the creation of a National Civil Police under the direction of civilian authorities independent of the armed forces, the establishment of the Office of the National Counsel for the Defence of Human Rights, an allocation to the judiciary from the State budget amounting to no less than 6 per cent of current income, the creation of a Supreme Electoral Tribunal and the redefinition of military jurisdiction as an exceptional procedure limited to dealing with purely military offences and misdemeanours. In this Mexico round it was also agreed to establish a Commission on the Truth to investigate serious acts of violence that had occurred since 1980 and whose impact on society demanded that the public should know the truth.

124/ El Salvador Peace Agreement, Chapultepec, 16 January 1992, 5, *End to Impunity*: "The parties recognize the need to clarify and put an end to any indication of impunity on the part of officers of the armed forces, particularly in cases where respect for human rights is jeopardized. To that end, the Parties refer this issue to the Commission on the Truth for consideration and resolution".

125/ In investigating and resolving the cases referred to below, Commission members examined documents in El Salvador and other countries; interviewed numerous participants, witnesses, victims and relatives; requested information from Government bodies; consulted court dossiers; visited places where incidents had occurred; and requested copies of instructions and orders given. Requests for precise information on various cases were transmitted to Ministers and heads of Government departments, and to what is now the former FMLN Command.

In the case of requests for reports from the Ministry of Defence, the Commission received replies to some of its inquiries. However, many of the replies were incomplete.

With regard to requests for reports that were not met and that in some cases referred to events prior to 1984, the Ministry of Defence informed the Commission that "no records exist since the General Staff was completely restructured in that year" (letter No. 10692, 27 November 1992). The Armed Forces Press Committee (COPREFA) told the Commission that it did not have any information for the period from January 1980 onwards and currently had available only the archive of press releases from January 1988 onwards (letter of 29 October 1992).

The replies to requests made to FMLN were also, in some cases, incomplete. the former Command attributed the inability to provide precise information to the Commission to the irregular nature of the war and the consequent lack of records.

126/ A detailed analysis of complaints and lists of victims are to be found in the annexes. More than 18,000 complaints from indirect sources were also registered, of which over 13,000 were analysed. The figures for direct and indirect sources have not been added to-gether. It is estimated that as many as 3,000 complaints were duplicated in the two sources. In any event the Commission believes that the total number of complaints registered is at least 22,000.

127/ The Commission also received thousands of other complaints from institutions which, once registered, could not be analysed either because they did not meet the corresponding minimum requirements, even though institutions had been informed of these in good time, or because the incidents reported had occurred outside the period covered by the mandate.

128/ For the investigation of this case, the Commission interviewed many witnesses, reviewed the court dossier and other documents and reports on the case, and visited the scene of the murders.

129/ The Commission received testimony from survivors and eyewitnesses. The accounts agree and are consistent with one another in describing the circumstances and indicating who was responsible. The relevant documentation was also reviewed. The court records and the forensic examination confirm that the incident occurred.

Belén Güijat canton was under the military jurisdiction of the Second Military Brigade which, in 1980, was under the command of Colonel Servio Tulio Figueroa. The Commission issued a summons to that officer through the Ministry of Defence. The only response it received—belated at that—was that he had retired. Information was also requested from the Minister of Defence concerning military operations carried out at the time in the district where the incident occurred; that request went unanswered. Despite repeated requests to the Minister of Defence for the names of those in charge of the security forces in Santa Ana and for information on military operations in Metapán in May 1980, no answer was received.

Another request to the present Commander of the Second Infantry Brigade went unheeded. A visit to Brigade headquarters to consult the records proved fruitless. Generally speaking, the competent military authorities did not cooperate in the investigation of this case.

130/ According to witnesses, he died a few years after the incident.

131/ The report on the medical examination of the bodies states specifically that a number of the bodies had what are known as powder burns. The forensic interpretation of this type of wound refers to the carbon ring that impregnates the skin when a person is shot at close range (under 30 centimetres). This carbon ring is caused by the deflagration of the powder when a shot is fired, leaving an indelible mark on the deceased's skin; in other words, the shot "burns the skin".

132/ When a person is shot, it is usually quite simple to determine where the bullet entered the body and where it exited, since the dimensions and characteristics of the two holes are quite different. Accordingly, the only logical interpretation of the statement that the forensic doctor was unable to make this determination is that the deceased were shot at such close range and with weapons of such large calibre that the bodies were literally destroyed.

133/ Enrique Alvarez Córdoba, former Minister of Agriculture and Livestock and President of the Frente Democrático Revolucionario (FDR). There were two bullet holes in his body. *El Diario de Hoy*, 29 November 1980.

134/ Juan Chácon, age 28, General Secretary of the Bloque Popular Revolucionario (BPR). There were three bullet holes in his body, one in the ear, another in the forehead and one in the thorax, and signs of strangulation. F. 7, court dossier No. 600, Fourth Criminal Court of San Salvador.

135/ Enrique Escobar Barrera, age 35, a member of the Movimiento Nacional Revolucionario (MNR). There were two bullet holes in his temple and signs of strangulation. F. 5, court dossier, quotation 2.

136/ Manuel de Jesús Franco Ramírez, age 35, a graduate in international relations and a member of the Partido Unión Democrática Nacionalista (UDN). There were four bullet wounds in his thorax and signs of strangulation. F. 6, court dossier, quotation 2.

137/ Humberto Mendoza, age 30, a member of the Movimiento de Liberación Popular (MLP). There were two bullet wounds in his body, one in the temple and the other in the thorax, and signs of strangulation. F. 4 court dossier, quotation 2.

138/ Doroteo Hernández, journalist and trade union leader of the Unión de Pobladores de Tugurios (UPT). At the time, he was not identified as a leader of FDR; however, the UCA Human Rights Institute/Christian Legal Aid document sent to the Commission on the Truth states that he was a leader of that organization.

139/ The Frente Democrático Revolucionario (FDR) came into being on 18 April 1980 as a result of a political agreement between the Frente Democrático (FD) and the Coordinadora Revolucionaria de Masas (CRM). It was formally established on 18 April 1980 by various political, popular and mass organizations. A number of its leaders had held prominent government posts in the first Revolutionary Junta which had overthrown General Romero on 15 October 1979. At the time, the leadership of FDR consisted of the five victims, Leoncio Pichinte and Juan José Martel.

140/ The National University of El Salvador was militarized on 26 June 1980, along with the Western University Centre and the Eastern University Centre, *Revista ECA*, No. 389, March 1981, p. 240. Other human rights organizations were also persecuted.

141/ "G3" rifles were the regulation weapon of the security forces at the time and were used by the armed forces of El Salvador in the war against Honduras in 1969.

142/ The JRG communiqué speaks of 13, a UPI cable mentions 200, *Prensa Gráfica*, 28 November 1980.

143/ The dossier notes that the justice of the peace made a visual inspection, that the bodies were identified and that two death certificates were issued. There was no police report of any kind, and nothing at all was done

by the judicial authorities; the case was finally closed because no proceedings had been carried out during a given period of time. This case clearly demonstrates the failure of the judiciary to function.

144/ Major Roberto D'Aubuisson stated publicly in a communiqué "Right now, based on the information available to us, we attribute responsibility to DRU, acting on direct orders from Colonel Majano ...".

145/ Communiqués of the Brigada Maximiliano Hernández Martínez, the Revolutionary Government Junta, the armed forces, Major Roberto D'Aubuisson, FDR, FMLN, *Revista ECA* No. 386, December 1980.

146/ Another significant point is that neither President Duarte nor other important Christian Democratic leaders were in the country, nor was Colonel Majano.

147/ Letter dated 9 December 1992 from the Commission on the Truth to the Chief of the National Police.

148/ The funeral itself turned into another act of violence when an explosive device blew up.

149/ The Commission on the Truth interviewed eyewitnesses, diplomats, senior commanders of the National Guard and the armed forces, members of the Maryknoll Order, relatives of the victims, lawyers for the defendants and the churchwomen's relatives, and a member of the court assigned to the case. In addition, the court dossier was reviewed and governmental and non-governmental reports were analysed. Colonel Zepeda Velasco was invited, unsuccessfully, to testify on several occasions.

150/ Rogers-Bowdler report, p. 10.

151/ Ibid., pp. 13-14.

152/ See the statement by Major Oscar Armando Carranza, who said that Colonel Eugenio Vides Casanova had ordered an investigation into the deaths of the churchwomen.

153/ Harold R. Tyler, Jr., *The Churchwomen Murders: A Report to the Secretary of State*, 2 December 1983 (known as the Tyler Report), p. 22.

154/ Ibid., pp. 29-30.

155/ Ibid., p. 24. See also the judicial statement by Lizandro Zepeda, vol. 2, f. 266, 23 June 1982, where he reports that he interviewed one person per day and that no conclusions were reached, although several people were interviewed.

156/ Judge Tyler concluded that Major Zepeda had probably informed Colonel Vides Casanova. Tyler Report, p. 26.

157/ Ibid., pp. 31-32.

158/ Ff. 102, 147-57.

159/ See President Duarte's speech, televised on 10 February 1982.

160/ Statement by Dagoberto Martínez, f. 132, vol. 3, 30 July 1983.

161/ See vol. 5 of the court dossier, f. 26, "Decision of the jury", 24 May 1983. See also ff. 26 and 65, 24 May and 20 June 1984.

162/ *The New York Times*, 25 May 1984, pp. 1 and 6.

163/ On 16 December 1980, United Nations Ambassador Jeane Kirkpatrick said: "I don't think the government (of El Salvador) was responsible. The nuns were not just nuns; the nuns were political activists. We ought to be a little more clear-cut about this than we usually are. They were political activists on behalf of the Frente and somebody who is using violence to oppose the Frente killed them." *Tampa Tribune*, 25 December 1980, pp. 23A and 24A, col. 1.

Secretary of State Alexander Haig testified as follows before the Foreign Affairs Committee of the House of Representatives: "I would like to suggest to you that some of the investigations would lead one to believe that perhaps the vehicle that the nuns were riding in may have tried to run a roadblock or may have accidentally been perceived to have been doing so, and there may have been an exchange of fire." See *Foreign Assistance Legislation for Fiscal Year 1982: Hearings before the House Committee on Foreign Affairs*, 97th Congress, First Session 163, 1981.

164/ The day after the deaths, President Jimmy Carter suspended aid to El Salvador, *The New York Times*, 14 January 1981.

In April 1981, the United States Congress was considering aid to El Salvador. On 26 April, Embassy officials met with the Minister of Defence García and with Vides Casanova and told them that the failure to investigate the case was jeopardizing United States aid. On 29 April, members of the National Guard were arrested and $25 million in military aid was approved the next day. See: Di Vicenzo, Janet, project ed., *El Salvador: The Making of U.S. Policy, 1984-1988*, vol. 1.

The day after members of the security forces were convicted, the United States Congress approved $62 million in emergency aid. See: *USA Today*, 25 May 1984, p. 9A. See also *The Boston Herald*, 25 May 1984, p. 5.

165/ Tyler Report, p. 63.

166/ Some of the evidence not included in the condensed version provided by the judge is as follows: (1) F. 68: judicial statement by José Dolores Meléndez, local commissioner, one of the first witnesses, who notified the justice of the peace and identified the bodies as "unknown"; (2) Ff. 111-115: statements made to the Medrano group by Santago Nonualca, who saw the white minibus going to and returning from the scene of the crime; (3) Ff. 120-133: statements made by National Guard members to the Medrano group concerning Colindres' actions before and after the murders; (4) F. 255: court order to take statements from Vides Casanova, Medrano and Zepeda Velasco; (5) F. 264: judicial statement by Medrano, who remembered little about his own investigation.

167/ In view of the total absence of investigations into the El Junquillo massacre, on 28 November 1992 the Commission on the Truth asked the Minister of Defence and Public Security, General René Emilio Ponce, to provide the Commission with the following information: details of the military units which took part in the military operation carried out between 10 and 12 March 1981 in the cantons of Agua Blanca and El Junquillo in the district of Cacaopera, Department of Morazán; the names of those responsible for ordering the operation and the orders they gave, together with the duties assigned to each military unit; the names of officers, non-commissioned officers and soldiers and the duties assigned to them; a copy of the operations report received by the Armed Forces General Staff and/or the Ministry of Defence concerning the results of the operation, together with the information available to the Ministry of Defence on the events which occurred in El Junquillo canton and in the hamlet of Flor Muerto in Agua Blanca canton, district of Cacaopera, Department of Morazán, between 10 and 12 March 1981.

At the time of drafting of this report, no reply to this request had been received from the Minister of Defence and Public Security.

The Commission received testimony from persons who made statements concerning the events that took place in El Junquillo canton and from other persons from whom the witnesses had sought assistance. It also requested information from the Government of El Salvador and from Military Detachment No. 6 at Sonsonate, and summoned an army officer. No reply was received to the request for information and the officer concerned failed to appear.

All the above factors were taken into consideration.

168/ During March 1982, there were some 700 journalists, photographers and television technicians in the country. Bonner, Raymond. *Weakness and Deceit*, Times Books, New York, 1984, p. 295.

169/ F. 252 of the dossier.

170/ Report I, p. 2.

171/ The Commission checked the video tapes and cassettes recorded by the journalists at the prison.

172/ According to official information transmitted to the Commission by the armed forces, there was no military detachment at Usulután at the time, only the Sixth Infantry Brigade, under the command of Lieutenant Colonel Elmer González Araujo.

173/ Record of the interrogation at Treasury Police headquarters. Annex II of report I.

174/ Ff. 73 et seq. of the dossier.

175/ F. 254 of the dossier.

176/ Interrogation record, annex II, report I.

177/ Report I, p. 3.

178/ Folio Ff. 73 et seq. of the dossier.

179/ A copy of the newspaper article can be found in annex III to report I. After studying the text of the press release, Colonel González denied that it was the work of COPREFA, saying that it has been written by the Treasury Police and passed on to COPREFA for publication, together with the photographs.

180/ F. 254 of the dossier.

181/ Report I, and f. 254 of the dossier.

182/ Ff. 246 et seq. of the dossier.

183/ F. 246 of the dossier.

184/ F. 246 of the dossier.

185/ Supplementary report of the investigation into the circumstances surrounding the events which led to the death of four Dutch journalists on 17 March 1982 in El Salvador, Ministry of Foreign Affairs of the Kingdom of the Netherlands, The Hague, 28 May 1982 (hereinafter referred to as report II).

186/ Report II, p. 7.

187/ Ff. 246 and 254 of the dossier. A Norwegian journalist staying in the same house as Wertz spoke to him as he was coming out of the shower, at 6.30 p.m.

188/ Report II, p. 1.

189/ Report II, p. 2.

190/ Ff. 117 et seq. of the dossier. Pseudonym of Napoleón Romero García.

191/ "Martín" said that, about 50 metres from the meeting point, he saw a blue pick-up truck with two people in it on the road to Santa Rita (report II, p. 4). Wertz, who was driving the minibus along the same road at the time, made no mention of this vehicle in any of his statements.

192/ Report II, p. 4. The sergeant also said that a number of men were hit by the first shots fired. Report II, p. 14.

193/ Report II, p. 6.

194/ Report II.

195/ Statement by the sergeant, report II, pp. 12 ff.

196/ Sergeant Canizales, report II, p. 13.

197/ According to information received by the Commission on the Truth from a number of sources, the intelligence data came from the Treasury Police, which had had the journalists under surveillance. Bonner, Raymond. *Weakness and Deceit*, p. 295.

198/ Report II, p. 15.

199/ F. 76 of the dossier.

200/ Report I, p. 11.

201/ Report II, p. 15. Dossier of the Office of the Attorney-General of the Republic, ff. 1, et seq.

202/ F. 254 of the dossier.

203/ F. 254 of the dossier.

204/ Report II, p. 9.

205/ Report II, pp. 12 ff.

206/ The Commission on the Truth received complaints on the case and interviewed witnesses, survivors and eyewitnesses, members of the Asociación Nacional de Indígenas (ANIS), members of the armed forces, civil defence members, members of popular organizations, members of the governmental Human Rights Commission and others. The dossier of the criminal proceedings was reviewed. The place of the arrests and the massacre was visited. Reports were also received from diplomatic and news sources, and governmental and non-governmental reports were reviewed. Carlos Sasso Landaverry, who was summonsed, did not appear before the Commission.

207/ Statement by Captain Figueroa Morales, Ministry of Defence investigation. F. 428.

208/ Judicial statement by Florencia Cruz Sánchez, mother of Gerardo Cruz Sandoval, 3 March 1983. F. 28.

209/ Statement by María Isabel Arevalo Moz, companion of José Guido García, 28 February 1983.

210/ Judicial statement by Nicolasa Zetino de Pérez, mother of Pedro Pérez Zetino and Benito Pérez Zetino, 28 February 1983. Ff. 19-20.

211/ Ibid.

212/ Statement by Felipa Bonilla, companion of Marcelino Sánchez Viscarra. Ff. 20-21.

213/ Judicial statement by Francisca Jiménez de Mártir, wife of Juan Bautista Mártir Pérez, 28 February 1983. Ff. 22-23.

214/ Judicial statement by Santos Márquez, wife of Héctor Manuel Márquez. Ff. 21-22.

215/ Judicial statement by eyewitnesses Aminta Ayala de Ayala (f. 16) and Candelario Elena (f. 26). See also statements by Adán Mejía Nataren (f. 15), Hortensia Dubón Ayala (f. 17), Ubaldo Mejía (ff. 18-19), Evangelina Escobar Mejía de Alemán (f. 25) and Rubenia López Morales (f. 27).

216/ Statement by Hortensia Dubón Ayala, companion of Antonio Mejía Alvarado (f. 17).

217/ Judicial statement by Adán Mejía Nataren, father of Lorenzo Mejía Carabante and uncle of Romelio Mejía Alvarado, 26 February 1983. F. 15.

218/ Ibid.

219/ Judicial statement by Candelario Elena, father of Ricardo García Elena, 1 March 1983. F. 26.

220/ Judicial statement by Evangelina Escobar Mejía de Alemán, wife of Francisco Alemán Mejía, 1 March 1983. F. 25.

221/ Judicial statement by Rebenia López Morales, sister of Leonardo López Morales, 2 March 1983. F. 27.

222/ Judicial statement by Aminta Ayala de Ayala, wife of Alfredo Ayala, 26 February 1983. F. 16.

223/ Statement by Ubaldo Mejía, father of Martín Mejía Castillio. Ff. 18-19.

224/ Colonel Elmer González Araujo is also referred to indiscriminately as Colonel Aráujo throughout the case.

225/ Inspection of the body of Alfredo Ayala, ff. 4-5.

226/ Statement by Captain Figueroa Morales, f. 428.

227/ According to all the soldiers who made depositions, they did not take anyone living in Las Hojas canton from their homes at any time, and they were not aware that any of their colleagues or superiors had done so. Ff. 424, 426, 432, 433 and 434. See also: statements by Rufino Raymundo Ruíz, José Reyes Pérez Ponce, José Sermeño, René Arevalo Moz, Teodoro Rodríguez Pérez and the Ministry of Defence investigation.

228/ Statement by Captain Figueroa Morales, f. 429.

229/ Letter from Infantry Colonel Napoleón Alvarado to the Minister of Defence, 20 April 1983, f. 411.

230/ Ibid., f. 442. This report was not submitted to the court until 15 December 1986, more than three years later, under the instructions of the Vice-Minister for Defence. F. 443.

231/ On 16 February 1984, the Attorney-General gave his opinion on the merits of the evidence, and took the view that the *corpus delicti* had been established by the inspection and identification of the bodies and that the criminal responsibility of the defendants had been established with the testimony of the witnesses. See: f. 317.

The defendants included Vicente Sermeño, Salvador Sermeño, Juan Aquilino Sermeño, Mario Pérez, René Arevalo Moz, Santiago Sermeño, Marcial Cáceres, Ileandro Pérez, Pedro Pérez, Vicente Sermeño, Alonso Inocente Cáceres and José Domingo Cáceres.

232/ The accused were Marcial Cáceres Rosa, René Arevalo Moz, Mario Arias Pérez, Pedro Pérez González, Leandro Pérez González, Salvador José Sermeño and Vicente Sermeño. At that time, there were no eyewitnesses to the participation of identified members of the armed forces. F. 318.

233/ F. 381.

234/ F. 382.

235/ F. 397.

236/ He said, "... since all the proceedings requested by the Office have been carried out ... without bringing about any change in the situation of the dismissed defendants in the case ... the case is dismissed in favour of the defendants ...". F. 471.

237/ F. 486.

238/ Article 1 of the Amnesty Act provided: "Art. 1.—Absolute and full amnesty shall be granted to all persons, whether nationals or aliens, who participated as direct or indirect perpetrators or as accomplices in committing political crimes, related common crimes or common crimes carried out by at least 20 persons ...". The Act contained a provision on pending cases. Article 4 (3) provided that "In the case of accused persons whose cases are pending, the competent judge shall of his own motion decree a general dismissal of proceedings in favour of the defendants without abatement of the action at law and shall order their immediate release." Article 4 (4) states: "In the situations regulated in paragraph 3, a judge or court that is for any reason hearing trials or proceedings brought for crimes indicated in this Act must refer them back within a period not exceeding 72 hours to the competent judge of first instance who was originally hearing those trials." Decree No. 805, vol. No. 297, *Official Gazette* No. 199, 28 October 1987.

239/ Ff. 546 et seq. The Court determined, on the basis of the testimony of the injured parties and of Figueroa Morales, that more than 20 people had participated in the operation carried out on 22 February 1983 in Las Hojas canton, although only 14 of them had been identified. The Court also noted that the Legislative Assembly had considered the possibility of making an exception for the Las Hojas case, so that the accused would not benefit from the special amnesty, but that in the end the Legislative Assembly had tacitly included it in the amnesty by not treating it as an exception. Ff. 551-52.

240/ El Salvador, Inter-American Commission on Human Rights, 24 September 1992. Report No. 26/92, case No. 10,278, para. 1.

241/ Report No. 26/92, para. 1.

242/ Ibid., para. 11.

243/ Ibid., para. 4.

244/ Ibid., para. 5.

245/ The Commission reviewed the complaints submitted by Americas Watch, the Archdiocesan Legal Protection Office and the non-governmental Human Rights Commission, the dossier of the criminal case and the report of the Commission for the Investigation of Criminal Acts. It also received information from diplomatic sources and from witnesses.

The Commission asked Colonel René Arnoldo Majano for official information on the activities of the Fifth Brigade on the date of the incident, in particular the name of the officer who was acting as Chief of Service. There was no response to this request for information.

246/ Statement by Second Lieutenant Arnoldo Vásquez Alvarenga and Deputy Sergeant Hernán Ayala Arias, at the offices of the Vice-Ministry of Public Security of the Ministry of Defence.

247/ Statement by Lieutenant Gálvez Gálvez and Second Lieutenant Vásquez Alvarenga at the offices of the Vice-Ministry of Public Security.

248/ Statement by Deputy Sergeant Hernán Ayala Arias and Second Lieutenant Vásquez Alvarenga at the offices of the Vice-Ministry of Public Security.

249/ Statement by Second Lieutenant Vásquez Alvarenga at the offices of the Vice-Ministry of Public Security.

250/ Statement by Lieutenant Gálvez Gálvez at the offices of the Vice-Ministry of Public Security.

251/ Statement by Lieutenant Gálvez Gálvez at the offices of the Vice-Ministry of Public Security.

252/ Statement by Captain Peña Durán and Major Beltrán Granados at the offices of the Vice-Ministry of Public Security. The latter said that he refused permission because he had to consult the commanding officers to see what they felt about that possibility. Beltrán also said that Peña had informed him that units of the Jiboa Battalion had arrested several people and confiscated subversive material, and that he had added that the arrests had been witnessed by the villagers and that the previous night he had been ordered to eliminate the detainees.

253/ Statement by Captain Peña and Lieutenant Gálvez at the offices of the Vice-Ministry of Public Security.

254/ In his statement at the offices of the Vice-Ministry of Public Security, Captain Peña Durán said that he had contacted the Brigade a second time and had spoken with then Major Rodríguez Molina, requesting and receiving his permission to go to Brigade headquarters. Captain Peña said in his statement at the offices of the

255/ Vice-Ministry of Public Security that he had spoken to the officers mentioned above in the order indicated. However, in the statement taken from him on this occasion, it was noted only that he had reported "on the situation" in San Francisco canton but not on the existence of the order to execute the detainee. When he testified before the Commission on the Truth, Captain Peña Durán said that he had expressly informed Rodríguez Molina, Turcios and Chávez Cáceres of the existence of the order. However, he said that when he informed Chávez, the latter simultaneously received the report that the detainees had died in an ambush. Colonel Chávez Cáceres said in his statement to the Commission on the Truth that Captain Peña had only informed him of the general situation in San Francisco canton. Colonel Turcios said that Captain Peña had reported to Major Rodríguez Molina, who had gone to the office of Lieutenant Colonel Turcios. They had then both gone to report to Colonel Chávez Cáceres. He does not recall having received as part of Peña's report the information that the detainee was going to be executed.

256/ Statement by Lieutenant Gálvez Gálvez at the offices of the Vice-Ministry of Public Security.

257/ Statements by Lieutenant Gálvez Gálvez, Reynaldo Aguilar Hernández and Oscar Cerón Sánchez at the offices of the Vice-Ministry of Public Security. Cerón Sánchez said that he heard Corporal Hernán Ayala Arias say that Lieutenant Gálvez had handed over command to Major Beltrán so as not to have problems with his soldiers. Corporal Ayala Arias did not refer to this fact.

258/ They were, including the four persons detained earlier, the following: José Félix Alfaro, Jesús Zepeda Rivas, María Zoila Rivas, Nicolás Flóres Alfaro, José Ulises Sibrián Rivas, Teresa de Jesús Argueta, José María Flóres, José Atilio Rivas, María de Jesús Sibrián and José Francisco Alfaro.

259/ Statement by Lieutenant Gálvez Gálvez at the offices of the Vice-Ministry of Public Security.

260/ Statements by Second Lieutenant Vásquez Alvarenga and Francisco Monzón Solis at the offices of the Vice-Ministry of Public Security.

On 6 March, at the offices of the Vice-Ministry of Public Security, Silverio Menjívar García said that Sergeant Tobar Guzmán had told him and other soldiers that "Major Beltrán had ordered him to lay the mines in order to kill the detainees".

261/ Statement by Sergeant Tobar at the offices of the Vice-Ministry of Public Security.

262/ Statement by private Manuel de Jesús Herrera Rivera at the offices of the Vice-Ministry of Public Security. In his judicial statement, Hernández Matute also said that Vásquez had designated Churute (Cruz Castro), Beltrán and himself to finish off the detainees. In his statement in the offices of the Vice-Ministry, Cruz Castro said that Vásquez designated him, (Méndez) Beltrán and (Hernández) Matute to finish off the detainees.

263/ Statement by Sergeant Jorge Alberto Tobar Guzmán and Napoleón Antonio Merino at the offices of the Vice-Ministry of Public Security of the Ministry of Defence, on 3 and 6 March 1989 respectively, and statement by Manuel de Jesús Herrera at the offices of the Vice-Ministry of Public Security.

264/ Statement by Francisco de Jesús Monzón Solís at the offices of the Vice-Ministry of Public Security. Judicial statement by Francisco Ponce Ramírez. Sergeant Tobar said in the same offices that a soldier had told him

that the officers had ordered them to shoot after the mines were detonated, but not more than one round. Second Lieutenant Vásquez said that Major Beltrán ordered the soldiers to shoot to simulate an ambush.

265/ Statements by Manuel de Jesús Herrera Rivera, Napoleón Merino Martínez, Fermín Cruz Castro and Santos Victorino Díaz at the offices of the Vice-Ministry of Public Security. The first of these said that he saw Cruz Castro, Ponce Ramírez and Hernández Matute. The second said that he saw Cruz Castro, Ponce Ramírez, Hernández Matute and Méndez Beltrán. In his statement, Fermín Cruz Castro mentioned himself, Hernández Matute and Méndez Beltrán. Santos Victorino Díaz said that he saw soldiers "Churute" (Cruz Castro), "Ciguanabo" (Méndez Beltrán), "Chico Balazo" (Ponce Ramírez), Matute (Hernández Matute) and Corporal Ayala Arias shoot the wounded detainees.

266/ Statement by Lieutenant Gálvez Gálvez.

267/ Statement by Lucio de Jesús Escoto Córdova at the offices of the Vice-Ministry of Public Security. After 3 March 1989, a document sent by the Fifth Brigade, based in San Vicente, listing the names of personnel in active service who had been in San Francisco canton, was added to the dossier of the court case. The name of Escoto Córdova was on the list (cf. folio 826).

268/ Folios 53 et seq. of the dossier.

269/ Report of the Commission for the Investigation of Criminal Acts.

270/ Ff. 867 and 966 of the dossier of the court case on the San Francisco massacre. He was also told that the accused were in custody at his disposal in the Vice-Ministry of Public Security.

271/ Sixth document, f. 1180 of the dossier.

272/ On 26 June 1990, the Supreme Court approved a motion by the Attorney-General to transfer the case against Major Beltrán from the San Vicente court to the Sixth Criminal Court in San Salvador. Seventh document, f. 1326 of the dossier.

273/ Seventh document, f. 1243 of the dossier.

274/ Seventh document, f. 1284 of the dossier.

275/ Located on the Catarina estate, Department of San Vicente.

276/ The operation began at 8 a.m. and ended at 4 p.m. CIHD report, p. 1.

277/ The following items were seized in the operation: Military *matériel*: 3 machine-guns, 5 machine-gun magazines, 1 M-16 rifle, 1 AR-15 rifle, 8 M-16 magazines, 17 9-millimetre cartridges, 3 40-millimetre grenades, 1 YAESU radio, 1 Sony mini tape recorder, 2 flashlights, 4 rucksacks and 2 soldier's canteens.

Medicines and medical equipment: 30 injections, 3 antibodies for clinical use, a minor surgery kit, 1 sphygmomanometer and an unspecified quantity of antibiotics. CIHD report, p. 3.

It should be noted that COPREFA news bulletins Nos. 114 and 115 of 17 and 18 April 1989 did not indicate that the equipment seized included medicines and medical equipment.

278/ Madeleine Lagadec's body was fully clothed in the photographs allegedly taken shortly after the executions and published by COPREFA.

279/ Juan Antonio's skull had been smashed by a stone, the skulls of Clelia Concepción Díaz Salazar and Isla Casares had bullet exit wounds in the occipital area, María Cristina's body had, in addition to a shrapnel wound in the stomach, a bullet wound in the forehead with an exit wound in the back of the head.

280/ The autopsy was performed by Dr. Baccino and Dr. Quillien at the morgue of the Keufatras cemetery, Brest, France, at the request of the Public Prosecutor of the Court of First Instance of Brest.

281/ "... the bullet penetrated the skull through the right temple and exited through the left temple; the trajectory was virtually within a frontal and nearly horizontal plane at the level of the base of the skull." Autopsy report signed by Dr. Baccino E. of the SEBILAU Service, Morvan Hospital Research Centre, Brest, and Dr. Quillien J., commissioned by the Public Prosecutor of the Brest Court of First Instance (2 May 1989).

282/ Robert H. Kirschner, MD. Deputy Chief Medical Examiner, Office of the Medical Examiner, Cook County, Chicago, Illinois. Physicians for Human Rights (Board of Directors, Executive Committee).

283/ Report on the autopsy of Madeleine Lagadec. Robert H. Kirschner, MD, Chicago, 10 January 1993.

284/ Ibid.

285/ Report of the Centre d'Applications et de Recherches en Microscopie Electronique. Prepared by Mr. Le Ribault, Doctor of Science, Chairman and Director of the Centre, assisted by Mrs. Monique Roze, whose expert opinions were requested by the Public Prosecutor of the Court of First Instance of Brest, France, 11 May 1989.

286/ It is clear that Madeleine Lagadec was half-naked when she was shot, that she was dressed when her body was photographed by COPREFA, and that her trousers had been pulled down and she did not have any underwear on two days later when she was found by the witnesses who testified to the Commission.

287/ Given the difficulty of analysing the residues of the impact of bullets and also the significant amount of phosphorus present, the Centre d'Applications et de Recherches en Microscopie Electronique puts forward two theories: if the phosphorus was from the explosive, its presence would mean that the shot was fired at close range. It is impossible to determine the range of the shot since neither the type of firearm nor the type of ammunition used is known. The second theory suggests that, if the phosphorus was not from the explosive, it could have been from incendiary bullets based on white phosphorus which ignites in contact with the air. In that case the absence of traces of explosive would indicate that the shot was fired at intermediate range (5 metres or more). It would thus be neither a close-range (point-blank) nor a long-distance shot.

288/ The Commission on the Truth reviewed all the relevant

documentation on the case of Dr. Begoña García and obtained testimony from an expert forensic pathologist as to the validity of and the conclusions reached by the official examination of the corpse and the clinical autopsy.

289/ Statement made by Lieutenant Colonel José Antonio Almendáriz Rivas to the First Criminal Court of Santa Ana at 12.30 p.m. on 19 August 1991.

290/ Letter No. 0630, dated 12 September 1990, from Lieutenant Gilberto García Cisneros of the National Police Third Command to the Commander of the Second Infantry Brigade.

The two judges of the respective district stated that they had never received notice or a summons to examine any corpse. Letter No. 320, dated 28 August 1991, sent by the Second Justice of the Peace of Chalchuapa, Raúl García Morales, and letter No. 457, dated 29 August 1991, sent by the First Justice of the Peace of Chalchuapa, Gloria Macal de Fajardo. Court dossier.

291/ Examination made in the First Criminal Court, Santa Ana, at 5.15 p.m. on 14 September 1990.

292/ Autopsy report, Pathology Department, Navarra Government Hospital, Navarra, Spain, 22 September 1990. Report prepared by the National Toxicology Institute, Ministry of Justice, Department of Madrid, at the request of the Second Court of Investigation of Pamplona (Navarra), Madrid, 30 October 1990. Report on the death of Dr. Begoña García Arandigoyen on 10 September 1990. Dr. Carlos Martín Beristaín, November 1990.

293/ The Commission on the Truth reviewed the dossiers of the investigations carried out by CIHD, the Second Justice of the Peace and the National Police in the case of the attack on FENASTRAS premises. It requested the armed forces, the National Police, the Treasury Police, the National Guard and CIHD to provide all relevant information on the 31 October 1989 bomb attacks. CIHD, the National Police and the National Guard provided the Commission with copies of the official dossiers and other documents concerning these incidents.

The Commission interviewed military officers, CIHD investigators, National Police agents, including the Chief of the Explosives Unit, leaders of FENASTRAS, COMADRES staff and numerous victims and witnesses. It summonsed Colonel Iván Reynaldo Díaz, Colonel Juan Vicente Eguizábal, Colonel Dionisio Ismael Muchuca, Colonel Carlos Mauricio Guzmán Aguilar and Colonel José Antonio Almendáriz Rivas, none of whom appeared.

294/ National Police patrol headquarters informed the Police Operations Centre that "D/T NI" (unidentified terrorist criminals) had "planted and detonated an explosive device". (Police Operations Centre news summary for the period from 6 p.m. on 30 October 1989 to 6 a.m. on 31 October 1989, National Police.)

295/ A report provided to the Commission on the Truth by the National Police stated that FENASTRAS "is organically linked to the clandestine organization Fuerzas Armadas de la Resistencia Nacional (FARN/RN) and its aim is to organize the working class to support FMLN ideological plans for destabilizing the Government of El Salvador by raising political, social and economic issues and the issue of human rights violations at the national and international levels, thereby mobilizing the working class to fight against the Government".

296/ On 18 September, National Police agents arrested 64 members of FENASTRAS who had taken part in a demonstration; some of them were tortured in police custody. *El Mundo*, 19 September 1989; confidential memorandum from Americas Watch. According to reports, one of those arrested, Julia Tatiana Mendoza Aguirre, later sued the National Police for alleged rape. She was one of those who died in the attack. The Commission received direct testimony from 364 people concerning cases of violence against trade unionists.

297/ On 19 October 1989, persons unknown carried out an attack on the homes of Rubén Zamora and Aronette Díaz, widow of Mario Zamora. On 17 October, Ana Isabel Casanova Porras, the daughter of Colonel Edgardo Casanova Vejar, was murdered.

298/ The attack left one civilian dead and more than five people injured. (Police Operations Centre news summary for the period 6 a.m.-6 p.m. on 30 October 1989, National Police.)

299/ According to article 149 of the Code of Criminal Procedure, in the case of offences "which have caused serious public outrage because of the circumstances of the crime or the status of the persons involved in them, either as victims or as suspects, the judge of first instance shall, under penalty of incurring a fine of 200 colones, personally carry out all the investigation proceedings ...". However, the proceedings were carried out by the justice of the peace, without any involvement of the judge of first instance.

300/ Inspection required by law, 31 October 1989, court dossier, folio 15.

301/ Report by Lieutenant Juan Antonio Aguirre Guerra, Commander of the Investigation Battalion, 31 October 1989, CIHD dossier, folio 10.

302/ Letter to the chief of the Investigations Section of the CIHD Executive Unit, signed by Detective Sergeant Juan Orlando Ramos Arevalo, dossier, folio 2.

303/ It was also determined that the explosion occurred in the passageway between the access wall and the wall of the FENASTRAS offices. The final report ruled out the possibility that the explosive device had been thrown from the street or that it had been a car bomb. See the report of the Technical Assistance Department of the Explosives Unit of the National Police, undated, CIHD dossier, folio 11.

304/ Letters to Colonel Héctor Heriberto Hernández, Director of the Treasury Police, Colonel Carlos Armando Carrillo Schlenker, Director of the National Guard, and Colonel Dionisio Ismael Machuca, Director of the National Police, dated 7 November 1989, CIHD dossier. The Treasury Police sent a reply to CIHD, describing nine of the victims as members of Restistencia Nacional.

305/ FBI report, 24 January 1990, court dossier, folio 50.

306/ Ibid.

307/ Ibid.

308/ At the time, the Movimiento Nacional Revolucionario (MNR) was a member of the political alliance Convergencia Democrática, which was part of the Frente Democrático Revolucionario (FDR).

309/ The Socialist International is a world-wide grouping of social-democratic, labour and socialist parties.

310/ Guillermo Ungo died a few months later in Mexico after a long illness.

311/ Objectively speaking, the Republic of Guatemala was not a safe place for the Salvadorian opposition to engage in political activity, mainly because of the domestic situation in Guatemala itself and the long-standing close ties between extreme right-wing Salvadorian groups and similar groups in Guatemala.

312/ Office of the President of the Republic. Presidential Staff. Security Department. *Caso: Oquelí Colindres*, Guatemala, May 1990, p. 2.

313/ Statement by Mario Antonio Sánchez Urizar, *Letter No. 093 from the Mixco National Police substation to the magistrate of the First Criminal Court*, 12 January 1990.

314/ *Autopsy report No. 045-90 from Dr. Julio Cesar Pivaral Santos to the judge of the Jutiapa Court of First Instance*, Jalpatagua, 15 January 1990.

315/ Office of the President of the Republic, Presidential Staff. Security Department. *Caso: Oquelí Colindres*, Guatemala, May 1990, p. 10.

316/ Ibid., p. 10.

317/ Robert Goldman and Tom Farer, *Evaluation of the investigation and reports made by the Government of the Republic of Guatemala*, October 1990, p. 32.

318/ A source reported that the Presidential Staff of the Republic of Guatemala obtained transcripts of routinely traced and recorded radio broadcasts which would have shed light on the incident. One expert in Guatemala confirmed that, technically speaking at least, the Presidential Staff itself could have made the recordings. The same expert confirmed that the basic errors in the police investigation were unusual, unless there was a definite unwillingness to make an investigation in this case.

319/ Letters sent to the President of the Republic of Guatemala, Mr. Serrano and to the Minister of Labour, Mr. Zolórzano. Interview with the Ambassador of Guatemala to the Republic of El Salvador. Visit by the Chairman of the Commission on the Truth to Guatemala City on 14 December 1992. Telephone request to President Serrano in January 1993.

320/ Dossier No. 73-DD H-90 of the office of the Attorney-General of the Republic of El Salvador.

321/ The Commission on the Truth interviewed eyewitnesses and a number of officials who had been working at the United States Embassy at the time. It also reviewed the dossier of the criminal proceedings and inspected the scene of the arrest and disappearance of the students. In order to protect confidential sources, such sources are not quoted in this report.

322/

323/ All the testimony indicates that at least one car entered the Embassy courtyard. There are indications that more than one car entered.

324/ Judicial statements by Mr. Florentín Meléndez, dossier, f. 39, and Mr. Santiago Orellana Amador, ff. 41-42.

325/ Dossier, ff. 50, 52.

326/ See the report on the case in this chapter.

327/ On 31 January, the National Guard central barracks was searched, but the disappeared students were not found. F. 43. Cells at the central barracks of the Treasury Police, the Municipal Police and the National Police were searched without success. Ff. 39-40. Both the Chief of the National Police and the Director-General of the Treasury Police denied having detained the students. Ff. 52, 55.

328/ Declaration by the "Ejército Secreto Anti-Communista", 11 May 1980.

329/ Inter-American Commission on Human Rights. Case No. 9844, El Salvador.

330/ Ibid., Letter from Jemera Rone (Americas Watch) to the Commission on the Truth, dated 26 August 1992. Statement made by Cruz Antonio López Hernández to

331/ the Human Rights Commission of El Salvador (governmental) on 1 April 1987.

332/ Letter dated 23 February 1987 to Edwin Corr, United States Ambassador to El Salvador, from Congressman James L. Obestar et al.

333/ Letter dated 26 February 1987 to José Napoleon Duarte, President of El Salvador, from Congressman James L. Obestar et al.

334/ Regular meeting of CIHD, 1987, record No. 12, p. 22. According to the summary, the investigation was made "at the request of the Human Rights Commission (governmental)"; however, the Head of CIHD at the time, Mr. Julio Alfredo Samayoa, says that it was made at the request of the Ministry of Foreign Affairs.

335/ CIHD has informed us that he submitted his resignation approximately six months ago and has probably left the country.

336/ "Summary of the investigations conducted during the period from 15 May 1987 to 30 May 1987". CIHD, 30 May 1987, pp. 2-3.

337/ Ibid., p. 3.

338/ Regular meeting of CIHD, 1987, record No. 16, p. 26. That same day, CIHD administered a lie detector test to its source. The result was favourable. "Summary of the investigations conducted during the period from 15 May 1987 to 30 May 1987", CIHD, 30 May 1987, pp. 3-4. CIHD then planned to summons and take statements from the members of the air force and the National Guard implicated in the arrest and transfer and referred to in the reports identifying Rivas Hernández. "Work plan", CIHD, 30 May 1987, pp. 1-2.

339/ Regular meeting of CIHD, 1987, record No. 17, p. 27. There is no new report on the case until 11 August 1987. Ibid., 1987, record No. 27, p. 40. Thereafter, there are no further reports in 1987. The records of CIHD meetings for 1988 were not transmitted to the Commission on the Truth.

340/ The Commission interviewed many witnesses, civilian and military, and vetted public documents on the case.

341/ Copy of the Paratroop Battalion log of incoming and outgoing vehicles, provided to the Commission on the Truth on 5 December 1992.

342/ The Commission on the Truth had access to official documents confirming that Colonel Rodríguez was on duty on 18 and 19 August 1989.

343/ Copy of the Paratroop Battalion log of incoming and outgoing vehicles. Information available to the Commission on the Truth shows that it was common practice, in cases of disappearance, not to keep official records of arrests.

344/ El Mundo, 21 August 1989, 4 September 1989 and 6 September 1989.

345/ On 5 September 1989, through the Archdiocesan Legal Protection Office, a sister of Juan Francisco filed a writ of habeas corpus with the Supreme Court of Justice. Sara Cristina's mother also requested a remedy of habeas corpus for her daughter, but the Court never dealt with the case.

346/ Letter dated 23 August 1989 from the Director-General of the Treasury Police to the Archdiocesan Legal Protection Office, contained in the Massi Chávez case file, Archdiocesan Legal Protection Office.

347/ Case No. 1906, Human Rights Commission of El Salvador.

348/ To date, the armed forces have not transmitted the information requested from the Treasury Police.

349/ National Police report transmitted to the Commission on the Truth, 23 December 1992.

350/ Report of the former National Guard transmitted to the Commission on the Truth on 20 January 1993.

351/ The convent was—in the words of the experts—a "primary synchronous common grave". Patricia Bernardi, Mercedes Doretti and Luis Fondebrider, Archaeological Report, p. 15.

352/ Archaeological Report, p. 18.

353/ When the exhumed bone remains were analysed, the expert anthropologists were able to identify 117 anatomically articulated skeletons, as indicated in their report. After the laboratory analysis was done, it was possible to identify at least 143 skeletons. See Clyde Snow, John Fitzpatrick, Robert H. Kirschner and Douglas Scott, Report of Forensic Investigation.

354/ Report of Forensic Investigation, p. 1.

355/ The basis for this assertion is "the simultaneous presence of both deciduous and permanent teeth" and "the fact that their primary and/or secondary centres of ossification had not fused" (Archaeological Report, pp. 17-18; cf. ibid., p. 8).

356/ Ibid., p. 18.

357/ Report of Forensic Investigation, p. 1.

358/ "... The remains of a foetus were wedged in the pelvic region, with the head between the two coxal bones and on the sacrum" (*Archaeological Report*, p. 8). As indicated in the laboratory report, it was determined that the mother "was in the third trimester of pregnancy" (*Report of Forensic Investigation*, p. 1).

359/ *Archaeological Report*, p. 16.

360/ Ibid., p. 16.

361/ Ibid., p. 11.

362/ Ibid., p. 11. The report went on to say: "We are referring to grid squares B2, B3, C3 and the south-west corner of C2, where 82 bodies—almost 70 per cent of the skeletons—and 18 of the 24 concentrations of bone remains—almost 80 per cent—were found. In these grid squares, 159 bullet fragments were found: 102 fragments in B3; 13 fragments in B2; 30 fragments in C3; and 14 fragments in C2. In these grid squares, all these bullet fragments were in direct contact with bone remains. In other words, 159 bullet fragments had struck a large proportion of the 82 skeletons and 18 concentrations discovered in this zone."

363/ Ibid., p. 17.

364/ Ibid., p. 16. The report supported this assertion as follows:
"(1) Observation of peri-mortem lesions, together with bullet fragments and holes in the floor underneath such fragments. This observation applies to skeletons 2, 5, 9, 10, 26, 57, 92, 110 and 113, located in grid squares C1, C2, C1, D2, B4, C3, B2, B3-C3 and B3 respectively ...;
"(2) The only way such shots could have produced holes in the floor is by shooting downwards, either straight down or diagonally;
"(3) In the case of skeletons 2, 10, 92, 110 and 57, the bullets which made the holes in the floor were found in the area of the skull; in the case of skeleton 26, in the cervical vertebrae (very close to the skull)".

365/ *Report of Forensic Investigation*, p. 2.

366/ *Report of Forensic Investigation*, p. 3.

367/ "24 separate weapons were identified, consistent with at least 24 individual shooters" (*Report of Forensic Investigation*, p. 3).

368/ Ibid., p. 3. The experts who exhumed the bone remains reached the same conclusion. Cf. *Archaeological Report*, p. 17.

369/ *Archaeological Report*, p. 17.

370/ *Archaeological Report*, p. 18.

371/ *Report of Forensic Investigation*, p. 1.

372/ They also stated that all their conclusions "are stated with a reasonable degree of medical and scientific certainty" and that they were willing to testify in a court of law regarding these conclusions. See *Report of Forensic Investigation*, p. 3.

373/ *The Washington Post*, 29 April 1981.

374/ *United Church Observer*, October 1980, p. 40. *Report on Human Rights in El Salvador*, compiled by Americas Watch and the American Civil Liberties Union, 26 January 1982.

375/ Statement by the Government and armed forces of Honduras, 24 June 1980.

376/ Judicial Case No. 218-92, folio 4. Chalatenango Court of First Instance, 26 October 1992.

377/ To investigate the case, the Commission on the Truth reviewed the previous investigations and the court dossier, as well as documents from various other sources, and interviewed many confidential witnesses. For their protection, these sources are not quoted in this report.

378/ The mass, at 6 p.m., was in memory of the mother of a friend of his, Jorge Pinto, Jr., owner of the opposition newspaper *El Independiente*. Announcements of the mass had been published in two newspapers, *La Prensa Gráfica* and *El Diario de Hoy*, on Monday, 24 March 1980. Court dossier, ff. 42-43.

379/ Monsignor Romero lived in a small house on the grounds of the Hospital de la Divina Providencia.

380/ *El Diario de Hoy*, San Salvador, 11 February 1980, p. 53. Signed article.

381/ *El Diario de Hoy*, San Salvador, 23 February 1980, p. 34. Signed article.

382/ Sermon delivered on 17 February 1980.

383/ He and several colleagues met in late February 1980 with Héctor Dada, one of the new members of the second Junta. Dada mentioned the death on 23 February of one of the leaders of the Christian Democratic party, Mario Zamora (see report in this chapter on the assassination of Zamora). He also mentioned that he was aware of death threats against himself and the Archbishop, among others. Interview with priest Rafael Urrutia.
Monsignor Romero said that he took the threat seriously, and even said privately that "... I have never been so afraid, not even in the time of General Romero ...". Interview with Roberto Cuéllar.
Interview with Héctor Dada.
Monsignor Romero received warning of equally serious death threats from the Papal Nuncio in Costa Rica, Monsignor Lajos Kada. Diary of Monsignor Romero. Subsequently, on Saturday 22 and Sunday 23 March, the nuns working in the Hospital de la Divina Providencia, where the Archbishop lived, received anonymous telephone calls threatening his life.

384/ Interview with Roberto Cuéllar.
Interview with priest Rafael Urrutia.
In the first week of March, Monsignor Romero met with the United States Ambassador to El Salvador, Robert White, whom he told of the threats on his life. Although the Archbishop did not give any specifics, he was keenly aware of the imminent danger and even confided to Ambassador White that: "My only hope is that when they kill me they don't kill many of us". Interview with Robert White.

385/ See report in this chapter.

386/ Statement made to the Commission for the Investigation of Criminal Acts by priest Fabián Conrado Amaya Torres. Court dossier on the investigation of the death of Monsignor Oscar Arnulfo Romero, case No. 134/80, Fourth Criminal Court, ff. 592 et seq.

387/ Police investigation conducted on 10 March 1980,

transmitted to the courts on 14 March 1986. The bomb was made of 72 sticks of commercial dynamite which could be activated either by a timing device or by radio and were sufficient to kill several of those officiating at the altar and those sitting in the front pews. "(...) Moreover, it is a device which has never been planted by subversives who have always been active in our country, unless it is true that they have new experts, for two Japanese are known to have arrived (...). There is no supply in the country of electric detonators of the type used". Court dossier, ff. 494 et seq.

Neither the authorities of the Catholic Church nor the Archdiocesan Legal Aid Office received any official communication on the results of police action and all indications are that there were no further investigations. Interview with Roberto Cuéllar. Interview with Monsignor Ricardo Urioste.

388/ Sermon of 23 March 1980.

389/ Court dossier, f. 4.

390/ Interview with Judge Atilio Ramírez Amaya.

391/ The dossier does not contain the record of this inquiry, or the X-rays. Ibid.

392/ Ibid.

393/ Majors Roberto D'Aubuisson, Jorge Adalberto Cruz Reyes, Roberto Mauricio Staben; Captains Alvaro Rafael Saravia, José Alfredo Jiménez, Víctor Hugo Vega Valencia, Eduardo Ernesto Alfonso Avila; Lieutenants Federico Chacón, Miguel Francisco Bennet Escobar, Rodolfo Isidro López Sibrián, Carlos Hernán Morales Estupinián, Jaime René Alvarado y Alvarado; Antonio Cornejo Jr., Ricardo Valdivieso, Roberto Muyshondt, Fernando Sagrera, Amado Antonio Garay, Nelson Enrique Morales, Andrés Antonio Córdova López, Herbert Romeo Escobar, Fredy Salomón Chávez Guevara, Marco Antonio Quintanilla, José Joaquín Larios and Julián García Jiménez. Order of 12 May 1980 issued by Major José Francisco Samayoa, Acting Commander of CITFA, placing the detainees at the disposal of the Military Examining Judge.

394/ cf. Chronology.

395/ Order of 12 May 1980 issued by Major José Francisco Samayoa, Acting Commander of CITFA, placing the detainees at the disposal of the Military Examining Judge. Exhibit No. 10 (contents not recorded).

396/ Ibid. Exhibit No. 7.

397/ The diary contains notes on "223 ammunition", a type of .22 calibre bullet and "2 Bushmasters" and "5 AR-15s", both of these being types of rifles that fire .22 and .223 calibre bullets.

398/ For example, "Amado" refers to Amado Garay; "Avila", "el pelón Avila", "Eduardo Av." and "Eduardo A." refer to Captain Eduardo Avila; "Negro", "Nando Sagrera" and "Nando S." refer to Fernando Sagrera; and "Saravia" refers to Captain Alvaro Rafael Saravia himself. For the involvement of all of these persons, see below.

399/ "General Framework for the Organization of the Anti-Marxist Struggle in El Salvador", document seized at

the San Luis estate on 7 May 1980. Arrest warrant of 12 May 1980 placing the detainees at the disposal of the Military Examining Judge, exhibit No. 4.

400/ Mr. Rey Prendes, a leader of the Christian Democratic party, made a statement to the press a few days after the video was shown; he denounced the simulation of "Commander Pedro Lobo" and revealed the criminal's true identity and background. Court dossier, ff. 152 et seq.

401/ In August 1985, the Office of the Attorney-General presented the statement of Roberto Adalberto Salazar Collier, "Pedro Lobo", to the Fourth Criminal Court. On that occasion, he made the same allegations but did not mention D'Aubuisson's name. One of the alleged conspirators presented a written statement in February 1986 denying the allegations against him. Court dossier ff. 152 et seq. and f. 241. Judge Zamora's official requests to television stations to supply him with a copy of the video with Salazar Collier's statements were denied. The Attorney-General's Office insisted that the stations reveal who had delivered and picked up the video, but the judge declared that there were no grounds for such a request. Court dossier, ff. 189, 200, 210, 212.

402/ Major D'Aubuisson cited a book entitled *La conspiración del silencio* by Manuel de Armas, which claimed that Cuban agents carried out the murder. *La Prensa Gráfica*, "Hace revelaciones mayor D'Aubuisson" (The revelations of Major D'Aubuisson), Friday, 6 September 1985, p. 2. *El Diario de Hoy*, Friday, 6 September 1985, p. 3.

403/ The armed forces appeared officially before the Commission on the Truth in October 1992 and alleged that FMLN had been responsible for the Archbishop's assassination without offering any evidence to back that assertion.

404/ Court dossier, f. 389.

405/ Statement by Amado Antonio Garay to CIHD on 19 November 1987. Court dossier, f. 274.

406/ Ibid.

407/ Ibid., f. 270.

408/ Ibid.

409/ Ibid., ff. 269 and 285.

410/ Court dossier, f. 289.

411/ Court dossier, f. 299.

412/ Public letter of Mr. Héctor Antonio Regalado dated 13 March 1989.

413/ He later became Chief of Security of the Legislative Assembly when D'Aubuisson was President of the Assembly.

414/ When he appeared before the Commission, Mr. Sagrera denied all involvement.

415/ Of these 817 cases, 644 (79 per cent) were extrajudicial executions.

416/ Left-wing actions that fell into the same category as violence perpetrated by the death squads are dealt with in the section of this report on abuses committed by the guerrillas.

417/ For details of how the death squads operated, see the account in this report of the assassinations of Monsignor Oscar Arnulfo Romero and Mario Zamora and the Sheraton case.

418/ The Organización Democrática Nacionalista, founded in 1963 by General José Alberto Medrano. Its network was national in scope, with representatives in each municipality, canton and community, and it had from 50,000 to 100,000 members. Members of ORDEN cooperated closely with security forces. One of their main tasks was to "detect" and report to the authorities the presence and activities of "subversives". They also took part in direct operations designed to intimidate those perceived to be enemies.

419/ See Chronology.

420/ After the 1979 coup, about 80 armed forces and security forces officers were retired. Interview with Héctor Dada.

421/ "General framework for the Organization of the Anti-Marxist Struggle in El Salvador", document confiscated at the San Luis estate on 7 May 1980, order of 12 May 1980 placing the detainees at the disposal of the Military Examining Judge, exhibit No. 4.
D'Aubuisson received military training in Taiwan.

422/ Ibid.

423/ Ibid.

424/ For those involved in the D'Aubuisson group, see the Archbishop Romero assassination case.

425/ The Commission interviewed witnesses and reviewed relevant documents from both confidential and public sources. To protect confidential sources, these are not quoted in this report.

426/ A witness maintains that, when they took this attitude, Zamora began to get up to leave and the meeting was on the verge of ending. Another leader, however, suggested that not everything in the document was necessarily true; after that, the meeting continued and the PDC political position became more flexible, at least as far as the document submitted to the armed forces was concerned.

427/ FPL leader who committed suicide in Managua.

428/ Napoléon Duarte was the most important leader of the Christian Democratic Party and his leadership extended beyond the party. He was a candidate for President with the Alliance in 1972, then exiled to Venezuela, a member of the third Revolutionary Junta, Provisional President in 1980 and finally elected President from 1984 to 1989. He died in 1989 after a long illness.

429/ The accusations were made in paid advertisements on television and in the press and in speeches broadcast on radio and television.

430/ Aronette Zamora is the current leader of the Unión Democrática Nacionalista (UDN) Party.

431/ Rubén Zamora was also a Christian Democratic leader at the time. He then left the party and was one of the founders of the Movimiento Popular Social Cristiano (MPSC).

432/ The line was dead for approximately 15 minutes.

433/ The Commission received testimony about the incident. This included testimony from people who cor-

roborated the statements of the surviving witnesses. The Commission went to the village of San Juan Opico and made various inquiries.
The military authorities that were asked by the Commission to provide information did not do so. The Artillery Brigade informed it that it did not have the relevant file. Not all the officers summonsed appeared before the Commission.

434/ Slang name given to villagers who collaborated with the security forces or the military by providing them with information about activities going on in the area or the personal activities of villagers. During these operations, they accompanied the soldiers and pointed people out to them.

435/ By law, it is the justice of the peace who must make the preliminary inquiries, that is, conduct a medical examination of the victims' bodies, assisted by a forensic expert, order the bodies handed over to the families for burial and take the first statements from witnesses.

436/ The Commission received public information from governmental and non-governmental sources and from individuals.

437/ An attempt was made on 23 September, when Viera and Francisco Menjívar, an official of the Ministry of Agriculture, were gunned down in front of the UCS offices in Nueva San Salvador. Viera was wounded and his companion killed.

438/ A review of existing testimony and other evidence, including the confessions of the two gunmen, statements by witnesses and by other members of the Intelligence Section of the National Guard and information received from governmental and non-governmental authorities, provides sufficient evidence that the events occurred as described below.

439/ Statement by José Dimas Valle Acevedo, 23 August 1982, f. 793. Also 23 September 1982, f. 831.

440/ He was nicknamed "fosforito".

441/ Statement by Valle Acevedo, f. 793.

442/ Statement by José Luis Sánchez, 18 August 1982, f. 755. See also statement by Amílcar Ruiz Linares, 19 August 1982, f. 757. A statement by Roque González, 19 August 1982, f. 758, indicates that López Sibrián usually carried an Ingram or a sub-machine-gun.

443/ Statement by Captain Eduardo Avila, 21 September 1982, f. 806. Statement by James Kevin Murphy, 30 October 1986. Statement by Gordon Fitch Ellison, 30 October 1986. A hotel employee also remembers having heard these words, although he did not make a statement to the judicial authorities.
See also statement by Teresa de Jesús Torres, 9 June 1981, f. 481. She noted that Christ's group made derogatory comments about Viera's group.

444/ Statement by Avila, f. 806.

445/ Statements by James Kevin Murphy and Gordon Fitch Ellison, 30 and 31 October 1986, regarding what Avila told both of them when he was given the lie detector test on 21 September 1982 at the General Staff. See also the statement by Torres, 24 June 1981, f. 480.

446/ Statement by Torres, f. 481.

447/ Statement by Valle Acevedo, f. 793.

448/ Ibid.

449/ Statement by Gómez González, 23 August 1982, f. 760. Statement by Uribe López, 27 August 1982, f. 767.

450/ Statement by Gómez González, f. 760. See also statement by Uribe López, 29 September 1982, f. 887.

451/ Statement by Gómez González, f. 760. He said he did not believe that López Sibrián had actually consulted Morán since López Sibrián had returned so quickly. Uribe López said that López Sibrián had been away for only three minutes. Statement by Uribe López, f. 887.

452/ Statement by Gómez González, f. 760.

453/ Statement by Gómez González, f. 760. Statement by Valle Acevedo, f. 794.

454/ Statement by Gómez González, f. 760. Statement by Valle Acevedo, f. 794. Other statements indicate that Avila handed over a 9-millimetre weapon. See, for example, statement by José Dagoberto Sambrano to the Commission for the Investigation of Criminal Acts on 29 October 1986.

455/ Statement by Gómez González, f. 760. Statement by Valle Acevedo, f. 794. Both González and Valle Acevedo identified photographs of Hans Christ as the person who had taken them to where the victims were.

456/ Statement by Gómez González, f. 760. Statement by Valle Acevedo, f. 794. Statement by Torres, f. 482.

457/ Marroquín Lara, the waiter who actually saw the two men shooting, told a witness that immediately after the murder, one of the gunmen stood over Viera's head and fired several bullets directly into it. Statement by Carlos Alfredo Portillo Morales, 11 June 1982, f. 717.

458/ The gunmen thought the house was Avila's, but Avila said that it was his brother's. See statement by Avila, f. 86.

459/ Statement by Valle Acevedo, f. 794. Statement by Gómez González, f. 760.

460/ Ibid.
Statement by Sánchez on f. 755. Statement by Salvador

461/ Raymundo, 19 August 1982, f. 789. See also the interview with Valle Acevedo in the Commission for the Investigation of Criminal Acts, 24 January 1986, and the interview with Sánchez by that Commission on 27 January 1986. The day after the murders, Gómez González told him that he had killed Viera, but Sánchez could not recall any more details of the conversation because he took it as a routine matter typical of the missions entrusted to them.

462/ Avila was summonsed before the Commission on the Truth but did not appear.

463/ Morán was summonsed before the Commission on the Truth but did not appear.

464/ This instruction was given in the course of apparently aggressive and harsh interrogations involving threats, deprivation of food and use of drugs to which both Valle Acevedo and Gómez González alleged they were subjected.
See interview with Valle Acevedo and Gómez González in the Commission for the Investigation of Criminal Acts, 24 January 1986, para. 3.

465/ On 17 September 1982, Morán was questioned by the Medrano commission. On that occasion, he said that he had never seen López Sibrián about the matter and that there had been no discussion about the perpetrators. He then said that although he "definitely" knew Gómez González, he could not remember whether Gómez González had been his bodyguard on the night of the murders.
Statement by Denis Morán, f. 790. There is no question that Gómez González was Morán's bodyguard on the night of the murders.

466/ His ginger hair was dyed black, his moustache was shaved off, he wore make-up, he was in uniform and he had a hat like the others.

467/ López Sibrián remained in the armed forces until President Duarte, under pressure from the United States Government, discharged him on 30 November 1984. He was then arrested for running a kidnapping ring and is still in prison. López Sibrián has consistently maintained his innocence, even to the Commission on the Truth.

468/ The Commission could not locate Mr. Christ to request him to appear before it.

469/ The Commission received information from various sources concerning the execution of mayors by FMLN. In the two cases which are described in detail, the Commission received from witnesses direct testimony which it proceeded to substantiate. With regard to the other cases, it requested information from FMLN; in its reply, the latter conceded that the execution of mayors was a policy approved by FMLN, and it supplied the names of some of the mayors who had been executed.

470/ FMLN, *La legitimidad de nuestros métodos de lucha*, El Salvador, Central America, 30 October 1988, p. 15.

471/ The Commission reviewed the trial records, interviewed the accused and requested information from both FMLN and the Government.

472/ In order to prove to the Commission that there was a directive from the General Command that advisers and military personnel should be considered legitimate targets, FMLN supplied the following information: (a) a list of names of United States advisers and military personnel killed in El Salvador between February 1983 and March 1987; (b) copies of reports in the newspaper *Venceremos* (official FMLN newspaper) concerning United States intervention in the armed conflict and the death or execution of some of those advisers; and (c) a copy of a press release containing a statement by United States Senator Edward M. Kennedy. According to the press release, the Senator was concerned at the number of United States advisers and military personnel assigned to the country. The statement was dated 1990.

473/ According to the statements made by Juan Miguel García Meléndez and Abraham Dimas Aguilar in trial No. 42/86 before the First Military Court, they had only very general prior knowledge of the attack before it was carried out.

474/ According to information from the testimony on

ff. 365 and 531 of trial dossier No. 42/86 of the First Military Court.

475/ According to cross-checking of the testimony on ff. 343, 365, 449, 485 and 531 of the trial dossier No. 42/86 of the First Military Court.

476/ According to cross-checking of the statements on f. 8 from trial dossier No. 67/A-89 of the Fifth Criminal Court.

477/ During trial No. 42/86 in the First Military Court, witnesses made the following statements: the shots were coming from all sides (f. 46); the first shots were fired by a United States marine sitting in the Flashback restaurant and he was the one who shot the guerrilla (f. 365); one American was carrying a firearm at the time (ff. 155 and 449); one marine had a firearm in his hands at the time (f. 453); the shot which wounded the guerrilla was fired by one of the marines (f. 512); one individual fled through the rear of Chili's restaurant (f. 531).

478/ In addition to testimony asserting that there was cross-fire, we find, attached to ff. 48, 305 and 308, reports concerning 34 spent cartridges found inside the Mediterranée and Chili's and the results of examinations of vehicles which were at the scene at the time of the attack. The latter established that two vehicles, one of them the attackers' vehicle, had bullet holes in their bodywork.

479/ Ff. 2 to 23 of trial dossier No. 42/86 of the First Military Court.

480/ According to the police report on f. 139 and witnesses' statements in ff. 453 and 531 of trial dossier No. 42/86 of the First Military Court.

481/ Police report on f. 139 of trial dossier No. 42/86 of the First Military Court.

482/ F. 285 of trial dossier No. 42/86 of the First Military Court.

483/ *La Prensa Gráfica*, 22 June 1985; f. 357 of trial dossier No. 42/86 of the First Military Court.

FMLN leaders maintained that the categorization of the executed United States marines as a military target had been the responsibility of members of the commando who planned the action. The latter, they said, had sufficient evidence to demonstrate that the four United States marines were in El Salvador to carry out military intelligence work. The information was obtained by means of:

1. Full-time personal monitoring of the activities of each marine;

2. Radio intercepts of the armed forces communication system; they said that the names of the executed persons came up constantly in these communications. The Commission asked for written evidence to back up the statements, but was informed that they were not in a position to provide such material since, owing to the nature of the action and the fact that it had taken place during a conflict, it was extremely difficult to have documentation regarding that type of decision.

FMLN also informed the Commission that, in the subsequent evaluation of the operation, it had been determined that the commando had erred in the "choice of place" because the possibility that civilians might be endangered had not been taken into consideration. For that reason, orders had been issued to suspend attacks on that type of objective in similar places.

484/ Ismael Dimas was interviewed by Radio Venceremos of FMLN the week after the attack. His pseudonym was "Ulises". In the interview, he acknowledged having been the military chief who directed the operation and one of those who fired on the marines. This is corroborated by the information provided by the Government of El Salvador, FMLN and the witnesses who were interviewed. According to the information obtained as a result of the Commission's investigation, Ismael Dimas died later in combat.

485/ In this extrajudicial confession, the defendants also confessed to having participated in a series of incidents that they said took place between 1979 and 1985, but did not give any places or specific dates (ff. 108, 122 and 130 of trial dossier No. 42/86 of the First Military Court).

486/ For example, at the trial, no judicial statement was taken from the defendants. Instead, there is a document "confirming" the statements they had made to the National Guard. The document does not specify what statements the defendants had made and had therefore confirmed.

487/ The 1987 Amnesty Act was enacted in October 1987 by Legislative Decree No. 805.

488/ F. 742 of trial dossier No. 42/86 of the First Military Court.

489/ F. 752 of trial dossier No. 42/86 of the First Military Court. His appeal was rejected on the grounds that he was not a party to the criminal proceedings.

490/ F. 770 of trial dossier No. 42/86 of the First Military Court. Several newspapers published the reactions of United States officials who warned that it jeopardized $18.5 million in aid to El Salvador which was in the process of being approved by Congress.

491/ F. 770 of trial dossier No. 86 of the First Military Court.

Under Salvadorian law, in certain situations the General Command of the Armed Forces acts as a special court. When the decision regarding amnesty was brought to that court, it determined that the Convention to Prevent and Punish Acts of Terrorism Taking the Form of Crimes against Persons and Related Extortion that are of International Significance and the Convention on the Prevention and Punishment of Crimes against Internationally Protected Persons, including Diplomatic Agents, were applicable to the case.

492/ F. 937 of trial dossier No. 42/86 of the First Military Court.

493/ There is insufficient evidence for the Commission to be able to say whether or not he participated in the operation. As in the case of the other defendants, he too, at his trial, was denied the benefit of the National Reconciliation Act.

494/ Andrade was arrested in 1989. FMLN leaders say that he was responsible, *inter alia*, for having given Government forces information about the biggest arms shipment ever seized from FMLN during the conflict. FMLN considers Andrade a traitor for having revealed this information to the Government of El Salvador and the United States Government, which he did while under arrest.

495/ To investigate this incident, the Commission interviewed some 70 individuals, many of them confidentially. The Commission has checked the information provided by witnesses against that obtained in other interviews and against court, police, newspaper, governmental, non-governmental and private sources.

496/ In his first two statements, Miranda said that his pseudonym was "José". On 3 February 1988, Miranda identified Romualdo Alberto Zelaya, who died on 27 January 1988 in a clash with National Police, as "José". F. 750.

497/ The number of men involved has been confirmed by what several witnesses saw. Vicente Vazquez and José Mejía saw the driver of the pick-up truck first, and a few minutes later saw two people boarding the same vehicle. Manuel de Jesús Serrano observed two individuals sitting on the sidewalk of the parking lot minutes before the murder. Aminta Pérez saw two individuals by a lamp post next to the parking lot minutes before the murder. F. 187.

498/ F. 94N, letter from Noé Antonio González, ballistics expert, to the chief of the CIHD Unit, 1 November 1987.

499/ F. 96N, letter from Noé Antonio González, ballistics expert, to the chief of the CIHD Unit, 1 November 1987.

500/ The National Police informed the Commission that ballistics experts do not have information on armed forces ammunition. See letter from the Director-General, Francisco Salinas, 23 February 1993.

501/ Anaya was the fourth member of CDHES-NG to be murdered; three of them had disappeared. See Lawyers Committee for Human Rights, *Underwriting Injustice: AID and El Salvador's Judicial Reform Program*, April 1989, p. 135.

502/ One of the five factions in the Frente Farabundo Martí para la Liberación Nacional (FMLN).

503/ See testimony of Herbert Anaya, 7 March 1986.

504/ See f. 508N, note by Corporal Adán de Jesús Morán Rivera, 26 May 1986. Complaint by Mirna Perla de Anaya to the Archdiocesan Legal Protection Office, 27 May 1986. He was one of a number of people belonging to popular organizations whom the Treasury Police arrested around that time.

505/ F. 527, statement by Herbert Anaya, 8 July 1986. Anaya says that he was subjected to physical and mental ill-treatment during his detention. See testimony of Herbert Anaya, 7 March 1986.

506/ See, for example, the paid announcement placed by Christian Legal Aid in *El Mundo* on 27 October 1987, "CGT también condena asesinato" (CGT also condemns murder), *El Mundo*, 27 October 1987. Paid announcement placed by the Human Rights Commission (governmental) in *La Prensa Gráfica*, 27 October 1987. Paid announcement placed by the Danish and Swedish sections of Amnesty International in *El Mundo*, November 1987. P. Glickman, "El Salvador: US Mildly Condemns Rights Figure's Assassination", 26 October 1987.

507/ *El Diario de Hoy*, "50 mil colones ofrece Duarte por Asesinos de Anaya" (Duarte offers 50,000 colones for Anaya's murderers), 26 October 1987.

508/ Members of ERP confirmed that he was a member of that organization.

509/ Interview with Miranda. F. 677, statement by Officer Miguel Antonio Pineda Varela of the Technical Operations Department of the National Police, 18 January 1988.

510/ According to newspaper reports, the International Committee of the Red Cross (ICRC) did not visit him until 4 January, after the initial period of 72 hours in detention was over. See D. Farah, "Salvadoran Expands on Role in Killing; Prisoner Rebuts Family, Reaffirms Rebels Ordered Rights Death", *The Washington Post*, 8 January 1988, see also f. 775, Miranda's retraction before the court.

511/ F. 708. He does not remember when and said it had no effect. F. 775, Miranda's retraction. He told the Commission that once he had been given one or two tablets which he could not identify.

512/ See "Samayoa Denies Miranda Bribed", translation and transcript of a report by Guevara, M. A., *Canal 12 Televisión*, 8 January 1988, in *Foreign Broadcast Information Service* (FBIS), 12 January 1988, p. 12.

513/ See D. Farah, "Salvadoran Expands on Role in Killing", *The Washington Post*, 8 January 1988. J. LeMoyne, "Salvadoran in Jail Talk, Tells of Assassination", *The New York Times*, 8 January 1988. M. Miller, "Jailed Salvadoran Student Tells Disputed Version of Killing of a Rights Activist", *The Los Angeles Times*, 9 January 1988.

514/ Interview with Miranda. See also f. 708. According to Miranda, those same people took the comforts away when he retracted his statement. The former Minister of Justice has denied that members of the National Police were able to visit him, stating that the only people who were able to visit him were those whom Miranda agreed to see.

515/ The then Minister of Justice, Julio Samayoa, attributed the delay to the fact that court personnel were on holiday and therefore the defendant could not be handed over. See: "Duarte Comments on Case", translation and transcript of a report by M. A. Guevara, *Canal 12 Televisión*, 6 January 1988, in FBIS, 12 January 1988, p. 11; recording of the press conference. President Duarte stated that the delay was permissible because Miranda had been arrested for one offence and his participation in the murder had emerged later. See *El Diario de Hoy*, "Dice Reo Confeso: el ERP 'Purgó' a Anaya Sanabria Para Culpar F.A." ("Prisoner confesses: ERP 'purged' Anaya Sanabria in order to put the blame on the armed forces"), 6 January 1988. Recording of the press conference.

516/ Judge Luis Edgar Morales Joya fled El Salvador after an attempt on his life on 9 August 1991.

517/ See f. 775.

518/ F. 937N. The judge's decision reads as follows: "There is no doubt that ... the confessions of the accused ... do not meet the intrinsic requirements of any confession ...". He found that Miranda's statement was "the only incriminating evidence against him" and was thus not sufficient to move on to the adversary stage.

519/ F. 943-53. It argued that the confession "is sufficient evidence because it is consistent with the facts and with the accounts given by [three] witnesses" and because "it has not been established in the trial that the defendant confessed because he had been tortured, and the [first] two confessions are consistent with one another. See f. 951.

520/ In July 1991, the First Criminal Chamber of the Supreme Court of Justice reported a decision to change the venue of the trial to the Fifth Criminal Court of San Salvador, f. 1046. It had already been transferred to the Mejicanos Criminal Court.

521/ F. 1133. Civil penalties—the payment of 20,000 colones in compensation to Mirna Perla, Anaya's widow, and the corresponding loss of a number of political and civil rights—were also imposed. With respect to Anaya's murder, the judge decided to leave the final decision, on whether or not to apply the Amnesty Act, to the Commission on the Truth.

522/ The Commission dismisses, for lack of evidence, the theory that the murder was an ordinary crime.

523/ It is necessary to take into account how much time had elapsed between the murder and the time the photos were shown, and the fact that the witness only caught a glimpse of the murderers.

524/ Moreover, according to a lie detector test carried out by CIHD on 1 January 1988, Miranda was not lying when he said that he had participated. F. 889.

525/ The Archdiocesan Legal Protection Office has claimed that the armed forces were responsible. Americas Watch expressed concern that the murder might point to a reactivation of the death squads. L. Gruson, "Killing in Salvador Imperils Peace Talks", *The New York Times*, 28 October 1987. "La viuda de Anaya culpa a la Policía de Hacienda" (Anaya's widow blames the Treasury Police). "Dirigentes del ERP también culpan a las fuerzas armadas salvadoreñas, o a escuadrones de la muerte" (ERP leaders also blame the Salvadorian armed forces or death squads for the murder).

526/ According to a colleague at CDHES-NG, Anaya reported that while being held by the Treasury Police he had received a death threat from a senior officer of that force. In Mariona, Anaya was warned by a prisoner that prison guards were saying that they would kill him once he got out. F. 694, statement by Reynaldo Blanco in the First Criminal Court, 6 February 1988.

Anaya's father was arrested by the National Guard in March 1987 and interrogated about his son's activities. Anaya denounced his father's detention publicly. F. 707, paid advertisement in *El Mundo*, 21 March 1987. After his release from Mariona, complained that he was being watched constantly by unknown persons, including some people using a vehicle with the registration number P-50-200. F. 702, paid advertisement by CDHES-NG on 3 June 1987. It never received an answer from the security forces to its request for information about the vehicle.

Radio Verdad, a clandestine right-wing station, denounced Anaya, apparently on 25 July 1987, as the "pernicious and corrupt head of the unofficial Human Rights Commission" and reported that "this Mr. Anaya, who does so much harm with so much disinformation about the country, will soon be exposed; Salvadorians must know who are the charlatans who head the groups which are seeking to destroy the Republic". F. 701, transcript of the broadcast.

On 3 August 1987, *El Diario de Hoy* reported that military intelligence had demonstrated the link between FMLN and humanitarian groups. According to the newspaper, a military source had said that "the people must know ... the real truth about the conflict in our country, but must not allow themselves to be misled by those false Salvadorians who are only doing grave harm to the population". F. 706.

527/ F. 694, statement by Reynaldo Blanco, 6 January 1988.

528/ A few months before the murder, CDHES-NG complained that some 10 heavily armed men had tried to force their way into its headquarters. F. 703, paid advertisement in *El Mundo*, 3 June 1987.

529/ Letter from Mirna Perla de Anaya to Mr. Edmundo Vargas Carreño, Executive Secretary of the Inter-American Commission on Human Rights, 15 April 1988. She also stated that the night before the murder, the house was watched by unknown persons in civilian clothing driving a blue pick-up truck and a silver-coloured Toyota limousine.

530/ In addition to examining the contents of the judicial dossier, as well as publications and reports on the case, the Commission interviewed many witnesses. It also obtained part of Mr. Guerrero's personal files on the assassination of the Jesuit priests.

531/ He was one of the founders of the Partido de Conciliación Nacional in 1962 and a co-author of the 1952 Constitution, President of the Legislative Assembly (1962-1965), Minister for Foreign Affairs (1969-1971), Chief of Staff for the President (1982), PCN Presidential candidate (1984) and President of the Supreme Court (1984-1989).

532/ *El Diario de Hoy*, "Asesinan a balazos al Dr. Francisco José Guerrero" (Dr. Francisco José Guerrero shot to death), 29 November 1989.

533/ Judicial statements by Víctor Manuel Rivera Monterrosa and Lilia del Milagro Avendaño de Guerrero.

534/ Statement by Víctor Manuel Rivera Monterrosa, 1 December 1989. Folio 173 of the dossier.

535/ Statement by witness Marcelino Antonio Hernández Ayala, 11 December 1989. Folio 228 of the dossier. Testimony of Manuel de Jesús Maldonado, on-the-spot police inspection, 28 November 1989, Folio 88 of the dossier. See also *La Prensa Gráfica*, "Asesinado ayer ex-presidente de la corte Dr. Francisco José Guerrero" (Dr. José Guerrero, former President of the Court, assassinated yesterday), 29 November 1989. *Diario Latino* (San Salvador), "Asesinan a 'Chachi' Guerrero" (Chachi Guerrero assassinated), 28 November 1989.

536/ Police report. Folio 79 of the dossier.

537/ Statement by Víctor Manuel Rivera Monterrosa, 1 December 1989. Folio 173 of the dossier.

538/ Report on the forensic medical examination, undated. Folio 84 of the dossier.

539/ Report of the Ballistic Technical Section of the National Police, 1 December 1989. Folio 168 of the dossier.

540/ Ibid., statement by Otto René Rodríguez. Folio 145 of the dossier.

541/ Testimony of Elías Cruz Perla, police report. Folio 88 of the dossier. Statement by Marcelino Antonio Hernández Ayala. Folio 228 of the dossier. A number of spent cartridges were found some 20 metres behind Mr. Guerrero's car. Sketch of the site, folio 43 of the dossier.

542/ Examination of the body of Angel Aníbal Alvarez Martínez. Folio 8 of the dossier.

543/ Examination, 4 April 1990. Folio 276 of the dossier.

544/ Police report. Folio 168 of the dossier. The judicial dossier contains no information on the bullets that hit Erazo Cruz.

545/ Testimony of Elías Cruz Perla to CIHD, 28 November 1989. Folio 88 of the dossier.

546/ The paraffin test is a technical chemical analysis used to determine whether a person has fired a weapon. The test is based on the presence of nitrate products deposited on the back of the hands when a firearm is fired.

547/ Statement by Erazo Cruz at the National Police medical clinic, 30 November 1989. Folio 153 of the dossier.

548/ Accused's statement by Erazo Cruz, 5 December 1989. Folio 193 of the dossier. Erazo Cruz recanted these statements before the court and also before the Commission on the Truth. Furthermore, "Efraín" had no known ties to the guerrillas (see below).

549/ Order for detention pending trial, 7 December 1989. Folio 219 of the dossier. The judge subsequently added the offences of causing grievous bodily harm, being a member of a subversive association and escape involving the use of violence (see below).

550/ Accused's statement by Erazo Cruz, 7 February 1992 (folio 405 of the dossier) confirmed by his testimony before the Commission, 4 September 1992.

551/ Penal Code, article 152.

552/ Penal Code, article 171.

553/ Penal Code, article 375.

554/ Penal Code, article 480.

555/ The charges of escape involving the use of violence and being a member of a subversive association remained pending in the Sixth Criminal Court. Then, at the end of July, the defence requested application of the National Reconciliation Act with a view to abatement of the criminal action at law relating to the subversive association charge. Article 1 of the Act states that amnesty shall be granted to all persons who participated in committing political crimes. Article 7 (c) of the Act states that in the case of accused persons whose cases are pending, the judge shall of his own motion decree a general dismissal of proceedings in favour of the defendants. The defence also requested the judge to order Erazo Cruz's release with regard to the charge of escape involving the use of violence. According to article 250, a person held pending trial shall be released when the penalty for the offence is a fine or a custodial penalty not exceeding a maximum of three years' imprisonment. The judge accepted the position of the defence and ordered a general dismissal of proceedings.

556/ Statement by Erazo Cruz to CIHD, 4 September 1989.

557/ *El Mundo*, "Hija de 'Chachi' Guerrero relaciona muerte de su padre con caso jesuitas" (daughter of Chachi Guerrero links her father's death with the Jesuit case), 30 January 1992.

558/ Description of the incident by José Napoleón Duarte: *Duarte: Mi Historia*, pp. 185-186. This version does not contradict the accounts of the incident subsequently published by FMLN.

559/ Originally the FMLN list contained the names of 34 people, nine of whom had disappeared after they were captured by Government forces. Likewise, in the active and secret negotiations, FMLN insisted on linking the release of Inés Duarte to that of 25 mayors and 96 war-wounded guerrillas (the latter finally totalled 101). It is important to mention the significant mediating role played by the Salvadorian church in the persons of Monsignor Rivera y Damas and Father Ignacio Ellacuría. The documents of FMLN and the Government of El Salvador likewise reveal clearly the mediating role played by Governments such as those of Colombia, Panama, Mexico and France, and by individuals such as Chancellor Willy Brandt and Hans Wischnewski of the Socialist International.

560/ Translated from English. British Broadcasting Corporation, "Release of Duarte's Daughter and Other Hostages in El Salvador". Source: Radio Venceremos 0045 GMT, 25 October 1985.
Another piece of information indicating FMLN involvement is to be found in the account of a guerrilla who says: "16 September ... Schafik Handal also got up early. He had spent a few days with us and was now hurrying to participate in the negotiations concerning Duarte's daughter". *Las Mil y Una Historias de Radio Venceremos*, José Ignacio López Vigil, UCA Editores, p. 401.

561/ The Supreme Court referred to the Commission 30 cases involving the death of judges, but according to the information received, two of the judges had died of natural causes.

Document 68

Letter dated 30 March 1993 from President Cristiani to the Secretary-General concerning the report of the Commission on the Truth

Not issued as a United Nations document; original in Spanish

With reference to the report of the Commission on the Truth, delivered and made public on 15 March 1993, we have analysed the various recommendations formulated therein in the light of the constitutional framework, our legal order and our institutional system, and in the context of the series of Peace Agreements reached through direct negotiations, of a section of which the Commission on the Truth is the executing agency.

The Geneva Agreement constituted the matrix within which the negotiating process was to develop to put a definitive end to the armed conflict in the country and it, in turn, established the other objectives of the peace process, which were to consolidate democracy, guarantee unlimited respect for human rights and REUNIFY SALVADORIAN SOCIETY.

Within this framework and with these aims, on 27 April 1991 the parties reached the Mexico Agreement, which comprised constitutional reforms and the establishment of the Commission on the Truth.

Constitutional reform thus constituted the basic agreement of the peace negotiations, the preamble to which clearly indicates that all the political agreements adopted would be incorporated in, and would be in harmony with, such constitutional reform.

The Commission on the Truth was established as a mechanism in the search for the historical truth in the armed conflict and, as stated in the introductory portion of the Agreement which established it, its fundamental purpose was "to contribute to the reconciliation of Salvadorian society". On this basis, the Commission was given a mandate to investigate serious acts of violence committed since 1980 and to recommend measures which could be inferred from the results of the investigation, and it was specified that "the Commission shall not function in the manner of a judicial body". This means that it was not given the power to judge and impose sanctions and it was inhibited from classifying criminal acts, evaluating evidence or elements of proof and establishing degrees of participation in such acts, since these attributes are exclusive to courts of justice. In the case of the agreement on the Commission on the Truth, this situation was clearly acknowledged in the reference in two sections of that agreement to the recognition and application of the ordinary system of justice in our country. These sections are included under the heading "FUNCTIONS", paragraph 6, and the heading "REPORT", paragraph 14.

The Government of the Republic has unequivocally demonstrated its political will to further the process of changes flowing from the Peace Agreements, assuming the largest share of the responsibility under those Agreements and making possible their complex and successful implementation, a fact which has been attested to most reliably and in the most laudatory terms. If situations were to arise, outside the framework of direct negotiations, which could be detrimental to the development of the process or the objectives set therein, we would be compelled to act to preserve their stability and thereby to consolidate democracy, respect for human rights and the aspiration of Salvadorian society for reconciliation.

We made a commitment to comply with the recommendations of the Commission on the Truth, well aware of what this responsibility meant. Today we reaffirm this commitment, as we accepted it, within a specific framework and context and for a specific purpose, and in accordance with the terms of the mandate which we gave to the Commission.

Accordingly, we will, within the sphere of our competence, comply strictly with the recommendations of the Commission on the Truth in so far as they are in accordance with the Constitution of the Republic, are in harmony with the Agreements resulting from the direct negotiations, contribute to the reconciliation of Salvadorian society and do not involve the exercise of any jurisdiction which infringes on our system and established institutional order.

Furthermore, our Government will as soon as possible state its overall position on the report of the Commission on the Truth as a whole, which we will in due course transmit to you for your information.

Accept, Sir, the assurances of the our highest consideration.

(Signed) A. CRISTIANI

Document 69

Letter dated 2 April 1993 from the Secretary-General to the President of the Security Council concerning the purification of the armed forces

S/25516, 2 April 1993

I have the honour to refer to my letter of 7 January 1993 (S/25078) in which I reported to the members of the Security Council on the latest developments relating to the implementation of the provisions of the Peace Accords for El Salvador concerning the purification of the Armed Forces (S/23501, Annex Chapter I, Section III).

In that letter I stated that I had asked President Cristiani to take early action to regularize the position of 15 officers in respect of whom the Ad Hoc Commission's recommendations had not yet been implemented. I have since raised this matter on a number of occasions with President Cristiani.

On 31 March 1993 I received a visit from Dr. Oscar Santamaria, Minister of the Presidency of El Salvador, who had been sent by President Cristiani to New York to communicate to me the President's plan for regularizing the position of the 15 officers concerned. The following day my comments were communicated to President Cristiani who thereupon revised the plan. It now provides that all the officers concerned will, by 30 June 1993 at the latest, have been placed on leave with pay pending completion of the procedures for their retirement which will take place not later than 31 December 1993. While on leave with pay they will not perform any official functions.

I have again concluded that this arrangement would, when implemented, bring the Government into broad compliance with the Ad Hoc Commission's recommendations, though I regret that this will not occur until a date several months later than that foreseen in the Agreements. However, I look forward to being able to confirm to the Security Council, shortly after 30 June 1993, that all the recommendations have finally been put into effect.

I should be grateful if you would bring this letter to the attention of the members of the Security Council.

(Signed) Boutros BOUTROS-GHALI

Document 70

Report of the ONUSAL Human Rights Division for the period from 1 July 1992 to 31 January 1993 (extract)

A/47/912-S/25521, 5 April 1993

I. Introduction

1. This report has been prepared in accordance with the decision concerning the verification of the human rights situation in El Salvador, contained in the report of the Secretary-General dated 26 May 1992 (S/23999 and Corr.1 and Add.1), that human rights would be the subject of a separate series of reports. The period covered by this report runs from 1 July 1992 to 31 January 1993. Mr. Philippe Texier ceased to be Director of the Division in July 1992. Some weeks later, the Secretary-General appointed as his replacement Mr. Diego García-Sayán, who took up his duties in mid-October 1992.

2. During the period under consideration, the peace process in El Salvador moved ahead, creating enhanced conditions for the enjoyment of human rights, especially after 15 December 1992 when the period of the cessation of the armed conflict ended and the conflict itself came to an end both formally and physically. This will have a definitely favourable impact on enhancing the protection of human rights in the country. However, the effective enjoyment of those rights will be assured only when the structural changes provided for in the peace agreements with a view to consolidating the rule of law, democratic life and the reconciliation of Salvadorian society are fully implemented.

3. In this report, the Director of the Human Rights Division submits to the Secretary-General and, through him, to the Security Council and the General Assembly an overall assessment of the situation up to January 1993; an evaluation of active verification as a means of promoting and protecting human rights; an analysis of active verification of the human rights situation; and, lastly, the results of verification of the human rights components of

other commitments made in the peace agreements (functioning of the judiciary and administration of justice, reform of the armed forces and the police, and action to provide information and education on human rights).

4. The report ends with a series of conclusions and recommendations, especially on matters requiring immediate action by the Government or legislative action to solve outstanding problems so that the peace process can be consolidated.

5. Starting in February 1993 and with a view to reporting more regularly to the Secretary-General and the General Assembly on the implementation of the San José Agreement (A/44/971-S/21541, annex) and of the human rights components of the other peace agreements, the Human Rights Division will submit quarterly reports.

6. The magnitude of this report, which covers an eight-month period, can be explained by two factors: first, the need to include in it both the results of the verification carried out since the appointment of the new Director of the Human Rights Division (October 1992) and those for the period immediately prior to his appointment, which were not covered by the fifth report (June to September 1992); secondly, because a number of adjustments in verification procedures, including revised methodologies, were introduced in November 1992 to enhance the efficiency of the Division's work. As a result, while the report covers a considerable period of time, this has allowed actual trends in the situation to be analysed in greater depth.

7. Lastly, it should be mentioned that the basic frame of reference for drafting the report was the idea that active verification of human rights in El Salvador, as part of an unprecedented, integrated peace-keeping operation, is intended not only to provide information on the existing human rights situation and to verify implementation of the agreements in this area, but also to contribute to efforts by the parties, the State and society to adopt consensus approaches and methods which will make it possible to reverse and overcome those situations in which the effective enjoyment of human rights is still not assured, even though the country has come a long way from the situation that existed prior to the conclusion of the peace agreements.

II. Overall assessment of the situation

8. Since the signing of the peace agreements, the question of human rights in El Salvador has been viewed in the context of a new political situation characterized, by contrast with the pre-existing situation, by the shared determination of all domestic forces to make the institutional changes needed to carry out a process establishing the full applicability of the rule of law, put an end to the armed conflict and reconcile Salvadorian society.

9. Accordingly, the analysis and evaluation of the human rights situation in the country following the signing of the peace agreements must fall within this frame of reference, in other words, it must be seen as an integral part of a process in which the parties to the conflict and the other political forces in the country undertook to ensure the enjoyment of human rights and fundamental freedoms as an essential component of peace and democracy.

10. On 15 December 1992, peace became a reality in El Salvador. The cease-fire period established in the agreements came to an end, and with it the armed conflict signalling the attainment of one of the goals of the Geneva Agreement of 4 April 1990 (A/46/551-S/23128, annex), that of ending an armed conflict that for over a decade had kept the population under fire from a civil war which claimed tens of thousands of lives.

11. With peace restored, this leaves the commitments aimed at achieving the other three goals agreed on by the Government of El Salvador and the Frente Farabundo Martí para la Liberación Nacional for the peace process (FMLN): promoting the democratization of the country, guaranteeing unrestricted respect for human rights and reunifying Salvadorian society.

12. Ending the conflict was not a process limited to halting the fighting, it was a comprehensive process for establishing a democratic order based on a series of substantive changes in national institutions, including the armed forces. These changes have been taking place as part of the implementation of the peace agreements. A variety of difficulties have arisen, some of them quite substantial, and these continue to affect the process, but experience has shown that the political will of the parties and the pressure of the legitimacy gained by the peace process generally prevail over problems which were, moreover, to be expected in a United Nations-verified peace-keeping operation whose magnitude and procedures are without historical precedent.

13. As the Secretary-General, Mr. Boutros Boutros-Ghali, has said, for the United Nations, "involvement in El Salvador has been a pioneering experience. It is the first in a new generation of United Nations operations whose purpose is post-conflict peace-building." [1]

14. In the new international post-cold-war situation, the integrated peace-keeping operation in El Salvador has indeed been a pioneering experience, in that it goes beyond the already important task of ending conflict and making peace. Precisely what distinguishes peacemaking and peace-keeping in El Salvador is the fact that the peace agreements provide for an interrelated series of tasks to be carried out by internal actors, and verified by

1/ S/25006, annex I, p. 6, second paragraph.

the United Nations, with a view to generating within the State and society the necessary institutional and political conditions for the effective functioning of democracy in accordance with the rule of law while, at the same time, promoting changes in the relationship between the State and society with the ultimate goal of achieving national reconciliation and reunification.

15. This integrated approach to the peace process explains the diversity of the specific agreements reached by the parties, agreements which they are implementing, in a major effort of national consultation with all political forces, through the National Commission for the Consolidation of Peace (COPAZ).

16. It is not in the nature of this report or within the mandate of the Director of the Human Rights Division to make specific assessments of compliance with the political and military agreements under the peace process. It is, however, essential to take those agreements as the appropriate, indispensable frame of reference for analysing trends in the human rights situation in the country, since the enjoyment of those rights depends in large measure on the proper functioning of the rule of law and, more specifically, on effective compliance with the peace agreements in the institutional, political and socio-economic spheres.

17. From this standpoint, we can see that both parties' strict observance of the cease-fire throughout its duration and their fulfilment of the outstanding obligations that were prerequisites for completing the cease-fire period had a decisive impact on trends in the human rights situation during the period covered by this report. The end of the armed conflict and the attainment of peace, in the context of the implementation of the agreements, are laying firm foundations in El Salvador for the consolidation of democratic life and the effective functioning of the rule of law. This in turn is creating for human rights a socio-political environment that is without precedent in the country's history.

18. After several decades of political instability and the alternation of periods of democracy with periods of authoritarian rule, the socio-political conditions now exist for the historical consolidation of democratic institutions. The amended Constitution responds to the modern conception of a State governed by the rule of law and provides basic guarantees for the constitutional and judicial protection of human rights in El Salvador. A consensus also exists among political forces in supporting democratic institutions, giving them greater legitimacy and stability.

19. At the same time, advances have been made in the secondary legislation envisaged by the peace agreements, especially as regards the Office of the National Counsel for the Defence of Human Rights, the restruc-

turing of the armed forces, the creation of the National Civil Police (PNC), land transfers 2/ and the administration of justice. These legislative advances have kept pace with the implementation of the agreements. However, laws on their own do not solve problems and a complicated working agenda thus remains pending, especially as regards the land problem, the start-up of the National Civil Police and the effective, independent functioning of the judiciary.

20. The enjoyment of human rights, especially in societies of the kind found in a large number of developing countries, does not depend only on their substantive protection under the law but also on the functioning of democratic institutions. More than in any other sphere, in the human rights sphere it is necessary to have applicable norms to guarantee those rights and efficient, democratic institutional mechanisms. This explains the practical interrelationship that exists between democracy and the enjoyment of human rights. The judicial system has a decisive role to play here: only a strong administration of justice that is both effective and politically independent can ensure the judicial protection of human rights. Without this, democracy cannot be complete.

21. Another substantive factor in the historical experience of the relationship between democracy and human rights is the exercise of power in both formal and practical terms. Democracy cannot be completed unless lawfully constituted civilian authority exercises its constitutional powers fully and, conversely, unless the armed forces are fully subordinated to civilian authority, in conformity with the Constitution and with the very structure of a State governed by the rule of law.

22. One additional element in the relationship between democracy and human rights is the role played by mechanisms for overseeing security and public order. Far from undermining public order, the enjoyment of human rights does the opposite: it enables the State and society to protect the safety of citizens and the institutional and legal order using the means of coercion provided by law. Thus, the protection of human rights does not only mean that the State fulfils its duty to guarantee those rights but also that citizens, their organizations and institutions duly fulfil a number of duties.

23. As a result, in order to ensure the full exercise of human rights, democratic life must be accompanied by the strengthening of civilian society so that individuals, institutions and non-governmental organizations are able to perform fully their duty of protecting human rights,

2/ Notwithstanding the adoption of the law on measures and guarantees for the implementation of the land-transfer and farmland-tenure security programme and the interim law giving former combatants beneficiary status, it is in fact the agreements pertaining to land that are proving most difficult to implement.

which means ensuring that they are not subject to any kind of intimidation, coercion or reprisals because of their individual or collective action.

24. In the case of El Salvador, the peace agreements, their progressive implementation, the end of the armed conflict and the establishment of peace as of 15 December 1992 have created the necessary legal, institutional, political and social conditions for democratic life to become a reality in which human rights can be exercised fully. However, the practical attainment of democracy is a more complex and contradictory process: it does not follow automatically from peace, but is a gradual process in which a variety of interests and wishes must be accommodated. The transition from an authoritarian society to a democracy, from war to peace, from a system in which human rights are violated to one in which they are protected and guaranteed is complex, difficult and fraught with contradictions.

25. The country is now embarking on this process. The basic trends are promising, but Salvadorians still have a long way to go before their chosen model of a democratic, reconciled society in which human rights are respected becomes a reality.

26. Problems exist, and for the foreseeable future complex situations will continue to arise whose solution will require a renewed expression of political will on the part of all sectors and forces committed to the peace agreements.

27. It is essential to maintain the credibility and strength of the peace process. At the time of final drafting of this report (late February 1993), questions remained about the incomplete implementation of the recommendations of the Ad Hoc Commission on the purification of the armed forces, a situation which aroused the concern not only of the Secretary-General but also of the Security Council. As the Secretary-General has said, full implementation of the recommendations emanating from the Ad Hoc Commission's report is not just a substantive issue in the process of restructuring the armed forces, it has a direct bearing on the armed forces' obedience and constitutional subordination to civilian authority and is therefore a test of the development and consolidation of the rule of law in El Salvador.

28. The publication of the report of the Commission on the Truth will be equally significant, since the effective enjoyment of human rights in El Salvador's emerging democracy presupposes a spirit of national reunification and reconciliation. As the Secretary-General has said, the watershed in the process of reuniting Salvadorian society will come when the report of the Commission on the Truth becomes available, since "Salvadorians will only put the past behind them once the truth about the past is brought to light". 3/ Once the

Commission's report is published, the Human Rights Division will give top priority to verifying effective implementation of its recommendations.

29. Moreover, the transition from war to peace brings with it a number of phenomena specific to situations of peace in which the end of armed conflict coincides with a reordering of legal, political and institutional structures. All these processes always carry within themselves the seeds of violence.

30. Personnel trained to see the use of force against internal enemies as legitimate, accustomed to handling military weapons and lacking the skills and opportunities for productive reintegration into civilian life may easily resort to different forms of anti-social violence. At the same time, lingering vestiges of politically motivated violence may find in such situations a breeding ground for the revival of serious human rights violations.

31. In the specific case of El Salvador, this phenomenon has coincided with difficulties and indecisiveness in moving ahead, with the urgency and efficiency that circumstances demanded, with the formation of the PNC and the start-up of its activities. The situation has been aggravated by the fact that no public security plan was designed and therefore implemented for the transitional period which, as soon as the cessation of the armed conflict began, should have been accompanied by, *inter alia*, effective measures for the voluntary surrender or requisition of any military weapons in the possession of civilians, including private security personnel, former members of the armed forces and individuals who belonged to FMLN, as well as emergency measures for combating ordinary crime. At the time of final drafting of this report, the Government announced a national anti-crime emergency plan, the content and application of which will be considered in the next report of the Director of the Human Rights Division.

32. The lack of public safety as a result of ordinary crime has reached disturbing levels which, although not dramatic, are causing a pervasive feeling of insecurity among the population. Among other positive consequences, peace should have brought greater public safety. This was something the population could legitimately expect. However, the widespread perception of insecurity and the magnitude of the crime wave may inhibit the feeling of safety that peace was expected to bring, thereby hindering the process—necessary to the consolidation of democracy—of overcoming the culture of fear and intimidation.

33. The Director of the ONUSAL Human Rights Division is seriously concerned at this situation, although the seeds of violence are always present in such transition processes. History has shown that situations of more or

3/ S/25006, annex I, p. 6, first paragraph.

less generalized criminal violence can, if not properly tackled, trigger a social context and subjective attitudes conducive to a resurgence of serious violations of human rights and fundamental freedoms.

34. What is more, trends such as those described above may give rise to currents of opinion which are opposed to key aspects of the model of democratic organization which Salvadorians chose through the peace agreements. This is foreseeable at least as regards the promotion of unconstitutional methods of combating crime or methods which depart significantly from the role which the armed forces should play in a State governed by the rule of law.

35. For these reasons, the report includes a section on violence and human rights which analyses this situation in greater detail while emphasizing that the violence in the country, although disturbing, is such that it can be controlled.

36. Despite this emerging situation, there is a definite trend towards an overall improvement in the human rights situation in the country, although some disturbing practices still persist. However, these positive trends in the situation of human rights in El Salvador must first grow and then be consolidated as part of the effective functioning of democracy if they are to be lasting and not just passing phenomena.

37. Above and beyond the specific evolution of the human rights situation, the enjoyment of human rights is always dependent on the legal, political and social environment which serves as their institutional context. As a result, even the progress we are now seeing is not necessarily irreversible, since it is linked to the consolidation of the rule of law, the dynamic of democratic life and, in particular, the process of demilitarization of the State and society.

38. That is why the human rights situation in El Salvador must be assessed in the broader context of violence and the functioning of the rule of law. Accordingly, the Human Rights Division has adopted provisions in its procedures and working methods in the belief that the effective enjoyment of human rights in El Salvador is still an objective goal which will be achieved only with the consolidation of the institutions of the rule of law as defined by the peace agreements and with the strengthening of democratic life as the ultimate guarantor of the process. This involves the convergence of two elements: on the one hand, fulfilment by the State of its duty to provide guarantees and, on the other, the effective exercise of rights and duties by all citizens of El Salvador.

III. Active verification as a means of promoting and protecting human rights

39. An appropriate methodology is fundamental for verifying human rights objectively. Methodological shortcomings can distort basic data and result in a failure to make a rigorous analysis of existing human rights violations or of the extent to which the enjoyment of those rights is guaranteed or undermined.

40. As a result, the active verification carried out by ONUSAL, through its physical presence in El Salvador and the systematic nature of its fieldwork, combined with its investigatory powers, is a procedure whose distinctive feature is that it has the necessary means to corroborate the existence or otherwise of a violation.

41. Active verification is a systematic investigatory procedure designed to gather objective evidence to corroborate the existence of human rights violations. It is carried out through a process comprising various phases: first, the receipt of complaints or the reporting of a violation on the Mission's own initiative; second, the investigation or inquiry proper, which comprises a detailed follow-up of the facts, police and judicial investigations and the exercise of the Mission's fact-finding powers; third, if the facts are corroborated and it is found that there was no violation of human rights, the case is closed, but if verification reveals the opposite, recommendations are made either for compensating the injury done or for rectifying the situation which gave rise to or facilitated the violation; fourth, throughout the process, active verification involves using the Mission's good offices to contribute to the transparency and efficiency of police investigations, due process, safety of witnesses, etc., and its power of initiative to assist in overcoming existing situations of human rights violations.

42. In this connection, it must be pointed out that complaints, and statistics on complaints declared admissible, while indicative of the existence of violations and the starting point for verification procedures, do not necessarily presuppose the existence of a violation. There is no direct correlation between the number of complaints declared admissible and the number of violations that occurred. Quite the opposite: the number of complaints usually exceeds the number of proven violations.

43. In order to apply more effective criteria, the Human Rights Division introduced, on 15 November 1992, a methodological guide for active verification. The guide contains standard operational definitions for each category of right observed and uniform criteria for the classification of complaints. Its use ensures that the entire process is conducted more rigorously and it is expected to permit a more objective analysis of trends in the human rights situation in El Salvador.

44. It will also make it possible to present statistics and trends not only for complaints declared admissible but also for the findings of verification, in other words, for proven violations.

...

VI. Conclusions and recommendations

A. *Conclusions*

273. Looking objectively at developments in the human rights situation in El Salvador during the eight months covered by this report, it would seem that the situation is gradually improving. If one compares the current situation with the situation that existed prior to the signing of the peace agreements, the progress is obvious. It is reflected in certain definite trends, such as the virtual absence of enforced disappearances or instances of torture during the period covered by this report. Nevertheless, disturbing violations, made all the more serious by their intensity and the means by which they are committed, persist, especially violations involving the right to life, integrity of person and liberty. All of this is taking place in an atmosphere of public insecurity created by such unlawful activities and the high number of concomitant fatalities.

274. Violations of the right to life can be seen in the many cases in which evidence of criminal acts coincides with political motives, making their classification difficult. Instances of death continue to occur which, while considerably fewer in number, can reasonably be shown to have had political motives and can be equated with summary executions. However, there is no government policy of complicity with such acts. Violations of the right to life are also evident in the criminal behaviour displayed by illegal organizations that dispense "private justice".

275. Death threats have been uncommonly frequent as peace takes hold in El Salvador. Arbitrary detentions for petty misdemeanours are also widespread and systematic, as are violations of due process.

276. In a society with no strong tradition of balanced labour relations, infringement of the right to trade-union freedom and recurrent regulatory and procedural obstacles to labour rights have continued to affect the enjoyment of these rights, seriously prejudicing the rights of workers. Yet, in another indication of the catalytic effect of the peace agreements, the Government, workers and employers have agreed on a social contract calling for significant changes in labour relations, which, when implemented, should do much to reverse the trend observed during the period covered by this report.

277. In a State governed by the rule of law, the effective and independent administration of justice is the essential means of guaranteeing the legality of human rights. ONUSAL has verified that the administration of justice continues to be woefully inadequate and totally incapable of ensuring fulfilment by the State of its duty to guarantee those rights or respect for the right of citizens to due process of law (despite some progress in the regulatory area, evidenced by the legislative implementation of the constitutional reform of the judiciary).

278. The existence of certain isolated violations notwithstanding, the freedoms of expression and assembly and the exercise of political rights are widely enjoyed with State guarantees that are consistent with international standards.

279. An overview of the political, social and economic process in El Salvador shows that the peace agreements have had a decisive influence on the human rights situation. This improvement should be extended to the rights that continue to suffer significant and, in some cases, systematic violations. For the enjoyment of human rights, then, the State must fulfil its duties as guarantor, while citizens, both individually and collectively, must exercise their rights and duties.

280. The consolidation of current positive trends and the elimination of persistent violations will depend largely on the effective implementation of the peace agreements and consolidation of the structural and institutional reforms aimed at enabling the rule of law to function effectively in a demilitarized, reunified, reconciled and tolerant society schooled in democratic values and human dignity.

B. *Recommendations*

281. In the San José Agreement, the parties pledged to give prompt consideration to any recommendations made by ONUSAL. In the five preceding reports submitted by the Director of the Human Rights Division to the Secretary-General and the General Assembly, a comprehensive set of recommendations was made, the implementation of which was and is indispensable to the protection and promotion of human rights in El Salvador.

282. The Government has accepted some of these recommendations on an ad hoc basis, but the recommendations as a whole have yet to be dealt with in a manner consistent with the provisions of the San José Agreement. Most of the recommendations have not received due attention. This situation, which is hardly conducive to the promotion of human rights, was reviewed by ONUSAL and the parties to the San José Agreement. As a result of recent consultations, the Human Rights Division has identified a readiness on the part of both the Government and FMLN to appropriately and effectively address the recommendations contained in the various reports. In the short term, there are plans for establishing the consultative mechanisms required for systematic, effective and mutually agreed follow-up to the recommendations.

283. Given that most of the recommendations made by the Human Rights Division in its previous reports have yet to be dealt with properly, the Director of the Division considers it necessary to reiterate here that the recommendations continue to apply and must be

implemented as a matter of urgency. The active verification carried out during the period covered by this report also prompts the following additional recommendations:

(a) In keeping with the thrust of the peace process, it is imperative that the Government complete, as soon as possible, the formalities required for the ratification of or accession to, as appropriate, the Convention against Torture and Other Cruel, Inhuman or Degrading Treatment or Punishment; the Inter-American Convention to Prevent and Punish Torture; the Additional Protocol to the American Convention on Human Rights in the Area of Economic, Social and Cultural Rights; and the Convention on the Political Rights of Women. Likewise, the necessary steps should be taken for the ratification of Conventions Nos. 87 and 93 of the International Labour Organisation, on freedom of association and the right to organize;

(b) To enhance the effectiveness of international norms for the protection of human rights, the Optional Protocol to the International Covenant on Civil and Political Rights should be ratified and the compulsory jurisdiction of the Inter-American Court of Human Rights should be recognized;

(c) Bearing in mind the structural weaknesses in the administration of justice, and in keeping with the spirit of the peace agreements, a structural and functional reform of the judiciary is called for. This reform should entail a review of the functional structures of the judiciary, an immediate evaluation of all judicial officials, inculcation of a sense of ethics within the judiciary, a review of judicial procedures, a re-evaluation of court administrative norms and the creation of a court inspection system;

(d) To improve criminal investigation in cases involving summary or arbitrary executions, and until the Criminal Investigation Division of the National Civil Police begins to function, immediate transitional measures are necessary. It would be useful, for example, to set up a special commission of inquiry devoted exclusively to the investigation of homicides in which there is a reasonable likelihood of political motives, including those classified as political murders as a result of ONUSAL verification. The commission could draw on the existing technical capacity of the Commission for the Investigation of Criminal Acts; it should be placed under the authority of the National Civil Police, in keeping with the spirit of the peace agreements, and should enjoy the support of the Office of the Attorney-General of the Republic, the Office of the National Counsel for the Defence of Human Rights and the Institute of Forensic medicine. In view of its purpose, the commission should conduct its investigations taking into account the relevant norms and the Model Protocol for the Legal Investigation of Extra-legal, Arbitrary or Summary Executions, adopted by the United Nations;

(e) The effective functioning of the remedy of *habeas corpus* is essential to the protection of human rights in El Salvador. To this end, legislative reforms and an information and education campaign are vital. Legislative reforms should focus on the notion that *habeas corpus* is guided expressly by the principles of speed, timeliness and effectiveness. As this remedy is supposed to give applicants full access to the courts, jurisdictional oversight which is broader and more accessible than that currently provided (by the Constitutional Chamber of the Supreme Court) must be ensured. Urgent revision of the Constitutional Procedures Act on the basis of existing bills is not inconsistent with the planned amendment of the Constitution. In accordance with the international agreements to which El Salvador is a party, specific provision should be made to ensure that remedies (*habeas corpus* and *amparo*) cannot be suspended or their use curtailed under any circumstances, including during states of emergency;

(f) Bearing in mind the positive trends that have emerged in the area of enforced disappearances and torture and the need to adopt measures to consolidate these trends, special criminal legislation must be drafted and adopted which defines both of these offences and establishes penalties and procedures commensurate with their seriousness when the perpetrators are members of the security forces or the authorities;

(g) In order to reduce and eliminate ill-treatment, legislation must be drafted which regulates clearly the official conduct of law enforcement officials. In addition, abuses of power must be punished, limits must be placed on the use of force and firearms by such officials and behaviour considered to constitute a criminal act by a public official must be more clearly defined. Such officials must also receive systematic and ongoing instruction in the exercise of police functions and the rights of detainees;

(h) Concerning the need to abolish the systematic practice of arbitrary detention for petty misdemeanours, the following steps are recommended:

(i) The Police Act of 21 July 1886, which remains in force, should be repealed, as it perpetuates a penal law which focuses on the author of an act rather than on the act itself; it is this latter concept that applies in democratic countries, where a perpetrator is punished for his actions, not his personal characteristics. The punishment of vagrancy and other petty misdemeanours listed in this Act is unconstitutional and runs counter to international rights norms. Once the Act has been repealed, all petty misdemeanours should be investigated and punished by magistrates;

(ii) Until the necessary changes are made to bring

Salvadorian legislation into line with the constitutional and international order, judges trying petty misdemeanours should apply Decree No. 457 (Act governing the procedure for administrative detention or the imposition of administrative fines). Another temporary measure would be the drafting of an administrative regulation that would complement the aforesaid Decree by giving priority to some of the most common and serious petty misdemeanours, spelling out the functional competence of the authorities, ordering full respect and guarantees for the rights of perpetrators and specifying the penalties applicable to police and municipal authorities who fail to follow the procedure stipulated in Decree No. 457 or exceed their authority;

(i) A compensation fund for the victims of serious human rights violations must be established. This fund should be funded from State resources, national and international donations and other resources as appropriate. In addition, a brief procedure will have to be established for determining the type of compensation to be awarded and who the recipient(s) shall be;

(j) Criteria for membership on the National Council of the Judiciary and the responsibilities of the Council must be stated more clearly and the necessary legislative changes made. Council members should be appointed directly by the institutional or social sector they represent and not by the Legislative Assembly. Both the selection and the appointment of magistrates and judges should be the exclusive domain of the National Council of the Judiciary. In order to give the Council greater latitude in choosing Supreme Court judges, it is proposed that the requirement that at least half of the names on the list of candidates be put forward by lawyers' associations should be abolished;

(k) The provisions of the National Council of the Judiciary Act which place the Judicial Training School entirely under the authority of the Council must be fully implemented. The School's administrative and budgetary independence from the Supreme Court of Justice must be ensured. The School must be able to provide magistrates and judges with academic and specialized training that will foster a critical approach to the problems encountered in the administration of justice. Judicial officials must also be provided with all elements required to foster concern and respect for the human rights of both the accused and the victim as well as other considerations that will enable them to grasp the social function of the administration of justice;

(l) A criminal procedures code that reflects basic human rights principles is incompatible with the so-called extralegal confessions made to auxiliary organs. To eliminate this practice, the adoption by the Legislative Assembly of the bill drafted for this purpose by the Ministry of Justice must be promoted;

(m) The disciplinary regime provided for under the Career Judicial Service Act should regulate the obligation of the Supreme Court of Justice of its President, as appropriate, to investigate formally and promptly any irregularities or violations of the guarantee of due process of law, particularly those identified by the National Counsel for the Defence of Human Rights in the determinations issued by him in accordance with the law;

(n) Since violations of due process tend to be systematic, it is imperative that the Supreme Court of Justice or its President, as appropriate, act on violations verified by ONUSAL and brought to its attention by the Human Rights Division by taking the necessary steps to investigate and punish violations provided for in the Career Judicial Service Act for which responsibility has been established, particularly in the case of the following violations:

(i) Failure by judges of first instance personally to conduct the requisite pre-trial proceedings in all cases giving rise to serious social unrest and especially in cases of attempted murder;

(ii) Failure to observe the rules invalidating any statements made under threat or any type of duress;

(iii) Illegal or arbitrary detention, and particularly any failure to perform duties by omission;

(iv) Failure to order judicial inspections, forensic examinations or autopsies in cases of violent or sudden death, as required by law;

(v) Serious irregularities or violations of the rights of prison inmates and detainees in general;

(vi) Serious delays in the administration of justice occasioned by pre-trial detention for periods exceeding the time-limits set for proceedings;

(o) Bearing in mind the restrictions placed on freedom of association, trade union freedoms and the enjoyment of workers' rights, as well as the expressed readiness of the State, employers and workers to rectify this situation within a framework of economic and social consultation, it is imperative that the Ministry of Labour, as a necessary expression of its confidence in labour consultation, help ensure the granting of legal recognition to trade unions. In general, restrictive and discriminatory practices affecting the exercise of trade union freedoms and labour rights must be eliminated;

(p) Bearing in mind the important role played by the International Labour Organisation and, in particular, its Committee on Freedom of Association in safeguarding trade union rights, the Government is urged to authorize a mission of direct contact between El Salvador and that Committee, in accordance with the Committee's repeated requests;

(q) Ongoing efforts to formulate the new armed forces doctrine and modify military training in the various military schools must be developed and pursued. In stating the objectives and anticipated results in both areas, it would be useful to know what progress has been made and what the ultimate goals of such reforms are. At the same time, it is imperative that the human rights component not be reduced to the mere provision of basic information about the ethical and legal aspects of human rights, but that it be an integral part of officer training; this means that human rights should not be viewed only as an academic course but as a qualitative component of the new military training;

(r) The recovery of military weapons that have fallen into the hands of private individuals and are generally used for criminal purposes must be expedited. Likewise, it is essential that greater control be exerted over the use of military weapons by personnel on active duty. In this connection, programmes to reintegrate former members of the armed forces and demobilized members of FMLN must also be expedited;

(s) In the new era created by the ending of the armed conflict, the development of a human rights culture is seen as vital to the consolidation of civilian society and the rule of law. Thus, the introduction into the formal educational system of a human rights education policy and specific projects in that field is indispensable. The ONUSAL Human Rights Division appeals to the international community to provide financial and technical cooperation for the efforts which the Ministry of Education has begun in this area with the help of various development cooperation agencies;

(t) The expansion and strengthening of the Office of the National Counsel for the Defence of Human Rights is essential to the consolidation of the peace process and the affirmation of the rule of law. The Human Rights Division urges the executive and legislative authorities to give the Counsel's Office adequate budgetary autonomy. At the same time, the international community is urged to pay special attention to the Office's projects, particularly those aimed at enhancing its investigative capacity and expanding its presence throughout the country;

(u) With regard to human rights education in the informal sector, the State must lift all restrictions on the work of non-governmental organizations while granting them all facilities and support for their activities in the field of human rights education, especially among the most vulnerable groups of society;

(v) The Human Rights Division also urges international organizations and development agencies to extend technical and financial cooperation to Salvadorian non-governmental organizations to help make civilian society a more vital force for the protection and promotion of human rights. At the same time, the Government must respond to applications by non-governmental organizations for legal recognition as quickly and positively as possible, granting such organizations particularly those active in the field of human rights all facilities and protection for them to do their job properly. Similarly, priority should be given to the investigation and punishment of any act of intimidation and coercion against non-governmental organizations.

Document 71

Letter dated 20 May 1993 from the Secretary-General to President Cristiani concerning an analysis by the United Nations of the recommendations of the Commission on the Truth

Not issued as a United Nations document

I write with reference to your letter of 30 March 1993 about the report of the Commission on the Truth. I also refer to the meeting which subsequently took place on 1 April 1993 between Dr. Oscar Santamaría, your Minister of the Presidency, and Mr. Marrack Goulding, Under-Secretary-General for Political Affairs.

As Mr. Goulding told Dr. Santamaría on that occasion, I had instructed that the United Nations undertake a detailed analysis of the Commission's recommendations in order to identify the action which would need to be taken by the various parties concerned and thus provide a basis for the verification functions entrusted to the United Nations by the Peace Accords and approved by the Security Council.

I now enclose the result of our analysis. [See Document 77, page 447.] It takes the form of a list of the Commission's recommendations, specifying in each case the entity or entities responsible for taking action, the form of that action and its timing. Also enclosed are two annexes. The first annex lists the recommendations of

ONUSAL's Human Rights Division which the Commission recommended should be immediately implemented; the second summarizes the changes required to the Constitution and existing legislation to achieve full implementation of the Commission's recommendations.

In carrying out this exercise, I have proceeded from the principle that the Commission on the Truth and its recommendations form an integral part of the Peace Accords, both parties having undertaken without qualification to implement the recommendations.

As far as the Government is concerned, this commitment requires it not only to implement the recommendations which fall within its competence but also to take the necessary political action to promote implementation of recommendations which may require amendment to the Constitution or existing legislation or which are the primary responsibility of other entities.

It seems to me of the greatest importance that as far as possible implementation of all the recommendations should be completed before the elections which are scheduled to take place next March, though I am aware that this will not be possible in the case of Constitutional amendments which would require action by two consecutive Legislative Assemblies. It is also important that priority be given to implementation of those recommendations which the Commission has identified as being of a particularly pressing and urgent nature.

Given the United Nations' responsibility for verifying the implementation of the Peace Accords, it will be necessary for me to inform the Security Council on a regular basis about the progress made with regard to the Commission's recommendations. It is my intention to submit my first report on this subject to the Council not later than 30 June 1993. I should accordingly be grateful, Mr. President, if you would be kind enough to inform me, by 20 June 1993, of the action which has been taken, or is planned, by the Government in order (a) to implement each of the recommendations for which, in the attached list, the Government is designated as an addressee (*destinatario*) and (b) to promote implementation of the other recommendations in the list.

I am writing in similar terms to the Coordinator-General of the FMLN and to the current Coordinator of COPAZ.

I am confident, Mr. President, that I can again rely on your cooperation in faithfully implementing this important component of the Peace Accords to which you have contributed so much and which are a lasting monument to your statesmanship.

Please accept, Mr. President, the assurances of my highest consideration.

(*Signed*) Boutros BOUTROS-GHALI

Document 72

Letter dated 20 May 1993 from the Secretary-General to Mr. Schafik Handal of the FMLN concerning an analysis by the United Nations of the recommendations of the Commission on the Truth

Not issued as a United Nations document

I write with reference to the report of the Commission on the Truth and to your letter of 5 April 1993 to General Suanzes on that subject.

After receiving the report in March, I instructed that the United Nations undertake a detailed analysis of the Commission's recommendations in order to identify the action which would need to be taken by the various parties concerned and thus provide a basis for the verification functions entrusted to the United Nations by the Peace Accords and approved by the Security Council.

I now enclose the result of our analysis. [See Document 77, page 447.] It takes the form of a list of the Commission's recommendations, specifying in each case the entity or entities responsible for taking action, the form of that action and its timing. Also enclosed are two annexes. The first annex lists the recommendations of UNUSAL's Human Rights Division which the Commission recommended should be immediately implemented; the second summarizes the changes required to the Constitution and existing legislation to achieve full implementation of the Commission's recommendations.

In carrying out this exercise, I have proceeded from the principle that the Commission on the Truth and its recommendations form an integral part of the Peace Accords, both parties having undertaken without qualification to implement the recommendations. This commitment requires each of the parties not only to implement the recommendations which fall within its competence but also to take political action, as appropriate, to assist and support implementation of recommendations which are the primary responsibility of other entities.

It seems to me of the greatest importance that as far as possible implementation of all the recommendations should be completed before the elections which are scheduled to take place next March, though I am aware that this will not be possible in the case of Constitutional amendments which would require action by two consecutive Legislative Assemblies. It is also important that priority be given to implementation of those recommendations which the Commission has identified as being of a particularly pressing and urgent nature.

Given the United Nations' responsibility for verifying the implementation of the Peace Accords, it will be necessary for me to inform the Security Council on a regular basis about the progress made with regard to the Commission's recommendations. It is my intention to submit my first report on this subject to the Council not later than 30 June 1993. I should accordingly be grateful, Mr. Coordinator-General, if you would be kind enough to inform me, by 20 June 1993, of the action which has been taken, or is planned, by the FMLN in order (a) to implement each of the recommendations for which, in the attached list, the FMLN is designated as an addressee (*destinatorio*) and (b) to promote implementation of the other recommendations in the list, especially those for which COPAZ is an addressee.

I am writing in similar terms to President Cristiani and to the current Coordinator of COPAZ.

I am confident, Mr. Coordinator-General, that I can rely on your cooperation in faithfully implementing this important component of the Peace Accords.

Please accept, Mr. Coordinator-General, the assurances of my highest consideration.

(*Signed*) Boutros BOUTROS-GHALI

Document 73

Letter dated 20 May 1993 from the Secretary-General to Mrs. Gloria Salguero Grosso, Coordinator pro tempore *of the National Commission for the Consolidation of Peace (COPAZ), concerning an analysis by the United Nations of the recommendations of the Commission on the Truth*

Not issued as a United Nations document

I write with reference to the report of the Commission on the Truth.

After receiving the report in March, I instructed that the United Nations undertake a detailed analysis of the Commission's recommendations in order to identify the action which would need to be taken by the various parties concerned and thus provide a basis for the verification functions entrusted to the United Nations by the Peace Accords and approved by the Security Council.

I now enclose the result of our analysis. [See Document 77, page 447.] It takes the form of a list of the Commission's recommendations, specifying in each case the entity or entities responsible for taking action, the form of that action and its timing. Also enclosed are two annexes. The first annex lists the recommendations of UNUSAL's Human Rights Division which the Commission recommended should be immediately implemented; the second summarizes the changes required to the Constitution and existing legislation to achieve full implementation of the Commission's recommendations.

In carrying out this exercise, I have proceeded from the principle that the Commission on the Truth and its recommendations form an integral part of the Peace Accords, both parties having undertaken without qualification to implement the recommendations. This commitment requires each of the parties not only to implement the recommendations which fall within its competence but also to take political action, as appropriate, to assist and support implementation of recommendations which are the primary responsibility of other entities. It is evident that the considerable volume of legislative action required of the Legislative Assembly gives COPAZ an especially important role in this process and it is for this reason that I am writing to you.

It also seems to me of the greatest importance that as far as possible implementation of all the recommendations should be completed before the elections which are scheduled to take place next March, though I am aware that this will not be possible in the case of those which require action by two consecutive Legislative Assemblies. It is also important that priority be given to implementation of those recommendations which the Commission has identified as being of a particularly pressing and urgent nature.

Given the United Nations' responsibility for verifying the implementation of the Peace Accords, it will be necessary for me to inform the Security Council on a regular basis about the progress made with regard to the Commission's recommendations. It is my intention to submit my first report on this subject to the Council not later than 30 June 1993. I should accordingly be grateful, Madam Coordinator, if you would be kind enough to inform me, by 20 June 1993, of the action which has been taken, or is planned, by COPAZ in order (a) to implement each of the recommendations for which, in the attached list, COPAZ is designated as an addressee (*destinatorio*) and (b) to promote implementation of the other recommendations in the list.

I am writing in similar terms to the President of the Republic and to the Coordinator-General of the FMLN.

I am confident, Madame Coordinator, that I can rely on the cooperation of COPAZ in helping implement this important component of the Peace Accords.

Please accept, Madam Coordinator, the assurances of my highest consideration.

(*Signed*) Boutros BOUTROS-GHALI

Document 74

Report of the Secretary-General on all aspects of ONUSAL's operations

S/25812, 21 May 1993

I. Introduction

1. The present report is submitted to the Security Council in compliance with resolution 791 (1992), by which the Council decided to extend the mandate of the United Nations Observer Mission in El Salvador (ONUSAL) for a further period of six months ending on 31 May 1992 and requested me to report as necessary on all aspects of ONUSAL's operations, at the latest before the expiry of the new mandate period. It follows my reports of 23 November 1992 (S/24833) on the overall implementation of the agreements signed between the Government of El Salvador and the Frente Farabundo Martí para la Liberación Nacional (FMLN), and of 23 December 1993 (S/25006), by which I informed the Council that the armed conflict in El Salvador had been brought formally to an end on 15 December 1992. Subsequently, in letters dated 7, 26 and 29 January and 2 April 1993 (S/25078, S/25241, S/25200 and S/25516), I informed the members of the Security Council of developments relating to specific aspects of the implementation of the Peace Accords.

2. ONUSAL continued to carry out the verification and related functions assigned to it under the direction of Mr. Iqbal Riza, my Special Representative, until 6 March 1993. As Mr. Riza assumed new responsibilities at United Nations Headquarters, I appointed Mr. Augusto Ramírez-Ocampo as my Special Representative and Chief of the Mission. Brigadier-General Victor Suanzes Pardo, Chief of the Military Division, served as the Interim Chief of Mission until Mr. Ramírez-Ocampo assumed his post in El Salvador on 14 April 1993.

3. The first phase of the timetable for implementation of the agreement signed in Mexico City on 16 January 1992 (see S/23501, annex) having successfully been brought to a close, the priority assigned to military aspects in the preceding period moved to other provisions of the agreements. These provisions will continue to be binding on both the Government and FMLN until their full implementation.

4. Difficulties arose in January 1993 after both sides failed to comply with some of their commitments. On 6 November 1992, the Government had undertaken to implement fully by 1 January 1993 the recommendations contained in the report of the Ad Hoc Commission on the purification (*depuración*) of the armed forces. However, this undertaking was only partially complied with and on 7 January 1993 I informed the Council (see S/25078) that in respect of 15 of the 102 officers mentioned in the report the Government had not taken measures in accordance with the Commission's recommendations and was thus not in compliance with the Peace Accords. As I reported then and in subsequent communications, I repeatedly urged President Cristiani to regularize that situation and to take the necessary action in respect of these officers. Only on 2 April 1993 was I in a position to report to the Council (S/25516) that the Government had made a commitment which, when implemented, would bring it into broad compliance with the recommendations of the Ad Hoc Commission.

5. The question of the purification of the armed forces had not been settled when the Commission on the Truth, which was to investigate the most serious acts of violence committed during the conflict, submitted its report on 15 March 1993 (see section V). Extreme posi-

tions were adopted and tension mounted as the High Command of the armed forces, the President of the Supreme Court, highly placed government officials and some political leaders, as well as segments of the media, vehemently and publicly rejected the findings and recommendations of the Commission on the Truth. There was strident criticism of the United Nations and renewed publication of anonymous threats against ONUSAL.

6. A week after the report was published, a general amnesty was approved by simple majority in the Legislative Assembly. I expressed my concern at the haste with which this step had been taken and my view that it would have been preferable if the amnesty had been promulgated after creating a broad degree of national consensus in its favour. The amnesty was criticized by sectors of the opposition and by FMLN for the same reasons as well as for certain specific provisions it contained. The Government countered that the political parties represented in the Legislative Assembly had agreed to a possible amnesty in a document signed hours before the approval, on 23 January 1992, of the law on national reconciliation, under which FMLN members were able to re-enter El Salvador legally—though this document was cast in very broad terms and did not specify when the amnesty should be enacted.

7. For its part FMLN, after starting the destruction of the arms it had concentrated in designated locations under ONUSAL's supervision, slowed this process which, by the end of December, had come to a virtual standstill. FMLN conditioned the resumption of destruction on the outcome of discussions which it was holding directly with the Government on a number of undertakings relating to the implementation of the Peace Accords, on which agreements were finally reached on 4 February. FMLN thereupon resumed destruction of its weapons in the designated zones and the process concluded on 11 February. On 29 January I had reported to the Council on this delay (S/25200). Destruction of FMLN weapons located outside El Salvador and of other categories of weapons was carried out subsequently (see para. 15).

8. Despite these complications, implementation of several key commitments under the Accords has continued to progress: the programme for the transfer of lands, although proceeding at a slow pace and with serious financial difficulties, is now well under way; deployment of the National Civil Police (PNC) started after the first classes graduated from the National Academy for Public Security in February 1993. Further, at the Government's request, ONUSAL has taken on the additional task of providing professional assistance to the National Civil Police. Given the considerable delays in these areas, an extraordinary effort will have to be made to ensure substantial advances before the general elections of March

1994. As was evident during the last World Bank Consultative Group meeting in April this year (see section X), the main constraint in this regard has been the preference of the donor community to finance infrastructural and environmental programmes rather than the above-mentioned peace-related programmes, crucial though they are to the successful implementation of the Accords.

9. Important progress in the implementation of other key commitments has also been made since my last report. For example, the restoration of public administration in the former zones of conflict, in particular the return of mayors and judges who had to leave their jurisdictions during the conflict, was a major achievement (see section VIII). The enactment of legislative reforms on the judiciary, the electoral system and other vital issues of the peace process was also important. In the area of human rights, the National Counsel for the Defence of Human Rights (Ombudsman) (*Procuraduría Nacional para la Defensa de los Derechos Humanos*) has opened regional offices to discharge his duties more effectively.

10. The National Commission for the Consolidation of Peace (*Comisión Nacional para la Consolidación de la Paz*) (COPAZ), where the Government, FMLN and political parties are represented, has continued to seek consensus on various draft laws and other measures related to the Peace Accords. Although in disagreement over its mandate at this stage of the peace process, the entities that comprise COPAZ have continued to participate in plenary sessions, albeit at times at a level lower than in the past. Work has likewise proceeded in the various subcommissions of COPAZ. COPAZ has also been discussing implementation of the recommendations of the Commission on the Truth. Progress has been very slow, however, and it has not yet been possible to agree on an overall unified proposal.

11. As I informed the Security Council (see S/25241), on 8 January 1993 the Government officially requested the United Nations to observe the general elections scheduled for March 1994, which should mark the culmination of the peace process. Since March, attention has increasingly been focused on these elections as, in the prevailing atmosphere of freedom of expression and respect for political rights, the political parties have engaged in a lively public debate over issues, candidates and alliances. Some parties have already selected their presidential candidates. A United Nations technical mission visited El Salvador in April in order to assess requirements, in the expectation that the Council will accede to the Government's request for observation of the elections by the United Nations.

12. It is in this context that the work of ONUSAL during the current mandate period is described below, followed by my observations and recommendations.

II. Military aspects

A. *Military Division*

13. Since the formal end of the armed conflict, ONUSAL's Military Division, which remains under the command of Brigadier-General Victor Suanzes Pardo until 31 May 1993, has continued to verify the remaining aspects of the cease-fire process, including the destruction of FMLN weapons and the reduction of the Armed Forces of El Salvador (FAES). It also monitors the recovery of military weapons held by private individuals, the introduction of the new armed forces reserve system and relevant aspects of other pending commitments under the armed forces chapter of the Peace Accords. In addition, the Division has contributed to the consolidation of peaceful conditions by its presence throughout the territory, particularly in the former zones of conflict and through the deployment and patrols of its military observer groups. The Division has also facilitated meetings between the teams involved in the Plan for the Prevention of Accidents from Mines (*Plan de Prevención de Accidentes de Minas*) and monitors its execution (see para. 22). There will be a continuing need for military observers in the field, should the Council decide to renew ONUSAL's mandate.

14. In May 1993, the Military Division had a strength of 74 military observers from Brazil, Canada, Colombia, Ecuador, India, Ireland, Spain, Sweden and Venezuela and 7 medical officers from Argentina. Following the end of the armed conflict and the subsequent reduction in the number of military observers in line with the intention expressed in my report of 23 November 1992 (S/24833, para. 13), the Division was restructured and redeployed in two regional offices in the eastern and western parts of the country. Given the advances in the peace process, the military component of the Mission will be further reorganized and reduced after 31 May 1993. In view of the tasks still to be carried out, it would be my recommendation that the number of observers be reduced to 38, including the 7 medical officers, and headed at the level of colonel.

B. *Cessation of the armed conflict*

15. Following the formal end of the armed conflict, the Division closed its 15 verification centres, 6 of which were transferred to the Police Division for use by the Auxiliary Transitory Police (see para. 38). That same day saw the final demobilization and incorporation into civilian life of the remaining FMLN ex-combatants, although the destruction of their arms, which at that time stood at 65 per cent of the inventory presented by FMLN, was delayed in some verification centres since FMLN conditioned their destruction on the implementation of complementary commitments undertaken by the Government. Subsequently, the gradual destruction of conventional and sophisticated FMLN weapons, which were concentrated in El Salvador under ONUSAL control, as well as that of weapons deposited outside the country, resumed under ONUSAL's verification. By 11 February, all the arms stored in the FMLN concentration areas had been destroyed and on 1 April the destruction of arms in deposits outside El Salvador was completed. Thus effectively the arms listed in the FMLN inventory presented to ONUSAL have been destroyed, except for a small quantity of individual weapons—about 3.5 per cent of the total—which were reported lost or stolen before their scheduled destruction. ONUSAL now has in its custody a very small number of sophisticated FMLN weapons, the destruction of which FMLN had scheduled to coincide with full compliance by the Government with the recommendations of the Ad Hoc Commission, due at the end of June. This arrangement has been understood and accepted by the Government. The Military Division is currently investigating the discovery of small caches of weapons presumed to have belonged to FMLN, which have drawn strong protest from the Government.

C. *Reduction of the Armed Forces of El Salvador (FAES)*

16. Pursuant to the New York Agreement of 25 September 1991 (A/46/502-S/23082, annex), the Government submitted a plan for the reduction of FAES to a size which it judged appropriate to its new doctrine and functions, as established in amendments to the Constitution that were agreed upon in April 1991. This plan provided for a 50.2 per cent reduction of FAES combatants, including demobilization of the 5 rapid reaction infantry battalions (*batallones de infantería de reacción inmediata*) (known as BIRIs). The reduction was to begin on 1 February 1992 and was scheduled to end in January 1994.

17. At the end of December 1992, FAES decided to accelerate the process of reduction of the infantry battalions and to complete it ahead of schedule. As a result, the demobilization of 15 battalions which was to have been effected during the whole of 1993 was carried out in January alone. The last BIRI was demobilized on 6 February 1993 and the overall process of reduction of FAES was completed on 31 March 1993.

18. The effective reduction of FAES personnel has been greater than the 50.2 per cent envisaged in the Government's original plan and in fact has reached 54.4 per cent. A further reduction in officers is envisaged, although this is subject to the development of plans for their reincorporation in civilian life.

D. *Introduction of the new armed forces reserve system*

19. In accordance with the new law governing military service and reserve service adopted on 30 July 1992 (see S/24833, para. 25), 14 departmental recruitment and reserve centres have been established. Of the planned 30 subsidiary offices, only 3 will be set up during 1993, reportedly owing to lack of resources.

E. *Recovery of military weapons held by private individuals*

20. Under the Peace Accords the recovery of military weapons held by private individuals was to have been finalized by 28 October 1992. In fact, by the time the armed conflict ended on 15 December 1992, this process had barely started. On 22 December, the Government and FMLN established a new deadline of 31 March 1993 for compliance with this commitment, under the verification of ONUSAL. The fact that, two months later, the process remains at a virtual standstill is a source of grave concern.

21. Only 40 per cent of the arms included on the lists provided by FAES have been recovered and the number of weapons that the Division has been able to verify is even smaller. Even more disturbing is the likelihood that the FAES inventory does not include all the weapons that were distributed by FAES during the years of conflict. The Government has given various explanations for the delay in implementation, but these do not lessen the seriousness of non-compliance which engenders a sense of insecurity in the population and may even be a factor in the high level of crime in the country (see para. 44). The assurances given by the Government and FAES that they genuinely wish to move ahead on this subject must be translated into more energetic measures that will permit the full implementation of this part of the Agreement as soon as possible. This will require continuing follow-up on the part of the Military Division of ONUSAL.

F. *Coordination of the clearing of minefields*

22. After participating in the working group that carried out the marking of minefields (see S/24833, para. 21), the Military Division is now engaged in the coordination of the Plan for the Prevention of Accidents from Mines. Under the Plan, mines and other explosive artifacts found in locations indicated by FMLN under ONUSAL supervision are being destroyed by a civilian company with which FAES members and FMLN ex-combatants are cooperating. Military observers are present in the area during the clearing of the minefields and issue records of proceedings on the artifacts destroyed.

The European Community (EC) and countries providing funds for the Plan have expressed the desire that the execution of the programme and resulting expenditures be cleared through ONUSAL, which is considering the practicability of this request.

G. *Other matters*

23. According to the 22 December 1992 agreement, the Government should have published the new FAES doctrine twice in all newspapers and by way of radio commercials, so that society as a whole might be informed of it. This has not been done and therefore constitutes an unfulfilled commitment.

24. After lengthy discussions in COPAZ, it is expected that a draft law on the regulation of private security services will be submitted soon to the Legislative Assembly for approval.

III. Public security matters

A. *Police Division*

25. The Police Division continues to perform its assigned role of monitoring and assisting the National Police during the period of transition until its replacement by the new police force established by the Accords, the National Civil Police (PNC). Since October of last year, the Division has also been supervising and supporting the Auxiliary Transitory Police (*Policía Auxiliar Transitoria*) (PAT), which is responsible for maintaining public order and security in the former zones of conflict until its replacement by the new police force. The Division has assumed additional functions as a result of the deployment of the National Civil Police in 3 of the 14 departments. In response to a request submitted by the Government and in close coordination with the international technical team that provides advice to the Director-General of PNC, the Division is evaluating the performance of the new police force in the field and providing it with technical advice and logistical support.

26. The Division has continued to assist in efforts to locate illegal arms caches and to support the Human Rights Division, to which 18 police observers are seconded. Police observers conduct special inquiries when required and ensure that appropriate security measures are provided for FMLN leaders, as established by the Accords. The Division also provides observers for the admission examinations to the National Public Security Academy.

27. The strength of the Division, which continues to be commanded by General Homero Vaz Bresque (Uruguay), is currently 315 police observers. They are contributed by Austria, Chile, Colombia, France, Guyana, Italy, Mexico, Norway, Spain and Sweden.

B. *National Public Security Academy*

28. The Academy, which trains the new National Civil Police (PNC), started its activities on 1 September 1992. The first two classes graduated simultaneously on 5 February 1993 and the third on 17 May 1993. Graduates have already joined PNC. Delays in the refurbishment of the premises of the Academy account at least in part for the three-month gap between the graduation of the first two classes and the third one. The Academy has announced that, henceforth, the completion of future courses, each comprised of some 300 graduates, will take place once a month. The Academy currently houses five full basic-level classes (about 1,800 trainees), one executive-level class (78 trainees) and one senior-level class (34 trainees). It has taken steps to train six full basic-level classes simultaneously. Thus, by the end of the year, about 5,500 students are expected to have joined the Academy and approximately 3,000 should have graduated.

29. The Academy has been functioning in temporary premises pending construction of permanent premises on a site which the Government purchased in December 1992. Financing will be needed for such requirements as a laboratory, library and sports and recreational facilities. Further, the Academy has to complete the construction of a firing range and facilities for practical training in police techniques, and to purchase training weapons and ammunition.

30. As I reported to the Security Council last November (S/24833, para. 37), the Academic Council accepted for the senior and executive levels 10 candidates from the National Police to which they had been transferred from the National Guard (*Guardia Nacional*) and the Treasury Police (*Policía de Hacienda*) after the signing of the Peace Agreement on 16 January 1992. This was done despite ONUSAL objections that this action contravened the Accords and subsequent undertakings by the Government. After undergoing four months of training abroad, these candidates joined the PNC as provisional commands (*mandos provisionales*). ONUSAL has held several discussions with the Government on this subject and has recommended that the admission of these officers be deemed exceptional so that it will not create a precedent. In order to eliminate such problems in the future, ONUSAL has recommended that a specially designed test be prepared for candidates from the National Police and for FMLN ex-combatants for the next admission examinations for the executive and senior levels.

31. The Academy has continued to receive the support of an international technical team of experts from Spain and the United States of America which provides the Director and the Academic Council with advice on aspects such as the recruitment and selection process, curricula, finances and the disciplinary regime of the Academy. Instructors from Chile, Norway, Spain and the United States of America are fully involved in training activities. Currently, the Academy has a total of 33 international experts and instructors.

32. Since January 1993, the effective monitoring of the functioning of the Academy has been strengthened by the presence of an ONUSAL observer in the Academic Council. The Mission has also continued to monitor the admission examinations and to recommend improvements where necessary. ONUSAL is also providing support to the Academy to strengthen its training courses on human rights.

33. As the Security Council is aware, I have appealed to the international community for financial support for the Academy, which has a crucial role to play in preparing the personnel for the new police force, a key component of the Peace Accords. Although valuable, the support received so far remains insufficient and a major effort by donor Governments is required. At the same time, however, it is incumbent on the Government of El Salvador to marshal its own resources and give the Academy the necessary budgetary priority to place it on a solid footing for attracting external assistance.

C. *National Civil Police*

34. The territorial deployment of the National Civil Police (PNC) started in March 1993 with the establishment of 18 police stations in one department. It has now reached a total of 34 stations, in 3 departments. The Government is committed to effecting monthly deployments this year in seven more departments, leaving deployments in the remaining four for 1994. It is also committed to organizing and deploying this year most of the functional divisions of the PNC. This will require additional international support, mostly in training and equipment. According to the Government's timetable, the PNC could be fully deployed and functional by September 1994. By then, the National Police should have been entirely phased out and replaced by the new police force.

35. The Government and FMLN agreed on 22 December 1992 that the personnel and equipment of the Criminal Investigation Commission (*Comisión de Investigación de Hechos Delictivos*) and the Special Anti-narcotics Unit (*Unidad Especial Antinarcotráfico*) would be gradually transferred to the Criminal Investigation Division (*División de Investigación Criminal*) and the Anti-narcotics Division (*División Antinarcotráfica*) of the PNC, respectively. The Director-General of the PNC, under the supervision of ONUSAL, will evaluate the professional competence and the capacity to function in the new police force of the personnel of these bodies, who will also have to undergo a special training course in the

Academy on the new police doctrine. The planned transfer has not yet taken place.

36. The Director-General of the PNC receives advice from a technical team from the United States on the organization and territorial and functional deployment of the PNC. ONUSAL, in coordination with the team when necessary, provides the new police force with technical advice and logistical support and evaluates its performance in the field. The evaluations are transmitted to the PNC and to the Academy. It has become evident that the PNC requires additional international support in the form of specialized equipment and training expertise.

37. In order to ensure that the PNC assumes the role assigned to it in the Peace Agreement, the Director-General should continue to work closely with the COPAZ subcommittee for the PNC, which serves as his advisory body in the adoption of relevant decisions or measures concerning the new police force, including those not expressly addressed in the Accords. The subcommittee should also continue its overall supervision of the establishment of the PNC until it has fully replaced the National Police.

D. *Special regime*

38. The Auxiliary Transitory Police (PAT) started its activities in early October 1992 and was deployed in 20 posts in 9 departments by the end of February. The deployment of PNC in three departments has resulted in the closure of nine of these posts. The remaining 11 will be phased out gradually as PNC continues its territorial deployment. PAT may be phased out completely if the recommendation by the Academic Council of the National Public Security Academy to replace it with PNC contingents is accepted by the Director-General of PNC.

39. The Director-General of PNC also has command of PAT. Each of its contingents is under the constant supervision and guidance of ONUSAL police observers, who also provide daily academic instruction. The Police Division provides PAT with logistical support.

E. *National Police*

40. The Peace Agreement stipulated that the National Police should be responsible for public order and security during the transition period until its complete replacement by PNC. Although such replacement has already taken place in 3 out of 14 departments, the reduction of the National Police has not yet begun. Rather, as I reported to the Security Council in May (S/23999, para. 30) and November 1992 (S/24833, para. 43), the National Police has been strengthened with personnel from the two former public security forces, the National Guard and the Treasury Police, and with self-contained units from one of the demobilized rapid reaction infantry battalions. The Government defends these transfers on the grounds that they are not expressly prohibited by the accords and that the rise in common crime requires it to strengthen the National Police. However, it is ONUSAL's view, which it has communicated to the Government, that such transfers are incompatible with the thrust of the accords and contravene their spirit, particularly when considered in the light of the slowness, in the early phases, in launching preparations for the Academy and PNC.

41. This situation results in a contradiction. The National Police was meant to be phased out gradually as the National Civil Police was deployed. Instead, it has increased significantly, not only as a result of these transfers, but also through the monthly graduation of some 60 to 100 police officers from the National Police training school which, ONUSAL recently found out, continues to operate. ONUSAL has been informed by the Government that the members of the National Police already replaced by PNC will be redeployed to areas of the country with higher crime rates. While the Agreement did not expressly establish that the reduction of the National Police should be synchronized with the deployment of PNC, it did state very clearly that the new police force should replace the old one. For this reason, it is necessary that, at a minimum, the Government respond to ONUSAL's request for its plan for the reduction of the National Police and, in that connection, that it inform ONUSAL of its plans for the closing of the National Police training school. The Government should also inform the Mission about its plans to dissolve certain police structures, mainly the *Batallón Fiscal* (the former Customs Police), whose continued existence is evidently incompatible with that of the Finance Division of the National Civil Police.

42. Resources are available for the integration into civilian life of those members of the National Police who will be phased out as the force is reduced. Such personnel will have access to the various reintegration programmes for ex-combatants of both sides. This will help them to adjust to their new circumstances.

43. One of the avenues open to members of the National Police is that of joining PNC through the Academy. On 17 June 1992, the Government and FMLN agreed that up to 20 per cent of the vacancies could be filled by serving National Police and FMLN ex-combatants, in order to maintain a balance between candidates from both sources. It was envisaged that these candidates would be carefully screened. However, during the last admission examination, ONUSAL ascertained that a large number of National Police candidates had left that force four to six years ago, in many cases after being dismissed for disciplinary reasons, and had only rejoined after the Peace Agreement was signed. This is clearly not what was intended in the Peace Agreement and is espe-

cially disturbing when linked to the apparent reinforcement, rather than reduction, of the National Police.

F. Problems of common crime

44. In February 1993 the Government, responding to growing public concern, outlined a programme for combating common crime. Although the figures at ONUSAL's disposal do not indicate a dramatic increase in common crime since the Peace Agreement was signed, it is indisputable that the rate is very high and that the end of the armed conflict may have contributed to its being brought to the public's attention. Indeed, common crime is the single most important matter of concern in El Salvador, according to a recent opinion poll. In this light, the Government's programme is seen as a timely one. A further positive aspect is that the programme limits the participation of the armed forces to the provision of logistical support to the police forces.

IV. Human rights and the administration of justice

45. As pointed out in the sixth report of the Director of the ONUSAL Human Rights Division (S/25521, annex), a factual analysis of respect for human rights in El Salvador reveals a gradual improvement, particularly when compared with that prevailing before the signing of the peace accords. Evidence of that improvement is the fact that not a single case of forced disappearance or torture was recorded during the reporting period (June 1992-January 1993). However, serious violations still persist with regard to the right to life, personal integrity and liberty. The gravity of these violations is underscored by their frequency and gruesome nature. They take place against a background of public insecurity generated by common crime and a high murder rate.

46. The active verification carried out by the Human Rights Division is directed not only at an objective recording of facts, but also at the exercise of good offices aimed at assisting efforts by Salvadorians to find a remedy to violations—some of them systematic—that still persist. In his sixth report, the Director of the Human Rights Division reiterated recommendations made in his previous reports and added 22 new recommendations. ONUSAL and the Government of El Salvador are currently discussing the modalities for full implementation of those recommendations which have not yet been implemented.

47. In carrying out its tasks, the Division cooperates with Salvadorian institutions to strengthen their ability to work in promoting human rights. ONUSAL is thus actively supporting the National Counsel for the Defence of Human Rights in his effort to improve his Office's investigative capacity and to establish regional offices in order to cover the needs of the entire Salvadorian population. In addition, the Division seeks to strengthen its relations with human rights non-governmental organizations that have been working for years under difficult conditions.

48. In the immediate future, in the context of the forthcoming electoral process, the promotion of human rights will require a greater effort from the State and society at large. Full observance of civil and political rights will require the consolidation of the rule of law, one of the ultimate objectives of the Peace Accords.

V. Report of the Commission on the Truth

49. The Commission on the Truth was established in accordance with the Mexico Agreements of 27 April 1991 (S/23130, pp. 5 and 16-18). It was entrusted with the task of investigating serious acts of violence that had occurred since 1980 and whose impact on society was deemed to require an urgent public knowledge of the truth. The Commission was composed of three international personalities appointed by the Secretary-General after consultation with the parties: Belisario Betancur, former President of Colombia; Reinaldo Figueredo Planchart, former Foreign Minister of Venezuela; and Thomas Buergenthal, former President of the Inter-American Court of Human Rights and of the Inter-American Institute for Human Rights. Within six months of starting its work, the Commission was to transmit a final report with its conclusions and recommendations to the parties and to the Secretary-General, who would make it public and would take the decisions and initiatives that he deemed appropriate. The parties undertook to carry out the Commission's recommendations.

50. The handing over of the report, a document of over 200 pages plus annexes of several hundred pages, was originally due in January but, with the parties' agreement, was postponed until 15 March 1993. The report is currently being translated into the official languages and it is hoped that it will be available for circulation as a document of the Security Council in early June.

51. The Commission received over 22,000 complaints of serious acts of violence which had occurred between January 1980 and July 1991. More than 60 per cent of the complaints referred to extrajudicial executions and more than 25 per cent to forced disappearances; more than 20 per cent included complaints of torture. The Commission's report describes about 30 cases which it deemed to fall into the category of serious acts of violence, as described in paragraph 49 above, and which were chosen to illustrate the different patterns of violence. These are classified as violence by agents of the State; massacres of peasants by the Armed Forces; assassinations by death squads; violence by the FMLN; and assassinations of judges.

52. The Commission listed its recommendations under four headings:

I. Recommendations arising directly from the results of the Commission's investigations: these relate to persons found to have been involved in the cases investigated and to certain aspects of the judicial system in El Salvador;

II. Eradication of structural causes directly connected with the incidents investigated: these recommendations include full implementation of the Peace Accords; reforms in the Armed Forces and in the arrangements for public security; and the investigation of illegal groups;

III. Institutional reforms to prevent the repetition of such events: these recommendations relate to the administration of justice; the protection of human rights (including the immediate implementation of some 19 recommendations already made by ONUSAL's Human Rights Division); and the new National Civil Police;

IV. Measures for national reconciliation.

53. The Commission's recommendations require a wide range of administrative, legislative and constitutional measures, as well as certain actions by individuals. Action is required not only from the Government and FMLN but also, in particular, from the Legislative Assembly which will have to adopt new laws or revise existing ones, as well as approving and ratifying the necessary constitutional amendments (requiring majority in one legislature and ratification by a two-thirds vote in the subsequent legislature) in order to implement the recommendations. The Government and COPAZ will have an important role in promoting the necessary legislation. The time-frame for implementation varies from recommendation to recommendation.

54. Shortly after receipt of the Commission's report, President Cristiani said, in a public statement and in a letter addressed to me, that he was willing to comply strictly with those of the Commission's recommendations which fell within his competence, were consistent with the Constitution, were in harmony with the Peace Accords and contributed to national reconciliation. At the same time, spokesmen of the Government accused the members of the Commission of having exceeded their mandate and in particular of having purported to assume judicial functions. In a letter dated 5 April 1993, Mr. Schafik Handal, the Coordinator-General of the FMLN, stated that, notwithstanding a number of reservations about the Commission's report, the FMLN accepted in their entirety the recommendations it contained. In some cases, however, FMLN implementation of those recommendations was conditioned on the Government's doing likewise.

55. In the light of this reaction, I instructed that a detailed analysis be made of the Commission's recommendations, examining whether any of them was outside the Commission's mandate or incompatible with the Constitution and identifying what action was required by whom and in what time-frame. I will shortly transmit this analysis to President Cristiani, to Mr. Handal as Coordinator-General of the FMLN, and to the current Coordinator of COPAZ. I shall draw their attention to my obligation to verify implementation of the Commission's recommendations and to report thereon at regular intervals to the Security Council, it being my hope to submit the first such report by the end of June. I shall ask President Cristiani, Mr. Handal and the Coordinator of COPAZ to provide me with information, before then, about action which has been taken, or is planned, by the Government, the FMLN and COPAZ, respectively, to implement each of the recommendations for whose implementation the United Nations analysis identifies it as having responsibility. As soon as this action has been taken, I shall circulate the analysis as a document of the Security Council.

VI. Economic and social matters

A. *Transfer of land programme*

56. My 13 October 1992 proposal for land transfer (see S/24833, paras. 55-60), by virtue of its acceptance by the two parties soon afterwards, in effect constitutes an addendum to the Peace Agreement. (The proposal is referred to below as the 13 October agreement.) The programme to transfer up to 237,000 mz* of land to a maximum of 47,500 people, including ex-combatants of both sides and landholders (people who had occupied land without title during the conflict years), was divided into three phases. These were determined by the availability of financial and land resources.

57. For the first phase, considered an emergency one, resources were expected to be made available from October 1992 to January 1993 since the Government was providing State lands and USAID was providing financial resources. At the time the agreement was negotiated, it already was anticipated that the implementation of this phase would take significantly longer, given the numerous logistical problems involved in carrying out such a complex programme. In the first phase 15,400 beneficiaries were to receive 77,000 mz. Priority was to be given to demobilized FMLN combatants by giving them all available land that had not been legally transferred to landholders.

58. The second phase was to start as soon as the

* 1 mz (manzana) equals 0.7 hectare.

European Community (EC) made resources available, which was anticipated for February 1993. This phase was distinct from the first due to the EC requirement for equal benefit for FMLN ex-combatants and former members of the Armed Forces from all the land that had not been legally transferred to current landholders. The second phase was to end when 20,000 mz could be purchased with the EC funds. It was expected to benefit about 4,000 recipients.

59. For the third phase, which is to provide some 28,100 recipients with 140,500 mz, representing 60 per cent of the total, there are at present neither available financial resources nor land. It was roughly estimated that at the average price at which the Lands Bank had transferred comparable land during the previous year, $85 million was needed for this phase.

60. The land transfer programme has progressed, albeit at a slow pace. The transfer of 36 State properties and 196 private properties, totalling an area of approximately 45,000 mz, has been negotiated with resources from the first phase. Once handed over, these properties will benefit 10,000 FMLN ex-combatants and landholders. This represents slightly less than 60 per cent of the area to be handed over during the first phase and covers somewhat more than 60 per cent of the beneficiaries. However, only 13 of the private properties whose transfer has been negotiated thus far, which benefit about 200 persons, have been registered; the remaining 183 are still in one of the various legal stages that precede the issuing of titles. With resources from the second phase, over 600 FAES ex-combatants have already benefited from the handing over and final registration of 11 properties totalling an area of 1,400 mz.

61. Much tension has resulted from the delays, the most serious consequence of which is that many beneficiaries will not be able to begin cultivation this planting season, which began in May. The timely granting of loans for agricultural activities is another problem, since the majority of beneficiaries have not yet received deeds to their properties and there are formal difficulties in granting them credit. Although the Government has agreed to provide credit to landholders who have already negotiated the acquisition of land, it has so far not yet agreed to provide the credit necessary for production this season to about 80 per cent of those who have not yet negotiated such acquisitions. This is a clear departure from the Peace Agreement which establishes not only that landholders shall not be evicted pending agreement on a solution to their land tenure, but that, moreover, they shall be given financial support to increase agricultural production. Furthermore, this implies, *inter alia*, that greater international food assistance over a more extended time than originally anticipated will be required.

62. Both sides have contributed to the delays. The original contracts for land legalization did not conform to the agreements and had to be changed. The number of landholders is likely to be significantly higher than the ceiling of 25,000 stipulated in the agreement. Not all plots of land identified meet expectations—in fact some of them have been rejected by FMLN. FMLN, on its part, has experienced a variety of difficulties in submitting the required lists of names and identification numbers of their demobilized recipients. Six months after the programme started, lists have yet to be presented for 97 of the 196 properties negotiated.

63. Another serious problem causing delay has been the slow and complicated procedure for the legal transfer of land under the direction of the Lands Bank (*Banco de Tierras*). Consisting of 17 stages, the procedure derives from laws which in some cases are 50 years old and requires some very time-consuming steps. The Government has been working with ONUSAL and FMLN, and USAID and EC as donors, to accelerate the procedure.

64. Another source of concern is that to date the Government, despite several requests, has still not provided ONUSAL with information on the process as it relates to FAES, in particular on the negotiations between FAES and the Lands Bank. Consequently, the Mission has neither been able to verify the lists of beneficiaries nor observe the negotiations related to the buying and selling of properties and the determination of the number of beneficiaries, as it has done in the case of FMLN ex-combatants. ONUSAL has received assurances from the Government that it will provide such information.

65. The issue of greatest concern refers to the relocation of landholders occupying plots of land whose owners do not wish to sell. This practice departs from the letter, and is certainly inconsistent with the intention and the spirit, of the 13 October agreement which provides that landholders occupying lands which cannot be purchased will be relocated last. The rationale for this was based on the Peace Agreement, which stipulates that combatants of both sides were to have priority and were to be given land as they demobilized, and that landholders were not to be evicted from the land they presently occupied until a solution could be found to relocate them.

66. For different reasons, both the Government and FMLN have chosen instead to relocate landholders on land whose owners are not willing to sell. Given the financial and land constraints, this is detrimental to other potential beneficiaries. The Government is under pressure from landowners who want to recover their land after so many years of not having access to it. FMLN has been under pressure from those occupying plots of land whose owners do not want to sell, because they cannot produce without access to credit and feel pressured to leave the

land. At the same time some FMLN ex-combatants have not been willing to accept State lands offered by the Government in the expectation of getting private land closer to their families who live elsewhere. Thus, for reasons which may be expedient in the short term both sides have accepted a reversal of the sequence and an alteration of the logic of the 13 October agreement by giving priority to the relocation of landholders. This could well compromise the success of a programme which was already quite ambitious in its original conception.

67. The relocation of landholders at this stage, when hardly 22 per cent of the potential beneficiaries have negotiated the purchase of land, will put unnecessary pressure on the land transfer programme and might even cause its failure. If landowners perceive that they can get rid of people occupying their land, they will be less likely to sell or they might demand higher prices (prices more in keeping with those of unoccupied land). This is likely to create four types of problems: (a) insufficient land for all prospective beneficiaries; (b) an increased need for financial resources to finance the programme; (c) if beneficiaries have to pay very high prices for their land, servicing their debt will become very difficult; and (d) transfer of land to demobilized members of FMLN and the Armed Forces will have to be delayed because of lack of financial resources.

68. Given the prices negotiated to date with private owners ($750 on average and rising, in comparison with the $600 prevailing before the programme started), there will not be enough financial resources available to carry out the first two phases. For the third phase $105 million will be needed rather than the $85 million estimated earlier. The distortion which is occurring in the implementation of the land programme will inevitably have a deleterious effect on efforts to obtain external financial assistance, which are already proving exceedingly difficult, a problem which will be addressed in section X.

69. The credit available has not only been insufficient for the purchase of land but also for housing and crop-raising. A recent study conducted by ECLAC at my request has found that even under the most optimistic assumptions regarding productivity, production costs and market prices, the vast majority of beneficiaries of land transfers who limit land use to grain production could not generate enough income on their plots to cover the basic needs of their families and the servicing of their debt. This means that most beneficiaries of land transfers who do not diversify into more productive crops will have to look for additional income during the fallow months, mostly as wage earners in labour-intensive export crops during the harvest period. Medium-term credit and technical assistance would allow beneficiaries to diversify into more profitable activities.

B. *Forum for Economic and Social Consultation*

70. On 22 February 1993, a landmark agreement was signed at the Forum by representatives of the Government, business and labour, whereby the right of labour to associate was effectively recognized for the first time. The agreement also established the principle of a tripartite mechanism for agreeing on ways to deal with labour conflicts. On 14 April, the Forum created a commission to facilitate the examination of 29 International Labour Organisation conventions proposed for adoption by the labour sector. Unfortunately, a stalemate has developed on four of the conventions being analysed for subsequent ratification; these relate to the right of labour to organize. This set-back threatens to obstruct work at the Forum, where discussions on the Labour Code are still pending.

C. *Reintegration programmes*

71. The Peace Agreement established that the main objective of the National Reconstruction Plan would be the development of the former zones of conflict, satisfaction of the most immediate needs of the population hardest hit by the conflict, and the reconstruction of damaged infrastructure. The Reconstruction Plan also provides for the taking of measures to facilitate the reintegration into civilian life of FMLN ex-combatants and war-disabled. In this context, the programmes set up by the Government for the reintegration of close to 11,000 FMLN ex-combatants in the above two categories are under way, as outlined below.

72. Concerning short-term programmes, the distribution of agricultural tools and basic household goods was completed at the end of April 1993; the agricultural training programme, coordinated by UNDP, was completed in mid-April; and the programme for industrial and services training, temporarily suspended pending the allocation of more funds, is likely to continue up to August 1993.

73. As regards other programmes, the Government and FMLN have agreed to an interest rate of 14 per cent, which is below market rates, for micro-business ventures and agricultural activities. Agricultural credit will be granted to all beneficiaries who have completed negotiations for the purchase of land, even if they have not yet received their final deed. Discussions held between the Government and potential donors, with ONUSAL participation, on the funding of fellowships for high-level studies resulted in an agreement to start the programme with available AID funds while pledged resources from Germany are being transferred. The programme for housing is not yet under way.

74. Programmes for the war-disabled have encountered difficulties stemming from the failure of both sides to agree on ways to provide long-term rehabilitation. The

urgency of agreeing on and implementing such programmes was highlighted by the tragic events of 20 May in San Salvador. The medical programme suffered a three-month interruption (from February to April) as a result of disagreements between the two sides on the selection of personnel for the running of the programme and of the delay in equipping the hospital. The implementation of the Law on the Fund for the Protection of War Disabled is dependent on the Government's handing over its initial financial contribution on 22 June, to the Board of Directors, which should have been sworn in at the end of April. The European Community is also contributing approximately $46,000 to the project on registration of potential beneficiaries of the Fund. ONUSAL has had no access to the implementation of programmes for the reintegration of FAES ex-combatants nor to information as to the financial compensation established for troops discharged as a result of the Peace Agreement.

75. A programme for the reintegration of former officers and medium-rank commanders of FMLN was agreed on 4 February 1993. It covers a maximum of 600 beneficiaries and provides for training, subsistence allowance, credit for production ventures and housing. UNDP, which is administering the training and technical assistance part of this programme, began its work in April with a view to effecting the final phase of the programme by 14 June.

VII. Political participation by FMLN

76. Soon after being granted full legal status as a political party, FMLN ended its former military structure and adopted that of a political organization. A national committee of 15 members—three for each of the five groups—took over the leadership from the former five-member General Command (*Comandancia General*). A Coordinator General, Mr. Schafik Handal, was appointed with authority to represent FMLN as a political party.

77. FMLN has established a large number of party offices in municipalities throughout El Salvador. It has also held meetings to enrol new members. Local assemblies have been held and departmental conventions are to commence towards the beginning of June. At a national convention scheduled for the end of June, decisions will be taken concerning campaign strategy and tactics for the forthcoming elections, including party alliances and selection of candidates. This consultation process is developing in an atmosphere where freedom of expression is fully respected.

78. Draft legislation on special protection for high-risk personalities, which will provide appropriate security to the leadership of FMLN as well as that of other parties, was unanimously approved in COPAZ but is still await-ing consideration by the Legislative Assembly. The Government has given approval to the import of vehicles by FMLN, but action is still pending on the issuance of the required permits (*franquicias*).

79. Under the agreement of 22 December 1992, the Government had undertaken to assign to FMLN a series of radio and television frequencies by 15 January 1993. This has been partially implemented with the assignment of four frequencies (three FM and one AM), two of which have been activated. However, FMLN has not been assigned any frequencies for UHF television or short-wave radio broadcasts.

VIII. Restoration of public administration in the former zones of conflict

80. An advance of special significance is that public administration has now been fully restored in the former zones of conflict. As the members of the Council will recall, this process took place in two stages. When the Peace Agreement was signed, 68 of the 262 mayors of El Salvador were away from their jurisdictions. Soon after the signing of the Agreement, 24 of them returned to these and were followed soon afterwards by almost the same number of judges. Opposition by local community organizations to the return of the remainder of the mayors and resistance by the latter to negotiating with the former on a framework for their return effectively halted the process. Under arrangements subsequently negotiated by ONUSAL, 42 of the 44 mayors returned to their jurisdictions by mid-February 1993. Similarly, most of the judges have also returned, with the exception of a few who have been unable to do so for lack of adequate premises in which to carry out their functions.

81. By mid-April 1993 all the mayors who had returned had organized public town meetings (*cabildos abiertos*) for the purpose of identifying projects for the reconstruction of their communities. In addition, these meetings served to elect representatives to municipal reconstruction and development commissions (*comisiones de reconstrucción y desarrollo*) made up of the mayor and his municipal council and an equal number of members elected by the community. One of the commissions' main functions is to select for financing by the Secretariat for National Reconstruction the most important reconstruction projects from among those put forward by the townspeople. Through this procedure, nearly 400 projects were submitted to the Secretariat for National Reconstruction between 15 October 1992 and 16 April 1993. Funds have been earmarked for this purpose in the National Reconstruction Plan. However, according to information received by ONUSAL, the Secretariat has to date disbursed funds for only a small number of the projects requested. ONUSAL expects the Government to

take urgent steps to accelerate the feasibility studies for these projects and their financing, as delays are creating resentment and frustration among those who have helped to reconcile the communities most divided by the war but are unable to initiate reconstruction for lack of support.

IX. Electoral system

82.   In December 1992, the Legislative Assembly approved by consensus a new Electoral Code the text of which had required protracted discussions in COPAZ. In a letter addressed to me by President Cristiani on 8 January 1993, the Government of El Salvador formally requested United Nations observation of the elections for the presidency, the Legislative Assembly, mayors and municipal councils, due in March 1994. The process would encompass the period prior to, during and after the elections. On 26 January, I informed the Security Council of the request (S/25241), pointing out that these would be the first elections to be held after the end of the armed conflict and that they would mark the culmination of the peace process. I urged the Security Council to accede to this request.

83.   A technical mission visited El Salvador from 18 to 28 April. The purpose of the mission was to define the terms of reference, concept of operations and financial implications of expanding the ONUSAL mandate to include the observation of the electoral process. During its visit, the technical mission held several meetings with the Supreme Electoral Tribunal, COPAZ and the political parties. Its report—the main findings of which are summarized below—is available to the Council upon request.

A. *Main findings of the mission*

84.   Based on prior experience in Nicaragua, Haiti, Angola and Eritrea, United Nations observation requires wide geographical and chronological coverage in order to monitor the conformity of electoral practice to patterns implicit in free and fair elections. This fosters acceptance among all concerned of the legitimacy of the process and its final outcome. In El Salvador, the task will be greatly facilitated by the knowledge and experience that ONUSAL has accumulated since its inception in July 1991.

85.   The main areas of concern identified by the technical mission revolve around the serious inadequacies of the existing electoral roll and the difficulties encumbering the timely issue of electoral documents. The foremost deficiencies are:

(a)   The large number of names belonging to expatriates or to dead persons; and insufficient controls at the national level to avoid double registration. Although both factors could result in multiple voting, that risk can be minimized through controls made possible by the new

equipment available to the Data Processing Centre, and through procedures that effectively prevent any person from voting more than once, such as the use of indelible ink.

(b)   Differences between the names included in the electoral rolls and those in the electoral cards, and/or persons with valid electoral cards whose names did not appear in the electoral rolls. These resulted in a considerable number of citizens not being able to exercise their right to vote at the legislative and municipal elections of March 1991.

(c)   There is a large number of citizens who are not included in the electoral roster. Although no reliable data are available, it is estimated that about one third of the potential voters are not included in the electoral rolls or do not have a valid electoral card. As electoral registration is voluntary in El Salvador, it would be unrealistic to expect the electoral rolls to provide a full coverage. However, there are clear indications that this large percentage of non-registered voters cannot be attributed to lack of interest, but rather to problems in the registration process. Abundant circumstantial evidence exists that problems in this area are massive. In many cases, potential voters are required to go to the registration centres repeatedly before obtaining their document which, despite the 30-day time-limit established by law, is frequently issued with several months' delay. In some cases, registration is denied because validation cannot be achieved owing to the fact that the electoral authorities have not been able to obtain or process the person's birth certificate.

(d)   In order to detect and correct existing mistakes, the Supreme Electoral Tribunal launched a campaign which failed to produce significant results. However, although the campaign was not aimed at increasing registration, the number of requests for registration more than tripled during the campaign. This unexpected result indicates what could be achieved by a massive effort to increase the number of registered voters. Operational adjustments to registration procedures and a well-designed campaign conceived to reduce drastically the number of non-registered citizens are essential pre-conditions for achieving a broad consensus on the legitimacy of the electoral process.

86.   One of the daunting problems faced by both the electoral authorities and the observation mission is the scarcity of reliable data. Adequate data on the number of non-registered voters would be available through questions included in the sample (*muestra de verificación*) used by the census authorities to verify the census data. But it will be necessary to improve the information on the factors restricting registration so that the registration drives organized by the electoral authorities are based on solid grounds. It would also be important to improve the

knowledge and understanding of the registration process. This would allow the electoral authorities to improve their case when explaining to the public the reasons for the failure to provide adequate responses to requests for registration. The improved information will also help to avoid a large number of requests in the few weeks before the closing of registration. It will also permit the establishment of a factual starting-point for the observation process.

87. Political parties represented by their Secretaries-General in the inter-party commission (*Interpartidaria*) have conveyed their concerns about the registration process to the Supreme Electoral Tribunal and urged the establishment and effective functioning of the Board of Vigilance of the political parties which, in accordance with the Electoral Code, should closely monitor the work of the Tribunal.

B. *Terms of reference*

88. The electoral component of ONUSAL should observe the electoral process before, during and after the elections in order to:

(a) Verify that measures and decisions taken by all electoral authorities are impartial and consistent with the holding of free and fair elections;

(b) Verify that appropriate steps are taken so that qualified citizens are included in the electoral roster, thus enabling them to exercise their right to vote;

(c) Verify that mechanisms are in place effectively to prevent multiple voting, given the unfeasibility of screening of the electoral roll prior to the elections;

(d) Verify that freedom of expression, organization, movement and assembly are respected without restrictions;

(e) Verify that potential voters have sufficient knowledge of the mechanisms for participating in the election;

(f) Examine, analyse and assess criticisms made, objections raised and attempts undertaken to de-legitimize the electoral process and, when required, convey such information to the Supreme Electoral Tribunal;

(g) Inform the Supreme Electoral Tribunal of complaints received regarding irregularities in electoral advertising or possible interferences with the electoral process; when appropriate, require information on corrective measures taken;

(h) Place observers at every polling site on election day to verify that the right to vote is fully respected;

(i) Assist the Special Representative of the Secretary-General in preparing periodic reports to the Secretary-General, who will in turn inform the Supreme Electoral Tribunal and report to the Security Council as necessary.

89. In carrying out its functions, the Electoral Division, under the overall authority of my Special Representative, will coordinate its activities with those of the Human Rights, Police and Military Divisions in their respective spheres of competence.

C. *Concept of operations*

90. In order to carry out these duties, I recommend that an Electoral Division be established as part of ONUSAL in five stages, as follows:

1. 1 to 30 June 1993. Preparatory stage, devoted to organization at the central and regional levels;

2. 1 July to 15 December 1993. Main tasks would be verifying citizens' registration and following political activities;

3. 16 December 1993 to 14 March 1994. Efforts should concentrate on observation of the electoral campaign;

4. 15 to 31 March 1994. Observation of the elections, counting of votes and announcement of results;

5. 1 to 30 April. Observation of a possible second round of elections for the presidency. (Should the first round yield a definitive result, the activities of the Division would conclude on 31 March 1994.)

91. The main tasks of the electoral observers would be to monitor electoral irregularities, receive complaints and convey them, as appropriate, to electoral authorities; observe political meetings and demonstrations; follow up and assess electoral advertising and electoral-related reporting in the media. The information thus collected should be the basis for analysing trends and acting upon them as required. These activities should be carried out in close coordination with the Human Rights and Police Divisions.

92. On election day, the number of observers should increase so as to permit monitoring at every polling site. The mission should verify the counting of votes and make projections for its own use and possibly for sharing with the Supreme Electoral Tribunal.

93. The electoral observation would continue after election day to cover all aspects related to the counting of votes and possible challenges to results. The observation would conclude with the official proclamation of final results by the Supreme Electoral Tribunal.

X. Economic and financial implications of implementing the peace accords: the need to support post-conflict peace-building

94. National reconciliation and the consolidation of peace in El Salvador demand that the Peace Accords be implemented. While this requires the political will of

the parties, financing is also critical to the success of programmes directly related to the Accords whose objective is to consolidate the peace. This applies particularly to programmes for the reintegration of ex-combatants into the economic, social and political life of the country; the creation of new institutions and the modernization of others that are essential for the construction and strengthening of a democratic society; emergency aid to poverty-ridden sectors of the population, especially in the former conflict areas; and the rehabilitation of infrastructure and basic services damaged or interrupted as a result of the conflict.

95.   At the same time as El Salvador is consolidating peace on the basis of the Peace Accords, it is carrying out a stabilization and structural reform programme to improve its productive capacity and the welfare of a large segment of the population which has been severely affected by years of war. Reconciling the two processes is problematical since the financing of the many peace-related programmes has economic and financial implications that often conflict with efforts to stabilize the economy.

96.   At the Consultative Group Meeting of donor countries that took place in Paris in April this year, the Government requested financing for priority programmes which are an integral and indispensable component of the framework for peace. These included programmes for the reinsertion of ex-combatants into productive activities and those relating to the strengthening of democratic institutions. The Government also requested financing for poverty alleviation, both in areas covered by the National Reconstruction Plan and in others. Excluding the latter, the financing needed for programmes directly related to the Peace Agreement amounts to close to $1.2 billion. Of this total the Government had already committed over $300 million and the international community less than $300 million and there was a gap of about $600 million that remained to be filled.

97.   Because of the urgency of financing these projects, the Government requested quick-disbursing funds which could be channelled directly or through "cofinancing" or "parallel financing" of policy-based loans. In addition to the advantage of quick financing, this would have given the Government flexibility in financing its priority projects. At the request of the parties, I wrote to the foreign ministers of donor countries supporting the Government's request and reaffirming my belief that the success of the programmes to which the Government must attribute high priority and for which financing has been requested is essential to the building and consolidation of peace.

98.   The response of the donor community has not yet lived up to expectations. Although pledges were slightly more than the $800 million gap which the Government was trying to finance in the period 1993-1996, donors showed a clear preference for financing specific projects, mostly in infrastructure and the environment. Thus, of the close to $600 million gap for programmes resulting from the Peace Accords, very little external financing is envisioned. For this year alone, $220 million will be needed for the reinsertion of ex-combatants into productive activities (purchase of land, agricultural credit, housing, credit for small enterprises, pensions for the disabled, etc.) and for the promotion of democratic institutions (National Civil Police, National Public Security Academy, human-rights-related activities, the judiciary, and activities related to the coming elections).

99.   Implementation of the agreements should not, however, be conditioned on the availability of foreign financing. Should there be a shortfall in this type of financing, as there will probably be, the Government will need to make adjustments in its economic programme. The study by ECLAC (see para. 69 above) found that there seems to be some room for flexibility as regards some of the targets imposed by the stabilization programme. In particular, a less restrictive ceiling on public expenditures and on the use of international monetary reserves could be adopted. At the same time, the Government needs to strengthen its fragile fiscal situation, particularly by discouraging tax evasion and reallocating expenditure, so as to make it more compatible with times of peace. While it is clear that the Government needs to make a further effort, the support of the international community in this post-conflict peace-building phase is essential.

XI. Financial aspects

100.   By its resolution 47/223 of 16 March 1993, the General Assembly authorized the Secretary-General to enter into commitments for the operation of ONUSAL, subject to the review by the Security Council of the mandate of the Mission, at a rate not to exceed $2.9 million gross ($2.7 million net) per month for the period beyond 31 May 1993. This authorization is subject to the prior concurrence of the Advisory Committee on Administrative and Budgetary Questions.

101.   The cost of maintaining ONUSAL during the extension period, including the strengthening of the Mission to include verification of the general elections, will entail additional expenses. A preliminary cost estimate of the establishment of the electoral component of the Mission will be provided in an addendum to the present report.

102.   As of 7 May 1993, unpaid assessed contributions to the ONUCA/ONUSAL special account for the period from inception through 31 May 1993 amounted to $26,762,272.

XII. Observations

103. I am glad to be able to report to the Security Council that, 16 months after the cease-fire took effect, the peace process in El Salvador has advanced significantly and is on course. Among its achievements are full respect by both parties for a prolonged cease-fire, the celebration of the formal end of the armed conflict on 15 December 1992, and the conversion of FMLN from an armed movement into a political party. As a result, two of the major goals of the Peace Accords were achieved.

104. This success has been accompanied by significant progress towards other principal objectives—the establishment of civilian control over the military, the beginnings of the establishment of a civilian police force, the reunification of Salvadorian society and the democratization of national institutions, with full respect for human rights. Both the Government of El Salvador and FMLN have demonstrated will and determination to resolve their country's problems democratically through political means, abandoning armed confrontation and conflict. They deserve recognition for accepting what seemed to both of them at times the risks of ending the armed conflict and allowing the Salvadorian people to decide democratically how they should be governed.

105. As the preceding sections of this report indicate, the path to national reconciliation has not been without difficulties. These have arisen partly from the inevitable polarization and distrust, partly from conflicting interpretations of the Peace Accords, partly from efforts by each side to extract the maximum advantage from implementation of these accords and partly from the inability of administrative structures on both sides to handle the demands of implementing complex agreements which reach into the very heart of the country's society and economy. Yet the predominating characteristic of the Salvadorian peace process has been its irreversibility.

106. At the same time, problems still exist. Efforts are required to ensure that they do not become obstacles to the continuing fulfilment of the two parties' undertakings. Both sides must intensify their joint efforts, with the support of ONUSAL, to accelerate the lands transfer programme so that the reintegration of former combatants into civilian life is expeditiously effected and a fair solution is found for those who occupied land during the war years. The establishment of a major new national institution, the National Civil Police, which has been bedeviled by delays, uncertainties and departures from the Accords, must also proceed quickly.

107. In the field of law and order, there are two points where special efforts are required from the Government. One is to begin the phasing out of the National Police, to which the Peace Agreement assigned only a transitory role, pending deployment of the National Civil Police. As indicated above, the continued strengthening of the National Police is inconsistent with the Accords and with the role of the National Civil Police as the only police authority in the country. This is a particularly sensitive issue in the context of the forthcoming elections.

108. The second is the recovery of assault weapons, of which large numbers remain in unauthorized hands. This aspect, too, could raise tensions during the electoral process, apart from contributing unnecessarily to the high level of common crime. I call upon the Government of El Salvador to fulfil both of these undertakings. They are major elements of the Peace Accords and their neglect would endanger the country's democratization and stability.

109. I am glad to be able to confirm to the Council that the long-delayed implementation of the recommendations of the Ad Hoc Commission on the purification of the Armed Forces is now on its way to completion, as reported to the Security Council in my letter of 2 April 1993 (S/25516). I wish to express my high appreciation to the members of the Commission, Dr. Abraham Rodriguez, Dr. Eduardo Molina Olivares and Dr. Reynaldo Galindo Pohl for having so conscientiously discharged a difficult duty to their country.

110. The question of implementing the recommendations of the Commission on the Truth has given rise to controversy and remains outstanding. This is another central element of the Peace Accords and is essential to the sometimes painful process of national reconciliation which is so vital to the building of peace. It is critical to the process that the parties should exercise leadership in this regard, in conformity with their commitment under the Peace Accords. As reported above, I am communicating to the Government and FMLN, as well as to COPAZ, which has a central role in this matter, my analysis of the action which has to be taken if I am to be able to confirm to the Security Council that the parties have fulfilled their solemn commitment to carry out the Commission's recommendations. Meanwhile, I wish to express my gratitude to the members of the Commission, Dr. Belisario Betancur, Dr. Reinaldo Figueredo and Prof. Thomas Buergenthal, for their singular devotion to their complex and delicate task.

111. The Commission on the Truth has drawn attention to flaws which still exist in the judicial system. These inhibited the Commission from recommending that the results of its investigation should be referred to the judiciary. While some reforms have been carried out, the Constitutional and legislative reforms enacted since April 1991 did not fully reflect the agreements reached in Mexico that month. The implementation of the recommendations of the Commission on the Truth in this

respect will go a long way to repairing this problem and should be given priority.

112. The elections in 1994 are likely to be the culminating point of the entire peace process. It is only when the Salvadorian people have been able to choose their President, their representatives in the Legislative Assembly and their mayors, through free and fair elections, that peace will have been consolidated in El Salvador. This presupposes an electoral process which enables all qualified Salvadorians to vote and which is free of any intimidation against parties or voters. The Supreme Electoral Tribunal has a heavy responsibility to ensure the registration of all who want to vote, the ability of all parties to campaign freely and the impartial conduct of a fair election. Much remains to be done, especially as regards registration, and the Tribunal will receive full cooperation from ONUSAL should the Security Council approve my recommendation that the Mission be authorized to observe the electoral process.

113. It is to be emphasized, however, that the successful conclusion of this peace process can be achieved only if the necessary financing is forthcoming. As has been made clear in various sections of the present report, two of the programmes—those relating to land and the new police force—do not at present have an adequate basis of financial support. Yet they are central to the Peace Accords and their failure or curtailment could threaten all that has been achieved. This state of affairs requires an urgent response both from the international donor community and from the Government. The Government's request at the Consultative Group Meeting in Paris last month for peace-related projects, which had my full support, did not receive the response which had been hoped, with the result that the problem has become acute. Further appeals for international support will be made. But this situation will have underlined to the Government that the implementation of the Peace Accords cannot depend entirely on external financing; it is the Government's responsibility, both as signatory to the Accords and as the Government of El Salvador, to define fiscal policies and public expenditure priorities which will enable it to fulfil its commitment to full implementation of the Accords.

114. In the light of the considerations and observations presented in this report, I recommend to the Security Council that it renew until 30 November 1993 the mandate of ONUSAL, and that it authorize the addition to it of an Electoral Division to observe the elections. It would be my intention to recommend, by that date, a further renewal of the Mission's mandate to enable it to complete its verification of the elections and to remain in El Salvador for a short transition period immediately thereafter.

115. At a time when all other continents are experiencing savage conflict and massive violation of human rights, the reconciliation and acceptance of pluralism in El Salvador is a remarkable example to the world. I pay tribute to the parties to the Peace Accords, especially to President Cristiani and the FMLN leadership, and to all Salvadorians, for their response to the opportunity now offered to them to escape from the suffering and losses of long years of war and to rebuild peace in their country.

116. I also wish to express my appreciation to the United Nations agencies in El Salvador and to the non-governmental organizations that have contributed to the peace process, as well as to all the members of ONUSAL for their dedicated efforts, under the direction of my Special Representatives, Mr. Iqbal Riza and, now, Mr. Augusto Ramírez-Ocampo, to restore peace and reconciliation in El Salvador.

Document 75

Report of the Secretary-General concerning the expansion of ONUSAL's mandate to include an Electoral Division

S/25812/Add.1, 24 May 1993

Addendum

1. As I indicated in the main part of the present report, it is my intention to enlarge the United Nations Observer Mission in El Salvador (ONUSAL) to include an electoral component for the purpose of observing and verifying the Salvadorian general elections scheduled for March 1994 until the proclamation of final results by the Supreme Electoral Tribunal of El Salvador. This is in response, as outlined in the main report, to the request of the Government of El Salvador.

2. In order to permit ONUSAL to carry out these expanded responsibilities it will be necessary to add an Electoral Division which will operate within the framework of the existing regional offices. These offices will require a total of 38 international personnel, including administrative support staff, and 7 local staff.

3. During the polling itself, 900 electoral observers will be required. Of these, it is anticipated that 320 will come from existing personnel of ONUSAL, 330 from the United Nations Development Programme (UNDP), other United Nations agency personnel in El Salvador and volunteers from selected non-governmental organizations, and the remaining 250 from the United Nations Secretariat and/or Member States. There will also be additional requirements for premises, transport operations, communication and miscellaneous equipment, supplies and services, and public information programmes.

4. Should the Security Council decide to expand the mandate of ONUSAL as set out in the main part of the present report, it is estimated that the additional cost of the expansion for the 11-month period from 1 June 1993 until 30 April 1994 would be approximately $7 million. A breakdown of the estimated cost by main categories of expenditure is provided for information purposes in the annex to the present addendum.

5. It would be my recommendation to the General Assembly, should the Security Council decide to expand the mandate of ONUSAL, that the additional cost relating thereto should be considered an expense to the Organization to be borne by Member States in accordance with Article 17, paragraph 2, of the Charter of the United Nations and that the assessments to be levied on Member States should be credited to the ONUSAL special account.

Annex

Cost estimates of the expansion of the United Nations Observer Mission in El Salvador (ONUSAL) from 1 June 1993 to 30 April 1994

(Thousands of United States dollars)

Civilian personnel, including travel to the mission area	5 940
Premises, rental and maintenance	50
Vehicle operations	65
Communications	50
Miscellaneous equipment	40
Miscellaneous supplies, services, freight and support costs	525
Public information programmes	350
TOTAL	7 020

Document 76

Report of the Secretary-General containing a summary of proposals relating to land transfers

S/25812/Add.2, 25 May 1993

Addendum

1. Part VI A of the Secretaty-General's report dated 21 May 1993 (S/25812) contains a number of references to the proposal of 13 October 1992 on land transfers. This proposal was made to the Government and to the Frente Farabundo Martí para la Liberación Nacional (FMLN) and accepted separately within a few days by each of the two parties. It is a supplement to the peace accords signed in Mexico City on 16 January 1992 and should be deemed an integral part of those accords.

2. In order to facilitate the Security Council's consideration of the report, the text of the proposal, together with a summary, is circulated herewith for the information of the members of the Security Council.

Annex I

I. *Introduction*

1. The proposal in this document is being made within the framework of United Nations verification of compliance by both Parties with the agreements between the Government of El Salvador and the Frente Farabundo Martí para la Liberación Nacional (FMLN) as at 15 September 1992, according to the timetable adjusted on 19 August 1992.

2. After examining the agricultural situation in El Salvador, the short-term availability of and future prospects for land and financial resources, the economic constraints facing the country and the conditions imposed by donor countries, and taking into account the needs of former combatants of both parties and of current landholders in conflict zones, the Secretary-General is submitting the following proposal for the implementation of the relevant parts of the agreements.

II. *Considerations*

A. *Potential beneficiaries*

3. Former combatants of FMLN and the Salvadorian armed forces aged 16 years or over on D-Day (1 February 1992) will be beneficiaries of the land trans-

fer, irrespective of their family situation. Landholders of lands within former conflict zones, as defined in the Agreement, including returnees living in these zones, would also be beneficiaries.

4. Land will be transferred to a maximum of 47,500 people (broken down approximately as follows: 7,500 former combatants of FMLN, including the war-disabled; 15,000 former combatants of the Salvadorian armed forces; and 25,000 landholders).

B. *Size of lots*

5. Taking into account the various factors which determine the viability of a plot of land for supporting a family, such as soil type, productive potential, type of production, technology, employment, market, infrastructure, etc., it has been decided to apply the criterion of the Salvadorian Institute for Agrarian Reform (ISTA) whereby the size of a lot varies according to soil type as follows:

Type of soil	Size
I-II	2 manzanas
III-IV	3 manzanas
V-VI	5 manzanas
VII-VIII	7 manzanas

According to this criterion, 2 manzanas of soil types I and II would be equivalent to 5 manzanas of types V and VI.

6. If landowners are willing to sell, landholders will remain on the lots they currently occupy, provided these are no larger than the maximum established in the above table and no smaller than half that size. If they are resettled, they would be assigned equivalent land using the same criteria.

C. *Payment terms and award of land*

7. The Government of El Salvador will have to ensure that former combatants of both Parties and landholders are able to secure the amount of land indicated above.

8. Based on the average price paid by the Land Bank, total estimated resources will be sufficient to purchase the amounts of land specified. Measures would be taken to protect the market against speculation.

9. With regard to the payment terms for beneficiaries, the terms laid down by the agrarian reform (payment over 30 years, 6 per cent annual interest rate and 4-year grace period) are considered acceptable. If revolving funds are established, efforts will be made to ensure that the benefits are distributed equitably.

10. The decision as to whether land should be awarded on an individual or group basis should, in principle, rest with beneficiaries, bearing in mind that beneficiaries of the agrarian reform are clearly given this choice. In the case of lands purchased through the Land Bank, the *pro indiviso* formula could be used if some

buyers want to form associations. Both the associative and the *pro indiviso* formulas will expedite the transfer and assignment of lands. However, in some cases it may be necessary to comply with the conditions laid down by donor countries for the use of resources.

III. *Consequences*

A. *Total land required and land currently available*

11. For the purpose of calculating land requirements and taking into account the distribution of the different lands in El Salvador, the average size of the lots to be awarded will be taken to be 5 manzanas. Given the number of potential beneficiaries, between 175,000 and 237,500 manzanas would be required, depending on whether landholders have, on average, the minimum or the maximum permitted number of manzanas.

12. Available land is estimated at 85,000 manzanas. This includes State lands already verified (25,000 manzanas), lands in excess of 245 hectares (13,000 manzanas), lands offered for sale to the Land Bank in the municipalities given priority under the National Reconstruction Plan (27,000 manzanas) and lands offered for sale to the Land Bank in the rest of the country (20,000 manzanas).

13. The total land available will be determined once the Special Agrarian Commission of the National Commission for the Consolidation of Peace (COPAZ) has completed verification of the land inventory submitted by FMLN.

B. *Total resources required and resources currently available*

14. Using as a basis the average price of sales conducted through the Land Bank up to 31 August 1992, namely $600 per manzana, the total resources required would be between $105 million and $143 million. The amount actually disbursed will be less if more State lands become available.

15. Resources of approximately $46 million will become available between now and February 1993, comprising external funding ($23 million) and internal funding equivalent to the estimated value of State lands ($23 million). Additional external resources totalling $12 million would become available in February 1993.

16. As the programme advances and lands are transferred, the Secretary-General will use his good offices to support efforts to obtain additional financial resources as a substantive contribution to the peace process.

C. *Phases for the land transfer*

17. The Government of El Salvador will draw up a land transfer programme immediately according to the following timetable:

(a) *First phase (emergency plan)*: October 1992 to January 1993. During the first phase, which would cover approximately 15,400 beneficiaries, priority will be given to former combatants of FMLN, who would obtain all the land still available once the situation of current landholders had been legalized. Land would be assigned to former combatants in the following order:

(i) Forty-two State properties which have already been verified (where there are already landholders);

(ii) Other State properties (ISTA or others);

(iii) At the same time, negotiations would be conducted for private properties: those already verified (63 out of 115), those on the FMLN inventory giving priority to the list of 537) and those already offered to the Land Bank.

The $46 million available in this phase would make it possible to transfer 77,000 manzanas at an average price of $600 per manzana. This involves 38,000 manzanas of State-owned land of an estimated value of $23 million and the purchase of 38,500 manzanas.

(b) *Second phase*: February to April 1993, subject to land availability. During this phase, $12 million would be available for the purchase of 20,000 manzanas. Lands totalling 8,000 manzanas would be available and an additional 12,000 manzanas would be required. Using the same average price, it would be possible to transfer land to a maximum of 4,000 beneficiaries, of whom 1,600 could be settled immediately while the remaining 2,400 would have to wait until the additional 12,000 manzanas became available. On lands where the situation of current landholders has not been legalized, land would be divided equally between former combatants of FMLN, if there are any left over from the first phase, and former combatants of the Salvadorian armed forces.

(c) The *third phase* would begin once the second phase was complete. In this phase, land would be assigned to the remaining 28,100 beneficiaries. Approximately 140,500 manzanas would have to be purchased, for which $85 million in additional funding would be required.

Former combatants of the Salvadorian armed forces will obtain land where there are no landholders until they have all been settled. Thereafter, landholders on lands whose owners do not wish to sell will be resettled.

18. In order to guarantee the tenure of beneficiaries who have been awarded land, pending completion of the entire legalization process, it is recommended that all beneficiaries be given temporary deeds of transfer as provisional title to the land.

19. Vigorous efforts and good faith on the Government's part will be needed to meet these targets. To permit the rapid transfer of lands, mainly through purchase and

sale contracts, it is recommended that the operational capacity of the Land Bank and ISTA and of the Financiera Nacional de Tierras Agrícolas (FINATA) be strengthened if necessary. It is assumed that the Government of El Salvador would bear the operating costs. Technical assistance in implementing the land transfer programme could be requested from the World Bank and the Food and Agriculture Organization of the United Nations (FAO).

D. *Organizational plan*

20. In view of the exceptional nature of the land transfer programme under the Peace Agreement and the urgent need to implement it, a management and coordination unit should be set up as the executive authority for directing and coordinating the action of the Ministry of Agriculture and Livestock. ISTA, the Land Bank and FINATA in all matters related to the implementation of the land transfer programme.

21. In addition, to facilitate implementation of the programme, an oversight committee will have to be set up comprising representatives of the Parties (the Government of El Salvador and FMLN) and of COPAZ (in the person of the acting coordinator of the Special Agrarian Commission). The United Nations Observer Mission in El Salvador (ONUSAL) will also be represented on the committee in order to provide verification and advisory services. The committee's functions will include cross-checking information on landholders and former combatants and monitoring implementation of the programme. It may need an auxiliary body to assist it in identifying lands for purchase and sale and may propose legal, administrative or other measures to facilitate the land transfer.

22. The activities of this committee are without prejudice to the mandate of the Special Agrarian Commission of COPAZ, whose verification work it complements.

23. The chief of the management and coordination unit will immediately begin drawing up the emergency plan to implement the land transfer programme without delay, setting targets and deadlines. This plan, and the overall programme, will be submitted to the above-mentioned oversight committee for consideration to ensure the full cooperation of all parties concerned.

E. *Guarantees after the cessation of the armed conflict*

24. Since the land transfer process will continue after the cessation of the armed conflict is complete, pending a satisfactory legal solution of the definitive land tenure system in conflict zones, the Government will guarantee landholders in these zones that they will not be evicted and that the status quo will be preserved until the situation is resolved. It will inform landowners of this decision, taken within the framework of the Peace Agree-

ment, by means of a widely circulated public notice and, if necessary, will issue a decree to this effect. FMLN, for its part, will do its utmost to prevent any illegal occupation of lands.

25. Former combatants of FMLN will receive a certificate of land transfer entitlement when they are reintegrated into civil, institutional and political life. Former combatants will be able to apply to the oversight committee, through their representatives, to settle any outstanding cases of land transfer.

Annex II

Summary of the land transfer proposal

Relevant considerations

Total number of potential beneficiaries

47,500 maximum (7,500 former combatants of FMLN, 15,000 former combatants of the Salvadorian armed forces, 25,000 landholders).

Size of lots

Type of soil	Size (in manzanas)
I-II	2
III-IV	3
V-VI	5
VII-VIII	7

If landowners are willing to sell, landholders will remain on the lots they currently occupy, provided these are no larger than the maximum size given in the above table and no smaller than half that size.

Total land required (for purposes of calculation, the average size of the lots to be awarded to former combatants will be taken to be 5 manzanas and the average size of landholders' lots will be taken to be between 5 manzanas maximum and 2.5 manzanas minimum):

175,000 to 237,500 manzanas (depending on the average maximum and minimum size of the lots occupied by landholders):

(a) 112,500 manzanas (22,500 x 5 manzanas, taken to be the average size of lots for former combatants);

(b) 62,500 manzanas (25,000 x 2.5 manzanas, taken to be the minimum size of landholders' lots;

(c) 125,000 manzanas (25,000 x 5 manzanas, taken to be the maximum size of landholders' lots).

Value of the land to be transferred (for purposes of calculation, the average price of sales conducted through the Land Bank up to 31 August 1992 will be used.

Namely, $600 at an exchange rate of $1 = 8.5 colones): *$105 to $142 million*

Land available or which could be purchased:

Approximately 85,000 manzanas in four categories:

(a) Verified State lands (25,000 manzanas);

(b) Lands in excess of 245 hectares (13,000 manzanas);

(c) Lands offered to the Land Bank (27,000 manzanas in conflict zones);

(d) Lands offered to the Land Bank (20,000 manzanas outside conflict zones).

Resources which will become available between now and February 1993

External resources:
Immediately available: $23 million (United States Agency for International Development)

Available in February 1993: $12 million (European Economic Community)

Internal resources:
State lands and lands in excess of 245 hectares (38,000 manzanas at $600): $23 million

Three phases of programme implementation:

(a) *First phase*: October 1992-January 1993
Resources available: $46 million

Land which can be purchased: 77,000 manzanas

Beneficiaries: 15,400 people

Distribution of land: Former combatants of FMLN will obtain all land where there are no landholders.

Note: 8,000 manzanas remain available for the second phase (85,000 manzanas minus the 77,000 manzanas used in this phase).

(b) *Second phase*: February to April 1993, subject to land availability.
Resources available: $12 million

Land which can be purchased: 20,000 manzanas

Beneficiaries: A maximum of 4,000 people (of whom 1,600 can be settled immediately on the 8,000 manzanas available; the remaining 2,400 will have to wait until an additional 12,000 manzanas become available).

Distribution of land: All land where there are no landholders will be divided equally between FMLN and the Salvadorian armed forces.

(c) *Third phase*: following completion of the second phase.
Remaining beneficiaries: 28,100 people

Land needing to be purchased: 140,500 manzanas

Additional resources required: $85 million

Distribution of land: Former combatants of the Salvadorian armed forces will obtain land where there are no landholders until they have all been settled. Thereafter, landholders on lands whose owners do not wish to sell will be resettled.

Document 77

Report of the Secretary-General containing an analysis of the recommendations of the Commission on the Truth

S/25812/Add.3, 25 May 1993

Addendum

Section V of the Secretary-General's report dated 21 May 1993 (S/25812) describes the action taken by the Secretary-General in connection with the report of the Commission on the Truth following its submission by the Commission on 15 March 1993. As foreseen in paragraph 55 of the Secretary-General's report, the United Nations analysis of the Commission's recommendations is circulated herewith as a document of the Security Council.

Annex

Analysis of the recommendations contained in the report of the Commission on the Truth

The recommendations contained in the report of the Commission on the Truth are set out below, together with a brief analysis of the measures needed to implement them. In the interests of clarity, the recommendations are listed in the order in which they appear in the report. Each recommendation is accompanied by details of the persons or institutions to whom it is addressed and who would be responsible for its implementation or for taking the appropriate action (for instance, a legislative proposal by the Government; action proposed by the Frente Farabundo Martí para la Liberación Nacional (FMLN) in the National Commission for the Consolidation of Peace (COPAZ)), legislative action required and the time-frame necessary for its implementation.

There are two appendices to this document. The first gives details of the human rights recommendations made by the United Nations Observer Mission in El Salvador (ONUSAL) and taken up in turn by the report of the Commission on the Truth, which calls for their implementation. The second is a working paper listing the principal constitutional or legal provisions that would need to be amended in order to comply with the recommendations.

I. Recommendations inferred directly from the results of the investigation

1. Dismissal from their posts and discharge from the armed forces of officers whose names appear in the report and who are personally implicated in the perpetration or cover-up of the cases reported, or who did not fulfil their professional obligation to initiate or cooperate in the investigation and punishment of serious acts of violence (I.A)

(a) Addressed to: the Government of El Salvador

(b) Legislative action required: an administrative measure

(c) Time-frame: immediate

Remarks: It is our understanding that only 10 of the officers mentioned in the report will remain in active service once implementation of the Ad Hoc Commission's recommendations is complete.

2. Dismissal of civilian officials in the civil service and the judiciary who are named in the report and who, acting in their professional capacity, covered up serious acts of violence or failed to discharge their responsibilities in the investigation of such acts (I.B)

(a) Addressed to: the Government of El Salvador (for civil service officials) and the judiciary (for officials of the judiciary)

(b) Legislative action required: an administrative measure

(c) Time-frame: immediate

Remarks: Three officials of the judiciary are involved: one senior official employed on a temporary contract and two judges.

3. Disqualification by law from holding public office for persons referred to in the above recommendations, and for any other persons implicated in the perpetration of the acts of violence described, including the civilians and members of the FMLN Command named in the findings on individual cases. The persons concerned should be disqualified from holding any public post or office for a period of not less than 10 years, and

should be disqualified permanently from any activity related to public security or national defence (I.C)

(a) Addressed to: the Government of El Salvador, FMLN, COPAZ and the Legislative Assembly.

(b) Legislative action required: no legislative measures possible, only a political decision. Some people have suggested the possibility of a constitutional amendment.

(c) Time-frame: only a political solution is appropriate, possibly in the form of an undertaking adopted within COPAZ or an agreement by COPAZ itself urging the persons named to refrain from holding or applying for any public post.

Remarks: Although the report recommends that COPAZ should prepare a preliminary legislative draft to be submitted to the Legislative Assembly for early approval, such an approach would affect essential provisions of the Constitution relating to political rights. This recommendation conflicts with that made in section III.B.8 of the report, concerning the ratification of international human rights instruments under which citizens cannot be deprived of their political rights in the manner recommended by the Commission on the Truth.

4. Resignation of the current members of the Supreme Court of Justice to enable the constitutional reform concerning the election of judges to the Court to be implemented immediately (I.D.(a))

(a) Addressed to: members of the Supreme Court of Justice

(b) Legislative action required: the resignation of members of the Court

(c) Time-frame: immediate

Remarks: The recommendation is not worded in such a way as to make it binding on the Government of El Salvador. Its implementation depends entirely on the willingness of the members of the Court to resign from their posts; for its part, the full Court has already announced that its members will not resign.

5. Amendment of the National Council of the Judiciary Act so that members of the Council can be dismissed by the Legislative Assembly only for precise legal causes (I.D.(b))

(a) Addressed to: the Government of El Salvador, COPAZ and the Legislative Assembly

(b) Legislative action required: amendment of the National Council of the Judiciary Act

(c) Time-frame: medium term

6. Amendment of the Career Judicial Service Act so that only those judges who, according to a rigorous evaluation made by the National Council of the Judiciary, have demonstrated judicial aptitude, efficiency and concern for human rights and offer every guarantee of independence, judicial discretion, honesty and impartiality in their actions, may remain in the career judicial service (I.E)

(a) Addressed to: the Government of El Salvador, the Legislative Assembly and COPAZ

(b) Legislative action required: inclusion of an appropriate provision in the new Career Judicial Service Act

(c) Time-frame: medium term

Remarks: Under the Constitution, it is the Supreme Court that punishes judges. The Council could only recommend to the Court that penalties be applied.

II. *Eradication of structural causes linked directly to the acts examined*

1. Full implementation of the peace agreements (II)

(a) Addressed to: the Government of El Salvador and FMLN

(b) Legislative action required: none

(c) Time-frame: none

2. Reforms in the armed forces (II.A.)

2.1 Appointment of a special committee of the Legislative Assembly to supervise the transition to the new model of the armed forces (II.A.1,2)

(a) Addressed to: the Legislative Assembly and COPAZ

(b) Legislative action required: a political decision by the Legislative Assembly

(c) Time-frame: immediate

2.2 Comprehensive review of the military legislation in force (II.A.2,3,4)

(a) Addressed to: COPAZ and the Legislative Assembly

(b) Legislative action required: a legislative decree and administrative measures

(c) Time-frame: immediate

Remarks: Legislative measures have already been adopted which include amendments to the relevant articles of the Constitution. Laws have also been adopted on military service and armed forces reserves, the National Public Security Academy, the National Civil Police, the State Intelligence Agency and the Ad Hoc Commission on the armed forces. In addition, the relevant articles of the procedural law applicable to states of emergency and the Code of Military Justice have been repealed. On 12 November 1992, ONUSAL sent the Ministry of Defence a list of the additional legislative amendments that need to be adopted in order to conclude the process of adapting existing armed forces legislation. Copies of that letter were sent to the Minister of the Presidency, the Minister of Justice and COPAZ. The matter is still pending on the agenda of COPAZ. In addition to the legislative amendments already proposed by ONUSAL, there are the recommendations made in the report of the Commission on the Truth concerning the amendment of other aspects of army regulations and the Code of Military Justice.

2.3 Inclusion of the study of human rights in the curricula of military schools (II.A.5)

(a) Addressed to: the Government of El Salvador

(b) Legislative action required: an administrative decision

(c) Time-frame: immediate

2.4 Military training abroad, on courses based on a doctrine of democracy and respect for human rights (II.A.6)

(a) Addressed to: the Government of El Salvador

(b) Legislative action required: an administrative decision

(c) Time-frame: immediate

2.5 Priority to be given to the eradication of any relationship between members of the armed forces and paramilitary or illegal groups (II.A.7)

(a) Addressed to: the Government of El Salvador

(b) Legislative action required: an administrative decision

(c) Time-frame: immediate

Remarks: It should be noted that, as stipulated in the agreements, civil defence units have been duly disbanded and the new system of armed forces reserves has already replaced the territorial service, which has also been disbanded. COPAZ is currently considering the preliminary bill for the regulation of private security services.

3. Reforms in the area of public security (II.B)

Scrupulous observance of the guidelines for the National Civil Police

(a) Addressed to: the Government of El Salvador

(b) Legislative action required: an administrative decision

(c) Time-frame: immediate

Remarks: It should be noted that the constitutional reforms have already relieved the armed forces of public security tasks, which will be the responsibility of the National Civil Police. The territorial deployment of the latter has already begun. However, the National Police, which is responsible for public security during the transitional period, is still run by military personnel in active service, even though it is answerable to the President of the Republic. Moreover, its ranks have been supplemented with former members of the public security forces that have been disbanded (the National Guard and the Treasury Police) and with soldiers demobilized from the rapid deployment infantry battalions. Many of these soldiers are joining the National Public Security Academy.

4. Investigation of illegal groups (II.C)

Investigation, with outside assistance, to ensure that they are disbanded

(a) Addressed to: the Government of El Salvador

(b) Legislative action required: an administrative decision

(c) Time-frame: immediate

Remarks: It should be noted that, as stipulated in the agreements, civil defence units have been duly disbanded and the new system of armed forces reserves has already replaced the territorial service, which has also been disbanded. COPAZ is currently considering the preliminary bill for the regulation of private security services.

III. Institutional reforms to prevent the repetition of such acts

A. Administration of justice

1. Further judicial reform (III)

(a) Addressed to: the Government of El Salvador, the Legislative Assembly and the Supreme Court

(b) Legislative action required: various constitutional amendments and amendments to secondary legislation which derive from all the specific recommendations. Discussion and adoption of a new Penal Code and Code of Criminal Procedure on the basis of the preliminary drafts already submitted to the Legislative Assembly. Administrative measures within the judicial system

(c) Time-frame: immediate and medium term

Remarks: In the third week of April 1993, the 11 members of the National Council of the Judiciary were elected, by consensus, in the Legislative Assembly. On beginning their work, they announced that they would carry out an investigation of the competence of judges.

2. De-concentration of functions of the Supreme Court and its President: analysis of whether the Constitution should be amended (III.A.1)

(a) Addressed to: the Government of El Salvador and COPAZ

(b) Legislative action required: consideration of the need for a constitutional amendment

(c) Time-frame: immediate and medium term

3. Appointment and removal of judges by the National Council of the Judiciary (III.A.2)

(a) Addressed to: the Government of El Salvador, COPAZ and the Legislative Assembly

(b) Legislative action required: a constitutional amendment, National Council of the Judiciary Act and Career Judicial Service Act

(c) Time-frame: immediate and medium term

4. Administrative accountability of judges to the National Council of the Judiciary (III.A.3)

(a) Addressed to: the Government of El Salvador, COPAZ and the Legislative Assembly

(b) Legislative action required: amendment of the Organic Law of the Judiciary and adoption of a new Career Judicial Service Act

(c) Time-frame: Immediate and medium term

5. Special independent body responsible for authorizing and regulating the professions of lawyer and notary (III.A.4)

(a) Addressed to: the Government of El Salvador, COPAZ and the Legislative Assembly

(b) Legislative action required: amendment of the Organic Law of the Judiciary

(c) Time-frame: immediate

6. Creation of new courts and improvement of judges' salaries (III.A.5)

(a) Addressed to: the Government of El Salvador, COPAZ, the Legislative Assembly and the judiciary

(b) Legislative action required: amendment of the Organic Law of the judiciary or adoption of a legislative decree creating new courts

(c) Time-frame: immediate

7. Reinforcement of the application of the right to due process (III.A.6)

(a) Addressed to: the Government of El Salvador, COPAZ, the Legislative Assembly and the judiciary

(b) Legislative action required: adoption of a new Penal Code and a new Code of Criminal Procedure. Administrative oversight measures (in the police and in the judicial system)

(c) Time-frame: immediate

Remarks: Preliminary drafts of both Codes have already been submitted by the Government of El Salvador to the Legislative Assembly

8. Priority to be given to the Judicial Training School (III.A.7)

(a) Addressed to: the Government of El Salvador, COPAZ and the Legislative Assembly

(b) Legislative action required: amendment of the National Council of the Judiciary Act and adoption of a new Career Judicial Service Act

(c) Time-frame: immediate

B. *Protection of human rights*

1. Implementation of ONUSAL recommendations (III.B)

The recommendations made by the ONUSAL Human Rights Division must be implemented by the parties as stipulated in the San José Agreement. Appendix I summarizes the relevant recommendations made in the sixth report of the ONUSAL Human Rights Division.

2. Strengthening of the Office of the National Counsel for the Defence of Human Rights (III.B.1)

(a) Addressed to: the Office of the National Counsel for the Defence of Human Rights

(b) Legislative action required: none; administrative measures

(c) Time-frame: immediate

Remarks: The Office of the National Counsel for the Defence of Human Rights has announced to the public its commitment to comply with the recommendations addressed to it. The National Counsel has sent the Secretary-General a letter to this effect. The Human Rights Division will liaise directly with the National Counsel in implementing this recommendation.

3. Measures to make the remedies of *amparo* and *habeas corpus* truly effective: broadening the competence of judges and making express provision that these remedies cannot be suspended as guarantees under any circumstances (III.B.2)

(a) Addressed to: the Government of El Salvador, COPAZ and the Legislative Assembly

(b) Legislative action required: a constitutional amendment for the first (competence of judges). Amendment of the Constitutional Procedures Act

(c) Time-frame: immediate

4. Constitutional force of human rights provisions and of international human rights instruments (III.B.3)

(a) Addressed to: the Government of El Salvador, COPAZ and the Legislative Assembly

(b) Legislative action required: a constitutional amendment and/or ratification of or accession to the international human rights treaties referred to in the report

(c) Time-frame: medium term

5. Changes in the system of administrative detention (III.B.4)

(a) Addressed to: the Government of El Salvador, COPAZ and the Legislative Assembly

(b) Legislative action required: adoption of a new Penal Code and Code of Criminal Procedure. Repeal of the 1886 Police Act

(c) Time-frame: immediate

6. Expansion of the system of information on detainees with the participation of the Office of the National Counsel for the Defence of Human Rights (III.B.5)

(a) Addressed to: the Office of the National Counsel for the Defence of Human Rights

(b) Legislative action required: only administrative measures

(c) Time-frame: immediate

7. New categories of crimes (III.B.6)

(a) Addressed to: the Government of El Salvador, COPAZ and the Legislative Assembly

(b) Legislative action required: adoption of a new Penal Code covering such crimes

(c) Time-frame: immediate

8. Material compensation for victims of human rights violations (III.B.7)

(a) Addressed to: the Government of El Salvador, COPAZ and the Legislative Assembly

(b) Legislative action required: adoption of a new Code of Criminal Procedure providing for an expeditious procedure. Special fund

(c) Time-frame: immediate

9. Ratification of international instruments and recognition of the compulsory jurisdiction of the Inter-American Court of Human Rights (III.B.8)

(a) Addressed to: the Government of El Salvador and the Legislative Assembly

(b) Legislative action required: resolutions of the Legislative Assembly

(c) Time-frame: immediate

C. *National Civil Police*

1. Putting into practice the investigation mechanism within the National Civil Police and dissolving the Commission for the Investigation of Criminal Acts (III.C)

(a) Addressed to: the Government of El Salvador, COPAZ and the Legislative Assembly

(b) Legislative action required: administrative measures

(c) Time-frame: immediate

IV. *Steps towards national reconciliation*

1. Special fund for the compensation of victims (IV.A.1,2,3,4)

(a) Addressed to: the Government of El Salvador; the United Nations (which should promote and coordinate action to obtain international contributions)

(b) Legislative action required: a legislative decree (art. 167, para. 4, of the Constitution) or an act adopted by the Legislative Assembly

(c) Time-frame: immediate (one month)

Remarks: The Commission establishes some characteristics of the Fund, *inter alia*, that 1 per cent of all external assistance should be set aside for this purpose. The Government cannot be required to comply with this recommendation, since it is not within its powers but depends on donor States. A formula reflecting this situation must be explored in order to ensure its implementation.

2. Forum for Truth and Reconciliation

(a) Addressed to: COPAZ

(b) Legislative action required: secondary legislation or an administrative order

(c) Time-frame: immediate (one month)

3. Construction of a national monument bearing the names of the victims, recognition of the good name of the victims and institution of a national holiday

(a) Addressed to: the Government of El Salvador and the Legislative Assembly

(b) Legislative action required: a legislative decree and/or an act

(c) Time-frame: immediate.

Appendix I

Recommendations of the ONUSAL Human Rights Division

1. Ratification of international human rights instruments

(a) Addressed to: the Government of El Salvador and the Legislative Assembly

(b) Legislative action required: resolutions of the Legislative Assembly

(c) Time-frame: immediate

Remarks: Some people consider certain provisions of the instruments in question to be incompatible with the Constitution (for example, ILO Convention No. 87). In this case, on depositing the instrument of ratification, a declaration of safeguards can be made, based on wording agreed to in the tripartite commission of the Forum For Economic and Social Consultation.

2. Structural and functional reform of the judiciary

(a) Addressed to: the Government of El Salvador, the Legislative Assembly and the judiciary

(b) Legislative action required: to be considered in terms of the specifics of the reform. Some amendments to the Constitution and to secondary legislation will be needed as a result of specific aspects of these recommendations.

(c) Time-frame: medium term

3. Establishment of a special commission of inquiry to investigate summary executions

(a) Addressed to: the Government of El Salvador

(b) Legislative action required: a legislative decree

(c) Time-frame: immediate

4. Measures to make *habeas corpus* and *amparo* effective and accessible

(a) Addressed to: the Government of El Salvador and the Legislative Assembly

(b) Legislative action required: amendment of the Constitution and of the Constitutional Procedures Act

(c) Time-frame: medium term

5. Compensation fund for victims

Remarks: Totally in line with the corresponding recommendation of the Commission on the Truth.

6. Improvement of the composition and powers of the National Council of the Judiciary and independence of the Judicial Training School

(a) Addressed to: the Government of El Salvador and the Legislative Assembly

(b) Legislative action required: amendment of the Constitution and of the National Council of the Judiciary Act

(c) Time-frame: immediate and medium term

7. Elimination of extrajudicial confession

(a) Addressed to: the Government of El Salvador and the Legislative Assembly

(b) Legislative action required: to be considered in the new Code of Criminal Procedure

(c) Time-frame: immediate

8. Definition of torture and enforced disappearance as offences in special criminal legislation

(a) Addressed to: the Government of El Salvador and the Legislative Assembly

(b) Action required: to be included in the new Penal Code

(c) Time-frame: immediate

9. Legislation regulating the conduct of law enforcement officials

(a) Addressed to: the Government of El Salvador and the Legislative Assembly

(b) Legislative action required: secondary legislation

(c) Time-frame: immediate

10. Abolition of the practice of arbitrary detention for petty misdemeanours

(a) Addressed to: the Government of El Salvador and the Legislative Assembly

(b) Legislative action required: repeal of the 1886 Police Act

(c) Time-frame: immediate

11. Temporary application of the Act governing the procedure for administrative detention or the imposition of administrative fines

(a) Addressed to: the Government of El Salvador

(b) Legislative action required: an administrative decision

(c) Time-frame: immediate

12. Amendment of the disciplinary regime under the Career Judicial Service Act so that the Court or its President can investigate formally any irregularities or violations of due process

(a) Addressed to: the Government of El Salvador and the Legislative Assembly

(b) Legislative action required: secondary legislation

(c) Time-frame: immediate

13. Authorization of a visit by the ILO Committee on Freedom of Association

(a) Addressed to: the Government of El Salvador

(b) Action required: an administrative order

(c) Time-frame: immediate

14. Investigations by the Supreme Court of Justice of violations of due process

(a) Addressed to: the Supreme Court of Justice

(b) Legislative action required: an administrative order

(c) Time-frame: immediate

15. Granting of legal recognition to associations and trade unions

(a) Addressed to: the Government of El Salvador

(b) Legislative action required: an administrative decision

(c) Time-frame: immediate/ongoing

16. Military training

(a) Addressed to: the armed forces

(b) Legislative action required: an administrative order

(c) Time-frame: immediate/ongoing

17. Recovery of military weapons

(a) Addressed to: the Government of El Salvador

(b) Legislative action required: a legislative decree

(c) Time-frame: immediate

18. Budgetary autonomy of the National Counsel's Office

(a) Addressed to: the Government of El Salvador and the Legislative Assembly

(b) Legislative action required: secondary legislation

(c) Time-frame: immediate

19. Facilities for and non-obstruction of NGO activities

(a) Addressed to: the Government of El Salvador

(b) Legislative action required: an administrative order

(c) Time-frame: immediate/ongoing

Appendix II

Principal legal provisions to be amended

1. Constitutional amendments

1. Competence of judges and magistrates to hear the remedy of *habeas corpus*: amend article 174, article 182 (1) and article 247.

2. Constitutional force of human rights provisions. Two non-exclusive alternatives: ratify pending treaties or introduce a constitutional provision giving constitutional force to the international human rights instruments to which El Salvador is a party.

3. Disciplinary regime of the National Council of the Judiciary: amend article 187 to give the Legislative Assembly the authority to remove or dismiss members of the Council by a specified majority.

4. System of administrative detention: amend article 14 by deleting administrative arrest.

5. ONUSAL recommendations: some recommendations coincide (i.e., *habeas corpus*). Also consider possible amendments to articles 131 and 182 with respect to the appointment of magistrates and judges.

2. Amendments to secondary legislation

1. Disciplinary regime of the National Council of the Judiciary. Amend articles 11 and 49 of the National Council of the Judiciary Act by specifying the legal causes for dismissal of members of the Council and establishing a special procedure in the Legislative Assembly in keeping with the powers conferred upon the Assembly by article 132 of the Constitution.

2. Evaluation of judges:

(a) Adoption of the new Career Judicial Service Act that incorporates suitable criteria for evaluating judges and magistrates, taking into account the role of the Judicial Training School. Moreover, the new Act should specify more precise legal causes for the dismissal or removal of judges and magistrates;

(b) Adoption of a special provisional legislative decree that would make it possible to conduct an immediate evaluation of judicial officials with a view to ascertaining whether current officials are really suited for service in the judiciary, whether their work is independent and efficient and whether they have demonstrated a concern for human rights.

3. Comprehensive review of military legislation: consider amendments to various military laws, in particular the Organic Law on National Defence, the Code of Military Justice and the laws on control of arms and explosives.

4. "Due obedience":

(a) Repeal article 173 of army regulations;

(b) Amend the Code of Military Justice by expressly incorporating article 40 (2) (c) of the Penal Code;

(c) Repeal paragraphs 4 and 10 of article 166 of the Code of Military Justice.

5. Punishment of abuses of military authority:

(a) Amend the Code of Military Justice by incorporating a new penal category for punishing military leaders and commanders who force their subordinates, through "due obedience", to act in violation of the law and of human rights;

(b) Incorporate in such amendments, as accessory penalties, discharge from military service and ineligibility to resume military functions for the duration of the penalty.

6. Disbanding of illegal armed groups:

(a) Adoption of a new act on private security bodies or an act regulating private security services. A bill is being considered in the Legislative Assembly;

(b) Adoption of a new act on the special protection of high-risk persons. A bill is being considered in the Legislative Assembly.

7. Administration of court resources:

(a) Amend the Organic Law of the Judiciary in order to give judges the authority to administer the resources of their courts;

(b) Amend the National Council of the Judiciary Act by expanding the Council's powers so that its members can oversee the administration of resources;

(c) The foregoing involves amending the legislation on the supervision of State property, the budgetary system and the Organic Law of the Court of Audit.

8. Concentration of functions in the Supreme Court of Justice and in its President:

(a) Amend the Organic Law of the Judiciary;

(b) Adoption of the new Career Judicial Service Act.

9. Appointment and removal of judges and magistrates: adoption of the new Career Judicial Service Act that will establish, on the basis of the necessary constitutional reform, the competence of the National Council of the Judiciary to appoint, remove or dismiss judges and magistrates.

10. Granting authorization to practise as a lawyer or notary: amend article 51, paragraph 3, of the Organic Law of the Judiciary to give the National Council of the Judiciary the power to do this.

11. Creation of new courts (two alternatives):

(a) Amend article 146 of the Organic Law of the Judiciary;

(b) Adopt a legislative decree creating new courts.

12. Extrajudicial confession: adoption of the new Code of Criminal Procedure.

13. Judicial Training School: amend the National Council of the Judiciary Act and adopt the new Career Judicial Service Act in order to strengthen the Judicial Training School by giving it the authority to evaluate judicial officials with a view to the admission to the career judicial service, promotion, suspension, transfer, removal or dismissal of judges and magistrates. This involves the corresponding constitutional reform.

14. Competence of judges and magistrates to hear remedies of *habeas corpus* and *amparo*: in addition to amending the Constitution, amend the Constitutional Procedures Act.

15. System of administrative detention: promulgate, with the appropriate contents, the new Code of Criminal Procedure and repeal the 1886 Police Act. Amend articles 496 ff. of the Penal Code on the regime for misdemeanours in order to give justices of the peace the competence to consider all categories of misdemeanours.

16. Establishment of new categories of crimes: amend the Penal Code.

17. Establishment of a simple, swift and accessible remedy for material compensation for harm suffered as a result of a human rights violation: amend the Code of Criminal Procedure so that the criminal proceedings

guarantee the speedy and effective exercise of criminal indemnity action and the speed of the criminal trial.

18. Material compensation: adoption of the new act establishing the fund for the protection of victims of violence.

19. Commission for the Investigation of Criminal Acts: repeal the Act establishing the Commission for the Investigation of Criminal Acts.

20. Ratification of human rights instruments.

21. Declaration of a national holiday: adopt a legislative decree declaring the national holiday recommended by the Commission.

Document 78

Security Council resolution concerning the enlargement of ONUSAL's mandate

S/RES/832, 27 May 1993

The Security Council,

Recalling its resolution 637 (1989) of 27 July 1989,

Recalling also its resolutions 693 (1991) of 20 May 1991, 714 (1991) of 30 September 1991, 729 (1992) of 14 January 1992, 784 (1992) of 30 October 1992 and 791 (1992) of 30 November 1992,

Having studied the report of the Secretary-General of 21, 24 and 25 May, 1/

Noting with appreciation the continuing efforts of the Secretary-General to support the full implementation of the agreements signed by the Government of El Salvador and the Frente Farabundo Martí para la Liberacíon Nacional to re-establish peace and promote reconciliation in El Salvador,

Welcoming the observation by the Secretary-General that sixteen months after the cease-fire, the peace process in El Salvador has advanced significantly and is on course, and that significant progress has also been made towards other principal objectives of the Peace Accords,

Emphasizing that determined efforts are required of both parties to ensure that the remaining problems do not become obstacles to the continuing fulfilment of their undertakings,

Noting that the Government of El Salvador has requested the United Nations to verify the next general elections scheduled to be held in March 1994 and that the Secretary-General has recommended that this request be accepted,

Stressing the necessity, in this as in other peace-keeping operations, to continue to monitor expenditures carefully during this period of increasing demands on peace-keeping resources,

1. *Approves* the report of the Secretary-General;

2. *Welcomes* the continuing adaptation by the Secretary-General of the activities and strength of the United Nations Observer Mission in El Salvador, taking into account progress made in implementing the peace process;

3. *Decides,* on the basis of the report of the Secretary-General and in accordance with the provisions of resolution 693 (1991), to enlarge the mandate of the Observer Mission to include the observation of the electoral process due to conclude with the general elections in El Salvador in March 1994, and requests the Secretary-General to take the necessary measures to this effect;

4. *Also decides* that the mandate of the Observer Mission, enlarged in accordance with the present resolution, will be extended until 30 November 1993 and that it will be reviewed at that time on the basis of recommendations to be presented by the Secretary-General;

5. *Endorses* the view of the Secretary-General, contained in his letter of 26 January 1993 to the President of the Security Council, 2/ that the general elections of March 1994 should constitute the logical culmination of the entire peace process in El Salvador;

6. *Urges* the Government of El Salvador and the Frente Farabundo Martí para la Liberacíon Nacional to respect and implement fully all the commitments they assumed under the Peace Accords, including, *inter alia*, those related to the transfer of lands, the reinsertion into civilian society of ex-combatants and war wounded, the deployment of the National Civil Police and the phasing out of the National Police, and the recommendations of the Ad Hoc Commission on the purification of the Armed Forces and the Commission on the Truth;

7. *Reaffirms its support* for the Secretary-General's use of his good offices in the El Salvador peace process;

8. *Calls upon* both parties to cooperate fully with the Secretary-General's Special Representative and the Observer Mission in their task of assisting and verifying the parties' implementation of their commitments and requests the parties to continue to exercise utmost moderation and restraint, especially in the former zones of

1/ S/25812 and Adds.1 to 3.
2/ S/25241.

conflict, in order to promote the process of national reconciliation;

9. *Urges* all States, as well as the international institutions in the fields of development and finance, to contribute generously in support of the execution of the peace accords and the consolidation of peace in El Salvador;

10. Requests the Secretary-General to keep the Security Council fully informed of further developments in the El Salvador peace process and to report on the operations of the Observer Mission at the latest before the expiry of the new mandate period;

11. *Decides* to remain seized of the matter.

Document 79

Letter dated 8 June 1993 from the Secretary-General to the President of the Security Council concerning the discovery of an FMLN weapons cache

S/25901, 8 June 1993

The purpose of this letter is to report to you about developments relating to implementation of the provisions of the Peace Accords for El Salvador as they pertain to the end of the military structure of the Frente Farabundo Martí para la Liberación Nacional (FMLN) and the destruction of its remaining weapons and equipment.

As the members of the Security Council were informed during informal consultations on 1 June 1993, an explosion at an automobile repair shop in Managua, Nicaragua, on 23 May led to the discovery of a weapons cache containing, among other things, a number of surface-to-air missiles, large quantities of ammunition and military weapons, as well as plastic and other explosives. A number of documents were also found, including over 300 passports of various nationalities. On the strength of the evidence found at the shop, the Nicaraguan authorities linked the *Fuerzas Populares de Liberación* (FPL), one of the constituent groups of the FMLN, to the presence of these illegal weapons on Nicaraguan territory. Although the leadership of the group at first denied any connection to the incident, it quickly acknowledged its responsibility for the existence of the cache, which it explained as an unfortunate by-product of the years of conflict. At the same time, however, it steadfastly denied any intention of reverting to the use of arms as an instrument of political pressure. It also offered its full cooperation in clarifying the facts.

At the invitation of the Nicaraguan Government, my Special Representative in El Salvador, accompanied by several members of ONUSAL, travelled to Managua on 29 May to cooperate in the investigation launched by the Nicaraguan authorities. Although Mr. Ramírez-Ocampo has now returned to El Salvador, the ONUSAL team has remained in Nicaragua to assist in the disposal of the arms and in the investigation of the facts surrounding their discovery. Evidence collected so far, together with the explicit acknowledgement by the leadership of the responsible FMLN group, has confirmed that the arms were the property of that group and that some of its members were involved in their maintenance. Enquiries continue with a view to assigning responsibilities more precisely. These enquiries will also examine the possible involvement of organizations or persons foreign to El Salvador. Leaders of the same FMLN group have provided information about the existence in Nicaragua of other clandestine deposits containing considerable amounts of weapons. Specialists from ONUSAL are working with a Nicaraguan team to itemize the war *matériel* found in those deposits and dispose of it.

Regardless of the results of the ongoing investigation, I must emphasize that the maintenance of clandestine arms deposits, for whatever reason, is a cause of serious concern and that the non-inclusion of these arms in the final inventory presented by the FMLN to ONUSAL raises serious questions of confidence and trust. It should be clear to those responsible that the peace process itself could be placed in jeopardy if such damaging incidents should again occur. In this regard I note with satisfaction that the FMLN is cooperating with ONUSAL to locate and eliminate possible remaining arms caches in El Salvador. It is also worth noting that, at ONUSAL's request, the FMLN agreed to the destruction, carried out on 4 June, of the sophisticated weapons located in El Salvador, which are referred to in paragraph 15 of my last report to the Security Council (S/25812 and Add.1-3). As will be recalled, the destruction of these weapons had been scheduled to coincide with full compliance by the Government with the recommendations of the Ad Hoc Commission, due at the end of June. It is hoped that these events will bring to a close the process of the destruction of all FMLN weapons, thus eliminating a source of distrust that has been affecting the peace process.

The swift resolution of this episode should serve to encourage the Government to accelerate the collection of the large number of assault weapons still in private hands in El Salvador. This would imbue a greater sense of confidence in the Salvadorian population and thus strengthen the process of national reconciliation, which is the overriding goal of the Peace Accords.

I should be grateful if you would bring this letter to the attention of the members of the Security Council.

(*Signed*) Boutros BOUTROS-GHALI

Document 80

Statement by the President of the Security Council concerning the FMLN *weapons cache*

S/25929, 11 June 1993

The Security Council takes note with concern of the letter of the Secretary-General dated 8 June 1993 regarding the existence in Nicaragua of a weapons cache belonging to the Frente Farabundo Martí para la Liberación Nacional (FMLN), discovered on 23 May 1993. 1/

The Security Council considers that the maintenance of clandestine arms deposits is the most serious violation to date of the commitments assumed under the peace accords signed at Mexico City on 16 January 1992 2/ and agrees with the Secretary-General that this is a cause of serious concern.

The Council reiterates its demand that the peace accords be complied with fully and promptly. In this context, the Council again urges FMLN to comply fully with its obligation to provide a complete inventory of its arms and munitions both inside and outside El Salvador and surrender them in accordance with the provisions of the peace accords, and to continue to cooperate in this regard with the United Nations Observer Mission in El Salvador.

The Security Council takes note with satisfaction of the cooperation of the Government of Nicaragua in itemizing and disposing of the war *matériel* found.

The Security Council expects that the parties to the Peace Accords will continue their efforts to complete the peace process and achieve national reconciliation in El Salvador.

1/ S/25901.
2/ S/23501.

Document 81

Letter dated 28 June 1993 from Nicaragua concerning cooperation by the Government of Nicaragua in itemizing and disposing of FMLN arms caches discovered in Nicaragua

A/47/970-S/26008, 2 July 1993

I have the honour to transmit to you herewith a letter from His Excellency Ernesto Leal, Minister for Foreign Affairs of the Republic of Nicaragua, informing you of the various actions taken by the Government of our country following the discovery on national territory of secret arms caches belonging to the Salvadorian guerrillas (see annex).

I should be grateful if you would have the text of this letter and its annex circulated as an official document of the General Assembly, under agenda item 36, and of the Security Council.

(*Signed*) Erich VÍLCHEZ ASHER
Minister Counsellor
Chargé d'affaires a.i.

Annex

Letter dated 22 June 1993 from the Minister for Foreign Affairs addressed to the Secretary-General

The Government of the Republic of Nicaragua, consistent with its political intent not to permit the use of its territory by irregular forces to destabilize other countries, and in fulfilment of the regional undertakings entered into in respect of disarmament and illicit arms transfers, informs the Secretary-General of the United Nations, Mr. Boutros Boutros-Ghali, of the various actions it has taken following the discovery on national territory of secret arms caches belonging to the Salvadorian guerrillas:

1. As you correctly mentioned in your letter to the President of the Security Council dated 8 June 1993, the Government of Nicaragua, following the explosion of a secret arms cache located in the Santa Rosa repair shop, north of the city of Managua, requested the United Nations Observer Mission in El Salvador (ONUSAL)—the organ entrusted with verifying compliance with the Peace Agreement in that country—to send a delegation forthwith to conduct an on-site investigation into the circumstances surrounding these events and to confirm the destruction of the armaments found.

2. Accordingly, the national authorities, with the support of ONUSAL experts and with the collaboration of the Fuerzas Populares de Liberación—the Salvadorian guerrilla faction which has assumed total and absolute responsibility for the existence in Nicaragua of these secret caches—began an investigation which led to the determination that there were 15 premises which were being used to store arms and documents, or as safe houses.

This war *matériel* was duly itemized and promptly destroyed in the presence and with the collaboration of ONUSAL experts. Immediately thereafter, a conclusive report was prepared, giving the details of the various activities carried out, and a detailed inventory of the arms, instruments and equipment found in the various caches and safe-houses; this was drawn up by the national authorities, together with the special envoys from ONUSAL.

3. The Government of the Republic of Nicaragua considers it appropriate to underscore the promptness, diligence and transparency of the action taken in the face of this situation, as was recognized by the President of the Security Council himself in his statement of 11 June 1993 (S/25929) following consideration of the item entitled "Central America: efforts towards peace", when he said:

"The Security Council takes note with satisfaction of the cooperation of the Government of Nicaragua in itemizing and disposing of the war *matériel* found."

4. The Government of Nicaragua likewise can not fail to point out that the corresponding criminal proceedings have been instituted against the various persons linked to the existence in Nicaragua of the secret war weapons. As stated in the said conclusive report, this is a criminal case which is being heard in the Managua Fifth District Criminal Court.

5. Finally, the Government of the Republic of Nicaragua ventures to reiterate that it fully supports existing regional agreements concerning subversive activities and illicit armaments transfers, such as the Procedure for the establishment of a firm and lasting peace in Central America (known as the Esquipulas II Agreement, of 7 August 1987), sections 5 and 6, respectively entitled "termination of aid for irregular forces and insurrectionist movements" and "non-use of territory to attack other States"; and the more recent preliminary mechanism on assistance, cooperation and coordination for the elimination of illicit arms traffic in Central America, signed on 16 June 1992, by the Central American security commission in San Salvador, which contains specific measures for proper compliance with the security commitments of the Esquipulas procedure.

6. Thus, to comply with these regional undertakings, the Government of Nicaragua has promulgated, in accordance with those agreements, legislation designed specifically to prevent and punish anyone who supports irregular forces or who transfers arms. Act No. 122 of 4 October 1990 adds to the Penal Code a new offence, which reads as follows:

"*Addendum to the offence against the peace of the Republic*

"*Article 1.* Add to article 546 of the Penal Code a sixth paragraph, reading as follows:

"*Paragraph 6.* Anyone who, within the national territory, promotes, assists or organizes foreign irregular forces, forms part thereof or uses or permits the use of national territory to instigate, assist or lend military or logistic assistance to such forces or to those organized in another country, by trafficking in, storing and transferring arms, equipment or military supplies; recruiting nationals and foreigners, billeting or training military personnel; installing and operating radio transmitters, television or radio-communication stations or who assists or collaborates with them in any other manner, shall be liable to imprisonment from 3 to 10 years and confiscation of the arms, supplies and other property used to commit the offence."

7. Thus, by adopting domestic or international legislation; by inviting international bodies to verify the itemizing and disposal of war *matériel*; and by instituting criminal proceedings against those accused, the Government of the Republic of Nicaragua is demonstrating its indisputable devotion to peace and its attachment to international law, as a contribution to the peace process in the Central American region.

(*Signed*) Ernesto LEAL SÁNCHEZ
Minister for Foreign Affairs

Document 82

Report of the Secretary-General concerning illegal arms deposits belonging to the FMLN

S/26005, 29 June 1993

1. The purpose of the present report is to update the Security Council on the recent discovery, at various locations inside and outside of El Salvador, of illegal arms deposits belonging to the *Frente Farabundo Martí para la Liberación Nacional* (FMLN). Following my letter of 8 June 1993 to the President of the Security Council on this issue (S/25901), the Council issued a statement on 11 June (S/25929) in which it expressed serious concern at the maintenance of such clandestine arms deposits, which it considered the most serious violation to date of the commitments assumed under the Peace Accords. The Council also urged FMLN to comply with its obligation to provide a complete inventory of its arms and munitions, both inside and outside El Salvador and surrender them in accordance with the provisions of the Peace Accords, and to continue to cooperate in this regard with the United Nations Observer Mission in El Salvador (ONUSAL). Ever since the discovery of the first illegal arms cache in Managua on 23 May, I have made continuous efforts directly and through ONUSAL to establish the facts, to ensure that all remaining clandestine caches are declared to it and their contents destroyed and to limit the repercussions on the peace process of this very serious violation of the Peace Accords.

2. On 12 June 1993, I addressed a letter to the Coordinator-General of FMLN, Mr. Schafik Handal, in which, among other things, I expressed my distress at learning that, contrary to the assurances he had given me, the final inventory of weapons presented to ONUSAL by FMLN had been grossly inaccurate. I reminded Mr. Handal that it was on the basis of ONUSAL's confirmation that all the items in the inventory had been accounted for and were being destroyed that FMLN had been legalized as a political party by the Supreme Electoral Tribunal (*Tribunal Supremo Electoral*) of El Salvador. I emphasized that such a deliberate attempt to mislead me placed my credibility in doubt and raised very serious questions of confidence and trust. I accordingly urged FMLN to

demonstrate in words and deeds that it remained committed to the peace process and also requested Mr. Handal to inform me, by 20 June 1993, of the action taken by FMLN to ensure that all arms caches in El Salvador and in neighbouring countries were located and their contents destroyed, and that any weapons still in possession of FMLN militants were similarly handed over to ONUSAL for destruction. The full text of my letter to Mr. Handal is annexed to this report (annex I).

3. On 17 June 1993, I received Mr. Handal's reply, dated 16 June, together with another letter, dated 11 June, addressed to me by Mr. Salvador Sánchez Cerén, Secretary-General of the FMLN constituent group which had acknowledged responsibility for the existence of the Managua arms cache, the Popular Liberation Forces (*Fuerzas Populares de Liberación*) (FPL). Both letters are annexed to the present report as annexes II A and B. Mr. Handal stressed that, notwithstanding the existence of undeclared war-related *matériel*, whose purpose had been "to keep a last negotiating card in order to guarantee peace and the conclusion of the agreements", FMLN had at no time considered resuming the armed struggle in El Salvador and unreservedly reaffirmed its commitment to the peace process. He also stated categorically that FMLN had no armed groups under its command. Finally, he referred to FPL's readiness to "clean up its house", adding that the FMLN leadership was considering how best to carry out the collection of arms which might have been dispersed and concealed. He also promised to inform me as soon as possible of the conclusions reached in this regard (see para. 5 below).

4. For his part, Mr. Sánchez Cerén apologized for having misled me and the United Nations, stating that FPL had not inventoried nor destroyed all its arms owing to its profound mistrust of the Armed Forces. This mistrust had grown with the Government's delays and failure to meet its commitments. Although various reschedulings had prevented the collapse of the process, the balance

reflected in the initial implementation timetable had been radically upset. He further stated that, as FMLN developed as a political party and its chances of expansion were increasing, the maintenance of those arms had become an onerous and unnecessary burden, incompatible with its new status. Consequently, FPL had already decided to hand over its caches to the Nicaraguan Government and to ONUSAL when the explosion occurred. He further stated that FPL had taken all the necessary steps to rid itself of all arms and that, once the total destruction of the weapons in Nicaragua was completed, it would inform ONUSAL about the location of the remaining caches in El Salvador. Shortly after this letter, FPL contacted ONUSAL with a view to setting up a schedule, not to exceed 45 days, for the location and destruction of the caches. This was followed, on 18 June, by a letter addressed to my Special Representative, in which Mr. Sánchez Cerén indicated FPL's willingness to begin working immediately with ONUSAL on this process. In his letter Mr. Sánchez Cerén also appointed an FPL liaison officer for the purpose of drawing up with ONUSAL the operational plan for the location and destruction, by 4 August 1993, of the above-mentioned weapons.

5. On 19 June 1993, Mr. Handal, complying with his promise to me, informed me that FMLN would cooperate with ONUSAL in locating and destroying all of its remaining weapons within a period of 45 days beginning on 21 June 1993 (i.e. by 4 August). Any weapons confiscated after the expiry of that period would be accounted for solely by the persons in whose possession they were found and would not be FMLN's responsibility. Finally, expressing concern for delays and non-compliance by the Government with its obligations under the Peace Accords, Mr. Handal stressed the need for the establishment of specific time-limits to assure full implementation of pending commitments. The need for such a timetable has been repeatedly raised by FMLN, particularly last March when Mr. Handal visited United Nations Headquarters on the occasion of the presentation of the report of the Commission on the Truth. In this regard, he emphasized the importance of renewed direct communication between the parties. The full text of Mr. Handal's letter is included in annex III.

6. On 17 June 1993, the ONUSAL technical team that had travelled to Managua on 29 May, at the invitation of the Government of Nicaragua, to work jointly with the Government's Special Disarmament Brigade (*Brigada Especial de Desarme*) on the establishment of the facts surrounding the 23 May explosion reported that the task of itemizing and destroying weapons and war-related *matériel* that were under the control of FPL had been completed. Based on the information provided by FPL, which cooperated fully in the investigation,

ONUSAL and the Nicaraguan authorities verified 16 "safe houses" (*casas de seguridad*), including the automobile-repair shop that was the scene of the 23 May incident. Five of those houses contained armament which was mostly in good condition, and which included some 1,240 rifles, 2,025 kilogrammes of explosives, 1,406,300 rounds of ammunition, 1,300 mortar grenades, 3,970 assorted grenades, 350 rockets (LAW), 35,700 detonators, 42 machine-guns and 19 surface-to-air missiles. No weapons or war *matériel* were found in the other "safe houses". The Nicaraguan authorities are continuing their inquiries into the possible involvement of parties foreign to El Salvador.

7. Another constituent group of FMLN, the former People's Revolutionary Army (*Ejército Revolucionario del Pueblo*), now renamed *Expresión Renovadora del Pueblo* (ERP), separately handed over to ONUSAL in San Salvador, on 17 June 1993, some 2-3 tons of *matériel* consisting primarily of small-arms ammunition and explosives, some of them in poor condition. ERP has also informed ONUSAL about the existence of another clandestine deposit in the eastern part of the country, which it will soon transfer to ONUSAL for destruction. Furthermore, ONUSAL has been informed by a third FMLN group, the National Resistance (*Resistencia Nacional*) (RN), that various caches of arms and ammunition located in the country would be transferred to it for destruction within the next few days. A fourth FMLN faction, the Liberation Armed Forces (*Fuerzas Armadas de Liberación*) (FAL), has also informed ONUSAL that it will soon provide information on its own holdings of war *matériel*.

8. On 11 June 1993, I received a letter from President Cristiani in which, among other things, he stated that the conduct of FMLN, in addition to being in violation of the commitments it had assumed, violated the constitutional provision prohibiting the existence of armed groups and might therefore be a reason to disband FMLN as a political party. In this connection, the President requested that the 14 December 1992 ONUSAL certification of complete disarmament on the part of FMLN be left in abeyance until FMLN had handed over all its war-related *matériel* for destruction. In the same letter, President Cristiani also demanded that FMLN demobilize armed groups of its members or sympathizers, or declare that it had severed links with such groups. The President also expressed the view that the gravity of the breach by FMLN warranted that the Security Council pass a resolution on the matter. President Cristiani's letter appears in annex IV to this report.

9. The right of FMLN to maintain its status as a political party in the current circumstances has also been questioned in other quarters and the view expressed that

this status should be cancelled or suspended. On 14 June 1993, the Supreme Electoral Tribunal (*Tribunal Supremo Electoral*), which, on the basis of ONUSAL's certification, had granted to FMLN its present status, requested from ONUSAL a full report on the discovery of arms caches in Nicaragua.

10. As indicated above (see para. 3), FMLN has categorically denied that it is supporting any armed groups or that it has any such groups under its command. However, it has not discarded the possibility that some of its former combatants belong to groups of delinquents and has requested that a professional investigation be conducted with the support of ONUSAL. It has also offered its full cooperation in dealing with this problem. ONUSAL has been investigating the issue for some time and has found no evidence of armed groups under the command of FMLN. It has, however, confirmed the existence of a number of armed criminal bands varying in size from 20 to 50 members and composed not only of ex-combatants of FMLN, but also of former members of the Armed Forces and civilians equipped with military weapons. ONUSAL has for its part ascertained that these bands are fully autonomous and that their behaviour is of a criminal and non-political nature. It has been able to identify members of one of those groups and has turned this information over to the Government. ONUSAL will continue to gather information on the activities of these criminal groups and to cooperate with the authorities on this matter. No direct relationship has been established between these groups and the arms caches recently discovered.

11. The seriousness of the situation which was revealed by the explosion of 23 May 1993 in Managua cannot be overemphasized. It has raised questions of confidence and trust and could have seriously undermined the peace process. However, the cancellation or suspension of FMLN's status as a political party could in my view place in jeopardy the progress which has so far been achieved and could itself deal a severe blow to the peace process. The transformation of FMLN into a political party and the full reintegration of its members, within a framework of full legality, into the civil, political and institutional life of the country, are at the very core of the Peace Accords. Indeed, this process constitutes the ultimate goal of the entire process as envisaged in the Geneva Agreement of 4 April 1990. It is likewise imperative to avoid a disruption of the electoral process, in which it is essential that FMLN have every opportunity to participate. Fortunately, FMLN's prompt and complete acceptance of its responsibility for the events and its full cooperation in the ensuing investigation have paved the way for a restoration of the confidence that should accompany the peace process. It is clear however that FMLN now has to demonstrate anew its commitment to

that process and that confidence will only be fully restored upon the complete disclosure, as promised, by FMLN of all its holdings in arms and munitions and their subsequent destruction by the date indicated. I shall keep the Security Council informed of further developments.

12. It is an indication of the strength and irreversibility of the peace process and a credit to both parties that a serious incident of this nature has not been allowed to derail the implementation of the Peace Accords. In this regard, I wish to commend President Cristiani for the statesmanship he has demonstrated and to exhort the Government and FMLN to make every effort in the months ahead to restore confidence in the peace process and to ensure its successful completion. I also wish to record my gratitude to the Government of Nicaragua for the cooperation and support it has given ONUSAL in this matter.

Annex I

Letter dated 12 June 1993 from the Secretary-General addressed to the Coordinator-General of the Frente Farabundo Martí para la Liberación Nacional (FMLN)

I write with reference to the recent discovery in Nicaragua of important quantities of military weapons and related items belonging to one of the constituent groups of the FMLN. You will already have seen the statement made on this matter by the President of the Security Council on behalf of the Council.

As you are well aware, it is on the basis of (a) repeated assurances by the FMLN that the inventory it had presented to ONUSAL was a full statement of its holdings of military *matériel* and (b) confirmation by ONUSAL that all the items in that inventory had been accounted for and were being destroyed, that the FMLN became a political party on 14 December 1992 and the armed conflict in El Salvador was brought formally to an end on the following day. It is because I was convinced that such indeed was the case that I stated then that El Salvador had crossed the line from armed peace into a new era. With this in mind, I am distressed to learn that, contrary to your assurances which I had accepted in good faith, the inventory presented to ONUSAL by the FMLN was grossly inaccurate and failed to include large quantities of warlike *matériel*. Such a deliberate attempt to mislead me places my credibility in doubt and raises in my mind very serious questions of confidence and trust which, in the absence of any communication from you, I am unable to answer at this time.

Recent pronouncements in El Salvador clearly show the damaging effects of the recent incident in Nicaragua and the very serious consequences that it could have for the peace process itself. I would urge you to take the necessary steps to demonstrate, in words and in deeds, that the FMLN, notwithstanding the damage done, continues to be committed to the Peace Accords and to the process of national reconciliation.

Given the United Nations responsibility for verifying the implementation of the Peace Accords, it will be necessary for me to keep the Security Council informed about developments in regard to this issue. I should accordingly be grateful if you would inform me by 20 June 1993 of the action which has been taken by the FMLN to ensure that all arms caches in El Salvador and neighbouring countries are located and their contents destroyed and that any weapons remaining in the hands of FMLN militants are similarly handed over to ONUSAL for destruction.

(*Signed*) Boutros BOUTROS-GHALI

Annex II (A)

[Original: Spanish]

*Letter dated 16 June 1993 from the Coordinator-
General of the Frente Farabundo Martí para
la Liberación Nacional (FMLN)
addressed to the Secretary-General*

In reply to your letter of 12 June 1993, I should like first of all to state that the Frente Farabundo Martí para la Liberación Nacional (FMLN) has at no time considered resuming the armed conflict. On behalf of all the comrades of the former General Command, I can assure you that we all remain committed to continuing to develop and consolidate the peace process. No one is supporting or is in command of armed groups.

While this does not rule out the possibility that there may be groups which include persons who at one point were FMLN combatants—just as it has been determined that there are armed groups made up of former members of the armed forces and security bodies, at the present time they have no connection with us. As you know, this is a frequent and almost inevitable phenomenon in post-war periods, but it, I repeat, does not mean that FMLN is supporting, organizing or concealing the existence of such groups.

Consequently, you may rest assured that the view which you expressed at the ceremony marking the cessation of the armed confrontation to the effect that "El Salvador has crossed the line from armed peace into a new era" is completely valid and objective as far as FMLN is concerned, today as it was on 15 December.

Comrade Salvador Sánchez Cerén, in his letter of 11 June, which I have attached, explains clearly the reason why a certain quantity of arms was withheld without informing ONUSAL about this fact. The purpose of this was to keep a last negotiating card in order to guarantee peace and the conclusion of the agreements. The need for this card derives from a profound mistrust of the armed forces. This mistrust is based on both the reluctance of the armed forces to adapt to change and accept the new doctrine, their new role in a democratic society, as well as the military capability which this armed institution still has and which is sufficient to reverse the process, in spite of the measures and commitment by the United Nations to prevent them from doing so.

I understand perfectly that since I have not communicated with you until now you feel unable to respond to the doubts and questions which the discovery of the arms stockpile in Santa Rosa has given rise to. I did not contact you earlier because I had assumed that the free-flowing communication and full collaboration which our comrades in the Popular Liberation Forces (FPL) have had with ONUSAL were sufficient. In any event, I accept your views on the matter and apologize for this oversight. At the same time, I should like to reiterate that I feel personally committed to do everything incumbent upon me to move forward through this critical period.

With regard to the information which you have requested from me concerning the measures which FMLN is taking in order to ensure that any further arms stockpiles which might exist in El Salvador or a neighbouring country are located and destroyed, I should like to indicate the following: as comrade Salvador Sánchez Cerén informs you, FPL has already taken the necessary steps to "clean up its house". The rest of us in the former General Command are considering the way in which arms which may have been dispersed and concealed could be recollected. I plan to return from Mexico City to San Salvador next Friday, 18 June. I shall then contact the other comrades and inform you as speedily as possible of the conclusions which we have reached. In the meantime, I am sending you a copy of the FMLN communiqué on the subject, which we issued yesterday.

I learned through the press that President Cristiani has requested you to suspend ONUSAL certification of the complete disarmament and demobilization of FMLN. The President intends to use this action by the United Nations to justify suspending the legal status of FMLN as a political party.

I am concerned at the fact that President Cristiani is taking these positions now. At first, he assumed a moderate stance with regard to the discovery in Santa Rosa. He espoused a position rather in defence of the peace process. Last Friday, however, he used the incident as a pretext for cancelling a high-level meeting between the parties which had been agreed upon after the discovery for the purpose of promoting compliance with the agreements to be carried out in order to reduce the negative impact of the incident. This change is probably due to the fact that President Cristiani is being subjected to strong pressure by those who are opposed to the peace process.

They know that the armed conflict came about because the political avenues were closed. They are aware that an attempt to close them again now, if only temporarily, may have serious implications for the process, which has not encountered any setback. Suspending the legal status of FMLN would be the first step backwards in the implementation of the agreements. Without any doubt, such a measure, instead of restoring trust between the parties, would enormously increase the feelings of mistrust.

Accordingly, I feel on the contrary that the United Nations should take extraordinary steps to re-establish communication between the parties and ensure that this stumbling block does not degenerate into an obstacle that paralyses and undermines the progress that has already been achieved or is close at hand. The Salvadorian people deserve the successful completion of this process, which began well and has proceeded well.

In view of the importance of the matter, you are at liberty to include a copy of this letter together with that of comrade Sánchez Cerén as an annex to your report to the Security Council.

I take this opportunity to convey to you the assurances of my highest consideration and once again reaffirm our commitment to proceeding forward in the peace process.

(*Signed*) Schafik Jorge HÁNDAL

Annex II (B)

[Original: Spanish]

Letter dated 11 June 1993 from the Secretary-General of the Fuerzas Populares de Liberación (FPL) addressed to the Secretary-General

I am writing to you in my capacity as Secretary-General of the Fuerzas Populares de Liberación Farabundo Martí (FPL), and as a member of the Political Committee and of the former General Command of FMLN, with reference to the stockpiles of arms which we did not destroy earlier.

I believe that we owe you, your closest colleagues, the Group of Friends of the Secretary-General and members of the Security Council an explanation because of the very significant contribution which you have made, and can continue to make, to the process of implementation of the agreements and consolidation of peace in El Salvador. Please forward a copy of this letter to them all.

In explaining the viewpoint of FPL, I am not seeking to be exhaustive, to evade responsibilities or to deny the seriousness of this. I am trying to place it in proper perspective, to maintain your confidence and that of the others for whom this letter is intended and, above all, to ensure that those who have always opposed the peace process do not seize this opportunity to reduce substantially the achievements of the Salvadorian people.

First of all I should like to assure you that the reason we did not take an inventory of or destroy these arms was at no time because we were thinking of using them to conduct a further military offensive. As you yourself can confirm, ever since we opted to seek a political solution to the Salvadorian conflict, FPL—as part of FMLN—has been working hard in the negotiations, contributing to the search for formulas that have helped us to untie the "Gordian knots". After the signing of the peace agreements, we have been endeavouring to move ahead constructively with their implementation while, at the same time, devoting ourselves wholeheartedly to transforming our secret political-military structure into an open political organization with an expanding popular base.

The results of these efforts became clear at the close of the first FPL Congress, which was an expression of the vitality and political strength which we have built up and the occasion for the highest governing body of FPL to ratify, by unanimously approving the strategy for this new period, the historic decision which our Central Committee had taken, namely, to replace the political and military struggle by an exclusively political struggle. Our current strategy is aimed entirely at achieving the implementation of the agreements, electoral victory, promotion of overall development and the growth and consolidation of our political party.

The real reason we did not make an inventory of or destroy all our arms was simply that we had profound mistrust of the armed forces. This forced us to keep one last negotiating card up our sleeve in order to guarantee the full execution of all agreements. As you know, even though the process was put back on track by means of various reschedulings which averted a major crisis in the peace process, the Government's delays and failure to meet commitments considerably increased our mistrust and definitively upset the balance achieved in the initial schedule. As a result, destruction of FMLN's military apparatus was carried out under circumstances substantially different from those which were initially agreed on. It was done before the arms for the exclusive use of the armed forces had been collected, before land ownership in the conflict areas had been legalized, before the functional structure of PNC had been created, before the purification of the armed forces had been completed, and so forth.

For this reason, although we were fully confident that after 15 December you and your colleagues would continue to press for full implementation of the agreements, we had serious grounds for believing that after that date the resistance of certain sectors of the armed forces would increase, which might reduce the latitude for United Nations mediation. As you are well aware, the effectiveness of the United Nations observer missions does not depend only on the sincerity, dedication and commitment of the Secretary-General and his colleagues. If that were so, all the peace processes which are currently being verified by the United Nations would be as successful as that of El Salvador.

After 15 December, we were able to confirm, on the one hand, that the resistance of those sectors of the armed forces which opposed the peace agreement did increase and, at the same time, our own capacity to press for compliance with the agreements was substantially weakened. This contributed, *inter alia*, to a significant slowing down of the pace of execution of agreements that were incomplete or outstanding.

As you know, most of the agreements which were rescheduled on 22 December and 4 February 1993 were not implemented on the agreed new dates. Up to now they have not been implemented. This non-fulfilment is correctly reflected in the report you presented, on 21 May, to the Security Council, in which it is stated that some 30 government commitments have not been fully met. This is without listing all the recommendations of the Commission on the Truth and the Human Rights Division of ONUSAL which the Government has not acted on.

Moreover, we were also able to confirm that, after 15 December, you, your colleagues and the Security Council continued to press insistently for full implementation of the recommendations of the ad hoc Commission, the Commission on the Truth and all other agreements.

Inasmuch as we were continuing to develop as a legal political party and as our prospects of continuing to do so were expanding apace, it became incompatible, burdensome and unnecessary for us to have these stockpiles of arms. For that reason, those in charge of maintaining the stockpiles had already decided to hand them over privately to the Government of Nicaragua and to ONUSAL, as had been done with the stockpiles we had in Honduras. Unfortunately this new decision was not carried out because all the active members of FPL were engrossed in preparing for Congress and the Congress itself, and in the immediate tasks following therefrom.

The discovery of the stockpile at Santa Rosa in Nicaragua and all the implications of that event convinced us that the decision to rid ourselves of all arms was the correct one. Unfortunately, we had to do it after the events of 23 May.

I should like to take this opportunity to apologize for concealing the existence of these stockpiles from you and your colleagues. For the reasons set out above, we were convinced of the need to keep them, but decided to do so without informing you of the fact, since we were aware of the impartiality with which you and your colleagues had acted in the Salvadorian peace process.

The above explanations relate to the past. As to the present and the future, we have already publicly acknowledged responsibility for the arms found at Santa Rosa and are handing over to the Nicaraguan Government and ONUSAL other stockpiles we had kept in that country. Once they have been destroyed, we shall inform ONUSAL of the whereabouts of the stockpiles we have maintained in El Salvador so that they can be immediately destroyed. In short, we have already undertaken the necessary measures to "clean up our house", in other words to comply with the undertakings we gave in the peace agreements. We are also cooperating with the Nicaraguan Government to settle the legal proceedings currently in progress.

However, we are concerned that all these actions have served to fan, rather than extinguish, the flames. Because of the domestic political situation in Nicaragua and the forthcoming elections in El Salvador, these actions are continually being distorted in an attempt to further damage FPL, reduce the prospects of an electoral victory by the Salvadorian left, create a climate in which attacks on the opposition can be stepped up and, above all, diminish past prospective gains under the peace agreements, which are the heritage not of FMLN, but of the Salvadorian people.

For almost a month the local press has focused attention on the arms hidden by FPL. Scant mention has been made of the arms for the exclusive use of the armed forces which are still in the hands of civilians. It has overlooked the fact that many of the commitments given by the Government have not been met, including the land transfer programme, the agreement to deploy the National Civil Police, the gradual disbanding of the national police, implementation of the medium-term programme for the reintegration of former combatants into civilian life, compliance with the recommendations of the Commission on the Truth, and so on.

Even your letter to the Security Council and the latter's subsequent declaration have been manipulated by certain sectors. Instead of serving to accelerate confidence-building and relaunch the process by urging full and immediate compliance with all the agreements, they are being used to promote mistrust and justify the failure to comply with the remaining agreements.

The fact that attention has been focused solely on the arms in the possession of FPL has today been used by the Government as a pretext for cancelling a high-level meeting at the eleventh hour. The meeting had been called by ONUSAL in the wake of the events in Nicaragua. It would have been very useful in seeking ways of rebuilding confidence, reopening communications, curbing the current increase in the dirty war, and speeding up implementation of the agreements.

It is clear that the extreme right is aggressively attacking the FPL leaders and prospective candidates not only from a desire to halt the implementation of the agreements once and for all, but also because they want to distort and reverse them. They know that FPL is the majority component of FMLN and one of its most dynamic forces. They know that by weakening FPL they can damage the prospects of the Salvadorian left winning the elections. They want to prevent the new Government from continuing to extend and consolidate the gains achieved by the negotiations. They want to ensure victory for ARENA in order to reverse the process of demilitarization and democratization carried out under the agreements.

In conclusion, I am convinced of the urgent need to put the transgression by FPL in a proper perspective, recognize that it has already been rectified and give rapid impetus to the process of implementing the agreements. It would be very useful if the chief of ONUSAL could call, privately as well as publicly, for efforts to overcome the crisis and the swift resumption of the process of complying fully with the agreements. Otherwise, that process will be seriously and irreparably damaged, with the main loser being not FPL but the Salvadorian people.

Without wishing to exonerate FPL, FMLN or the Government, we hope that in the interest of the Salvadorian people you will again be able to foster the resumption and consolidation of the peace process and prevent the current crisis from escalating and resulting in deadlock. There is an urgent need to refocus attention and efforts on meeting the outstanding commitments. Time is running out.

I take this opportunity to convey the assurances of my highest consideration, and to reaffirm our complete readiness to continue promoting the consolidation of peace through full compliance with all the agreements.

(*Signed*) Salvador SÁNCHEZ CERÉN

Annex III

[Original: Spanish]

Letter dated 19 June 1993 from the Coordinator-General of the Frente Farabundo Martí para la Liberación Nacional (FMLN) addressed to the Secretary-General

Further to my letter of 16 June 1993, I am writing to inform you that, after my return from Mexico yesterday I met with my comrades of the former General Command and we adopted decisions and measures concerning the arms of the Frente Farabundo Martí para la Liberación Nacional (FMLN) that remain to be collected and destroyed. The decisions and measures are the following:

1. Collect and destroy, in close cooperation with the United Nations Observer Mission in El Salvador (ONUSAL), arms still held by FMLN, within a period of 45 days beginning on 21 June. We believe that this is sufficient time for us and we hope that it will also be sufficient for ONUSAL with its reduced military staff.

2. We cannot specify in advance the number and type of these arms, since there may be scattered and concealed weapons stockpiles over which we have no firm control. We have taken the necessary measures to determine the existence and whereabouts of such weapons stockpiles. We believe that, at the end of the aforementioned period, we will be in a position to specify the number and type of weapons that were collected.

3. The Fuerzas Populares de Liberación (FPL) has informed us of its decision to reveal the location of and destroy the weapons stockpiles that it still maintains in El Salvador, once it has finished destroying, with the cooperation and supervision of ONUSAL, its stockpiles of weapons in Nicaragua. FPL has already submitted the plan for its operation in El Salvador to ONUSAL.

The Ejército Revolucionario del Pueblo (ERP) has also informed us that last week it provided ONUSAL with information about arms still in its possession with a view to their destruction.

We believe that all these arms should be accounted for at the end of the 45 days.

4. The collection of FMLN arms during this time period should proceed without publicity, in private, in accordance with a plan that each member organization of FMLN will submit to ONUSAL. This operation can begin immediately, with the plan already submitted by FPL. ONUSAL would publicize the final results. The Armed Forces of El Salvador (FAES) and the National Police should not participate in this operation in any way. Since the operation involves former areas of conflict that are subject to a special security regime, the participation of the National Civil Police would be acceptable only when ONUSAL considers it necessary.

5. The arms confiscated after the expiry of the 45-day period shall be accounted for solely by the persons in whose possession they are found. FMLN disclaims all responsibility. We have expressly agreed to this arrangement.

6. We have carefully examined the case of the arms that disappeared, after having been inspected and itemized by ONUSAL, at the 15 points at which our forces were concentrated during the period of the "armed peace", and we have concluded that:

(a) These arms were taken from under our control; to put it bluntly, they were stolen;

(b) It is clear that, since the arms formed part of the inventories that we turned over to ONUSAL and were inspected by its Military Division, there is no reason to suppose that we removed them ourselves for the purpose of concealing them;

(c) We are unable to recover these arms and, if they are confiscated in the future by the competent authorities, those persons in whose possession the arms are found shall be held accountable.

The developments that have prompted me to write this letter are, as you well understand, typical of a post-war situation and the complex process of dealing with the consequences of a long war that has had political, economic, moral, material and psychological repercussions and has left mistrust and anxiety in its wake. We cannot allow any of these difficulties and, at times, complications affect the peace or hinder the process of democratization. This is our firm conviction and resolve.

The peace process in El Salvador, despite these incidents, is a tangible fact, and it must be continued and encouraged. The strength of that process derives from each party's compliance with the agreements and commitments it has undertaken. This is also the source of its credibility.

FMLN has paid a high political price for not having complied fully with its obligation to submit accurate inventories of its arms. However, by taking the measures set out in this letter, it is making an extraordinary effort to normalize its situation within a short period of time— by 4 August 1993—and thereby give new impetus to the Chapultepec process.

In your report of 21 May 1993, you informed the Security Council of a considerable and disturbing number of cases of non-compliance or distortions of its obligations on the part of the Government of President Cristiani, which form a truly dramatic panorama. We see no reason for considering such cases of non-compliance as any less serious than ours, which we are currently rectifying. This situation continues to give rise to mistrust among our member organizations and also among broad sectors of the population. Mistrust is increasing as the date of the elections— which will be held in March 1994—approaches and the time remaining in the term of President Alfredo Cristiani is growing shorter; at the same time, the many cases of non-compliance that you referred to in your report have not been substantially redressed.

We are convinced of the need for extraordinary measures and efforts to ensure that the Government fulfils all its obligations in what remains of the current year, in any case before the March 1994 elections, except in those cases in which it was agreed that full compliance would take place at a later date.

We believe that the Government must agree on specific time-limits that will enable it to end its dilatory behaviour and comply fully with its obligations that it has undertaken. We hope that you obtain specific commit-

ments and measures from the Government of El Salvador so that the peace and democratization process can be brought to a satisfactory conclusion. It is particularly important, as I mentioned in my previous letter, to re-establish direct communication between the parties.

I should like to reiterate, on behalf of all the members of FMLN, our strong desire to continue and promote the Chapultepec process, our firm resolve not to resume the armed struggle, and our assurances that we wish to cooperate in overcoming current difficulties without jeopardizing the peace process in any way.

Finally, I should like to draw your attention to the efforts being made to ban or suspend the legality of FMLN as a political party:

On 14 June, the Supreme Electoral Tribunal decided to request ONUSAL to provide information relating to the discovery of a FPL weapons cache in Managua, "since, in order to register the Partido Farabundo Martí para la Liberación Nacional on 14 December 1992, it was required that the aforementioned party should be a 'truly disarmed organization', as the aforementioned Mission certified on that same day".

The reply of ONUSAL will undoubtedly be of legal significance, since it can be used as evidence against the legality of FMLN, with consequences that could greatly damage the peace process, to which I referred in my previous letter. The manner and terms in which ONUSAL replies to the request of the Supreme Electoral Tribunal will therefore be of the utmost importance. We believe that this situation should be dealt with very carefully.

(*Signed*) Schafik Jorge HÁNDAL

Annex IV

[Original: Spanish]

Letter dated 11 June 1993 from the President of the Republic of El Salvador addressed to the Secretary-General

I am writing to convey to you the deep concern of the Government of the Republic of El Salvador at the large quantities of arms, ammunition and explosives belonging to FMLN recently discovered in Nicaragua, and at the other large quantities which might be present in Nicaragua and about which there is hard information. This should be investigated and verified in the next few days.

The aforementioned discoveries are in addition to the discoveries in El Salvador that we reported earlier to ONUSAL, and demonstrate unequivocally that FMLN has consciously violated its fundamental commitment to hand over all weapons, munitions, mines, other explosives and military equipment of its forces, including those located in other countries. Moreover, it has called into question your statement in the report to the Security Council dated 21 May 1993 (S/25812) that "by 11 February, all the arms stored in the FMLN concentration areas had been destroyed and on 1 April the destruction of arms in deposits outside El Salvador was completed".

The aforementioned violation becomes even more serious if one considers all the efforts you made before 15 December 1992 to ensure that FMLN included in the inventory submitted to ONUSAL large quantities of weapons in its possession that had not been included in the inventory submitted at the beginning of the cease-fire—conduct that was also in violation of the commitments assumed. Furthermore, it confirms the opinion of the Government of El Salvador, which is shared by other Governments, that the weapons and war *matériel* declared by FMLN differed substantially from what was actually its arsenal, a fact which was reported to ONUSAL on many occasions before 15 December 1992, the date on which you certified as satisfactory the inventory of arms and war *matériel* submitted by FMLN.

The conduct of FMLN is extremely serious and could affect the credibility of the entire peace process, but it is also a violation of the constitutional provision prohibiting the existence of armed groups, and it might be a reason to disband FMLN as a political party. In addition, that breach has been described as a serious development by the national supervisory body—COPAZ—as witness the accompanying document.

Our commitment is to consolidate peace in El Sal-

vador; accordingly, the word pledged before you in the Geneva agreement must be honoured. We therefore respectfully request that you give a clear indication that there has been a serious breach of the commitment undertaken by FMLN as described above, and that the ONUSAL certification of complete disarmament on the part of FMLN be left in abeyance, until FMLN has handed over—and made available to ONUSAL for complete destruction—all war *matériel* in its possession either in El Salvador or in other countries. We believe that the gravity of the breach warrants a resolution by the United Nations Security Council; we are calling for a resolution because we think it is necessary in order to safeguard the prestige of a process which, as you stated in the report, constitutes a notable example for the world.

We also believe that the time is ripe for FMLN to be required to disarm the armed groups of members or sympathizers (we have reported them to ONUSAL and it has verified the reports in some cases), or declare that it has severed links with such groups, so that the means afforded by legislation might come into play, with a view to safeguarding the lives and property of the peaceful inhabitants of El Salvador.

Please find attached a copy of all the reports sent to ONUSAL on the question that has prompted this letter, as well as the aforementioned COPAZ statement and documents confirming what we are now reporting.*

(*Signed*) Alfredo CRISTIANI

*These attachments are not included in this report.

Document 83

Report of the ONUSAL Human Rights Division for the period from 1 February to 30 April 1993 (extract)

A/47/968-S/26033, 2 July 1993

I. Introduction

1. In the sixth report it was stated that, starting in February 1993, "with a view to reporting more regularly to the Secretary-General and the General Assembly on the implementation of the San José Agreement (A/44/971-S/21541, annex) and of the human rights components of the other peace agreements, the Human Rights Division [of the United Nations Observer Mission in El Salvador] will submit quarterly reports" (A/47/912-S/25521, para. 5). The seventh report, which covers the period from February to April 1993, is being submitted in compliance with that decision by the Director of the Division, Mr. Diego García-Sayán.

2. During the period under review, the Commission on the Truth released its report on the investigation of serious acts of violence that have occurred since 1980, in accordance with the mandate given to it under the Mexico and Chapultepec peace agreements. The impact of the report of the Commission on the Truth on Salvadorian society has perhaps been the most important human rights development during the period covered by this report (February, March and April), demonstrating yet again that peace and democracy presuppose a system which guarantees the effective exercise of human rights. Above and beyond reactions resulting from a report of this nature, what is important is that the Parties should

fully keep their promise to implement forthwith the recommendations of the report, which are mandatory in nature, as are the other undertakings assumed by the parties under the various peace agreements. ONUSAL will verify the implementation of these obligations.

3. The structure of the present report does not differ substantially from that of the sixth report. With regard to the administration of justice it includes two situation analyses relating to *habeas corpus* and violations of the guarantee of due process which have been identified in judicial practice as major areas. Both analyses were carried out with a positive aim, namely to contribute, at the diagnostic level, to the task of modernizing and reforming the administration of justice which was established by the peace agreements and started with the constitutional reforms adopted in 1991.

4. With respect to the verification of individual freedoms and fundamental rights, the report confirms the trend towards a progressive improvement in the enjoyment of human rights together with the subsistence of violations—some of them serious and systematic—in certain categories of rights.

5. In accordance with the provisions of the San José Agreement, the Parties undertook to give their earliest consideration to any recommendations made to them by the Mission. This provision of the San José Agreement has a decisive impact on the perception of active verification as practical and useful work, a perception which is, quite rightly, sustained by the possibility that the findings may lead to normative changes, administrative arrangements, alternative policies or conducts which may help overcome the problems and expand the level of enjoyment of human rights. Viewed thus, the recommendations of the Human Rights Division are not acts which are isolated from the shared concern of the Parties and of Salvadorian society as a whole. They are, on the contrary, a reflection of the general national consensus regarding the need for legislative changes, political or administrative decisions and lines of institutional conduct all aimed at moving forward towards building a State that will be a guarantor of human rights.

6. Accordingly, it has been deemed advisable, on this occasion, not to include further recommendations in addition to those already made—which are, in themselves, numerous—but to put the emphasis on defining specific lines of action to facilitate implementation of those recommendations, that being the first priority of ONUSAL's active verification.

II. Overall assessment of the situation

7. In reviewing overall trends of human rights in El Salvador, the Human Rights Division, referred, in its previous report, to two aspects which appear to have a sub-stantive impact on implementation of the peace agreements in terms of the promotion and protection of human rights.

8. First of all, the interrelationship that exists between full implementation of the peace agreements, consolidation of democratic life and the rule of law as essential components of the social, political and institutional "environment", is a prerequisite if monitoring of the legality of human rights is to function effectively.

9. Secondly, and as a conclusion derived from the preceding premise, it was pointed out that the continuation over time of existing trends towards improvement, and their extension to categories of rights which still present disturbing violations, depends on a sustained pace in the execution of the peace agreements. That is particularly important if we take into account that the positive trends that have been noted may be related to the system of protection which ONUSAL's presence in itself signifies.

10. The evolution of developments subsequent to the sixth report corroborates the validity of these remarks. The basic trends noted during the months of February, March and April continue to point to the existence of an ambivalent situation, for although progress is being made, at the same time there are still incidents and situations—some of them serious—which disturb ONUSAL, the human rights community of El Salvador and the international community.

11. On the positive side, we see continuation of the improvement noted in respect of cases of torture and enforced disappearances. In the sixth report, the verification carried out by the Human Rights Division established that no violations of that kind were recorded during the period from June 1992 to January 1993. This positive development confirmed trends which had been noted some months earlier.

12. During the months of February, March and April 1993, these very encouraging results were confirmed in the case of enforced disappearances. However, one case of torture has been confirmed and also a number of homicides in which the victims showed clear signs of torture prior to their death. These acts have aroused the concern of the Salvadorian church and of non-governmental organizations; the Government also has expressed consternation because of the assumption that these practices might herald a return to old ways.

13. Continuing with the positive trends, it is well known that the Office of the National Counsel for the defence of human rights is becoming increasingly active and that its autonomy, which is necessary if it is to perform its functions appears to be growing; what is more important, it has begun to win the confidence of the population.

14. In addition, attention should be drawn to the commendable promotion of judicial reform, which began with the constitutional reforms in pursuance of the provisions contained in the peace agreements. The Ministry of Justice's normative proposals, which include not only specific initiatives but also substantive reforms, reflect a willingness not only to comply with the agreements but also to modernize the administration of justice with a view to guaranteeing human rights.

15. On the side of the scale which is still clearly disturbing we find a variety of acts. They range from those relating to specific categories of rights in which there is a downward trend in the number of violations (right to life, right to integrity, right to security, arbitrary detention, violation of due process of law), to more general aspects relating to the resurgence of intolerant attitudes that are incompatible with the view of the Peace Agreements as an instrument for promoting national consensus in order to consolidate the rule of law and democratic life.

16. Of these acts and situations two have had an impact on national life during the period covered by this report. On the one hand, there have been more than a dozen homicides which bear clear signs of having been organized and, on the other, following publication of the report of the Commission on the Truth, there have been some reactions openly opposed to the peace agreements.

17. Concerning the extreme violations of the right to life which have occurred, the Salvadorian Church and non-governmental organizations have sounded the alarm regarding the possibility of a reactivation of the so-called death squads.

18. Notwithstanding the fact that, in the majority of cases, ONUSAL verification has ruled out the presence of squads, there is no doubt that there have been homicides which bear the signs of having been organized and involving methods and procedures similar to those which, in the past, were used by the death squads.

19. With regard to the impact which the report of the Commission on the Truth has had on the State and on society, reactions varied. There were public threats made through paid advertisements sponsored by the intolerant sectors. Some institutions representative of the State also adopted a confrontational attitude. All this generated a relatively tense climate which the Office of the National Counsel for the Defence of Human Rights referred to as a disturbing resurgence of social polarization.

20. However, the parties, through their highest representatives, in their official statement adopted an attitude consistent with the obligations stemming from the peace process. The President of the Republic pointed out that the recommendations of the report were mandatory and that the Government would therefore carry them out, as is natural, within the framework of the Constitutional provisions. The Frente Farabundo Martí para la Liberación Nacional (FMLN) expressed its determination to carry out the recommendations fully. Thus, the parties once again charted a course of conciliation and national understanding as the sole means of giving renewed impetus to the implementation of the peace agreements.

21. The fact that there are strengths and weaknesses in the enjoyment of human rights does not mean that the current situation resembles that of Scylla and Charybdis. It is rather an expression of the complexity of the transition towards democracy, a process in which progress has been made towards a significant improvement in the enjoyment of human rights, particularly when compared to the situation that existed prior to the peace agreements; however, at the same time, it shows that there are deficiencies and difficulties in dealing with equal vigour with problems and conducts shaped over a long period of time during which violence was a sign of the times.

...

VI. Assessment of the recommendations by the Human Rights Division

324. Under the San José Agreement, the parties pledged to implement promptly the recommendations of the ONUSAL Human Rights Division. This provision is rooted in the conviction of both the Government of El Salvador and FMLN that international verification of the enjoyment of human rights in El Salvador should not be limited to mere observation but should promote and influence changes in the structural, legal, institutional and social conditions that had led to widespread serious violations during the armed conflict.

325. Accordingly, active verification in El Salvador was devised as a means of promoting and protecting human rights on a level never before experienced in the United Nations system. The only viable and effective means of ensuring that active verification had an impact on the real situation, in keeping with the desire of the parties, was to have the findings of the monitoring process reflected in concrete and specific recommendations to be implemented by the parties.

326. The recommendations thus express the will of the parties, which have conferred an authority on the ONUSAL Human Rights Division that must be exercised with the overall rationale of the peace process in mind. The recommendations are teleological in nature because they seek to promote the achievement of the ultimate objectives of the peace process. Yet their implementation does not necessarily imply literal response. In some cases, such a response may be necessary, but in others the

recommendation's objective, significance and practical execution can be approached in a number of ways.

327. Beginning with its second report, the Human Rights Division has been formulating a series of recommendations. However, no specific mechanism has been envisaged for their implementation, which has been somewhat ad hoc. As noted in the sixth report, the Government "has accepted some of these recommendations on an ad hoc basis, but the recommendations as a whole ... have not received due attention". The sixth report went on to add that: "As a result of recent consultations, the Human Rights Division has identified a readiness on the part of both the Government and FMLN to appropriately and effectively address the recommendations contained in the various reports. In the short term, there are plans for establishing the consultative mechanisms required for systematic, effective and mutually agreed follow-up to the recommendations" (A/47/912-S/25521, para. 282).

328. The favourable prospects for action indicated in the sixth report have become a reality, for the Minister of the Presidency, Dr. Oscar Alfredo Santamaría, and the Special Representative of the Secretary-General of the United Nations and head of ONUSAL, Dr. Augusto Ramírez Ocampo, have agreed that the subject of human rights and, specifically, the recommendations of the Human Rights Division should be periodically evaluated at joint meetings at the highest level. The outcome of the initial meetings has been highly satisfactory, since they have made it possible not only to initiate the process for full implementation of the recommendations but to review the entire human rights situation as well. It is in this context that the Human Rights Division has submitted to the Government a report of violations calling for a thorough investigation.

329. At the same time, the Government and ONUSAL have agreed on the establishment of executive machinery to implement agreements reached in the context of the joint periodic evaluations at the highest political level referred to in the paragraph above. This executive machinery is constituted by the Presidential Commissioner for Human Rights and the Director of the ONUSAL Human Rights Division, with their respective teams of technical consultants. The establishment of this executive machinery is a sign that the political will required for the implementation of the ONUSAL recommendations exists.

330. In connection with the establishment of the machinery to follow up the recommendations of the Human Rights Division, section V of the report which the Secretary-General of the United Nations submitted to the Security Council on 21 May 1993 (S/25812) referred to an appendix (S/25812/Add.3) containing a full list of the recommendations of the ONUSAL Human Rights Division, to be implemented in fulfilment of the obligations resulting both from the San José Agreement and from the report of the Commission on the Truth. The recommendations are as follows:

1. Ratification of international human rights instruments to which the Government of El Salvador has not acceded or that it has not ratified as yet (listed in the sixth report);

2. Structural and functional reform of the judiciary;

3. Establishment of a special commission of inquiry to investigate arbitrary and extralegal executions;

4. Amendment of the legislation governing the remedies of *habeas corpus* and *amparo* to make them effective;

5. Establishment of a compensation fund for victims of human rights violations;

6. Improvement of the composition and powers of the National Council of the Judiciary and ensuring the independence of the Judicial Training School;

7. Elimination of extrajudicial confession;

8. Definition of torture and enforced disappearance as offences in special criminal legislation;

9. Drafting and passing legislation regulating the conduct of law enforcement officials;

10. Abolition of the practice of arbitrary detention for petty misdemeanours and repeal of the 1886 Police Act;

11. Temporary application of the Act governing the procedure for administrative detention or the imposition of administrative fines;

12. Amendment of the disciplinary regime under the Career Judicial Service Act so that the Supreme Court of Justice or its President can investigate formally any irregularities or violations of due process;

13. Authorization of a visit to El Salvador by the ILO Committee on Freedom of Association;

14. Investigations by the Supreme Court of violations of due process;

15. Prompt legal recognition of associations and trade unions.

331. At the initiative of the Executive—to be exact, the Ministry of Justice—a start has been made on the process of implementing a great number of recommendations, through the global and sectoral reforms that the Ministry of Justice is preparing with a view to eliminating the flaws that continue to exist in the administration of justice. Examples of such action are the elimination of extrajudicial confession, the definition of torture and

enforced disappearance as offences, and the commencement of the reform of the legislation on *habeas corpus.*

332. Furthermore, as already indicated in this report, in the period under review developments with regard to the issue of arbitrary detention for petty misdemeanours appear to have begun to lead to action representing a promising start on the implementation of the relevant recommendation. Once implementation of the relevant new plan begins, the situation will have to be assessed again. The recommendations on military training and a new military doctrine are being implemented properly. As of the completion of this report, the Armed Forces have begun to fulfil their undertakings with regard to the issuance of a new military doctrine.

333. Generally speaking, in the context of the bilateral meetings being held both in the area of the political consultation mechanism and in the operational area, ongoing implementation of recommendations is being assessed and the establishment of criteria for implementing recommendations whose implementation has not yet begun is being considered. As a result of this work, the eighth report of the Human Rights Division will contain a specific assessment of the implementation of each individual recommendation.

VII. Conclusions

334. In general, with some slight variations, the trend towards a definite improvement compared with the situation that existed prior to the signing of the peace agreements continues. At the same time, the situation remains very mixed, in that violations—some of them serious and systematic—involving essentially the right to life, security, integrity of person, liberty and due process of law continue to occur.

335. The trend towards the absence of enforced disappearances and torture, already referred to in the sixth report, has continued (although one instance of torture was reported during the period covered by this report); at the same time, arbitrary and extralegal executions and organized acts of "private justice" have been committed using methods and practices displayed by irregular groups, whose possible resurgence has generated considerable alarm in the church, the Office of the National Counsel for the Defence of Human Rights and other representative institutions.

336. The right to liberty continues to be affected by arbitrary detentions for "petty misdemeanours", although the competent authorities, in coordination with ONUSAL, have begun to adopt corrective measures which should mitigate the severity of this problem.

337. With regard to the administration of justice, the problems analysed in the Division's earlier reports on the subject have persisted. At the same time, however, the executive branch, proceeding in a manner consistent with initiatives under way in civilian society, has encouraged significant judicial reforms which reflect modern doctrines that guarantee human rights. Violations of the due process of law continue to be widespread.

338. The right to freedom of association as it pertains to trade union freedoms, and the effective enjoyment of workers' rights, continue to be subject to the limitations and restrictions outlined in the sixth report. Moreover, the promising agreements reached within the framework of the Forum for Economic and Social Consultation have encountered serious obstacles, given the momentary paralysis in consultations between Government, management and labour.

339. Freedom of expression and political rights are not subject to any restriction and are guaranteed by the State.

340. The activities of the Office of the National Counsel for the Defence of Human Rights have entered a qualitatively advanced stage, and the Office is emerging as an institution with the autonomy and political will required for it to fulfil its constitutional mandates to promote and safeguard human rights. In that connection, oversight of legality in respect of human rights in El Salvador, through the quasi-jurisdictional mechanism of the Ombudsman, is beginning to have a beneficial impact on the rights of the population.

341. Although ordinary violence has not increased disproportionately compared to the period before peace was established, it is exerting a negative impact on society that clearly is not conducive to the enjoyment of human rights. The weight of ordinary violence, measured in terms of the deaths caused and the calibre of weapons used, continues to generate a growing feeling of insecurity in the population. The steps taken by the Government to collect weapons from the population have not produced significant results. As long as that situation continues, not only will ordinary violence continue to pose a serious problem, but also, the latent conditions for a resurgence of selective acts of political violence will persist.

342. It is necessary to point out that the violations currently being reported are occurring in a qualitatively different framework from the serious human rights situation which existed in El Salvador in the past. The violations being committed today are not a reflection of the will of the State, but rather, are acts which must be interpreted as carry-overs from the situation that existed prior to the signing of the peace agreements. At the present time, the political, institutional and social changes taking place in El Salvador are, on the contrary, characterized by the affirmation of the rule of law, democratic life and the protection and promotion of human rights. This process cannot unfold in a linear fashion, and by its very nature gives rise to a series of contradictions

and encounters various difficulties. The essential factor here is that the momentum of the peace process gradually overcomes problems, even those arising from the fact that certain agreements are not yet being observed. The will of the parties to honour the human rights agreements plays a fundamental role in this positive process; it deserves the support of the international community.

343. The agreement reached with the Government of El Salvador concerning the assessment of the human rights situation and follow-up to the rcommendations of ONUSAL, through machinery for consultation at both the political and executive levels, is an example of political will that is fully consistent with the spirit and the letter of the peace agreements.

Document 84

Letter dated 7 July 1993 from the Secretary-General to the President of the Security Council concerning the purification of the armed forces

S/26052, 8 July 1993

I refer to my letter of 2 April 1993 (S/25516), by which I informed the Security Council about recent developments in the implementation of the provisions of the Peace Accords for El Salvador relating to the purification of the Armed Forces (see S/23501, annex, chap. I, sect. 3).

In that letter, I informed the Security Council that President Cristiani had agreed to a plan under which, at the latest by 30 June 1993, the last 15 high-ranking officers whose situation had not yet been regularized would be placed on leave with pay pending completion of the procedures for their retirement, which would take place not later than 31 December 1993. Under the plan, it was also agreed that, while on leave with pay, these 15 officers would not perform any official functions.

In my letter, I also stated that, when implemented, the above-mentioned arrangement would bring the Gov-

ernment of El Salvador into broad compliance with the Ad Hoc Commission's recommendations, although with a delay of several months in relation to the date established by the Accords.

Following publication of the General Order of 30 June 1993 by the High Command of the Armed Forces of El Salvador, ONUSAL has verified that the 15 officers have been placed on leave with pay, as envisaged in the plan presented by President Cristiani. I am therefore in a position to confirm that the Government of El Salvador has now taken the steps that it promised to comply with the Ad Hoc Commission's recommendations.

I would be grateful if you would bring this letter to the attention of the members of the Security Council.

(*Signed*) Boutros BOUTROS-GHALI

Document 85

Letter dated 12 July 1993 from the President of the Security Council to the Secretary-General concerning the discovery of illegal arms deposits belonging to the FMLN

S/26071, 12 July 1993

I have the honour to inform you that the members of the Security Council have taken note with appreciation of your report of 29 June 1993 (S/26005) regarding the recent discovery, at locations inside and outside El Salvador, of illegal arms deposits belonging to the Frente Farabundo Martí para la Liberación Nacional (FMLN).

The members of the Security Council express their continuing concern regarding this grave violation of the Peace Accords, and agree with your opinion that the maintenance of clandestine arms deposits by the FMLN

has raised questions of confidence and trust and that the seriousness of this situation cannot be over-emphasized.

The members of the Council reiterate their view that both parties should comply fully with their respective obligations under the Peace Accords, and especially that the FMLN should provide a complete inventory of all its arms and munitions both inside and outside El Salvador and deliver them to ONUSAL for their destruction in accordance with the provisions of the Peace Accords.

The members of the Council note the FMLN's promise to disclose all its holdings of arms and munitions and subsequently to destroy them by 4 August 1993. The members of the Council stress that the complete disarmament of the FMLN, and the reintegration of its members into the civil, political and institutional life of the country, form an essential part of the peace process.

The members of the Security Council share your assessment that it is an indication of the strength and irreversibility of the peace process that a serious incident of this nature has not been allowed to derail the implementation of the Peace Accords. The members of the Council also agree with your view that the cancellation or suspension of the FMLN's status as a political party could deal a severe blow to the peace process.

The members of the Council welcome the letter from the Minister for Foreign Affairs of the Republic of Nicaragua addressed to you on 22 June 1993 (S/26008), and expect that the Government of Nicaragua will comply with its international obligations to prevent the use of its territory for the illegal storage or transshipment of arms and other war *matériel* and to investigate fully all the illegal arms deposits discovered in Nicaragua, including possible links to international terrorism.

The members of the Council welcome your intention to keep the Council informed of further developments, especially the actions the FMLN has promised to complete by 4 August 1993.

(*Signed*) Sir David HANNAY
President of the Security Council

Document 86

Letter dated 13 July 1993 from President Cristiani to the Secretary-General concerning the recommendations of the Commission on the Truth

Not issued as a United Nations document; original in Spanish

We respectfully refer, in the context of compliance with the Peace Agreements, to the recommendations of the Commission on the Truth. As we have stated in the past, we shall comply with those recommendations as far as we are competent to do so, in accordance with the Constitution of the Republic and in conformity with the spirit and the letter of the said Agreements.

On this basis, the Government has, in close communication with the Director of ONUSAL, embarked on a programme of work which has enabled comprehensive analysis of the subject. The analysis has yielded highly satisfactory results in terms of a recognition that the Government is in a position to promote fulfilment of all but the three following objectives: separations from public office and factors disqualifying an individual from exercising such office; constitutional reforms and matters in which initiative and action must come from the judicial authority through the Supreme Court of Justice. In this connection, it will be a pleasure to speak with you at our meeting during the Third Ibero-American Summit, to be held at Salvador, Bahía, Brazil, on 15 July.

In the hope that we shall meet very soon, we are pleased to convey to you the renewed assurances of our highest consideration.

(*Signed*) Alfredo CRISTIANI

Document 87

Letter dated 13 July 1993 from the President of the Security Council to the Secretary-General welcoming confirmation of El Salvador's compliance with the Ad Hoc Commission's recommendations regarding the armed forces

S/26077, 13 July 1993

I have the honour to inform you that your letter dated 7 July 1993 (S/26052) concerning the implementation of the provisions of the Peace Accords for El Salvador relating to the Ad Hoc Commission's recommendations regarding the Armed Forces has been brought to the attention of the members of the Council.

The members of the Council welcome your confirmation that the Government of El Salvador has now complied with the Ad Hoc Commission's recommendations. They believe that the actions taken by the Government of El Salvador represent a significant achievement in the consolidation of the peace process in El Salvador.

(Signed) Sir David HANNAY
President of the Security Council

Document 88

Report of the Secretary-General on developments concerning the identification and destruction of clandestine arms deposits belonging to the FMLN

S/26371, 30 August 1993

1. The present report is submitted in pursuance of my report of 29 June 1993 (S/26005) in which I undertook to keep the Security Council informed of developments concerning the identification and destruction of clandestine arms deposits belonging to the Frente Farabundo Martí para la Liberación Nacional (FMLN), the presence of which in the territory of El Salvador and that of certain neighbouring countries had been acknowledged by FMLN. It will be recalled that, as reported in the above-mentioned document (para. 5), FMLN had informed me that it would cooperate with ONUSAL in locating and destroying all such remaining weapons within a period of 45 days beginning on 21 June 1993, i.e., by 4 August 1993.

2. In the wake of that commitment, continuous and systematic operations were carried out by ONUSAL, on the basis of information provided by FMLN and with its active cooperation, to complete the destruction of the contents of all illegal caches by the above-mentioned deadline. By that date, however, only 85 per cent of the clandestine arms located had been destroyed. The delay was due mainly to logistical and operational difficulties, arising in particular from the dispersion of what turned out to be a large number of small deposits; the difficulties of the terrain; the poor condition and resulting instability of the explosives; the independent handling of relevant information by the various constituent groups of FMLN; and the need to coordinate with the national authorities in Nicaragua and Honduras. Further, a new list of clandestine arms was presented to ONUSAL on 3 August by one of the FMLN constituent groups.

3. The overall process of verification and destruction of FMLN weapons and equipment mandated by the Peace Accords, which was finally completed on 18 August 1993, includes two distinct phases. The first covers the period until the accidental explosion of the illegal arms cache in Managua on 23 May 1993 (see S/25901). Weapons verified and destroyed during that period include those that were turned in at 15 ONUSAL verification centres in El Salvador by 15 December 1992, as well as those voluntarily declared later, prior to the Managua explosion, which were held in Honduras, Nicaragua and El Salvador. The second phase covers ONUSAL's operations with respect to arms discovered in the immediate aftermath of the Managua incident and those declared by FMLN in compliance with its renewed commitment to disclose all its remaining weapons. These operations were carried out in El Salvador, Nicaragua and Honduras.

4. Weapons and war-related *matériel* verified and destroyed during the first phase represent approximately 70 per cent of the total quantity located during both phases. Figures for items turned in by 15 December 1992 and in later voluntary declarations prior to the Managua explosion include, respectively: 5,929 and 1,216 individual arms; 334 and 26 support weapons; 163,891 and 219,080 rounds of ammunition; 25 and 7 rockets; and 756 and 1,632 grenades. In addition, 687 kilograms of explosives, 54 surface-to-air missiles and 29 pieces of communications equipment were also located and destroyed.

5. In the second phase, ONUSAL verified and destroyed approximately 30 per cent of the total FMLN weapons and munitions, representing those discovered or turned in as a consequence of the Managua explosion (20 per cent) and those declared following FMLN's commitment to me (10 per cent). They include, respectively: 1,701 and 1,005 individual arms; 3 and 16 support weapons; 1,413,380 and 2,236,255 rounds of ammunition; 1 and 107 rockets; 2,880 and 3,960 grenades; 2,026 and 2,394 kilograms of explosives and 34 pieces of communications equipment; as well as 19 and 1 surface-to-air missiles.

6. In addition to the armament found in the five safe houses in Nicaragua, of which I informed the Council in my report of 29 June 1993 (see S/26005, para. 6), the second phase entailed the uncovering, with the help of FMLN, of 114 arms caches in and outside El Salvador. The actual destruction of the *matériel* found in those caches which, owing to the difficulties mentioned above was an arduous and challenging task, was carried out by the military component of ONUSAL with the support of the civilian police component.

7. The condition and operational utility of the armament identified in the second phase varies. While the weapons and munitions encountered in Honduras and Nicaragua were in an advanced state of deterioration, those found in El Salvador, although fewer in number, had operative and logistic value. Arms were in good condition, ammunition was accessible, storage techniques were good and caches were distributed throughout 10 of the 14 geographical departments of the country.

8. Total figures for the complete inventory of FMLN arms and munitions identified since the cease-fire came into effect on 1 February 1992 thus include 10,230 arms (9,851 individual and 379 support weapons); 4,032,606 rounds of ammunition, 140 rockets, 9,228 grenades; 5,107 kilograms of explosives and 63 pieces of communications equipment; as well as 74 surface-to-air missiles. The number of identified arms caches belonging to all five constituent groups of FMLN is 128, of which 109 were in El Salvador, 14 in Nicaragua and 5 in Honduras.

9. Since, in accordance with the agreements, ONUSAL had to rely on the data voluntarily provided by the parties as its main source of information, a comparative analysis based on other official and unofficial sources was made in order to make a realistic assessment of FMLN inventory. The criteria considered included: estimates by well-known international and national research institutions on military matters; number of demobilization certificates issued by ONUSAL to ex-FMLN combatants (totalling 8,430 individuals, of whom 1,018 are war-disabled); and acquisition and operative plans disclosed. Furthermore, it should be noted that, according to Salvadorian Army press bulletins issued throughout the war, the Armed Forces captured more than 4,000 individual weapons (some unofficial sources put this figure at 7,000), 270 support weapons and some 4,500,000 rounds of ammunition, as well as 31 surface-to-air missiles.

10. Taking these elements as a point of reference and on the basis of ONUSAL's verification of the destruction of weapons discovered or declared by FMLN, I am in a position to state that by all available indications its military structure has now been effectively dismantled and that its former combatants have been demobilized and have been reintegrated, within a framework of full legality, into the civil, institutional and political life of the country, as established in the Peace Accords. With the closing down of this delicate process, the apprehensions raised by the discovery of large quantities of undeclared weapons still in FMLN possession seem now to have been surmounted.

11. Despite some delays in providing all the lists of arms declared by each of its constituent groups, FMLN was forthcoming and cooperative during the entire operation. Attached to the present report as annex I is the text of a certificate subscribed by the five members of the former General Command and addressed to my Special Representative in El Salvador to the effect that, to the best of their knowledge, all weapons, ammunition, mines, other explosives and military equipment belonging to FMLN have now been located, collected and destroyed. The five further state that any weapons confiscated in future should be accounted for solely by the persons in whose possession they are found and will not be FMLN's responsibility. In a public statement to this effect, which is also attached to the present report as annex II, FMLN again reaffirms that it has definitively given up arms as a means to achieve its goals and is determined to undertake political action only within the legal and institutional framework of the country. On 23 August 1993, I received from the Coordinator General of FMLN, Mr. Schafik Handal, a letter dated 21 August in which, *inter alia*, he expresses on behalf of the FMLN leadership the view that they have now complied fully with their undertaking to end the military structure of FMLN.

12. The Salvadorian Supreme Electoral Tribunal (Tribunal Supremo Electoral) has been duly informed of the foregoing by my Special Representative. It will be recalled that the Tribunal, which, on the basis of ONUSAL's certification that all the items in the FMLN inventory had been accounted for and were being destroyed, had granted to it the status of a political party, had requested from ONUSAL a full report on the discovery of undeclared arms.

13. There is little doubt that, due to the circumstances surrounding a bitter armed conflict such as the one which prevailed in El Salvador for 12 years, the irregular nature of the war and the sense of insecurity inherent to a post-war period in any country, an unknown number of weapons and remnants of war-related *matériel* are likely to remain for some time in the hands of individuals or groups, including criminal ones. As announced by FMLN, these cases should be dealt with in accordance with the laws of the country. In addition, there could still be cases of individuals willingly handing in arms, or of the chance discovery of isolated arms caches which were at one time under

the responsibility of individuals who subsequently lost their lives in the conflict, unbeknownst to FMLN.

14. The facts reported have brought into sharp focus the public's condemnation of armed groups and the futility of arms as a viable means to achieve political aims. In this climate, various groups and individuals have come forward spontaneously to declare unregistered weapons. The Government of El Salvador, the Commission for the Consolidation of Peace (COPAZ) and the Legislative Assembly should accelerate action in order to put into effect as quickly as possible regulations regarding private security services and the effective registration, possession and bearing of firearms. Such measures would enable the authorities to conduct a systematic and permanent campaign to recover all unregistered military weapons currently in the hands of private entities or individuals, thus contributing to the effective disarming of Salvadorian society.

15. I should like to commend the restraint exercised by President Cristiani during this delicate period. I should also like to thank the Governments of Nicaragua and Honduras for their full cooperation with ONUSAL in this matter. The United Nations will continue to lend its full support to the Salvadorian peace process, whose resilience and irreversibility have again been demonstrated during this difficult test. It is to be hoped that the activities leading to the March 1994 elections now will develop in an atmosphere of normality, thus reinforcing the peace process which in general has been exemplary.

Annex I

[Original: Spanish]

Certification

We, Schafik Jorge Handal, José Eduardo Sancho Castañeda, Joaquín Villalobos Huezo, Salvador Sánchez Cerén and Francisco Alberto Jovel Urquilla, members of the former General Command of the Frente Farabundo Martí para la Liberación Nacional,

HEREBY CERTIFY:

That, as we offered to do in our letter of 19 June, addressed to the Secretary-General, we the members of the former FMLN General Command have expedited and completed the task of locating, collecting and destroying, in close cooperation with ONUSAL, the remaining weapons held in scattered stockpiles over which we had no firm control.

That having completed the activities implied by this commitment, we are able to certify to you that to our knowledge there are no weapons, ammunition, mines, other explosives or military equipment belonging to FMLN remaining to be handed over and destroyed.

Consequently, the arms confiscated after this date shall be accounted for solely by the persons in whose possession

they are found. FMLN disclaims all responsibility.

In order that this may be placed on record with the United Nations in the person of the Special Representative of the Secretary-General, Mr. Augusto Ramírez Ocampo, we hereby issue and sign this document in San Salvador, on 17 August 1993.

(*Signed*) Schafik Jorge HÁNDAL

(*Signed*) José Eduardo SANCHO CASTAÑEDA

(*Signed*) Joaquín VILLALOBOS HUEZO

(*Signed*) Salvador SÁNCHEZ CERÉN

(*Signed*) Francisco Alberto JOVEL URQUILLA

Annex II

[Original: Spanish]

FMLN *communiqué*

We, the political leaders of the five organizations making up the party, meeting in assembly on 14 August at the El Espino estate, hereby declare:

1. We are a new party, democratic and pluralistic, in which various revolutionary political tendencies coexist and will continue to coexist.

2. The full implementation of the Chapultepec Agreements, which embodies our objectives of demilitarization, democratization and social development, constitutes the basis of our programmatic platform.

3. We have unanimously reaffirmed our total commitment to the peace and democratization process initiated with the signing of the Agreements and, hence, our firm determination to strive, wholeheartedly and exclusively, for the consolidation of that process in the political, institutional and legal fields. Armed conflict is a thing of the past; we have completely abandoned it and do not consider it a valid option in this new phase.

4. We emphatically reject the activities of armed groups, whatever justification they may claim. We continue fighting for the establishment of a State in which the rule of law truly prevails and within that context we support the just struggles of the people's movement and civilian society.

5. We have completed the process of handing over and destroying all the weapons that were still in our possession. We consider that this chapter in the implementation of the Agreements by FMLN is closed.

As we have already stated to the Secretary-General of the United Nations, any further weapons that may be discovered will be the individual responsibility of those concerned.

6. We are moving forward as a party, united in an

intensive electoral political effort with a single list of candidates and one strategy, in coalition with Convergencia Democrática. We shall continue striving to broaden this coalition.

7. We are aware that we represent hope to broad sections of the population and we shall pursue with responsibility, enthusiasm and energy our historic task of achieving, through political struggle, the establishment of a regime that guarantees, for all Salvadorians, economic development with democracy and social justice.

San Salvador, 16 August 1993

FMLN POLITICAL COMMITTEE

Document 89

Report of the ONUSAL Human Rights Division for the period from 1 May to 31 July 1993 (extract)

A/47/1012-S/26416, 15 September 1993

I. Introduction

1. This report contains an evaluation of the human rights situation in El Salvador during the period from 1 May to 31 July 1993. The text follows the basic structure of previous reports, although it has been deemed appropriate to group the summary accounts of some representative cases of existing violations in a supplementary document.

2. Furthermore, in order to ensure that the work of active verification receives the necessary public dissemination, which in itself is a means of promotion and protection, beginning with this report it has been deemed appropriate to include an account of all complaints declared admissible by the Human Rights Division during the period under consideration.

3. The report contains, in addition, the results of a study examining the degree of effectiveness or ineffectiveness of the application of the remedy of *amparo* in judicial practice, the goal, as always, being to contribute to the judicial reform process and to help improve the administration of justice.

4. As stated in the previous report, the section on ONUSAL recommendations contains a detailed analysis of the compliance or non-compliance with those recommendations.

5. The methodology used in the reports takes as a point of reference the changes in the human rights situation over the three months analysed in each report. Thus, the reports do not necessarily reflect trends, but rather, situations at different points in time. Analysis of trends will be included in the ninth report on the basis of cumulative data over nine months.

II. Overall assessment of the situation

6. The human rights situation in El Salvador continues to evolve in an ambivalent manner. On the one hand, signs of improvement are continuing while, on the other, grave violations, especially in relation to the right to life, persist and are even growing worse. The fact that there have been no reports of enforced disappearances over a total period of 13 months illustrates the former; the existence of politically motivated arbitrary executions and torture, the latter.

7. In the context of the implementation of the peace agreements, this reality calls for greater responsibility on the part of the State in fulfilling its obligation to provide guarantees, especially with regard to ensuring that the perpetrators of violations do not go unpunished. The fact that a large part of the complaints verified by ONUSAL, the Office of the National Counsel for the Defence of Human Rights and non-governmental organizations continue to go unpunished, notwithstanding the institutional reforms undertaken, is due to the limited ability of the competent bodies to investigate offences and punish offenders. This situation brings with it negative consequences that can result in an increase in violations and can jeopardize existing improvements.

8. At the same time the violence continues, and no overall solution has been found for dealing with the real causes of the problem. There is a pressing need to disarm civilians who are in possession of military weapons, and this calls for the immediate approval of appropriate legislation so that the necessary administrative measures may be taken for the recovery of these weapons.

9. With regard to the situation of trade union rights and freedom of association, there are growing problems that require fundamental solutions both within the Forum for Economic and Social Consultation and with respect to the labour conflicts which have just arisen. Dialogue and negotiation are indispensable tools of a labour policy compatible with the peace agreements and existing international norms. The State, the business community and workers must continue on this path in search of negotiated agreements.

...

V. Assessment of the recommendations by the Human Rights Division

111. In its seventh report, the Human Rights Division gave an account of the establishment of a mechanism for consultations between the Government of El Salvador and ONUSAL for the proper implementation of recommendations by the Human Rights Division. At the same time, a list was made of the recommendations which the Government of El Salvador is responsible for implementing in accordance with provisions of the San José agreement.

112. In this connection, a concise assessment is given of the implementation process relating to the aforementioned recommendations:

1. Ratification of or accession to international instruments, including the Conventions of the International Labour Organisation mentioned in the sixth report.

Implementation:

The Government has expressed its willingness to ratify or accede very shortly, to the human rights conventions save for the one concerning recognition of the compulsory jurisdiction of the Inter-American Court of Human Rights. The Government has stated that the ILO Conventions will be dealt with within the framework of consultations held in the Forum for Economic and Social Consultation.

2. Structural and functional reform of the judiciary.

Implementation:

The implementation of this recommendation entails necessary constitutional reforms. However, normative reforms are being carried out towards this end. Those reforms which are particularly relevant are the substantive and sectoral reforms promoted by the Ministry of Justice. Some of these reforms, such as elimination of the automatic reviews and amendments already adopted with respect to the public defender, have already been adopted by the Legislative Assembly. Other amendments to the institution of *habeas corpus* and the draft new code of criminal procedure are being discussed with the legal community.

There are plans to adopt a new penal code and a code of penal procedure, as well as specific legislation to abolish extrajudicial confession, eliminate the presumption of guilt, shorten administrative detention, transfer petty misdemeanours from police jurisdiction to the magistrate's courts, introduce new regulations covering investigations and searches and amend the code of military justice.

3. Establishment of a special commission of inquiry to investigate arbitrary and extralegal executions.

Implementation:

The Government has stated that it is prepared to give priority to the investigation of cases brought to its attention by ONUSAL, as well as by non-governmental organizations, as possible summary or arbitrary executions. At the same time it has stated that it would not be possible to establish a special commission, since the structure of the country's institutions does not allow for such investigative bodies. Accordingly, it has been agreed that the main purpose of the recommendation, which is to ensure that investigations are independent, prompt and efficient as a means of avoiding impunity, will be borne in mind.

The efficiency of a mechanism whereby the Criminal Investigation Commission undertakes—independently of any proceedings which the relevant organs may be required to institute—to investigate cases of violent or presumed politically motivated deaths brought to the Government's attention by the Human Rights Division, is being explored. Under this mechanism ONUSAL is to put before the Criminal Investigation Commission and the National Police, via the Minister for the Presidency and the Ministry of Justice, priority cases of deaths requiring prompt, independent and efficient investigation. An account of these is to be found in the supplement to this report. The initial experience with this procedure indicates that specific criteria—both technical and with respect to duration—must be established for investigations by the Criminal Investigation Commission, so that the investigations may fulfil the requirements of promptness, independence and efficiency, it being understood that, if they do not, it would mean the recommendation was not being implemented.

4. Amendment to the legislation governing remedies of *habeas corpus* and *amparo* to make them effective.

Implementation:

The Government has submitted to national debate a draft bill which amends the legislation regarding *habeas corpus*. In general terms said draft is a positive step, although there may be further amendments to enhance its effectiveness. The Human Rights Division will present to the Ministry of Justice an analysis of the above-mentioned draft with specific proposals. Nevertheless, as has been stated in previous reports, and specifically in the recommendation on the subject, in order properly to guarantee the remedy of *habeas corpus*, constitutional reforms are needed in order to ensure that applicants have full access to the courts; at present this is limited to the Constitutional Chamber of the Supreme Court.

No initiative has yet been taken with respect to the

remedy of *amparo*; the recommendation consequently has yet to be implemented.

5. Establishment of a compensation fund for victims of human rights violations.

Implementation:

Preliminary steps have been taken to implement this recommendation; they include an examination of different modalities for the establishment of the fund, such as criteria for determining the number of potential beneficiaries and the identification of the necessary financial resources. The Human Rights Commission of El Salvador (CDHES) has drawn up a plan for the creation of a special national reparation and reconciliation fund and has submitted the text of the draft bill to the Legislative Assembly. The CDHES plan contains many constructive and suitable elements which should be taken into account; the Human Rights Division considers that implementation of this recommendation is a matter of urgency that can no longer be postponed.

6. Improvement of the composition and powers of the National Council of the Judiciary and independence of the Judicial Training School.

Implementation:

This recommendation entails amending the Act on the National Council of the Judiciary and also the Constitution. Nothing has been done as yet to implement it.

7. Elimination of extrajudicial confession.

Implementation:

With the new Public Defenders Act and the amendments to the Code of Criminal Procedure and to the Act organizing the Public Prosecutor's Office, regulating the right of the accused to legal defence, the practice of extrajudicial confession has decreased. Nevertheless, the Ministry of Justice has submitted a preliminary bill specifically prohibiting extrajudicial confessions, and designed also to safeguard the constitutional provision which provides that statements obtained against the will of the individual shall be invalid and that anyone who obtains and uses such statements shall be held criminally liable.

The purpose of this text is to protect the right of the accused not to be forced to incriminate himself or herself, and to disallow the use of extrajudicial confession as evidence.

Once this bill is adopted, after it has been discussed with the legal community and submitted to the Legislative Assembly, this recommendation will have been implemented. There will, however, remain one additional task, namely, monitoring the effective implementation of the laws by the police and judges.

8. Definition of torture and enforced disappearance as offences in special criminal legislation.

Implementation:

The preliminary bill of a new Penal Code submitted by the Minister of Justice defines torture as an offence against the fundamental right to security and integrity of person. It likewise defines enforced disappearance as an offence, stating that any official who legally or illegally detains an individual without indicating the latter's whereabouts shall be liable to imprisonment from four to eight years, a fine for a period of 180 to 250 days at the prescribed rate and general disqualification for a period of six to ten years, providing that the offence is not one punishable by a heavier penalty. The bill defines the offences of enforced disappearance proper, enforced disappearance carried out by individuals following orders and enforced disappearance entailing culpable responsibility for allowing or agreeing to the commission of the offence.

Implementation of the recommendation began with the initiative of the Ministry of Justice; implementation will be completed once the relevant corresponding legislation has been adopted.

9. Legislation regulating the conduct of law enforcement officials in terms of ensuring respect for human rights.

Implementation:

The Ministry of Justice has drafted a preliminary bill concerning regulations for administrative detention aimed at averting excess and abuse in the use of force during detention by adopting the Code of Conduct for Law Enforcement Officials, adopted by the General Assembly of the United Nations, as part of domestic legislation.

The passing of this preliminary bill will mean that the corresponding recommendation is being implemented; other partial reforms, such as those referred to in the regulation covering investigations and searches, will also contribute to this objective. Once the corresponding legislation has been passed after consultation with the legal community and the citizenry, it will be indispensable to set up machinery for cooperation and evaluation of its implementation with the Civil Police, the National Police and the Anti-Drug-Trafficking Unit.

10. Abolition of the practice of arbitrary detention for petty misdemeanours.

Implementation:

ONUSAL has been encouraging implementation of this recommendation in coordination with the National Police, the National Civil Police, the Supreme Court and the municipalities. Towards this end, certain verification procedures have been worked out and a set of instructions have been issued to the police force to decrease the number of such arbitrary detentions while legislative reforms are being adopted.

Assessment of the implementation of the instructions indicates that implementation is not yet satisfactory. A programme to encourage proper implementation has been developed in cooperation with the courts. Similar action is to be taken with the municipalities. Arbitrary detention for petty misdemeanours is the main cause of the violation of the right to liberty in this country. By dealing with the problems and shortcomings identified in the execution of the instructions it will be possible to move towards reducing the high incidence of arbitrary detention. However implementation of the recommendation requires, as a matter of urgency, the repeal of the Police Act of 1896 and adoption of the preliminary bills on regulations governing detention by the police authorities and transfer of petty misdemeanours from police jurisdiction to the magistrate's courts.

11. Temporary application of the Act governing the procedure for administrative detention or the imposition of administrative fines.

Implementation:

This recommendation is linked to the previous one as a temporary means of lowering the high incidence of arbitrary detentions for petty misdemeanours. The police instructions regarding misdemeanours were designed with a view to applying the Act governing the procedure for administrative detention or the imposition of administrative fines (Legislative Decree No. 457) instead of resorting to obsolete provisions of the Police Act of 1886 or illegal proceedings. Although marked progress has been made, the Act is not being adequately implemented as yet. A programme for the National Civil Police, the National Police, the Municipal Police, and the Anti-Drug-Trafficking Unit must be set up as a matter of urgency in order to establish that, during the transition period prior to repeal of the Police Act of 1886 and the transfer of petty misdemeanour cases from police jurisdiction to the magistrate's courts, the provisions of Legislative Decree No. 457 must be applied in cases of administrative arrest.

12. Amendment to the disciplinary regime under the Career Judicial Service Act so that the Supreme Court of Justice or its President can investigate formally any irregularities or violations of due process.

Implementation:

ONUSAL has been holding consultations with the Supreme Court of Justice on the implementation of this recommendation which is essential in assuring the effectiveness of the guarantees of due legal process, especially *vis-à-vis* the right to legal counsel, the right to be tried by a competent tribunal within a reasonable period of time and the right to a fair trial.

13. Legal recognition of associations and trade unions.

Implementation:

Although some progress has been achieved under the consultation mechanism, this recommendation has yet to be implemented.

14. Visit by the ILO Committee on Freedom of Association.

Implementation:

The Committee will undertake the proposed visit to El Salvador pursuant to the recommendation.

15. Inclusion of a human rights component as a substantive and permanent feature of military training.

Implementation:

This recommendation, which is already being implemented must, by its very nature, be a continuing process. In this regard, the Human Rights Division will submit a specific cooperation programme to the Armed Forces.

16. Recovery of weapons which are intended exclusively for Armed Forces personnel but which are in the possession of individuals and tighter monitoring of the use of arms by military officers in active service.

Implementation:

Notwithstanding the steps taken, this recommendation has yet to be implemented because of the ineffectiveness of the measures; as a result, a situation which is propitious to human rights violations still persists. Legislation must be drafted to define the legal framework for the possession of weapons and empower the competent authorities to collect weapons in the possession of the civilian population.

17. Budget autonomy for the Office of the National Counsel for the Defence of Human Rights.

Implementation:

This recommendation should be implemented in accordance with the general rules governing the auditing of State accounts. However, consultations between the Government and the Office with regard to its implementation have not yet begun.

18. Lifting of any restrictions on NGO activities and support for their work programmes.

Implementation:

The legal status of some non-governmental organizations is still undetermined.

VI. *Conclusions*

1. During the three months under review, there have been definite improvements as well as serious violations in the human rights situation; this is evidenced by the persistence of the alarming trends with respect to the right to life, the confirmation of one case of torture that must not go unpunished and by the fact that once again no disappearances have occurred, the latter being the most tangible proof of progress. The perpetrators of human rights violations, especially the right to life, still go unpunished in a substantial number of cases. This is all the more serious when those involved are members of the armed forces, the police or State organs. This situation casts doubts on the State's ability to guarantee respect for human rights.

2. Politically motivated human rights violations have been more open and are rendered more serious because of the electoral context the country has entered.

3. At the same time, common violence and an unfavourable climate for the protection of human rights have created a complex and precarious situation charac-terized by the presence of a hodgepodge of armed groups and gangs that must be investigated and punished according to the law.

4. In this regard, the various State bodies and civilian society will have to reaffirm the consensus, conciliation and spirit of reconciliation not only as a substantive goal of the peace but also as daily components of political life and social intercourse.

5. The generally positive trends that the peace has brought about in the area of human rights are not yet—they could not be—irreversible. Such trends can endure only if the institutions established as a result of the peace function effectively, if State institutions observe the law scrupulously, if the judiciary has the authority and autonomy to carry out investigations and mete out appropriate punishment, if the Office of the National Counsel for the Defence of Human Rights is strengthened and its constitutional functions respected by State agencies and if civilian society is strengthened; non-governmental organizations must play a key role in the latter process.

Document 90

Report of the Secretary-General on the implementation of the recommendations of the Commission on the Truth

S/26581, 14 October 1993

Introduction

1. The purpose of the present report is to update the Security Council on the implementation of the recommendations of the Commission on the Truth, which forms part of the Peace Accords for El Salvador. The Commission on the Truth was established in accordance with the Mexico agreements of 27 April 1991 (S/23130) and was entrusted with the task of investigating serious acts of violence that had occurred since 1980 and whose impact on society was deemed to require an urgent and public knowledge of the truth. Under the Mexico agreements, the parties undertook to implement the Commission's recommendations.

2. The Commission released its report on 15 March 1993 (S/25500, annex). It contained some 40 recommendations, listed under four headings:

(a) Recommendations arising directly from the results of the Commission's investigations;

(b) Eradication of structural causes directly connected with the incidents investigated;

(c) Institutional reforms to prevent the repetition of such events;

(d) Measures for national reconciliation.

3. As I pointed out in my report of 21 May 1993 (S/25812, para. 53), the Commission's recommendations require a wide range of administrative, legislative and constitutional measures. Action is required not only from the Government of El Salvador and the Frente Farabundo Martí para la Liberación Nacional (FMLN), but also from individuals and institutions, in particular from the Legislative Assembly and the Commission for the Consolidation of Peace (COPAZ). COPAZ was established by the Peace Accords as a national institution responsible for overseeing implementation of all the agreements and comprises representatives of the Government, FMLN and all political parties represented in the current Legislative Assembly.

4. Following the release of the Commission's report, serious reservations were expressed by the Government regarding the applicability of the Commission's recommendations. Taking into account these reservations and also the number of institutions involved in the process of implementation, I instructed that a detailed analysis of the recommendations be made. The resulting report,

which was made available to the Security Council on 25 May 1993 (S/25812/Add.3), examined whether any of the recommendations was outside the Commission's mandate or incompatible with the Constitution and identified what action was required and by whom (the "addressees") and in what time-frame. On 20 May 1993, I conveyed that analysis to the Government, FMLN and COPAZ and requested each of them to inform me by 20 June 1993 of the action it had taken or planned to take to implement the recommendations for which it was designated as an addressee and to promote the implementation of the other recommendations. In my letters to the Government and FMLN, I stressed the actions which each of them should take to promote those recommendations for which COPAZ is an addressee.

5. The United Nations analysis found that only one of the Commission's recommendations, that concerning disqualification by law from holding public office, could not be implemented as it was at variance with fundamental provisions of the Constitution and conflicted with another recommendation made by the Commission concerning the ratification of international human rights instruments under which citizens cannot be deprived of their political rights in the manner recommended by the Commission.

Positions of the Government, FMLN and COPAZ

6. Since my last report, the Commission's recommendations have been the subject of active exchanges of views and communications between the Secretariat and the Government, FMLN and COPAZ. These have not succeeded in disposing of all the Government's initial reservations. However, I have consistently stressed the unqualified commitment given by the signatories of the Mexico agreements to implement the Commission's recommendations; the United Nations own obligation to verify the signatories' compliance with that commitment; and the need for concrete action by them in implementing measures whose thrust is not the sanctioning of individuals but the prevention of impunity, strengthening the judicial system and promoting the observance of human rights and national reconciliation. ONUSAL has been encouraging the signatories to take that approach and has assisted the various institutions involved in the implementation process. The Human Rights Division, in particular, has been in close contact with the Government on matters related to the implementation of 19 earlier recommendations by the Division, which were endorsed by the Commission on the Truth.

7. The current status of implementation of each of the Commission's recommendations is outlined in a progress report by ONUSAL, which is annexed to the present report. Where implementation of a recommendation involves legislative action, the report indicates whether, in ONUSAL's view, the proposed action fully reflects the Commission's intent.

8. Following my letter of 20 May 1993, the Government, FMLN and COPAZ informed me of their positions with respect to the Commission's recommendations. In a letter dated 11 June 1993, the Coordinator General of FMLN, Mr. Schafik Handal, outlined FMLN's approach to the two recommendations applicable to it. He said that, while disqualification by law from holding public office appeared impossible, FMLN would be ready to accept a procedure of "self-disqualification" by those FMLN members referred to in the recommendation, provided that the government officials and military officers concerned did likewise. Mr. Handal also referred to efforts made by FMLN to promote the implementation of recommendations addressed to COPAZ.

9. In a letter dated 23 June 1993, the *pro tempore* Coordinator of COPAZ informed me that, while COPAZ had begun considering the Commission's recommendations in March, a number of issues required further analysis before COPAZ could pronounce itself. However, COPAZ intended to accelerate consideration of the report in order to be able to convey its position to me as soon as possible. Subsequently, on 10 September 1993, I received a preliminary report from COPAZ outlining action taken on all recommendations under headings I and II (see S/25500, annex, sect. V). That report is reflected in ONUSAL's progress report. Another report from COPAZ on the remaining recommendations is expected shortly.

10. Following several exchanges of view between ONUSAL and the Government of El Salvador, President Cristiani stated, in a letter to me dated 13 July 1993, that a comprehensive analysis by the Government of the Commission's recommendations had shown that the Government would be in a position to implement all of them with the exception of those falling in three categories, namely: (a) those involving dismissal from the civil service and disqualification from holding public office; (b) those implying constitutional reforms; and (c) those recommendations whose implementation would have to be initiated and carried out by the Judiciary through the Supreme Court of Justice. These three categories are discussed below.

A. *Dismissal and disqualification by law from holding public office*

11. COPAZ considered at length the recommendations on these points and reached a common conclusion on them. In a letter dated 9 August 1993, the *pro tempore* Coordinator of COPAZ informed me that it had agreed "that any solution regarding implementation should be within the framework of guaranteeing full participation

by all Salvadorians, without exception, in the country's future and with a view to the broader objective of national reconciliation". Based on that conclusion, COPAZ requested me "to help this institution, created by the Peace Accords as a mechanism representing Salvadorian civil society, to attain the above-mentioned goals".

12. I subsequently received a letter dated 19 September 1993 from FMLN's Coordinator General, in which he stressed that the recommendations on dismissals and disqualification from holding public office were independent of each other. In his opinion, therefore, while disqualification from holding public office was inapplicable, the recommendation regarding dismissal of officers should be carried out. His letter did not express a view about the applicability of the dismissal of civil servants.

13. The mandate entrusted to the United Nations in El Salvador is to verify the parties' compliance with the commitments accepted by them in the Peace Accords and the recommendations of the Commission on the Truth are an integral part of those Accords. While insisting on the signatories' obligation to honour their commitments under the Accords, I have indicated that, if they and Salvadorian society at large (as represented through CO-PAZ, for instance) were to agree that specific provisions should not be implemented, I would be prepared to recommend to the Security Council that non-implementation of those provisions should not be regarded as a violation of the Accords. Although not entirely clear, the terms of the letter addressed to me by COPAZ seemed to indicate that a consensus existed that the recommendations contained in sections I A, B and C of the Commission on the Truth's report should not be implemented. However, the subsequent letter of FMLN's Coordinator General raised doubts on this score. I have accordingly decided to seek clarification from COPAZ.

B. *Constitutional reform*

14. Under the Salvadorian Constitution, constitutional reform requires ratification by two successive legislatures. Therefore, unless the current Legislative Assembly ratifies the constitutional reforms required by the Commission on the Truth, the earliest time they could be implemented would be in 1997, on the assumption that they would be ratified both by the Legislative Assembly that will be elected in March 1994 and by its successor, to be elected three years later. It is therefore imperative that action be initiated during the life-time of the current Legislative Assembly.

15. An additional complication is that, under the Salvadorian Constitution, the executive branch may not initiate constitutional reforms. There are thus limits to the ability of the Government to ensure implementation of constitutional amendments. However, in my letter dated 20 May 1993, I insisted on the Government's obligation to take the necessary political action to promote implementation of those recommendations which required amendment to the Constitution. On 9 August 1993, President Cristiani informed the President of the Legislative Assembly of the Government's commitment to promote four constitutional reforms required by the Commission's recommendations (recommendations III A 1, 2 and 4 and III B 2). He indicated that he had informed the United Nations that it was not within the competence or authority of the executive branch to initiate constitutional reforms; he was accordingly referring the matter to the Legislative Assembly for its consideration.

16. While I understand the institutional limitations on the executive branch's ability to promote constitutional reforms before the legislature, I hope that the four constitutional amendments concerned, which address the need to decentralize powers and competence concentrated in the Supreme Court, will receive strong support from the Government. Reform of the Supreme Court is a significant element in the judicial reform recommended by the Commission on the Truth in order to ensure that never again will those responsible for acts of violence enjoy the impunity that characterized the recent conflict. I therefore urge the signatories of the Peace Accords, and the Government in particular, to take full advantage of the power given to COPAZ to prepare legislative drafts related to the Accords.

C. *Recommendations to be implemented by the judiciary through the Supreme Court of Justice*

17. The Commission on the Truth specifically referred to the point that some of its recommendations required action or initiatives by State organs other than the executive branch. The Commission stressed that the Government's undertaking to implement the recommendations meant that in such cases it must take the necessary action and initiatives to ensure that recommendations are put into practice by the appropriate State machinery (S/25500, annex, sect. V 3).

Observations

18. As is evident from the ONUSAL progress report, some action has been taken on a large number of the recommendations made by the Commission on the Truth. No implementation has, however, been reported with regard to the recommendations concerning dismissal and disqualification, those involving constitutional amendments and those on *amparo* (III B 2) and the jurisdiction of the Inter-American Court of Human Rights (III B 3). In most cases, only partial implementation has been effected as draft legislation is under consideration by Government agencies or legislative bodies or because pre-

liminary action is being taken by the Government.

19. At a high-level meeting on 8 September 1993, in which ONUSAL participated, the Government and FMLN agreed on the need to step up the implementation process with a view to "sweeping the table clean" before 20 November 1993, when the electoral campaign is to start. I urge the Government, FMLN, COPAZ and other institutions involved in the implementation of the Commission's recommendations to make every effort to achieve this goal. To this end, I have asked my Special Representative, Mr. Ramirez-Ocampo, to assist those concerned in reaching agreement on target dates for the implementation of as many as possible of the outstanding recommendations.

20. I shall report further on this matter to the Security Council in due course.

Annex

Progress report on the implementation of the recommendations of the Commission on the Truth

I. *Recommendations arising directly from the results of the investigation**

I.A. *Dismissal from their posts and discharge from the armed forces of officers who are named in the report and who are personally implicated in the perpetration or cover-up of the cases reported, or who did not fulfil their professional obligation to initiate or cooperate in the investigation and punishment of serious acts of violence*

1. Eight military officers who fall within this category are still holding their positions (see paras. 11 to 13 of the main body of this report on the issue of dismissal and disqualification).

I.B. *Dismissal of civilian officials in the civil service and the judiciary who are named in the report and who, acting in their professional capacity, covered up serious acts of violence or failed to discharge their responsibilities in the investigation of such acts*

2. One civilian mentioned by the report is not at present an official of the civil service, although he represents the Government at COPAZ. Two judges and one forensic doctor were also mentioned in the report. Their dismissal falls within the jurisdiction of the judiciary (see paras. 11 to 13 of the main body of this report on the issue of dismissal and disqualification. It should also be noted that the evaluation of all judges by the National Council of the Judiciary has begun).

I.C. *Disqualification by law from holding public office for persons referred to in the above recommendations and for any other persons implicated in the perpetration of the acts of violence described, including the civilians and members of the FMLN Command named in the findings on individual cases. The persons concerned should be disqualified from holding any public post or office for a period of not less than 10 years, and should be disqualified permanently from any activity related to public security or national defence*

3. Under heading I C, the Commission also recommended that the bodies authorized to make appointments to public office refrain from appointing the persons referred to in section I C. In that respect, the nomination by the Government of the President of the Supreme Court of Justice to the Inter-American Legal Committee seems inconsistent with the spirit, if not the letter, of the Commission's recommendation (see paras. 11 to 13 of the main body of this report on dismissal and disqualification).

I.D.(a). *Resignation of the current members of the Supreme Court of Justice to enable the constitutional reform concerning the election of judges to the Court to be implemented immediately*

4. This recommendation is not binding on the Government, as it depends entirely on the willingness of the members of the Court to resign from their posts. They have publicly stated that they will not resign. It should be noted that the term of office of the present Court expires in June 1994. At that time the newly elected Legislative Assembly will designate the new Court in accordance with the provisions of the relevant articles of the Constitution, which are to be revised on the basis of the Peace Accords.

5. COPAZ has requested the Supreme Court to report on the legal foundations on which it bases its position regarding the issue.

I.D.(b). *Amendment of the National Council of the Judiciary Act so that members of the Council can be dismissed only by the Legislative Assembly for precise legal causes*

6. An inter-agency government team is preparing a draft amendment to the current law of the National Council of the Judiciary that sets precise legal causes for the dismissal of Council members but does not transfer this responsibility to the Legislative Assembly. The Government's interpretation is that such a transfer would

---

* The headings refer to the relevant sections of document S/25500, annex, section V.

require a constitutional amendment. ONUSAL is of the view, however, that a change in the National Council of the Judiciary Act (rather than in the Constitution) could resolve the problem raised in the recommendation, as the question at stake is addressed in article 49 of that Act.

7. COPAZ has decided to define precisely the causes for dismissal of members of the National Council of the Judiciary.

I.E.   *Amendment of the Career Judicial Service Act so that only those judges who, according to a rigorous evaluation made by the National Council of the Judiciary, have demonstrated judicial aptitude, efficiency and concern for human rights and offer every guarantee of independence, judicial discretion, honesty and impartiality in their actions, may remain in the career judicial service*

8. A technical commission has been set up by the Legislative Assembly to introduce new amendments in the Career Judicial Service Act, which was partially reformed in 1992. It is still not possible to provide a definitive statement regarding the amendment of the Act, since the Commission entrusted with its formulation has not yet produced a draft.

9. It should be noted that the National Council of the Judiciary, which was elected by consensus and has been fully operational since June 1993, has recently begun to evaluate judges, having requested ONUSAL's cooperation in providing information about those who have incurred irregularities. The Supreme Court of Justice has stated that the evaluation undertaken by the Council strengthens the Judiciary and that it will be receptive to its conclusions.

10. COPAZ has requested the National Council of the Judiciary to report on the elements or criteria taken into consideration in the evaluation of judges.

II.   *Eradication of structural causes linked directly to the acts examined*

Full implementation of the peace agreements

11. The Secretary-General of the United Nations reports regularly to the Security Council and the General Assembly on the implementation of the peace agreements. In his last report to the Security Council, issued on 21 May 1993 (S/25812), he noted, among the achievements of the peace process, full respect by both parties for a prolonged cease-fire, the celebration of the formal end of the armed conflict and the conversion of FMLN into a political party. He also noted that significant progress had been made towards the establishment of civilian control over the military, the beginnings of the establishment of a civilian police force, the reunification of Salvadorian society and the democratization of na-

tional institutions. However, the Secretary-General also pointed out the need for further efforts to deal with several important components of the peace agreements, in particular the land transfer programme, the full establishment of the National Civilian Police and the recovery of assault weapons. The Secretary-General will submit his next report to the Security Council on implementation of the peace agreements in November 1993.

II.A.   *Reforms in the armed forces*

12. Structural reforms of the armed forces have already been carried out in compliance with the peace agreements and following constitutional amendments, whose basic purpose has been to ensure their subordination to civilian power within the rule of law. Such reforms include mainly the removal of police functions from the military sphere of competence; the purification of the armed forces based on an evaluation of its members by an ad hoc commission; the establishment of new doctrinal principles and a new educational system; its reduction by approximately half the original size; the abolishment of the National Intelligence Department and its substitution by a new State Intelligence Agency under civilian control; the disbandment of rapid deployment infantry battalions that had been established as a consequence of the armed conflict; and the proscription of paramilitary forces or groups, including the disbandment of the civil defence and suppression of the territorial service, which has been replaced by a new system of reserves. These reforms have included a number of legal measures.

II.A.1.   *Appointment of a special committee of the Legislative Assembly to supervise the transition to the new model of the armed forces*

13. As established in the Legislative Assembly's rules of procedure, the Assembly has the capacity to appoint special committees to investigate matters of national interest and to adopt the conclusions or recommendations it deems appropriate on the basis of their reports. No such special committee has been set up to fulfil the task mentioned in paragraph II A 1, but COPAZ has formally recommended to the Legislative Assembly that the existing Public Security and Defence Committee carry out that task on a priority basis.

II.A.2,   *Comprehensive review of the military legislation*
3 and   *in force*
4.

14. This recommendation is being implemented through the amendments and/or other legal measures already approved by the Legislative Assembly at the initiative of the Executive. At present the Assembly has before it a draft for a new Basic Law of National Defence submitted by the Executive. With respect to paragraphs

II A 2 and 3, the draft under consideration meets the requirements of the peace agreements and includes the establishment of legal limits to the rule of due obedience. As far as paragraph II A 4 is concerned the Code of Military Justice, which would be the relevant law in this case, does not contain specific references to sanctions against the violations of human rights.

15. COPAZ has set itself the task of revising the current military legislation in order to ascertain whether any of its provisions contradicts the Constitution. COPAZ has also agreed to make proposals for legal amendments with respect to paragraphs II A 3 and 4, which include the establishment of a mechanism to deal with disobedience of illegal orders and sanctions against abuses of power and violations of human rights.

II.A.5. *Inclusion of the study of human rights in the curricula of military schools*

16. Studies of human rights, constitutional law and international humanitarian law have been included in the curricula of military schools and post-graduate military courses. The Human Rights Division of ONUSAL will provide cooperation for a global revision of existing curricula with a view to ensuring their overall compatibility with the new courses. The Human Rights Division actively participates in the holding of courses and seminars designed, *inter alia*, for military officers. These courses focus on human rights, military sociology and army-society relations. They are held at the Ministry of Defence, the Joint General Staff Headquarters, the College of Advanced Strategic Studies and other institutions. They enjoy the personal support of the new Minister of Defence who was, before assuming his present post, responsible for the development and implementation of these critical components of the Peace Accords.

17. On 20 September 1993, the Division of Human Rights submitted to the Minister of Defence for his consideration a project entitled "Project of cooperation between the Division of Human Rights of ONUSAL and the Doctrine and Military Training Command". Through this project, the Human Rights Division would provide technical support to the military and civilian faculty of the military training centres. It would also organize conferences and an international seminar with the participation of foreign experts.

18. Finally, an in-depth revision of military curricula (see also sect. III B, recommendation 15 of the Human Rights Division) has been undertaken by the Academic Council of the Military College. As agreed in COPAZ, the Academic Council of the Military College consists of four military members and four civilian members, in addition to the Director of the College who presides over the Council.

19. COPAZ has requested from the Minister of Defence a report on the issue referred to in this recommendation.

II.A.6. *Military training courses abroad based on a doctrine of democracy and respect for human rights*

20. This recommendation is being implemented as part of the reforms of the armed forces, through training courses in several democratic countries. COPAZ took note of information provided by the Government on existing agreements with several countries regarding technical training of military personnel.

II.A.7. *Priority to be given to the eradication of any relationship between members of the armed forces and paramilitary or illegal groups*

21. The armed forces Court of Honour was created as stipulated in the peace agreements (chap. I 12 C). Composed of seven officers (one of each rank, starting with general and ending with second lieutenant), with a one-year mandate, the Court's internal by-laws were submitted to ONUSAL in 1992. As stipulated in the agreements, the Court tries acts that are contrary to military honour without prejudice to the judicial system.

22. ONUSAL has not detected any institutional relationship between members of the armed forces and paramilitary or illegal groups.

23. COPAZ has requested a report from the Government on this issue.

II.B. *Reforms in the area of public security*

24. Important reforms in the area of public security have been or are being implemented in compliance with the peace agreements.

25. Since its establishment, the functioning of the National Academy for Public Security has improved. At present, six classes at the basic level have graduated from the Academy. As a consequence, approximately 2,000 officers of the National Civil Police are now deployed in five departments of El Salvador. Partial deployment has also taken place in the capital and in Usulután. These officers are now under the orders of permanent commanders.

26. A monthly admission of approximately 400 students at the basic level is planned for the remainder of the transition period until the National Civil Police is fully deployed. As a result, a total of about 5,700 police will have graduated by July 1994. The second Academy course at the executive and senior levels will begin shortly. It will train a total of 240 police officers.

27. According to a plan presented by the Government, the National Civil Police will be deployed in 8 to 10 departments by the end of 1993. Its complete deploy-

ment throughout the 14 departments of El Salvador is expected to conclude between August and October 1994. The Government has informed COPAZ of its plan for the deployment of the functional divisions of the National Civil Police. Training of the future personnel of the Traffic and Finance Divisions has already started at the Academy. Their deployment should start in October and November 1993, respectively. An operational plan for the phasing out of the National Police was submitted by the Government on 11 October 1993.

28. An adequate allocation of resources, properly supported by continuous technical and financial assistance from the international community, is necessary to ensure completion of this key element of the peace agreements.

29. In recruiting members of the National Civil Police, a balance is being maintained between candidates from the FMLN and from the National Police. Each category has a 20 per cent representation, at the basic, executive and senior levels. The remaining 60 per cent of candidates are made up of personnel that is entirely civilian in character. The appointment on 1 June 1993 of a former army captain and Head of the Executive Antinarcotics Unit to the position of Deputy Director of the National Civil Police was a cause for concern. The Government informed ONUSAL that the ex-captain had resigned from the army prior to his appointment, which was political and did not constitute a career post. It also pointed out his extensive police training, an important factor given the requirements of his post. FMLN objected to the appointment. The matter was settled on 8 September when FMLN accepted the appointment on an exceptional basis and on the condition that it should not set a precedent. The two other political appointees of the National Civil Police, namely the Director-General and the Deputy for Management, are civilians.

30. In accordance with the supplementary agreements reached on 22 December 1992, members of the Executive Antinarcotics Unit and the Criminal Investigation Commission could be transferred to the corresponding National Civil Police functional divisions after an evaluation to be verified by ONUSAL and additional courses at the National Academy for Public Security. Evaluation of personnel and additional courses started in August. ONUSAL began verification of that process at the request of the Government on 10 September. Some members of the Executive Antinarcotics Unit have already joined the National Civil Police even though ONUSAL has not yet been able to conclude its verification task. In particular, information requested from the Government

such as the list of Executive Antinarcotics Unit and Criminal Investigation Commission members as of 22 December 1993 and other documentation have not yet been handed over to ONUSAL. ONUSAL has also made recommendations regarding the transfer process, to which no answer has been given yet.

31. COPAZ has called on the Government to continue with efforts to respect the civilian character of the National Civil Police.

II.C. *Investigation of illegal groups*

32. Cases of arbitrary executions over the past few months have given ground for concern that illegal groups are operating, whose methods seem to repeat behavioural patterns prevailing in the past. As explained below, the Government has agreed to give priority to the investigation of arbitrary executions. In compliance with this decision, a mechanism has been set up whereby the ONUSAL Division of Human Rights provides the list of cases requiring special investigation to the Minister of the Presidency, the Minister of Justice and the Criminal Investigation Commission.

33. It should be noted that the Criminal Investigation Commission will be dissolved shortly and integrated into the National Civil Police as the "Division for Criminal Investigation". Its members are to be transferred to the National Civil Police according to a procedure outlined in section II B above. The Division of Criminal Investigation of the National Civil Police, under the functional direction of the Attorney-General's Office and in coordination with ONUSAL, will give high priority to investigating illegal groups.

34. Measures helping to prevent the reappearance of illegal groups included the disbanding of the Civil Defence and the former territorial service, which is to be replaced by a new system of armed forces reserves. Discussions within COPAZ on a draft law regulating private security entities, which have been temporarily set aside owing to other priorities, are expected to resume shortly and produce a draft to be submitted to the Legislative Assembly. Prior to this, COPAZ is concluding a draft law for the control of arms. The Government has prepared its own draft, which was recently sent to the Legislative Assembly for approval (see also sect. III B).

35. An in-depth investigation of the phenomenon of illegal groups, with a view to impeding its resurgence, constitutes a priority that has been consistently considered by COPAZ. This was reflected in its recent communication to the President of the Republic, in which COPAZ requested that the President use all the means at his disposal speedily to address the issue.

III. *Institutional reforms to prevent the repetition of such acts*

III.A. *Administration of justice*

Further judicial reform

36. Several recommendations under this heading require constitutional amendments. A letter from the President has been sent to the Legislative Assembly requesting consideration of recommendations III A 1, 2, 4 and III B 2. According to the Salvadorian Constitution, amendments to the fundamental law of the country can only be proposed by a minimum of 10 members of the legislature. On the issue of constitutional reforms, see paragraphs 14-17 of the main body of the report.

37. However, as far as the issue of administrative accountability of judges to the National Council of the Judiciary (III A 3) is concerned, contrary to ONUSAL's point of view that a constitutional amendment would be required, the President is of the opinion that the recommendation could be satisfied through legal reforms.

38. Other recommendations for judicial reforms that do not require constitutional amendments are being gradually implemented. Drafts prepared by the Ministry of Justice for a new Code of Criminal Procedure and for a law regarding juvenile delinquents are being submitted to public consultation. The proposed Procedural Code provides for oral arguments and public access to all phases of the judicial process, which guarantees the accused's right to defence. Drafts for a new Criminal Code and a new penitentiary law are currently under consideration. Several amendments to existing laws have been approved by the Legislative Assembly. Others are under discussion or in the process of being submitted by the Executive for approval.

III.A.1. *Deconcentration of functions vested in the Supreme Court and its President*

39. Implementation of this recommendation requires constitutional amendments (see paras. 14-16 of the main body of this report on the issue of constitutional reform).

40. The Government has informed ONUSAL that a commission was set up by the judiciary to promote administrative reforms aimed at the decentralization of the Supreme Court's functions.

III.A.2. *Appointment and removal of judges by the National Council of the Judiciary*

41. Implementation of this recommendation requires a constitutional amendment (see paras. 14-16 of the main body of this report on the issue of constitutional reform).

42. However, the process for the selection of lawyers for their subsequent appointment as judges of peace by the Supreme Court of Justice has already been undertaken by the newly appointed National Council for the Judiciary.

III.A.3. *Administrative accountability of judges to the National Council of the Judiciary*

43. Implementation of this recommendation would require constitutional amendments to the Basic Law of the Judiciary—on which no initiative has been taken—and the Career Judicial Act, which is being studied by the Technical Commission set up to this effect by the Legislative Assembly and mentioned in section I E above.

III.A.4. *Special independent body responsible for authorizing and regulating the professions of lawyer and notary*

44. Implementation of this recommendation requires a constitutional amendment (see paras. 14-16 of the main body of this report on the issue of constitutional reform).

III.A.5. *Creation of new courts and improvement of judges' salaries*

45. The Supreme Court of Justice had been setting up new courts and improving the salaries of judges before the release of the report of the Commission on the Truth. The number of courts has increased considerably since 1989. For example, Courts of first instance, totalling a number of 87 in 1989, reached 120 in March 1993. The salaries of judges have almost doubled since 1989. Budget allocations to the judiciary are being gradually increased as required by the peace accords.

46. During 1992, district courts (*juzgados de paz*) Nos. 9 and 10 were created in San Salvador and juvenile and civil courts in the surrounding areas (Soyapango and San Marcos); also created were the third civil chamber (first central sector), the third penal chamber (first central sector), two chambers of the second instance (second and third eastern sector), the second civil court in San Miguel and the third criminal court in San Miguel.

III.A.6. *Reinforcement of the application of the right to (a)-(d). due process*

47. Implementation of this recommendation is a continuous process. Important steps in this direction have been approved by the Legislative Assembly at the Executive's recommendation, such as removing the requirement for consultations by judges of a lower court to those of a higher rank, and approving reforms proposed by the Ministry of Justice in the current Code of Criminal Procedure with regard to the rights of the accused. The right to due process is further reinforced in the drafts for the new Criminal Code and Code of Criminal Procedure. Several administrative measures are being implemented or in the process of being approved for the same purpose.

48. With regard to subparagraph (a), the *Ley de Defensoría Pública* prohibits police interrogations in the absence of lawyers. Furthermore, the Ministry of Justice has prepared a draft law expressly invalidating extrajudicial confessions; subparagraph (b) is included in the draft Code of Criminal Procedure; with regard to subparagraph (c), although progress is being made, the National Police is not complying fully with the requirements concerning maximum time-limits; subparagraph (d) is covered by the instruments referred to in connection with subparagraphs (a) and (b).

III.A.7. *Priority to be given to the Judicial Training School*

49. The Judicial Training School is now under the jurisdiction of the National Council for the Judiciary, which has actively undertaken its improvement and strengthening and is seeking international technical assistance. The Government has supported these efforts.

50. The National Reconstruction Programme projects external financial requirements for the School for the period 1993-1996 in the amount of $12 million, of which $3.9 million is available ($0.9 million from the Government of El Salvador and $3 million from USAID), leaving a financial gap of $8.1 million.

III.B. *Protection of human rights*

51. As indicated below, a good number of these recommendations are in the process of being implemented and others are the subject of ongoing consultations. The Government and the ONUSAL Human Rights Division hold regular bilateral meetings to discuss these issues.

52. Following is a detailed evaluation of the state of implementation of the recommendations of the ONUSAL Human Rights Division:

(a) *Ratification or adherence to international human rights instruments, including the conventions of the International Labour Organization (ILO)*. The Government has expressed its willingness to ratify or adhere to human rights conventions in the near future, with the exception of the one recognizing the compulsory jurisdiction of the Inter-American Court of Human Rights. With regard to the ILO conventions, the Government has indicated that they will be processed within the framework of the consultations being carried out in the Forum for Economic and Social Consultation;

(b) *Structural and functional reform of the judiciary*. Although implementation implies constitutional reforms, some policy-setting reforms are being effected in that direction, of which some have already been approved by the Legislative Assembly and others are being debated within the judicial community (see also sect. III A 6);

(c) *Establishment of a special commission of in-quiry to investigate arbitrary executions*. While the Government has expressed its willingness to give priority to the investigation of those cases indicated by ONUSAL and NGOs as possible arbitrary executions, it has stated the impossibility of creating a special commission, given the fact that such an investigative mechanism is not provided for in the country's institutional structure. It has therefore been agreed to address the substance of the recommendation by establishing a mechanism of investigation of those cases which, in the opinion of ONUSAL, warrant it;

(d) *Measures to make* habeas corpus *and* amparo *effective and accessible*. The Government has submitted for national debate a draft law amending the legislation on *habeas corpus*. In general terms, the draft represents a positive step, although it could be expanded to offer more effective protection. A regulation that would fully guarantee *habeas corpus* would imply constitutional reforms to guarantee wide access by those affected to the jurisdictional organ that is currently limited to the Constitutional Hall of the Supreme Court. Implementation of the recommendation on *amparo* is pending, as no proposals have as yet been made;

(e) *Compensation fund for victims*. The Government is now carrying out a preliminary evaluation of this recommendation, which includes a study of the various ways of establishing the Fund (see also sect. IV below). The non-governmental Human Rights Commission of El Salvador has prepared a draft law for the creation for a special fund for reparation and national reconciliation, which it has submitted to the Legislative Assembly. The draft contains constructive elements that should be taken into account in the recommendation's implementation;

(f) *Improvement of the composition and powers of the National Council of the Judiciary and independence of the Judicial Training School*. This recommendation implies amendments to the National Council of the Judiciary Act and to the Constitution. The procedure for its implementation is yet to be initiated;

(g) *Elimination of extrajudicial confession*. The new *Ley de Defensoria Publica* and the changes in the Procedural Criminal Code and the Basic Law of the Public Ministry in relation to the control of the defence of the accused has resulted in a lessening of the incidence of extrajudicial confessions. The Ministry of Justice has also prepared a draft law specifically on the invalidation of extrajudicial confession, the adoption of which, following consultations with the judicial community and its presentation to the Legislative Assembly, would constitute an important step towards the implementation of this recommendation (see also sect. III A 6);

(h) *Definition of torture and enforced disappearance as offences in special criminal legislation*. The draft new Criminal Code, prepared by the Ministry of Justice, defines torture as a crime against the fundamental rights of the individual. Also defined as a crime is enforced disappearance itself, enforced disappearance carried out by individuals in compliance with official orders and enforced disappearance that implies responsibility for allowing or agreeing to the commission of that crime. Implementation of the recommendation began with the proposal of the Ministry of Justice and will culminate in the adoption of the corresponding law (see sect. III B 6);

(i) *Legislation regulating the conduct of law enforcement officials.* The Ministry of Justice has taken a first step by preparing the draft law on Rules for Administrative Detention aimed at avoiding excesses and abuses in the use of physical force in detention through the adoption as internal law of the Republic of the Code of Conduct for Law Enforcement Officials, adopted by the United Nations General Assembly (see also sect. II B 4 (a));

(j) *Abolition of the practice of arbitrary detention for petty misdemeanours.* The implementation of this recommendation is being prompted by ONUSAL in coordination with the National Police, the National Civil Police, the Supreme Court and the municipalities. Pending the adoption of legal reforms, various verification processes have been carried out and a police instructive was adopted with a view to diminishing this type of arbitrary detention (see also sect. III B 4 (a));

(k) *Temporary application of the Act governing the procedure for administrative detention or the imposition of administrative fines.* The police instructive mentioned in the previous point was conceived with a view to applying the law on procedures for the imposition of arrest or administrative fine (Legislative Decree No. 457) instead of obsolete provisions of the Police Law of 1886 or illegal procedures. A programme for the National Civil Police, National Police, Municipal Police and the Executive Antinarcotics Unit establishing compulsory application of Decree No. 457 in the transition period pending the repeal of the Police Law of 1886 and the removal from the jurisdiction of the police of petty misdemeanors is urgently needed;

(l) *Amendment of the disciplinary regime under the Career Judicial Service Act so that the Court or its President can investigate formally any irregularities or violations of due process.* ONUSAL has been carrying out consultations with the Supreme Court of Justice for the application of this recommendation, the implementation of which is indispensable for assuring the effectiveness of the guarantees for due process, especially with regard to the right to a defence, to be judged by a competent court in a reasonable time-frame and to an impartial trial;

(m) *Authorization of a visit by the ILO Committee on Freedom of Association.* The Committee will carry out the pending visit, which will mean compliance with the recommendation;

(n) *Investigations by the Supreme Court of Justice of violations of due process.* The disciplinary regime under the Career Judicial Service Act has not yet been modified with a view to allowing the Supreme Court of Justice or its President to investigate ex officio and efficiently the irregularities or violations of the right to due process, particularly those pointed out by the National Counsel for the Defence of Human Rights Office. The Human Rights Division has conveyed to the Supreme Court a list of cases in which the responsibility of some judges appears involved. The Court is currently investigating them;

(o) *Granting of legal recognition to associations and trade unions.* In spite of some advances within the framework of the consulting mechanism, compliance with this recommendation is still pending;

(p) *Military training.* This recommendation is being applied and by its very nature is a process which should be ongoing. The Human Rights Division will propose a specific cooperation programme to the Armed Forces in this regard (see also sect. II A 5);

(q) *Recovery of military weapons.* Partial implementation of this recommendation has begun. The Government has committed itself to collecting the remaining arms, which are located in various institutions, and to replacing them by other, appropriate ones, by 20 November. The remaining military arms in the possession of civilians or ex-military personnel will be collected following the adoption of the "Law for the control of arms, munitions, explosives and similar articles", a draft of which was submitted by the Government to the Legislative Assembly on 25 August 1993. Another draft for the same law, prepared by COPAZ, is being debated for subsequent submission to the Assembly;

(r) *Budgetary autonomy of the National Counsel's Office.* This recommendation should be carried out within the general accounting norms of the State. Nevertheless consultations between the Government and the Counsel for compliance have not yet begun;

(s) *Facilities for and non-obstruction of NGO activities.* Cases of NGOs seeking legal recognition are still pending.

III.B.1. *Strengthening of the Office of the National Counsel for the Defence of Human Rights*

53. The National Counsel for the Defence of Human Rights is implementing the recommendations according to its established timetable. Regional offices have already been established in three cities (Santa Ana, San Vicente and San Miguel). A formal cooperation agreement has been signed with ONUSAL.

III.B.2. *Measures to make the remedies of* amparo *and* habeas corpus *truly effective: broadening the competence of judges and making express provision that these remedies cannot be suspended as guarantees under any circumstances*

54. In accordance with existing constitutional provisions (art. 29), the guarantee of *amparo* and *habeas corpus* cannot be suspended even in a state of emergency.

55. With regard to *habeas corpus*, draft legislation on this remedy has been prepared by the Ministry of Justice. It meets the requirements regarding protection of personal freedom and other related fundamental rights and extends the jurisdiction of *habeas corpus* to courts of appeal.

56. An amendment to the Constitution is required to extend such jurisdiction to courts of first instance and justices of the peace (see paras. 14-16 of the main body of this report on the issue of constitutional reform).

57. Since no proposal has been adopted to date on *amparo*, the implementation of this recommendation is pending in its entirety (see also sect. III B, recommendation 4).

III.B.3. *Constitutional force of human rights provisions and of international human rights instruments*

58. The Government has informed ONUSAL that it will promote ratification, with the reservations that may apply on constitutional grounds, to the following international human rights instruments: Optional Protocol of the International Covenant on Civil and Political Rights; Convention against Torture and Other Cruel, Inhuman or Degrading Treatment or Punishment; Inter-American Convention on the Prevention and Punishment of Torture; Supplementary Protocol to the Inter-American Convention on Human Rights regarding economic, social and cultural rights and Inter-American Convention on Political Rights of Women.

59. ONUSAL has also been informed by the Government that it will not promote acceptance of the jurisdiction of the Inter-American Court of Human Rights.

60. Section III B, recommendation 1, also refers.

III.B.4. *Changes in the system of administrative detention* (a)-(c).

61. The Minister of Justice has informed the Legislative Assembly that a drastic reduction of administrative detention is proposed in draft legislation to be submitted to the Assembly shortly.

62. With regard to subparagraphs (a) and (b), the Ministry of Justice has prepared the following two drafts: the draft rules for detention by police (which seeks to avoid excessive use of violence during arrests). The draft reflects the Code of Conduct for Law Enforcement Officials; and the draft on the reduction of time-limits for

administrative detention so that the suspect can be handed over to judicial authorities within 24 hours.

63. The objective set forth in subparagraph (c) can be reached only by repealing the Police Act of 1886. The Government has agreed to it, but no draft legislation has been prepared yet. On the other hand, the Ministry of Justice has proposed drafting a law whereby the jurisdiction of the police for petty misdemeanors would be attributed exclusively to the justices of the peace, in an effort to preserve the principle of monopoly of jurisdiction. The Human Rights Division is cooperating with the Ministry in this regard.

III.B.5. *Expansion of the system of information on detainees with the participation of the Office of the National Counsel for the Defence of Human Rights*

64. The present information system of the Supreme Court is considered to reflect the state of the art. The extension of this system to the National Counsel for the Defence of Human Rights should be coordinated with the Court.

65. The computerized system of the Supreme Court concerns all judicial and non-judicial detainees in the country. It is available to the National Counsel for the Defence of Human Rights, which is organizing its own system. However, the Counsel is not being informed of all arrests, as stipulated by the Constitution of the Republic (art. 194.I.5).

III.B.6. *New categories of crimes*

66. The draft Criminal Code being prepared by the Ministry of Justice includes new criminal offences committed with the direct or indirect support of the State apparatus. Among the crimes relating to the fundamental guarantees of persons is torture by officials. It provides for the case when an official having the power to avoid or prevent torture fails to do so. Also proscribed are genocide and enforced disappearance of a person by an official. Sanctions are provided for anyone guilty of permitting the commission of these crimes by others. ONUSAL is evaluating these amendments.

III.B.7. *Material compensation for victims of human rights violations*

67. The existing Criminal Code envisages compensation for damages caused by the commission of a crime through the "civil consequences of a crime" following the established norms for attachment. Under the draft Criminal Code, compensation for damages will be made through the so-called "civil consequences of a punishable act".

68. The draft Code of Criminal Procedure establishes a procedure for compensation through petitioning the court that handed down the sentence following the criminal process. If the court considers the procedure

admissible, it will give the order for compensation of damages, following a settlement hearing. Although the proposed reform does not in itself constitute "a simple, swift and accessible remedy", as recommended by the Commission on the Truth, it does have the advantage over the existing procedure that, being a special process, indemnization can be better evaluated and can even result in settlement in specific cases.

69. Notwithstanding the above, it would be desirable that, as recommended by the Commission, legislation could be passed differentiating between the procedure for compensation as envisaged in the Codes and that dealing with compensation resulting from human rights violations.

III.B.8. *Ratification of international instruments and recognition of the compulsory jurisdiction of the Inter-American Court of Human Rights*

70. Comment on section III B 3 applies.

III.C. *National Civil Police*

III.C.1. *Putting into practice the investigation mechanism within the National Civil Police and dissolving the Commission for the Investigation of Criminal Acts*

71. Comment on section II C applies.

IV. *Steps towards national reconciliation*

IV.A. *Special fund for the compensation of victims*

72. Before taking a final decision, the Government is currently engaged in carrying out a feasibility study aimed at (a) identifying potential beneficiaries of a special fund; (b) determining the cost of such a fund; and (c) investigating the possibility of obtaining the required resources (see sect. III B, recommendation 5).

IV.B. *Construction of a national monument bearing the names of the victims, recognition of the good name of the victims and institution of a national holiday*

73. The Government is selecting a site for the construction of a national monument. The good name of the victims and the message of reconciliation is reflected in public statements by both parties. The Legislative Assembly has instituted 16 January as a national holiday.

IV.C. *Forum for Truth and Reconciliation*

74. In its consideration of the recommendations, COPAZ is likely to take a decision shortly.

IV.D. *International follow-up action*

75. The United Nations is providing constant follow-up action and will continue to do so.

Document 91

Report of the Secretary-General on the activities of the ONUSAL Electoral Division

S/26606, 20 October 1993

Introduction

1. This is the first of a series of periodic reports that I intend to submit to the Security Council concerning the activities of the Electoral Division until the elections scheduled for 20 March 1994 are held.

2. The installation of the Electoral Division of the United Nations Observer Mission in El Salvador (ONUSAL) is practically completed. In the initial stage, the Division's chief task is to verify the registration of citizens on the electoral rolls and to observe the political activities of the period preceding the electoral campaign, as was explained in my earlier report dated 21 May 1993 (S/25812). This stage will extend until the beginning of December 1993 when the time-limit for applying to register on the electoral rolls will have expired. Electoral observers have been stationed in all the regional offices of the Mission and by the end of October the Division is expected to have its full complement of electoral officials.

I. The pre-electoral framework

3. The institutional framework in which the electoral process will go forward has already been established. On 20 March 1994 four elections will be held simultaneously: elections for President, with a second round within the ensuing 30 days if no candidate has obtained an absolute majority in the first round; parliamentary elections for the 84 seats in the National Assembly on the basis of proportional representation; municipal elections in 262 mayoral districts on the basis of a simple majority (the party obtaining the most votes will win the office of mayor and all the posts in the municipal corporation); and for the Central American Parliament, treated

as a single national district, for which 20 deputies will be elected on the basis of proportional representation.

4. The Supreme Electoral Tribunal has already set up offices in all the departments and municipalities of the country. The Electoral Law calls for a Board of Vigilance consisting of representatives of all the political parties, with authority to supervise the work of all Supreme Electoral Tribunal offices. Although it has already been established, it has not yet been allocated all the resources necessary for the effective exercise of its functions. For its part, the Supreme Electoral Tribunal is also seriously lacking in the funds necessary for its operations. Although the Supreme Electoral Tribunal budget and the external aid provided are sufficient to finance the activities proposed for that purpose, most of those funds have not yet been disbursed. Among the main reasons for that delay is the slowness on the part of the Supreme Electoral Tribunal in taking operational decisions.

5. Twelve political parties will be competing in the forthcoming elections. For the first time the Frente Farabundo Martí para la Liberación Nacional (FMLN) is participating. Most of the parties registered enjoy parliamentary representation in the present National Assembly: the Alianza Republicana Nacionalista (ARENA) now represented in the government with 39 seats; the Partido Demócrata Cristiano (PDC), with 26 seats; the Partido de Conciliación Nacional (PCN), with 9 seats; the three parties of the old coalition, Democratic Convergence (Movimiento Nacional Revolucionario (MNR), Movimiento Popular Social Cristiano (MPSC) and Partido Social Demócrata (PSD)), with 8 seats; Movimiento Auténtico Cristiano (MAC), with 1 seat; Unión Democrática Nacionalista (UDN) with 1 seat. Among the parties not represented in the present Assembly the following will be competing in the elections: Movimiento de Solidaridad Nacional (MSN); Pueblo Libre (PL) and Movimiento de Unidad (MU). In mid-September the MPSC, PSD and UDN parties announced their intention to constitute a single fusion party which would again use the name Democratic Convergence.

6. Thus far five candidates have announced for the office of President: Armando Calderón Sol for ARENA; Fidel Chávez Mena for PDC; Rubén Zamora for FMLN, MPSC, PSD and UDN; Víctor Manuel Valle for MNR and Edgardo Rodríguez for MSN. PCN had announced General Rafael Bustillo as its candidate for President, but on 1 September the General renounced his candidacy as well as his membership in the party.

7. The exercise of freedom of expression and of the press is satisfactorily regulated by the laws now in force. There is a communications network, mainly in private hands, expressing a diversity of views and with sufficient technical coverage for the effective exercise of that freedom. The radio is the medium with the widest coverage. There are 85 radio stations, 73 of them commercial, 2 State-operated, 1 of the Armed Forces of El Salvador, 7 religious and 2 FMLN. There are six television channels, only one of which, channel 10, is State operated. The Salvadorian Telecorporation, owned by the man who inaugurated television in El Salvador in 1956, includes channels 2, 4 and 6. Channels 12 and 21, which are also privately owned, have been operating since 1984 and March of 1993 respectively.

8. Access of political parties to the media is regulated by the Electoral Law. The parties are entitled to disseminate electoral propaganda in all the media. The latter are under obligation to keep the Supreme Electoral Tribunal informed about the normal rates for their services, which should apply to electoral propaganda. Private communication enterprises are obligated to provide services to all parties on an equal basis and cannot claim the conclusion of prior contracts or payment of instalment, as excuses for failure to comply with the equal treatment rule. The space and time allotted for electoral propaganda should be programmed according to the rules of the Supreme Electoral Tribunal, in coordination with the Board of Vigilance and the National Secretariat for Communications.

II. The situation of the electoral roles

9. Problems relating to voter registration continue to be a major concern although there has been a significant improvement in recent weeks. More than 100,000 requests for registration have been received in the first 21 days of September. This is a significant increase over the 40,000 requests received in August or the 10,000 received in July. Several opposition parties and some international aid agencies have criticized the efficiency of the registration operation, attributing it to possible lack of political will on the part of the Supreme Electoral Tribunal. Despite persisting difficulties, which will have to be overcome if the target of an adequate electoral roll is to be achieved, ONUSAL, for its part, has been able to verify improvements in the operational situation.

10. My previous report drew attention to some serious deficiencies in the electoral rolls, some of which still persist. First of all, there are a large number of citizens who have not yet been registered or who do not yet have an electoral card. According to a study conducted by the United Nations Development Programme (UNDP)/ ONUSAL, 27 per cent of Salvadorians of voting age— some 700,000 people—do not have an electoral card. Failure to register is commonest in those departments which experienced the highest levels of armed conflict in the past. Nevertheless, the failure to register would ap-

pear to be due more to lethargy on the part of the citizens and technical inefficiency on the part of the Supreme Electoral Tribunal than to a deliberate effort to exclude certain sectors of the population for political reasons. There are numerous problems which limit the possibility of achieving a high percentage of registration.

11. First of all, as voter registration is voluntary in El Salvador it would be too much to expect that all potential voters would register. Added to this is the complexity of the system and the serious difficulties in the registration process. The starting-point in this process is presentation of a request for registration by the voter, who must return a month later to collect his electoral card. If the information on the request tallies with that on the birth certificate stored in the registry files, the card will be ready. However, responsibility for sending the birth certificates to the registry lies with the mayoral offices and some offices tend to send them late or not at all. Often, upon going to collect his card a person discovers that the request has not been validated, and it is quite common not even to be given any explanation. This problem must be remedied in the next few weeks in order to avoid a situation such as that which occurred in 1991, when thousands of citizens were not duly registered even though their requests for inclusion in the register had been submitted in time and in the proper form. For that reason appeals to the citizenry to come forward and register must necessarily be accompanied by an improvement in the mechanism for the issuance of electoral cards. One ground for concern, in this connection, is the fact that in recent weeks whereas the number of requests for registration has risen considerably, the number of cards issued has remained fairly constant.

12. Another problem which affects the registration process is the large number of names corresponding to people who are abroad or who are deceased and the inadequacy of controls to avoid double registration. Both factors make it easy for a person to register more than once. The availability of larger capacity equipment will enable the Supreme Electoral Tribunal to check double registrations nationwide. There is little that can be done, for the time being, about the registration of persons who are deceased, given the deficiencies of the information available to the Supreme Electoral Tribunal. Nevertheless, it will be possible to prevent anyone from voting twice by proper use of indelible ink.

13. Another persisting problem relates to discrep-ancies between the names included in the electoral rolls and those on the electoral cards. There are also cases of people with valid cards but whose names do not appear in the register at the polling station at which they are to vote. Although the magnitude of these problems is not clear, it may be considerable, judging from the number of complaints concerning citizens who were unable to exercise their right to vote in the legislative and municipal elections of 1991. The difficulty can be minimized by improving the card issuance process and by periodically providing parties and citizens with lists of registered voters in order to check that the information on a card tallies with that on a register.

14. In addition, it should be pointed out that there are serious deficiencies with regard to the training of Supreme Electoral Tribunal personnel; limited transportation for transporting the mobile registration teams and shortcomings in the public information campaign. The search for solutions has not been facilitated by the manner in which the Tribunal takes decisions (a vote by four of the five members is needed even on matters of limited political consequence). This system is unlikely to change in the short term. Accordingly, only an awareness of the difficulties that this creates and the noble aims of the members can facilitate achievement of the necessary consensus among members of the Tribunal. Given that the Tribunal's political legitimacy derives from its technical effectiveness and the impartiality of its decisions, whether the elections are viewed as free and fair by all contending parties will depend greatly on the manner in which the registration process is conducted. The main danger is that if, owing to a failure to resolve the technical problems, the Supreme Electoral Tribunal ceases to be regarded as legitimate, this will taint the entire electoral process. For that reason it is vital that the authorities, the parties and other external institutions which are supporting the electoral process in El Salvador should collaborate and coordinate their activities with a realistic vision and should make constructive criticisms which will facilitate the task of drawing up the electoral rolls.

15. Finally, it should be recalled that voter registration is a principal element in shaping the political atmosphere. If properly carried out it will benefit the entire political process and will facilitate the development of a favourable context for the forthcoming electoral campaign.

Document 92

Letter dated 3 November 1993 from the Secretary-General to the President of the Security Council concerning the persistence of human rights violations in El Salvador

S/26689, 3 November 1993

In recent reports to the Security Council concerning the work of the United Nations Observer Mission in El Salvador (ONUSAL), I have brought to the attention of the Council some worrying developments in the implementation of the Peace Accords between the Government of El Salvador and the Frente Farabundo Martí para la Liberación Nacional (FMLN), as well as in the electoral process, which ONUSAL was mandated to observe by the Security Council in resolution 832 (1993).

Among these developments has been the persistence of serious human rights violations which was reported by the Division of Human Rights of ONUSAL in its eighth report covering the period from 1 May to 31 July 1993 (S/26416 of 15 September 1993, para. VI, 1). In that report, the Director of the Division noted in particular that politically motivated violations had become more open, a development made more serious in view of the forthcoming electoral process (ibid., para. VI, 2). These concerns about the human rights situation were also mentioned in my report on the implementation of the recommendations of the Commission on the Truth (S/26581 of 14 October 1993). In the context of the Commission's recommendation for the investigation of illegal groups (S/25500, annex, V, II, C.), the report noted that cases of arbitrary executions over the past few months gave ground for concern that illegal groups were operating, whose methods seemed to repeat behavioural patterns prevailing in the past (S/26581, annex, para. 32).

On 25 October, I learned with shock and profound sadness of the execution, in death-squad style, of a leader of the FMLN. That assassination was followed on 30 October by the murder of another leading member of the FMLN. These killings have generated apprehension in El Salvador and the international community at large. They substantiate the concerns referred to in the above-mentioned reports and call for vigorous investigation. They also confirm the need for immediate implementation of the recommendation of the Commission on the Truth regarding investigation of illegal groups. I have, therefore, decided to instruct the Director of the Division of Human Rights of ONUSAL, with supplementary expert assistance as needed, to work with those concerned in order to assist the Government in implementing the recommendation of the Commission on the Truth that a thorough investigation of private armed groups be undertaken

immediately. While the responsibility for implementation of that recommendation lies with the Government, it is my view that the National Counsel for the Defence of Human Rights, within its responsibilities under the Constitution, could also play an important role.

Recent developments have also brought out the need to accelerate the implementation of other recommendations of the Commission on the Truth relating to the eradication of structural causes linked to human rights violations that occurred during the civil war and also to institutional reforms to prevent the repetition of such acts.

I should also like to recall the difficulties relating to the formation and deployment of the National Civil Police which I described in my report on the implementation of the recommendations of the Commission on the Truth (S/25500, annex, para. 30). In addition to the fact that the deployment of the new police is far behind the schedule established in the Peace Accords, ONUSAL has met with persistent difficulties in carrying out its task of verifying that only individuals meeting certain criteria are recruited to the National Civil Police. Furthermore, the above-mentioned report stated that members of the Special Antidrug Unit of the National Police had already joined the National Civil Police even though ONUSAL had not yet been able to verify their suitability.

I should like to stress that the agreements relating to the creation of an exclusively civilian police are a key component of the Peace Accords. The Truth Commission also emphasized the need to ensure that there were no links between the National Civil Police and the former security bodies or any other branch of the armed forces (S/25500, annex, II.B). It is therefore essential that the provisions of the Peace Accords regarding the National Academy for Public Security and the National Civil Police should be scrupulously fulfilled. Together with other reforms, they will establish a framework conducive to national reconciliation and observance of human rights. ONUSAL must be allowed to carry out its verification mandate unimpeded.

Finally, I should like to recall the delays and difficulties which I described in my first periodic report on the electoral process (S/26606 of 20 October). The forthcoming elections in El Salvador are to be the culmination of the whole peace process. It is essential to the credibility of the electoral process that the registration of voters should be as comprehensive as possible. Accordingly, it is my hope that the Government of El Salvador and the institutions involved in the registration process will make every effort, with the assistance of ONUSAL, to overcome existing deficiencies and ensure that all eligible Salvadorians have an opportunity to be duly registered so that they can play a full part in deciding the future of their country.

Under the timetable initially agreed upon by the parties, implementation of most provisions of the Peace Accords should have been completed before the general elections in March 1994. Delays in implementation will, however, make it impossible to reach that objective in some areas, in particular the phasing out of the National Police and full deployment of the National Civil Police. There are also considerable delays in the transfer of lands and other reintegration programmes. But the recent mur-

ders have brought into sharper focus the need to accelerate the implementation of the Accords in order to set the stage for a genuinely free and fair electoral process. At a high-level meeting on 8 September 1993, in which ONUSAL participated, the Government and the FMLN agreed on the need to step up the implementation process with a view to "sweeping the table clean" before 20 November 1993, when the electoral campaign will begin. I fully share that sense of urgency and have requested my Special Representative in El Salvador to exercise the utmost diligence in promoting a comprehensive implementation of the Peace Accords by the target dates agreed upon by the parties.

I would be grateful if you would be kind enough to bring this information to the attention of the Members of the Security Council.

(*Signed*) Boutros BOUTROS-GHALI

Document 93

Statement by the President of the Security Council concerning the violent deaths of two FMLN leaders and other members of the FMLN

S/26695, 5 November 1993

The Security Council has learned with shock and concern of the violent deaths in recent days in El Salvador of two leaders and other members of the Frente Farabundo Martí para la Liberacion Nacional (FMLN), as well as one member of the Alianza Republicana Nacionalista (ARENA) party. It notes, in this respect, that the Director of the Human Rights Division of the United Nations Observer Mission in El Salvador (ONUSAL) has referred in its last two reports 1/ to what appears to be a pattern of politically motivated murders, a development all the more serious in light of the upcoming electoral process. The Council insists that this violence has to stop.

The Council deems it essential that the authorities of El Salvador take all necessary measures so that those responsible for the killings be promptly brought to justice, with a view to preventing such events from occurring in the future. It welcomes the technical cooperation that Member States are extending to the competent Salvadorian authorities, at their request, in order to assist them in the investigation of these criminal acts.

The Council notes with particular concern that the Secretary-General, in his report on the implementation of the recommendations of the Commission on the Truth, 2/ underscored the significance of cases of killings over the past few months that seemed to follow patterns that could indicate a resurgence of illegal armed groups, whose

activities had diminished following the signature of the peace accords in January 1992.

In this regard, the Council takes note, with approval, of the Secretary-General's decision, as reported in his letter dated 3 November 1993 to the President of the Council, 3/ to direct the Human Rights Division of ONUSAL to work with the El Salvador Human Rights Prosecutor in order to assist the Government of El Salvador in implementing the recommendation of the Commission on the Truth that a thorough investigation of illegal armed groups be undertaken immediately.

The Council further underlines the importance of full and timely implementation of all the provisions of the peace accords. It remains concerned about delays occurring in several instances, namely, the phasing out of the National Police and full deployment of the National Civil Police, the implementation of the recommendations of the Commission on the Truth and the transfer of lands and other reintegration programmes, which are essential for the development of a solid framework and a new climate for the respect of human rights in El Salvador.

The Council also calls upon all parties to continue

1/ S/26416.
2/ S/26581.
3/ S/26689.

their efforts to make the March 1994 elections representative and successful. It recognizes the progress that has been made in registering thousands of voters, but, taking into account the delays and problems reported by the Secretary-General in his report of 20 October 1993, 4/ it calls upon the Government and all concerned to ensure that all qualified voters who have applied will receive the necessary documents in time to vote. It welcomes the steps taken by the Secretary-General to assist in this process through the Electoral Division of ONUSAL.

The Council welcomes the agreement reached between the Government and the FMLN on the need to speed up the implementation of the provisions of the peace accords and, accordingly, urges all parties concerned to accelerate the fulfilment of their commitments under those accords before the electoral campaign gets under way. It expects ONUSAL to be allowed fully to carry out its verification mandate unimpeded. The Council will continue to follow developments in El Salvador with close attention.

4/ S/26606.

Document 94

Report of the Secretary-General on ONUSAL's activities from 22 May to 20 November 1993

S/26790, 23 November 1993

Introduction

1. The present report is submitted to the Security Council in compliance with resolution 832 (1993). It describes the activities of the United Nations Observer Mission in El Salvador (ONUSAL) for the period from 22 May to 20 November 1993.

2. Since my report of 21 May 1993 (S/25812 and Add.1-3) on the overall implementation of the Peace Accords signed between the Government of El Salvador and the Frente Farabundo Martí para la Liberación Nacional (FMLN), I have submitted a number of reports on specific aspects of the implementation process. These include my letter of 8 June (S/25901) and my reports of 29 June and 30 August (S/26005 and S/26371) on the discovery and destruction of illegal arms deposits belonging to FMLN, my report of 14 October 1993 regarding the implementation of the recommendations of the Commission on the Truth (S/26581) and my report of 20 October (S/26606) on the activities of the Electoral Division of ONUSAL. In addition, the seventh and eighth reports of the ONUSAL Human Rights Division are contained in documents S/26033 and S/26416 and Add.1.

3. Mr. Augusto Ramirez-Ocampo has continued to serve as my Special Representative and Chief of Mission. The ONUSAL Electoral Division began operating in September 1993.

4. The discovery in Nicaragua on 23 May 1993 of an illegal arms cache belonging to FMLN and the latter's subsequent admission that it had maintained large quantities of weapons both within and outside El Salvador marked a serious violation of the Peace Accords. The United Nations Observer Mission in El Salvador (ONUSAL), in collaboration with the Governments concerned and with the full cooperation of FMLN, undertook the complicated task of verifying and destroying the undeclared arms. On 30 August, I confirmed to the Council (S/26371) that the military structure of FMLN had been effectively dismantled and that its former combatants had been demobilized and reintegrated into the civil, institutional and political life of the country.

5. At the end of July, after a delay of several months, I was in a position to report to the Council (S/26052) that the Government had taken the necessary steps to comply with the provisions of the Peace Accords relating to the recommendations of the Ad Hoc Commission on the Purification of the Armed Forces of El Salvador.

6. Several other key aspects of the Peace Accords continued to suffer serious delays. The programme for the transfer of lands fell further behind the targets agreed in October 1992. Delays also affected the reintegration programmes for ex-combatants and war-disabled. Serious difficulties affected the operations of the National Public Security Academy and the deployment of the National Civil Police. Additional problems arose over the lack of a plan for phasing-out the National Police and the establishment of the functional divisions of the National Civil Police, including the transfer to them of members of the Criminal Investigation Commission and the Special Antinarcotics Unit. The collection of weapons previously issued for the exclusive use of personnel of the Armed Forces of El Salvador remained far from incomplete.

7. In late August, ONUSAL held a series of meetings with each of the parties in an effort to find ways of tackling these delays. There followed, on 8 September 1993, a meeting at the highest level between the two parties and ONUSAL, at which it was agreed to "sweep the table clean" with respect to outstanding agreements before the start of the electoral campaign on 20 November 1993. Commitments were undertaken on the adoption of draft laws on the possession of weapons and the regulation of private security services; the submission of a plan for the phasing-out of the National Police; measures to ensure the civilian character of the National Civil Police and its autonomy from the Armed Forces of El Salvador; deployment of the National Civil Police; the admission of former FMLN combatants at the executive and senior levels of the National Public Security Academy; and plans to accelerate the transfer of land and the reintegration programmes. Agreement was reached on measures aimed at strengthening the climate of reconciliation, including cooperation in eradicating armed illegal groups and a pledge to refrain from mutual accusations in cases of serious incidents. A timetable was devised by ONUSAL for implementation of these commitments and joint government-FMLN-ONUSAL working groups were created or reinforced to deal with various of them.

8. The National Commission for the Consolidation of Peace (COPAZ), with its subcommissions, has continued to exercise its function of supervising implementation of the Peace Accords, with ONUSAL present as an observer. Despite the slowness of its decision-making process, which requires consensus, COPAZ has continued to play a useful role.

9. In August, the Forum for Economic and Social Consultation reached agreement on an agenda for its discussion of reforms of El Salvador's labour legislation. This came after several weeks of stalemate caused by disagreements among government, business and labour representatives on International Labour Organization (ILO) conventions relating to collective labour rights. The creation of a Labour Council within the Ministry of Labour, which institutionalizes consultations among the three parties, is a positive development. However, ILO conventions on collective rights have yet to be ratified.

10. In response to increasing crime and growing public concern about security, the Government has deployed the Armed Forces in several parts of the country in a deterrent role. A key provision of the Peace Accords is that the Armed Forces should be used for public security functions only in exceptional circumstances, which should be reported to the Legislative Assembly. ONUSAL has pressed the Government, so far without success, to make such a report in order to respect this constitutional provision.

11. In recent weeks, a number of murders and assaults have raised fears about the possible resurgence of illegal armed groups with political objectives, including the so-called death squads. In October, the Division of Human Rights of ONUSAL alerted the Government to this danger and stressed the usefulness of establishing an autonomous mechanism for the investigation of these incidents. The subsequent killings of two senior FMLN leaders, a member of the governing party (ARENA) and two former municipal officials belonging to that party, brought this issue into sharper focus. In view of these killings and the ONUSAL position as expressed by its Human Rights Division, the Government created an Interinstitutional Commission to investigate this type of crime. At a meeting between the President and the FMLN leadership (with ONUSAL present), it was decided to invite foreign experts to cooperate in the investigation of the cases of the two senior FMLN leaders. This led to the creation of a subgroup of the Commission, the Interinstitutional Investigation Group for that purpose. On 29 October, ONUSAL informed the Government that the Interinstitutional Commission did not meet United Nations criteria for the investigation of summary executions. Nevertheless, in compliance with its observation function, ONUSAL has been following closely the work of the subgroup. On 3 November 1993 I conveyed my concerns in a letter to the President of the Security Council (S/26689), to which the Council responded with the President's statement of 5 November 1993 (S/26695).

I. Military aspects

A. *Matters relating to the end of the armed confrontation*

12. As at 1 November 1993, ONUSAL had a strength of 31 military observers from Brazil, Canada, Colombia, Ecuador, Spain, India, Ireland, Sweden and Venezuela and 7 medical officers from Argentina, deployed in two regional offices in the western and eastern parts of the country, from which they patrol, in particular, the former zones of conflict. During the period under review they were concerned mainly with the aftermath of the explosion in Managua on 23 May 1993 of an arsenal belonging to the FMLN faction "Fuerzas Populares de Liberación". The incident was covered in my reports to the Council dated 8 June, 29 June and 30 August 1993 (S/25901, S/26005 and S/26371) and by the Council itself in its statement of 11 June 1993 (S/25929). It required ONUSAL to verify and destroy the 128 widely dispersed caches declared by FMLN in El Salvador (109), Nicaragua (14) and Honduras (5), containing 38 missiles and approximately 3,000 individual and collective weapons.

13. The Armed Forces of El Salvador, which, as I

reported in May, had completed the reduction of its troops in March 1993, developed plans for the reduction of its officer strength. However, the reintegration programmes for demobilized soldiers have been seriously delayed. The payment of compensation (one year's wages) stipulated by the Peace Accords has not yet begun and the land transfer and training programmes cover only a very small percentage of the potential beneficiaries.

14. In November 1992 (see S/24833, para. 28), ONUSAL verified, from documentation and various personal interviews, the disbanding of the former National Intelligence Department and the handover of all its premises to other units of the Armed Forces of El Salvador, in accordance with the Peace Accords. The Government stated that the Department's files would remain in the care of the Armed Forces of El Salvador Joint Chiefs of Staff but has not yet clarified how they will ultimately be disposed of. Department files that could allude to persons reintegrated into the civil, political and institutional life of the country are supposed to be destroyed or transferred to the State Intelligence Agency. ONUSAL also verified the creation of that Agency and the appointment of its Director, in keeping with the Peace Accords. The intelligence activities of the Armed Forces should now be carried out within the framework of the doctrinal principles that appear in chapter I.3 of the Peace Accords and derive from the reformed Constitution. It is not fully clear that the above provisions have been adequately complied with and ONUSAL is pursuing this matter with the Government.

B. Recovery of weapons of the Armed Forces held by private individuals

15. The recovery by the Government of Armed Forces of El Salvador weapons held by private individuals has been very seriously delayed and cannot be fully implemented until two laws regulating the use and possession of arms by individuals and by security institutions are enacted and in force. The first of these is before the Legislative Assembly and close to being approved. The second has not yet been submitted by COPAZ to the Legislative Assembly. At the high-level meeting on 8 September 1993, the Government undertook to collect these weapons and substitute others for them by 20 November 1993. This has not happened, although work is under way to verify the weapons concerned with a view to establishing a comprehensive inventory of them.

C. Clearing of minefields

16. After collaborating with the working group that prepared the demining programme for El Salvador (S/25812, para. 22), ONUSAL military observers helped to coordinate and control the clearing of 425 minefields.

Contractual problems between the Government of El Salvador, which assumed financial responsibility for the project in the absence of a commitment by international aid organizations, and an international company have prevented the completion of the programme, although it is 80 per cent complete and is expected to be terminated before year's end.

D. Other matters

17. During the period under review, and in compliance with the Accords, the Armed Forces of El Salvador has disseminated its new doctrine. It has likewise initiated courses, seminars and conferences for its members and for other sectors of Salvadorian society in accordance with this new doctrine. Worthy of note is the organization of the first advanced strategic studies course in which, for the first time, military officers and civilians from a broad range of institutions and political parties, including FMLN, study and analyse security and national defence problems and the new role of the Armed Forces of El Salvador in Salvadorian society.

18. Military observers have been monitoring the deployment of the Armed Forces of El Salvador for public security duties ("plan vigilante"). According to the Government, the plan is aimed at completing the training of the Armed Forces of El Salvador and deterring crime by deploying the Forces on roads in high-crime areas that are not in former conflict or urban zones. ONUSAL's reaction to this move is described in paragraph 10 above.

II. Public security matters

A. Police Division

19. The Police Division, which has a current strength of 277 police observers contributed by Austria, Brazil, Chile, Colombia, France, Guyana, Italy, Mexico, Norway, Spain and Sweden, continues to perform its task of monitoring and assisting the National Police during the period of transition until its complete replacement by the National Civil Police, which should take place by 1 September 1994, as established in the Organic Law of the National Civil Police. Between October 1992 and July 1993, police observers also supervised and supported the Auxiliary Transitory Police, which was responsible for maintaining public order and security in the former zones of conflict during those months. In response to a government request that ONUSAL provide support to the National Civil Police for a six-month period and in close coordination with the international technical team that advises the Director-General of the National Civil Police, the Division carried out, between 1 April and 30 September 1993, an evaluation of the performance of the new police force in the field and provided it with technical

advice and logistical support. The Government did not request an extension of this support and the Division has had to limit its involvement with the National Civil Police to observation of its performance in order to verify compliance with the Peace Accords. ONUSAL remains ready to help the Government to complete the territorial and functional deployment of the National Civil Police on time.

20. The Division also supports the Human Rights Division, to which 19 police observers are seconded, and the Electoral Division. Police observers conduct special inquiries when required and verify that appropriate security measures are provided for FMLN leaders, as established by the Accords. The Division also provides observers for the admission examinations to the National Public Security Academy.

B. *National Public Security Academy*

21. The Academy, which is responsible for the training of recruits to the National Civil Police, celebrated its first anniversary on 1 September 1993. In 14 months it has graduated eight basic-level classes with a total of about 2,306 students, of whom 44 are National Civil Police officers. It is now training an additional 2,200 basic-level students and nearly 200 executive and senior-level students and intends to graduate a total of 5,700 agents and 240 officers by end-July 1994, as envisaged in the Peace Accords and in the supplementary agreements of August 1992. In order to attain that target the Academy has increased its monthly recruitment from the 330 established in the Accords to more than 400. It may be advisable to maintain the monthly intake of 400 after July 1994 in order to reach the tentative goal of around 10,000 agents and 500 officers before the target date of mid-1999 set by the Peace Accords.

22. Perhaps the greatest challenge that the Academy faces in the coming months is that of simultaneously training by end-July 1994 both agents and officers required by the National Civil Police for its territorial deployment and specialists to staff its various functional divisions. It has already begun training the first members of the Transit and Finance Divisions, although the number planned for the latter Division would seem insufficient to replace the 1,200-strong Customs Police. The training of officers for the Division for the Protection of Eminent Persons and the Borders Division will take place between February and July 1994. During the second half of 1994, the Academy will train experts in arms and explosives and the environment. The plan envisages the training of a total of 810 specialists by November 1994. It does not, however, include the training of specialists in criminal and antinarcotics investigations, as those two divisions will initially be staffed with personnel transferred from the existing Criminal Investigation Commission and the Special Antinarcotics Unit.

23. The complementary accords of June 1992 established that, during the transition period, 20 per cent of entrants to the Academy would be from FMLN and 20 per cent from the National Police and the remaining 60 per cent would be persons who had not participated in the armed conflict. The National Police has already filled its quota and FMLN has committed itself to doing so before the end of the transition period. More and more of the new recruits will thus have to be persons who did not participate directly in the armed conflict. The Academy will accordingly have to increase its recruitment campaign among the civilian population.

24. The Academy has discovered that some 40 candidates who requested admission as civilians had been former FMLN combatants. FMLN stated that that did not result from a deliberate policy on its part but from the decisions of individual candidates and requested that the persons concerned be counted as part of its 20 per cent quota.

25. In order to verify whether former members of the Treasury Police, National Guard and élite battalions (immediate reaction infantry battalions) have also been admitted to the Academy as civilians, ONUSAL asked the Government in October to provide the Academy with lists of the personnel of those bodies prior to their dissolution and demobilization. The Government has not yet responded to that request, thus preventing this verification from being carried out. I must also reiterate the concern expressed in my previous report (S/25812, para. 43), regarding some candidates submitted by the National Police to the National Civil Police. The problems referred to in my reports of November 1992 and May 1993 (S/24833, para. 37, and S/25812, para. 30) that resulted from the incorporation in the executive and senior levels of the Academy of 10 former officers of the National Guard and the Treasury Police have finally been overcome.

26. The Academy has continued to receive the support of an international team of experts from Spain and the United States of America that provides the Director and the Academic Council with advice on aspects such as the recruitment and selection process, curricula, finances and discipline. Instructors from Chile, Norway, Spain and the United States play a full part in the training. Currently, the Academy has a total of 38 international experts and instructors, and three new instructors from Sweden are expected to join soon. It is essential that this international support be maintained. At the same time, the Academy should begin training Salvadorian instructors, chosen from among its own graduates.

27. ONUSAL continues to monitor the functioning

of the Academy and is represented by an observer at its Academic Council. It also monitors the admissions examinations and recommends improvements when necessary. Its Human Rights Division is organizing, jointly with the Academy, seminars and workshops on human rights and provides literature on the subject. ONUSAL remains ready to provide personnel from its Police Division to support and complement the efforts of the international technical team.

28. In the Government's budget for 1994, recently presented to the Legislative Assembly, about $ 10 million has been assigned to the Academy, a slightly higher level than in the current year. This will need to be complemented by continuing support from the international community. In addition to the Governments of Spain, the United States and Norway, which have been involved in the project from the outset, Germany and Sweden have recently contributed to it. I appeal to other Member States to follow suit.

C. National Civil Police

29. The National Civil Police, which began operating in March 1993, is currently deployed in six departments. By year's end, it will have replaced the National Police in 9 of the 10 departments where its deployment was planned for 1993. During the first half of 1994, it will begin operations in all remaining parts of the country except the capital, San Salvador, where it will initiate its deployment in July 1994, where, it should be noted, a partial deployment took place in early October 1993 as part of a plan to combat the high level of delinquency.

30. As regards the National Civil Police's functional divisions, the deployment of its Territorial Traffic Division began in October and that of the Finance Division in November. The Protection of Eminent Persons Division will follow in February 1994, the Border Division in April, the Arms and Explosives Division in June and the Environmental Division in the second half of 1994. The Criminal Investigation and Antinarcotics Divisions should be constituted before the end of 1993 with the integration of personnel from the Criminal Investigation Commission and the Special Antinarcotics Unit, respectively.

31. However, as I informed the Council in May (S/25812, para. 35), the integration of former Criminal Investigation Commission and Special Antinarcotics Unit personnel into the National Civil Police must be carried out in accordance with the complementary agreements of 22 December 1992, which establish that personnel of those bodies wishing to join the National Civil Police must first be evaluated by its Director-General, under ONUSAL verification and based on criteria of professional competence and suitability to join the new civilian

police force. They must also pass a special course on the new National Civil Police doctrine at the National Public Security Academy. As indicated in my report to the Council on the implementation of the recommendations of the Commission on the Truth (S/26581, annex, para. 30), ONUSAL is still not in receipt of all the information that it has requested on the candidates, nor have its recommendations for improving the procedures for transferring personnel from those units to the National Civil Police been given due consideration. These include psycho-technical tests and conceptual tests on the new National Civil Police doctrine. Moreover, under the complementary agreement of 22 December 1992, those members of the Special Antinarcotics Unit and the Criminal Investigation Commission who were at the same time members of the Armed Forces should have resigned from the Armed Forces of El Salvador before joining the National Civil Police. ONUSAL has not so far succeeded in obtaining the necessary documentation to verify that this provision was complied with.

32. A further cause for concern is that, although ONUSAL has not yet been able to verify the manner in which this transfer is being carried out, Special Antinarcotics Unit and Criminal Investigation Commission personnel have already joined the National Civil Police. Moreover, contrary to the complementary agreement of 22 December 1992, which provided that Special Antinarcotics Unit personnel would be incorporated only into the National Civil Police's Antinarcotics Division, Special Antinarcotics Unit personnel have already begun fulfilling other functions, for example, those of Chief of the National Civil Police detachment in San Miguel, which is the second most important detachment in the country.

33. It is also a matter of concern that the Government submitted the relevant legislation regarding Criminal Investigation Commission and Special Antinarcotics Unit transfers directly to the Legislative Assembly, bypassing COPAZ, and that some of the provisions in one of the new laws are not consistent with the Organic Law of the National Civil Police or some international instruments on human rights. It is essential that other laws and regulations relating to National Civil Police be discussed by COPAZ before being submitted to the Legislative Assembly.

34. Nor has the subcommission of COPAZ for the National Civil Police been permitted to function as a consultative body to the Director-General. Contrary to the Peace Accords and the renewed commitment made by the Government at the high-level meeting of 8 September 1993, the Director-General has not been requesting its opinion before adopting relevant decisions or measures regarding the organization and deployment of the National Civil Police.

35. It is also essential that the National Civil Po-

lice's organic structure be completed with the immediate appointment of its Inspector-General, whose responsibilities include monitoring and controlling the activities of the force's operational and management services, as well as its respect for human rights. The units on control and disciplinary investigation should also be established without further delay.

36. The Government's failure to provide the National Civil Police with adequate logistical and technical support is another factor that is compromising the new force's ability to perform its functions. In early November 1993, the 1,740 civilian policemen deployed in 5 departments and partially in another 3 had only 67 vehicles (one third of which were in the capital), 31 motorcycles (all in San Salvador) and 134 portable radios. This is blatantly insufficient. In addition, working conditions in National Civil Police stations are generally very poor. This lack of support imposes considerable strain on the civilian policemen, taxes their morale and hampers their performance, in spite of their best efforts. It is important that the Government immediately make available to the National Civil Police resources previously assigned to the National Police and other public security bodies.

37. It is also necessary for the Government to provide the National Civil Police with an adequate budget. It has asked the Legislative Assembly for an increase from $12 million for 1993 to $33 million for 1994. However, the Director-General of the National Civil Police has told ONUSAL that this is still $20 million short of what is technically necessary and this shortfall could affect future National Civil Police deployment. While the primary responsibility must rest with the Government, I hope that the international community will support the Government's efforts, especially by providing the National Civil Police with some of the equipment it needs. The United States and Sweden have set an encouraging example in this regard.

D. National Police

38. In early October the Government presented its plan for the phasing out of the National Police, for which ONUSAL had been pressing since February. It consists of two phases: during the first phase (October 1993-May 1994) 2,400 policemen will be demobilized at a monthly rate of 300; during the second phase (May-October 1994), 6,850 will be demobilized at a monthly rate of 1,370. The plan also establishes that the Customs Police, comprising 1,211 policemen, will be demobilized when the National Civil Police Finance Division becomes operational. A total of 10,461 National Police will thus be demobilized. The National Police training school, which currently graduates between 60 and 100 agents per month, will be closed at the end of 1993.

39. The figures contained in the Government's plan confirm my statements in previous reports that the National Police was significantly strengthened after the signing of the Peace Accords. The insistence of the Government on this policy, and in particular on keeping the National Police training school in operation until the end of 1993, is difficult to reconcile with the Peace Accords. As the National Police's 20 per cent quota has already been filled, graduates from the National Police school will not be qualified to join the National Civil Police; this means that the effect of its continued operation has been to deprive the National Civil Police of potential recruits.

40. The Government's plan is at variance with the Organic Law of the National Civil Police, which provides that the National Police should disappear by 1 September 1994. Moreover the plan to maintain the bulk of the National Police after the deployment of the National Civil Police is virtually complete would be inconsistent with the principle contained in the Accords that the National Civil Police should progressively replace the National Police as it deploys throughout the country. ONUSAL is therefore pressing the Government to accelerate the reduction of the National Police and bring its phasing-out into line with the rate of deployment of the National Civil Police.

41. It will be evident from this section of the report that there are many causes for concern about the way in which the police and public security provisions of the Peace Accords are being implemented. I accordingly decided to send to El Salvador a small police mission to assess the current state of implementation and make recommendations on how the United Nations can further support this vital part of the Peace Accords. The mission arrived in San Salvador on 16 November 1993.

III. Human rights and the administration of justice

42. During the period under review, reports covering ONUSAL's work in the area of human rights were submitted to the General Assembly and the Security Council under my notes of 2 July, 15 September and 27 October 1993 (S/26033, S/26416 and Add.1). The Human Rights Division continues its active verification and its programmes in support of the institutions responsible for the administration of justice and protection of human rights. Of special relevance are activities being carried out with the Supreme Court of Justice for the training of judges and magistrates and support to the Armed Forces of El Salvador in the development of a new democratic doctrine and the revision of curricula in the military academies relating to human rights and constitutional law. The Division cooperates with the Office of the National Counsel for the Defence of Human Rights, with which it signed an agreement aimed at the transfer to the

Counsel's Office of experience and investigative technology when ONUSAL withdraws from El Salvador. A permanent consultative mechanism exists at the highest level between the Division and the Counsel's Office with a view to conducting joint verification activities in the near future.

43. During the period covered by the Division's most recent report (S/26416), the human rights situation has evolved in a somewhat ambivalent fashion, showing in some areas signs of improvement and in others an increase in serious violations. Problems relating to the right to life, individual liberty, personal integrity and due process have intensified. There has been a troubling 34 per cent rise in complaints of arbitrary executions: 43 in the current quarter, as compared with 32 in the preceding one.

44. Particularly worrying are the activities of the so-called "death squads". Taking on names used in the past, or using newly created ones, these illegal groups have been the authors of numerous death-threats with clearly political connotations. At the same time, groups who purport to take the law into their own hands against supposed common delinquents have also been making death-threats and carrying out murders. The emergence of criminal organizations of this type seriously affects the stability of the peace process by eroding confidence and security, which are its fundamental bases.

45. The assassination on 25 October 1993 of Francisco Velis, a member of the FMLN National Council and a candidate for the forthcoming elections, was a particularly grave occurrence that added force to fears about the resurgence of death squads. The murder, five days later, of Eleno Castro, another member of the FMLN National Council, and the subsequent discovery of the bodies of several FMLN supporters killed in a style reminiscent of the death squads that operated with impunity during the years of armed conflict raised political tension and led many to fear a new human rights crisis in El Salvador. At the same time at least three members of the governing party (ARENA) have also been murdered in recent weeks. All these murders have been very widely repudiated within El Salvador and the international community has expressed its concern over the possible consequences for implementation of the Peace Accords, respect for human rights being a *sine qua non* for the success of the peace process and for the consolidation of a democratic society. It is to be hoped that the investigation that is being carried out with international assistance can quickly lead to the identification and punishment of those responsible. It is particularly important that, as endorsed by the Security Council in its statement of 5 November 1993, arrangements should be agreed for the Human Rights Division of ONUSAL to work with the National Counsel for the Defence of Human Rights to help the Government to carry out the relevant recommendation of the Commission on the Truth. By 20 November, such arrangements had not yet been agreed, although considerable progress had been made towards an agreement.

IV. Commission on the Truth

46. The progress report that I submitted on 14 October (S/26581) described the measures taken on some of the recommendations of the Commission on the Truth and the action required on several outstanding points of great importance, namely the dismissal of officials mentioned in connection with the serious acts of violence investigated by the Commission; recommendations requiring constitutional amendments, particularly with regard to the decentralization of powers and competence of the Supreme Court; and recommendations on *amparo* and the recognition of the jurisdiction of the Inter-American Court of Human Rights. Progress on these issues depends not only on action by the Government and FMLN, but also by individuals and institutions, in particular, COPAZ and the Legislative Assembly.

47. Since the above-mentioned progress report, there has been one important development that merits the attention of the Council. In October, the Ministry of Justice submitted six draft laws to the Legislative Assembly. These were aimed at perfecting the guarantees for due process through reforms to the Criminal Code and the Code of Criminal Procedure and the invalidation of extrajudicial confessions. The package also contained the proposed repeal of the law of dangerous condition (*estado peligroso*), which violates some of the fundamental rights enshrined in international instruments. To this is annexed a proposal for modification of article 13.4 of the Constitution, which represents an important precedent. This is a very positive step in the implementation of the recommendations of the Commission on the Truth and, at the same time, of those of the ONUSAL Human Rights Division, which were endorsed by the Commission.

V. Economic and social matters

A. *Transfer of land programme*

48. In my last report I was able to point to progress, albeit slow, in the implementation of the land transfer programme of 13 October 1992. Six months later I regret to report that, in spite of commitments by the two parties to accelerate the process, very little progress was made until very recently. A year after agreement was reached on the land programme, land titles had been issued to less than 10 per cent of the potential beneficiaries. This was discouraging land owners from selling since they could not receive payment until the legal transfer was finalized.

The difficulties encountered and the slow rate of progress were also discouraging potential donors from making new commitments to the programme. This was particularly true of the United States Agency for International Development (USAID) and European Community (EC) donors, who noted that funds previously committed by them were still partially unused. It was also worrying that both parties had entered into new agreements to accelerate the programme but had had difficulty in putting them into practice.

49. The main problem still related to determining who should be entitled to land. The agreement stipulated that ex-combatants of both sides and landholders who had occupied land during the conflict and had been "verified" by the Special Agrarian Commission of CO-PAZ would be entitled to land. However, FMLN had questioned the way the verification was made. For example, the verification as reflected in the Commission's records often included the names of those on the board of a cooperative but not all of its members, although they had filled out forms for verification purposes (boletas). Thus the Commission's verification underestimated the total number of potential beneficiaries. In the Follow-up and Supervision Committee, a tripartite (Government/FMLN/ONUSAL) mechanism to accelerate the land programme, it was agreed that those who had filled out boletas would also be included. These, however, had not been accepted at the 42 government offices that were established in October 1993 to undertake the reverification nor had they been included in the Government's total of persons to whom it contemplated transferring land.

50. The FMLN, for its part, had also failed to comply with certain commitments. At the high-level tripartite meeting of 8 September 1993, the Government proposed and FMLN accepted that land would be transferred first to those who had been reverified. Those who had not been verified, as well as minors, would receive land at the end of the programme, if additional financing was available. The total number of beneficiaries, however, could not exceed the total contemplated in the 13 October 1992 land programme. For this sequence to begin, FMLN would have had to "clean up" the lists of beneficiaries it had submitted to the Government so as to eliminate those who had not been verified. Although the difficulties of doing this should not be underestimated, FMLN's failure to comply with the 8 September Agreement was being interpreted by the Government and by some donors as reflecting a desire to exploit the non-implementation of this programme for political purposes.

51. The land programme needed to be reactivated as soon as possible and in a dynamic way, and I appealed to the two parties to exercise flexibility in the belief that the remaining technical, financial and legal difficulties could be solved if the political will to do so existed. There was an urgent need to reduce tension among those ex-combatants whose justified expectations of getting land, credit and housing had been largely unfulfilled. Credit for agricultural production and for housing could not be obtained unless borrowers held title to, or a promise of, land. Thus, problems in land transfer had seriously delayed the reintegration of former combatants and landholders into productive activity.

52. To get the programme moving and facilitate the search for new financing, the Government had offered to issue certificates (Certificados de asignación) by 31 December for all verified people in FMLN lists for 50 State properties and also to transfer 120 negotiated private properties, provided that FMLN agreed to include only verified beneficiaries. For FMLN to clean up these lists would have been very difficult. For this reason I requested the Government to show flexibility by accepting as many non-verified people on these properties as possible.

53. I am pleased to report that on 17 November the Government agreed to accept the lists presented by the FMLN for the 120 private properties and for the 50 State properties already negotiated, so that they could be transferred before 15 December. I now urge FMLN to honour its commitment to prepare lists for the remaining properties with ex-combatants and landholders who have been verified. This would be on the understanding that a solution will be found for the unverified ones after the verified persons have received land and as resources become available, as had been agreed at the 8 September meeting.

54. The Government's willingness to accept the lists that FMLN had presented for those 170 properties will make it possible for 12,000 beneficiaries to gain access to credit for production by the end of the year. The Agricultural Development Bank, which needs to be strengthened for this purpose, would have time to establish its eligibility criteria, specify the different types of credit for different types of crops, train people, establish the necessary documentation, etc. The Bank needs to be ready to advertise its credit line by January and February so that borrowers can start getting credit in March, in time for the planting season.

55. A solution also needs to be found to the problem of human settlements (referred to in the agreements as predios e immuebles). Although at the 8 September meeting it was agreed that those in rural areas would be included in the land programme, no transfers have yet taken place. FMLN wants them transferred as they exist, with all the infrastructure and en bloc. Since approximately 750 beneficiaries of FMLN live in these settlements, breaking them up would have complex political and social consequences. The Government will

also need to show flexibility and political will to solve this problem.

56. The follow-up to land transfers is extremely important. Although some beneficiaries have received training before obtaining land, it is important that specific training relating to different crops be provided when the transfer takes place so that they can put the credit to use as productively as possible. Technical expertise to help beneficiaries to diversify production will also be needed. This is an area in which the international community could make a significant impact.

B. *Forum for Economic and Social Consultation*

57. In May 1993, I reported that, although the representatives of Government, business and labour had agreed, in February 1993, on the principle of the right of labour to associate, there had been, in April, a set-back in the work of the Forum with regard to the adoption of the ILO conventions relating to these rights (see S/25 812, para. 70). This stalemate was compounded by a month-long health-care workers' strike, which generated tension, as workers from other sectors stopped work or threatened to do so to show solidarity.

58. On 25 August 1993, the Forum emerged from this impasse and approved a new agenda, which included the reform of primary national laws on labour issues, without eliminating the issue of the ILO conventions. The agenda included the Labour Code, the Organic Law of the Ministry of Labour and Social Welfare and the Social Security Law.

59. The presentation and discussion of proposals by ILO experts to reform the labour code have contributed greatly to a new dynamism in the Forum. Most of the changes concerning the individual rights of workers were adopted and, since 25 October, the parties have been discussing collective rights and freedom to form and join unions.

60. I am glad to be able to report that, as a result of the discussions, restrictions on the unionization of rural workers have been removed and the three parties have agreed on the creation of a Labour Council within the Ministry of Labour, which will institutionalize consultation between all three parties on labour issues. Unfortunately the business sector decided to suspend its participation in the Forum as of 20 November 1993, the date of initiation of the electoral campaign.

C. *Reintegration programmes*

61. ONUSAL has continued to work with the parties and with the United Nations Development Programme (UNDP) with a view to stimulating the implementation of various programmes designed to facilitate the economic and social reintegration into civilian life of former FMLN and Armed Forces of El Salvador combatants.

FMLN ex-combatants

62. As reported in May, all the short-term programmes (agricultural training, distribution of agricultural tools, basic household goods and academic instruction) have been completed, with the exception of the industrial training programme, which is now scheduled to end in April 1994.

63. Among the many problems the following are worth mentioning. First, a global strategy is lacking in the formulation of the programmes, and this has affected their design and planning. Second, short-term training programmes did not start at the same time and were not synchronized with the dates of demobilization, with the result that some beneficiaries registered in programmes because of economic need rather than preference or vocation to learn. Third, there was no overall planning and the same mistakes were repeated in the different programmes.

64. In spite of the many problems, short-term programmes served an important purpose. They reduced the risk that demobilized people would resort to crime as a means of survival. They also helped to ensure respect for the cease-fire and thus played a crucial role in the peace process.

65. There is now a need to focus and expand on medium- and longer-term programmes, including credit for micro-enterprises, agriculture and housing, technical assistance and scholarships. As with the short-term programmes, there has not been a clear overall strategy to ensure that ex-combatants can be reintegrated into the productive life of the country. The programmes for micro-enterprises, technical assistance and scholarships have suffered serious delays, partly as a result of administrative problems but also for lack of immediate financing and political will. Those for agricultural credit and housing have been delayed by the lack of progress in the transfer of land. These delays have disrupted the continuum between short- and medium-term programmes and generated scepticism and tension among the beneficiaries, who have had to find other ways to meet their socio-economic needs.

66. At the end of October, a German-financed project for the construction of 2,000 houses for FMLN ex-combatants was inaugurated in eight departments. This represents an important start, though the number of houses to be provided meets only one third of the total demand.

67. The non-governmental organization (NGO) *Fundación 16 de enero* needs to be strengthened in order to enable it to comply with its given role in the agreed programmes of representing, organizing and informing potential beneficiaries among ex-combatants of the five FMLN groups. The fact that it has not had the necessary support or the funding to do this has weakened FMLN's

capacity to participate successfully in these programmes and has added to the administrative difficulties of implementing them.

Armed Forces of El Salvador ex-combatants

68. These programmes are similar to those envisaged for FMLN. While short-term reintegration programmes for the demobilized members of the Armed Forces of El Salvador have started, they cover only part of the target group. In addition, most of the medium-term programmes are still in the preparatory phase. ONUSAL continues to offer its help in overcoming the existing problems so that all these programmes can be implemented. A German-financed housing project similar to that inaugurated for FMLN ex-combatants is being prepared for demobilized members of the Armed Forces of El Salvador.

69. The Peace Accords stipulate that those members of the Armed Forces of El Salvador who are demobilized as a result of the Accords are entitled to an indemnity of one year's salary (chap. I.13.B). ONUSAL is still unable to obtain from the Government the information it needs on reintegration programmes (including land transfer) for ex-combatants of the Armed Forces of El Salvador (see S/25812, para. 74).

War-disabled

70. The Fund for the Protection of Wounded and War-disabled as a Consequence of the Armed Conflict was created by Decree No. 416 of 13 December 1992 in compliance with the New York Agreement, which stipulated that the Government would provide the resources to enable its Board of Directors to function. The swearing in of the Fund's Board of Directors was postponed several times, but finally took place at the end of June after a demonstration in San Salvador in which at least one life was lost. However, the emergency budget presented by the Board to permit the disbursement of funds established by the Law, which should have started in June, still awaits the approval of the Ministry of Finance. Nor has the Government yet fulfilled its obligation to make an initial contribution to the Fund, which is an important condition for the start of contributions from donors.

VI. Political participation by FMLN

71. As I informed the Council on 29 June (S/26005), the discovery of undeclared FMLN arms caches raised questions in certain quarters about the legality of FMLN as a political party. After I had reported to the Council on 30 August (S/26371) that the residual arms deposits declared by FMLN had been verified and destroyed by ONUSAL, the Supreme Electoral Tribunal of El Salvador was duly informed, in accordance with its

request. This enabled FMLN to continue as a legally recognized political party. On 5 September 1993, FMLN held its national convention at which it decided to participate in the elections and chose its candidates.

72. At the high-level meeting of 8 September 1993 between the Government, FMLN and ONUSAL, the Government undertook to assign two television frequencies and one short-wave frequency to the institution or persons designated by FMLN. This, added to the AM and FM frequencies previously assigned, fulfils the commitment entered into by the Government in the complementary agreements of 22 December 1992. The Government also agreed to grant tax exemptions for the vehicles imported by FMLN for use by its leaders; these are still being processed.

73. Likewise, the approval by the Legislative Assembly on 17 June 1993 of the Law for the Protection of Individuals Subject to Special Security now permits its application to FMLN, whose bodyguards are being incorporated into the National Civil Police as supernumeraries, although not in the numbers originally envisaged. FMLN leaders have hitherto been protected by ex-combatants chosen by them and armed with their own weapons verified by ONUSAL and authorized by the Government. The recent murders of two FMLN leaders highlight the need for the provision of adequate security to the FMLN leadership which, under the Peace Accords, is the responsibility of the Government.

VII. Restoration of public administration in the former zones of conflict

74. As I reported to the Council in May, all mayors and judges returned to their jurisdictions at the beginning of the year. However, some of them are still not living in their municipalities, which limits to some extent the services they can provide to their communities. Neither mayors nor judges have faced political obstacles in the exercise of their functions and relations between them and local communities have on the whole been positive. The re-establishment of public services has, however, been slow and the disbursement of funds for the reconstruction of the areas most devastated by the conflict has still not been made in the amount and with the urgency that the situation demands. I again urge the Government to accord higher priority to the reconstruction of the former zones of conflict.

VIII. Electoral process

75. The Council has recently received a detailed report (S/26606) on the activities of the ONUSAL Electoral Division. The Division's mandate is being carried out in five stages: during the first stage, from 1 to 30 June 1993, offices at the central and regional levels were

established; the second stage, from 1 July to 18 December 1993, entails, *inter alia*, the verification of the registration of voters and subsequent political activities; the third stage, from 19 December to 14 March 1994, will be devoted to the observation of the electoral campaign; and the fourth stage, from 15 to 31 March 1994, will cover observation of the elections, the counting of votes and the announcement of results. The fifth and final stage will run from 1 to 30 April 1994, if a second round of voting is required for the election of the President.

76. The Division is now concentrating on verifying that steps are taken to permit the inclusion of all qualified citizens in the electoral register. Major progress had been made in mobilizing citizens to apply to register. By 19 November the Supreme Electoral Tribunal had received over 785,000 registration forms. There nevertheless remains a problem of transforming these applications into voter registration and electoral cards and serious technical difficulties have not yet been fully overcome.

77. One problem is that many municipalities are failing to send applicants' birth certificates to the Tribunal, a legal requirement for the transformation of application forms into electoral cards. A second problem is the limited capacity of the Tribunal for the timely computerization of voters' application forms and the birth certificates needed for their validation. A third problem relates to the transmission of information between the Tribunal on the one hand, and the political parties and Board of Vigilance on the other. At the time of writing, the Tribunal had not yet complied with its legal obligation to provide the parties with computer terminals connected to the centre that produces the voters' register or with lists of electoral cards available for delivery to applicants. The availability of this information would be useful in helping the parties to check how many prospective voters are still not registered. ONUSAL continues to support the Tribunal in its efforts to resolve these problems.

IX. The financial needs of post-conflict peace-building

78. As I pointed out in my last report, the international community responded generously during the last Consultative Group meeting in Paris in April 1993 to the Government's request for financing for the national reconstruction plan during the period 1993-1996. However, donors showed a clear preference for financing specific projects, mostly in infrastructure and the environment. As a result, commitments for peace-related programmes for the reintegration of ex-combatants into productive activities (purchase of land, agricultural credit, housing, credit for small enterprises, pensions for disabled, etc.) and for the promotion of democratic institutions (National Civil Police, National Public Security Academy, human-rights-related activities, the Judiciary and activities related to the coming elections) fell short of expectations.

79. In my efforts to promote financing for peace-related programmes in El Salvador, I have found that many donors condition their assistance on the Government's compliance with the Peace Accords and on stronger commitments to implement the specific programmes quickly and to give them priority in the government budget. It is thus with satisfaction that I am now able to report that the Government has begun to allocate some funds that could have been used for other purposes to some of the peace-related projects. For example, of the approximately $71 million committed to the land programme from its inception, the Government has committed about 35 per cent of the total ($25 million), with the remainder being provided by USAID ($34 million) and EC ($12 million). At the same time, its 1994 general budget allocates $10 million to the Academy and $33 million to the National Civil Police. The Government continues to mobilize external financing, especially in the form of grants and/or highly concessional loans, and has indicated its willingness to use some of the quick-disbursement funds that it obtains for these programmes.

80. Additional resources are required rather urgently for the strengthening of the Judiciary and other democratic institutions, including the National Civil Police, and for crucial programmes for the reintegration of ex-combatants and for continuing support in the area of human rights, including the National Counsel for the Defence of Human Rights. Financing is also critical for key programmes for the reintegration of ex-combatants and their supporters into the civilian and productive life of the country.

X. Financial aspects

81. By its resolution 47/234 of 14 September 1993, the General Assembly authorized the Secretary-General to enter into commitments for the operation of ONUSAL at a rate not to exceed $3 million gross ($2,720,000 net) per month for the four-month period from 1 December 1993 to 31 March 1994, should the Council decide to continue the Mission beyond 30 November 1993. This authorization is subject to the prior concurrence of the Advisory Committee on Administrative and Budgetary Questions. Should the Security Council continue the mandate of ONUSAL beyond 30 November 1993, the monthly cost of maintaining the Mission through 31 March 1994 will be limited to the commitment authority contained in General Assembly resolution 47/234. I shall report to the Advisory Committee and to the General Assembly on the additional requirements needed for the maintenance of the Mission beyond 31 March 1994.

82. As of 15 November 1993, unpaid assessed contributions to the ONUSAL special account for the period since the inception of the Mission to 30 November 1993 amount to some $25.5 million.

XI. Observations

83. The Peace Accords signed at Chapultepec on 16 January 1992 were a historic achievement of the Salvadorian people. President Cristiani and his Government and the leaders of FMLN and their supporters responded to the historic need to bring to an end a long period of civil strife, which had culminated in 11 years of bloody armed conflict. The settlement which they negotiated with the help of the United Nations was not just a cease-fire. It was a comprehensive package of interrelated agreements designed to address and resolve the many issues that had created economic, social and political tensions and finally erupted into armed conflict. It is important to remember that every element in the interrelated agreements was negotiated with the two sides and freely accepted by each of them.

84. Implementation of the Peace Accords has on the whole progressed well. Enormous advances have been achieved, advances that it would have been difficult to imagine when the United Nations first became involved in the effort to make peace in El Salvador four years ago. The elections that are to take place in March 1994 should represent the culminating point in the whole process. It had been envisaged that the vast majority of the provisions of the Peace Accords would have been implemented well before the elections. The timetable that forms part of the Accords was drafted on this basis. It was thought important that implementation of the Accords should not be caught up in the electoral campaign and that the electorate should be able to make its democratic choice at a time when the full dimensions of the new El Salvador created by the Accords were already apparent to it.

85. The electoral campaign officially began a few days ago, on 20 November 1993, preceded, during recent weeks, by a distinct polarization of political positions. The present state of implementation is described in some detail in the previous sections of this report. Much has been achieved. But it is a matter of considerable concern to me that the electoral campaign should have begun when some very important elements in the Accords remain only partially implemented and when there are disturbing signs of the reappearance of some ugly features of El Salvador's past.

86. I should like in particular to draw the Security Council's attention to three aspects: human rights, police matters and the economic and social programmes for the reintegration of both sides' ex-combatants into civil society.

87. The Human Rights Division of ONUSAL had expressed concern, in its last two reports, about a possible re-emergence of "death squads", whose contribution to the horrors of the Salvadorian civil war, and prior to it, have been amply described by the Commission on the Truth. While it would be wrong to prejudge the outcome of investigations that are under way, the recent series of murders must at least create a strong supposition that the Human Rights Division's fears were well founded. Be that as it may, those murders have had a nefarious impact on the political climate and have undermined confidence in the peace process. It is therefore essential that there should be, as soon as possible, an impartial, independent and credible investigation into illegal armed groups, as recommended by the Commission on the Truth. On 5 November 1993, the Council approved my ideas about how the United Nations should help in such an investigation. I regret that, in spite of the dispatch to El Salvador of a mission led by Under-Secretary-General Goulding from 8 to 15 November, it has not yet proved possible to reach agreement on the establishment of the investigation. Consultations, however, continue with all concerned and I hope soon to be able to report a favourable outcome.

88. Meanwhile the human rights components of the Peace Accords have been implemented in varying degrees. Important legal reforms, such as those to the Penal Code and the Code of Criminal Procedure, the elimination of extrajudicial confessions and the modification of regulations with respect to *habeas corpus*, are in progress, although many of them are only in the proposal stage and deficiencies in judicial practice persist. Within the Armed Forces, the development of human rights components both in the new military structure and in the new doctrine have been conducted consistently in cooperation with the ONUSAL Human Rights Division. The consolidation and extension of this progress will depend on the country's capacity to reverse the regressive trends that have been detected in recent months, on the effective operation of the institutions created by the Peace Accords, especially the National Counsel for the Defence of Human Rights, and on the effective deployment of the National Civil Police. Progress will also depend on the implementation of the pending recommendations of the Commission on the Truth concerning the judiciary.

89. The section on public security matters in this report (paras. 19-41) paints a somewhat disturbing picture. The civilianization of the police function was a central principle of the whole settlement. Only thus could the Armed Forces be reduced, remodelled and given the role normally performed by the military in democratic societies. I acknowledge the complexity of establishing a completely new police force and transferring responsibil-

ity for public order to it in the aftermath of a long civil war and in the middle of a crime wave. But ONUSAL's reports create the impression that at some levels in the Government there may be a lack of commitment to the objective enshrined in the Peace Accords. This is reflected in the denial to the National Civil Police of the necessary logistical and technical resources, the introduction into that force of military personnel, the prolongation of the existence of the National Police and the denial to ONUSAL of the information it requires for verification purposes. Concerns also persist that the military intelligence establishment may still be involving itself with internal security matters.

90. The severe delays in fulfilling the promises of land and other benefits that were made to ex-combatants of both sides has given rise to tension which, as the situation in a neighbouring country has shown, can become a dangerous source of instability. As regards land, both the Government and FMLN should respect their agreements and resolve to accelerate their implementation. The Government should also show flexibility in solving the human settlements problem and avoid threatening to evict landholders before the programme has been finalized and a solution is found to the problem of non-verified landholders. The medium-term programmes of reintegration also need to be accelerated through more financing, more technical assistance and, most importantly, more political will.

91. Full compliance with the Peace Accords will strengthen my efforts to obtain external financial assistance in support of peace-related programmes. The parties must show a continued commitment to the rapid implementation of these programmes in order to sustain the interest and support of the international community. A third factor that could stimulate external support would be a clear demonstration of the Government's political will by giving these programmes the high priority they deserve and require in its budget.

92. For my part, I have asked my Special Representative to obtain the Government's and the FMLN's agreement to a new timetable that will set the firmest possible dates for completing the implementation of the most important outstanding points in the Peace Accords. Even so, it is clear that it will not be possible to complete implementation of all such points before the elections. It is important therefore that the new Government should maintain its predecessor's commitment to implement the Accords in their entirety. In this context, an important step was taken on 5 November 1993 when, in response to an initiative by my Special Representative, six of the seven presidential candidates signed a statement, entitled "Commitment of the presidential candidates to peace and stability in El Salvador", in which they *inter alia* solemnly committed themselves to maintain the constructive evolution of the peace process and to implement all the commitments contained in the Peace Accords and rejected any politically motivated violence or intimidation. I subsequently received a letter from the candidate who declined to sign the statement, in which he explained that, although he agreed with its objectives, he had not signed it because he believed that it should have contained more detailed commitments to specific measures. It is important that all those taking part in the election campaign should demonstrate their commitment to the peace process and, in particular, their commitment to the implementation of the Accords in full.

93. Until a short while ago, impressive progress had been made in implementing the Accords despite a number of obstacles, which could usually be overcome through supplementary negotiations and agreements. But recent developments described in this report have caused serious worry as to whether previous achievements are now threatened, especially as the electoral campaign gets under way. Both President Cristiani and the leadership of FMLN have been commended in the past for their determination to ensure that peace is consolidated. I exhort them to overcome these new challenges and make sure that the peace process continues on its course.

94. The elections and the transition to the administration of the newly elected President, who will be inaugurated on 1 June 1994, will be a critically important period and it is clearly necessary for ONUSAL to continue to carry out its verification and good offices functions throughout it. I accordingly recommend that the Security Council extend ONUSAL's mandate for a further period of six months, that is until 31 May 1994.

95. I have just received a recommendation from my Special Representative for some additional police observers to be assigned to ONUSAL and for a modest increase in the Mission's economic and political staff. This recommendation is currently under study and I shall revert to the Council, as necessary.

96. As regards the future of ONUSAL beyond 31 May 1994, my present thinking is that it will probably be desirable to keep the Mission in existence, at reduced strength, for a further period of a few months to verify the full deployment of the National Civil Police and the phasing-out of the National Police, together with implementation of any other major points in the Peace Accords, such as those relating to land and other reintegration programmes, which remain outstanding at that time. I shall revert to the Council with a considered recommendation on this matter well before the expiry of the mandate extension recommended in the present report.

97. In conclusion, I should like to pay tribute to

my Special Representative, Mr. Augusto Ramirez-Ocampo, and to all the personnel of ONUSAL, for the exemplary manner in which they are assisting the Government and people of El Salvador to consolidate peace in their country through full implementation of the Peace Accords.

Document 95

Security Council resolution concerning the peace process in El Salvador and the extension of ONUSAL's mandate

S/RES/888, 30 November 1993

The Security Council,

Recalling its resolution 637 (1989) of 27 July 1989,

Recalling also its resolutions 693 (1991) of 20 May 1991, 714 (1991) of 30 September 1991, 729 (1992) of 14 January 1992, 784 (1992) of 30 October 1992, 791 (1992) of 30 November 1992 and 832 (1993) of 27 May 1993,

Recalling further the presidential statements by the President of the Security Council of 18 March 1993, 1/ 11 June 1993 2/ and 5 November 1993, 3/

Having studied the further report of the Secretary-General of 23 November 1993, 4/

Noting with appreciation the continuing efforts of the Secretary-General to support the full and timely implementation of the agreements signed by the Government of El Salvador and the Frente Farabundo Martí para la Liberación Nacional (FMLN) to maintain and consolidate peace and promote reconciliation in El Salvador,

Welcoming the Secretary-General's observation that the peace process in El Salvador has advanced, and that significant progress has been made towards other objectives of the peace accords,

Concerned at the continuing problems and delays in implementing several important components of the peace accords, including *inter alia* those related to the transfer of lands, the reintegration into civilian society of ex-combatants and war-disabled, the deployment of the National Civil Police and the phasing out of the National Police, and the recommendations of the Commission on the Truth,

Noting with concern the recent acts of violence in El Salvador, which may indicate renewed activity by illegal armed groups, and which could, if unchecked, negatively affect the peace process in El Salvador, including the elections scheduled for March 1994,

Welcoming in this regard the efforts of the Secretary-General in cooperation with the Government of El Salvador towards the establishment of a mechanism to investigate illegal armed groups and their possible connection with renewed political violence,

Also noting with concern the seemingly politically motivated murders of members of the different political parties, including the Frente Farabundo Martí para la Liberación Nacional and the Alianza Republicana Nacionalista,

Noting that El Salvador has entered a critical phase in the peace process and that political parties have just begun a campaign for the March 1994 elections, which should take place in a peaceful environment,

Stressing the importance of free and fair elections as an essential element of the entire peace process in El Salvador,

Noting recent progress in voter registration and stressing the importance of all registered voters being issued relevant credentials so as to enable broad participation in the elections,

Welcoming the commitment of the presidential candidates to peace and stability in El Salvador of 5 November 1993, as referred to in paragraph 92 of the further report of the Secretary-General,

Welcoming also the recent announcement by the Government of El Salvador to expedite the implementation of the land transfer programme,

Welcoming further the work of the United Nations Observer Mission in El Salvador and noting its vital importance to the entire peace and reconciliation process in El Salvador,

Reiterating the need, in this as in all peace-keeping operations, to continue to monitor expenditures carefully during this period of increasing demands on peace-keeping resources,

1. *Welcomes* the further report of the Secretary-General of 23 November 1993;

2. *Condemns* recent acts of violence in El Salvador;

3. *Expresses concern* that important elements of the peace accords remain only partially implemented;

4. *Urges* the Government of El Salvador and the Frente Farabundo Martí para la Liberación Nacional to

1/ S/25427.
2/ S/25929.
3/ S/26695.
4/ S/26790.

make determined efforts to prevent political violence and accelerate compliance with their commitments under the peace accords;

5. *Reaffirms its support* for the Secretary-General's use of his good offices in the El Salvador peace process;

6. *Also reaffirms its support*, in this context, for the efforts of the Secretary-General, in cooperation with the Government of El Salvador, aimed at the immediate launching of an impartial, independent and credible investigation into illegal armed groups, and urges all sectors of society in El Salvador to cooperate in such an investigation;

7. *Calls upon* all parties concerned to cooperate fully with the Secretary-General's Special Representative and the United Nations Observer Mission in El Salvador in their task of verifying the parties' implementation of their commitments and urges them to complete such implementation within the framework of the agreed calendar and the new timetable proposed by the Observer Mission;

8. *Stresses* the need to ensure that the police and public security provisions of the peace accords are scrupulously observed, with full Observer Mission verification, and that necessary steps are taken to complete the recovery of all weapons held by private individuals in contravention of the peace accords;

9. *Urges* the Government of El Salvador and the Frente Farabundo Martí to remove all obstacles facing implementation of the land transfer programme and stresses the need to accelerate reintegration programmes for ex-combatants of both sides in conformity with the peace accords;

10. *Reaffirms* the need for full and timely implementation of the recommendations of the Commission on the Truth;

11. *Calls upon* the relevant authorities in El Salvador to take all necessary measures to ensure that the elections to be held in March 1994 be free and fair and requests the Secretary-General to continue to provide assistance in this regard;

12. *Urges* all States, as well as the international institutions engaged in the fields of development and finance, to contribute promptly and generously in support of the implementation of all aspects of the peace accords;

13. *Decides* to extend the mandate of the Observer Mission to 31 May 1994;

14. *Requests* the Secretary-General to keep the Security Council fully informed of further developments in the El Salvador peace process;

15. *Requests* the Secretary-General to report by 1 May 1994 on the operations of the Observer Mission so that the Council may review the Mission's size and scope for the period after 31 May 1994, taking into account the Secretary-General's relevant recommendations for the fulfilment and completion of its mandate;

16. *Decides* to remain seized of the matter.

Document 96

Letter dated 7 December 1993 from the Secretary-General to the President of the Security Council concerning implementation of the recommendations of the Commission on the Truth regarding the investigation of illegal groups

S/26865, 11 December 1993

In my letter to the President of the Security Council (S/26689) of 3 November 1993, I expressed the concern that recent cases of arbitrary execution in El Salvador confirmed the need for the immediate implementation of the recommendations of the Commission on the Truth regarding the investigation of illegal groups. I stated that I had decided to instruct the Director of the Division of Human Rights of ONUSAL, with supplementary expert assistance as needed, to work with those concerned in order to assist the Government in implementing this recommendation. I added that the National Counsel for the Defence of Human Rights, within his constitutional responsibilities, could also play an important role in the investigation.

The Security Council approved my ideas about how the United Nations should help in such an investigation in its statement (S/26695) of 5 November 1993. From 8 to 15 November 1993 I dispatched a mission to El Salvador led by Under-Secretary-General Marrack Goulding. Extensive consultations were held with all concerned and considerable progress was made towards an agreement on the principles for the establishment of a Joint Group for the investigation of politically motivated illegal armed groups. In later consultations, it was agreed that the members of the Joint Group would be two independent representatives of the Government of El Salvador nominated by the President of the Republic, the National Counsel for the Defence of Human Rights and the Director of the Division of Human Rights of ONUSAL.

I have been informed by my Special Representative in El Salvador, Mr. Augusto Ramirez-Ocampo, that President Cristiani has now nominated the two independent Government representatives to the Joint Group. Mr. Ramirez-Ocampo has informed me that both persons nominated, Dr. José Leandro Echevarría and Dr. Juan Jerónomo Castillo, are independent lawyers of longstanding prestige and that he is satisfied that they are well qualified for the task at hand. In addition, the nominations have the approval of the National Counsel for the Defence of Human Rights.

The text of the Principles for the establishment of the Joint Group is attached to this letter. The mechanism for the investigation of illegal armed groups has thus been duly conformed and may commence its work immediately.

I would be grateful if you would be kind enough to bring this information to the attention of the members of the Security Council.

(Signed) Boutros BOUTROS-GHALI

Annex

Principles for the establishment of a joint group for the investigation of politically motivated illegal armed groups

1. A Joint Group will be formed for the investigation of politically motivated illegal armed groups. The members of the Group will be the following:

(a) Two representatives of the Government of the Republic of El Salvador, nominated by the President;

(b) The National Counsel for the Defence of Human Rights;

(c) The Director of the Division of Human Rights of ONUSAL.

The participation of the National Counsel for the Defence of Human Rights and the Director of the Division of Human Rights of ONUSAL, will be without prejudice to their mandates under the Constitution of El Salvador and the San José Agreement, respectively.

2. The Joint Group will have its own institutional identity and its purpose will be to assist the Government in applying the recommendations of the Commission on the Truth with respect to carrying out an in-depth investigation into illegal armed groups. The definition of illegal armed groups will be that of the phenomenon described in the recommendations of the Report of the Commission on the Truth. The investigation will cover the activities of such groups from 16 January 1992, the date on which the Peace Accords were signed.

3. The Joint Group will have the following faculties:

(a) To organize, conduct and supervise a technical team composed of Salvadorian and foreign investigators of renowned competence, impartiality and respect for human rights.

(b) To present a report to the President of the Republic and to the Secretary-General of the United Nations which will include conclusions and recommendations and the reports received from the technical team. The report of the Joint Group will be public.

4. The Joint Group will endeavour to adopt its decisions by consensus. However, if this consensus is not reached, the case will be referred to the President of the Republic and the Secretary-General of the United Nations, for its resolution in a manner which will guarantee the effectiveness and credibility of the investigation.

5. The Joint Group and the technical team will have no jurisdictional functions and will work within a framework which will be:

(a) Autonomous;

(b) Impartial and apolitical;

(c) Confidential, except when criminal acts committed by individuals or groups are uncovered. In these cases, information regarding these criminal acts will be immediately referred to the attention of the Public Prosecutor, who will carry out the appropriate investigation.

6. The Joint Group will be established on 8 December 1993 and will have a mandate of six months' period during which the members of the Joint Group will remain in office. At the end of its mandate, it will present the report referred to in paragraph 3 (b).

7. The Joint Group will have its own budget and an autonomous administration.

8. The Secretary-General of the United Nations will convey these Principles to the Security Council and will request from the Council a statement of support.

Document 97

Letter dated 10 December 1993 from the President of the Security Council to the Secretary-General concerning the establishment of a Joint Group for the investigation of politically motivated illegal armed groups

S/26866, 11 December 1993

The members of the Security Council welcome your letter of 7 December 1993 (S/26865), concerning the establishment of a Joint Group for the investigation of politically motivated illegal armed groups, composed of two independent representatives of the Government of El Salvador nominated by the President of the Republic, the National Counsel for the Defence of Human Rights and the Director of the Division of Human Rights of the United Nations Observer Mission in El Salvador (ONUSAL).

The members of the Council support the "Principles", attached to your letter, which will give the group an independent, impartial and non-political character. The members of the Council also support your role in ensuring the effectiveness and credibility of the investigation.

The members of the Council consider it of the utmost importance that all necessary measures are taken to facilitate the task of the Joint Group so that the recommendations of the Commission on the Truth regarding the full investigation of the illegal armed groups is promptly implemented. They call upon all parties in El Salvador to cooperate fully in this respect.

The members of the Council will continue to follow closely the situation in El Salvador and request you to keep them informed on developments on this matter.

(*Signed*) LI Zhaoxing
President of the Security Council

Document 98

Report of the ONUSAL Human Rights Division covering the period from 1 August to 31 October 1993 (extract)

A/49/59-S/1994/47, 18 January 1994

I. *Introduction*

1. In order that the reports of the Human Rights Division would appear at intervals that would enable the Secretary-General, the Security Council and the General Assembly systematically to monitor the developments in the human rights situation in El Salvador, the Director of the Human Rights Division decided that, starting in January 1993, the Division's reports would be submitted quarterly. The sixth, seventh and eighth reports were prepared on this basis and as they covered a 90-day period they were bound to reflect an analysis of the short-term situation.

2. This approach was described in the Division's eighth report in the following terms: "the methodology used in the reports takes as a point of reference the changes in the human rights situation over the three months analysed in each report. Thus, the reports do not necessarily reflect trends, but rather, situations at different points in time. Analysis of trends will be included in the ninth report ...". This intention was based on the need to couple short-term analysis with a broader vision examining the quantitative data on a composite basis and making possible a qualitative approach to identifying trends in the evolution of the human rights situation in the country.

3. This report has been written with this purpose in mind. It therefore has a twofold aim of providing an analysis of the short-term situation during the three-month period from August to October 1993 and assessing trends in the human rights situation over a combined ten-month period (January to October 1993).

II. *Analysis of the situation in August and September 1993*

II.1 *Overall assessment of the situation: a serious deterioration*

4. The ambivalent human rights situation in El Salvador described in the eighth report, which was a cause for concern owing to the increase in arbitrary executions and the activities of illegal armed groups, including the

so-called death squads, took a serious turn for the worse between August and October. As regards institutional developments, however, the Government continues to make considerable efforts in the area of legal reform by promoting laws that guarantee respect for human rights.

5. Over the past few months, various national institutions, especially the archbishopric, repeatedly reported killings attributed to the so-called "death squads".

6. Similarly, in its seventh report issued on 2 July 1993, the Human Rights Division of ONUSAL had noted that "concerning the extreme violations of the right to life which have occurred, the Salvadorian Church and non-governmental organizations have sounded the alarm regarding the possibility of a reactivation of the so-called "death squads" (A/47/968, para. 17), adding that "... there is no doubt that there have been homicides which bear the signs of having been organized and involving methods and procedures similar to those which, in the past, were used by the death squads" (ibid., para. 18).

7. In the press release on the eighth report, issued on 22 October 1993, the Human Rights Division expressed its profound concern about "the activities of death squads" adding that such groups went by names used in the past such as "Ejército Secreto Anticomunista" and "Brigada Maximiliano Hernández Martínez"; at the same time, other organizations such as the self-styled "Frente Revolucionario Salvadoreño" (that have thus far issued only death threats) and "Escuadrón los Angeles de la Muerte" (responsible for various threats, including some of the recent ones in Chalchuapa, and two "private justice" murders in La Fosa community). In the eighth report, the Division recalled that "politically motivated human rights violations have been more open and are rendered more serious because of the electoral context the country has entered" (A/47/1012-S/26146, para. 112).

8. A few days later, on 25 October, while he was dropping his youngest daughter at a day-care centre, Mr. Francisco Ernesto Velis, former guerrilla commander and member of the National Council of the Frente Farabundo Martí para la Liberación Nacional (FMLN) party was violently killed when three shots were fired at his head. On 26 October, in the locality of Guazapa, Mr. Medardo Brisuela Hernández and his wife Justa Victoria Orellana Ortiz were killed at their home. The wife was shot to death while breast-feeding her baby daughter, who escaped unscathed. The murdered couple were FMLN militants. On 26 October, Mr. Salvador Guzmán Pérez, a suspect in the murder of Mr. Oscar Grimaldi, FMLN member and logistics officer of the Fuerzas Populares de Liberación (FPL), was found murdered at Los Planes de Renderos. The order for his arrest had been received the previous day by the Criminal Investigation Commission. On Saturday, 30 October,

Mr. Eleno Hernán Castro, alias "Comandante Carmelo", was shot to death on the coast road near Santa Cruz Portillo. At the time of his death he was a member of the National Council of FMLN, the National Subcommission on Lands and of the Political Committee of the Partido Revolucionario Salvadoreño (PRS)—Ejército Revolucionario del Pueblo (ERP). On 3 November, Mr. José Gabriel Quintanilla, FMLN coordinator in the Department of San Miguel was attacked by three persons dressed in black who tried to execute him when he came out of his house in the town of San Jorge. The assailants riddled their victims with bullets. Although he was hit by four bullets in the chest and thorax he did not die but was seriously wounded. On 2 November, Mr. Sebastián Araniva Salamanca, member of the Alianza Republicana Nacionalista (ARENA) party and municipal councillor of the Municipality of Chinameca was assassinated.

9. This list of complaints of killings which were accepted by ONUSAL as arbitrary or extralegal executions forms part of a series of violations of human rights that include the attack on Dr. Vásquez Sosa, Minister of Health, on 7 December; the death threats issued on 21 October by the Brigada Maximiliano Hernández Martínez against Dr. José María Méndez, a distinguished Salvadorian lawyer and Dr. Francisco Lima, candidate of Convergencia—FMLN for vice-president; the anonymous death threats against Dr. Juan Mateu Llort, Director of the Institute for Forensic Medicine, reported by the victim on 1 November; and the complaints made by Mr. Humberto Centeno about the tapping of the telephones of some members of parliament and other prominent people.

10. Reports of acts of intimidation against national institutions and diplomatic missions have also begun to be received. Unidentified persons placed explosives on the premises of the National Public Security Academy and the Embassy of Mexico; they also sent threatening messages to the office of the Pan American Health Organization and to a female staff member of the International Organization for Migration. On 1 November, following the burial of Eleno Castro, demonstrators burned tyres and threw Molotov cocktails at the premises of *El Diario de Hoy*. Those events were also unanimously condemned by all the country's political and social sectors, as well as by the international community including the Inter-American Press Association (IAPA). On 25 September, the self-styled "Escuadrón Los Angeles de la Muerte" distributed pamphlets in Chalchuapa that warned ONUSAL in a threatening manner not to interfere in its activities.

11. Between 1 August and the time when the drafting of the present report was completed (15 November) the active verification conducted by ONUSAL dealt with

47 complaints of human rights violations which adduced evidence and information pointing to the possibility of political motivation either because of the victim's position, the methods used or the material characteristics of the violation. The investigation of those cases must necessarily consider the assumption of political motivation as a reasonable one that could establish the motives or give the investigation the necessary breadth to clarify any doubts about the facts. Of the complaints 10 related to arbitrary or extralegal executions (José Santos Vásquez, Oscar Grimaldi Gutiérrez, Rafael A. Nolasco Acosta, Angel Alfaro Enríquez, Francisco Velis Castellanos, Joel Antonio Hernández, Medardo Brizuela Hernández, Odil Miranda, Manuel de Jesús Acevedo, Eleno Castro Guevara); 3 related to attempted arbitrary executions (Humberto Solórzano Cerén, Osmín Machado and José Gabriel Quintanilla); 14 related to death threats (Francisco Lima, José María Méndez (members of the Fundación 16 de Enero), René Mercadel Perla Jiménez, Israel Aguilar Payés, José Alberto Morales, José Francisco Valdez (members of the San Miguel FPL), Porfirio Pérez, Miguel Angel Hernández, Enrique Ardón Martínez, José Tránsito Alas Regalado, Agustín Barrera, Oscar Manuel Ortiz, Jesús Amado Pérez Marro, Celina Yolanda Díaz García, Lorena Peña Mendoza, Luis Enrique López Díaz, José Antonio Cornejo and Mario García Cortés); 9 related to intimidatory threats (Francisco Arévalo, Reinaldo Castaneda, Nélida Elizabeth Martínez, Nelson Napoleón García, Fredy Rosas Alvarado, José A. Rivera Velázquez, Carolina Guardado and members of the Santa Tecla and Soyapango FMLN); 1 related to arbitrary detention (Luis Antonio Menjívar); 1 related to a case of ill-treatment (Walter Gómez); 2 related to abductions (Medardo Alfredo Quijano Arriola and José Alberto Orellana); and 1 related to violation of the right to freedom of association (various teachers). The possible political motivation in some of those cases, such as that of Eleno Castro, "Comandante Carmelo", may be ruled out by the findings of the investigation. However, as in this case, such a conclusion must be the outcome of the investigation and not an a priori assertion. This is vital for the transparency and credibility of the investigation.

12. These acts of selective violence have undoubtedly been a significant political factor in the life of the nation. They had a profound impact both on developments in the human rights situation and on important aspects of the peace agreements and the recommendations of the Commission on the Truth which, having a bearing on the protection of human rights, are encountering obstacles to implementation or concerning which no decisions regarding implementation have yet been taken.

13. All the cases referred to in the preceding paragraphs show how serious and widespread the deterioration of the human rights situation in El Salvador is. An analysis of these cases indicates that there is an upsurge in political violence including the activities of illegal armed groups known in the country as "death squads" and that this upsurge coincides, on the one hand, with the formal launching of the electoral campaign and, on the other hand, with the final phase of the implementation of the peace agreements and the presence of ONUSAL as the institutional expression of international verification. However, it is encouraging that the Government itself has not only condemned such acts but has also taken a number of decisions that demonstrate the political will of the President of the Republic to investigate each case and mete out appropriate punishment to those found responsible for violations. The Government's initiative to allow criminal investigation bodies from the United States of America, the United Kingdom and Spain, to collaborate in the investigations, as well as its manifest willingness to set up a unit to investigate illegal armed groups, as suggested by the Secretary-General, are clear indications of its commitment to clarify the facts.

14. The elections planned for March 1994 represent a unique and decisive milestone in the history of the country and in the process of implementing the peace agreements. In a way, for the first time in the political history of El Salvador, the electoral process will be conducted on the basis of standards reflecting the rule of law, without excluding any social sector or political force, and under the international monitoring of the United Nations. From this point of view, whatever the election results, they will confirm in practice the new political and institutional system arising out of the peace agreements. The transparency with which the competent authorities have been organizing the elections constitutes a safeguard that should be mirrored in the field of human rights.

15. In this context, the current violence with its evident political repercussions and the acts of the so-called "death squads" are not directed against broad social sectors and political groupings, as in the past. This violence is not like that of the 1980s, when one group defended the established system and the other fought to change it. That situation was expressly resolved by the peace agreements, through the constitutional, political and institutional reforms that the parties formerly in conflict agreed to by consensus, with the support of all other political forces.

16. Rather, the current violence is directed against the democratic political system which has been worked out by the Government and FMLN, with the support of all political forces, with the aim of building up through consensus the rule of law and a stable and functioning democracy. Thus, the acts of political violence which have

occurred during the period covered by this report reflect the intransigence of fringe elements attacking the Salvadorian nation as a whole, all national political forces and the democracy proposed in the peace agreements. The Human Rights Division must state that, in the active verification process it has conducted in investigating the cases referred to it, it did not find any indication or evidence of any institutional involvement of the State in these violations. Therefore, it can affirm that they do not compromise the Government as an institution; on the contrary, this selective violence seems to be directed against all democratic political forces, including the Government of El Salvador itself, which, as a party to the agreements to which the substantive obligations of the peace process were assigned, has taken historic steps, together with FMLN and the other political forces in the country, towards the progressive establishment of an effective democratic political system based on the rule of law.

17. The nation-wide rejection of political violence clearly bears out this judgement. Political violence has been unanimously rejected throughout the country, including by the Government and all political parties, the Catholic Church, non-governmental organizations, labour organizations and trade unions. As the broad majority was turning against the resurgence of political violence, the Secretary-General, in a letter to the Security Council dated 3 November 1993, wrote concerning the Velis case: "On 25 October, I learned with shock and profound sadness of the execution, in death-squad style, of a leader of FMLN". He further noted that the deaths of Francisco Ernesto Velis and Eleno Castro followed other acts of violence and human rights violations in recent months, thus increasing concerns that illegal groups had resumed their activities. Summing up the impact of those killings, the Secretary-General wrote "Be that as it may, those murders have had a nefarious impact on the political climate and have undermined confidence in the peace process" (S/26790, para. 87).

18. Subsequently, from 8 to 11 November, the Under-Secretary-General for Political Affairs, Mr. Marrack Goulding, visited San Salvador to assist in working out the structure of the mechanism for investigation of illegal armed groups in accordance with the frame of reference provided by the Secretary-General in his report to the Security Council. The establishment of this mechanism embodies the national Salvadorian view that the activities of such groups should be brought to light and their leaders punished, as a welcome expression of the strength of the democratic process and the authority of the law in a State governed by the rule of law.

19. In unison with the national consensus that has emerged regarding the need to stop all acts of political violence and to conduct an immediate and independent investigation of the activities of illegal armed groups, the international community has also expressed its profound concern over the events which rocked the country in October and warned of the consequences that political violence could entail for the process of implementing the peace agreements. Undoubtedly, situations such as those reported are related to the difficulties encountered in recent months in properly implementing the recommendations of the Commission on the Truth and the agreements on which action has yet to be taken. In a commendable reaction, broad support has emerged for more rigorous steps to implement the peace agreements and the recommendations of the Commission on the Truth, as part of a process intended ultimately to provide the legal and institutional means to eradicate violence through the vigorous exercise of a democratic legal system.

...

III. Analysis of trends in the human rights situation in El Salvador

1. General observations

81. As noted in the introduction to this report, the methodology which the Director of the Human Rights Division has been using in order to keep the Secretary-General informed of developments in active verification, in compliance with the mandate contained in the San José Agreement, consists of the preparation, every three months, of status reports and, following aggregate periods, the presentation of evaluations designed to identify broader trends in the human rights situation in El Salvador. This report presents a summary of the analysis of trends for the period of 10 months from January to October 1994.

2. Peace has created improved conditions for the observance of human rights, whose enjoyment depends on strict implementation of the agreements

82. An initial evaluation involves comparing the human rights situation during the armed conflict with the situation existing after the signing of the peace agreements. This point of view makes it possible to determine the impact of the peace agreements and their implementation on the reality of human rights, and to establish the scope of the changes in the social, political and legal environment, which affects the exercise by the population of its rights.

83. During the conflict in El Salvador, grave, systematic and mass violations of human rights were perpetrated. Between 1980 and 1990, the situation in El Salvador attracted the attention of the international

community, and the United Nations system of international protection, through the Sub-Commission on Prevention of Discrimination and Protection of Minorities, the Commission on Human Rights and the General Assembly, adopted a number of measures in response to that extremely serious situation. The end of the armed conflict, the restructuring of the State and society, including the political system, initiated by the peace agreements, have opened the way for a substantive and positive change in the protection and exercise of human rights. It is an incontrovertible fact that the grave and systematic violations of human rights, which gave rise to international monitoring, are no longer a fact of life in El Salvador. The conflict has given way to peace. A political regime that excluded important sectors of society has been replaced by a democratic process that has enlisted the former guerrilla forces as a legitimate political party. Moreover, the peace agreements, which have brought constitutional, institutional and structural reforms, are currently being implemented; all the reforms are designed to establish a State based on rule of law, and the legitimacy of the State is the best guarantee for the protection of human rights. Generally speaking, there has been a qualitative change in the social, legal and political conditions in which Salvadorians can exercise their rights. In that regard, the structural situation that led to grave and systematic violations in the 1980s, which resulted in the establishment of international monitoring mechanisms under the auspices of the Economic and Social Council of the United Nations, has been replaced by the construction of a democratic society based on national reconciliation.

84. Although the implementation of the peace agreements is a process whose end results will be apparent only when the institutions and the democratic rule of law are functioning efficiently, there is no doubt that the human rights situation in the post-conflict era has, in general, significantly improved and the current institutional, political and legal "environment" is much more favourable than was the case during the armed conflict. This first criterion for analysis makes it possible to state that the peace agreements and their implementation have had, and continue to have, an exceptionally important and wide-ranging impact on the improvement of the human rights situation in El Salvador.

3. Human rights during the implementation of the peace agreements: a disturbing backsliding trend

85. However, a second criterion for evaluating the trends in the human rights situation is not concerned with an overall comparison of the situation that existed during the war and the positive changes that have taken place since the signing of the peace agreements but with the specific assessment of the enjoyment of human rights in the context of peace, national reconciliation, the implementation of structural and institutional reforms and, in general, the building of a State based on the rule of law and democracy. In this respect, the evaluation should be conducted on the basis of specific events and situations and the imperative demand for respect for human rights required by the democratic institutions that have been established as a result of the peace accords.

86. Based on this criterion, a composite analysis of developments in the human rights situation during the past 10 months makes it possible to discern two quite distinct phases. The first phase covers the period from January to May, during which the situation evolved unevenly, with strengths and weaknesses; there was a clear downward trend in the commission of such acts as forced disappearances or torture, and an improvement in the overall political situation. The second phase, covering the period from June to October, was marked by a progressive worsening of the situation leading to a grave deterioration of the situation in October, characterized by an upsurge of selective violence against citizens who were openly engaged in politics, as well as death-squad-style murders.

87. In the context of the transition from an uneven situation, which was marked by some positive developments, to a serious deterioration that has alarmed the citizens of El Salvador and the international community, the quantitative indicators are quite telling. Thus, the average monthly number of extralegal executions, attempted arbitrary executions and death threats was greater during the period from June to October than during the preceding five months. The indicators are similar in the cases of undue use of force, kidnappings, other kinds of threats, violations of due process of law and arbitrary detention. The statistical annex to this report contains composite statistics for January-October.

4. Persons presumed responsible for human rights violations: the case of the National Police

88. With regard to complaints concerning persons presumed responsible, the situation of the National Police is extremely serious, since 478 complaints out of a total of 1,357 were made against it. The large number of complaints made against the National Police, almost all of which were verified by ONUSAL, dramatically reveals the negative effect that delays in disbanding the National Police and the deployment of the National Civil Police have had on the human rights situation.

89. The peace agreements established the National Civil Police in the belief that, in order to guarantee peace, El Salvador must have a security body which has a new institutional mandate and operates in accordance with democratic principles and the concept of public security

as a service provided by the State to its citizens: a body that is free of any considerations based on politics, ideology, social position or any other bias, respects human rights and is subordinate to the constitutional authorities. In other words, a police force that is subject to a State based on the rule of law and to legality and replaces the National Police, whose distinguishing trait up to now has been its arbitrary and discriminatory behaviour, which is on the margin of legality and violates basic rights.

90. The active verification carried out by ONUSAL clearly shows that the National Police, throughout the transition process, has been continuing to behave in a manner which is not in keeping with legality and systematically results in human rights violations. During the period from June to September of this year, it was verified that the National Police continues to be responsible for arbitrary executions, such as the one carried out against Héctor David Segovia Verillos, who was executed on 9 July following his arrest. Police officers Enrique Cerna, Dagoberto Estrada Saravia, Luis Armando Laurea and Rudy Sánchez Escobar, from the National Police at San Miguel (Fifth Command), were responsible and, to date, have not been punished. It was also verified that there had been an attempted arbitrary execution of José Antonio Pérez Hernández when he sustained a bullet wound as a result of an attack carried out by two officers of the National Police in Aguilares.

91. It is a matter of particular concern to the Division that in recent months the National Police has again resorted to practices involving torture, as were verified in the case of Manuel de Jesús Hernández, who, while under arrest, was tortured early in the morning of 19 August by officers of the National Police from the Fifth Command Headquarters in San Miguel. According to testimony, they were reproached for "not having killed" the victim when they had the opportunity. Mauricio Gómez Campos was also tortured by officers of the National Police while he was being held arbitrarily in the cells of the Fifth Command Headquarters in San Miguel on 6 September. The motive for using torture was to find grounds for convicting him.

92. In the same way, the recurrent practice of ill-treatment by officers of the National Police demonstrates once more the arbitrariness and unlawfulness with which that body operates as well as the repressive and intimidatory attitude that underlies the training given to its members. The following cases illustrate this situation: José Ismael Ochoa Cruz, who was beaten in the street on 12 August by officers from the Fifth Command Headquarters of the National Police in San Miguel because he had tattoos on his arms and chest, was subsequently arrested arbitrarily; Marlon Giovani Hernández Campos, who, after being arbitrarily arrested, was punched, kicked

and struck with rifle butts on 6 June while he was in handcuffs in front of and inside the National Police unit in Lolotique; Abel José Padilla, who was attacked on 29 August by the National Police commander in Chalcuapa, Santa Ana; Lieutenant Adolfo Martínez Zetino, who, under similar circumstances, beat five other persons and was transferred to that post from the town of Metapán for repeated misconduct.

93. There is a very similar situation in the cases of excessive use of force. During the period referred to in this analysis of trends, the cases involving Ricardo Orellana Valencia stand out: when captured on 1 July, he was severely beaten by officers of the National Police in Berlín. The officers who participated in his arrest were: Jorge Alberto Pameres Mendoza, Ramón Antonio Rivera, Jorge Alberto Ramos Galán, Gerardo Eliseo Quintanilla, Rubén Antonio Guevara Vásquez, Pablo Vitelio Mendoza and Jorge Antonio Reyes Granados. In addition, there are a number of cases that are particularly serious because they involve abuse by National Police officers of the weapons assigned to them. Two of these cases are reported to have resulted in the death of the victim: Carlos Alberto Deras Rivas, who was shot on 7 July by officers of the National Police in Mejicanos and subsequently died; and Angel Mendoza Villatoro, who was killed on 19 July by Guillermo Antonio Ortega Campos, an officer of the National Police in Yucuaiquín. Other cases of excessive use of force by officers of the National Police were reported against Julio César Mena Girón on 13 September by the National Police in San Salvador; José Enrique Santo, by National Police officers from the Fifth Command Headquarters in San Miguel; and Oscar Amaya Guardado, on 3 July, by Juan Pablo Araniva, a National Police officer in Mejicanos.

94. Likewise, officers of the National Police abuse their authority and regularly threaten citizens. The following cases are representative: Jorge Alberto Morales Duarte, who, because of his trade union and political activities, was subjected to intimidatory acts by the National Police in Santa Tecla, on 28 August when National Police officers illegally entered the house of his mother-in-law, Mrs. Marina Zúñiga, causing material damage (Mrs. Zúñiga was subsequently threatened); Idalia del Carmen Guerrero Cruz and Hilda Maribel Carillo Escobar, victims of threats by Alfaro Serrano, a National Police officer in Zacatecoluca, who warned them not to pursue legal action for rape that they had initiated against Rodolfo Ramírez, a bodyguard of a colonel in the Armed Forces of El Salvador, Oscar Rodezno.

95. The National Police systematically make arbitrary arrests. The following arrests can be cited as examples: Betty del Carmen Alvarado Díaz, by the Lourdes National Police on 1 August; Juan Diego Aguilar Flores, by the

Zacamil National Police on 1 June; Marvin Arnoldo Alvarez Sánchez and José María Hernández, by the San Miguel National Police (Fifth Command) on 24 August.

96. Fulfilment of the commitment regarding the complete disbandment of the Salvadorian National Police has repeatedly been postponed, which has undoubtedly been a factor generating human rights violations. There is an urgent need to expedite the disbandment of the National Police. That will mean substantial progress in the implementation of the peace agreements; such a decision will, through the deployment of the National Civil Police, result in conditions more conducive to respect for human rights on the part of the security forces. However, in what remains of the transitional period, the Government has a responsibility to ensure that the National Police acts strictly in conformity with law and order, since there are indications and evidence that, as the date of its complete disbandment draws nearer, a higher number of illegal acts and human rights violations are being committed by the National Police.

5. The reactivation of illegal groups known as "death squads"

97. As the final phase of the peace agreements draws near—especially the entry into force of the new political system, characterized by the participation of all national sectors, without discrimination of any kind, which will mean the final reintegration of former guerrilla fighters into the democratic life of the country—the illegal armed groups known in El Salvador as "death squads" have been reactivated. This situation has been a source of concern to the Secretary-General, who, in his most recent report to the Security Council, noted that "[p]articularly worrying are the activities of the so-called 'death squads'. Taking on names used in the past, or using newly created ones, these illegal groups have been the authors of numerous death-threats with clearly political connotations. At the same time, groups who purport to take the law into their own hands against supposed common delinquents have also been making death-threats and carrying out murders. The emergence of criminal organizations of this type seriously affects the stability of the peace process by eroding confidence and security, which are its fundamental bases" (S/26790, para. 44).

98. The Commission on the Truth recommended, as a preventive measure, an investigation of these groups with a view to their elimination. In the section of its report entitled "The death squad pattern", the Commission noted that these illegal armed groups have been one of "the most horrendous sources of the violence which swept the country in recent years ... All necessary measures must be taken to ensure that they are disbanded. Given the country's history, prevention is essential in this

area" (S/25500, p. 180). In the section on "Findings" relating to that subject, the Commission listed a number of criteria which, because of their relevance for the future, should be part of the background to the investigation of the activities of these illegal armed groups.

99. The Human Rights Division has verified activities of the "death squads" "Ejército Secreto Salvadoreño", "Brigada Maximiliano Hernández Martínez" and "Escuadrón Los Angeles de la Muerte", in the terms referred to in this report. In addition, there have been reports of some surviving structures of organizations which spread terror in the past; they are being investigated. Some of the military personnel held in Santa Ana prison for crimes committed as members of "death squads" during the past decade have also claimed to have information regarding activities and current leaders of these illegal armed groups.

100. The decision to establish a joint unit to investigate illegal armed groups, suggested by the Secretary-General and the Security Council, has long been awaited by the Salvadorian people. The "death squads", meaning organized groups which carry out selective violence in a clandestine manner, concealing the identity of their members, for the purpose of acquiring or maintaining political or social control, are criminal organizations incompatible with the peace agreements, a democratic legal system and the commitment of the parties to consolidate law and order. The fact that the Government has welcomed the Secretary-General's proposal and has worked constructively to establish a joint investigation unit constitutes a wholesome example of political transparency, commitment to law and order and an institutional will to carry out an effective and independent investigation, which should be assessed in a positive light by domestic political forces and the international community.

IV. Findings

101. The status report for the period from August to October 1993 indicates a serious regression in the human rights situation in El Salvador, especially because of the increase in politically motivated violations and the perpetration of crimes similar to those committed in the past by "death squads", which have been reactivated as described in paragraph 7 of this report.

102. The analysis of trends during the aggregate period from January to October 1993 reveals a complex situation, in that an ambiguous trend with clearly positive aspects has been taking a regressive turn, which has become serious in recent months. This situation, with the trends identified by the Human Rights Division of ONUSAL, could be further aggravated during the electoral process and in the immediate post-electoral period. Should this assumption prove correct, the situation would be extremely serious, and all political forces have a duty to prevent that from happening, since, as the Secretary-General has recalled,

"respect for human rights [is] a *sine qua non* for the success of the peace process and for the consolidation of a democratic society" (S/26790, para. 45).

103. Preventing this situation is the responsibility of the State, the judicial branch, the Office of the National Counsel for the Defence of Human Rights, political and social forces and the population as a whole. The violence which has emerged in El Salvador in recent months is not aimed at any one social and political sector, but at the entire nation, in that it threatens the peace agreements and the building of a democratic society, on which there is a firm national consensus involving all political forces and the public at large.

104. An effective method of isolating and eliminating these sources of violence should be accompanied by strict implementation of the peace agreements, especially those which have a direct and indirect impact on the situation of human rights or common violence. In that connection, as the Secretary-General has pointed out, establishing a timetable for the effective implementation of the pending agreements is essential. As the Secretary-General has stated, the immediate future of the human rights situation will depend "on the country's capacity to reverse the regressive trends that have been detected in recent months, on the effective operation of the institutions created by the Peace Accords, especially the National Counsel for the Defence of Human Rights, and on the effective deployment of the National Civil Police. Progress will also depend on the implementation of the pending recommendations of the Commission on the Truth concerning the judiciary" (S/26790, para. 88).

105. Encouraging signs, in that connection, are the Government's positive response to these developments, especially the fact that it invited the Federal Bureau of Investigation (FBI), Scotland Yard and Spanish police experts to advise national bodies in the investigation of assassinations of political leaders, and the establishment of a joint unit to investigate illegal armed groups. Another positive sign is the unanimous pledge by the Salvadorian presidential candidates to shoulder full responsibility for the commitments contained in the peace agreements. It is also urgent and essential for the Secretary-General's proposed investigation of illegal armed groups in El Salvador to be initiated as soon as possible and to be provided with a legitimate, reliable and credible investigation mechanism.

106. The serious regression seen in the period under review reveals the accuracy of some assessments made by non-governmental organizations, namely, that the progress achieved in relation to the past could easily be reversed, since the effective functioning of institutions linked to public security, the administration of justice and the protection of constitutional respect for human rights is still insufficient. From that standpoint, the work of non-governmental organizations emerges, once again, as an irreplaceable guarantee of proven effectiveness in protecting human rights and reporting violations. The Salvadorian non-governmental organizations constitute a guarantee of protection with which society has provided itself; because of their efficiency, independence and freedom of conscience, they are the most functional means of supplementing international verification procedures.

107. The developments reported above have, to some extent, tested the strength of the human rights components of the peace agreements. Over and above any redressable situation to which attention has been drawn in the preceding paragraphs, the response of the State and society, the Government and the opposition political parties, public opinion and the public at large has been a unanimous rejection of violence and, in particular, violence which is politically motivated. That, together with the common will of the Government, FMLN and other political institutions to investigate the activities of illegal armed groups through the Joint Investigation Group, constitutes a firm reality which should make it possible, in the immediate future, to overcome the problems identified in this report.

Document 99

Letter dated 15 February 1994 from the Secretary-General to President Cristiani about concerns relating to implementation of the peace accords

Not issued as a United Nations document

I very much regret that I will not be able to join you this week in San Salvador on the occasion of the inauguration of the First International Forum of Culture of Peace. As you know, there are pressing matters before the United Nations that compel me to remain at Headquarters at this time.

I want to assure you that the pressure on my time in no way diminishes my interest in the affairs of your country and the role of the United Nations in assisting it at this moment of transition and hope. I continue to attribute the highest importance to the process under way in El Salvador, epitomizing as it does the continuum of this Organizations's activities in the fields of peace-making, peace-keeping and post-conflict peace-building.

You have presided over the destiny of your nation at a crucial moment, and you have ably and courageously seized upon the overwhelming wish of your countrymen to bring the decade-long conflict to an end by addressing its root causes through negotiation. I have no doubt that you will long be remembered for your accomplishments, which include an essentially incident-free cease-fire period during which long-fighting adversaries managed to disengage and initiate a period of transition to reconciliation: the goal stated in the Geneva Agreement of "reunifying Salvadorian society".

The opportunity to pay tribute to you will shortly be upon us when your term as President comes to an end following a closely watched electoral process. I very much hope that continuing difficulties will be sorted out and that the unfolding of the process, thanks in no small part to your leadership, will be the most successful in El Salvador's history, at a crucial moment in the peace process launched under the auspices of the United Nations.

I should, however, like to raise directly with you certain lingering concerns which have been the subject of continuing contact and written communication between my Special Representative and members of your Government. I do so because I believe that your justly earned personal authority, in addition to that which you command as President of the Republic, can spur movement, even at this late stage in your tenure, where the tasks your people set for themselves are still incomplete.

My areas of concern relate principally to the maintenance of internal order and to the reintegration into society of estranged groups including former combatants. I need not go into detail regarding either of these two issues. Both were discussed in my last report to the Security Council, and were singled out for emphasis in the concluding Observations section. They have furthermore been amply discussed with your collaborators. In neither of these two areas was implementation of the agreements expected to be completed before the expiry of your term in office, though at this stage both should have been considerably more advanced than they are. I trouble you with them, in addition to the above stated reasons, because I believe that your personal leadership is needed in order to put them back on track and facilitate the task of your succesor.

Establishing the civilian character of the police function was a fundamental tenet and objective of the entire peace agreement, coupled with the new role attributed to the Armed Forces and their reduction in size. However, there continue to be disquieting signs of reluctance to comply with these objectives and, especially, of an attempt to re-militarize the National Civil Police (PNC).

This is certainly inconsistent with the Peace Accords. The PNC is still denied resources, there is as yet no clear accounting of the transfer to the PNC of military personnel, and your collaborators have expressed to my special Representative a desire to de-link the deployment of the PNC from the phasing out of the National Police (PN). ONUSAL continues to be prevented from properly carrying out its verification responsibilites in this regard. In addition, there remains concern about activities by the military intelligence bodies which are contrary to the Peace Accords.

The incorporation of members of the FMLN into the new National Academy for Public Security (ANSP), together with former members of the Armed Forces and fresh recruits who had participated in neither structure, provides the basis for a well-integrated force which, if distortions are corrected, can provide a strictly civilian public security body which other nations of the Americas can look to as an inspiring model. For this El Salvador is to be congratulated and you, Mr. President, for your foresight, deserve much credit. I need hardly underscore, therefore, the importance of the issues relating to public security being sorted out urgently. Together with those relating to the reform of the Judiciary, which are still largely pending, as well as the recommendations of the Commission on the Truth, they lie at the core of the primary goal which was set forth in the Geneva Agreement of ensuring unrestricted respect for human rights.

The reintegration of the members of the FMLN, within a framework of full legality, into the civil, institutional and political life of the country was the ultimate objective of the peace process as set forth in the Geneva Agreement of 4 April 1990. The establishment of the necessary guarantees and conditions for achieving this objective was the main purpose of the second stage of the negotiations as laid down in the Caracas Agreement of 21 May 1990. A new thrust in this direction was established when the parties agreed in New York, on 25 September 1991, to compress the negotiations which in due course led to the Chapultepec Agreement of 16 January 1992.

Progress in reintegration of the FMLN into the political life of El Salvador is nothing short of astonishing. It was hard to imagine, less than two years ago, that the FMLN could be participating in the electoral campaign to the extent that it is doing today—with the very same name under which it waged war for over a decade. However, violent deaths of FMLN leaders, and leaders of your own party and others, are a source of great concern, and the work of the Joint Group investigating the illegal armed groups is of enormous importance in this regard. Let us hope that this ugly phenomenon can be nipped in the bud.

Notwithstanding positive developments, much remains to be done in other, critical areas of reintegration. The main one is the transfer of land, through which most former combatants and supporters of the FMLN are to be reintegrated. The compromise reached when the parties accepted my proposal of 13 October 1992 raised the hope that this difficult and complex question could be put back on the way to resolution, thus easing the predicament of up to 47,500 potential beneficiaries. Efforts were set in train, despite serious obstacles, to mobilize international assistance.

In November 1993, when Under-Secretary-General Marrack Goulding visited San Salvador leading a special mission, transfers had come to a virtual standstill, and it was agreed to set a goal of transfers of land to 12,000 beneficiaries by the end of the year. In mid-February, transfers have barely reached 10,500 well short of that goal. It is not merely a problem of numerical objectives: at this pace, the bulk of potential beneficiaries will once again miss the planting season in May as a result of lack of access to credit. Similarly, other reintegration programmes are moving extremely slowly, and the terms of some of the programmes, including that for former guerilla sub-commanders, raise concern as to their viability. During his November mission, Mr. Goulding expressed to you the concern, which I entirely share, that these programmes, if they are not given the priority which they deserve, could lead to the kind of crisis which has bedev-illed neighbouring countries and nullify the objective of reintegration. Here again, your personal leadership is needed in light of signs that the political commitment which your authority embodies has not been reflected in governmental agencies whose role in implementing programmes is crucial to their success.

Starting from the Geneva Agreement, the parties requested the United Nations to verify compliance with the implementation of accords reached in the negotiation. For this purpose, the Security Council established ONUSAL. In the New York Agreement, the parties decided to establish COPAZ, as the national mechanism for overseeing the implementation of all the agreements. There is an essential complementarity between the work of these two bodies. It is my duty to keep the Security Council, under whose authority ONUSAL was established, informed about progress made on the basis of the Chapultepec and other agreements. Nothing would please me more than to be able to report that before leaving office you, Mr. President, had chosen to bring your authority to bear in order to ensure that problems are ironed out and the process in all its aspects is reinvigorated and accelerated. I can think of no more admirable legacy for you to leave to your country.

Please accept, Mr. President, the assurances of my highest consideration and my warmest regards.

(*Signed*) Boutros BOUTROS-GHALI

Document 100

Report of the Secretary-General on the activities of the ONUSAL Electoral Division

S/1994/179, 16 February 1994

Introduction

1. The present report is the second in a series of reports on the activities of the Electoral Division of the United Nations Observer Mission in El Salvador (ONUSAL) that I intend to submit to the Security Council until the elections scheduled for 20 March 1994 are held. My previous report (S/26606) was issued on 20 October 1993.

2. The activities of the Electoral Division during the period from November 1993 to January 1994 have focused on observing voter registration, which was closed on 20 November 1993, monitoring the election campaign and providing assistance in the drawing up of an electoral roll, in keeping with the appeal made by the Security Council on 5 November 1993 (S/26695). The Electoral Division holds regular joint meetings with the Supreme Electoral Tribunal, the Board of Vigilance, which is made up of representatives of all political parties, and the party campaign managers with a view to solving any problems that may arise during the campaign. In order to monitor the campaign, the Division is asking the parties to provide a schedule of their campaign activities. In addition, a system has been set up to receive and process allegations of violations of the Electoral Code. These allegations are transmitted in writing to the Supreme Electoral Tribunal, which is asked to report on the follow-up action taken. The Division has already prepared a plan for the reception and deployment of the international observers who, working with current Mission staff, and thus bringing the total number to 900, are to monitor the events on election day. In the area of foreign affairs, the Division has met with more than

60 delegations from embassies, international organizations, non-governmental organizations (NGOs) and universities, as well as numerous researchers and journalists seeking information about the electoral process.

I. Institutional framework of the election

3. On 20 March 1994, four elections will be held simultaneously in El Salvador: elections for President, with a second round if no candidate obtains an absolute majority in the first round; parliamentary elections for the 84 seats in the National Assembly on the basis of proportional representation; municipal elections in 262 mayoral districts on the basis of a simple majority (the party obtaining the most votes will win the office of mayor and all the posts in the municipal corporation); and for the Central American Parliament, to which 20 deputies will be elected on the basis of proportional representation.

4. Six parties and one coalition have registered to run in the presidential election, headed by the following candidates: Armando Calderón Sol for the Alianza Republicana Nacionalista (ARENA); Fidel Chávez Mena for the Partido Demócrata Cristiano (PDC); Rubén Zamora for the coalition composed of the Movimiento Nacional Revolucionario (MNR), the Convergencia Democrática (CD) and the Frente Farabundo Martí para la Liberación Nacional (FMLN); Edgardo Rodríguez for the Movimiento de Solidaridad Nacional (MSN); Jorge Martínez for the Movimiento de Unidad (MU); Rina de Rey Prendes for the Movimiento Auténtico Cristiano (MAC); and Roberto Escobar García for the Partido de Conciliación Nacional (PCN). The number of parties running in the elections for the National Assembly and municipal councils was reduced to nine following the merging of the Movimiento Popular Social Cristiano (MPSC), the Partido Social Demócrata (PSD) and the Unión Democrática Nacionalista (UDN) into a single party called Convergencia Democrática and the failure of the Pueblo Libre (PL) party to put forward any candidates.

5. In the Legislative Assembly elections, the parties are running in all departments without forming coalitions. In the municipal elections, the parties are most often running on their own, although the situation varies from region to region. In general, no coalition candidates are running in the cities, with the exception of San Salvador, where a coalition candidate has been put up by FMLN and MNR. In smaller towns, the most common coalition is FMLN/CD.

6. Recent months have seen a number of reforms in electoral legislation; generally speaking, these tend to be inclusive in nature, facilitating the participation both of political parties and of Salvadorian citizens. Mention should be made of the following measures: the deadline for the closure of voter registration was extended by one month to 19 January 1994, thereby facilitating the issuing of voter registration cards; the deadline for registering candidates for the office of Deputy and for the municipal councils was extended from 19 to 31 January 1994; and publishing the results of surveys or projections of possible voting outcome was prohibited during the period running from 15 days prior to the election until the final results are made public.

7. Lastly, a major reform of the Electoral Code succeeded in resolving the dispute between the Supreme Electoral Tribunal and the parties comprising the MNR/CD/FMLN coalition with regard to the composition of the departmental and municipal election boards, a dispute caused by the Tribunal's decision to reduce the number of representatives of the coalition parties to one when the coalition was legally registered. ONUSAL voiced its concern publicly at the difficult situation thus created and asked that the problem be resolved by means of a broad interpretation of the law that would allow all parties running in the four elections to participate. The legislative reform of 19 January unequivocally calls for all parties registering candidates to be represented on the departmental and municipal election boards.

8. The Supreme Electoral Tribunal, the highest authority and the general overseer of the electoral process, has improved its organization, its management capacity and its ability to deal flexibly with problems that have arisen in recent months. In spite of the Tribunal's outdated computer equipment and initial problems of transport and communication, the work of registering voters and issuing voter registration documents has been achieved with technical and logistical support from ONUSAL and the contracting of private computing and photocopying companies. These companies also entered data in digital form from birth certificates that were collected to validate the maximum possible number of voter registration requests that had been rejected for want of a birth certificate.

9. Notwithstanding these improvements, the Tribunal has yet to have an office in the town of Concepción de Oriente and maintains a presence only sporadically in other small towns such as Nuevo Edén de San Juan and San Luis de la Reina. In eight towns in Chalatenango which had been involved in the conflict, the cameras used in processing voter registration cards were returned to the departmental seat, contrary to the Tribunal's plan. This violation was reported to the Tribunal, but the cameras have yet to be returned to the towns in question. There are still many towns in which the Tribunal office is closed over the weekend, preventing citizens from smaller towns and villages from obtaining their cards. Although this

problem is related to the use of municipal facilities, which are closed on weekends, it is the Tribunal's responsibility to provide this service without interruption.

10. During the next five weeks, when hundreds of thousands of voter registration cards are to be issued, it is important that the Tribunal's offices remain open throughout the country seven days a week, as originally planned. The issuing of cards is being promoted by the holding of special weekend days similar to those organized for voter registration, with the participation of the Tribunal, municipal governments, ONUSAL and NGOs.

11. The Supreme Electoral Tribunal has not been able to meet the 30-day deadline for issuing registration cards or notifying individuals why they have not received them. Of the 40 alleged violations relating to the issuing of voter registration cards, 13 related to this fact. Now that special days for the issuing of registration cards are being held, the Tribunal, with the help of NGOs, has begun to reply within 10 days by telegram to those citizens who have not received cards even though they had filled out a request.

12. In December 1993, departmental election boards were set up; these are mid-level electoral authorities with important functions in the areas of election monitoring, reporting violations of electoral legislation, delivering all election material to the municipal boards and collecting ballots. All political parties taking part in the election are represented on both the departmental and the municipal boards. The composition of these boards reflects the multiparty nature of the electoral authority. The elected chairmen of the departmental electoral boards come from FMLN in 7 of the country's 14 departments; from PDC in 4 departments; from ARENA in 2 departments; and from MSN in 1. Although the Boards are formally established, they have scant resources with which to operate. As a result, during January 1994 ONUSAL received numerous requests from the boards for resources from the Supreme Electoral Tribunal.

13. The Board of Vigilance, composed of representatives of all parties fielding candidates in the election, acquired its own facilities during December 1993 and now has its own computers. To support the work of the Supreme Electoral Tribunal, the Board is helping to provide advisory services to citizens who encounter problems in obtaining voter registration cards. In addition, the Board of Vigilance and the political parties now possess copies of the electoral roll updated as of 19 January 1994, which replaces the previous list dating from May 1993.

14. An Electoral Counsel was appointed by the Attorney-General of the Republic in January 1994. The incumbent of this position, which is called for by law, is responsible for investigations and questions of *amparo* associated with the electoral process. However, as of the end of January an Auditor-General for Elections had yet to be appointed. The Auditor-General must be appointed by the Tribunal and is responsible for the administrative, financial and technical aspects of all legal matters pertaining to the electoral process. In both cases, the need for the appointment has been publicly stressed by certain opposition parties, particularly FMLN. With the appointment of the Auditor-General in the near future, the institutional structure of the electoral authority should be complete.

II. Closure of voter registration

15. My report of October 1993 concluded with the hope that the authorities, the parties and other external institutions that are supporting the electoral process in El Salvador would collaborate and coordinate their activities with a realistic vision and offer constructive criticism that would facilitate the preparation of the electoral rolls, given that voter registration was a principal element in shaping the political atmosphere and the context of the election campaign. Following the closure of voter registration on 19 January 1994 and the drawing up of the provisional electoral rolls, major improvement in registration conditions has been observed. Here the work done by the Tribunal must be acknowledged, both in making its procedures more flexible and in remaining open to criticism and to suggestions from the Board of Vigilance, the political parties and the foreign agencies providing support for the electoral process. In addition, owing to the strategic and logistical support from the Electoral Division, with the help of the other components of ONUSAL, the joint efforts of various agencies and individuals resulted in a voter registration exercise that was more inclusive and free of flaws than might have been predicted a few months earlier.

16. During this period, the ONUSAL teams made an average of six observation visits to each of the country's 262 towns, or more than 1,700 visits. ONUSAL also provided support for the Tribunal plan during this period by dispatching some 2,500 mobile team visits, involving more than 5,000 trips by Mission staff. In the course of providing this support, some 297,000 kilometres of travel and roughly 180 hours of helicopter flying time were logged. ONUSAL put forward and supported two plans for locating birth certificates in every town in the country so that requests for inclusion in the electoral rolls could be validated.

17. Quantitatively speaking, the registration exercise can be counted a success. With regard to the registration phase, when the deadline for submitting registration requests was reached on 19 November 1993, the outcome of the campaign launched by the Tribunal in July of that year was generally commended in political circles. The official figure of 787,834 registration requests re-

flects a high degree of citizen mobilization. Of the requests submitted between 1 July and 19 November 1993, some 469,098 were for new registrations, 85,560 were for changes and 229,800 were for reinstatement.

18. As for the number of actual registrations, when the electoral rolls were closed on 19 January 1994, the total stood at 2,653,871, of which 2,171,805 corresponded to voter registration cards issued in previous years and 482,066 for temporary cards that could be converted into permanent cards once they became available in the distribution centres and were claimed by the individuals concerned. By 19 January, voter registration cards had been issued to approximately 80 per cent of the estimated population of voting age. Once the temporary cards are converted into permanent cards, as many as 2.3 million Salvadorians may appear on the final electoral rolls and possess a registration card that will allow them to vote, according to projections made in September 1993 by the ONUSAL Electoral Division. This is equivalent to 85 per cent of the estimated voting-age population.

19. It should be borne in mind, however, that the electoral rolls will list approximately 2.7 million names. The discrepancy of 400,000 registrations between the Electoral Division's estimate of 2.3 million potential voters and the 2.7 million listed in the rolls, according to reliable estimates, may be ascribed to the following factors: (a) an indeterminate number of deceased persons holding voter registration cards may remain on the rolls, their definitive removal having been prevented by inadequacies in the system of death certificates; (b) at the same time, some 300,000 temporary cards issued in the field since 1991 that have been neither claimed nor converted into permanent cards may still exist, so that the individuals in whose names they were issued will remain on the rolls; and (c) an element that is the most difficult to quantify, is that there may be many Salvadorians still residing outside the country who, while possessing voter registration cards, are highly unlikely to return to the country to vote.

20. The various plans for locating birth certificates succeeded in obtaining certificates to validate some 60,000 requests for registration, with another 80,000 remaining invalid at the time registration was closed. It is probable that most of these requests would require a more detailed and time-consuming effort at validation owing to problems, *inter alia*, in identifying the place and date of birth and relating to the nature and order of names and surnames of the individuals concerned. El Salvador has no civil registry *per se*, and the relevant legislation affords great latitude in the use of surnames. These factors are compounded by distortions, both of a physical nature and in the identification of birth places, caused by migration from rural areas to towns and displacements caused

by the armed conflict. One legal way of validating the requests that were rejected when registration was closed remains open, and the citizens concerned may make use of it until 19 February 1994, when the final rolls are to be issued: articles 51 and 48 of the Electoral Code, and the Supreme Electoral Tribunal has upheld this in joint meetings with ONUSAL, the Board of Vigilance and donor organizations, permits any citizen whose name has not been included in the provisional rolls to submit a valid request accompanied by the corresponding birth certificate, whereupon he shall be included in the rolls.

21. With the closure of voter registration and the completion of work on the provisional electoral roll, certain difficulties persist that will have to be overcome if citizen participation is to proceed smoothly on election day. In the first place, it is necessary to ensure that all the temporary cards issued duly reach the Tribunal offices in the towns in which the voters have stated that they wish to vote, so that each of the voters goes to the expected site and no local community, however small, is faced with significant electoral gaps in its register. This last point is of particular importance in the municipal elections, where a small number of votes can decide the result of the election.

22. Secondly, citizens must verify that the information given on their card tallies exactly with the information included in the electoral roll. In accordance with article 30 of the Electoral Code, requests for corrections and adjustments to the provisional electoral roll may be legally submitted for up to 30 days before the election, until 19 February. This deadline was altered after the deadline for the closure of registration was legally changed to 60 days before the election. Some requests, for example those concerning the loss of a voter registration card, can be submitted even a few days before the election, as provided by article 48 of the Code. In practice, the Supreme Electoral Tribunal has not included in its extensive instructions any specific directives on deadlines by which citizens are to submit various types of applications. ONUSAL has emphasized the need to provide unambiguous publicity where deadlines are concerned. Proper enforcement of the law requires that the Tribunal indicate the new deadlines for the implementation of articles 30 and 51 and determine the precise deadline for the implementation of article 48. If the provisional roll is to be corrected satisfactorily, not only the Tribunal but also the political parties and NGOs must be involved in helping the voters to verify whether the registration entry is correct and to submit the appropriate request.

23. Even when the final electoral roll is available on 19 February, some of the problems mentioned in my October 1993 report will persist and will have to be faced on election day by the electoral authorities at all levels and by the political party monitors and the international

observers. For example, it will be impossible to determine the number of persons in possession of two or more voter registration cards, each with a different identity, obtained through the improper use of officially valid documentation. This situation is due to the legal framework within which the register was drawn up and the attention paid to certain exceptional circumstances; it is almost impossible to remedy. Every precaution must therefore be taken to ensure that such persons vote only once. Multiple voting by persons with several cards using different identities can be prevented only by an appropriate use of indelible ink at the time of voting. In this matter, the electoral authorities and also the party monitors and international observers will have to take special care to ensure that the ink does not become mingled with products other than those from the official supplier or with supplies left over from previous elections, that only officially provided bottles are used and that voters are not allowed to depart from the voting site until they have received the ink mark.

III. The electoral campaign

24. The electoral campaign opened officially on 20 November for the election of the President and on 20 January for the election of the Legislative Assembly. The electoral campaign for the municipal elections begins officially on 20 February. In practice, campaign activities started before the dates indicated and there is some discreet overlap between them. The political climate of the campaign is calm in institutional terms—relations between the contending parties, organization of public events, access to the media, content of publicity, and so forth—despite some incidents of political violence and intimidation and the persistence of high rates of common crimes and ordinary offences. ONUSAL teams have attended approximately 200 electoral events throughout El Salvador, in all the departments, without coming across any incidents of importance.

25. At the institutional level, campaign activities are proceeding without major incident, although the extent of compliance with the electoral norms can and must be improved in the time remaining before the elections. Under the auspices of ONUSAL and the Tribunal, the political parties have signed pacts of honour about the conduct of the campaign in 12 of the 14 departments of El Salvador, and similar pacts are under discussion in the remaining 2 departments. The parties hold joint meetings at regular intervals to discuss campaign developments. These meetings are sponsored by ONUSAL.

26. Generally speaking, the public part of the campaign and the display of posters, flags and wall paintings have proceeded smoothly, although there have been reports of incidents in which activists have destroyed or pasted over a political party's mural propaganda. Thus far, none of these incidents has been serious. All the parties are being granted access to the media, although the frequency of access and the extent of coverage depend on the medium concerned. As to the content of the publicity, the Electoral Division of ONUSAL has received a number of complaints regarding the use of public resources to promote indirectly the party of the Government in power. In addition, the Electoral Division itself, in monitoring the media, has noticed two pieces of televised publicity by the ARENA party containing elements that may violate article 18 of the electoral propaganda rules. That article provides that no party shall include in its publicity emblems and insignia used by other parties.

27. There are some incidents that are not at all conducive to an atmosphere of civil tranquillity and political freedom. First and foremost, there are the murders in recent months of at least 15 persons of some political importance, concerning which suspicions or allegations of political motivation have been expressed. Two former commanders and four ex-combatants of FMLN were murdered in the last week of October 1993. During November 1993, four ARENA activists (a councilman, a former mayor, the brother of a mayor and a grass-roots activist) and two FMLN activists were murdered, and an FMLN activist and an ARENA activist were injured. In the first week of December, a former commander of FMLN and the brother of an FMLN candidate for mayor were murdered. In January 1994, a young MSN activist was murdered while painting political graffiti. During the same period, the Human Rights Division of ONUSAL received 46 reports of murders, initially described as summary executions, including the 15 murders already cited, whose perpetrators are not identified. In addition to these incidents of extreme violence, there have been public reports in the media describing approximately 15 acts of intimidation, attempted violence or threats against political persons or facilities; they relate mostly to FMLN and to a lesser extent to PDC and ARENA. The deep concern caused by the resurgence of violence in El Salvador was reflected in my letter to the President of the Security Council of 3 November 1993 (S/26689), his reply in a note of 5 November (S/26695), my report on ONUSAL of 23 November (S/26790) and Security Council resolution 888 (1993) of 30 November 1993. Although the murders alluded to are not fully elucidated in terms of police investigation or judicial outcome, they do have a direct political relevance in an electoral campaign and should be regarded as incidents with a political impact, even though assessing that impact would be highly problematical at this stage of the electoral process.

28. However, while the personal unhappiness and the social failure that are implicit in the loss of human

life, bodily assaults and violations of personal safety are to be deplored, it is encouraging to note that the frequency of this type of incident has diminished during December and January, and that the Joint Group for the investigation of politically motivated illegal armed groups, which was established on the initiative of the United Nations, is already meeting and is discharging its mandate. Moreover, the aforementioned acts of violence and intimidation against political persons occurred outside the framework of the electoral campaign proper and of the dialogue, both institutional and informal, between the contending parties. Thus far, they do not seem to have affected in a relevant or visible way the relatively normal climate in which the electoral process is unfolding, particularly in the light of the country's recent emergence from a long internal conflict and the extremely harsh environment of crime, unemployment and lack of basic social services with which Salvadorians have to contend daily.

IV. Observations

29. The Salvadorian people have travelled a long and arduous path to reach the current stage in their quest for peace and national reconciliation. The elections on 20 March represent an opportunity to establish a new political framework that will include the forces formerly in opposition which refused to resolve their differences by means of civil discourse and dialogue between Government and opposition and between parliamentary majority and parliamentary minorities. Travelling this path could not have been without difficulties and risks. It is to the credit of the Salvadorian people and their leaders of all persuasions that they were able to overcome the obstacles through courage and political wisdom and to advance to the stage of holding elections. Further difficulties must be expected; it is to be hoped that they are few and of little importance. What is essential, however, is that the political leaders should not lose sight of the noble objectives set and should remain steadfast in working towards those objectives, while the citizens must not find pretexts to lose their trust in the leaders or the feeling of security and political freedom. These are the circumstances that will enable the voters to cast an individual, free and secret ballot on 20 March and accept as valid the election result.

Document 101

Letter dated 3 March 1994 from the Secretary-General to President Cristiani about concerns relating to implementation of the peace accords

Not issued as a United Nations document

I wish to refer to my letter of 15 February 1994, in which I reviewed some issues concerning the implementation of the Peace Accords between the Government of El Salvador and the Frente Farabundo Martí para la Liberación Nacional (FMLN). In that letter, I put to Your Excellency certain concerns which I believed then, and still believe, can be successfully tackled within the next few weeks under your personal leadership. These concerns relate principally to the maintenance of internal order and to the reintegration into society of estranged groups, including former combatants. I remain concerned about these issues and I would value an early reply to my letter, so that I can assure the Security Council that appropriate steps are being taken.

I understand from my Special Representative that preparations are under way for a high-level meeting at which you personally and the leadership of the FMLN would attempt to settle pending matters, and specifically to agree on a calendar of implementation. It seems to me important that this meeting should take place very soon. A further pending matter which my Special Representative is pursuing with COPAZ is the submission to the Legislative Assembly of Constitutional reforms which are essential to complete the reform of the Judiciary. Failure to get these approved in the present Legislature would be a serious setback to the consolidation of what has been achieved in El Salvador under your Presidency.

I very much look forward to hearing from you soon on these matters and I hope to be able to celebrate these major steps forward with you when you hand over the Presidency to your successor.

Please accept, Mr. President, the assurances of my highest consideration and my warmest regards.

Document 102

Report of the Secretary-General on the activities of the ONUSAL Electoral Division

S/1994/304, 16 March 1994

I. Introduction

1. The present report is the third in a series of reports that I have been submitting to the Security Council on the activities of the Electoral Division of the United Nations Observer Mission in El Salvador (ONUSAL) until the elections scheduled for 20 March 1994 are held. This is a special report that summarizes the activities of the Electoral Division and attempts to provide an overview of the unfolding of the electoral process up to election day. My last report (S/1994/179) was issued on 16 February 1994 and there will be another report issued immediately after the elections that will include comments on the events on election day and an assessment of the overall conduct of the election as monitored by international observers of the United Nations.

II. Deployment of the electoral component

2. The Electoral Division of ONUSAL was established in September 1993 with a mandate to observe the electoral process before, during and after the elections under the following terms of reference:

(a) To observe that measures and decisions made by all electoral authorities are impartial and consistent with the holding of free and fair elections;

(b) To observe that appropriate steps are taken to ensure that eligible voters are included in the electoral rolls, thus enabling them to exercise their right to vote;

(c) To observe that mechanisms are in place effectively to prevent multiple voting, given that a complete screening of the electoral rolls prior to the elections is not feasible;

(d) To observe that freedom of expression, organization, movement and assembly are respected without restrictions;

(e) To observe that potential voters have sufficient knowledge of the mechanisms for participating in the election;

(f) To examine, analyse and assess criticisms made, objections raised and attempts undertaken to delegitimize the electoral process and, if required, to convey such information to the Supreme Electoral Tribunal;

(g) To inform the Supreme Electoral Tribunal of complaints received regarding irregularities in electoral advertising or possible interferences with the electoral process; when appropriate, to request information on corrective measures taken by the Tribunal;

(h) To place observers at all polling sites on election day to verify that the right to vote is fully respected.

3. The Electoral Division has been functioning for six months with 36 Professional staff deployed through six regional offices. In spite of the rather small number of staff, the electoral component has been able to perform the observation duties assigned to it on the basis of coordination with, and the close collaboration of, the other components of ONUSAL. In addition to observing the activities of the Supreme Electoral Tribunal, the political parties, other public organizations and the mass media, the ONUSAL teams have been providing technical and logistic support in the preparation of the register of voters in all regions of the country. By the end of the campaign period, the ONUSAL teams had made an average of nine observation visits to each of the country's 262 towns, or more than 2,350 visits, and had also dispatched a total of 3,700 patrols. In the course of providing this support, some 437,000 kilometres of travel and roughly 270 hours of helicopter flying time were logged.

III. Observation activities

4. ONUSAL promoted discussions with a view to obtaining the signing of codes of conduct by political parties. Pacts of this kind were signed by all contending parties in each of the 14 departments of El Salvador as well as in a number of municipalities. On 10 March, at ONUSAL headquarters, all presidential candidates signed a declaration in which they declared their rejection of violence and their commitment to respect the results of the elections and to comply with the Peace Accords. Periodic meetings with political parties were held at the central and local levels in order to discuss ongoing problems and viable solutions. The Electoral Division held joint meetings on a regular basis with the Supreme Electoral Tribunal, the Board of Vigilance, which is made up of representatives of all political parties, and the party campaign managers with a view to solving any possible problem arising during the electoral process. It was at these meetings that technical proposals to improve the registration process were discussed and evaluated.

5. The Division has met with more than 70 delegations from Governments, non-governmental organizations (NGOs), international organizations, universities and the media seeking information about the electoral

process. During the months preceding the elections, ONUSAL has been approached by representatives of various organizations which intend to monitor the elections by mobilizing some 2,000 international observers, in addition to ONUSAL's own observers. The Electoral Division has prepared a kit containing documents on electoral procedures and international observation, as well as reports of the Secretary-General. These documents are available to those delegations and reporters who seek information at ONUSAL.

6. ONUSAL has mobilized 900 international observers to be deployed prior to election day in all of the 262 municipalities of El Salvador. There will be an observer team at each of the 355 polling centres, which constitute a total of 6,970 polling stations. The number of observers per team will vary according to the size of the polling centre at a ratio of approximately 10 stations per observer. The ONUSAL observers will cover the conduct of the polls on 20 March as well as the counting of votes both at the polling station and at the Supreme Electoral Tribunal later that day and over the following days. After election day, a public statement will be made by ONUSAL on the conduct of the election.

IV. Registration of voters

7. The preparation of the electoral register was a central issue from the beginning of the process. As stated in my last report (S/1994/179, para. 17), at the closure of the register, and in overall quantitative terms, the registration of voters can be considered satisfactory. The electoral lists include the names of over 2,700,000 Salvadorians, of whom more than 2,350,000 may be in possession of a voting card when the deadline period for delivery of cards closes on 12 March. This figure amounts to over 85 per cent of the estimated voting-age population. Some flaws and outstanding difficulties with regard to registration and the lists of voters are described below.

8. One major flaw of the Register is that over 74,000 persons requesting registration have not been included because their application could not be validated by a birth certificate. At the national level, that figure amounts to 2.8 per cent of the entire register of voters. Nevertheless, there are 35 municipalities in former conflict zones where the average of non-validated applications amounts to 10.4 per cent, more than triple the national average. In absolute terms, the number of those applications translates to over 10,000. This occurred in spite of the fact that two extensive plans for the recovery of more than 360,000 birth certificates from municipal offices were implemented with the assistance of ONUSAL and the United States Agency for International Development (USAID), concentrating more intensively in the former conflict zones. Nearly 60,000 applications for

registration were validated on the results of those plans. Since destruction of registers was particularly frequent in these areas, it was there that an exceptionality decree for the redocumentation of citizens was more broadly applied.

9. A way to solve the problem of the remaining non-validated applications was provided for in articles 30, 48 and 51 of the Electoral Code, whereby corrections and claims may be made with regard to the Register during a time period to be established by the Supreme Electoral Tribunal. In practice, although the Tribunal issued instructions on this matter via the media, it failed to include specific deadlines for citizens to submit complaints. During the last days of February and up to 6 March, ONUSAL teams observed that requests for corrections and submission of birth certificates for the validation of voter applications were being accepted by the Tribunal. Approximately 5,000 claims of citizens who did not have a voting card owing to the lack of a birth certificate were processed by the Tribunal.

10. Another problem that still persists with regard to the Register is the possibility of multiple voting by persons in possession of several voter cards under the same or different identities. It is impossible to determine the number of persons in such circumstances. On the one hand, the names of deceased citizens were not removed from the Register for technical reasons. On the other hand, double registration of the same person under different identities was made possible by the legal framework that was designed to deal with certain exceptional circumstances of displaced populations and destroyed registries. Multiple voting by persons with several cards can be prevented only by appropriate use of indelible ink at the time of voting. In this matter, the electoral authorities, as well as the party monitors and international observers, will have to take special care to ensure that the ink is preserved and properly utilized.

11. ONUSAL teams have observed cases of citizens who, despite the appearance of their names on the voter lists, were unable to obtain their voter cards because their registration card was not available even after all cards had been sent to the field. There were also citizens who had a voter card, but whose names did not appear on the list of the municipality where they had chosen to vote. While at least some of these cases may have been corrected by the Tribunal in response to claimants, the extent of the problem could not be quantified and difficulties may arise on election day.

V. Electoral campaign and respect of basic freedoms

12. Under the terms of reference of its electoral component, ONUSAL was asked to observe whether freedom of expression, movement, organization and as-

sembly were being respected without restrictions. In monitoring campaign activities, ONUSAL teams have attended more than 800 events, mainly political meetings and demonstrations, that have generally taken place in an orderly, well-organized manner. Despite the absence of security forces at two thirds of the events, only a few serious incidents have occurred. Although some persons were seriously injured, no fatalities have been reported from campaign activities. Approximately 34 per cent of events monitored by ONUSAL were organized by the Alianza Republicana Nacionalista (ARENA); 32 per cent by the coalition composed of the Convergencia Democrática (CD), the Movimiento Nacional Revolucionario (MNR) and the Frente Farabundo Martí para la Liberación Nacional (FMLN); 16 per cent by the Christian Democratic Party; and 18 per cent by other parties. These activities were proof that freedom of movement, demonstration and expression were respected in a way that contributes to the holding of an election in a free manner.

13. Political advertising through the mass media has also been monitored by ONUSAL. All the parties are present in most media, although with different intensity. ARENA has consistently taken the lead in advertising time, on both radio and television, followed closely by the Christian Democratic Party, and at a further distance by the CD/MNR/FMLN coalition and other parties. As for the content of political advertising, it has been found to be generally congenial to the prescriptions of electoral legislation. Nevertheless, the Electoral Division of ONUSAL has received a number of complaints from different political parties regarding the use of public resources to promote indirectly the governing party. In addition, although there is a ban on publicity of government programmes 30 days prior to the elections, in monitoring the media the Electoral Division itself has ascertained that several ministries and governmental agencies were advertising their own programmes up to the time of the drafting of the present report.

14. There has been publicity on television and the radio and in newspapers by a private institute and also by anonymous advertisers, the content of which is strongly hostile to FMLN and to the presidential candidate of the CD/MNR/FMLN coalition. Besides violating article 4 of the electoral propaganda rules, whereby only political parties and coalitions may make use of electoral propaganda, this publicity also violates article 18 of the rules, which stipulates that no party shall include in its publicity emblems, symbols and insignia used by other parties. Although the Supreme Electoral Tribunal ordered these advertisements to be withdrawn, they continued to be published. In all cases, the content of this publicity runs counter to the spirit of peace and reconciliation that

should preside over the elections. There has also been some publicity by ARENA and the Convergencia Democrática with elements that may violate article 18 of the electoral propaganda rules.

15. Complaints of irregularities in electoral publicity and other aspects of the electoral process were in a timely manner transmitted by ONUSAL to the Supreme Electoral Tribunal in accordance with the terms of reference of the Electoral Division. Communication with the Tribunal included not only complaints presented to ONUSAL by claimants from different sources, mostly political parties, but also reports on problems identified in the field by ONUSAL observers. These communications covered most of the issues subject to public discussion. In some cases, they were solved by action from the Tribunal. In this connection, ONUSAL made recommendations to the Tribunal as appropriate. Some 300 complaints were presented to ONUSAL during the campaign period, most of them (23 per cent) dealing with arbitrary or illegitimate action by public authorities. The remainder consisted of acts of intimidation (21 per cent), destruction of propaganda materials (18 per cent), aggression (9 per cent), murder (7 per cent) and miscellaneous complaints (22 per cent).

16. With regard to civic education, extensive media advertising was undertaken by the Supreme Electoral Tribunal during the registration process and in the final phase of the campaign, at which time emphasis was placed on how to vote. In addition, a number of well-funded NGOs were very active in the field of civic education. Their activities concentrated on the production and massive distribution of materials, such as pamphlets and brochures. Massive civic education campaigns were of the utmost importance, as in elections held in the past decade an average of 10 per cent of the ballots were void and blank.

17. Among the problems remaining to be resolved is the issue of location of polling stations in some of the former areas of conflict. In accordance with the law, polling stations have been established in the municipalities throughout the country. But a decision taken by the Supreme Electoral Tribunal has resulted in the relocation of four polling stations from their respective municipalities to the departmental capital of Chalatenango. The decision of the Supreme Electoral Tribunal is based on its perception that there exists a lack of security and minimal population in these municipalities. This perception is not upheld by ONUSAL observers. The decision of the Supreme Electoral Tribunal has provoked major discussion and strong opposition from political parties and the citizens of these municipalities, including a demonstration of 600 to 700 people in front of the Tribunal offices. ONUSAL has

reiterated, in conversations with the Tribunal and in public statements, that the decision to relocate polling stations violates articles 125 and 241 of the Electoral Code. In spite of ongoing protests, the Supreme Electoral Tribunal to date maintains its position.

VI. Observations

18. El Salvador is approaching these elections under political conditions that were unthinkable three years ago. Despite remaining difficulties with the registration of voters and a political climate where mistrust among contenders still persists, the conditions for the holding of free and fair elections are generally adequate. The fact that all political forces are participating for the first time, that basic political freedoms are respected and that the number of violent incidents during the campaign has been limited leads to the expectation that voter turnout will be substantially higher than in previous elections. Furthermore, never before have the rules governing the issuance of the ballot and the counting of the vote been as congenial to democratic standards. There is good reason to expect that these elections will be a crucial stepping-stone in the consolidation of peace and national reconciliation among the Salvadorian people.

Document 103

Letter dated 28 March 1994 from the Secretary-General to the President of the Security Council concerning implementation of the peace accords

S/1994/361, 30 March 1994

I am reporting separately to the Security Council on the activities of the United Nations Observer Mission in El Salvador (ONUSAL) in relation to the elections held on 20 March 1994. The purpose of this letter is to raise with the members of the Council continuing concerns regarding the implementation of certain aspects of the original Peace Accords signed by the Government of El Salvador and the Frente Farabundo Martí para la Liberación Nacional (FMLN), following negotiations held under United Nations auspices. These concerns relate to public security, including the deployment of new National Civil Police (PNC) and the phasing out of the old National Police (PN); the reintegration into society, through transfers of land and other programmes, of estranged groups including former combatants; and the constitutional reforms recommended by the Commission on the Truth.

All of these issues were discussed in the report which I submitted to the Council on 23 November 1993 (S/26790). At that time I had expressed my considerable concern that some very important elements in the Accords remained only partially implemented, when they should have been completed or well on the way to completion before the elections. My preoccupation today stems from the fact that, four months after that report, little progress has been achieved in the above-mentioned areas.

Establishing the civilian character of the police function was a fundamental tenet and objective of the entire peace agreement, coupled with the new role attributed to the Armed Forces and their reduction in size. However, there continue to be disquieting signs of reluctance to comply with these objectives. There have been developments which, if they remain uncorrected, would produce a result inconsistent with the Peace Accords. The PNC is still denied resources, there is as yet no clear accounting of the transfer to the PNC of military personnel, and there seems to be a desire to de-link the deployment of the PNC from the phasing out of the PN. ONUSAL continues to be hindered from properly carrying out its verification responsibilities in this regard. In addition, there remains concern about activities by the military intelligence bodies which are contrary to the Peace Accords.

The incorporation of members of the FMLN into the new National Academy for Public Security (ANSP), together with former members of the Armed Forces and fresh recruits who had participated in neither structure, provides the basis for a well integrated force which, if distortions are corrected, can provide a strictly civilian public security body which can yet serve as an inspiring model. It is important that the issues relating to public security be sorted out urgently as part of the effort to ensure a framework for the respect of human rights, one of the principal goals of the peace negotiations.

The reintegration of the members of the FMLN, within a framework of full legality, into the civil, institutional and political life of the country was the ultimate objective of the peace process as set forth in the Geneva Agreement of 4 April 1990. Progress in reintegration of the FMLN into the political life of El Salvador is astonishing, as witnessed by the significant number of seats which they recently gained in the Legislative Assembly. Notwithstanding positive developments, much remains to be done in other, critical areas of reintegration. The main one is the transfer of land, through which most former combatants and supporters of the FMLN are to be reintegrated. The compromise reached when the parties accepted my proposal of 13 October 1992 raised the hope that this difficult and complex question could be put back on the way to resolution, thus easing the predicament of up to 47,500 potential beneficiaries. Efforts were set in train, despite serious obstacles, to mobilize international assistance.

In November 1993, when Under-Secretary-General Marrack Goulding visited San Salvador leading a special mission, transferring had come to a virtual standstill, and it was agreed to set a goal of transferring of land to 12,000 beneficiaries by the end of the year. Three months later, in mid-March, transfers had not yet reached 11,000, and thus remained delayed and short of that goal. It is not merely a problem of numerical objectives: at this pace, the bulk of potential beneficiaries will once again miss the planting season in May as a result of lack of access to credit. Similarly, other reintegration programmes are moving extremely slowly, and the terms of some of the programmes including those relating to lack of satisfactory credit facilities, raise concern as to their viability.

A particularly urgent matter, which I recently mentioned to the members of the Council, is that of recommendations of the Commission on the Truth requiring constitutional amendments, particularly with regard to the decentralization of powers and competence of the Supreme Court. Members of the Council will recall that the recommendations of the Commission on the Truth were accepted as binding in the Peace Accords. The urgency is due to the fact that in El Salvador constitutional amendments must be approved by a simple majority in one legislature and ratified by the following legislature by a two-thirds majority. Thus, unless the amendments are approved by 30 April 1994, the date of expiry of the current legislature, they cannot enter into force before 1997. Urgent action to implement these amendments is needed in order to ensure that the long-delayed reform of the judiciary takes place.

In recent correspondence, through my Special Representative, and through my Senior Political Adviser who travelled to San Salvador last week, I have taken up these matters with President Cristiani, under whose leadership I am convinced that the remaining problems can be put on the way to a solution. I believe it is essential to have an updated agreement between the parties on a timetable for the implementation of pending matters so that the process should suffer no further delays during the transition to the new Government. I hope that the Council can support my efforts in these areas on which action to put the process back on track is urgently required.

(*Signed*) Boutros BOUTROS-GHALI

Document 104

Report of the Secretary-General concerning elections held on 20 March 1994

S/1994/375, 31 March 1994

I. Introduction

1. The present report is the fourth in a series of reports that I have been submitting to the Security Council on the activities of the Electoral Division of the United Nations Observer Mission in El Salvador (ONUSAL) concerning the elections of 20 March 1994. My most recent report (S/1994/304) of 16 March 1994 contained a summary of the activities of the Electoral Division and an overview of the conduct of the electoral process up till election day. The purpose of this report is to provide a general assessment of election day.

II. Participation in the elections

2. At the time of writing the present report, it is estimated that some 1,500,000 voters participated in the election, which would be an increase of nearly 400,000 compared with the elections of 1991 and 1989. This amounts to 55 per cent of the 2,722,000 persons on the electoral rolls. Although it is substantially higher than in earlier elections, this participation is lower than what many had been hoping for. It is attributable, at least in part, to some structural problems of the system which were pointed out in earlier reports. First of all, the complex system of Salvadorian registration means that citizens must invest a considerable amount of time in order to obtain a voter card. Secondly, the limited number of polling centres means that voters must travel considerable distances in order to be able to vote. These drawbacks of an electoral system that was inaugurated in the early 1980s were not corrected in time for these elections. To this must be added other specific problems observed on

election day, 20 March, about which more will be said later on.

III. The results of the election

3. In order to provide the population quickly with information regarding the election results, the Supreme Electoral Tribunal organized a provisional count of the votes. The system was based on transporting a copy of the tally sheets from the polling stations directly to San Salvador by car and helicopter. The tally sheets were processed at the operations centre set up for that purpose by a specialized company which had recently carried out the same type of work in other countries in the region. The system was tried out on four successive Sundays and, during the last two trials, the coverage was 100 per cent and success complete. However, the actual operation of the system appears to have presented difficulties since, three days after the polls closed, the provisional count was still not complete. The greatest difficulty was found in transporting the data to the place where the count was being taken, since there were no problems with the computing system. The provisional count was suspended on Wednesday, 23 March, when some 82 per cent of the votes had been computed. On the basis of these data, the results of the presidential election published by the Tribunal are as follows: Alianza Republicana Nacionalista (ARENA) 49.26 per cent; Movimiento Nacional Revolucionario (MNR)—Convergencia Democrática (CD)—Frente Farabundo Martí para la Liberación Nacional (FMLN) coalition 25.29 per cent; Partido Demócrata Cristiano (PDC) 16.01 per cent; Partido Conciliación Nacional (PCN) 5.23 per cent; Partido Movimiento de Unidad (PMU) 2.39 per cent; Movimiento de Solidaridad Nacional (MSN) 1 per cent and Movimiento Auténtico Cristiano (MAC) 0.82 per cent. These results basically tally with the quick count carried out by ONUSAL and with the count carried out by the principal political parties.

4. Based on these results, the President of the Tribunal declared that since no candidate obtained more than 50 per cent of the votes, there would be a second round, however, a definitive, official announcement has yet to be made. That same day, 23 March, the final count of the presidential votes began and continued until Monday, 28 March. It will be some time before the complete results of the elections for the Legislative Assembly and the municipalities are known, although available data would seem to indicate that ARENA will have a relative majority in the Assembly and that it has won most of the mayoral districts.

5. No party has challenged the results of the presidential election but, at the time of writing this report, the results of the municipal elections have been challenged in more than 40 mayoral districts. Most of the challenges have been made by FMLN, and a lesser number by the Partido Demócrata Cristiano, the Partido Movimiento de Unidad and ARENA. These challenges are based on disagreements regarding the count, especially the characterization of certain votes as invalid. In several cases the grounds for the challenge is the absence of the Partido Movimiento de Unidad symbol from the ballot papers of some municipalities. The election to the Legislative Assembly has been challenged by FMLN in La Unión department, on the grounds that the count was interrupted the night of 20 March, in the capital of the department. It is likely that many of these challenges will be resolved by mutual agreement in the course of the final count. Those that are not will have to be resolved by the Tribunal, against whose decisions there is no appeal.

IV. The conduct of the election

6. In El Salvador, the only persons able to vote are those whose names are on the electoral roll and who, when they come to vote, are able to produce an identity document issued by the Supreme Electoral Tribunal, the data on which must tally with those on the electoral roll. In each municipality, the electoral roll is divided into lists of 400 persons for each polling station in alphabetical order. In each municipality the polling stations are concentrated in a small number of polling centres. For the elections of 20 March, there were 355 such centres which contained anywhere from one polling station in two small municipalities to 280 in the gigantic centre set up in the international fairground in San Salvador. One practical consequence of this system of organization was that most voters had to travel a considerable distance in order to exercise their right to vote. As was pointed out in earlier reports, given the practical impossibility of screening the electoral roll to remove the names of deceased voters and to identify possible double registrations, voters had their fingers stamped with indelible ink so as to preclude the possibility of anyone voting twice.

7. ONUSAL monitored proceedings on election day by deploying nearly 900 observers of 56 nationalities who covered all polling centres with teams of between 2 and 30 observers. The observation continued for a total of more than 15 hours from the time the polling stations were set up to the completion of the count. This massive presence of ONUSAL made it possible throughout election day to resolve countless practical problems of organization of the voting. A team of 40 specialized observers is currently monitoring the official count of the votes in the Supreme Electoral Tribunal. The observers collected information on the events of election day on more than 7,000 forms (one for each of the 6,984 polling stations and the 355 polling centres) which were subsequently

compiled by the Electoral Division and which constitute the basic documentary source for evaluating the conduct of the elections on election day.

8. ONUSAL made a quick count based on a random sample of 291 polling stations, which made it possible to have a reliable projection of the outcome of the presidential election two hours after the polls closed. As is customary in such cases, the information was transmitted by the head of the Mission to the Supreme Electoral Tribunal. The difference between the quick count and the provisional results provided by the Tribunal is 0.5 per cent.

9. In general, there were no serious incidents affecting law and order on election day, and no ballot-rigging. The trend towards fewer violent incidents in recent months culminated in complete calm on election day. The security forces had a normal day, carrying out their duties at election rallies and other activities, and patrolling polling centres. As provided for in the legislation—and unlike what happened during earlier elections—the armed forces did not take part in election security operations; they confined themselves to performing their routine duties.

10. There was political pluralism in the constitution of the electoral authorities at all operational levels, and the parties were all represented on such electoral agencies as the Monitoring Board, the departmental electoral boards, the municipal electoral boards and the polling station teams. ONUSAL observers noted the presence of monitors from the main political parties at all polling stations, and noted no interference with their work. This massive presence of monitors and the ease with which they were able to convey their concerns to ONUSAL observers made it difficult for serious irregularities to occur without being documented on the forms which the observers completed for each polling station. Only eight reports of serious incidents were received, none of them of such a nature or on such a scale as to make the problem intractable or to have a significant effect on the results of the election. The most serious incidents had to do with the large number of voters with voter cards whose names were not on the register. This happened in two municipalities of San Salvador (Zacamil and Soyapango) and in one municipality of San Miguel (Nueva Guadalupe). In these three cases, the interim solution was to prepare a special ballot box for those voters.

11. For the most part, the polling stations operated normally, although quite often they opened after 7 a.m.— because some of the voting material was missing, because members of the polling station team were late or because there was too large a crowd of voters at locations that did not have the capacity to handle them. The indelible ink, which is of considerable importance in preventing people from voting more than once, was, in general, applied properly. There were no reports to the contrary.

12. Up to the night before the elections, there had still been no solution to the problem of the four municipalities of Chalatenango (Arcatao, San José Las Flores, San Isidro Labrador and Nueva Trinidad) from which the Supreme Electoral Tribunal had decided that voting should be moved to the departmental capital, citing security considerations and the scarce population, which were described as reasons of *force majeure*. On the night of 19 March, the Tribunal ruled that the election for each of these municipalities would be held simultaneously at two locations, the municipality itself and the capital of the department. All the parties accepted this ruling. Voting took place normally, and the votes were counted in the city of Chalatenango, to which the ballot boxes from the four municipalities were transported. ONUSAL observers accompanied the materials being delivered, and were in attendance when the elections were conducted and when the votes were counted.

13. In addition to the positive factors described above, there were serious difficulties in organizing the voting and preparing the electoral roll. Because of the over-concentration of polling stations at the few polling centres, it was very difficult for voters to find the tables where they were supposed to vote. The problem was particularly serious in the urban areas, especially in the greater San Salvador area, where 30 per cent of the electorate is concentrated. There was also insufficient public transport, especially in the urban areas, and that made it difficult for many voters to reach polling centres far from their homes. It seems that a considerable number of electors gave up because they could not easily find a polling centre or because there was no transport; but it is difficult to say exactly how many, and all the parties were affected.

14. In addition, many citizens with voter cards were unable to vote, because their names were not on the list, save for those voters who were able to vote at the specially equipped tables in the municipalities of Zacamil, Soyapango and Nueva Guadalupe. ONUSAL estimates that over 25,000 people, i.e. nearly 2 per cent of the electorate, were thus affected. There were also citizens who were unable to vote because others had used their names to vote. ONUSAL has determined that a very small number was involved. It is regrettable that despite the strenuous efforts to register new voters made by ONUSAL, the donor countries and non-governmental organizations, the Supreme Electoral Tribunal failed to produce a more adequate electoral roll.

15. The training provided to members of the polling station teams and to party monitors was clearly inadequate. The Tribunal was late in starting the training seminars, and training materials became available only a few days before election day. This happened even though support from the international community and assistance from the Centre

for Advisory Services and Electoral Promotion were available long enough in advance to guarantee adequate training in good time and in due form.

V. Practical recommendations

16. Since there is soon to be a second round for the presidential election, the anomalies recorded in the first round should be eliminated, in the light of the experience gained by the Supreme Electoral Tribunal from the process that took place on Sunday, 20 March. In a letter dated 24 March to the Supreme Electoral Tribunal ONUSAL expressed its views regarding what measures could be taken prior to the second round in order to deal with the shortcomings identified.

17. A number of measures have already been taken as of the completion of this report, including the reform of the Electoral Code by the Legislative Assembly, thus permitting the issuance of voter cards between the first and second rounds. Another step that should be taken is to increase the number of polling centres, particularly in urban areas and especially in San Salvador. Even though the experience gained on 20 March has improved the operational capacity of the electoral personnel, their training must be strengthened. Properly trained, clearly identified personnel must provide citizens with appropriate guidance at polling locations so that they can participate in an effective and orderly manner.

18. Since the rainy season is approaching, the polling centres for the second round should be sheltered from the rain. It is also necessary to ensure that public transport functions normally, both in terms of number of vehicles and frequency of circulation.

19. The electoral rolls must be reviewed to ensure that the names of all citizens with voter cards appear on the electoral lists and that the rolls displayed publicly at polling locations correspond exactly to the polling teams' lists. The Supreme Electoral Tribunal must therefore permit the citizens concerned to lodge complaints within a period of not less than one week. In addition, the Tribunal's computation centre must verify that the general electoral rolls and the polling teams' lists match.

20. With regard to electoral publicity, the Supreme Electoral Tribunal must take the necessary steps to ensure that there is no publicity that violates articles 4 and 18 of the electoral propaganda rules or that is not in keeping with the spirit of reconciliation of the peace agreements. Article 4 prohibits organizations that are not political parties from engaging in electoral publicity, and article 18 prohibits the use of the names, symbols and emblems of other parties. Clear instructions must therefore be given in order to prevent a recurrence of the situation that arose in the previous electoral campaign. In the event of illegal publicity, the Tribunal must be more energetic in applying sanctions and ensuring that the sanctions are applied by all the legal means at its disposal.

21. The Supreme Electoral Tribunal must conduct a massive public information campaign emphasizing the following: specific deadlines for the review of the electoral rolls and collection of voter cards; motivation of the electorate to participate in the second electoral round, and provision of information on the location of polling centres, with an indication that public transport will be available.

22. The Supreme Electoral Tribunal must give the Monitoring Board and the political parties greater access to information on the operation of the computation centre, the register and the electoral project unit. Only thus will it be possible to implement effectively the provisions of the Electoral Code on the monitoring of and provision of information on the electoral process.

23. The adoption of measures such as those mentioned above will undoubtedly help to ensure that the second round is better organized. However, the experience gained from the elections already held has shown that there are very serious flaws in the methods used, which indicates that some aspects of the methods should be reconsidered: functioning of the Supreme Electoral Tribunal, organization of the electoral register and rolls, organizational methods at polling locations and their geographical distribution. The Legislative Assembly could consider a complete reorganization of the current system, including the creation of a single civil identity and voter document, as well as a civil register that would facilitate automatic preparation of the electoral roll so that citizens would not have to request inclusion of their names on the rolls.

VI. Final considerations

24. As pointed out in previous reports, the general conduct of the electoral process and the campaign has many positive aspects: massive expansion of the electoral rolls; participation by the political parties throughout the process and at all levels of the electoral authorities; peaceful exercise of the right to organize, of the right to freedom of expression and of the right of assembly; publicity by the parties in all the media; conduct of campaign activities without violent incidents; and proper functioning on the part of the security forces and the armed forces. Unfortunately, the high visibility and frequency of the problems observed on election day, discussed throughout this report, may have helped to leave a particularly negative impression of the overall process, especially with observers, who were concentrated in the final stage.

25. However, the irregularities noted must not be mistaken for significant manipulation of the election by

means of fraudulent interference with its essential components, such as ballot boxes, ballot papers and tally sheets. In fact, where the presidential election is concerned, no party has rejected the results and the ONUSAL observers did not record any fraudulent acts that could have a significant impact on the outcome. Moreover, the fact that the provisional count by the Supreme Electoral Tribunal, the quick count by ONUSAL, the count by the principal political parties and the voting trends identified by pre-electoral surveys all basically tally with one another constitutes an additional technical element confirming that there was no significant manipulation of the election.

26. In general, the Assembly and municipal elections were conducted under the same conditions as the presidential election. The foregoing remarks therefore remain valid in general. However, the smaller size of constituencies at this electoral level means that problems affecting a small number of votes can have a significant impact on the outcome and give rise to challenges such as those mentioned earlier. Such challenges will be dealt with in the manner laid down by the legislation, and

ONUSAL will continue to observe how cases evolve until definitive solutions are found. There is no reason why local challenges should affect the overall validity of the electoral process.

27. In view of the foregoing considerations, on 21 March my Special Representative stated:

In the light of the information gathered by the observers on election day, and in view of the systematic observation of the electoral process that has taken place over the past six months, ONUSAL believes that in general the elections on 20 March took place under appropriate conditions in terms of freedom, competitiveness and security. Despite the serious flaws regarding organization and transparency already referred to, the elections can be considered acceptable.

28. I shall issue a fifth report on the eve of the second round and a sixth immediately after the second round of the presidential elections, probably on 24 April.

Document 105

Report of the ONUSAL Human Rights Division covering the period from 1 November 1993 to 28 February 1994 (extract)

A/49/116-S/1994/385, 5 April 1994

I. Introduction

1. In order to provide the Secretary-General with a broad overview of developments in the human rights situation in El Salvador during the pre-election period which culminated on 20 March in the elections to the Presidency of the Republic, the collegial bodies and the municipal mayoralties, the first to be held in the country since the peace agreements (S/23501, annex), the present report analyses the period from November 1993 to February 1994.

2. The active verification of human rights is a part of the provisions adopted by the Government of El Salvador and the Frente Farabundo Martí para la Liberación Nacional (FMLN) in order to implement the peace agreements, which comprise a great number of commitments linked directly or indirectly with the subject of human rights. Verification is substantively carried out in relation to the fulfilment of the San José Agreement on Human Rights, signed on 26 July 1990 (S/21541, annex). This is in addition to human-rights-related commitments which are part of the other political agreements comprising the overall framework of the peace process, especially those involving judicial reform, reforms in the armed forces and

the establishment of the National Civil Police, as well as the recommendations made by the Commission on the Truth and those formulated by the Human Rights Division.

3. The ensemble of commitments contained in these agreements and recommendations include several dozen specific objectives which, together, are gradually generating conditions for the enjoyment of human rights in El Salvador which are different from those that existed in the past. In their totality, these human-rights-linked commitments thus constitute the most substantive and most far-reaching process for the promotion and protection of human rights to have been carried out to date in a country which is a Member of the United Nations. This is largely to the credit of the Salvadorian people, the Government—in whose name, given the structure of the State system, the great majority of the commitments have been undertaken—FMLN and the other political forces in the country represented in the National Commission for the Consolidation of Peace (COPAZ), the national organ supervising the execution of the agreements.

4. With this in mind, the Human Rights Division must point out that the specific development of the

situation of each one of the rights under verification must be evaluated and interpreted on its merits, and also in the context of the peace process, which is itself the most transcendent and decisive choice ever made in the country's history to build, by means of consensus, dialogue and negotiation, a State based on the rule of law, whose institutions express respect for human rights and the free exercise of democratic life. From the perspective of the international system, it is an entirely new process in the history of United Nations peace-keeping activities, the grandest and vastest operation for the promotion and protection of human rights ever undertaken by any Government with the endorsement and validation of the international community.

II. Analysis of the situation from November 1993 to February 1994

A. *Overall assessment of the situation*

5. In my ninth report to the Secretary-General, I noted that the human rights situation in El Salvador during the months of August, September and October "took a serious turn for the worse between August and October" (A/49/59-S/1994/47, annex, para. 4). In analysing the overall situation, I said that "a composite analysis of developments in the human rights situation during the past 10 months makes it possible to discern two quite distinct phases. The first phase covers the period from January to May, during which the situation evolved unevenly, with strengths and weaknesses; there was a clear downward trend in the commission of such acts as forced disappearance or torture, and an improvement in the overall political [*and juridical*] situation. The second phase, covering the period from June to October, was marked by a progressive worsening of the situation leading to a grave deterioration of the situation in October, characterized by an upsurge of selective violence against citizens who were openly engaged in politics, as well as death-squad-style murders" (ibid., para. 86).

6. Analysing the situation during the period from August to October, I stated that "the current violence is directed against the democratic political system which has been worked out by the Government and FMLN, with the support of all political forces, with the aim of building up through consensus the rule of law and a stable and functioning democracy. Thus, the acts of political violence which have occurred during the period covered by this report reflect the intransigence of fringe elements attacking the Salvadorian nation as a whole, all national political forces and the democracy proposed in the peace agreements. The Human Rights Division must state that, in the active verification process it has conducted in investigating the cases referred to it, it did not find any

indication or evidence of any institutional involvement of the State in these violations. Therefore, it can affirm that they do not compromise the Government as an institution; on the contrary, this selective violence seems to be directed against all democratic political forces, including the Government of El Salvador itself, which, as a party to the agreements to which the substantive obligations of the peace process were assigned, has taken historic steps, together with FMLN and the other political forces in the country, towards the progressive establishment of an effective democratic political system based on the rule of law" (ibid., para. 16).

7. The acts of violence described in the ninth report constituted a sort of decisive test of the vitality of the peace process and of the will of the parties, especially the Government of El Salvador, to ensure that the law is being observed in respect of human rights. The response of the State, society and the international community has been generally positive. It has been expressed, in the first place, in the Government's invitation to foreign investigators (Scotland Yard, the Federal Bureau of Investigation and the Spanish police) to participate in the investigations together with a governmental inter-agency commission so as to further the corresponding police inquiries. And secondly, by the constructive attitude adopted by the Government, as well as by FMLN, in the process of consultations which led to the organization of the Joint Unit for the Investigation of Illegal Armed Groups having Political Motivations, whose establishment was suggested by the Secretary-General to comply with the relevant recommendation of the Commission on the Truth.

8. The Joint Unit, comprised of Mr. Carlos Mauricio Molina Fonseca, the National Counsel for the Defence of Human Rights, Messrs. José Leandro Echeverría and Juan Jerónimo Castillo, representing the President of the Republic, and Mr. Diego García-Sayán, director of the ONUSAL Human Rights Division, has now begun its activities with the financial collaboration of a group of friendly countries. Its activities are being carried out with the most absolute freedom of action and autonomy; on the level of civil society, the response has also been encouraging since all national sectors, institutions, churches and political forces have expressed their unanimous rejection of any form of violence, especially that which could be politically motivated. In this regard, the candidates for the presidency of the Republic have expressed their intention to support and respect the investigations of the Joint Unit, as well as to implement the peace agreements whatever the outcome of elections.

9. At the same time, the Human Rights Division of ONUSAL proceeded, in accordance with the provisions

of the San José Agreement, to carry out the corresponding investigations, especially those connected with the deaths of the FMLN leaders Francisco Vélis Castellanos, Eleno Castro and José Mario López Alvarenga, as well as the attempt perpetrated on 24 February 1994 on the life of Marta Valladares (Nidia Díaz, former commander of FMLN).

10. The investigation into the death of Francisco Vélis Castellanos is not yet complete. Nevertheless, given the characteristics of the crime, the likeliest explanation seems to be that it was politically motivated. Following investigation into the other cases, it has been determined that the murder of Eleno Castro was a criminal act resulting from an altercation and that responsibility can be attributed to common criminals; and that the killing of José Mario López Alvarenga, according to the current status of the investigations, could have been triggered by an unrelated incident, in that the FMLN leader now appears to have been killed when he went to the defence of an elderly woman who was being attacked by common criminals on leaving a bank.

11. The basically encouraging responses to the grave situation of the previous three months, the findings of some of the investigations, and the developments over the course of the four months (November, December, January and February) analysed in this report do not, on the whole, suggest that the grave deterioration described in the ninth report is continuing at the present point in time; rather, the characteristics of the overall trends of the process seem to be reasserting themselves. In sum, the November-February period shows a certain improvement, in contrast to the serious problems warned of in the ninth report.

...

III. Analysis of the implementation of the recommendations of the Human Rights Division

136. In the eighth report, the Director of the Human Rights Division assessed the implementation of the Division's recommendations with a view to helping to remove some of the remaining constitutional and legal obstacles to the protection of human rights.

137. This report will seek to update that assessment not only because some time has elapsed but also, and in particular, because given the present stage of the peace process and the evolution of the human rights situation, the political community views the implementation of the recommendations of the Human Rights Division and the Commission on the Truth as crucial to the further legal development of procedures for constitutional and legal protection.

138. A status report on the implementation of the recommendations is given below.

A. Recommendations involving constitutional reforms

139. The Division's recommendations concerning the structural and functional reform of the judiciary and amendments to the regulations governing the remedies of *habeas corpus* and *amparo* would entail constitutional reform. There are two substantive aspects to these reforms. First, there is the decentralization of the functions of the Supreme Court of Justice, which involves transferring authority for appointing and removing justices of the peace, judges of first instance and magistrates to the National Council of the Judiciary and making an independent body responsible for authorizing lawyers and notaries to practise as such and suspending them. Second, there are the constitutional amendments, whereby judges of first instance would be competent to deal with issues of *habeas corpus* and *amparo*.

140. The President of the Republic duly sent a message to the Legislative Assembly requesting it to consider those recommendations of the Commission on the Truth involving constitutional amendments—which echo and endorse the recommendations of the Human Rights Division. In accordance with the Constitution of El Salvador, a constitutional amendment must be petitioned by a minimum of 10 legislators and the procedure for adopting it extends over two legislative sessions.

141. ONUSAL believes that the implementation, during the legislative session ending on 30 April, of the constitutional amendments concerning decentralization of the power of the Supreme Court of Justice is a key and decisive element in the judicial reform process in El Salvador. Without a truly independent judiciary, whose administrative structure does not compromise the judges' freedom and independence of judgement and the lawyers' action, the entire legal reform effort being promoted by the Ministry of Justice itself would be devoid of meaning. Modern legislation which provides basic guarantees of human rights cannot be effective if it is administered by a judiciary which has the power to influence the conduct of judges and lawyers either directly or indirectly. In this context, it is equally important to carry out reforms aimed at making the remedy of *habeas corpus* effective and easily accessible to the citizens by giving judges of first instance and justices of the peace competence to hear such remedies.

142. In this context, it would seem self-evident that the success of all the efforts being made in the legislative sphere will depend on the existence of the political capacity to promote the independence and effectiveness of the judiciary through constitutional reform, which thus becomes an urgent and immediate task. ONUSAL believes that, although the current Legislative Assembly is about to conclude its activities, it should initiate a constitutional reform process that would culminate during the first

session of the new Legislative Assembly to be installed on 1 May 1994.

B. *Recommendations which do not involve constitutional amendments*

1. *Establishment of a special commission of inquiry to investigate arbitrary and extra-legal executions*

143. In the wake of the assassinations of FMLN leaders in October and November 1993, the Government decided to establish an Interinstitutional Investigation Commission headed by the Minister and Chief of Staff in the office of the President and composed of representatives of the Office of the Attorney-General, the National Civil Police, the Criminal Investigation Commission, the State Intelligence Agency and the Presidential Commissioner for Human Rights. This Commission worked on the investigation into the cases of Eleno Castro, Ernesto Vélis and Mario López and continues to assume responsibility for the investigation of other assassinations of political leaders or attempted arbitrary executions, such as the attempt on the life of national FMLN leader Marta Valladares (Nidia Díaz). ONUSAL is monitoring the investigations being conducted by the Interinstitutional Commission. The existence of a special entity to investigate cases of assassinations of political leaders in which not only must the possibility of political motivation not be ruled out *a priori*, but be given serious consideration, is certainly a major improvement over the former situation. The fact that, in the investigation of some of these cases, advice was sought from investigators belonging to prestigious foreign investigation bureaus, is added proof that there is a political will which recognizes the need for effective and independent investigation.

144. However, as indicated in the ninth report of the Human Rights division and without prejudice in any way to the outcome of the investigations being conducted by the Interinstitutional Commission, "the Human Rights Division feels constrained to point out that the composition of the Commission does not necessarily reflect the desired independence of judgement. There is, for example, the involvement of the political power of the State in the bodies legally responsible for criminal investigation, while the Office of the National Counsel for the Defence of Human Rights, which has broad constitutional powers to investigate human rights violations on a quasi-jurisdictional basis, is not represented. In that connection, the Secretary-General reported to the Security Council on 29 October that the Interinstitutional Commission 'did not meet the United Nations criteria for the investigation of summary executions' (S/26790, para. 11), but that, in compliance with its observation function, ONUSAL has none the less been closely following the work of the subgroup" (A/49/59-S/1994/47, annex, para. 23).

2. *Ratification of or accession to international instruments, including the Conventions of the International Labour Organization mentioned in the sixth report*

145. In compliance with this recommendation, the executive branch has transmitted the relevant instruments to the Legislative Assembly for the adoption of the instruments of ratification and/or accession to the Convention against Torture and Other Cruel, Inhuman or Degrading Treatment or Punishment; the Additional Protocol to the American Convention on Human Rights in the Area of Economic, Social and Cultural Rights (Protocol of San Salvador) and the Inter-American Convention to Prevent and Punish torture. The Legislative Assembly must adopt those instruments and thereby give full effect to the recommendation concerning them. They should be adopted before the end of the current legislative session.

146. A similar constructive attitude must be taken towards the Optional Protocol to the International Covenant on Civil and Political Rights and recognition of the compulsory jurisdiction of the Inter-American Court of Human Rights. Such recognition is essential if El Salvador's participation in international mechanisms for the protection of human rights is to comply with international standards and be consistent with the spirit that informs the peace process taking place in the country. There is no constitutional or legal impediment to prevent El Salvador from recognizing the compulsory jurisdiction of the Court. This option would be available in addition to domestic jurisdictional remedies and is consistent with a broad view of the democratic system rooted in the very spirit of the Salvadorian Constitution, which affirms the functional principle of non-exclusion from national and international protection mechanisms.

147. The Forum for Economic and Social Consultation has decided to ratify 14 of the ILO conventions. Those procedures should be completed in the immediate future.

3. *Establishment of a compensation fund for victims of human rights violations*

148. This recommendation is vital to the firm establishment of a culture of peace and reconciliation. The compensation of victims of human rights violations is not only a matter of ethics, justice and equity but is also necessary for establishing credibility in the administration of justice. Finally, it would demonstrate genuine political will in respect of the task of reconciliation. The Human Rights Commission of El Salvador (CDHES) submitted a draft from a civilian standpoint which the Human Rights Division has characterized as a sound proposal and which could be the point of

departure for legislative action. Unfortunately, the executive has made no progress at all in this regard and the Human Rights Division has not been informed of the results of the preliminary studies which the Government told ONUSAL it had launched several months ago. The Human Rights Division believes that it is essential for the Government authorities to submit the appropriate draft legislative decree to the Legislative Assembly. Given the nature of the institution to which the regulations would apply, a national consensus should be sought on the text.

4. Improvement of the composition and powers of the National Council of the Judiciary and independence of the Judicial Training School

149. The National Council of the Judiciary and the Supreme Court of Justice each submitted preliminary bills to the Legislative Assembly which, at least on paper, appear to be aimed at implementing the recommendation. However, despite some of their positive provisions, these preliminary bills do not comply with the substantive aspects of the recommendation, namely, granting the National Council of the Judiciary authority to appoint and remove judges and magistrates. In that sense, this recommendation has not been implemented and cannot be said to be in the process of being implemented, for, as has already been indicated, that would require a constitutional amendment.

5. Elimination of extrajudicial confession

150. As indicated in the eighth report, the provisions of the new Public Defender's Act and the amendments already introduced in the Code of Criminal Procedure and the Act organizing the Public Prosecutor's Office have virtually eliminated from the legislation any legal possibility of using extrajudicial confession. However, as its express abolition is necessary, the Ministry of Justice has submitted to the Legislative Assembly a draft legislative decree abolishing extrajudicial confession. Although some time has elapsed since the submission of this proposal, the Legislative Assembly has not yet adopted it. It is essential that it be adopted before the end of the current legislative session. COPAZ has a special responsibility in this connection.

6. Definition of torture and enforced disappearance as offences in special criminal legislation

151. The executive branch has added these two violations to the offences defined in the preliminary bill of the new Penal Code. The public has now been consulted on the text of the new code. The Ministry of Justice, according to the methodology used to promote the initial reforms, is all set to submit the draft legislative decree for adoption by the current Legislative Assembly.

7. Legislation regulating the conduct of law enforcement officials in terms of ensuring respect for human rights

152. This recommendation has been incorporated in a draft legislative decree elaborated by the Ministry of Justice, which gives legal effect to the provisions of the Code of Conduct for Law Enforcement Officials, adopted by the General Assembly of the United Nations. Accordingly, the draft text is eminently satisfactory. It has been transmitted by the executive branch to the Legislative Assembly for adoption, but no action has been taken yet. Its adoption by the Assembly is of the utmost importance.

8. Abolition of the practice of arbitrary detention for petty misdemeanours

153. Beyond the efforts made by ONUSAL, the National Police and the National Civil Police to reduce the number of arbitrary detentions for petty misdemeanours, which have had uneven results, implementation of this recommendation means repealing the 1886 Police Act, transferring jurisdiction over petty misdemeanours to the judicial authorities and expressly regulating the powers and functions of the Municipal Police, which should not be competent to make arrests and determine punishment for petty misdemeanours. It is regrettable that there has been no initiative thus far to abolish the 1886 Police Act outright. This should be done in the immediate future.

9. Temporary application of the Act governing the procedure for administrative detention or the imposition of administrative fines

154. This recommendation is linked to the preceding one, as a temporary means of reducing the high incidence of arbitrary detentions for petty misdemeanours. Since March 1993, the National Police and, subsequently, the National Civil Police have been following a set of instructions on petty misdemeanours which brings the law into compliance with the recommendation. The instructions seek to have the police force apply the "Act governing the procedure for administrative detention or the imposition of administrative fines" (Decree No. 457) in place of the obsolete provisions of the 1886 Police Act or illegal procedures. Despite the efforts made and the measure of progress achieved, its application is still incomplete.

10. Visit by the ILO Committee on Freedom of Association

155. This recommendation has been fully implemented. Professor José Vida Soria headed the ILO mission of direct contact which visited El Salvador between 27 September and 1 October 1993 within the framework of the activity of the Committee on Freedom of Associa-

tion. In its report to the Committee, the mission pointed out that it had also found that following the recent establishment of peace (January 1993), there was a real desire by all to put the past behind them, and that, in fact, the main concern was not to dwell on the past but rather to build the present and the future without minimizing the seriousness of the past situation. The report went on to say that the mission had found a society attempting to forget the past through the use of its freedom of expression, its capacity for dialogue and its other democratic freedoms, and that, in that connection, the activities of the United Nations and, in particular, those of ONUSAL could not be overlooked.

156. The implementation of this recommendation has been beneficial to both the Government and to labour and management. Additionally, it has helped to overcome a number of obstacles which had been mounting for many years in the relationship between the Salvadorian State and ILO, with obvious negative effects on the interrelationship between domestic and international labour law. Referring to the new situation that has emerged with the implementation of the recommendation, the mission of direct contact pointed out that in any case, the country and ILO could be said to have entered a new phase in their relationship, as evidenced by the fact that the Forum for Economic and Social Consultation had approved ratification of 14 major ILO Conventions and had promised to submit them to the Legislative Assembly, that the mission was permitted to visit and that the Government had provided it with substantial information concerning the alleged acts.

11. Legal recognition of associations and trade unions

157. By its very nature this is an ongoing recommendation, and refers to the State's responsibility to apply the law on a non-discriminatory basis and to respect pre-established procedures and deadlines in dealing with all applications for legal recognition, particularly from trade unions, associations and non-governmental organizations. During the period covered by this report, commendable progress has been achieved in this respect, for example, the legal recognition, on 10 December 1993, of the Fundación para la Autogestión y Solidaridad de los Trabajadores Salvadoreños (FASTRAS).

158. Beyond these successful cases, it seems necessary to make some effort to go beyond case-by-case treatment of non-governmental organizations (NGOs) and establish a legal framework and procedure that would provide legal safeguards in connection with the legal requirements and procedures for their establishment. This implies the need to elaborate and adopt a law establishing procedures for the legal recognition of non-governmental organizations. The Ministry of the Interior could also brief NGOs regularly in order to ensure that they have a clear understanding of the required procedures and that they avoid situations which, in practice, affect the legitimate interest of NGOs seeking legal recognition within the framework of a pre-established, efficient procedure. The NGOs themselves should be consulted in the elaboration of the above-mentioned legal procedures.

12. Budget autonomy for the Office of the National Counsel for the Defence of Human Rights

159. The implementation of this recommendation is related to the need to allow the Office of the National Counsel for the Defence of Human Rights, which is currently part of the Public Prosecutor's Office, greater autonomy. However, this would entail a constitutional amendment. The Office of the National Counsel is drawing up a proposal that would ensure it an acceptable degree of autonomy and effectiveness in the use of its budgetary resources, without resorting to constitutional reforms for the time being.

13. Preliminary bills relating to the Penal Code, the Code of Criminal Procedure and the prison act

160. In accordance with the methodology used by the Ministry of Justice for its legislative initiatives, the preliminary bills on both the prison act and the Code of Criminal Procedure are awaiting Government approval. Consultation of the public on the preliminary bill concerning the Penal Code has been in progress since January 1994. These processes, which are undoubtedly vital, should not, however, delay the submission of preliminary bills to the current Legislative Assembly for adoption at the earliest possible date. In that connection, it would be useful to establish a timetable for the consultation processes on these preliminary bills, and for their approval by the President and submission to the Legislative Assembly before the Assembly concludes its activities on 30 April 1994.

14. Amendments to the Career Judicial Service Act

161. A Commission was established within the Legislative Assembly to study amendments to the Career Judicial Service Act. Thus far, it has not submitted any findings. This is disturbing, for the suggestions made by the Human Rights Division and the Commission on the Truth in this area are crucial to the integrity of the judicial branch in El Salvador.

IV. Conclusions

162. The evolution of the human rights situation during the four-month period covered by this report (November-February) does not present all the characteristics of deterioration that were evident during the period immediately preceding it (August-October) and

conforms more to the trends described in previous reports. This seems to confirm the general theory that clear responses which express a political will to investigate complaints are the best way to dispel or confirm suspicions of human rights violations. At the same time, they are the chief deterrent to human rights violations. In order to give unequivocal expression to such capacities, it will be necessary, however, to do something about impunity, which is still very much a reality both in police inquiries and in most judicial proceedings.

163. The active verification carried out by the Human Rights Division into the acts of violence perpetrated by organized criminal groups many of which are composed of former members of the armed forces and former FMLN combatants, appears to confirm the theory that some of the crimes against individuals who are or have been linked to FMLN or the army, are politically motivated. In many of the violent acts that occurred during the period of conflict, the victims were able to identify the perpetrators; it could therefore be concluded that as a direct consequence of the war, crimes with a private political component are being perpetrated to settle scores.

164. The right to life is still the most vulnerable category. While violations of the right to life during the period, covered by this report do not reflect the same characteristics as those that were verified during the previous period, arbitrary executions and attempted arbitrary executions still account for the majority of complaints received. The inability of the investigations branch of the police to apprehend those responsible and the subsequent inability of the judiciary to punish them, continue to be a fundamental reason for the high incidence of violations of the right to life and especially of the sense of impunity that continues to prevail.

165. During the period covered by this report, complaints of death threats continued to increase. This serious situation could be directly related to the high rates of ordinary crime—especially crimes of extortion involving money—that characterized the previous period. However, the only explanation for many of these crimes appears to be that they are politically motivated. This is especially true of a large number of complaints that seem to be closely tied in with the electoral campaign.

166. The active verification carried out during the period covered by the report, has clearly established the fact that the National Police continues to carry out many of its activities in flagrant breach of legality and in violation of human rights as reflected by the statistics included in this report. That notwithstanding, the new Director of the National Police has adopted crucial measures to deal with that serious situation and to shake the commanding officers from their lethargy. While the Human Rights Division hails the policy imposed by the new

Director of the National Police since 1 January, it would like to reiterate the need to fulfil the commitment established under the peace agreements to completely disband this security body and to deploy the National Civil Police throughout the country within the deadlines provided for in the agreements.

167. The Human Rights Division has repeatedly complained about the seriousness of the situation with regard to ordinary violence. It has also warned about the possible links between ordinary violence and human rights violations, and about factors that contribute to violence which are linked to the non-fulfilment, delay in or partial fulfilment of commitments stemming from the peace agreements. Nevertheless, the actions taken by the Government to deal with crime appear to play down such warnings and tend to continue the policy of prolonging the existence of the National Police whose activities in respect of public security not only have not produced satisfactory results, but have also failed to stem the increase in ordinary violence especially in those areas where the National Civil Police has not yet been deployed.

168. The systematic practice of arbitrary detention in El Salvador—particularly administrative detention for petty misdemeanours, which are a violation of the principle of legality, a violation of the right to minimum procedural guarantees or which are carried out by bodies that are not specifically authorized by law to do so—can only be stopped by abrogating the 1886 Police Act, transferring jurisdiction for misdemeanours to the courts and by clearly regulating the power of auxiliary bodies to carry out such detentions.

169. The incidents of violence that occurred during the period covered by the report in the San Francisco Gotera, Sensuntepeque and Santa Ana penitentiaries have highlighted the serious crisis in El Salvador's penitentiary system and the failure of the prison authorities to carry out their duty to provide guarantees regarding human rights. These events also underscore the need to modernize the prison system as soon as possible and to allocate more resources to that sector. In that connection, the consideration and adoption of the prisons bill is an urgent task.

170. In the last few months, the National Civil Police has no doubt had a positive impact on the human rights situation in those areas where it has been deployed. However, it is essential that the shortcomings that have been identified during the active verification concerning, basically, the process whereby its members are selected, the inadequacy of resources and the inadequate training in police procedures that leads to arbitrary practices, be corrected promptly.

171. The immediate implementation of the constitutional reforms relating to the decentralization of the Supreme Court of Justice is crucial to the independence

that should be enjoyed by the judiciary in El Salvador. In that respect, the Human Rights Division is of the opinion that it is incumbent upon the current Legislative Assembly to initiate constitutional reforms that should be completed during the first session of the new Legislative Assembly to be installed on 1 May 1994.

Document 106

Statement by the President of the Security Council concerning elections held on 20 March 1994

S/PRST/1994/15, 7 April 1994

The Security Council has received the Secretary-General's report on the observation by ONUSAL of the elections in El Salvador on 20 March 1994 (S/1994/375). It has also received the Secretary-General's letter of 28 March 1994 (S/1994/361) drawing to the attention of the Security Council his continuing concerns regarding problems in the implementation of the Peace Accords in El Salvador.

The Security Council congratulates the people of El Salvador on the peaceful and historic elections held on 20 March 1994. It notes that the Special Representative of the Secretary-General stated on 21 March 1994 that in general the elections on 20 March 1994 took place under appropriate conditions in terms of freedom, competitiveness and security and that, despite serious flaws regarding organization and transparency, the elections can be considered acceptable. The Security Council calls upon those concerned to take the necessary measures, as recommended by the Secretary-General, to correct those shortcomings which appeared in the first round and thus to guarantee a genuine and indisputable expression of the will of the people in the second round of the presidential elections on 24 April 1994.

The Security Council calls for the full implementation of the Peace Accords. It shares the concerns expressed by the Secretary-General that progress is still required regarding the implementation of the points highlighted in his letter of 28 March 1994 (S/1994/361), particularly in relation to public security, including the deployment of the new National Civil Police (PNC) and the phasing out of the National Police (PN); the reintegration into society through transfers of land and other programmes of estranged groups, including former combatants; and the constitutional reforms recommended by the Commission on the Truth, especially as they relate to the reform of the judiciary. The Security Council urges those concerned to make every effort to ensure that further delays in those areas are avoided and distortions corrected, so that the process can gain momentum, the provisions of the Peace Accords be duly implemented and the goals of the peace process be fully achieved.

Document 107

Letter dated 21 April 1994 from the Secretary-General to the President of the Security Council concerning the pre-electoral situation as of 20 April 1994

S/1994/486, 21 April 1994

I have the honour to transmit to you the text of the progress report on the pre-electoral situation in El Salvador as at 20 April 1994, prepared by the Electoral Division of the United Nations Observer Mission in El Salvador (ONUSAL). The report was made public in El Salvador on 20 April 1994, the last day on which, according to the Electoral Law of El Salvador, public comments were allowed with regard to the electoral process.

I should be grateful if the attached text could be circulated to the members of the Security Council for their information.

(*Signed*) Boutros BOUTROS-GHALI

Annex

*Balance sheet of the pre-electoral situation
as of 20 April 1994*

1. This is a situation report on the monitoring in the last few weeks by the United Nations Observer Mission in El Salvador (ONUSAL) of the conditions for holding the second round of voting in the presidential election next Sunday, 24 April. When the Secretary-General's fourth report on the activities of ONUSAL's Electoral Division was issued (S/1994/375), the official results of the first round were still not known. The results of the voting in the presidential election were as follows: Alianza Republicana Nacionalista (ARENA), 49.03 per cent; Coalition Convergencia Democratica (CD)—Frente Farabundo Martí para la Liberación Nacional (FMLN)—Movimiento Nacional Revolucionaria (MNR), 24.9 per cent; Partido Democrata Cristiano (PDC), 17.87 per cent; Partido Conciliación Nacional (PCN), 5.39 per cent; Partido Movimiento de Unidad (PMU), 2.41 per cent; Movimiento de Solidaridad Nacional (MSN), 1.06 per cent; and Movimiento Autentico Cristiano (MAC), 0.83 per cent. In view of those results and according to Salvadorian electoral law since no candidate had obtained a simple majority, a second round of voting in the presidential election had to be held between the two candidates having obtained the highest number of votes. Moreover, having failed to obtain 1 per cent of the votes and in accordance with article 261 of the Electoral Code, the MSN, MAC and MNR parties will be eliminated. As a result of the election for the Legislative Assembly, the 84 seats have been allocated as follows: ARENA 39; FMLN 21; PDC 18; PCN 4; CD 1; PMU 1. Finally the 262 mayoralties are distributed as follows: ARENA 206; PDC 29; FMLN 16; PCN 10; MAC 1.

2. While the series of irregularities noted in the Secretary-General's previous report (S/1994/375) did not represent any significant manipulation and had no impact on the outcome of the presidential election, those irregularities could have influenced some results in the elections for the Assembly and the Municipal Councils, given the smaller size of the electoral districts, and might give rise to a substantial number of challenges.

3. In line with the foregoing and in a letter addressed to the Supreme Electoral Tribunal on 24 March, ONUSAL made recommendations pointing out the most relevant flaws that should be rectified in the second round of voting. Some referred to the organization of the elections: the number of polling centres, transportation for the voters, guidance and training of the election officers at the polling stations and electoral publicity. With regard to the Electoral Register, it was recommended that par-

ticular attention should be paid to ensuring that the lists of eligible voters publicly posted and those at the polling stations were identical. A consensus was reached on those aspects shortly thereafter between the candidates (ARENA and the CD/FMLN/MNR Coalition) and the Supreme Electoral Tribunal in the course of meetings to consider the problem, based on a previously agreed timetable.

4. The ONUSAL Electoral Division assigned observers to the five areas of work which the candidates and the Tribunal regarded as most important, namely, the Electoral Roll, Computation, Printing, the Electoral Project and Training. ONUSAL verified that the ballot papers were printed in its presence and that of representatives of the parties, with the exception of the first 10,000 or so test ballots that were not numbered. No numbered ballots were printed when the ONUSAL observers were not present and they reported that the printing of the ballot papers was completed without incident.

5. It is hoped that the increase in the number of polling centres to 35, in particular in the area of greater San Salvador, will serve to relieve the congestion caused by crowds of voters on 24 April. However, this measure may not be sufficient to solve the problem of access to the polling centres experienced on 20 March. Furthermore, in light of the upcoming rainy season, the installation of hundreds of open air polling centres continues to be very risky.

6. There is concern about the limited and uneven success of the training programme for members of polling centres and stations. With the exception of the Department of Chalatenango, ONUSAL observers have reported irregular attendance by members of ARENA and the Coalition at the Tribunal's training sessions.

7. By the same token, there is no evidence that information officers are being groomed to guide voters at the polling centres, as the Tribunal has been advertising. There is still enough time to attend to this need. It is imperative that the Tribunal designate these officials as soon as possible and that it place big signs at the entrance to the polling centres indicating the first and last names of each polling station.

8. It is cause for concern that it is taking so long to find an arrangement acceptable to the Tribunal for dealing with the problem of transportation despite the availability of financial resources from various donors. A formula is being finalized that would offer free transportation in the rural areas and an agreement is being negotiated with the urban bus companies guaranteeing that all lines that normally operate in the city will be functioning. Since the polling centres in El Salvador are arranged in alphabetical order, not on the basis of proximity to the voters, which is unusual in such cases, it is essential that

transportation be provided. It is clear that the supreme electoral authority cannot relinquish that responsibility.

9. ONUSAL has been informed that around 30,000 persons have been listed in the electoral roll, two thirds of whom had asked to be registered but had failed to submit the necessary birth certificates to support their requests. The remaining third consisted of replacements or changes. The Mission has also been informed that each polling station will receive two identical copies of the electoral roll. Previously, the rolls were different, in that the one at the polling table provided space for the voters to sign and make comments whereas the one posted for the public was more condensed. ONUSAL cannot but express its regret that, despite the amount of time and resources invested in registering voters, there continue to be problems that adversely affect the transparency of the electoral roll and the exercise of the right to vote.

10. With regard to the provisional count and the transmission of the results on the night of 24 April, it would be advisable for the Tribunal to do its utmost to avoid a recurrence of the information vacuum witnessed during the March election. It is obvious that for a number of reasons with which the Tribunal is familiar and which could recur on 24 April, the arrangements for collecting information were not workable. In this connection, ONUSAL has once again offered the Tribunal its technical services to collaborate with the staff resources available to the Tribunal in designing a system of information collection and phased counting of votes with a view to avoiding a recurrence of the distressing situation created during the first electoral round on 20 March. Together with the lack of information, that situation gave rise to speculation as to the fairness of the election, which the United Nations defended from the outset on the basis of the results of a "quick count".

11. With regard to challenges to the results of the voting, ONUSAL is concerned at the manner in which the file on the FMLN's protest against the electoral results in 37 municipalities was closed. It is the opinion of the Mission's legal services that those protests should have

been examined more carefully. At the same time it regrets that, to date, no meeting has been held, as initially agreed by the Tribunal, between the legal experts of the challenging party, ONUSAL and the Tribunal, in order to study in detail the legal basis for the Tribunal's decision.

12. ONUSAL welcomed as a very positive move, the signing of the declaration by the two presidential candidates on Monday, 18 April, in which they express their faith in the country's governability, they pledge to conduct a dignified campaign and they promise to work during the next two years towards comprehensive reform of the electoral system. The Secretary-General also referred to electoral reform in his report of 31 March (S/1994/375). The United Nations will always stand ready to provide technical support for a thoroughgoing reform of the electoral system that includes a single identity document, voting in the area of residence and a closer relationship between the formulas for representation in the Assembly and in the municipalities.

13. Before the signing of the declaration by the presidential candidates, their respective campaign managers met and sent a joint letter to all the national media asking them not to accept electoral publicity from organizations or individuals other than those affiliated with the political parties of the candidates. The monitoring by the Tribunal of compliance with the law governing this matter will be of paramount importance.

14. With regard to the atmosphere in which the campaign is developing, the Electoral Division has received complaints of acts of intimidation and attempts to buy votes, especially in the Department of Sonsonate. It is regrettable that there have been a few isolated acts of violence during the electoral campaign.

15. As to publicity in the media, during the past two weeks ONUSAL has detected some advertising "spots" that violate the electoral law and the spirit of reconciliation of the Peace Agreements. The Mission is gratified that the agreement between the two candidates and their respective campaign managers has elevated the tone of the campaign.

Document 108

Report of the Secretary-General concerning the second round of elections, held on 24 April 1994

S/1994/536, 4 May 1994

I. Introduction

1. The present report is the fifth in a series of reports that I have submitted to the Security Council on the activities of the Electoral Division of the United

Nations Observer Mission in El Salvador (ONUSAL), in connection with the elections of 20 March 1994 and the second presidential round thereof, held on 24 April 1994. My latest report of 31 March 1994 (S/1994/375) contained a general evaluation of the elections of 20 March. The purpose of the present report is to provide an evaluation of the second round of 24 April.

II. Preparation of the second round

2. In order to help overcome the serious irregularities detected on 20 March, the Electoral Division made a series of recommendations to the Supreme Electoral Tribunal on 24 March. Some of them related to the organization of the election: number of polling centres, transport for voters, guidance and training of electoral officials on the polling station teams and electoral publicity. With regard to the electoral roll, it was recommended that particular attention be given to ensuring that the lists that were displayed matched those at the polling tables. Consensus on these aspects was reached a few days later between the contending parties (Alianza Republicana Nacionalista (ARENA) and the MNR-CD-FMLN Coalition) and the Supreme Electoral Tribunal; the latter pledged to take steps to correct the difficulties noted.

3. In monitoring the implementation of these measures, the Electoral Division posted observers in the five areas of work which the contending parties and the Supreme Electoral Tribunal designated as most important: registration, computation, printing, electoral project unit and training. It was noted that the printing of the ballot papers was carried out in the presence of representatives of the parties and of ONUSAL, save for the first tens of thousands which were the results of trial runs and were unnumbered. No numbered ballot paper was produced without said observers being present.

4. An additional 35 polling centres were set up, the biggest increase being in the greater San Salvador area where the largest crowds had occurred on 20 March. This decision undoubtedly helped ensure that everything proceeded in a more orderly fashion on 24 April.

5. As for the training of members of the polling station teams, ONUSAL observed that the training programme prepared by the Tribunal had had uneven success. Save in the Department of Chalatenango, attendance at the Tribunal's training sessions by members of ARENA and the Coalition parties was irregular; those parties decided to train their own representatives separately.

6. Furthermore, the personnel assigned to give guidance to voters at the polling centres were selected by the contending parties from among their own members. By mutual agreement between the two candidates, and even though the Electoral Code did not provide for this, such personnel were identified with the distinctive marks of their respective parties. Some of them did useful work in providing guidance to voters at the polling centres. However, in many centres the use of party symbols by such personnel led to tension and confrontations.

7. Reasonable solutions were sought to the problem of transport for the voters. With the assistance of USAID and UNDP, arrangements were made to provide free transport in rural areas and to establish two free transport circuits in the San Salvador metropolitan area, using 130 buses bearing the logo of the Supreme Electoral Tribunal.

8. With regard to the electoral roll, a series of changes were made. On the one hand some 15,000 names were added to it; two thirds were people who had asked to be included on the roll but could not produce a birth certificate in support of their request, the remainder involved reinstatements and changes. In addition, the polling station teams received two identical copies of the electoral roll. Previously the copies were different; the lists at the polling tables had spaces so voters could sign, and to allow for comments, whereas those which were displayed in public were printed in smaller type. Finally, voters were given more information to enable them to find the proper polling place. A list of polling centres and polling stations, together with the full names of the first and last persons on the electoral list at each polling station was published in the newspapers.

III. The electoral campaign

9. The second round was preceded by an electoral campaign which lasted just over two weeks. ONUSAL observers were present at campaign activities; these were fewer in number and were attended by fewer people than those that preceded the first round. On the whole, there were no incidents affecting law and order although, regrettably, there were some isolated acts of violence. Nationwide, the Electoral Division verified some 50 acts.

10. We view as extremely positive the signing of the joint statement by the two presidential candidates on the morning of Monday, 18 April, expressing their commitment to the future governance of El Salvador, their determination to conduct a decent campaign and their pledge to make every effort during the next two years to overhaul the electoral system completely. I referred to the subject of electoral reform in my report of 31 March, following the first electoral round. Prior to the signing of the statement by the presidential candidates, their respective campaign managers had met and sent a joint letter to all the mass media in El Salvador, requesting them not to accept publicity from organizations or persons other than the contenders' political parties.

11. As of the signing of the statement, the tone of the electoral publicity improved. Until that time, the campaign had been taking place in a tense atmosphere, with plenty of electoral publicity, on the part of both contenders, of a kind that violated the electoral propaganda rules and the spirit of national reconciliation em-

bodied in the peace agreements. Moreover, the Electoral Division had received 16 complaints, some of them about acts of intimidation and attempts to buy votes.

IV. The conduct of the election

12. ONUSAL monitored proceedings on election day, 24 April, by posting 900 observers to cover all polling centres in the country, from the time the polling stations opened until the first vote count was completed. ONUSAL continued to observe the official vote-counting process in the Supreme Electoral Tribunal. Generally speaking, election day proceeded virtually without serious incidents affecting law and order or ballot-rigging, and there was a distinct improvement in the organization of the election, including the layout of the polling centres, the stationing of personnel to direct voters to the proper polling places, the finding of names on the electoral roll, free public transport and, on the night of 24 April, early broadcasts of the election results. All these factors contributed to a more organized election day, thanks to the joint efforts of both presidential candidates, the political parties which had nominated them, the Supreme Electoral Tribunal and the donor countries.

13. Throughout election day, ONUSAL observers noted the following kinds of irregularities: while most polling stations were open from 7 a.m. until 5 p.m., as provided by law, there were some which opened after 7 a.m. or closed before 5 p.m. In the Municipality of Pasaquina, 18 of the 23 polling stations ceased to be monitored by representatives of one of the candidates. Many complaints were received from both parties about Electoral Code violations by party members who were campaigning at polling centres. There were two complaints about armed civilians. The National Civil Police also detained two persons who voted twice. As in the first round, ONUSAL observers confirmed that a considerable number of citizens were unable to exercise their right to vote even though they had voter cards.

V. The results of the election

14. According to the final count by the Supreme Electoral Tribunal, announced at a press conference on 27 April at 5 p.m., the results of the second round of the presidential election were as follows: ARENA - 818,264 votes (68.35 per cent); Coalition - 378,980 votes (31.65 per cent); making a total of 1,197,244 valid votes. The total number of votes cast was 1,246,220, of which 3,467 were challenged, 40,048 were invalid and 5,461 were abstentions. The results were predicted on the night of 24 April by the Tribunal on the basis of a provisional count of more than 90 per cent of the votes. ONUSAL organized its own quick count, based on a sample of 294 polling stations, which showed, at 7.15 p.m. on 24 April, that ARENA had won 67.88 per cent of the votes cast and the Coalition 32.12 per cent.

15. At the time of issuance of my fourth report on the activities of the Electoral Division of ONUSAL (S/1994/375) the official results of the first round were not yet known. Voting in the presidential election gave the following results: ARENA 49.03 per cent, Coalition 24.9 per cent, PDC 17.87 per cent, PCN 5.39 per cent, PMU 2.41 per cent, MSN 1.06 per cent and MAC 0.83 per cent. The 84 seats contested in the election for the Legislative Assembly were distributed as follows: ARENA 39, FMLN 21, PDC 18, PCN 4, PMU 1 and CD 1. Lastly, the 262 mayoral districts were distributed as follows: ARENA 206, PDC 29, FMLN 16, PCN 10 and MAC 1.

16. The results of the presidential, legislative and municipal elections of 20 March may be considered final. The irregularities in the elections, referred to in my previous report (S/1994/375), did not constitute ballot-rigging and thus had no impact on the election results as a whole. Nevertheless, given that the electoral constituencies for the municipal councils are smaller, the irregularities may have affected some results there; they did give rise to a significant number of challenges. In some instances the Supreme Electoral Tribunal reached a decision after examining the evidence cited by the complainant. In other instances, such as the electoral challenges made by FMLN in 37 municipalities, the Tribunal agreed to hear the appeals but the evidence was not examined since it was decided that the appeal was not valid. ONUSAL legal officers determined that both the submissions and the Tribunal's decisions not to examine the evidence were tainted by procedural flaws. We expressed our concern at the manner in which these cases were closed. Given the political importance of the challenges and the need for transparency in elections of such significance it would have been wiser to deal more carefully with these appeals. In any event there is no appeal against Tribunal decisions on such matters, although the remedy of *amparo* under ordinary jurisdiction remains available to the individual.

VI. Final considerations

17. Subsequent to these elections problems remain in terms of the organization of elections, in particular concerning the preparation of the electoral roll, and there is an evident need for a thorough reform of the electoral system. The two candidates in the presidential election of 24 April have committed themselves to such a reform. The reform should not only resolve outstanding problems concerning the organization of the elections but also establish a new system offering better safeguards to ensure that all citizens are able to exercise their right to vote. The United Nations remains ready to provide technical

support in connection with such a reform, which should include as key elements a single identity document, provision for voting in the area of residence of the voter, standardization of the formula for representation in the Assembly and municipalities, and depoliticization of the Supreme Electoral Tribunal.

Document 109

Report of the Secretary-General on ONUSAL's activities from 21 November 1993 to 30 April 1994

S/1994/561, 11 May 1994, and addendum, S/1994/561/Add.1, 25 May 1994

I. Introduction

1. The present report, which describes the activities of the United Nations Observer Mission in El Salvador (ONUSAL) for the period from 21 November 1993 to 30 April 1994, is submitted to the Security Council in compliance with resolution 888 (1993), in which the Council, in extending the mandate of ONUSAL until 31 May 1994, requested me to report by 1 May 1/ on the operations of the Mission so that the Council might review its size and scope for the period after 31 May 1994, taking into account my recommendations for the fulfilment and completion of its mandate. The report follows my report of 23 November 1993 (S/26790) on the overall implementation of the Peace Accords between the Government of El Salvador and the Frente Farabundo Martí para la Liberación Nacional (FMLN).

2. With effect from 1 April 1994, I appointed Mr. Enrique ter Horst to serve as my Special Representative and Chief of Mission of ONUSAL as successor to Mr. Augusto Ramírez-Ocampo (see S/1994/288 and S/1994/289). I should like to take this opportunity to pay tribute to Mr. Ramírez-Ocampo's deep commitment to the cause of peace and reconciliation in El Salvador.

3. The work of ONUSAL during the period under review is described below in five sections devoted respectively to military matters; public security matters; the Commission on the Truth; economic and social matters; and the financial needs of post-conflict peace-building. The Mission's work in the area of human rights has continued to be the subject of a separate series of reports, the two most recent of which were submitted to the General Assembly and the Security Council as annexes to my notes of 18 January and 29 April 1994 (A/49/59-S/1994/47 and A/49/116-S/1994/385). Given the fact that the last report of ONUSAL on the question of human rights was issued only a few days ago, the present report does not contain a section devoted exclusively to that question. However, references are made whenever necessary to specific aspects of the work of the Division of Human Rights during the period. Since my report of 23 November, I have also submitted to the Security Council three reports and one progress report on the activities of the Electoral Division of ONUSAL (S/1994/179, S/1994/304, S/1994/375 and S/1994/486). I have also informed the members of the Council from time to time of developments relating to specific aspects of implementation of the Peace Accords and I recently raised with them my continuing concerns regarding certain problems in that connection (see S/1994/361 and S/PRST/1994/15). These problems relate especially to public security matters, the recommendations of the Commission on the Truth, the land transfer programme and other programmes for the reintegration of ex-combatants into civilian life. These aspects of the Peace Accords are accordingly discussed in some detail in sections III, IV and V of the present report.

4. In my November report, I shared with the Security Council my grave concerns with regard to the assassination of several political leaders, a development that had given rise to apprehensions that illegal armed groups with political objectives—the so-called death squads—were re-emerging. In the light of the recommendation of the Commission on the Truth that a thorough investigation of private armed groups be undertaken, I instructed the Director of the Division of Human Rights of ONUSAL to assist the Government in implementing the Commission's recommendation (see S/26689), a decision that was subsequently endorsed by the Council (see S/26695).

5. Intensive negotiations with the Government and FMLN by Under-Secretary-General Marrack Goulding and Mr. Ramírez-Ocampo culminated in the establishment on 8 December 1993 of a Joint Group for the Investigation of Politically Motivated Illegal Armed Groups composed of the National Counsel for the Defence of Human Rights, the Director of the Division of Human Rights of ONUSAL and two representatives of the Government of El Salvador nominated by the President (see S/26865 and S/26866). The Joint Group is to present a report with its findings and recommendations at the end of May 1994.

1/ The report is being submitted after the 1 May deadline with the consent of the Security Council.

6. Since the establishment of the Joint Group, several acts of violence have been committed against representatives of political or social organizations, including the assassination, immediately after the establishment of the Joint Group, of a member of the highest decision-making body of FMLN. Investigations are under way in an effort to clarify the motives for these acts and to identify the culprits. It is encouraging that, according to the most recent report of the Division of Human Rights, murders analogous to those committed during the final months of 1993 have not recurred. Notwithstanding this relative improvement in the human rights situation, violations of the right to life, due process and other fundamental rights have continued. It is to be hoped that the continuing efforts to investigate and punish crime and to strengthen democratic institutions will result in progress in the fight against impunity.

7. On 20 March 1994, the first post-conflict elections were held in El Salvador for the presidency, the vice-presidency, all members of the Legislative Assembly and the municipal councils, as well as representatives to the Central American Parliament. For the first time FMLN participated as a political party. The Electoral Division of ONUSAL verified the electoral campaign, which officially opened on 20 November 1993. The Division also observed, and provided support for, the Supreme Electoral Tribunal's registration of voters and delivery of voter cards.

8. As I reported to the Security Council, the elections were held under generally acceptable conditions, without any major acts of violence, although serious flaws regarding organization and transparency were detected (see S/1994/375). These were not, however, deemed to have had an effect on the final outcome. Since none of the candidates obtained the required absolute majority in the presidential race, a second round was held on 24 April 1994 between the two candidates with the highest number of votes, namely, those of the Alianza Republicana Nacionalista (ARENA) and the Convergencia Democrática/FMLN/ Movimiento Nacional Revolucionario (CD/FMLN/MNR) coalition. This second round resulted in the election of the ARENA candidate, Mr. A. Calderón Sol, who will take office on 1 June 1994. In view of the fact that a fourth and final report on the activities of the Electoral Division of ONUSAL, covering the second round, will be before the Security Council when it takes up the present report, the matter is not further discussed here.

9. The National Commission for the Consolidation of Peace (COPAZ) has continued its work with the presence of an ONUSAL observer. It has presented to the Legislative Assembly draft laws on the regulation of the holding of weapons and on private security bodies. Hav-ing been adopted by the Assembly, both laws are now being enacted. COPAZ has also recently recommended to the Assembly a number of constitutional reforms to deconcentrate the functions of the Supreme Court of Justice and further protect individual rights, in compliance with the relevant recommendations of the Commission on the Truth. Some constitutional amendments were eventually approved before the expiry of the Assembly's mandate on 30 April 1994. Although making some progress on both matters, they fall short of both the Commission's recommendations and the COPAZ proposals.

10. Work in the Forum for Economic and Social Consultation continued until mid-December, although its plenary sessions were suspended in November upon the withdrawal of the business sector. Having failed to reach a consensus on reforms to the Labour Code, the Government presented to the Legislative Assembly a draft that included some, though not all, of the points suggested by the International Labour Organization (ILO). The draft became law on 21 April 1994. Following the elections, intentions regarding resumption of the Forum's work remain unclear.

II. Military aspects

A. *Organic structure*

11. On 1 May 1994, ONUSAL had a strength of 22 military observers from Brazil, Canada, Colombia, Ireland, Spain, Sweden and Venezuela, and 7 medical officers from Argentina and Spain, deployed at headquarters and at two regional offices covering the entire territory of El Salvador. The corresponding strength on 1 November 1993 was 31 military observers and 7 medical officers.

B. *Recovery of military weapons held by private individuals*

12. Since the entry into force on 11 January 1994 of the Law for the Control of Weapons, Munitions, Explosives and Related Artifacts approved by the Legislative Assembly on 9 December 1993, ONUSAL has been verifying the replacement by the Armed Forces of El Salvador of registered military weapons in the hands of state authorities or institutions with other arms authorized by the above-mentioned law. Weapons in the possession of penitentiaries and a small number still in the hands of Salvadorian personalities remain to be replaced.

13. With regard to unregistered military weapons held by private individuals—civilians or discharged military personnel—the Government had undertaken to recover them through an information campaign that would begin immediately after approval of the relevant law. However, very few weapons were surrendered to the Armed Forces of El Salvador during the period stipulated

by the law. It is clear that a great many such weapons remain in the hands of individuals, either because insufficient information was provided or because of reluctance to hand them over. Because of repeated delays, what should have been an urgent process has been extremely slow and as a result the problem of arms proliferation continues to be a source of concern in El Salvador. Because of the relevance of the problem to the current crime wave, it is imperative that the Government take urgent concerted action to ensure the handing over of those weapons to the authorities.

C. *Clearing of minefields*

14. After various interruptions, the demining process, which began on 15 March 1993, concluded on 30 January 1994 with the clearing of some 425 minefields and the disposal of over 9,500 mines of various types. ONUSAL military observers participated actively in helping to overcome the problems that arose in the programme and in ensuring its successful completion.

15. ONUSAL military and police observers are taking part in a follow-up programme for the destruction of explosive artifacts, organized jointly by the Government of El Salvador, the United Nations Children's Fund (UNICEF), FMLN, the Armed Forces of El Salvador and the National Civil Police. To date, 845 of the roughly 900 artifacts uncovered so far have been destroyed. Current financial problems in the programme are being resolved by the Government with external financial assistance.

D. *Compensation of demobilized members of the Armed Forces of El Salvador*

16. As a result of an agreement signed on 15 December 1993 between the Government and the Association of Demobilized Personnel of the Armed Forces of El Salvador, compensation equivalent to one year's pay, as stipulated in the Peace Accords, has been made to 6,000 of the 18,000 demobilized members of the Armed Forces of El Salvador. Agreement was reached on 28 January 1994 to continue with the indemnities and to conclude payments on 30 June 1994. In subsequent conversations between the Government and the Association, with ONUSAL mediation, it was agreed to accept 31 December 1993 as the final demobilization date; to include certain administrative personnel of the Armed Forces of El Salvador as beneficiaries; and to establish a mechanism for the investigation of complaints. The agreement is, however, awaiting the written government ratification requested by the Association.

E. *Other matters*

17. As anticipated in November 1993 (see S/26790, para. 14), ONUSAL has continued to follow up

intelligence activities of the Armed Forces of El Salvador to verify that they conform with the doctrinal principles set forth in the Peace Accords and derived from the amended Constitution. Frequent contacts with both the Joint Chiefs of Staff of the Armed Forces and the State Intelligence Agency have enabled ONUSAL to verify the existence of an increasing delimitation and specialization of functions in each of these services. It is important that ONUSAL sustain its verification activities in this area.

18. With regard to the files of the disbanded National Intelligence Department, it has been verified that these continue to be in the care of the Joint Chiefs of Staff of the Armed Forces. This body, however, has informed ONUSAL that it can review the contents of the files.

19. ONUSAL military observers maintain their contacts with the Armed Forces at various levels and, as requested by the Government, continue to verify and destroy arms. They also collaborate with the Police and Human Rights Divisions on various issues, such as the investigation of armed bands in the country, and they maintain a reassuring presence in former conflict areas.

III. Public security matters

A. *Police Division*

20. The Police Division, which has an authorized strength of 353, has a current strength of 268 police observers from Austria, Brazil, Chile, Colombia, France, Guyana, Italy, Mexico, Spain and Sweden. Its task remains to monitor and assist the National Police until its complete replacement by the National Civil Police (see para. 47).

21. The Division has also sought actively to observe the performance of the National Civil Police in order to verify compliance with the Peace Accords. For some months after October 1993, it was not able to carry out this task satisfactorily owing to a lack of cooperation by the National Civil Police (see also paras. 30 and 42). However, in early March 1994, a small cooperation programme was started with the provision by ONUSAL police observers of training and advice to the National Civil Police Highway Patrol Unit. Arrangements are also now being made to establish a technical assistance programme that will enable recent graduates of the National Public Security Academy to benefit from the expertise and experience of the ONUSAL Police Division in a variety of subjects. This support will complement that currently being provided by the team from the United States of America that advises and assists the National Civil Police.

22. The Police Division also supports the Division of Human Rights, to which 20 police observers are seconded. Police observers conduct special inquiries when required and verify that appropriate security measures are

provided for FMLN leaders, as established by the Accords. Police Division personnel also oversee the admission examinations at the Academy and from late 1993 they supported the activities of the Electoral Division.

B. *National Public Security Academy*

23. The National Public Security Academy, which is responsible for the training of recruits to the National Civil Police, started its activities on 1 September 1992, four months behind schedule. Following the recent graduation of its thirteenth basic-level class, the Academy has produced a total of 3,923 basic-level and 102 executive and senior-level police. It is now training an additional 2,218 basic-level and 131 executive and senior-level students and it intends to graduate a total of 5,700 agents by 20 September 1994. About 240 officers will have graduated by late July 1994, as envisaged in the Accords. While the Government devoted 97,708,574 colones ($11,230,870) of its own resources to the Academy in 1992 and 1993, the budgetary allocation for 1994 is 89,760,970 colones ($10,317,351).

24. The Government will soon need to take important decisions regarding the pace of monthly intakes and graduations and the duration of the training courses at the Academy after the transition period, which should expire on 31 October 1994. The length of training courses could be increased in the future to improve academic quality. Simultaneously, the Academy will probably need to give increasing importance to further specialized training and to the retraining of those National Civil Police officers and agents who were deployed in the first two years with only very basic academic preparation. These retraining courses would be of special value for officers and agents with military backgrounds (especially those originating from the Criminal Investigation Commission and the Special Antinarcotics Unit), who did not attend the normal courses at the Academy. Special courses will have to be designed to train the basic-level commanders who will replace those personnel who have been carrying out those tasks on a provisional basis.

25. During the month of May, the Academy will carry out its first annual evaluation of the members of the new police force, as mandated by the Accords. This evaluation will provide the Academy, *inter alia*, with an indication of its own strengths and weaknesses, thus enabling it to undertake a thorough revision of its study plans and an assessment of its teaching staff. ONUSAL has identified consistent deficiencies in the training of members of the civil police in legal matters and the use of force and firearms. It has also observed a considerable imbalance in favour of former members of the National Police in the composition of the team of National Civil Police monitors responsible for discipline at the Academy.

ONUSAL's position is that if this imbalance is not addressed it could jeopardize the civilian character of the new police force, notwithstanding the Government's recent insistence that the idea of militarizing the National Civil Police has never arisen.

26. The Academy has continued to receive the support of an international team of experts from Spain and the United States of America that advises the Director and the Academic Council on aspects such as the recruitment and selection process, curricula, finances and discipline. Instructors from Chile, Norway, Spain, Sweden and the United States play a full part in the training. Currently, the Academy has a total of 40 international experts and instructors. Since it is essential that this international support be maintained, ONUSAL has, at the Government's request, asked those countries providing technical cooperation to extend it at least until December 1994. One of the most important tasks of the international team in the coming months will be to train the Salvadorian instructors who will replace it.

27. ONUSAL continues to monitor the functioning of the Academy and is represented at its Academic Council by an observer who speaks when important matters related to the Accords are raised. ONUSAL also cooperates with the Academy at other levels, especially with its Admissions and Selection Committee. It monitors the admission examinations and recommends improvements when necessary. The Division of Human Rights organizes, jointly with the Academy, seminars and workshops on human rights, and continues to provide literature on the subject. ONUSAL remains ready to provide personnel from its Police and Human Rights Divisions to support and complement the efforts of the international technical team and, at the request of the Academy, will provide support to the first annual evaluation of the National Civil Police.

C. *National Civil Police*

28. The National Civil Police, which began operating in March 1993, is now deployed in seven departments, in the urban areas of two more departments and in large sections of San Salvador. Deployment in the last four departments and in other rural areas where the National Police is still in charge of public security is to take place by the end of September 1994. At that date the National Civil Police should have replaced the National Police in all 14 departments of El Salvador, though this is two months later than envisaged in the Peace Accords. However, the Government recently indicated that the National Police would not be phased out until March 1995 as current crime levels in the country required more than the 5,700 National Civil Police agents envisaged in the Peace Accords (see para. 47).

29. The National Civil Police Divisions of Public Security, Antinarcotics, Criminal Investigations and Protection of Eminent Persons are currently operational, although the last three function largely with agents who are not graduates of the Academy. The Government should therefore encourage the specialized training of Academy graduates in order to incorporate them into these divisions. Although close to 250 agents have already undergone specialized training in traffic control and finance, both divisions are far from being fully operational. While members of the former are currently receiving additional training from ONUSAL (see para. 21), the Finance Division only deployed its first contingent on 11 May, over five months behind schedule. The deployment of the Finance Division must be accelerated as the Division should gradually replace the Customs Police, which is due to be demobilized on 31 October 1994 at the latest (see para. 45). The training of members of the Border Division has begun belatedly, given that its deployment should have started in early April; and the training of members of the Arms and Explosives and Environmental Divisions needs to be initiated if they are to begin their planned deployment in early June and during the second semester of 1994, respectively. ONUSAL has offered the Government the assistance of its police observers in the organization and implementation of the functional deployment of the National Civil Police and a response is awaited.

30. As I informed the Council in my November 1993 report (S/26790, paras. 31 and 32), ONUSAL has received little cooperation from the Government and the National Civil Police in its efforts to verify the incorporation, in accordance with the complementary agreement of 22 December 1992, of former Special Narcotics Unit and Criminal Investigation Commission personnel into the Antinarcotics and Criminal Investigations Divisions of the National Civil Police.

31. In order to correct the irregularities in the transfer to the National Civil Police of these personnel with military backgrounds, ONUSAL reached an agreement with the Government on the setting up of a Select Review Committee composed of the Directors-General of the National Civil Police and the Academy and the United States technical adviser to the National Civil Police. An ONUSAL representative participated in the Committee as a verifier. On 10 February 1994, the Committee decided that the Government should provide a complete list of the candidates for incorporation into both units, indicating whether or not they had attended the special Academy course, and the marks obtained in the psychotechnical and conceptual examinations, which they had taken on the recommendation of ONUSAL. Only those candidates who had attended the special course and

passed the examinations could be accepted into the National Civil Police. ONUSAL has not yet received that list.

32. The Select Review Committee also decided that, before joining the National Civil Police, officers of the Special Antinarcotics Unit and Criminal Investigation Commission would have to pass a special resident course at the Academy on the new civil police doctrine. Attendance at an additional special resident course would be required from agents who had joined both units after the complementary agreement of 22 December 1992. On 11 April 1994, the first two courses for officers and agents, of five and two weeks' duration respectively, started at the Academy. Similar courses were recommended by the Select Review Committee for the remaining members of both units.

33. The Committee also agreed to take necessary action if charges of serious human rights violations raised by FMLN against 46 members of the Special Antinarcotics Unit were corroborated. Thus far, no evidence has been produced.

34. The Committee also stated that former members of the Special Antinarcotics Unit and the Criminal Investigation Commission could join only the Antinarcotics and the Criminal Investigations Divisions of the National Civil Police and could not be assigned to duties outside those divisions until after December 1994. For its part, ONUSAL has made it clear that the officers of those units can at no time hold command positions in other divisions or in the departmental delegations of the National Civil Police without undergoing the regular Academy courses for officers. Furthermore, the Committee recommended that the Government start to train Academy graduates in antinarcotics and criminal investigation so as to incorporate them into the corresponding divisions of the National Civil Police. ONUSAL has recently ascertained that many of the former sergeants of the Special Antinarcotics Unit enrolled in the National Civil Police as sub-inspectors are now responsible for criminal investigations in a number of delegations of the National Civil Police, instead of working in their area of specialist expertise.

35. The appointments given to former personnel of the Special Antinarcotics Unit and the Criminal Investigation Commission also suggest discrimination against those personnel who joined the National Civil Police in compliance with all the requirements established by the Peace Accords. Although they did not undergo the normal course for senior-level officers at the Academy, the current chiefs of the Antinarcotics and Criminal Investigations Divisions, both of them former members of the Special Antinarcotics Unit and the Criminal Investigation Commission respectively, have been enrolled into the National Civil Police as Commissioners. With the Deputy-Director for Operations, there are now three commissioners in the National Civil Police, all of them former members of the Special Antinar-

cotics Unit and the Criminal Investigation Commission. 2/ So far, no Academy graduates have been granted the rank of commissioner. Likewise, 12 Special Antinarcotics Unit officers and 7 from the Criminal Investigation Commission have been enrolled as subcommissioners, while 44 sergeants of the former unit have joined as sub-inspectors (see para. 34). It must be noted that it is only after successfully undergoing a one-year course at the Academy that senior and executive-level graduates become subcommissioners and sub-inspectors, respectively. FMLN has objected to these appointments, indicating its understanding that under the complementary agreement of 22 December 1992 such personnel should join the National Civil Police only as specialists.

36. These developments have affected the delicate balance in the command structure of the police, which constitutes a key element in the Accords, under which 60 per cent of all positions should be occupied by personnel who did not participate directly in the armed conflict, 20 per cent by former National Police (military) members and 20 per cent by FMLN ex-combatants. Indeed, as a result of the above-mentioned enrolments, 30 subcommissioners in the new police force belonged to the old public security system, while only 7 are from FMLN and only 17 are civilians. Recent appointments of division and departmental chiefs also appear to favour former personnel of the previous security bodies. ONUSAL has raised this matter with the Government.

37. Similar imbalances exist at the basic level of the new police. While the National Police filled its 20 per cent share at the Academy months ago, FMLN has not been able to present enough candidates to fill its 20 per cent quota, and as a result only 13 per cent of Academy recruits are from FMLN. The incorporation into the National Civil Police of former Special Antinarcotics Unit and Criminal Investigation Commission members who had previously been part of the National Police has increased the latter's share significantly.

38. All these imbalances run counter to the letter and spirit of the Peace Accords and need to be urgently redressed in order to avoid further militarization of the new civil police. As requested by ONUSAL, it is essential that the Government provide the Academy with lists of former personnel of the Treasury Police, National Guard and élite battalions (immediate reaction infantry battalions) to enable ONUSAL to verify whether or not members of those bodies have been admitted to the Academy as civilians (see S/26790, para. 25). The Government should also provide ONUSAL with complete lists of current members of the National Police in order to verify that they do not join the Academy as civilians. This is especially important in view of information received by ONUSAL that former National Police personnel are being hired to fill technical posts within the National Civil Police.

39. In my November 1993 report (S/26790, para. 35), I informed the Council that it was essential to complete the organic structure of the new police with the immediate appointment of its Inspector-General and the establishment of the disciplinary and control units. The Government has indicated that the Inspector-General will be appointed by the new Minister for the Interior and Public Security who will assume his functions with the next administration. Since it is to this Ministry that the civil police will be subordinated in the future, its creation and the appointment to its higher posts of civilians with impeccable credentials will be among the most important tasks of the new Government.

40. The Director-General has now appointed the heads of the units on disciplinary investigation and control and the former unit has been operational for two months. ONUSAL, however, has received complaints that the National Civil Police has failed to take forceful action and to cooperate with the judiciary when its agents are reported to have been involved in unlawful behaviour. The Director-General of the National Civil Police has been meeting with the heads of the two units, in the presence of ONUSAL, with a view to correcting this situation. The control unit has yet to be provided with the human and material resources and legal framework that will permit it to begin the important task of supervising all police services.

41. The budget allocation of the National Civil Police for 1994 is 291,826,360 colones ($33,543,259), compared with expenses of 84,267,524 colones ($9,685,922) for the years 1992 and 1993. This represents a sizeable increase in the last six months in the resources provided to the National Civil Police by the Government. While in November 1993 the National Civil Police had 67 vehicles, 31 motorcycles and 134 portable radios, it now has 257 vehicles (30 of them donated by the United States Government, which has offered to deliver an additional 170), 35 motorcycles and 670 portable radios. The National Civil Police is in the process of installing a very modern communications system and most of its vehicles contain mobile radios. Having purchased a total of 4,000 handguns and 1,000 rifles, it now has at its disposal some 4,440 guns and 1,020 rifles, including those on loan from the Armed Forces of El Salvador. This equipment, which does not include that belonging to the Antinarcotics and Criminal Investigations Divisions, is considered to be sufficient to meet the needs of the 4,000 graduates currently deployed. Nevertheless, civil police premises still need considerable improvement.

2/ The Deputy-Director for Operations, a former army major, resigned on 3 May 1994.

42. ONUSAL has detected the following four main weaknesses in the functioning of the National Civil Police:

(a) There is an absence of clear guidelines and criteria regarding legal and police procedures, a problem that is compounded by deficiencies in the legal instruction received at the Academy. The unit for control of the National Civil Police should play an important role in providing such guidelines and supervising their implementation;

(b) There is insufficient coordination between the police and the Academy. One way to improve this could be to set up a permanent coordinating mechanism between the two institutions. The forthcoming evaluation of National Civil Police members by the Academy should be useful in bringing both institutions closer;

(c) There is a lack of coordination in the activities of the police, the judiciary, the Attorney-General's Office and the National Counsel for the Defence of Human Rights. The fight against crime and the simultaneous strengthening of democratic institutions can only be successful if there is a joint inter-institutional effort;

(d) In September 1993, in what can only be termed a self-defeating move, the Government did not request the extension of the technical assistance that ONUSAL had provided to the National Civil Police since April (see S/26790, para. 19), thereby depriving the new police of valuable support. Since then, in contrast to the welcome initially given to the new corps by the population, complaints of human rights violations by the National Civil Police have increased. In addition, both the Police and Human Rights Divisions of ONUSAL have faced serious difficulties in carrying out their verification activities as police units have been instructed not to cooperate with ONUSAL.

43. With a view to overcoming these weaknesses, ONUSAL has offered to resume the provision of technical assistance to the civil police and the terms of reference for the provision of such assistance are currently being discussed. It is encouraging that the Government has expressed interest in taking advantage of the experience and expertise of ONUSAL personnel in the field. The Director-General of the National Civil Police has recently asked ONUSAL to contribute to the legal training of his personnel and has produced jointly with the Division of Human Rights a set of guidelines on legal and police procedures to serve as a basis for the training of the National Civil Police officers and agents. This training is to be carried out jointly by the National Civil Police and ONUSAL, which have also established a coordinating mechanism for processing complaints of human rights violations and facilitating the Mission's verification duties.

D. *National Police*

44. Between October and December 1993, the National Police demobilized 900 agents. In January 1994, the Government announced the suspension of demobilization but subsequently informed ONUSAL of the demobilization of a further 900 agents between January and March. ONUSAL has requested an explanation of this apparent contradiction. Thus far, only around 10 per cent of all demobilized personnel have registered for reintegration programmes (see para. 46). According to the Government's phasing-out plan, a further 5,900 agents and over 1,000 administrative personnel currently deployed in four departments and parts of three other departments will have to be discharged before the 31 October 1994 deadline established by the Accords. ONUSAL has continued to urge the Government to accelerate the reduction of the National Police and to bring its phasing-out into line with the deployment rate of the National Civil Police.

45. The Peace Accords also call for the dissolution of the 1,211-strong Customs Police. The Government has committed itself to its demobilization, once the Finance Division of the National Civil Police becomes operational. As indicated above (para. 29), the first contingent of the Finance Division has been deployed. However, the Government has yet to announce its plan for the demobilization of the Customs Police.

46. The initiation of reintegration programmes for demobilized National Police personnel has suffered very serious delays (see also para. 86). Thus far, only 15 per cent of potential beneficiaries have participated in the counselling phase of the programmes and, as noted above, only 10 per cent of the reported 1,800 demobilized agents have registered in programmes. Decisive action will be needed by the agencies involved and by the National Police itself to ensure successful implementation of the programmes. In compliance with the Accords, a special effort by the Government will be required in order to ensure compensation equivalent to one year's pay to every demobilized National Police member.

47. Recently, the Government has proposed a redefinition of the agreed arrangements governing public security during the transition period, in order to ensure that when the National Civil Police replaces the National Police completely it will have more than the 5,700 agents referred to in the Accords. The changes proposed by the Government would delay until at least 31 March 1995 the full deployment of the National Civil Police scheduled for September 1994 and the parallel phasing-out of the National Police, which in conformity with the Peace Accords should be concluded by 31 October 1994. It has also expressed interest in negotiating with FMLN the incorporation into the National Civil Police of more

National Police, whose quota has already been exceeded (see para. 37). ONUSAL insists that any such alterations must be previously agreed between the parties to the Accords and must be implemented in a way that preserves the fundamental characteristic of the National Civil Police as a single and truly civilian police force nationwide.

IV. Commission on the Truth

48. Some progress has been achieved since my last report towards compliance with the recommendations of the Commission on the Truth. Before expiry of its term on 30 April 1994, the Legislative Assembly approved several constitutional reforms regarding the judiciary, which include the deconcentration of some of the functions held by the Supreme Court and the protection of individual rights. The amendments should be ratified by the current legislature, which initiated its work on 1 May.

49. In November 1993, the Christian Democratic Party had presented several draft reforms that would have complied with the Commission's recommendations. The initiative was not successful, however, since a majority of the Assembly was then opposed to discussing constitutional reforms during the electoral campaign, which opened on 20 November. The question was revived as the campaign drew to a close in March 1994. In April 1994, a number of legislators from the Christian Democratic Party and the Democratic Convergence, as well as independent legislators, agreed to promote reforms on the basis of drafts submitted to them by the Federation of Lawyers Associations. Proposals were soon put forward by various other organizations.

50. Significant progress was also achieved in CO-PAZ, which for several months had been unable to tackle the question because of lack of consensus. In a letter sent to me on 14 April 1993, COPAZ reported that it had recommended to the Legislative Assembly a number of constitutional amendments whose approval would have entailed a significant devolution of the Court's functions and improvement in the guarantees of due process.

51. Several reforms were finally approved by the Legislative Assembly on 29 April, but they fell short of the Commission's recommendations and the COPAZ proposals. No amendments were made to provisions regarding the appointment of judges and magistrates and their dismissal. These remain functions of the Court. According to the recommendations, these functions were to be removed from the Court and become the responsibility of the National Council of the Judiciary.

52. The power to suspend lawyers and notaries in the exercise of their profession was removed from the Court, as recommended, and assigned to a new entity, the National Council of Lawyers and Notaries. The five members who will constitute this Council will be elected by a two-thirds vote by the Legislative Assembly. Three of them will be elected from candidates put forward by the Supreme Court of Justice (one), the National Council of the Judiciary (one) and the Federation of Lawyers Associations (one). The remaining two will be elected directly by the Assembly from among professionals meeting the requirements established by the Constitution. The authorization of lawyers and notaries, however, which was also to be transferred to an independent entity, remains within the Court's responsibility.

53. Authority as regards granting *habeas corpus* was assigned to lower courts, as recommended. The Supreme Court is henceforth to deal only with those cases involving the trial of high government officials or revisions of lower judges' decisions denying the release of detained or arrested persons. The right to *habeas corpus* is applicable in cases of violations against the dignity or physical integrity of detainees and, in general, to all illegal or arbitrary detentions.

54. Authority concerning *amparo*, until now a function of the Court's Constitutional Division, has now been expanded to its other Divisions, depending upon the matter under consideration. No provision has been made, however, to extend it to lower courts, as recommended.

55. The Legislative Assembly is to approve an allocation of not less than 4 per cent of the national budget to the Judicial Organ. This allocation will also include the National Council of the Judiciary and the National Council of Lawyers and Notaries. The Assembly will also approve a 2 per cent minimum budgetary allocation to be distributed among the institutions comprising the Public Ministry.

56. The provision that dismissal of members of the National Council of the Judiciary requires a two-thirds majority of the legislature, which had already been approved through a reform of the relevant law, has now been incorporated into the Constitution.

57. Several amendments have been approved with regard to due process. They include, among others, the maximum period for detentions due to administrative misdemeanours, which has been reduced from 15 to 5 days. Although an improvement in comparison with the previous stipulation, this amendment falls short of recommendations made by the Commission on the Truth and the Division of Human Rights of ONUSAL.

58. Detainees' rights have been reinforced, in particular the right to be notified by the authority responsible for their detention, to refrain from self-incrimination and to a timely and appropriate defence. Extrajudicial confessions have also been eliminated, as a specific provision was made to the effect that detainees' confessions will have legal consequences only when made in the presence of the competent judicial authority and according to law.

59. Amendments involving individual rights were in general approved in the Legislative Assembly by consensus. Amendments relating to the judiciary did not obtain the favourable vote of all legislators belonging to the Christian Democratic Party or the Democratic Convergence, who had proposed more drastic reforms. In addition to those amendments, the Legislative Assembly, by a majority of votes, modified the terms of state grants for public services and the functioning of the Court of Accounts.

60. The amendments approved, which imply a partial reduction of the Supreme Court's highly concentrated power and considerable improvement in the guarantees of due process, do not, however, entail the in-depth institutional overhaul of the judicial system recommended by the Commission on the Truth. It is to be hoped that, following prompt ratification by the current Legislative Assembly, secondary legislation as well as administrative and budgetary measures will be adopted to put into practice the progress achieved. This, however, does not obviate the need to revert to further constitutional reform if full compliance with the recommendations of the Commission on the Truth is to be achieved. It is regrettable that this opportunity has been lost and that such compliance will have to wait another three years.

61. The Legislative Assembly has recently adopted the Convention against Torture and Other Cruel, Inhuman or Degrading Treatment or Punishment. However, reservations were expressed with regard to the competence of the Committee against Torture to investigate reliable information about the systematic practice of torture, to transmit its findings and the suggestions it deems pertinent, and to include a summary thereof in its annual report to the States parties and to the General Assembly. It is essential that this competence of the Committee against Torture be recognized as part of the monitoring of legality and of mechanisms for the protection of human rights. Reservations also apply to the recognition of the competence of the International Court of Justice to deal with controversies in relation to the interpretation or application of the Convention. El Salvador's adherence to the Convention is therefore partial and the recommendation of the Commission on the Truth on this point has not been satisfied.

62. Still to be ratified are the Optional Protocol to the International Covenant on Civil and Political Rights, the American Convention for the Prevention and Punishment of Torture and the Additional Protocol to the American Convention on Human Rights relative to Economic, Social and Cultural Rights (San Salvador Protocol), which should be effected as soon as possible. Furthermore, El Salvador is the only Central American country that has not recognized the mandatory competence of the Inter-American Court of Human Rights, the importance of which ONUSAL has consistently underlined.

63. Other recommendations of the Commission on the Truth and by the Division of Human Rights of ONUSAL that have not yet been implemented include the endowment of the National Counsel for the Protection of Human Rights with budgetary autonomy and the creation of a fund for the compensation of victims of human rights violations.

64. The Division of Human Rights has underlined the importance of following a strict timetable for the adoption in the Legislative Assembly of the drafts proposed by the Government relating to the criminal and criminal procedural codes, and draft laws on penitentiaries, a code of conduct for officials responsible for law enforcement, and other reforms that are important for the protection of human rights.

65. With respect to the dismissal of military or civilian officials and their disqualification from holding public office, clarification from COPAZ was sought regarding a letter it had sent to me on 9 August 1993 (see S/26581, para. 11) stating its position on these provisions. In a letter dated 31 January 1994 addressed to the Under-Secretary-General for Political Affairs, the *pro tempore* Coordinator of COPAZ stated that its previous communication should be interpreted as a request that non-implementation of those recommendations not be regarded as a violation of the Accords.

V. Economic and social issues

A. *Land transfer programme*

66. In my last report, I pointed out that the land programme, as agreed by the parties on the basis of the Secretary-General's proposal of 13 October 1992, had been proceeding at a very slow pace. In August 1993, the Government presented a plan to accelerate land transfers to former combatants of FMLN and landholders, the Acceleration Plan. It is evident that while the Government's wish to overcome the delays that had beset the programme must be welcomed, the Acceleration Plan can be a positive contribution to the overall peace process only if it is conceived as a means of implementing existing agreements—Chapultepec and the 13 October programme—rather than as a substitute for them.

67. The Acceleration Plan was supplemented in mid-November with operative guidelines, which spelt out in concrete terms how the Plan would be implemented. By that time, only 4,424 persons had received title to land. This represented less than 10 per cent of the maximum 47,500 potential beneficiaries from FMLN and the Armed Forces of El Salvador contemplated in

the 13 October programme. In spite of some progress, the target of providing titles to 12,000 persons by the end of the year, which had been accepted as feasible by both the Government and FMLN, was not met. In fact, by 31 December 1993 only 6,261 persons, slightly over half the target, had received title. Four months later, at the end of April 1994, this figure had reached 11,585, representing an increase from 10 to 24 per cent of the maximum number of beneficiaries, but still below the end-of-year target.

68.   Although the Acceleration Plan has facilitated land transfer in the short run, it has raised new problems for completion of the programme in the longer term. The main objection raised by FMLN to the operative guidelines presented in November 1993 was the fact that, as a result of the new verification rules imposed by the Government, potential beneficiaries were losing the rights recognized for them in the 13 October programme. The total number of FMLN beneficiaries contemplated in the Plan was approximately 25,000 instead of the 32,500 (7,500 ex-combatants and 25,000 landholders) contemplated in the 13 October programme. The latter programme is still the only valid agreement between the two parties and it must therefore remain the basis on which ONUSAL verifies compliance.

69.   More worrying was the provision in the operative guidelines for eviction of those who were occupying properties that had not been applied for by the 25,000 beneficiaries envisaged. FMLN objected to this as contrary to the Chapultepec and 13 October agreements, which stipulated that landholders occupying land at the end of the conflict would not be evicted until the Government had found an acceptable solution to their land tenure problem.

70.   In addition to those left out of the programme as a result of the new verification rules, there remained the problem of the so-called "non-verified" landholders. With regard to these, the Government had agreed at the 8 September 1993 high-level trilateral meeting (Government/FMLN/ONUSAL) that non-verified landholders would be dealt with at the end of the programme, as resources became available. FMLN accepted this at the time. In November 1993, the difficulty of transferring properties on which there were non-verified occupants (and the impossibility in most cases of relocating them), led me to ask the Government to show flexibility by accepting as many non-verified people on the negotiated properties as possible (S/26790, para. 52). The Government subsequently accepted all non-verified landholders (2,900 people) on the properties that were transferred during the first phase of the Acceleration Plan. This welcome flexibility unquestionably provided some impetus to the programme.

71.   In February 1994, although the first phase of the Acceleration Plan had not yet been fully implemented, the Government presented a second phase. This has raised a number of problems, which are discussed below.

72.   The problem of the non-verified landholders has surfaced again and with a new dimension. On 13 April 1994, after much delay, FMLN finally presented a list of all landholders whom they wanted included as beneficiaries in the programme, in addition to the 25,000 who had earlier been reverified by the Government. These "non-verified" landholders amount to 7,285 people. The total of beneficiaries would still be below the maximum of 32,500 for FMLN ex-combatants and landholders specified in the 13 October programme.

73.   The Government was under no obligation to include them now because of the agreement that they would be dealt with at the end of the programme, as accepted by FMLN on 8 September 1993. However, the impossibility of proceeding with the transfer of properties containing non-verified landholders has again brought the programme to a virtual standstill. In search of a solution, my Special Representative has been meeting with government officials and representatives of major donor countries to find ways to finance the early transfer of land to non-verified landholders. I am glad to report that, in its letter dated 5 May 1994, the Government has informed my Special Representative that financing is now available to cover transfer of land to all potential beneficiaries, including the non-verified landholders, thus removing one of the most serious obstacles to the implementation of this programme.

74.   The second phase of the Acceleration Plan has raised new problems by contemplating the issue by the Land Bank of credit certificates to potential beneficiaries. The latter would then negotiate terms for purchase of the land directly with landowners. FMLN has objected to the fact that these certificates have an expiry date (30 April 1995). Given past problems with land transfers and the fear that these might now worsen (since FMLN beneficiaries will be negotiating directly with the landowner without much technical assistance), the possibility that beneficiaries' entitlement might expire at a fixed date would be most disturbing. ONUSAL has reported the reaching of an understanding that the certificates could be renewed upon expiry. Justifiable concerns would be alleviated further and compliance with the 13 October programme restored if this understanding were to be made explicit in the certificates.

75.   The ceiling specified in the certificates for the credit to be provided is also at variance with the 13 October programme and requires a formal agreement by the parties to be amended. In that programme, the Government committed itself to transfer certain quan-

tities of land to FMLN beneficiaries, following the criterion of the Salvadorian Institute for Agrarian Reform whereby the size of a lot varies according to soil type. At current prices and exchange rates, the ceiling of 30,000 colones specified in the certification may be sufficient. However, in the event of a large devaluation or increases in land prices, the potential beneficiaries would not have access even to the small plots provided for in the programme. Though such an eventuality may be unlikely, it would be prudent to make provisions to safeguard against it.

76. A solution needs also to be found for the problem of human settlements (referred to in the agreements as *predios e inmuebles*). As stated in my last report (S/26790, para. 55), FMLN wants them transferred as they exist, with all the infrastructure and *en bloc*. This is a pressing issue since as many as 60 per cent of the properties to be distributed under the second phase of the Acceleration Plan fall into this category. These communities have an important infrastructure built up over the years, which their members would lose by relocating to other rural areas. For this reason, they would refuse to leave if owners did not want to sell, could not be found or had no title to the land to be transferred. A solution that does not entail breaking up these communities therefore needs to be found. The Government has agreed to present a plan to this effect two weeks after FMLN submits relevant information from these communities concerning the number of people and properties that they want included in the land programme.

77. Various points of tension extraneous to the land programme persist, especially in the properties contemplated in the agreement signed on 3 July 1991 between the Government and the peasant organizations and incorporated into the land programme, for which a satisfactory solution has not been found. This has led many owners to initiate legal actions for eviction and has resulted in land occupations by various peasant groups. Early in May, new tensions arose following the eviction of peasants from a property in Sonsonate.

B. *Reintegration programmes*

78. With considerable difficulty, ONUSAL has continued to work with the parties and with the United Nations Development Programme (UNDP) to promote implementation of the various medium-term programmes designed for ex-combatants of the Armed Forces of El Salvador and FMLN, as well as supporters of the latter who became landholders in the former zones of conflict. The many problems besetting these programmes were analysed in some detail in my last report. Administrative problems, financial constraints and lack of full cooperation apparently reflecting a lack of political will in the

mid-level bureaucracy have contributed in different degrees to serious delays.

1. *FMLN ex-combatants*

79. After much delay, all medium-term programmes for FMLN ex-combatants have now started. At weekly coordination meetings, the parties and ONUSAL are trying to improve communication and facilitate the solution of problems as they arise. The programme providing credits for small business has begun only recently, and only 322 of the 1,597 potential beneficiaries who were scheduled to receive credit by June 1994 have so far benefited from the programme. Those who have received credit are now supported by a two-year technical assistance programme.

80. On 31 December 1993, 3,634 agricultural credits for ex-combatants of both sides had been disbursed. The number of beneficiaries in the first three months of 1994 was only 271, in spite of the fact that this was a crucial period, just before the planting season started. The separate credit line for landholders was equally sluggish. As at 31 December 1993, 1,446 credits had been disbursed. In spite of ONUSAL's repeated requests, the Banco de Fomento Agropecuario has not provided updated information.

81. In addition to the lack of credit, the majority of demobilized Armed Forces of El Salvador and FMLN personnel who received title to land are still not able to cultivate in an effective way as a result of problems with the existing technical assistance programme. A new programme has been designed for the 1994/95 agricultural cycle, to be executed by the National Centre for Agricultural Technology. Since the Centre lacks the capacity to meet in full the demand for technical assistance, UNDP is preparing a proposal for a complementary programme that would make it possible to accommodate all beneficiaries of the land programme.

82. With regard to the programme for the 600 medium-level commanders (Plan 600), its training component has been completed and requests for small-business credit are now being formulated. Although agreement has been reached on the terms of the credits, communication and coordination problems between the participating organizations have delayed the process. By 3 May, the first two credits had been disbursed, but the Government announced at the same time severe restrictions on technical assistance as a result of budgetary constraints. This is a matter of great concern since technical assistance is a crucial component of the programme. Without it the chances of success are minimal.

83. As to other programmes, that for medical care for the war-wounded and disabled ex-combatants concluded in March 1994, after several extensions. Those who require continuous care will be referred to the Pro-

tection Fund (see para. 85). The credit programme for housing is seriously delayed as a result of funding shortages.

2. Ex-combatants of the Armed Forces of El Salvador

84. The programmes for demobilized members of the Armed Forces of El Salvador were initiated later than those for FMLN ex-combatants. The short-term programmes are scheduled to end during the first six months of 1994. With regard to medium-term programmes, the most advanced are those for agricultural credit and technical assistance. Nevertheless, credit has been disbursed to only 712 beneficiaries and 1,182 have received technical assistance. Within the scholarship programme, 381 out of the 600 potential beneficiaries have started their studies. With regard to the credit programme for small business, 6,131 demobilized members of the Armed Forces of El Salvador have received training that makes them eligible to receive credit, but the credit programme contemplates only 1,597 beneficiaries. So far only 154 credits have been disbursed.

3. War-disabled

85. Implementation of the law creating the Fund for the Protection of Wounded and War-disabled as a Consequence of the Armed Conflict is still in the preparatory phase, although some progress has been made since my last report (S/26790, para. 70). Its Board of Directors started to function with considerable delay upon the late disbursement by the Government of funds required for pre-operational activities. The Board has thus been enabled to begin the setting up of its administrative structure and to proceed with the additional registration of potential beneficiaries. The Board will also revise the existing actuarial study to define the resources required to finance the benefits contemplated in the law. The budgetary allocation for the Fund's full operation should be approved upon completion of the study.

4. Demobilized National Police personnel

86. Reintegration programmes for the National Police, which are similar to those for demobilized FMLN and Armed Forces of El Salvador members, consist of three phases, namely, counselling, training and credit and technical assistance. The first of these started on 15 February 1994 in six offices throughout the country. It was planned that programmes should begin with demobilized National Police, but when demobilization was suspended it was agreed that agents in active service could also enrol. As at 30 April, only 192 of the 1,800 demobilized agents had attended the counselling sessions. The National Police has not provided ONUSAL with concrete information on the whereabouts of the rest of those demobilized. Some 1,174 agents in active service entered the counselling phase.

C. Urban human settlements

87. The matter of urban human settlements, which involves houses vacated by their owners during the conflict and presently occupied by others, was dealt with at the high-level trilateral meeting of 8 September 1993. The Government agreed to address the problem outside the land programme and with additional financing after completion of a census carried out by COPAZ. In the census presented on 15 December 1993, COPAZ registered 1,373 houses, of which 752 are within the land transfer programme, thus reducing the problem of human urban settlements to the remaining 621 cases. The Government has since acquiesced in the design of a plan that could provide a solution to this delicate problem.

D. Forum for Economic and Social Consultation

88. In August 1993, the Forum agreed on an agenda that included the revision of several national laws related to labour conditions. They were the Labour Code, the Organic Law of the Ministry of Labour and Social Welfare, the Social Security Law and the status of public workers (see S/26790, para. 58).

89. Until the end of November 1993, the Forum concentrated on discussion of an International Labour Organization (ILO) proposal to reform the Labour Code. Although the three parties (representatives of Government, business and labour) came to an agreement on most of the proposals, 9 of the 49 points under discussion, which referred to important aspects of the right of labour to associate freely, remained unsettled. As I reported at the time (S/26790, para. 60), the business sector ceased its participation in the Forum when the electoral campaign began. Plenary sessions were thus suspended, although some work continued until mid-December.

90. On 13 December 1993, the Government presented to the Legislative Assembly a draft law to reform the Labour Code. It included most of the agreements achieved in the Forum while introducing new provisions and proposed to settle the nine disputed articles in a way that was considered unsatisfactory by the labour sector. The law was nevertheless passed with virtually no change on 21 April 1994. It provides for the establishment of a Labour Board with equal representation of the three parties but presided over by the Minister for Labour and limited to consultative functions within the structure of the Ministry of Labour.

91. With the conclusion of the elections, the future of the Forum remains unclear. Despite previous statements that it would return to the Forum after the elections, the private sector now appears to consider the new Labour Board a substitute for the Forum. Contacts with the Government are under way to establish feasible alternatives. In any case, the agenda of August 1993 remains

practically unchanged and the specific point on the status of public workers needs to be addressed as a matter of priority, since this group has been the source of most of the labour unrest in El Salvador in the past eight months.

VI. Financial needs of post-conflict peace-building

92. In my last report I pointed to the urgent need for additional resources to finance peace-related programmes in El Salvador, in particular those relating to the strengthening of the judiciary and other democratic institutions, including the National Civil Police, and those in support of human rights, including the National Counsel for the Defence of Human Rights. The need to finance crucial programmes for the reintegration of ex-combatants and their supporters into the civilian and productive life of the country was also mentioned in that context.

93. During the meeting of the Consultative Group held in Paris in April 1993, the Government reported a shortfall of $476 million to cover financial needs arising from the Peace Accords during the period from 1993 to 1996. In the Government's report to the Government Donors Meeting in March 1994, the shortfall for the same needs was shown to be some $376 million, distributed as follows: $51.1 million for the National Public Security Academy, $116 million for the National Civil Police, $7.8 million for the National Counsel for the Defence of Human Rights, $34.4 million for strengthening the justice system, $7.3 million for the National Council of the Judiciary and Judicial Training School, $6.8 million for the Supreme Electoral Tribunal, $37.5 million for compensation for the disabled, $63.7 million for the Land Bank, $18.7 million for housing, $14.2 million for agricultural credit and $17.9 million for small-business credit.

94. As I also indicated in my last report, donors have been generous in financing infrastructural and environmental projects but they have often been reluctant to finance some programmes directly related to the Accords that are crucial for peace consolidation. The Government's efforts in that regard, involving a total of $375 million, and those of the international community, involving grants or loans for an estimated total of $140 million for the period from 1993 to 1996, have been insufficient to cover all needs.

95. Although, as reported above (see para. 73), ONUSAL received a letter dated 5 May 1994 from the Government indicating that additional financing is now available for the transfer of land to all potential beneficiaries, including the 7,285 non-verified landholders, this will be effective only if it is integrated with agricultural credits and technical assistance for which additional financing is necessary. Other commitments undertaken by the Government in the context of the Peace Accords, such as the payment of financial compensation to demobilized Armed Forces of El Salvador and National Police personnel and credit for housing, still fall short of requirements.

VII. Financial aspects

96. In its resolution 48/243 of 5 April 1994, the General Assembly, *inter alia*, authorized the Secretary-General to enter into commitments for ONUSAL in an amount not to exceed $3,895,900 gross ($3,612,300 net) for the period from 1 June to 15 September 1994, subject to the decision to be taken by the Security Council in respect of the Mission. Should the Council decide to continue the mandate of ONUSAL as recommended in paragraph 100 below, I will seek any additional resources required for the operation of the Mission during the extension period.

97. The cash flow situation of the ONUSAL special account remains critical. As at 15 April 1994, unpaid assessed contributions to that account amounted to some $24 million for the period from inception until 28 February 1994. In order to provide the necessary cash flow requirements of the Mission, a total of $9 million has been borrowed from the Peace-keeping Reserve Fund ($6 million) and from other peace-keeping accounts ($3 million). These amounts have not yet been repaid.

VIII. Observations

98. The timetable that forms part of the Chapultepec Accords provided that almost all aspects of the Peace Accords would have been implemented before the new Government emerging from the elections of March/April 1994 assumed office on 1 June 1994. The main exceptions were deployment of the National Civil Police and demobilization of the National Police, which were to be completed later, on 28 July and 31 October 1994 respectively. As to the land transfer programme, it became clear that it would have to be extended into 1995. It was therefore expected that at least a vestigial presence of ONUSAL would be required after 1 June 1994. As is evident from the present report, serious shortcomings in implementation of the Accords mean that on 1 June 1994 much will remain to be done, in spite of all the efforts in recent months to make up for lost time.

99. My concerns on this score were expressed in a letter I addressed to President Cristiani on 15 February 1994. In that letter I touched especially on delays in the programmes relating to public security, land transfer and other aspects of the reintegration of ex-combatants into civil society. I raised these concerns, as well as non-compliance with the recommendations of the Commission on the Truth, in my letter of 28 March to the President of the Security Council (S/1994/361). On 22 April 1994, I received a detailed reply from President Cristiani, in which he assured me, *inter alia*, of the Government's

intention to comply fully with all the pending provisions of the Peace Accords and reaffirmed the irreversibility of the peace process. The President also offered explanations with regard to delays and difficulties experienced in the areas of concern mentioned in my letter to him, as well as in my letter to the President of the Security Council. It is nevertheless clear that the unresolved issues are of such importance as to make it even more necessary for ONUSAL to remain in existence for a further period with sufficient capacity to verify implementation of the outstanding provisions of the Accords and to make its good offices available to help resolve difficulties that may arise in that regard.

100. In this connection, it will be recalled that when the Government of El Salvador and FMLN asked the Secretary-General, in early 1990, to assist them in their efforts to achieve a negotiated solution to their long conflict, they set as goals not only the cessation of the armed confrontation but also the promotion of democracy, unrestricted respect for human rights and the reunification of Salvadorian society through the reintegration of the members of FMLN, within a framework of full legality, into the civil, institutional and political life of the country. 3/ The United Nations was asked to verify compliance with the agreements entered into by the parties. ONUSAL was established by the Security Council in order to conduct this verification and to use its good offices to promote compliance with the agreements, beginning with the San José Agreement on Human Rights of 26 July 1990 (A/44/971-S/21541, annex). The agreements include not only the Peace Accords taken as a whole but also the recommendations of the Commission on the Truth, which are mandatory under the Accords. I believe that the United Nations has a continuing responsibility, notwithstanding the delays that have occurred, to honour its undertaking to verify compliance with the Peace Accords, which were reached in negotiations carried out under its auspices, and that it is therefore necessary to extend the mandate of ONUSAL for a further six months, that is, until 30 November 1994.

101. During this period, I shall continue to reduce the size of ONUSAL as rapidly as implementation of the outstanding agreements permits. The Electoral Division has already been disbanded and the military component, which at its peak had a strength of 368, will be reduced by the end of May from 23 to 12 military observers. The main burden during the coming six months will fall on the core civilian staff in the Chief of Mission's office who are responsible for the all-important land transfer and reintegration programmes, on the Police Division, which has to verify the transfer of functions from the National Police to the National Civil Police throughout El Salvador, and on the Division of Human Rights, which, in

addition to its tasks of verification, is already helping the National Counsel for the Defence of Human Rights to build up its capacity to assume responsibility for those functions when ONUSAL is withdrawn. The Chief of Mission's office and the Division of Human Rights will probably have to remain at more or less their current strength (16 and 30 international staff respectively) for the new mandate period, but I have approved a plan that envisages a progressive reduction in the strength of the Police Division from its current 268 to 145 by 1 October 1994. I shall of course keep this matter under constant review.

102. Meanwhile, I appeal to the Government of El Salvador, both the outgoing and incoming administrations, and to all others concerned, to make the effort necessary to ensure that their remaining commitments are implemented with the least possible delay, in order to consolidate peace and prosperity in El Salvador. There are four areas that seem to me to require especially urgent attention:

(a) Agreement on measures to enhance the civilian character of the National Civil Police and to increase its strength;

(b) Accelerated demobilization of the National Police and its completion by the end of 1994, rather than extending it to March 1995; further transfers of National Police personnel to the National Civil Police, as proposed in the President's letter of 22 April, to be effected only with the concurrence of FMLN, as such transfers are not envisaged in the Peace Accords;

(c) A solution to the pressing problem of human settlements;

(d) Arrangements to ensure that those who have title to land under the land transfer programme also have access to agricultural credit and technical assistance in time for the current planting season.

103. In this critical phase of peace consolidation, I also appeal again to the international community for continued financial support for the peace-related programmes, which are so vital to national reconciliation, democratization and prosperity in El Salvador.

104. The present report unavoidably has highlighted the points where compliance has been lacking or incomplete. This is because the agreed timetable for the implementation process has been delayed and this must be rectified. Yet there have been notable advances, above all in the integration of FMLN into the political life of El Salvador. While the electoral process has shown major defects and these need to be corrected, the elections themselves were completed without violence—a significant achievement. I am confident that I speak for all

3/ Geneva Agreement, 4 April 1990.

Member States of the United Nations who have supported the Salvadorian peace process when I commend all the political parties and their leaders who ensured orderly elections. A heavy responsibility now lies upon the majority party, ARENA, and the leading opposition party, FMLN, to maintain their dedication to the political process and to strengthen the institutions of democracy in El Salvador. Only this effort can make possible the consolidation of lasting peace in their country.

105. It is with gratification that I commend the vital roles played by President Alfredo Cristiani and by the leadership of FMLN, headed by Mr. Schafick Handal. It is their strong conviction that arms must be abandoned and national reconciliation embraced that has restored peace to El Salvador. After he hands over his high office on 1 June 1994 to President-elect Calderón Sol, I have no doubt that President Cristiani, as President of ARENA, will not flag in his demonstrated commitment to preserve a lasting peace in his country.

106. In concluding, I wish to express my highest appreciation for the dedication and perseverance of all personnel of ONUSAL, led by my Special Representatives, who have spared no effort to restore hope to the Salvadorian people.

Addendum (S/1994/561/Add.1)

1. As I indicated in paragraph 96 of my main report (S/1994/561), I wish to inform the Council that the estimated cost of extending the United Nations Observer Mission in El Salvador (ONUSAL) for the six-month period from 1 June to 30 November 1994 would be approximately $14 million. The staffing component of the Mission would include a civilian staff of up to 92 international and 166 locally recruited staff, 12 military personnel and, initially 268 police personnel, who will be reduced to 145 by 1 October 1994. A breakdown of the estimated cost by main categories of expenditure is provided for information purposes in the annex to the present addendum.

2. It would be my recommendation to the General Assembly, should the Council decide to extend the mandate of ONUSAL, that the additional cost relating thereto should be considered an expense of the Organization to be borne by Member States in accordance with Article 17, paragraph 2, of the Charter of the United Nations and that the assessments to be levied on Member States should be credited to the ONUSAL special account.

Annex

Cost estimates for the extension of the United Nations Observer Mission in El Salvador for the period from 1 June to 30 November 1994

(In thousands of United States dollars)

		Amount
1.	Military personnel costs	170
2.	Civilian personnel costs	10 500
3.	Premises/accommodation	430
4.	Infrastructure repairs	-
5.	Transport operations	500
6.	Air operations	400
7.	Naval operation	-
8.	Communications	45
9.	Other equipment	20
10.	Supplies and services	250
11.	Election-related supplies and services	-
12.	Public information programmes	-
13.	Training programmes	-
14.	Mine-clearing programmes	-
15.	Assistance for disarmament and demobilization	-
16.	Air and surface freight	-
17.	Integrated Management Information System	-
18.	Support account for peace-keeping operations	685
19.	Staff assessment	1 000
	Total	14 000

Document 110

Letter dated 24 May 1994 from the Secretary-General to the President of the Security Council concerning agreement on a new "Timetable for the implementation of the most important outstanding agreements"

S/1994/612, 24 May 1994

Further to my report of 11 May 1994 on the United Nations Observer Mission in El Salvador (ONUSAL) (S/1994/561 and Add.1), I have the honour to inform you that on 19 May the two parties in the El Salvador peace process reached agreement on a new "Timetable for the implementation of the most important outstanding agreements". The text of that timetable is attached.

In connection with the above, I should also like to inform you that in the course of his visit today the President-elect of El Salvador, Mr. Armando Calderón Sol, reiterated to me his personal commitment to the terms of the Peace Accords and his desire to see these accords implemented without delay for the benefit of all Salvadorians.

I should be grateful if this information could be brought to the attention of the members of the Security Council.

(*Signed*) Boutros BOUTROS-GHALI

Annex

Timetable for the implementation of the most important agreements pending

19 May 1994

Armed Forces

1. The 289 weapons registered as belonging to the Armed Forces of El Salvador in the possession of penitentiaries and 11 of the 45 that are in State institutions shall be collected and replaced, in compliance with the Law for the Control of Weapons, Munitions, Explosives and Related Artifacts, by 20 May 1994 at the latest. The Government shall submit a report to ONUSAL concerning the 34 weapons still in the possession of State officials.

2. In view of the entry into force on 11 January 1994 of the Law for the Control of Weapons, Munitions, Explosives and Related Artifacts, and since the two-month period for the voluntary surrender of weapons intended for exclusive use by the Armed Forces of El Salvador in civilian hands has expired, the Government, with United Nations support, shall draw up, by 30 May 1994 at the latest, practical measures for the collection of such weapons. These measures may include extension of the period for voluntary surrender of weapons, accompanied by a broad publicity campaign, and the possible purchase of weapons with international financial support.

Public security 1/

3. With a view to ensuring full compliance with the Peace Accords, the parties agree to reschedule the following items pending in the area of public security:

A. *Deployment of the National Civil Police*

The National Civil Police shall complete its replacement of the National Police, wherever the latter are deployed, with a view to filling the vacancies by 31 January and, at the latest, by 31 March 1995. Following partial deployment in Ahuachapán and Sonsonate by the end of the present month, the replacement of the National Police by the National Civil Police shall be carried out in the following order: La Paz, Cuscatlán, Santa Ana, Ahuachapán and Sonsonate, La Libertad, rural San Salvador and metropolitan San Salvador.

The functional deployment of the Border, Environmental and Arms and Explosives Divisions shall begin on 2 June, 1 July and 1 August 1994, respectively. The deployment of all the functional divisions of the National Civil Police shall be concluded by 31 January and, at the latest, by 31 March 1995.

B. *Demobilization of the National Police*

The demobilization of the National Police shall be concluded by 31 January and, at the latest, by 31 March 1995. The Customs Police shall be disbanded once the Finance Division of the National Civil Police becomes operational, but in no case after that date.

C. Restructuring of the Ministry of the Interior and Public Security

The Government of El Salvador shall establish at the earliest possible time the office of the new Deputy Minister for Public Security. The Deputy Minister shall enjoy autonomy of administration and shall have political responsibility for directing the National Civil Police and the National Public Security Academy. He shall ensure, in particular, appropriate operational and doctrinal coordination between the two institutions.

D. *Regulatory machinery*

The Government undertakes to appoint the Inspector-General during the month of June 1994. The person appointed shall have legal training and experience, and special knowledge of human rights. The Government shall provide the General Inspectorate with the human and material resources for the proper performance of its duties, and shall ensure that its organic and functional structure are developed in accordance with the rules and that it becomes operational before 30 September 1994.

The Government shall provide the Control and Disciplinary Investigation Units with the human and material resources to enable them to be developed and put into service before 31 July 1994.

Two subcommissioners and the necessary administrative staff shall be appointed to the Control Unit.

The Disciplinary Investigation Unit shall consist of two sections. In the case of the first, dealing with investigation, there shall be appointed one subcommissioner,

1/ The parties undertake to comply with this complementary agreement without prejudice to their commitments under the remaining provisions of the Peace Accords relating to public security.

two sub-inspectors and six sergeants. In the case of the second, dealing with procedure, there shall be appointed one subcommissioner, two sub-inspectors and three secretaries with the rank of sergeant.

The Government shall request the necessary international technical assistance, in coordination with the United Nations, in order to ensure the full institutional consolidation of the General Inspectorate and the Control and Disciplinary Investigation Units.

E. Irregularities in the National Civil Police and the functioning of the National Public Security Academy

With the collaboration of the Government, the United Nations shall verify, in the National Civil Police, *inter alia*, the granting of ranks to ex-members of the Special Antinarcotics Unit and the Criminal Investigation Commission and the functioning of the Antinarcotics and Criminal Investigations Divisions, and the assignment of duties to the National Civil Police and the necessary balance between personnel of different origins. In addition, with the collaboration of the Government, the United Nations shall verify, *inter alia*, the functioning of the Academic Council, the teaching staff, the team of monitors and the recruitment and selection machinery of the National Public Security Academy. It shall also verify the study plans and the disciplinary regime.

In accordance with the results of that verification, the United Nations may, where necessary, make recommendations to the Deputy Minister for Public Security, by 30 June 1994 at the latest, with a view to ensuring that the appropriate corrective action is taken.

F. *Measures for promoting additional recruitment to the National Civil Police*

F.1. With a view to promoting the admission of qualified civilian personnel to the National Public Security Academy and the National Civil Police, the Government commits itself to the following actions:

(a) To raise the level of grants in the National Public Security Academy, especially those awarded to students at the executive and higher levels;

(b) To establish a specific budgeting system for the National Civil Police;

(c) To establish, without any discrimination on political grounds, cooperation agreements between the National Public Security Academy and non-governmental organizations in such a way as to ensure the active participation of those organizations in the campaign to promote civilian recruitment to the National Public Security Academy of persons so entitled, consisting of verified non-combatants of the Frente Farabundo Martí para la Liberación Nacional (FMLN), providing that all the necessary regulatory requirements are fulfilled.

F.2. If, despite the measures described above, the National Public Security Academy is unable to restrict its recruitment entirely to persons who did not participate directly in the armed conflict, the Government may favour the recruitment of members of the National Police to the National Civil Police, subject to the following requirements:

(a) The admission of such persons to the National Public Security Academy may be commenced only after compliance with any recommendations that may be made by ONUSAL as referred to in section E.

(b) This recruitment shall be limited to a maximum of 1,000 agents at the basic level, including technical and administrative personnel.

(c) It shall be carried out in a regular and gradual manner, with full compliance with admission requirements, including approval of the entrance examinations and attendance at and completion of the regular six-months' course at the National Public Security Academy, without prejudice to the independent candidates admitted to the relevant course at the National Public Security Academy.

(d) Before submission of an application for entry to the National Public Security Academy, the conduct of the candidates shall be assessed by a committee composed of the Directors of the National Civil Police, the National Public Security Academy and the National Police, a subcommissioner of the National Civil Police who did not participate directly in the armed conflict, and a representative of ONUSAL. The committee shall interview each candidate and review the original documents submitted by each of them.

(e) The Government shall provide the United Nations with complete lists of the current personnel of the National Police and of the demobilized personnel of the Treasury Police, the National Guard and the Immediate-Reaction Infantry Battalions.

G. Verification

The United Nations shall verify compliance with this agreement, for which purpose it shall have unrestricted access to all documentation and information that it might request from the competent authorities.

Land-transfer programme

4. The Government shall institute the measures provided for in the second phase of the Acceleration Plan which it has submitted, including the amendments agreed to in the Joint Working Group. In the light of the financial commitments undertaken by the international community, the Government has decided to proceed concurrently with the transfer of land to beneficiaries verified by the Office for Agrarian Coordination, and to the list of landholders submitted by FMLN on 13 April 1994. In order to accelerate the execution of the Plan, which shall be concluded by 30 April 1995, the parties agree to take

the necessary steps to achieve approval of the legislative decree embodied in it, within the shortest possible time.

5. The Government shall put forward a special scheme for the transfer of land in the rural human settlements of Morazán and Chalatenango in the Joint Working Group on land, within 15 days after FMLN has provided the relevant information.

Reintegration programmes

6. The Government shall implement the reintegration programmes by the dates laid down by the General Coordination Bureau and shall ensure its efficient functioning (see note, annex II, d.).

7. Within the normal guidelines and programmes, the Government shall implement programmes of basic and middle-level education for the 800 young persons who were under 16 years of age on 1 February 1992, with the support of food programmes, and shall appeal to international organizations for additional sets of tools. If the beneficiaries do not want a formal education, appeals shall be made to the European Union and the Gesellschaft für Technische Zusammenarbeit, for support to vocational programmes. These programmes must be drawn up by 30 June 1994 at the latest.

8. The Government, as part of its overall budget for 1995, shall propose to the Legislative Assembly the opening of a budgetary item entitled "Fund for the Protection of Wounded and War-disabled as a Consequence of the Armed Conflict".

Recommendations of the Commission on the Truth

9. The Government shall promote the necessary action, by 30 May 1994, at the latest, to enable the Legislative Assembly to approve, at the earliest possible date, the legislative measures set forth in annex I, which shall reflect the relevant recommendations of the Commission on the Truth.

10. The Government shall take the necessary measures to ensure that the Legislative Assembly approves the instruments of ratification of the international human rights instruments, on the basis of the recommendations of the Commission on the Truth. (See annex I.)

Follow-up

11. The parties and the United Nations shall hold tripartite meetings every two weeks in order to follow up the actions described in this timetable and its annexes.

Annex I

a. *Draft laws submitted to the Legislative Assembly for its approval*:

1. Reform of the Code of Criminal Procedure in order to lay down the basic principles to be followed in procedures for arrest;

2. Elimination of extrajudicial confession (embodied in the constitutional reform recently approved, which required ratification);

3. Reform of the Code of Criminal Procedure in order to reduce administrative detention to 24 hours;

4. A draft law on penitentiaries.

b. *Draft laws to be submitted to the Legislative Assembly*:

1. A new Penal Code;

2. A new Code of Criminal Procedure;

3. Reform of the rules for provisional detention and release on bail during the proceedings;

4. A draft law on *habeas corpus*.

c. *Laws now being drafted in the context of the judicial reform being instituted by the Ministry of Justice*:

1. Repeal of the 1886 Law on the Police and, as a consequence, replacement of police jurisdiction over minor offences, which shall be assigned to justices of the peace;

2. Regulations on house searches;

3. Rules of conduct for police detention, in accordance with the Code of Conduct adopted by the United Nations;

4. Measures to secure compliance with procedural deadlines (the Government states that they are envisaged as part of the draft new Code of Criminal Procedure).

d. *Draft laws the formulation of which is currently in the preliminary stage*:

1. A new law on the judicial profession, including provisions on the decentralization of powers of the Supreme Court of Justice;

2. Measures to render effective the recourse to *amparo*;

3. The establishment of a special procedure for rendering effective material compensation for victims of human rights violations (the Government states that this is envisaged as part of the draft new Code of Criminal Procedure);

4. The creation of a fund for the compensation of victims of human rights violations (the Government has informed the Secretary-General with a view to obtaining the assistance of the international community).

e. *Ratification of international instruments*:

1. Signed by the Government and not yet submitted to the Legislative Assembly:

-Optional Protocol to the International Covenant on Civil and Political Rights;

2. Submitted by the Government and approved with reservation by the Legislative Assembly:

-United Nations Convention against Torture and Other Cruel, Inhuman or Degrading Treatment or Punishment;

3. Submitted by the Government and awaiting approval by the Legislative Assembly:

-Optional Protocol to the American Convention on Human Rights (San Salvador Protocol);

-Convention on the Political Rights of Women;

4. Not submitted by the Government to the Legislative Assembly as being considered contrary to the Constitution, or for other reasons:

-Conventions Nos. 87 and 98 of the International Labour Organization;

-Convention on the Non-applicability of Statutory Limitations to War Crimes and Crimes against Humanity;

-Inter-American Convention to Prevent and Punish Torture;

-Acceptance of the compulsory jurisdiction of the Inter-American Court of Human Rights established under the American Convention on Human Rights.

FMLN considers that all the above instruments, which are included in the recommendations of the Commission on the Truth, should be ratified.

Annex II

Action arising from the Peace Accords which should be concluded

Land-transfer programme

a. The Government shall take the appropriate steps to ensure that Decree No. 385 remains in force until the land-transfer programme has been finalized. Decree No. 403 shall also remain in force.

b. The land credit certificates may, if necessary, be extended beyond 30 April 1995, as agreed in the Joint Working Group.

c. The Government shall complete the formalities for the transfer of the 17 properties pending among those provided for in the Agreement of 3 July 1991 by 30 June 1994 at the latest. To that end, the Government,

through the Salvadorian Institute for Agrarian Reform, shall continue the relevant negotiations, in which the landowners, the beneficiaries and ONUSAL shall participate, by 30 May 1994 at the latest.

d. The Government shall facilitate verification by the United Nations of compliance with the constitutional principle governing the allocation of surplus land from properties that exceed 245 hectares.

Integration programmes

Ex-combatants of FMLN and landholders

a. The Government shall guarantee access by the beneficiaries of the land-transfer programme to agricultural and livestock credit.

Ex-combatants of the Armed Forces

b. Demobilized members of the Armed Forces shall continue to be compensated, as laid down in the Peace Accords and in compliance with Decree No. 784 approved by the Legislative Assembly and the agreement of 23 March 1994, by 15 June 1996 at the latest.

Disabled

c. Until the approval of the special budget for the operational stage of the Fund for the Protection of Wounded and War-disabled as a Consequence of the Armed Conflict, the Government shall ensure the provision of funds to meet their most urgent needs.

Table of reintegration programmes

d. [See table on page 566.]

Urban human settlements

As agreed at the tripartite meeting of 8 September 1993, and as soon as COPAZ has carried out a census of 621 units, the Government shall conduct the corresponding study in order to solve the problem, which shall be submitted to ONUSAL by 30 June 1994 at the latest. The parties and the United Nations shall make efforts to encourage the international community to participate in the financing of the solution chosen.

Forum for Economic and Social Consultation

The parties shall exercise their best offices to have the Forum reconstituted by 30 June 1994 at the latest, since it has not completed the tasks assigned to it, yet they continue to be necessary for the stability and economic development of the country.

Timetable for reintegration of FMLN

Programme	Starting date	Ending date	Length	Activity
Credit for microbusinesses	21 Feb. 94	31 Oct. 94	8 months	Drawing up of profiles Provision of credit
Technical assistance	15 May 94	15 Dec. 95	19 months	Technical assistance for profiles and projects
Agricultural and livestock credit	28 Feb. 94	31 May 94		Disbursement of credit for crops and livestock production in winter
	28 Feb. 94	31 Aug. 94		Approval of remainder of requests for credit
Technical assistance I	1 Apr. 94	31 May 94	2 months	Consultancy services for credit
Technical assistance II	1 May 94			Start of technical assistance*
Programme for middle-level leadership (plan 600)	15 Feb. 94	31 Aug. 94	5.5 months	Drawing up of profiles of credit projects
	1 Mar. 94	30 Sep. 94	7 months	Analysis of request and granting of credit
	15 May 94	31 Jan. 95	7 months	Provision of consultancy services for setting up micro-enterprises
		15 Jun. 94		Provision of funds to provide credit for housing
	15 Jun. 94			Start on operational provision of credit for housing
Scholarships	13 Aug. 93	Aug. 98		Granting of scholarships
Emergency housing (UNDP)	Nov. 93	30 Jun. 94	7 months	Completion of construction process, first phase
(UNDP)	Jul. 94	May 95		Second phase of programme
(SAN/HABITAT)	15 Dec. 93	30 Jun. 94	6.5 months	Delivery of sets of building materials
Permanent housing	Jun. 93	Jun. 95	24 months	Construction of permanent housing
Medical care	Nov. 92	30 Jun. 94		Administrative closure AMED**

Note: It should be understood that any change in the starting date will cause a corresponding change in the date for the conclusion of the programme.

* Executed by the National Centre for Agricultural and Forestry Technology (CENTA) and non-governmental organizations.

** Programme of medical care for the disabled.

Document 111

Security Council resolution concerning the peace process in El Salvador and the extension of ONUSAL's mandate

S/RES/920, 26 May 1994

The Security Council,

Recalling its resolution 637 (1989) of 27 July 1989,

Recalling also its resolutions 693 (1991) of 20 May 1991, 714 (1991) of 30 September 1991, 729 (1992) of 14 January 1992, 784 (1992) of 30 October 1992, 791 (1992) of 30 November 1992, 832 (1993) of 27 May 1993 and 888 (1993) of 30 November 1993,

Recalling also its presidential statements of 18 March 1993, 1/ 11 June 1993, 2/ 5 November 1993 3/ and 7 April 1994, 4/

Having considered the report of the Secretary-General of 11 May 1994, 5/

Having considered also the reports of the Secretary-General of 31 March 1994 6/ and 4 May 1994, 7/ on the observation of the electoral process,

Noting with satisfaction the successful completion of the electoral process in El Salvador, despite irregularities that had no impact on the election results as a whole,

Noting with appreciation the continuing efforts of the Secretary-General to support the full and early implementation of the agreements signed by the Government of El Salvador and the Frente Farabundo Martí para la Liberación Nacional (FMLN) to maintain and consolidate peace and promote reconciliation in El Salvador,

Welcoming the Secretary-General's observation that there have been notable advances in the process of national reconciliation, particularly the integration of the FMLN into the political life of El Salvador,

Concerned at the continuing delays in fully implementing several important components of the peace accords, including *inter alia* the deployment of the National Civil Police and the phasing out of the National Police, the questions related to the transfer of lands, the reintegration into civilian society of ex-combatants and war disabled and several recommendations of the Commission on the Truth,

Noting with satisfaction, in this context, the conclusion, on 19 May 1994, of an "Agreement on a timetable for the implementation of the most important agreements pending" 8/ between the Government of El Salvador and the FMLN,

Welcoming the commitment of the President-elect of El Salvador, reiterated before the Secretary-General, to comply fully with all Peace Accords and to consolidate national reconciliation as reported in the Secretary-General's letter of 24 May 1994, 9/

Welcoming also the work of the United Nations Observer Mission in El Salvador (ONUSAL) and noting its vital importance to the peace and reconciliation process in El Salvador,

Reiterating the necessity, in this as in all peace-keeping operations, to continue to monitor expenditures carefully during this period of increasing demands on peace-keeping resources,

1. *Welcomes* the reports of the Secretary-General of 31 March 1994, 6/ 4 May 1994 7/ and 11 May 1994; 10/

2. *Welcomes* the fact that both the first and the second round of the elections took place under appropriate conditions in terms of freedom, competitiveness and security;

3. *Expresses concern* that important elements of the peace accords remain only partially implemented;

4. *Reaffirms* its support for the Secretary-General's use of his good offices towards the early completion of the El Salvador peace process;

5. *Calls upon* all concerned to cooperate fully with the Secretary-General's Special Representative and the Observer Mission in their task of verifying implementation by the parties of their commitments;

6. *Urges* the Government of El Salvador and the FMLN strictly to comply with the "Agreement on a timetable for the implementation of the most important agreements pending";

7. *Requests* the Secretary-General, in this context, to keep the Security Council informed, as appropriate, on progress made on the implementation of the above-mentioned Agreement, and to report no later than 31 August 1994 on compliance with its timetable and on other relevant issues including measures undertaken to contain the costs of the Observer Mission;

8. *Stresses* the need to ensure that, under appropriate verification by the United Nations, the police and public security provisions of the peace accords are scrupulously observed, in particular the completion of the demobilization of the National Police, as well as the enhancement of the civilian character of the National

1/ S/25427.
2/ S/25929.
3/ S/26695.
4/ S/PRST/1994/15.
5/ S/1994/561, Add.1.
6/ S/1994/375.
7/ S/1994/536.
8/ S/1994/612, annex.
9/ S/1994/612.
10/ S/1994/561.

Civil Police, in accordance with the timetable agreed by the Government of El Salvador and the FMLN;

9. *Urges* all concerned to remove all obstacles facing implementation of all aspects of the land transfer programmes, so that they are completed within the timetable agreed by the parties;

10. *Stresses* the need to accelerate reintegration programmes for ex-combatants of both sides in conformity with the timetable agreed by the parties;

11. *Reaffirms* the need for full and timely implementation of the recommendations of the Commission on the Truth;

12. *Urges* all States, as well as the international institutions engaged in the fields of development and finance, to contribute promptly and generously in support of the implementation of all aspects of the peace accords;

13. *Decides* to extend the mandate of the Observer Mission until 30 November 1994 in the terms recommended by the Secretary-General in his report of 11 May 1994; 10/

14. *Requests* the Secretary-General to report by 1 November 1994 on the Mission, including on the fulfilment and completion of its mandate and on modalities for its progressive withdrawal; and invites the Secretary-General, in consultation with competent specialized agencies, to prepare modalities for assistance to El Salvador, within the framework of the peace accords, for the post-Observer Mission period;

15. *Decides* to remain seized of the matter.

Document 112

Letter dated 31 May 1994 from the Secretary-General to President Cristiani conveying his regrets that he will be unable to attend the ceremony inaugurating President Cristiani's successor

Not issued as a United Nations document

I deeply regret that I will be unable to join you on the occasion of the inauguration of Dr. Armando Calderón Sol as your successor in the Presidency of El Salvador.

Until the very last minute, I had hoped to be able to join you at this culminating moment in your Presidency. I would very much have appreciated the opportunity of your departure from office to pay homage once again to the role that you played at a crucial period in your country's history. You took over the Presidency in 1989 determined to achieve peace by negotiation, and with the strong support of your countrymen you succeeded. In your memorable speech at the signature of the Peace Accords at Chapultepec, you acknowledged that the causes of the conflict that had torn your nation for over a decade were profound, and that much had to be done to remove those causes. Remarkable progress has been made to this end, and you can view your accomplishments with great satisfaction. I have no doubt that your name will be permanently and justly linked to the noble cause of peace in El Salvador.

I wish you all success in your future endeavours.

Please accept, Mr. President, the assurances of my highest consideration.

(Signed) Boutros BOUTROS-GHALI

Document 113

Report issued on 28 July 1994 by the Joint Group for the Investigation of Politically Motivated Illegal Armed Groups (extract: conclusions and recommendations)

S/1994/989, 22 October 1994

I have the honour to transmit herewith the report presented in El Salvador on 28 July 1994 by the Joint Group for the Investigation of Politically Motivated Illegal Armed Groups.

As you are aware, in November 1993, gravely concerned by the assassination of several political leaders in El Salvador, I instructed the Director of the Division of Human Rights of the United Nations Observer Mission in El Salvador (ONUSAL) to assist the Government in implementing the recommendations of the Commission on the Truth regarding the investigation of illegal groups (S/26689). As a result of this initiative, the Joint Group, composed of the National Counsel for the Defence of Human Rights, the Director of the Division of Human Rights of ONUSAL and two representatives of the Government of El Salvador nominated by the President, was established on 8 December 1993 (S/26865).

The creation of the Joint Group was endorsed by the Security Council (S/26695, S/26866) and the Council requested me to keep it informed of developments on this matter.

The Joint Group conducted investigations throughout the first half of 1994. At the end of May, the members of the Group requested that their six-month mandate be extended by a further two months, that is until 31 July 1994, in order to allow them sufficient time to follow up on their findings and to begin planning procedures for the transfer of unfinished investigations to the appropriate national institutions. This extension was agreed to by the President of El Salvador and by myself.

The attached report contains the Joint Group's findings regarding politically-motivated violence in El Salvador and its recommendations for the strengthening of the investigative structures of the new National Civil Police and for appropriate reforms within the judicial system. In addition to this report, the Joint Group has made available to the Salvadorian authorities, to the National Counsel for the Defence of Human Rights and to ONUSAL, a Restricted Annex of evidence which requires further investigation. Now that the authorities are in possession of this information, it is my strong conviction that efforts to investigate and eradicate illegal armed gorups should continue as a necessary prerequisite for the consolidation of peace and democracy in El Salvador.

I should be grateful if you could bring this information to the attention of the members of the Security Council.

(*Signed*) Boutros BOUTROS-GHALI

Annex
Letter dated 28 July 1994 from the Joint Group for the Investigation of Politically Motivated Illegal Armed Groups addressed to the Special Representative of the Secretary-General for El Salvador and Chief of Mission of ONUSAL

We officially deliver herewith the Final Report of the Joint Group for the Investigation of Politically Motivated

Illegal Armed Groups, in compliance with your mandate of 8 December 1993.

(Signed) Carlos Mauricio MOLINA FONSECA

(*Signed*) Juán Jerónimo CASTILLO

(*Signed*) Diego GARCIA SAYÁN

...

V. *Conclusions and recommendations*

A. *Considerations regarding the execution of the mandate*

1. The Joint Group has exhaustively analysed the information gathered during the period covered by its mandate. The evidence thus collected, consisting of inputs of various natures and origins, is considered sufficient to establish an adequate characterization of the phenomenon of politically motivated violence in El Salvador at present. Nevertheless, evidence that would enable one to point to individual responsibilities to the extent of making it public is limited. As previously mentioned, the evidence is being delivered to the competent authorities in a confidential annex together with the present report.

2. In carrying out its investigations, the Joint Group encountered various types of difficulties and obstacles that stood in the way of its arriving at more concrete results. Its findings, it is believed, are only part of the complex phenomenon that constituted the object of the task undertaken. Without question, the subject dealt with by the Joint Group continues to arouse great apprehension in various segments of Salvadorian society, a situation that renders it difficult, if not downright impossible, to approach.

3. The Joint Group feels compelled to mention that the collaboration received did not measure up to expectations or, in some cases, promises made. This assessment applies to the official sector, political parties and non-governmental organizations and is not intended to imply that the investigations were deliberately blocked. Yet it must be recognized that in some cases an active approach that would have imparted the necessary momentum to the investigations was not forthcoming.

4. It is obvious that among the population, the wounds of the recent past connected with the drama of political violence are still fresh. Fear, mistrust of institutions charged with conducting investigations, and impunity have a decisive impact on the will of the citizens, causing them to hold back from behaviour that might bring subsequent reprisals. Unfortunately, owing to the still existing conditions of insecurity, the attitude of "looking the other way" continues to guide the responses of many individuals and institutions that might possess

relevant information for an investigation of this type. This is especially true when the events or situations to be investigated are very near in time and consequently pose, for those in possession of information, far greater threats and risks.

5. The mandate given to the Joint Group was "to assist the Government in applying the recommendation of the Commission on the Truth with respect to carrying out an in-depth investigation into illegal armed groups". This mandate, despite its original operating and time limitations, was, in the opinion of the Group, duly accomplished. It is now time for the investigation and subsequent punishment of the type of criminal acts involved here to be fully taken up by the component national institutions, with the committed support of Salvadorian society as a whole. A context in which a new National Civil Police is being built with effort and the foundations are being laid for a reform of the Judicial Organ is more than adequate for successfully meeting this immense challenge.

6. The international community provided the initial impulse for this task, which by its very nature must be ongoing and long-term. Such cooperation will no doubt continue to be offered to the extent necessary, but will be directed toward assisting permanent institutions, which must assume unwavering responsibility for the task. The Joint Group is convinced that the new political times in which the country is living will enable the entire national community to take up a vigilant attitude toward those institutions, which will acquire their legitimacy through their actions and the results that they gradually show to society.

B. Conclusions based on the results of the investigations

7. On the basis of the mass of information handled by the Joint Group, it can be concluded that the so-called "death squads", with the characteristics they had in the 1980s—as described in Chapter II (Background) of this report—represented a phenomenon different from the politically motivated violence existing at present in El Salvador.

8. Those structures, as organized in the past, answered to the political and social situation prevailing at the time, which is unquestionably not the same today. The Joint Group concluded that maintaining the contrary will irremediably lead the wrong way in terms of orienting investigations so as to make it possible to define the phenomenon properly today and thus be in a position to eradicate it. The conflict has ended and the overwhelming majority in terms of sectors, groups and individuals have redefined their roles in society, opting in favour of the exercise and practice of democracy as mechanisms of political action and struggle.

9. The results of the work undertaken by the Joint Group pursuant to its mandate do not allow it to present any categorical conclusions to the Salvadorian people. The Group can affirm, however, that it gathered sufficient evidence pointing beyond a reasonable doubt to the action of groups and persons who continue at present to choose the path of violence for achieving political results. That information, which identifies concrete individuals and situations, is a fundamental starting point for enabling the competent national institutions, in exercise of their legal powers, to go deeper into the investigations and, where appropriate, determine criminal responsibilities.

10. On the strength of the investigations conducted, the Joint Group feels that the phenomenon of political violence has at present its own characteristics, which can be identified, notwithstanding all the complexity of the subject. On the basis of the information gathered, it can be affirmed that there exist solid grounds for asserting that the broad network of organized crime that flails the country, in which, the evidence shows, there is active participation of members of the armed forces of El Salvador and the National Police, cannot be divorced from many acts of politically motivated violence.

To be sure, political motives do not seem to constitute the sole or even the essential driving force behind these structures, which engage predominantly in acts coming under the label of "common crime", but with a high degree of organization and infrastructure. Yet important questions arise concerning the present ties of persons earlier identified with the activities of the "death squads" to highly organized criminal structures that devote themselves in particular to bank robberies, car theft and traffic in arms and drugs, among other illicit activities.

11. The substantial change in the political situation—due to the transition from war to peace—has left no operating room for persons who participated in the armed conflict and members of the "death squads", who have had to seek other structures and *modi vivendi* to which to transfer the methods and procedures used in the recent past.

What is apparently taking place is a shift toward more decentralized structures geared primarily to common crime and exhibiting a high degree of organization. Nevertheless, those same structures no doubt maintain intact their ability to assume, when circumstances require, the role of perpetrators of politically motivated criminal acts. The process of political transition seems, then, to leave no room for structures that might be referred to as "classic"; many of their members as well as individuals who find it difficult to adapt to new conditions become a focus of new and powerful organized criminal structures. They are presumably joined by persons affected by dramatic changes in the country's institutional landscape, such as the reduction of the armed forces of El Salvador, the demobilization of FMLN and the dismantling of the old security bodies and the National Police.

12. Furthermore, to the metamorphosis of the "death squads" as a result of the peace process must be added another characteristic that appears to emerge from the investigations: the fragmentation of earlier structures. Locally, one can see signs of the action of groups that pursue political objectives, using violent means for that purpose. Such groups tend to be closely connected with acts of common crime and are characterized by a high degree of organization, logistics and the support, in certain cases, of State agents.

13. To these factors one must add another that proves to be an effect of inertia in a post-war situation, namely so-called "private political violence": in other words, the phenomenon whereby certain acts of violence occur which are politically motivated but in the commission of which neither criminal structures nor agents of the State play a role. These apparently relate more to situations in which "accounts to be settled" explain specific criminal acts. To the extent that such acts are properly investigated and punished, and in view of the spirit of national reconciliation that is flowing in from various sectors of the society, one may hope that such a phenomenon will gradually spend itself.

14. The Joint Group, in its investigations, collected information on specific situations and cases. The information includes evidence relating to the alleged participation of private persons and State employees in criminal acts that fall within the limits of its mandate. Nevertheless, as mentioned earlier in this report, the data obtained do not constitute full evidence on the basis of which one might publicly point to personal responsibility in respect of those implicated in the information received. For that reason, that information is being turned over on a confidential basis to the competent authorities in order to enable them to utilize it in accordance with the law.

15. The Joint Group concludes that, despite the great strides in the process of pacification and the efforts made by Salvadorian society to consolidate a climate of national reconciliation, there still exist data that support the well-founded suspicion that recourse to violence in order to solve political differences has not yet been definitively eradicated. The universe of cases analysed by the Joint Group yields sufficient evidence to back up that affirmation.

Political violence, either organized or in the form of "private political violence", as a way of settling old disputes is still present. The gravity of this situation

demands that each and every Salvadorian, and even more so those with institutional responsibilities, make every possible resource available for the great national task of eradicating once and for all this phenomenon that has caused, and still causes, so much harm to the country.

C. Recommendations

16. The Joint Group deems it opportune, based on the analysis of political violence in El Salvador, to propose to the official institutions and the different sectors of society a series of recommendations intended to guarantee a proper system for the prevention/punishment of this type of crime.

17. It is obvious that the grave problem of the persistence of recourse to violence as a means for settling political differences affects the entire Salvadorian community, irrespective of political or social status. Beyond the direct victims, the country's authorities and the Government of the Republic, in particular, find themselves sorely affected in their legitimacy and their ability to bring the society together within the perspective of consolidation of peace and reconciliation among Salvadorians. The sinister phenomenon described in this report undermines the stability of the peace process and, in an endless chain, nourishes attitudes of violence, generates mistrust in democratic institutions and discourages the productive sectors.

18. As stated earlier in this report, the Joint Group expresses its conviction that a situation having the scope of that covered by its mandate requires permanent activity. Taking on and resolving such issues in a consistent manner must be guided not by time-limits but by results, for which a sophisticated process urgently needs to be carried out. It will require appropriate technical and human resources and a juridical framework that grants the bodies charged with conducting it all procedural and substantive powers conducive to a consistent result. A task of this type must necessarily, by its very nature, be carried out by the competent national institutions, within a context of support and supervision by all sectors of society.

19. Here the new National Civil Police has an unusually important role. In order for this experiment, in itself a challenge, to have proper results in a situation as complex as that of El Salvador today, it is absolutely essential to provide it with the necessary resources for carrying out the job of criminal investigation in such a way as to offer the citizens the certainty that political violence and organized crime in the country will be definitively extirpated.

20. With this in view, the Joint Group considers it necessary, first and foremost, to strengthen the mechanisms of police investigation, creating within the PNC Criminal Investigation Division a special unit for dealing

with the phenomenon in question. Such a unit might have the following characteristics:

(a) The criteria for the selection of its staff would have to ensure much-needed confidence among the various social and political sectors, in addition to technical efficiency in the performance of its investigatory functions. Due examination of the previous histories of the members of the unit is deemed advisable if the citizens are to have the proper trust in the special unit;

(b) Its members must receive thorough and proper specialized training, in view of the complexity of the subject with which they will be working. Politically motivated crime has special characteristics, which means that investigation must be broader than is required in cases of common criminality. For that purpose, appropriate specialized courses might be introduced within the National Public Security Academy, along with continuous updating and refresher training within the National Civil Police. In this regard, technical assistance and advanced training courses abroad might be especially useful.

(c) The special unit must also have all the requisite technical and logistic means for properly performing its task of investigation. This means not only the support of a qualified technical crime investigation laboratory—which basically already exists—but also efficient information systems, a communications network that functions properly, transport means that match service needs and modern weapons to enable the unit to deal when necessary with situations of extreme danger. The high efficiency required of the members of the unit, in view of the nature of the material with which they will be working, and the high risk involved in that work make it advisable for the agents and leaders of such a special unit to receive a remuneration commensurate with the importance of their job.

(d) For the purposes mentioned above, the international community must render to the Government of El Salvador the necessary technical and financial cooperation, in a manner to be determined, so as to qualify the members of the special unit and equip the unit with the requisite material resources to enable it to become an efficient, solid body respected by the citizenry.

(e) In the area of institutional relations, it is essential that the Attorney-General's Office fully assume its constitutional mandate to direct criminal investigations, in cooperation with the National Civil Police. Consequently, the new special unit must firmly establish a connection with that Office so as to permit efficient investigation of politically motivated criminal cases within the institutional framework. Thus, the entire State machinery qualified to conduct criminal investigations must operate in a harmonious, transparent manner.

(f) Given the grave situation faced by El Salvador owing to the activities of organized crime—a situation that constitutes a serious menace to the social and political stability of the country—and in view of what has been stated in this report regarding the possible relationship between those powerful structures and politically motivated crime, such a PNC special unit can also be highly effective in fighting organized crime.

21. With regard to the judicial system, the Joint Group feels that it is necessary to advance further with its reform so as to impart to that system the degree of efficiency demanded for trying cases of politically motivated crime. The Joint Group expresses its favourable expectations regarding the new dynamics that the Judicial Organ will acquire with the entry into operation of the new Supreme Court of Justice. In the way of more concrete mechanisms for consideration, the Joint Group strongly recommends the following:

(a) The new Supreme Court of Justice should definitively undertake a proper "purification" of the court system in respect of magistrates and judges who, based on the assessments made by the National Council of the Judiciary, have been found guilty of violations of the law or misuse of authority or do not measure up to the high responsibilities that their office implies. This will give a crushing blow to the enormous vices that have marked the Judicial Organ in recent years, the most serious of which include impunity and corruption.

(b) From the standpoint of organic law, the Joint Group considers that it is essential to adopt, within a framework of respect for due process of law and human rights, the necessary legal reforms to provide a special procedure for those cases in which there come to light criminal acts involving either alleged political motives or ties to organized crime. This would make it possible to provide, in such cases, sufficient guarantees of the safety of any victims, their relatives or witnesses, and would at the same time constitute a clear statement of the priority accorded by the State to such situations, which directly affect national stability.

For that purpose, the Joint Group suggests that an appropriate solution would be to appoint, in accordance with the law, designated or special judges to try criminal cases of the type in question. Such a solution might be made viable through the reform of secondary legislation, especially the Basic Law of the Judiciary, the National Council of the Judiciary Act and the Career Judicial Act.

From the procedural standpoint, the legal reform should empower the Supreme Court of Justice to attribute competence to the designated or special judge in cases involving possible political motives or organized crime, in view of the serious consequences they entail for a climate of normal peaceful coexistence in the country.

The power to assign a criminal case to a designated

or special judge would belong to the Supreme Court of Justice, though any interested person or institution might, in exercise of the right of petition, request such assignment. Once such assignment was made, the original trial judge would be declared incompetent and would transfer all records and documents relating to the proceedings to the designated or special judge. The trial of the case, down to its final resolution, would take place in the capital of the Republic, where the designated or special judge would set up his office.

(c) Serious consideration should be given to the possibility of issuing, for a transitory period, bounty legislation permitting release from or reduction of criminal responsibility in exchange for important, duly corroborated information containing substantial evidence for the detection and arrest of the actual perpetrators and, in particular, the persons responsible for the planning of the criminal acts referred to in this report. In a manner that must be clearly set out in the law, the authority might even order a change of identity, material support and the departure to another country of the person or persons concerned.

(d) Finally, the Joint Group stresses the need for the Judicial Organ to establish the necessary coordination with the Attorney-General's Office and the National Civil Police for laying down unified criteria for the investigation of crimes and the interpretation of the different types of evidence and establishing the formalities of extrajudicial procedures, so as to prevent the occurrence of irregularities that subsequently entail the nullity of important police operations. to achieve this, it is considered necessary to set up a permanent mechanism of high-level coordination among the hierarchies of the different organs involved in this process, possibly including, among other things, periodic refresher courses for the officials concerned.

22. The Joint Group requests the National Counsel for the Defence of Human Rights to create a technical verification mechanism relating to everything involved in the investigation of common crime in which political motivation is assumed to exist. For that purpose, the institution in question must be provided with a technical team and the necessary instrumentation, inasmuch as those resources do not exist at present.

23. The Joint Group views in a positive light the current policy of the Government of the Republic on security bodies. It is felt that, as the process of demobilization of the National Police is accelerated, the situation will evolve even more favourably, in view of the fact that the participation of members of that institution in incidents investigated by the Joint Group and in other recent occurrences connected with organized crime has been established.

Similarly, the Joint Group deems the strengthening of internal controls within the armed forces necessary with a view to preventing conduct in violation of the law on the part of any of its members and, should it occur, detecting such conduct, so that measures can be taken to turn those allegedly responsible over to the ordinary courts of law.

24. In addition, the Joint Group considers that the Salvadorian State must increase its supervision of information and intelligence activities in conformity with the new policy on such matters arising from the Peace Accords.

In this regard, it is stressed that the existence of evidence that intelligence work is being done by units of the armed forces in clear violation of the constitution is a matter of deep concern. It is obvious that such activities, in addition to being outside the legal system of the State, involve the permanent risk of being used for the political control of certain sectors of the population. What is more, as the legal framework indispensable for the indispensable supervision of an activity of that kind does not exist, the result of such intelligence work can be used by groups or individuals, either within the State apparatus or without, for the achievement of their own political interests.

25. The State Intelligence Agency (OIE), moreover, must assume fully its constitutional function. It is essential—for the security not only of the State itself, but also, and fundamentally, of its citizens—that the State Intelligence Agency should have the political and technical capacity to centralize intelligence concerning situations and cases such as those analysed in this report, for the proper handling of such intelligence is essential to institutional stability and the climate of peace in favour of which Salvadorians have chosen.

26. As stated before, the persistence of a situation in which violence for political ends is not properly combated and eradicated has a marked effect on the climate of pacification and reconciliation for which so many sacrifices were made by the entire Salvadorian people. The task of uprooting this phenomenon must be taken on by the entire community as a major national endeavour. At present, no one can ultimately benefit from criminal acts of this kind.

Consequently, every individual, each as befits him, must make the necessary contribution for challenging the climate of dread, insecurity and resentment that political violence generates:

- The Government of El Salvador must exercise within the State constant vigilance in order to detect possible illicit acts on the part of its employees, whether committed for political ends or connected with organized crime. This will make it possible to purge the State machinery definitively, offering the citizens an exemplary message that will generate security and trust. The different State organs (Judicial Organ, Attorney-General's Office and National Civil Police) will thus be able to shape a picture combining modernity, efficiency and firm, democratic exercise of their respective authority.

- The political parties are under an obligation publicly to declare recourse to violence permanently out of bounds, so as to discourage any of their possible adherents who may still place their trust in repudiable methods of that kind. It would be most favourable for El Salvador if the rejection of politically motivated violence were to become a theme agreed on by all political forces and those forces gave the citizens clear and definite signals to that effect. In this respect the mass media can play a crucial role.

- Social organizations and non-governmental organizations, especially those for the protection of human rights, have a unique part to play in this new phase of El Salvador's history. The laudable role of the human rights organizations during the painful years of systematic violations that the country experienced is undeniable. They must continue and strengthen that work and maintain their watchfulness over State institutions; moreover, when conditions permit, they should assume a task of coordination and collaboration in investigations and the proposing of solutions. The gravity of the subject of this report makes that essential.

Document 114

Report of the ONUSAL Human Rights Division covering the period from 1 March to 30 June 1994 (extract)

A/49/281-S/1994/886, 28 July 1994

I. *Introduction*

1. The Peace Accords signed between the Government of El Salvador and the Frente Farabundo Martí para la Liberación Nacional (FMLN) assigned the Human Rights Division responsibility for carrying out the active verification of the human rights situation and for cooperating with national bodies in order to contribute to the improvement of mechanisms for protecting human rights and to help ensure respect for the rules of due process of law.

2. In this context, the Human Rights Division has been periodically providing the Secretary-General and, through him the Security Council and the General Assembly with information concerning human rights developments in El Salvador. Its reports have also contained a status report on the implementation of the other commitments set forth in the various agreements, particularly those concerning the establishment, reform or consolidation of the institutions responsible for the protection and monitoring of the legal guarantees of human rights. As the departure of the United Nations Observer Mission in El Salvador (ONUSAL) draws near, it is becoming urgent that these commitments should be honoured.

3. Accordingly, this report, which covers the months of March, April, May and June 1994, again contains an analysis of the functioning of some of the institutions which are part of the justice system in El Salvador—a subject on whose active verification the Human Rights Division has gradually placed increased emphasis—and of the process of legislative reforms deriving from the obligations contained in the Peace Accords.

II. *Analysis of the situation from March to June 1994*

A. *Overall assessment of the situation*

4. In my tenth report to the Secretary-General (A/49/116-S/1994/385), I stated that the human rights situation from November 1993 to February 1994 showed "a certain improvement, in contrast to the serious problems warned of in the ninth report", an indication that the overall trends of the process seemed to be reasserting themselves. In the period covered by this report, these trends continued.

5. The 1993 period prior to the first and second months of electoral rounds, held during the period covered by this report, were marked by a climate of growing political violence, a trend which some thought might affect the electoral process. Except in a few isolated cases, however, the final stages of the electoral campaign were not disrupted by acts of violence.

6. None the less, the increase during recent months in violence related to common crimes has attained very disturbing proportions; the high crime indexes, particularly the proven existence of complex organized-crime

networks, coupled with the impunity resulting from the inadequate functioning of the justice system, are currently the greatest obstacles to the effective exercise of human rights in El Salvador.

7. In this connection, I must express my particular concern at indications that active-duty members of the Armed Forces and the National Police are participating in criminal activities. This situation, in addition to its inherently serious implications for the establishment of the rule of law, could easily conceal or lead to the formation of structures which perpetrate political violence disguised as common crime. In this same vein, we must reiterate our concern at the growing presence of armed gangs which are the main perpetrators of various criminal activities in some rural areas of El Salvador. On a number of occasions, I have pointed out that the existence of such illegal groups is a latent threat to the enjoyment of human rights.

8. The Government has been taking appropriate measures to deal with this difficult situation of lack of public safety. The President of the Republic, Mr. Armando Calderón Sol, not only has publicly acknowledged the existence of organized crime and vowed to combat it but has also been formulating a public-safety policy in the spirit of the peace agreements—that is to say, by giving his firm support to the National Civil Police as the sole organ legally responsible for ensuring the public peace and internal law and order.

9. A healthy expression of this political will is the recent deployment of the National Civil Police in the departments of La Paz, Cuscatlán, Santa Ana, the northern part of San Salvador, Ahuachapán and Sonsonate. The National Civil Police is now deployed in all departments of El Salvador, although in some departments its presence is confined to department capitals or major cities, while the National Police continues its activities in the other areas. During the period covered by this report, Mr. Victor Hugo Barrera was appointed Deputy Minister of Public Safety and Mr. Rodrigo Avila was appointed Director of the National Civil Police. They have reaffirmed their commitment to elaborating a reform process in the institution in order to ensure its maximum efficiency.

10. These positive responses by the Government also resulted in the President's decision to advance the date of the demobilization of the National Police to next December. His decision was precipitated by the involvement of an active-duty National Police officer in a bank hold-up, an incident which highlighted the participation of members of the National Police in organized crime. The President also decided to disband the Criminal Investigation Section of the National Police.

11. The number of complaints received by the Hu-

man Rights Division in the four-month period covered by this report was smaller than that recorded in the preceding four-month period (a decrease from 437 to 333). During the period analysed there was a monthly decline, with the number of complaints dropping from 100 in March to 90 in April, 82 in May and 61 in June. It should be stressed, however, that the number of complaints received by the Office of the National Counsel for the Defence of Human Rights is beginning to increase, reflecting a natural and desirable transfer of the tasks of verification to that Office.

12. Moreover, it is not enough that the complaint figures should be lower during a given period. This is encouraging, but the situation is still precarious if State institutions do not have the professionalism and the degree of efficiency necessary to prevent and punish human rights violations.

13. A significant number of complaints received by ONUSAL contain evidence or information which clearly suggests political motives. The recent attempt on the life of former FMLN Commander and current Legislative Assembly Deputy María Marta Valladares (Nidia Díaz) and the assassinations of Jorge Bill Martínez Zaldaña, José Isaías Calzada Mejías and Heriberto Galicia Sánchez, all opposition members, give cause for concern, since they seem to indicate that there are still groups in El Salvador which resort to violence as a means of resolving political disputes. This is also reflected by the large number of threats against persons engaged in political activities.

14. The Legislative Assembly also adopted in the first round of voting a number of constitutional reforms which incorporate some of the recommendations formulated by the Human Rights Division and the Commission on the Truth. Other recommendations, however, went unheeded.

...

III. *Conclusions and recommendations*

127. While the general trend of the process has been maintained, the increase in acts of common violence in the country and the clear involvement of members of law-enforcement bodies in criminal acts, together with the impunity which results from the deficit operation of the justice system, are major obstacles to the effective exercise of human rights in El Salvador.

128. Faced with the problem of the lack of public security, the Government has begun adopting appropriate measures. The President of the Republic has firmly supported the National Civil Police as the only agency legally entrusted with ensuring public security and internal law and order. There has been increased deployment of the National Civil Police. Individuals committed to

increasing the efficiency of the National Civil Police have been named to the posts of Deputy Minister of Public Security and Director of the National Civil Police. It has been announced that the demobilization of the National Police will be carried forward, and the Criminal Investigation Section of the National Police was dissolved ahead of schedule. The Division concurs with the view of the President of the Republic that the demobilization of the National Police should be accelerated even further.

129. Although there were fewer complaints received than during earlier periods, many of them involve indications or elements of judgement which make the consideration of possible political motivation unavoidable and which seem to suggest that there are still groups that resort to violence as a means of resolving political conflicts. This is harmful to the peace process and hampers the Government's efforts to consolidate a State based on the rule of law.

130. Despite the remarkable progress made by the armed forces in developing the new military doctrine, the evidence of participation of active-duty military men in criminal acts makes it indispensable to press the investigation and to bring those involved before the courts of ordinary justice.

131. The human rights situation in El Salvador will remain precarious until State institutions are efficient enough to prevent and to punish human rights violations. The impunity of the perpetrators is, in fact, still the main cause of human rights violations in El Salvador. It is therefore essential to accelerate the reform of the judicial system. The new Supreme Court of Justice has the necessary tools for undertaking an internal purge of the Judicial Organ, on the basis of the studies made by the National Council of the Judiciary.

132. The anticipated departure of ONUSAL demonstrates the importance of the work of permanent national bodies such as the Office of the National Counsel for the Defence of Human Rights and non-governmental human rights organizations for the protection and promotion of human rights. It is to be hoped that the Office of the National Counsel will be able to assume the task of active verification fully when ONUSAL terminates its activities.

133. The non-governmental organizations have been adapting their activities to the new situation in the country and have been contributing to the construction of a democratic State, but since human rights violations are not occurring on such a massive scale as in the past, they are finding it difficult to obtain the funding necessary to their work. An appeal is being made to the international community to assist the non-governmental organizations in playing their role, which is, in a sense, more important than ever.

134. The penitentiary system is experiencing a serious crisis. The prison regime must be modernized as soon as possible, and more resources must be allocated to the problem. It is important to move forward on the adoption of the Prison Act, which has already been submitted to the Legislative Assembly.

135. Some of the recommendations for improving the justice system which were made by the Human Rights Division and the Commission on the Truth are now being put into practice, among them the granting of *habeas corpus* and the invalidation of extrajudicial confession. It is important that the new Legislative Assembly should ratify the constitutional reforms which are in the process of approval and the pending reforms of secondary legislation.

136. Other recommendations for the process of constitutional reform have not yet been implemented. Of particular importance are the proposal that the National Council of the Judiciary should be granted the power to appoint and dismiss judges, the expansion of authority concerning *amparo*, the reduction of the maximum period for detentions due to administrative misdemeanours, and the repeal of the Police Act. The Legislative Assembly should take up these matters as soon as possible.

137. As regards the international standards for human rights, the Legislative Assembly ratified only the Convention against Torture and Other Cruel, Inhuman or Degrading Treatment or Punishment; however, serious reservations were expressed regarding the competence of the Committee against Torture to receive complaints concerning systematic violations. Furthermore, El Salvador is the only Central American country that has not recognized the mandatory competence of the Inter-American Court of Human Rights. Among those instruments still pending, ratification of the Additional Protocol to the American Convention on Human Rights relative to Economic, Social and Cultural Rights, of the Optional Protocol to the International Covenant on Civil and Political Rights, and of the American Convention for the Prevention and Punishment of Torture would be particularly important.

Document 115

Report of the Secretary-General on ONUSAL's activities

S/1994/1000, 26 August 1994

I. Introduction

Shortly after the issuance of my report to the Security Council on 11 May 1994 (S/1994/561 and Add.1), the Government of El Salvador and the Frente Farabundo Martí para la Liberación Nacional (FMLN) reached agreement on 19 May on a new "Timetable for the implementation of the most important outstanding agreements" emanating from the peace accords. I brought that agreement to the attention of the Security Council in my letter of 24 May to the President of the Council (S/1994/612). The present report is submitted pursuant to resolution 920 (1994), in which the Council, *inter alia*, urged the Government and FMLN to comply strictly with the 19 May agreement and requested me to report, no later than 31 August 1994, on compliance with the timetable and on other relevant issues, including measures undertaken to contain the costs of the United Nations Observer Mission in El Salvador (ONUSAL).

Since his inauguration on 1 June 1994, President Calderón Sol has taken steps to ensure compliance with the outstanding provisions of the peace accords. The high-level governmental team responsible for follow-up activities at the political level has been maintained, the fortnightly tripartite meetings envisaged by the 19 May agreement are held regularly and joint working groups on various outstanding issues continue to function.

A turning-point appears to have been reached in the area of public security. After recent events revealed the involvement in criminal activities of individuals or groups within the public security apparatus, 1/ the Government promptly denounced the existence of organized crime and expressed its determination to take decisive action against all those involved regardless of their origin, thus squarely confronting an issue that had not hitherto been openly addressed. The appointment of the new Vice-Minister for Public Security and the new Director-General of the National Civil Police should help strengthen that institution and improve its performance.

After a two-month extension of its mandate, the Joint Group established in December 1993 to investigate politically motivated illegal armed groups completed its work and submitted its report to President Calderón Sol and to myself on 28 July 1994. The report is being issued as an official document of the United Nations.

Since 1 May 1994, the Legislative Assembly has functioned with the participation of FMLN as the country's second political force, as well as with that of other political parties. Despite a four-week delay, the election by consensus of the new Supreme Court of Justice, after a painstaking process of negotiations which had tested the political parties' capacity to compromise, was a laudable achievement. The National Commission for the Consolidation of Peace (COPAZ) and several of its sub-commissions also continue to function. Talks are under way on its possible transformation into a peace foundation.

II. Implementation of outstanding agreements

This section deals with the implementation of the 19 May timetable and accordingly examines matters relating to the armed forces, public security, the land-transfer programme, reintegration programmes and the recommendations of the Commission on the Truth.

A. Armed forces

While military weapons in the possession of penitentiaries have been replaced in a number of cases with arms authorized by the 9 December 1993 law (see S/1994/561, para. 12), the Government has proposed that the collection of such weapons be temporarily suspended in view of the insecurity prevailing at several penal institutions where violent rioting has occurred recently. It was agreed that the situation would be reviewed on 28 August 1994. As regards other registered military weapons, a list of which has been provided by the Government, security considerations have led to an agreement that action on those weapons will also be reviewed on 28 August.

Concerning the voluntary surrender of unregistered military weapons and the registration of other weapons, a reform of the relevant law has extended the applicable deadlines, and regulations on the application of the law have been approved. Offices are scheduled to open before the end of August for the registration or collection of these weapons. However, a forceful and effective publicity campaign to promote compliance with the law has yet to begin and practical measures for its implementation have yet to be announced.

There are indications that certain members of the armed forces on active duty continue to carry out internal intelligence activities, contrary to the new mandate of the

---

1/ On 22 June 1994, an armed robbery that claimed the lives of five citizens was filmed by a television crew and led to the arrest of the Chief of the Investigative Department of the National Police.

armed forces as set out in the Constitution. It is imperative that the Inspector-General and his office carry out their duties efficiently to ensure strict compliance with the law and the peace accords in this regard.

B. *Public security*

Deployment of the National Civil Police

Since I last reported on this subject to the Security Council, the National Civil Police has been fully deployed in the departments of La Paz and Cuscatlán and partially deployed in those of Ahuachapán and Sonsonate, thus leaving the departments of San Salvador and La Libertad still under the jurisdiction of the National Police. With the start-up of the Environmental and Border divisions in June, eight of the National Civil Police's nine functional divisions are now technically operational. The deployment of the Arms and Explosives Division, originally scheduled for 1 August, has been rescheduled for the end of the month.

Demobilization of the National Police

Information received by ONUSAL indicates that approximately 1,900 National Police personnel have now been demobilized or dismissed. According to the Director of the National Police, personnel under his command now total some 4,800. While the Government has publicly announced its intention to complete the demobilization of the National Police before the deadline established in the timetable (i.e., 31 January, and at the latest, 31 March 1995), no final decision has yet been taken. Moreover, applications for reintegration programmes for the National Police have dwindled considerably and ONUSAL has been informed that they will soon be discontinued. ONUSAL has requested a detailed phasing-out plan for the coming months, as well as information on the future of National Police agents.

On 1 July, in the wake of the arrest of the Chief of the Investigative Department of the National Police on grounds of involvement in criminal activities (see para. 3 and note 1), the Government decided to demobilize the unit's 732 members effective 1 August and to transfer its functions to the National Civil Police. However, a new 750-member anti-crime unit was subsequently established within the National Police. According to information received by ONUSAL, the members of this unit are to form part of the group of up to 1,000 former National Police agents who may enter the National Public Security Academy under the terms of the 19 May 1994 agreement (see para. 26). ONUSAL has requested more precise information about the functions of the unit and the background of its personnel.

As to the former Customs Police, which had been incorporated into the National Police, the Government has announced that its personnel would be absorbed by the Treasury Ministry as a fiscal control unit whose duties would include the control of smuggling. Armed police functions would be exercised exclusively by the Finance Division of the National Civil Police. However, having verified that members of the former Customs Police deployed in border and other areas carry military and light weapons, ONUSAL has called the Government's attention to this apparent contradiction with the principle of a single police body with national jurisdiction laid down in the peace accords.

Restructuring of the Ministry of the Interior and Public Security

The Government has established the office of the new Vice-Minister for Public Security and, on 1 June, appointed Mr. Hugo Barrera to that position, where he will be responsible for directing the National Civil Police and the National Public Security Academy. He will also have authority over the National Police until its final demobilization.

Regulatory machinery

Consultations are continuing with the Attorney-General of the Republic and the National Counsel for the Defence of Human Rights on the appointment of the Inspector-General of the National Civil Police, which should have taken place in June 1994. The Control and Disciplinary Investigation units are being provided with the necessary human and material resources. Agreement has been reached on international technical assistance with the participation of ONUSAL, which submitted a technical cooperation plan at the beginning of August.

Irregularities in the National Civil Police and the functioning of the National Public Security Academy

In accordance with the 19 May timetable, ONUSAL has made recommendations (which are binding) and suggestions to the Vice-Minister for Public Security. Some of these are summarized in the following paragraphs. Measures towards compliance with the recommendations, the purpose of which is to bring the Government into compliance with the letter and the spirit of the peace accords, should be taken by 30 August and implementation completed before 30 October 1994, except for those recommendations requiring a longer period for full application.

Concerning irregularities in the Anti-narcotics Division of the National Civil Police, ONUSAL has ascertained that a large portion of the Division's members carry out activities unrelated to anti-narcotics work. This is contrary to agreements reached earlier. ONUSAL has accordingly recommended that the Division limit its activities to that area and adjust its structure accordingly. It has also recommended that personnel incorporated into the former Special Anti-narcotics Unit after the complementary agreement of 22 December 1992 (which allowed members of the unit to enter the National Civil Police on an exceptional basis and under certain conditions) be returned to their earlier positions. A revision of the law on the fight against drugs (*Ley Reguladora de las Actividades relativas a las Drogas*) to ensure that it conforms with the Constitution and the Organic Law of the National Civil Police has been suggested.

Given that the Criminal Investigations Division lacks the necessary resources and personnel to carry out all criminal investigations in the country, as established in the Organic Law of the National Civil Police, ONUSAL has recommended that it be strengthened with graduates from the Academy. The transfer of National Police files to the National Civil Police, including those of its investigative department, should take place as soon as possible.

The Anti-narcotics and Criminal Investigations divisions continue to operate with excessive autonomy within the National Civil Police. ONUSAL has recommended that appropriate steps be taken to ensure subordination to the hierarchy, coordination with other divisions and submission to internal regulatory machinery. It has also recommended that both divisions coordinate their activities with the Attorney-General's office and the judicial branch.

Problems with the assignment of ranks have been confirmed in both divisions: in the case of the Anti-narcotics Division, ranks have been assigned arbitrarily, while in the Criminal Investigations Division no ranks have been assigned. ONUSAL has recommended that members of both divisions be evaluated in order to determine their provisional ranks and that they enrol in regular courses at the Academy at the appropriate levels. This will help to correct the existing anomalies and will facilitate the integration of both divisions into the National Civil Police.

In order to safeguard the entitlement of the five best students in each Academy promotion to choose their place of assignment among existing vacancies, ONUSAL has recommended that clear and objective criteria be established to evaluate their academic performance. Moreover, given that frequent changes in command positions in the National Civil Police have affected efficiency, a system should be established to ensure continuity of service while providing more stable working conditions. In this regard, the prompt approval of a law regulating the police career would be essential.

With respect to the functioning of the National Public Security Academy, ONUSAL has recommended that a permanent mechanism for the evaluation of teachers be established and that every effort be made to retain international instructors at least until 1995. In line with

ONUSAL's recommendations, a Chief of Studies has been appointed and the present curriculum is being revised to make the Academy more responsive to the needs of the National Civil Police, particularly as regards judicial procedures, the use of firearms and training in the field. Following the transition period, the duration of basic-level courses should be extended.

ONUSAL has also recommended that, in coordination with the National Civil Police, the Academy carry out an evaluation of that institution's personnel before 15 September 1994. Measures supplementing ONUSAL's recommendations in respect of the Academy should be adopted by the Academic Council before 20 October 1994. The Council should submit its first annual report, which will include its evaluation of the National Civil Police and will assess the implementation of ONUSAL's recommendations, to the Minister of the Interior and Public Security on 30 October 1994. As recommended by ONUSAL, representatives of the Director of the National Civil Police now regularly attend the meetings of the Academic Council.

As regards the recruitment and selection process, ONUSAL has suggested that the current recruitment campaign be complemented by field visits, in particular to those areas where the turnout of applicants has been low, and that the participation of the National Civil Police be enlisted. It has further recommended that more time be devoted to individual interviews with candidates and that the selection process be reviewed in the light of accumulated experience.

The current team of Academy monitors (*monitores*) consists of 17 former National Police members, 6 FMLN ex-combatants and 25 other individuals who did not participate in the armed conflict. ONUSAL has recommended that, for the remainder of the transition period, personnel from every origin be considered for such positions, due account being taken of their professional merits. ONUSAL has also noted that the supervision of the more than 2,000 students at the Academy requires an increased number of monitors, in respect of whose activities, selection, training and rotation appropriate rules should be devised. The disciplinary regime should be enforced only by the relevant authorities and the files of students who were sanctioned by unqualified authorities should be cleared.

Measures for promoting additional recruitment to the National Civil Police

At the Government's request, ONUSAL has submitted a document containing a proposal for an increase in grants given to Academy students, information on pensions and other benefits for National Civil Police personnel, and the related budgetary implications. The Government has informed ONUSAL that a special budget allocation has been requested in order to increase Academy grants retroactively to 1 July. A response is pending on the question of benefits for National Civil Police personnel. With regard to the promotion of civilian recruitment to the Academy, progress has been made towards the signing of an agreement between the Academy and the Asociación Salvadoreña de Apoyo a la Democracia (ASPAD), representing the non-governmental sector. It should be borne in mind that in addition to the requirement that ONUSAL's recommendations in this regard be implemented, the possible admission to the Academy of up to 1,000 additional former members of the National Police (see para. 12) could only take place if the Academy were unable to recruit enough candidates who had not taken part in the armed conflict.

C. *Land-transfer programme*

Regrettably, there is little progress to report with regard to the effective transfer of land to former combatants of the Armed Forces of El Salvador (FAES) and the FMLN as well as to landholders, as contemplated in the peace agreements. The acceptance last May by the Government, at my request, to include the so-called "non-verified" landholders in the programme removed one of the main impediments to its implementation (see S/1994/561, para. 70). At that time I also urged the FMLN to make the utmost effort to overcome some of the impediments to the transfer of land for which they were responsible. Among these, some of the most serious were the need to stop putting additional people on the land or relocating them from one place to another; to facilitate the process by being present with the appropriate documentation at the different stages and at the specified time and place; and to make sure that all potential beneficiaries signed the deeds on time so that owners could be paid for their land. The response of FMLN in this regard has been disappointing and many of these problems continue to paralyse the land programme. It should be pointed out, however, that although in some cases non-compliance clearly reflects a lack of political will on the part of FMLN, in others it is a consequence of their weak organizational structure and lack of resources.

In terms of what has been achieved and what remains to be done, the picture is as follows. The total number of potential beneficiaries of the land-transfer programme has not yet been determined since FMLN has not provided the relevant information on rural human settlements (referred to in the agreements as *predios e inmuebles*) which, according to the 8 September 1993 high-level tripartite meeting (Government/FMLN/ONUSAL), are to be included in the land programme (see S/26790, para. 55). Pending a solution to this problem,

there is agreement to transfer land to 28,648 former combatants of FMLN and landholders and 12,000 former combatants of the armed forces, amounting to a total of 40,648, which is below the maximum number of 47,500 contemplated in the agreement. Of these, only 8,936 of the FMLN beneficiaries (31 per cent) and about 3,000 of the FAES beneficiaries (25 per cent) have so far completed the legal process. These data illustrate that the programme is once again at a standstill: by the end of April 11,585 persons had received title to the land and by mid-August this figure had only increased to 11,936, still below the end-1993 target of 12,000, a figure that had been accepted as feasible by both the Government and FMLN (see S/1994/561, para. 67).

Delays in the transfer of land are impeding the reintegration of potential beneficiaries into productive activities and are creating other kinds of problems that are likely to complicate the implementation of the agreements. In many cases land deeds cannot be finalized because a few beneficiaries have not signed. Under such conditions, restrictions imposed by donors prevent the Lands Bank from paying owners for their land. Delays in payments are discouraging landowners from selling, and the resulting land shortages are likely to put upward pressure on prices. At the same time, the paralysis in the programme has resulted in committed funds remaining undisbursed. This in turn is discouraging donors from committing the necessary additional funding, not only for the land-transfer programme, but also for programmes relating to the provision of agricultural credit and technical assistance, which are conditional on the legalization of land tenure and are seriously under-financed.

On 18 August the Government submitted a new plan to accelerate the transfer of land to former combatants of FMLN and landholders, in an attempt to overcome the many operational problems that had inhibited its implementation so far. The most noteworthy point in the plan is the commitment of the Government to strengthen the legal and administrative capacity of the regional offices of the executing agency so as to facilitate the measurement, appraisal, negotiation and legalization of properties, as well as to organize a publicity campaign through regional radio stations to inform potential beneficiaries of their rights and of the different steps they need to take if they want to participate in the programme.

If these shortcomings can be overcome by the new measures to be adopted by the Government and with the full cooperation of FMLN, the main issue to be resolved in this regard relates to human settlements. Human settlements were established after the Government of El Salvador agreed to the return of refugees that had fled to Honduras during the years of conflict. Over the years, with the financial and technical support of the international community, these settlements of returnees and displaced persons have built an important social infrastructure and productive capacity in agro-industry in relatively small areas of land. In a country with such land scarcity these settlements constitute an alternative model to purely agricultural activities. Because of the social and political implications of breaking up these communities and the fact that their members strongly oppose relocation, a solution will have to be found to transfer these settlements under a special regime and *en bloc*, with compensation to the original owners, as proposed by FMLN. The situation has been complicated by the fact that it has become clear that it is not always possible to separate the rural from the urban settlements and a solution will have to encompass both. At the 8 September 1993 meeting the Government also agreed to work on a solution to urban human settlements, albeit outside the land-transfer programme, once COPAZ completed an inventory. That inventory was presented on 15 December 1993, registering 1,373 houses, of which 752 were included within the land-transfer programme, thus reducing the problem of urban human settlements to the remaining 621 cases (see S/1994/561, paras. 76 and 87).

The transfer of land to former members of the armed forces also presents serious difficulties which ONUSAL cannot fully evaluate since it continues to lack full information on this issue. The programme is under-financed and additional funding is needed to cover 8,000 of the 9,000 remaining potential beneficiaries. The situation has been aggravated by the delays in indemnization to demobilized members of the armed forces, the growing links between indemnization and land transfer and the increasing threat of an organization which includes some disgruntled former combatants of the armed forces. Members of that organization recently occupied the National Assembly, the Lands Bank and the Instituto Salvadoreño de Transformación Agraria as a way to exert pressure on the Government to accept their demands. Their main claim is that members of paramilitary forces demobilized because of the peace agreements should also be entitled to the same programmes. These forces have been estimated as low as 50,000 and as high as 250,000. Even if these forces had a valid claim, the fact remains that the agreements only contemplate the transfer of land to former combatants of the armed forces and the 13 October 1992 programme establishes a maximum figure of 15,000 for them. Pressure to include those not contemplated in the programme has detracted from the real problem which is the sluggishness and inadequacy with which the programme has been carried out and the need to accelerate its implementation.

D. *Reintegration programmes*

ONUSAL has continued to work with the parties and with the United Nations Development Programme (UNDP) on the implementation of the medium-term programmes for former combatants of the armed forces and FMLN, supporters of the latter who became landholders in the former zones of conflict and demobilized members of the National Police. Progress can be reported in spite of the many operational and administrative problems and the lack of financing, which have resulted in serious delays in some programmes.

Given the restrictions imposed by the small size of the plots being transferred, the only possibility of making agricultural production sustainable is by strong support through training, technical assistance and credit. To start with, agricultural training programmes, which are by now completed, did not cover a large number of potential beneficiaries of the land-transfer programme. The first technical assistance programme coordinated by UNDP and executed by non-governmental organizations has also been completed. A new programme for the 1994/95 agricultural cycle will be carried out through a Government agency, the National Centre for Agricultural Technology (CENTA). This programme will need to be strengthened technically and financially and supplemented by the work of non-governmental organizations earmarking technical assistance for the former zones of conflict, as proposed by FMLN.

Technical assistance is essential to ensure the optimal use of credit. The programme for agricultural credit is severely under-capitalized, and this has had a negative impact, primarily upon potential beneficiaries from among the armed forces and landholders.

The training programme for micro-enterprises has also concluded and credit has been provided to about half of the potential beneficiaries. There are indications, however, that a majority of beneficiaries are not productively investing these funds. This creates a double problem: on the one hand, the programme will not achieve its main objective, which is the successful reintegration of these people into productive activities. On the other, borrowers will soon afterwards be in default, limiting the Government's ability and/or willingness to give them new loans in the future.

With regard to the programme for the 600 medium-level commanders ("Plan 600"), implementation is taking place with delays, inadequate technical assistance and a shortage of funds for housing. Problems related to the lack of coordination and joint programming between beneficiaries and the executing agencies have not been resolved (S/1991/561, para. 82).

The number of members of the National Police

attending the first phase of the reintegration programme (the counselling phase) is less than expected (about 3,400 of the expected 4,800). The following phases (training, credit and technical assistance) will be impeded by the lack of financing.

E. *Recommendations of the Commission on the Truth*

Having agreed upon a plan of action to promote the early approval of legislative measures emanating from the recommendations of the Commission on the Truth, which are binding, the parties and ONUSAL have discussed these issues in separate meetings with the Legislative Assembly. The Assembly is now proceeding to study the relevant draft legislation.

Regarding the final approval of pending international human rights instruments, the Government maintains its objection to their approval but is continuing to hold consultations of a technical nature. Other specific non-legislative measures recommended by the Commission are still pending.

F. *Other items in the timetable*

No progress has been achieved on the question of human urban settlements and resumption of work by the Forum for Economic and Social Consultation.

III. Other relevant issues

The election of the new Supreme Electoral Tribunal, which took place on 30 July 1994, will provide an opportunity for the much-needed reform of the Tribunal's internal organization and personnel structure in a way that should strengthen professional and technical merit. Other reforms to be tackled in the electoral system include the establishment of a new electoral roll and the possible issuance of a single personal identity and voting card; proportional representation in municipal councils; and provision for voting in the area of a citizen's residence. All these reforms should be in force well in advance of the next legislative elections, to be held in 1997, and should therefore be agreed upon before the end of 1994.

ONUSAL has increased its technical support to national institutions and other entities. The Human Rights Division has given priority to cooperation with the National Counsel for the Defence of Human Rights, the importance of which cannot be overemphasized in view of the fact that the Counsel is scheduled to take over all the Division's functions after ONUSAL's departure. Seminars have also been held with non-governmental organizations active in the field of human rights.

In view of the limited resources available to the National Counsel for the Defence of Human Rights, the international donor community has repeatedly been asked to cooperate with that institution. While this appeal has, in general, met with a favourable response, it is imperative that the National Counsel concentrate on consolidating investigations, particularly of human rights violations, as recommended by various international experts and actively called for by non-governmental organizations concerned with human rights. It is significant in this context that the Counsel has expressed its desire to receive the technical cooperation that ONUSAL has always stood ready to provide.

A technical cooperation agreement has been signed between ONUSAL and the Vice-Minister for Public Security for the provision of assistance by ONUSAL to the National Civil Police in such areas as regulatory machinery (i.e., the Control and Disciplinary Investigation units), transit, environment, arms and explosives, and in the elaboration of an operational guide. ONUSAL will also serve as the catalyst in obtaining international technical assistance for the two above-mentioned units.

The lack of financing for peace-related programmes is critical. It has been estimated that to conclude the land programme $32 million will be needed ($1 million for the programme for FMLN and landholders, which has been generously financed by the United States Agency for International Development (USAID), and $31 million for FAES). The programme for agricultural credit to former combatants of FMLN, the armed forces and landholders currently has a deficit of $17 million and the one for credit to micro-enterprises has a deficit of close to $4 million. Programmes to reintegrate demobilized members of the National Police require $14 million. The financial needs resulting from the reintegration programmes are in addition to those required to cover the indemnization of the demobilized members of the armed forces ($6 million) and those of the National Police ($9 million). In order to implement these programmes it is imperative that the Government and the international community find ways to finance the existing deficit of over $80 million as soon as possible. A total assessment of additional requirements will not be possible until estimates are provided to cover the transfer of human settlements, the Fund for the Protection of the War-disabled and housing needs for people who have not been covered by existing programmes.

IV. Measures taken to contain the costs of ONUSAL

In my report of 11 May 1994 (S/1994/561, para. 101), I stated that the size of ONUSAL would be reduced as rapidly as implementation of the outstanding agreements permitted. Consequently, bearing in mind the progress made to date, I have already reduced the military component to 12 military observers and 7 medical personnel from a total of 30 on 1 May. By 1 October, I expect the medical personnel to be further reduced to 3 and during November all the military observers will be phased out. The reduction in the size of the police division is in accordance with my earlier plans (see S/1994/561/Add.1) and I intend to bring the level down to 145 by 1 October (excluding 15 police instructors posted to the National Police Academy). In the same manner, I intend to start the progressive phasing out of the substantive civilian staff in the light of developments over the coming months.

In addition, the operational requirements of ONUSAL have been reviewed with the intention of taking additional measures to contain the costs of the Mission. As a result, the air transport expenses have been reduced drastically by replacing the two full-time helicopters previously used by the Mission with one aircraft that is now being hired only on an as-required basis. Similarly, a substantial reduction of the vehicle fleet is under way, concomitant with the staffing reduction. I expect the vehicle fleet to be reduced by at least 170 by 1 October 1994. This reduction will make possible the use of the surplus in other missions which are short of vehicles. I should mention that the phasing out of personnel and equipment is being closely correlated with the needs of existing missions, as well as with the planning for new missions.

Against this background, I have submitted a report to the General Assembly containing cost estimates for the period until November. I am pleased to report that this represents a substantial savings when compared to the previous mandate period.

V. Observations

The establishment of FMLN as a fully legal party in the political and civil life of the country provides striking evidence of El Salvador's transformation from a country riven by conflict into a nation on the path to reconciliation. Despite formidable difficulties, it has come to constitute a credible opposition in the National Assembly and maintains a presence at the regional and municipal levels. Much will depend upon the commitment of the majority party, the Alianza Republicana Nacionalista (ARENA), to govern wisely and with moderation, so that plurality becomes an integral feature of Salvadorian politics.

Despite delays, progress achieved in those areas of the 19 May timetable which are most relevant to the strengthening and modernization of democratic institutions reflects the new Government's decision to establish firmly the rule of law in El Salvador. While this attitude is an encouraging indication of its commitment to the peace process, several difficult issues remain to be resolved in order to ensure compliance with pending obligations under the peace accords.

The new appointments in the public security sector and the Government's resolve to fight organized crime constitute a significant step in correcting the irregularities and deficiencies affecting the new police, of which I informed the Security Council in my last report. The President's decision to accelerate the demobilization of the National Police, though still to be implemented, is consistent with the new Government's attitude and has received support from important sectors of Salvadorian society.

The unanimous election of an independent Supreme Court of Justice paves the way for the much-needed reform of the judicial system, including the approval of speedier procedures and the removal of corrupt judges. The changes in the police and in the justice system finally offer hope that El Salvador will see the end of impunity, one of the root causes of the war.

During this last phase of the Mission, in which institution-building and strengthening are being emphasized, the justice and police sectors will continue to require careful attention. This also applies to the ability of the institution of the armed forces to abide fully by its new mandate under the Constitution, including ending all intelligence activities relating to domestic objectives. The strengthening of internal supervisory mechanisms, and particularly of the Inspector-General's functions, is also of supreme importance at this stage. Some of the experts presently with ONUSAL might be retained after the closing of the Mission in the framework of a broad technical assistance programme to the relevant national institutions.

The virtual paralysis of the land-transfer programme, delays and distortions in other reintegration programmes and the unresolved problem of the human settlements are a source of increasing concern. Although the peace agreements stipulated that landholders occupying land at the end of the conflict would not be evicted until the Government could find an acceptable solution to their land tenure problem (S/1994/561, para. 69), delays in the implementation of the programme are giving rise to tension between landowners and landholders. Tensions are also rising among former combatants whose justified expectations of receiving land, credit and housing have been largely unfulfilled (see S/26790, para. 51).

To solve the critical problem of the human settlements, FMLN must provide once and for all the necessary information on these settlements. The Government must exercise once more its flexibility and vision in solving this potentially explosive problem. The international community, which has invested so heavily in the establishment of these settlements over the last four years, should extend its support in this crucial phase to ensure their consolidation and long-term sustainability. This matter requires the formation of a tripartite commission to analyse the issue in greater detail and make proposals for a special regime without which the transfer of these properties will not be possible.

Concerns about reintegration programmes relate not only to their completion but also to their success and long-term sustainability. Success will be measured in terms of the original objective of reintegrating into productive activities those groups that had been marginalized during the conflict years. This would not only contribute to strengthening the domestic economy but would also allow beneficiaries to service the debt they have incurred with the Government by agreeing to participate in the programmes. In this regard, the beneficiaries should respect the terms specified in the contracts they have entered

into. However, given the serious limitations of existing reintegration programmes, in order for them to be sustainable over time they will need to be supplemented by further technical assistance and additional credit. The assistance of the programmes and agencies of the United Nations system, the regional development banks and bilateral donors will be essential to achieve this goal.

The conditions necessary to ensure the full and final implementation of the peace accords seem to be in place, although difficulties in carrying out outstanding obligations should not be underestimated. The Security Council should be in a position to evaluate progress in this regard on the basis of the report that I shall present to it at the end of October 1994.

Document 116

Statement by the President of the Security Council concerning compliance with outstanding provisions of the peace accords

S/PRST/1994/54, 16 September 1994

The Security Council has received the Secretary-General's report of 26 August 1994 1/ on the United Nations Observer Mission in El Salvador, submitted pursuant to resolution 920 (1994). The Council is encouraged by the Secretary-General's observation regarding El Salvador's transformation from a country riven by conflict into a nation on the path to reconciliation.

The Security Council welcomes the steps taken by the President of El Salvador, since his inauguration on 1 June 1994, to ensure compliance with the outstanding provisions of the peace accords. It notes that, while some delays and difficulties still persist, progress has been achieved in areas of the "Agreement on a timetable for the implementation of the most important agreements pending" of 19 May 1994 relevant to the strengthening and modernization of the democratic institutions of El Salvador.

The Security Council reaffirms the need to ensure that, under appropriate verification by the Observer Mission, the police and public security provisions of the peace accords are scrupulously observed. In particular, the Council expects that the Government of El Salvador will accelerate the demobilization of the National Police, as foreseen in the peace accords and as announced by the President of El Salvador.

The Security Council also shares the Secretary-General's concern at the limited progress of the land-transfer

programme, delays and distortions in other reintegration programmes and the unresolved problem of the human settlements, which was originated in the course of the conflict. The Council calls for the removal of remaining obstacles and the prompt fulfilment of the programmes, in conformity with the timetable agreed by the parties. It calls upon States, as well as international institutions, to contribute promptly and generously in support of those programmes.

The Security Council reiterates the need for full implementation of the recommendations of the Commission on the Truth. In this regard, it welcomes the unanimous election of an independent Supreme Court of Justice as an important step in the process of reform of the judicial system.

The Security Council welcomes the steps taken by the Secretary-General to reduce the size of the Observer Mission to the lowest possible level of personnel and to contain its costs, consistent with the effective performance of its duties. The Council reaffirms the commitment undertaken by the United Nations to verify the implementation of the peace accords and, in this context, expresses the hope that significant further progress will be made in implementing the accords.

1/ S/1994/1000.

Document 117

Letter dated 6 October 1994 from the Secretary-General to the President of the Security Council transmitting the text of a joint declaration on compliance with the peace accords signed on 4 October 1994 by the Government of El Salvador and the FMLN

S/1994/1144, 10 October 1994

In the context of the Security Council's efforts to ensure compliance by the parties in El Salvador with their commitments under the Peace Accords, I have the honour to inform you that, on 4 October 1994, representatives of the Government of El Salvador and the Frente Farabundo Martí para la Liberación Nacional (FMLN) signed a joint declaration reflecting their determination to see these Accords implemented fully and urgently for the benefit of all Salvadorians.

I attach the text of the joint declaration. I should be grateful if it could be brought to the attention of the members of the Security Council.

(*Signed*) Boutros BOUTROS-GHALI

Annex

Joint declaration signed on 4 October 1994 by the representatives of the Government of El Salvador and the Frente Farabundo Martí para la Liberación Nacional (FMLN)

The Government of El Salvador,

Aware of its responsibilities under the Peace Agreement,

Encouraged by the tangible progress achieved in transforming the Salvadorian State and society since the signing of the Agreement in Chapultepec,

Resolved to consolidate and strengthen peace, democracy and a State based on the rule of law, which the Salvadorian people is building,

Aware of the need to comply fully and promptly with pending commitments,

Convinced, in this final and decisive stage of the process, that the national interest requires a special and concerted effort to attain this objective,

And the Frente Farabundo Martí para la Liberación Nacional (FMLN), for these same reasons and objectives,

Decide:

1. To cooperate closely and actively in order to ensure full compliance with all the Peace Accords, both those pending and those being carried out, by no later than 30 April 1995.

2. To establish, to this end, joint mechanisms with the participation of the Government, FMLN and the United Nations Observer Mission in El Salvador (ONUSAL), and to determine the specific measures necessary for the rapid fulfilment of the aforementioned commitments. FMLN supports the Government's efforts to obtain financing for the fulfilment of pending commitments. Once the programme for speeding up the implementation of the Accords has been decided, the Government and FMLN shall together take measures to obtain from the international community any resources that may still be required.

3. To keep the Salvadorian people and the international community informed of any decisions and steps that they take.

4. To reiterate the request of both the Government and FMLN to the United Nations to extend the mandate of ONUSAL until 30 April 1995.

SIGNED at San Salvador on 4 October 1994 in the presence of the President of the Republic, Dr. Armando Calderón Sol.

(*Signed*) General Mauricio Ernesto VARGAS

(*Signed*) Schafik Jorge HÁNDAL

Document 118

Report of the Secretary-General on ONUSAL's activities

S/1994/1212, 31 October 1994, and addendum, S/1994/1212/Add.1, 14 November 1994

I. Introduction

1. The present report is submitted in compliance with paragraph 14 of resolution 920 (1994), by which the Security Council requested me to report by 1 November 1994 on the United Nations Observer Mission in El Salvador (ONUSAL), including on the fulfilment and completion of its mandate and on modalities for its progressive withdrawal. In the same paragraph, the Council invited me to prepare modalities for assistance to El Salvador, within the framework of the peace accords, for the post-ONUSAL period.

2. As members of the Security Council will recall, I last reported on ONUSAL on 26 August 1994 (see S/1994/1000). Given that my report contained a detailed account of the state of implementation of outstanding commitments under the peace accords, the present report provides an overall assessment of the process in its political, institutional and socio-economic dimensions and evaluates the effort required to build a solid basis that will ensure, as far as possible, its irreversibility.

3. Political life in El Salvador continues to adjust to the rules of democracy, as embodied in the Constitution which has been reformed in accordance with the peace accords. The legislative, executive and judicial branches of the State respect their respective attributions, public security and national defence are exercised through separate institutional structures and all major political parties have entered a process of internal discussion to adjust to the new parameters created by the transition from a society divided by a prolonged civil war to a democratic system directed towards reconciliation, stability and development.

4. Helped by political stability, the Salvadorian economy continued to grow at over 5 per cent in 1993, reflecting strength in construction and commerce in the private sector. The fall in the budget deficit to 3 per cent of gross domestic product (GDP) in 1993 can be explained by increased tax revenue and the rationalization of expenditure. The rate of inflation fell to 12 per cent, the lowest level in the last five years. In spite of the real appreciation of the colón, non-traditional exports grew by about 18 per cent, probably helped by increases in productivity. A rise in the volume of coffee production also contributed to export growth. In spite of export growth, the trade deficit reached $1.2 billion in 1993. Economic growth has been even more dynamic during the first half of 1994.

The increase in the price of coffee in 1994 is expected to increase export revenue in 1995.

5. Despite this real progress, certain issues remain to be resolved before all pending commitments under the peace accords can be said to have been met. These issues relate to the full deployment of the National Civil Police; the completion of the demobilization of the National Police; the reform of the judicial and electoral systems; the transfer of land to former combatants and the conclusion of some important economic reintegration programmes for their benefit; the implementation of the recommendations of the Commission on the Truth; and the completion of the ongoing process to extend all public services to the former conflict zones.

II. Issues relating to public security

6. Since I last reported to the Security Council, the territorial deployment of the National Civil Police has continued, leaving only parts of 2 of the country's 14 departments without full coverage. While all nine functional divisions of the National Civil Police are now deployed, some of them are not yet fully operational. Increasing disciplinary problems, combined with continued deficiencies in training and gaps in the legal framework that governs the operations of the National Civil Police, underline again the need for a more expeditious and effective implementation of ONUSAL's recommendations for the correction of irregularities in the National Civil Police and the functioning of the National Public Security Academy (see S/1994/1000, paras. 16-25) in order to avoid a further erosion of public confidence in the new force. Until this is done, the National Civil Police will remain fragile and unable to develop as an effective enforcer of the law. This could result in a tendency to establish order through practices outside the legal framework. It is hoped that the recently appointed Inspector-General who, as provided by the peace agreement (see S/23501, annex, chap. II, 3, B, (b)), will be responsible for monitoring and supervising the operations of the National Civil Police, will be provided with the necessary means to address these negative trends.

7. While demobilization of the National Police has accelerated and the Government has informed ONUSAL that the process will be largely completed by 31 December 1994, a detailed plan for phasing out the remaining personnel has not yet been received by ONUSAL. It is still unclear whether the requirements set out in the 19 May 1994

timetable for the implementation of the most important outstanding agreements (see S/1994/612, annex, para. 3.F.2) will be met for the admission into the Academy of additional National Police candidates. In addition, the Customs Police will not be fully demobilized until 31 March 1995, the final deadline envisaged under the 19 May timetable (see ibid., para. 3.B).

III. Human rights and the judicial system

8. The human rights situation in El Salvador has improved markedly during ONUSAL's three years of operation. The work of the Mission's Human Rights Division has been the subject of periodic reports by its Director, the next one of which will be submitted shortly. The Division's verification has been implemented by investigation of human rights violations and the strengthening of national institutions, so as to overcome deficiencies and leave these institutions with the capacity to meet the demands of the peace accords.

9. In the past six months, ONUSAL's Human Rights Division has emphasized the strengthening of national institutions such as the National Council of the Judiciary, the office of the Attorney-General of the Republic, the National Civil Police and the National Public Security Academy, as well as the development of a new doctrine for the Armed Forces. In July, a mechanism for the joint verification of human rights violations was established with the National Counsel for the Defence of Human Rights, together with a training and specialization programme for officials of the National Counsel. The Division has also continued to conduct seminars and specialized workshops on human rights for members of the judicial system, the Armed Forces and non-governmental organizations (NGOs) active in the field of human rights. These activities have been complemented by the publication of a series of books and pamphlets on human rights.

10. In this phase of the peace process, institution-building is crucial for the consolidation of the progress achieved in the protection of human rights and due process. In view of the future winding-up of ONUSAL, programmes to ensure continuous support for institution-building are being prepared.

11. Progress in the strengthening of the judiciary has been achieved through the adoption of legislation that enhances the protection of human rights and seeks a more independent and efficient judicial system. However, serious deficiencies still exist that prevent the eradication of impunity. With the establishment of the new Supreme Court of Justice (see S/1994/1000, para. 5), conditions are in place for the required reform of the judicial system, an issue that must be promptly and effectively addressed by the new Court, together with the adequate training of judges. While initial progress has been made on the latter issue through specialized courses for judges sponsored by ONUSAL, this task should now be assumed on a permanent basis by the Supreme Court and the Judicial Training School, with the support of the international community. Without the completion of judicial reform, the institutional framework for guaranteeing the rule of law and respect for human rights will remain weak, notwithstanding the development of the National Civil Police and parallel efforts to strengthen the National Counsel for the Defence of Human Rights.

IV. Electoral system

12. Following its election in July 1994 (see S/1994/1000, para. 42), the new Supreme Electoral Tribunal has begun discussing reform. A commission of members from various political parties, serving in their individual capacity, has been set up at the Government's initiative. The Tribunal has focused on the preparation of a single identity and voting document, a task in which it has received the technical support of the Electoral Advisory and Promotion Centre of the Inter-American Human Rights Institute (IIDH/CAPEL). Should the IIDH/CAPEL proposal be implemented, a new electoral roll could be in place in time for the 1997 legislative elections, while the new identity/voting document would be ready for the 1999 presidential elections. Other reforms under discussion relate to measures for voting in the area of residence and provisions to ensure some form of representation in municipal councils for parties in addition to the one obtaining the largest number of votes.

13. A thorny issue, which stems from the politicization of the Tribunal, is the assignment of quotas to the largest political parties for the recruitment of the Tribunal's personnel. Continued resistance by some members to modification of this rule could undermine the Tribunal's professionalism. Repairing this basic flaw in the system is essential if the Tribunal is to be truly independent and reliable.

V. Recommendations of the Commission on the Truth

14. ONUSAL continues to insist on the implementation of the judicial reforms and other recommendations of the Commission on the Truth, which are binding upon the parties under the peace accords, especially those referring to the ratification of international human rights treaties, including recognition of the compulsory jurisdiction of the Inter-American Court of Human Rights. A number of recommendations not requiring legislative action are also still pending.

VI. Socio-economic matters

A. *Land-transfer programme*

15. I am pleased to report that 1,006 beneficiaries have received title to land since mid-August. However, in spite of a number of measures taken by the Government to accelerate the land-transfer programme through decentralization of decision-making and streamlining of procedures, exactly two years after the land programme was accepted by the parties only 32 per cent of the established total of 40,648 potential beneficiaries (see S/1994/1000, para. 28) have received land. These 12,942 beneficiaries have received a total of 51,303 *manzanas*, the average per beneficiary thus being slightly less than 4 *manzanas* (2.8 hectares). The remaining operational problems should not be underestimated since the land to be transferred is in smaller plots and it will therefore be necessary to deal with a larger number of landowners; the land is of lower quality and therefore more of it will be needed; and it is located in areas without a dependable registry of properties. The relocation of an estimated 8,000 landholders, which should be left for the end of the programme as stipulated in the 13 October 1992 agreement, will also be a problem not only because of the psychological difficulties associated with relocation but also because of the lack of adequate alternatives in a country with such an acute land shortage. Given the delay in the implementation of this programme and the difficulties that lie ahead, I made a personal appeal to President Calderón Sol last month to adopt measures to facilitate the rapid completion of this programme. I have also urged both the Frente Farabundo Martí para la Liberación Nacional (FMLN) and the Armed Forces to refrain from any further effort to revise and/or add to the list of potential beneficiaries.

16. The expiry earlier this year of a decree which, pursuant to the peace accords, barred eviction of landholders in the former conflict zones, has been a source of concern, particularly because of the expectations of eviction that it created among landowners. However, on 1 September the Legislative Assembly extended landholders' protection from eviction. Another welcome development was the adoption on 11 October of a decree to expedite procedures for the legalization of unregistered properties and for the solution of several other problems affecting lands to be transferred. On the other hand, the adoption on 22 September of a decree by which only titled landowners are allowed to sell their coffee beans is a new source of concern.

17. In addition to the problem of transferring land, there is the problem of human settlements (referred to in the agreements as *predios e inmuebles*), which is the most serious problem that remains to be resolved. At my request, my Special Representative has urged the Government to adopt a flexible policy to ensure that the settlements can be easily and quickly transferred. Such flexibility is called for because strict interpretation of the rules of the 13 October 1992 land programme would prevent such transfer. The socio-political consequences of breaking up these settlements would be serious (see S/1994/561, paras. 76 and 87 and S/1994/1000, para. 56), and it was for this reason that the Government had agreed to adopt a new policy.

B. *Reintegration programmes*

18. Although progress can be reported with regard to some reintegration programmes, there are still delays. The programme for agricultural credit, which is essential to reactivate production in the zones of conflict, is still paralysed. Another matter of concern is the Government's unilateral decision to reduce credit to landholders from 10,000 to 4,000 colones. This will deprive them of the ability to produce the minimum required for subsistence and servicing their debts. At the same time, the agricultural technical assistance programme to beneficiaries of the land programme continues to cover only a small number of properties. Without agricultural credit and technical assistance, there is no possibility that the few who have benefited from the land programme will be able to become successful producers and service their debt, particularly in view of the small amount of land to which they have been entitled.

19. Delays in housing programmes, including those targeted for middle-level former commanders of FMLN ("Plan 600"), are also a source of concern, as is the lack of adequate resources for the Fund for the Protection of the Wounded and War-Disabled as a Consequence of the Armed Conflict (see S/26790, para. 70).

20. Also disturbing is the announcement by the National Reconstruction Secretariat of the closure of reintegration programmes for demobilized personnel of the Armed Forces, owing to lack of financial resources.

21. Understandably, these situations are creating serious discontent among the affected groups. The recent takeover of the Legislative Assembly, not for the first time, by a group of disgruntled former combatants of the armed forces who held hostage 27 legislators from various parties from 26 to 28 September has brought these tensions into focus. With ONUSAL as intermediary, talks were arranged and agreement was reached on ways to accelerate the completion of compensation payments, the implementation of established programmes and the incorporation of former members of paramilitary bodies in regular social programmes.

VII. Public administration

22. The restoration of public administration in former conflict zones has been virtually completed as regards the return of mayors and judges, but education, health care and other basic services are still lacking in several areas. Thorough reconstruction of the areas most ravaged by the war can be achieved only by making a decisive effort to extend these essential services to them. The Government has been urged repeatedly to give priority to these needs. It argues, however, that shortages in funding and resources have prevented the provision of basic services even in areas that were not affected by the conflict.

VIII. Financial aspects

23. The Fifth Committee, by its draft decision contained in document A/C.5/49/L.3 of 11 October 1994, recommended to the General Assembly that the Secretary-General be given authority to enter into commitments for the operation of ONUSAL in the amount of $5,643,700 gross ($5,040,800 net) for the period ending 30 November 1994. Therefore, should the Security Council decide to extend the current mandate of the Observer Mission beyond 30 November 1994, I shall request the General Assembly at its current session to make adequate financial provisions for the extension of the Mission.

24. As at 24 October 1994, unpaid assessed contributions to the ONUSAL special account (including the United Nations Observer Group for Central America) since the inception of the mission amounted to $23.8 million. In order to provide ONUSAL with the necessary cash-flow, a total of $9 million has been borrowed from other peace-keeping accounts. These loans remain unpaid. The total outstanding assessed contributions for all peace-keeping operations on 24 October 1994 amounted to $1,630.9 million.

IX. Observations

25. The Government of President Armando Calderón Sol has repeatedly confirmed its commitment to comply fully with those elements of the peace accords that remain to be implemented. The leadership and a large majority of the Armed Forces have also expressed the same commitment, even though a relatively small political sector continues to regard the armed forces as having made a disproportionate sacrifice as a consequence of the peace accords. This evidence of sustained political will is encouraging. However, it must be matched by concrete action and the capacity to activate still recalcitrant sectors within the administration. Delay in implementation of the outstanding commitments has also been due to lack of organization and expertise—a common phenomenon in developing countries—and, in some instances, to lack of financing. Furthermore, in compliance with the peace accords, some crucial elements still require the presence and assistance of the United Nations playing its verification and good offices role.

26. The joint declaration made on 4 October 1994 by the Government and FMLN, which reconfirmed the commitment of both signatories to complete implementation of the peace accords (see S/1994/1144), bears witness to the political will mentioned above. The parties intend to work out promptly specific agreements to accelerate implementation of the outstanding issues and to send a joint mission to donor countries and institutions to seek the funds still required to finance the programmes.

27. In addition to the delays in implementing the land and other reintegration programmes, inadequacies in the provision of credit and technical assistance are endangering their success and sustainability. United Nations agencies and programmes need to become more involved, but with a common design and strategy. Success of the reintegration programmes is critical to the consolidation of the peace process. Failure or continued delays could give rise to serious upheaval, as has been the case in other countries, including neighbouring ones. Promises have been made and they must be kept. A strong and urgent push to these programmes as well as to the problem of human settlements is imperative.

28. The United Nations undertaking in El Salvador has been innovative in a variety of ways. The Organization played a central role in the negotiation of the peace accords from start to finish and has overseen a multidimensional peace-keeping and peace-building operation in whose design it played a key part. It remains engaged in the transition from peace-keeping to post-conflict peace-building. This involves not only security-related aspects such as the abolition of the old military-controlled National Police and the creation of a new National Civil Police, following the reform of the Armed Forces in a role confined to defence against external threat, but also key institutional reforms designed to entrench the rule of law and provide a solid framework to guarantee respect for human rights. Last but not least, the United Nations supports a complex set of programmes for the reintegration into society of former combatants of both sides and of the rural populations who occupied land in conflict zones during the years of armed confrontation. In endorsing the Secretary-General's negotiating efforts and subsequently the peace accords themselves, the Security Council accepted the request of the parties that the United Nations verify compliance with all the agreements reached therein. The Council has confirmed this acceptance and did so again recently when it adopted the statement made on its behalf by the President on 16 September 1994 (S/PRST/1994/54).

29. The Salvadorian peace process holds the promise of being a remarkably successful achievement once it is completed. However, certain key undertakings have yet to be fully implemented, although it is expected that this can be done within a reasonable period of time. Both the Government of El Salvador and FMLN have stressed to me that, if that goal is to be achieved, it is essential for the United Nations to fulfil its commitment to the Salvadorian people to verify the full implementation of the peace accords. To this end I am exercising maximum suasion on the parties, both directly and through my Special Representative, reminding them of the international community's expectation that each will honour its commitments in full and promptly. In these circumstances, I believe that it is essential to retain ONUSAL in existence for one further mandate period, albeit at much reduced strength not exceeding a total of 100 international staff, to ensure that the incomplete undertakings are fully implemented, particularly until such a time as the National Police is completely disbanded and the National Civil Police is fully deployed and operational. These goals in the public security field should be accomplished in about five months. At that time it would be possible to consider how best to approach the remaining verification duties incumbent upon the Organization, which, although they would not involve United Nations military or police personnel, nevertheless concern critical and sensitive components of the peace accords. These include the institutional reforms in the judiciary, the recommendations of the Commission on the Truth and, most of all, the reintegration programmes, especially the extremely slow-moving land programme, which are critical to a durable peace.

30. Accordingly, I recommend to the Security Council the extension of ONUSAL until 30 April 1995, at which date that part of its functions which require military and police personnel will have been completed. Before the Mission's termination, I would present to the Security Council my thoughts on mechanisms to maintain United Nations verification thereafter, as well as information on technical assistance programmes in the fields of human rights, the judiciary, the electoral system and reintegration, especially land transfers, that would contribute to long-term political and social stability in the country. This approach responds to the widely held view that the termination of ONUSAL should not mark the end of United Nations efforts to consolidate peace in El Salvador.

31. In concluding, I pay tribute to my Special Representative, Mr. Enrique ter Horst, and to all the personnel of ONUSAL for the dedication, perseverance and exemplary manner in which they are carrying out the mandate entrusted to them. They have spared no effort to restore hope to the people of El Salvador and consolidate peace in their long-suffering country.

Addendum (S/1994/1212/Add.1)

Pursuant to paragraph 30 of my main report (S/1994/1212), I wish to inform the Security Council that the estimated cost of extending the United Nations Observer Mission in El Salvador (ONUSAL) for the five-month period from 1 December 1994 to 30 April 1995 would be approximately $5.5 million. The staffing component of the Observer Mission would consist of 3 military observers, 46 civilian police monitors and instructors, 59 international staff and 86 locally recruited staff. A breakdown of the estimated cost by main categories of expenditure is provided for information purposes in the annex to the present addendum.

It would be my recommendation to the General Assembly, should the Security Council decide to extend the mandate of ONUSAL, that the additional cost relating thereto should be considered an expense of the Organization to be borne by Member States in accordance with Article 17, paragraph 2, of the Charter of the United Nations and that the assessments to be levied on Member States should be credited to the ONUSAL special account.

Annex

Cost estimates for the extension of the United Nations Observer Mission in El Salvador (ONUSAL) for the period from 1 December 1994 to 30 April 1995

(Thousands of United States dollars)

	Amount
Military personnel costs	37.1
Civilian personnel costs	3 698.1
Premises/accommodation	372.5
Infrastructure repairs	-
Transport operations	126.0
Air operations	120.5
Naval operations	-
Communications	35.0
Other equipment	20.0
Supplies and services	146.0
Election-related supplies and services	-
Public information programmes	30.0
Training programmes	-
Mine-clearing programmes	-
Assistance for disarmament and demobilization	-
Air and surface freight	7.5
Integrated Management Information System (IMIS)	-
Support account for peace-keeping operations	261.4
Staff assessment	636.2
Total	5 490.3

Document 119

Report of the ONUSAL Human Rights Division covering the period from 1 July to 30 September 1994 (extract)

A/49/585-S/1994/1220, 31 October 1994

I. Introduction

1. The Human Rights Division has been reporting regularly to the Secretary-General on the human rights situation in El Salvador, largely on the basis of active verification of cases or situations that constitute or are likely to constitute human rights violations. On the basis of complaints received by ONUSAL statistics have been compiled which have helped to identify trends in human rights situation during specific periods and to keep track of broader trends as well.

2. However, it should be pointed out that progress or the lack thereof in consolidating the system for the protection of human rights in El Salvador cannot be measured solely on the basis of case statistics. Numerical discrepancies can be attributed to many different factors and occur repeatedly. Such an evaluation, then, must deal essentially with the state of the legal and political institutions for the protection of human rights in El Salvador which, at this stage in the peace process, are capable of consolidating the progress made.

3. While ONUSAL has not neglected verification of complaints of human rights violations, it has, in preparation for its withdrawal from El Salvador, gradually been shifting the focus of its active verification to institutional support, which offers an opportunity for making an overall assessment of the situation and determining whether a degree of "sustainable development" in human rights protection has been achieved by the anticipated date of completion of the Mission. The justification for this emphasis lies in the fact that permanent national institutions must fully assume prime responsibility for defending and protecting human rights in El Salvador as ONUSAL, which is an ad hoc and temporary mechanism, gradually withdraws from national life.

4. With this prospect in mind, the Human Rights Division has since July been working even more closely with the Office of the National Counsel for the Defence of Human Rights in the receiving and investigation of complaints. At the same time, the Division has been expanding its cooperation programmes with institutions responsible for the protection of human rights and the administration of justice in El Salvador, in order to help reform and strengthen them, pursuant to the guidelines set out by the parties in the peace agreements.

5. With these considerations in mind, this report has been prepared to inform the Secretary-General, and through him the Security Council, of the human rights situation in El Salvador, specifically in terms of the level of development and maturity of institutions responsible for defending, protecting and promoting human rights. For this reason, it differs in structure from previous reports. It contains a second chapter on institution-building and a third chapter that reviews the active verification of human rights on the basis of the complaints handled by ONUSAL.

. . .

IV. Conclusions and recommendations

105. Progress in the transition to democracy and the consolidation of a State governed by law called for in the El Salvador peace agreements can be seen in the clearly visible change in the country's political and social climate. A gradual expansion of opportunities seems to be convincing people that dialogue and consultation are legitimate democratic vehicles for social relations and the settlement of disputes and to be discrediting the use of violence at all levels. The result is an atmosphere of diminished tension and renewed calm within which the rights and freedoms of the individual can be exercised.

106. The progressive decline in the number of complaints declared admissible by ONUSAL since September 1991 is a useful indicator of the overall gradual improvement in the human rights situation, notwithstanding the reservations I have expressed in past reports. In September 1993 alone, for example, ONUSAL received 163 complaints of violations of fundamental rights, as compared with 58 complaints in September 1994. It is noteworthy that there have been no enforced disappearances in El Salvador for over two years, an unprecedented absence in Latin America during transitions to democracy. It is also significant that in September 1991 alone ONUSAL declared 119 complaints of arbitrary detention admissible, but only 13 in September 1994.

107. With respect to the right to life, in addition to the gradual decrease in the number of complaints of arbitrary executions, there has been an obvious change in the nature of the violations reported, which less and less often present the shady characteristics of previous periods, such as political motivation and premeditation. The arbitrary executions reported during this period are explained chiefly by police inexperience in the legitimate exercise of force, a shortcoming that must be promptly corrected.

108. It is encouraging that during the reporting period no politically motivated violations of the right to life were noted. This can be explained in large measure by the political liberalization and democratization of the country, together with the response by the State, Salvadorian society and the international community to the ominous period of selective violence in the second half of 1993 directed at citizens who were openly involved in politics. The cooperation of the international community in looking into these incidents, as evidenced by the participation of foreign investigators in police investigations at the invitation of the Government and, at a very basic level, by the creation, at the suggestion of the Secretary-General, of the Joint Unit for the Investigation of Illegal Armed Groups having Political Motivations, seems to have served as a deterrent to political violence.

109. More importantly, however, it is necessary to eradicate definitively all vestiges of the practice of using violence for political purposes and to dismantle the mechanism through which it operates: organized crime. This can be accomplished only by strengthening and consolidating the institutions responsible for criminal investigation and the administration of justice, which will mean lifting the veil of impunity that currently conceals these crimes and makes a resurgence of politically motivated violence possible. For this reason the recommendations of the Joint Unit for the Investigation of Illegal Armed Groups having Political Motivations—that the Office of the Attorney-General continue its investigations of the cases before it and that it form a special unit for the investigation of politically motivated crimes within the Criminal Investigation Section of the National Civil Police—are indeed appropriate.

110. The continued existence of organized crime networks, some of which would appear to involve current members of security forces in cover-ups or their actual operations and enjoy a margin of impunity as a result of weaknesses in the judicial system, constitutes one of the most serious threats to the peace process and democracy in El Salvador. With their sophisticated organization and infrastructure, these criminal structures are not only able to operate in the everyday criminal world but, when necessary, can also direct their machinery against politically active groups or individuals. It is easy to find examples in Latin America of how serious the failure to combat and eradicate criminal organizations promptly can be for political and social stability.

111. The process of institution-building is beginning to overcome initial difficulties and get truly under way. During the reporting period, progress was achieved within the judicial system, the Office of the National Counsel for the Defence of Human Rights and the National Civil Police, and the prospects for carrying out hitherto unimplemented recommendations on the administration of justice and human rights have improved.

112. The Legislative Assembly's election by consensus of a new Supreme Court of Justice is an important step towards guaranteeing the autonomy and impartiality that the chief judicial body requires and will also foster further judicial reform. The new Court's determination to promote this process can already be seen in a number of measures to reorganize the court system and in the Court's manifest intention to purify the judiciary. The results of these efforts would have optimal effect if emphasis was placed on the ongoing professionalization of members of the judicial system and a strategy for the comprehensive training of judges and government procurators with a view to identifying the new qualifications such officials should possess in a democratic judicial system which deserves the support of the international community.

113. The biggest obstacle to the process of institution-building is the delay in enacting certain legal reforms. This view is corroborated by an anonymous survey conducted among government procurators, justices of the peace and judges of courts of first instance regarding the main deficiencies in the administration of justice. Similarly, the enhancing of measures for the protection of human rights in El Salvador is contingent upon the adoption of the various international instruments and acceptance of the competence of the Inter-American Court of Human Rights, neither of which has occurred despite repeated recommendations. All of this leads me to suggest that the members of the Supreme Court of Justice should press the Legislative Assembly to approve the pending reforms soon.

114. The Office of the National Counsel for the Defence of Human Rights has made progress in strengthening its institutional capacity. Its involvement in technical cooperation activities and its implementation in July with the Human Rights Division of a joint verification mechanism have been decisive in enabling the Office to broaden and strengthen human rights protection and in improving its ability to take over the verification activities currently performed by ONUSAL when ONUSAL leaves the country. However, the Government and the Legislative Assembly need to budget sufficient funds for the Office's requirements, given its cooperation with ONUSAL in the overhaul of the Office's monitoring system and the need for it to continue to operate throughout the country.

115. At this stage, the progress made in deploying the National Civil Police should be accompanied by increased professionalism and specialization in police activities, a strengthening of internal police control mechanisms and a clearer definition of the Force's chain of command. The appointment of an Inspector-General

of the National Civil Police during this period represents a significant advance. Changes in the National Civil Police must be accompanied by steps in the judiciary, the Office of the Chief State Counsel and the Office of the Attorney-General to overcome the deficiencies that hinder police activities, as well as by improving linkages between the National Civil Police and the National Public Security Academy.

116. The problems in the penitentiary system confirmed by ONUSAL two years ago have yet to be solved. This situation, coupled with the successive riots in the country's detention centres, led me to suggest the declaration of a state of emergency in the penitentiary system. I have submitted to various State entities a series of proposals for the joint implementation of solutions to the crisis that go beyond improving the prison infrastructure. I have suggested the establishment of a comprehensive

plan for reorienting Salvadorian criminal policy which would include the following measures. The Supreme Court of Justice should issue a series of instructions to judges regarding the discretional use of pre-trial detention, the notification of defendants of any circumstance which may affect their legal position and closer supervision over prison officials. The Office of the Attorney-General should instruct government procurators to be more selective in appealing pre-trial release orders and to the supervision and orientation of criminal investigations. The Office of the Chief State Counsel of the Republic should establish internal mechanisms for controlling the work of defence attorneys in trials where the defendant is present. These measures would complement others required of the central Government and the penitentiary system itself, such as increasing budget allocations and unifying the penitentiary regulations.

Document 120

Security Council resolution concerning the peace process in El Salvador and the extension of ONUSAL's mandate

S/RES/961, 23 November 1994

The Security Council,

Recalling its resolution 637 (1989) of 27 July 1989,

Recalling also its resolutions 693 (1991) of 20 May 1991, 714 (1991) of 30 September 1991, 729 (1992) of 14 January 1992, 784 (1992) of 30 October 1992, 791 (1992) of 30 November 1992, 832 (1993) of 27 May 1993, 888 (1993) of 30 November 1993 and 920 (1994) of 26 May 1994, and recalling also the statement of the President of the Council of 16 September 1994 , 1/

Having considered the report of the Secretary-General of 31 October 1994, 2/

Having considered also the report of the Joint Group for the Investigation of Politically Motivated Illegal Armed Groups of 28 July 1994, as contained in the letter of the Secretary-General dated 22 October 1994, 3/

Noting the request of the Government of El Salvador and the Frente Farabundo Martí para la Liberación Nacional (FMLN) for a further extension of the mandate of the United Nations Observer Mission in El Salvador in the joint declaration dated 4 October 1994, as contained in the letter of the Secretary-General of 10 October 1994, 4/

Concerned by delays in implementing several important elements of the peace accords, particularly those regarding the National Civil Police and the completion of demobilization of the National Police, as well as those related to: the transfer of lands, the implementation of programmes to facilitate the reintegration into civilian

society of ex-combatants and war-disabled, the problems of human settlements, the reform of the judicial and electoral systems, and several recommendations of the Commission on the Truth,

Noting with appreciation the accomplishments of the Observer Mission to date and the continuing efforts of the Secretary-General, his Special Representative and the Mission to support the full implementation of the agreements signed by the Government of El Salvador and FMLN to maintain and consolidate peace and promote reconciliation in El Salvador,

Welcoming the ongoing efforts of the Secretary-General to contain the costs of the Observer Mission,

Welcoming the continuing commitment by all concerned directed towards reconciliation, stability and development in political life in El Salvador, as noted by the Secretary-General in his report of 31 October 1994,

1. *Welcomes* the report of the Secretary-General of 31 October 1994;

2. *Reaffirms* the importance of full and timely implementation of all aspects of the peace accords, including the recommendations of the Commission on the Truth, and appropriate follow-up to the findings of the

1/ S/PRST/1994/54.
2/ S/PRST/212.
3/ S/1994/989.
4/ S/1994/1144.

Joint Group for Investigation of Politically Motivated Illegal Armed Groups;

3. *Expresses concern* that important elements of the peace accords remain only partially implemented;

4. *Calls upon* all concerned to cooperate fully with the Secretary-General's Special Representative and the Observer Mission in their task of verifying implementation by the parties of their commitments;

5. *Urges* the Government of El Salvador and the FMLN to redouble their efforts to comply with the "Agreement on a timetable for the implementation of the most important agreements pending" so as to complete implementation of all aspects of the peace accords within the period of the timetable and requests the Secretary-General to keep the Security Council informed on a regular basis of the status of implementation of outstanding commitments and the Observer Mission operations;

6. *Urges* all States and the international institutions engaged in the fields of development and finance to contribute promptly and generously in support of the implementation of all aspects of the peace accords, as requested jointly by the Government of El Salvador and FMLN;

7. *Approves* the recommendations by the Secretary-General in his report of 31 October 1994 regarding the implementation by the Observer Mission of its mandate;

8. *Decides* to extend the mandate of the Mission for one final period until 30 April 1995;

9. *Requests also* the Secretary-General to report by 31 March 1995 on the Mission, including on the fulfilment and completion of its mandate and on modalities for its withdrawal, to be completed by 30 April 1995, in a manner consistent with the effective performance of its duties;

10. *Reaffirms* the commitment undertaken by the United Nations to verify full implementation of the peace accords; welcomes the intention of the Secretary-General to consider ways for the United Nations to discharge its remaining verification duties; and invites the Secretary-General, in consultation with competent specialized agencies, regional organizations and Member States, to prepare modalities for further assistance to El Salvador, within the framework of the peace accords, for the period after 30 April 1995;

11. *Decides* to remain seized of the matter.

Document 121

Resolution of the General Assembly concerning the situation in Central America: procedures for the establishment of a firm and lasting peace and progress in fashioning a region of peace, freedom, democracy and development

A/RES/49/137, 19 December 1994

The General Assembly,

Recalling the relevant resolutions of the Security Council and its own resolutions, particularly resolutions 47/118 of 18 December 1992 and 48/161 of 20 December 1993, in which it recognized that there remained in Central America major obstacles to the full exercise of peace, freedom, democracy and development and the need for a global frame of reference that would enable the international community to channel support to the efforts of the Central American Governments, as well as the desirability of increasing support by providing resources for the consolidation of the objectives set, in order to prevent the region's material limitations from diminishing or reversing the progress made,

Recognizing the importance and validity of the commitments assumed by the Central American Presidents at the Esquipulas II summit meeting on 7 August 1987 and at their subsequent summit meetings, especially the fourteenth summit meeting, held at Guatemala City from 27 to 29 October 1993, the fifteenth summit meeting, held at Guácimo, Costa Rica, from 18 to 20 August 1994, the Central American Environment Summit for Sustainable Development, held at Managua on 12 and 13 October 1994, and the International Conference on Peace and Development in Central America, held at Tegucigalpa on 24 and 25 October 1994, at which a framework of priorities for the formulation and implementation of an integrated strategy for sustainable development covering political, moral, economic, social and ecological matters was established,

Aware of the importance of supporting the efforts of the Central American peoples and Governments for the consolidation of a firm and lasting peace in Central America, and bearing in mind that the Central American Integration System constitutes the institutional framework for subregional integration through which integrated development can be promoted in an effective, orderly and coherent manner,

Convinced of the hopes that inspire the peoples of Central America to achieve peace, reconciliation, development and social justice, as well as the commitment to settle their differences by means of dialogue, negotiation and respect for the legitimate interests of all States, in accordance with their own decision and their own historical experience, while fully respecting the principles of self-determination and non-intervention,

Recognizing the importance of the peace-keeping operations that have been carried out in Central America pursuant to the decisions of the Security Council and with the support of the Secretary-General,

Recognizing also the need to preserve and enhance the results obtained by means of new and innovative initiatives that take into account the new circumstances prevailing in the region, which necessitate a new course based on an integrated strategy for sustainable development in the region,

Reaffirming that there can be no peace in Central America without sustainable development or democracy, which are essential for transforming the region and realizing the hope of the Central American peoples and Governments that Central America may become a region of peace, freedom, democracy and sustainable development,

Emphasizing the important role of international cooperation in supporting the integrated proposal for sustainable development agreed on at the most recent meetings of Central American Presidents, in particular the Central American Environment Summit for Sustainable Development and the International Conference on Peace and Development in Central America,

Stressing the importance of honouring the commitments to accelerate the establishment of a new model of regional security in Central America, as established in the Tegucigalpa Protocol of 13 December 1991 1/ and the Agenda and Programme of Specific Action for Sustainable Development adopted at the fifteenth meeting of Central American Presidents, at Guácimo,

Noting with satisfaction the progress made in the peace negotiations between the Government of Guatemala and the Unidad Revolucionaria Nacional Guatemalteca, with the assistance of the Secretary-General and the support of the Group of Friends of the Guatemalan peace process (Colombia, Mexico, Norway, Spain, United States of America and Venezuela), and the contribution by the Assembly of Civil Society and other Guatemalans, within the constitutional framework and the peace agreements,

Recalling its resolution 48/267 of 19 September 1994, in which it decided to establish the United Nations Mission for the Verification of Human Rights and of Compliance with the Commitments of the Comprehensive Agreement on Human Rights in Guatemala, in accordance with the recommendations of the Secretary-General,

Stressing the great importance it attaches to the conclusion of the negotiations, the speedy termination of the internal armed conflict and the full compliance by both parties with the undertakings agreed to, all of which will help the people of Guatemala to overcome successfully the social and economic problems facing the country,

Taking into account the commitment expressed by both parties, the Government of Guatemala and the Unidad Revolucionaria Nacional Guatemalteca, to achieve the full exercise of human rights and to seek peace through dialogue and negotiation,

Noting with satisfaction the holding of free and democratic elections in El Salvador, the progress made towards fulfilment of the outstanding commitments assumed under the peace accord, the political will consistently expressed by the signatories thereto and the support of the various Salvadorian political forces for accelerating the resolution of crucial outstanding issues, which is essential to promote reconciliation and maintain and consolidate peace in El Salvador,

Also taking into account the efforts made by the Government of Nicaragua to promote broad national agreement as the best way of consolidating peace, national reconciliation, democracy and sustainable development with social justice,

Welcoming with satisfaction the adoption of resolution 49/16 of 17 November 1994, entitled "International assistance for the rehabilitation and reconstruction of Nicaragua: aftermath of the war and natural disasters", in which the exceptional circumstances prevailing in the case of Nicaragua are recognized,

Recognizing that the consolidation of peace in Nicaragua is a key factor in the Central American peace process, as well as the need for the international community and the United Nations system to continue providing Nicaragua with the support it needs to continue promoting its economic and social rehabilitation and reconstruction in order to strengthen democracy and overcome the aftermath of war and recent natural disasters,

Also recognizing the valuable and effective contribution of the United Nations and of various governmental and non-governmental mechanisms to the process of democratization, pacification and development in Central America, and the importance for the gradual transformation of Central America into a region of peace, freedom, democracy and development of both the political dialogue and the economic cooperation set in motion by the ministerial conference between the European Union and the Central American countries and the joint initiative of the industrialized countries (Group of Twenty-four) and the group of cooperating countries

1/ A/46/829-S/23310, annex III.

(Group of Three) 2/ through the Partnership for Democracy and Development in Central America,

Bearing in mind that the process established by the International Conference on Central American Refugees was completed in May 1994, that the United Nations Development Programme has assumed the role of lead agency which was formerly performed by the Office of the United Nations High Commissioner for Refugees and that the mandate of the Special Plan of Economic Cooperation for Central America, 3/ through which both the United Nations system and the international community, and especially the cooperating countries, have supported activities supplementing the Central American peace process, has come to an end,

Considering the Declaration of Commitments in favour of the populations affected both by uprootedness and by conflicts and extreme poverty in the framework of the consolidation of peace in Central America, adopted at Mexico City on 29 June 1994 at the final international meeting of the Follow-up Committee of the International Conference on Central American Refugees, in which the Governments of the convening States emphasized the need to give continuity to the treatment of uprooted populations by changing the emphasis from emergency programmes to sustainable human development strategies in areas or populations given priority by the countries concerned for the consolidation of peace and the eradication of extreme poverty,

Aware that the Central American countries have concluded the Alliance for the Sustainable Development of Central America, 4/ an initiative that inaugurates a promising phase involving the reordering of regional priorities, the effective implementation of which calls for maximum effort on the part of the Governments and the various sectors of the Central American countries, as well as the support of the international community, in order to overcome the underlying structural causes of the crisis in the region,

Taking note of the report of the Secretary-General of 7 October 1994 on the situation in Central America, 5/

Welcoming with deep satisfaction the Tegucigalpa Commitments on Peace and Development 6/ adopted at the International Conference on Peace and Development in Central America,

1. *Commends* the efforts of the Central American peoples and Governments to consolidate peace by implementing the agreements adopted at recent meetings of the Central American Presidents, especially their fifteenth meeting, held at Guácimo, Costa Rica, the Central American Environment Summit for Sustainable Development, held at Managua, and the International Conference on Peace and Development in Central America, held at Tegucigalpa, and requests the Secretary-General to continue to give the fullest possible support to the initiatives and activities of the Central American Governments;

2. *Supports* the decision of the Central American Presidents to declare Central America a region of peace, freedom, democracy and development, as set out in the Tegucigalpa Protocol, 1/ and encourages the initiatives of the Central American countries, in the framework of the integrated strategy for sustainable development and based on the latest Central American meetings, to consolidate Governments which base their development on democracy, peace, cooperation and full respect for human rights;

3. *Emphasizes* the decision of the Central American Presidents included in the Declaration of Guácimo 7/ and adopted at the Managua Environment Summit, in which the national and regional strategy known as the Alliance for Sustainable Development—a comprehensive Central American initiative in the political, moral, economic, social and environmental fields—was concretized, translating that strategy into a programme of immediate action through which the Central American countries hope to become, with the support of the international community, an example of sustainable development for other regions;

4. *Welcomes* the efforts of the Central American countries to promote economic growth within a context of human development, as well as the progress achieved in strengthening democracy and consolidating peace in the region, as amply demonstrated by the successful holding of fair and transparent electoral processes in Costa Rica, El Salvador, Honduras and Panama;

5. *Also emphasizes* the functioning of the Central American Integration System since 1 February 1993 and the registry of the Tegucigalpa Protocol with the United Nations Secretariat, expresses its full support for the efforts made by Central Americans, under the political leadership of their Presidents, to stimulate and broaden the integration process in the context of the Central American Integration System, and calls on Member States and international organizations to provide effective cooperation to Central America so that it can steadily promote and strengthen subregional integration in order to make it an effective mechanism for achieving sustainable development;

6. *Reaffirms* the importance of creating a new model of regional security based on a reasonable balance of forces, the pre-eminence of civil authority, the elimination of extreme poverty, the promotion of sustainable development, the protection of the environment and the eradication of violence, corruption, terrorism and trafficking in drugs and arms, a commitment made at the

---

2/ The group of cooperating countries, known as the "Group of Three", consists of Colombia, Mexico and Venezuela.
3/ A/42/949, annex.
4/ A/49/580-S/1994/1217, annex I.
5/ A/49/489 and Corr.1.
6/ A/49/639-S/1994/1247, annex II.
7/ A/49/340-S/1994/994, annex.

fifteenth meeting of Central American Presidents;

7. *Calls upon* the international community and the United Nations system to expand their technical and financial support for the professionalization of the police forces of the Central American countries in order to safeguard democratic institutions;

8. *Notes with satisfaction* the signing of the Framework Agreement for the Resumption of the Negotiating Process between the Government of Guatemala and the Unidad Revolucionaria Nacional Guatemalteca, 8/ the Comprehensive Agreement on Human Rights and the Agreement on a Timetable for the Negotiation of a Firm and Lasting Peace in Guatemala, 9/ the Agreement on Resettlement of the Population Groups Uprooted by the Armed Conflict and the Agreement on the Establishment of the Commission to Clarify Past Human Rights Violations and Acts of Violence that have Caused the Guatemalan Population to Suffer; 10/

9. *Recognizes* the importance of the decision of the Government of Guatemala and the Unidad Revolucionaria Nacional Guatemalteca to negotiate seriously and resolutely with a view to reaching peace agreements with no further delay;

10. *Calls upon* those concerned to advance speedily in the Guatemalan peace process in order to achieve, as close as possible to the 31 December deadline, agreement on a firm and lasting peace in keeping with the commitments made in the Framework Agreement;

11. *Reiterates its appreciation* to the Secretary-General and the Group of Friends for their efforts in support of the Guatemalan peace process, as well as its appreciation for the contribution of the Assembly of Civil Society and other Guatemalans, within the constitutional framework and the peace agreements, for their efforts in support of that process;

12. *Notes with satisfaction* the establishment of the United Nations Mission for the Verification of Human Rights and of Compliance with the Commitments of the Comprehensive Agreement on Human Rights in Guatemala, and, in the context of human rights, urges those concerned fully to comply with their commitments under the agreements already signed, including the agreement relating to the Mission;

13. *Also notes with satisfaction* the efforts of the Secretary-General, the agencies of the United Nations system and the international community as a whole to coordinate their support for the peace process and, in particular, for the implementation of the agreements, and encourages them to continue their assistance in favour of peace, national reconciliation, democracy and development in Guatemala;

14. *Requests* the Secretary-General to continue his support for the Guatemalan peace process, through his representative, and his assistance in implementing the agreements;

15. *Calls upon* the Government of El Salvador and all the political forces involved in the peace process to make all possible efforts to fulfil their vital outstanding commitments in accordance with the "Timetable for the implementation of the most important outstanding agreements" 11/ and fully to implement all aspects of the agreements, and requests the Secretary-General, in consultation with the Government of El Salvador, the Member States and the specialized agencies, to devise procedures for providing El Salvador, in the context of the peace accord, with the necessary cooperation and assistance in the period after the United Nations Observer Mission in El Salvador, in order to safeguard peace and the strengthening and consolidation of national reconciliation, democracy and sustainable development;

16. *Requests* all States and invites the international development and financing institutions to react quickly and generously to the joint appeal of the Government of El Salvador and the Frente Farabundo Martí para la Liberación Nacional to provide the additional resources required for the full implementation of the peace accord;

17. Reiterates its recognition of the effective and timely participation of the Secretary-General and his representatives and encourages them to continue to take all necessary steps to ensure the successful implementation of all the commitments made by the parties to the El Salvador peace accord, including efforts to mobilize the necessary resources for the reconstruction and development of the country, which are essential for the consolidation of peace and democracy in El Salvador;

18. *Recognizes* the achievements made by the people and Government of Nicaragua in their efforts to consolidate peace, democracy and reconciliation among Nicaraguans, as well as the political dialogue and process of economic and social consultation among all sectors of the country, in order to strengthen the bases for the country's reconstruction;

19. *Supports* the treatment accorded to Nicaragua in the light of its continuing exceptional circumstances, so that the international community and financial institutions can incorporate that treatment into programmes to support the country's economic recovery and social reconstruction;

20. *Expresses its approval* of the establishment of a support group for Nicaragua, which, under the coordination of the Secretary-General, is playing an active role in supporting the country's efforts towards economic recovery and social development, particularly with regard to solving the external debt problem and securing invest-

8/ A/49/61-S/1994/53, annex.
9/ A/48/928-S/1994/448, annexes I and II.
10/ A/48/954-S/1994/751, annexes I and II.
11/ See S/1994/612.

ments and new resources that will allow the country's economic and social reconstruction programmes to continue, and requests the Secretary-General to continue to support those efforts;

21. *Emphasizes* the importance that the political dialogue and economic cooperation under way within the ministerial conference between the European Union and its member States and the Central American countries, with the participation of the Group of Three 2/ as cooperating countries, have for the Central American countries' efforts to achieve peace, consolidate democracy and ensure sustainable development;

22. *Requests* the Secretary-General to give the Central American countries every possible assistance for the consolidation of peace and the strategy of sustainable development in the region;

23. *Recognizes* the importance of implemented, updated and pending programmes, and, in view of the fact that the resources assigned to the Special Plan of Economic Cooperation for Central America have been used up, requests the agencies of the United Nations system, in particular the United Nations Development Programme, and international institutions to mobilize the necessary resources to set in motion new national and regional programmes in support of the content of the Declaration of Guácimo, 7/ the Alliance for the Sustainable Development of Central America 4/ concluded at the Managua Summit, and the Tegucigalpa Commitments on Peace and Development 6/ adopted at the International Conference on Peace and Development in Central America, in order to prevent the progress made in Central America from being reversed and to ensure that peace is consolidated in the region by means of integrated, sustainable development;

24. *Reiterates its appreciation* to the United Na-

tions High Commissioner for Refugees and the United Nations Development Programme for carrying out their mandate under the International Conference on Central American Refugees, and requests the international community to continue supporting the region in the efforts needed to comply with the Declaration of Commitments adopted at Mexico City on 29 June 1994, as part of the new strategies for sustainable human development to eradicate extreme poverty and consolidate peace in the new Central American context;

25. *Emphasizes* the commitments on sustainable development adopted at the fifteenth meeting of Central American Presidents, the Central American Environment Summit for Sustainable Development and the International Conference on Peace and Development in Central America, and urges States Members and organs of the United Nations system to give them every support;

26. *Reiterates its full appreciation* to and thanks the Secretary-General for his efforts in favour of the pacification process in Central America, particularly in those countries where it is necessary to achieve and consolidate peace, national reconciliation, democracy and sustainable development, and to the groups of friendly countries which have made a direct contribution to attaining those ends;

27. *Decides* to include in the provisional agenda of its fiftieth session the item entitled "The situation in Central America: procedures for the establishment of a firm and lasting peace and progress in fashioning a region of peace, freedom, democracy and development";

28. *Requests* the Secretary-General to report to it at its fiftieth session on the implementation of the present resolution.

Document 122

Letter dated 6 February 1995 from the Secretary-General to the President of the Security Council concerning post-ONUSAL arrangements

S/1995/143, 17 February 1995

I would like to bring to the attention of the members of the Security Council certain concerns with regard to the forthcoming end of the mandate of the United Nations Observer Mission in El Salvador (ONUSAL).

It will be recalled that, in the report I submitted on 31 October 1994 (S/1994/1212) on the occasion of the expiry of ONUSAL's previous mandate period, I recommended to the Security Council the extension of

ONUSAL until 30 April 1995, at which date that part of its functions requiring military and police personnel would have been completed. I also informed the Council that, before the Mission's termination, I would present my thoughts on mechanisms to maintain the capacity of the United Nations to verify compliance with those parts of the peace accords whose implementation was still pending, in accordance with the commitment undertaken by the United Nations as reaffirmed by the Council.

In resolution 961 (1994), the Security Council approved my recommendations regarding ONUSAL's performance of its mandate and decided to renew the mandate "for one final period until 30 April 1995". The Council also requested me to "report by 31 March 1995 on ONUSAL, including on the fulfilment and completion of its mandate and on modalities for its withdrawal, to be completed by 30 April 1995, in a manner consistent with the effective performance of its duties".

Informal reports on the status of the 19 May 1994 timetable for the implementation of the most important outstanding agreements have been made available periodically to the members of the Security Council. As they will see from the latest report, which is submitted separately, a somewhat disquieting situation still obtains, particularly as regards the implementation of agreements concerning land and other reintegration programmes including the difficult issue of human settlements, as well as those related to the judiciary, electoral reform and the binding recommendations of the Commission on the Truth. The recent forcible takeover of the Legislative Assembly and the Ministry of Finance and of land by members of the Association of Demobilized Members of the Armed Forces, which was fortunately defused with the assistance of ONUSAL, is but one symptom of lingering discontent at the failure to implement some parts of the peace agreements.

These considerations reaffirm my conviction that it is essential to put in place, following the disbandment of ONUSAL *per se*, a mechanism to continue the verification responsibilities and the good offices function that ONUSAL has carried out to date. I am raising the matter at this time, without waiting until late March, because the Council's decision in resolution 961 (1994) that ONUSAL's withdrawal should be completed by 30 April 1995 has the practical effect of reducing, well before that date, ONUSAL's capability to perform its duties effectively. This is because measures have to be taken well in advance of that date to draw down the Mission's personnel. It therefore becomes urgent that decisions be taken to enable the United Nations to continue to discharge its responsibilities without interruption, as has been requested by the Government of El Salvador and the Frente Farabundo Martí para la Liberación Nacional (FMLN), the signatories to the peace agreements.

The arrangement that I propose to put in place would consist of a small team of about eight Professionals, with the necessary support staff. This team would have the capability to provide good offices, to verify implementation of the outstanding points on the peace agreements and to provide a continuing flow of accurate and reliable information so that I can keep the Security Council informed as necessary.

ONUSAL has been coordinating closely with the Resident Representative of the United Nations Development Programme (UNDP) in El Salvador in order to ensure that the latter is in a position to continue to help to consolidate peace. I would ensure that this cooperation continues so as to maintain a truly integrated approach in the post-conflict peace-building phase. I would hope to minimize the costs of the United Nations team by utilizing UNDP facilities. However, it would be necessary for the team to maintain a separate identity, given its inherently political tasks and responsibilities and the fact that verification and good offices require an independence and impartiality that could prove difficult to reconcile with UNDP's role as a partner of the Government. The United Nations team would of course advise UNDP on the execution of peace-related programmes.

I would propose to establish this team of Professionals for an initial period of six months from the end of ONUSAL's mandate.

(*Signed*) Boutros BOUTROS-GHALI

Document 123

Letter dated 17 February 1995 from the President of the Security Council to the Secretary-General concerning post-ONUSAL arrangements

S/1995/144, 17 February 1995

I have the honour to inform you that your letter dated 6 February 1995 (S/1995/143), concerning the arrangement that you propose to put in place following the termination of the United Nations Observer Mission in El Salvador (ONUSAL) has been brought to the attention of the members of the Council. They welcome the proposal contained in your letter that verification responsibilities and the good offices function be carried out under your authority, in the manner you propose.

(*Signed*) Legwaila Joseph LEGWAILA
President of the Security Council

V   Subject index to documents

*[This subject index to the documents reproduced in this book should be used
in conjunction with the index on pages 608-611. A complete listing of the documents
indexed below appears on pages 77-85.]*

A

Abduction.
– Document 67

Act of New York I (1991).
– Documents 34, 37

Act of New York II (1992).
– Document 37

Administration of justice.
– Documents 43, 70, 77, 83, 90, 93-94, 96-97, 105,
114, 119
See also: Due process of law. Judges. Judicial system.
Right to a fair trial. Right to counsel.

Agreement on Human Rights (1990).
– Documents 9, 30, 42-43, 45, 50, 53, 70

Agricultural land.
– Document 56
See also: Land reform. Land tenure.

Allotment of land.
See: Land allotment.

Amparo.
– Documents 89, 105
See also: Civil and political rights. Criminal
procedure. Detained persons.

Arbitrary executions.
See: Extralegal executions.

Armaments.
– Documents 56, 60, 79-82, 85, 95, 110
See also: Armed forces.

Armed conflicts.
– Document 8
See also: Armed incidents. Disputes. Human rights in
armed conflicts.

Armed forces.
– Documents 23, 29, 30, 38, 41, 44, 55-56, 58,
62, 67, 69-70, 74, 77-78, 84, 87, 90, 94, 99, 103,
109-111, 113-115, 118
See also: Armaments. Child soldiers. Military
demobilization. Military personnel. Military reform.
Troop withdrawal.

Armed incidents.
– Documents 7, 30
See also: Armed conflicts.

Arms transfers.
– Document 81

Arrest.
– Document 38
See also: Criminal procedure. Detained persons.

Assassination.
– Documents 67, 92
See also: Extralegal executions. Political violence.

B

Boutros-Ghali, Boutros.
–Documents 34, 39-42, 44, 46-53, 55-58, 60,
62-64, 68-69, 71-79, 82, 84-88, 90-92, 94-97,
99-104, 107-112, 115, 117-118, 122

C

Caracas Agreement (1990)
–Documents 11, 28, 99

Cease-fires.
–Documents 7, 11-12, 16, 20-21, 26, 34, 38, 41-42,
44, 50, 56-58, 60, 65, 70, 80, 82, 115, 118
See also: Truce supervision.

Central America situation.
–Documents 1-8, 11-13, 20, 26, 31, 35, 58, 80, 81,
106
See also: Nicaragua situation.

Charter of the United Nations (1945).
–Document 14

Child soldiers.
–Document 30
See also: Armed forces.

Civil and political rights.
–Documents 9, 67
See also: Amparo. Due process of law. Freedom of
association. Freedom of expression. Freedom of
movement. Right of assembly. Right to a fair trial.
Right to counsel. Right to life.

Civil liberties.
See: Civil and political rights.

Civil rights.
See: Civil and political rights.

Civil service.
– Documents 77, 86

Civilian persons.
– Documents 24, 30, 38, 110-111
See also: Human rights in armed conflicts.

Commission on the Truth.
See: UN Truth Commission to Investigate Serious Acts of Violence in El Salvador.

Commissions of inquiry.
– Documents 1, 67, 90, 92-94, 105
See also: Dispute settlement. Fact-finding missions. Special missions.

Compensation.
– Documents 89, 105, 109

Compressed Negotiations (1991).
– Documents 25

Conflict resolution.
See: Dispute settlement.

Constitutions.
– Documents 15, 17-18, 29, 68, 71-73, 77, 86, 90, 101, 105-106, 114

Consultations.
– Documents 7, 22-23, 111
See also: Dispute settlement. Negotiation.

Contadora Group.
– Document 2

Conventions.
See: Treaties.

Costs.
– Documents 109, 111, 115, 118

Crime.
– Document 70
See also: Criminal procedure. Drug traffic. Organized crime.

Criminal investigation.
– Documents 43, 45, 67-68, 70, 89, 92, 95, 97, 105, 113, 120
See also: Police.

Criminal procedure.
– Document 105
See also: Amparo. Arrest. Crime. Judicial system.

Cristiani, Alfredo.
– Documents 8, 14-15, 17-18, 22-23, 32, 46, 49, 51, 68, 71, 86, 99, 101, 112

D

Declaration of Puntarenas (1990).
– Document 12

Declaration of San Isidro de Coronado (1989).
– Document 8

Declarations.
– Documents 2-3, 6, 8, 12, 29

Detained persons.
– Documents 43, 45, 77, 89, 98, 105
See also: Amparo. Arrest. Disappearance of persons. Extralegal executions. Political prisoners. Prisoner treatment. Torture and other cruel treatment.

Development.
– Document 12
See also: Development assistance.

Development assistance.
– Documents 95, 111, 115, 118
See also: Development. Technical cooperation.

Disappearance of persons.
– Documents 45, 67
See also: Detained persons. Extralegal executions. Human rights violations. Torture and other cruel treatment.

Dismissal.
See: Employee dismissal.

Displaced persons.
– Document 30
See also: Humanitarian assistance. War victims.

Dispute settlement.
– Documents 3-5, 19-21, 25-28, 31, 33-37, 39, 42, 44, 50, 53-62, 65-66, 69, 99, 106, 110, 112
See also: Commissions of inquiry. Consultations. Disputes. Fact-finding missions. Mediation. Negotiation. Special missions.

Disputes.
– Document 5
See also: Armed conflicts. Dispute settlement.

Domestic security.
See: Internal security.

Drug traffic.
– Document 3
See also: Organized crime.

Due process of law.
– Documents 30, 38, 43, 45, 89
See also: Administration of justice. Civil and
political rights. Right to a fair trial.

E

Economic and social development.
See: Development.

Economic integration.
– Document 12

Economic planning.
– Document 12

Educational policy.
– Document 12

Election campaigns.
– Documents 102, 104, 108
See also: Election law. Elections.

Election law.
– Document 56
See also: Election campaigns. Elections.

Election verification.
– Documents 4, 7, 11, 14, 63, 74-75, 78, 91, 95,
  100, 102, 104, 106-108
See also: Elections. Technical cooperation. Voter
registration.

Elections.
– Documents 1, 4, 7, 11-12, 29, 41, 44, 63, 65,
  74-75, 78, 91, 93-95, 100, 102-104, 106-108, 111
See also: Election campaigns. Election law. Election
verification. Voter registration.

Electoral assistance.
See: Election verification.

Employee dismissal.
– Document 77

Environmental protection.
– Document 12

Extralegal executions.
– Documents 38, 45, 67, 83, 89, 98, 105
See also: Assassination. Detained persons. Disappearance of persons. Political prisoners. Right to life. Summary executions. Torture and other cruel treatment.

F

Fact-finding missions.
– Documents 9, 24, 34, 67
See also: Commissions of inquiry. Dispute
settlement. Special missions.

Financial assistance.
– Documents 78, 95, 111, 120

Financing.
– Documents 16, 41, 52, 56, 74-75, 109, 115, 118

FMLN.
See: Frente Farabundo Martí para la Liberación
Nacional.

Foreign trade.
– Document 12

Freedom of assembly.
See: Right of assembly.

Freedom of association.
– Documents 38, 70, 83, 102, 105
See also: Right of assembly. Trade union rights.

Freedom of expression.
– Documents 70, 102, 104
See also: Right of assembly.

Freedom of movement.
– Documents 38, 45, 83, 102, 104

Freedom of opinion.
See: Freedom of expression.

Freedom of speech.
See: Freedom of expression.

Freedom of travel.
See: Freedom of movement.

**Frente Farabundo Martí para la Liberación
Nacional-Frente Democrático Revolucionario
(FMLN) (El Salvador).**
– Documents 8, 10-11, 13, 15-19, 21-30, 32-39,
  41-42, 44-53, 55-58, 60-61, 64-67, 72, 74, 76,
  78-80, 82, 85, 90, 92, 95, 99, 101, 103, 109, 111,
  115, 117-118, 120

G

Geneva Agreement (1990).
– Documents 11, 27, 68, 99

Good offices.
– Documents 2, 35, 57-58, 78, 95, 111, 122

Government personnel.
See: Civil service.

Guatemala—Dispute settlement.
– Document 31

Guatemala—Human rights.
– Document 58

L

Land.
– Documents 95, 106
See also: Agricultural land.

Land allotment.
– Documents 46-49, 51-52, 99
See also: Land reform.

Land mines.
– Document 56
See also: Mine clearance.

Land reform.
– Documents 76, 78, 109-111, 115-116, 118
See also: Agricultural land. Land allotment. Land tenure.

Land registration.
– Documents 74, 94, 103, 109
See also: Land tenure.

Land tenure.
– Documents 41, 44, 50, 56
See also: Agricultural land. Land reform. Land registration.

Law enforcement officials.
– Documents 70, 89, 105, 109-110
See also: Judges. Police.

Law reform.
– Documents 29, 43, 45, 68, 70-73, 77, 83, 89-90, 101, 103, 105, 114, 119

Laws and regulations.
– Documents 24, 67, 110
See also: Legislative process.

Legal profession.
– Document 77
See also: Judges.

Legal remedies.
– Documents 43, 45, 89

Legislation.
See: Laws and regulations. Legislative process.

Legislative process.
– Document 81
See also: Laws and regulations.

M

Maps.
– Documents 16, 24, 41

Mediation.
– Document 18
See also: Good offices. Negotiation.

Mexico Agreements (El Salvador) (1991).
– Document 29

Military demobilization.
– Documents 49, 51, 56, 58, 60, 111, 115-116, 118
See also: Armed forces. Military personnel. Troop withdrawal.

Military education.
– Documents 70, 89

Military personnel.
– Documents 11, 34, 39-42, 44, 55, 58, 84, 103, 109, 111
See also: Armed forces. Child soldiers. Military demobilization. Military reform.

Military reform.
– Document 87
See also: Armed forces. Military personnel.

Mine clearance.
– Documents 94, 109
See also: Land mines.

Missing persons.
See: Disappearance of persons.

Munitions.
See: Armaments.

N

National Commission for the Consolidation of Peace (El Salvador).
– Documents 51, 73, 101

National human rights commissions.
See: Human rights institutions.

Negotiation.
– Documents 5, 7-8, 10-13, 15, 17-18, 20-23, 25-28, 31-35, 37, 39, 58, 60-61, 112
See also: Consultations. Dispute settlement. Mediation.

New York Act I (1991).
– Documents 34, 37

New York Act II (1992).
– Document 37

New York Agreement (1991).
– Document 25

Nicaragua—Armaments.
– Documents 79-82, 85

Nicaragua—Armed incidents.
– Document 7

Public international law.
See: International law.

Q

Querétaro Agreement (Guatemala) (1991).
– Documents 31, 58

R

Reconstruction.
– Documents 41, 56, 61, 77

Recruitment.
– Document 30

Regional cooperation.
– Documents 3, 12

Regional disarmament.
– Documents 12, 20

Regional economic integration.
See: Economic integration.

Regional security.
– Documents 12, 20

Regulations.
See: Laws and regulations.

Rehabilitation projects.
– Document 118

Repatriation.
– Documents 3-4, 7, 11, 51

Report preparation.
– Document 111

Right of assembly.
– Documents 102, 104
See also: Freedom of association. Freedom of expression.

Right to a fair trial.
– Document 70
See also: Administration of justice. Due process of law. Right to counsel.

Right to counsel.
– Document 43
See also: Administration of justice. Right to a fair trial.

Right to life.
– Documents 30, 38, 43, 45, 70, 89, 105, 119
See also: Extralegal executions. Human rights in armed conflicts.

S

San José Agreement (1990).
– Documents 9, 30, 42-43, 45, 50, 53, 70

Security Commission established under the Esquipulas II Agreement.
– Document 31

Signatures, accessions, ratifications.
– Documents 89, 105, 114
See also: Treaties.

Social and economic development.
See: Development.

Soldiers.
See: Military personnel.

Special missions.
– Documents 42, 50, 53, 55, 95, 99, 106, 111, 120
See also: Commissions of inquiry. Dispute settlement. Fact-finding missions. Humanitarian assistance. Visiting missions.

Staff security.
– Documents 42, 58

Staffing.
– Document 118

Summary executions.
– Documents 30, 38, 43, 45, 67
See also: Extralegal executions. Torture and other cruel treatment.

T

Technical cooperation.
– Document 110
See also: Development assistance. Election verification.

Tela Declaration (1989).
– Document 3

Torture and other cruel treatment.
– Documents 38, 45, 70, 83, 89, 98, 105
See also: Detained persons. Disappearance of persons. Extralegal executions. Political prisoners. Prisoner treatment. Summary executions.

Trade.
See: Foreign trade.

Trade union rights.
– Documents 89, 105
See also: Freedom of association.

Training programmes.
– Documents 41, 44, 70, 107, 109

Treaties.
– Documents 2-3, 7, 40-42, 53
See also: Peace treaties. Signatures, accessions, ratifications. Verification.

Treatment of detained persons.
See: Prisoner treatment.

Trials.
See: Criminal procedure. Right to a fair trial.

Troop withdrawal.
– Document 120
See also: Armed forces. Military demobilization.

Truce supervision.
– Documents 16, 19, 34-35, 39, 41, 44, 53, 81-82, 85
See also: Cease-fires.

Truces.
See: Cease-fires.

U

United Nations.
– Documents 1, 120

UN. Ad Hoc Commission to Evaluate the Officer Corps of the Armed Forces of El Salvador.
– Document 84, 87

UN. Commission on Human Rights. Special Representative on the Situation of Human Rights in El Salvador.
– Document 57

UN. Secretary-General.
See: Boutros-Ghali, Boutros. Pérez de Cuéllar, Javier.

UN. Special Representative of the Secretary-General in El Salvador.
– Documents 17-18, 78, 95, 106, 111, 120

UN Development Programme
– Document 122

UN Observer Group in Central America.
– Documents 4-5, 7-8, 11-12, 31, 58

UN Observer Mission for the Verification of the Electoral Process in Nicaragua.
– Documents 4, 7, 11

UN Observer Mission in El Salvador.
– Documents 10, 16, 21, 24, 26, 31, 33-35, 39-42, 44, 50, 53-58, 60, 63-64, 74-75, 78-79, 82, 85, 88, 90-92, 95, 99-100, 102-104, 106-111, 115-118, 120, 122-123

UN Observer Mission in El Salvador—Activities (1993).
– Document 94

UN Observer Mission in El Salvador—Budget Contributions.
– Document 56

UN Observer Mission in El Salvador—Establishment.
– Document 19

UN Observer Mission in El Salvador—Financing.
– Documents 16, 41, 56, 74-75, 109, 115, 118

UN Observer Mission in El Salvador—Recommendations.
– Document 30

UN Observer Mission in El Salvador. Chief Military Observer.
– Document 40

UN Observer Mission in El Salvador. Human Rights Division.
– Documents 30, 38, 43, 45, 70, 83, 89, 93, 98, 105, 114, 119

UN Observer Mission in El Salvador. Human Rights Division—Recommendations.
– Documents 38, 43, 45, 70-73, 83, 89, 105, 114, 119

UN Truth Commission to Investigate Serious Acts of Violence in El Salvador.
– Documents 66-68, 71-74, 77-78, 86, 90, 92, 94-95, 109-111, 115-116, 118, 120

V

Verification.
– Documents 30, 56-58, 70-73, 81, 83, 94-95, 98-99, 105, 119-120, 122
See also: On-site inspection. Treaties.

Visiting missions.
– Document 13
See also: Special missions.

Voter registration.
– Documents 74, 91, 100, 102, 104, 108, 118
See also: Election verification. Elections.

W

War victims.
– Document 77
See also: Displaced persons. Human rights in armed conflicts.

Weapons destruction.
– Documents 55, 60, 64, 74, 79-82, 85, 88-89

VI Index

[The numbers following the entries refer to paragraph numbers in the Introduction.]

O

Office of the United Nations High Commissioner for Refugees, 22, 144

ONUCA.
See UN Observer Group in Central America

Organization of American States (OAS), 18-19, 33

Organized crime, 175

P

Pan American Health Organization, 17, 75

Partido de Conciliación Nacional, 162-163

Partido Democráta Cristiano, 161-163

Partido Movimiento de Unidad, 162-163

Peace Accords
challenges and delays, 73-91, 121-129, 147-148
financing, 135-137
implementation, 4, 63-68, 73, 133, 145-146, 168, 177-178, 183-184

Peace corridors, 17

Peace process, 4, 19-22, 23-31, 44, 174

Peace-keeping operations, 2-3, 5, 20.
See also UN Observer Mission in El Salvador

Pérez de Cuéllar, Javier, 16, 18, 24, 26-28, 36-37, 44-45, 52-53, 57, 98

Police, 71, 95, 120.
See also National Civil Police; National Guard; National Police; National Public Security Academy; Treasury Police

Political parties, 88, 128, 161-163

Political violence, 103, 175.
See also Assassination; Massacres; Violence

Polling stations, 156-158

Procedure for the Establishment of a Firm and Lasting Peace in Central America (1987), 19-22

Public administration, 117

Public information, 50, 94, 151-152

R

Ramirez-Ocampo, Augusto, 124, 165

Reconstruction, 67, 117, 189

Refugees, 14, 144.
See also International Conference on Central American Refugees

Reintegration of ex-combatants.
See Combatants

Rivera y Damas, Arturo, Monsignor, 10, 17

Riza, Iqbal, 47, 124

Romero, Oscar Arnulfo, Archbishop, 9-10

S

San Isidro de Coronado Declaration (1989), 26

San José Agreement on Human Rights (1990), 34-37, 46

Sánchez Cerén, Salvador, 58, 127

Soto, Alvaro de, 27-28, 90

Special Plan of Economic Cooperation for Central America, 22

Special Representative of the Secretary-General in El Salvador, 47, 124, 165

Special Representative on the Situation of Human Rights in El Salvador, 96-97, 173

Stabilization programme, 131-132, 134

Support Group, 15-16, 18-19

T

Tela Declaration (1989), 23

ter Horst, Enrique, 165

Trade unions, 26

U

UN
& Organization of American States, 18-19, 33
role, 2, 34-35, 186
technical mission, 106

UN Children's Fund, 17, 75, 95

UN Development Programme, 22, 75-76, 132, 144, 184

UN Educational, Scientific and Cultural Organization, 75

UN Observer Group in Central America, 20, 32-33, 48

UN Observer Mission for the Verification of the Electoral Process in Nicaragua, 32

UN Observer Mission in El Salvador, 3-6, 43-50, 176
deployment, page, 46-47
Electoral Division, 107, 141, 143-145, 150-151, 165
good offices, 81
Human Rights Division, 71, 96, 114, 141, 180
mandate, 46, 50, 69-70, 91-92, 105-108, 124, 177, 182, 183-184, 189
Military Division, 69-71, 81, 95, 119
Police Division, 69-71, 95
post-ONUSAL arrangements, 183-184
recommendations, 164
staff security, 81
staffing, 47, 70-71, 182
withdrawal, 189

UN. Commission on Human Rights, 15, 96-97
Independent Expert on the Situation of Human Rights in El Salvador, 96-97, 173
res.1992/62, 97
Special Representative on the Situation of Human Rights in El Salvador, 15, 45, 49

UN. Economic Commission for Latin America and the Caribbean, 137

UN. General Assembly
res.35/192, 8

UN. Secretary-General, 16, 18-19
good offices, 22, 31

UN. Security Council
res.530(1983), 15
res.644(1989), 20
res.693(1991), 46
res.714(1991), 56

United Nations publications of related interest

The following UN publications may be obtained from the addresses indicated below, or at your local distributor:

An Agenda for Peace
Second edition, 1995
By Boutros Boutros-Ghali,
Secretary-General of the United Nations
E.95.I.15   92-1-100555-8   155 pp. $7.50

An Agenda for Development
By Boutros Boutros-Ghali,
Secretary-General of the United Nations
E.95.I.16   92-1-100556-6   132 pp. $7.50

Building Peace and Development, 1994
Annual Report of the Work of the Organization
By Boutros Boutros-Ghali,
Secretary-General of the United Nations
E.95.I.3   92-1-100541-8   299pp. $9.95

New Dimensions of Arms Regulation snd
Disarmament in the Post–Cold War Era
By Boutros Boutros-Ghali,
Secretary-General of the United Nations
E.93.IX.8   92-1-142192-6   53pp. $9.95

Basic Facts About the United Nations
E.93.I.2   92-1-100499-3   290pp. $5.00

Demographic Yearbook, Vol. 44
B.94.XIII.1   92-1-051083-6   1992   823pp.
$125.00

Disarmament—New Realities:
Disarmament, Peace-Building and Global
Security
E.93.IX.14   92-1-142199-3   397pp. $35.00

United Nations Disarmament Yearbook, Vol. 18
E.94.IX.1   92-1-142204-3 1993   419pp.
$50.00

Statistical Yearbook, 39th Edition
B.94.XVII.1 H   92-1-061159-4   1992/93
1,174pp. $110.00

Women: Challenges to the Year 2000
E.91.I.21   92-1-100458-6   96pp. $12.95

World Economic and Social Survey 1994
E.94.II.C.1   92-1-109128-4   308pp. $55.00

World Investment Report 1994—
Transnational Corporations, Employment
and the Work Place
E.94.II.A.14   92-1-104435-9   446pp.
$45.00

Yearbook of the United Nations, Vol. 47
E.94.I.1   0-7923-3077-3   1993   1,428pp.
$150.00

The United Nations Blue Books Series
The United Nations and Apartheid, 1948-1994
E.95.I.7 (Soft)   92-1-100546-9   565 pp. $29.95

The United Nations and Cambodia, 1991-1995
E.95.I.9 (Soft)   92-1-100548-5   352 pp. $29.95

The United Nations and Nuclear Non-Proliferation
E.95.I.17 (Soft)   92-1-100557-4   199pp. $29.95

United Nations Publications
2 United Nations Plaza, Room DC2-853
New York, NY 10017
United States of America

United Nations Publications
Sales Office and Bookshop
CH-1211 Geneva 10
Switzerland

Printed on recycled paper